W9-APR-250

second edition

AMERICAN GOVERNMENT

Strategies and Outcomes

Stephen E. Frantzich
U.S. Naval Academy

Stephen L. Percy
University of Wisconsin-Milwaukee

BOOK ACTIVATION KEY
124 OKWQE6
This key activates your online textbook.
Scratch off gray area above to see your BOOK ACTIVATION KEY.
If the key is already visible, then it has been used and is no longer valid. Contact us at www.atomicdog.com or 800-310-5661 x8 to purchase your Online Edition.
Refer to the booklet, How to Use Your Online Edition, for further instructions.

ATOMICdogPUBLISHING

Cincinnati, Ohio
www.atomicdog.com

To our students, who frequently challenge but occasionally disappoint, who generally impress but sometimes depress, yet whose potential makes the development of a textbook a worthwhile investment of our time. Little do they know how much we have learned while teaching them.

Book Team

Vice President/Publisher: Laura Pearson
Managing Editor: Kendra Leonard
Director of Interactive Media and Design: Joe Devine
Director of Quality Assurance: Tim Bair
Production Coordinator: Kathy Davis
Web Production Editor: Angela Makowski
Quality Assurance Editor: Dan Horton
Marketing Manager: Mikka Baker

When ordering this title use ISBN 1-59260-096-4.

ISBN 1-59260-095-6

Library of Congress Control Number: 2005921873

Printed in the United States of America by Atomic Dog Publishing, 35 East Seventh Street, Fourth Floor, Suite 405, Cincinnati, OH 45202.

10 9 8 7 6 5 4 3 2 1

Contents

Preface

Introduction

American government encompasses an exciting and important set of institutions and processes that have life and death implications for both American citizens and the world as a whole. We as authors believe that a textbook should try to capture some of that excitement.

In writing a textbook, we readily recognize that the reading material is seldom—and probably should not be—the heart of a course. Most learning occurs from personal interaction between a qualified instructor and interested students. We designed this text to support that interaction. We approached our task as authors with considerable trepidation, recognizing the complexity of the subject and the wide variety of competing texts.

This is a comprehensive text covering the basic institutions and processes of American government. It is designed to create well-educated individuals who can understand the American political process and to provide potentially active citizens with the tools to help make their policy preferences into law.

Using a Game Analogy to Study Politics

In our attempt to increase understanding, we have used a carefully crafted game analogy to organize our examination of American government and politics. The analogy is meant to enliven the study of American government by recognizing that politics occur as self-interested individuals and organizations compete with each other within pre-established political arenas and rules to affect political outcomes. Thus, we find game-related concepts, such as players, teams, arenas, rules, strategies, and outcomes, to be very useful organizing tools to describe American politics and governmental institutions. We are careful to ensure that the judicious use of the analogy does not trivialize politics or offer an overly complex, game-theoretic perspective.

Organization of the Book

After a brief introduction to the game theme in Chapter 1, Chapters 2–5 establish the context of American government, looking at the legal, cultural, and economic environment in which political institutions and processes operate. Chapters 6–8 focus on the organized groups and institutions (the media, interest groups, and political parties) that inform and draw together citizens in preparation for political action. Chapters 9–11 deal with the types of political activity (public opinion, political participation, and elections) that make the American political process democratic. Chapters 12–18 deal with the institutions of government (Congress, the presidency, the bureaucracy, the judiciary, and state and local government).

While public policy, the ultimate consequence of political decisions, is infused throughout all chapters, Chapters 19–21 focus in more detail on various policy areas. The Epilogue returns to many of the themes throughout the book and places them in broader context. We recognize that instructors of introductory courses in American politics have multiple ways to organize the progression of course topics. The chapters to this text are designed so that they may be read in any order determined by the instructor. With the exception of the first and last chapters, the book's chapters can be explored using a variety of ordering schemes.

Pedagogical Features

Harnessing Technology

Aside from the necessity of meeting the minimal standard for any text of including comprehensive and up-to-date scholarship, we approached the project with the strong assumption that more learning occurs when students are actively involved. This edition of the text comes with its own history. The first edition included, as this one does, print-based Time Out Boxes where students are asked to take a break from reading the text and think about a related issue. The first edition, published a decade ago, also took advantage of existing technology to be the first American Government text available on CD-ROM. The current edition allows authors enamored with the judicious use of technology to partner with Atomic Dog Publishing, a leading provider of interactive learning online textbooks. Their design template offers students the best of both the traditional and e-book world. While the book can be effectively used as a stand-alone hard-copy text, we believe that the interactive segments significantly enhance the potential for learning.

A Note to the Student

While you probably had little choice about which text to use for this course, we appreciate your using the text, as evidenced by your reading of this preface. Learning seldom occurs unless a willing student actively involves him- or herself by interacting with high-quality content. Whether you use this text in hard copy, online, or some combination of the two, we have designed it to increase the potential for meaningful involvement. In the short term your job as a student is to absorb, evaluate, and make use of the information we supply to help make generalizations to describe and explain the complex world of politics and government. In the long run, we anticipate that many of you will use your newly acquired knowledge to become active citizens, attempting to mold the process and policy outcomes of politics and government.

Pedagogical Material in the Text

Several pedagogical devices are included within each chapter of this text as a means of enhancing student learning experiences. We have included video segments, interactive polls and a few interactive figures and boxes to enhance your experience using this text—we urge you to utilize these features to the fullest extent possible.

***Key Points*:** Each chapter begins with a brief list of key points to help orient students to the upcoming material.

Chapter Previews: The substance of each chapter begins with a brief vignette from the real world of politics and government designed to highlight some of the key aspects of the chapter to follow.

***Time Out Boxes*:** Clearly identified boxes in the text ask students to stop reading for a moment and to consider a question, an issue, or an exercise related to the chapter discussion. The Time Outs are intended to highlight key chapter issues and make them more relevant to student experiences. Answers to some of the questions posed in the Time Out features are provided in the chapters in boxes appropriately called *Answers to Time Out*.

Chapter Boxes: Text boxes present relevant information on specific issues or real-life examples of the processes, players, or institutions being examined. Boxes on technology indicate the recognition that technology is changing the political process, and these boxes highlight some of the most important changes. Other in-depth boxes go beyond what is discussed in the text on various topics.

***Glossary Terms*:** Chapter glossary terms, which are indicated with boldfaced type in the text, are listed at the end of each chapter. In the online version, users can click on a glossary term for a quick definition check.

Further Reading: A list of books, journal articles, and other materials provide further information and background on topics included in the chapter.

***Practice Quiz*:** Students can check their retention of key chapter material in end-of-chapter questions. The quizzes are interactive, which means that the students can take the quiz online and are given feedback on their answers. Errors are explained and students are referred back to appropriate sections for reexamination.

Important Documents in American Politics in Annotated Form: Included are the Declaration of Independence, the Articles of Confederation, a carefully annotated version of the U.S. Constitution, and Federalist Papers No. 10 and 51.

VIDEO

Videos: Several videos have been included in the online version that further enhance the concepts discussed in text. You will see a still of each video in this print version, with an icon similar to the one shown on the left next to the still. This icon indicates that a video is available in the online version.

Critical Thinking

Throughout the text you will be encouraged to approach the topics as a political *scientist.* Science in this context refers to an approach to understanding, not a particular body of knowledge. Political scientists attempt to objectively describe and explain how the political process *actually operates* using facts, rather than relying on personal values to make judgments as to how the process *should* work.

As citizens, we legitimately use values (un-provable preferences) to choose between candidates and/or to decide which policy options we prefer. As political analysts we must attempt to hold our values in check and provide factually based descriptions and explanations of the operations of political processes and institutions.

Using the Online Edition

American Government: Strategies and Outcomes, Second Edition, is available online as well as in print. The online chapters demonstrate how the interactive media components of the text enhance presentation and understanding. For example,

- Animated illustrations help clarify concepts.
- QuickCheck interactive questions and chapter quizzes test your knowledge of various topics and provide immediate feedback.
- Clickable glossary terms provide immediate definitions of key concepts.
- The search function allows you to quickly locate discussions of specific topics throughout the text.
- Highlighting capabilities allow you to emphasize main ideas. You can also add personal notes in the margin.

You may choose to use just the online version of the text, or both the online and the print versions together. This gives you the flexibility to choose which combination of resources works best for you. To assist those who use the online and print versions together, the primary heads and subheads in each chapter are numbered the same. For example, the first primary head in Chapter 1 is labeled 1-1, the second primary head in this chapter is labeled 1-2, and so on. The subheads build from the designation of their corresponding primary head: 1-1a, 1-1b, etc. This numbering system is designed to make moving between the online and print versions as seamless as possible.

Finally, next to a number of figures and boxes in the print version of the text, you will see icons similar to the ones on the left. These icons indicate that these figures and boxes in the online version of the text are interactive in a way that applies, illustrates, or reinforces the concept.

Supplements

A comprehensive set of instructional materials has been prepared by Professor Stephen L. Percy to accompany this textbook.

An *Instructor's Manual* equips course instructors with chapter outlines and learning objectives, annotated questions for further thought, discussion and follow-up ideas for the Time Outs included in textbook chapters, and annotated research and paper topics.

A *Test Bank,* organized by chapter, provides instructors with multiple-choice questions they may use for examinations; this ancillary collection includes approximately 100 questions per chapter.

A full set of *PowerPoint® Presentations* is available for this text. This is designed to provide instructors with comprehensive visual aids for each chapter in the book. These slides include outlines of each chapter, highlighting important terms, concepts, and discussion points.

A Final Thought

As authors we know that the experience of writing and revising this book made us both better teachers and scholars. The response to the first edition was heartening. It is up to the readers to determine whether we have been able to translate our enthusiasm for the chosen approach into a useful contribution to their education.

In the end, the responsibility for any books falls on its authors. The substantive chapters were divided evenly according to the authors' interests and backgrounds. Steve Percy took on the task of developing the test bank. Steve Frantzich created the conceptual ideas for the interactive segments for the online version. In the end, it was the continuation of a collaboration that began over thirty years ago, when a young Assistant Professor Frantzich looked out over his class at Hamilton College to quickly recognize sophomore student Steve Percy as a bright and capable individual. We have continued to learn from each other ever since.

Acknowledgments

In previous editions we have thanked a large contingent of editors, reviewers, and colleagues who contributed significantly to the development of this book. We continue to appreciate their efforts. For this edition, we owe special appreciation to Jane Frantzich, who continued as unofficial copy editor. Howard Ernst provided wise counsel and created a set of annotated documents that improve the text greatly. Barbara Breeden of the U.S. Naval Academy's Nimitz Library sought out necessary material with a vengeance. Many of Professor Frantzich's students at the Naval Academy suffered through evaluations of initial drafts of the interactive segments, providing frank and helpful evaluations. Jarad Parker at the Center for Urban Initiatives and Research at the University of Wisconsin-Milwaukee provided quality assistance in overseeing the production of chapters. This text would not have appeared in its exciting online format without the help and encouragement of the Atomic Dog Staff. Ed Laube, Publisher, pursued the authors relentlessly and provided constant encouragement. Kendra Leonard, Developmental Editor, not only managed the project, but also added significantly to the creative design.

Reviewer Acknowledgments

We would like to thank the following reviewers for their helpful suggestions and comments:

Arthur Belonzi, St. John's University, (NY)
Susan Burgess, University of Wisconsin–Milwaukee
Chris Cooper, Western Carolina University
Jimmy Davis, Oklahoma State
Anne Freedman, Roosevelt University
David Garnham, University of Wisconsin–Milwaukee
Ramon Gonzales, Albuquerque, New Mexico
Harvey Grody, California State–Fullerton
Sara Ann Grove, Shippensburg University
Timothy M. Hagle, University of Iowa
Beth Henschen, Loyola University of Chicago
Thomas Holbrook, University of Wisconsin–Milwaukee
Daniel Kempton, Northern Illinois University
Matthew Kerbel, Villanova University
Donald Kettl, University of Wisconsin–Milwaukee
Mary Kweit, University of North Dakota
Jarol Manheim, George Washington University
William Mclauchlan, Purdue University
Joan Mclean, Ohio Wesleyan
David Nice, Washington State University
Norm Ornstein, American Enterprise Institute
Christine Pappas, East Central University
Steven Shier, Carleton College
JoAnn Scott, Ohio Northern University
Stephen Wasby, SUNY–Albany
Laura Woliver, University of South Carolina

About the Authors

Stephen E. Frantzich

U.S. Naval Academy

Stephen Frantzich is Professor of Political Science at the U.S. Naval Academy in Annapolis, Maryland. A graduate of Hamline University (B.A.) and the University of Minnesota (Ph.D.), his 14 books and numerous articles and book chapters have focused on the impact of new technologies on American political institutions and processes. He serves as a consultant to various congressional committees, C-SPAN, the Dirksen Center, foreign parliaments, and a number of foundations. Long an advocate of innovative teaching, Frantzich was chosen as the outstanding professor at the U.S. Naval Academy and recognized for his creative teaching by the American Political Science Association, C-SPAN, and the Center for Civic Education. He has received two senior Fulbright scholarships to teach overseas (in Denmark and the Czech Republic) and runs an all-volunteer project (Books for International Goodwill) that has shipped over 1.9 million books to developing countries. His most recent books include: *Citizen Democracy: Political Activists in a Cynical Age* (Rowman and Littlefield), *Cyberage Politics 101: Mobility, Technology and Democracy* (Peter Lang Publishers), and *Congress: Games and Strategies* (Atomic Dog Publishing).

Stephen L. Percy

University of Wisconsin–Milwaukee

Stephen L. Percy is Professor of Political Science, Director of the Center for Urban Initiatives and Research, and the Chancellor's Deputy for the Milwaukee Idea at the University of Wisconsin–Milwaukee, where he teaches courses in American government, urban politics, and public administration. He received his B.A. degree in government from Hamilton College and his Ph.D. in political science from Indiana University. Among his publications are *A Time for Boldness: A Story of Institutional Change* (co-authored with Nancy Zimpher and Mary Jane Brukardt, Anker Publishing, 2002), *Disability, Civil Rights and Public Policy: The Politics of Implementation* (University of Alabama Press, 1989), *Demand Processing and Performance in Public Service Agencies* (co-authored with Eric J. Scott, University of Alabama Press, 1985), and numerous journal articles that have appeared in *Journal of Politics, Western Political Quarterly, Public Administration Review, Social Science Quarterly*, and *Urban Affairs Quarterly*.

1

The Game of American Politics

Key Points

- **Why we speak of American politics as a series of games**
- **Concepts such as the playing field, rules, strategies, and winners and losers applied to a real case scenario**
- **How power is distributed in a democracy**
- **Impacts of new technology on the political game**

Preview: Passage of the North American Free Trade Agreement

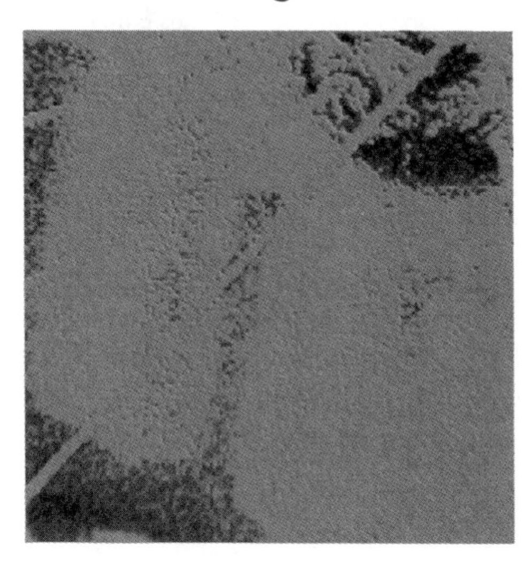

Uncharacteristically, cheers erupted in the House of Representatives chamber on the night of November 20, 1993, as the tote board indicated a vote of 234–230 approving the North American Free Trade Agreement (NAFTA). This long-sought treaty between the United States, Canada, and Mexico (see Table 1-1) would remove most of the trade barriers between the three countries. A few minutes later in the White House, President Clinton, watching the proceedings on C-SPAN, excitedly responded to the media:

> *Tonight's vote is a defining moment for our nation. At a time when many of our people are hurting from the strains of this tough global economy, we chose to compete, not retreat—to lead a new world economy.*[1]

What led up to this exultant moment? Over the preceding years, in spite of the close proximity of the United States, Canada, and Mexico, numerous trade and investment restrictions had developed in an attempt to protect businesses in each country. But by 1989, the United States and Canada had finally entered a free trade agreement, successfully expanding markets for each country's goods. Then, in 1990, the United States and Mexico opened up their own free trade agreement discussions. In 1991, when Canada joined them, the goal became three-way cooperation and the creation of the world's largest free trade zone.

The differences between the countries, however, created some major problems. Mexico's weaker economy did not guarantee an immediate market for Canadian and U.S. goods, and its lower wages and more limited environmental restrictions gave Mexico a competitive advantage in producing some goods and services. Both opposition and support for NAFTA in the United States tended to be associated with the expected impact on the goods, services, and labor forces that dominated various specific North American economies. For example, high-tech businesses—confident that they could sell to Mexico—were very supportive of NAFTA, while labor-intensive agricultural businesses—such as flower growers—were opposed to the agreement. Labor unions representing less-skilled workers, who would have more difficulty competing with the lower wages of Mexican workers, feared the agreement more than did organizations representing more-skilled workers.

In general, proponents harbored a philosophical and economic commitment to free trade and were able to see the long-term economic benefits of creating a powerful North American trading bloc. Opponents feared the short-term economic impact on employment and wages. By 1992, to reduce both political opposition and potential negative impact on the economy, an agreement was reached between Canada, Mexico, and the United States to eliminate ***tariffs*** *and other trade barriers over a fifteen-year period. One by one, numerous other issues entered the debate*

tariff A tax levied on products being imported into the country.

Table 1-1 **Key U.S. Dates in the North American Free Trade Agreement**

Date	Event
The Game Begins: June 11, 1990	President George H. Bush and President Carlos Salinas de Gortari of Mexico announce that they will open preliminary discussions toward negotiating a free trade agreement between the two nations.
Another Nation Joins the Game: February 5, 1991	George H. Bush announces that Canada, which already has a free trade agreement with the U.S., will join the negotiations with Mexico. The goal: an agreement that will create the world's largest free trade zone.
The Rules Are Established: May 1991	Congress gives George H. Bush the authority to negotiate the free trade agreement under fast-track procedures requiring an up-or-down vote on the completed deal without amendments.
The International Strategies Are Employed: August 12, 1992	After 14 months of bargaining, the U.S., Mexico, and Canada reach agreement on a 2,000-page pact eliminating tariffs and other barriers to trade over a 15-year period.
A New Player Enters the Game: October 4, 1992	Democratic presidential candidate Bill Clinton ends months of speculation by announcing his support for NAFTA. He says, however, that if elected he will demand that supplemental agreements be negotiated to provide greater protection for worker rights, the environment, and sudden import surges.
The Legislative Strategies Begin: November 4, 1993	President Bill Clinton sends to Congress legislation to implement NAFTA. Because of strong opposition from labor groups and Ross Perot, Clinton concedes facing an uphill battle to win passage. He negotiates treaty changes with key opponents.
The Game Continues: November 9, 1993	Ross Perot and Vice President Al Gore increase public involvement by appearing on "Larry King Live" and debating the merits of NAFTA before a TV audience of 18 million households.
A Winner Emerges: November 17, 1993	The U.S. House of Representatives approves NAFTA, 234–200.

Source: Adapted from Associated Press Worldstream, "NAFTA Chronology: U.S.–NAFTA Debate," November 18, 1993, LEXIS-NEXIS database.

Getty Images

U.S. Naval Academy Photo Lab

Players play games with similar rules but different results because of differences in abilities and training.

and were dealt with in such a way that the idea of NAFTA was kept alive politically. Changes in immigration laws were specifically excluded. A North American Development Bank was created to provide loans for economic expansion. In an attempt to even the playing field among the nations, stronger protection of labor and the environment was also included in the final agreement.

As is often the case in ***politics,*** *no one could predict the precise consequences of NAFTA. Proponents and opponents in Congress assumed different scenarios concerning the ultimate impact and voted accordingly. By just four votes, the "ayes" won the game.*

politics Efforts of individuals and groups to secure the benefits, services, and protections provided by governments.

With those congressional votes, politicians in Ottawa and in Mexico City, who had put their careers on the line, were finally vindicated. Their plan to gradually eliminate almost all trade and investment restrictions between the United States, Canada, and Mexico over the next fifteen years was about to become a reality.

Around Washington, some political activists were more somber. They grieved that they had been unable to stop what they believed was a bad agreement. They were also critical of the way President Clinton and the pro-NAFTA forces had secured victory. Predictions by them of American job loss, threats to the environment, and a decline in American autonomy had been to no avail.

What really happened on November 20, 1993? Who were the key players? By what rules were they forced to play? What strategies did NAFTA supporters and opponents use to gain their goals? Were the winners and losers on predictably composed teams?

1-1 Gaining Insight through Comparison

> So it seems only natural to look at how we are governed—the way Washington really works today—as a power game, not in some belittling sense, but as a way of understanding how government actually works and why it does not work better. For the game is sometimes glorious and uplifting, at other times aggravating or disenchanting. It obviously is a serious game with high stakes, one in which the winners and losers affect many lives—yours, mine, those of people down the street, and of people all over the world.[2]

The terms and concepts used to describe a game are easily—often unconsciously—applied to the process of government. American government and American politics are the intertwined subjects of this book, and for both, the analogy of a game is apt and useful.

Clearly, much about politics resembles a game. Players and observers often use the language of gaming when describing politics. Presidential candidates join the "race" for the White House by entering the election "arena" and throwing their hat into the "ring." Politicians "score" points in policy debates, and a "victor" often emerges. The president's staff is viewed as a "team" locked in a "contest" with the opposing "teams" in Congress, the bureaucracy, or even the general public. Interest groups adopt "strategies" designed to influence the votes of members of Congress.

Describing politics as a game does not imply a lack of seriousness ("Oh, it's nothing but a game"). Politics in the United States is a game with very important consequences. The game consists of important decisions about the collective action of society made by the **government.** Whether public funds will be spent on schools or missiles, whether tax laws will favor the rich or the poor, and whether racial or gender discrimination will be opposed or tolerated are but a few of the issues that hang in the balance. In the game of politics, the participants individually and collectively use their power to help assure that their preferences are reflected in new laws and regulations that affect the lives of many citizens. At stake is personal and social survival.

government *The formal set of institutions having the legitimate right to make collective decisions on the part of an organized society.*

In some respects the game analogy used in this book may prove to be imperfect. American politics is not one but *many* games, a series of contests related to one another in sometimes obvious and sometimes not so obvious ways, all being played more or less simultaneously. But the game analogy serves well in making the political process easier to understand. It makes a complex series of events into something we have all participated in at some time or other, which is undoubtedly one reason game terminology has been used so frequently by observers and participants in American politics (see Box 1-1: The Players Speak). Using the game analogy effectively draws attention to an essential aspect of American government: the *dynamic* nature of the process.

1-2 The Dynamics of American Government

A game is not static, but full of action. So it is with American politics: the action is non-stop and played out in numerous simultaneous contests. Political games overlap, and they are generally **continuous** rather than **discrete.** A discrete game is a one-time contest in which the players are unlikely to face each other again. Such games are rare in politics, where there are continuous rounds of confrontation. Opposing players expect to face one another again in the future. These players realize that whatever they do during this particular contest will be remembered the next time they meet.

continuous games *Games with no clear ending point and with many rounds.*

discrete games *Games that have a clear ending point; games with either one or a limited number of rounds.*

Political games are also often highly interconnected. Observing American politics is something like watching football, baseball, and basketball games, with all the players sharing the same field with a track meet and bridge tournament. To further complicate the picture, some of the players participate in more than one of the games taking place, and what happens in one game affects the other games. As one game becomes more exciting or rewarding, players gravitate toward it. During a "hot" presidential contest, for example, congressional and local candidates may find it harder to attract volunteer workers and funding for their campaign. The "action" focuses on the game with the highest stakes.

The game analogy provides a way of organizing the diversity of action taking place within what we call politics. It offers a set of categories for describing the elements of political activity. It helps point out the interrelationships among the rules, the strategies, the major players and their objectives, and the nature of the playing fields. The game analogy also can help us understand more about who wins and who loses in politics, and why.

1-3 The Context of Play

In this chapter we explore the context of American government. All games have a **playing field**—that is, a context in which they are played—and the nature of the playing field can influence the outcome of the game. Those familiar with the condition of the playing field have an advantage over opponents who do not. For example, the **lobbyist** who

playing field *Context in which political games are played, including political culture and public opinion.*

lobbyists *Individuals, often paid by interest groups, who communicate group interests to government officials. The term originates from the practice of waiting in the lobby of the legislative chambers when attempting to persuade legislators before a vote.*

Box 1-1 The Players Speak

A look at daily media coverage of politics and activities on all levels of government reveals frequent use of gaming terminology as part of political phrases and analogies:

> I have a history of negotiating, of bringing people together. When the game's on the line, you give the ball to your best player. I want the ball.
>
> —*Jesse Jackson, Washington Post, August 15, 1987.*

> It [Washington politics] reminds me of a bunch of little boys playing a game. They're all so enthralled and enraptured and they think the whole world is watching, and it is not. It really is an inside-the-Beltway game. . . . It reminds me of a description I once heard of Washington—30 square miles surrounded by reality.
>
> —*Senator Jake Garn, R-Utah, Washington Post, November 13, 1986.*

> Public service can be tough, and even ugly sometimes, but that doesn't mean we shouldn't dust ourselves off, get back in the game.
>
> —*President George W. Bush, Dallas Morning News, April 25, 2001.*

> While they turn civil rights into a political game, the majority of our constituents—women, racial and religious minorities, older Americans, and the disabled—lack basic protections from employer discrimination. Let's stop the games and work together to resolve this important issue.
>
> —*Representative Jolene Unsoeld, D-Wash., Congressional Record, April 25, 1991, E-1477.*

> Mr. Speaker, the biggest shell game, the biggest con game going on in this country today is being done by federal agencies which grossly underestimate the cost of some programs so they can be approved. Then the cost overruns and expenses in future years are just unbelievable.
>
> —*Representative John Duncan, R-Tenn., Congressional Record, May 2, 1991, H-2691.*

> Under that agreement . . . the playing field will be a level one in 1999, but unless we do something today to help our shipyards, there will not be very many of them around to compete on that level playing field in 1999. It is about as fair as ensuring an evenly matched baseball game between teams only to find that when the first inning starts that you've sent team USA out to the plates with broken bats.
>
> —*Representative Joseph Moakley, D-Mass., Congressional Record, August 2, 1994, H-6565.*

> George (H.) Bush talks a good game, but he has no game plan to rebuild America from the cities to the suburbs to the countryside so that we can compete and win again in the global economy. I do.
>
> —*Presidential candidate Bill Clinton, Acceptance Speech, Democratic National Convention, July 16, 1992, LEXIS-NEXIS database.*

> Politics is a game of addition, not subtraction.
>
> —*Representative Thomas Davis (R-Va), chairman of the Republican Congressional Campaign Committee discussing reaching out to groups that don't normally support Republicans, Denver Post, May 15, 2001.*

understands how congressional committees operate and has a sense of the relationships among legislative players on a specific subcommittee is likely to be more effective than lobbyists who lack this knowledge. Incumbent office holders have a "home team advantage" when it comes to winning office. Incumbents are familiar with the rules, know the other key players, and have experience with putting together a successful winning strategy in a particular political setting.

We tend to think of playing fields in physical terms—the baseball diamond, the chessboard, hopscotch marks on the sidewalk. But in most games, as we shall see, the playing field also has a nonphysical component in the form of the players' expectations and the cultural norms defining "fair play."

1-3a Playing Field Boundaries

The "physical" boundaries of political playing fields significantly affect strategies and outcomes, and they vary from game to game. Some, such as the three levels of government—

the federal, state, and local levels—are defined with relative clarity. Increasingly, political problems such as pollution and crime control cross established political boundaries, forcing different levels of government to work together. The impact of new communications technologies, a continuing theme throughout this book, redefines the importance of many of the physical boundaries and forces governments to interact both globally and nationally.

federalism *Pattern of government in which a national, overarching government shares power with subnational or state governments.*

We will start with the constitutionally defined contexts of government. According to the principles of **federalism** governing powers are not concentrated in one central, national government. Instead, governments at three levels govern simultaneously, making decisions that distribute benefits, services, and regulatory protections. Politics is usually conducted very differently on each of the three levels of play, based on their differing rules, traditions, and needs. The federal government attempts to bring about some uniformity and deal with problems that defy physical boundaries. In an even broader context, Chapter 21, "American Politics in an Interdependent World: International Economics, Foreign Policy, and National Defense" discusses the United States' role in the international community.

The physical boundaries of political playing fields are significant, vary from game to game, and affect outcomes and strategies. A campaign for student body president involves a very different playing field than that of a campaign to secure the nation's presidential nomination. A personable young campus politician may wage a successful campaign at virtually no cost by simply going door to door. An alternate strategy for a campus election is described in LearnMore: Campus Elections, Media, and Late-Night Television. In a small community, posters placed in front yards may be enough to elect an individual as mayor.

technology *Specialized knowledge and tools, often scientific in nature, facilitating the conduct of everyday life and activities, including politics.*

Technology has changed the strategies candidates can use to overcome physical barriers to communication. The "whistle-stop" campaigns of the past, which brought candidates directly to the voters, have been superseded by high-tech campaigns, reducing the need for physical travel. Today presidential candidates rely on polished television advertisements and appearances on cable TV to make an impact on voters in fifty widespread states. New technologies, such as email and the Internet, create a virtually borderless playing field for the politics of future decades. Box 1-2: Campus Elections, Media and Late-Night Television shows how technological innovation applies to all levels of politics.

1-3b Political Arenas

arena *Location where a game is played. Often tied directly to political institutions, such as the presidency or Congress, where players make policy.*

Arenas are the more circumscribed places where political decisions are made. Most arenas are institutional "decision points" created as part of our governmental system. Arenas can be found at all levels of the American political system, from local governments to the national government in Washington, D.C. Each of the branches of government and the institutions of which they are composed form a different decision-making arena.

Box 1-2 Campus Elections, Media, and Late-Night Television

Even candidates for campus elections have used the media as a means to reach voters and get their point across. An enterprising candidate for student government at the University of Virginia (UVA) discovered a unique and relatively inexpensive way to reach his fellow students through television.

Wanting to go beyond the usual tactic of mounting campaign posters across campus, and noting that many UVA students regularly watched "Late Night with David Letterman," the student candidate contacted the local television station and found that he could afford a fifteen-second spot during Letterman's show. (Late-night spots on local stations are relatively inexpensive.) With the help of friends, he put together a short campaign video and arranged to run it during Letterman's program. While he lost the election, he became an instant campus celebrity, enhancing his name recognition and establishing himself as a strong candidate for future student council elections.

It is no accident that the American political system contains many political arenas. Wishing to avoid the autocratic rule of European monarchies, which concentrated political power in the hands of one or a few, the Founders responsible for drafting the U.S. Constitution sought to design a political system in which political power was widely diffused. One means of dispersing power was to create a system with multiple decision points.

The existence of many arenas—each with its own players, decision-making rules, and acceptable strategies—inspires frequent attempts to shift or move decision making from one arena to another. Clever players determine the arena in which they are most likely to be successful and shift their efforts to that arena to maximize an advantage. For example, in the 1950s, African-American civil rights activists shifted their efforts from the legislative branch to the courts, where their lack of electoral clout proved less of a handicap. In later years, other civil rights activists, persuaded that their cause had gained as much as it could through the courts, took to the streets, engaging in mass protest. This, in turn, opened the door to the legislative arena, where new laws—notably, the Civil Rights Act of 1964 and the Voting Rights Act of 1965—strengthened the ability of African Americans to have an impact on the electoral game.

1-3c Human Factors

In politics, as in other games, the playing field has an important human dimension. In political games, two important human elements are political culture and public opinion.

Political culture refers to the political values and attitudes prevalent in society. Distinctive features of the American political culture include deeply held beliefs regarding the principle of majority rule, the value of citizen participation in policy decisions, and respect for the U.S. Constitution. Such beliefs are the product of our political history and are passed along from one generation of Americans to the next. Political culture is a long-term influence; it is part of the basic context of American government. [While the family and local community were once almost the sole source of an individual's basic beliefs, such influences must now compete with divergent messages from the media.

political culture *Widely shared fundamental beliefs, attitudes, and perspectives regarding political activity.*

Public opinion concerns short-term attitudes and beliefs held by American citizens about contemporary issues, problems, and personalities. Public opinion changes frequently as the result of dramatic events, new leadership, or media attention to political issues or public problems. Technologies such as television and computer-based communication have changed the speed with which opinions are formed and the methods by which those opinions are communicated to political leaders. Most often, though, short-term opinions are based on longer-term cultural beliefs.

public opinion *Short-term attitudes about political players or particular public policies that are important enough to generate widespread interest.*

Let's try to clarify the distinction between political culture and public opinion. Are you, for example, uncomfortable with the fact that poor people in the United States are much less likely to seek or win political office than are wealthier citizens? If so, you are reflecting a typically American cultural expectation that politics should be an open and fair process played on an "even" or "level" playing field in which everyone is able to participate. This attitude is part of the political culture because it is widely accepted by most Americans, had its origins long ago, and is passed down from generation to generation through traditional stories and myths. The idea of equal opportunity is reflected in the "log cabin to White House" stories emphasizing the humble origins of many U.S. presidents. Public opinion is a more short-term application of a broad attitude to a narrow issue or political leader that is shared by many other individuals. For example, if most Americans accept the often-discussed proposals for public financing of electoral campaigns, the object of which is to increase political opportunities for those who could otherwise not afford to wage campaigns, we would say that public opinion is on the side of this policy initiative.

Although Americans as a whole share many values as part of the national political culture, the political cultures of regions, states, localities, and social sub-groups may differ significantly. While the state of Massachusetts, for example, regularly reelected Senator Edward Kennedy, a recognized political liberal, this senator would clearly have had little political chance for election in many conservative states in the South and West.

One reason for this is that the political culture—the political values and attitudes—of the citizens of Massachusetts is decidedly more liberal than that of citizens in many other states.

1-4 The NAFTA Vote Reexamined

The House vote on NAFTA—the North American Free Trade Agreement case study that opened this chapter—is more easily understood through the use of the game analogy. The vote was part of a much larger game involving many rounds of play. Previous rounds included negotiations with Canada and Mexico during the George H. Bush administration and a court challenge regarding President Bill Clinton's right to bring the agreement to Congress without submitting an environmental impact statement. Subsequent to the House vote, the agreement had to be approved by the U.S. Senate and the Mexican government. In the midst of all this, the crucial decision in the NAFTA battle occurred on the House floor. Our analysis will include a series of questions that will be used throughout this book to guide us through the complexities of American politics and government.

1-5 The Playing Field

The playing field defines where the game is played. It is the physical, technological, and attitudinal context of the game. Thinking about the playing field triggers questions such as:

- How does the nature of the playing field affect the way the game is played?
- Does the playing field encourage "fair" play?
- What other arenas affect how this game is played?

1-5a The NAFTA Playing Field

How might we describe the NAFTA playing field? In the broadest sense, the NAFTA game was played in an international diplomatic culture defined by values and attitudes such as "remaining faithful to one's agreements," "supporting one's leaders," and "having consistency in one's commitments." Faced with the vote on NAFTA, many members of the House recognized that the United States would look weak if a trade agreement negotiated by their president was not approved. Most members understood that once agreed upon, NAFTA was not subject to continuous revision.

At the same time, NAFTA was being debated in the arena of American political culture, which includes deeply held beliefs in principles such as respect for the Constitution,

NAFTA initialing ceremony, October 1992

George Bush Presidential Library

the value of citizen participation in politics, the right to freely express one's beliefs, and the value of decisions made by majority rule. More specifically, the NAFTA vote was taking place in the congressional arena. Remember, each decision-making setting has its own culture. The congressional culture recognizes the responsibility of its members to represent the interests of their constituents and views compromise as a desirable way of ameliorating conflict. The NAFTA vote had to be consistent with these expectations in order to be accepted.

Apart from attitudes and values, physical characteristics also define and affect how a game is played. The geographic proximity of Canada, Mexico, and the United States, with their common borders, made the trade pact desirable. It was easy to see the three countries as one large economic market as opposed to three separate physical entities. Many previously restricted transfers of goods, services, and labor would be legal under NAFTA. To some degree, the necessity of a North American Free Trade Zone was driven by technological changes in transportation and communication that reduced the importance of physical distances. Citizens of Mexico or Canada become potential customers for U.S. goods as they see our products on television.

The NAFTA decision itself was affected by the openness of the congressional decision-making process and the skills of opponents and proponents whose positions were heard via television advertising and programming. One of the defining moments of the battle was a cable television debate between Vice President Al Gore and NAFTA opponent Ross Perot on "Larry King Live."

1-6 The Rules

A deck of cards on a table does not by itself tell us much about how a particular game is played. The same deck of cards could be used to play poker, blackjack, "52 pick-up," or more complex games such as bridge. What distinguishes one game from another are the **rules.** In any game, the rules perform several vital functions:

rules *Guidelines that determine how political games will be conducted, who gets to play, and the information the players will receive during the game.*

- First and foremost, the rules explain the object of the game and how we can win, for example, by receiving the most points, pinning an opponent to the mat, or being the first over the finish line.
- Often, rules define who is allowed to play. For example, professional athletes may not compete in amateur athletics, and welterweight boxers do not fight heavyweights.
- Rules determine acceptable strategies, the moves that players are allowed to make within the context of the game. The rules of football limit the kinds of tackles one may use, while those of bridge define appropriate bids.

As with any rules, those governing political games tell us what is permissible and what is not. In the United States, for example, Congress can pass laws making certain behaviors illegal, but it cannot apply new laws retroactively. Nor can Congress interfere with the role of the courts by punishing those who violate the law. Because American politics involves more than one game, *more than one set of rules apply*. The rules that apply to play in the congressional arena do not necessarily hold when dealing with the courts or the executive branch. For example, it is legal and acceptable to give campaign contributions to members of Congress and later contact them about your preference on legislation, but giving such contributions to a judge would be seen as an illegal bribe. Despite significant variations depending on the institution, there is, nonetheless, a primary rulebook: the U.S. Constitution. In American politics, all other sets of formal rules—and some informal rules as well—are subordinate to those established in the Constitution and must be consistent with its requirements.

1-6a Not All Rules Are Written Ones

Standards of fair play and acceptable behaviors in politics are often determined by unwritten or informal rules, which can have important consequences. For example, no written laws prohibit presidential candidates from committing adultery or misrepresenting their credentials. Nonetheless, as many recent political candidates have learned, unwritten rules about morality and ethics do exist, and candidates who are perceived as violating them suffer politically.

At times, the rules can be changed between games, but it is not seen as legitimate to change in the middle of a game. Although Al Gore might have felt that the rules giving George W. Bush the presidency after the 2000 election based on the electoral college were unfair given Gore's popular vote victory, he was willing to accept the outcome. Both George W. Bush and Al Gore planned their electoral strategies around existing rules. Some of the fiercest battles in politics are over the rules that will govern the next rounds of play. No one wants to go into battle at a disadvantage.

Finally, rules are seldom completely neutral. In most cases, they give an advantage to some players and present a disadvantage to others. For example, federal campaign financing rules, which place few limits on the amount of money spent as long as it is publicly reported, work to the benefit of congressional candidates who are able to raise a large amount of funds. Public financing of elections, on the other hand, would pave the way for a very different set of candidates, including many who are less able to raise funds on their own.

1-6b NAFTA and the Rules

norms *The informal social rules that guide the behavior of an institution and its members.*

Rules may emerge from formal agreements such as constitutions or laws or may be based on more informal agreements such as social **norms.** Consideration of the rules raises these questions:

- What formal and informal rules are operative in this particular game?
- How are the rules enforced?
- What difference do the rules make in terms of the outcome of the game?

The House vote on NAFTA occurred under two broad sets of formal rules. The U.S. Constitution serves as the basic rulebook for all of American government, and it required that the president submit such a trade agreement to the House. The House itself operates in accordance with rules that define its membership, who may speak, and the conditions for voting. For example, House rules allow members fifteen minutes to cast their votes using the electronic voting terminals. Any time during the fifteen-minute period, a vote may be changed. During the NAFTA vote, the White House had agreed to "release" some members if their vote was not needed for passage. That is, these members could initially vote to support NAFTA and then change their vote at the last minute. The NAFTA vote was conducted under a specific set of "fast-track" rules. The House had agreed prior to the debate to limit the time they would spend on NAFTA and to make delaying amendments out of order. As one trade expert saw it, "If we didn't have fast track, NAFTA wouldn't have even gotten to a final vote."[3]

Groups and individuals who cannot win under the current rules often try to change them. When NAFTA got to the Senate, there was an unsuccessful attempt to ignore the fast-track agreement that would have doomed NAFTA. Another group of opponents tried to appeal to an outside "referee," the Supreme Court, arguing that NAFTA violates the Constitution.

Since gathering votes for NAFTA required striking bargains with individual members, informal norms legitimizing such behavior came into play. Tom Lewis (R-Fla.), an undecided member who was finally convinced to support NAFTA, explained:

> [The White House representatives] have gone more miles in order to satisfy the concerns of Florida agriculture than anybody else has. If you ask for a number of things and get most of all that you asked for, then you certainly can't turn your back.[4]

During the debate, the formal rules were enforced by the presiding officer in the chamber, who relied on a detailed book of precedents. Attempts to change the content of NAFTA and delay its passage were ruled out of order. The applicability of constitutional rules falls to the federal courts and ultimately the Supreme Court. The courts did not agree with the charges that NAFTA was unconstitutional. Informal norms are enforced by social sanctions, such as ignoring the offender or refusing to deal with them during the next round. A member agreeing to support NAFTA and then breaking his or her word would not have been trusted the next time.

It is hard to overestimate the importance of rules. Without the fast-track agreement, delaying tactics would have killed NAFTA. If the House had been working under the rules of the Mexican parliament, which requires a two-thirds vote as opposed to a simple majority, NAFTA would have gone down to defeat.

1-7 The Players

How a game is played depends on the players' goals and abilities. The pickup basketball game or sandlot softball game may be played with rules very similar to those used in professional sports, but the nature of the **players** makes it a very different type of contest. Who gets involved in the game? Why? What resources do they bring?

players *Persons who actively participate in political games.*

The answer to the first of these questions is in part determined by legal considerations. Certain activities, such as running for office and voting, have age or residency requirements. But legal restrictions today have a relatively minor impact on political involvement. Changing social traditions often determine the acceptability of participation by various groups of individuals. For example, the feminist movement in the United States changed attitudes toward women candidates and increased the acceptance of women as equal players in political games. On the individual level, resources—time, money, knowledge, and experience—and personal motivation have a large impact on involvement.

1-7a Joining the Game

Playing the political game in America is largely voluntary (with the exception of a few responsibilities, such as paying taxes and serving on a jury). No one is required to vote, attend political meetings, or run for office. The large number of overlapping games in our political system allows many opportunities for citizen involvement and participation. But most citizens are little more than spectators, cheering or booing from the sidelines, while many others are simply unaware of the games being played. Answer the questions in Time Out 1-1 to find out what sort of player you are in the American political scene.

As we shall see, those who choose to participate in the political process are not a random sample of U.S. citizens. This is significant, because the political system responds more favorably to those who participate than to those who do not. In the end, public policy tends to reflect the interests of those who influence that policy through continuous participation in political games.

Players bring different amounts and types of resources to the game. The options available to a well-financed interest group with many members and a large staff are different from those available to a less well endowed and unorganized group. The experienced candidate whose name is well known can approach the campaign in a manner quite different from that of a newcomer with plenty of new ideas but little name recognition and experience.

Resources alone, however, do not tell the whole story. Some potential players with seemingly abundant resources have neither the skill nor the motivation to make use of them, while other players parlay limited resources into significant political power through hard work and skill.

1-7b Changing the Pool of Players

While relatively well defined patterns of political involvement develop over time, these patterns are not permanent. New groups and individuals frequently enter the game as they discover the advantages of political involvement. Others, frustrated by a lack of success, withdraw. This pattern is found frequently on the local level. A group of neighbors concerned about an immediate and common problem—an increase in burglaries or unsightly litter—often form an informal association to deal with the problem. They might, for example, form a "neighborhood watch" program to fight crime or organize a

Time Out 1-1

INTERACTIVE BOX

What Type of Player Are You?

Are you a player? Look at the following list of political activities and check those that apply.

Have you ever . . .

A1. Registered to vote? ____

A2. Voted in an election? ____

A3. Tried to persuade others how to vote? ____

B1. Worn a political button? ____

B2. Attended a political meeting? ____

B3. Contributed to a candidate? ____

B4. Contacted a public official? ____

C1. Worked in a political campaign? ____

C2. Solicited campaign funds? ____

C3. Been active in a political party? ____

C4. Run for political office? ____

cleanup campaign. Sustaining such associations has proven difficult over time, however, since interest often wanes as the motivating problem begins to diminish and the initial excitement of participation wears off.

The movement of people in and out of political games is evident in many political campaigns. On occasion, individuals become excited about a particular candidate. Their enthusiasm leads them to take such actions as contributing to campaigns, distributing campaign leaflets, and attending political rallies. After the election, whether or not their candidate has won, interest in the candidate tends to wane, and their political participation resumes a less active pattern.

Often, the entrance of new players into political games alters political outcomes. In recent years, increased participation by groups as disparate as gays, Native Americans, and Christian fundamentalists has affected both election results and the content of public policy. In studying American politics, you need to understand who the players are, what public policies they favor or oppose, and the strategies they use to influence governmental decisions.

Political players find it useful to join with other players to pool resources and exert greater political power; in other words, they form a team. The major political parties—the Democrats and Republicans—represent some of the most important and stable teams in American politics. Interest groups are another important type of political team; they represent individuals or organizations who share similar interests and policy preferences.

__coalition__ A temporary group of often diverse members who agree to support a particular policy position.

Many of the teams that form in American politics are so temporary and so unstable and share so few interests that they are best thought of as temporary **coalitions** rather than permanent teams. During electoral campaigns, the supporters who come together on behalf of a particular candidate represent a political coalition. Another form of political coalition is the clustering of members of Congress who choose to support a particular piece of legislation. These legislative coalitions are often quite transitory and can bring together a group of legislators who oppose each other on most other issues. These types of coalitions inspired the phrase "Politics makes for strange bedfellows."

1-7c The NAFTA Vote Players

Not everyone plays in every game. Identifying who chooses or who is allowed to play often has a dramatic impact on how the game is played and who wins. Thinking in these terms invites questions such as:

- Who are the players?
- What motivations, resources, and skills do the players bring to the playing field?
- How might the strategies and outcome of the game be different if the players changed?

In a formal sense, the ultimate players in the NAFTA vote were the 434 members of the House of Representatives (one seat was vacant). Although not granted a formal vote, President Clinton put himself in the middle of the game by proposing the treaty and fighting for its passage. One member of Congress recognized the importance of Clinton's role by asserting, "We just had an excellent bipartisan meeting with the president. You know, he's our quarterback in this NAFTA game" (Representative Henry Bonilla [R-Tex.]).[5] A variety of interest groups joined the game on both sides of the issue and tried to mobilize the public by encouraging supporters to contact their members of Congress.

Members of Congress desire reelection. Being chosen by the voters provides them a position of power and validates their past. A number of House members were torn between the good NAFTA was expected to do for the national economy and the threat it posed to local industries. Norman Mineta (R-Calif.) agonized over what Mexican competition would do to the flower-growing industry in his district. In announcing his support for NAFTA, he argued, "I have been a friend of labor for my entire public life. . . . I have also been bothered by the fact that certain workers and industries have been underrepresented on this issue, such as my friends in the cut-flower business. . . . [But] in the big picture, we're better off in the long run with NAFTA."[6]

Many Republicans in the House found their decision eased by the fact that supporting free trade fit nicely with their capitalist ideology. Once in the game, President Clinton recognized that his leadership would be damaged by a loss and knew he would have to use the resources of the presidency to help promote the agreement. Unfortunately, he did not have the resource of a united party. Both the Democratic majority leader (Dick Gephart [D-Mo.]) and the majority whip (David Bonior [D-Mich.]) actively opposed NAFTA, as did a majority of Democrats. External interest groups possessed money and access to the media but tended to cancel each other out.

Although the complexion of Congress is changing slowly, its players are largely well-educated, white, upper-middle-class males. Most of them depended on campaign contributions from the business community, which tended to support NAFTA. One key opponent chided his colleagues during the debate by asking, "Are you on the side of the Fortune 500? Or are you on the side of the unfortunate 500,000 Americans who will lose their jobs because of this agreement?" (David Bonior [D-Mich.])[7] If Congress were populated by more members dependent on the support of labor unions who largely opposed NAFTA, the outcome might have been very different.

We have been discussing players and rules, but players and rules alone do not make a game. Action begins when players implement a plan for winning. In section 1-8 we will examine game strategy.

1-8 Strategies

A plan of action designed to win a game is a **strategy.** If we exclude games of chance (where luck, not skill, dominate), the essence of game playing involves choosing an appropriate strategy. Such strategy makes the most advantageous use of your resources to allow you to win the game without running afoul of the rules.

strategy *Preconceived plan of action intended to achieve victory in political games; action taken to enhance the probability of winning. Also called a game plan, tactic, or procedure.*

Interesting games are those that provide ample opportunity for countering an opponent's strategy, keeping the game's outcome in doubt for many moves. What constitutes a winning strategy in politics varies from game to game and from arena to arena. A highly successful strategy for winning votes during an election campaign is unlikely to work equally well in a courtroom or in a congressional committee hearing. In any game, success or failure depends not only on your strategic choices but also on those of your opponents. The more you know about the motivation and available options of the other players, the more likely that you can affect their behavior.

Answers to Time Out 1-1

Responses

If you checked one or more of activities C1–C4, so you qualify as a player. Less than 5% of the U.S. population fall into this category.

If you checked one or more of activities B1–B4 (but none from C1-C4), so you are an activist, along with less than 15% of the U.S. population.

If you checked one or more of activities A1–A3 and nothing else, so you are basically a spectator, along with about 60% of the U.S. population. You are a "fan in the stands" most of the time.

If you checked none of the preceding activities, so you fall into the apathetic category, along with about 30% of the U.S. population.

1-8a Strategies for Using Power

power The ability to get others to follow your wishes by employing resources such as threats, promises, personal charisma, or information.

At the heart of the political game is **power.** Power is the ability to induce others to change their behavior in some desired direction. Candidates who persuade voters to vote for them, or interest groups that threaten to withhold future campaign funds from a legislator to persuade her to vote on behalf of a measure she initially opposed, have wielded power.

In politics, players seldom seek power simply for its own sake. Instead, they value power as a means to an end—namely, influencing the outcome of the game at hand in a desired direction. In other words, they use power to increase the chances of winning something important to them. Power in politics is valuable not so much for what it is as for what it can do. Time Out 1-2: "Political Power and You: A Textbook Case" shows how the concepts of politics apply to everyday life.

There are various strategies for using power, each requiring a different set of resources or skills. Note in the following discussion that each may be ranked in terms of its relative "cost."

rewards Positive payoffs received for successfully playing political games.

sanctions Negative payoffs received for playing political games.

The use of **rewards** or **sanctions** is the most blunt and expensive form of power: "You voted against my bill yesterday, so you can forget my vote on the bill you want to pass today," or, "Here is $5,000 for your campaign. I know we can count on your continued support." The successful use of rewards or sanctions requires that you possess:

- Something of value needed by the other player
- An awareness of that need
- The ability to wield the rewards or sanctions involved in an effective manner

Because rewards and sanctions are limited in nature and can be quickly used up, they are a relatively expensive form of power. There are, of course, some legal limits on the use of financial rewards to influence political behavior. Outright political bribes and influence peddling, for example, are illegal.

Time Out 1-2

Political Power and You: A Textbook Case

Why are you reading this book? Chances are that you did not just pick it up as a result of your own choice. Rather, someone exercised power over you and got you to do something you would not otherwise have done. And so, instead of going to bed, going out for a pizza, or studying for your English test, here you are reading this book.

Jot down the key reasons why you are reading about American government right now. Next, read the kinds of answers you might have written, and find out what they mean with respect to the subject of power when you read the upcoming answers to Time Out 1-2.

The most effective use of rewards and sanctions often comes from the threat that they will be used: "If you don't vote with the president on this one, you can forget his support on your education bill," or, "If Congress passes that bill with the provision I oppose, I will veto that bill." If opposing players accept the threat and change their behavior, then the person making the political threat is able to change the behavior of others without actually expending political resources. Political threats about the applications of rewards or sanctions are most effective when they are credible—that is, when opponents recognize potential power and believe it will be applied unless they acquiesce.

Persuasion involves convincing someone that, based on its substantive merits, what you want is something they should support: "This bill is really the most favorable to union members for these reasons. . . ," or, "Failure to support this policy will weaken the president's position as a world leader and, in turn, weaken the United States." Persuasion is particularly important in politics, since politics generally deals with issues about which reasonable people can disagree. There is often no one right answer. Successful persuasion requires an understanding of other players' goals, a firm grasp of the relevant facts, and the ability to communicate those facts in a forceful and effective manner. The cost of persuasion is best measured in terms of the time and effort involved in convincing others to support you or your position.

persuasion *The ability to convince others to follow a desired course of action.*

Leadership refers to the personal respect, or trust, granted to some players because of their demeanor, seniority, personal charisma, and/or behavior. The successful exercise of leadership results in players supporting the leader's suggestions on the basis of trust or respect. Leaders build trust by establishing a reputation for consistently taking the interests of their followers into account and for making good decisions. As with persuasion, the cost of leadership can be measured in terms of the time and effort required to employ it successfully.

leadership *Ability to influence others as a result of demeanor, trust, or personal charisma.*

Authority is the power granted some players as a result of their formal position or rank: "I may not agree completely with him, but he is president and has the right to make such an appointment," or, "The majority of Congress has spoken, and that is the end of it," or, "The head of the agency wants it this way, and we are here to carry out her wishes." Leaders employing authority often gently—and sometimes not so gently—remind those they want to influence of their "rightful" authority. The effective use of authority requires knowing the legal basis of your positional rights, understanding others' perceptions of those rights, and employing them in a judicious manner.

authority *Power that some players have over others as the result of their rank or position.*

1-8b Finding the Best Strategy

Careful use of resources is crucial to the effective exercise of power. A basic strategy in the political game involves first trying the least expensive tactics before resorting to more expensive methods. If, for example, a president can get the Senate to approve an appointment simply because he is president (that is, he wields authority), why spend the time trying to persuade the senators or threatening them? Efficient use of resources is important because resources not used in playing one game are then available for playing the next round of the game or for playing a game in another political arena. Effective players recognize that power resources are limited.

Encouraging spectators to join the players on the field is a common political strategy. Jesse Jackson and other African-American leaders have worked diligently to increase the voter registration and turnout of African Americans to expand that group's power in American politics. In 1992 and 1996, Ross Perot attempted to activate dissatisfied voters from both parties. Candidates of all types frequently urge potential supporters to join their campaign effort, to make contributions, and to vote; often this means drawing them away from other political games. These new players represent additional resources to electoral candidates.

In analyzing political games, the goal is to discover the types of strategies that work best or are used most frequently in specific settings. The task is complicated by the varying conditions that influence strategy effectiveness. Because of the wide reach of modern communications technology, candidates unwilling or unable to adapt to the use of television, direct

Answer to Time Out 1-2

Political Power and You: A Textbook Case

- If you are reading this text because your professor told you to do so, you have been subjected to *authority* ("I am expected to do what my professor says").
- If you have developed respect for your professor or roommate and are reading this text because they said, "Hey, this is good stuff," you are responding to *leadership*.
- If your professor has convinced you that this book includes information that will be of value to you either now or in the future, you have been subjected to *persuasion*.
- If you have a test coming up and your professor has made it clear that "much of the material will come directly from the text," or if you have been told that "those who cannot discuss the text material in class will fail," you are being influenced by *rewards and sanctions*.

Your reasons for reading the text may include multiple categories or may not fit neatly into one of the previous categories. This is often true of the uses of and responses to power in the political world as well.

mail, voter profiling, the Internet, or other popular campaign methods are at a disadvantage in today's political arena. As in most competitive games, outcomes in the political game are often determined by the players' ability to adapt old strategies to new situations and ever-changing technologies.

The continuous nature of political games also affects players' behavior, sometimes constraining them. The late political activist Lawrence O'Brien took as the title of his autobiography *No Final Victories*. In politics, you must often play the game in such a way as to "live to play another day." Each conflict is only one round in a much longer game; this discourages unreasonable strategies that might create more ill will than immediate political gain.

Failure to recognize this limitation on acceptable behavior often results in spectacular failure. The Watergate scandal that led to President Richard Nixon's 1974 resignation and the Iran-Contra affair during the Reagan administration were both perpetrated by "true believers" who felt that the ends justified the means and that their actions represented a "final" solution to the perceived problem. The players involved failed to consider adequately not only the consequences of failure but also the long-term impact of their strategies in the event of success. Had the strategies involved in either incident become an accepted rule change, the nature of the American political game would have changed. It is a credit to the political system that the strategies involved in these cases were publicized and condemned, thereby discouraging corruption of the system.

The interrelatedness of political games also complicates players' choices of strategies. The strategies and behavior appropriate for one game may be less so for another. Consider the incumbent city council member who is simultaneously seeking reelection while serving as district chair for his party's relatively unpopular presidential candidate. If he decides to make a full-scale effort on behalf of the presidential candidate, he may well damage his own prospects for reelection or his ability to get things done in the city council.

One further consequence of this interrelatedness of political games is that, while we can readily identify and isolate individual games for purposes of analysis, it is important to remember that each may be a cause or effect (or even both) of others. President George W. Bush will likely appoint at least one Supreme Court justice and has appointed numerous federal court nominees. Thus, voters who entered the voting booth in November 2000 not only helped select a president but also indirectly determined several major federal court appointments.

1-8c Strategies Used in Passing NAFTA

Players employed a number of strategies in the NAFTA game. They employed power resources such as authority, leadership, persuasion, and rewards and sanctions to encourage others to do their bidding. The ultimate strategy of the proponents in the House NAFTA game was to create a coalition of at least 218 members (a majority) who may not have agreed on everything in the agreement but who were willing to cast a positive vote. The opponents, of course, were trying to build their own coalition of at least 218 negative votes. Thinking in terms of strategies raises these questions:

- Which strategies are allowable and effective in this political arena?
- Which players have the capacity to employ which strategies?

The key coalition builder in support of the NAFTA vote was President Clinton. Opponents included labor union leaders, Ross Perot, and some key Democratic Party congressional leaders. President Clinton began building the coalition by drawing on the authority of the presidency. In a rare display of agreement, he held a press conference with all living previous presidents endorsing NAFTA. He essentially argued, 'I am the president and have the legitimate right to negotiate such trade agreements.' Some members of the House bought this argument and provided an initial block of support. Opponents had a difficult time effectively using their authority.

Leadership involves convincing others to personally trust you. President Clinton met with numerous members of Congress to convince them that he was well informed on the issue and that he would not ask them to do anything foolish. In this case, President Clinton could not draw solely on his role as party leader. From the outset, much of the opposition came from within his own Democratic Party, so he needed Republican votes to win. Republicans are normally less likely to follow the leadership of a Democratic president than are Democrats. In this case, however, President Clinton used leadership effectively. Ross Perot had some ability to lead the public, but it did not translate into congressional support.

President Clinton then tried to use logic and data to persuade members of Congress that NAFTA was good for the country and good for them. He and his supporters employed public opinion polls and economic projections to argue that "what the president wants is really what you want." The opponents, of course, were simultaneously using their own information to argue for the opposite conclusion through press conferences and extensive paid advertising. The president's advantage as a persuader lay in his ability to get free media coverage for the pro-NAFTA arguments. Box 1-3: Trading in on Talk Show Politics reveals the importance of the strategy of following the audience.

Box 1-3 *Trading in on Talk Show Politics*

It was a strange place for a key policy debate and an odd line-up of participants. The debaters were not confronting each other on the floor of Congress, where the ultimate decision would be made, and, in fact, neither of the participants would vote on the policy. Instead, Vice President Al Gore and private citizen H. Ross Perot met in a sterile television studio from which the major networks were barred. Bracketing CNN television talk-show host Larry King, the two contenders argued with each other and responded to viewer calls for 90 minutes in the crucial days before the congressional vote on the North American Free Trade Agreement (NAFTA).

The televised debate over NAFTA told us as much about the changing technology of political persuasion as it did about the issue itself. By 1993 cable television had arrived, and it already reached more than 62 percent of the 94 million American homes with television sets. The major network share of prime-time television audiences declined to about 50 percent.[a] Above and beyond the domestic audience, the signal of a major cable station, CNN, reached viewers around the world. Public interest in talk shows had increased dramatically. Almost half of American adults indicated that they listen to call-in shows "regularly" or "sometimes." [b] Larry King had earlier built up his own audience and carved out his own niche as a relatively safe venue for political debate. In 1992 H. Ross Perot had announced his intention to seek the presidency on "Larry King

continued

Box 1–3 Trading in on Talk Show Politics

—Continued

Live," and both George H. Bush and Bill Clinton took their turns before his microphones.

The White House decision to challenge Perot over NAFTA was risky. The Democrats were behind in the vote tally in Congress, and presidential speeches and arm-twisting seemed to have reached their limit. Perot was a made-by-television political force, while adjectives such as "wooden" and "boring" were generally used to describe Al Gore. But the White House hoped to beat Perot at his own game by provoking him "into blowing his cool, into getting visibly mean and verbally abusive when cornered." [c] Gore was a good choice for this task. Verbal aggressiveness would not be expected, and if the strategy backfired, the president would not be tainted. The White House, therefore, had a many-sided agenda. They wanted to rescue NAFTA. And they also hoped to discredit Perot, who it was expected would challenge Clinton again for the presidency in 1996.

The first sign that the strategy was working showed up in the audience figures. The debate drew the highest rating in history of any regularly scheduled cable television program. Almost twelve million households tuned in—almost ten times Larry King's average audience at that time. AT&T estimated an astonishing 2.2 million phone calls to the program. More than 17,000 of them came from outside the United States.

Consistent with White House expectations, testy Ross Perot came out swinging. According to more than one commentator, he "shot off his mouth and shot himself in the foot."[d] He began by ridiculing former presidents and secretaries of state who supported NAFTA. He spent much of the evening complaining that he was not being allowed to answer the questions. His constant whine of "Are you gonna listen? Work on it!" came off as petty.

For his part, Vice President Gore "conducted himself like a talk show thug, continually interrupting, stepping on the other fellow's lines. . . . Instead of dry facts, he took command of the low ground where Perot is often found. . . . He resorted to personal attacks, answering the wild charges about lobbyists with personal experiences dealing with Perot as a lobbyist." [e] Perot seemed to have found his match and was forced to resort to calling Gore a "liar," the clear "cry of a stymied debater."[f]

The "food fight between Vice President Gore and Ross Perot" [g] may not have raised the substantive level of debate, but it had clear political payoffs. Gore was almost universally declared the winner by the media. Public opinion polls also indicated that 59 percent of the viewers scored the vice president as the winner compared to 32 percent for Perot. More importantly, support for NAFTA in the population increased from 34 percent to 57 percent.[h] Immediately after the debate, telephone calls to congressional offices that had been lopsidedly opposed to NAFTA reversed their preferences, and at least seven formerly undecided House members announced that they would support the agreement.[i]

When the NAFTA vote finally occurred, participants and observers alike credited the debate on "Larry King Live" with being a significant factor in the president's victory. In the broader sense, choosing to debate on a cable talk show demonstrated that Clinton and Gore had "learned to exploit the new media." This event was "just the latest sign that American politics has been unalterably changed by new techniques of communication."[j]

a. "NAFTA Debate Tops Cable Ratings," *The Plain Dealer*, November 12, 1993, 13C.
b. Times Mirror Center for the People & the Press, "The New Political Landscape," press release, October 1994.
c. William Safire, "A Sputtering Perot Gets Gored," *The Atlanta Journal and Constitution*, November 12, 1993, A13.
d. Matt Roush, "Words with Staying Power," *USA Today*, December 27, 1993, 3D.
e. Marvin Kitman, "Gore's NAFTA Knockout," *Newsday*, November 11, 1993, 121.
f. Safire, A13.
g. David Broder, "Country Saw the Wrong Debate," *The Plain Dealer*, November 13, 1993, 7B.
h. *Business Times*, November 12, 1993.
i. Ed Siegel, "Camera Ready," *The Boston Globe*, November 14, 1993, 73.
j. John Jacobs, "Perot Loses at His Own Game," *Sacramento Bee*, November 11, 1993, B6.

As the final vote approached and the strategies of authority, leadership, and persuasion had not created a winning coalition for either side, both sides relied on the strategy of rewards and sanctions. The anti-NAFTA forces had to rely on future threats. Capitol Hill was bombarded with letters, telegrams, telephone calls, and emails in which people argued that NAFTA would lead to economic hardships and the voters would punish supporters at the polls. Labor leaders were more specific, threatening to go after NAFTA supporters in the 1994 election.

The president, however, had more immediate rewards to distribute. To blunt the electoral threats, President Clinton sent supporters a "cover" letter, indicating that he would "discourage NAFTA opponents from using this issue against pro-NAFTA Members, regardless of party, in the coming election."[8] He then broadened support for NAFTA by changing the content of the agreement to include specific protection for crops such as sugar, citrus, and wheat, picking up crucial support from members in such states as Florida. He gained support from some key southern members by extending the phase-out of textile quotas. While President Clinton could not make specific commitments to changing NAFTA itself, he promised to "do what he could" to protect various industries, put pressure on organizations to assure environmental cleanup, and enforce labor standards.

While most of the concessions from the president were related to trade with Canada and Mexico, he did troop out some benefits that had no relation to the issue at hand. For example, one member received a commitment to have military cargo planes built in her district and three others were promised international air routes from their districts to London.[9] One congressional NAFTA supporter argued that toward the end the White House dealt like "a bazaar, open for business to buy favors."[10]

In the end, the president and his supporters simply had more resources and a broader range of strategies to use. The opposition's foreboding predictions and vague threats could not compete with the president's immediate promises and rewards.

1-9 Winning, Losing, and the Object of the Game

It is often said, "It doesn't matter whether you win or lose, but how you play the game." Even so, for individual players the object of most games is to win. In most political games, the object of players is to assure that a particular government policy, or set of policies, will be favorable to themselves, their families, or their organization.

1-9a Types of Games

The definition of winning varies from game to game. In the game of checkers you either win or lose, and the winner does so at the expense of the loser. Two winners and no losers is not possible. Such games are called **zero-sum games**. In these games, the payoff for the winner is absolute and comes from the loser; that is, what the winner wins the loser loses. Most recreational games fall into the zero-sum category, as do some political games—notably, elections. The electoral contest between presidential candidates, for example, is a zero-sum game in which one candidate's victory comes at the direct expense of the other candidates.

zero-sum games *Games with a finite payoff in which a player's winnings are gained at the expense of the other player or players*

Many political games are not zero-sum but **positive-sum games** in that more than one player can "win." A congressional compromise that allows the passage of a public law that meets some of the needs of all or most of the players involved is an example of a positive-sum game.

positive-sum games *Games in which most, if not all, of the players gain as a result of playing the game.*

In politics, a **negative-sum game** is also possible. In such games, all or most of the players are likely to lose something. Thus, "winning" becomes a matter of losing less, rather than gaining more. Battles over budget cuts are classic examples of negative-sum games. The players who "win" are those whose budgets are cut the least.

negative-sum games *Games in which most, if not all, the players lose something as a result of playing the game.*

Another complicating characteristic of political games is that players are often not the only ones affected by the outcome. Political decisions often affect nonplayers, whose interests may not have been taken into account by decision makers. The decision to close a military base, for example, may be made by a few players within the military bureaucracy whose primary goals are to increase military effectiveness and to save money. That decision, however, is likely to have an adverse impact on the owners of the restaurants and convenience stores near the base, as well as on civilian employees at the base, none of whom may have been aware the game was being played. These spillover effects,

externalities *Consequences of political strategies and games that affect other players not directly involved in the game.*

whether negative or positive, are called **externalities** and will be further discussed in Chapter 19, "Domestic Policy: Social Programs and Regulatory Policy."

Throughout this book, as we consider who wins and who loses in American politics, we will look for ways in which the game's basic elements—the playing field, the players and arenas, the rules and strategies—determine the outcomes. We will concentrate particularly on discovering *patterns* of winning and losing, and the ways in which these patterns can or should be changed. The ultimate winners or losers, of course, are the American people, whether they are active players, interested spectators, or unaware bystanders.

1-9b Winning and Losing the NAFTA Game

The object of all serious games is to win. The assessment of winners and losers in politics invites questions such as:

- Who are the winners and losers in this round?
- Just what do the winners win?
- What role do resources, skills, and/or luck play in winning or losing?
- To what degree is there a consistent pattern of winning and losing?

The headlines largely tell the story of the immediate winners and losers in the NAFTA battle:

- **"Vote Deals Big Defeat to Labor"** (*The Cleveland Plain Dealer*, November 18, 1993)
- **"Clinton Wins Major Battle on Free Trade"** (*The Arizona Republic*, November 18, 1993)
- **"House Gives Trade-Pact Victory to Clinton With 16 Votes to Spare"** (*Minneapolis Star Tribune*, November 18, 1993)

Subsequently, many of the Democrats in strong labor union areas had their political base weakened in the 1994 election because of their support for NAFTA. A large percentage of the more than fifty House Democratic incumbents who lost in 1994 could blame part of their defeat on their NAFTA vote. The long-range impact of NAFTA on the U.S. economy will determine the ultimate winners and losers.

The NAFTA vote in the House was largely the result of the skillful use of resources by the president. He was lucky that the ideology and previous commitments of many Republicans led them to support NAFTA without inducements. It was, however, a costly victory. New expectations were created concerning the president's willingness to bargain. When it came to subsequent policy initiatives, such as health care reform, President Clinton was not able to repeat his performance.

The policy process is a continuous game. There was little time for NAFTA supporters to glory in their victory. New policy battles needed to be fought on different playing fields, with new sets of players, under different rules, employing distinct strategies, and resulting in widely differing winners and losers. Box 1-4: The NAFTA Game Checklist summarizes the NAFTA battle and applies the key concepts of the game analogy.

1-10 Theories of the Game

In any game, the various players and spectators tend to have their own theories of how the game really works. These explanations do not always coincide. Your cousin, for example, may believe that owning Boardwalk is the key to winning at Monopoly®, while your sister may be certain that victory depends on acquiring all four railroads, and as early as possible. (If that's what they really think, it should be easy for you to beat them!)

Observers of American politics, including political scientists, have advanced a number of competing explanations of how the American political game works. These theo-

Box 1-4 The NAFTA Game Checklist

The Playing Field
The congressional vote on NAFTA was played out in an international and domestic and institutional culture that defined acceptable behavior.

The Rules
NAFTA was subject to the general rules of Congress, with the exception that implementation of the fast-track provision reduced some of the potential for delaying tactics.

The Players
Officially, NAFTA involved players from three countries and all three branches of American government.

A variety of unofficial players representing interest groups and the media became deeply involved.

Players brought with them personal ideologies and political goals that affected how they interpreted the facts surrounding NAFTA.

The Strategies
The passage of NAFTA involved building a political coalition in Congress.

As coalition manager, President Bill Clinton utilized a wide array of power resources.

The Winners and Losers
In the short term, President Clinton was the big winner by being able to deliver on his campaign promise, while Republicans were able to satisfy the interests of their business constituency.

Mexico won a new lease on life for its shaky economy.

Labor unions lost both on the substantive issue and in their image as critical players.

Some Democratic members of Congress paid a political price for their support of NAFTA in the 1994 elections.

In the long run, the actual economic and social impact of NAFTA will determine the ultimate winners and losers.

ries of the game offer quite different explanations for who, in the words of well-known political scientist Harold Lasswell, "gets what, when, and how." [11]

While there are many forms of democratic political systems, they all have rules that clearly limit the power of the rulers, and they all emphasize citizen involvement in governmental decisions. The most commonly advanced theories of how democratic politics works are:

- Elitism
- Pluralism
- Republicanism
- Participatory democracy

Table 1-3 shows these four theories arranged along a continuum, from least democratic to most democratic. The **authoritarian system** is included as a point of contrast for all forms of democracy.

authoritarian system *System of government whereby power is concentrated in a leader or an elite group without accountability.*

Classification is an important part of developing knowledge. While no actual political system absolutely fits any of the theoretical classifications shown in Table 1-2, they do serve as benchmarks for distinguishing between differing views of government. Each idealized model of the democratic political game embodies a different set of rules. These rules lead to variations in terms of players, arenas, acceptable strategies, and the pattern of winning and losing.

1-10a Elitism

elitism *Theory of political power in which key political decisions are made by a small number of skilled, committed persons.*

Elitism is the system in which most, if not all, key political decisions are made by a relatively few powerful individuals who have similar social characteristics and outlooks. This

Table 1-2 Theories of the Political Game

Least Democratic				Most Democratic
Autocracy (Authoritarianism)	**Elitism**	**Pluralism**	**Representative Democracy**	**Participatory or Direct Democracy**
Citizens are not involved in the selection of governmental leaders or in the decisions made by government. Decisions are made by an autocrat or dictator.	A single set of leaders controls all games and determines governmental decisions. Leaders seek to be self-perpetuating.	Multiple political games encourage different levels of citizen involvement. Different sets of leaders are influential in different policy areas.	Government officials are responsible to the constituents who elect them. Through the electoral process, constituents communicate their interests and concerns to governmental leaders.	Citizens serve as governmental leaders and make policy decisions through meetings of all citizens.

group is known as the political elite.[12] In the elitist view of the political game, there are few players and many spectators. The players determine not only the outcome of the game but also the rules.

Those who believe that the elitist view is the most accurate description of the American political system argue that most citizens have little real interest in politics and are, at best, spectators. These citizens are content to leave control of the game to a relative handful of more skillful, able players. Thus, while the elites must attend to public opinion to retain popular support, they have considerable leeway in choosing their policies. Their fundamental problem, in fact, is maintaining the elite group. For this reason, current elites carefully screen all future members of the elite to ensure their "acceptability."

Dramatic shifts in public policy are uncommon in an elitist system. Elites fear such shifts, especially those caused by popular passions or the short-term perspective of the average citizen. They go to great lengths to maintain control over the outcome of important political games. Because, under ordinary circumstances, this desire of the elites meshes well with the political apathy of most citizens, an elitist system is highly stable.

1-10b Pluralism

pluralism *Theory of political power in which there are multiple opportunities for participation.*

Pluralism offers a different theory of the political game.[13] Where elitists see one game controlled by a small group of players who are only broadly accountable to the mass of citizens, pluralists see many games—so many games, in fact, at so many levels, that virtually everyone can play if they so choose. To be sure, most of those who play involve themselves with only a few of the possible games, but everyone has the opportunity to play at some level.

Pluralists recognize that not all games are equally accessible or of interest to all potential players. Some games clearly are more open than others, and many require a particular kind of skill to be played successfully. Thus, while those interested in a particular kind of policy—public education, for example—may have little influence on, or interest in, another kind of policy—say, defense—so their place in the defense policy game is taken over by others who do and who have the necessary skills and motivation.

Pluralists are not concerned with the dominance of any specific elite. They contend that the elites who exercise power in one area of public policy seldom have similar power in other areas. In the pluralist view, different elites are more likely to be in competition—for scarce government funds, for example—than in league with one another. From this perspective, the existence of conflict encourages compromise, makes for better policy, and motivates the players most involved in any particular policy area to reach out for public support. Pluralism encourages grassroots participation and ensures that the game remains democratic overall.

1-10c Representative Government

A third explanation of the American political game is known as **representative government.** Those who explain the game in this fashion believe, somewhat as elitists do, that relatively few citizens participate in the day-to-day business of government. Unlike elitists, however, representative theorists believe that the primary cause of citizen nonparticipation lies not in apathy but in the pressures of everyday life. These pressures, they argue, all but force average citizens to leave politics to others while they concentrate on meeting the demands of their career, family, education, or social life. As a result, they delegate responsibility for political decision making to their elected officials, who are, in turn, directly responsible to those from whom they receive their mandate, the public. Some observers call this a "small 'r' republican" form of government to distinguish it from purer forms of democracy.

representative government *Theory of political power in which citizens or constituents choose others to represent their interests in government decision making.*

A representative system is democratic because the leading players are chosen by and are directly accountable to their **constituents**—the groups and individuals whose interests they represent and are expected to protect. Elections are the most important mechanism whereby public officials are held accountable. If dissatisfied, constituents can vote an incumbent out of office at the next election. In his or her place, they can elect a new representative they believe will be more attuned to their interests and needs. Public opinion polls and direct communications with policymakers also serve to keep policymakers aware of and attuned to the wishes of the people.

constituents *Persons who elect a person to office or to whom an appointed official is accountable.*

Policymakers in a representative system think in terms of constituents whom they must "look out" for. While we normally think of only elected officials as having constituencies, appointed officials—bureaucrats and judges, for example—also have individuals, groups, or sets of interests to whom they feel accountable. In this sense, they, too, have constituencies. Thus, in a republican system, there may be relatively few players who are active on a day-to-day level, but most are accountable to others in the public. For such a system to be truly democratic, the playing field must be designed so that all citizens have relatively equal access to some appropriate set of political decision makers.

1-10d Participatory or Direct Democracy

The simplest, most familiar—and, in some ways, most radical—theory of the democratic game is known as **participatory** or **direct democracy.** Few believe that participatory democracy accurately describes how the American political game operates today. Yet, it represents the "purest" form of democracy and is the model from which all other forms of democracy have evolved.

participatory (direct) democracy *Theory of political power in which all or most players participate directly in all political decisions.*

In a participatory democracy, all citizens are players. Everyone plays the game, regularly participating in day-to-day political decisions. The New England town meeting, where all of the citizens meet to thrash out local issues and to make local policy, is the classic example of participatory democracy.

1-10e NAFTA and Theories of the Game

One could describe the NAFTA battle using any of the theories of the game. Much of the initial negotiation between top national leaders looked pretty elitist, involving a relatively narrow set of perspectives. As the issue developed, people representing a large number of competing interests began to get involved and pluralism was evident. As the issue moved to Congress and members attempted to protect the economic and environmental interests of their constituents, the representative tendencies held sway. In attempting to create a winning coalition, both sides used public opinion polls and the media, which created a more participatory democracy. The debate between Vice President Al Gore and Ross Perot on "Larry King Live" attempted to move the process in the same direction.

Characterizing the entire process into one of the categories is difficult and reflects the complexity of the political game.

1-10f Evaluating the Theories of the Game

The theories of the democratic game provide quite different descriptions of the game, as well as different predictions concerning who plays and where, how they play, and who wins and who loses. They also suggest different descriptions of the game's character: An elitist game is highly stable. Pluralist politics, on the other hand, is often dynamic and unpredictable, precisely because the coalitions that are its dominant feature tend to be unstable. The same is largely true in a representative system, although the degree of unpredictability is somewhat less, given the more limited number and more permanent nature of the players.

Regarding these theories, two quite different questions may be asked:

- Which offers the most accurate description of the way the American political game is played?
- Which offers the best description of the game as it should be played?

The same person could answer these two questions in altogether different ways.

You might feel, for example, that pluralism offers the best overall description of how the American political game is actually played, while you might also believe that direct democracy is the way it should be played.

The primary drawback of direct democracy is that it requires so much work from all players. Assembling the hundred or so citizens of a small New England town and conducting a discussion of local issues—during which each citizen may conceivably express an opinion on each issue and react to the ideas offered by other participants—is difficult enough. As the numbers involved grow larger, the effort needed to organize discussion and the time required for all to speak increase dramatically. The idea of the town meeting is a notion that lies at the heart of the American political game, but it no longer describes the way the game is played except in a few small communities where issues and players are limited.

1-11 Technology and the Changing Game

For some, technology holds the promise of a return to something approaching a town meeting. Communication and electronic technology could one day allow everyone to participate in the day-to-day decisions of a democratic government. The American political game might come to resemble direct democracy far more closely than it does at present.

Presidential candidate Ross Perot raised this issue in the 1992 election campaign, suggesting that "electronic town meetings" might be organized, and that suggestion has become a reality in recent elections. In such meetings, citizens vote via two-way television cable or telephone lines on policy proposals being debated in Washington. President Clinton and Vice President Gore regularly used **teleconferencing** to interact with citizens. In the NAFTA battle, both sides attempted to use talk-show radio and television to stimulate public concern, concluding with a highly publicized debate on the issue between Vice President Gore and Ross Perot. After the 1994 elections, newly selected House Speaker Newt Gingrich (R-Ga.) began his term of office with a commitment to more computerized citizen access to Congress. The 2000 and 2004 presidential election processes were marked by extensive use of the Internet for fundraising and communications. Cable television technology allows for two-way communication between voters and their candidates. The primary motivation behind such technology was to allow consumers who see products marketed on television to purchase them through the cable system. Citizens could use this same technology to vote on issues under consideration by policymakers or candidates for office. Today's candidates use cell phones and palm pilots extensively to communicate with their staff; eventually they may use them to communicate with voters as well.

teleconferencing *An interactive technology using computer-based digitized video to allow a two-way conversation between individuals or groups.*

The 2004 presidential contest saw former Vermont governor Howard Dean race to the front of the pack of Democratic candidates by urging his supporters to use the Internet to arrange face-to-face "meet-up" events and to raise funds. Both George W. Bush and Senator John Kerry recognized the potential and quickly began tapping the Internet for fund raising and as an unregulated vehicle for distributing their hardest-hitting political advertisements to their most ardent supporters.

1-11a The Role of Technology: Catalyst, Player, Issue

Even if we do not now have direct democracy, technology is changing the game of politics and raising new issues for politicians to consider. Of prime importance is the role that technology plays in the collection, storage, and dissemination of information relevant to political games and the implementation of public policies. Information transfer is the core technology of politics. As such, it is central to the efforts of all players who try to influence the outcomes of games through communication.

Technologies such as the electronic media and computers of all sorts alter the playing field and influence the likelihood of player success, the applicability of old rules, and the effectiveness of new strategies. In these ways, technology can change both the nature of the game and its outcome.

The impact of technology on the political game is not a new phenomenon. However, the pace of technology-induced changes continues to accelerate with each passing year. Such terms as the **new politics, teledemocracy,** and **cyberdemocracy** have become part of the political lexicon as computers and television have come to play an increasing role in American politics.

new politics *A set of political strategies relying on new communication technologies and the personal appeal of candidates.*

teledemocracy *The harnessing of techniques, such as televised town meetings with the capability of two-way communication and remote voting, to increase citizen participation.*

cyberdemocracy *Political strategies using new computer-based technological tools, such as email and the Internet.*

Many important questions arise. Some have to do with the degree to which government should promote or control technology:

- Do computer data banks threaten individual privacy?
- Does government have a responsibility to provide equal access to technology?
- Do candidates have a right to free television time?
- Is the public really competent to participate in the political game electronically or in any other way?
- Should political activists be allowed to purchase all the technology their resources allow?
- Should all aspects of the game, as it is played in the legislature executive offices and the courts, be televised live?
- Does technology even the playing field or exacerbate current inequalities?

Such issues are discussed where relevant throughout this book.

1-12 Looking Back at the NAFTA Vote

In this chapter's attempt to apply the game analogy to a particular political decision, we hope to have convinced you that the game analogy is a good tool for understanding American politics and government. We view the analogy as a "checklist" of factors that help assure that our analysis will not miss anything important. Forgetting to analyze the formal and informal rules would have given us an imperfect picture of the NAFTA battle. Identifying the players helped us understand who would have influence on the decision and who would not. Recognizing the variety of political strategies applicable to this case indicated both the range of strategies available and the fact that only certain strategies work in specific settings. Distinguishing the winners in the NAFTA battle revealed a great deal about the skill of players and the utility of strategies but also pointed out the initial setting for the next round of play.

1-13 Looking Ahead: The Plan of the Book

In the chapters that follow, we examine the processes and institutions of American politics by discussing the nature of the playing field, the arenas, the rules, the players, the relevant strategies, and the winners and losers.

1-13a The Context of American Government

In Part 2 (Chapters 2-5) we will examine the context of American government. Chapter 2, "The American Constitution," focuses on the framework the Constitution provides for the American political system. The various arenas prescribed in the Constitution are examined, along with the rules associated with decision making in each arena. Chapter 3, "Federalism," describes the legal basis of American federalism and changing patterns in federal, state, and local relationships. The question of civil liberties as a prerequisite for democracy is considered in Chapter 4, "Constitutional Rights and Civil Liberties." In Chapter 5, "American Political and Economic Culture," the basic elements of political culture—that is, long-standing beliefs about how the political system should function—are examined. This chapter also outlines the basic character of the American economic system, which affects, and is affected by, the political system.

1-13b Mediating Institutions

Part 3 (Chapters 6-8) focuses on some of the ways the primary players in American politics come together to inform the public and organize their political wishes. Chapter 6, "The Mass Media," considers the modern media that both report on the conduct of American politics and influence governmental decision making. Included in that chapter is a description of how electoral candidates and representatives of political causes use the media to convey their messages to potential voters and decision makers. Chapter 7, "Interest Groups," explores the ways individuals organize into interest groups, making it possible for them to either directly or indirectly become players. Once organized, interest groups attempt to win victories for their policy preferences. Political parties are the focus of Chapter 8, "Political Parties." Parties concentrate players into teams and employ strategies designed to win elections.

1-13c The Process of American Government

Democracy involves individuals taking action on their beliefs. Part 4 (Chapters 9-11) focuses on these processes. Chapter 9, "Public Opinion," explores the aggregate beliefs and opinions of the U.S. population. The wishes of its citizens are the basis of a democratic government. In Chapter 10, "Political Participation," we look at the varieties of options for political participation and explore the nature of participants and non-participants in each realm. The hallmark of democratic government is free elections. The campaign and election process is analyzed in Chapter 11, "Campaigns and Elections."

1-13d Policy-Making Institutions

In Part 5 (Chapters 12-18) our attention shifts to the institutional arenas in which governmental decisions are made. Later chapters focus on the Congress, the presidency, the federal bureaucracy, the courts, and state and local governments. In examining each of these arenas, we discuss the rules that govern decision making, the unique way in which players are selected, the strategies commonly employed by the players involved, and the patterns of winning and losing. The chapter examines the uniqueness of each, while attempting to outline ways in which institutions cooperate and compete for predominance in the political game.

1-13e Public Policy

The final set of chapters in Part 6 (Chapters 19-21) draws upon the material presented in earlier chapters to explore the evolution and impact of important policies enacted by the federal government. The ultimate test of who wins and who loses in American politics and government involves the policies that are adopted and rejected. Chapter 19, "Domestic Policy," presents an overview of the public policy process, tracing the evolution of policies from preliminary ideas through legislative enactment and implementation to impacts and evaluation. Chapter 20, "Civil Rights," explores civil rights in America, documenting the means through which many groups of Americans fought for and achieved their political rights. The next two chapters, on redistributive and regulatory domestic policies, consider important domestic policy issues, including social and welfare policy, regulation of the economy, environmental protection, and labor policy. Chapter 21, "American Politics in an Interdependent World," examines the interdependency of the American political system with the politics of other nations, including consideration of both foreign policy and national defense. The final chapter reexamines the principal features of the game of American politics, including playing fields, arenas, rules, and strategies, and considers future developments in the playing of political games.

Key Terms

arena
authoritarian system
authority
coalition
constituents
continuous games
cyberdemocracy
discrete games
elitism
externalities
Federalism
government
leadership
lobbyists
negative-sum games
new politics
norms
participatory (direct) democracy
persuasion
players
playing field
pluralism
political culture
politics
positive-sum games
power
public opinion
representative government
rewards
rules
sanctions
strategy
tariff
technology
teleconferencing
teledemocracy
zero-sum games

Practice Quiz

1. The attitudes reflected in political culture and public opinion differ largely in terms of their
a. time perspective.
b. intensity.
c. substantive content.
d. correctness.

2. The key distinguishing factor of a game is its
a. players.
b. rules.
c. winners.
d. length.

3. Power granted to some participants in the political process based on their formal position is called
a. leadership.
b. persuasion.
c. efficacy.
d. authority.

4. As defined in the chapter, the power resource of personal trust is most important when using
a. persuasion.
b. authority.
c. leadership.
d. influence.

5. Threats are a power resource relevant to the use of
a. leadership.
b. persuasion.
c. authority.
d. rewards and sanctions.

6. Games in which one player wins at the expense of others are called ______ games.
a. positive-sum
b. negative-sum
c. zero-sum
d. continuous

7. One would expect the greatest amount of political involvement by citizens in a democratic political system described as
a. elitist.
b. pluralist.
c. idealist.
e. direct.

8. ______ is the core technology of politics.
a. Monetary favoritism
b. Logical calculation
c. Emotive assessment
d. Information transfer

9. Most U.S. citizens can best be called ______ in terms of their involvement in the political game.
a. spectators
b. players
c. apathetics
d. elitists

10. Persuasion is important in politics, since politics deals with
a. absolutes that must be ingrained through culture.
b. issues over which reasonable people can disagree.
c. emotions that are either suppressed or expressed.
d. republican principles as old as the nation itself.

You can find the correct answers to these questions by taking the quiz and then submitting your answers in the Online Edition. The program will automatically score your submission. Where you miss a question, the program will provide the correct answer, a rationale for the answer, and the section number in the chapter where the topic is discussed.

Further Reading

A fascinating account of American politics that uses the game approach is presented by noted journalist Hedrick Smith in his book *The Power Game: How Washington Works* (New York: Random House, 1988).

Descriptions of different approaches to the game of politics are presented by Willis D. Hawley and Frederick M. Wirt in *The Search for Community Power* (Engelwood Cliffs, NJ: Prentice-Hall, 1968).

For classic discussions of elitist approaches to political power, consult Floyd Hunter, *Community Power Structures* (Chapel Hill, N.C.: University of North Carolina Press, 1953) and C. Wright Mills, *The Power Elite* (New York: Oxford University Press, 1956, 1963). The pluralist perspective is reflected in Robert A. Dahl's *Who Governs?* (New Haven, CT: Yale University Press, 1961).

An interesting treatment of the impact of technology on the future of humanity is presented in Albert H. Teich (ed.), *Technology and the Future* (Belmont, CA: Thompson/Wadsworth, 2003).

An engaging insight into the role of image-making in the political game is presented by Michael Kelly in "David Gergen: Master of the Political Game," *New York Times Magazine*, October 31, 1993, 62-71.

For discussions of the Impact of the Internet on politics see: Richard Davis, *The Web of Politics* (New York, Oxford University Press, 1999) and Peter M. Shane, *Democracy Online* (New York: Routledge, 2004).

For a current rationale for pluralism, see William A. Galston, *The Practice of Liberal Pluralism* (New York: Cambridge University Press, 2004).

Endnotes

1. Marc Sandalow, "House Approves NAFTA," *The San Francisco Chronicle*, November 18, 1993, A1.
2. Hedrick Smith, *The Power Game: How Washington Works* (New York: Random House, 1988), xiv.
3. Richard Alm, "U.S. Trade Negotiations Veering Off the Fast Track," *The Dallas Morning News*, September 19, 1994, 1D.
4. John Aloysius Farrell and Michael Putzel, "House Gives Clinton Win," *The Boston Globe*, November 18, 1993, 1.
5. Federal News Service transcript, White House press stakeout, 1 October 1993, LEXIS-NEXIS database.
6. Federal News Service transcript, November 15, 1993, LEXIS-NEXIS database, and Gary Marsh, "Norman Mineta: World War II Injustice Drives His Political Life," *Business Journal—San Jose*, May 2, 1994, 12.
7. Quoted in Farrell and Putzel.
8. Ann Devroy and Kenneth Cooper, "Hopeful White House Edges Toward NAFTA Win," *Washington Post*, November 17, 1993, A1.
9. Sarah Anderson and Ken Silverstein, "All the President's Handouts," *Harper's Magazine*, March 1944, vol. 288, no. 1726, 21.
10. Farrell and Putzel.
11. Harold D. Lasswell, *Politics: Who Gets What, When, How* (New York: Smith, 1950).
12. See, for example, Floyd Hunter, *Community Power Structures* (Chapel Hill, N.C.: University of North Carolina Press, 1953), and C. Wright Mills, *The Power Elite* (New York: Oxford University Press, 1956, 1963).
13. See, for example, Robert A. Dahl, *Who Governs?* (New Haven, CT: Yale University Press, 1961).

2

The American Constitution: Establishing the Rules of the Game

Key Points

- The origins of American government in the colonies.
- First efforts to create a united government under the Articles of Confederation.
- The components of the U.S. Constitution of 1787 and the rules about citizen participation, the powers of the national government, and the system of checks and balances.
- The contents of and purposes for the Bill of Rights.
- The reasons for and the process of amending the Constitution.

Preview: The Founders and Their Challenge

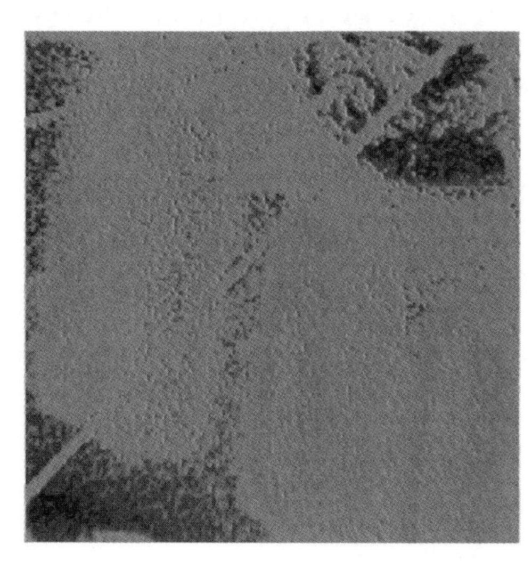

The players were experienced professionals of the day. The rules were quite explicit: maintain secrecy, avoid the media, and work in private. The strategy was to come to decisions without the help or interference of those most likely to be affected by the decisions. Day after day, the selected few trudged to the meetings for prolonged and often rancorous discussion. They arrived with their personal agendas and biases, and they acted on their explicit desires to protect and promote the interests of those who sent them. Heated debates over basic principles occurred regularly, requiring seri-

Scene at the Signing of the Constitution, by Howard Chandler Christy
Library of Congress, Prints & Photographs Division [LC-USA7-575]

ous compromise. The final product of their secret efforts would have to be sold to a much larger group.

The scene just sketched has been repeated millions of times as corporate boards of directors plan strategies for new products, as coaching staffs outline their approaches to next year's season, as editorial boards plan what will be reported in the next day's news, and as criminals scheme their next set of drug deals. What was different about the meetings in Philadelphia in 1787 was that these secretive strategists were planning nothing less than a new government. Furthermore, it was a new democratic government, one that would be based on broad public participation and that would require forfeiting much of the emphasis on secrecy. The strategy of secrecy was used at this convention so that all points of view could be expressed by participants and so that many different types of compromises could be debated—all free of immediate public scrutiny. The Founders that met in Philadelphia sought to make their plans known only after they had a complete new plan for government drafted and ready to present to the people.

The new constitutional rulebook (and its initial amendments) undermined secrecy by encouraging a free press and by dividing power among competing institutions that might use and/or threaten public disclosure as an effective political strategy. Ironically, the U.S. Constitution, forged in secrecy, came to establish a government in which official secrecy became less acceptable than in virtually any other country. The shift to open government was not complete or immediate. Seldom again, however, would such complete secrecy legitimately dominate the American political decision-making process. It was behind closed doors that the basic American principle of "open covenants openly agreed to"—the assurance of open government in the future—emerged.

When Americans think about the Constitution and the founding of their nation, they probably picture a group of immortal figures meeting in the redbrick statehouse in Philadelphia to write a legendary document. While the Founders were talented individuals made larger than life by history, they were also real people. They differed in their views about how a new government should be designed. The Constitution, which has served as the guiding force of our democratic political system for more than two centuries, did not emerge easily from quiet discussions among those who shared identical views about governing. Instead, it was created through a process of argument, discussion, debate, and compromise.

Americans may know the names of some delegates to the Constitutional Convention, but who were they? What do we know about their backgrounds? Box 2-1:Who Designed the Constitution? presents information on the social and economic backgrounds of these political players.

In creating the Constitution, the Founders recognized that they were designing the rules that would govern how future political games would be played. Whatever they came up with had to take into account the American states and their citizens. From the outset, the players at the convention in Philadelphia saw the advantage of a national government handling those responsibilities that were too big for individual states to resolve. Primarily these were defense from foreign invasion, regulation of trade among states, and creation of a standard national currency. However, the national government was not to intrude on the governing authority of states or on the basic rights of citizens.

The Founders thus faced the fundamental challenge of creating a national government strong enough to handle its responsibilities but restrained enough to not overpower state

Box 2–1 *Who Designed the Constitution?*

Of the forty-two delegates who attended most of the meetings, thirty-nine signed the Constitution. How representative of American citizens were the Founders in the late 1700s? An overview of the occupations, economic positions, education, and political experiences of members of this group reveals some important characteristics about the players who designed the fundamental rulebook of American government:[a]

Age

The average age of the fifty-five men who attended the Constitutional Convention was 42 at a time when the median age in the country was 16 (today it is 33). Benjamin Franklin of Pennsylvania was the oldest delegate at 81 years of age, and Jonathan Dayton of Jersey (who later had the city of Dayton, Ohio, named after him) was the youngest at 26.

Attendance

Nineteen of the delegates chosen to represent their state never attended a meeting. James Madison was the only delegate to attend every meeting. His notes on the debates serve as the primary record of what went on. His journal was kept secret until after his death in 1836 and along with other papers was sold to the government in 1837 for $30,000 (the equivalent of over $400,000 today).

Occupation

The 55 Founders who met in Philadelphia represented a privileged group of Americans. Almost two-thirds of the delegates to the convention were lawyers. Smaller numbers were farmers (most with large-scale farms) and merchants.

Economic Position

The Founders were men with property. Almost all of them owned their homes, and several owned country estates or held land for speculation and profit. Three delegates held investments in manufacturing companies, and 12 had investments in banking companies. Nineteen of the Founders were slave owners.

Political Experience

Many of the Founders were not new to national politics. Three had attended the Stamp Act Congress, 7 had been present at the First Continental Congress, and 8 had signed the Declaration of Independence. Perhaps most importantly, 42 delegates had served in the Confederation Congress under the Articles of Confederation, and almost all had served in elected offices at the state level.

Education

The Founders were well educated in a period when a college education was not widely pursued. Over half the delegates to the Constitutional Convention had attended a college or university, including such schools as Princeton, Yale, William and Mary, Harvard, and the University of Pennsylvania. Other delegates were self-educated, studying the law and other professions on their own.

---

a. The descriptions of the Founders are based on data presented in Clinton Rossiter, *The Grand Convention* (London: MacGibbon & Kee, 1968), Forrest MacDonald, *We the People: The Economic Origins of the Constitution* (Chicago: University of Chicago Press, 1958), and "Fascinating Facts About the Constitution" at www.constitutionalfacts.com).

governments. As we shall see, the Founders created an American "experiment." This constitutional experiment granted powers to the national government while at the same time providing limits on that power. In other words, some, but definitely not all, governing authority was vested in a national government to be known as the United States of America. A subsequent challenge was to ensure that none of the institutions created within the national government—the Congress, presidency, and federal courts—would dominate the others.

To understand the founding of the nation, one needs first a description of how America moved from a set of loosely connected European colonies to a group of states with common concerns and interests. When they broke away from England, the colonists needed to create a new governing structure. Their first effort, the Articles of Confederation, helped them through the Revolutionary War. Soon afterward, however, the representatives of the states created by the Articles recognized that the new government was too weak to cope with the severe problems facing the new nation. Representatives of the states came together a second time in order to craft a more effective plan for a national government. This great effort produced the set of governing principles and rules known as the Constitution of the United States, which for over 200 years has provided the framework within which the games of American politics are played.

2-1 The American Colonies

In about 1600, after a long period of exploration, England and other European nations began to establish settlements in the New World. Throughout the 17th century, new colonies sprung up along the eastern coast of North America. In 1607 a shipload of settlers arrived in the New World and established Jamestown on the marshy banks of the James River in what is now Virginia. The next colonial settlement was founded in 1620 at Plymouth in New England by a group of religious separatists, the Pilgrims. They had been persecuted in England and had failed to find a suitable haven in Holland. When their ship, the *Mayflower*, was blown off course and arrived farther north than they expected, the colonists decided to create a new community at this location.

The number of colonies grew, even though harsh weather and the lack of food and other necessities made the early years difficult. Within New England, settlements arose in the areas of Maine, Massachusetts, and New Hampshire. Farther south, the colony of Maryland was created in 1634 by Cecilius Calvert, Second Baron of Baltimore, who sought both a refuge for his fellow English Catholics and a profitable venture. Settlements that began in the Carolinas in the mid-1600s eventually separated into a northern and a southern colony. Georgia, viewed by England as a buffer between the colonies and Spanish Florida, was settled by John Oglethorpe and followers in 1733.

The Landing of the Pilgrims
In 1620, the *Mayflower* carried a band of religious separatists who were blown off course to Plymouth, New England, where they created a new community.
Library of Congress, Prints & Photographs Division [LC-USCZC4-4311]

Depiction of sailing vessel used for early colonial trade.
Yanker Poster Collection, Library of Congress, Prints & Photographs Division [LC-USZC4-12371]

Increasingly, New World colonies engaged in important trade with the mother country. They provided raw materials—including lumber, indigo (a dye), furs, and, later, tobacco—that were vital for the burgeoning industries in the mother country on the other side of the Atlantic. Over time, England (Great Britain, after the union with Scotland in 1707) adopted a policy of **mercantilism,** whereby the colonies performed two functions vital to the British economy. They both provided raw materials to England and consumed goods manufactured in England. Mercantilism was an economic game with political consequences. The success of the mercantile policy for Great Britain made the colonies increasingly important to the British, who, as the 1700s progressed, took a more active role in governing colonial America.

mercantilism *Philosophy that colonies perform a subservient role to the economy of the mother country by providing raw materials and by serving as a base for the purchase of manufactured goods.*

2-1a Governing the American Colonies

Rules established by Parliament and the British Crown long before the United States was created governed the territories. Some of the colonies were initially governed by companies that received a royal charter and financed settlement. This was the case in Virginia, which was created and governed by the Virginia Company of London, and also in the Massachusetts Bay colony. Other colonies, particularly those in New England, were largely self-governing at the start.

Setting an example for government by the people, the Pilgrims, before disembarking from their ship, agreed in the **Mayflower Compact** to create a common **polity** and to abide by majority rule. Following the tradition of Parliament, representative assemblies were created in the colonies. Members of these assemblies were popularly elected. The first of these was the House of Burgesses, founded in Virginia in 1619.

Mayflower Compact *Agreement signed by the Pilgrims on the Mayflower in 1620 concerning the governance by majority rule of the Plymouth Plantation.*

polity *An organization with an agreed-upon form of government.*

By the mid-1700s, the British Crown had assumed direct responsibility for governing the colonies. The British monarch appointed colonial governors who carried out the decisions of the Crown. Assemblies representing colonial residents met to discuss issues of common concern and to provide advice to the governors. Sometimes, the governors listened to the ideas and counsel expressed in the assemblies; other times, they did not. In this political game, the colonial representatives were relatively weak players. Most of the power resided with the governors and with the British king and Parliament.

Throughout the first half of the 1700s, tensions grew between the colonies and the mother country. The colonists increasingly resented the operation of a political game in which they had little right or opportunity to participate. British authorities regulated trade and commerce to ensure a steady flow of raw materials to Britain and of manufactured goods to the colonies. The repeated efforts of Parliament and the British

Crown to tax the colonies left the colonists without a voice in the creation of tax policies. During much of the 1700s, Britain sent a military force to protect the colonists from attacks by Indians as well as by French and Spanish settlers, and the presence of these troops also served to temper early thoughts of rebellion in the colonies. But the growing presence of British authorities, along with efforts to regulate commerce and impose new taxes, caused colonists to question more forcefully the fairness of British rule.

2-1b Movement toward Unification

Tensions between Great Britain and the colonies escalated as a result of the French and Indian War, which began in 1754 and was settled by the Treaty of Paris in 1763. In spite of the British victory over the French, the war proved costly. To reduce the war debt, the British Parliament levied a tax on the colonies through the Stamp Act of 1765. The stamp tax was levied on all court documents, newspapers, periodicals, contracts, and other printed matter. For documents to be legal and for printed matter to be sold, stamps sold by British authorities had to be attached to them.

Sons of Liberty *Groups of colonists who protested coercive acts of Parliament in the period prior to the American Revolution.*

While the stamp tax had been used in England since 1694, it was immediately unpopular with the colonists. Protest groups, including the **Sons of Liberty,** formed in the colonies to oppose British taxation and oppressive rule. Their strategies included public protests and behind-the-scenes work to defeat the tax.

Responding to public resentment over the Stamp Act, the colonies sent representatives to a meeting in New York City in October 1765. This meeting was a first effort to form a political coalition to complain about British actions and taxes. This Stamp Act Congress protested to London, requesting that the stamp tax be repealed. While at first unsympathetic, Parliament reconsidered the stamp tax after the American colonists initiated a political strategy intended to cause economic harm. The tactic was **boycotting** the purchase of goods manufactured in Great Britain. Colonial women participated in this protest by refusing to purchase English-made goods and instead relied upon goods produced through their own spinning and weaving. These boycott actions hurt British merchants, who pressed Parliament to repeal the tax. Parliament did so, but, at the same time, it restated its full authority to govern the colonies.

boycott *Political action of not purchasing the goods of a nation, group, or individual, to protest its policies; the use of economic pressure to exert political influence.*

The British Parliament rubbed salt in this festering wound in 1767, when it passed the Townsend Act. This act levied duties (taxes) on paper, paint, glass, tea, and other commodities that the colonists routinely imported from Britain. The colonists were incensed at still another effort to tax without representation. Once more they boycotted British goods and organized public protests. As the boycott grew, British merchants again pressed Parliament to remove the duties. In 1770 Parliament repealed all the duties except the one on tea, which it retained to make its point that Parliament had the lawful power to tax the colonies.

The outrage sparked by this tax was magnified when Parliament enacted the Tea Act of 1773, granting the British East India Company the right to export surplus tea to the colonies, and levied a duty (import tax) on the sale of tea in the colonies. Faced with the threat of monopoly by this large British company and the prospect of being taxed on the tea without any representation in Parliament, the colonists demonstrated against British controls over the tea trade. The most dramatic protest was the well-known Boston Tea Party, in which members of the Sons of Liberty, disguised as Indians, boarded the British ship *Dartmouth*, broke chests of imported tea, and dumped the contents into Boston Harbor.

Great Britain responded harshly to the rebellion by passing the Coercive Acts of 1774. These acts (1) closed Boston Harbor until the East India Company was paid for the destroyed tea, (2) restricted the power of local meetings and of the Massachusetts House of Representatives, (3) required colonists to "quarter" (house and feed) British troops, and (4) gave colonial governors the power to relocate the trials of those accused of capital offenses to other colonies or to Great Britain.

Participants in the Boston Tea Party protested the tax on tea and British rule without colonial representation in Parliament.

Yanker Poster Collection, Library of Congress, Prints & Photographs Division [LC-USZ62-134553]

2-1c The First and Second Continental Congresses

Reminded by these strong British actions of their disadvantaged position in political games concerning colonial governance, representatives from all the colonies except Georgia met in Philadelphia in 1774.

Acting as the **First Continental Congress,** they decided to protest the heavy-handed British rule of the colonies that allowed them no representation. Great Britain ignored their protest and restated its view that Parliament had full authority to levy taxes and to take what other actions it deemed appropriate. By late 1774 the colonies had organized militias that became involved in skirmishes with British troops. The most famous of these clashes occurred in Lexington and Concord, Massachusetts, in April 1775

First Continental Congress *The 1774 meeting of delegates from the colonies to discuss what were seen as negative actions by Parliament.*

In the spring of 1775, colonial representatives met again at the **Second Continental Congress** to discuss a plan to create a formal union among the colonies. Moderates were able to persuade the more radical representatives to send an "Olive Branch Petition" directly to the king. The petition expressed colonial loyalty to the king and requested his help in convincing Parliament, the growing center of political power in Great Britain, to take back its measures against the colonies. This step was in vain, for the king refused to accept the petition. From this point on, the American Revolution was inevitable.

Second Continental Congress *Second meeting of colonial delegates; 1775, voted to send the "Olive Branch Petition" to the king; 1776, approved the Declaration of Independence; 1777, approved the Articles of Confederation.*

The Second Continental Congress reconvened in the spring of 1776. It declared the colonies independent from the mother country. This formal repudiation of Great Britain's right to rule the colonies represented nothing less than revolution. The colonial leaders sought to stake out a new political playing field where the colonies would be able to govern themselves. The Second Continental Congress created a Continental Army and appointed George Washington its commander-in-chief. It also appointed two committees, each with important responsibilities. One was given the task of drafting a statement justifying the movement for independence, while the other was charged with preparing a plan to unify the colonies under a single government. The colonies, in turn, were called on to prepare state constitutions to replace existing royal charters.

2-1d The Declaration of Independence

The first committee appointed by the Second Continental Congress produced the Declaration of Independence, which was authored primarily by Thomas Jefferson. It presented the reasons why the colonies sought to separate themselves from British rule. The document listed specific complaints about British actions and laid the roots of democracy by stating that governments derive their power from the "consent of the governed." It declared that when a government becomes destructive to individual rights, it is the right of the people to establish a new government.

The declaration's assertion that "all men are created equal" was a revolutionary expression in the political world of the 18th century. This concept of human equality opposed the customary practices of the time, which gave superior status to those with hereditary standing.[1] Throughout American history, this statement of equality has served as a basic underpinning of American democracy.

Underlying the Declaration of Independence specifically, and the American Revolution more generally, were important philosophical ideas about citizens and government. The well-educated Founders had access to the thinking of the philosophers who were the intellectual leaders of the Enlightenment in Europe. (The Enlightenment refers to 18th century Europe, a period when art flourished and philosophers created new ideas about the nature of man, the role of government, and rights of humans.) This led them to another important idea, the **social contract,** the concept that civil society results from a voluntary agreement between naturally free and equal citizens. This social contract theory is attributed to Jean-Jacques Rousseau (1712–1778), a noted French philosopher. He argued that acceptance of government and laws should be based on a common agreement of free individuals who share basic rights by nature of their humanity.[2]

social contract *Agreement among individuals to form a polity.*

The Intellectual Founding Fathers

The Founders were well read in the political philosophers of Europe and were not above borrowing their ideas with or without directly giving them credit. The following philosophers were particularly important:

John Locke (1632–1704) was an English physician and philosopher. His ideas served as the basis for Jefferson's introduction to the Declaration of Independence, which justified dissolving a government when it breaks the trust of the people by working against their will, since government originates when a free people enter into a joint contract for their collective good. Jefferson recognized the Declaration as "pure Locke."

In Locke's words:

> Whenever the legislators endeavor to take away and destroy the property of the people, or to reduce them to slavery under arbitrary power, they put themselves in a state of war with the people, who are thereupon absolved from any further obedience (*Two Treatises of Government*, 1689).[3]

John Locke (1632–1704) *English writer and philosopher who espoused the belief that men are born with inalienable rights—including rights to life, liberty and property—that the government should not have the power to restrict. Locke's work heavily influenced Thomas Jefferson as he crafted the American Declaration of Independence.*

Jean-Jacques Rousseau (1712–1778), a Swiss-born French philosopher, began his most important book, *The Social Contract*, by asserting that "Man is born free, and everywhere he is in chains." He challenged the divine right of kings as corrupting society and running counter to the social contract. He carried his ideas into education, arguing for extensive freedom for students in designing the pace and content of their learning (see his *Emile*). In the social realm, Rousseau boldly asserted that ordinary people had the right to govern themselves. His ideas reverberate through both the Declaration of Independence and the Constitution.[4]

Jean-Jacques Rousseau (1712–1778) *European philosopher who articulated the concept of a "social contract," that is, an agreement among people that sets the conditions and expectations for being a member of a society.*

Charles de Montesquieu (1689–1755) expressed a deep concern about the concentration of power, arguing for a separation of powers among the various branches of government. His ideas of "checks and balances," expressed in *The Spirit of the Laws* (1734), were further developed by Thomas Jefferson (*Notes on the State of Virginia*, 1984) and by James Madison (*Federalist 51*).

Charles Montesquieu (1689–1755) *French philosopher and jurist who proposed that governments be created with a formal separation of executive, legislative, and judicial powers.*

Also fundamental to the Declaration of Independence was the notion of **natural rights,** another contribution of John Locke, who argued that, prior to the advent of government, human beings were governed by "natural" laws that conveyed certain rights on all individuals.[5]According to Locke, these natural rights included the rights to life, liberty, and property. In addition, Locke believed that government should be built upon the consent of the governed. Governing authorities should have limited, rather than absolute, powers.

natural rights *Rights to life, liberty, property, and pursuit of happiness; based on the philosophical position that every individual is entitled to them.*

In writing the Declaration of Independence, Thomas Jefferson used the logic of both Locke and Rousseau. He directly borrowed Locke's concept of natural rights in contending that individuals have "certain unalienable Rights, that among these are Life, Liberty, and the pursuit of Happiness" (note that Jefferson substituted "pursuit of happiness" for Locke's "property"). Rousseau's social contract theory is evident in the words of the Declaration of Independence that proclaim:

> That whenever any Form of Government becomes destructive of these ends [protecting unalienable rights], it is the Right of the People to alter or to abolish it, and to institute new Government, laying its foundation on such principles and organizing its powers in such form, as to them shall seem most likely to effect their Safety and Happiness.

The important principles outlined in the Declaration of Independence continue, to this day, to serve as the philosophical foundations of American politics. (The full text of the Declaration of Independence is presented in Appendix 1; it can also be read at http://memory.loc.gov/const/declar.html.)

2-2 First Attempt at a National Government: The Articles of Confederation

To fulfill the second charge of the Second Continental Congress, John Dickinson of Delaware took the lead in drafting "The Articles of Confederation and Perpetual Union Between the States," which was considered by the Congress in closed session in 1777. After some revisions, the Congress approved the **Articles of Confederation** and forwarded this plan for a united government to the state legislatures for ratification. (The full text of the Articles of Confederation is presented in Appendix 2; it can also be read at http://www.usconstitution.net/articles.html.)

Articles of Confederation *Legal basis for the first plan of government for the United States (1776; replaced by the Constitution upon its ratification in 1788).*

The plan for a new government was based on the principle of **confederation,** whereby the balance of power lies with the states. Under this plan, the powers of the central government are weak in comparison to those of the states, who wish to retain their own governing power.

confederation *A plan by which a league of sovereign states delegates limited powers to a central government.*

As the delegates to the Second Continental Congress—and, later, the state legislatures—scrutinized and debated the Articles of Confederation, one immediate source of conflict was evident: How much power would be placed in the new confederated government? When the Declaration of Independence was issued, the colonies became independent states and their former colonial assemblies became state legislative bodies. Thus, the state governments were the first legally established form of government in the newly independent nation, and they were the primary players in building the new nation. The delegates recognized the need to create a new political game that included a national government capable of leading the revolution as well as of addressing common problems. At the same time, they wanted to protect their ability to govern their own residents.

2-2a Governing Rules in the Articles of Confederation

The Articles of Confederation specified which powers would be given to the new national government and which would be retained by the states. It proclaimed that each state would retain all powers, freedoms, and rights that were not clearly and expressly granted to the confederated government. The powers directly assigned to the confederated government included those related to national defense and foreign affairs.

The Articles of Confederation created a flawed political game. It failed to give the confederated government two important powers: levying taxes directly and regulating interstate commerce. According to the Articles of Confederation, the confederated government was to be funded through a system by which each state was given a tax quota and then was asked to pay its share voluntarily. This plan meant that the new government would depend upon the willingness of states to contribute to the national treasury. But, in making no provision to allow the new government to regulate trade among the states, the authors of the Articles of Confederation made an error that would ultimately render the Articles ineffective.

unicameral legislature *Legislature that has one house.*

The governing structure outlined in the Articles of Confederation was quite simple. The main governmental arena was the Confederation Congress, a **unicameral legislature.** The key rule for representation—determining the players—was also simple. Each state was entitled to send a delegation of representatives to the Congress, but each state would receive only one vote in the new legislature. Large states, such as New York and Virginia, had the same voting power as smaller states.

Unlike our current system, the government created by the Articles of Confederation did not have separate executive and judicial branches. However, the Confederation Congress was given power to hear disputes between states. Also, the Committee of the States, composed of 13 members (one from each state), was created to oversee day-to-day administration of the government. This body administered the affairs of the nation when the Confederation Congress was not in session. In addition, the Congress created executive departments to oversee such important functions as war, foreign affairs, and finance.

rule of unanimity *All eligible voters or voting units must vote in favor of a proposed measure before it is formally approved.*

The final provision of the Articles of Confederation concerned the method for revising the plan of confederation. Article 13 stated that the Articles of Confederation, once ratified, could be modified only through consent of all parties involved. This **rule of unanimity** concerning amendments gave each state the ability to veto any proposed modifications. This rule contributed to the eventual downfall of the Articles of Confederation, since the new government was not given the flexibility needed to deal with new and unfolding problems.

2-2b The Problems with Confederated Government

The Revolutionary War was a unifying event for the new nation. It gave the states a common purpose and required that they work together to defeat the British. When the war was formally concluded through the Treaty of Paris in 1783, the confederated government was faced with a true test of its effectiveness. Could this governing plan still work now that the common threat was eliminated and the states were returning to normal conditions? Before long, major problems with the new government were apparent.

As a result of the war, the national government had accumulated substantial debts that it found difficult to repay. The Confederation Congress, lacking the power to borrow funds or to impose taxes, struggled unsuccessfully to raise revenues and repay debts. Problems in debt repayment made other nations and private lenders reluctant to extend credit to the government.

During the post-Revolutionary War period, the nation also faced the serious instability of its currency. Much of this problem resulted from individual states printing their own paper currency, which had little or no real value—often in large amounts. Many creditors refused to accept the currency. This made it hard for people to repay debts. Because the confederated government was not empowered to issue currency or to regulate financial affairs, it could not deal with the crisis.

Another major problem facing the nation concerned trade among the states. Since declaring independence, each state had designed its own regulations about trade, commerce, tariffs, and navigation. These policies were often inconsistent across states, which made it difficult for merchants to conduct interstate trade. State policies became barriers to trade and thus hurt the development of the American economy. The Confederation Congress was largely powerless to deal with the trade problem.

These problems caused many leaders to question the ability of the government created through the Articles of Confederation to govern the new nation. The national government clearly lacked adequate powers to deal with the major crises facing the country. Calls for a convention to reconsider the structure and powers of the national government became louder.

2-3 Creating a New Constitution

The state of Virginia issued a call to other states to meet in Maryland in 1786 to discuss trade and commerce issues. Only five states sent representatives to this Annapolis Convention, where problems with governance under the Articles of Confederation were discussed. While no action was taken because so few states were in attendance, those present called for another meeting of state representatives to be held the next year in Philadelphia. After debate, the Confederation Congress agreed to the holding of a convention limited to considering revisions to the existing Articles of Confederation. However, state representatives arriving in Philadelphia in the summer of 1787 preferred a different strategy. They wanted to start from scratch and to devise an entirely new constitutional plan that would fundamentally revise the rules of the political game.[6] (Box 2-2: Faxes Take Aim at Constitutional Change explores a modern-day situation in which citizens used current technology to stop an attempt to change the Constitution. Games related to the Constitution will probably always be played as interested citizens seek to change it or preserve it intact.)

As the Preamble to the document that emerged from the Philadelphia meeting clearly states, its purpose was twofold. The representatives strove to create a "more perfect Union"—one more effective than that realized under the Articles of Confederation.

Box 2-2 *Faxes Take Aim at Constitutional Change*

Concerned citizens armed with fax machines successfully aborted what they perceived as a plot to strengthen global government, to weaken the power of the states, and to rewrite the U.S. Constitution. They took aim at a proposed Conference of the States, which had been supported by the nation's legislative leaders and states' governors. After the 1994 elections, two conservative governors proposed the conference, which was to be authorized by resolutions coming from all state legislatures. The goal was to find ways to reclaim power from the federal government, which they felt was too bureaucratic and outdated in the global marketplace. The sponsors hinted that if the federal players failed to respond, a constitutional convention might be necessary.

The very mention of a constitutional convention and of the importance of the global marketplace immediately rallied a group of citizens called "constitutionalists." Michael Kazin, a history professor at American University, viewed their concerns as stemming from three decades of social and economic upheaval. Globalization had cost them jobs and presented the menace of global government running American lives. Encroachment into civil liberties has created fear; expansion of federal regulations was just one sign of government going beyond the scope of the Constitution. They did not like the present state of federal government, but, unlike the conservative establishment, they saw a constitutional convention as an even bigger danger. The basic rulebook was not to be tampered with, they affirmed.

The group embraced a number of segments of the American population. It and its fight against the Conference of the States (among other causes) was not, however, dominated by extremist militias but by urban, educated, and nonviolent—although angry—men and women. Former PTA president Linda Liotta, whose home had become one of thousands of outposts of a new grassroots political movement, was one of them. Mrs. Liotta discovered that the Council of State Governments, a sponsor of the proposed Conference of the States, received backing from many multinational companies. This was a red flag that she felt proclaimed, "Big organizations, funded globally, can dictate the agenda in our states." Previously active in fighting the health care plan proposed by the Clinton administration, she formed Americans for America, one of the networks of fax machine users who made common cause out of what appears to be little common ground, building mushrooming fax and computer networks of angry taxpayers, property rights groups, states' rights groups, gun owners, home schoolers, right-to-lifers, John Birchers, and Christian patriots.

Joining Linda Liotta's network that was pressuring state legislators were several other grassroots groups and even the AFL-CIO labor organization, which viewed the anti-Washington tone of the Conference of the States proposal as a threat to workplace protections. The Conference was shelved after only 14 states passed resolutions supporting it. A new round of play was suggested by its advocates: a federalism summit—with no state legislature support requested.

Source: Dale Russakoff, "No-Name Movement Fed by Fax Expands," *Washington Post,* August 20, 1995, A1, 22.

They also wished to establish justice, maintain domestic peace and security, provide national defense, and secure the benefits of liberty for current and future citizens of the nation.

2-3a The American Experiment in Constitutional Design

The Founders recognized the importance of creating a new model of government. They understood that the rules and institutions they were creating through the Constitution would structure future political thought and action and would directly influence the roles and powers of the states they represented. The result of their work—the American "experiment" in democratic governance[7]—would stand eventually as a model for citizens of other nations who sought to fashion democratic government. Furthermore, the Founders were wise politicians and strategists. They approached the making of the Constitution from a strategic perspective. They sought to protect the interests of their states as they designed rules for future political efforts in the new nation. While they debated the Constitution, the Founders raised both broad and fundamental political issues as well as strategic issues related to the anticipated impact of constitutional provisions on future politics.

Early in the deliberations in Philadelphia, George Washington, the revered leader of the Revolutionary War, was selected as president of the convention. To encourage open debate on issues, convention members decided that their meetings would be held secretly.

As the convention progressed during that hot summer in Philadelphia, decisions were made about the structure of a new national government, the powers and functions

---

Questions for Thought
The Constitutional Text

The full text of the Constitution is included in Appendix 3; it can also be read at http://www.house.gov/Constitution/Constitution.html. Take some time to read through this important document, and then consider the following questions:

In the Preamble: What is the basic rationale and underlying philosophy in the Constitution for the new governmental system to be created through it?

In Article I: What are the primary powers and responsibilities granted to Congress? Who is eligible to serve in Congress? What are the similarities and differences in the two legislative branches, the House of Representatives and the Senate?

In Article II: What are the primary responsibilities of the president? Who is eligible to serve as president? How are presidents chosen?

In Article III: What are the primary responsibilities of the Supreme Court? How is the Supreme Court organized, and who is eligible to serve on the nation's highest court?

In Article IV: What process will be used to admit new states into the Union?

In Article V: How can the Constitution, once ratified, be amended?

In Article VI: What process is spelled out for the original ratification of the Constitution? What is the role of state ratifying conventions?

As the rulebook that guides the structure and operation of the U.S. government, the Constitution is amazingly brief. In comparison, the constitutional documents of most states are much longer and far more detailed than the U.S. Constitution. As you read through this text, you may wish to keep a bookmark in Appendix 3 so that you can refer to constitutional language relevant to discussions presented later in this section and to subsequent sections throughout the text.

---

of governmental institutions, the players who could participate in governmental institutions, and rules about how governmental decisions would be made. The Constitution established three branches within the national government. Congress, composed of two houses (a **bicameral legislature**), was given the responsibility for making laws. The presidency was designed primarily as an office to oversee the execution of public laws. The third institution, the federal judiciary, was empowered to judge conflicts that arose through the execution of laws. The Supreme Court was created to be the highest court in the nation. The first issue in creating a new national government involved its relationship to the states.

bicameral legislature *A legislature with two chambers.*

2-3b Rules about Representation

Determining how the various states would be represented in the national government was a difficult problem, but not a new one. When the states came together earlier to discuss and design the Articles of Confederation, the same question had arisen. The fundamental issue concerned whether states should be represented equally or proportionately, on the basis of population.

Delegates to the Constitutional Convention recognized that rules about representation would influence the relative powers of the states and their citizens. Two teams of players emerged concerning the representation issue: the larger states and the smaller states. The more populated states saw a strategic advantage in pressing for representation rules based on population, which would give larger states more representation than smaller ones. The states with smaller populations emphasized the tradition of the Articles of

Table 2-1

Key Features of the Virginia Plan, the New Jersey Plan, and the Constitution

Virginia Plan	*Issue*	*New Jersey Plan*	*End Compromise*
Bicameral Legislature	Structure of Congress	Unicameral Legislature	Bicameral Legislature
Both chambers to be based on state population	Representation in Congress	Each state to have equal representation	Each state equally represented in the Senate; representation in the House of Representatives based on state population
Single executive to be selected by Congress	Structure of executive	Multiple executives to be selected by Congress	Single executive selected by the Electoral College
Removal by Congress	Removal of executive	Removal by majority of state legislatures	Removal by Congress through bicameral impeachment procedure
National court system; judges appointed for life by Congress	The courts	No national court system	National court system; judges appointed for life by president with consent of the Senate

Confederation and pressed for the principle of equal representation, a plan that would prevent domination by larger states, such as New York, Pennsylvania, and Virginia.

Virginia Plan *Proposal drafted by James Madison and presented at the Constitutional Convention that reflected the interests of larger states.*

New Jersey Plan *Submitted by William Patterson of New Jersey on behalf of smaller states at the Constitutional Convention. It called for equal representation of states in a one-house legislature.*

Great Compromise *Agreement at the Constitutional Convention concerning representation of the states; creation of a two-house legislature, the Senate with equal representation and the House of Representatives with representation based on population.*

James Madison championed the cause of the larger states. Under the **Virginia Plan,** which he authored, the national legislature was to be composed of two houses (echoing the structure of the British Parliament), with the members of each house apportioned on the basis of population and selected for office by popular election. The smaller states countered with an alternative representation plan. Their design, known as the **New Jersey Plan,** called for a one-house legislature in which each state had equal representation (as under the Articles of Confederation). The question of representation was divisive and might even have scuttled the convention altogether if a compromise had not been forged. Fortunately, a resolution known as the **Great Compromise** was struck. Congress would be composed of two houses: a Senate and a House of Representatives. Representation in the House would be allocated proportionately among the states based on population. The Senate, on the other hand, would be a smaller body in which all states would be equally represented.

Acceptance of the Great Compromise allowed the convention to resolve what was probably the biggest point of contention. It was one of the first instances in American politics of a positive-sum game, where all sides won. The larger states would wield proportional political power in the House of Representatives, while the smaller states would share power equally in the Senate.

2-4 Governing Institutions: Powers and Functions

Besides grappling with the issue of representation, the Founders spent substantial energy in conceptualizing and designing the institutions of the new national government. The Constitution outlines the branches of the national government, the functions of these branches, and the rules for selecting persons to serve in these institutions.

2-4a Rules about Powers Granted to Congress

While state delegations were split with regard to representation, they were more united when it came to formulating rules that set out the legitimate powers of the national government. The Founders came to Philadelphia with a shared vision. They recognized the need to strengthen some powers of the national government while protecting the powers, rights, and privileges of state governments.

As shown in Appendix 3, Section 8 of the first article of the Constitution spells out the powers granted directly to Congress, as follows:

- Because convention delegates recognized that defense was most appropriately provided at the national level, the Constitution delegated to Congress the power to establish an army and a navy and to declare war (see Figure 2-1).
- To allow the national government to deal with the financial crisis facing the nation, the Constitution granted Congress the powers to levy taxes, borrow money, coin money, and punish counterfeiters.
- To resolve the chaos surrounding commerce among the states, the Constitution granted Congress the power to regulate interstate trade by devising and enforcing uniform regulations concerning trade, tariffs, and navigation.

necessary and proper clause *Provision of the Constitution empowering the national government to enact laws required to enforce the powers granted to it in Article I, Section 8; known also as the elastic clause.*

implied power *The authority that, though not explicitly granted by the U.S. Constitution, is inferred based on a broad interpretation of the necessary and proper clause.*

At the end of the list of powers granted to Congress, the Founders inserted a clause that stated that Congress shall have the power "to make all laws which shall be necessary and proper for carrying into execution the foregoing powers." This important provision, known as the **necessary and proper clause,** stipulated that Congress has the **implied power** to pass all laws necessary to exercise its powers.

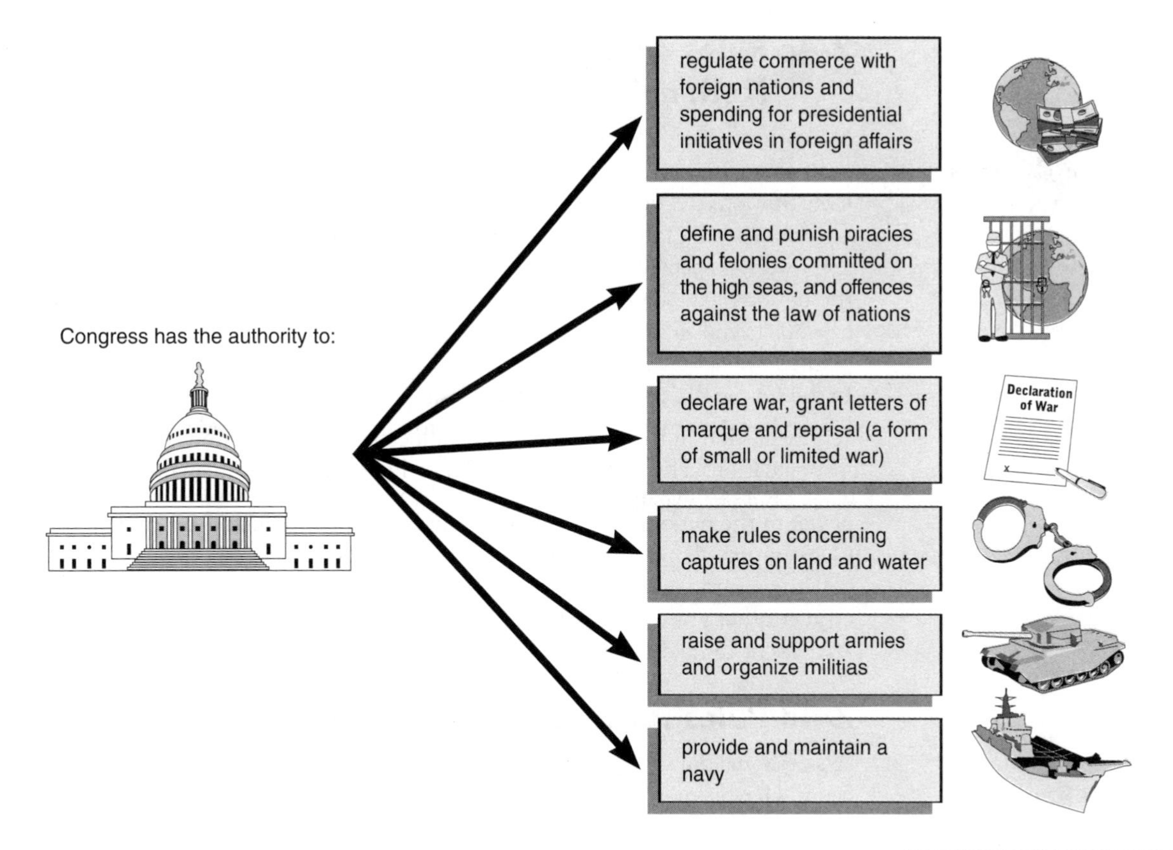
Congress has the authority to:
regulate commerce with foreign nations and spending for presidential initiatives in foreign affairs
define and punish piracies and felonies committed on the high seas, and offences against the law of nations
declare war, grant letters of marque and reprisal (a form of small or limited war)
Declaration of War
make rules concerning captures on land and water
raise and support armies and organize militias
provide and maintain a navy

Figure 2-1
Foreign Policy Powers of Congress

2-4b Rules Limiting Congressional Power

Section 9 of the first article of the Constitution includes provisions designed to protect personal liberties from encroachment by Congress. Among the powers denied to the national legislature is peacetime suspension of the **writ of habeas corpus.** This important provision protects persons from being arrested for a crime and left in prison indefinitely without having been formally charged. Similarly, the Constitution prevents Congress from passing a **bill of attainder** (a law declaring someone guilty of a crime without a trial) or an **ex post facto law** (a law that makes a past action illegal and punishable at the time the law is enacted).

writ of habeas corpus *Legal order directing a person or authority holding someone as prisoner to bring that person before judicial authority to determine the lawfulness of imprisonment.*

bill of attainder *Legislative act that declares an individual guilty of a crime without a trial and punishes the person.*

ex post facto law *Law that makes some action taken in the past illegal and punishable at the time the law is enacted.*

Convention delegates were deeply divided about the question of slavery. Two teams of players, divided along regional boundaries, emerged. The slave system was defended by representatives of southern states, where slaves were central to the plantation economy. The southern states preferred that the Constitution include no prohibitions against or interference with slavery. They also wanted to count slaves as part of the population figure that determined the state's proportionate membership in the House of Representatives. Many delegates from northern states argued that slavery should be either abolished or restricted.

The slavery issue was resolved with another compromise. Congress was prohibited for 20 years (until 1808) from passing laws about the importation of slaves. For the purpose of figuring the number of seats in the House of Representatives, states were allowed to count three-fifths of their slaves in the population.

Some historians have denounced the Founders for their unwillingness to deal more forthrightly with the issue of slavery. Others have suggested that direct confrontation on the slavery issue might have so divided the delegates that the convention would have been torn apart. The delegates clearly followed a strategy at the convention of deciding not to decide. To move the convention forward, the parties agreed to postpone the issue. That did not, however, end the quarrel for long, for within a few decades, the slavery issue was hotter than ever and sparked a civil war within the nation.

2-4c Rules about the Supremacy of National Government

supremacy clause *Constitutional provision declaring that, should the Constitution, treaties, or laws of the national government clash with those of state governments, the national ones shall be supreme.*

Notwithstanding the preceding prohibitions on governing power, the Constitution includes, within Article VI, the **supremacy clause,** which states that, when the Constitution, treaties, or laws of the national government conflict with those of a state government, the former are supreme. When Congress enacts a law that is clearly within its powers as specified in the Constitution and that law conflicts with a state law, then the national law shall be the supreme law of the land.

At several times in the nation's history, the supremacy clause of the Constitution has granted the national government superior status over the states in important policy issues. In the Voting Rights Act of 1964, for example, the national government banned the use of literacy tests in voter registration. This provision countered and nullified the laws in some states and localities that required those wishing to register for voting to pass a literacy test.

You might wonder why the Founders, ever concerned about amassing too much power in the national government, would decide to include the supremacy clause in the Constitution. Their intent was to strike a practical balance between giving the national government too much power, something they feared greatly, and creating a national government that was too weak to function effectively, as had been their experience with the Articles of Confederation.

2-4d Rules for Selecting Governmental Players

A simple maxim of most games is that you have to be able to play in order to win the game. Hence, rules about player participation are crucial to the outcome of political games. Several sections of the U.S. Constitution outline rules about selecting players for governmental institutions. These rules help determine who can be players and the process by which players are selected for office.

The Constitution places an age restriction on some players. To be eligible for election, members of the House of Representatives must be at least 25 years old, senators must be at least 30 years old, and the president must be at least 35. In addition, representatives and senators must have been citizens for 7 or 9 years, respectively, before their election. Also, the president must have been born in the United States.

Selecting Members of Congress

The rules about selecting players vary by governmental branch. For Congress, the Founders agreed that members of the House of Representatives would be popularly elected for 2-year terms. In this way, the House would reflect the direct will of the people. The theory was that frequent elections would require representatives to meet regularly with their constituents (people who live in their legislative district) during election campaigns and to consider constituent opinions between elections.

Despite their belief in democracy and government by the people, the Founders were concerned about the force of the public will. They feared that the mass of voters might have their passions "whipped up," that they would be incautious and perhaps demand actions they would later regret. For this reason, the Senate was designed as a body that would deliberate slowly and thoroughly. It would be partially insulated from rapid swings of public opinion. In the words of Thomas Jefferson, "We pour legislation into the Senatorial Chamber to cool it [of the public passions]."[8] To achieve this end, senators were given longer terms of office (6 years). Senatorial terms were also staggered so that one-third of the members would stand for election every 2 years. Thus, it would take 6 years and three different elections to unseat the entire Senate.

The Founders decided that senators would be selected by their respective state legislatures. By so doing the Founders intended to forge a link between the state and the national legislatures. This provision of the Constitution was changed in 1913 through the 17th Amendment, which stipulated that senators be selected by popular elections in each state. By this time there was strong sentiment in the nation that members of each House of Congress should be selected by popular election.

Selecting the President

Constitutional Convention delegates proposed many different plans for choosing the president. These included presidential selection by (1) popular election, (2) election by Congress, (3) election by state legislatures, and (4) election by a group of electors selected within each state.

In an effort to conclude their business, but without much enthusiasm, convention delegates accepted the fourth option, a plan for an **Electoral College.** Under this plan, each state selects a number of electors equal to the total number of senators and representatives from the state. Today, electors are chosen by popular elections held in each state. The electors meet in their respective states, vote for presidential candidates, and forward tallies to the president of the Senate. The individual receiving a majority of the electoral votes is elected president. Should no person receive a majority, the election is decided in the House of Representatives. (This system is discussed in more detail in Chapter 11, "Campaigns and Elections," and Chapter 14, "Presidency: Selection and Structure.")

Electoral College *The collective name for individuals chosen by majority vote in each state to cast that state's ballots for president.*

2-4e Rules Designed to Balance the Powers of Governmental Branches

To control the power of the national government, the Founders designed a plan—called the system of **checks and balances**—to counterbalance the power of individual branches (see Figure 2-2). This system creates a political game in which each of the three branches of government has some ability to limit the power of the other two. This plan followed the theory of French philosopher Charles de Montesquieu (1689–1755), who argued that governing power could be effectively limited by dividing it among multiple branches and by making the power of the branches interdependent.[9]

checks and balances *Assignment of government powers so that the powers of one branch of government may be used to limit the powers of another branch.*

Perhaps the most prominent example of checks and balances is the power of the president to check the lawmaking powers of Congress by vetoing a law enacted by Congress.

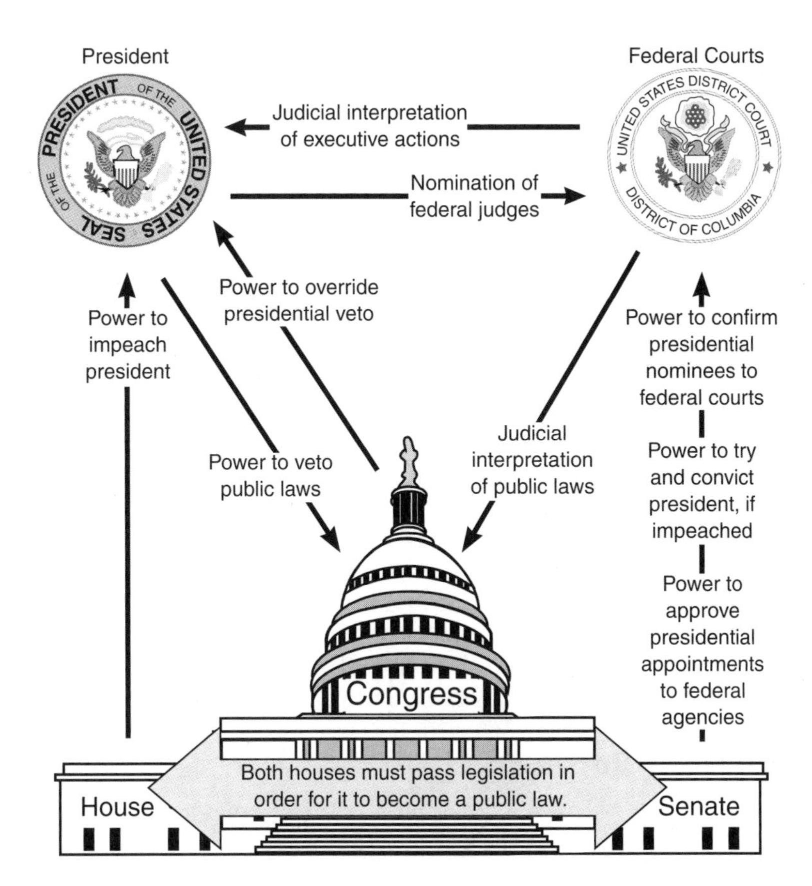

Figure 2-2
The System of Checks and Balances among Branches

The presidential veto is not absolute, however. Congress can respond to the veto check through an override vote that requires a two-thirds majority vote in both houses.

The Constitution also gives Congress the power to check the actions of the president. The Senate, for example, must approve—that is, give advice about and consent to—many types of presidential appointments, including appointments made to the federal courts and to top positions in the federal bureaucracy.

The Senate also must approve all foreign treaties negotiated by the president before they can take effect. In this regard, the Senate played a key role in considering and approving the North American Free Trade Agreement (NAFTA), analyzed in detail in Chapter 1. Both the Senate and the House can also check the president's power as commander in chief of the armed forces by limiting appropriations for military activities.

The federal courts, too, are involved in the system of checks and balances. Federal judges are appointed by the president and confirmed by the Senate, which allows the legislative and executive branches to determine judicial membership. Congress is empowered to remove from the bench, through impeachment and conviction, judges who have committed crimes or who have violated their oath of office. One balancing power that is not explicitly stated in the Constitution, but that has evolved in practice is the power of the federal courts to determine the constitutionality of laws passed by Congress or of actions taken by the executive branch (see Chapter 17).

Comprehending the purpose and structure of the system of checks and balances is fundamental to understanding the game of American politics. The system—part of a broad plan to create a national government with limited rather than dominant powers—was a relatively new invention at the time the nation was founded.

separation of powers *The allocation of governmental powers among the three branches of government so that they are a check on one another.*

James Madison wrote eloquently about the system of checks and balances, defending the **separation of powers** as a means to keep the overall power of the national government in check:

> It is agreed on all sides that the powers properly belonging to one of the departments [branches] ought not to be directly and completely administered by either of the other departments [branches]. It is equally evident that none of them ought to possess, directly or indirectly, an overruling influence over the others in the administration of their respective powers.[10]

2-5 Amending and Ratifying the Constitution

One of the profound weaknesses of the Articles of Confederation was its provision that changes required unanimous consent by all the states. The Founders sought to avoid this problem without making it too easy to change the Constitution. They feared that frequent modification could create instability and uncertainty in the political game.

2-5a Rules about Amending the Constitution

The delegates to the convention decided on two alternate methods for amending the Constitution. One requires both the House of Representatives and the Senate to approve constitutional changes by a two-thirds vote. If this vote is achieved, the amendment must be forwarded to and approved by three-fourths of the states, either in their state legislatures or in special conventions.

Under the second plan, a constitutional convention is called if requested by two-thirds of the states. This convention proposes amendments to be submitted to the states. Again, three-fourths of the states must approve the amendments before they are formally accepted as part of the Constitution. Thus, in both plans, the states play a primary role in approving changes to the Constitution, the nation's fundamental rulebook.

ratification *Formal approval of a legal document, for example, the Constitution.*

2-5b Rules for Ratification

A final issue to be resolved by the attendees at the Constitutional Convention concerned a process for **ratification** of the proposed Constitution. Remember, the delegates themselves were empowered by their states to meet in Philadelphia only to discuss *modifying* the Articles of Confederation. They did not have the power to formally accept the Constitution on behalf of their states. The states themselves needed to give their approval.

According to the last provision, Article VII, the proposed Constitution was to be submitted to each state, which would then call a special constitutional convention. Each state convention, to be composed of citizens of the state, would be charged with the tasks of reviewing the proposed constitutional language and making the decision about ratification for the state. Approval by nine state conventions (representing acceptance by nine of the thirteen colonies) would ratify the Constitution, thereby creating the new government of the United States.

Political interests motivated the decision to use special conventions to ratify the Constitution. Many of the delegates in Philadelphia feared that political leaders in their states, especially those in state legislatures, would oppose some or all of the provisions of the proposed Constitution. The delegates anticipated that some ensconced politicians would be jealous of the powers being granted to the national government. The Founders therefore preferred a plan whereby the Constitution would ultimately be approved by the people rather than by state government officials. The special ratification conventions were an answer to these worries, placing the ratification decision in the hands of individual citizens outside of formal institutions of state government.

2-5c The Struggle for Ratification: Federalists versus Anti-Federalists

The plan for the national government outlined in the Constitution faced multiple hurdles before being formally adopted. The first hurdle was review by the Confederation Congress. Next, the Constitution was scrutinized by the states. Opinions in the nation were divided, and it was unclear, at the start, whether there was sufficient support in the country to ratify this new plan for a United States.

As debate and discussion about the newly drafted Constitution ensued, two teams of players emerged. The **Federalists** felt the Constitution would create a political situation with a stronger and more effective national (or federal) government. The **Anti-Federalists,** fearing the national government would be too powerful and infringe upon state and individual rights, opposed all or part of the governing plan outlined in the proposed Constitution. These opposing forces lobbied on behalf of their positions at both state and national levels. In the end, the Federalists were victorious, but only after a long and often bitter struggle.

Federalists *Individuals who supported the ratification of the Constitution as drafted in Philadelphia in 1787.*

Anti-Federalists *Individuals who opposed all or portions of the proposed Constitution and encroachment on local power.*

2-5d Review of the Proposed Constitution by the Confederation Congress

The Confederation Congress was the first battleground for the Federalists and Anti-Federalists. Following the lead of Richard Henry Lee of Virginia and Nathan Dane of Massachusetts, the Anti-Federalists made two proposals. They urged the Confederation Congress either to refuse to send the proposed Constitution to the states or to forward it with a letter describing how the convention had violated its mandate to revise the Articles of Confederation. This group also recommended that the Confederation Congress modify the Constitution, including the addition of a "bill of rights." The Federalists strongly opposed these actions, arguing that the Constitution should be forwarded directly to the states with a resolution of approval and without any amendments.

This conflict, like so many during the drafting of the Constitution, was resolved through a strategy of compromise that gave something to both sides. The Confederation Congress voted to send the proposed Constitution to the states with no resolution, either favorable or unfavorable. With this move, the ratification was thrown into the laps of the states.

2-5e Ratification Struggles in the States

For the next 4 years, the states debated ratification. Some—including Delaware, Pennsylvania, and New Jersey—ratified the Constitution before the end of 1787. The strategy of the Federalists was to push for rapid action, with the intent of creating momentum toward ratification. Generally, the smaller states were the first to ratify because they often saw advantages in a stronger national government. Residents of Georgia, for example, felt that a stronger national government would be able to provide protection from Indian attacks.

The strategy of the Anti-Federalists was to slow down the decision process. They believed that, upon reflection, the American people would see beyond their enthusiasm for ratification and develop doubts about the proposed powerful national government. They argued that violations of personal liberty could result from the powers granted to the national government in the proposed Constitution.

Besides oral discussions and debates, arguments about the proposed Constitution were presented in pamphlets designed to sway citizen views about the Constitution. While there were many such pamphlets, perhaps the most well known and influential were the essays known as *The Federalist*, which presented forceful arguments in support of ratification (see Box 2-3: Persuasion as Political Strategy for excerpts from writings by Federalists and Anti-Federalists). Although written by Alexander Hamilton, James Madison, and John Jay, the essays were signed only "Publius" so that the arguments contained within them would be judged without regard to the reputation and political positions of the authors. Today, *The Federalist* is a primary source of theoretical justification for the provisions of the U.S. Constitution. (The full texts of *Federalist* No. 10 and *Federalist* No. 5 are presented in Appendices 4 and 5, respectively.)

While ratification moved forward relatively quickly in the smaller states, the larger states, with the exception of Pennsylvania, were slower to act. These states had more power and wealth and thus had more to risk through federation. On June 21, 1788, the Constitution was formally adopted when New Hampshire became the ninth state to ratify it.

At about the same time, and without knowledge of the vote in New Hampshire, Virginia voted to ratify the Constitution—but only after long debate and with reservations. In this state, the debate concerning ratification centered on the fiery oratory of Patrick Henry, an Anti-Federalist, versus the studied logic and wisdom of James Madison, who strongly supported ratification.

Perhaps the most heated battle for ratification took place in New York, where, at the start, it appeared that the Anti-Federalists would win the day. The news that another large state, Virginia, had voted to ratify the Constitution was, however, a blow to the Anti-Federalists. While it was hard to conceive of a United States without New York, it was also difficult for New Yorkers to picture themselves outside of the Union. After further debate, New York agreed to ratify the Constitution while expressing dissatisfaction that no declaration of citizen rights was included.

By the end of 1788, 11 states had ratified the Constitution, and plans were initiated to elect the first U.S. Congress. Two of the original 13 states—North Carolina and Rhode Island—took several more months before finally ratifying the Constitution.

2-6 The Bill of Rights: Initial Changes to the Constitution

The ratification of the Constitution did not resolve all controversies. Several states had ratified the Constitution with the recommendation (but not the requirement) that changes should be made, or a second constitutional convention would have to be called to consider amendments.

The concerns that remained about the Constitution were basically those raised by the Anti-Federalists during ratification debates. First, many people were unhappy that

Box 2–3 Persuasion as Political Strategy—Arguments for and Against the Proposed Constitution

After the proposed Constitution was completed in Philadelphia in 1787, it moved to the states, where special conventions considered ratification. During this period, proponents (known as the "Federalists") worked on the side of ratification, while their opponents (the "Anti-Federalists") argued that constitutional ratification would create a dangerously powerful national government. Debates about ratification were carried out in newspapers and pamphlets. Prominent among published treatises representing the pro-ratification side were a series of essays together known as *The Federalist*. On the opposing side, essays were written against ratification, including those written by George Mason and Richard Henry Lee of Virginia and Robert Yates of New York.

The paragraphs below present a few quotations from these pro- and anti-ratification essays. As you read through these contrasting passages, ask yourself about the key differences in the positions of the two sets of players, the Federalists and the Anti-Federalists. Consider the following questions:

> What were the principal reasons the Federalists supported ratification? What did the Anti-Federalists fear about ratification?
>
> What did each side think about the potential for the system of checks and balances to curb national governmental power?
>
> What position did each side take concerning the impact of population size and diversity on the creation of a new national government?
>
> What did the Federalists and Anti-Federalists think about the powers being granted in the Constitution to the national government?

The Pro-Ratification Position

Introducing the *Federalist* essays (Alexander Hamilton addresses the question of whether good government can be created through reflection and choice):

> It has been frequently remarked that it seems to have been reserved to the people of this country, by their conduct and example, to decide the important question, whether societies of men are really capable or not of establishing good government from reflection and choice, or whether they are forever destined to depend for their political constitutions on accident and force. If there be any truth in the remark, the crisis at which we are arrived may with propriety be regarded as the era in which that decision is to be made... (Alexander Hamilton, *Federalist* No. 1, 1787)

On the system of checks and balances (James Madison notes that the system protects against one branch usurping inordinate power):

> But the great security against a gradual concentration of the several powers in the same department consists in giving to those who administer in each department the necessary constitutional means and personal motives to resist encroachments of the others...Ambition must be made to counteract ambition. (James Madison, *Federalist* No. 51, 1787)

On the impact of population size and diversity (Madison declares that size and diversity prevent against tyranny of the majority and oppression):

> The smaller the society, the fewer probably will be the distinct parties and interests composing it; the fewer the distinct parties and interests, the more frequently will a majority be found of the same party; and the smaller the number of individuals composing a majority, and the smaller the compass within which they are placed, the more easily will they concert and execute their plans of oppression. Extend the sphere and you take in a greater variety of parties and interests; you make it less probable that a majority of the whole will have a common motive to invade the rights of other citizens. (James Madison, *Federalist* No. 10, 1787)

On the powers granted to the national government (Madison supports the Constitution's list of powers necessary for effective operation of the national government):

> We have now reviewed, in detail, all the articles composing the sum or quantity of power delegated by the proposed Constitution to the federal government, and are brought to this undeniable conclusion that no part of the power is unnecessary or

continued

Box 2–3 Persuasion as Political Strategy—Arguments for and Against the Proposed Constitution

—Continued

> improper for accomplishing the necessary objects of the Union. The question, therefore, whether this amount of power shall be granted or not resolves itself into another question, whether or not a government commensurate to the exigencies of the Union shall be established; or, in other words, whether the Union itself shall be preserved. (James Madison, *Federalist* No. 44, 1787)

The Anti-Ratification Position

Introducing the Anti-Federalist position (the author reminds readers that the important question of ratification has substantial future implications):

> The most important question that was ever proposed to your decision, or to the decision of any people under heaven, is before you, and you are to decide upon it by men of your own election, chosen specially for this purpose. If the constitution, offered to your acceptance, be a wise one, calculated to preserve the invaluable blessing of liberty, to secure the inestimable rights of mankind, and promote human happiness, then, if you accept it, you will lay a lasting foundation of happiness for millions yet unborn; generations to come will rise up and call you blessed... But if, on the other hand, this form of government contains principles that will lead to the subversion of liberty—if it tends to establish a despotism, or what [is] worse, a tyrannic aristocracy; then, if you adopt it, this only remaining asylum for liberty will be shut up, and posterity will execrate your memory. (Attributed to Robert Yates, *Brutus* I, 1787)

On legislative checks and balances (the author warns that legislative bodies will be so similar in terms of composition that little effective checking of power will result):

> To produce a balance and checks, the Constitution proposes two branches in the legislature; but they are so formed, that the members of both must generally be the same kind of men—men having similar interests and views, feelings and connections—men of the same grade in society, and who associate on all occasions... Senators and representatives thus circumscribed, as men, though convened in two rooms, to make laws, must be governed by the same system of politics; the partitions between the two branches will be merely those of the building in which they sit: there will not be found in them any of those genuine checks and balances... (Attributed to Richard Henry Lee, *Letters from the Federal Farmer XI*, 1788)

On the impact of population size and diversity (the author sees differences regarding population size and diversity as threatening to effective governance):

> The territory of the United States is of vast extent; it now contains near three millions of souls, and is capable of containing much more than ten times that number. Is it practicable for a country, so large and so numerous as they will soon become, to elect a representation, that will speak their sentiments, without their becoming so numerous as to be incapable of transacting public business? It certainly is not.
>
> In a republic, the manners, sentiments, and interests of the people should be similar. If this be not the case, there will be a constant clashing of opinions; and the representatives of one part will be continually clashing against those of another. (Attributed to Robert Yates, *Brutus*, I, 1787)

On powers granted to the national government (the author expresses concerns about the potential for national government to threaten liberty):

> There appears to me to be not only a premature deposit of some important powers in the general [national] government—but many of those deposited there are undefined, and may be used to good or bad purposes as honest or designing men shall prevail. (Attributed to Richard Henry Lee, *Letters from the Federal Farmer IV*, 1787)

the Constitution did not include a declaration that specified the rights of individuals and prohibited governmental actions that infringed on those rights. While the concept of inalienable or natural rights was espoused in the Declaration of Independence, such rights were, for the most part, not directly addressed in the Constitution. Second, critics of the Constitution feared that the powers granted to the national government threatened state sovereignty.

During its first session, the new Congress addressed these persistent concerns about the Constitution. James Madison took the lead in drafting an initial set of constitutional amendments that were scrutinized, debated, and reworded. Eventually, the Congress approved 10 amendments that we now refer to as the **Bill of Rights.**

Bill of Rights *The first ten amendments to the Constitution that spell out many civil rights and liberties of citizens.*

Most of the 10 amendments focus on rights that American citizens now take for granted: freedom of speech, religion, and the press, protection from unreasonable searches, and due process protection when governmental action affects life, liberty, and property (see Box 2-4: Components of the Bill of Rights; these civil liberties are discussed in more detail in Chapter 4, "Constitutional Rights and Civil Liberties").

Box 2-4 Components of the Bill of Rights

The Bill of Rights was enacted by Congress in 1789 and ratified in 1791.

Amendment 1: Freedom of Religion, Freedom of Press, Freedom of Assembly, Freedom to Petition Government

Congress may not:

a. Establish an official religion
b. Interfere with religious freedom
c. Prohibit free speech
d. Abridge the right to a free press
e. Abridge the right to peaceably assemble
f. Prevent people from petitioning the government for redress of grievances

Amendment 2: Right to Bear Arms

Since a well-armed militia is necessary for the security of a free state, the right to bear arms will be guaranteed.

Amendment 3: No Quartering of Soldiers

In peacetime, no soldier may be quartered in a home without the consent of the home owner. In time of war, soldiers may be quartered only in a manner prescribed by law.

Amendment 4: Protection from Unreasonable Searches and Seizures

Citizens have the right to be secure in their persons and property against unreasonable searches and seizures. Search warrants shall not be issued without probable cause.

Amendment 5: Right to Life, Liberty, Property

Individuals may be held to answer for capital offenses or serious crimes only if indicted by a grand jury. No person shall be tried for the same crime twice. Individuals may not be compelled to serve as witnesses against themselves. No individual shall be deprived of life, liberty, or property without due process of law. The owners of private property taken for public use shall receive just compensation.

Amendment 6: Protections in Criminal Trials

Accused persons in criminal trials shall have the right to a speedy and public trial by an impartial jury. These persons have the right to be informed of the nature of the accusation against them, to obtain witnesses in their favor, and to have the assistance of legal counsel.

Amendment 7: Suits at Common Law

In civil suits at common law, the right to a trial by jury is preserved. Examination of facts in jury trials shall be conducted by the rules of common law.

Amendment 8: No Excessive Fines or Bails; No Cruel or Unusual Punishment

Excessive fines are forbidden. Cruel and unusual punishments shall not be inflicted.

Amendment 9: Protecting Rights Not Enumerated

The assignment of rights in the Constitution does not deny other rights retained by the people.

Amendment 10: Powers Reserved to the States and to the People

The powers not delegated to the United States government by the Constitution, nor prohibited to the states, are reserved to the states or to the people.

Note: The precise wording of the amendments contained in the Bill of Rights is included in Appendix 3, "The Constitution."

Two of the amendments in the Bill of Rights seek to constrain the power of the national government. The 9th Amendment states that the assignment in the Constitution and the Bill of Rights of particular rights to the people (for example, freedom of speech or freedom of religion) does not deny to citizens other rights that are not specifically mentioned in the fundamental rule book. Citizens of the nation, therefore, retain other unspecified rights not addressed in the Constitution.

reserve powers *Powers not granted to the national government in the Constitution and retained by the states and the people..*

The 10th Amendment covers the **reserve powers;** it declares that those powers not given to the national government nor prohibited to the states are reserved for (or held by) the states and the people of the nation. This provision was intended to remind national leaders that the national government is entitled to exercise *only* those powers granted to it by the Constitution and that the states have legitimate legislative powers of their own. Other powers and responsibilities are retained by the states and, ultimately, by the people. This amendment explicitly acknowledges the basic American constitutional arrangement we refer to as *federalism*, which allows national, state, and local governments to share governing power. It is the subject of Chapter 3.

Like the provisions of the Constitution, the amendments in the Bill of Rights first required passage by both houses of Congress (by a two-thirds vote in each) and then by at least three-quarters of the states. Congress approved the amendments in September 1789 and forwarded them to the states. As with ratification of the Constitution, the states debated the proposed amendments. By 1791 nine states had officially ratified the amendments, thus formally adding them to the Constitution.

2-7 Amendments since the Bill of Rights

The Constitution has been amended infrequently since passage of the Bill of Rights. Amendments have been proposed for three reasons.

First, some constitutional changes have been proposed because of unforeseen problems that arose in governmental structures and processes. One such problem became apparent in the bitterly contested presidential election of 1796, in which John Adams of Massachusetts ran against Thomas Jefferson of Virginia. By the time of this election, two political parties had emerged (the Federalist Party and the Democrat-Republican Party). In designing the electoral college, the Founders had not clearly anticipated the rise of political parties and the impact such parties would have on electoral outcomes.

According to the Constitution, the president was the individual who received the highest number of electoral votes (as long as it constituted a majority) and the vice president was the person who received the next highest number. This system worked to place two opponents in the highest offices of the executive branch: John Adams, a Federalist, was elected president, and Thomas Jefferson, a Democrat-Republican, was elected vice president. It was apparent to many in the nation that placing opponents in the top two executive positions would be neither harmonious nor productive. The 12th Amendment, ratified in 1804, changed the system so that the president and vice president are elected in separate ballots.

A second reason amendments were added to the Constitution was to give the national government the powers it needed to deal with new issues not originally contemplated by the Founders. One such issue was the prohibition of alcoholic beverages. In the early 1900s, temperance reformers sought to prevent the sale of "evil alcohol." This movement was sufficiently strong in 1919 to convince Congress and a large majority of states to ban the manufacture, sale, and transportation of intoxicating beverages.

Prohibition did not last long, however. Within a few years, a thriving illegal and underground market for alcohol developed. Within a decade, enforcement problems became so great that Congress and the states voted to repeal the 18th Amendment. This is the only instance of one amendment being enacted to repeal an earlier one.

A third reason for constitutional amendments has been to expand the protection of individual rights and liberties. Beyond the Bill of Rights, individual rights were involved in the 13th, 14th, 15th, 19th, 24th, and 26th Amendments. They, respectively, prohibited slavery, required due process and equal protection of the law for all citizens, forbade denial of voting rights on the basis of race or color, prohibited denial of the right to vote on the basis of gender, outlawed the poll tax, and allowed those 18 years of age or older to vote (see Table 2–2).

Table 2-2

Subjects of Constitutional Amendments beyond the Bill of Rights

Amendment	Year	Amendment Subject
Amendment 11	1795	The judicial power of the federal courts shall not extend to lawsuits made against a state government by a citizen of another state or a foreign nation.
Amendment 12	1804	The president and vice president shall be elected on separate ballots in the Electoral College.
Amendment 13	1865	Slavery shall be abolished in the nation.
Amendment 14	1868	State governments are prohibited from (1) making any law that abridges the rights of a citizen of the United States; (2) depriving any person of life, liberty, or property without the process of law; or (3) denying its residents equal protection under the law.
Amendment 15	1870	The rights of citizens may not be denied or abridged on the basis of race, color, or previous condition of servitude.
Amendment 16	1913	Congress is given the power to levy an income tax.
Amendment 17	1913	Senators are elected by popular vote in states.
Amendment 18	1919	The sale, manufacture, or transportation of alcoholic beverages is prohibited.
Amendment 19	1920	The rights of citizens may not be denied on the basis of sex.
Amendment 20	1933	The beginning of congressional and presidential terms of office is moved to the month of January in the year the term begins.
Amendment 21	1933	The 18th Amendment is repealed.
Amendment 22	1951	Presidents may serve no more than two terms of office.
Amendment 23	1961	Residents of the District of Columbia may be represented in the electoral college.
Amendment 24	1964	The right of citizens to vote in a primary or other federal election may not be abridged because of failure to pay a poll tax or other tax.
Amendment 25	1967	Rules for succession in case of removal, death, or resignation of a president are defined.
Amendment 26	1971	The rights of citizens 18 years of age or older to vote may not be denied on the basis of age.
Amendment 27	1992	No law changing the pay received by senators or Members of the House of Representatives shall take effect until after the next election of the House of Representatives.

Box 2-5 The ERA: Time Ran Out

The ERA, the Equal Rights Amendment, is an example of a proposed constitutional amendment that was approved by both houses of Congress but failed to obtain approval at the state level. Stated simply, the ERA says that *"Equality of rights under the law shall not be denied or abridged by the United States or by any state on account of sex."*

The ERA was passed by more than the requisite two-thirds vote by the House of Representatives in 1971 and the Senate in 1972. Congress then transmitted the ERA to the states and gave them 7 years to consider ratification. President Richard Nixon, a conservative, hailed the ERA, stating, "I have not altered my belief that equal rights for women warrant a constitutional guarantee."[a]

ERA supporters claimed that the amendment was needed to end the discrimination that women faced in the economic, social, political, and cultural life of the nation. Perceived discrimination against women in the workforce was of particular concern to ERA supporters. After congressional passage of the ERA, many states quickly followed suit and ratified the amendment.

Despite strong initial support for the ERA, serious controversy arose as the state legislatures reviewed the amendment and considered its ratification. Many opponents asserted that equality was already protected by existing laws. One specific argument made against the ERA was that it would require women to serve in the armed forces. Senator Sam J. Ervin, Jr. (D-NC) argued that, under the ERA, women could be "sent into battle to have their fair forms blasted into fragments by the bombs and shells of the enemy."[b] Another area of controversy surrounded the issue of abortion. Some analysts claimed that ERA passage would lead the courts to strike down laws banning federal funding of abortions because denial of this funding would apply only to women and amount to sex discrimination. More outrageous opponents asserted that the amendment would require unisex bathrooms and locker rooms.

By 1982, after a 10-year struggle (the period for ratification was extended 3 additional years), only 35 states had ratified the ERA, 3 short of the 38 needed. The ERA failed as a constitutional amendment at this point. Since then, Congress has considered relaunching the ERA, but a two-thirds vote of both houses has not been obtained.

a. Letter from Richard M. Nixon to Senate minority leader Hugh Scott concerning support for the Equal Rights Amendment, HJ Res 208, dated March 18, 1972.

b. Statement made by Senator Sam J. Ervin Jr. at hearings held on the Equal Rights Amendment, HJ Res 208, March 20, 1972.

Constitutional history is full of interesting stories about politics in American life. Box 2-5: The ERA: Time Ran Out provides information on the Equal Rights Amendment, a political struggle to amend the Constitution that failed despite hard-fought efforts. Box 2-6: A Forgotten Amendment Comes Alive tells the story of a constitutional amendment enacted after laying dormant for two centuries.

The U.S. Constitution and its 27 amendments, with a total of approximately 7,700 words (4,600 words, with 3,300 words in the amendments), is very short and relatively stable compared with state constitutions. Table 2-3 shows a comparison of lengths among the state constitutions. Some states have had a series of constitutions over time, changing them to suit changing needs within the state.

Box 2–6 A Forgotten Amendment Comes Alive

When James Madison proposed a series of constitutional amendments in the first Congress, he included one that stated that no law changing the pay received by members of Congress could take effect until after the next election of the House of Representatives. In effect, the amendment did not allow members of Congress to change their pay during the 2-year congressional session: *"No law varying the compensation for the services of the Senators and Representatives shall take effect, until an election of Representatives shall have intervened."*

While most of the other amendments offered by Madison were debated, enacted, and ratified as the Bill of Rights, the amendment concerning pay increases was not quickly ratified. Six states ratified the amendment by 1792, another in 1873, and 32 more by 1992. When Michigan ratified the amendment in May 1992, 38 out of the 50 states had approved the amendment, thereby meeting the requirement that constitutional amendments be ratified by three-quarters of the states.

When Congress has enacted more recent laws presenting constitutional amendments, it has included time limits for state ratification (as discussed in the Equal Rights case discussed in Box 2-5). Earlier amendments, including this one concerning pay increases, did not have any time limits.

When Illinois ratified the amendment, some debate arose over whether the current Congress would accept an amendment originally enacted by a Congress 203 years previously. At first, some congressional leaders appeared willing to challenge the validity of the amendment's ratification. However, after the amendment was formally certified by the archivist of the United States, Congress backed down and accepted the amendment as ratified. Congressional leaders feared that the electorate—already suspicious of federal government spending and worried about ethics violations by members of Congress—would not react favorably, especially in an election year, to congressional actions to block the amendment's ratification.

Source: For a more detailed discussion, see Stephen Frantzich, *Citizen Democracy: Political Activists in a Cynical Age*, Lanham, MD: Rowman and Littlefield Publishing Co., 1999, pp. 11–20.

Table 2-3

The U.S Constitution in Comparative Context

	Number of Constitutions	Length (in words)	Number of amendments
Alabama	6	310,296	664
Alaska	1	15,988	28
Arizona	1	28,876	125
Arkansas	5	40,720	85
California	2	54,645	500
Colorado	1	45,679	135
Connecticut	4	16,608	29
Delaware	4	19,000	132
Florida	6	38,000	86
Georgia	10	37,894	51
Hawaii	1	20,774	95
Idaho	1	23,442	115
Illinois	4	13,700	11
Indiana	2	19,315	42

continued

Table 2-3

The U.S Constitution in Comparative Context—*continued*

	Number of Constitutions	Length (in words)	Number of amendments
Iowa	2	12,616	52
Kansas	1	12,616	91
Kentucky	4	23,911	36
Louisiana	11	54,112	107
Maine	1	13,500	168
Maryland	4	41,349	214
Massachusetts	1	36,700	118
Michigan	4	25,530	23
Minnesota	1	11,547	118
Mississippi	4	24,323	121
Missouri	4	42,000	99
Montana	2	13,726	23
Nebraska	2	20,048	213
Nevada	1	20,700	128
New Hampshire	2	9,200	143
New Jersey	3	17,800	52
New Mexico	1	27,200	139
New York	4	51,700	217
North Carolina	3	11,000	30
North Dakota	1	20,564	137
Ohio	2	36,900	159
Oklahoma	1	79,153	161
Oregon	1	49,326	220
Pennsylvania	5	27,503	26
Rhode Island	2	10,233	59
South Carolina	7	22,500	480
South Dakota	1	25,315	105
Tennessee	3	15,300	34
Texas	5	80,806	390
Utah	1	11,000	96
Vermont	3	8,295	52
Virginia	6	21,092	34
Washington	1	50, 237	92
West Virginia	2	26,000	67
Wisconsin	1	14,392	133
Wyoming	1	31,800	68

Source: The Book of the States, Council of State Governments, 2001

Conclusion

The Constitution is the primary rulebook for American politics and government. It created the primary arenas for governmental decision making: Congress, the presidency, and the federal courts. It stipulates rules about who is eligible to serve as players in each of these arenas and about how the players are selected. The provisions of the Constitution also seek to limit the power of the national government through (1) a careful listing of what powers are granted to the government and which are prohibited to it, and (2) a system of checks and balances through which governmental arenas share power and exercise it in an interdependent fashion.

The struggles to create first the Articles of Confederation and then the Constitution were political games themselves. In both cases, delegates from the states met to consider proposals for forming a national government. Both times, delegates sought to grant sufficient power to the national government to deal with problems of concern to all states while retaining substantial governing powers for the states.

Compromise was the key strategy in formulating the Articles of Confederation and the Constitution. Representatives of the various states disagreed on many key issues, including representation in the legislature, selection of the president, and the scope of power to be granted to the national government. In all cases, the delegates were able to reach an agreement that was mutually satisfactory. When they could not reach agreement—for example, in the instance of slavery—the Founders decided to postpone the debate until after the new union had been created.

The Constitution is not a stagnant document; it continues to be an evolving rulebook. What is important is not only the language of the Constitution itself but also its interpretation. Such interpretations, rendered by the Supreme Court and other federal courts, provide guidance about how the Constitution applies to modern problems, many of which the Founders never envisioned. Debates continue, however, about constitutional interpretation. Those holding the strict constructionist view of interpretation see the need for a literal reading of the Constitution, whereas those with the broad constructionist view see the necessity of applying the Constitution to new issues it has not previously addressed. Whichever view one holds, constitutional interpretation is relevant to such diverse policy issues as abortion, the rights of individuals with disabilities, and the legality of burning the American flag, even though the Constitution does not explicitly address any of these issues. The next two chapters examine ramifications of the Constitution by exploring questions related to the national and state governments in the intergovernmental system (Chapter 3) and the evolution of individual rights and liberties (Chapter 4).

Key Terms

Anti-Federalists
Articles of Confederation
bicameral legislature
bill of attainder
Bill of Rights
boycott
Charles Montesquieu (1689–1755)
checks and balances
confederation
Electoral College
ex post facto law
Federalists
First Continental Congress
Great Compromise
implied power
Jean-Jacques Rousseau (1712–1778)
John Lock (1632–1704)
Mayflower Compact
mercantilism
natural rights
necessary and proper clause
New Jersey Plan
polity
ratification
reserve powers
rule of unanimity
Second Continental Congress
separation of powers
social contract
Sons of Liberty
supremacy clause
unicameral legislature
Virginia Plan
writ of habeas corpus

Practice Quiz

1. When they arrived in the New World, the Pilgrims created a governing plan for themselves that is known as the
- **a.** Articles of Confederation.
- **b.** First Continental Congress.
- **c.** Bill of Rights.
- **d.** Mayflower Compact.

2. A key strategy used by people living in the American colonies to protest what they felt were unfair British policies was
- **a.** boycotting the purchase of goods manufactured in Britain.
- **b.** nullifying laws enacted in Britain.
- **c.** large-scale migration to French-controlled Canada.
- **d.** rewriting the Mayflower Compact.

3. A key theme expressed in the Declaration of Independence was
- **a.** the equality of people.
- **b.** government that has the consent of the governed.
- **c.** fundamental rights of all citizens.
- **d.** all of the above.

4. A fundamental weakness of the Articles of Confederation was
- **a.** that they conflicted with provisions of the Mayflower Compact.

b. the inability of the Confederated Congress to manage currency and interstate trade.
c. its establishment of two-house legislation.
d. all of the above.

5. Under the Virginia Plan, the legislative body of the proposed U.S. government would be composed of
a. one house.
b. two houses.
c. one house and one Supreme Court.
d. one house plus the electoral college.

6. The supremacy clause of the U.S. Constitution holds that
a. when federal laws clash with those of states, state laws rule over federal laws.
b. when federal laws clash with those of the states, federal laws rule over those of states.
c. the Supreme Court decides whether federal laws rule over state laws.
d. the president is the chief executive with supreme power over the executive branch.

7. The Founders felt the U.S. Senate would be a more cautious and deliberate body, slower to be swayed by popular pressures because
a. its members serve longer terms in office with only one-third of the body up for election in any two-year period.
b. its members were to be nominated by the president and continued by the House of Representatives.
c. its members are confirmed by Supreme Court Justices who serve for life.
d. the electoral college mediated the Senate from popular votes.

8. Which is *not* a feature of the system of "checks and balances" in the national government as structured by the U.S. Constitution?
a. The president nominates federal judges who are then confirmed by the Senate.
b. Both houses of Congress must pass laws for them to be enacted.
c. The president can veto laws enacted by Congress.
d. The Supreme Court can override presidential veto of laws enacted by Congress.

9. The U.S. Constitution was ratified by
a. a majority of votes of adults in each of the states.
b. the state legislatures of the states.
c. ratifying conventions organized in each state.
d. a national vote of U.S. citizens.

10. The Anti-Federalists argued that the Constitution was dangerous because it would allow the national government to have
a. too much power over the individual state governments.
b. power that would infringe upon the rights and liberties of individuals.
c. powers that were not well defined, threatening state government power.
d. all of the above.

11. Which of the following was *not* included in the Bill of Rights?
a. Freedom of religion
b. Freedom of speech
c. Right to bear arms
d. Supremacy clause

12. The 10th Amendment, known as the reserve clause, holds that any governing powers not granted to the national government nor prohibited to the states were reserved for
a. states and people of the nation.
b. national government and people of the nation.
c. the federal judiciary.
d. the U.S. Congress.

You can find the correct answers to these questions by taking the quiz and then submitting your answers in the Online Edition. The program will automatically score your submission. Where you miss a question, the program will provide the correct answer, a rationale for the answer, and the section number in the chapter where the topic is discussed.

Further Reading

Some useful background works on the Constitution include: Phill B. Kurland and Ralph Lerner (eds.), *The Founders' Constitution* (Five volume set) (Indianapolis, IN: Liberty Fund, Inc., 2000); Terry L. Jordan, *The U.S. Constitution: And Fascinating Facts About It* (Oak Hill Publishers, 1999); and Floyd G. Cullop, *The Constitution of the United States: An Introduction* (New York: New American Library, 1999).

A book that describes in detail the debates and discussions that led to the writing of the Constitution is Richard B. Bernstein with Kym S. Rice, *Are We to Be a Nation? The Making of the Constitution* (Cambridge, MA: Harvard University Press, 1987).

An interesting discussion of early American history is presented in James A. Henretta, W. Elliot Brownlee, David Brody, and Susan Ware, *America's History* (Chicago, IL: Dorsey Press, 1987).

Two other sources that analyze the origins of American democracy and the writing of the Constitution are: Gordon S. Wood, *The Creation of the American Republic, 1776–1787* (New York: W. W. Norton, 1969); and Richard Beeman, Stephen Botein, and Edward C. Carter II, eds., *Beyond Confederation: Origins of the Constitution and American National Identity* (Chapel Hill, NC: University of North Carolina Press, 1987).

An examination of the origins of the Constitution and its development over time is presented in Alfred H. Kelly, Winfred A. Harbison, and Herman Belz, *The American Constitution: Its Origins and Development*, 6th ed. (New York: W. W. Norton, 1983). See also William Peters, *A More Perfect Union: The Making of the United States Constitution* (New York: Crown, 1987); and Charles Beard, *An Economic Interpretation of the Constitution of the United States* (New York: Macmillan, 1935).

An easily accessible introduction to the Constitution is presented in Mort Gerberg, *The U.S. Constitution for Everyone* (New York: Putnam, 1991). Another useful source is Jack Peltason, *Understanding the Constitution* (San Diego, CA: Harcourt, Brace, Jovanovich, 1991).

Several sources present the arguments for and against ratification of the Constitution (the Federalist and Anti-Federalist positions). The arguments for ratification are presented in *The Federalist* (New York: Crown, 1966); these essays, initially penned under the name "Publius," were actually written by Alexander Hamilton, James Madison, and John Jay. For a detailed discussion of the Anti-Federalist positions, see Herbert J. Storing, *What the Anti-Federalists Were For: The Political Thought of the Opponents of the Constitution* (Chicago, IL: University of Chicago Press, 1981). A thorough reference to Anti-Federalist writings is presented in the six-volume set by Herbert J. Storing, *The Complete Anti-Federalist* (Chicago, IL: University of Chicago Press, 1981).

For background on the intellectual contributions of Thomas Jefferson and James Madison to the founding of the American Republic, see a book that provides correspondence between the two: James Morton Smith, ed., *The Republic of Letters: The Correspondence between Thomas Jefferson and James Madison 1776–1836* (New York: W. W. Norton, 1995).

For another useful book that explores debates about Constitutional ratification, see Saul Cornell, *The Other Founders: Anti-Federalism and the Dissenting Tradition in America, 1788–1828* (Chapel Hill, NC: University of North Carolina Press, 1999).

Endnotes

1. Alfred H. Kelly, Winfred Harbison, and Herman Belz, *The American Constitution: Its Origins and Development*, 6th ed. (New York: W. W. Norton, 1983), 63.
2. Jean-Jacques Rousseau, *On the Social Contract*, ed. Roger D. Masters (1762; reprint, New York: St. Martin's Press, 1978). See also Richard Fralin, "The Evolution of Rousseau's View of Representative Government," *Political Theory* 6 (November 1978), 517-36.
3. See Jack Plano and Milton Greenberg, *The American Political Dictionary*, Harcourt Publishers, 2002, p. 9, and Jay Shafritz *The Harper Collins Dictionary of American Politics*, 1993, p. 280.)
4. See Jay Shafritz, *The Harper Collins Dictionary of American Politics*, 1993, p. 428.)
5. John Locke, *Treatise of Civil Government*, 1689.
6. Charles de Montesquieu, *The Spirit of Natural Laws*, 1734. See also E. P. Panagopoulos, *Essays on the Meaning of Checks and Balances* (Lanham, MD: University Press of America, 1986).
7. Vincent Ostrom, *The Political Theory of a Compound Republic: Designing the American Experiment*, rev. ed. (Lincoln, NE: University of Nebraska Press, 1987).
8. This phrase is attributed to Thomas Jefferson by Suzy Platt, *Respectfully Quoted* (Washington, D. C.: Library of Congress, 1988), 60.
9. *The Spirit of Natural Laws*, 1734.
10. James Madison, "Federalist No. 48," *The Federalist Papers* (New York: Mentor Books, 1961).

3

Federalism: The Complex Structure of American Government

Key Points

- **How the Constitution establishes power sharing between the national and state governments**
- **Constitutional and political reasons for the evolution of American federalism**
- **The elements and operation of fiscal federalism, including the patterns of federal grants to states and localities**
- **The changing state of regulatory federalism; the imposition of mandates on state and local governments**
- **The rising power of state governments and the shifting of program design and operation**

Preview: Politics at Multiple Levels

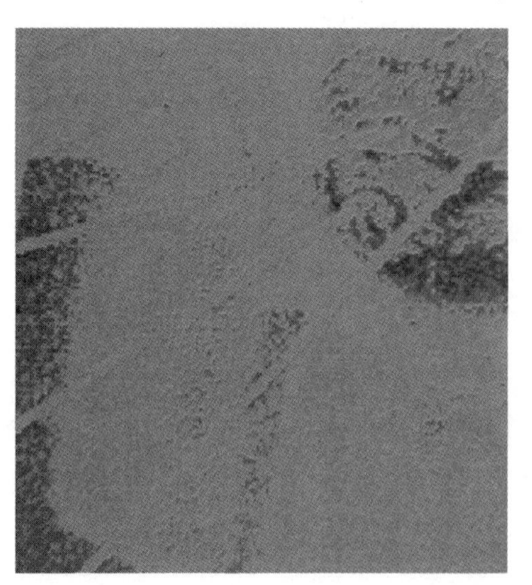

Thomas Grasso was executed in Oklahoma in 1995, and so ended a debate that had been played out between two states about the appropriateness of the death penalty. Grasso's story began in December of 1990 when, in the course of a robbery, he strangled an 87-year-old woman in Tulsa with a strand of Christmas tree lights and smashed her head with an iron. Grasso then fled to New York where, in 1991, he robbed and strangled an 81-year-old Staten Island woman. He was arrested in New York and convicted in 1992 and given a sentence of 20 years to life in prison. New York did not have the death penalty at this time.

In spite of his conviction, the warrant for Grasso's arrest as a murder suspect in Oklahoma remained outstanding. Under an interstate agreement, signed by forty-seven states including these two states, New York was required to return Grasso to Oklahoma on a temporary basis so that he could stand trial for murder there. Under the agreement, however, even if Grasso was found guilty of murder in Oklahoma, he would have to be returned to New York to serve his sentence before Oklahoma could carry out its punishment.

USDA

In the Oklahoma trial, Grasso pleaded guilty. He asked for and received the death penalty, and the interstate conflict began at this point. Governor David Walters of Oklahoma refused to return the convicted murderer to New York, claiming that Grasso's wish to die superseded Oklahoma's responsibility to return him to New York. The Governor of New York, Mario Cuomo, an opponent of the death penalty (he had repeatedly vetoed bills passed by the state legislature to enact a death penalty), brought suit in federal court to rule on the legality of Oklahoma's refusal to return Grasso. The federal court for the Eastern District of Oklahoma ruled that Oklahoma had to return Grasso to New York. It also stated, however, that Cuomo could waive New York's right to demand Grasso's return.

Cuomo faced a personal moral dilemma. He had argued for the return of Grasso based on the law, not on his own moral opposition to the death penalty. Now the law could no longer be used as the argument for Grasso's return because the court allowed Cuomo to waive the law. Oklahoma's governor asked Cuomo, a fellow Democrat, to waive Grasso's return to New York. Cuomo refused, stating that waiving the return would negate the sentence of the New York State courts.

This was how matters stood until the political game changed again with Cuomo's defeat at the polls in the 1994 gubernatorial election. George E. Pataki, a Republican, was elected governor. Unlike Cuomo, Pataki was an advocate of the death penalty. One of his first acts as governor was to arrange for the return of Grasso to Oklahoma, where he was subsequently executed by chemical injection in March 1995.

The Grasso case says much about federalism and political games, which literally have life or death importance at times. Under the Constitution, states reserve the right to enact laws concerning most criminal matters, including the legal penalties associated with criminal convictions. Prior to 1995, Oklahoma allowed the death penalty in murder cases and New York did not. When Grasso was tried and convicted of murder in two states, he set off several political controversies. Which state had the fundamental right to enact a murder sentence? What is the moral appropriateness of the death sentence as a penalty for murder? Does the convict have the right to choose the penalty? Ultimately, this interstate conflict was resolved through a federal court ruling (concerning an interpretation of the interstate agreement) and by a change in New York's office of governor. Although the stakes are not often so high, interstate conflicts such as those demonstrated in the Grasso case are not uncommon. While unitary political systems, such as that of Great Britain, provide for uniform laws across the nation, a federal system, such as that in the United States, allows for diversity in laws and public policies throughout the nation. Conflict among states is a price paid for a federal system that allows states to enact laws that reflect the interests of residents but that do not necessarily match the laws and policies of other states.

Sources: John Kifner, "A Distant State Watches a Killer Waiting to Die," *New York Times*, March 19, 1995, L37, and Robert D. McFadden, "Principles and Politics Collide in Tangled Execution Dispute," *New York Times*, November 6, 1994, A1.

unitary political system *Governing system in which a national government governs with little or no use of regional or state governments.*

In any federal system, the responsibility for governing is shared between one national government and multiple subnational units. In the American system, *federalism* involves the sharing of governing powers between the national government in Washington, D.C. and the 50 state governments. Federal systems contrast with **unitary political systems,** like that of Great Britain, where one central government wields practically all governing authority throughout the nation.

The use of the term *federal* has led to some confusion. Sometimes, the word refers to the national government in Washington, D.C. For example, the "federal grant program" refers to the program operated by the national government. At other times, federal refers to the system of federalism in the United States, including the legal and political relationships among the national, state, and local governments. The "federal character of our political system," for example, alludes to relationships among governments at different levels in the American political system. *Intergovernmental relations* is another term that refers to the relationships and interactions among players at different governmental levels. Because there is no conformity of use, the meaning of the word *federal* must be determined from the context of the discussion.

Federalism can be clarified by thinking of it as a political game between national and state players. The national players include the president, officials in the executive branch, Congress, and the federal courts. The players at the state level include governors, state government agencies, state legislatures, and state courts. In more recent times, local governments have joined states as active players in the game of intergovernmental relations.

secession *Move of states to formally and legally become separate from the Union.*

The resolution of disputes between national and state governments about governing power has been a key part of the evolution of American government. As seen in Chapter 1, the issue of slavery introduced conflict early in the nation's history. It contributed to the southern states' **secession** and to a civil war that forced these states back into the Union. During this century, the national government became the stronger, if not the dominant, player in the federal system. Nonetheless, state governments have always performed important governing roles. Today, as the national government moves to shrink its spending and responsibilities, states are re-emerging as far stronger players in the federal system.

In this chapter we review the fundamental tenets of federalism that are the legal basis for political games between the national and state governments. The chapter traces the evolution of federal relationships and notes the emergence of another set of intergovernmental players: local governments. The chapter also examines fiscal federalism (financial relationships with the states), as well as regulatory federalism (the efforts of the national government to regulate the activities of state and local governments). Chapter 18 examines the structures and operations of state and local governments in the United States.

3-1 The Rules of Federalism

To clarify the underlying rules of federalism—the rules that give powers to various governments and structure their interactions—we return briefly to certain provisions of the U.S. Constitution that were outlined in Chapter 2. Recall how rules about federalism, as designed by the Founders, sought balance between the powers of the national and state governments.

3-1a Empowering the National Government

Article I, Section 8 of the Constitution outlines the powers directly granted to the national government. They are powers to provide a national defense, coin money, and regulate interstate commerce. Of prime importance is the necessary and proper clause, which grants Congress the power to enact laws required for executing the powers granted to the national government. In addition, the supremacy clause, included in Article VI, holds that when the Constitution, laws, and treaties of the national government conflict with those of the states in areas where the national government is empowered, the national laws shall be the supreme law of the land.

The Constitution prohibits the states from taking certain actions. Some of these prohibitions enhance national government power, whereas others limit the powers of states in their relations with other states. For example, the Constitution forbids state governments from entering into formal treaties with foreign nations, coining money, or granting titles of nobility. Box 3-1: The Founders' View of Federalism presents some of the Founders' views about federalism as expressed in *The Federalist.*

3-1b Empowering the States

Because state governments existed before the Constitution was written, it was not necessary to spell out in that document all of the powers that state governments could exercise. Instead, the Founders presumed that all powers not given to the national government

Box 3-1 The Founders' View of Federalism

Contained within *The Federalist*—the essays by Alexander Hamilton, John Jay, and James Madison advocating ratification of the Constitution and written in Philadelphia in 1787—are many ideas about the principles of federalism and the operation of a federal system in America.

Logic of the federal system:

> This form of government is a convention by which several smaller states agree to become members of a larger one, which they intend to form. It is a kind of assemblage of societies that constitute a new one, capable of increasing, by means of new associations, until they arrive to such a degree of power as to be able to provide for the security of the united body. (Alexander Hamilton, *Federalist* No. 9)

Limits on national government power:

> In the first place it is to be remembered that the general government is not to be charged with the whole power of making and administering laws. Its jurisdiction is limited to certain enumerated objects, which concern all the members of the republic, but which are not to be attained by the separate provisions of any. The subordinate governments, which can extend their care to all those other objects which can be separately provided for, will retain their due authority and activity. (James Madison, *Federalist* No. 14)

States more likely to encroach on national government than the reverse:

> It will always be far more easy for the State governments to encroach upon the national authorities than for the national government to encroach upon the State authorities. The proof of this proposition turns upon the greater degree of influence which the State governments, if they administer their affairs with uprightness and prudence, will generally possess over the people...Upon the same principle that a man is more attached to his family than to his neighborhood, to his neighborhood than to the community at large, the people of each State would be apt to feel a stronger bias towards their local governments than towards the government of the Union; unless the force of that principle should be destroyed by a much better administration of the latter. (Alexander Hamilton, *Federalist* No. 17)

Interestingly, the last proposition—that states are more likely to encroach upon national government authority than the reverse—has proven to be factually incorrect, at least in terms of the American experience. Until recently, as described later in the chapter, the long-term tendency within the American system of federalism has been for the national government to become the more dominant player in games of intergovernmental politics. In the last few years, the state governments have become more active and vital players in the game of American politics as the federal government has moved to reduce its expenditures, programs, and governmental agencies. In the wake of federal cutbacks, the states have assumed more responsibilities in designing and implementing many key programs, including major social welfare programs.

would be retained by the states. Many Anti-Federalists were uncomfortable with this important principle operating only as a presumption. Therefore, they championed the idea of including the reserve powers within the Bill of Rights. The 10th Amendment states that any powers not given to the national government remain the authority of state governments or of the people. Box 3-2: Competing Theories of Federalism explores two points of view regarding whether the power of the national government originated from the states or from the consent of all the people.

3-2 States' Rights, Crisis, and Rebellion

Not long after the Constitution was ratified, lingering tensions over the power of the national government erupted into political disputes about federalism. These disputes usually involved national players on one side and state players on the other.

3-2a Early Disputes over States' Rights

In the late 1700s, the United States unofficially sided with Great Britain in the latter country's war with France. During this conflict, Congress enacted four laws under the Alien and Sedition Acts of 1798. These laws allowed deportation of foreigners and prohibited the publication of false or malicious attacks against the president, Congress, or the nation. These laws were enacted with the strong support of President John Adams (a Federalist) who sought to discourage political activity by pro-French immigrants to the United States, whose anti-British protests were embarrassing to the Federalists. The Alien and Sedition Acts were also intended to weaken the political power of the opposing party, the Democrat Republicans, by reducing the opportunities for public criticism of President Adams. One way to accomplish this, the Federalists felt, was to threaten new aliens immigrating to the United States with the possibility of deportation if they were suspected of **sedition.** Because new immigrants typically aligned themselves with the Democrat Republicans, deporting some would also reduce the strength of the opposition to the Federalists.

sedition *Incitement of rebellion against governmental authority.*

Opposition to the Alien and Sedition Acts was championed by the state legislature of Kentucky, which declared the laws to be "unauthoritative, void, and of no force." The argument used to defend the practice of voiding national government laws thus became known as the **Kentucky Resolution.** It stated that the national government consisted of a compact of states in which "each party has an equal right to judge for itself." This resolution was a clear exposition of the **compact theory** of federalism and a firm argument for **states' rights** (see Box 3-2: Competing Theories of Federalism). The state of Virginia enacted a similar nullification of the Alien and Sedition Acts. With the election in 1800 of Thomas Jefferson, a Democrat Republican and an opponent of the Alien and Sedition Acts, tensions subsided and the acts were never enforced.

Kentucky Resolution Law *Passed by the Kentucky State Legislature in 1798 that held that the Alien and Sedition Acts were void and of no force; an early expression of the states' rights philosophy.*

compact theory *Theory of federalism that sees the national government and the U.S. Constitution as legally based on the consent of sovereign state governments.*

states' rights *The position that states have clear rights and privileges under the Constitution, onto which actions of the federal government may not infringe.*

The issue of states' rights soon rose again, this time over the creation of a national bank. In 1816, Congress chartered the Second National Bank and gave it certain powers over state banks. Many states opposed this action, which they felt conflicted with their right to charter banks. To show its displeasure, the Maryland legislature enacted a law that placed a state tax on the Second National Bank and limited its power to issue notes. The bank's cashier refused to pay the tax, an act that led to the important Supreme Court case *McCulloch v. Maryland* (1819).

The Supreme Court under Chief Justice John Marshall, a proponent of a strong central government, ruled against Maryland and held that the action of Congress to charter a national bank was constitutional. This decision was based on two important interpretations of the Constitution. First, the Court held that the necessary and proper clause empowered the Congress to take actions other than those expressly listed in the Constitution. Second, the Court noted that the Constitution granted Congress the power to collect taxes, borrow money, and regulate commerce.

In this case, the Supreme Court also responded to Maryland's claim that, since the Constitution was created by an agreement among **sovereign** state governments (that is,

sovereign *Undisputed, supreme power as a political unit.*

Box 3-2 Competing Theories of Federalism

Our federal system rests not only on constitutional provisions but also on an underlying theory of federal arrangements. Two theories about the fundamental nature of American federalism dominate. One view—the **compact theory**—sees the federal system as created through a formal agreement among the original thirteen sovereign state governments. From this perspective, the power of the national government arises from the consent of the state governments. The other view—termed the **contract theory**—holds that American federalism is based on the consent of the whole people.

Both points of view have some legitimacy. On the one hand, state governments were sovereign political entities prior to the writing of the Constitution, and all but Rhode Island sent delegates to participate in the Constitutional Convention in Philadelphia. This would suggest that state governments had a formal role in creating the Constitution. On the other hand, the states ratified the Constitution not through an act of the state legislatures, but instead through ratification conventions composed of citizens of the state. Ratification by convention, it is argued, means that approval of the Constitution was made by, and rests with, the people.

The compact theory approach to federalism is evident in the language of the Articles of Confederation, which state that "Each state retains its sovereignty, freedom, and independence, and every Power, Jurisdiction and right, which is not by this confederation expressly delegated to the United States." Here, the Articles of Confederation stress state sovereignty and delegation of power from the confederation of states. Reflecting a contract theory approach to federalism, the Constitution begins with the well-known statement, "We the People of the United States, in Order to form a more perfect Union, establish Justice, insure domestic Tranquility, provide for the common defense...do ordain and establish this Constitution for the United States of America." Here, "the people" are mentioned prior to any notion of state sovereignty or confederation.

governments acting as political units with undisputed power), the laws of these governments should have higher power than federal laws. Writing for the Court, Chief Justice John Marshall dismissed Maryland's compact view of federalism. He argued instead for the **contract theory,** the view that the Constitution derives its authority directly from the people through the state ratifying conventions.[1]

contract theory *Theory of federalism that sees the national government and Constitution as legally based on the consent of the people.*

3-2b Sectional Differences within the Nation

Rivalries among the states grew throughout the 1800s and threatened the underlying foundations of American democracy. In part, these rivalries, which developed along regional lines, resulted from different paths of economic development. The southern states of the early 19th century retained much of their colonial character. The plantation economy, where agriculture was organized around large farms owned by a small group of families, remained dominant. The plantations produced cash crops for marketing in European nations. Open and unrestricted foreign trade was therefore important for the continued economic vitality of the southern states.

Slaves were central to the plantations because they provided cheap labor to plant and harvest such crops as tobacco and cotton. Several early American presidents, including George Washington and Thomas Jefferson, owned slaves. Although many people in the North and South questioned the morality of slavery, the practice was defended in the South as necessary for maintaining the plantation economy. Wealthy established families dominated political life in the South, maintaining a pattern of government by aristocracy.

Life in the northern states was quite different. The northern economy was centered on small, family-owned farms and the production of manufactured goods. The spread of the Industrial Revolution from England through the northern states led to the development of a large class of workers who toiled not on farms but in urban factories.

Also during the 19th century, waves of emigrants from Ireland, Germany, Italy, Scandinavia, and other European nations came to America to escape poverty, war, and famine and to find new opportunities. These emigrants settled in the rapidly growing northern cities, which contributed to social diversity. By the mid-19th century, both immigration and industrial growth had fostered the development of many large urban centers in the North. The South remained largely rural in character.

3-2c Political Conflicts Generated by Sectional Differences

The economic and social differences between the North and South resulted in a series of political controversies. The issue of slavery was regional, dividing the nation almost from the start. The Founders, who included a stipulation in the Constitution that no law about slavery could be enacted for 20 years after ratification, initially sidestepped it. The first crisis came in 1820, when the Missouri Territory petitioned for entry into the Union as a slave state. Some in Congress sought to admit Missouri to the Union but to include provisions that would ultimately abolish slavery there. The southern states saw this as a direct threat to the slavery system.

Missouri Compromise of 1820 *Agreement reached in Congress allowing the admission of Missouri as a slave state and Maine as a free state and prohibiting slavery north of the 36_30' parallel line.*

This dispute between regional state players was temporarily resolved through the **Missouri Compromise of 1820.** Balanced by the entry of Maine as a free state, Missouri was allowed to enter the Union as a slave state. Slaves were, however, prohibited in the other territories north of the 36 x 30 parallel line. This compromise, which prevented the spread of slavery into many future states, proved to be but an early round of a protracted political game concerning slavery.

Another troublesome issue concerned the tariffs levied by the national government on imports and exports. In 1828 Congress imposed stiff tariffs on manufactured goods imported into the country and on raw materials exported abroad. While protecting manufacturing industries in the North, this measure, known as the "Tariff of Abominations," was a significant burden on the South. The southern states' livelihoods depended on the uninhibited exportation of agricultural products to Great Britain and other nations.

nullification doctrine *Claim of some states that they had the right to review laws passed by Congress and to nullify those they felt were inappropriate.*

Responding to the tariff specifically, and to sectional tensions more generally, a state convention in South Carolina announced a doctrine of **nullification.** This doctrine said that any state finding a federal law to be unconstitutional could declare it "null and void" within the state. Unless three-quarters of the states ratified an amendment granting Congress the disputed power, the federal law would be nullified. Like the Kentucky Resolution of 1798, this doctrine was justified on the basis of the compact theory of federalism, which suggests that, as the ultimate authorities for the Constitution, the states have the power to review and nullify federal laws. Although few states formally embraced the nullification doctrine, its articulation and debate signified growing tensions about federalism.

Compromise of 1850 *Compromise reached by Congress, admitting California as a free state and including a strict policy regarding the return of runaway slaves.*

Another round of political games surrounding slavery began in 1850 as California sought entry into the Union as a free state. Again, the southern players feared that the nation was tipping away from slavery. Some southern leaders urged secession—that is, leaving the Union. After a grueling debate about the future of slavery, Congress enacted the **Compromise of 1850.** Pleasing to the North was California's entry into the Union as a free state and the ban against slave trade (but not ownership) in the nation's capital. To pacify the southern states, Congress enacted a more stringent law regarding the return of runaway slaves. Again, this serious skirmish over slavery was halted for the moment by the strategy of compromise, but the game was not over.

3-2d Sectionalism, Rebellion, and the Civil War

abolition *The complete removal of the practice of slavery.*

Regional tensions within the nation reached a crisis with the election of Abraham Lincoln as president in 1860. While campaigning for office, Lincoln spoke against the extension of slavery into new states and for a protective tariff to help the industries of the northern states. Southerners saw Lincoln as an **abolitionist** who, if elected, would seek to eliminate slavery and to support policies favoring northern states. In the election, Lincoln, as the Republican candidate, carried the North but not one state in the South.

The Union began to crumble just four days after Lincoln's election. South Carolina, ever the hotbed of the South's anger at the North, voted to call a special convention. Held in December 1860, delegates at the state convention voted to secede from the nation. By the following summer, ten other states had followed suit. After secession, the Southern states met and formed the Confederate States of America. Jefferson Davis, formerly a senator from Mississippi, was elected president.

The Civil War was ignited at Fort Sumter in South Carolina the following spring. Lying deep in the heart of the Confederacy, the fort contained federal troops and military supplies. Recognizing its strategic position, Lincoln announced that he would send provisions to the fort. Southerners responded in April 1861 by bombarding the fort, which, after 34 hours of attack, surrendered.

The attack on Fort Sumter rallied support in the North for armed reaction to secession, which was branded as a rebellion that justified military response. Lincoln's move to raise an army in the North generated a similar response in the South. Soon the armies began to clash, marking the start of the Civil War. Although the sides appeared roughly equal at the outset, the North's industrial capacity eventually tipped the scales in its favor. With time, the North's military and industrial power contributed to the defeat of Southern armies and to the subsequent end of the Confederacy.

In January 1863 President Lincoln announced the **Emancipation Proclamation,** declaring that slaves residing in the states still in rebellion would be free once those states came under Union military control. Two years later, in April 1965, the Confederate army surrendered, and the southern states began the process of readmission to the Union. Later, in December 1865, the 13th Amendment to the Constitution was ratified. It dealt the final deathblow to slavery: the practice was outlawed in the nation.

Emancipation Proclamation *Formal declaration by President Abraham Lincoln in 1863, freeing all slaves in the Confederate States; continuing rebellion prevented implementation.*

In 1868, immediately following the Civil War, the 14th Amendment was proposed by Congress and ratified by state legislatures. It defined citizenship and prohibited states from enacting or enforcing laws that abridge the rights of citizens (including former slaves). It also prohibited states from denying citizens equal protection under the law. The 15th Amendment, ratified in 1870, declared that the rights of citizens to vote should not be abridged on the basis of race, color, or previous condition of servitude. These amendments are important linchpins of civil rights protection in the United States.

3-3 The Evolving Patterns of Intergovernmental Relations: Change Affects the Game

The character of the relationship between the national and state governments has changed and evolved throughout the history of the country. The intergovernmental tensions that peaked during the Civil War subsequently settled down, and then they arose again. National growth, economic fluctuations, world wars, an enlarged national government, and other factors caused renewed frictions between American states and the national government. From the early days of the Republic until today, there have been primarily four kinds of federalism: dual, cooperative, creative, and competitive.

dual federalism *Each level of government operated more or less separately from the other.*

The earliest pattern of relationships, **dual federalism,** lasted from the creation of the nation through about 1930. During this period, the powers of the national government were exercised more or less independently from those of the states. The first half of the dual federalism period included battles over states' rights, nullification, and secession. After these issues were resolved through the Civil War, the national and state governments returned to separate governing activities. Political scientist Morton Grodzins has described this era of dual federalism as **layer-cake federalism.** In dual federalism, each layer of government performed its functions and exercised its powers for the most part separately from the other.[2]

layer-cake federalism *Period of dual federalism when the national and state governments operated separately from each other with little mixing of governing responsibilities.*

One interesting development during this period was the emergence of a new set of players in the federalism game: local governments. Throughout the early decades of the 19th century, American cities grew at a hectic pace, particularly as a result of immigration and the Industrial Revolution. As cities grew in population, local governments became necessary to maintain public order, build streets, and provide other services (see Chapter 18, "State and Local Governments"). State governments were too far from the local scene to provide these services effectively.

cooperative federalism *In response to the Depression and World War II, the national, state, and local levels of government exercised more direct cooperation.*

Beginning in the 1930s, the pattern of relationships among players in the federal system changed markedly. The period of **cooperative federalism,** lasting from 1930 to about 1960, saw interactions among national, state, and local governments increase. This move toward greater cooperation was facilitated by two major crises: the Great Depression and World War II. The depression caused unprecedented social and economic upheaval in the nation. Unemployment reached unparalleled levels. Efforts to revive the economy, increase employment, and reduce the impact of economic dislocations were pursued cooperatively at all governmental levels. One example was the large-scale public works projects commissioned during the depression. Parks, highways, and other projects were constructed with federal funds granted to states and localities for the purpose of creating jobs and easing unemployment. During World War II, states and localities cooperated with and administered programs that were designed at the national level to spur the war effort.

creative federalism *Period when national, state, and local governments cooperatively initiated bold and creative social programs.*

Great Society *Name for policies (such as the War on Poverty) in the 1960s advanced in the belief that social and economic problems can be solved by government programs.*

Starting in the early 1960s and lasting through the 1970s, the pattern of intergovernmental relations shifted to **creative federalism.**[3] This was the period of the **Great Society** programs. President Lyndon B. Johnson and Congress embarked upon bold new programs to fight poverty, hunger, crime, illness, and other social problems. These innovative programs were designed so that the national government provided most of the funding. The states and localities supplied the administrative support and personnel for execution. Direct cooperation among the national, state, and local governments was required to tackle enormous and widespread problems.

marble-cake federalism *Pattern of relationships among the national, state, and local governments that features extensive sharing and intermingling of governing responsibilities.*

Intergovernmental relations during the periods of cooperative and creative federalism have been referred to as **marble-cake federalism.** This denoted the extensive mixing and sharing of responsibilities for executing federally funded programs. The different governmental layers no longer performed governing responsibilities independently in the federal system. In programs like Medicaid, Head Start, and many others, the federal government contributed substantial funds to the states along with substantial rules about how programs should be operated. The states became the implementers of these federal programs, representing a new mixing of national and state government functions.

competitive federalism *Period of federal relationships, roughly 1980 to the present, characterized by cutbacks in federal aid, re-sorting of program responsibilities, and the increased use of regulatory mandates.*

Since 1980 American federalism has entered a period of **competitive federalism,** during which relations among the federal players are tense, unsettled, and sometimes combative. This competitive period emerged as the national and state governments began to rethink their patterns of relationships and raise major questions about the magnitude, funding, and responsibility for implementing federal programs. Most of the federal programs initiated during the period of creative federalism remain. The national government, however, has moved in the last three decades to reduce its financial support of long-standing federal programs. This move resulted, in part, from concerns about the size of federal spending and mounting federal deficits. It also stemmed from a growing commitment among politicians of both parties to shrink the size of the national government. State and local governments welcome greater flexibility in operating programs but worry about how they can operate programs with fewer federal dollars.

regulatory mandates *Actions either required of or prohibited to state and local governments if they are to receive federal funds or avoid legal penalties.*

Another dimension of competitive federalism concerns the growing use of **regulatory mandates** imposed by Congress. These mandates, explored in more detail later in this section, impose requirements and restrictions on the activities of state and local governments—often as a condition of receiving federal funds. Since the 1980s Congress has been less willing to increase funding of federal programs and more willing to create new regulatory mandates for states and localities to follow. The reaction from the states and cities—strong and negative against the financial burden of regulatory mandates—has resulted in substantial efforts to reduce or eliminate these mandates.

The period of competitive federalism has witnessed growing challenges from the states concerning the power and authority of the national government. Worried about the power of incumbency, for example, about half of the states during the 1990s enacted term-limit laws for members of Congress elected in their state (see Box 3-3: A Modern Issue of States' Rights). In other actions, states challenged the regulatory power of the

Box 3–3 A Modern Issue of States' Rights: The Case of Term Limits

Background

During the 1990s, several states across the nation enacted laws that set limits on the number of terms that members of Congress—both Senators and Representatives—representing their state could serve in Congress. By 1995, twenty-three states had enacted such term limit measures. The state of Arkansas, for example, enacted a law in 1992 stating that the names of any persons who had already served three or more terms in the House of Representatives or two or more terms in the Senate could not be placed on the election ballot. (The law did, however, allow citizens to write in the names of such candidates.)

In 1995 the Supreme Court considered a case that challenged the constitutionality of the Arkansas term limit law. The case was seen as setting a precedent against which the term limit laws of other states would be judged. After hearing oral arguments and debating the case, the Supreme Court, by a divided 5–4 vote, judged the Arkansas law to be unconstitutional. This decision—seen as a major blow by term-limits advocates—represents a contemporary example of a states' rights issue debated in the context of American federalism.

Questions raised

The question of term limits for Senators and Representatives raises important questions about federalism and constitutional interpretation. For instance, why did some states enact term limit laws for members of Congress? On what grounds did some parties question the constitutionality of state term-limits laws, and what key issues of federalism are involved in the term-limits issue? And finally, on what basis did the Supreme Court strike down the term-limits laws?

Analysis

At the root of concerns about term limits is the power of incumbency. The incumbents of political offices—including those in Congress—were seen as generally entrenched. Given their extensive name recognition and their ability to raise campaign funds, it became politically very difficult to defeat incumbents at the polls. Incumbents, therefore, tended to serve long terms of office and to develop extensive ties to key interest groups. In the eyes of many analysts, this pattern of long-term incumbency reduced the ability of the public to use competitive elections as a means to register support for or opposition to candidates and public policies.

Proponents of term limits expected that shorter tenures in office would reduce the power of special interests and increase the attention of elected officials to their constituents.

On what basis did the states propose to create term limits? Article I, Section 3 of the Constitution stipulates qualifications for Senators and Representatives. Senators are to be elected for 6-year terms; Senators must be 30 years of age or older and have been a citizen of the United States for at least 9 years. Representatives, who are to serve 2-year terms, must be 25 years of age or older and have been a U.S. citizen for at least 7 years. The Constitution contains no provisions about term limits. Qualified persons can run for office and serve in office as many times as they like.

In creating term limits, the states sought to add new qualifications concerning the eligibility of persons to serve in the Senate and House of Representatives. Persons who had served a set number of terms would be ineligible to be listed on an election ballot or to run for office. The key issue here is whether states have the authority to add eligibility requirements beyond those stipulated in the Constitution. Proponents of term limits argue that the language of the Constitution does not forbid states from adding eligibility criteria. In addition, they argue that the right to add eligibility requirements exists among the powers reserved to the states through the 10th Amendment to the Constitution. The reserve clause, as discussed in Chapter 2, states that powers

continued

Box 3-3 A Modern Issue of States' Rights: The Case of Term Limits

—Continued

not delegated to the national government in the Constitution, nor prohibited to the states, are reserved to the states or to the people.

In the majority opinion, authored by Justice John Paul Stevens, the Supreme Court held that term limits violate the intentions of the Founders for a uniformly elected national legislature of the people.[a] The majority held that the Founders intended for the Constitution alone to be the source of eligibility requirements. They disagreed with the proposition that setting eligibility requirements was among the powers reserved to the states (or, for that matter, a power granted to Congress). The majority opinion stated that if the people wish to introduce term limits, then the appropriate means to achieve this is through amendment of the Constitution. Four members of the Court disagreed with the majority. In a dissenting opinion, Justice Clarence Thomas supported the view of term-limits proponents, arguing "Nothing in the Constitution deprives the people of each state of the right to prescribe eligibility requirements for the candidates who seek to represent them in Congress. The Constitution is simply silent on this question. And where the Constitution is silent, it raises no bar to action by the states or the people."[b]

---

a. *U.S. Term Limits, Inc. v. Thornton,* 514 U.S. 779 (1995).

b. Minority Opinion by Justice Clarence Thomas, *U.S. Term Limits, Inc. v. Thornton,* 514 U.S. 779 (1995).

national government. The pressure for regulatory relief focuses on both relieving the financial pressures associated with regulatory compliance and the general belief that federal regulatory requirements unfairly eclipse state government power. Continual pressure points in regulatory tensions are federal clean air and water requirements that mean substantial state and local expenditures must be made to achieve compliance. Resentment about federal regulatory authority was evident in the summer of 2000 as residents of several Midwest states voiced complaints about Environmental Protection Agency requirements that cities with high ozone pollution sell only reformulated gasoline. A shortage of this special fuel caused a rapid rise in gas prices to over $2 per gallon in 2001, causing great concern, even anger, among motorists who saw their gas prices rise daily.

The period of competitive federalism represents a substantial rethinking of intergovernmental relations that results from significant tensions in the federal system. This rethinking sees expanded roles and responsibilities for state governments and a reduced role for the national government. To understand intergovernmental tensions, it is useful to understand how the federal government's power expanded throughout history, only to be challenged on many fronts today.

3-4 The National Government as Dominating Player

As the nation moved from dual to cooperative and then to creative federalism, the national government slowly but steadily emerged as the stronger player. Although calls for states' rights have never ceased, national government power over the affairs of the country has, until quite recently, increased substantially. This has occurred under the same Constitution that the Founders saw as guaranteeing a strong role for the states. Several factors explain how the balance of governing power within the federal system shifted toward the national government.

equal protection clause *The provision of the 14th Amendment that forbids states from abridging the constitutional rights of citizens and requires equal enforcement of the law for all citizens.*

First, the 14th Amendment and its **equal protection clause** have extended constitutional rights and responsibilities to the states. The equal protection clause was added to the Constitution as a means of compelling southern states to treat all citizens—including former slaves—equally under the law. Through a process known as **selective incorporation,** the rights and liberties of citizens outlined in the Constitution and the Bill of Rights have been coupled to the equal protection clause, thereby also extending protection of citizens from the actions of state and local governments. In this way, most of the rights and liberties articulated in the Bill of Rights have been "nationalized." (Selective incorporation is discussed in more detail in Chapter 4.)

selective incorporation *The process through which freedoms and protections of the Bill of Rights have been extended to state and local levels..*

This extension of civil rights protection has worked to limit some powers and activities of state and local governments. In a highly visible example, the power of states to regulate abortions has been affected by Supreme Court decisions. These rulings hold that the right to privacy constitutionally protects some abortions. Here we see an institution of the national government—the Supreme Court—deny states the right to legislate abortion policy. The grounds are that such policies can violate the privacy rights of individual citizens as outlined in the Constitution and Bill of Rights.

Second, the reach of national government power has been lengthened through elastic interpretations of the Constitution. Actions beyond those expressly listed in the Constitution have been judged permissible, often on the grounds of the necessary and proper clause (see Chapter 2). The first major example was the *McCulloch v. Maryland* case, in which the right of the national government to create a national bank was upheld as a power implied in the Constitution through the necessary and proper clause. Since that landmark decision, other cases have cumulatively allowed the national government to extend its functions beyond those directly spelled out in the Constitution, so that it can implement its proper powers.

Third, the **commerce clause** of the Constitution has increased national power. Given the nature of the modern economy, most goods and services produced in the country are transported across state boundaries. Using the commerce clause, Congress has enacted laws to regulate monopolies, clean the environment, and protect consumers. Such actions, not originally anticipated by the Founders, have been ruled as valid, given the power of the national government to regulate commercial activities that cross state lines.

commerce clause *Provision in the U.S. Constitution that empowers the national government to regulate interstate commerce.*

Fourth, the 16th Amendment, adopted in 1913, allows the national government to levy an income tax that provides the national government with an efficient and expandable source of revenue. Funds raised through the income tax, levied both on individuals and business corporations, financed new types of social welfare and environmental protection programs. The national government probably could not have afforded them without the revenues derived from the income tax.

Fifth, and very important, national government power has been enhanced by its **spending power.** The food stamp program demonstrates how this power works. During the Great Society years, Congress wished both to enhance the nutrition of poor persons and to help farmers by increasing food consumption. The plan provided poor persons with stamps that could be used to purchase food products at government expense. This program was seen as the best means to achieve congressional objectives. One major difficulty, however, was that Congress was not empowered in the Constitution to issue food stamps or to engage in social welfare. Since it could not simply pass a federal law to require all states to operate a food stamp program, how could Congress legally create one?

spending power *The ability of the federal government to influence the actions and programs of state and local governments because of the provision of federal funds to support such programs.*

The answer was simple: Allocate grants to the states to finance the establishment of a food stamp program. The large-scale federal monies made available through the food stamp program were too great for states to ignore. Thus the national government encouraged and facilitated states' operation of this program without requiring it. Federal financial transfers—the spending power of the national government—have been used to create a large number of other social welfare programs. These include aid to families with dependent children (AFDC) and Medicare (subsidized health care for senior citizens). Because state participation is legally optional, the Supreme Court has ruled that the federal spending power does not violate constitutional provisions.

News magazines showed the entire nation that some of its citizens lived in extremely impoverished conditions.
Library of Congress, Prints & Photographs Division [LC-USF34-061073-D]

Beyond affecting state policy and spending priorities, its spending power increases the power of the national government in another way. Most federal grants include stipulations that must be followed if the state wishes to participate in the program. For example, states and localities that receive federal funds are required to adopt affirmative action plans to increase the participation of minorities in the public work force. If a state or city does not follow federal affirmative action guidelines, it risks losing those funds. Box 3-4: The National Drinking Age Game presents an overview of how the federal spending power was used to raise the national minimum drinking age to 21.

One final factor that has increased the power of the national government has been the gradual recognition of some problems as inherently national in scope, requiring concerted effort throughout the country for solution. Television, which presents stories about people, issues, and problems from across the nation, has increased the tendency of people to adopt a national view about problems and government.

Relevant here is the issue of hunger. Before television reporting (and photographic displays in major magazines), few Americans realized the extent of hunger and malnutrition in Appalachia and urban ghettos. Faced with striking images of poverty and hunger, Americans during the 1960s came to recognize the problem and to press for its solution. The federal government was seen as the most appropriate unit to effectively organize an antipoverty policy throughout the country.[4] More recently, media stories have increased national awareness of such problems as homelessness in American communities, the spread of AIDS, and fighting terrorist acts targeted at the United States. The role of the media in the national culture is explored in Chapter 6.

3-5 Fiscal Federalism: Financial Relationships among Players

fiscal federalism *Financial arrangements and transfers among governments at different levels in the federal system.*

Fiscal federalism involves the financial arrangements and grants between different levels of government. In this section, we examine the different forms of fiscal federalism, as well as its magnitude and impact. Beginning with the New Deal in the 1930s, and expanding substantially through the programs initiated in the 1960s as part of the Great Society Program, fiscal federalism has become an integral part of American politics. Its principal mechanism has been federal grants, through which the national gov-

Box 3–4 The National Drinking Age Game

The Issue: In the early 1980s, Congress faced increasing pressure to respond to the growing incidence of alcohol-related traffic deaths. Such groups as Mothers Against Drunk Driving (MADD) lobbied diligently for congressional action to reduce the level of teenage alcohol consumption and the number of traffic accidents involving drunk drivers. They argued that a national minimum drinking age would eliminate many drunk-driving accidents involving teenagers who drove across state lines to purchase alcohol.

Congress Responds: In 1984 Congress enacted the National Minimum Drinking Age Amendment (amending an existing federal law, not the Constitution). This law authorized the Secretary of Transportation to withhold 5% of federal highway funds from any state that, by 1987, did not have or enact a law prohibiting the sale of alcohol to persons under the age of 21. This percentage was increased to 10% in 1988. This legislation also provided incentive funds to states that established a mandatory minimum sentence for persons convicted of drunk driving.

The States Respond: The response of state governments to this federal action was both vocal and negative. From their perspective, the regulation of alcohol sales was a power retained by the states through the reserved powers of the Constitution and the 21st Amendment, which repealed federal government authority to control the sale of alcohol.

Court Action: Unhappy about the federal action, the state of South Dakota filed suit against the national government. The state claimed that the plan to withhold federal highway funds from states that did not adopt a 21-year-old drinking age interfered with the state's power to regulate the sale of alcohol. In this case *South Dakota v. Dole* (1987), the Supreme Court held that the federal spending power made it constitutional for the national government to impose such a requirement as part of an intergovernmental grant.

The Result: While expressing anger and frustration, the states that had a minimum drinking age younger than 21 passed laws to raise the drinking age. Within 3 years, the objective of a national minimum drinking age of 21 had been achieved—not by a single national law but by a series of state laws and actions stimulated by the threat of reduced federal government dollars for highway construction and maintenance.

ernment provided financial incentives for states and localities to create and operate new programs.

3-5a Forms of Fiscal Federalism

The most common form of federal grant is the **categorical grant,** provided to states and localities so that specific programs can be performed. Categorical grants resemble a contract in which the federal government provides funds to state and local governments, which in turn are responsible for creating and operating programs as defined by the federal government. The AFDC, food stamp, and school lunch programs are among the many programs operated through federal categorical grants given to the states.

categorical grant *Common form of federal grant to state or local government for a specific purpose or objective. See also* **project grant** *and* **formula grant.**

In many grants, participating state and local governments are required to contribute funds toward the program. These are known as **matching funds.** While matching fund formulas vary from program to program, a typical pattern is for the federal government to provide 80% of the funds with states and localities covering remaining costs. The expectation is that their 20% matching requirements will increase state and local government commitment to program objectives and implementation. In this way, the subnational governments develop a vested interest in helping federal programs succeed.

matching funds *Monies that state and local governments are required to contribute to participate in federal grant programs; intended to increase state and local stake in federal programs.*

Categorical grants can be subdivided into two types: formula and project grants. **Formula grants** are allocated to state and local governments according to formulas that allow the federal government to target funds to specific areas or purposes. Thus, if Congress wished to finance an educational program in poor inner-city neighborhoods, it could include, within the formula, requirements about high population density, poverty,

formula grant *Federal grant to states or localities that is distributed on the basis of a prespecified formula.*

and unemployment. Because these conditions are found in many poor city neighborhoods, the formula would work to direct federal funds to targeted areas.

project grants *Federal grant programs that require states and localities to submit a project proposal for review by the federal agency overseeing the grant program.*

With **project grants,** individual state and local agencies must apply to participate in a federal program and receive federal funds. The application must outline how the agency will create or continue a program that complies with federal guidelines and objectives. These applications are routed to the appropriate federal agency, which examines and rates the quality of project proposals and determines which ones will be funded. Federal grants for the construction of facilities like hospitals or community health clinics are typically project grants.

block grants *Federal grants to state or local governments for a broad program area.*

Categorical grants represent the most prominent form of federal financial assistance to states and localities. Another form, however, is the **block grant,** through which the federal government provides funding for broad program areas instead of for specific programs. The Community Development Block Grant (CDBG) program, for example, allows local governments to design projects for economic or community development. The key difference between categorical (whether formula or project) and block grants is that the latter provide states and localities with greater discretion in spending program funds.

general revenue sharing *Federal grant with few strings attached; this type of grant was common from 1972 to 1986.*

From 1972 until 1986, another variant in federal financial assistance was **general revenue sharing (GRS).** Under this program, federal funds were given to states and localities on a formula basis, with almost no restrictions on the purposes for which the money could be spent. Even though the amount of federal dollars spent through GRS was consistently lower than that expended through categorical and block grants, GRS was popular with state and local officials, who appreciated having discretion in determining how federal funds were spent. In 1986, in an effort to reduce federal spending, the GRS program was terminated. Table 3-1 shows the impact of federal grants on state and local spending.

3-5b Magnitude and Impact of Fiscal Federalism

One way to describe the impact of federal grants is to consider the types of programs and activities they have funded. Figure 3-1 shows the major categories of federal grants to states and localities—health care; income security; education, training, employment, and social services; and transportation.

The impact of federal financial assistance can also be gauged by the magnitude of federal grants-in-aid to state and local governments (see Table 3-2). Federal grants rose from $7 billion in 1960 to almost $350 billion in 2002. Federal grants to states and localities in 2002 represented about 16% of all federal expenditures.

Another way to look at fiscal federalism is to measure the impact of federal spending on the expenditures of state and local governments. In 2001 federal grants represented almost one third of all state and local spending. Given the magnitude of federal grant dollars, federal spending cuts can have a strong and negative influence on states and localities.

Table 3-1

The Impact of Federal Grants on State and Local Spending

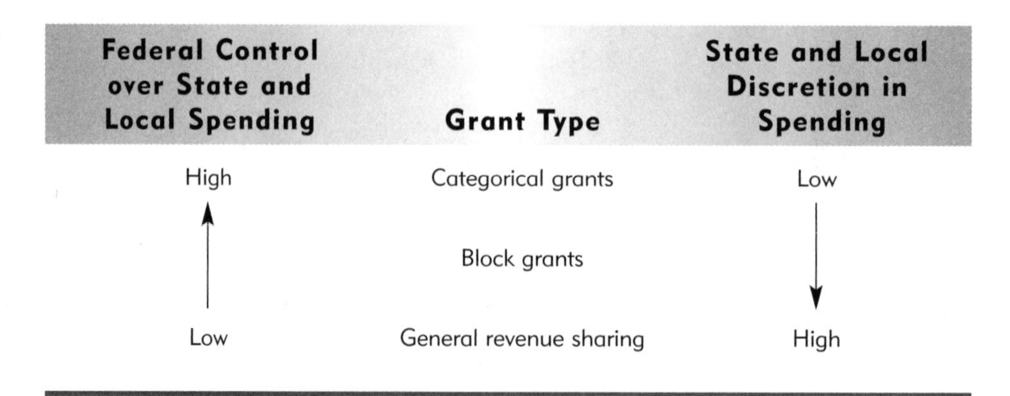

Federal Control over State and Local Spending	Grant Type	State and Local Discretion in Spending
High ↑	Categorical grants	Low ↓
	Block grants	
Low	General revenue sharing	High

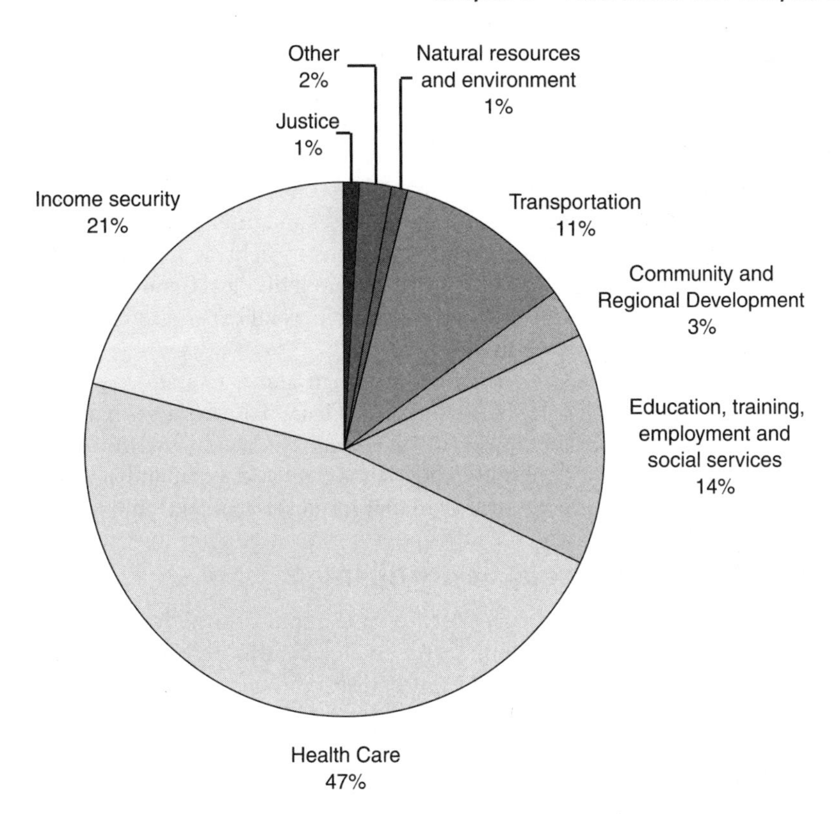

Figure 3-1

Allocation of Federal Grants to State and Local Governments by Function, 2005 (est).

Source: Office of Management and Budget, *Budget of the United States Government FY 2005. Analytical Perspectives,* Table 8-3, p. 120.

Table 3-2 **Federal Grants-in-Aid to State and Local Governments, 1960–2002 (est.)**

Year	Total Grants (in Billions)	Federal Grants as a Percentage of: All Federal Outlays	State and Local Expenditures	Gross Domestic Product
1960	7.0	7.6	14.6	1.4
1965	10.9	9.2	15.2	1.6
1970	24.1	12.3	19.2	2.4
1975	49.8	15.0	22.7	3.3
1980	91.4	15.5	25.8	3.4
1985	105.9	11.2	20.9	2.7
1990	135.3	10.7	18.1	2.3
1995	225.0	14.8	25.0	3.1
2000	284.6	15.9	30.7	2.9
2002 (est)	346.5	16.9	na	3.3

Source: Statistical Abstract of the United States, 2002, Table 411, p. 264.

When faced with federal cutbacks, state and local governments have two options: (1) apply more state and local revenues to make up the difference, or (2) cut back programs.

How Does Your State Stack Up?

Grants and federal expenditures to states depend on some factors such as population and the location of federal programs (such as military bases and interstate highways). Funding also depends on the effectiveness of state politicians in fighting for federal funds. Per capita expenditures include grants, direct payments to individuals, and other federal government program costs. Table 3-3 shows the per capita total expenditures for each of the states in the year 2000.

Still another way to consider federal government grants to state and local governments is by the purpose of the grants. As shown in Figure 3-1, the largest category of federal grants was for health-related programs including Medicaid (financial assistance to support health care of senior citizens). Other major categories of federal aid to states and localities include income security, education and social services, and transportation.

3-5c Reforming Fiscal Federalism

Federal grants lie at the heart of many debates at the start of the 21st century that concern the scaling back of federal spending and involvement in state and local level activities. These grants were one of the prime mechanisms through which the federal government expanded its powers in relation to states by stimulating the creation of many social welfare programs. Typically, state and local officials, as players in the federalism game, welcomed the flow of federal dollars—mainly in the form of categorical grants. They resented, however, the strict requirements governing program operations and spending. These officials frequently contended that "those folks in Washington" (i.e., members of Congress and federal officials—once called "pointy-headed bureaucrats" by Governor George Wallace of Alabama) did not understand needs and constraints at the local level. State and local leaders asserted that they could achieve federal objectives more effectively if there were fewer federal restrictions and greater flexibility in using federal dollars. These changes would allow them to tailor programs to the unique needs and problems of their state or community.

National government players have tended, until quite recently, to see things differently. Although they recognized that state and local players might have more detailed knowledge of local conditions, they were concerned, especially when they were a part of federal agencies responsible for monitoring programs, that state and local officials might not all share the same view concerning the objectives of federal programs. Without tight federal restrictions, these officials feared that state and local government would use federal monies for their own purposes and not necessarily as designed or intended by natural policy makers.

These contradictory views about the wisdom of tight federal controls have led to persistent strains within the federal system. State and local officials have followed a two-pronged strategy, pressing for both more federal monies and more discretion in spending these monies. Another strategy preferred by state and local governments calls for transforming categorical grants into block grants, thereby giving states more discretion in operating programs.

Most existing categorical grants in the social welfare area are entitlements, where the federal government agrees to provide payments to all eligible persons no matter how much funding is required. The shift to block grants would end the entitlement practice. The federal government under the block grant proposals would pay only the annual lump-sum payments, placing a financial limit on federal commitment to social welfare programs each year. Social welfare advocates worry that ending the practice of entitlements would leave many poor people without an adequate safety net. Another criticism of the block grant initiative concerns the capacity of states to take over and operate social welfare and other programs once the requirements associated with categorical grants are removed.

Some analysts argue that many states have insufficient experience and administrative capacity to take over primary responsibility for operating social welfare programs.

Table 3-3

How Does Your State Stack Up?

National Average	$6.6 billion (per state)	$6,268 (per person)
	Grants	**Per Capita Total Expenditures (2000)**
Alabama	5.3	7,128
Alaska	2.3	10,214
Arizona	5.2	5,921
Arkansas	3.4	6,221
California	39.8	5,566
Colorado	3.9	5,660
Connecticut	3.9	6,678
Delaware	.9	5,418
Florida	13.7	6,257
Georgia	7.9	5,780
Hawaii	1.5	8,025
Idaho	1.5	7,529
Illinois	11.8	5,237
Indiana	5.9	5,290
Iowa	3.1	5,946
Kansas	2.7	6,211
Kentucky	5.1	6,392
Louisiana	6.2	6,224
Maine	1.9	6,416
Maryland	7.6	9,094
Massachusetts	9.7	6,958
Michigan	10.9	5,195
Minnesota	5.3	5,069
Mississippi	4.2	7,105
Missouri	6.9	7,004
Montana	1.7	7,335
Nebraska	2.1	6,294
Nevada	1.4	4,816
New Hampshire	1.3	5,109
New Jersey	8.5	5,495
New Mexico	3.6	9,118
New York	32.9	6,132
North Carolina	9.1	5,536
North Dakota	1.3	9,262
Ohio	11.8	5,435
Oklahoma	4.1	6,570
Oregon	4.3	5,378
Pennsylvania	14.8	6,458
Rhode Island	1.6	6,666
South Carolina	4.7	6,150
South Dakota	1.3	7,693
Tennessee	7.0	6,461
Texas	21.7	5,397
Utah	2.2	5,095
Vermont	1.1	6,133
Virginia	5.9	10,067
Washington	6.8	6,261
West Virginia	3.0	6,935
Wisconsin	5.8	4,968
Wyoming	1.2	7,257

Source: U.S. Bureau of the Census, *Statistical Abstract of the United States*, 2002, Table 461, "Federal Funds—Summary Distribution by State."

Political scientist Donald F. Kettl has argued, for example, "In terms of administrative capacity, the states are all over the lot. Some are on the level of the federal government. Some are innovative and exciting. But some are a long way from that kind of competence."[5]

Leaders in many states reacted positively to the proposed shift from categorical to block grants for nutrition and other social welfare programs. As noted previously, they have argued that standard Washington-based solutions to problems (as designed through categorical grants) ignored differences in those problems across the states. These leaders believe in the ability of state and local governments to design and operate programs that will be better suited to local needs and circumstances.

State and local officials do worry that reduced federal involvement may mean fewer grant dollars. Sometimes when categorical grants are clumped together and transformed into block grants, the overall level of federal funding is reduced. When this occurs, states may be pressured by constituents to expand state funding of programs to make up the difference. This would tend to place substantial pressure on state budgets. Box 3-5: Playing Computer Politics with Intergovernmental Grants explains how computer technology now influences members of Congress in their decisions about formulas to distribute federal grant dollars.

Box 3–5 *Playing Computer Politics with Intergovernmental Grants*

Computer technology significantly influences the decisions made by Congress about formulas to distribute federal grant dollars. In the words of one analyst, "Members of Congress have a new weapon in their hands when they gather to vote on federal aid programs: thick computer printouts showing how much money their districts would receive under various proposals before them."[a]

When designing federal programs to distribute monies to states and localities, Congress creates allocation formulas that identify and weigh specific measurable indicators. For example, a program designed to improve the health of newborn children at health risk might include an allocation formula with such indicators as level of poverty, number of maternity care providers, use of illegal drugs in the community, and infant mortality rates. These indicators help legislators to target monies to those communities where infant health is most threatened and where more medical care facilities are needed.

All indicators, however, have allocative consequences, in that more monies will be allocated to some communities and less to others. According to the newborn children at health risk indicators, a city with high rates of infant mortality, drug use, and poverty, and with only a few maternity care providers, would receive more monies than other cities, while a formula with other indicators would result in a different distributional pattern.

Computers, combined with databases with hundreds of indicators for individual states and congressional districts, allow legislators and their staffs to determine quickly the allocative consequences of alternative distribution formulas. Congress has created a variety of databases and analysis programs that allow legislators to estimate the impact of proposed policies on each congressional district.[b]

Legislators, of course, want to ensure that their districts or states receive at least some financial assistance through intergovernmental grants. For this reason, the political games surrounding allocation formulas for intergovernmental grants tend to "spread the money around." Few legislators are willing to agree to formulas that target federal dollars to only a few communities, even if these communities are the neediest. Instead, legislators tend to support formulas that distribute funds widely, so that their constituents receive some support. Although this type of strategy is not new, the use of computers allows for rapid and precise estimates of allocative consequences and thus intensifies the quest for formulas that "spread the wealth."

---

a. Rochelle L. Stanfield, "Playing Computer Politics with Local Aid Formulas," *National Journal*, December 9, 1978, 1977.

b. Stephen E. Frantzich, *Computers in Congress: The Politics of Information*, Vol. 4 of *Managing Information: A Series of Books in Organization Studies and Decision Making* (Beverly Hills, CA: Sage, 1982).

3-6 Regulatory Federalism: Mandates and Power Relationships among Players

regulatory federalism *Pattern of regulatory requirements imposed by a government at a higher level in the federal system upon lower-level governments.*

Mandates imposed on lower levels of government by a higher one are examples of **regulatory federalism.** From the beginning of categorical grant programs, the federal government has specified requirements binding upon recipients of federal aid. Most stipulations pertain directly to the particular program or objective of the grant; these are referred to as the "strings" attached to federal grants. Other regulatory requirements represent the federal government's efforts to pursue objectives broader than individual programs. For example, federal requirements that state and local governments work toward environmental preservation, protect the safety of employees in the workplace, or take affirmative action in hiring women and people of color as a condition of receiving federal funds are regulatory mandates.

The U.S. Advisory Commission on Intergovernmental Relations (ACIR) has documented the forms and magnitude of regulatory mandates placed by the federal government upon states and localities. By the mid-1980s, ACIR counted over thirty-five major federal laws regulating state and local governments.[6] This number increased through the early 1990s. The breadth of regulatory power is evident in the number of different areas being regulated by the federal government, including environmental protection, civil rights, consumer protection, labor issues and workplace safety, and energy conservation (see Box 3-6: Examples of Major Federal Laws Regulating States and Localities).

In spite of efforts by the Republican presidential administration to scale back the growth of regulatory mandates, most of them continued to operate into the 1990s. Monitoring this trend toward expansion, the ACIR concluded in 1993 that

> For the first time in the nation's history, federal mandates and regulations rival grants and subsidies in importance as federal tools for influencing the behavior of state and local governments. In less than two decades, the Congress enacted dozens of statutes that utilized new and more coercive techniques to regulate state and local governments directly or sought to enlist them as administrative agents in regulating the private sector.[7]

Federal regulatory mandates force behavioral changes by state and local governments as well as by private companies and organizations. Illustrative of regulatory mandates was a directive issued by the Environmental Protection Agency (EPA) in 1991. It instructed public utilities to test all public water supplies for concentrations of lead. The EPA recognized that lead pipes were polluting water and potentially generating a public health hazard in many communities. The EPA directive also ordered utilities to reduce the levels of lead concentration when lead was detected in public water supplies. The order pertained to over 79,000 utility companies across the nation and demonstrates the reach of regulatory mandates imposed by the national government.

A key issue concerning federal mandates and regulations since 2000 has been affirmative action. Some conservatives, including the George W. Bush administration, have sought to challenge the use of race as a criteria that should be considered in college admissions or award of federal contracts. This question moved to the federal courts, which subsequently upheld some affirmative action policies and struck down others.

In many instances federal regulatory mandates are imposed on states and localities without any federal grant funds to help these governments comply with the mandates. State and local governments wish to retain federal funds and thus generally accept the fact that they must comply with regulatory mandates. They have generally been unhappy, however, with the prospect of having to pay compliance costs for mandates set nationally by Congress.

Consider two seemingly identical interstate highways. Both are constructed of the same materials, and both cross similar geographical areas. But wait: the speed limit signs are different. One indicates a 65 mile-per-hour limit, whereas the other warns "55 miles per hour: it's the law." What factors help explain the differences? For a discussion of this question, see Box 3-7: Why Do Speed Limits on Interstate Highways Vary across the States?

Box 3-6 Examples of Major Federal Laws Regulating States and Localities

Since the 1960s, the federal government has enacted a variety of federal laws that place regulatory mandates on state and local governments in such areas as environmental protection, civil rights, occupational safety, consumer protection, and energy conservation. Examples of federal laws that created regulatory mandates and the year of their initial passage are listed in this box. Regulatory mandates require that states and localities take actions and spend state and local monies to achieve nationally defined objectives. Once enacted, many of the federal laws that create regulatory mandates are revised by subsequent laws, many of which have expanded mandate scope. The Clean Air Act, for example, was amended in 1990 to require employers with more than one hundred employees to devise commuting options such as carpooling to reduce the number of auto trips to work and thus air pollution in major metropolitan areas.

These regulatory mandates have come under fire in the last decade as states and localities have pressed for relief from the mandate burden. Many proposals have been made to weaken regulatory mandates, notably in the area of environmental protection. Regulatory mandates are outlined in several federal government laws and policies.

Environmental Protection

The *Water Quality Act of 1965* establishes federal water quality standards for interstate waters.

The Clean Air Act Amendments of 1970 establish national air quality and emission standards.

The *Endangered Species Act of 1973* protects and conserves endangered and threatened species of animals.

The *Safe Drinking Water Act of 1974* assures drinking water purity.

Civil Rights

The *Civil Rights Act of 1964* prohibits discrimination on the basis of race, color, or national origin in programs receiving federal funds.

The *Civil Rights Act of 1968* prevents discrimination on the basis of race, color, national origin, sex, or religion in the sale or rental of federally assisted housing.

The *Education of All Handicapped Children Act of 1975* requires that all handicapped children receive a free educational program appropriate to their needs.

The *Age Discrimination Act of 1975* prevents discrimination on the basis of age for programs receiving federal funds.

The *Americans with Disabilities Act of 1990* requires that most public and private employers provide reasonable accommodations in the work place to employ people with disabilities.

Labor/Safety in the Workplace

The *Occupational Safety and Health Act of 1970* requires the elimination of unsafe and unhealthy working conditions.

The *Fair Labor Standards Act Amendments of 1974* extend federal minimum wage and overtime pay protections to state and local government employees.

Energy Conservation

The *Emergency Highway Energy Conservation Act of 1974* established a national maximum speed limit of 55 miles per hour. (This act has since been amended to allow higher speed limits in some areas.)

Sources: U.S. Advisory Commission on Intergovernmental Relations, *Regulatory Federalism: Policy, Process, Impact and Reform* (Washington, DC: ACIR, 1984); U.S. Advisory Commission on Intergovernmental Relations, *Federal Regulation of State and Local Governments* (Washington, DC: ACIR, 1993).

3-6a Reforming Regulatory Federalism

Complying with mandates is often costly and time-consuming. Mandates have been described as "millstones around the necks of local governments."[8] By the late 1980s, many state and local governments felt jilted by their federal partner. Once they had been "romanced with billions of dollars in grant money and promised an enduring commitment based on a sharing of responsibilities," but by the 1990s the subnational governments saw federal dollars shrinking and federally imposed mandates growing.[9]

Box 3–7 Why Do Speed Limits on Interstate Highways Vary across the States?

The nature of the federal relationship between the national and state governments explains the differences in interstate speed limits. During the 1970s, the national government, using its spending power, attached a provision to federal laws funding highway construction that required states to adopt a 55 mile-per-hour speed limit. States that refused to comply faced a substantial reduction in federal funds given to the state to build and repair highways. The states, therefore, complied with the mandate, although often unwillingly. Opposition to the 55 mile-per-hour limit, especially in the western states, caused Congress to modify federal highway legislation in the 1980s, allowing states the option of raising highway speed limits to 65 miles per hour except in congested urban areas. Many western states quickly raised their state's speed limits, while other states, like Connecticut, retained the standard 55 mile-per-hour limit on all state highways. Current federal law allows states flexibility in setting speed limits. States have used this flexibility differently, thereby accounting for differences in interstate highway speed limits.

Do you agree with this decision to give states the right to set their own speed limits on federal interstate highways? What do you think the effects have been on traffic fatalities, air pollution, and the commercial trucking industry?

Time Period

In 1970's, the federal government used funding of highway projects to enforce the 55 mile-per-hour speed limit. States failing to adopt the national speed limit faced substantial reduction in federal funds for highway construction and repair. This constraint was lifted during the 1980's.

Location

The greatest opposition to federally imposed speed limits came from the western states, where long distances between cities and relatively uncrowded highways made a high speed limit both desirable and relatively safe. They were the first to raise their limits during the 1980's.

Highway Construction Materials

While it may seem reasonable that speed limits would be linked to the physical character of the highway, this was not a major factor in determining speed limits.

Federalism

After experimenting with a uniform speed limit, the 1980's saw a return to the right of states to determine their own speed limits on non-urban interstate highways, even if the highways were funded by the federal government. Most western states raised their limits, while more urban states such as Connecticut retained the 55 mile-per-hour speed limit on all highways. Allowing states such power is a key example of federalism at work.

Regulatory mandates forced states and localities to start or expand programs that would comply, often causing increased spending to cover program creation or expansion. Even if the federal government did provide some monies to cover compliance activities, such as in the case of mandates to clear air and water, the monies did not cover all the costs necessary to achieve compliance, so states and localities were forced to pick up the balance. The private sector, too, was displeased with regulatory mandates placed on businesses. The business community typically saw governmental regulation as expensive—both with regard to mandated activities and to the large amount of paperwork required by the federal government to demonstrate compliance. Federal regulations were also seen as damaging to the ability of firms to compete in the worldwide marketplace.

The primary defenders of regulations have been those groups who directly benefit from strictly designed and enforced regulations. For example, environmentalists, who have sought to protect endangered species, wetlands, and national forests, argued that strong, nationwide regulations and restrictions are the most effective means to that end.

By the end of the twentieth century, Congress came under attack for creating regulatory burdens on state and local governments that it did not even impose on itself. This

Box 3-8 Which Do You Trust More, the Federal Government or Your State Government?

American federalism involves ongoing questions and debates about what level of government—national or state—should be responsible for specific governmental functions. Sometimes the federal government has assumed primary responsibility, sometimes the states take the lead, and often responsibilities are shared between the two.

Stop and think for a moment. Which level of government do you generally trust to do a better job of governing? In what policy areas do you trust your state government more, and in what areas would you trust the federal government to do a better job of running things? Your answers to these questions will likely influence your views about recent federalism debates that typically focus on a broader role for states in providing governmental services and a parallel reduction in federal responsibilities.

This same question was posed to a national sample of randomly selected Americans in a survey conducted by the *Washington Post-ABC News* in 1995.[a] Survey results demonstrate that most Americans trust their own state government far more than the national government. Almost 7 out of 10 respondents said they trusted their own states more to do a better job of running things. Only 27% said they would trust the federal government more. Relative trust in state government was consistent across party lines, with about 60% of Democrats, 70% of Independents, and 80% of Republicans saying they trusted their state governments over the federal government to run things better.

The poll respondents were asked if their state government or the federal government would do a better job in seven policy areas. In six of the areas—fighting crime, establishing rules about welfare, creating rules for workplace safety, setting Medicare and Medicaid regulations, designing environmental rules on clean air and water, and setting rules for civil lawsuits—respondents were more likely to trust their states over the federal government. In only one policy area, protection of civil rights, did survey respondents say they trusted the federal government more than the states.

How well did your answers match up with the national sample?

Most Americans trust state governments better than the federal government on many issues:

Fighting crime

Establishing rules about welfare

Creating rules for workplace safety

Setting Medicare and Medicaid regulations

Designing environmental rules for clean air and water

Setting rules for civil lawsuits

a. Richard Morin, "Power to the States: Almost Across the Board, Faith in the Federal Government's Ability Is Way Down," *Washington Post National Weekly Edition*, March 27–April 2, 1995, 37.

image of double standards prompted Congress to practice what it preached with regard to complying with regulatory mandates.[10] As one of its first actions, the 104th Congress in 1995 passed legislation that required both houses of Congress to conform to the regulatory mandates placed upon other branches of the federal government.

The question of which level of government does a better job is an ongoing consideration for many people. Box 3-8: Which Do You Trust More, the Federal Government of Your State Government discusses how your answers to this and related questions influences your views.

3-7 The Politics of Federalism

Controversies about federalism often become important political debates. States' rights, expansion of national government power, fiscal federalism, and regulatory mandates often become issues in political campaigns and on the floor of Congress. These controversies have also generated heated debates in the offices of mayors and governors, on the floors of state legislatures and city councils, and, sometimes, even in the living rooms of Americans. We will now look at how federalism affects partisan politics, the political power and recent revitalization of the states, and regional competition.

3-7a Federalism and Partisan Politics

Many national leaders have seized upon issues of federalism when seeking to win elective office or to develop a policy agenda. In formulating his Great Society program, President Lyndon B. Johnson (1963–1969) called for a new-shared commitment and cooperation among the national, state, and local governments in responding to such social problems as poverty, hunger, malnutrition, and inadequate health care. Like many liberals and Democrats, Johnson welcomed the use of federal power and influence to pursue social welfare policies throughout the nation.

President Richard M. Nixon (1969–1974), like most conservatives, did not share this enthusiasm for strong federal action to orchestrate a national response to social problems. Instead, Nixon preferred to give states and localities greater flexibility in crafting governmental programs to deal with social problems. Given this philosophy, Nixon pushed for general revenue sharing and block grants. As we have just seen, these forms of federal assistance provide states and localities with more discretion in spending than do categorical grants. Nixon also proposed a concept known as "New Federalism," which was intended to decentralize the administration of many programs. While never fully implemented (the plan was not adopted by a Democratic-controlled Congress), the thrust of this plan was to shift power away from the federal bureaucracy and toward state and local officials, who were seen as being closer to the problems that required solutions.

With the election of President Jimmy Carter (1977–1981), a Democrat, a return to Johnson-style enthusiasm for a strong categorical grant program was expected. Carter's response, however, was more complex. While he was the governor of Georgia, Carter had watched the implementation of federal grant programs from the state level. He believed in the capacity of state governments to deal effectively with social and economic programs. Carter, therefore, embraced block grant programs that provided states with flexibility in program design and spending.

As a conservative, President Ronald Reagan (1981–1989) sought to readjust federalism to diminish the power of the national government. A major thrust of the Reagan administration was **deregulation**—that is, modifying federalism by removing or loosening federal regulatory mandates. The aim was to reduce the regulatory burdens on states, localities, and private business. Under Reagan, indeed, regulation of telephone services, natural gas distribution, and the savings and loan industry was substantially reduced. President George H. Bush (1989–1993) followed this direction, calling for less governmental regulation and more state and local flexibility in spending federal funds.

deregulation *An initiative to lessen or remove the impact of regulatory mandates placed on the private sector and on state and local governments.*

Given his experience as the governor of Arkansas, President Bill Clinton, like his predecessor Jimmy Carter, had the opportunity to view the carrying out of federal programs from the statehouse perspective. This experience contributed to his approach to federalism in the 1990s. At about the midpoint of President Clinton's 8 years in office, Congress enacted (and Clinton signed into law) legislation that significantly transformed the nation's welfare program by transferring significant authority to state governments. Under the previous Aid to Families with Dependent Children (AFDC) program, the federal government directed the nation's welfare program with uniform guidelines and policies. In receiving AFDC funds, states were required to implement the program according to guidelines created by the national government. Through a broad-scale reform of the program enacted in 1996, state governments were given substantial authority concerning how to operate the welfare program in their state. The law also required that recipients find work within 2 years to remain eligible for the program and that welfare benefits would be limited to 5 years. Legislation like this signaled that, at the end of the 20th century, substantial rethinking about the federal partnership was underway, with the trend moving toward greater state authority to operate and manage programs financed heavily by the national

devolution *Movement of governing power away from the national government toward state and local governments.*

government. This trend, sometimes known as **devolution,** marked a significant change in the relative power relationship between the federal government on the one hand and state and local governments on the other.

Devolution and reducing regulatory barriers has been a hallmark of the George W. Bush administration, including some efforts to roll back regulatory requirements related to environmental projects. Strong pressure from environmental groups worked to block regulatory requirements from being weakened during Bush's first term.

3-7b The Courts and State Government Power

Since the mid-1980s, the most substantial debates about federalism and intergovernmental politics have focused on reforming patterns of fiscal and regulatory federalism. Other political issues have concerned long-standing questions about the constitutional reach of federal government powers. Such questions are often resolved in the federal judiciary system. Federal court decisions have had a mixed effect on the position of states in the federal system. Decisions such as *Garcia v. San Antonio Metropolitan Transit Authority* (1985)[11] and *South Carolina v. Baker (1988)*[12] have reaffirmed a strong federal role. These examples have, respectively, upheld the power of the national government to apply minimum wages to state and local employees and to regulate state and local government bonds.

Some judicial decisions of the past two decades, however, have expanded the role of state governments in the federal system by upholding state authority in matters that the Constitution does not clearly address. For example, while retaining the principle that some abortions are protected by the constitutional right to privacy,[13] the Supreme Court has indicated in recent cases that it sees a larger role for states in regulating abortions.[14]

3-7c Games of Regional Competition: Sun Belt vs. Frost Belt

Another issue in the game of intergovernmental politics concerns competition among the states for federal grant dollars. This competition has both political and economic ramifications. Beginning in the 1970s, states in the southern half of the nation, known as the Sun Belt, began to experience substantial population growth. Much of this growth resulted from the movement of Americans from northern states (the Frost Belt)—particularly from the Northeast and Midwest—to states in the Southeast and Southwest. Several economic factors motivated this population relocation in the 1970s, including the expansion of energy production industries in the South and declining industrial production in the Midwest. Many companies relocated to the South to take advantage of cheaper land, energy costs, and labor, and of lower taxes.

Lifestyle choices and immigration also have stimulated population shifts in a southerly direction. Senior citizens have sought warmer and more hospitable climates for their retirement, accounting for substantial population increases in Florida, Texas, and Arizona. The arrival of Latinos from Mexico and Central and South America and of Asians from Southeast Asia also has contributed to population increases in several states in the South and West.

The shift in population from the northern to the southern half of the nation was accompanied by an increased flow of federal dollars to Sun Belt states.[15] Recognizing that the flow of federal monies was tipping in favor of the Sun Belt, the states on both sides (Sun Belt and Frost Belt) have formed player teams to press for a flow of new federal dollars in their direction. The Sun Belt Institute and the Northeast-Midwest Institute serve as lobbies for their respective regions, tracking the regional flow of federal dollars and lobbying to attract monies in their direction.

Sun Belt growth likely means enhanced political power for conservatives, often Republicans, but sometimes moderate Democrats as well. The reapportionment of seats in the House of Representatives following the 2000 census has meant more districts in the Sun Belt and more seats for conservatives.

3-7d Revitalization of the States

One pronounced trend in federalism in the 1980s and 1990s was the resurgence of state governments as vibrant players (See Box 3-9: States as Policy Innovators: Learnfare and

Box 3–9 States as Policy Innovators: Learnfare and Welfare Reform

American states have played the role of policy innovator, devising public policies that, if successful, serve as models for other states to follow. On occasion, policies initiated at the state level have been adopted by Congress and implemented nationally.

An example of such policy innovation is Learnfare, created by the state of Wisconsin in 1988 to enhance the educational achievement of children in welfare families. Under Learnfare, a policy pushed strongly by Wisconsin's Republican governor Tommy Thompson, children whose families participate in the AFDC program (a joint federal-state program) have their attendance monitored in local schools. If the children have more than the allowable number of unexcused absences in a given month, their family's welfare payment is reduced. The Learnfare plan was endorsed by conservative president George H. Bush and activated through special permission granted by the Department of Health and Human Services. Initially, the program was limited to teenagers.

Learnfare designers expected that welfare parents would give greater attention to their children's school attendance if attendance was tied to welfare payments and that, subsequently, these children would attend school more regularly and increase their educational achievement.[a] In this way, they may decrease their likelihood of needing welfare assistance in the future.

Learnfare was an innovative program because it coupled the provision of public program benefits (welfare payments) with a behavioral requirement (regular school attendance). Few other social programs have linked the receipt of benefits to behavioral actions or changes.

Learnfare has been controversial in Wisconsin. Opponents object to the linkage of benefits to sanctions and argue that it is inappropriate to penalize an entire family that is already quite poor for the behavior of a child or young adult. Opponents have also expressed concerns that Learnfare may lead to greater family problems and possibly more child abuse.[b]

Proponents of the program counter that it is right and appropriate to link benefits to behavioral responsibility. They also argue that the contemporary welfare system is doing more to create dependency than to foster independence. In their view, Learnfare is one means to shift the balance toward greater independence.

Evidence on the implementation of the Learnfare program shows mixed results.[c] Accurate monitoring of the attendance of AFDC children has proven difficult; mistakes in the records have sometimes resulted in undeserved penalties. While early evaluations suggest that the school attendance patterns of some AFDC children have improved, Learnfare has yet to generate substantial improvements in school attendance patterns. A recent study, for example, found little difference between teens subject to Learnfare and other students with regard to enrollment in school or attendance.[d] The State of Wisconsin was sufficiently pleased with the program, however, that it decided to expand it, on a limited basis in a few areas, to all school-age children. This move expanded coverage to children in elementary and middle schools. While many states have expressed interest in Learnfare, most have chosen to await the results of Wisconsin's experiment before launching their own program.

a. Thomas Corbett, Jeannette Deloya, Wendy Manning, and Liz Uhr, "Learnfare: The Wisconsin Experience, in *Focus*, Vol. 12 (Madison, WI: Institute for Research on Poverty, University of Wisconsin-Madison, Fall 1989).

b. Bruce Murphy, "A Black Eye for Wisconsin?" *Milwaukee Magazine*, May 1990, 114.

c. Wisconsin Legislative Audit Bureau, *Learnfare Program Administration* (Madison, WI: Legislative Audit Bureau, 1990), Report 90-23; John Pawasarat and Lois Quinn, *The Impact of Learnfare on Milwaukee County Social Service Clients* (Milwaukee, WI: Employment and Training Institute, University of Wisconsin-Milwaukee, 1990); John Pawasarat, Lois Quinn, and Frank Stetzer, *Evaluation of the Impact of Wisconsin's Learnfare Experiment on the Attendance Patterns of Teenagers Receiving Aid to Families with Dependent Children*, report submitted to the Wisconsin Department of Health and Social Services and the U.S. Department of Health and Human Services (Milwaukee, WI: Employment and Training Institute, University of Wisconsin-Milwaukee, 1992).

d. Wisconsin Legislative Audit Bureau, *An Evaluation of Wisconsin's Learnfare Program: Summary of an Interim Report on First Semester Effects* (Madison, WI: Wisconsin Legislative Audit Bureau, 1994).

Welfare Reform). Several reasons account for this revitalization of the states. First, the states have increased their funding commitment to several social programs to prevent federal cutbacks from decimating existing programs. Second, many states are assisting localities facing dire budget situations. Faced with increasing demands for urban services and a reduction in federal grants, local officials have actively sought state assistance. Many states have responded by increasing funding of locally operated programs, noticeably those concerning the courts and social welfare.[16]

Enhanced state activism has taken forms other than increased financial grants to localities. During the last decade, policy innovation at the state level has markedly increased through the pursuit of new, often experimental, programs to cope with long-standing problems.[17] This innovation allows states to serve as laboratories for social experiments, which, if successful, can be adopted by other states. Prior to 1980, reformers in such areas as social welfare and environmental protection typically looked to the federal government for policy innovations and reforms. States today continue to serve as hosts for welfare reform policy that was, prior to welfare reforms during the Clinton administration, highly regulated by federal rules and guidelines.

In 2002 and 2003, questions of federalism focused upon financial issues. The economic recession of the period reduced state and local government revenues. Because states and localities are generally required to operate balanced budgets, reduced revenues cause major challenges and stimulate budget cuts. In 2003, state government made repeated calls to the president and Congress to increase general funding flows to the states, to help alleviate budget deficits. Facing its own deficit, the national government found it difficult to respond.

Conclusion

Federalism—a political game of sharing governing powers between the national and subnational units of government—is alive and well in the United States. Throughout most of the twentieth century, the power of the federal players grew at the expense of state and local players. Nonetheless, both cities and states performed important roles in governing their citizens, and they administered many programs designed and funded by the national government. Layer-cake federalism, where powers are exercised more or less separately, has given way to a more cooperative marble-cake federalism.

Important games of intergovernmental relations are played in the areas of fiscal and regulatory federalism. Through its spending and regulatory powers, the federal government has sought to influence the actions and programs of states and localities. State and city officials appreciate federal financial assistance, but they often complain, sometimes quite loudly, about the regulatory burdens associated with acceptance of federal dollars.

Persistent state and local complaints about federal mandates—particularly unfunded ones—were recognized by Congress in the late 1990s, which considered substantial reforms in both fiscal and regulatory federalism. On the fiscal front, Congress cut back some federal programs and transformed others from categorical to block grants. This increased state and local flexibility in designing and operating programs. Congress also created the principle that it will fund the compliance costs of any new regulatory mandates placed on states and localities. Concerning regulatory federalism, Congress debated multiple measures intended to reverse the trend of ever-increasing regulation of state and local governments and the private sector.

Throughout the 1990s and into the 2000s, state governments have been expected to play a more active role in governing the United States. Given greater flexibility in program operations, states have increasingly served as experimental sites for policy innovations that were not possible under the former system of universal national policy requirements.

Key Terms

abolition
block grants
categorical grant
commerce clause
compact theory
competitive federalism
Compromise of 1850
contract theory
cooperative federalism
creative federalism
deregulation
devolution
dual federalism
Emancipation Proclamation
equal protection clause
fiscal federalism
formula grant
general revenue sharing
Great Society
Kentucky Resolution Law
layer-cake federalism
marble-cake federalism
matching funds
Missouri Compromise of 1820
nullification doctrine
project grants
regulatory federalism
regulatory mandates
secession
sedition
selective incorporation
sovereign
spending power
states' rights
unitary political system

Practice Quiz

1. Unitary political systems are based upon
- **a.** the separation of powers.
- **b.** emancipation.
- **c.** federalism.
- **d.** political power concentrated in one national government.

2. The "reserve powers" of the Bill of Rights focus upon
- **a.** slavery.
- **b.** interstate commerce.
- **c.** the states and people retaining powers not granted to the national government.
- **d.** prohibiting states from leaving the union.

3. The Kentucky Resolution represented an effort by state governments to
- **a.** expand slavery.
- **b.** end slavery.
- **c.** secede from the Union.
- **d.** nullify a national government law.

4. The Missouri Compromise of 1820 dealt with
- **a.** admission of states supporting slavery into the Union.
- **b.** the Alien and Sedition Acts.
- **c.** the right of states to leave the Union.
- **d.** the selection of Supreme Court justices.

5. Through the Emancipation Proclamation in 1863, President Abraham Lincoln stated that
- **a.** southern states who seceded from the union would be brought back into the Union through military force.
- **b.** slaves living in states that left the union would be freed when the states were brought back into the union.
- **c.** the balance of "slave" and "free" states should be equal.
- **d.** states would be free to control the commerce within their boundaries.

6. "Layer-cake" federalism refers to a pattern of national-state government relations where the
- **a.** functions of national and state government are intertwined and fluid.
- **b.** functions of national and state governments are relatively separate from each other.
- **c.** rebellious Southern states were brought back into the nation.
- **d.** functions of national and state government are focused upon issues of slave and free states.

7. The Great Society programs are most closely associated with which president?
- **a.** James Madison
- **b.** Abraham Lincoln
- **c.** Lyndon B. Johnson
- **d.** Ronald Reagan

8. The Commerce Clause of the U.S. Constitution grants the national government the power to
- **a.** create a Department of Commerce.
- **b.** issue and regulate currency.
- **c.** regulate trade among the states.
- **d.** create social welfare programs.

9. The spending power of the national government allowed the U.S. Congress to
- **a.** create Great Society programs.
- **b.** regulate commerce.
- **c.** expand national government action in areas that are not directly empowered by the Constitution.
- **d.** do both a and c.

10. A categorized grant made by the national government operates as
- **a.** a contract, where states are funded to provide specific programs.
- **b.** a generally open-ended allocation of national government funds to states.
- **c.** an allocation of national government funds for broad-areas of service.
- **d.** a program to restore southern states after the Civil War for reconstruction.

11. State and local discretion in using and spending federal funds is greatest in which form of national government spending?
- **a.** Categorical grants
- **b.** General revenue sharing
- **c.** Block grants
- **d.** Project grants

12. Devolution refers to the transfer of governing powers from the
- **a.** states to the national government.
- **b.** states to the private sector.
- **c.** national government back to the states.
- **d.** state legislatures to state governors.

You can find the correct answers to these questions by taking the quiz and then submitting your answers in the Online Edition. The program will automatically score your submission. Where you miss a question, the program will provide the correct answer, a rationale for the answer, and the section number in the chapter where the topic is discussed.

Further Reading

One of the most thorough reviews of the origins, development, and current status of federalism and intergovernmental relations is presented in Deil S. Wright, *Understanding Intergovernmental Relations*, 3rd ed. (Pacific Grove, CA: Brooks/Cole Publishing, 1988).

For a discussion of the Constitution and federalism, see Chapter 8, "Federal-State Relations," in Louis Fisher, *Constitutional Structures: Separated Powers and Federalism* (New York: McGraw-Hill, 1990).

Among the classic treatments of American federalism are Morton Grodzins, *The American System: A New View of Government in the United States* (Chicago, IL: Rand McNally, 1966); William Riker, *Federalism: Origin, Operation, Significance* (Boston, MA: Little, Brown, 1964); and Samuel H. Beer, "Federalism, Nationalism, and Democracy in America," *American Political Science Review* 72 (1978), 9–21.

An excellent source on regulatory federalism is the U.S. Advisory Commission on Intergovernmental Relations (ACIR), *Regulatory Federalism: Policy Process, Impact and Reform*, Report A-95 (Washington, D.C.: ACIR, 1984).

For many different perspectives on the evolution of federalism during the 1980s, see the U.S. Advisory Commission on Intergovernmental Relations (ACIR), *Readings in Federalism: Perspectives on a Decade of Change*, Report SR-11 (Washington, D.C.: ACIR, 1989). For a report that sheds lights on the costs of federal mandates on states and localities, see the ACIR, *Federally Induced Costs Affecting State and Local Governments* (Washington, D.C.: ACIR, 1994).

The fiscal dimension of intergovernmental relations is analyzed in Teres Ter-Minasian, *Fiscal Federalism in Theory and Practice* (Washington, D.C.: International Monetary Fund, 1997).

The periodical *Governing*, published each month by Congressional Quarterly, Inc., is another excellent source on contemporary developments in intergovernmental relations.

While many academic journals in political science and public administration publish articles dealing with federalism, the journal *Publius* focuses primarily on the question of intergovernmental relations. *Publius* is published by the Center for the Study of Federalism and should be available in most college libraries.

An interesting examination of the impact of federal regulatory mandates is presented in Michael Fix and Daphne A. Kenyon, eds., *Coping with Mandates: What Are the Alternatives?* (Washington, D.C.: Urban Institute Press, 1990).

Detailed information on trends and patterns in intergovernmental aid is presented in the U.S. Advisory Commission on Intergovernmental Relations (ACIR), *Significant Trends of Fiscal Federalism*, Volumes I and II (Washington, D.C.: ACIR, 1992). See also Donald F. Kettl, *The Regulation of American Federalism*. Baton Rouge, LA: Louisiana State University Press, 1983).

For a perspective on shifts in the system of American intergovernmental relations, see David B. Walker, *The Rebirth of Federalism: Slouching toward Washington* (Chatham, NJ: Chatham House Publishers, 1995); Timothy Conlan, *From New Federalism to Devolution: Twenty-Five Years of Intergovernmental Reform* (Washington, D.C.: Brookings Institution, 1998); and David Shapiro, *Federalism: A Dialogue* (Evanston, IL: Northwestern University Press, 1995).

See also Paul L. Posner, *The Politics of Unfunded Mandates: Whither Federalism?* (Washington, D.C.: Georgetown University Press, 1998).

Endnotes

1. 17 U.S. (4 Wheat.) 315 (1819).
2. Morton Grodzins, *The American System: A New View of Government in the United States* (Chicago: Rand McNally, 1966).
3. These periods of federalism are drawn, in part, from the work of Deil Wright, *Understanding Intergovernmental Relations*, ed. (Pacific Grove, CA: Brooks/Cole, 1988), 66–112. Wright breaks down the different periods of federal relationships in more detail than has been presented in this textbook.
4. A cogent discussion of the evolution of hunger as a national issue is presented in Jeffrey M. Berry, *Feeding Hungry People: Rulemaking in the Food Stamp Program* (New Brunswick, NJ: Rutgers University Press, 1984).
5. Cited in David E. Rosenbaum, "Governor's Frustration Fuels Effort on Welfare Financing," *New York Times* (March 18, 1995), 1.
6. U.S. Advisory Commission on Intergovernmental Relations, *Regulatory Federalism: Policy, Process, Impact and Reform* (Washington, D.C.: ACIR, 1984).
7. U.S. Advisory Commission on Intergovernmental Relations, *Federal Regulation of State and Local Governments: The Mixed Record of the 1980s* (Washington, D.C.: ACIR, 1993), 1.
8. Edward Koch, "The Mandate Millstone," *The Public Interest*, Fall 1980, 43–44.
9. John Moore, "Mandates without Money," *National Journal*, October 4, 1986, 2366.
10. See, for example, the U.S. Advisory Commission on Intergovernmental Relations, *Disability Rights Mandates: Federal and State Compliance with Employment Protections and Architectural Barrier Removal* (Washington, D.C.: ACIR, 1989).
11. *Garcia v. San Antonio Metropolitan Transit Authority*, 105 S. Ct 1007 (1985).
12. *South Carolina v. Baker*, 11 L Ed 2d 595 (1988). For a review of the impact of this court decision, see Douglas J. Watson and Thomas Vocino, "Changing Intergovernmental Relationships: Impact of the 1986 Tax Reform Act on State and Local Governments," *Public Administration Review* 50 (July/August 1980): 427–34.
13. *Roe v. Wade*, 410 U.S. 113 (1973).
14. *Webster v. Reproductive Health Services*, 109 S. Ct. 3040 (1989).
15. "Federal Spending: The North's Loss Is the South's Gain," *National Journal*. June 26, 1976, 878–91. See also Ronald Brownstein, "Chasing the Sun," *National Journal*, September 10, 1988, 2236–41.
16. Steven D. Gold, *State and Local Fiscal Relations in the Early 1980s* (Washington, D.C.: The Urban Institute Press, 1983), Chapter 4.
17. Richard P. Nathan, "The Role of the States in American Federalism," in *The State of the States*, Carl E. Van Horn, ed. (Washington, D.C.: Congressional Quarterly, 1989), 15–32.

4

Constitutional Rights and Civil Liberties: A Prerequisite for Political Democracy

Key Points

- **The changeable nature of civil liberties.**
- **The potential for conflict between the individual rights of one person and those of others.**
- **The fundamental tension between public order and personal liberty.**
- **The nationalization of constitutional rights and liberties.**
- **Subtleties inherent in the freedoms of expression, assembly, and press; religious freedom; privacy rights; due process and the rights of the accused; and the right to vote.**

Preview: Constitutional Rights Are Not Etched in Stone

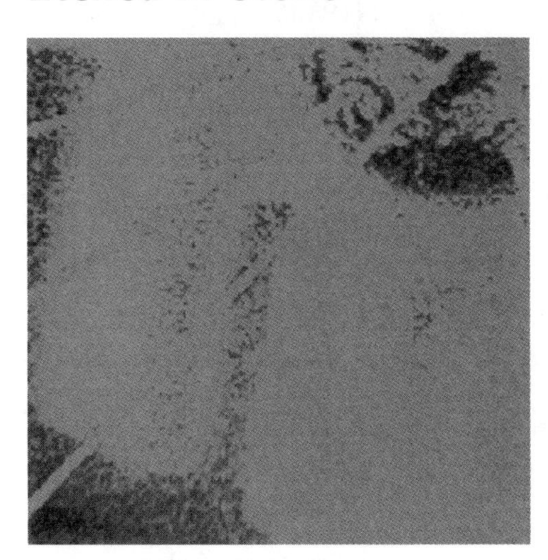

The two editors, each sitting on an extremely sensitive story, were tense as the final publication deadline approached. The first editor's story included plans for creating a homemade atomic bomb. The controversial subjects of the other editor's story were teenage pregnancies and the impact of divorce on high school students. Since both stories could be embarrassing and potentially even dangerous to publish, both editors were concerned, as journalists, about the consequences of printing their stories. The issue that troubled them was the impact their decisions to print might have on the rights of a free press and of freedom of expression that are guaranteed by the 1st Amendment to the Constitution.

Statue of Lincoln at the Lincoln Memorial
© Digital Stock 1996

*In each case, a government official stepped in to block publication. In the end, one story ran and the other did not. Contrary to what you might think, the story about high school pregnancies became more of a "bomb" than the story about building a bomb. Considerable objection was raised to the atomic bomb story on the grounds of protecting national security. Much of the objection dissipated, however, when it was reported that the plans had come from unclassified government documents and, indeed, had already been published. United States traditions of free expression and opposition to prior censorship removed any remaining threat to publication. When the case went to the courts (*United States v. The Progressive*), it languished, and the Supreme Court never formally ruled on it. The lesson seems to be that censorship in advance of publication is generally unwarranted and often impossible to enforce.*

*The high school pregnancy and divorce story, on the other hand, was killed—not by the editor but by the principal. Was the principal's action an unconstitutional act or a threat to the basic right of free expression? Not according to the federal courts (*Hazelwood School District v. Kuhlmeier*, 484 U.S. 260 [1988]).*

The editor of the bomb story worked for a regular newspaper, while the other editor was preparing a high school newspaper. The courts ruled that public school newspapers were subject to censorship prior to publication by school principals, who represent school district government. The courts viewed high school newspapers as teaching tools, not vehicles for informing the public. Free speech, therefore, was not an issue. As in many cases, the civil liberties of Americans are not absolute but rather are conditioned by the context.

The Constitution of the United States, including the Bill of Rights and other amendments, did more than establish a system of federal government and allot power among governmental branches. It also created a series of rights and liberties designed to protect the people from the power of government. Liberties such as the freedoms of press, speech, and religion empower individuals. They enable citizens to be effective players in political games and to protect themselves from onerous actions by those who exercise governmental power and authority. Civil rights are therefore important cornerstones in American democracy and its plan for national government with limited, rather than absolute, governing power.

Civil liberties protect both active and passive players in American politics from random use of power by government officials. This protects individuals when governments seek to make arrests, suppress publications, or take control of private property for public purposes. Government officials, when taking actions such as these, are prohibited from taking some measures, for example, illegally gathering evidence in criminal trials. In addition, officials must follow certain procedures to protect individual rights, as when suspects are read their rights prior to being questioned by the police.

Civil liberties are also intended to protect minorities from tyranny by the majority. Should a majority of citizens, for example, wish to silence the minority on some issue, the right of freedom of speech, firmly grounded in the Bill of Rights, protects the members of the minority's right to express themselves. Thus, while some Americans may wish to silence advocates of gay marriage, abortion rights, or bans on handguns, the freedoms of speech and of the press protect the open expression of views on these and other controversial issues.

With its focus on civil liberties and constitutional protection of individual rights, this section will examine the array of civil liberties provided through the U.S. Constitution. The basic freedoms of speech, press, and assembly will be analyzed as well as freedom of religion, separation of church and state, the right to privacy, and the rights of persons accused of committing crimes. The section will also explore the right of citizens to become political game participants by voting in elections.

4-1 Understanding Constitutional Rights and Civil Liberties: Six Fundamentals

Civil liberties are constitutionally based freedoms guaranteed to American citizens. Actually, the original Constitution, ratified in 1789, contained only a few of these civil liberties, such as the right to a trial by jury. Most of the civil liberties Americans today take for granted were added to the Constitution through the Bill of Rights, a set of amendments ratified in 1791.

civil liberties *Fundamental freedoms provided to American citizens in the Constitution and the Bill of Rights. Includes freedoms of speech, the press, religion, and assembly.*

In spite of concerted effort to outline basic constitutional rights and freedoms, the Founders recognized that the Constitution could not cover every possible question about civil rights and liberties. Much of the history of American government has involved efforts to clarify the meaning of the civil rights and liberties initially outlined in the Constitution. The following points highlight some fundamental characteristics of civil rights and liberties in America.

The first is that the rights of individuals in American political life have changed and evolved over time. At the end of the nineteenth century, **segregating** whites and African Americans in public education, housing, and public accommodations was still considered legal and constitutional. Until about 1920, most women were legally prohibited from voting. Landlords were mostly free to discriminate when leasing residential property. Through these and other practices, the rights and opportunities enjoyed by some Americans—to use public facilities, vote, and lease a home without discrimination—were denied to other citizens. Throughout the twentieth century, constitutional amendments and public laws have ended the legal basis of these discriminatory practices, generally following prolonged struggles by groups to push for legal prohibitions against discrimination. (Many of these struggles are described in Chapter 20.)

segregation *The enforced separation of a group (such as a racial one) from the rest of society.*

A second fundamental is that no rights are absolute. The rights and liberties of individual players and groups of players have some bounds, for if taken to the extreme, they could cause governmental instability and harm to other individuals. Americans, for example, diligently guard the right to free speech, but this right does not protect persons who shout "Fire!" in a crowded theater when no danger is present. Also unprotected by the Constitution are those who publicly make false and malicious statements about another person's character. Nor does freedom of speech protect a defense worker who wishes to sell military secrets to foreign nations. Even the right to own and sell private property, one of the most fundamental components of the American capitalistic system, is not unlimited. When an individual's property is needed to achieve some purpose that greatly benefits society—completing a major highway, for example—the government is empowered to take control of that property, provided that just compensation is given to the property holder.

A third fundamental is that rights are not always automatically recognized. Even when players or groups feel that they have a constitutional right, other persons or governmental authorities may not recognize that right. Players may be compelled to fight for their rights. One forum to assert one's rights is the courts, where disagreeing parties meet to formally resolve their conflicting rights. Public protest is another means of forcing the government—and sometimes society in general—to recognize rights.

A fourth fundamental is that it is a responsibility of government to determine whose rights prevail when the rights of one player or group clash with those of another. Within the framework of the U.S. Constitution, individual players or groups can claim rights that conflict in specific situations. For example, when a contagious disease begins spreading through a community, public health officials often require that all schoolchildren be inoculated. Some parents may seek to prevent their children from being inoculated on the grounds that such treatment violates their privacy or religious practice. Whose rights prevail in this situation, those of society or those of the parents? When rights conflict, the government, most often through the courts, determines whose rights prevail (see Time Out 4-1: "Noise Games": Conflicts over Rights).

due process *Legal proceedings conducted in a proper manner, ensuring protection of individual rights.*

A fifth fundamental is that the Constitution and the Bill of Rights require the government to proceed under **due process** of the law when it takes actions that might interfere with an individual's rights or liberties. That is, governmental actions must follow specified processes intended to protect individuals as much as possible from harm by government officials. When someone is arrested, for example, the police must follow a prescribed set of actions that include informing suspects of their rights.

A final fundamental is that most rights and liberties specified in the Constitution have been nationalized. The rights and liberties established in the Bill of Rights initially were designed to protect the people and the states from encroachments by the national government.[1]

The ratification of the 14th Amendment to the Constitution in 1868 provided the basis for also extending the rights and protections afforded by the Bill of Rights to the actions of state and local governments. This amendment prohibits states from (1) making or enforcing laws that abridge the rights and privileges of U.S. citizens; (2) depriving any persons of life, liberty, or property without due process of the law; and (3) denying any persons equal protection under the law. Through a series of Supreme Court decisions, the freedoms and protections of the Bill of Rights have been extended to states through a process known as selective incorporation (see Chapter 3). In each case of incorporation, the Court has coupled a specific (or selected) right (as outlined in the Bill of Rights) to the due process provision of the 14th Amendment. Since the beginning of the twentieth century, the Supreme Court has selectively incorporated most provisions of the Bill of Rights, thereby applying them to the actions of state and local governments.

Time Out 4-1

"Noise Games": Conflicts over Rights

Imagine for a moment the following situation (one you may well have faced many times if you live in a college dormitory): You have an important test to study for this evening. You are a bit behind in your studying, and you need to pull an "all-nighter" to be prepared. Also, you are the type of person who needs total quiet to study. Your dorm neighbor has just purchased a hot compact disc that he feels the need to play over and over all night long at maximum volume.

In this case, whose rights are more important—yours to have silence so you can study or his to play music?

In what ways are you likely to resolve this issue?

Consider the same situation outside of the college dorm. Imagine that you live in an apartment in a large city and that the noisemakers are residents of a nearby apartment building. In this case, whose right is more important—yours to study or theirs to listen to loud music? How could this problem be resolved?

4-2 Liberty and Public Order: Conflicting Values

Both personal liberty and public order are cherished values within American democracy. Without personal freedoms such as the freedoms of speech, the press, and the right to assemble, obtaining information about government, participating meaningfully in government, and making informed choices in elections would be inconceivable. Americans, like most other peoples of the world, also desire public order. They want to live peacefully, without worrying about crime, violence, and unwanted intrusions into their lives. Americans expect government to provide public order and to protect life and property. Locally, people expect their police departments and other law enforcement agencies to control crime effectively. Nationally, Americans expect that the military will prevent other nations from invading or inflicting harm.

Although personal liberty and public order are fundamental American political values, they are not always compatible. If a government enhances individual liberties, it often finds itself facing increased problems of public order. If, on the other hand, the government puts public order ahead of individual liberty, then personal freedoms may be violated. During protests against the Vietnam War, the values of free speech and public order collided. Individuals, using their free speech rights, engaged in strong and visible action to protest a governmental policy. Sometimes these protests obstructed public events; occasionally violence erupted. Seeking to restore public order and to protect life and property, law enforcement officials moved in and forcefully ended protests. Some Americans felt that the protesters were right in their position and should be allowed the full opportunity to express their dissatisfaction with the war. Others felt that the protests were harmful disruptions that threatened life and property. They urged government authorities to take firm action to end the protests.

More recently, protests about abortion have generated calls for greater public order. During the 1990s, pro-life (anti-abortion) groups organized large-scale protests at the sites of abortion clinics in many cities across the nation. The purpose of these protests was to intimidate women from entering the clinics. In some cases, protesters physically prevented anyone from entering the facility. In a few isolated instances (not supported by most pro-life groups) the protests have become violent. Doctors and other staff members at abortion clinics have been threatened and attacked. A doctor and two clinic workers were gunned down and killed in one city; there has been loss of life from such violent protests elsewhere as well.

A demonstrator offers a flower to military police on guard at the Pentagon during an anti-Vietnam War demonstration.

National Archives and Records Administration, Records of the Office of the Chief Signal Officer

Time Out 4-2

Where Do You Stand?

Choose the response to the following question that best reflects your view, and you will have a chance to see who among the public tends to agree or disagree with you in the Answers to Time Out 4-2 box on page 96.

A woman should always be able to obtain an abortion as a matter of personal choice (as opposed to there being specific legal limits or abortion being outlawed completely).

-YES
-NO

In response to the growing violence at abortion clinics, Congress, in 1994, enacted the Freedom of Access to Clinic Entrances Act with the intention of safeguarding access to abortion clinics. This legislation prohibits the use of force, threat of force, or physical obstruction—including sit-in demonstrations—to interfere with, injure, or intimidate any woman attempting to obtain an abortion. The prohibitions apply at both the clinic door and at women's and clinic workers' homes, which had also been targets of abortion protesters. The law also allowed civil and criminal actions to be brought by the national government and set penalties for destroying or damaging abortion clinics.

Pro-life groups have questioned the constitutionality of this law, which they see as infringing upon their right to protest governmental actions (in this case allowing abortions to be performed). These groups have staged protests that include actions in violation of the new law, in part to create legal cases designed to test its constitutionality. Proponents of the law believe that the maintenance of public order and the protection of the right of women to enter clinics are more fundamental rights than the free speech rights of the pro-life groups. Ultimately, the federal courts are being called upon to resolve this dispute as both sides seek to ascertain the constitutionality of the clinic access law. Proceed to Time Out 4-2: Where Do You Stand? and compare your position on abortion with those of others in the nation.

Many judicial decisions and governmental policies seek to balance the values of personal liberty and public order (see Time Out 4-3: Three Landmark Cases). Changing conditions, however, may work to favor one value over the other. During times of threatening conditions—such as natural disasters, riots, or wars—governments have pursued, and courts have upheld, policies that scale back personal freedoms in the name of national security or public safety. In more peaceful times, the courts have been much more reluctant to uphold laws that suspend personal freedoms.

Time Out 4-3

Three Landmark Cases

Background

Consider the following three cases and determine whether you think the actions of public officials were justified. In each case, decide whether the person in the case was treated fairly in your opinion. Then see the Answers to Time Out 4-3 box to compare your answers to the court rulings in the case. In preparation, you might want to take a look at the fifth and sixth amendments to the Constitution, which deal with the rights of the accused and one's rights when on trial.

continued

—Time Out 4-3 Continued

Cases

Case 1

A 51-year-old man who has been in and out of jail many times is charged by the police with having broken into a poolroom in Florida. He has no money and is unable to hire a lawyer. He asks the court to appoint a counsel to represent him. The judge refuses, saying that the laws of the State of Florida allow for courts to appoint and pay for counsel only in murder cases. At the trial the individual does the best he can to represent his own interests, even to the point of making opening arguments to the jury, cross-examining witnesses for the prosecution, and making a short summary at the end to defend his innocence. After the jury deliberates, it finds the defendant guilty. He is sentenced to serve 5 years in the state prison.

Poll: What do you think?

Was the defendant deprived of important constitutional rights when the judge did not provide him a lawyer?

Yes

No

The Rest of the Story

Gideon's story is made even more notable because he had to file his own appeal, printing it on a prison form (see the document reproduced in the photo shown below).

DIVISION OF CORRECTIONS
CORRESPONDENCE REGULATIONS

In The Supreme Court of The United States
October Term, 1961
No 890 Misc.
Clarence Earl Gideon, petitioner
—vs—
H.G. Cochran, Jr. Director, Divisions of corrections, State of Florida respondent.

"Answer to respondents, response to petition for writ of Certiorari."

Petitioner, Clarence Earl Gideon recieved a copy of the response of the respondent in the mail dated sixth day of april, 1962.
Petitioner, can not make any pretence of being able to answer the learned attorney General of the state of Florida because the petitioner is not a attorney or versed in law nor does not have the law books to copy down the decisions of this Court. But the petitioner knows there is many of them. Nor would the petitioner be allowed to do so.
according to the book of Revised Rules of the Supreme Court of The United States. Sent to me by Clerk of the same Court. The response of the respondent is out of time (Rule # 24)

After the Supreme Court ruled, Gideon was granted a new trial with a lawyer paid for by the state. In this trial he was acquitted and set free. In the process the right of the accused to a lawyer in all criminal cases was established.

Case 2

A 22-year-old man of Mexican descent is arrested in Illinois by the police in connection with the fatal shooting of his brother-in-law. While being held in police headquarters, the arrested man asks to see his lawyer, who is in the building. The police refuse. The man is told, however, that the police have solid evidence that he fired the fatal shots. Without informing him of his right to remain silent, the police urge him to make a statement. Eventually, the man gives the police a damaging statement that is used in the trial against him.

Poll: What do you think?

Were the man's constitutional rights violated when police refused him access to his lawyer?

Yes

No

The Rest of the Story

Constitutional protections do not only apply to the innocent or the law abiding. A recent wanted notice described Danny Escobedo this way:

> ESCOBEDO is wanted in the Northern District of Illinois for probation violation and weapons offenses. He is also wanted for questioning by the Cook County Sheriff's Department and the Chicago Police Department in regards to a homicide which occurred in 1983. He has a long criminal history dating back to 1957 and has been arrested 25 times for a myriad of violent offenses. ESCOBEDO has been convicted and incarcerated for homicide, rape, sexual assault and narcotics offenses. He is also believed to be a member of the Latin Kings street gang. (http://www.landmarkcases.org/landmark-frame_due1.html)

Case 3

The police in Arizona arrest a 23-year-old man who is accused of kidnap and rape of an 18-year-old woman. At the police station, the rape victim identifies the man in a lineup as the man who raped her. Two officers subsequently interrogate the man. At first the man, later diagnosed by a doctor as a schizophrenic, denies committing the offense. Under further questioning, he writes and signs a brief statement admitting and describing the crime. At trial, the man is convicted, in part on the basis of his confession.

continued

—Time Out 4-3 Continued

Poll: What do you think?

Were the man's constitutional rights violated?

Yes

No

The Rest of the Story

Ernesto Miranda received a second trial in which his confession was not presented. Based on the remaining evidence, he was again convicted of kidnapping and rape. After serving 14 years, he was paroled in 1972. Four years later, Miranda was stabbed to death in a barroom fight. Ironically, police arrested a suspect who, after choosing to exercise his Miranda right of silence, was released.

Conclusion

Together, these three Supreme Court cases represent important precedents that define the extent of constitutional rights of defendants in criminal cases. These cases have provided law enforcement officers and prosecutors with important information concerning how the constitutional rights of the accused, including the 5th Amendment's right to avoid self-incrimination and the 6th Amendment's right to counsel, will be viewed by the courts. These court rulings have substantially influenced the way police gather information and interrogate suspects.

Answers to Time Out 4-2

Where Do You Stand?

A woman should always be able to obtain an abortion as a matter of personal choice (as opposed to there being specific legal limits or abortion being outlawed completely).

-YES

-NO

If you said yes, you're in the minority overall. Based on the 2000 National Election Study, 43% of the respondents supported a woman's right to choose abortion. The type of people most likely to agree with your support of a woman's right to choose abortion were:

(percent **supporting** a woman's right to choose abortion)

Jewish*	67%
Liberals	62%
30–49 years of age	50%
Democrats	49%
Independents	47%
Moderates	45%
Women	44%
NATIONAL AVERAGE	43%

*among worship attendees

If you said no, you're in the majority. Here is the breakdown of those who agree with you:

(percent **opposing** a woman's right to choose abortion)

Republicans	70%
Conservatives	68%
Protestants*	66%
Catholics*	64%
People over 50 years of age	63%
People under 30 years of age	60%
Males	58%
NATIONAL AVERAGE	57%

*among those attending worship

Answers to Time Out 4-3

Case 1

Was the defendant deprived of important constitutional rights when the judge did not provide him a lawyer?

Yes

No

If you replied yes, the court agreed with you. This case occurred in Florida in 1963. After his conviction and sentencing, the defendant, Clarence Earl Gideon, filed a petition in the Florida Supreme Court attacking his conviction on the grounds that he had been deprived of his right to counsel, guaranteed by the Constitution and the Bill of Rights. This case eventually made its way to the U.S. Supreme Court. The Court ruled in favor of Gideon, holding that the 6th Amendment's stipulation that in criminal prosecutions the accused has the right to defense counsel applied not only to federal cases but also to criminal cases conducted in state courts (*Gideon v. Wainwright*, 372 U.S. 335 [1963]). Gideon's conviction was overturned.

If you replied no, the court disagreed with you. This case occurred in Florida in 1963. After his conviction and sentencing, the defendant, Clarence Earl Gideon, filed a petition in the Florida Supreme Court attacking his conviction on the grounds that he had been deprived of his right to counsel, guaranteed by the Constitution and the Bill of Rights. This case eventually made its way to the U.S. Supreme Court. The Court ruled in favor of Gideon, holding that the 6th Amendment's stipulation that in criminal prosecutions the accused has the right to defense counsel applied not only to federal cases but also to criminal cases conducted in state courts (*Gideon v. Wainwright*, 372 U.S. 335 [1963]). Gideon's conviction was overturned.

Case 2

Were the man's constitutional rights violated when police refused him access to his lawyer?

Yes

No

If you replied yes, the court agreed with you. The Supreme Court ruled in this case that Danny Escobedo had been denied his constitutional rights when the police refused to let him consult with his attorney. The Court held that the 6th Amendment's provision that accused parties have the right to the "assistance of counsel" for their defense applies to this case involving prosecution under laws of the State of Illinois (*Escobedo v. Illinois*, 378 U.S. 478 [1964]).

If you replied no, the court disagreed with you. The Supreme Court ruled in this case that Danny Escobedo had been denied his constitutional rights when the police refused to let him consult with his attorney. The Court held that the 6th Amendment's provision that accused parties have the right to the "assistance of counsel" for their defense applies to this case involving prosecution under laws of the State of Illinois (*Escobedo v. Illinois*, 378 U.S. 478 [1964]).

Case 3

Were the man's constitutional rights violated?

Yes

No

If you replied yes, the court agreed with you. Attorneys for the man in this case, Ernesto A. Miranda, appealed his conviction on the grounds that his confession had been coerced and that his 5th Amendment protection against self-incrimination had been violated. In an important case involving the rights of the accused, the Supreme Court agreed that Miranda's constitutional rights had been violated (*Miranda v. Arizona*, 384 U.S. 436 [1966]). Through this case, the Court established a set of warnings that persons accused of crimes must be given *before* being interrogated. These include the right to remain silent (and refuse to answer police questions), the fact that any statements given to police may be used in evidence during a subsequent trial, the right to consult with an attorney and to have an attorney present during questioning, and the right to have a lawyer appointed if the accused has no funds.

If you replied no, the court disagreed with you. Attorneys for the man in this case, Ernesto A. Miranda, appealed his conviction on the grounds that his confession had been coerced and that his 5th Amendment protection against self-incrimination had been violated. In an important case involving the rights of the accused, the Supreme Court agreed that Miranda's constitutional rights had been violated (*Miranda v. Arizona*, 384 U.S. 436 [1966]). Through this case, the Court established a set of warnings that persons accused of crimes must be given *before* being interrogated. These include the right to remain silent (and refuse to answer police questions), the fact that any statements given to police may be used in evidence during a subsequent trial, the right to consult with an attorney and to have an attorney present during questioning, and the right to have a lawyer appointed if the accused has no funds.

4-3 Freedom of Speech

The 1st Amendment states that "Congress shall make no law...abridging the freedom of speech, or of the press; or the right of the people peaceably to assemble, and to petition the Government for a redress of grievances." These few but important words establish the fundamental rights of individuals to free speech, a free press, and freedom of assembly. Throughout the twentieth century, hundreds of court cases have considered the extent and limits of protections under the 1st Amendment.

The rights outlined in the 1st Amendment sometimes conflict with each other. On the one hand, the freedoms of speech and the press are fundamental to the effective operation of democratic government. Only when people are free to express their beliefs and values, to question and criticize governmental policies and leaders, and to propose alternative courses of action can they make informed judgments during elections and meaningfully play the political game between elections. The right to free speech allows them to talk and debate with others, and freedom of the press enables the wide distribution of information and viewpoints.

On the other hand, statements or accusations may prove harmful to other individuals or to the nation as a whole. Telling people to jump off a bridge because it is about to collapse when the bridge is actually completely safe subjects the people who jump to severe harm. Similarly, purposely spreading false information to harm another person's reputation is a danger associated with free expression.

The boundaries of free expression rights sometimes need clarification. The arena for clarifying the meaning of these rights is generally the federal court system. The basic approach of the courts has been to extend the freedom of expression as far as possible, limiting it only when serious harm to others or to the nation could result. Principles for determining the limits of freedom emerged in the early twentieth century, initially in cases involving protests against World War I. (See Box 4-1: Gays and St. Patrick's Day Parades for an interesting case that concerns the rights of two opposing groups.)

4-3a The "Clear and Present Danger" Principle

In an important Supreme Court case in 1919, Justice Oliver Wendell Holmes, Jr., outlined a clear and present danger test to determine whether the exercise of free speech exceeded constitutional protection:

> The question in every case is whether the words used...create a clear and present danger that they will bring about the substantive evils that Congress has a right to prevent.[2]

This test, initially applied to a case involving a man jailed for urging young men to resist the draft during World War I, has served as an important guide to free speech cases.

Soon after Justice Holmes wrote this description, in *Gitlow v. New York* (1925) and other cases, the Supreme Court modified this standard, creating a bad tendency test that allowed speech to be prohibited if it posed threats to or endangered the public.[3]

From the bad tendency perspective, there need be no clear and present danger, only a substantial threat of danger to the public. The Supreme Court next expanded its free speech test to include the concept of imminence.[4] Thus, free speech was seen as protected by the 1st Amendment unless it represented a clear, present, and immediate threat.

The Supreme Court has distinguished between the abstract advocacy of force and language intended to incite people to use force. In *Brandenburg v. Ohio* (1969), the Court upheld the right to speech that abstractly mentions the use of force against the government. It simultaneously held that speech intended directly to incite the use of force was not protected under the 1st Amendment.[5]

symbolic speech *Expression of ideas and beliefs through symbols or symbolic actions.*

4-4 Defining Free Speech and Expression

Supreme Court decisions have extended free speech rights to **symbolic speech**—that is, nonverbal expression. The Court, for example, upheld the right of students to wear arm

Box 4–1 Gays and St. Patrick's Day Parades: A Conflict in Free Speech Rights?

Many U.S. cities—especially those that have a large population with Irish heritage—have a major parade each year celebrating St. Patrick's Day. New York and Boston are among the cities with prominent parades on this Irish holiday. In recent years, parades in both cities have encountered substantial controversy about whether gay and lesbian organizations are permitted to march in St. Patrick's Day parades with banners identifying their organizations. Organizations representing gay persons have claimed that these parades are public events and that on the base of free speech rights they have a right to participate.

Background

In Boston, the annual St. Patrick's Day parade is organized the by South Boston Allied War Veterans Council, a private organization that has obtained permission from the city to hold the parade each year.[a] This organization sought to ban the Irish American Gay, Lesbian and Bisexual Group of Boston (GLIB) from the parade, because they dislike the message of the organization that proclaims both same-gender orientation and Irish heritage. When they were first banned from the parade, GLIB sued in the Massachusetts courts. Based on state civil rights statutes, the courts upheld their right to march. The Supreme Judicial Court of Massachusetts held that under state civil rights laws, the gay, lesbian, and bisexual organization could not be banned from the parade. The sponsoring organization called off the parade in 1994 in protest, and in 1995 marchers carried black flags rather than the traditional green to protest the court decisions.

The U.S. Supreme Court ruled in 1995 that the private sponsors of the parade were within their rights to exclude the gay, lesbian, and bisexual organizations from marching in the parade.

Questions

What are the constitutional issues that the Supreme Court must consider when two organizations each demand their right to free speech?

Should a gay and lesbian organization have the right to march in holiday parades with banners proclaiming their organization?

What constitutional basis might these organizations give for the right to march in these parades?

What reasons might a sponsoring organization give for its legal right to ban such groups from parades?

Analysis

Both sets of players in this conflict argued that their claims were based upon free speech rights. GLIB argued that the parade was a public event in which they had a right to participate. The parade sponsors claimed that the parade itself represented their right to express their Irish heritage. This right included the possibility of banning organizations whose message the sponsors felt violated their expression in holding the parade.

The U.S. Supreme Court considered these questions in the Boston parade case in 1995. In a unanimous decision, the Supreme Court upheld that the state of Massachusetts did not have the right to require parade organizations to include among the marchers a group whose message the organizers do not wish to convey.[b] The Court's decision, written by Justice David H. Souter, viewed the parade as a private event. The opinion defined the word *parade* to indicate marchers who are making a collective point to each other and to bystanders along the route. In this way, parades are viewed as a form of expression organized by the parade sponsors. Because the parade constitutes private expression, the Court held that the Massachusetts statute requiring parade organizers to include groups whose messages they disagree with in the parade violates the organizer's 1st Amendment free expression rights. If the parade had been sponsored by the government rather than by a private organization, the Supreme Court decision would likely have supported the right of gay, lesbian, and bisexual organizations to participate in the parade, since no group's right of free expression would be involved.

---

a. Some material in this box was taken from Linda Greenhouse, "High Court Lets Parade in Boston Bar Homosexuals," *New York Times* (June 20, 1995), A1.

b. *Hurley v. Irish-American Gay, Lesbian and Bisexual Group of Boston* (1995).

Box 4–2 Is Burning the Flag Legal and Constitutional?

The burning of the American flag has been upheld as constitutional by the Supreme Court on the basis of the constitutional right to freedom of expression.
AP photo/FILE/Charles Tasnadi

One issue that has generated controversy concerns the constitutionality and legality of burning the American flag as a protest against government policies. One group of players views the flag as a vital symbol of the American nation and government. They see flag burning as an unacceptable action that defames the nation and everything the nation stands for. Other players feel that burning the American flag is a constitutionally protected form of free speech. While many who see flag burning as constitutional are upset by this action, they contend that free speech rights are fundamental and must be protected.

This issue came to a head in the Supreme Court decision in *Texas v. Johnson* (1989).[a] In this case, the Supreme Court overturned the conviction of Gregory Lee Johnson, who had burned a flag at the 1984 Republican National Convention. Johnson was convicted of violating a Texas law that forbade flag burning. The Supreme Court, by a close 5 to 4 decision, ruled that the Texas law was unconstitutional because it violated the 1st Amendment right to free speech.

President George H. Bush, many members of Congress, and others throughout the nation were angered by the Supreme Court decision. Some argued for a constitutional amendment that would prohibit flag burning. Congress decided, instead, to enact a federal law—the Flag Protection Act of 1989—that states that anyone who knowingly mutilates, defaces, physically defiles, burns, or tramples

bands and to fly the American flag upside down as protests against the Vietnam War.[6] In the 1970s, the Supreme Court, on the basis of free speech guarantees, upheld the right of individuals to burn the American flag as a form of political protest (see Box 4-2: Is Burning the Flag Legal and Constitutional?).[7] Other Supreme Court decisions have extended 1st Amendment protections to behavioral forms of protest, including participation at sit-in demonstrations.[8]

One person who tested the limits of free speech was Gregory Lee Johnson, who found little to like about the United States. Growing up as a military dependent, he gravitated toward black draftees disenchanted with the Vietnam conflict and convinced of American racism. As a leader in the Communist Youth Brigade, he described the country as "an imperialist system which dominates and exploits large segments of the world" and sought to bring down the American "empire." At the 1984 Republican National Convention in Dallas, Johnson organized protests against corporate domination and nuclear policy. In the heat of the moment, a flag was stolen and burned while Johnson and others chanted, "America, the red white and blue, we spit on you." Johnson willingly chose to accept the charges of "desecrating a venerated object" and fought them in the American flag shall be fined or imprisoned. This law was a direct message to the Supreme Court that Congress did not care much for the Court's interpretation of the 1st Amendment in the *Johnson* case.

The struggle did not end there. Shortly after Congress enacted the Flag Protection Act of 1989, some opponents set out to test the law's constitutionality. In both Washington, D.C., and Seattle, opponents openly burned the flag and were charged with violating the new federal law. Federal judges dismissed these cases, citing the Johnson decision. In June 1990 the Supreme Court upheld the lower court judges' decisions, ruling that the federal law violated the free speech guarantee of the 1st Amendment.[b]

The Court decision prompted calls from President George H. Bush and many members of Congress for a constitutional amendment to prohibit flag burning. Although a national poll by the *New York Times* showed that 59 percent of those surveyed favored a constitutional amendment, Congress did not immediately take action to begin the amendment process.

Five years later, Republican Senator Orrin Hatch (R-UT) and Democratic Senator Howell Heflin (D-AL) introduced legislation in Congress to start the process of enacting a constitutional amendment to ban flag burning. The senators argued that the American flag was a unique symbol of freedom that unified the nation and that as long as it was illegal to desecrate federal currency and property, it should also be a crime to desecrate the flag. Under the proposed amendment, the states would set criminal penalties for flag burning. Although there was support in the Republican-controlled Congress for the measure, not all senators agreed with a flag-burning amendment. Senator Bob Kerry (R-NE) argued that the "fabric of America is not threatened" and that there is "such a strong natural condemnation of people who burn flags that people don't burn flags."[c] Despite these opposing views, the amendment gained momentum and was approved by the House of Representatives in June 1995 by a 312 to 120 vote. In an impassioned floor debate, Representative Lindsay Graham (R-SC) implored: "If you need to burn something, burn your Congressman in effigy, but don't burn the flag."[d]

The issue of flag burning remains on the political "burner" with those opposed to it repeating calls for a constitutional amendment to ban flag burning. To date, there has been insufficient political support for Congress to enact legislation that would commence the amendment process.

---

a. *Texas v. Johnson*, 491 U.S. 397 (1989).

b. *United States v. Shawn D. Eichman, David Gerald Blalock, and Scott W. Tyler* and *United States v. Mark John Haggerty, Carlos Garza, Jennifer Proctor Campbell, and Darius Allen Strong*, 110 S. Ct. 2404 (1990).

c. Katherine Q. Seelye, "Conservatives Revive Bill on Protecting Flag," *New York Times* (March 22, 1995), A8.

d. Cited in Katherine Q. Seelye, "House Easily Passes Amendment to Ban Desecration of Flag," *New York Times* (June 29, 1995), A1.

court. Those who fight for their constitutional rights are often not people with whom many would wish to associate. Even his lawyer saw Johnson as a "punk anarchist," but argued that "a strong democracy should be able to tolerate this kind of dissent." The Supreme Court agreed. Johnson remains an angry critic of U.S. policy on issues such as racism, police brutality, challenges to affirmative action, and discrimination. (For more of the story, see Stephen Frantzich, *Citizen Democracy: Political Activists in a Cynical Age*, Lanham, MD: Roman and Littlefield Publishers, 1999: 43–49.)

While the 1st Amendment does not protect "fighting words," that is, speech intended to incite a fight or other violence among individuals, the Supreme Court has so narrowly applied the category that few verbal exchanges have ever been recognized as fighting words.[9] Words that one might see as inciting a fight could be seen by others as freedom to express distaste for someone or something. In the political world, what might be seen as fighting words could also be seen as an expression of political dissatisfaction or protest. In different cases, the Supreme Court has upheld the use of four-letter words (highly offensive to some but used as a means of protest by others)[10] and struck down local ordinances prohibiting people from cursing police officers.[11]

4-4a Free Speech versus Hate Speech

hate speech *Words related to race, religion, or creed intended to incite anger or violence.*

In an effort to curb racially motivated violence, many states and localities enacted laws and ordinances in the late 1980s and early 1990s related to **hate speech** and hate crimes, crimes where victims are selected on the basis of race, religion, or creed. Indeed, hate speech codes have been enacted on many college campuses across the United States in an effort to reduce racial tensions on campus. Laws related to hate speech and hate crimes have tended to come in two varieties. First, there are laws that make it a crime to arouse anger or resentment in others on the basis of language making reference to race, color, creed, gender, or religion. Second, there are laws that provide for stiffer penalties or longer prison sentences for those convicted of crimes where victims were selected on the basis of race, gender, creed, ethnic, or religious bias.

While deploring racial violence and recognizing the repugnance of some forms of hate speech, the Supreme Court has struck down many hate speech laws on the grounds that they violate the 1st Amendment. For example, the Court ruled as unconstitutional a hate speech law in St. Paul, Minnesota, which made it a crime to place on public or private property a burning cross, swastika, or other symbol likely to arouse anger, alarm, or resentment on the basis of race, color, gender, or religion.[12] On the other hand, the Supreme Court upheld the constitutionality of a State of Wisconsin law that provides heavier prison sentences when assailants chose their victims on the basis of race, religion, color, or other biases.[13] While the St. Paul law was judged unconstitutional because it sought to restrict expression, the Wisconsin law, which was focused on action, not expression, was not seen as violating constitutional protections.

4-4b Free Speech and National Security

National security is an area where the right to free speech can collide with America's broader security interests. One question is whether the 1st Amendment should protect those who would use the right of free speech to advocate the overthrow of the government. The Supreme Court has acknowledged that the government has the right to protect itself from those who advocate action to harm or overthrow it. It has upheld the constitutionality of such laws as the Smith Act of 1940 (which made it unlawful to advocate overthrowing the government "by violent force"[14]) and the McCarran Act, passed during the Korean War (which required Communist "front" organizations to register with the U.S. attorney general).[15]

It is, of course, fully constitutional to suggest "overthrowing" current government leaders through use of the ballot box. Except where speech or printed material clearly advocates the use of armed or violent means to overthrow the government, the Supreme Court has tended to protect the free speech rights of individuals. This has been true even in cases where the substance of public comments or printed materials has severely criticized the government or the overall American political system.

4-4c Campaign Spending, Expenditures, and Free Expression

The issue of freedom of expression has extended into many political games. Regarding political campaign contributions and campaign spending, Congress faces two conflicting interests: (1) the rights of private citizens and organizations to make financial contributions to candidates seeking office, and (2) the need to protect political campaigns from corrupting influences.[16] In the first half of this century, in ruling on constitutional challenges made to the Federal Corrupt Practices Act, the Supreme Court upheld the power of Congress to require political committees to maintain financial records of contributions and to file statements with Congress including the names and addresses of contributors.[17]

Following allegations of illegal fund raising by the Nixon reelection campaign in 1972, Congress enacted laws intended to limit the contributions made to electoral candidates and the expenditures made by candidates in election races. These campaign finance laws were challenged on the grounds that they violated the rights of contributors and candidates to freedom of expression in the form of giving contributions to candidates. The Supreme Court has upheld limits on direct campaign contributions to a candidate on the grounds that such limits reduce the potential for political corruption.[18] On the other hand, the Court ruled that overall limits on campaign expenditures violate the constitutional rights of candidates to express their positions and of individuals to support candidates.[19] The Court also ruled that candidates could not be limited in the amounts they wish to spend to support their own campaigns.

A more troublesome issue has concerned limits on indirect expenditures made on behalf of candidates, including organizations or groups, separate from the candidate's campaign organization, purchasing advertisements supporting the candidate. Following its logic that limits on campaign expenditures are generally a violation of free expression rights, the Supreme Court has struck down laws that limit the expenditures of outside groups on behalf of electoral candidates. (Campaign spending laws are described in more detail in Chapter 11.)

4-5 Freedom of the Press

It was not by accident that the freedoms of speech and the press were included together in the 1st Amendment. Both are intimately related to the unobstructed communication of ideas, and both are required conditions for an informed citizenry.

Freedom of the press and the possible curb on it can be understood in two ways:

- censorship (restraint prior to publication) and
- punishment after the fact for something already published.

As one constitutional scholar has noted, "At the least, the guarantee of freedom of the press means freedom from prior restraint or censorship. At the most the guarantee also means that governments may not punish the press for what it publishes."[20]

Freedom of the press faces new challenges as technology redefines the media and their message. Immediate, real-time coverage of events changes the information that is communicated and its impact. For example, both Israeli and American military officials became quickly concerned during the Persian Gulf War when CNN reporters issued almost instantaneous reports on the locations and the extent of damage caused by the Scud missiles launched by Iraq against Israeli cities. The officials recognized that such information could aid the Iraqis in pinpointing locations for future missile attacks. The Israeli censors moved quickly to convince CNN and other network reporters not to reveal the exact locations of missile hits. When "real-time" information poses a threat to national security, free press protections may be legally constricted.

4-5a Prior Restraint

Throughout its history, the Supreme Court has been extremely reluctant to uphold the practice of prior restraint—that is, to allow governments to prohibit material from being published. Although the Court has suggested that limitations on prior restraint are not absolute, it has seldom upheld governmental action to prevent the publication of newspapers, handbills, pamphlets, and other materials.

A prior restraint case that received substantial publicity in the early 1970s concerned the federal government's attempt to prevent the *New York Times* and the *Washington Post* in 1971 from printing excerpts from Department of Defense documents known as the "Pentagon Papers." Gathered together into a book published in 1972,[21] these papers documented the American role in the Vietnam War during the Truman, Eisenhower, Kennedy, and Johnson administrations and provided evidence that the United States was more deeply involved in Vietnam during these administrations than had been previously

Figure 4-1
Libel Choices

Imagine that you are the editor of your college paper. For every story you run, you must decide whether the content you publish could carry one of three levels of risk:

1. Virtually no risk of a successful libel charge
2. Only a moderate risk of a successful libel charge
3. High risk of a successful libel charge

What criteria will you use to decide to run a story? How will you prevent charges of libel?

acknowledged. The Pentagon Papers were based on classified documents obtained by antiwar activist Daniel Ellsberg.

The Nixon administration sought an injunction to stop the newspapers from printing stories based on the Pentagon Papers, arguing that the information had been illegally obtained and threatened national security.

By a 6 to 3 vote, the Supreme Court overturned a lower court injunction and allowed publication.[22] The majority opinion held that the government had failed to justify why censorship should be imposed or how national security would be substantially compromised.

4-5b Punishment after Publication

For a free press to operate, publishers must have extensive discretion in determining what to publish. In many totalitarian nations, the government becomes directly involved in deciding what is published, and a free press ceases to exist. At the other extreme, a government that places absolutely no restrictions on what is published is unheard of.

libel *Malicious and intentional use of untrue written statements that damage an individual's reputation.*

The Supreme Court has ruled that freedom of the press does not allow publishers to engage in **libel**—that is, spreading false and harmful information about individuals. Defining libel, however, has proved difficult. To protect the free press as much as possible, the American legal tradition has been prone to place the burden of proof on the person who feels libeled. According to judicial decisions, publishers can be punished for libel only if published statements are proved to be false, to cause damage, and to be printed with "actual malice."[23] Actual malice is found if it can be shown that statements were printed by a publisher who knew them to be false or if printed statements demonstrated a reckless disregard for the truth. (See Figure 4–1).

4-5c Obscenity

Obscenity is an issue that has troubled the American public, government officials, and the courts. Again, a tension exists between personal liberty (the right to print, purchase, and view obscene materials) and public order (the right to protect society from obscene materials seen as harmful and unpleasant). State and local governments, responding to cries from citizens, have devised many types of laws and policies that seek to ban the sale and distribution of obscene materials. The courts, in turn, have been asked to evaluate the constitutionality of these laws. Some contend that the laws violate the freedoms of speech and of the press.

The key problem with the obscenity issue is devising a workable definition of the word *obscene*. This is difficult because obscenity, like art, is in many ways in the eye of the beholder. Noted political scientist and legal scholar Henry Abraham has observed:

> What is 'obscenity' to some is merely 'realism' to others; what is 'lascivious' in the eyes of one reader is merely 'colorful' in those of another; what is 'lewd' to some parent may well be 'instructive' to another.[24]

Perceptions about what is obscene vary from person to person, city to city, and region to region, making it very difficult to craft a universal test of what is obscene.

The Supreme Court waded into the obscenity issue in 1957 and 1966 when, in two important cases, it repeated its view that obscenity is not a protected form of free speech or press.[25] The Court also outlined a test of obscenity. Something is obscene if, to the average person applying contemporary community standards, the dominant theme of the material taken as a whole appeals to prurient interests. While the Court did not provide a clear-cut statement of what constitutes prurient interests, it ruled that obscene materials were those without redeeming social importance.

In *Miller v. California* (1973), the Supreme Court, building from earlier obscenity decisions, developed a three-pronged test of obscenity concerning sexual-related materials. Materials could be judged obscene, and therefore without 1st Amendment protection, if:

- "Applying contemporary community standards," the average person would find that the work, taken as a whole, "appeals to prurient interests."
- The material depicts "in a patently offensive way" sexual conduct that is prohibited by state laws.
- As a whole, the material "lacks serious literary, artistic, political, or scientific value."[26]

This was a ground-breaking case, because it allowed community standards to play a key role in determining what material was obscene. In subsequent cases, the Court has retreated somewhat from allowing communities to have total say in defining obscenity.[27] In a 1987 case, the Court ruled that only the first two components of the *Miller* test could be decided on the basis of community values; the literary, artistic, political, or scientific value of the work was seen as not varying across communities.[28]

In at least one instance, the Supreme Court was willing to forego the community standards test and to rule material as obscene and not protected by the 1st Amendment. This involved a case of child pornography, against which the Court has taken a strong stand.[29]

4-6 Freedom of Assembly

Americans take for granted their right to assemble for such purposes as political discussion, debate, and protest. Thus they were shocked and dismayed to see the brutal means used by Chinese authorities to suppress the protest held in Tiananmen Square in Beijing in 1989. This incident reminded Americans that the right to assemble is not legally protected everywhere in the world.

Some Americans fear that assemblies of people—especially in times of civil unrest or crises—may erupt into disturbances that will violate public order. Particularly worrisome to advocates of public order are political protests, such as parades, demonstrations, and boycotts. In deciding cases involving protests at public gatherings, the Supreme Court again has faced the conflicting values of personal liberty and public order.

The Court has upheld many types of public protest, including parades and demonstrations. At the same time, however, the Court has allowed public authorities to regulate some of these activities in order to protect the public. Thus, local governments may require that groups planning parades obtain an official permit. Laws may also prohibit protesters from disrupting public functions and offices. And, in allowing regulation of public assembly, the Court has firmly held that such regulation must be limited to narrow situations that directly involve public order.

The May 17, 1989, rally held by students in Tiananmen Square, Beijing, China, attracted 3 million people, before the government brutally attacked the protesters.
Associated Press, AP

4-7 Separation of Church and State

establishment clause *Provision of the 1st Amendment that holds that "Congress shall make no law respecting an establishment of religion."*

free exercise clause *Provision of the 1st Amendment that prevents Congress from prohibiting the free exercise of religious practice.*

The 1st Amendment makes two stipulations about religion. Congress is prohibited from establishing a national religion (the **establishment clause**) and from interfering with religious practice (the **free exercise clause**). These stipulations are important in the United States, given the central role of religion in the lives of many Americans. While religion and government were intertwined in some of the early colonies, including Rhode Island and Maryland, the idea that government should be separated from religious practice was well established by the time of the American Revolution.

Questions about the separation of church and state have arisen over many policy issues, including tax exemptions for religious institutions, prayer in public schools, and public aid to parochial schools. In each of these issues, the Supreme Court has been asked to assess the constitutionality of government actions that affect religious practice. Like other 1st Amendment rights, the exercise of freedom of religion is not absolute. As one expert has noted, "Freedom to believe is absolute, but freedom to practice that belief may be circumscribed by government under certain conditions."[30] Box 4-3: Campus Debate: Free Speech versus Separation of Church and State describes a recent issue of separation of church and state concerning a public university refusing to fund a campus publication prepared by a student Christian group.

4-7a Public Responsibilities and the Free Exercise of Religion

The practice of religion has in certain situations run counter to public responsibilities and duties. When conflicts have arisen, the courts have been called upon to determine which religious practices are protected under the 1st Amendment. They have to decide when it is and when it is not appropriate for governments to take actions or make requirements that infringe upon the free practice of religious beliefs.

In several cases involving the free exercise clause, the courts have been asked to rule upon whether or not governmentally required actions can violate constitutionally protected freedoms. One such controversy concerned the requirements in some schools that students recite the pledge of allegiance at the start of each school day. Some groups, in particular the families of Jehovah's Witnesses, challenged this practice, which they

Box 4-3 A Campus Debate: Free Speech versus Separation of Church and State

Questions about the constitutionally defined principles of freedom of speech and separation of church and state were central issues in a 1995 case that involved the University of Virginia. After some internal debate, the school refused to subsidize a magazine entitled *Wide Awake*. This publication was written by a group of university students to provide a Christian perspective on both personal and community issues.[a] The university said that it would not finance the campus publication (as it does in the case of a variety of other magazines) on the grounds that it declined to subsidize religious speech in the same way as it declined to subsidize student political and lobbying activities. With limited resources to support campus publications, the university argued that it was right and proper to make choices about what types of publications it would financially support.

A case on behalf of the Christian students' group was brought to the federal courts. The students' side argued that the university suppressed the publication because of its religious views and that this action constituted discrimination on the basis of religion. The lawyer representing the students argued that if the clients had been vegetarians, African-American separatists, or members of the Students for a Democratic Society rather than Christians, they would have received funding.

A federal appeals court in Richmond ruled in favor of the university.

The Supreme Court, however, in a sharply divided 5–4 vote, overturned the appeals court ruling and held that the university was constitutionally required to subsidize the Christian magazine on the same basis as other student publications.[b] For the majority, important free speech principles were at stake in the case. The majority opinion, written by Justice Arthur M. Kennedy, held that the university could not silence the expression of selected viewpoints on the grounds that the expression is religious in content. The dissenting justices, led by David H. Souter, disagreed with this view. From their perspective, the Court's ruling would approve direct funding of religious activities by a governmental unit—in this case, the University of Virginia as a state institution. For the minority, the separation of church and state doctrine justified the university in refusing to fund the religious-based campus publication. This case clearly highlighted the potential conflict between two important 1st Amendment principles—freedom of expression and separation of church and state.

---

a. This material was drawn from Linda Greenhouse, "Justices Hear Campus Religious Case," *New York Times* (March 2, 1995), A11, and Linda Greenhouse, "Court Rules University Must Help Subsidize Religious Journal," *New York Times* (June 30, 1995), A1.

b. *Rosenberger v. The Rector and Board of Visitors of the University of Virginia*, No. 94-329.

claimed violated their religious beliefs. In 1943 the Supreme Court, reversing an earlier position,[31] judged the mandatory requirement that students salute the flag unconstitutional. Justice Robert Jackson, writing for the majority, stated that "If there is any fixed star in our constitutional constellation, it is that no official, high or petty, can prescribe what shall be orthodox in politics, nationalism, religion or other matters of opinion or force individuals to confess by word or act their faith therein."[32]

The Pledge of Allegiance became a focus of national debate in 2003 when the U.S. Supreme Court agreed to hear a case involving whether school requirements that students recite the pledge, with its phrase "under God," violates their constitutional rights. The phrase "under God" was added to the pledge in 1954 by an act of Congress. The atheist father of a daughter in a California public school sued the United States, Congress, the state of California, and two school districts, claiming that requiring students to recite this phrase was an undue government pressure to recognize a Supreme Being—a violation of the 1st Amendment. In June 2004 the Court dismissed the case on the grounds that the father, involved in a child custody case with the child's mother, did not have standing to bring the case on behalf of his daughter.

Nursery School Children Saluting the American Flag
The U.S. Supreme Court ruled in 1943 that it is unconstitutional to require students to state the pledge of allegiance.
Library of Congress, Prints & Photographs Division [LC-USW3-017675-E]

Compulsory education is one area where the free exercise principle has come into conflict with state and local laws. For example, the Supreme Court upheld the right of Amish people in Wisconsin not to send their children to school beyond the eighth grade because the teachings in high school curricula were contrary to Amish religious principles[33] (see Box 4-4: Freedom of Religious Practice vs. Compulsory Education Laws). Religious practice issues have arisen in other areas as well. The Supreme Court has upheld, for example, the right of religious groups to use public parks for their group's gatherings,[34] as well as the claim of Jehovah's Witnesses that they could not be compelled to bear license plates with the motto "Live Free or Die."[35] On the other hand, the Court overruled the claims of religious groups when it upheld governmental requirements that religious organizations must obey federal minimum wage laws,[36] that Islamic prisoners may be denied the right to attend religious services for security reasons,[37] and that the State of Minnesota can require the Amish to comply with highway safety laws.[38]

4-7b Prayer in School

One troublesome area concerning the separation of church and state has been the issue of school prayer. Until the 1960s, many schools opened their day with some form of prayer. Some of these prayers were Christian-based; others were unrelated to any specific religious denomination. While many Americans accepted school prayer, opponents, including atheists, argued that it represented governmental fostering of religion.

In a controversial decision, the Supreme Court ruled in 1963 that school prayer was an unwarranted intrusion of religious matters into public affairs. Justice Tom C. Clark, writing for the majority, defended the Court's decision on the separation of church and state:

> The constitutional prohibition against laws respecting an establishment of religion must at least mean that in this country it is no part of the business of government to compose official prayers for any group of the American people to recite as part of a religious program carried on by government.[39]

Using much the same argument, the Supreme Court declared the practice of daily Bible readings in public schools to be unconstitutional.[40]

Box 4–4 *Freedom of Religious Practice vs. Compulsory Education Laws*

As in many areas of constitutional interpretation, the courts often seek a balance between conflicting claims. The right of the state to regulate citizens may be in opposition to the rights of religious groups to exercise their religious practices without government interference. One area of disagreement is compulsory education. A 1972 case involved members of the Amish community who violated the compulsory education laws in Green County, Wisconsin, by refusing to send their 14- and 15-year-old children to public schools after they completed the eighth grade. Even though the Wisconsin law required students to attend school until reaching the age of 16, the Amish refused to comply. They argued that ideas and values taught in secondary education (grades 9 through 12) are markedly at variance with the Amish religious principles. The Amish society emphasizes informal learning-through-doing, a life of goodness rather than of intellect, wisdom rather than technical knowledge, and community welfare rather than individual competition. For the Amish, the principles taught in secondary public schools—including emphasis on intellectual and scientific accomplishments, self-distinction, competition, and worldly achievements—were completely antithetical to their own religious beliefs.

The Supreme Court was asked in this case to determine which rights were more prominent—those of the Wisconsin county to enforce compulsory education laws or those of the Amish parents to exercise their religion without government interference. Ultimately, the Court sided with the Amish and granted them exemption from the compulsory education law. In the majority opinion in this case, Chief Justice Warren Burger argued that "we see that the record in this case abundantly supports the claim that the traditional way of life of the Amish is not merely a matter of personal preference, but one of deep religious conviction, shared by an organized group and intimately related to daily living."[a] For this reason, the Court viewed the compulsory education requirement of Wisconsin beyond the eighth grade to be a violation of the religious rights of the Amish community.

---

a. *Wisconsin v. Yoder*, 406 U.S. 205 (1972).

Political debate about school prayer has continued despite Supreme Court rulings on the issue. Conservative religious groups in particular have continued to advocate for allowing prayer in schools. As a political strategy, these groups have sought a constitutional amendment that would expressly allow school prayer. Conservatives in the Republican Party have embraced the idea of a constitutional amendment. Controversy continues to surround the school prayer issue, and some conservative groups promise to keep the idea of a constitutional amendment that would allow school prayer on the political agenda.

4-7c State Aid to Religious Schools

Both local public education systems and various religious groups operate schools. While the curricula of both are similar, parochial schools include religious instruction, which is not provided in public schools. Questions have arisen about whether it is constitutional for state and local governments to provide any form of educational assistance to parochial schools. Those opposed to this aid hold that it represents governmental support of religious organizations and thus violates the principle of separation of church and state.

Supreme Court decisions about public assistance for religious schools have upheld the constitutionality of assistance that is secular (nonreligious) and that does not foster any religion. The Court upheld, for example, the state of New York's lending of secular textbooks to religious schools on the grounds that this activity benefited the parents and children, not the schools.[41] However, the Court ruled as unconstitutional state laws that provided financial aid to parochial schools for teachers[42] or for school maintenance.[43] In these areas the Court saw public assistance as aiding religion and inappropriately entangling governmental and religious activities.

In 2002 the Supreme Court considered the case of school vouchers, state programs that provide state aid vouchers to parents who can use them to enroll their children in private and, sometimes, parochial schools. The states creating these programs claimed that state tax dollars were not directly supporting religious institutions (parochial schools) because the vouchers were given to parents who could then choose what type of school their child could attend. Voucher opponents challenged this logic and argued that religious schools were receiving substantial state government support. The Supreme Court ruled 5–4 in 2003 in favor of the Cleveland voucher system, giving judicial support to voucher programs being implemented or planned in several communities.[44]

4-7d Tax Exemptions

Federal, state, and local governments have historically exempted churches from paying property and income taxes. These exemptions were challenged in the courts on the basis that they violated the principle of separation of church and state. The Supreme Court argued in 1970 that these tax exemptions were similar to those provided to other community organizations, such as hospitals, libraries, and museums. The Court upheld the practice of tax exemptions on the grounds that churches are a stabilizing influence in the community and that exemptions do not represent an inappropriate intermingling of government and religious functions.[45]

4-8 The Right to Privacy

Even though the right of an individual to pursue life free of intrusions by government or other people is strongly held in American society, it is often taken for granted. The desire for privacy is enhanced by the traditions of private property and a capitalist economy as free as possible from government control. Both emphasize individualism. Further discussion of these cultural principles will be found in Chapter 5.

4-8a Constitutional Basis of the Right to Privacy

In spite of the centrality of privacy to American life, neither the Constitution nor the Bill of Rights expressly states that privacy is a civil right. Some constitutional analysts, however, contend that the right to privacy is implied (if not expressly stated) in several provisions of the Bill of Rights. The 3rd Amendment, for example, prohibits the quartering of troops in homes without the owner's consent. The 4th Amendment states that individuals have the right to be secure in their persons and home. The 5th Amendment holds that individuals may not be required to give evidence against themselves. In addition, some analysts argue that the right to privacy is grounded in the 9th Amendment, which holds that the specific list of rights in the Constitution does not deny to individuals other rights that are not provided there. Still another argument is that the due process right to liberty, provided in the 14th Amendment, means that government does not have the unlimited right to interfere in the affairs of individuals.

Since 1965 federal courts have interpreted the Constitution as establishing a right to privacy. A privacy right was first recognized in the case of *Griswold v. Connecticut*, where the Supreme Court struck down a Connecticut law that prohibited the use of birth control devices.[46] The decision in *Griswold* was based on the view that the use of birth control devices was a private decision involving husband and wife. Given recognition of a right to privacy, the next question concerned the limits of this right. Box 4-5: The Battle for Privacy in the Electronic Age discusses how modern technologies can endanger individual privacy.

4-8b Privacy and Abortion

Roe *v.* Wade *Major Supreme Court decision in 1973 that upheld the right of women to have abortions.*

The issue of the right to privacy has been fundamental to judicial decisions concerning abortion. In one of the most controversial cases of the twentieth century, the Supreme Court held in ***Roe v. Wade*** (1973) that state laws that prohibited all abortions were

Box 4–5 The Battle for Privacy in the Electronic Age

The realization that civil rights and liberties are evolutionary and not stagnant is continually brought home in cases involving privacy rights. For example, tricky questions about an individual's right to privacy emerge in the workplace. One at-work issue concerns mandatory drug testing: Do employers have the right to require unscheduled drug testing? Thus far, in recognition of the major problems that drugs can cause in certain professions, the Court has allowed drug testing in such professions as law enforcement, air traffic control, and public transportation.

Another tricky issue concerns communications in the workplace: Should employees have the right to private communications while on the job? A modern example of this problem concerns email messages sent and stored in computer systems. Who owns these messages? Can companies use them to discipline employees? Employees and employers have been frequently involved, in recent years, in sorting out these questions.

Modern technologies may represent a danger to individual privacy. Computers and surveillance equipment allow for the collection and storage of vast amounts of data about individual persons. For example, credit rating services gather, store, and report upon the financial credit histories of most Americans. Both Congress and the courts are engaged in efforts to more clearly define the modern rights of privacy in the electronic age. Still another modern issue of technology and privacy is explored in Box 4-6: Of Cookies and Cookies.

Box 4–6 Of Cookies and Cookies

Think for a moment about cookies. What comes to mind? How might they be related to privacy?

Traditional Cookies

We give up personal information regularly. Have you ever gone shopping and received a store coupon at the register for your favorite kind of cookie and wondered, "How did they know?" Many supermarket chains use the data secured by product scanning to create profiles of individual customers to target them for future product promotions. While the impact of such profiling might save you money and is largely benign, some people feel uncomfortable about any type of profiling. It is not hard to imagine someone being able to monitor our movements and shopping patterns for purposes we find abhorrent. For example, what if insurance companies could raise our rates if we were not eating healthy diets? Or what if our boss found out we were shopping during business hours?

Cyberage Cookies

While on the Internet, have you ever had an unrequested box appear on your computer screen trying to sell you something? If so, you probably visited a website dealing with related material. The virtually infallible computer remembered your computer's address and created a "cookie" allowing advertisers to reach out to a select group of individuals to try to motivate them to buy a product or promote a cause. Cookies, lists of "favorites places," and website "history" logs all tell a great deal about a user. Law enforcement agencies often use such data to profile both crime victims and perpetrators. The degree to which such information is private is still being determined by the courts. The key point is that we increasingly leave an electronic trail and need to be vigilant about sharing information we deem private.

unconstitutional because they violated the right of pregnant women to privacy.[47] The Court ruled in this case that women's constitutionally protected right to privacy includes the decision to terminate a pregnancy during the first trimester (3 months) of pregnancy. After the 3-month mark, however, the Court recognized the right of states to regulate abortion (if they so wished) in order to protect a pregnant woman's health and the potential life of the fetus.

The Supreme Court has rendered decisions since *Roe* that have expanded the right of states to regulate abortion practices. This is a reflection of the conservative shift in judicial philosophy that resulted from appointments made by Presidents Ronald Reagan and George H. Bush. For example, the Court has validated requirements that minors have either parental or court consent before having an abortion.[48] In another landmark case—*Webster v. Reproductive Health Services* (1989)—the Court upheld several restrictions on abortions contained in a Missouri law. Specifically, it ruled as constitutional (1) state prohibitions on the use of public facilities and employees to perform abortions, and (2) state requirements that physicians conduct tests to determine the viability of fetuses prior to performing an abortion.

Judicial interpretation of privacy rights in the context of abortion continued in the 1990s when, in *Planned Parenthood v. Casey*, the Supreme Court reaffirmed *Roe v. Wade* and upheld additional regulations on abortion practices.[49] This case involved Pennsylvania's Abortion Control Act, which required (1) women seeking abortions to delay an abortion for 24 hours after being given information on abortion and its alternatives, (2) teens seeking abortions to have the consent of a parent or judge, and (3) a married woman to inform her husband about her intent to have an abortion. The Court upheld the 24-hour waiting period and teen consent requirements but struck down the spousal consent provision on the grounds that it imposed an undue burden on a woman's right to choose.

Privacy and Sexual Activity

The limits of the right to privacy remain an open question. Even though the courts have protected such practices as abortion and birth control, they have not traditionally viewed privacy rights as pertaining to sexual practices among consenting adults. The courts have, for example, upheld state sodomy laws, which prohibit such sexual actions between unmarried persons and between homosexuals.[50]

In a dramatic decision in 2003, however, the Supreme Court reversed its own 1986 ruling and struck down state laws that make it criminal for individuals of the same gender to engage in sexual relations. This ruling was hailed as a major victory for gay rights activists, who claimed that private sexual behavior was not a matter appropriately regulated by the government.[51]

By 2004 gay marriage entered the political scene as some communities began to issue either marriage licenses or certificates of civil union to same-sex couples. While this action was challenged under local and state law, some opponents on the national scene called for a Constitutional amendment against gay marriage. It is clear that unions between same-sex couples will be a significant political issue for some time.

4-9 Rights of the Accused

Two amendments to the Constitution—the 5th and the 14th—stipulate that government must adhere to due process of law. Procedural due process concerns the protections and privileges individuals have when the government acts to deprive them of life, liberty, or property. Vitally important to governmental actions during criminal prosecutions, the principle of due process is based on American values of fairness.[52] For example, while the Constitution offers no clear standards concerning convictions, the idea that the accused must be found to be guilty "beyond a reasonable doubt" has become deeply imbedded within the American judicial system.

Several amendments, together with other constitutional features, lay out an extensive series of other rights and protections for individuals accused of violating laws:

- The 4th Amendment protects individuals from unreasonable searches and seizures.
- The 5th Amendment prohibits individuals from being compelled to give evidence against themselves and requires Grand Jury indictment by the government prior to proceeding with criminal prosecution in court.
- The 6th Amendment requires that accused individuals receive a speedy and public trial.
- The 7th Amendment provides the right of trial by jury.
- The 8th Amendment stipulates that excessive bail shall not be required and that cruel and unusual punishments shall not be inflicted by the government.

4-9a Rules about Gathering Evidence

Among the civil liberties specified in the Bill of Rights is the 4th Amendment's stipulation that the people have a right "to be secure in their persons, houses, papers, and effects, against unreasonable searches and seizures." In interpreting the 4th Amendment, the Supreme Court has recognized the importance of private property in American society and the public expectation that such property will not at random be entered, searched, or taken by the government.

The Court has held that an individual's property can be searched only if an official search warrant is issued and signed by a neutral judicial officer on the condition of **probable cause.** Probable cause means that preliminary evidence suggests that a crime has been committed and that a property search will yield physical evidence related to this crime. Crafting a precise definition of probable cause has been difficult. The Court has ruled that sworn allegations without corroborating facts to back them up are insufficient to justify a probable cause conclusion. However, judicial officers may determine probable cause on the basis of hearsay (a statement based not on direct knowledge but on what was heard or reported) if they are satisfied that the informant is credible or has reliable information.

probable cause *Reasonable grounds that a criminal act has been committed.*

An important development in the interpretation of 4th Amendment protections was the **exclusionary rule,** first drafted by the Supreme Court in 1914.[53] According to this rule, defendants in federal cases may request that evidence obtained by means that violated their rights be excluded from their criminal trials. To avoid the exclusion of important evidence, public authorities have been encouraged to protect the due process rights of suspects when gathering evidence. The exclusionary rule was extended to state and local authorities through *Mapp v. Ohio* (1961).[54]

exclusionary rule *Constitutional ruling, premised on the 4th Amendment, that evidence obtained through an illegal search or seizure may not be used in a criminal trial.*

Reflecting a more conservative perspective, the Supreme Court under Chief Justices Warren Burger and William Rehnquist has chipped away at the exclusionary rule. In one 1984 case, the Court held that illegally obtained evidence could be admitted at a trial if it would inevitably have been discovered by lawful means.[55] In the same year, the Court permitted an exception to the exclusionary rule to allow evidence obtained using defective search warrants if the authorities acted in the "good faith" belief that the warrant was valid.[56]

The courts have generally allowed law enforcement officers to search suspects and the immediate premises without warrants during the process of arrest. However, if such searches go much beyond the place of arrest, the legality of the evidence becomes questionable. The Supreme Court has been more willing to allow automobile searches without warrants. Generally, the Court has allowed auto searches whenever police have probable cause to believe that cars have been involved in illegal activity such as the transport of illegal drugs.[57]

4-9b The Right to Counsel

The 6th Amendment requires that persons accused of crimes shall have the right to defense counsel. While an early federal law provided counsel to federal cases involving capital crimes, the Supreme Court in 1938 extended this right to persons accused of violating federal law.[58] The right to counsel was extended to defendants in state cases through the selective incorporation case of *Gideon v. Wainwright* in 1963.[59] Currently, if a defendant cannot afford legal counsel, the government arranges for such counsel at public expense.

4-9c The Right to Avoid Self-Incrimination

During major investigations of government scandals—including the McCarthy hearings on Communism in the United States, the Watergate break-in, and the Iran-Contra affair—witnesses commonly plead the 5th Amendment. In so doing, witnesses are invoking the constitutional right that protects them from being compelled to incriminate themselves. Suspects may not be required to confess, provide testimony, or supply evidence that could be used in their conviction. This privilege is accorded only to persons and not to corporations, labor unions, or other organizations.[60]

The 5th Amendment privilege against compelled self-incrimination was linked to the 6th Amendment right to legal counsel through the case of *Miranda v. Arizona* in 1966.[61] During Miranda's trial for kidnap and rape, Arizona authorities used as evidence statements that Miranda made during police interrogation, at which time he had not been advised of his 5th Amendment rights. The Supreme Court overturned Miranda's conviction on the basis that he had not been clearly informed that he had the right to remain silent and to have counsel present during interrogation.[62]

Miranda rules *Due process requirement that suspects be informed of their rights.*

As an outcome of this trial, law enforcement agencies adopted **Miranda rules.** These require police officers, at the time of arrest or interrogation, to read suspects a statement that informs them that they may remain silent and obtain legal counsel and that any statement made to police may be used as evidence against them in court. If arresting officers fail to inform suspects of their Miranda rights, information obtained during interrogations will be, in most cases, inadmissible as evidence.

4-9d Rules against Cruel and Unusual Punishment

While the 8th Amendment to the Constitution prohibits the use of "cruel and unusual" punishment, it provides little help in defining when punishment crosses that line. This determination has been left to interpretation by the federal courts. In assessing whether a punishment is cruel and unusual, the courts have generally sought to compare the severity of criminal sentences with so-called evolving standards of decency. The Supreme Court has overturned sentences where it has judged them to be extremely severe in contrast to punishments issued in similar cases.

The most controversial issue surrounding protection from cruel and unusual punishment concerns the death penalty, known as capital punishment. Critics have sought to have capital punishment ruled unconstitutional on the grounds that it represents a cruel and unusual punishment even in cases of murder. The Supreme Court has thus far not agreed with this line of reasoning and has held that the death penalty is constitutional as long as due process protections are carefully followed.

4-10 The Right to Bear Arms

One controversial issue of civil liberties concerns whether the Constitution provides all individuals with the right to bear arms. This question has taken on new importance in recent years as governments at all levels have considered gun control legislation to deal with rising urban crime and violence. Since America's founding, the technology of weapons production has changed dramatically, making for increasingly powerful and destructive weapons. Police officials across the nation report the use of sophisticated and powerful weapons such as "Saturday Night Special" handguns, submachine guns, and powerful rifles in the commission of violent crimes. The image of colonial militiamen with a one-shot, inaccurate musket bears little resemblance to the often well-armed modern criminal.

The 2nd Amendment to the Constitution states that "A well-regulated Militia, being necessary to the security of a free State, the right of the people to keep and bear

Arms, shall not be infringed." This amendment was motivated by two concerns: (1) the ability of states to counter the military force of the national government, should the national government begin to violate constitutional provisions and assume full governing power, and (2) the need for state governments to have a military force capable of suppressing riots or rebellions within their boundaries.

The traditional view of the 2nd Amendment has been that the right to bear arms, as articulated in the Constitution, is directly linked to the provision of a "well-regulated Militia" by the state. The Supreme Court has ruled that the 2nd Amendment protects only the right of states to maintain militias and not the inherent right of individuals to bear arms.

The most celebrated Court ruling concerning the 2nd Amendment was *United States v. Miller* (1939). This case involved two individuals charged with violating the National Firearms Act of 1934 by transporting a double-barreled shotgun across state lines. As one means of defense, the defendants charged that the firearms law violated the 2nd Amendment. The Supreme Court upheld the constitutionality of the federal law and stated that:

> In the absence of any evidence tending to show that possession or use of a 'shotgun having a barrel of less than 18 inches in length' at this time has some reasonable relationship to the preservation or efficiency of a well-regulated militia, we cannot say that the 2nd Amendment guarantees the right to keep and bear such an instrument. Certainly it is not within judicial notice that this weapon is any part of the ordinary equipment or that its use could contribute to the common defense.[63]

Because the Court could find no possible connection between the shotgun and the maintenance of a state militia, it found no constitutional protection of the individuals being prosecuted. It is not clear from this opinion how the Court would have ruled if the weapon in question had born some relationship to the weapons used by the militia.

Opponents of gun control legislation, including the powerful National Rifle Association (NRA), have not given up asserting the 2nd Amendment as a constitutional right to bear arms. While the Supreme Court and other federal courts have tended to uphold the constitutionality of gun control laws and sustain the view that the right to bear arms extends only to the context of state militias, major political battles about gun control clearly will continue. The courts will continue to serve as the primary arena for determining to what extent, if any at all, American citizens are entitled by the Constitution to bear arms. Congress, too, will serve as an arena for gun control disputes, witnessed by the crime bill enacted by Congress in 1994 to prohibit the sale of most assault weapons and the effort of conservatives in the Republican-controlled 104th Congress to repeal this measure. Read Time Out 4-4: Where Do You Stand on Gun Control? and consider your views on gun control today.

Where Do You Stand on Gun Control? **Time Out 4-4**

Choose the response to the following question that best reflects your view, and you will have a chance to see who among the public tends to agree and disagree with you in Answer to Time Out 4-4 box on page 116.

Do you think the federal government should make it more difficult for people to buy a gun than it is now?

-YES

-NO

Answer to Time Out 4-4

Do you think the federal government should make it more difficult for people to buy a gun than it is now?

-YES

-NO

If you replied yes, you're part of the majority. Based on the 2000 National Election Study, 59% of the respondents supported increased gun regulation. The type of people most likely to agree with your support of increased gun regulation were:

(percent **supporting** increased gun regulation)

Liberals	76%
Democrats	73%
Females	69%
Moderates	62%
People 30-49 years of age	62%
People under 30 years of age	60%
NATIONAL AVERAGE	59%

If you said no, you're in the minority. Based on the National Election Study for the 2000 election, 41% of the respondents opposed increased gun regulation. The type of people most likely to agree with your lack of support of increased gun regulation. were:

(percent **opposing** increased gun regulation)

Republicans	58%
Males	54%
Conservatives	53%
People over 50 years of age	44%
Independents	42%
NATIONAL AVERAGE	41%

4-11 The Right to Vote

franchise *The right to vote.*

populist *Member of a party claiming to represent the rights of the common people; formed in 1891 to further agrarian interests.*

suffragettes *Women advocating and demonstrating for extension of enfranchisement to women.*

poll tax *A special tax required before a person could vote; was often used to discourage low-income individuals, and particularly members of minorities, from voting.*

literacy test *Examinations of a potential voter's ability to read and write; was often used to deny the rights of members of minorities to vote.*

Despite Americans' strong heritage of popular government based on the will of the people, the **franchise** has only recently been extended to all adult citizens in the nation. This right to vote is central to American democracy, since it affects the selection of the president, members of Congress, and over 80,000 elected officials at the state and local levels. Because the Constitution contains no specific provisions about voting (the Founders decided to leave this responsibility in the hands of the states), the regulation of voting practices was traditionally viewed as a function of state governments. In the first decades of the nation's history, voting in many states was restricted to male property owners. By the administration of **populist** president Andrew Jackson, however, most states had enacted laws that allowed male citizens to vote.

The franchise was extended to women in 1920 after many years of protests by **suffragettes,** who argued that women were citizens and, therefore, deserved the right to vote (see Box 4-7: The Struggle for Women's Right to Vote). In response to their protests, the 19th Amendment, adopted in 1920, guarantees women's voting rights.

After Reconstruction (1865–1877), southern states faced the prospect of having large numbers of new African-American voters. Fearing the political power of these new citizens, several southern states enacted provisions that made it harder for African Americans and other poor individuals to vote in party primaries, in which candidates are selected for the general election. Some states allowed only whites to vote in party primaries. Some also used the **poll tax,** requiring that voters pay a nominal sum to vote, or the **literacy test** as mechanisms to restrict voting by African Americans and poor whites.

Box 4–7 The Struggle for Women's Right to Vote

The movement to enfranchise women—giving them the right to vote—dates back at least as far as the Civil War. Elizabeth Cady Stanton and Susan B. Anthony were supporters of women's rights prior to the Civil War and ardent supporters of the abolition of slavery. Following the Civil War, these two women hoped that their work with Republican abolitionists would enlist their support in return in the struggle to grant women the right to vote. They placed great hope on the 15th Amendment, ultimately ratified in 1870. This amendment was designed to ensure that African Americans freed from slavery would not be denied the right to vote. Stanton and Anthony, leaders of the women's suffrage movement, sought to have women included in the 15th Amendment. Fearing that there was insufficient public support for this move at the time, Republican leaders backed away from including women in this amendment.

About this time, the women's suffrage movement split into two camps. The National Woman Suffrage Association was formed in 1869, and Stanton was elected its first president. It relied upon the suffrage societies that Stanton and Cady had formed in communities across the nation. The members distrusted the Republicans, who had backed away from including women in the 15th Amendment. A rival organization, the American Woman Suffrage Association, was also formed in the same year. This group sought to develop strong ties with the Republicans and with male abolitionists, hoping that they would come to support a national measure to guarantee women the right to vote. Both groups pushed for women's suffrage and broader rights for women, albeit with different strategies. In 1890 they finally joined together as the National American Woman Suffrage Association (NAWSA).

The work of Cady and Stanton stimulated grassroots efforts to change state and local laws to allow women to vote. This was a hard struggle. By the turn of the century, only four western states—Colorado, Idaho, Utah, and Wyoming—had granted women the right to vote. In the next two decades, 12 more states enacted laws allowing women to vote.

The attention shifted back to the national scene about the time of World War I. Reflecting in part the contributions of women to the war effort, the support continued to grow for a constitutional amendment to grant women the vote. NAWSA, which by then numbered 75,000 members, threw its support behind the administration of Woodrow Wilson and the war effort, believing that demonstrations of patriotism would help their movement. Wilson was converted to the suffrage cause in 1916, but he believed the issue should be handled by the states. In 1918 he changed positions and supported a constitutional amendment. The House of Representatives quickly passed legislation to begin the process of a amending the Constitution to guarantee women the right to vote. The Senate action was slower, taking 18 months to win approval. It took another year for enough states to consider and approve the measure to achieve ratification. The 19th Amendment was ratified on August 20, 1920, when Tennessee gave the last vote needed for ratification. The amendment itself is brief—"The right of citizens of the United States to vote shall not be denied or abridged by the United States or by any State on account of sex"—but its impact on the rights of women is substantial.

Since the 1940s both judicial decisions and federal laws have eliminated these obstacles to participation in voting, thereby expanding the number of players in the American political game. In 1944 the Supreme Court considered the argument of the Democratic party of Texas that primaries were voluntary associations that had the right to exclude African-American participants. The Court ruled against the Texas political party and held that all-white primaries were unconstitutional.[64]

Federal legislation and a constitutional amendment have extended voting participation rights to African Americans. The 24th Amendment, ratified in 1964, struck down the poll tax. On the heels of the civil rights protests, Congress enacted the Voting Rights Act of 1965. This legislation, extended and strengthened since 1965, prohibits discrimination in registration and voting and forbids the use of literacy tests. In a move that extends the power of the federal government directly into state affairs, the act allows the federal government to register voters and to oversee voter participation in areas with a record of voting discrimination.

The political struggles by women and by members of minorities to acquire the right to vote are described in Chapter 20, and strategies for electoral participation are outlined in Chapter 10.

Conclusion

Constitutional rights and liberties were included in the Constitution, mostly in the Bill of Rights, to protect individuals and groups in American society from the powers of the national government. As hallmarks of democracy and limited government, the Constitution provides Americans with the freedoms of speech, the press, assembly, and religion; gives protection to those accused of violating the law; and now extends suffrage to all adults aged 18 and over. Constitutional rights and liberties, originally designed to protect against the encroachments of national government power, now include protection against the actions of state and local governments.

An important responsibility of the federal courts, including the Supreme Court, has been to interpret the meanings and boundaries of civil rights and liberties in the United States. The judicial interpretations that clarify rights and liberties have often sought to balance personal freedoms on one side with social and political order on the other. Questions about the exact bounds of civil rights and liberties remain unanswered as the federal courts continue to hear cases concerning alleged violations of constitutional rights. Because constitutional interpretation is never final, the courts play an ongoing role in determining the winners and losers in disputes involving constitutional principles.

The legacy of Supreme Court decisions is that they cumulatively provide a more precise meaning of the civil rights and liberties provided in the Constitution and the boundaries of legitimate actions that can be taken by government. Constitutional rights and liberties continue to protect players and nonplayers from many forms of encroachment by government leaders. They also protect players who are in a minority position with regard to a right or a liberty from domination by the majority. Players and player groups cannot always count on legal protections being immediately recognized by other players, including the national, state, or local governments. Sometimes they sue in federal courts to resolve conflicts when their rights clash with the purported rights of other players or of the government.

Changing technologies related to communication and information storage and retrieval will continue to pose new challenges to civil rights and liberties. For example, with the new capabilities to transmit information rapidly via computer and satellite networks, is it possible for governments to suppress effectively the publication of materials that they believe threaten national security? Similarly, can a person's right to privacy be protected as governments and others build sophisticated systems that track many types of data about individual citizens? These and other questions about civil liberties will be raised as technological advances change the context in which individual rights and liberties are exercised and protected.

Key Terms

civil liberties
due process
establishment clause
exclusionary rule
franchise
free exercise clause
hate speech
libel
literacy test
Miranda rules
poll tax
populist
probable cause
Roe v. Wade
segregation
suffragettes
symbolic speech

Practice Quiz

1. Which civil liberty is *not* included in the 1st Amendment to the U.S. Constitution?
a. Freedom of speech
b. The right to bear arms
c. Freedom of assembly
d. Freedom of the press

2. A key provision of the 14th Amendment to the U.S. Constitution guarantees:
a. the separation of church and state.
b. freedom of the press.
c. equal protection under the law.
d. trial by a jury of one's peers.

3. What is true of "symbolic speech"?
a. The courts have generally ruled it unconstitutional.
b. The federal courts have upheld it on the basis of the Supremacy Clause.
c. The federal courts have upheld it on the basis of the Reserve Clause.
d. The federal courts have upheld it on the basis of the 1st Amendment.

4. What is true of the U.S. Supreme Court's general attitude about prior restraint, that is, the ordering that information not be printed/published?
   a. The Supreme Court regularly engages in prior restraint.
   b. The Supreme Court seldom engages in prior restraint.
   c. The Supreme Court typically tries to protect the 1st Amendment.
   d. Both b and c.

5. In order to prove libel, one must show that a statement:
   a. is false.
   b. causes damage.
   c. was made with actual malice.
   d. All of the above

6. What is true about determining the constitutionality of obscenity?
   a. It is usually easy to determine what is obscene.
   b. The Supreme Court has transferred obscenity cases to state courts.
   c. Defining obscenity is a challenge, since what is "obscene" to one person is undisturbing or appreciated by others.
   d. Both b and c.

7. On what type of speech/publication has the Supreme Court taken a clear position in ruling that the 1st Amendment does *not* protect it?
   a. The right to bear arms
   b. Child pornography
   c. Protection of the environment
   d. The right to counsel

8. The "establishment clause" of the 1st Amendment to the U.S. Constitution holds that:
   a. accused individuals have rights.
   b. Congress is prohibited from creating a national religion.
   c. Congress shall not enact laws that interfere with religious practice.
   d. Congress shall establish fixed dates for presidential and legislative elections.

9. What is true about constitutional interpretation concerning public sector aid being given to religious-based schools?
   a. Public sector aid is prohibited in all cases.
   b. There is no conflict.
   c. Public aid is allowable so long as aid does no foster religious training in the school.
   d. The issue has not been examined much by the courts.

10. What is true about the "right to privacy"?
   a. It is explicitly granted in the 1st Amendment.
   b. It is explicitly granted in the 14th Amendment.
   c. It has no constitutional basis whatsoever.
   d. It is inferred from multiple amendments, including those that spell out rights against unreasonable search and seizure.

11. What did the *Roe v. Wade* decision do?
   a. It prohibited all abortions.
   b. It protected all abortions.
   c. It allowed abortion in many cases, especially during the early part of pregnancy.
   d. It left the decision about the constitutionality of abortion to the state courts.

12. Which amendment to the U.S. Constitution focuses on the right to carry a weapon?
   a. The 1st Amendment
   b. The 2nd Amendment
   c. The 5th Amendment
   d. The 14th Amendment

You can find the correct answers to these questions by taking the quiz and then submitting your answers in the Online Edition. The program will automatically score your submission. Where you miss a question, the program will provide the correct answer, a rationale for the answer, and the section number in the chapter where the topic is discussed.

Further Reading

For more detailed information on civil liberties, see John J. Dinan, *Keeping the People's Liberties: Legislators, Citizens, and Judges as Guardians of Rights* (Lexington, KY: University Press of Kentucky, 1998), Shmuel Lock, *Crime, Public Opinion, and Civil Liberties: The Tolerant Public* (Westport, CT: Praeger Publishers, 1999), William Lockhart, et al. (eds.) *Constitutional Rights and Liberties: Cases, Comments and Questions* (Florence, KY: West Wadsworth, 1996).

For a discussion of hate speech and civil liberties, see Henry Louis Gates, Jr., and Donald E. Lively, *Speaking of Race, Speaking of Sex: Hate Speech, Civil Rights, and Civil Liberties* (New York: New York University Press, 1994).

The topic of civil liberties during periods of war is examined by William H. Rehnquist in *All the Laws but One: Civil Liberties in Wartime* (New York: Knopf, 1998).

An excellent source on the evolution of American civil rights and liberties through Supreme Court decisions is presented by Henry J. Abraham in *Freedom and the Court: Civil Rights and Liberties in the United States*, 5th ed. (New York: Oxford University Press, 1988).

A well-organized and well-documented source on civil rights and liberties is Elder Witt, *The Supreme Court and Individual Rights*, 2nd ed. (Washington, DC: Congressional Quarterly, 1988). See also John Brigham, *Civil Rights & American Democracy* (Washington, DC: Congressional Quarterly, 1984).

For sources that include analysis and the text of key Supreme Court decisions, consult Louis Fisher, *Constitutional Rights: Civil Rights and Civil Liberties*, 2nd ed. (New York: McGraw-Hill, 1995) and David M. O'Brien, *Constitutional Law and Politics, Volume II: Civil Rights and Civil Liberties*, 2nd ed. (New York: W. W. Norton, 1995).

For a detailed discussion of constitutional controversies concerning racial discrimination, affirmative action, abortion, hate speech, and religious freedom, see H. L. Pohlman, *Constitutional Debate in Action: Civil Rights and Liberties* (New York: HarperCollins, 1995).

For a thorough discussion of the gun control issue and the protections offered by the 2nd Amendment, see Robert J. Spitzer, *The Politics of Gun Control* (Chatham, NJ: Chatham House Publishers, 1995).

Endnotes

1. This view was upheld by the Supreme Court under John Marshall in the case of *Barron v. Baltimore*, 32 U.S. (7 Pet.) 243.
2. *Schneck v. United States*, 249 U.S. 47 (1919).
3. *Gitlow v. New York*, 268 U.S. 652 (1925).
4. *Whitney v. California*, 247 U.S. 356 (1927).
5. *Brandenburg v. Ohio*, 395 U.S. 444 (1969). See also *Yates v. United States*, 354 U.S. 298 (1957).
6. *Tinker v. Des Moines School District*, 393 U.S. 503 (1969).
7. *Spence v. Washington*, 418 U.S. 405 (1974).
8. *Texas v. Johnson*, 491 U.S. 397 (1989).
9. *Garner v. Louisiana*, 368 U.S. 157 (1961).
10. David O'Brien, *Constitutional Law and Politics. Volume II: Civil Rights and Civil Liberties* (New York: W.W. Norton, 1995), 454.
11. *Cohen v. California*, 403 U.S. 15 (1971).
12. *Lewis v. New Orleans*, 415 U.S. 130 (1974).
13. *R.A.V. v. City of St. Paul, Minnesota*, 112 S. Ct. 2538 (1992).
14. *Wisconsin v. Mitchell*, 113 S. Ct. 2194 (1993).
15. *Dennis v. United States*, 341 U.S. 494 (1951).
16. *Communist Party v. Subversive Activities Control Board*, 367 U.S. 1 (1961).
17. Louis Fisher, *Constitutional Rights, Civil Rights and Civil Liberties*, Volume 2 of *American Constitutional Law*, 2d ed. (New York: McGraw-Hill, 1995), 1333.
18. *Burroughs v. United States*, 290 U.S. 534 (1934).
19. *Buckley v. Valeo*, 424 U.S. 1156 (1976).
20. As an exception to this principle, the Supreme Court has upheld the limits on campaign spending for presidential candidates who accept public funding for their campaign. See Chapter 14.
21. Elder Witt, *The Supreme Court and Individual Rights*, 2d ed. (Washington, D.C.: Congressional Quarterly, 1988), 53.
22. Daniel Ellsberg, *Papers on the War* (New York: Simon and Schuster, 1972).
23. *New York Times v. United States*, 403 U.S. 713 (1971).
24. *New York Times Co. v. Sullivan*, 376 U.S. 254 (1964).
25. Henry A. Abraham, *Freedom and the Court: Civil Rights and Liberties in the United States*, 5th ed. (New York: Oxford University Press, 1988), 252.
26. *Roth v. United States*, and *Alberts v. California*, 354 U.S. 476 (1957).
27. *Miller v. California*, 413 U.S. 15 (1973).
28. See, for example, *Jenkins v. Georgia*, 418 U.S. 153 (1974).
29. *Pope v. Illinois*, 481 U.S. 497 (1987).
30. *New York v. Ferber*, 458 U.S. 747 (1982).
31. Witt, *The Supreme Court*, 81.
32. *Minersville School District v. Gobitis*, 310 U.S. 586 (1940).
33. *West Virginia State Board of Education v. Barnette*, 319 U.S. 624 at 641-42 (1943).
34. *Wisconsin v. Yoder*, 406 U.S. 205 (1972).
35. *Niemotko v. Maryland*, 340 U.S. 268 (1951).
36. *Wooley v. Maryland*, 430 U.S. 705 (1977).
37. *Tony and Susan Alamo Foundation v. Secretary of Labor*, 471 U.S. 290 (1986).
38. *O'Lone v. Shabazz*, 482 U.S. 342 (1987).
39. *Minnesota v. Hershberger*, 110 S. Ct. 1918 (1990).
40. *Engel v. Vitale*, 370 U.S. 421, 425 (1962).
41. *Abington Township v. Schempp* and *Murray v. Curlett*, 374 U.S. 203 (1963).
42. *Board of Education v. Allen*, 392 U.S. 236 (1968).
43. *Lemon v. Kurtzman*, 403 U.S. 602 (1971).
44. *Committee for Public Education and Religious Liberty v. Nyquist*, 413 U.S. 756 (1973).
45. *Zelman v Simmons-Harris*
46. *Walz v. Tax Commission*, 397 U.S. 664 (1970).
47. *Griswold v. Connecticut*, 381 U.S. 479 (1965).
48. *Roe v. Wade*, 410 U.S. 113 (1973).
49. *Planned Parenthood Association v. Ashcroft*, 462 U.S. 476 (1983).
50. *Planned Parenthood of Southeastern Pennsylvania v. Casey*, 112 S. Ct. 2791 (1992).
51. *Lawrence and Garner v Texas*, 02-0102.
52. See, for example, *Bowers v. Hardwick*, 478 U.S. 186 (1986).
53. Louis Fisher, *Constitutional Rights: Civil Rights and Civil Liberties* (New York: McGraw-Hill, 1995), 818.
54. *Weeks v. United States*, 232 U.S. 383 (1914).
55. *Mapp v. Ohio*, 367 U.S. 643 (1961).
56. *Nix v. Williams*, 464 U.S. 417 (1984).
57. *United States v. Leon*, 468 U.S. 897 (1984).
58. *Carroll v. United States*, 267 U.S. 132 (1925).
59. *Johnson v. Zerbst*, 304 U.S. 458 (1938).
60. *Gideon v. Wainwright*, 372 U.S. 335 (1963).
61. Most recently, *Bellis v. United States*, 417 U.S. 85 (1974).
62. *Miranda v. Arizona*, 384 U.S. 436 (1966).
63. In an interesting sidebar to this case, the defendant was given a new trial and was once again found guilty of the crime he was charged with committing. *United States v. Miller*, 307 U.S. 174 (1939).
64. *Smith v. Allwright*, 321 U.S. 649 (1944).

5

American Political and Economic Culture: The Contexts of the Playing Field

Key Points

- **The importance of the physical characteristics of the political playing field.**
- **The role of political culture in American political attitudes and behavior.**
- **The process of political socialization.**
- **The content and implications of dominant American political values.**
- **The structure and political consequences of the American economic system.**

Preview: How Do We Define the American Way?

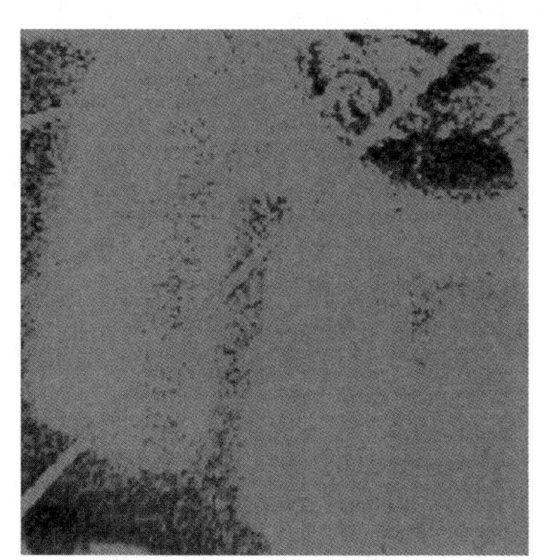

There is a pretty good chance that you have used one of the 2,500 libraries and/or listened to one of the 7,600 church organs donated by a Scottish immigrant who arrived in the United States in 1848 to work as a weaver's assistant for a dollar a week. He did not remain poor long. Capitalizing on the cultural values and economic opportunities of the nineteenth century, he worked himself up through a variety of jobs to become one of America's leading steel manufacturers and philanthropists. While tailored to new times and conditions, the threads of Andrew Carnegie's political and economic outlooks are still woven into American political and economic culture.

Having opened our doors to a succession of individuals looking for a better life, we are still a nation of immigrants. We have high regard still for the accumulation of property and would largely agree with Carnegie's view that "upon the sacredness of property civilization itself depends."[1] We continue to view hard work as the preferred way to prosper. As a society we have little argument with Carnegie's capitalist idea that "while the law [of competition] may sometimes be hard for the individual, it is best for the race."[2] Many of us tend to be uncomfortable with inherited as opposed to earned wealth. Finally, most Americans would agree with Carnegie that a child who inherits too much is likely to fall victim to sloth and indolence.

Carnegie also set the tone for reliance on volunteerism as opposed to government for civic projects. He argued that "Surplus wealth is a sacred trust which its possessor is bound to administer in his lifetime for the good of the community."[3] He opposed most forms of government control. In fact, he often attached strings to his contributions with which the receiving government would have to comply rather than vice versa.

There is clearly a danger in sanctifying an industrialist who made his fortune on the backs of workers who were largely unprotected and in an age before income tax and antitrust laws. Nevertheless, Andrew Carnegie's commitment to America as a land of material opportunity in an atmosphere of civic volunteerism and limited government control lives on as an ideal of the American way.

How do we define the "American way"? One cannot understand American politics without having a sense of the unique characteristics of the United States. The game of American politics takes place on a specific playing field that has distinctive characteristics. One of the relatively permanent aspects of the playing field of American politics is its distinctive *political culture*.

We have in earlier chapters considered the foundations of government as spelled out in the rules and structures established by the Constitution. American government is intended to be by and for the people. Now we turn to the elusive, changing human factors of American political culture—a distinctive set of American values and attitudes concerning government and the political process.

values *Attitudes referring to the desired goals for individual or societal accomplishment.*

Values can be viewed as the "master ideals" of a society—beliefs such as "all people are created equal" and a commitment to fair play. They define what the "good" society would look like. These values have broad applicability to many situations. We may place value in such abstract goals as equality, fairness, security, efficiency, hard work, family life, and economic success.

attitudes *Long-term and deeply held perspectives about what is important and how society works. See also* ***opinions*** *and* ***values****.*

Attitudes refer to broad and relatively permanent perspectives by which we interpret and evaluate specific areas of the political system. One author defines them as follows: "Attitudes are likes and dislikes. They are our affinities for and aversions to situations, objects, persons, groups, or any other identifiable aspects of our environment, including abstract ideas and social policies."[4] Attitudes also include our expectations about how the world should work. Some individuals distrust politics and see dastardly tricks behind every political decision. Their conversations are sprinkled with comments such as "You can't trust City Hall" and "What do you expect from politicians?" Others remain optimistic, praising the political process when it works and assuming that failures will eventually be corrected.

opinions *Short-term expressed preferences between alternative courses of action.*

Unlike values and attitudes, political **opinions** involve expressing short-term preferences, for example, among several candidates or policies. Opinions often emanate from our long-term preferences and outlooks (values and attitudes), but they involve short-term means for reaching those longer-range goals. Attitudes and opinions directly influence the nature of an individual's political activity. They even determine who decides to come in from the sidelines. That dynamic will be further explored in the last several chapters of this book. This chapter focuses on values as part of the context of American government.

The **economic culture** of the United States is another important part of the playing field. Historical commitments to values such as deep respect for private property rights undergird American capitalism and define many political issues. Most Americans believe that the free enterprise system and democratic government are inseparable and would accept the judgment that "business is the engine of society."[5] The economic culture involves public values, varying perspectives on how the economic system does or should work, and opinions, many of which find their way into public laws.

economic culture *Widely shared fundamental beliefs, attitudes, and perspectives about how the economy should work.*

Furthermore, political observers often argue that in order to understand American politics, one should "follow the money." As individuals, we spend much of our time attempting to attain economic security. Politics is often seen as the way by which we can increase our chances of economic well-being and protect our gains. Conversely, economic resources often determine who can play the political game—and their likelihood of success.

5-1 The Physical Playing Field

All established governmental units and most political organizations are defined by a set of physical boundaries, which in turn specify those individuals allowed to play a particular political game. For example, legal residents of Denver are entitled to vote in city elections but not in the elections of other cities in the state. Fixed election districts based on geographical boundaries link American voters to their elected representatives and serve as the basis of representative democracy. America's ocean boundaries on two sides and its common physical boundaries with only two other countries simplify our defense and limit our policy problems. The vastness and geographical variation of the United States add to both our strength and our potential for regional miscommunication and conflict.

The political playing field is comprised of much more than its physical components. Nevertheless, geography and the lay of the land do determine eligible players, raise issues that the political system must confront, and help to define many of the goals for which the game is played.

5-1a Unity Out of Diversity

Meaningful democracy requires effective two-way communication between the rulers and the ruled. Physical size and the nature of a political unit's terrain may affect such communication. America is a large and diverse country. Recognizing the diversity, understanding the limitations in communication, and fearful of national government power, the Founders opted for a federal system. This system gives the states considerable political control and the ability to fit political structures and policies to local needs. During the country's initial decades, most residents of the United States identified themselves much more with their state than with the emerging nation. It took more than the signing of documents to create either the feeling or the reality of nationhood.

The development of the United States as a unified nation, in which citizens identified themselves as Americans first, proceeded slowly. During the first decades of American history, the large plantation agricultural orientation of the southern states often came into conflict with the interests of merchants and small farmers in the North. Soil conditions, the contour of the land, and the climate of the South encouraged large cotton plantations based on cheap slave labor. Northern geography was more amenable to different crops and small family farms. The conflict of outlooks and economic needs eventually led to the Civil War in 1860. After the war, improvements in transportation and communication eventually tied the two regions more closely together despite physical barriers, distance, and differing geographically based interests.

The geographic regions of the United States still retain distinctive attitudes and outlooks. Differences between the rural South, the urban Northeast, and the small-town Midwest are as great as the differences between countries in many parts of the world. Issues such as a return to **"family values"** (support for the sanctity of marriage, protecting children from lewd entertainment, etc.) find their most favorable response in small-town and rural America. In large urban areas government involvement in such issues generally is seen as impinging on individual freedom.

"family values" *A set of moral principles that could include, but is not limited to, opposition to abortion, birth control, and premarital sex, and support for prayer in public schools, introduced as a political slogan by Dan Quayle.*

Internet technology allows the creation of non-geographic "virtual communities" as people with like interests and perspectives get together in chat rooms or post their views on bulletin boards. It is still unclear whether such communities will enhance democracy by bringing new people into the game, undermine democracy by fragmenting society into competing groups that don't communicate with each other, or simply be irrelevant to the political process.

5-1b Geographically Based Conflicts

Although less of an impediment to communication than in the past, geographical characteristics are still a source of conflict in American politics today. At the Constitutional Convention, as we learned in Chapter 2, states with extensive land yet low populations argued against representation by population alone. Similarly, an individual state's size and population affect the policy positions that its representatives are expected to take. For example, during the move toward business deregulation in the 1980s, representatives of sparsely populated areas attempted to use the political process to deny airlines the right to cut out less profitable routes. They wanted to guarantee continued airline service to their isolated citizens. Cities with large, concentrated populations, on the other hand, showed more interest in increasing flights to other major cities and worried less about cutting unprofitable routes.

Some of the major battles in the political game have involved the division of scarce resources. For example, cities facing water shortages often turn to Congress or the courts to guarantee the right to divert water from other political jurisdictions with an abundant supply (see Box 5-1: Water, Water, Not Everywhere). Differing needs based on geography are still a source of conflicts that must sometimes be solved in a political arena.

5-1c The Decline of Regionalism

Physical barriers such as mountains and rivers once limited the size of political systems, but new communication and transportation technologies make these traditional barriers less important. In the fourth century B.C., Aristotle asserted that democracies must be small enough that no citizen would have to travel more than one day to participate. Such a view has been overtaken by technologies that eliminate physical proximity as a requirement for communication.[6]

Despite America's size and geographic variations, few Americans live physically or socially isolated lives. Telephones, radios, and commercial and cable television are within the reach of almost every American (see Box 5-2: The Spread of Communication Technologies in America). The computer-based information superhighway reaches nearly everywhere in the country. More than half of employed Americans use a computer at work. Almost two-thirds have a computer at home to access the Internet and/or receive and send email. By 2004, at least 200 million Americans (almost 70%) were going online regularly to connect to free and commercial databases and to send email. Almost one-third were going online daily for news. During the 2002 midterm elections, 13% used the Internet to get political news.[7] Elected officials, once isolated in Washington, D.C., or in state capitals, now have little excuse for not knowing what is going on back in their

Box 5–1 *Water, Water, Not Everywhere*

In a state known for importing just about everything, from goods and services to the bulk of its population, it probably should come as no surprise that Los Angeles county supervisor Kenneth Hahn would repeatedly propose importing three billion gallons of water per day from more than one thousand miles away. Hahn argues that each day the Columbia River in the Pacific Northwest "dumps into the Pacific Ocean 90 billion gallons of fresh water. This is 3.7 billion gallons an hour, 61 million gallons a minute, and 1 million gallons a second. This is wasteful and sinful."

At the time, in reaction to Hahn's proposal to stick long "straws" into the resources of other states, Idaho governor Cecil D. Andrus said, "Ridiculous," Washington governor Booth Gardner exclaimed, "Neither desirable nor feasible," and Oregon governor Neil Goldschmidt retorted, "Hoping you're not serious." What Supervisor Hahn saw as the reasonable sharing of wasted resources, others saw as imperialism.[a]

One state official's imperialism is another's opportunity. While a number of adjacent states refused to sell water to California for fear that once California became dependent it would "then use its political muscle to steal it later,"[b] Alaskan officials sought the opportunity. Ric Davidge, an Alaskan entrepreneur, proposed transporting millions of tons of the precious liquid in water-gorged baggies. California officials began listening, seeing it as a way of getting around their selfish neighbors. The plan is still under technical development and political consideration.[c]

---

a. Jay Matthews, "County Supervisor Looks a Long Way North for Water," *Washington Post*, May 20, 1990, A23.
b. Steve LaRue, "Alaska Water Sales to California Could Just About Be in the Baggies," *San Diego Union-Tribune*, June 6, 1994, B2.
c. See Toni Rizzo, "Proposed Mendocino Water-Grab Threatens Californians' Control of Water," 2002, http://www.gualalariver.org/export/greenfuse.html, and Daniel B. Wood, "Latest Plan to Ease Water Woes: Big Baggies," *Christian Science Monitor*, http://www.csmonitor.com/2002/0312/p01s01-ussc.html.

districts. They face fewer limits on their ability to communicate with constituents, and vice versa. Such immediate access may be a mixed blessing if government officials are tempted to emphasize immediate responsiveness over careful consideration of policy options.

Increased physical mobility and technological innovations have also altered the homogeneity of political arenas based on geography. In previous times, physical characteristics determined land use much more than they do today. When transportation was more time-consuming, and effective communication could only take place face-to-face, maintaining business enterprises and other economic activities required participants to be closer together. Individuals in certain occupations tended to concentrate in the same areas.

Today, fax machines, overnight mail, cell phones, and computers allow many people to work wherever they want. No longer must companies be located in a few large urban areas. For example, the publisher of this book operates out of Cincinnati, Ohio, and employs freelancers around the country who communicate via fax and email from their electronic "cottages." It can successfully compete with other publishers without having to concentrate its operations in New York, formerly the unchallenged publishing capital. Similarly, legislative districts that were once composed primarily of farmers or of people dependent on the lumber industry have been invaded by small companies and self-employed individuals working out of their homes electronically. Diversity of land use confronts elected representatives with an increased variety of conflicting public demands.

The physical playing field continues to be a factor in American politics as it defines players, affects strategies, stimulates the issues over which political interests battle, and often determines winners and losers. Increasingly, though, the values and attitudes of

Box 5-2 The Spread of Communication Technologies in America

Modern information technology has made the United States an increasingly interconnected nation. Geographical barriers such as rivers, mountains, and even distance itself mean little to the exchange of information by telephone, radio, television, or the Internet. Once considered luxuries, it is hard to imagine a household lacking access to any one of these tools in our wired nation. These technologies have become vehicles for spreading political ideas. Change has become an abiding characteristic of modern life. Just as Americans became accustomed to radio, television replaced it. After a few decades of dominance, commercial broadcast television now faces a serious challenge from cable television. The expected merging of technologies in the near future will erase the line between audio, video, and text, again changing the way Americans gather information and surmount physical barriers.

American Households with Communication Technology Services

Source: U.S. Bureau of the Census, Statistical Abstract of the United States, Table 1126, p. 721, Washington, D.C., GPO, 2003.

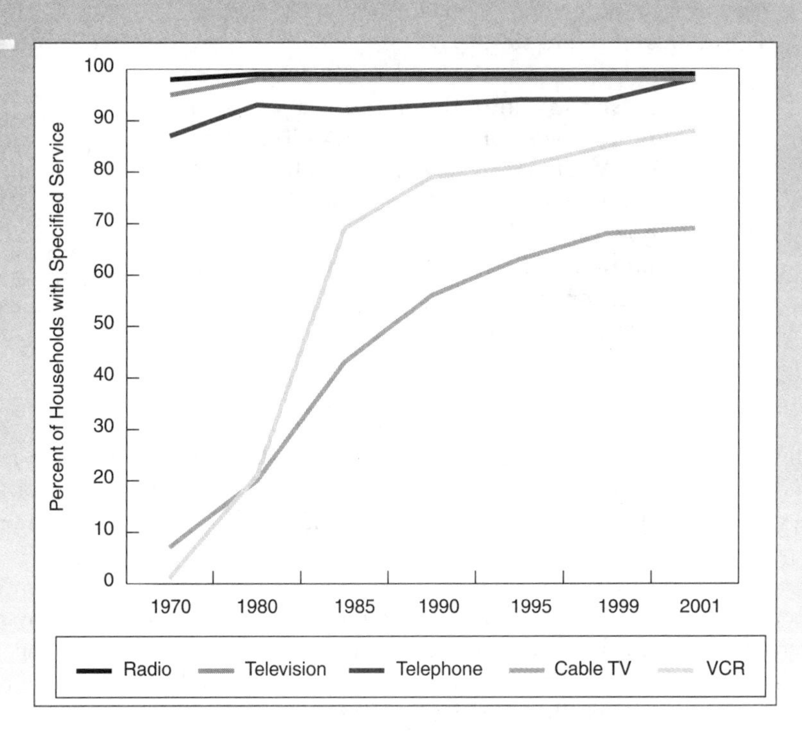

people—no matter where they may be physically located—define the nature and operation of American politics.

5-2 Political Culture

culture *Those aspects of a society's history, artistic accomplishment, and attitudes toward the world deemed worthy of transmission from one generation to the next.*

A society's **culture** includes those elements of its history, accomplishments, and attitudes about life that are passed down from one generation to the next by the family, schools, peers, social organizations, and mass media. Developments such as the American Revolution, jazz, television sitcoms, shopping malls, and baseball are all part of our culture. We have defined political culture as those aspects of the general culture that concern government and the political process.

American political culture includes:

- beliefs about the rules under which the game should be played,
- the esteem in which government is held,

- attitudes toward who should play the game of politics,
- definitions of acceptable strategies, and
- criteria for accepting or rejecting outcomes of the political game.

These attitudes are important because they precede—and may help to predict—political behavior. Pride in a democratic heritage, for example, would logically generate a sense of civic duty.

Astute political leaders often base their actions on widely held political values and attitudes. The civil rights movement, for example, effectively used the American commitment to equality in promoting its cause during the middle decades of this century. During the 1980s, President Reagan called the Nicaraguan Contras "freedom fighters" and evoked powerful symbolic images by likening them to America's "brave men at Valley Forge." President George H. Bush called U.S. military activity in Panama "Operation Just Cause." President Clinton named his initiative in Haiti "Operation Democracy" and referred to the Kosovo activity as "Operation Allied Forces" as strategies for showing broad support and expanding public approval. Who could oppose "just" causes in the pursuit of "democracy" fully supported by our military allies? In 2001, President George W. Bush used the relatively benign terminology of "Operation Southern Watch" and "Operation Northern Watch" when using U.S. bombs to enforce the Middle East no-fly zone on Iraq. He also reintroduced the appealing "Star Wars" analogy first used by President Reagan to describe his high-tech missile defense system. Star Wars implies use of high technology by the "good guys," with little risk to Americans.

By comparing Saddam Hussein to Adolf Hitler before the start of the Persian Gulf War, President George H. Bush provided the American public with a clear and personalized image of the enemy. A decade later, George W. Bush continued the pattern of framing a proposed war as a struggle with an individual, Saddam Hussein, rather than blaming the people of Iraq. This fit the American cultural premise that it is not appropriate to stereotype an entire nation. Demonizing the leadership made it easier to obtain public support for military action and facilitate attempts to reestablish relations with Iraq after the war.

5-2a The Transmission of Political Culture

Political culture is not inbred. Rather, it is something we learn. The process by which we acquire our values, attitudes, and outlooks about politics and government is known as **political socialization.** Political socialization refers primarily to the way in which children or new adult immigrants acquire values and attitudes about politics and the appropriate role of government. The term *socialization* is preferred to the term *learning*, since attitude development depends to a large degree on communication and interpretation by individuals in a larger social rather than only a school environment. Some observers believe that the pervasiveness of mass media technologies, such as radio and especially television, is undermining the influence of other individual and traditional sources on attitude formation. However, face-to-face communications continue to be important influences. Although socialization continues throughout our lifetime, early experiences leave a significant mark. Subsequent socialization in new social settings must modify the initial attitude before replacing it with another.

political socialization *The process by which political attitudes and outlooks of society are transmitted from one generation to the next through teaching or emulation.*

The instilling of these outlooks begins with the family and continues in school and in interactions with peers and others in a variety of social settings. Socialization may involve unintentional teaching through bedtime stories, intentional glorification of historical heroes in school, experiences such as saluting the flag, or informal discussions with friends and family. Socialization also results from **emulation.** Children follow the patterns set by parents, friends, teachers, and media heroes out of respect or admiration.

emulation *The patterning of one's attitudes, outlooks, and behavior after parents, friends, or other respected individuals.*

Often the primary agents of socialization—the socializers—are not directly aware of their impact. Individuals express their attitudes to those they respect and then observe reactions. Positive reactions result in strengthening a particular attitude, while negative reactions force rethinking it. The child from a family opposed to gun control who expresses her support for the right to bear arms gets a pat on the head or a smile of approval. The sibling who expresses concern about the rapidly increasing number of deaths from handguns subjects herself to a disapproving glance or direct confrontation.

People often apply their personal experiences to the larger political world. Children whose parents treat them with dignity, who go to schools that encourage individuality and participation, who observe few negative interactions with government, and whose peers have had similar experiences, generally emerge from childhood with a positive attitude toward government. Children with abusive parents, who attend schools that emphasize discipline, who observe government officials (that is, the police) as a threat, and who interact with peers having similar experiences, often view government authority negatively rather than as a potential force for good.[8]

Adults view some attitudes as so important that they teach them directly. Most children with affirmative role models develop positive attitudes toward one of the political parties by the time they leave grade school. Yet few of them sit down and consciously study the goals and positions of the parties before establishing their **party identification.** As the authors of a book about American public opinion noted:

party identification *The sense of affinity or feeling of belonging to one of the political parties.*

> Instead, they know they are Republicans or Democrats in much the same way they know they are Catholics, Episcopalians, Methodists, and so on. They are told by their parents. But they have little idea what the labels mean. Once the choice is made, however, it takes a sizeable amount of incongruous information before the particular party label is abandoned.[9]

For most people direct education concerning acceptable attitudes is confined to just a few areas. (A summary of socialization factors appears in Chapter 9, Box 9-1.) In addition to political party preference, there is religious affiliation, identification with a particular ethnic heritage, and adherence to basic moral views. For example, most parents attempt to teach a few basic values—such as that honesty is the best policy, that hard work is rewarded, and that education is the route to success—indirectly through stories with morals and directly through cautions and advice.

The Founders assumed that the family would be "the seed bed of virtue, undergirding democracy by building discipline."[10] The often heard cry to return to "family values" (as defined by the Religious Right in many cases) is a reaction to a perceived decline in the number of traditional households with the skill and ability to teach a relatively uniform set of moral principles. American families vary in competency, composition, and the nature of the values they impart.

The Institutional Basis of Political Culture

It was long assumed that the values and attitudes that children learned at home would be reinforced by churches and schools. The weakening of religious affiliation and the increasing **secularization** of America has perhaps made more of the Founders' desire to separate church and state than they intended. The Founders worried about favoring one religious denomination, but they assumed that religious values—in the sense of morality—would underlie political choices. For the past few years, the Religious Right has attempted to define the acceptable cultural values and to insert religious values into political debate. One observer noted:

secularization *Emphasizing worldly concerns as opposed to religious or moral ones.*

> Hardly anyone is ignoring the Religious Right these days. Elections are games of numbers, and the ascendancy of the movement in the Republican party has placed it at the fulcrum of American politics. Politicians in both parties are scrambling to define it and deal with its impact.[11]

The stubbornness and narrowness of the views of certain leaders of the Religious Right make some Americans uncomfortable, while other citizens applaud a return to basic Judeo-Christian principles in public life.[12]

At the same time, the contemporary American school system reflects our diverse political culture. It does not have a strong role in shaping a system of nationally shared values. As belief in strict discipline declines and diversity increases, the public schools marshal their resources to maintain order and reflect tolerance instead of teaching one set of values.

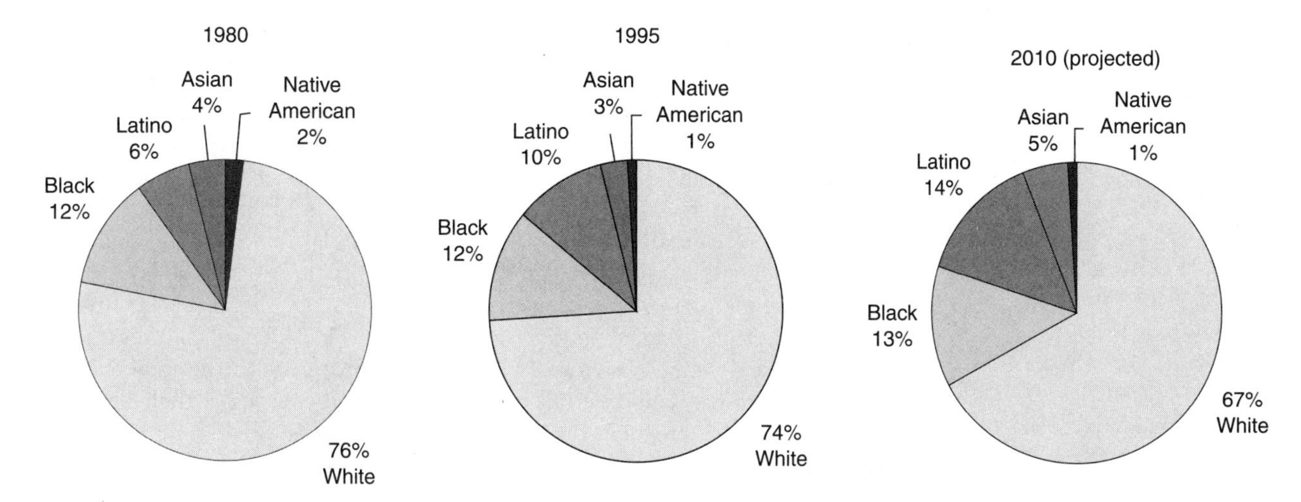

Figure 5-1
The Growing Ethnic Diversity of America, 1980–2010

Because of our relatively wide-open immigration policies and differential birth rates, the United States is becoming more ethnically diverse. Diversity influences the demands made on government and the ease with which compromises can be made.

Sources: Data from Barbara Vobejda "Asians, Hispanics Giving Nation More Diversity," *Washington Post*, June 12, 1991, p. A3; "Radical Change in Ethnic Population," *Evening Capital*, September 29, 1993, p. A3 (based on U.S. Census Bureau estimates).

Political Culture and Societal Diversity

Countries vary in both the content and homogeneity of their political cultures. A society composed of individuals from similar backgrounds, with a narrow range of lifestyles and a well-developed communication system, develops few **subcultures.** The United States, on the other hand, has long recognized itself as a nation of immigrants. President Franklin D. Roosevelt reinforced this point when he addressed the Daughters of the American Revolution, a group with great pride in its American roots, as "my fellow immigrants." Over the years we have opened our doors to seekers of freedom and economic opportunity from a series of countries going through political difficulty. Due to relatively open immigration policies and the higher birthrates among many immigrant groups, the United States has become increasingly diverse (see Figure 5-1).

The notion of America as a **melting pot** of immigrants from different races, nations, religions, and ethnic backgrounds was long a source of national pride. The earlier part of the twentieth century was marked by only sporadic conflicts between competing cultural influences. However, despite the promise of America as a melting pot of values and outlooks, with continuous waves of new immigrants and few experiences of ethnic conflict, "the confidence that they [the diverse immigrants] could be fused together waned" by mid-century.[13]

A reemergence of ethnic pride in the language, history, and artistic achievements of various groups has led to the contemporary emphasis on **cultural diversity,** which attempts to respect differences. Conflict has emerged on a number of different levels, including the viability of English as the only official language and the eligibility of immigrants to receive social welfare benefits. During the 1990s, citizens of some states with high levels of immigrants, such as California and Florida, attempted to both limit immigration and deny government benefits to illegal aliens.

subculture *A divergent set of social outlooks held by an identifiable minority group within a society.*

melting pot *A description of the American experience of welcoming successive waves of immigrants and integrating them into the dominant culture.*

cultural diversity *The coexistence of a variety of cultures that are accepted as worthy and legitimate.*

Recognizing the importance of Latino voters, both Al Gore and George W. Bush made special efforts to mobilize their support before the 2000 election. Each candidate attended Latino events and created commercials in which they spoke Spanish. George W. Bush ended up doing better among Latino voters in both 2000 and 2004 than have other Republican candidates, and the Latino votes proved crucial in a number of states such as Florida.

The various racial and ethnic groups in the United States view politics in unique ways. This vision is often based on how policy has treated their interests historically. As we shall see, minority groups are much more committed than is the majority to an activist national government, which will attempt to improve their social and economic conditions.

The process of socialization and the common outlooks and sources of conflict that it engenders are constantly changing. New social and technological conditions affect who is socialized, the content of the message, and the process of transmission.

New Agents of Socialization

Many people today spend more and more time watching television and less and less time with the family. Television's influence as a socializing agent, therefore, has increased. News programs provide direct information on how the political system works. Entertainment programs increasingly take up political issues. The visual component of television makes its messages particularly potent, and its immediacy accelerates the potential speed of cultural change. Clothing styles, social outlooks, and political perspectives transmitted by television can sweep the country in a matter of days.

The dominance of network television programming, at least until the 1990s, contributed to a basically national political culture with few localized subcultures. The emergence of top-rated shows has exposed millions of Americans to the same stories and images simultaneously. Children talk about or act out the antics of their favorite programs. Entertainment programs on television both reflect and help form contemporary political and social culture. More and more, they take up such topics as homosexuality, premarital sex, and drug use.

During the 1960s, *Father Knows Best, Leave It to Beaver,* and other programs glorified the family and especially the father's ability to solve knotty problems such as what to do about cheating on homework or how to get a date for the prom. By the early 1980s, *The Cosby Show* and *Family Ties* portrayed the father as a lovable but quite fallible individual, who was often outsmarted by his wife or family. The 1990s' *Home Improvement, King of the Hill* and *Dave's World* at best treated parents as funny "doofuses."[14] Other programs, such as, *The Simpsons, King of the Hill, Family Guy, That 70's show,* and *Titus* degraded parents and other authority figures even more by showing them as ignorant, ineffectual, and often ill-tempered. To the degree that children are exposed to the concepts of power and leadership through television, it is no surprise that contemporary children show considerable distrust of authority figures in general and for political leadership in society.

The impact of American television is not limited to socializing American children. American television programs dominate the airwaves in many countries of the world. Not only do audiences of these countries get a picture of the United States, but their children pick up expectations of how to act. A number of experts fear that the cultural imperialism of American television and movies will undermine indigenous local cultures and replace them with some of the worst aspects of American culture.

The emergence of cable television, with its broader range of programming aimed at narrower audiences, has the potential for increasing societal fragmentation. Individuals watching Spanish-language television, the Black Entertainment Network, National Empowerment Television (conservative), or Busnet (business) will receive very different views on the political process (see Box 5-3: Losing Control of Socialization in the MTV Generation). Specialized lines of communication supported by new technologies could feed the tendency for individuals to identify with ethnic, gender, or ideological groupings as opposed to seeing themselves as Americans. Many of the new subcultures are no longer geographically based.

The Internet provides an even more individualized method of socialization, and many parents lack the skills to monitor or block information on the web that could challenge the political perspectives they would prefer their children acquire. Children who "live" on the web are exposed to ideas that can help frame their view of reality.

5-2b Political Culture and the Rules of the Game

Political culture helps define acceptable ways of playing the game. Americans respect the basic political structure, support individual rights, and expect fairness.

Respect for the Basic Political Structure

Living in the oldest constitutional democracy in the world is a source of pride for many Americans. While citizens of other countries revel in their artistic or scientific heritages, Americans traditionally have been much more likely to identify their political system as

Box 5-3 *Losing Control of Socialization in the MTV Generation*

The popularity of MTV and its ability to spread both audio and video messages raises concern that parents have lost some control of what their children see and learn. The problem is compounded by the large percentage of parents who work outside the home and therefore are not there to monitor their children's after-school viewing habits. As with most communications technologies, MTV can be used to teach both widely accepted attitudes and those with a narrower base of support.

During the 1992 election, MTV's "Rock the Vote" videos used sophisticated graphics and rock star endorsements to encourage young voters to register and vote. MTV took some credit for the 18 percent increase in voter registration among 18- to 24-year-olds compared to the 1988 election. Bill Clinton's appearances on MTV proved to be an effective method of reaching younger voters: Clinton did better among young voters than had any previous Democratic candidate, and he credited MTV with much of his success. As a symbol of his appreciation, the MTV Inaugural Ball was the first one Clinton visited on Inaugural Day. After the 1992 election, the Rock the Vote organization went on to lobby effectively for the motor-voter bill, designed to make voter registration easier by linking it with applying for a driver's license. At the bill-signing ceremony, Bill Clinton recognized MTV's efforts and indicated that he first made his commitment to the bill when he signed a "Rock the Vote" card during the presidential primaries.

In a more questionable realm, many people (especially adults) feel that MTV programming of fare such as the *Beavis and Butt-Head, Jackass,* and *Spiderman,* programs glorify violence and encourage attitudes questioning all forms of authority. One set of parents in Montgomery County, Virginia, who refused to allow their children to watch MTV at home, organized politically when they realized that MTV was being beamed into their local library. They asked library officials either to pull the plug on MTV or to require library patrons under age eighteen to have parental permission to watch MTV. In another example, the city council in Sleepy Eye, Minnesota, was pressured by parents to support a resolution banning MTV from their cable system.

In both cases the parents saw MTV as potentially undermining their rightful control over how their children were socialized, and in both cases the affected teenagers and civil liberties advocates challenged such actions on the grounds of free speech. MTV remained available. In Sleepy Eye, parents were given the option of individually controlling their children's access by installing "traps" on their sets to block MTV, but only a handful took this option. Congress attempted to walk the fine line between protecting 1st Amendment rights to free speech and protecting children by requiring new television sets to be equipped with V Chips to allow parents to voluntarily block violent and offensive material.

Sources: Marilyn Achiron, "Motor-Vated," *People,* June 7, 1993, 53; LEXIS-NEXIS; Remarks by President Bill Clinton During the Signing Ceremony for the Motor-Voter bill, 20 May 1994; "Mother Wants MTV Out of Libraries," *Washington Times,* 15 October 1994, A11; William Souder, "We Don't Want Your MTV: A Town Trying to Unplug," *Washington Post,* June 29, 1994, D1.

their country's greatest accomplishment. In a five-country study of political culture in the 1960s, political scientists Gabriel Almond and Sidney Verba found that 85 percent of American respondents said that they were most proud of their governmental and political institutions. This figure was more than twice that of British, German, Mexican, or Italian respondents. Americans indicated more pride in government than in any other aspect of the country.[15]

Today many Americans continue to value the Constitution and the framework it establishes, but they do not feel the same way about the current state of the institutions it created. By the 1970s, scandals and policy failures significantly dampened the ardor for all three branches of government (see Figure 5-2). The upheavals in Eastern Europe in the early 1990s resulted in country after country scurrying for advice on how to build their new democracies after the U.S. model, yet this failed to reinforce Americans' pride

Figure 5-2
Public Confidence in American Political Institutions

Over time, Americans have generally lost confidence in political institutions, making it more difficult to govern though them.

Source: Louis Harris and Associates telephone surveys of 1,200–1,500 randomly selected American adults, LEXIS-NEXIS database.

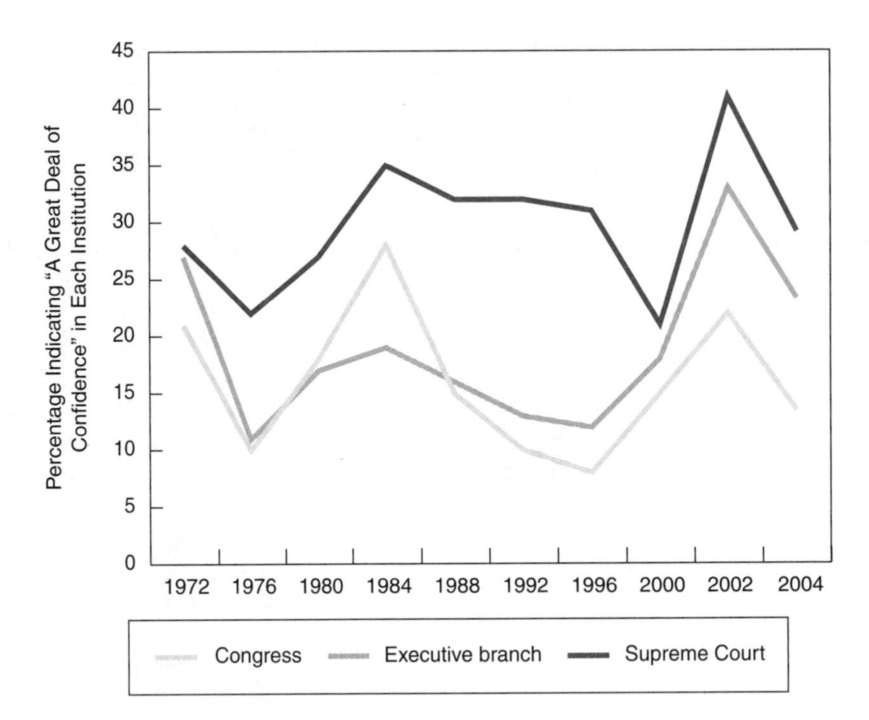

in their governmental institutions. The increasing depth of American cynicism was captured by national polls asking Americans whether the United States "is the greatest country in the world, better than all other countries in every possible way." In 1955 a total of 66 percent of Americans agreed that the United States was the greatest; by 1991 that figure had dropped to 37 percent, with a recovery to slightly more than 50 percent in 1996.[16] The fact that cynicism toward government was a worldwide phenomenon does little to lessen how far our institutions will have to go to regain high trust among the public. The terrorist attacks of September 11, 2001, did lead Americans to turn back to government institutions as positive forces in American society, but the staying power of that shift proved to be temporary.

Americans also feel significant dissatisfaction with government performance. By the 1980s many believed that "government is too intrusive, too profligate, and too inefficient."[17] Voters feeling that they could not "fight City Hall" initially focused on the inadequacies of the existing players. In the early 1990s, voters' disgust led to cries of "throw the rascals out" more than "cancel the game." But by the mid-1990s government shortcomings were no longer seen as the personal inadequacies of existing players. They were viewed, rather, as basic flaws in the rules of the game. Box 5-4, The Culture of Playing Politics provides data on how Americans view their government.

Current surveys seem to indicate that "Politicians and voters alike have decided for the time being that government is the enemy."[18] To some observers it appears that there has been a major "unraveling of political culture" and the development of a "cynicism industry. . . a cabal [secret plot] of political players who all have a vested interest in creating higher and higher levels of anxiety."[19] From candidates and the media to talk-show hosts and elected officials, anger at government and public officials is a commodity that strikes a responsive chord in audiences. The 2000 presidential election campaign saw virtually all the candidates—even existing officeholders—trying to run as outsiders to avoid the taint of association with existing officials.

Support of Basic Rights

The most fundamental and enduring values in American political culture are equality, individualism, and fairness. Most Americans completely accept and approve the basic constitutional rights of freedom of speech, freedom of religion, and freedom of association—at least in the abstract. In concrete situations they are somewhat more likely to curb these freedoms when the results of exercising them conflict with other deeply held beliefs. For example, groups advocating the overthrow of the government or the burning of the American flag—a sacred symbol of American political culture—are likely to face limitations on their rights of free speech. The more Americans perceive a group as a threat to their well-being or to the nation as a whole, the more likely they are to limit its freedoms.[20] Yet even in the most extreme cases, Americans hesitate to limit what are seen as basic freedoms.

The specific groups that Americans dislike or fear tend to change over time. With the dissolution of the Soviet Union, the once-feared Soviet communists are now little more than quaint relics of a failed political experiment. The Black Power movement associated with the urban riots of the 1960s eventually lost much of its power to instill fear as civil rights groups moved toward using more peaceful means of gaining their objectives. During the 1990s street gangs engendered more fear than did the organized political groups of an earlier era, such as the Black Panthers or the Ku Klux Klan.

Look at your responses to the poll in Time Out 5-1. In question 1, you probably agreed that "People should be allowed to express unpopular opinions." Such a view expresses a basic commitment to the constitutional guarantee of free speech. Now look at your responses to questions 4 through 9. When answering these questions, you probably found some place where you wanted to draw a line limiting free speech. Virtually all of us would agree that some behaviors simply do not deserve legal protection.

If your inconsistency makes you feel a bit uncomfortable, take some comfort in the fact that you are not alone. Many Americans temper their support for basic freedoms when confronted with specific, concrete applications.

Equity: Commitment to a Level Playing Field

According to former Senate majority leader George J. Mitchell (D-Maine) in a statement made at the Iran-Contra hearings in 1987, "The glue of nationhood for us is the American

An Opinion Poll

Time Out 5-1

Generally speaking, do you agree or disagree with these statements?

1. People should be allowed to express unpopular opinions	Agree	Disagree
2. People like me don't have any say about what the government does.	Agree	Disagree
3. Public officials care about what people like me think.	Agree	Disagree
4. A person should be allowed to make a speech in my community claiming that blacks are genetically inferior	Agree	Disagree
5. A person who advocates doing away with elections and letting the military run the government should be allowed to make a speech in my community.	Agree	Disagree
6. An admitted communist should be allowed to make a speech in my community	Agree	Disagree
7. People should be allowed to burn or deface the American flag as a political statement		
Musicians should be allowed to sing songs with lyrics others might find offensive	Agree	Disagree
8. People should be allowed to say things in public that might be offensive to religious groups	Agree	Disagree

Remember to write down your responses; we'll refer to them later in the chapter.

Sources: Questions 1 and 8–9: Center for Survey Research and Analysis, University of Connecticut, June 2001. Questions 4–6: National personal survey of 2,817 adults carried out by the National Opinion Research Center as part of the General Social Survey, 2002.

Box 5-4 The Culture of Playing Politics

One of the key questions about the political game is "Who are the players?" This question can be approached in different ways. In later chapters we will look at the rules that determine who can play and who cannot. We will also analyze the social and political characteristics of those who choose to participate. At this point, we will consider the values and attitudes that underlie involvement.

In the broadest sense, America's democratic political culture assumes that at a minimum everyone should have the opportunity to participate in politics at a relatively equal level. In reality, however, we know that not everyone has the skills or motivation to be involved.

The acceptance or rejection of particular cultural outlooks helps explain which members of the public will take an active role in playing the political game and which will remain on the sidelines. The sense of political efficacy is not simply an orientation to politics retained in a person's head. Such attitudes underlie political behavior. Attitudes about how the political system works serve as either arguments for involvement or excuses for staying out of the process. As the data in the charts in this box indicate, individuals who feel their efforts will have a positive impact, and who perceive decision makers as responsive to their demands, are much more likely to make the effort.

As with many games, potential players may lack or lose confidence in their ability to play or be unwilling to get involved. As the song from the musical *Damn Yankees* goes, "You Gotta Have Heart." Participants in games requiring high levels of concentration such as golf or chess often find that the mind game is as important as the physical process of playing. In politics, if cultural norms begin either to undermine individual feelings of competence or to create attitudes that the game is rigged, is it any wonder that it has become more difficult to get more individuals to play?

The high level of cynicism of the American public threatens the political game. As the charts indicate, a significant percentage of the U.S. population harbors attitudes detrimental to full participation in the political game. As with previous measures of political satisfaction (see Figure 5-2), there was considerable improvement after the terrorist attacks in 2001, which lacked staying power.

It is quite probable that individuals who accept attitudes supportive of government are more likely to participate in the political process. Since these individuals are not a random sample of the U.S. population, this has the potential for distorting whose voice gets heard and whose preferences prevail. It is also clear that such supportive attitudes have declined in recent years, sending up a signal that without a reversal the game could be called for lack of interest.

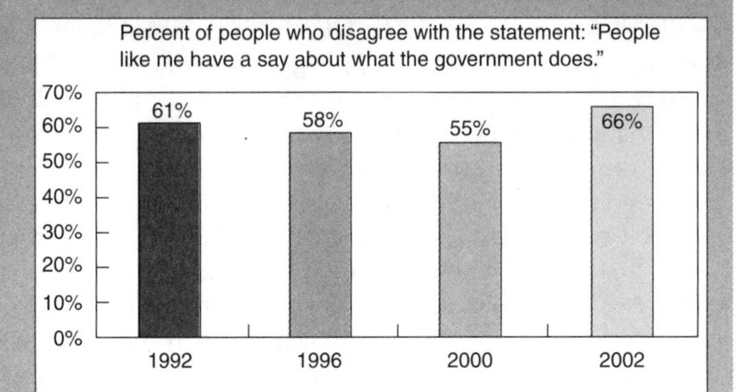

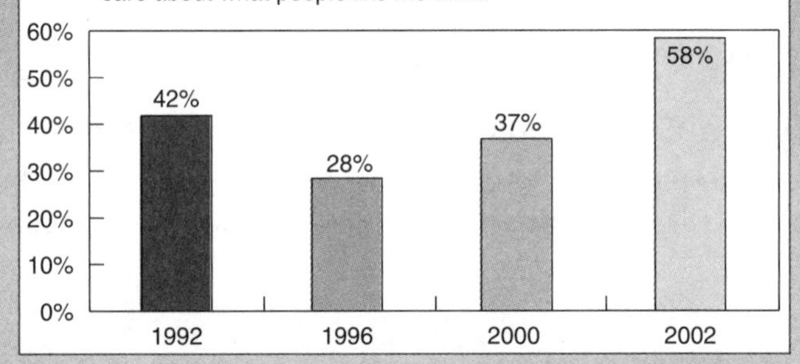

Note: Only those having an opinion are included.
Source: National Election Studies, University of Michigan.

Source: "Trust in Government Survey" based on national adult samples of 1,500–1,800 respondents for the Pew Research Center by Princeton Survey Research Associates, and Gallup and New York Times polls from 1997–2003 reported in the LEXIS-NEXIS database.

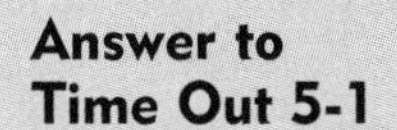

Political Power and You: A Textbook Case

Consider the results of nationwide polls* that requested the same information as you were asked to provide in the poll in Time Out 5-1:

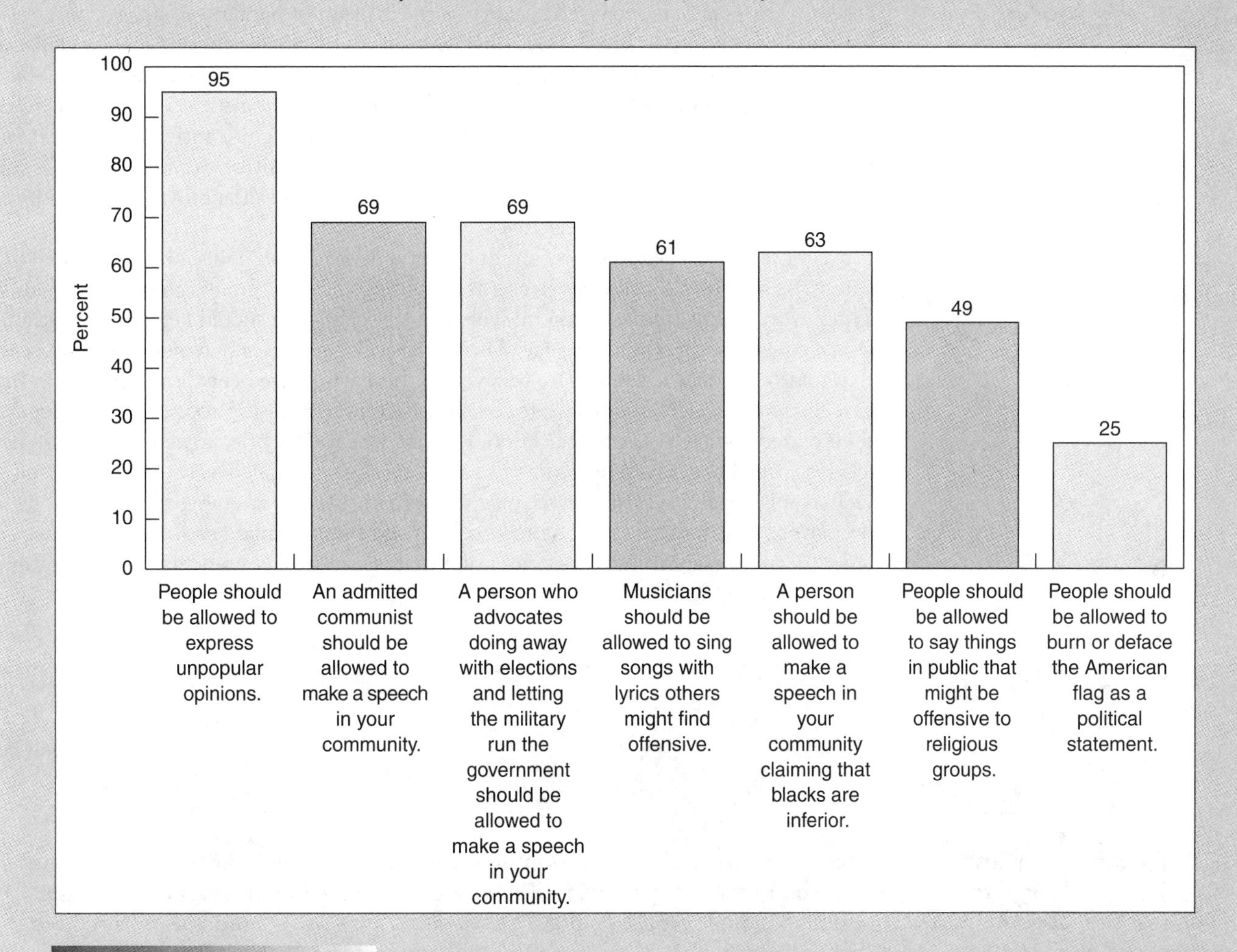

*Poll Sources: Question 1 and questions 7–9, national telephone survey of 1,012 adults carried out by the Center for Survey Research and Analysis, University of Connecticut, June 2003. Questions 4–6, national personal survey of 2,817 adults carried out by the National Opinion Research Center as part of the General Social Survey, February 2002.

ideal of individual liberty and equal justice. The rule of law is critical in our society. The law is the great equalizer, because everybody in America is equal before the law."

A fair playing field has rules and conditions that guarantee all players the same potential to win. Most Americans believe that the United States should be a country of laws, not simply assembled people, and that everyone deserves to be treated equally. The American Dream includes a belief that anyone should realistically be able to strive for the highest levels of accomplishment in government, business, and the arts.

Despite widespread support for the basic ideal of equality, however, the nature of the equality on the playing field is subject to considerable disagreement. Virtually everyone agrees with the concept of **equality of opportunity**—that rules should not disadvantage specific groups of individuals from participating. Without equality of opportunity, some groups of individuals are perpetually doomed to lose. Others win, however, regardless of

equality of opportunity *The guarantee that all participants in the political process begin with an equal chance to win.*

their skill, effort, and/or motivation. Lack of equal opportunity breeds resentment and lessens motivation among the predestined losers.

equality of outcome (or condition) The result of a political (or economic) game in which all players end up the same.

Yet few of us completely accept the idea of **equality of outcome,** which guarantees everyone, no matter what their skill or efforts, the same rewards from the political process. The Founders promised equality in the "pursuit of happiness" but not necessarily its attainment [21] (see Box 5-5: Dealing with Equality). Subgroups in America view the governmental role in promoting equality differently. In 1997 half of Caucasians believed that "We have gone too far in pushing equal rights in this country." Only 18 percent of African Americans agreed. Men and women also differed significantly, with 51 percent of men feeling we had gone too far compared to 39 percent of women. Both the gap between African Americans and Caucasians and the overall disapproval of the push for equal rights increased during the 1990s.[22]

For the last few decades, a recurrent question in American politics has concerned the extent to which the rules governing the political process should guarantee equality. Those who benefit from existing rules argue that each game should begin anew without regard paid to the previous outcome. Those who seek equality of outcome agree but assert that some consideration must also be given to those who have been disadvantaged in the past. Incumbent elected officials, for example, see no reason not to use the resources of their current office to assure reelection. Challengers, meanwhile, argue that they should receive special benefits to overcome the advantages of incumbency. (Some sports games, such as golf and horse racing, make playing more interesting by giving a handicap to better players, thus forcing everyone to excel beyond their normal level of performance in order to win.) Establishing rules that ensure that all political contenders start at the same point, however, is difficult.

Box 5-5 Dealing with Equality

Supreme Court justice Clarence Thomas used a game analogy to explain his commitment to equality of opportunity as opposed to equality of condition as it relates to minorities in America:

> [As a boy growing up in the South, Thomas] was on the back porch playing blackjack for pennies with some other boys. As the game went on, one boy kept winning. Thomas finally saw how: The cards were marked. The game was stopped. There were angry words. Cards were thrown. From all sides, fast fists snatched back lost money. There could be no equitable redistribution of the pot. The strongest, fastest hands, including those of the boy who had been cheating, got most of the money in the pile.
>
> Some of the boys didn't get their money back. The cheater was threatened. The boys who snatched pennies that they had not lost were also threatened. But no one really wanted to fight—they wanted to keep playing cards. So a different deck was brought out and shuffled, and the game resumed with a simple promise of no more cheating.

That story, Thomas said, is a lot like the story of race relations in America. Whites had an unfair advantage. But in 1964, with the passage of the Civil Rights Act, the government stopped the cheating. The question now is, should the government return the ill-gotten gains to the losers—the blacks, the Latinos, and the women who were cheated by racism and sexism? Does fairness mean reaching back into the nation's past to undo the damage?

Thomas believes that government simply cannot make amends and therefore should not try. The best it can do is to deal a clean deck and let the game resume, enforcing the rules as they have now come to be understood.[a]

Dealing a clean deck is Justice Thomas's analogy for equality of opportunity, while making amends for past injustices reflects an attempt to bring about equality of condition. Not everyone agrees with his conception of the problem, but as a member of the Supreme Court, he is in a better position than most to see that his viewpoint wins the game.

a. Juan Williams, "A Question of Fairness," *Atlantic*, vol. 29 (February 1987), 78–79.

Despite a legal commitment to equality of opportunity, American political culture still contains significant racist and sexist attitudes that handicap some potential participants in politics. Such attitudes have softened over time, but a nation's culture is slow to change. Legal attempts to reduce discrimination reflect changing political culture and also serve as stimuli for further cultural change. **Affirmative action** legislation arose after the civil rights movement of the 1960s. Its purpose was to compensate groups such as women and other minorities for admissions and hiring procedures that discriminated against them in the past. Affirmative action has become an explosive issue. While supporters continue to argue that preferential mandates are both fair and necessary, critics argue that they are neither. Claims of perceived **reverse discrimination** have led to arguments that affirmative action programs violate a more fundamental constitutional right—equality and justice *for all*. Box 5-6: A Woman's Place Is in the Workplace and the

affirmative action *Policies designed to enhance the employment of women and members of minorities and to undo past discriminatory practices.*

reverse discrimination *Hurting one group in society in the process of attempting to help another group by giving them a special preference.*

Box 5-6 A Woman's Place Is in the Workplace and the Polling Place

Money and politics have always been closely intertwined. Earlier this decade, when the right of women to vote was being debated, one of the arguments against granting the right to participate was the fact that nonparticipants in the economic realms should not have a role in deciding on the collection and distribution of taxes. During this period, relatively few women worked outside the home, and those who did largely saw their salaries as supplementary.

The percentage of women who joined the workforce grew gradually, initially taking off during World War II. By the 1970s women began simultaneously to reach both their political and economic maturity. Economically, more women saw their job as a career rather than as a short-term activity to fill the time between school graduation and marriage. "DINK" families (double income/no kids) became a conscious plan as husbands and wives chose to put off having children, at least temporarily, while building their assets. Politically, the gap in participation between men and women began to erode. Women matched men's voting participation, and an increasing percentage of women became candidates for public office.

By the 1990s the economic importance of women reached new levels. More than 60% of the women between eighteen and fifty-five were employed outside the home at least part-time. By 2002, 30% of women were either single wage earners or sole providers for their families. Women earned an average of 77 cents for every dollar earned by a man. Men were three times as likely to earn more than $75,000 than women were (15.8% versus 5.5%) and almost half as likely to earn less than $10,000 (2.8% versus 4.4%). Women contributed an average of over 40% of their families' incomes.[a] Such figures clearly "challenge(s) the persistent notion that women's earnings are supplemental."[b]

In the political realm, similar trends became evident. An increasing number of women ran for office in contests in which they had some chance of winning. The fund-raising gap between men and women began to disappear, and adequately funded female candidates were just as likely to win as were their male counterparts. The actual increase in the number of female elected officials at the national level grew more slowly (see Chapters 11 and 12), but women had become established in state and local offices from which national candidates are recruited.

The social implications of women's increasing opportunity to play in both the economic and political games are less clear. New issues concerning day care, family leave, the division of domestic responsibilities, and the ownership of assets have edged their way onto personal and societal agendas. For the foreseeable future, however, an increasing number of women will attempt to balance a variety of demanding roles. The accomplishment of a greater degree of gender equality in both the economic and political realms will force adjustments by women, men, and society as a whole.

---

a. See Current Population Report, P60-221, U.S. Census Bureau, 2003, http://www.census.gov/prod/2003pubs/p60-221.pdf, Current Population Report, P20-544, 2003, http://www.census.gov/prod/2003pubs/p20-544.pdf, and Tamar Lewis, "Women Are Becoming Equal Providers," *New York Times*, 11 May 1995, A27.
b. Arlene A. Johnson for the Families and Work Institute, quoted in *Ibid.*

Polling Place points out the improving, but continuing, disadvantage of women in the economic and political realm.

The Civil Rights Act of 1964 sought to eliminate not only discriminatory hiring practices but also practices that limited political participation. In response to complaints from women and members of minorities, the Democratic Party changed its presidential nominating convention rules during the 1960s and 1970s to establish quotas for these previously disadvantaged groups. These changes resulted in an increased percentage of women, youth, and blacks attending political conventions. They also had the undesired result of putting at a disadvantage such groups as elected officials, union members, and longtime party workers. The Democrats spent almost two decades adjusting their rules to ensure what they felt was true equality in the party's delegate selection process (see Chapter 8).

Numerous other examples of attempts to make the playing field level abound. The fact that people who would vote as Democrats were less likely to register to vote encouraged the Democratic Party to support simplified registration procedures. They supported programs such as postcard and Election Day registration. After gaining the presidency in 1992, the Democrats endorsed the motor-voter plan, which allows individuals to register to vote at the same time that they get a driver's license.

Changes in the rules get entangled in perceived partisan advantages. Republicans strongly supported term limits to help even the playing field while in the minority, but cooled to the issue significantly when holding the majority of seats in Congress and many state legislatures. The Democrats had little time for Republican-backed campaign finance reform, which would reduce the role of interest group contributions, as long as they received a majority of the funds. Once in the minority, Democrats took up the campaign finance battle and Republicans who had begun reaping the benefits of the existing laws backed off. During the 2000 Republican nomination race, Senator John McCain (R-Ariz.) found little support for his attempts at reforming campaign finance from his Republican challengers who frankly admitted they would not support a change in the rules that would hurt Republicans.[23] In 2001, McCain lead a successful effort in Congress for campaign reform, backed largely by Democrats and loudly objected to by most of his fellow Republicans.

Rules that appear equal on the surface may, in fact, actually increase inequality. For example, both challengers and those in office raise funds under the same set of rules. The results of their efforts, however, differ significantly (see Chapter 11). The ability of incumbents to raise more funds than challengers undermines equality. It is regularly suggested that congressional candidates each receive a relatively modest federal grant to run their campaigns. Since challengers generally must spend a great deal more money than incumbents to get themselves known, such "equality" would actually protect incumbents.

While a truly "equal" set of rules remains beyond us, an abstract commitment to the concept of equality remains deeply embedded in American political culture.[24]

5-2c Political Culture and the Political Players

Political culture affects the behavior of both possible players and observers. It determines who will play and how they will be evaluated.

American Individualism and the Desire to Be Part of the Game

Individualism and collective action through politics seem to be conflicting concepts, but Americans have found creative ways to accommodate each. As one journalist notes:

> Our politics today reinforces a vision of society inhabited by unencumbered private individuals, pampered with promises, fortified with multiplying legal rights, and awash in consumer choices. . . . The very definition of a good society is one in which large majorities of adults are citizens, capable of self-governance and prepared to display a regard for others.[25]

The concept of rugged individualism, Yankee ingenuity, and a can-do attitude—these are the things that make this country great in the eyes of many. The idea that individual people are responsible for their own well-being and destiny has been preserved in American culture and the mass media. While some cultures value group efforts, sharing, and communal relations, Americans tend to believe in the power of the individual human spirit and the inherent tendencies toward competition and conflict. Given this belief, Americans are quick to oppose any governmental actions that might get in the way of individualism. Such an outlook seems to work against involvement in the communal activity of governing.

After their colonial experiences, the Founders clearly feared government. Echoing this sentiment, Henry David Thoreau in 1849 argued, "That Government is best which governs least."[26] This continues to be a major theme in American political culture, as witnessed by Ronald Reagan's assertion, "Government is not the solution; government is the problem."[27] According to then Senate majority leader Bob Dole (R-Kans.), the Republicans were elected in 1994 to evaluate "the alphabet soup of government" using the criterion, "Is this program a basic function of limited government? Or is it another example of how Government has lost faith in the judgments of our people and the potential of our markets?"[28] Responding to Bill Clinton's State of the Union message, Dole argued, "It is time to carry out the mandate the American People gave us. . . . And that means limited government, less spending, fewer regulations, lower taxes, and more freedom and opportunity for all Americans."[29] President Clinton took up the cause of more limited government by supporting major reforms in welfare policy, balancing the budget, and reducing the **deficit.**

deficit *The shortfall between government expenditures and income.*

Americans like the idea of limited government. Federalism and the separation of powers fit well with Americans' basic mistrust of government, unless such limitations threaten programs from which they benefit. Most Americans believe that if governmental power is not concentrated, it will be less intrusive. Ideas such as national identification cards, common in many European democracies, send shivers down the spines of most Americans. Americans accept government help for their individual problems but rail against the general intrusiveness of government, retaining special ill will toward national government intervention.

If Americans cannot solve a social problem themselves, they prefer government action at the local level. If local players cannot take on the task, they look to the state level. Most Americans view action by the national government as a last resort. Figure 5-3 reveals the degree to which support varies.

Americans' Sense of Political Efficacy

In spite of past causes for disillusionment—for example, the Watergate scandal, the Vietnam War, the Iran-Contra situation, and President Bill Clinton's personal behavior—most Americans are still relatively optimistic about their government. Although support

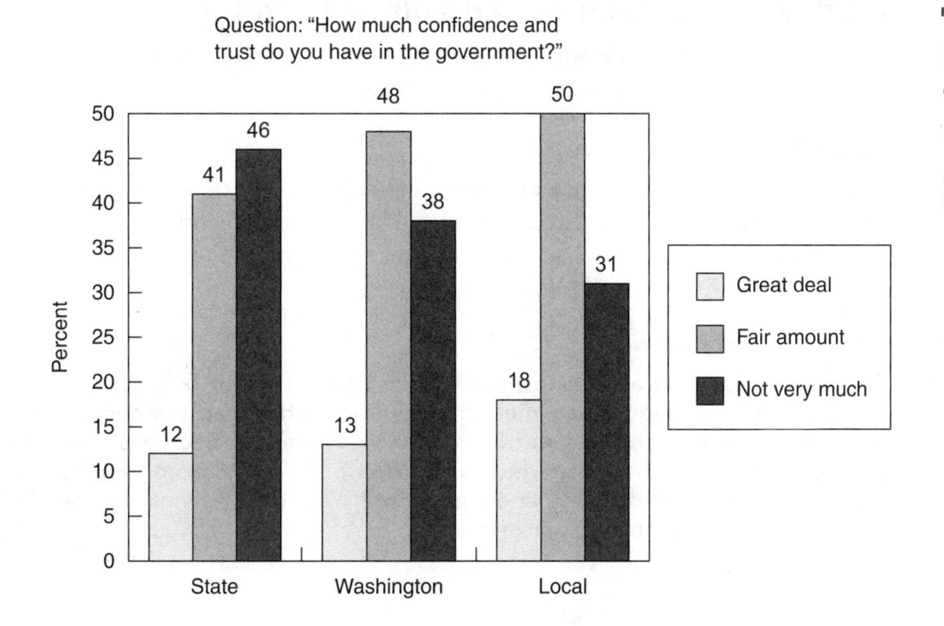

Figure 5-3
Trust in Various Levels of Government

Source: Gallup poll September/October 2003, LEXIS-NEXIS database.

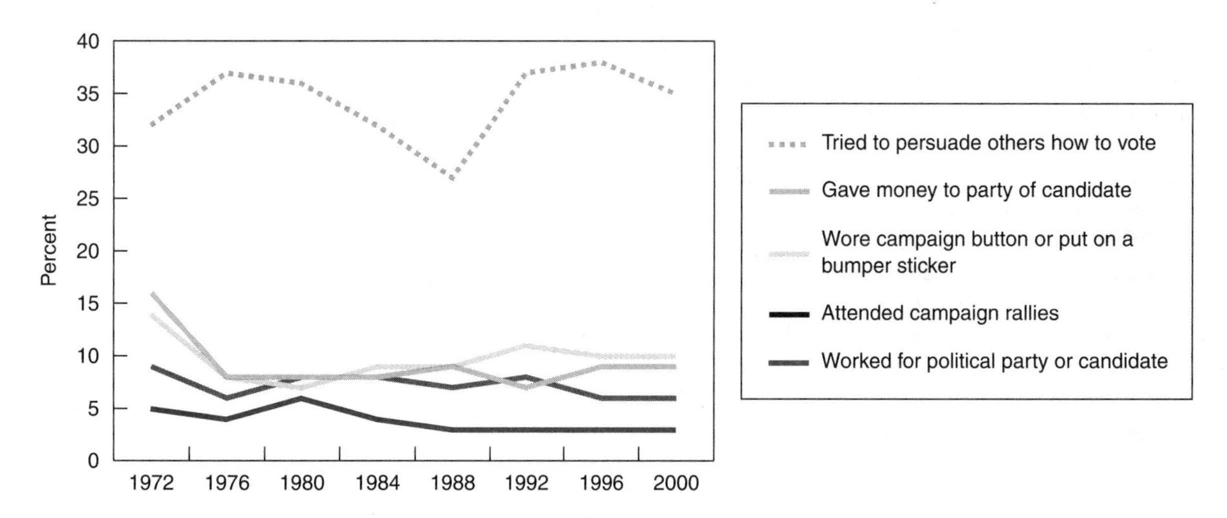

Figure 5-4
Nonvoting Forms of Political Participation

Source: National Election Study data reported in M. Margaret Conway, *Political Participation in the United States*, Washington, D.C.: Congressional Quarterly, Inc., 2000, p. 8.

efficacy *The feeling that involvement in politics makes sense and is an efficient use of one's time.*

for political institutions and leaders has declined, they still believe in the rights and responsibilities of citizenship. Americans are an example to the world in their feelings of **efficacy,** the sense that joining in the political process is worthwhile.

Relatively high levels of efficacy, however, are not enough to overcome restrictive laws and limited motivation. Americans exhibit relatively low levels of voter participation (see Chapter 10). Non-electoral ways of participating, such as joining groups and communicating with public officials, have decreased more modestly[30] (see Figure 5-4). Most Americans feel that if they became involved, their efforts would be both welcomed and rewarded.

Gender does not seem to play a big role in determining levels of political efficacy. Feelings of efficacy are lower for minorities, who have had fewer opportunities to participate and have been rewarded less in the political game.[31] Feelings of efficacy are one of the key factors that divide players from observers in the American political system.

Evaluating the Key Players

Americans have become increasingly frustrated with government in recent years. More than 60 percent believe that "Dealing with a federal government agency is often not worth the trouble."[32] Most citizens personalize their political opinions. They tend to support their local elected representatives while being highly critical of politicians in general and the institutions of which they are a part. Public support for the Congress, for example, is much lower than support given to individual members by their constituents.[33]

5-2d Political Culture and Political Strategies

Political culture helps to determine acceptable strategies. Americans prefer joint efforts, moral leaders, and open decision-making processes.

In Unity There Is Strength

Side by side with American commitment to individualism lies the common tendency to join together with others to gain a strategic advantage in the political game. As inconsistent as it may seem, Americans often join groups in order to protect their individual

Time Out 5-2

Trust in the Game

Look at your responses to questions 2 and 3 in Time Out 5-1, in which you expressed your feelings about whether government officials cared about people like you and when you felt you had a say in government decisions. Compare your responses with those reported. Which group of Americans do you fit into? Are you trusting or distrusting of government? What elements of your political socialization might explain your answers?

freedoms. When French writer Alexis de Tocqueville wandered around America in the early 1800s to study the new democracy, he concluded that "in no country in the world has the principle of association been more successfully used, or applied to a greater multitude of objects, than in America."[34] Voluntary associations are primarily extensions or enlargements of individuals' interests.

America's reputation as a nation of joiners continues. From community associations and campus petition drives to political parties and interest groups, Americans join more groups, on the average, than citizens from any other nation.[35] Many of the thousands of computer bulletin boards and electronic mail networks deal with political issues. Clearinghouses for information on presidential campaign choices began to emerge in 1996 and have expanded since then. To a large degree, the American system is not a democracy of individuals but, rather, a democracy of groups or teams.

In the pluralistic view of government described in Chapter 1, individuals identify themselves politically and expand their potential power by forming and joining groups.[36] The great number of organized teams makes a mixture of noisy demands on the political system. Far from undermining democracy and individual interests, such a variety supports the impact of the individual on government and moderates the danger of excessive government control over individuals. James Madison asserted in *Federalist* No. 10 that a diversity of organized interests is a safeguard against the domination or abuse by any one team of players.

Moralistic Expectations of Leadership Strategies

Americans view politics in moralistic terms. Broad commitments to traditional, often idealized family values affect how we evaluate politicians. The personal morality of political leaders is expected to be much higher than that of business or entertainment leaders. Even though almost half of U.S. marriages involve at least one divorced partner,[37] it took until 1980 for a divorced presidential contender—Ronald Reagan—to win. Less than two decades earlier, Nelson Rockefeller had lost his bid for the Republican presidential nomination partly because of his highly publicized divorce.

Public officials were once relatively immune from questions about their personal lives, but the barriers of acceptable media coverage have been lowered significantly.[38] For example, fifty years ago, the press never showed pictures of Franklin Roosevelt in his wheelchair. Nor did the press mention other personal shortcomings of key officials. Today's aggressive media places few limits on their investigation of the personal lives of public officials. Americans see no inconsistency in condemning political leaders for actions that they accept in others. They do not seem to object to—in fact, they may even relish—learning the details of the romantic alliances of presidents John F. Kennedy and Bill Clinton, the alleged drug use by former Texas governor Ann D. Richards, the Playboy Bunny massages of former Virginia senator Charles S. Robb, or the alleged extramarital affairs of presidential candidates and congressional leaders.

President Clinton's universally characterized "inappropriate personal relationship" with a White House intern raised a moral and political debate among citizens and officeholders over the proper balance of evaluating presidents on their public accomplishments versus their personal behavior. On the one hand President Clinton was given significant credit for a booming economy, a balanced budget, and a number of foreign policy successes, but on the other hand, most Americans found his behavior reprehensible and his attempts at a cover-up inappropriate. In a largely partisan vote, the House of Representatives eventually **impeached** (presented formal charges to) the president for lying in an attempt to cover up the affair. In the heat of the impeachment battle, House Speaker-elect Bob Livingston (R-La.) found it necessary to resign after admitting an adulterous personal affair, shocking his Republican colleagues who were strongly pushing for President Clinton's removal. The Senate, in another largely partisan vote, failed to muster the necessary two-thirds vote for conviction. While some concluded that the situation with President Clinton reduced the role of personal morality in evaluating public officials, President Clinton redirected the moral considerations to other criteria, explaining, "Why should you be cynical? If someone makes a mistake, and they say they make a mistake, and they do their best to atone for it then you can say, 'Well, people

> **impeach** *To indict a government official for improper acts and in the process to verify that enough evidence exists to go forward with a proceeding that could lead to removal from office. In the case of federal government officials such as the president and judges, the House of Representatives impeaches and the Senate tries the case.*

aren't perfect, and I'm disappointed,' but that shouldn't make you cynical."[39] For politicians the line between public and private life has largely been erased.

The sense of political morality carries over into policy making. Americans have never been very comfortable supporting government strategies based on deceit. "Hardball" politics of intelligence gathering (spying) or of intervention into the affairs of other countries requires political players to engage in fancy footwork or intentional cover-ups. The testimony of Colonel Oliver North in the Iran-Contra hearings demonstrated that government officials often feel held back by what they see as the public's naïve and overly moralistic expectations.

Political Strategies Based on Openness

In negotiating the end of World War I, President Woodrow Wilson captured the American faith in the basic good judgment of the people when he fought for "open covenants openly arrived at."[40] A progression of procedures has opened the American political process to the public and the press to a degree that surpasses that of most other countries. Since the earliest days, Congress maintained open galleries for the press and public. Its deliberations were also reported in the *Congressional Record*. More recently, Congress has expanded the definition of the visitors' gallery by allowing television cameras to cover its procedures gavel-to-gavel. Modern presidents have seen it as their duty to report regularly to the public either through press conferences or speeches. The courts, especially those (such as the Supreme Court) involved in the appeals process, justify their actions publicly, although they still confer in private.

During the last two decades, "Government in Sunshine" rules (also called "Sunshine laws") opened up to public view committee deliberations in Congress and in the federal bureaucracy. Similar laws apply to state and local governments. The Freedom of Information Act allows public access to government records. It and the Federal Election Campaign Financing Act, which requires federal candidates to report campaign contributions and expenditures, are the most obvious attempts to open the political process to public scrutiny. Significant evidence in the Watergate break-in, proof of illegal actions during the Vietnam War, confirmation of mishandling of the Iran-Contra affair, and some of the information related to the Clintons' financial dealings in the Whitewater investment scheme stemmed from access provided by these new laws. More recently, computerized databases have begun to allow individual citizens, the media, and interest groups to monitor governmental processes more effectively. The White House, Congress, and many executive agencies provide tracking information via the Internet (see Chapters 13, 15, and 16 for electronic addresses).

5-2e The Political Culture of Winning and Losing

No one likes to lose—in politics or any other game. The impact of losing in American politics is lessened because groups and/or individuals losing one round often have the opportunity to win another. In a number of cases, limits are placed on penalties that losers must pay and/or the frequency with which laws can be changed. The political game fits the American cultural desire to give everyone plenty of chances to win.

Lack of Finality of the Political Game

Few political issues are ever settled once and for all. Political games are continuous. Americans are a practical people who recognize both the inevitability and the advantages of change. Groups and individuals losing the political game in one arena are allowed—almost encouraged—to carry on the fight either at another time or in another place. Opponents of abortion, for example, after losing battles in state legislatures and the courts, turned to Congress to try to stop government funding for abortions.

Even the Constitution has been amended twenty-seven times, although most of the public disapproves of frequent tampering. Despite this cultural hesitation, activists of all political stripes have pursued changes in the basic rulebook. Frustration with court rulings on prayer in schools, abortion, gay marriage, flag burning, and the need for a balanced budget has stirred conservatives to "perfect" the Constitution. Liberals, on the other hand, reject the conservatives' suggested adjustments. Liberals have not widely supported amending the Constitution since their unsuccessful battle to pass the Equal Rights Amendment beginning in the 1970s. It is the liberals who now glory in the sanctity of the Constitution.

Accepting the Results of the Game

Americans don't like sore losers. Election contests end generally with the winner graciously asserting that the people have spoken and wishing the winner the best. When supporters of H. Ross Perot began to boo at the mention of Bill Clinton's name on election night in 1992, losing candidate Perot hushed the crowd, telling them, "The only way we're going to make it work is if we all team up together."[41] A few minutes later, George H. Bush graciously conceded, saying "The people have spoken, and we respect the majesty of the democratic system. Our entire administration will work closely with his team to ensure the smooth transition of power. America must always come first . . . and now I ask that we stand behind our new president."[42]

After his bitterly contested campaign for a third term as governor of New York, Mario M. Cuomo stood before his supporters on election night to congratulate the winner and express an upbeat theme, saying "I had great plans for this state in the coming years and I have great hope for her still. . . . We've been given too much, we have been too fortunate to become bitter and negative. . . . My greatest hope is that this state will grow together."[43]

After an historical delay of over three weeks to recount votes and requiring the extraordinary involvement of the Supreme Court, Vice President Al Gore, narrow winner of the popular vote but loser in the electoral college, put aside his frustration and conceded the 2000 election by saying, "I say to President-elect Bush that what remains of partisan rancor must now be put aside, and may God bless his stewardship of this country . . . Now the Supreme Court has spoken. Let there be no doubt, while I strongly disagree with the court's decision, I accept it . . . for the sake of unity of the people and the strength of our democracy, I offer my concession."[44]

Losers in other arenas, such as Congress and the courts, usually congratulate the winners on a game well fought and, without bitterness, pledge themselves to try harder the next time.

Social Values That Make the Game's Outcome Better

Some goals and groups are protected to some degree from the results of the political game. Most Americans see some value in helping those who cannot help themselves. Children, the homeless, and the economically downtrodden—groups who have little hope of affecting the political game directly—sometimes find political champions who draw support from the cultural attitude that such groups deserve protection. While they may rail against welfare cheats and other groups that they view as using the government, most Americans accept the notion of helping less fortunate citizens.

5-2f Importance of Political Culture

Political culture fulfills important needs for individual citizens, political institutions, and society in general. Individuals receive a series of standards by which to judge politics and guide their behavior. Political institutions and their leaders gain an understanding of public expectations and see more clearly the contours of acceptable behavior. The continuity of political culture brings predictability to politics and supports the stability of the political system. How political culture undergirds public opinion will be discussed in Chapter 9, where we explore the process of democracy.

5-3 Economic Culture

Political orientations and economic conditions are closely related. Political culture sets the stage for a country's economic system, while the economic culture undergirds the political system. English theorist John Locke asserted that individuals should have the inalienable rights of "life, liberty, and estate (property)." When writing the Declaration of Independence, Thomas Jefferson substituted "pursuit of happiness" for "property." Few of Jefferson's contemporaries misunderstood his meaning. He was emphasizing the means rather than the ends. Property *rights* were sacrosanct to most colonial Americans.

During America's early years, the concept of property extended to owning people (slavery). Voting was often limited to property owners. By the time of the American Revolution, the fortunate combination of a large, sparsely settled continent, a resourceful people, and favorable laws regarding taxation and inheritance resulted in the relatively wide distribution of private property among white males. These conditions also led to an almost universal respect for the rights of property owners. The Constitution affirmed the right to vote as one of those rights. The Revolution was essentially a property holders' revolt against England, whose taxation policies and regulation of trade threatened property rights.[45]

capitalism *An economic system based on the widespread belief in private ownership of production and trade, combined with an unrestricted marketplace.*

Protestant ethic *The theologically supported precepts of individualism, hard work, frugality, and respect for material success as a sign of God's favor.*

In the nineteenth century, deep respect for the rights of private property supported the development of American **capitalism,** which emphasized private ownership of the means of production and trade, combined with a free marketplace of goods and services. The emphasis on individual property rights in the economic realm fit well with the cultural expectation of individualism in the political arena.

Other aspects of American political culture also supported the economic culture. In one of the most influential and controversial theories of social science, Max Weber asserted that the **Protestant ethic,** emphasizing hard work, facilitated the capitalistic system.[46] Protestant political thought affects Americans' view of the government's role in the economy. Although government regulation of business and trade has increased significantly, the antipathy toward deep and direct government involvement in the American economy prevails. Government intervention is viewed as an exceptional step, taken only to preserve the free enterprise system. It may be needed, for example, to regulate business monopolies that threaten competition and to protect consumer and worker safety.

5-3a Rules of the Economic Game

One strain of American political thought argues that democracy and capitalism are inseparable. Governmental policies attempt to bring some predictability to economic relationships by enforcing contracts and maintaining civil order during conflicts among the players. Licensing and regulatory powers seek to protect consumers from fraudulent advertising and dangerous products. Both the advertising for and the content of the toothpaste you used this morning, for example, were subject to government regulation. In many cases, regulation also protects business interests by guaranteeing prices and requiring common standards.

price fixing *A conspiracy among companies to subvert the free market and agree on a price for a product or service.*

The U.S. Constitution grants persons special rights and responsibilities that do not apply to other things. The courts' definition of business corporations as "persons," however, provides corporations with a range of constitutional protections uncommon in many political systems. Rules against monopolies and **price fixing** limit the collective strategies of business.

Most U.S. economic policies are more indirect. Few formal rules dictate when and how players in the economic game must act. Policies that regulate interest rates or encourage individual savings and spending set the stage for private-sector economic decisions. But they do not predetermine them. Consumers, producers, and marketers are left on their own to make the economic decisions that best contribute to their goals. Part of President Bill Clinton's difficulty in getting health care reform passed was based on the hesitancy of all players. They did not want to intervene in private contracts between employers and employees and between employees and their health care providers. Commitment to the free market came into conflict with the desire to guarantee all citizens adequate health care.

5-3b The Economic Players

All Americans play a role in the economic system as a producer and/or consumer. They vote with their dollars on the products they like and the quality that they will accept, rather than allowing some government agency to tell producers what to sell. The planned economies that dominated Eastern Europe for much of this century remain alien to Americans. Whenever Americans buy a product, they send a signal to producers about their desires. The more positive signals that are sent, the more products are produced and sent to store shelves. As long as fraud, unfair competition, or threats to health or safety do not arise, the government generally sits back. Americans can buy whatever products they want, even cans of "mountain air," pieces of the Berlin Wall, Pokemon cards, and other fad items. Unlike many countries, the U.S. government usually regulates private corporations delivering public utilities (electricity, telephones, television, and so on) rather than providing such services directly.

In recent years pressure has built to privatize a number of government services. The federal government now uses private contractors to do such things as clean government buildings and repair equipment. Some localities are experimenting with allowing private corporations to run schools and prisons. Republicans tend to like privatization, since it provides opportunities for businesses. Democrats fear its impact on unions and government workers.

After taking over Congress in 1995, the Republicans began a move to limit restraints on business. They attempted to respond to business and public concerns about huge jury awards for victims of medical malpractice and faulty products. The Republican House voted to impose limits on damages for virtually all civil litigation. The Senate took a more tempered view, opting for balancing victims' rights against outrageous claims.

The American economy is not static. Changes in resources, technology, and demands for goods and services affect the role and strength of various players. Three stages in American economic history stand out:

- the preindustrial period,
- the industrial period, and
- the postindustrial age.

The Preindustrial Period

Until the middle of the 1800s, the majority of Americans made their living from the land (see Figure 5-5). This agricultural age was largely marked by plantation agriculture in the South and small family farms throughout the rest of the country. Thomas Jefferson glorified farmers and viewed their control over property as the basis for political independence: "Mobs of the cities were to be feared because of the dependence upon others for their bread, opinions, and political leadership."[47]

The exportation of agricultural products from rural areas to urban centers dominated domestic economic activity. In addition, southern plantations exported agricultural produce, and other regions traded raw materials, such as lumber and minerals, to foreign customers. Concerned about taxes and transporting their crops, farmers in the 1830s organized the Grange, one of the first national political interest groups.[48]

Agriculture remains an important, although not dominant, part of the American economy. In recent years, new technologies of planting, harvesting, and management have allowed **economies of scale,** in which larger farms reduce their overhead and produce more products at a lower price. This has led to the reduced importance of the family farm and an increase in corporate agriculture. The efficiency of contemporary American agriculture allows significant foreign trade of agricultural products while requiring programs to discourage farm surpluses, such as government subsidies for not growing certain crops.

economies of scale *The ability to reduce the per unit cost of a produced item by expanding the size of the production process and thus reducing administrative overhead, equipment, and other fixed costs.*

The Industrial Period

By the end of the Civil War, a growing percentage of Americans made their living producing manufactured goods. This industrial age led to the growth of corporations able to accumulate financial backing (**capital**) to fund large-scale manufacturing. The increase in large-scale corporations and poor working conditions gave rise to a labor force that had to organize into unions to protect the individual workers.

Given the demand for capital by corporations, financial investing in corporate stocks became a method of increasing personal wealth. Advances in communications

capital *The private accumulation of goods used in the production of derivative goods.*

Figure 5-5
Employment by Sectors

This empirical data reinforces the assertions of Alvin and Heidi Toffler that the United States is on the edge of a "third wave" of development. In their view, the first wave in which agriculture dominated is long past. The second wave, marked by assembly-line manufacture of identical products and a similar development of homogenized political outlooks, is dead or dying. The third wave is a brain-based service economy facilitated by computers and other technology; here customized products and fragmented political outlooks will dominate. The Tofflers argued that political leaders would either have to ride the new wave or become engulfed by it.

Sources: Alvin and Heidi Toffler, *Creating a New Civilization: The Politics of the Third Wave.* Atlanta, GA: Turner Publishing, 1995. Marc Porat, *The Information Economy,* p. 189. Copyright © 1976. Stanford University Institute for Communications Research.

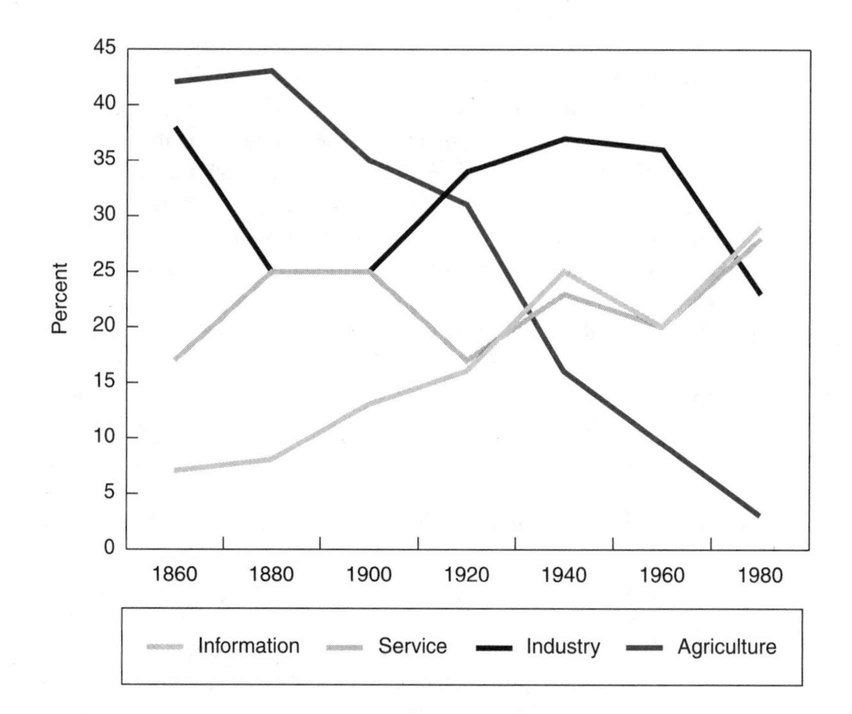

and transportation technologies allowed corporations to grow into national and, starting in the twentieth century, multinational organizations. Large corporations dominated both the political and economic scene during the late 1800s. This, in turn, led to governmental reaction against their excesses in the form of antitrust legislation that challenged monopolistic practices.

The stock market crash in 1929 shocked investors and led to increased government regulation of business. The government stepped in to insure bank deposits and to influence interest rates. Because of the threat of government intervention, business officials took a more active role in politics, contributing to election campaigns and lobbying government. Labor unions also developed into significant political forces during the early 1900s, often influencing Democratic Party nominations and affecting election outcomes. By 1950 almost one-third of nonfarm workers belonged to unions. After peaking about 1960, union membership has steadily declined to less than 20 percent due to the movement toward a more service-oriented economy.[49]

The Postindustrial Age

postindustrial society *Economy based on the production of services rather than goods, where the professional and technical classes dominate and where new technologies change the nature of social interaction.*

The years shortly after World War II ushered in the **postindustrial** age, in which the majority of workers made their living by providing information or services.[50] Fewer jobs were available in factories and more were possible in education, restaurants, real estate, health care, and banking. Because of the instant availability of information and communication technologies, service and information workers could be spread throughout the entire country rather than having to be concentrated in manufacturing centers. This dispersion encouraged less permanent political organizations, because service and information workers tend to create political organizations to deal with specific problems and then let them die when the problem is solved.

Changes in the workforce also affected traditional political organizations. As unionization dwindled, the importance of unions as either economic or political players also declined. Corporations and individual businesspersons continued to play important roles in American politics, both through political campaign contributions (see Chapter 7) and because of the high level of prestige they traditionally commanded in American society. President Calvin Coolidge set the stage for contemporary attitudes in 1925 when he asserted that "the chief business of the American people is business." In 1952 President Dwight D. Eisenhower's secretary of defense, Charles Wilson, legitimized the premier role of business when he argued that "what's good for General Motors is good for the country." Eisenhower's successor, John F. Kennedy, chose the president of General Motors,

Robert McNamara, as his secretary of defense. National surveys consistently show that more than three-quarters of Americans agree with the statement that "the strength of this country today is mostly based on the success of American business."[51]

On the other hand, less than half of Americans (45 percent) agree with the statement that "Business corporations generally strike a fair balance between making profits and serving the public interest."[52] The accounting scandals that came to light in 2002 clearly had an impact on business, as public respect for businesses dropped to record levels (see Figure 5-6).

The 1970s was a rough period for all organized entities in America. Cynicism toward "the establishment" grew. While organized labor reacted to its decline in membership and public support by scaling back its public demands and exposure, business reacted with increased activity and organization. Business interest groups are the most numerous, best financed, and most effective in the policy process (see Chapter 7).

Although remaining the premier exporter of information, services, and intellectual products during the extension of the postindustrial period, the U.S. economy became more dependent on foreign sources for raw materials and finished goods. Contemporary battles have emerged over the outsourcing of technical services and jobs to foreign countries. The most visible impact of dependence involves energy, where U.S. dependence on foreign oil led to major changes in foreign policy that favored oil-producing nations. The growing **balance of trade** problem limited the potential for keeping American capital within the country.

balance of trade *The sum total of imports and exports, with special concern for the degree to which a country spends more on importing goods and services than it earns from other nations.*

During the first half of this century, the United States was clearly a creditor nation, being owed more by foreign countries than it owed to them. More recently, the United States has shifted to a debtor nation position, with other nations profiting from America's need to borrow and purchase their goods. While the United States once largely imported raw materials and turned a profit by making them into manufactured goods, it now imports significant amounts of high-cost foreign goods, such as automobiles and electronics. During the 1992 presidential primaries, "Japan bashing" became an issue as many Americans blamed Japan for U.S. economic difficulties. Many see the increased foreign investment in the United States as a threat to American economic independence, because business decisions are based on the corporate or national needs of U.S. creditors rather than being made to promote American companies or national economic well-being.

The 1996 presidential election revealed significant improper campaign contributions by Chinese businessmen through a Democratic National Committee official. Scandals involving illegal involvement by foreigners in the U.S. political process[53] are worrisome,

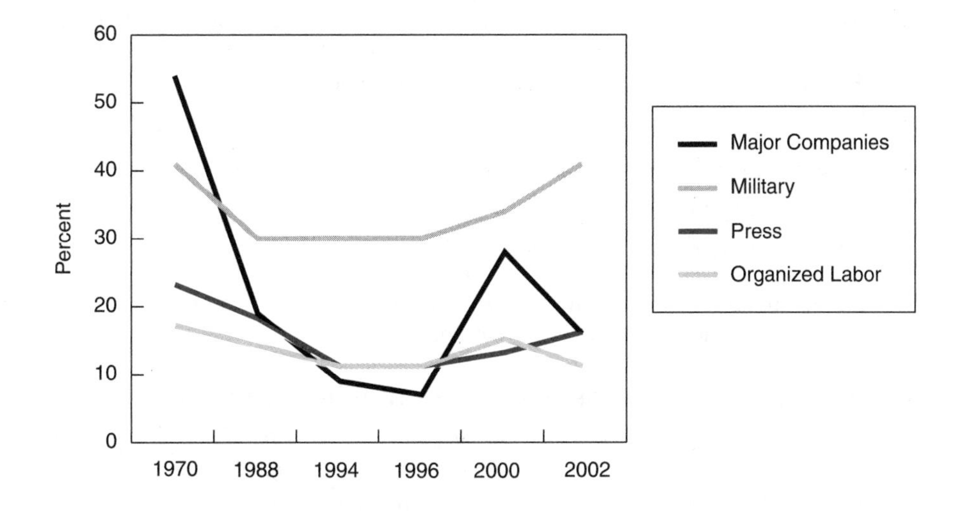

Figure 5-6

Percentage of Public Indicating "A great deal of Confidence" in American Institutions

Public distrust of societal institutions is not limited to governmental entities. Polls indicate a more general frustration with all institutions. Despite some improvement for the military and the press after the terrorist attacks of September 11, 2001, the general trend remains downward.

Source: Louis Harris and Associates and Gallup Organization telephone surveys of 1,000–1,500 randomly selected American adults, LEXIS-NEXIS database, 1970–2002.

but they are probably less important than the legal involvement of multinational and foreign investors in the U.S. economic system and political process. Global corporations and the growth of foreign ownership of U.S. businesses affect life in the United States. The linking of world financial markets through communication and transportation technology limits the United States' ability to act independently in the economic arena. The 1989 New York Stock Exchange crash, caused by computerized trading, echoed and re-echoed through stock markets around the world. In addition, fluctuations in foreign stock markets increasingly have had an impact on the U.S. economy. Even more recently, **insider trading,** revelations of enormous salaries for executives, entertainers, and athletes, and a series of accounting scandals further reduced the prestige of business and expanded the role of government agencies as watchdogs over business dealings.

insider trading *The illegal use of inside information by corporate officials to plan effective investment strategies.*

The fortunes of individual sets of players in the economic game have changed, and along with them, their fortunes in the political game:

- Organized labor has moved from a position of dominance to that of a minor player.
- American business aggressively plays to win the game.
- Government agencies act as umpires, keeping watch over the shoulders of all economic players.

5-3c Strategies of Economic Policy

Most participants in the political process desire a strong American economy benefiting all players. Few issues, however, divide both private- and public-sector decision makers more than those associated with the economy. Policies affecting taxes and government regulation have a direct economic impact on individuals and organizations. Differing views of basic cultural values, such as equality of opportunity, equality of outcome, and the desire for limited government, are basic to many of the conflicts. Elected officials realize that they will be judged most harshly on their handling of the economy. In the 1992 presidential election, Bill Clinton used the slogan "It's the economy, stupid" to help himself keep his campaign focused on this major issue.

Until the Great Depression of the 1930s, government intervention in the economy was limited. Franklin Roosevelt's **New Deal,** a series of programs designed to deal actively with the economic dislocation of the Depression, established a new level of public expectations. The battle over an activist government versus one that accepts the status quo has been won largely by those who promote continuous, if indirect, government involvement. No one expects the government to simply sit by and watch. Agreement on the need for intervention, though, is one thing. Agreement on where and when such intervention should occur is another.

New Deal *Series of policy initiatives proposed by President Franklin D. Roosevelt to lead the nation out of the Great Depression, regulate the economy, and stimulate economic growth.*

American policy makers have three basic policy options for influencing the economy. They can:

- increase demand for goods and services by government spending,
- extract money through taxes, or
- control activity through regulation.

The contemporary debate over economic policy is dominated by two opposing perspectives: demand-side and supply-side economics.

demand-side economic policy *Policies benefiting the demand segments of the economy (workers, consumers, and so on) to stimulate economic growth starting at the bottom and working its way up.*

Demand-Side Economics: Nurturing the Tree from the Bottom

Political players with deep loyalties to workers and consumers support policies designed to directly increase the economic well-being of those groups. **Demand-side economic policy** emphasizes such policies as increased minimum wages, lower and more **progressive tax rates** to help middle- and low-income workers, and low personal interest rates. Democrats and economic liberals assert that only if the "little guys" in the economic system are taken care of will they be able to purchase goods and services. These purchases eventually benefit the corporations, which supply goods and services. This, in turn,

progressive tax rates *Tax rates requiring wealthier individuals and corporations to pay a higher percentage of their income than poorer individuals and corporations do.*

increases the number of jobs and the levels of income, thereby benefiting the economy for everyone.

Supply-Side Economics: Trickle Down the Nutrients

Most recently associated with Ronald Reagan, **supply-side economics** asserts, by contrast, that the most efficient way to improve the economy is to reward those who increase productivity and capital investment. Advocates of supply-side economics tend to be Republicans and economic conservatives. They push for lower tax rates for corporations and investors, flat tax rates for individuals, government subsidies for corporate expansion, limits on government regulation, and the transfer of more governmental functions to the private sector.

supply-side economic policy *Policies benefiting the supply segments of the economy (investors, corporations) to stimulate economic growth by having the results "trickle down."*

Proponents of supply-side economics argue that such strategies result in increased motivation and productivity, which then generate economic growth, new jobs, and increased tax revenue. The benefits starting out at the top supposedly "trickle down" throughout the entire economy.

No matter what the theory of economic intervention, the political calendar often determines economic policy. The strategy is to expand government spending and reduce interest rates and taxes before elections to please the voters. In non-election years, the strategy of adopting new taxes and higher interest rates leads to a series of politically motivated business cycles.[54]

5-3d Determining the Economic Winners and Losers

Most observers assume that those economic interests with the largest monetary stake in economic policy should have the largest say in its development. Businesses that can argue that a policy will have a life-or-death impact on their economic well-being usually gain their objective. Even though the aggregate impact of an economic policy on consumers often supersedes the impact on the corporation, corporate interests generally win out. Thus, government often protects American industries from competition from imports, such as current quotas on the importation of Japanese cars, even though this policy drives up the sticker prices of all cars for the individual consumer.

Financial considerations are not, however, the only factors driving economic policy. The government's responsibility to protect the health and safety of individuals often conflicts with business interests. Policies concerning workplace safety and protection of the environment drive up the cost of doing business. Government attempts to serve as a referee balancing societal and business needs.

Some patterns of policy preferences with regard to American economic culture include low-tax orientation and wide variations in societal income distribution. Table 5-1 reveals that America is leading the pack in terms of low taxes.

Table 5-1

Comparative Individual Income Tax Rates of Selected Developed Countries

For Income tax and employer and employee social security contributions (as a percentage of labor costs, 2004).

US	30%
Great Britain	30%
Canada	30%
Denmark	44%
Austria	45%
Italy	46%
France	48%
Sweden	49%
Germany	51%
Belgium	56%

Source: http://www.oecd.org accessed May 2004.

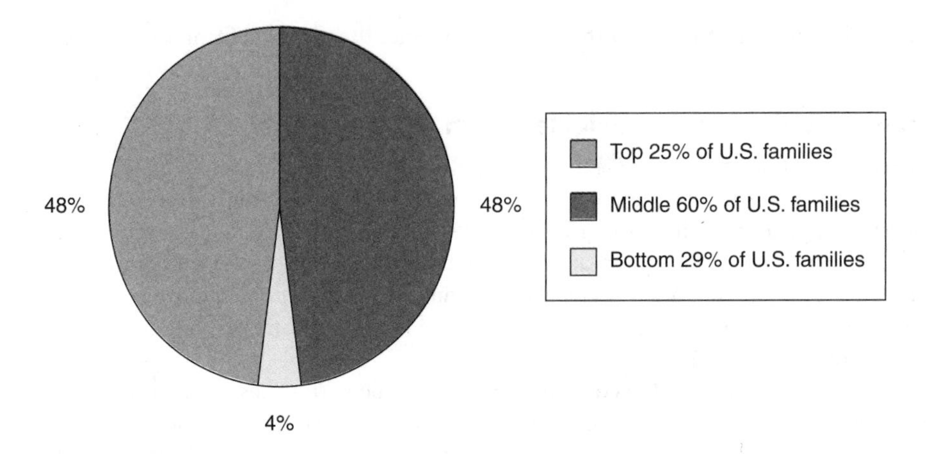

Figure 5-7

Share of Aggregate Family Income by American Economic Groupings, 2003

Income is clearly not evenly divided in the United States. More than 50 percent of the families exist on less than 20 percent of the income.

Source: U.S. Bureau of the Census, *Statistical Abstract of the United States*, Table 688, p. 459. Washington, D.C.: GPO, 2003. http://www.census.gov/prod/www/statistical-abstract-us.html.

Low Tax Orientation

The revolutionary cry of "no taxation without representation" has led to limited taxation with representation (see Figure 5-7). Elected officials are hesitant to propose tax increases, and candidates on all levels have won by promising tax decreases. Despite growing federal budget deficits, in 1981 Congress passed Ronald Reagan's tax-cut package. It emphasized relief for businesses and individuals in higher income groups.[55] Five years later, the burden was shifted a bit from individuals to corporations.

In the 1988 campaign, candidate George H. Bush's resounding assertion of "no new taxes" served as a significant policy difference from the ideas of Massachusetts's governor Michael S. Dukakis. Early in his term, however, the stark realities of the budget deficit required George H. Bush as president to alter his tax pledge, a shift that eventually was held against him when he attempted to win another term in office.

President Bill Clinton and the Democratic Party were politically punished in 1994 for the moderate tax increases they passed in 1993. The 1994 congressional elections sent the signal that the public preferred lower taxes and less government activity. By early 1995, congressional leaders, Republican candidates posturing for the 1996 presidential nomination, and even President Clinton scrambled to wear the label "middle-class tax cutter." On the state level, candidates such as New Jersey's Christine Todd Whitman won based on a commitment to significant tax cuts. They instantly became national leaders.

During the 2000 presidential race, the candidates stumbled over each other to present their version of lower taxes. Republican tax plans tended to favor their supporters in business and people in the middle to upper tax brackets, while Democrats placed their emphasis on cuts for lower-income individuals. All claimed that despite the emphasis of the cuts they proposed, segments of the economy would benefit. One of President George W. Bush's initial legislative victories in 2001 was a major across-the-board tax reduction. Despite heavy anticipated military expenditures, President Bush stuck with his commitment to tax cuts, and many observers saw the 2002 and 2004 elections as a mandate for his tax policy.

Societal Income Distribution

America has one of the world's highest standards of living. Thus, the American definition of living in poverty refers to a relatively comfortable lifestyle compared to poverty in many other parts of the world. Yet the distribution of income among groupings in the United States varies widely (see Figure 5-7). During the 1980s, lower-income individuals actually lost ground in relation to wealthier individuals (see Figure 5-8).

The political implications of unequal income distribution are heightened by the identifiable groups, such as racial minorities, who consistently find it more difficult to

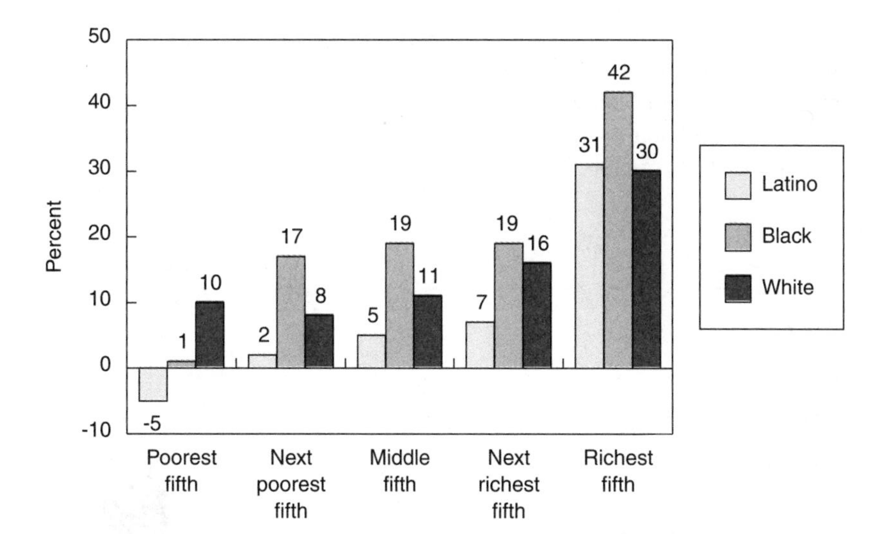

Figure 5-8
1980-1998 Change in Mean Household Income

During the 1980s and 1990s, wealthier families increased their income at a higher percentage rate than did poorer families, with poorer Latino families actually losing ground. Black families did better than whites in the middle income groups.

Source: Data calculated from U.S. Census Bureau historical mean income tables using 1998 dollars. Raw data available at http://www.census.gov.

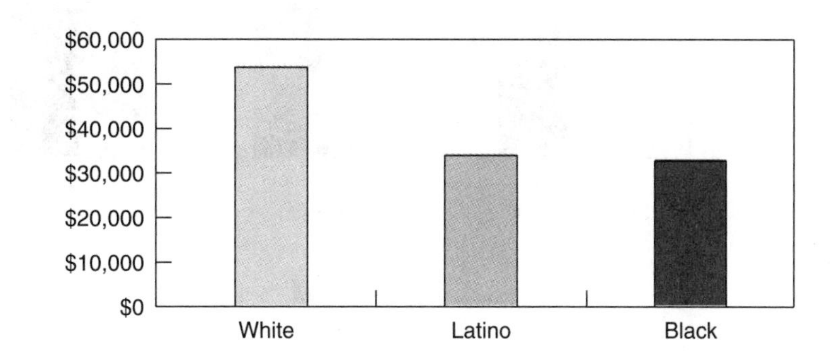

Figure 5-9
Household Income of Ethnic Groups in 2003

Source: U.S. Bureau of the Census, Statistical Abstract of the United States 2003, Table 671. http://census.gov/prod/www/statistical-abstracts-us.html.

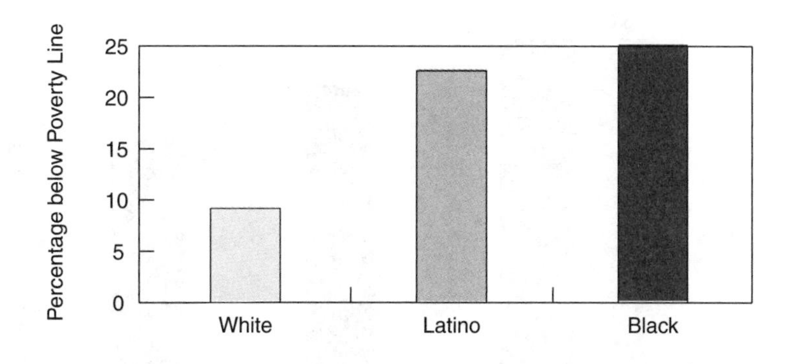

Figure 5-10
Percentage of White, Latino, and African-American Households below the Poverty Line in 2003

Economic well-being in the United States is still clearly differentiated by ethnic background.

Source: U.S. Bureau of the Census, *Statistical Abstract of the United States,* 2003, Table 697, p. 463. http://www.census.gov/prod/www/statistical-abstract-us.html

earn incomes comparable to that of nonminorities. African-American family net worth—that is, the total accumulation of savings and property—averages about 10 percent that of white families. Although the gap in yearly income is less dramatic, it remains significant. Women remain concentrated in lower-paying jobs. Women doing work equal to that done by men often find their salaries 25 percent or more behind that of their male counterparts. Women's groups point out that there has tended to be a feminization of poverty. Figures 5-9 through 5-12 reveal income disparities between major demographic groups in the United States.

Economic resources often determine who can play the political game and the strategies they can pursue. Financially comfortable individuals often feel they have a greater stake in the outcome of the policy process and possess the necessary resources to become involved. For most people, committing resources to play in the political game is secondary to acquiring necessities such as food and shelter. Winners in the American political game often look much like winners in the economic game. Underlying both the decision to play and the available strategies is a unique economic culture.

Figure 5-11
Comparative Income of Men and Women

In 1999 women earned an average of 74 cents for each dollar earned by a man. This figure is up from 59 cents on the dollar in 1963, when the federal Equal Pay Act was signed. While the gap is narrowing, women earn less based on their lower education, concentration in low-paying jobs, more limited tenure, and unequal salary scales.

Source: U.S. Bureau of the Census, *Statistical Abstract of the United States 2003,* Table 693, p. 461. http://www.census.gov/prod/www/statistical-abstract-us.html

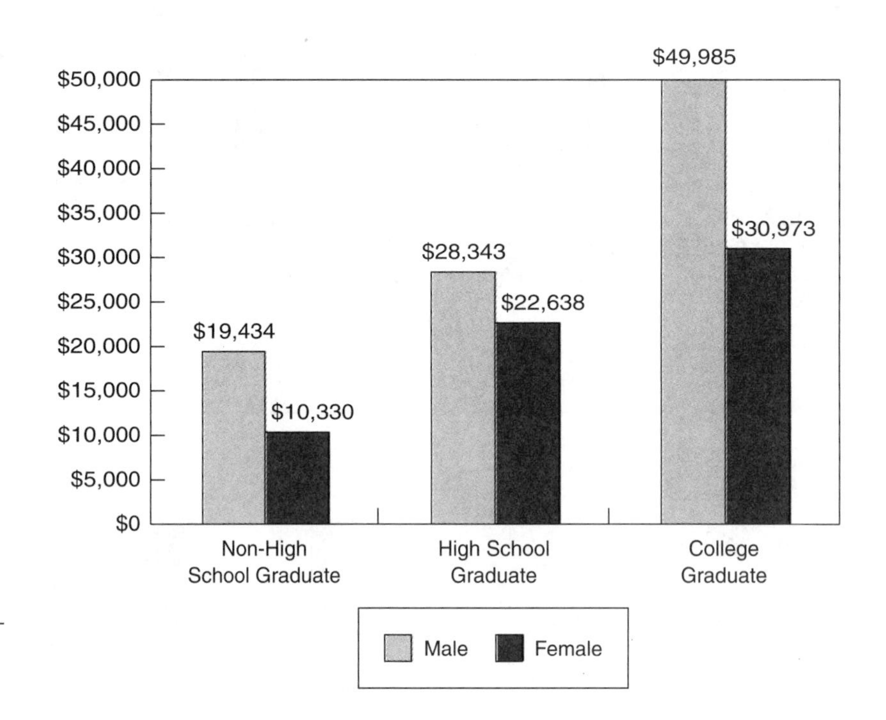

Figure 5-12
Comparative Unemployment of Men and Women 1995–2000

Source: U.S. Bureau of the Census, *Statistical Abstract of the United States 2001,* Table 674. http://www.census.gov/prod/www/statistical-abstract-us.html

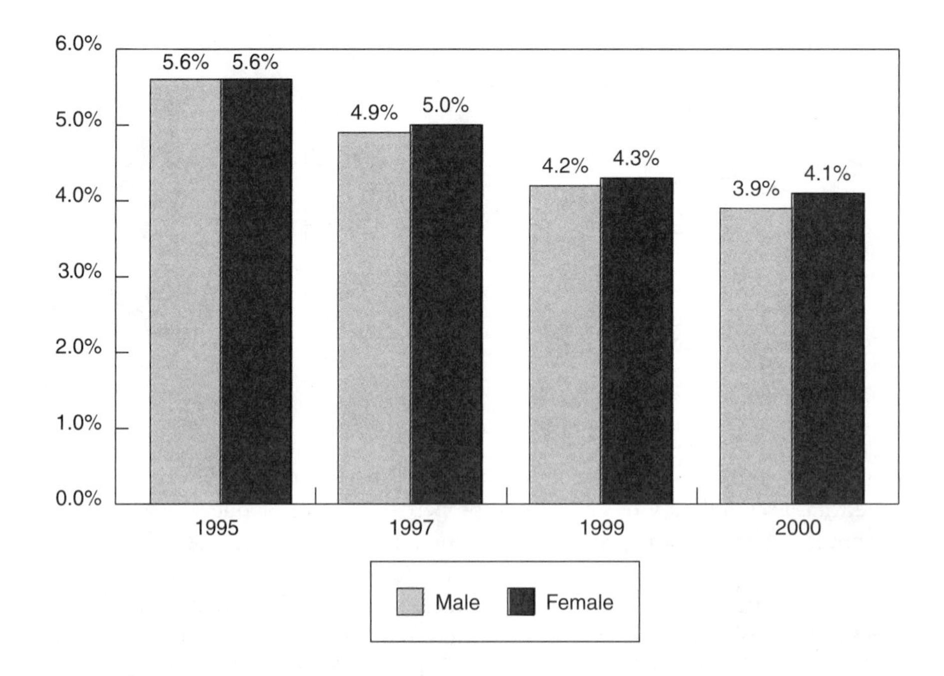

Conclusion

The political and economic cultures of the United States establish the particular character of the American political playing field, encouraging some players and discouraging others. Acceptance of many political rules emanates from their association with cultural expectations. Political culture encompasses public expectations concerning the performance of government and suggests acceptable political strategies.

The economic system involves one of the most important sets of issues over which the political game is fought. It also distributes societal resources, some of which can be directed toward future rounds of the political game. Winning or losing in the political arena often determines the degree to which one wins or loses economically and vice versa.

Although political and economic cultures evolve over time, the change is extremely slow. When determining strategy, effective players in the political process must take into account the relatively stable nature of the playing field.

Values and attitudes undergird political outlooks. They provide a foundation for democracy in the United States—one as important as the Constitution. Both are subject to change, but both are enduring. The cultural and economic playing fields create opportunities for action, the essence of the political game. The next set of chapters looks at the mediating institutions that motivate individual players to enter the fray and that make it possible for players to join together to affect the outcome.

Key Terms

affirmative action
attitudes
balance of trade
capital
capitalism
cultural diversity
culture
deficit
demand-side economic policy
economic culture
economies of scale
efficacy
emulation
equality of opportunity
equality of outcome (or condition)
"family values"
impeach
insider trading
melting pot
New Deal
opinions
party identification
political socialization
postindustrial society
price fixing
progressive tax rates
Protestant ethic
reverse discrimination
secularization
subculture
supply-side economic policy
values

Practice Quiz

1. Attitudes about life passed down from one generation to the next are a part of
a. manifest destiny.
b. pluralism.
c. political culture.
d. positive sum games.

2. The sting of losing in American politics is ameliorated by the fact that it is a _____ game.
a. discrete
b. continuous
c. zero-sum
d. largely irrelevant

3. Political culture can be best explained as
a. inbred.
b. a part of our cosmic being.
c. now limited to artistic and musical components of American life.
d. learned.

4. The notion of socialization implies that political outlooks are
a. dominated by liberal (socialist) perspectives.
b. learned in a social setting.
c. influenced by the special status of the public persuaders.
d. both a and b.

5. Public policies which guarantee that the rules should not disadvantage particular groups in society emphasize
a. equality of outcome.
b. equality of opportunity.
c. socialism.
d. social Darwinism.

6. The sense that joining the political game is worthwhile is called
a. efficacy.
b. ideology.
c. idealism.
d. civic pride.

7. American cultural expectations of morality in the behavior of public leaders can best be described as
a. rigid.
b. nonexistent.
c. inconsistent.
d. irrelevant.

8. _____ rights were especially sacrosanct to the Founders.
a. Environmental
b. Property
c. Civil
d. Bargaining

9. Democrats tend to support _____ economic policy.
a. supply-side
b. demand-side
c. flat tax
d. free trade

10. Compared to most countries, the United States tends to have particularly _____ taxes.
a. high personal and high business
b. low personal and low sales
c. high personal and low business
d. high sales and low business

You can find the correct answers to these questions by taking the quiz and then submitting your answers in the Online Edition. The program will automatically score your submission. Where you miss a question, the program will provide the correct answer, a rationale for the answer, and the section number in the chapter where the topic is discussed.

Further Reading

Gabriel Almond and Sidney Verba's book *The Civic Culture* (Boston, MA: Little, Brown, 1963) is the classic study of political culture based on national surveys in five countries.

A series of essays on political culture with an attempt to update the original findings without the benefit of a comparable five-nation survey is found in *The Civic Culture Revisited*, edited by Gabriel Almond and Sidney Verba (Newbury Park, CA: Sage, 1989).

Charles O. Jones edited *The Reagan Legacy: Promise and Performance* (Chatham, NJ: Chatham House, 1988), which is a series of essays on the Reagan period, with an especially useful analysis by Paul E. Peterson and Mark Rom of the economic implications of that era.

For an insightful look at the role of religion in the contemporary American political process, see Richard John Neuhaus, *The Naked Public Square: Religion and Democracy in America* (Grand Rapids, MI: William B. Erdmans, 1991).

For an analysis of the political socialization process, see Jarol Manheim, *The Politics Within* (New York: Longman, 1982).

For an extensive look at socialization with particular emphasis on democratic values, see James G. Gimpel, J. Celeste Lay, and Jason E. Schuknecht, *Cultivating Democracy: Civic Environments and Political Socialization in America* (Washington, D.C.: Brookings Institution, 2003).

For a look at the gulf between rich and poor, see Edward N. Wolff, *Top Heavy: A Study of Increasing Inequality of Wealth in America* (New York: Twentieth Century Fund, 2002).

Endnotes

1. Andrew Carnegie, *North American Review*, June 1889.
2. *Ibid.*
3. *Ibid.*
4. Daryl J. Bem, *Beliefs, Attitudes and Human Affairs* (Belmont, CA: Brooks/Cole, 1970), 5.
5. This characterization of business appeared on CNN, March 7, 1995.
6. Benjamin R. Barber, "Pangloss, Pandora or Jefferson: Three Scenarios for the Future of Technology and Democracy," in *Information Technology, the Public Issue*, ed. R. Plant (New York: St. Martin's Press, 1988). See also Richard Davis, *The Web of Politics* (New York: Oxford University Press, 1999), 18.
7. *Gallup*, Harris and Princeton Research Associates polls from 2002 and 2003, LEXIS-NEXIS database.
8. See Robert S. Erickson, Norman R. Luttbeg, and Kent L. Tedin, *American Public Opinion: Its Origins, Content and Impact* (New York: Macmillan, 1988), 136, 146–47.
9. Erickson, Luttbeg, and Tedin, *American Public Opinion*, 137.
10. Montesquieu paraphrased in "On Values: Talking with Peggy Noonan," PBS, February 17, 1995.
11. James A. Barnes, "Rightward March?" *National Journal*, August 6, 1994, 1847.
12. See Richard John Neuhaus, *The Naked Public Square* (Grand Rapids, MI: William B. Erdmans, 1991), 263–64.
13. Nathan Glaser and Daniel Patrick Moynihan, *Beyond the Melting Pot* (Cambridge, MA: MIT Press, 1964), 288–89.
14. Megan Rosenfeld, "Father Knows Squat," *Washington Post*, November 13, 1994, G1. A 1999 study by the National Fatherhood Initiative found most prime-time programs portrayed fathers as bumblers. See David Peterson, "TV Fatherhood Has Degenerated from Wise to Witless," *Star Tribune* (Minneapolis), June 20, 1999, 1A.
15. Gabriel Almond and Sidney Verba, *The Civic Culture* (Princeton, NJ: Princeton University Press, 1963), 102.
16. The Gallup Poll, May 12, 1955 , July 1, 1991 and January 1996. Based on national polls of 1,504, 1,003, and 2,047 adults, respectively. LEXIS-NEXIS database.
17. Everett Carl Ladd, Jr., and Seymour Martin Lipset, "Anatomy of a Decade," *Public Opinion* 3 (1980): 2–4.
18. A. M. Rosenthal, "What Americans Want," *New York Times*, January 31, 1995, A21.
19. Thomas Mann quoted in Cokie Roberts and Steven Roberts, "Cynicism Sends America Along an Uncertain Path," *Rocky Mountain News*, November 13, 1994, 97A.
20. See James L. Gibson, "Pluralism and the Protection of Civil Liberties," *Western Political Quarterly* 43 (September 1990): 511–33; and James L. Gibson and Richard D. Bingham, *Civil Liberties and Nazis: Attitudinal, Behavioral and Policy Linkages in the Skokie Free Speech Controversy* (New York: Praeger, 1985).
21. Jarol Manheim, *The Politics Within* (New York: Longman, 1982), 58.
22. Pew Research Center poll of 1,165 adults, November 1997. LEXIS-NEXIS database. See also Lincoln Caplan, "The Civil Rights Tug of War," *Newsweek*, February 13, 1995.
23. Jennifer Holland, "McCain Vows to Keep Campaign Clean," AP Online, December 22, 1999, LEXIS-NEXIS database.
24. For an interesting discussion of equality and an analysis asserting that Americans do not seem to be willing to take action, at least in terms of economic equality, see Jennifer Hochschild, *What's Fair: American*

Beliefs about Distributive Justice (Cambridge, MA: Harvard University Press, 1981).

25. Don Eberly, "Even Newt Can't Save Us," *Wall Street Journal*, February 3, 1995, A12.
26. Henry David Thoreau, *Civil Disobedience*, 1849.
27. Ronald Reagan's 1980 inaugural address, quoted in *Vital Speeches*, XLVII (February 15, 1981): 258.
28. Robert Dole, *Congressional Record*, January 4, 1995, S-12.
29. Robert Dole, *Congressional Record*, January 25, 1995, S-1484.
30. Alan I. Abramowitz, "The United States: Political Culture Under Stress," in *The Civic Culture Revisited*, ed. Gabriel Almond and Sidney Verba (Newbury Park, CA: Sage, 1989), 196.
31. Abramowitz, "The United States," 182. See also Dwaine Marvick, "The Political Socialization of the American Negro," in *Public Opinion and Behavior: Essays and Studies*, eds. Edward C. Dreyer and Walter A. Rosenbaum (Belmont, CA: Wadsworth, 1970), 161–79.
32. National adult poll of 985 respondents carried out by the Pew Research Center, November 1999, LEXIS-NEXIS database.
33. Glenn R. Parker and Roger H. Davidson, "Why Do Americans Love Their Congressmen So Much More Than Their Congress?" *Legislative Studies Quarterly* 4 (February 1979): 54–61. See also "Congress, My Congressman," *Public Perspective* 3 (May/June 1992).
34. Alexis de Tocqueville, *Democracy in America* (1835; reprint, New York: Mentor, 1956), 95–96.
35. Ronald J. Hrebenar, *Interest Group Politics in America* (Armonk, NY: M. E. Sharpe, 1997), 9.
36. Manheim, *The Politics Within*, 59.
37. By 2001, it was estimated by the Census Bureau that 40 percent of first marriages would end in divorce. National Center for Health Statistics, 2001, http://www.cdc.gov/nchs/pressroom/01news/firstmarr.htm.
38. See Larry Sabato, *Feeding Frenzy: How Attack Journalism Has Transformed American Politics* (New York: Free Press, 1991).
39. ABC News, *World News Tonight*, December 17, 1999, LEXIS-NEXIS database.
40. Woodrow Wilson, "Address to the Congress on the Fourteen Points," January 8, 1918.
41. Quoted in Thomas J. Brazaitis, "Clinton Wins," *The Plain Dealer*, November 4, 1992, 1A.
42. Quoted in Dan Balz and Ann Devroy, "Clinton Sweeps In," *Washington Post*, November 4, 1992, A1.
43. "The 1994 Elections: New York Governor," *New York Times*, November 9, 1994, B11.
44. Manheim, *The Politics Within*, 64.
45. Alan P. Grimes, "Conservative Revolution and Liberal Rhetoric: The Declaration of Independence," in *200 Years of the Republic in Retrospect*, eds. William C. Havard and Joseph L. Bernd (Charlottesville, VA.: University Press of Virginia, 1976), 16–17.
46. Max Weber, *The Protestant Ethic and the Spirit of Capitalism* (trans. Talcott Parsons) (New York: Scribner's Sons, 1931).
47. Robert J. Morgan, "'Time Hath Found Us': The Jeffersonian Revolutionary Vision," in *200 Years of the Republic in Retrospect*, eds. William C. Havard and Joseph L. Bernd (Charlottesville, VA: University Press of Virginia, 1976), 33.
48. Jack C. Plano and Milton Greenberg, *The American Political Dictionary* (Fort Worth, TX: Harcourt Brace, 1997), 484.
49. *The World Almanac 1994* (New York: Pharos Books), 141.
50. Daniel Bell, *The Coming of the Post-Industrial Society: A Venture in Social Forecasting* (New York: Basic Books, 1973).
51. Based on a 1999 national survey of 895 for the Pew Research Center, LEXIS-NEXIS database.
52. *Ibid.*
53. U.S. campaign law makes it illegal to accept contributions from non-citizens and foreign corporations. In the 1970s a number of congressmen were punished for taking contributions from a Korean businessman. After the 1996 election, the Justice Department and Congress investigated Chinese contributions to the Clinton campaign.
54. See Edward R. Tufte, *Political Control of the Economy* (Princeton, NJ: Princeton University Press, 1978), 55–64.
55. Paul E. Peterson and Mark Rom, "Lower Taxes, More Spending, and Budget Deficits," in *The Reagan Legacy: Promise and Performance*, ed. Charles O. Jones (Chatham, NJ: Chatham House, 1988), 218.

6

The Mass Media: The Player Observers

Key Points

- **The development of American mass media and its relation to the political process.**
- **The rules under which the media operate.**
- **The criteria by which events are defined as newsworthy.**
- **Bias emanating from the media, the individuals being covered, and the consumers of news.**
- **The role of the media in agenda setting.**
- **The challenges of the news media.**

Preview: Mediating the Mediators

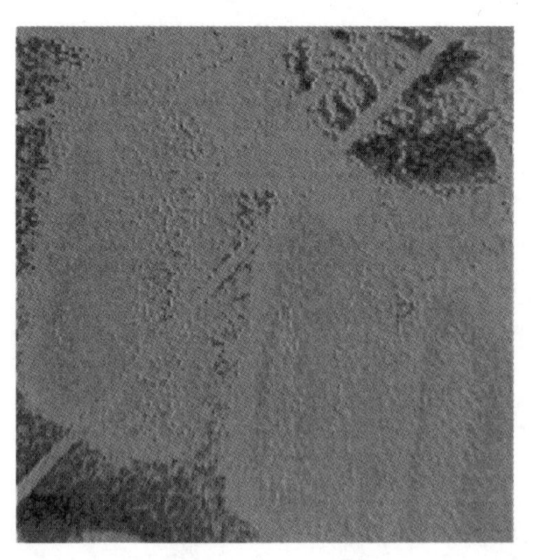

On the surface it looked like a ludicrous way for a young and ideologically driven politician to make a name for himself and to become a real player in the political process. Rather than focusing his efforts on the major newspapers or television stations with audiences in the millions, he chose a medium that seldom had an audience of more than 500,000. Furthermore, the medium of choice had no fixed schedule and often required its viewers to wait through hours of boring proceedings for something of interest. To make the choice even more outrageous, the young politician decided not to latch onto the main events of the day. Instead he focused his efforts on a time period added to the end of the day, when even the most interested official participants did not bother to stay around to watch.

The strategy seemed doomed to failure, but things are not always what they seem. Congressman Newt Gingrich's (R-Ga.) strategy was to use the "special orders" period of the House of Representatives. During special orders, there is virtually no one else in the chamber, yet a member is allowed to reserve a block of time to speak on any topic. As an official part of House proceedings, these speeches are carried over

President Truman holds up the *Chicago Daily Tribune* headline, "Dewey Defeats Truman" in St. Louis, Missouri, November 3, 1948.

Library of Congress, Prints & Photographs Division [LC-USZC4-607504]

C-SPAN (the Cable Satellite Public Affairs Network). Thus they provided Gingrich a national audience and a means to affect American politics.

Gingrich realized that despite the relatively small size of its audience, C-SPAN reached political "movers and shakers," whose opinions carried weight. He also realized that C-SPAN would not edit his remarks. This would give him and his conservative colleagues the ability to transmit extensive information to their followers. Gingrich's performance on C-SPAN brought him to the attention of his fellow Republicans, who were looking for a leader for the television age. At the same time it gained him considerable coverage on the more traditional media—major newspapers and the commercial television networks—that monitored C-SPAN.

Starting back in 1984, Gingrich's efforts helped bring down three Democratic Speakers of the House and put the Republican Party in a position to become the majority party. In 1994 Gingrich's efforts made him the first Republican Speaker of the House in 40 years.

How did it happen? First Gingrich and his colleagues used the after-hours special orders speeches back in 1984 to take on Speaker Thomas P. (Tip) O'Neill (D-Mass.). The Democratic leader's violent verbal reaction led to an embarrassing reprimand by the chamber and contributed to his decision to retire. Once again, in 1988, Gingrich and his colleagues used special orders speeches to question the ethics of the next Speaker, Jim Wright (D-Tex.), who eventually was forced to resign.

Later, cries by Gingrich and his supporters for term limits for members of Congress were again broadcast by C-SPAN. This fanned the issue and forced the Democratic Congress and its Speaker Tom Foley (D-Wa.) to go on the defensive. The image of a permanent and unresponsive Congress contributed to unprecedented Democratic losses in the 1994 election. Then, in a classic case of "live by the sword, die by the sword," Speaker Gingrich's high media visibility, his questionable ethics concerning a book deal, and his explanations of fund-raising issues made him a prime target for Democratic media attacks. Although he survived a House ethics probe with an apology and a fine, his highly publicized projections of major Republican victories in 1998 set the stage for his resignation as Speaker and from the House. In the attempt to replace Speaker Gingrich, the bright glare of media attention forced the leading candidate, Bob Livingston (R-LA), to resign after the media carried a story about his extramarital affair. Under the increasing attention of the media, a Speaker-designate and three House Speakers in a row had paid the price of having the traditional insider game of Congress being played out on the front pages of newspapers and the evening news lead stories.

Newt Gingrich had something in common with Bill Clinton, who used the new media environment effectively on the presidential level. He recognized that in the era of expanding channels and increasingly differentiated audiences, the traditional conception of broadcasting had been replaced by the increased use of "narrowcasting." Finding a receptive audience and presenting a powerful message has become a successful strategy for determining winners and losers.

Few of us experience political events directly. Because political arenas lie beyond our direct vision, we depend on intermediaries to report and interpret the wider political worlds. The **formats** of the **media** vary, and as they evolve, their relative influence changes. Traditionally, the media were referred to as the "press," due to the domination of print journalism: newspapers, magazines, and books. Now a distinction is made between print and electronic journalism, and the "press" is no longer the public's main source of news. Radio and television are the dominant sources of political information for most Americans, with newspapers and magazines supplementing the electronic media for the more politically informed citizens. We are on the cutting edge of a new media revolution. Computerized bulletin boards and digitized versions of media resources are widely available on the Internet, and marriages of new communication capabilities leave the future wide open. Regardless of the format, the media deliver the information that the public gets indirectly, as opposed to what it experiences in person.

format *The manner of presentation distinctive for each medium, which affects its use and impact.*

media *The generalized term for all commercial communications that attempt to reach a mass audience with newsworthy information or entertainment.*

Some media professionals downplay their role by describing it as simply reporting newsworthy stories. However, patterns of information selection and methods of presentation help to determine the context of American politics. The media help to interpret the playing field by explaining the rules, identifying the players, exposing the strategies, and revealing the winners and losers. The media also find themselves becoming an integral part of political strategies as they themselves intentionally and unintentionally become players.

In studying the role of the media in American politics, one recognizes that there are basically four groups of players:

- the media themselves, as producers;
- the public, as receivers;
- the organizations and individuals whose actions the media cover, as subjects of news stories; and
- the government regulators.

Each of the players maintains different goals and strategies. The continuing success of many political players, especially elected officials, depends on their ability to use media coverage for their own purposes. Political players who are the subjects of news coverage attempt to control the timing, substance, and **spin** of the stories about their activities. We, the consumers of the news, develop patterns of selecting the news necessary to inform our decisions. Those individuals and causes that win the battle for media coverage generally win the political game as well.

spin *The attempt to portray potentially negative events in the most positive light so that they won't "spin out of control."*

This chapter outlines the nature of the various media players, the rules under which they work, the strategies that the various players use in relation to the media, and the ultimate winners and losers—those who get media attention and those who do not.

6-1 The Players: A Variety of Media Voices

Contemporary America is blessed with a large and growing variety of news media sources. The nature, reach, and influence of the media have changed since the inception of the Republic, as the following survey documents.

6-1a The Early Newspaper Era

During the first century and a half of America's existence, newspapers were the dominant news media. Although the direct audience of literate citizens was relatively small, ideas in newspapers spread by word of mouth. The proponents of rebellion against England used newspapers to arouse public opinion against abuses of British authority. Later, Alexander Hamilton, James Madison, and John Jay turned to writing "letters to the editor" to argue for the ratification of the Constitution. We now call that collection of letters *The Federalist*.

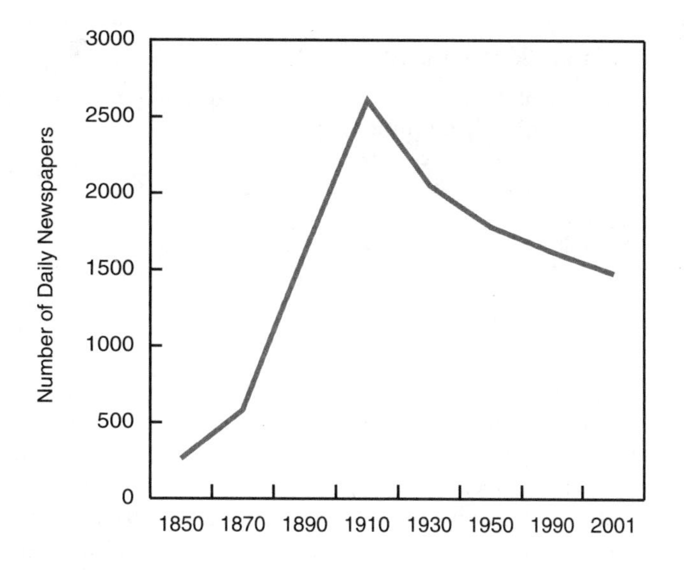

Figure 6-1
Number of Daily Newspapers, 1850–2001

Source: Data from Harold W. Stanley and Richard G. Niemi, *Vital Statistics on American Politics, 2003-2004,* (Washington, D.C., Congressional Quarterly, Inc., 2003), pp. 174–175.

As American political institutions developed, early newspapers received subsidies from political parties and acted as little more than promoters of **partisan** positions. President Thomas Jefferson, for example, funneled all news to party papers and froze out opposition-party reporters. Once a party reached power, its newspaper also received subsidies in the form of contracts to print government documents.

partisan *Favoring the interests of one party over another.*

Several factors led to the decline of the partisan press. Abraham Lincoln rejected the idea of an administration newspaper and later created the U.S. Government Printing Office to handle government printing contracts.[1] The growth of commercial advertising in the late 1800s subsidized the development of independent large-circulation newspapers. Most cities attracted competing newspapers, with both morning and evening publication times. The number of daily newspapers peaked in the early 1900s (see Figure 6-1). Availability of newspapers grew continuously from the 1850s to the 1940s and then began a slow decline. No longer dependent on party subsidies and aware of the economic advantage of impartiality, newspapers developed the unique American commitment to objective news reporting.[2] "Opinion pages" with clearly partisan editorials, editorial cartoons, and political essays were separated from the professional news reporting that begins on page 1. Until recently, most local papers operated independently, with a primary commitment to local coverage. They relied on national **wire services** to provide a page or two of national and international news. As we will see, the emergence of newspaper chains—the first media conglomerates—forever changed the media's influence on political behavior.

wire services *Commercial reporting services, such as the Associated Press (AP) and United Press International (UPI), that provide objective stories focusing on national and international events. Local editors choose which stories to include, edit their length, and introduce them with headlines.*

6-1b Emergence of the Electronic Media

Technology has dramatically altered the form, substance, and timeliness of the information that the media provide to spectators and other players, and these changes have affected both the political game and the role of contemporary media. Frederick Williams dramatically illustrates the quickening pace of technological change in communications with the following analogy:

> Imagine that the history of human communications from Cro-Magnon times to the present were squeezed into the 24 hours of a single day. We would spend the morning hours with little change. Writing (Egyptian hieroglyphics) would appear as late as 8:40 in the evening, followed by the Phoenician alphabet at 9:28. It is not until 11:38 P.M. that the first Gutenberg Bible would be printed. The pace begins to quicken as the steam press appears at 11:53 P.M., then the telegraph 24 seconds later, the telephone at 11:55:02 and the phonograph 2 milliseconds later. The last 5 minutes, a mere speck of time in the history of human communications, virtually explode with new communications technologies: commercial radio, motion pictures, computers, xerography, transistors, television, satellites, microelectronic circuitry, and all the rest.[3]

Time Out 6-1

Let's Look at your Media Usage

1. How often do you watch the national nightly news on CBS, ABC, or NBC?
   a. Regularly or sometimes
   b. Hardly ever or never
2. Do you go online to get news every day?
   YES
   NO

Radio and then television revolutionized the way individuals received political news. Ease of use and the emphasis on entertainment made the electronic media more appealing to individuals who are less interested in receiving in-depth information. Radio made a valiant attempt to challenge the dominance of newspapers during the 1930s and 1940s, but it found itself displaced by television in the 1950s. By the 1960s, television had displaced newspapers as the primary medium for transmitting political news to citizens. (See Table 6-1). Now the Cable News Network (CNN), MSNBC, and other more specialized sources such as C-SPAN and Court TV provide 24-hour, in-depth news coverage. Take the poll in Time Out 6-1: Let's Look at Your Media Usage, and then compare your media usage with others' in the Answers to Time Out 6-1 box on page 162.

The Internet emerged on the scene in the 1990s and quickly became a player in the media game. Use of the new media varies considerably across different segments of the population. Younger citizens are much more likely to turn to the Internet and less likely to turn to newspapers, particularly for news.

One of the more fascinating changes in the contemporary media mix is the growing audience for public affairs and news programming on cable television. CNN actually involves three channels of all-news programming. The original CNN prides itself on its "long-form" in-depth programming. It had the luxury, in 1994, of covering events such as the O. J. Simpson trial and, in 1995, extensive on-site specials on the Oklahoma City bombing in their entirety. CNN's hourly "Headline News" provides a fixed sequence of news, weather, business, and sports. Its international coverage brings the all-news format to worldwide subscribers.

Ted Turner's experiment in 24-hour-a-day news programming clearly reached its stride during the Persian Gulf War, when public officials, such as President George H. Bush, Saddam Hussein, and Defense Secretary Richard Cheney, admitted that much of their information came from CNN. As CNN International Director Peter Vessey saw it, "We cut the world in on the diplomatic process. And Bush and Hussein can talk at or by each other on television."[4]

C-SPAN was created in 1979 by cable television network operators to broadcast gavel-to-gavel coverage of the House of Representatives. Because they feared embarrassing pictures of an empty chamber or of unruly members, the House decided to control the cameras and to limit what might be shown. Eventually C-SPAN began using its cameras to cover such events as selected committee meetings, speeches, call-in programs, and public affairs conferences. When the U.S. Senate and the British House of Commons installed their own cameras, C-SPAN created a second network to provide gavel-to-gavel coverage of the Senate and selective coverage of the House of Commons and other foreign legislatures.

C-SPAN emphasizes long-form programming. Although it reaches a relatively small audience (compared with the major networks), C-SPAN tends to draw the players in American politics who use its programs to monitor the game and to prepare their own participation. Audience analyses indicate that C-SPAN viewers are much more likely than are members of the general population to vote, to contribute to campaigns, and to communicate with their elected officials. C-SPAN offers a unique window on the political process. From the outset, high television production costs, especially for news programming, ensured a place for national network news programming, but local stations generally could not afford to send reporters and camera crews around the country to cover national news for their relatively small audiences. Local network affiliates focused on the local scene and depended on the networks for other stories. The network news programs were aimed at a large, diverse, national audience. They emphasized short, objective stories of general interest designed to offend neither viewers nor advertisers.

Table 6-1 Milestones in the Development of Television as a News Source

1939	Television is first demonstrated at the New York World's Fair.
1947	"Meet the Press" debuts on NBC.
1951	NBC launches "The Today Show."
1951	CBS transmits first program in color.
1952	First gavel-to-gavel coverage of national party convention begins.
1954	The congressional Army-McCarthy hearings are televised live on ABC.
Late 1950s	CBS and NBC begin 15-minute national evening news.
1960	Presidential debate between John F. Kennedy and Richard M. Nixon is televised.
1961	John F. Kennedy allows the unrestricted televising of White House press conferences.
1961	Noncommercial, public television broadcasts begin.
1963	All three networks begin half-hour evening news programs.
1963	Four days of live coverage chronicle the Kennedy assassination and funeral; Jack Ruby kills alleged Kennedy assassin Lee Harvey Oswald on live television.
1965	Network newscasts convert to color.
1967	PBS (the Public Broadcasting Service) launched.
1968	"60 Minutes" premieres on CBS.
1973	Live telecasts of the Watergate hearings dominate ratings.
1974	Richard Nixon's resignation as president covered live on television.
1975	America's so-called "living-room war" ends as U.S. troops pull out of Vietnam.
1975	Videocassette recorders first become available on the home market.
1979	C-SPAN (Cable-Satellite Public Affairs Network) begins live coverage of the House of Representatives.
1980	CNN (Cable News Network) begins 24-hour news broadcasting; "Nightline" begins on ABC, providing late-night, in-depth news story coverage.
1981	MTV goes on the air.
Early 1980s	Networks begin late-night and early-morning news programs to counter 24-hour cable news services.
1982	*USA Today* debuts and is sold in boxes that look like televisions.
1983	The Pentagon places strict limits on news access to "Operation Just Cause," involving the U.S. invasion of Grenada; external criticism leads to loosened rules for future operations.
1984	Major networks drop gavel-to-gavel coverage of the national party conventions.
1986	C-SPAN begins live coverage of the Senate.
1991	The beginning of the Persian Gulf War is seen live as CNN reporters give a real-time play-by-play description and view of the bombing of Baghdad.
1991	Network evening news is expanded to one hour for the duration of the Persian Gulf War.
1991	Live TV coverage of capital punishment approved.
1991	Unsuccessful Soviet coup is covered live, and ABC presents a live call-in program featuring Boris Yeltsin and Mikhail Gorbachev.
1992	Bill Clinton campaigns on MTV.
1992	CNN and network cameras greet the Navy Seals as they assault the beaches in Somalia.
1992	Congress passes new legislation regulating cable television.
1993	President Bill Clinton and Vice President Al Gore use national town meetings to communicate with the American public.
1993	The White House offers speeches and press releases on the Internet.
1994	Cable and telephone companies begin to position themselves to deliver a wide variety of information on the Information Superhighway.
1995	Republicans open the House and Senate to broader television access and increase access to congressional information via the Internet.
1995	Gavel-to-gavel coverage of the O. J. Simpson trial garners a significant audience and expands interest in televised court proceedings.
1996	NBC launches MSNBC to create a major network presence on cable television.
Late 1990s	Major television networks launch their own websites as an alternative method of distributing selections of their programming.
2004	Iraq War covered in real time with "embedded" journalists traveling with the troops. Time delay: none.

Sources: Bill Thomas, "Finding the Truth in the Age of Infotainment," *Editorial Research Reports,* January 19, 1990, 34; Ed Papazian, *TV Dimensions* (New York: Media Dynamics, Inc., 1986), 106.

Answer to Time Out 6-1

If you answered A to question 1 in Time Out 6-1, you joined with about half (58%) of Americans who watch network news regularly or sometimes. Significantly fewer younger citizens watch new programs on television. If you answered B, you joined with the 42% of American adults who seldom watch network news. Significantly fewer younger citizens watch news programs on television. See Figure 6-2.

If you answered YES to question 2, you are in the minority. Only about one-quarter (27%) of Americans get their news online every day. That figure is increasing annually and is significantly higher for younger citizens. If you answered NO, you are in the majority. Only about one quarter (27%) of Americans get their news online every day. See Figures 6-3 and 6-4.

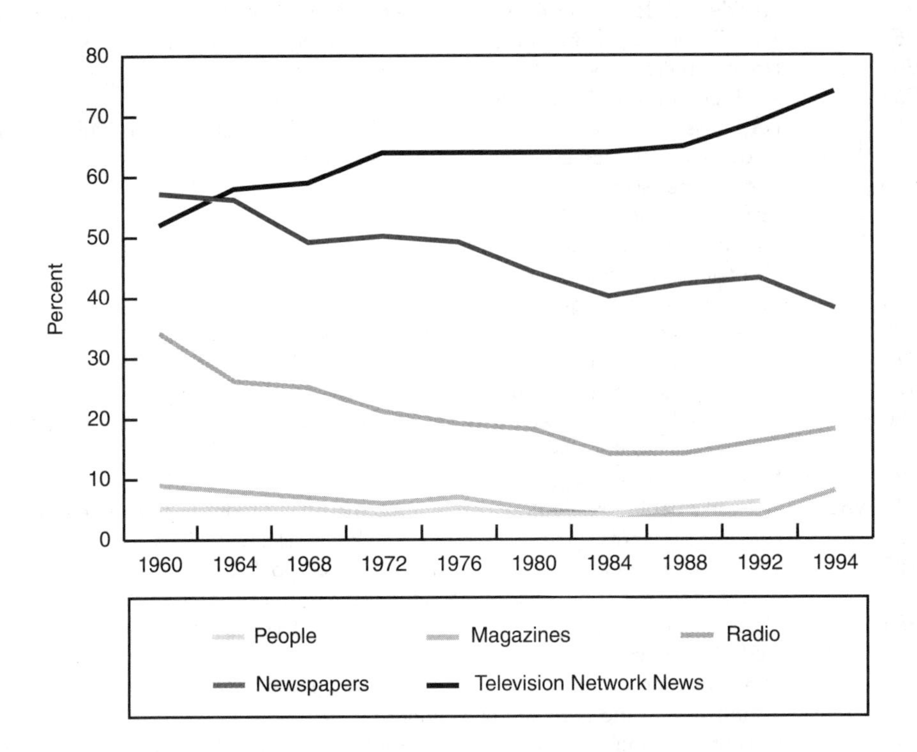

Figure 6-2
The Spread of Internet Availability and Usage for News

Sources: Data from "America's Watching—Public Attitudes Toward Television 1993," (New York: The Network Television Association and the National Association of Broadcasters, 1993), pp. 29, 31; Harold W. Stanley and Richard G. Niemi, *Vital Statistics on American Politics, 2001–2002* (Washington, D.C.: Congressional Quarterly, Inc., 2001.)

ratings *The measurement of the relative size and composition of the audience watching or listening to a particular network or station.*

The media are ever wary of losing audience. Stories about extreme political groups from both sides of the political spectrum—such as neo-Nazis and communists—often find it difficult to get the coverage they would like in the mainstream national media. After the 1995 bombing of the Alfred P. Murrah Federal Building in Oklahoma City, a national discussion of hate talk emerged, and some of the more extreme right-wing radio talk shows were canceled. A loss of audience means lower **ratings,** which means lower advertising income. Without their sponsors, media cannot survive. When evidence first began to mount years ago linking cigarettes to numerous health problems, the networks downplayed the findings in order not to offend cigarette advertisers, who were responsible at that time for significant portions of network revenue.

Television links a substantial political populace through instantaneous communication. In the 1960s, a large proportion of the American population experienced at the same moment events such as the civil rights protests, the events following the assassinations of John F. Kennedy and Martin Luther King, Jr., and the landing of U.S. astronauts on the moon. In the following decades, Americans watched together the release of American hostages in Iran, the student protests in China's Tiananmen Square, the fall of the Berlin Wall, the bombing in Baghdad, the fall of the Soviet Union's Communist government, and the terrorist attacks on the World Trade Center and the Pentagon (see Table 6-2). Worldwide television coverage of New Year's celebrations marking the new millennium helped establish feelings of a world community as time marched across the planet. Television's visual potency and immediacy challenged old-fashioned outlooks on

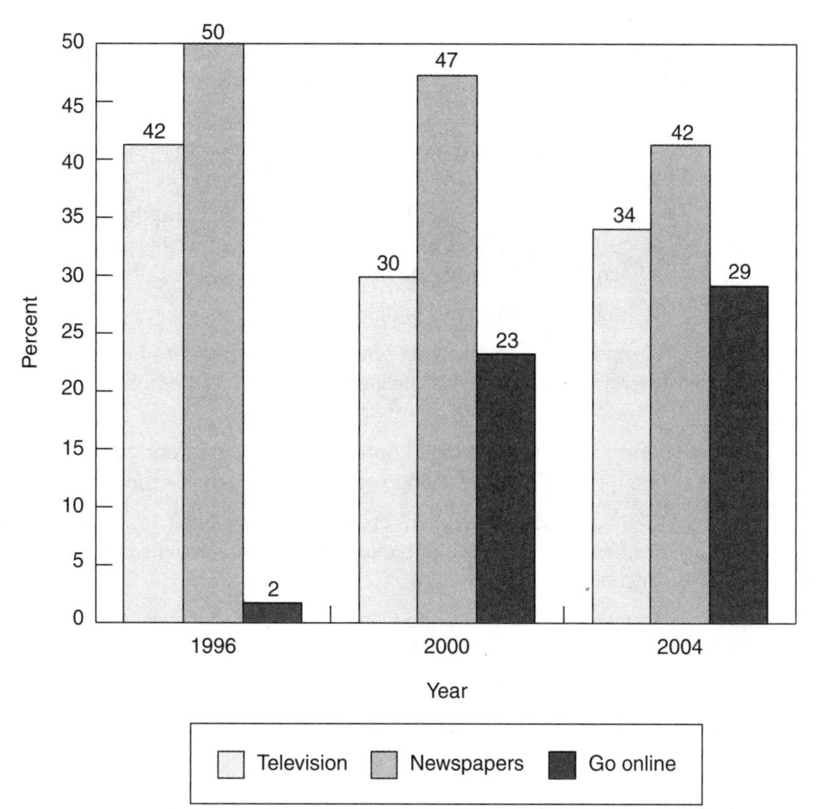

Figure 6-3

Regular* Sources of Political News

*"Regular" consumers use television and newspapers daily and the internet three or more times a week.

Source: Pew Research Center for the People and the Press, "Online Audience Larger, More Diverse," June 2004. Available at www. people-press.org.

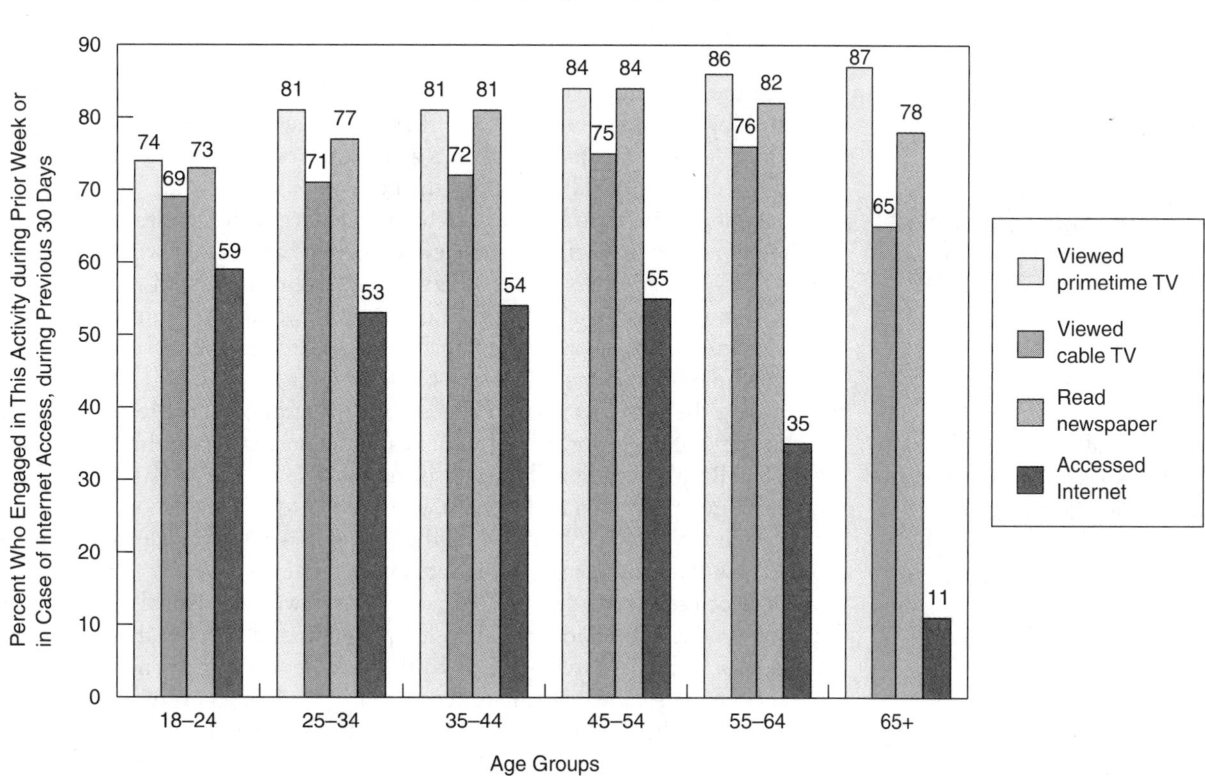

Figure 6-4

Age and the New Media Audience (2000)

Sources: U.S. Bureau of the Census, *Statistical Abstract of the United States,* Table 1127, Washington, D.C.: GPO, 2001.

Table 6-2

Increasing the Speed of Covering the Game of War, 1776–2001

Year	Event
1776	Correspondent reports on the reaction of the king of England to the American colonists' Declaration of Independence. Time delay: 50 days.
1815	Treaty of Ghent leaves London on January 2, 1815, by boat and arrives in New York on February 11. The treaty travels by post rider to Boston, which takes 32 hours. Andrew Jackson has been fighting the Battle of New Orleans since January 8, because he does not know that the peace treaty has been signed. Time delay: 41 days.
1950	Korean War begins. Time delay: 24 hours.
1968	A reporter covers the Vietnam War: the film is sent by land to Saigon and then is transmitted via satellite to New York to be broadcast. Time delay: 12 hours.
1991	A reporter films the initial bombing of Baghdad and sends live shots via satellite that are put directly on the air. Time delay: Seconds.
1992	CNN and network camera crews beat Navy Seals to the beaches in Somalia and broadcast real-time pictures of the assault via satellite. Time delay: Seconds.
2001	Cameras capture a plane flying into the World Trade Center and camera crews rush to the sites of terrorist attacks for live reports. Time delay: Virtual real-time coverage.

political events. Feelings of physical isolation were dispelled, and a national community was created. Traditional biases and ignorance were shaken as television brought home the wider political world.

By the 1980s, low-cost Minicams and satellite feeds changed the playing field once again, allowing some well-financed affiliates to assign their own reporters to cover stories in remote regions. Such coverage can add a local twist to stories. For example, the networks covered the broad contours of the Persian Gulf War, while local reporters followed military units from their own regions to provide **local color** stories about the experiences of hometown servicemen and servicewomen. This also occurs within the boundaries of the United States. CNN and the networks covered the general rescue efforts following the Oklahoma City bombing and focused on the worldwide hunt for the bomber. Local stations interviewed local residents who were related to the victims or produced stories on search-and-rescue specialists sent out from their locality.

local color *Aspects of a story that have special meaning for a local rather than a national audience.*

Just as the networks reached almost total penetration of the television audience, new technologies brought forces that would cause **fragmentation** within the market (see Box 6-1: The Ratings Game). The rapid spread of cable television has provided a wide array of specialized programming for those who can afford it. News and government "junkies" can watch CNN or C-SPAN, while their neighbors might be glued to a sports network or MTV and remain completely isolated from public affairs.

fragmentation *The breaking of a society (or audience) into groups of individuals with narrow and competing interests.*

Videocassette recorders (VCRs) added a new twist: individuals became their own television producers, picking and choosing programs and viewing them according to their personal schedules. Wireless access to the Internet on cell phones and palm-sized personal computers allow immediate access to text and video even when one is away from the home or office, adding a new dimension to the "digital divide" between those members of society who are wired and those who lack access.

With the arrival of satellite transmissions and videotapes, political candidates and elected officials recognized the advantages of aiming specialized programs at specific audiences. Presidential candidate Bill Clinton used televised town meetings sent to targeted audiences extensively in 1992. In his attempt to win the 1996 Republican nomination, former governor Lamar Alexander of Tennessee created his own monthly television show beamed by satellite to party workers' homes.

Box 6–1 The Ratings Game

Ratings of Evening News Programs

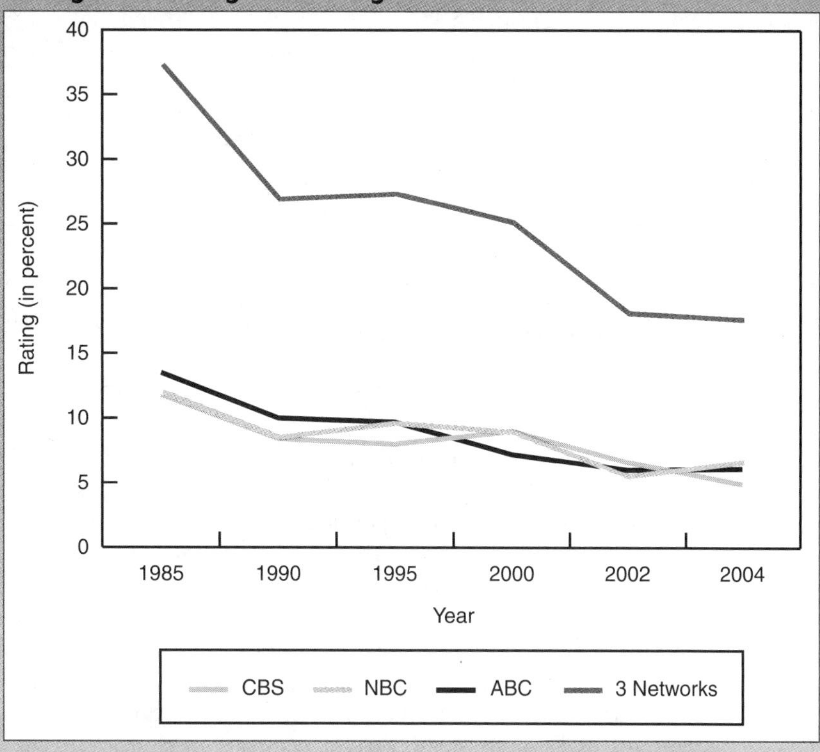

Source: 2002 BPI Entertainment News Wire—LEXIS-NEXIS, September 17, 2002 and www.mercurynews.com, accessed May 2004.

Figures regarding television set ownership and cable television subscriptions tell little about the size and makeup of television audiences. When television networks and individual stations attempt to sell their advertising time, potential advertisers want to know who is watching. The Nielsen Corporation uses such methods as viewing logs and electronic monitors to measure the ratings of each program and station. These ratings tell the proportion of households viewing and provide demographic characteristics, such as age, economic status, and educational attainment of the viewers. The higher the ratings, the more a station can charge for advertising time.

In the last few decades, viewing patterns have changed significantly. In 1980, 90 percent of households viewing television were tuned into one of the three major networks (ABC, CBS, and NBC) during prime time.[a] By 1990, with the arrival of widespread cable subscriptions, this figure had dropped to 60 percent. By the end of the decade, the major networks could only garner about 45 percent of the prime time audience. (See Figure 6-5.)

The turnaround is most dramatic for the viewing of evening news programs. Although there is no evidence that people are watching less news, the percentage tuning into the network news programs is declining. Viewing of cable and public television news programming has increased.

a. In strict terms, "ratings" are the percentage of *all* homes where the occupants are viewing a particular program or network, while a "share" is the percentage of homes with the television *on* where the occupants are viewing a program or network. Each rating point translates into approximately 1 million homes. The percentage figures reported here are ratings of the viewing audience.

Sources: A. C. Nielsen Media Research reports cited in Richard Zoglin, "Caught in the Crossfire," *Time*, September 3, 1990, 69; Brian Donlon, "Movies Are NBC's Ace," *USA Today*, May 15, 1991, 3D; Lynn Elber, "Television," Associated Press Newswire, December 18, 1995; and Frazier Moore, "Business as Usual in 'ER'," AP Online, December 22, 1999, LEXIS-NEXIS database.

Figure 6-5
The Growing Use of the Internet for News

Source: Surveys conducted by the Pew Research Center for the People and the Press, "Public's News Habits Little Changed by September 11," http://people-press.org.

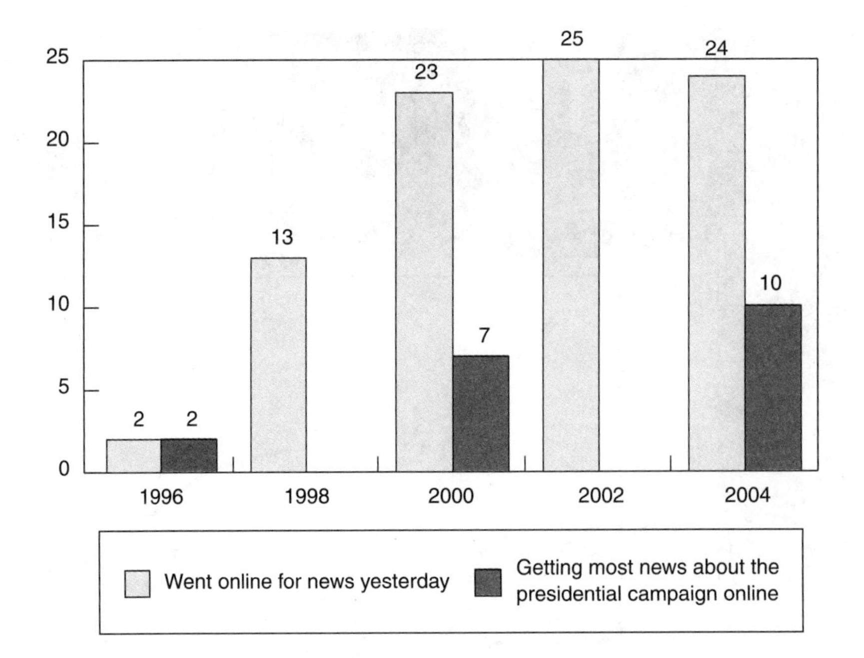

Although the average adult watches more than 20 hours of television a week, the current array of programming no longer assures our earlier shared experiences, especially when it comes to receiving political information. In the mid-1990s, political candidates such as Bill Clinton realized that it was important to go where the audiences were. They downplayed national network news coverage in favor of capturing the attention of individuals who watched cable television or who avoided network news. By going on programs such as "Larry King Live," "Arsenio Hall," and "Donahue," Clinton's actions were themselves then newsworthy and generated coverage in the more traditional media. The 2000 presidential campaign saw both candidates following the audience, appearing on late-night TV with David Letterman and attempting to capture the daytime audience on "Oprah." The crowning visual image of the 2000 campaign may well be Al Gore and George W. Bush opening a special broadcast of "Saturday Night Live" with parodies of themselves. Al Gore repeated his much-commented-on deep sighs from the first presidential debate, and George Bush intentionally mispronounced words, as often became the staple of his coverage during the campaign. The line between politics and entertainment became even more blurred in 2002, when Senator John McCain (R-Ariz) hosted "Saturday Night Live." During the 2004 Democratic nomination battle, John Edwards officially announced his campaign on Comedy Central, Al Sharpton appeared on "Saturday Night Live," Howard Dean lampooned himself on "David Letterman," and John Kerry rode onto the "Jay Leno" set on a motorcycle.

During the 1990s, an older technology, radio and radio programming, emerged in a new form to affect the political process. Radio talk shows with large national audiences served to spread new information and reinforce existing attitudes. Hosts such as conservative Rush Limbaugh avoided traditional journalistic objectivity and represented media with an agenda. By 1994 almost half of the American public reported that they listened at least occasionally to radio shows that encourage listeners to call in and discuss politics. More than 20 percent of the public listened to such programs regularly.[5] Short-wave radio showed the adaptability of technology—once a relatively harmless hobby for personal interaction, it emerged in the mid-1990s as a vehicle for right-wing groups to communicate worldwide.[6]

The Internet became an important political tool beginning with the 1996 presidential contest when all the major candidates produced websites and Bob Dole promoted his during a presidential debate. Jesse Ventura, the surprise 1998 Reform Party gubernatorial winner in Minnesota, used the Internet as a low-cost organizing tool to activate his supporters. Although on a typical day, only about 12% of Americans go online to visit political websites and less than half have ever done so, those who do have a deep interest in politics and are more likely to vote and give money to campaigns (see Figures 6-5 and 6-6). For

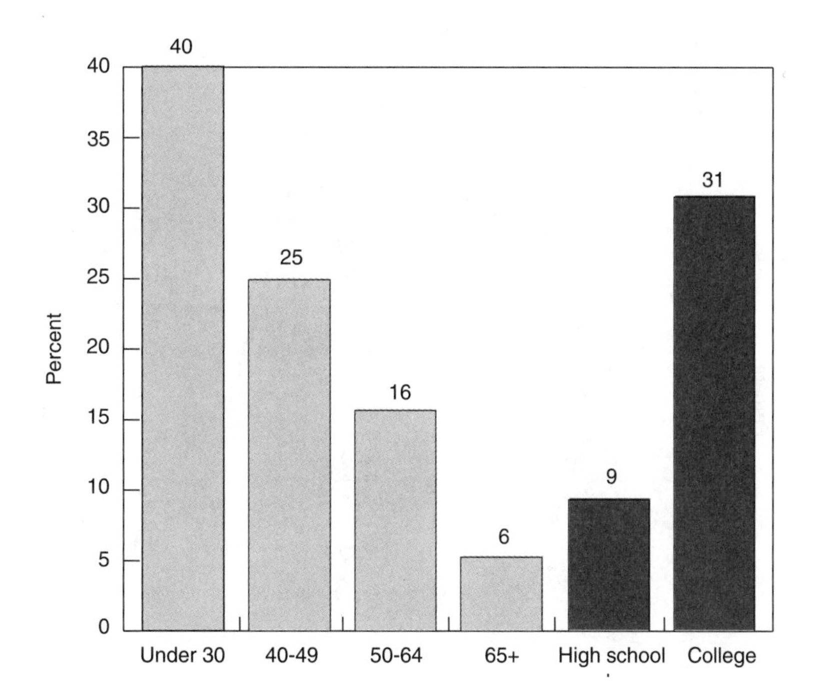

Figure 6-6
The Demographics of Internet Usage for Political News

Percent of demographic group who used the Internet to get most of their news about the 2004 election.

Source: Pew Research Center for the People and the Press, 2004. www.people-press.org

politicians looking toward the future, the percentage of the population relying on the web for political information is increasing rapidly, especially among younger voters. Recognizing the importance of this activist segment of the population, the presidential primary contenders in 2000 and 2004 effectively tapped the Internet as an effective fund-raising and communicating vehicle[7] New Hampshire governor Howard Dean used meetup.org to motivate face-to-face meetings of his supporters in hundreds of localities, harnessing the potentially impersonal web to facilitate traditional campaign activity.

6-1c Contemporary Print Media

Increasing production costs and competition from the electronic media for advertising revenue threatened the existence of many newspapers after World War II. The total number of newspapers continued to decline (see Figure 6-1). Most cities lost the services of competing newspapers, and many newspapers were bought by large chains. By 1984, 79 percent of the daily newspapers and 84 percent of Sunday papers were owned by chains. In the 1920s, 502 cities boasted at least two competing newspapers. By 1978 that number had dropped to 35, and today there are fewer than 25.[8]

To gain a larger share of a more heterogeneous readership, newspapers decreased their partisanship even more. An increasing number refused to endorse presidential candidates (see Figure 6-7). When endorsements were made, though, the Republican orientation of publishers became evident. Since 1932 only two elections saw a majority of newspapers endorsing the Democratic candidate. In 1964, Republican Barry M. Goldwater lost the endorsement battle to Democratic incumbent Lyndon B. Johnson, and in 1992 Democrat Bill Clinton picked up more newspaper endorsements than did Republican incumbent George H. Bush. In 1996, 111 newspapers endorsed Bob Dole, 65 supported Bill Clinton, and 415 remained uncommitted. In the 2000 race, the pace of endorsements increased, with over three-quarters of newspapers making a pick. George W. Bush gained a 2-to-1 endorsement margin nationally, with a 3-to-1 margin among small papers in medium and small towns. Even among large papers, Vice President Al Gore trailed slightly in endorsements.[9]

Newspaper circulation figures expanded until the early 1970s, in spite of the decline in the number of daily newspapers published. Since the early 1970s, the actual number of copies of the surviving newspapers that were printed also began to drop (see Figure 6-8). During the 1950s, one newspaper was printed for every three people in the United States, but this figure had dropped to one copy for every four persons by the 1980s.

Figure 6-7
Daily Newspaper Endorsements of Presidential Candidates, 1932–2000

*In 2004, George W. Bush received endorsements from 48% of the papers giving endorsements and John Kerry received 52%.

Source: Harold W. Stanley and Richard G. Niemi, *Vital Statistics on American Politics* (Washington, D.C.: Congressional Quarterly, Inc., 2001), pp. 194–195; http://toys.jacobian.org/endorsements/full.html.

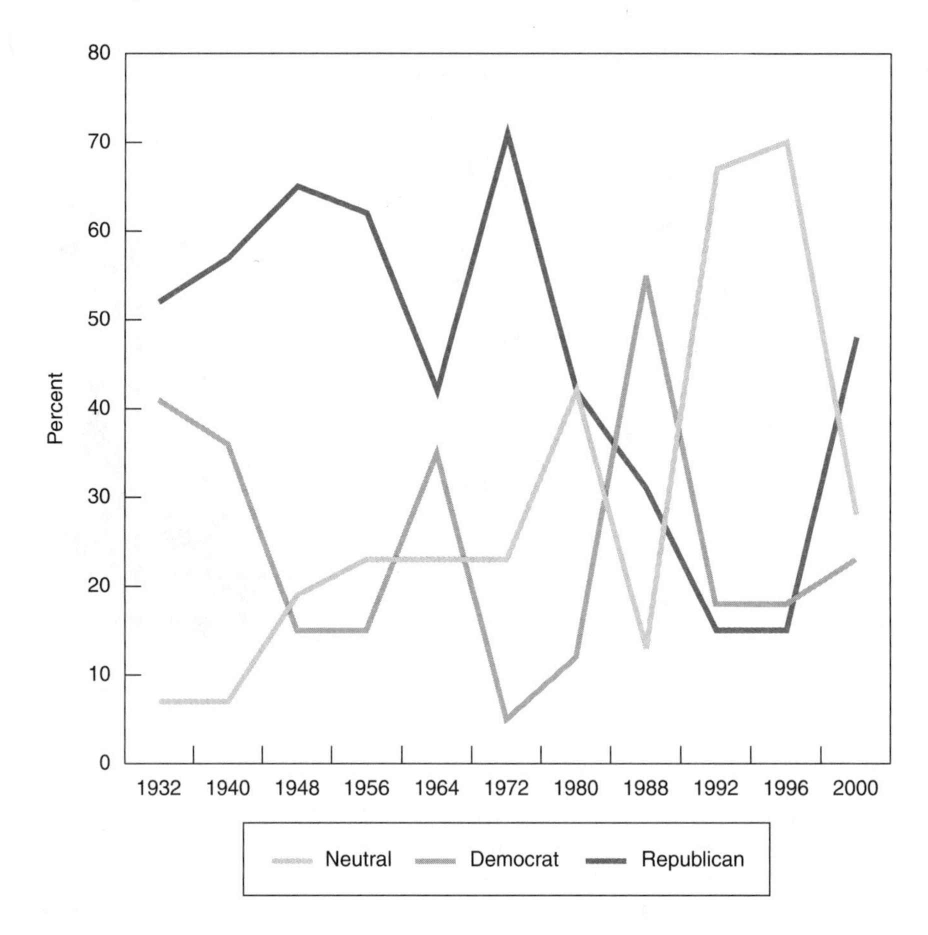

Figure 6-8
Total Circulation of U.S. Daily Newspapers, 1850–1999

Source: Harold W. Stanley and Richard G. Niemi, *Vital Statistics on American Politics 2003–2004* (Washington, D.C.: Congressional Quarterly, Inc., 2003), p. 174.

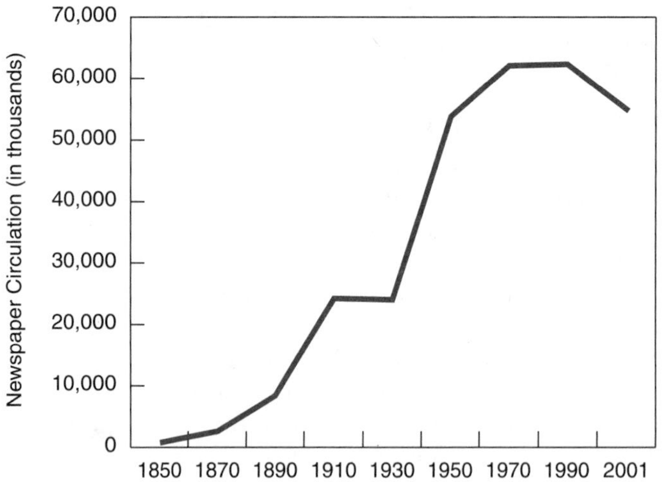

While there has been an overall decline in newspaper readership, the most dramatic decline has been among younger citizens, especially when it comes to using newspapers for political news. As Figure 6-9 shows, during political campaigns, younger voters are less than half as likely to rely on newspapers than older voters are, a gap that is relatively recent. While younger voters are going elsewhere for news, the results show up in terms of their more limited grasp of political information. As Figure 6-10 shows, the knowledge gap between younger and older voters has grown along with the gap in using newspapers during campaigns.

Computerized production and satellite transmission in the 1980s ushered in the era of nationalized newspapers such as the *Wall Street Journal* and *USA Today*. Stories began to be sent via satellite to printing plants around the country, allowing rapid delivery to the reader. Newspapers are now available via fax machines and online for more immediate reading. These same technologies increased the timeliness of stories and photos in both local newspapers and national news magazines. A number of newspapers and magazines

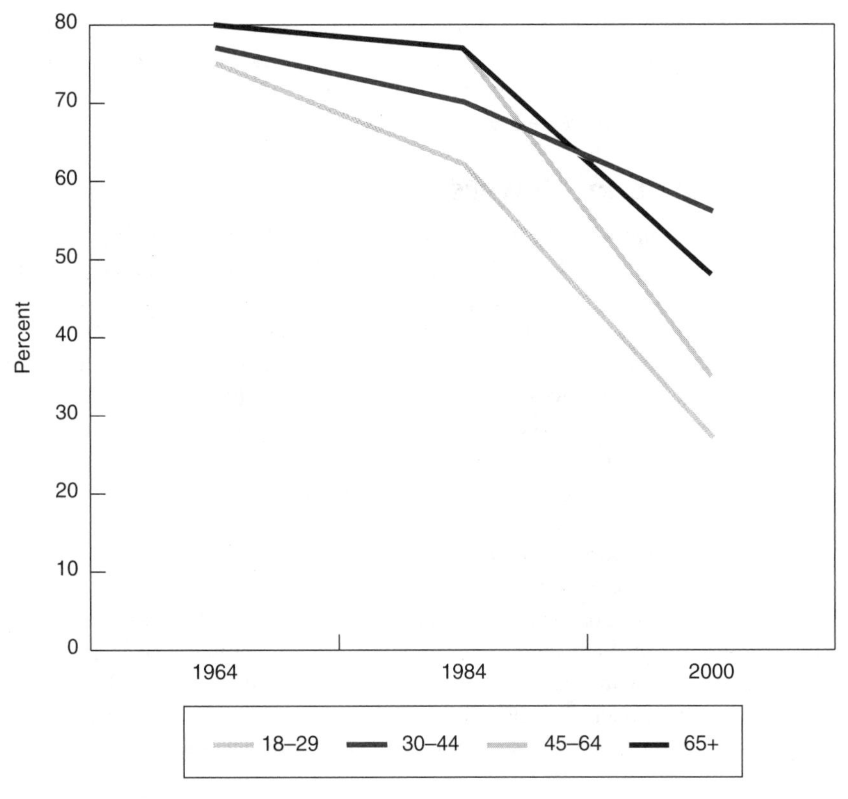

Figure 6-9
Reliance on Newspapers for Campaign Coverage by Age Groups

Note: Respondents were asked whether they read newspaper articles about the campaign.

Source: National Election Studies quoted in Martin P. Wattenberg, *Where Have All the Voters Gone?* Cambridge, MA: Harvard University Press, 2002, p. 92.

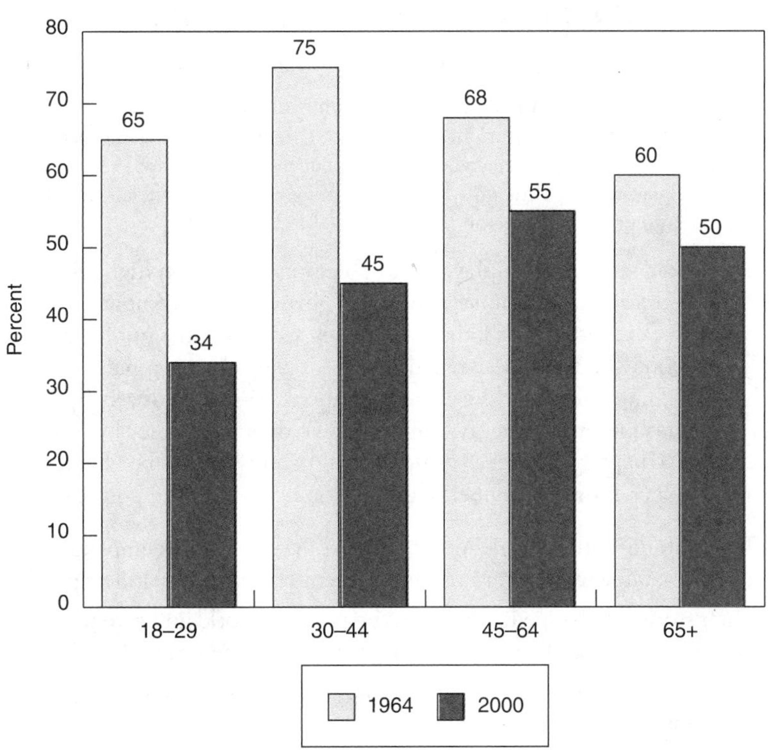

Figure 6-10
Age and Political Knowledge, 1964 and 2000

Note: Entries are the percentage of accurate responses to a series of basic questions about the campaign such as the state each presidential candidate was from.

Source: National Election Studies quoted in Martin P. Wattenberg, *Where Have All the Voters Gone?* Cambridge, MA: Harvard University Press, 2002, p. 94.

harnessed the new technologies to create local versions of the national publications with localized advertising and stories.

Also in the 1980s, the greatly reduced costs of computerized desktop publishing reversed the trend of a declining number of publications. More than 2,800 new magazines were launched between 1980 and 1990, many focusing on specialized hobbies, alternative lifestyles, or local interests.[10] Computerized online databases and electronic bulletin boards allow interested individuals to create their own electronic newspapers, filled with immediate news of specialized interest. All of these trends result in a "breakup of the mass mind . . . and pump a diversity of images . . . and values into society."[11] Differing information and expectations inject conflict into the political game. The breaking up of the media market has significantly affected both how short-term opinions are formed and the ability of the media to create a uniform political culture (see Chapter 5).

6-1d Individual Players

In spite of the domination of television networks and newspaper chains, news-reporting decisions still depend on the judgment of individual reporters, producers, and publishers (see the opening narrative in Chapter 4). Journalists are not typical of the population as a whole in terms of education, life experiences, and professional goals. Like other American elites, reporters are highly educated. They also have backgrounds usually in the humanities or social sciences and earn a relatively high income once they have acquired a few years' experience. This combination creates both support for social welfare and the desire to maintain the financial rewards of their own accomplishments. There is considerable disagreement as to how well journalists are able to carry out their professional responsibilities without allowing their personal biases to intrude. The question of objectivity is addressed again at the end of this chapter.

Journalists do not, however, march in lockstep. Differing responsibilities within the profession color perceptions of how the news should be reported. Newspaper owners and the editors reporting to them must protect their papers' economic well-being. Therefore they traditionally take a more conservative outlook than reporters do. Television producers attempt to play a moderating role similar to that of newspaper editors, but the time pressures of television production make screening the final content before broadcast more difficult.

6-1e The Role of the Media in the Game

Consider the following statement by television journalist John Chancellor:

> The American press, set free in the eighteenth century, entered the twentieth as a strong and generally responsible institution...We got into this craft to be scorekeepers, not players of the game...Journalists may want to be observers, but they are regarded as participants in the game by other players: by politicians, Presidents, and government officials on all levels. We didn't ask to play, but there we are on the field, The Media Team.[12]

The media serve as both players and observers, a position highlighted by their informal characterization as the "fourth branch of government," comparable in importance to the legislative, executive, and judicial branches. Counting the unofficial branches of government beyond the three designated in the Constitution is a matter of preference and emphasis. Calling the press the "fourth branch" was popularized by Douglas Cater,[13] while other authors emphasize the importance of the bureaucracy by calling it the "fourth branch" (see Chapter 16). Let's consider why the press might be characterized this way.

The media perform a number of different functions in the political game:

- They inform both players and observers of politics about impending as well as past activities, allowing them to make judgments about issues and to plan strategies.
- Their stories in the media interpret the political world and give it meaning by revealing patterns and linking individual events to broader symbols.
- By choosing issues to cover, the media help to set the agenda for politics by defining problems and pointing out possible solutions.
- The media monitor other players (especially elected and appointed officials). They expose other players' compliance (or lack of it) with the rules and their strategies for gaining political office and for deciding on policy.
- In a democracy, the media's granting of visibility to persons and causes often determines who wins and who loses. According to author Michael Parenti, "For many people an issue does not exist until it appears in the news media."[14]
- In the longer term, the media are one agent of socialization, helping individuals to establish their long-term orientations to the game (see Chapters 5 and 9).

6-2 Media Rules

The media function under a number of political rules. There are things they are not allowed to communicate, and there is information they must disperse.

As far as American print media are concerned, they are probably the most free of government control of any media in the world. No one needs a license or permit to begin publishing a newspaper, newsletter, magazine, or web page. Only economic constraints and motivation limit the number of printed publications. Content, however, may be subject to regulation under special circumstances.

The first wave of electronic mass media (radio and television) was heavily regulated by the national government. Radio and television developed at a time when technology limited the number of channels and interference-free frequencies. The government interposed itself as a referee, regulating the distribution of this once-scarce resource. The Federal Communications Commission (FCC), created by Congress to regulate radio and television, has spent half a century granting licenses to television and radio stations and monitoring their moral and civic contributions. The arrival of cable and satellite systems with hundreds of channels eliminated the scarcity argument for media regulation and tempered FCC responsibilities, but a number of the rules affecting the media remain in effect. The Internet, on the other hand, was treated like print and granted the "free expression" guarantees of the Constitution.

6-2a Government Secrecy and Prior Restraint

There is often tense disagreement about what the government wants covered versus what the media wants to expose. The American legal and social tradition discourages censorship and encourages government to distribute information widely.

To a large degree, judgments about media content come after the fact. If television programming or a publication fails to find an audience, then low ratings or poor sales send the appropriate message. Some potential media content, however, is canceled before it airs. All governments draw a line at types of information that would not be appropriate to share with the public, particularly in relation to national security. Government reports on troop levels, contingency defense plans, intelligence agency staffs, and plans for new weapons systems all stand high on the list of information that no government wishes to have distributed to the public. Government employees classify some documents as secret and thereby limit their distribution. In doing so they exercise **prior restraint.** Journalists often go to court to get such documents declassified. The courts have tended to side with journalists when government officials deny access primarily to avoid embarrassment. Such was the case when the public gained access to the tapes made in Richard Nixon's White House during the Watergate scandal (more fully discussed in Chapter 15).

prior restraint *Forbidding the publication or broadcast of material before it is written or aired.*

The level of official secrecy in the U.S. government remains significantly lower than that in most other countries. Journalists usually voluntarily accept standards for not publishing certain information. Government officials sometimes successfully request delays in publication when publicity might endanger lives or national security.

The Challenge of the New Media

The ever-evolving alternate media, joined with the importance of freedom of speech, pose new challenges. Short-wave radio, the Internet, and other means of communication have had virtually no bounds in terms of government control. In 1994 federal efforts to monitor computer communication that could threaten national security caved in before grassroots outrage (see Box 7-3: Creating an Interest Group Out of Thin Air in Chapter 7).

After the bombing of the federal building in Oklahoma City and the tragic loss of life, public attention was drawn to the fact that even a child could learn how to build a bomb via information offered on the Internet. Extremists and paramilitary organizations are among the groups that have long been plugged into networks in the United States. Simply sharing information comes under constitutionally protected speech. However, as discussed in Chapter 4, the U.S. system must sometimes delicately balance liberties with other rights and with public safety.

cyberspace *The area of communication created by new computer-based technologies.*

In 1995 legislators began to take a closer look at **cyberspace,** short-wave, and emerging technologies. Politicians from the whole spectrum of political philosophies were involved in grappling with phenomena such as "mayhem manuals." As Democratic senator Dianne Feinstein (Calif.) put it:

> Enough is enough. Common sense should tell us that the first amendment does not give someone the right to teach others how to kill people. The right to free speech in the first amendment is not absolute, and there are several well-known exceptions to the first amendment which limit free speech...I do not for 1 minute believe that anyone writing the Constitution of the United States some 200 years ago wanted to see the first amendment used to directly aid one in how to learn to injure and kill others.[15]

The terrorist events of September 11, 2001, created concern over the use of the Internet to undermine national security. The passage of the "Patriot Act" allowed the government, under certain conditions, to use technology to monitor communicating, buying, and library borrowing patterns of individuals. Both the courts and elected officials have tried to balance the desire for personal privacy and freedom with the need to protect the nation.

6-2b After-the-Fact Regulation

Not stopping a publication or broadcast does not eliminate governmental control: knowing that the courts lie in the wings tempers the urge to publish or broadcast some materials. For example, although the First Amendment guarantees freedom of the press, the Supreme Court has allowed local government to define what is obscene in their jurisdiction (see Chapter 4).

libel *Malicious and intentional use of untrue written statements that damage an individual's reputation.*

slander *Malicious and intentional use of untrue verbal statements that damage an individual's reputation.*

Prohibitions against the use of malicious and untrue statements (called **libel** in printed publications and **slander** in verbal broadcasts) protect individuals from false threats to their reputations. Actually, libel and slander laws protect politicians relatively little. The publication or broadcast of false information is not enough to win a libel or slander suit. The victim also must prove that the journalist acted intentionally out of malice, showed a "reckless disregard for the truth," and made no attempt to correct the error.[16]

6-2c Opening up the Government

Most government agencies do not regularly limit information access. In fact, many pursue explicit missions to inform the public. The U.S. government remains the largest publisher and distributor of information in the world. The danger for both the press and the public lies more in being inundated than in being starved for government information.

Virtually every government agency has a set of officials whose task is to disseminate information to the media and eventually to the public. Variously called press secretaries, public affairs officers, and government information specialists, these individuals launch public relations campaigns to disseminate information to the public (and in the process make their agencies look good). They work on the principle that "to know us is to love us" and assume that a positive public image will pay off in terms of budget allocations and freedom from attack. Far from avoiding the media, most agencies and individuals in government realize that they need the media to get out their message. The media in turn recognize dependence on these officials to provide the information they need to write and produce stories.

Freedom of Information Act *Legislation requiring agencies to publish a classification scheme for their documents and to establish a procedure for requesting documents that does not compromise national security, trade secrets, or personal privacy.*

government-in-sunshine laws *Laws that require government agencies to conduct their meetings open to the public, except in specified situations such as discussions that might violate national security interests or the privacy of individuals.*

Since access is generally expected, explicit limitations become more noticeable. In reaction to increased access limitations, Congress passed in 1966, and strengthened in 1974, the **Freedom of Information Act,** which established procedures for identifying and accessing most government documents. Most states subsequently passed laws even more favorable to the public's access to state government information. In reality, the cost, knowledge, and motivation required to request access mean that journalists, rather than individuals, use these laws more often and more effectively.

At times, government officials have to be pushed a bit to open up their meetings and records. A variety of **government-in-sunshine laws** require open meetings except under unusual circumstances. The presence of television cameras in city councils, in both houses of the U.S. Congress, and in a number of state and local courts have redefined the concept of open government.

Government documents, once available only in printed form, are now distributed on compact disks and via online data services. (Electronic addresses for receiving this information are found in appropriate chapters.) The potential for more effective distribution of government information is great. The increasing tendency of government to create and send out its information via computer could also limit access, however, since computer access requires skill, equipment, and resources not available to everyone. There is a danger of creating two classes of citizens in the age of the Information Superhighway—information "haves" and "have nots." Those without access to timely and complete information will be greatly hampered in playing the political game. Government officials currently show a new interest in adjusting information access laws and procedures to better fit contemporary technology and to have it serve the goal of a better-informed citizenry.[17]

6-2d Government-Required Coverage

Government regulation of the media was intended to encourage public access to a wide variety of information, but mandated coverage often became the maximum as well as the minimum amount of political coverage provided. The contemporary movement away from government regulation has emphasized the free flow of information motivated by market competition. The following discussion traces some of the key issues as they have changed over time.

Public Interest Broadcasting

Until the 1980s, the FCC, through its power of license renewal, encouraged public interest and especially news programming in the electronic media. Stations were required to submit programming logs (plans of events), and local individuals were encouraged to comment on the contributions that specific stations made to the public interest. In light of expanded outlets and the mood of deregulation, the FCC dropped these requirements during the 1980s. The 1992 cable television bill included a "must-carry" provision, which required local cable companies to include the major networks in their offerings. Later legislation expanded the must-carry provision, requiring the distribution of high-density programming on cable. While FCC regulation of program substance has diminished, local government regulation has increased. Local government bodies, which control cable television licenses, often include requirements for public interest programming and public access channels. In general, however, content for all the electronic media stems more from audience demand than from regulation.

Fairness

Another requirement imposed on the electronic media by Congress and regulated by the FCC was the **Fairness Doctrine.** Because radio and television stations were seen as having a monopolistic control over information, they were required to treat issues objectively by presenting opposing views. Such fairness was difficult to measure and administer. Opponents argued that the policy stifled debate by discouraging reports on any policy position. They further stated that the idea of monopoly control had lost its meaning. The proliferation of channels due to the arrival of cable television and expanded broadcast bands provided more consumer options.

fairness doctrine *Enforced by the Federal Communications Commission until 1987, this rule required radio and television stations to be fair to all sides of political issues by fairly presenting opposing views.*

Criticism of electronic media regulation emerged at a time when conservatives such as Ronald Reagan were taking up policies aimed at limiting government involvement in Americans' lives. From a purely political perspective, many conservatives felt that the requirement of fairness provided liberals with more access to the airwaves than would be the case without such regulation. The Fairness Doctrine, a victim of the deregulation movement, was eliminated in the 1980s. The 1990s saw an explosion of programming—such as Rush Limbaugh (conservative), John Hightower (liberal), the Black Entertainment

Network, and National Empowerment Television (conservative)—each with a clear political agenda.

Equal Time

equal time rule Legislation enforced by the Federal Communications Commission that requires radio and television stations offering or selling time to one candidate or party to offer equal time at equal rates to all other candidates or parties in a particular race.

To reduce the potential of media broadcasts favoring one political candidate over another, the **Equal Time Rule** requires a station to provide equal time at the same rate to all candidates or parties. Under this rule, the key limitation on candidates is their financial resources for buying advertising time.

The Equal Time Rule, however, applies only to broadcasts controlled by the candidate and not to normal news coverage. To avoid the participation by a myriad of minor party candidates, Congress by special law exempted the 1960 Nixon-Kennedy debates from the rule, and the media simply defined the debates as news events in later years.

Government Subsidies

The federal government subsidizes public television and public radio to a much smaller degree than do most other countries. The Corporation for Public Broadcasting (CPB) encourages diversity and cultural programming by contributing about 15 percent of the budgets of local public radio and television stations. The remainder of the stations' funds come from private contributions and corporate grants. In 1995 House Speaker Newt Gingrich (R-Ga.) labeled the CPB as a type of government waste that should be cut. He and a number of his conservative colleagues argued that, even though public radio and television programming was excellent, it was time for public radio and TV to fend for themselves in the commercial marketplace. The threat to federal financing of public broadcasting subsided and then flared up again in 1999 when it was found that individual stations were sharing fund-raising lists with the Democratic Party, starting a new round of partisan criticism calling into question the ideological bias of public broadcasting.[18]

6-2e Business Constraints

As business enterprises, the media are subject to a variety of rules which, in general, attempt to increase the flow of information. For example, the courts have protected media when local politicians have attempted to hinder opposing newspapers through unfair taxation.[19] Working from the premise that diversity and competition serve the public interest, FCC rules limit the number of local stations that a national network or corporation may own. The rules also limit the ability of the same corporation to own a newspaper and a television station in the same town. The increasing dominance of foreign-owned media empires presents a potential threat to domestic control of American media sources. Rupert Murdoch, as an Australian citizen, was thwarted by U.S. laws from expanding his U.S. holdings. With great fanfare he became a U.S. citizen and continued to expand his Fox Network and other ventures.

Audiences in most parts of the world depend heavily on government-owned or government-subsidized media outlets. Privately owned stations are clearly the exception. The absence of dominant, government-owned media and the fact of relatively limited regulation motivate U.S. media to respond to public desire. The media must always keep in mind that their audiences "vote" with subscription forms, channel changers, and computer mice.

6-3 Strategies of Media Players

Apart from the government itself, each set of players in the media game uses different strategies to reach their goals. In this section, we will look at the strategies of each of the following players:

- the media producers,
- the subjects of media coverage, and
- the media consumers.

6-3a Producer Strategies

American media are impossible to understand without recognition of their commercial nature. Success for all but a narrow portion of the media translates into profits or losses, determined by audience size and subscription totals. As reporter Linda Ellerbee put it:

> In television the product is not the program, the product is the audience and the consumer of that product is the advertiser. The advertiser does not "buy" a news program. He buys an audience. The manufacturer (network) that gets the highest price for its product is the one that produces the most product (audience).[20]

Ellerbee's critique suggests that we must look carefully at the motivations of the media as they define what is news.

Defining Political Newsworthiness

Media producers define newsworthiness partly in terms of inherent characteristics of particular media. Some events, such as an attempted presidential assassination or the passage of an important bill, require coverage. Otherwise, the media have considerable leeway in choosing what is newsworthy. The nature of the audience targeted by a radio or television station or a newspaper becomes a significant factor in that choice. *The Wall Street Journal*, for example, emphasizes business news. The *Washington Post* caters to its subscribers by covering domestic politics extensively. The *New York Times*, on the other hand, recognizes the interest of its readership in international stories by emphasizing their prominence and frequency.

Audience Characteristics

Both the media and their advertisers expend considerable effort determining the size and characteristics (e.g., lifestyles, buying habits, and attitudes) of audiences and subscribers. The relationship between a medium and its consumers is also important. Newspaper readers are "intentional" audiences who choose to read a particular paper. They tend to focus on the same sections and types of stories day after day. Television audiences, and especially radio audiences, are much more inadvertent or casual. Most often they use the radio or television as background noise to accompany other activities rather than choose one of these media to acquire specific information. The expansion of options on cable television resulted in the phenomenon of "channel surfing." Many individuals do not watch entire programs or wait for a commercial to switch but instead use their remote control to zip through a series of channels, watching snippets of programs. In effect, they become their own program producers. Surfing on the Internet takes individualizing information reception one step further. Such approaches to newsgathering do not guarantee that the mass of the public will be broadly or similarly informed on politics.

Within specific media, each outlet has some idea of its target audience. The local weekly newspaper appeals to a more homogeneous set of subscribers than a national newspaper such as the *New York Times*, which views itself as a historical record of the nation. Television networks transcend geographic boundaries and focus more on national stories than do local stations. Because news and public affairs programming—as compared to entertainment programs—appeals to the more upscale segments of the population, television news focuses on topics of most interest to the better educated and better off.[21]

Media Characteristics

The format or physical characteristics of each type of media help to define its unique patterns of news coverage. Newspapers, for example, have many large pages and can be read at leisure. Consequently they have a relatively large **news hole,** or area devoted to news, and can cover stories in more depth. On the other hand, the standard 22-minute evening news program consists of fewer than 20 stories, each between 1 and 2 minutes in length. Television attempts to capitalize on its immediacy and visual characteristics. Yesterday's news is not news on television but might be perfectly appropriate for a newspaper or weekly newsmagazine. Many stories thought to be newsworthy for the print media never

news hole *The amount of room in a publication or in a broadcast given over to covering the news.*

Box 6-2 Let a Million Television Crews Bloom

Philosophers often puzzle over whether there is any sound if a tree falls in the middle of a forest and no one is there to hear it. For television news, the comparable question is whether any news exists if no camera is there to record it.

Capturing news footage on video is not always intentional. The camera crew that captured the plane crashing into the World Trade Center was filming the skyline for another purpose. The rapid spread of surveillance and home video cameras have dramatically expanded the number of amateur news crews capturing events and making them potentially newsworthy for television journalists. Home recordings of tornadoes, airplane crashes, and other events show up regularly on both local and national news programs.

The 1991 beating of Rodney King by members of the Los Angeles Police Department after an alleged traffic violation would have remained a local story if the scene had not been captured by an amateur cameraman. It was no longer a case of pitting the word of one poor, minority ex-convict against a group of police officers. The tape dominated news programs and spurred investigations of racism and excessive use of force by police departments around the nation. A number of police departments explored the idea of wiring their officers for sound and installing minicameras in all police vehicles to gather evidence, to record confrontations, and to make sure that proper procedures were followed.[a] Although the camera does not lie and truth should prevail, the pervasive use of such new technologies, especially if they end up on the news or in the courtroom, also raises some significant questions of privacy.

a. Jay Matthews and Jill Walker, "L.A. Beating Case May Boost Police Use of Videotape," *Washington Post*, April 24, 1991, A3.

make it into a television newscast if videotape of the event is lacking (see Box 6-2: Let a Million Television Crews Bloom).

In the search for larger audiences and greater profits, media producers use a number of simple rules of thumb in choosing which events to select for coverage. The media formula rests on the desire to guarantee stories that are interesting to the audience and capable of being covered at a reasonable cost.[22] Television's small news hole offers limited time to provide the background material necessary to evaluate emerging political players. This forces it to rely most heavily on a few well-known spokespersons. A president gets on the air, both because he or she is important and because he or she does not have to be introduced to the bulk of the audience. Spokespersons for extreme causes or emerging issues get bypassed in favor of celebrities or established authorities on the major networks.[23] However, the increasing popularity of hour-long television news magazines such as ABC's "20/20" or "Dateline" and tabloid television may well challenge this tendency.

On television, abstract analysis gives way to personalized political issues.[24] The domination of the news by the O. J. Simpson trial in 1995 is a prime example. Above and beyond Simpson's celebrity status, the media justified the extensive coverage by arguing that it would inform the American public about the judicial process. The **news hook** was Simpson; the subsidiary effect might be a better-informed population. In some viewers' minds the coverage raised questions about the competency of the police, the effectiveness of the jury system, the role of money in getting "the best justice one can afford," and potential racism on the part of police officers. The untimely deaths of Princess Diana and John F. Kennedy, Jr., pushed politics as usual off the front pages and raised issues about the media-hounding of celebrities and air safety, respectively.

news hook *The characteristic of a news event on which one hangs the story. This is often an individual whom the media feel is newsworthy.*

sound bite *A short segment of a speech or an interview used in a radio or television news story—usually with strong symbolism and/or wording.*

Conflict makes better news than compromise, especially when the conflict can be made dramatic through visual presentations and **sound bites** (see Time Out 6-2: Selling Yourself by Sound Bite, and Figure 6-11).

Selling Yourself by Sound Bite

Time Out 6-2

Assume that you have stepped into an elevator along with a professor who is looking for someone to fill a job that you want. You know that you will lose your audience when the elevator stops. Frame a short response to her question, "Why should I hire you?" Express your response and time it on your watch. It probably took you a couple of minutes to sell yourself.

The media do not give politicians even that much time. Rather than providing uninterrupted time blocks controlled by the candidate, the media offer sound bites of a speech or an interview (see Figure 6-11). Generally, the segments selected are not those that the candidate would have chosen.

Equally important, the length of sound bites has decreased in recent years. When Hubert H. Humphrey faced Richard M. Nixon in 1968, the average sound bite of the candidate speaking lasted about 43 seconds. In the 2000 presidential campaign, George W. Bush and Al Gore were allowed sound bites averaging only about 8 seconds in length. The remainders of most stories were devoted to visuals of the candidates, unaccompanied by their words.[a] It is not surprising, then, that issues, substance, and qualifications decline in importance.

a. Kiku Adatto, "The Incredible Shrinking Sound Bite," *The New Republic*, May 25, 1990, 20–23, and Stephen J. Farnsworth and S. Robert Lichter, *The Nightly News Nightmare*, Lanham, MD: Rowman and Littlefield, 2003, p. 81.

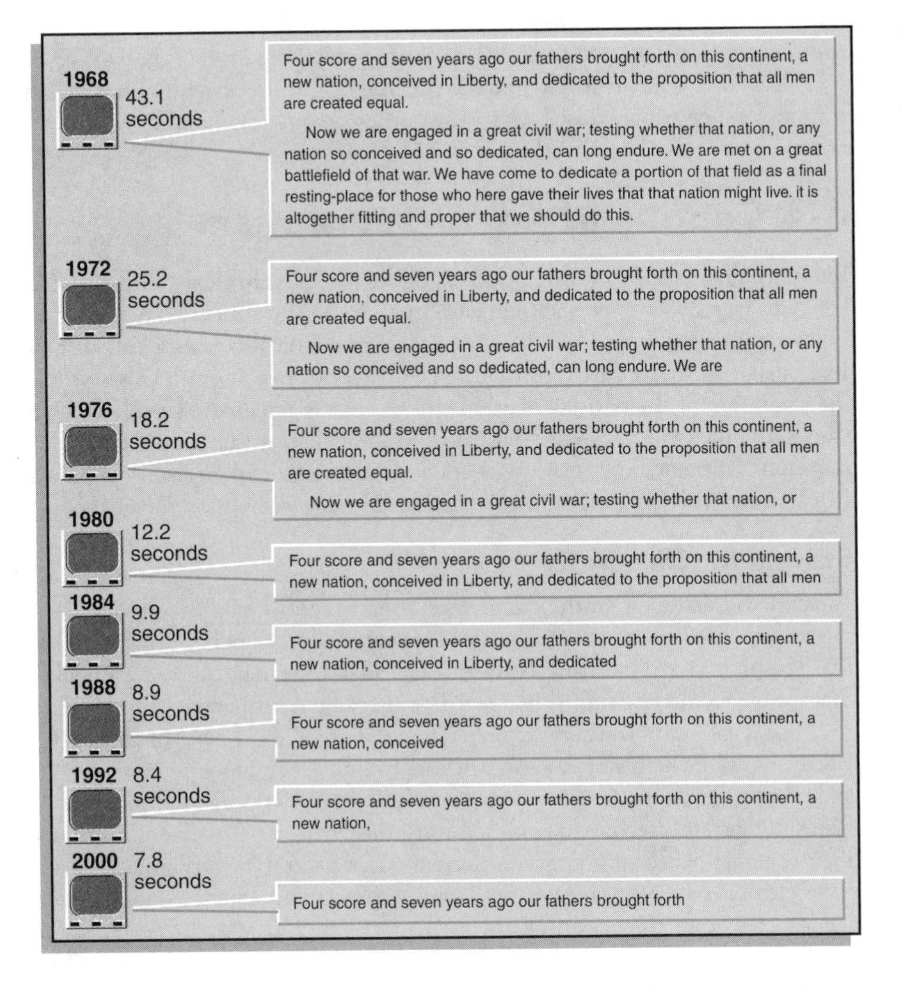

Figure 6-11
The Incredible Shrinking Sound Bite

Sources: Adapted from Kiku Adatto, "The Incredible Shrinking Sound Bite," *The New Republic* 3932, May 25, 1990, pp. 20–23; John Carmody, "The TV Column," *Washington Post*, November 18, 1992, p. 66; Vital Speeches of the Day, vol. 64, no. 22, pp. 684–89 and Stephen J. Farnsworth and S. Robert Lichter, *The Nightly News Nightmare*. Lanham, MD: Rowman and Littlefield, 2003, p. 21.

As one former presidential press secretary and journalist pointed out, the strategic rules that guide politicians and the journalistic rules that guide television are at odds:

> The rules of politics are negotiation, weaving, subtlety, nuance, trading, advancing, retreating, and so on...But television doesn't like nuance. And television doesn't like subtlety...Television deals in a world of simplicity.[25]

Another common television technique is the use of labels. Labels such as *liberal, conservative, feminist,* and *environmentalist* simplify issue stands and allow journalists to go on with a story without giving the audience much context for interpretation.[26]

As business enterprises, American media find cost a significant factor in defining news. Few individual newspapers have resources to directly cover national events. They rely instead on national news services such as the Associated Press (AP) or the resources of the chain of which they may be a part. Local editors tailor stories through choices, placement, and assignment of headlines, while using their reporters to develop stories on the local implications of national stories.

Television networks locate production crews in the large cities where they expect to find major news (New York, Washington, D.C., Chicago, Los Angeles) and then attempt to cover stories from these locations. Covering stories on taxes, crises in health care, and government inefficiency from the urban news hubs is economical. Natural disasters and other obvious news stories force the assignment of production crews to other areas. To some degree, political news follows the journalists, rather than vice versa. The permanent assignment of a network camera crew to the White House almost guarantees daily coverage even if more newsworthy events occur elsewhere.

Competition among media sources within markets invites comparisons of their news-gathering results. Editors dislike going out on a limb either by covering stories that the competition has not included or by not covering stories that everyone else has included. This leads to **pack journalism.** Reporters check with colleagues from other stations or newspapers to see what stories they are covering and how they are covering them.

pack journalism *A defensive strategy used by journalists comparing their coverage with that of competing media, which results in uniformity of coverage.*

6-4 Canons of Good Journalism

canon *An accepted rule, standard, or criterion.*

Journalism has developed into a profession with relatively clear standards of appropriate behavior (see Box 6-3: News Rules and Strategies). The American Society of Newspaper Editors, for example, in 1993 developed a code of ethical behavior called the **Canons** of Journalism. Journalists attempt to provide objective coverage and help to simplify public interpretation of the political world by using widely understood symbols. Fourth of July stories are filled with flags and fireworks to imply patriotism. Candidate political orientations are intimated by showing them with members of their political base supporters: Republicans with business audiences and Democrats with union members.

Striving for Objectivity

After the breakaway from the dominance of party control of media during the late 1800s, objective journalism became the goal accepted both by the public and by working journalists. The professional standards of the media lead to the public and professional expectation that the media will be neutral observers, not intentional participants in the political process.

The goal of objectivity remains more elusive than you might at first expect. Decisions as to which story to cover, whom to interview, which pictures or visuals to use, and what conclusions to draw are influenced by personal, organizational, and economic biases. Reporters often cover stories, for instance, from a particular angle that stems from their personal biases and/or assumptions about the interests of their audience.

Television aspires to greater impartiality because its audience is more diverse and less self-selected than that of the print media.[27] One drawback, however, is that its very attempt to stay in the mainstream often results in defense of the status quo.[28] That is, simply standing back and allowing the news to emerge may mean that the networks ignore important issues. Defining all issues as having two competing sides, and then publicizing

Box 6–3 News Rules and Strategies

A key aspect of any game is its rules. Some rules are formal and encoded in laws and regulations, while other rules are more informal, a simple ordering from years of experience. In either case, the rules provide guidance about how to proceed. Most of the day-to-day rules affecting the media fall into the more informal realm.

The free enterprise basis of the American news media based on guarantees given by the 1st Amendment to the Constitution may suggest that the media are free in a one-sided way to unilaterally define what is news. While it is true that few formal laws regulate the news media, it is not true that there are no rules. As we walk a story through the process, some of the more informal rules of news definition and the strategies they bring about become clearer.

Assume that you are the editor of a national evening television news program, deciding what goes on the air. You will have to juggle legal requirements, economic necessities, and news-making principles. In order to follow acceptable strategies, you and your colleagues have devised a set of shorthand rules to apply to each situation.

At the morning editorial meeting, you get a tip from one of your reporters that an elected official is going to be charged with sexual harassment and you must decide whether to send a news crew to cover the press conference. You have a limited number of news crews. Not sending the crew will assure that the story does not go on the air. Five basic rules guide your strategy:

IS-THERE-AN-AUDIENCE-FOR-THIS-STUFF-RULE: Commercial networks count eyeballs. Advertising rates are based on the size of the audience. If the audience will not be interested, the news media is seldom interested.

NEWS-HOOK RULE: Is the politician important enough and well known enough for coverage on a national news program? You can't spend most of the story explaining who the person is.

LAUGH-TEST RULE: Is there any chance that the charges are true? Is this a credible source, or is it some demented soul trying to get attention? Would a reasonable person trust this source?

COVER-YOURSELF RULE: Can you report on the news conference without being charged with slander? As long as you can say, "So and so said...," you are probably off the hook.

WHO-ELSE-WILL-COVER-IT-RULE: Newspeople do not like to get scooped. If others are going to cover a story, it's better to cover it just in case.

You decide to send out the crew but leave open the question about using the story. When the news crew comes back for the mid-afternoon editorial meeting, they have good news and bad news. The source seems credible, but she talked for a long time. Microphone feedback made some of the tape unusable. Four more rules kick in.

IF-IT-CAN'T-BE-SEEN-IT-IS-NOT-NEWS-RULE: Television almost demands pictures. Lacking good pictures, the story may just as well not have happened.

THE-BREVITY-IS-NEXT-TO-GODLINESS-RULE: Since most news stories are less than 2 minutes in length, individuals who cannot have their words edited into a sound bite will find their words missing from the story.

YOU-CAN'T-SAY-THAT-ON-TELEVISION-RULE: While standards continually change, the networks censor themselves when it comes to profanity and graphic descriptions of a sexual nature.

CAN-WE-LOOK-FAIR-RULE: The perception of fair coverage is more important than actual fair coverage. Unless the media can either get a response from the person charged or get a flat refusal to respond, the story might be dropped.

The editorial committee meeting breaks up. The decision is to use the story. Now how and when it will appear need to be decided. Three final rules determine that.

LEAD-WITH-THE-HARD-NEWS-AND-LEAVE-THEM-SMILING-RULE: The first story on most national news broadcasts is usually reserved for hard news that has national or international implications. If a president or a leading presidential candidate were involved in this story, it would be the lead. The last story on most news programs is a softball or feel-good story, designed to leave pleasant memories in the viewers' minds. The harassment story does not seem to fit either model.

KEEP-THEM-FROM-USING-THE-REMOTE-RULE: American viewers are increasingly becoming channel surfers, moving from one program to the next, especially during commercials. Stations have about 5 seconds to grab the attention of a surfing viewer. A sexual harassment charge against a prominent politician might work as a good teaser, urging viewers to "stay tuned" after the break for a hot-breaking story.

A-BREAKING-STORY-IS-THE-NEWS-RULE: The shelf life for television news is relatively short. A hot-breaking story, especially if there is good visual footage, may well drive out a story that is only a few hours old. Our worried politician charged with harassment may have to hope for a good earthquake, flood, or airplane crash to push his story off the air. Remember, you only have time for about 20 stories each night.

The above rules are clearly not hard-and-fast components of a formula for deciding what is news. There is a great deal of personal judgment as to what gets on the air. Network news executives do tend to think alike, though. On the average night about one-third of the stories on all three networks are the same, about one-third appear on two of the three networks, and one-third of the stories are unique to one network.

each side's position, appears objective, when actually it clouds the complexity of most issues. One critic points out:

> In practice...journalistic neutrality means that groups with the loudest, best-financed, and most-rehearsed voices get their message across more effectively and more often. The result of journalism's unwillingness to develop a voice for democracy is that the news has become virtually a direct pipeline for propaganda from powerful organizations to the people.[29]

The rise of tabloid journalism, represented by programs such as "A Current Affair," blurs the line between objective journalism and sensationalism in pursuit of an audience. Even the mainstream media have approached—if not crossed—the line. On the day Newt Gingrich was to be sworn in as Speaker of the House, CBS's Connie Chung ran a controversial clip from an interview in which Gingrich's mother—after being assured that the comments were "just between us"—called Hillary Clinton a "bitch." Chung was accused of breaking a confidence, and CBS was chastised at the time for extensively promoting the interview. Chung's aggressiveness was thought to be a major reason for her later losing her news anchor position. Despite criticism, the gambit worked for CBS, however, when its ratings soared—at least for a while.

adversarial reporting *An approach to covering news stories in which the reporter refuses to accept the position expressed by the participants and, instead, aggressively delves into the situation, with little regard for embarrassing the subjects.*

In recent years, some journalists have become more aggressive by including more news interpretation and developing a style of **adversarial reporting** (see Box 6-4: Finding the Rotten Apple in the Barrel). As journalist Eleanor Clift put it, "The press always plays the game of 'gotcha.' . . . You try to trap the person into saying something that will make news, and news by definition tends to be negative."[30] By revealing the Watergate, Iran-Contra, Whitewater, and Clinton Impeachment scandals, journalists reinforced their position as separate players in the game of power politics.

The depth to which journalists should delve when covering politics is constantly reinterpreted. The private lives of public officials were once beyond the boundaries of reporting unless the actions directly affected the official's public position. Today the erasing of that line leads to entertaining stories but calls into question personal rights of privacy (see Box 6-5: Discovering the "Vice" of Vice Presidential and Presidential Candidates).[31] As political consultant Robert Squire put it:

> Now, more than ever in the past, ethics as an issue is fair game...The rules of the game have changed. The private lives of public figures...are now within the legitimate purview of the news media, thus theoretically providing a key to their offstage character, potential capabilities and likely performance.[32]

The Politics of Symbolism

The political world is extremely complex. The media use such symbols as flags, the Bill of Rights, the peace sign, the Capitol dome, and clenched fists to simplify issues and to help the public interpret abstract political notions.[33] Since a picture is often worth a

Box 6-4 *Finding the Rotten Apple in the Barrel*

ABC newsman Sam Donaldson, one of the most aggressive investigative television journalists, justified his approach by commenting:

> If you send me to cover a pie-baking contest on Mother's Day, I'm going to ask dear old Mom why she used artificial sweetener in violation of the rules, and while she's at it, could I see the receipt for the apples to prove that she didn't steal them. I maintain that if Mom has nothing to hide, no harm will have been done. But the questions should be asked. Too often, Mom, and presidents—behind those sweet faces—turn out to have stuffed a few rotten apples into the public barrel.[a]

a. Quoted in *Newsweek*, March 2, 1987, 59.

Box 6–5 Discovering the "Vice" of Vice Presidential and Presidential Candidates

The media have shown particular aggressiveness in scrutinizing the backgrounds of recent vice presidential candidates. In 1972 investigative reporter Jack Anderson reported and then recanted a story about Democratic nominee Senator Thomas Eagleton's drunk-driving record, while other reporters revealed his psychiatric treatment for depression. After backing his choice "1,000 percent," presidential nominee Senator George McGovern dropped Eagleton from the ticket. In 1984 the business dealings of Democratic nominee Representative Geraldine Ferraro's husband dominated the headlines and eventually led to a post-election court case. The extensive publicity about her son's later arrest and conviction on drug charges stemmed from her political fame. In the 1988 election, it was the Republicans' turn. Vice presidential nominee Senator Dan Quayle's record of avoiding the military draft—by allegedly using his father's political connections to get into the Indiana National Guard—led to derisive commentary. George Bush's attempt to "pass the torch to a new generation of political leaders" got caught in a hailstorm of criticism. Both the media and members of his own party questioned whether Quayle should be replaced on the ticket.

During the 2000 campaign, Republican vice presidential candidate Dick Cheney was criticized for his ultra-conservative voting record while in Congress, a very generous separation payment from his employer who had benefited from government contracts, and for a drunk-driving conviction. Democratic candidate Joseph Lieberman was questioned about seeming duplicity because of his policy switches on issues such as school vouchers in order to become consistent with the views of presidential candidate Al Gore and for inappropriately interjecting religion into the campaign. During his time as vice president, Dick Cheney's heart condition has raised questions about his suitability for the job and trailed him almost constantly. In 2004, Dick Cheney's prior association with Haliburton Corporation, a major recipient of government contracts in Iraq, raised questions of ethics, while Democratic nominee John Edwards received criticism for his prior success as a trial lawyer allegedly driving up medical malpractice costs.

Presidential candidates are not immune to scrutiny of their personal lives by the media. In 1988 Senator Gary Hart (D-Colo.) was pushed from the race after charges of marital infidelity. In 1992 presidential candidate Bill Clinton was dogged by questions from the press about his draft record and personal morality. The media also pursued an unproven story about a romantic liaison of President George H. Bush. Early in the 1996 presidential campaign, Senator Robert Dole was questioned about his use of corporate jets, and California Governor Pete Wilson faced tough questioning about his hiring of an undocumented alien. The 2000 presidential race was rife with charges about Governor George W. Bush's alleged cocaine use, Vice President Al Gore's involvement in illegal fund raising, and Senator John McCain's temper.

In 2004, John Kerry was forced to confront his abandoning support for the War in Vietnam and publicly throwing military medals over the White House fence over thirty years earlier. George W. Bush again faced criticism for his pre-presidential business and personal behavior.

By increasing the scrutiny of candidates, the media may well raise the level of honesty and provide voters with the information necessary to make a reasoned choice. On the other hand, it could also dampen the willingness of capable candidates to put themselves and their families through such an ordeal, even if they have nothing to hide. Such emphasis on personal characteristics also takes time and attention away from more in-depth coverage of other important aspects of the campaign, such as issues, platforms, and beliefs.

thousand words, television, with its limited news hole, uses visual symbols to establish the context of a story and to prepare the audience for a message. Some symbols, such as the flag, take on an almost sacred quality. Its respectful display in a news story enhances the image of the political players associated with it. The camera zooming in on a peace sign or a clenched fist prepares viewers to consider their own views about the legitimacy and desirability of political protest.

Myths concerning political leaders, such as George Washington's honesty ("Father, I cannot tell a lie—I cut down the cherry tree") or Abraham Lincoln's rise from a log cabin to the White House, are used to inspire the public and to serve as cultural benchmarks against which to judge the behavior of subsequent leaders. The media are primary vehicles for reinforcing the symbols by which we make sense out of the political world.

6-4a Political Player Strategies

After analyzing the strategies of elected and appointed government officials, one media analyst concluded:

> Politicians, governments, and others have become increasingly sophisticated in their ability to anticipate how the news media will report their words and deeds, and how the public will respond to those reports. They have developed increasingly effective strategies for managing or circumventing the news, shaping their images, and channeling public perceptions...The result is a democracy of the uninformed, one that is ever more vulnerable to the wispiest breezes of political expediency.[34]

Journalists cover politicians, and politicians pursue personal and policy goals that can be furthered by news coverage. In the pursuit of favorable coverage, all sorts of clever players accommodate their messages to the needs and strategies of various media. Groups hold demonstrations in Washington or state capitals, not only because the policy makers are there but also because the journalists are there. Officials create photo opportunities to provide the visual images that help to assure them of television airtime. Bill Clinton jogs with famous Americans and almost always gets coverage. Politicians and journalists have a **symbiotic** relationship. Journalists need politicians for stories, and politicians need the coverage that journalists provide.

symbiotic *A relationship between two entities in which each needs the other for some purpose.*

Politicians who are getting bad press coverage often make themselves unavailable to the media. Bill Clinton refused to have a formal press conference for three months after the Republican gains in the 1994 midterm election (which the media interpreted as largely his fault).

Despite avowals of secrecy, officials strategically **leak** information to favored reporters. Leaks have the effect of allowing officials to gauge public reaction or to affect the policy process. Interviews are often given under elaborate rules that deny the reporter the right to attribute statements to any individual for similar reasons.

leak (news) *A government official's deliberate disclosure of secret information to embarrass others or to promote a particular policy.*

Although it does not totally upset the special relationship between journalists and their sources, television does give politicians additional options for control. News conferences are scheduled to allow coverage on the evening news. Jimmy Carter held off his press conference on the Camp David Accords on peace in the Middle East until prime time. The houses of Congress allow permanent television coverage as a way of bypassing the selectivity of journalists and communicating directly with the public.

Political decision makers not only generate news; they are themselves users of media information. The players in the political game use the media to monitor the political process and to anticipate the reactions of other players and of the general public. Images of presidents and other key decision makers sitting around their television sets heighten the importance of the media and increase the impact of their biases. As former Secretary of Defense Richard Cheney said during the Persian Gulf War:

> We have been very sensitive to collateral damage in the Baghdad area and I think the best source of how careful we have been is listening to the CNN reporters who were watching the story unfold.[35]

The availability of television—and especially instantaneous news programming such as CNN—has reduced the time between news events and public reaction. Players are beginning to understand that they are living in the era of **real-time politics**—a change that has quickened the pace of the political game.

real-time politics *Monitoring political events as they happen without delay or mediation.*

6-4b Receiver (Consumer) Strategies

It is hard to imagine anyone feeling starved for political information in contemporary America. Political "junkies" have almost limitless media sources from which to choose to stay abreast of political developments. Most of us face the reality of too much information. In response, we use explicit and implicit techniques to tame the volume and content of media information.

Selective Exposure

Arthur Sulzberger, former publisher of the *New York Times*, wrote:

> Along with responsible newspapers we must have responsible readers...the fountain serves no useful purpose if the horse refuses to drink.[36]

selective exposure *The decision to use a particular mass communications medium or source.*

Consumer decisions about using various media lead to **selective exposure.** Not all individuals are spectators in the political game. Some simply avoid political programming or decide not to use the media at all. Television and radio are low-effort media. They allow passive information consumption: An inadvertent audience gets political information even though it is not specifically "tuned in."[37] Heavy television viewers, as compared with newspaper readers, seem to be more politically confused and cynical than are low-to-moderate viewers.[38] Reading a newspaper takes more effort. Individuals reading news or political opinion magazines exhibit significantly higher motivation and interest than does the average citizen. As we will see, there are significant differences in the United States as to which media various segments of the population use, the degree to which users of different media are informed, and the political outlooks that each segment develops.

Because the media seek to maintain and expand their audiences and make a profit, the volume and content of political information in individual media outlets vary. Media serving audiences that are higher on the socioeconomic scale tend to portray political news in a more sophisticated manner. Even the television networks allow local affiliates a choice of versions of a particularly sensitive story in the evening news.

To some degree, the nature and availability of media coverage are beyond the individual's control. Individuals in urban areas make up a more reachable market. Thus they are more likely to have the broadest range of newspapers, magazines, and television stations from which to choose. For example, cable television companies wire the physically concentrated and more affluent suburbs well before they begin in urban and remote areas. The appearance of satellite dishes in rural areas arose to fill the need for choice. Furthermore, the cost of cable hookups could lead to a growing gap between the politically informed and uninformed that is based on economic status.[39] As cable television and telephone services expand to provide a wider—but more expensive and skill-dependent—range of information as components of the information superhighway, the potential for an information underclass increases.

Selective Attention

selective attention *The process of picking and choosing among sources and messages in a consistently biased manner.*

Access to a particular medium does not guarantee equal attention to all of its content. Viewers and readers pay **selective attention** to the content of the media they use. They exclude two out of every three newspaper articles and read fewer than 20 percent of them in full. An even smaller percentage of television news stories receives enough concentrated attention to be recalled in any fashion shortly after the newscast.[40]

Individuals tend to specialize, focusing their attention on certain subjects or individuals of personal interest (see Box 6-6: Different Strokes for Different Folks). People do not automatically reject ideas contradicting their beliefs and values, yet the more firmly they hold certain beliefs, the more they tend not to select media stories challenging those views (see Chapter 5).[41]

The rapidly expanding range of media access and, especially, electronic options promises to increase user selectivity. The mass audiences that emerged in the twentieth century may well be replaced by smaller, more homogeneous audiences in the future. Society could fragment into specialized groups that pay attention only to specific areas of interest.[42] The growth of talk radio programs and short-wave programs with ideological hosts and loyal listeners provides political activists with an echo chamber that amplifies

Box 6–6 Different Strokes for Different Folks

The news stories to which Americans pay attention involve a combination of what is happening in the world, what is reported, and what people are interested in. National poll results indicate that domestic events are generally followed more closely than are foreign ones, that men follow the news more closely than women do, and that attention to the news generally increases with age and education. As the following graphs indicate, demographic characteristics are often related to one's attention to the news, especially when the stories are perceived as having a personal impact (see figures).

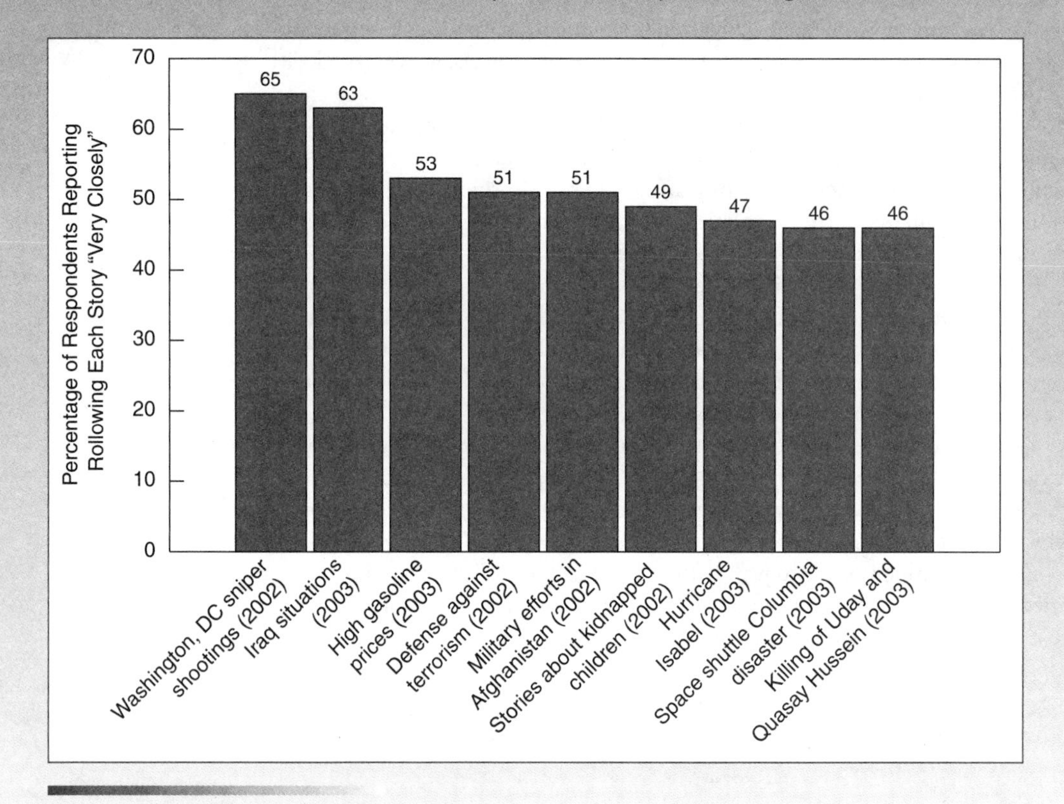

Top News Stories of 2002–2003

Source: Pew Research Center, http://people-press.org/nii/.

their own views. Similarly, computer bulletin boards, email discussion groups, and chat rooms often draw together individuals with comparable outlooks who share and reinforce their biases. Increasingly, media use is more important for reinforcing attitudes than for changing them.[43]

Selective Perception

selective perception *The way in which an individual interprets and categorizes the content of new information.*

Individuals who view or read the same information emerge from the experience with different lessons. Through **selective perception,** people attempt to categorize new information into familiar categories and to relate it to current attitudes.[44] Two people seeing a story about the resignation of a public official accused of fraud might perceive the facts in different ways. An individual with a cynical attitude toward government would file it away as "another example of untrustworthy politicians." An individual with a deep sense of empathy might think, "What a blow to his family."

The public differentiates among the various media. Television, with the power of visual evidence, confident anchorpersons, and a format that emphasizes stories with firm

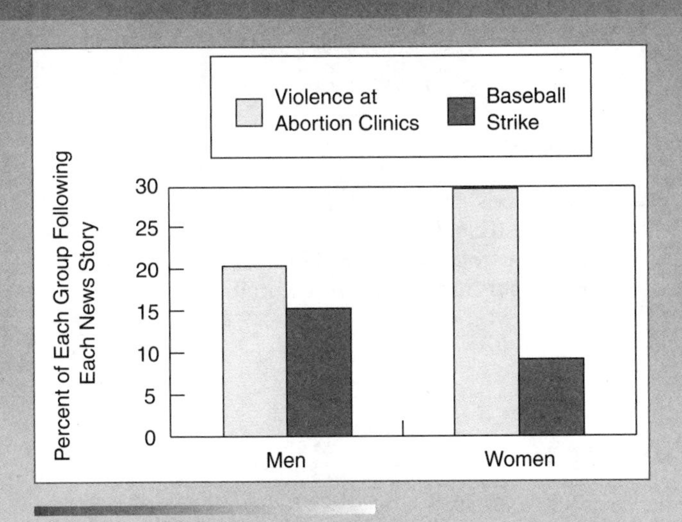

Violence at Abortion Clinics vs. Baseball Strike

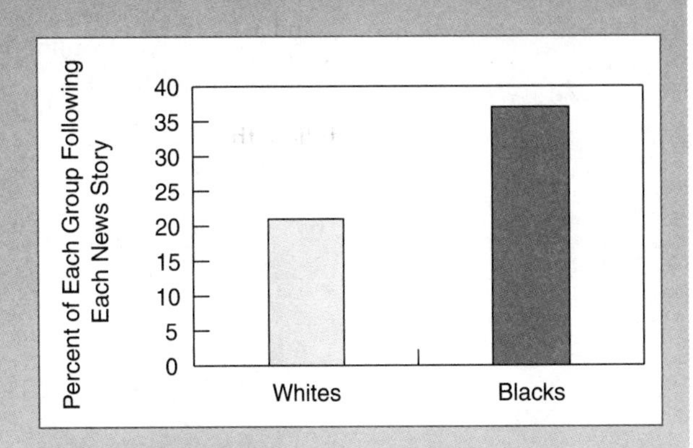

O. J. Simpson Trial

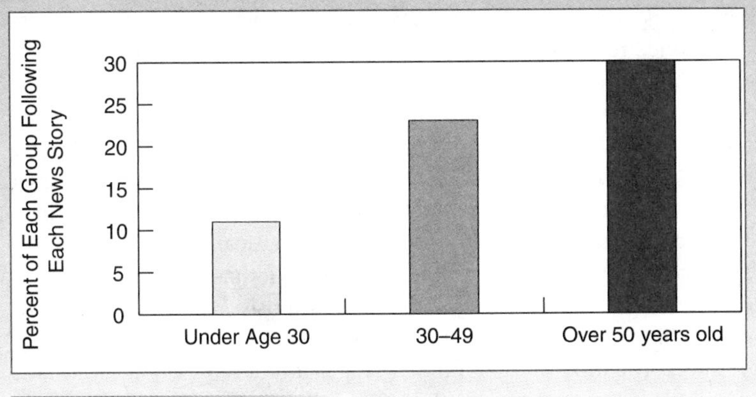

Condition of the U.S. Economy

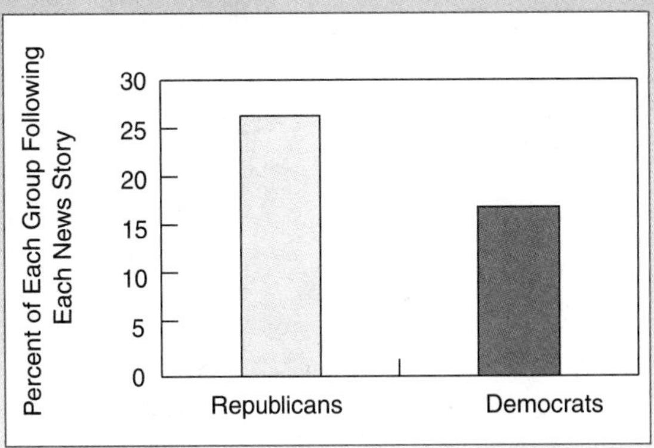

Activities of the New Republican Leaders

conclusions, is perceived as uniquely authoritative and objective (see Time Out 6-3: Time Spent Viewing Television, and Figure 6-12).[45] Print sources are regarded as being less objective although they constitute a source of more in-depth coverage. Contemporary mass media have nationalized politics and have made political information more accessible to the American public. Even so, the patterns of selectivity mean variation in the messages that individuals absorb.

6-5 Winners and Losers in the Media Game

The mass media contribute to the political agenda in several ways. Rather than changing our attitudes toward events, they suggest what we should think about. The information selected by the media forms the raw material from which citizens and politicians alike weave their cases. The media often spotlight the problems to which political bodies should pay attention. Political activists who seek to include their favorite issues on the political agenda urge the media to communicate information favorable to their cause.

Time Out 6-3

Time Spent Viewing Television

Take a moment to answer the following poll.

1. **Have you done any of the following?**
   - **Read the daily newspaper yesterday**
     Yes No
   - **Watched any nightly network television news program yesterday**
     Yes No
   - **Went online for news yesterday**
     Yes No
2. **How many hours did you watch television yesterday?**
   Less than 1 1-3 3-6 more than 6
3. **Some people like to switch channels frequently with their remote control as they watch television. Does this describe the way you watch?**
   Yes No

6-5a Who Gets Coverage?

Insufficient media coverage may doom a candidate or a political cause. In most cases even negative coverage is better than being ignored. Contemporary media practices benefit some causes while crippling others.

Individuals once knew more about local public affairs than about events associated with the remote national government. Today, however, the nationalizing effect of network television, wire service reporting, and chain ownership of print media emphasizes national politics almost to the exclusion of local politics.[46] Local politicians take their cues about important issues as well as possible solutions to them from national news programs.[47] Non-national network stories tend to focus on the East Coast, where the largest audiences and concentrations of media producers are. Even international events have become a part of our daily experiences. For example, the Vietnam War and the conflicts and revolts in Eastern Europe and Africa were played out dramatically on our home television screens. Visuals of Chechen citizens in the streets and victims of the civil wars in Bosnia and Rwanda drive home the agony of real people in crisis. Such images lead to public demands for U.S. involvement to ease the suffering.

Media coverage affects the international image of nations and causes. The aftermath of the War in Iraq included images that tarnished the efforts of both the U.S. and its adversaries. Pictures of prisoner abuse undermined the image of the United States as a protector of freedom and promoter of human rights. Gruesome footage of the beheading of U.S. and foreign nationals painted U.S opponents as barbarians.

Media coverage grants individuals and organizations access to the public mind. The ease of covering an individual president rather than the institution, Congress, accounts for some of Congress's decrease in visibility in relation to the executive branch (see Chapter 14). Increased public awareness of the House of Representatives and its leaders after television coverage in its chambers began was one of the primary reasons why the U.S. Senate allowed cameras to cover its proceedings. The expansion of media sources sped up the decline of political parties by allowing candidate-centered campaigns (Chapters 7 and 8). It also hastened the mobilization of the public into interest groups (Chapter 7).

As we have seen, television favors causes and campaigns with a clearly identified leader and a visual component. Candidates who do not perform well on television begin their campaigns at a disadvantage. Complex issues, such as the failures of savings and loan institutions, show up less often in the televised media than do visually dramatic natural disasters or political causes with photogenic leaders. The focus of television on immediacy and personality emphasizes emotional issues rather than issues based on logic, facts, and reason.[48] Television favors stories with good guys, bad guys, and clear victories or defeats. Election campaign stories are a perfect example. Rather than focus on issues and on candidate qualifications, most stories emphasize the game aspects of politics—who is ahead, who is behind, and who is gaining on the field.

Two important characteristics of contemporary television are the speed and pervasiveness of coverage. As one political strategist put it, "People get indicted on the *Today* show, tried on CNN, and sentenced on *Nightline*."[49] With the advent of continuous real-time news programming such as CNN, and the willingness to break into regular news programs to cover emerging stories, there is less time for the media to reflect on the legitimacy or the proper way to cover particular stories. The decision by most networks to spend a number of hours covering the slow-speed chase of O. J. Simpson as it happened is just one example of this new media immediacy and timeliness.

6-5b Biased Coverage

Although charges of consistent bias fill pages of commentary both within the press and among media critics (academic analysts and media watch groups), convincing evidence of such bias is difficult to come by. Research indicates bias against both liberals and conservatives, but whether this bias was intentional remains difficult to prove.[50]

Intentional bias fades in comparison to **structural bias.** Patterns of newsroom staffing, news gathering, and reporting may lead unintentionally to unfair coverage. Economic considerations and personal outlooks may undermine objective decisions based on newsworthiness. Nonmainstream issues and powerless individuals get relatively little attention. Journalists view them as having little interest for their audience and as unlikely to increase their revenues. Commercial competition and pack journalism result in the tendency for all the media to sound alike for fear of being viewed as out of step.

structural bias *Potential distortion that is built into the news gathering and reporting process but that is not intended by the journalists or editors.*

With their large audiences, the national media attempt to generalize all stories to increase audience appeal. They leave the impression that what they are reporting may be happening in one particular locality but that similar events have happened, or will happen, in anyone's town or neighborhood. The national emphasis of the news media emerges from economic realities, not from an attempt to diminish the importance of state and local government. While economic necessities and perceptions of who is newsworthy push the media to focus attention on incumbent power holders, the nature of their attention is often not neutral. Most journalists view newsmakers with considerable cynicism, looking for foibles and failures more than for achievements and accomplishments.[51]

Local media labor under a different set of structural biases. They have a mutually rewarding relationship with the politicians they cover, often needing them as sources as much as the politicians need the media for exposure. Under such conditions, the local media tend to be less harsh on their local politicians. They tend to hold state and national politicians and political institutions as a whole to a higher standard.

From a broader perspective, because they too are products of this society, members of the media reflect considerable **ethnocentrism.** They often fail to force us to recognize the basic inadequacies in our society.[52] Most news stories are written from the American perspective, often simply applying American standards and definitions of national interest to other countries.

ethnocentrism *The emphasis on and unthinking support for the values and institutions of one's own society to the exclusion of the contributions of other societies.*

6-6 The Media and Democracy

Modern large-scale democracies require effective and aggressive media that support democratic procedures and legitimize current regimes. Within the benefits of contemporary media lie a number of potential dangers. The sheer volume and variety of contemporary media coverage of politics overwhelm some individuals and may be one source of apathy.[53] Television coverage is criticized extensively for its superficiality, stereotypes, and lack of coherent explanations, which limit its contributions to democratic debate.[54] But many citizens have little interest in the details of politics and complain little about the nature of coverage. While television makes it easy and pleasant to monitor politics, it also disengages people from the political game. It turns politics into

Answer to Time Out 6-3

If you have done all of the activities mentioned in Time Out 6-3, you expose yourself to considerably more media than the average American, as the following data indicate:

Percentage of U.S. adults (over age 18) in 2002 who

Read the daily newspaper yesterday:	41%
Watched any TV news program yesterday:	32%
Went online for news yesterday:	25%

If you watched fewer than 4 hours of television yesterday, you fall below the national average. According to a recent Gallup Poll, the average American watches 4.1 hours of television per day during the week and 3.5 hours on the weekend.

The figures for media usage have dropped considerably in the last two decades, especially for reading newspapers. Individuals under age 35 are both less likely to read newspapers and less likely to watch television news, and members of this age group have shown the greatest decline in these areas since the 1960s.

There is also a considerable difference in the way different groups watch television. As Figure 6-13 indicates, younger viewers and men of all ages are more likely to be "channel surfers," skipping commercials and viewing only segments of programs. As the Jerry Seinfeld joke goes, "Women nest and men hunt."[a]

a. Quoted in "The Battle (Zap! Click!) of the Sexes," *New York Times*, July 7, 1991, d1.

Source: Pew Research Center for the People and the Press. June 9, 2002 survey of adults, "Public's New Habits Little Changed by September 11, http://people-press.org.

Figure 6-12
Total Hours Viewed Per Day, 2003

Source: Nielsen ratings data reported at www.tvb.org.

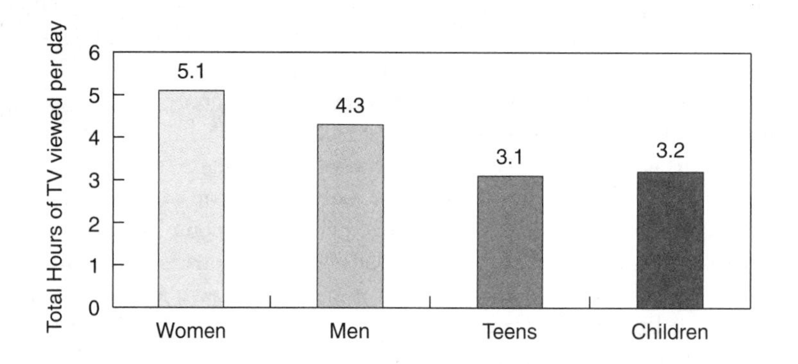

Figure 6-13
Channel Surfing by Demographic Groups

Source: National poll results reported in "The Role of Technology in American Life," *Times Mirror Center for the People and the Press*, May 1994, 1.

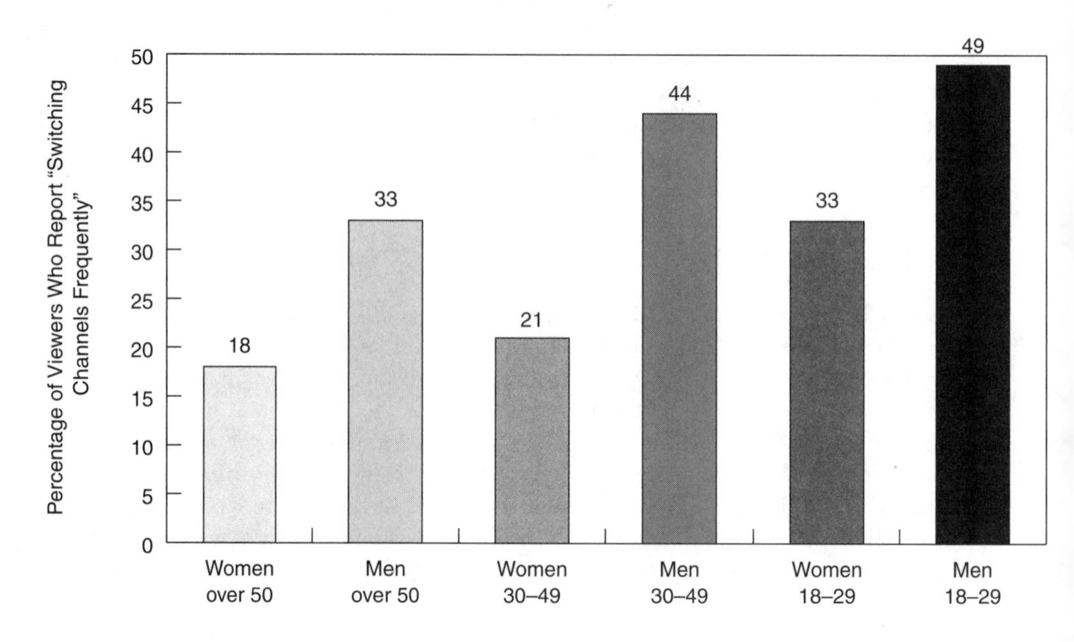

an isolated and entertaining spectator sport that requires no citizen commitment, preparation, or skill.[55] Newscaster Paul Harvey drove this point home with the story about the little boy who, when told that the Persian Gulf War was over, asked, "Will there be reruns of the war on this summer?"[56] (see Box 6-7: Viewing the Plays in the Nintendo War).

With its commitment to objectivity and its diverse audience, television injects conflict into people's political outlooks by showing different sides of political arguments.[57] Within limits, such conflict vitalizes the political contest and gives players goals. Constant turmoil, however, can undermine both individual and societal stability. The power of the contemporary media to inform and to activate is a two-edged sword capable of both supporting and undermining democracy.

Box 6–7 *Viewing the Plays in the Nintendo War*

During the Gulf War one editorialist noted:

> The war in the Gulf is being portrayed, perceived, underestimated and/or disparaged as a kind of electronic board game. (*Washington Post* editorial[a])

> I realize the desire to score this [war] like a football game and report the score this period. (Pete Williams, Assistant Secretary of Defense for Public Affairs[b])

The combination of sophisticated military technology and the use of satellite and graphics technologies by the news media changed the nature of war reporting during the war in the Persian Gulf. "Smart" bombs armed with television cameras gave instant pictures that confirmed U.S. military successes. Press spokespersons for the military and public affairs officers suppressed some information and put limits on what could be covered. Recognizing the power of the press, the military began giving its own battle "chalk talks," complete with maps and clips of the battle highlights, emphasizing the information it wanted reported. Military experts hired by the networks used light pens to describe the military "plays," in much the same way that sportscaster John Madden debriefed fans during National Football League games. Both the electronic and print media continually kept "score" of equipment destroyed and lives lost.

Some observers expressed discomfort that such coverage sanitized the war and made people forget that the lives of real people on both sides were at stake. Rather than encouraging serious consideration of the human and political stakes, media coverage of the war had the potential for lulling citizens into the view that war was "easy, riskless, [a] kind of child's play."[c] Congressman Joe Serrano (D-New York) reminded his fellow representatives:

> Let's not forget that we are destroying a culture here. Our sons should be made aware that this isn't a Nintendo game. When that electronic sight bears down and the flash confirms the detonation, there are children, mothers and fathers dying. Poor people, innocent people.[d]

Congressman Ron Dellums cautioned:

> We are looking at war as if it were a Nintendo game. We have not seen the stench, the pain, the bleeding, the dying, the broken bodies and spirits that are the reality of war.[e]

After the fighting stopped, the electronic media lost interest in the important—but visually less appealing—political results of the Persian Gulf War. The lack of good pictures resulted largely in the disappearance of the ongoing story of the Middle East from the evening news. Television journalists quickly turned their attention to the failed coup in the Soviet Union. Live pictures from the front of the Russian Parliament building with Russian president Boris Yeltsin facing down the approaching tanks made a better television story.

---

a. Editorial, "The Nintendo Issue," *Washington Post*, January 23, 1991, A16.

b. Quoted in Brent Baker, "Desert Storm: The Difficult Business of Fighting a TV War," *Trident*, February 15, 1991, 10.

c. Quoted in Brent Baker, "Desert Storm."

d. *Congressional Record*, February 5, 1991, E-478.

e. *Congressional Record*, February 6, 1991, H-953.

Conclusion

Entrenched American traditions along with continuing contemporary technological advances place the media in a position to affect the outcome of the political game. Although the media do not in the main pursue their own agendas, they are used strategically by various other players to improve their chances of winning. Far from being objective, external spectators of the game, however, the media have earned their characterization as the fourth branch of government. The media help to determine the players while playing the game themselves. They publicize the strategies of other players while employing their own set of strategies. As one of the freest institutions in the world, the American media pursue their mainly profit-making strategies. At the same time they force political activists and interested citizens alike to develop strategies for capitalizing on media power in order to set policy agendas and to transmit information. Technology continually changes the content, reach, timeliness, and impact of the media, which, in turn, changes the political playing field for players and spectators alike.

Key Terms

adversarial reporting
canon
cyberspace
equal time rule
ethnocentrism
fairness doctrine
format
fragmentation
Freedom of Information Act
government-in-sunshine laws
leak (news)
libel
local color
media
news hole
news hook
pack journalism
partisan
prior restraint
ratings
real-time politics
selective attention
selective exposure
selective perception
slander
sound bite
spin
structural bias
symbiotic
wire services

Practice Quiz

1. The media during the first century of America's existence consisted primarily of newspapers that were
 a. dominated by professionals.
 b. dominated by partisan presses.
 c. committed to objective reporting.
 d. based in Washington, D.C.

2. What led to the decline of the partisan press?
 a. The invention of television
 b. The decline of partisanship in the public
 c. The growth of commercial advertising
 d. The decrease in the use of wire services

3. What has happened to newspapers since World War II?
 a. The number of newspapers has increased.
 b. Newspapers have become more partisan.
 c. Newspapers have increased political endorsements.
 d. The number of competing newspapers has decreased.

4. What do "government-in-sunshine" laws require?
 a. That all government meetings be open
 b. That procedures be developed to determine which documents are classified
 c. That all judicial proceedings be open
 d. That government meetings be open except under unusual circumstances

5. The process by which individuals can emerge from the same experience with different understandings is selective
 a. attention.
 b. exposure.
 c. perception.
 d. retention.

6. The fact that the American news media is a commercial enterprise that must show a profit is an example of
 a. pack journalism.
 b. structural bias.
 c. intentional bias.
 d. cognitive dissonance.

7. In order to pursue a case of libel against someone the statements must have been all of the following except:
 a. spoken out loud.
 b. false.
 c. motivated by maliciousness.
 d. clearly harmful.

8. The average American adult watches over _____ hours of television per week.
 a. 3
 b. 7
 c. 14
 d. 20

9. National evening network news programs date back to
a. 1944.
b. 1952.
c. 1963.
d. 1972.

10. The more aggressive reporting style associated with Watergate and continuing to the present is called _____ journalism.
a. adversarial
b. pack
c. civic
d. yellow

You can find the correct answers to these questions by taking the quiz and then submitting your answers in the Online Edition. The program will automatically score your submission. Where you miss a question, the program will provide the correct answer, a rationale for the answer, and the section number in the chapter where the topic is discussed.

Further Reading

To get a better feel for the relationship between journalists and politicians, see Charles Press and Kenneth Verburg, *American Politicians and Journalists* (Glenview, IL: Scott, Foresman/Little, Brown, 1988); and W. Lance Bennett, *News: The Politics of Illusion* (New York: Longman, 1988). Jarol Manheim's *All of the People All of the Time: Strategic Communications and American Politics* (Armonk, NY: M. E. Sharpe, 1991) provides an excellent look at how politicians and government use media for their own purposes.

For a critical challenge encouraging journalists to do a better job of reporting public affairs, look at Lewis W. Wolfson's *The Untapped Power of the Press: Explaining Government to the People* (New York: Praeger, 1985). For a criticism from the left of the political spectrum, see Michael Parenti, *Inventing Reality: The Politics of the Mass Media* (New York: St. Martin's Press, 1986). Tom Patterson takes on the media for being too critical in *Out of Order* (New York: Alfred A. Knopf, 1993), while Larry Sabato sounds a similar theme in *Feeding Frenzy: How Attack Journalism Has Transformed American Politics* (New York: The Free Press, 1991).

Paul Weaver makes the most extreme argument that the news media have incentives to intentionally mislead the American public in *News and the Culture of Lying* (New York: The Free Press, 1994).

Doris Graber's *Mass Media and American Politics* (Washington, D.C.: Congressional Quarterly, Inc., 1997) and Dean Alger's *The Media and Politics* (Englewood Cliffs, NJ: Prentice-Hall, 1989) provide broad coverage of media strategies. Graber's *Processing the News: How People Tame the Information Tide* (New York: Longman, 1988) focuses on audience strategies for media use.

For a look at the new media, see Richard Davis's *The Web of Politics* (New York: Oxford University Press, 1999); Richard Davis and Diana Owen, *New Media and American Politics* (New York: Oxford, 1998); and Wayne Rash, Jr., *Politics on the Nets* (New York: W. H. Freeman, 1997).

Endnotes

1. Charles Press and Kenneth Verburg, *American Politicians and Journalists* (Glenview, IL: Scott, Foresman/Little, Brown, 1988), 30–36.
2. Daniel J. Boorstin, *The Americans: The Democratic Experience* (New York: Random House, 1973), 106.
3. Frederick Williams, *Communications Revolution* (Beverly Hills, CA: Sage, 1982), 28–33.
4. Sarah Booth Conroy, "Diplomacy: Is It Down the Tube?" *Washington Post*, March 10, 1991, F1.
5. Based on a December 1994 Times Mirror Center for the People and The Press national poll of 1,511 adults. Reported in *The New Political Landscape* press release.
6. Sara Rimer, "Terror in Oklahoma: On the Air and On the Net," *New York Times*, March 27, 1995, A22.
7. For information on the use of political sites, see www.pewinternet.org studies. In 2004, Republican John McCain was particularly successful with Internet fund raising, especially after his surprise win in the New Hampshire primary in 2000, and Howard Dean led the way in Internet creativity in 2004. See Ben White, "The Cyber Stump," *Washington Post*, May 17, 2000, G18.
8. Junko Fujita, "Two Boston Dailies Battle It Out," *Christian Science Monitor*, August 11, 1994, 14.
9. Harold W. Stanley and Richard G. Niemi, *Vital Statistics on American Politics* (Washington, D.C.: Congressional Quarterly, Inc., 2000), 193. 2000 data come from a survey of newspapers in *Editor and Publisher Magazine*, November 6, 2000, p. 24.
10. Stephen Pomper, "The Big Shake-Out Begins," *Newsweek*, July 2, 1990, 50.
11. Alvin Toffler, *The Third Wave* (New York: William Morrow, 1980), x.
12. Quoted in Lewis W. Wolfson, *The Untapped Power of the Press: Explaining Government to the People* (New York: Praeger, 1985), viii.
13. Douglas Cater, *The Fourth Branch of Government* (New York: Knopf, 1959).
14. Michael Parenti, *Inventing Reality: The Politics of the Mass Media* (New York: St. Martin's Press, 1986), ix.
15. U.S. Congress, Senate, *Congressional Record*, June 5, 1995, vol. 141, no. 90, S7683.
16. Press and Verburg, *American Politicians and Journalists*, 52.
17. See U.S. Congress, Office of Technology Assessment, *Informing the Nation: Federal Information Dissemination in an Electronic Age* (Washington, D.C.: U.S. Government Printing Office, October 1988).
18. Ann Hodges, "PBS Tries to Defuse List-Sharing Issue," *Houston Chronicle*, August 3, 1999, 4.
19. Press and Verburg, *American Politicians and Journalists*, 55.
20. Quoted in W. Lance Bennett, *News: The Politics of Illusion* (New York: Longman, 1988), 3.
21. Benjamin Ginsberg, *The Captive Public: How Mass Opinion Promotes State Power* (New York: Basic Books, 1986), 140.
22. See Press and Verburg, *American Politicians and Journalists*, 71–78.
23. Bennett, *News*, 95.

24. Bennett, *News*, 22–26.
25. Bill Moyers quoted by Tom Shales in "Petty or Teddy," *The Washington Post*, January 30, 1980, B11.
26. See Kathleen Hall Jamieson, *Eloquence in an Electronic Age* (New York: Oxford University Press, 1988), 248; and Neil Postman, "Critical Thinking in the Electronic Age," *Kettering Review* (Winter 1988): 40–48.
27. Anthony Smith, "Mass Communications," in *Democracy at the Polls*, eds. David Butler, Howard R. Penniman, and Austin Ranney (Washington, D.C.: American Enterprise Institute, 1981), 178.
28. See Shanto Iyengar and Donald Kinder, *News That Matters* (Chicago: The University of Chicago Press, 1988).
29. Bennett, *News*, 13.
30. Eleanor Clift on "The McLaughlin Group," December 4, 1993, LEXIS-NEXIS database.
31. For a journalist's statement of concern, see David Broder, "The Press Is on Shaky Ground," *Washington Post*, November 15, 1987, C7.
32. "Ethics and the 88 Race," *National Journal*, August 1, 1987.
33. See Dean E. Alger, *The Media and Politics* (Englewood Cliffs, NJ: Prentice-Hall, 1989), 45–56; and Murray Edelman, *The Symbolic Uses of Politics* (Urbana, IL: University of Illinois Press, 1967).
34. Jarol B. Manheim, *All of the People All of the Time: Strategic Communications and American Politics* (Armonk, NY: M. E. Sharpe, 1991), 5.
35. Press conference, Secretary of Defense Richard Cheney, January 17, 1991. LEXIS-NEXIS database, Federal News Service transcript.
36. Quoted in Max Frankel, "Beyond the Shroud," *New York Times Magazine*, March 19, 1995, 30.
37. Austin Ranney, *Channels of Power* (New York: Basic Books, 1983), 12. The term *inadvertent audience* comes from Michael Robinson, "Television and American Politics, 1956–1976," *The Public Interest*, Summer 1976, 3–39.
38. Ronald Berkman and Laura Kitch, *Politics in the Media Age* (New York: McGraw-Hill, 1986), 314.
39. Todd Gitlin, "New Video Technology: Pluralism or Banality," *Democracy*, October 1981, 70.
40. Doris Graber, *Processing the News: How People Tame the Information Tide* (New York: Longman, 1988), 249–50.
41. Graber, *Processing the News*, 258.
42. Christopher Arterton, *Teledemocracy: Can Technology Protect Democracy?* (Newbury Park, CA: Sage, 1987), 34.
43. Robert S. Lichter and Linda S. Lichter, "Does TV Shape Ethnic Images?" *Media and Values*, Spring 1988, 7.
44. Graber, *Processing the News*, 250.
45. Iyengar and Kinder, *News That Matters*, 15, 127.
46. Herbert Simon, "The Consequences of Computers for Centralization and Decentralization," in *The Computer Age*, eds. Michael Dertouzos and Joel Moses (Cambridge, MA: MIT Press, 1983), 223.
47. See Richard Hollander, *Video Democracy* (Mount Airy, MD: Lomond Press, 1985), 34; and Paul H. Weaver, "Newspaper News and Television News," in *Television as a Social Force*, eds. Douglas Cater and Richard Adler (New York: Praeger, 1975), 94.
48. Hedrick Smith, *The Power Game* (New York: Random House, 1988), 399.
49. Political strategist Tony Podesta quoted in Steven V. Roberts et al., "Why Are We So Angry?" *U.S. News and World Report*, November 7, 1994, 36.
50. Press and Verburg, *American Politicians and Journalists*, 92–94.
51. See Stephen Hess, *Washington Reporters* (Washington, D.C.: Brookings Institution, 1981).
52. See Herbert J. Gans, *Deciding What's News* (New York: Random House, 1980).
53. See Jeffrey Abramson, F. Christopher Arterton, and Gary R. Orren, *The Electronic Commonwealth: The Impact of Media Technologies on Democratic Politics* (New York: Basic Books, 1988), 109; and Ronald Berkman and Laura Kitch, *Politics in the Media Age* (New York: McGraw-Hill, 1986), 321.
54. Bennett, *News*, 9.
55. Albert Borgman, "Technology and Democracy," in *Technology and Politics*, eds. Michael Kraft and Norman Vig (Raleigh-Durham, NC: Duke University Press, 1988), 199.
56. "Paul Harvey News," March 1, 1991.
57. Ranney, *Channels of Power*, 187.

7

Interest Groups: Organizing the Players around Narrow Themes

Key Points

- **The role of interest groups in a pluralistic democracy.**
- **Why individuals organize.**
- **The paths from latent interest and categoric groups to potential groups and organized interest groups.**
- **Rules that hold back interest group development and action.**
- **Differences between public and private interest groups.**
- **Strategies used by interest groups.**

Preview: Getting MADD or Getting Even

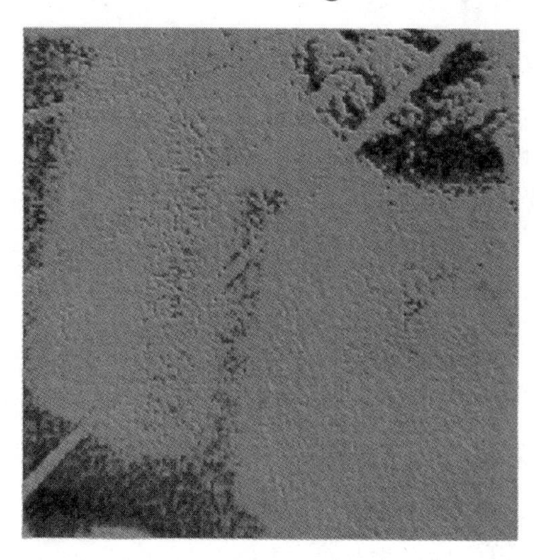

A poised and confident middle-aged woman faced the bank of TV cameras as the spokesperson for the American Beverage Institute, an organization of restaurant, hotel, and liquor industry executives opposed to new measures limiting drinking and driving. She had become accustomed to the cameras and the shouted questions after years of sessions such as this. Now she vigorously pressed the point that new initiatives to reduce the standard for declaring an individual legally drunk went too far and limited the rights of American citizens.[1] Groups such as Mothers Against Drunk Drivers (MADD) had shifted to an anti-alcohol agenda and were pushing for what she called "de facto prohibition." She asserted that being vengeful toward moderate social drinkers had little to do with solving the drunk driving problem.

The scene might have been passed off by the media and the public as just another interest group representative doing her job. There is, however, more to the story. A decade earlier this same woman, Candy Lightner, was grieving the death of her daughter at the hands of a drunk driver. She took action to galvanize the families of other victims to do something. Sitting at her kitchen table, she scanned obituaries and news articles for the ominous words "killed by a drunk driver." She wrote letters to the families inviting them to capitalize on the benefits of democracy and join together to stop this national tragedy. Thousands of individuals emerged from their private grief as victims and became participants in the political process. Mothers Against Drunk Drivers moved with moral force and organizational skill to secure tougher drunk driving laws and to increase the drinking age.

Over the years, however, Candy Lightner, no longer able to control her creation, disassociated herself from it. Organized political effort generally wins out over individual activity. And so her press conference, opposing the organization she had founded, was more of an odd footnote to history than a reversal of political fortunes. MADD continues to prosper politically without her.

Former Senate majority leader Robert Dole (R-Kan.) once said: "This is the game. This is a political game. You can hear the thunder or the roar out in the hall, after the score, after the touchdown, after the victory."[2] Policy making is not simply an insider's game among elected and appointed officials played without an active audience. Interested individuals, who carefully watch and react to the actions of such officials, often join together to influence the kinds of policy decisions that are made. **Interest groups** are mediating institutions that monitor politics, raise questions for the political agenda, outline acceptable alternatives on behalf of their members, and fight for their preferred proposals.

interest group *Individuals who are aware of the interests they share with others and who have expended the resources necessary to create an organization that attempts to influence government policy. See also* **categoric group** *and* **potential group.**

Indeed, while there are hundreds of thousands of organized groups in the United States, a group is not considered a political interest group unless it attempts to influence the policies enacted by government. Political parties (discussed in detail in Chapter 8) must deal with a wide range of policy issues, but they emphasize getting their members elected. Interest groups, on the other hand, generally represent narrower interests and are more concerned with affecting policy than with controlling who is elected.

This chapter will outline the rules under which interest groups operate in the United States and assess the motivations of players in the interest group process. We will then turn to the strategies these groups use to affect policy and to an assessment of who wins and who loses in this endeavor.

7-1 The Spectrum of Interest Groups

American interest groups come in many sizes and represent various levels of organization. Long-standing groups, such as the Chamber of Commerce of the United States, the National Rifle Association (NRA), and the Teamsters Union, have dues-paying members, employ large professional staffs, perform a number of nonpolitical activities, and consistently intervene in the selection of policy makers and in the policy process. Other groups spring up more informally around a contemporary issue, represent relatively fewer people, struggle along with a small number of volunteer leaders, and fade away after the issue becomes irrelevant. Most interest groups fall somewhere between these two extremes. They are generally sorted out by the primary motivation of their members.

7-1a Private Interest Groups

There are two main types of private interest groups—those who are tied together primarily by financial interests and those with noneconomic ties.

Economic Groups

Economic groups look out for the financial interests of a people in a particular occupation or profession, for example:

- Business/Professional/Trade Associations (e.g., Tobacco Institute, National Education Association (NEA), American Medical Association (AMA)
- Unions (e.g., Teamsters, American Federation of Labor-Congress of Industrial Organizations (AFL-CIO)
- Aggregates (looking out for the economic interests of an entire industry or a collection of businesses; e.g., Chamber of Commerce, National Association of Manufacturers)

Noneconomic Groups

Noneconomic groups strive for the betterment of one segment of society or promote a particular cause, for example:

- Cause groups [promoting their preferences of what a "good" society would look like; e.g., National Rifle Association (NRA), American Civil Liberties Union (ACLU)]
- Status groups [promoting benefits for individuals with a particular status in society; e.g., National Organization for Women (NOW), National Association for the Advancement of Colored People (NAACP)]
- Victim groups [friends, relatives, or actual casualties of unfortunate events; e.g., Mothers Against Drunk Driving (MADD), American Cancer Society]
- Public interest groups [promoting purportedly societywide benefits; e.g., Common Cause, Public Citizen, Sierra Club, Consumer Federation of America]

private interest group *A group looking out for the interests of one segment of society.*

Private interest groups recognize that the public goals they wish to pursue either affect only a certain segment of the population or are not shared by everyone. They view the political game as a competitive process in which they hope to win benefits for their supporters. The causes they promote include such things as increased wages, changed government regulations, and increased government expenditures that benefit a specific group. Private interest groups recognize that being viewed as "selfish" may work against their cause, so they often publicly frame their goals in terms of doing what is right or of benefiting the larger society. For example, the Tobacco Institute and the National Rifle Association promote smokers' and gun owners' rights not only as benefits to smokers and gun owners but as a way to protect the American tradition of individual freedom.

7-1b Public Interest Groups

public interest group *A group advocating the broader interests of society as opposed to the narrower economic interests promoted by most business and professional interest groups.*

Groups that describe themselves as **public interest groups** attempt to establish their legitimacy by arguing that they facilitate the acquisition of collective benefits that will be universally held. Groups such as Common Cause, Ralph Nader's Public Citizen, and the Sierra Club attempt to organize individuals around largely noneconomic issues, such as citizenship rights, product safety, and the environment. These groups are characterized by low membership fees and large memberships. They argue that they represent the broader interests of society, interests that do not specifically benefit their membership only.[3]

The positions taken by public interest groups are not always more legitimate or more broadly held than the positions taken by the so-called private interest groups with whom they compete over public policy. Neither private nor public interest groups include more than a very small proportion of individuals either interested in or affected by particular sets of policies. The existence of a universally held public interest gets called into question when conflicts arise. Supporting the environment sounds good, for example, until it prevents a new highway from being built because it would disturb the nesting area of an endangered species, at which time certain members of the public fall on one side of the issue, at odds with other members of the public, depending on how the highway will affect them personally.

Part of the problem of sorting out and discussing interest groups stems from the difficulty of defining exactly what an interest group is. Some organizations, such as the NRA, MADD, and the American Association of Retired Persons (AARP), clearly fit the definition of a political interest group. Their primary purpose lies in influencing public policy. Other groups, such as labor unions (including, e.g., the NEA) and professional associations (e.g., the AMA and the Chamber of Commerce of the United States), serve other important purposes as well. They negotiate contracts and educate their members. They also attempt to influence governmental officials and decisions. Still other entities, such as national religious organizations (e.g., the National Council of Churches or the American Jewish Congress) and service clubs (e.g., Rotary Clubs or the American Association of University Women), serve largely nonpolitical purposes. At times, however, they use some of their resources to influence policies of direct relevance to their membership. In 2001, there was considerable discussion about the Salvation Army's decision to step out of its traditional role as a religious denomination and welfare agency to lobby heavily in support of portions of President George W. Bush's faith-based initiative proposal concerning the right of organizations receiving federal funds to disqualify gays for employment in their programs. AARP, the largest organization in the United States, has a great deal of political clout, leading opponents to challenge its nonprofit status based on its numerous commercial services such as financial, insurance, and travel programs. Such questioning has tarnished the image of AARP but will probably not limit their political activity. Powerful groups whose primary purpose is not lobbying often do not register as political players and are not treated as interest groups.

Individuals join interest groups for many reasons, from deep concern for the policies that a group promotes to the social and material benefits that membership provides. Members interested in policy changes recognize that in unity there is strength (see Time Out 7-1: Creating an Interest Group). Interest group leaders often speak both for their formal members and for a wider group of individuals with similar outlooks whom they claim to represent. Interest groups often provide useful information to decision makers, as noted in a pamphlet from the Kettering Foundation:

> Policymakers have an easier time dealing with the clear, concise, and forceful views put forth by organized groups . . . Many citizens feel that these groups have a louder and stronger voice in the policy process than the general public.[4]

Time Out 7-1

Creating an Interest Group

Assume you want to create an interest group around one of the issues that divides the American public. You have data from public opinion polls where respondents took positions on the following issues:

1. **Federal spending on tightening border security to prevent illegal immigration should be increased.**
2. **The government should make it more difficult for people to buy a gun.**
3. **Companies that have a history of discriminating against blacks when making hiring decisions should have an affirmative action program.**

Assume you have no personal preference and simply want your group to take the most popular position on these issues. Which position would you choose to retain the highest level of support from the public on each issue? (See Figures 7-1 and 7-2.)

1. **Federal spending on tightening border security to prevent illegal immigration should be increased.**

   AGREE .....
   DISAGREE .....

2. **The government should make it more difficult for people to buy a gun.**

   AGREE .....
   DISAGREE .....

3. Companies that have a history of discriminating against African Americans when making hiring decisions should have an affirmative action program.

AGREE .....
DISAGREE .....

How would your group have fared?

Although the public is divided, support of gun control will retain 55% of the voters.

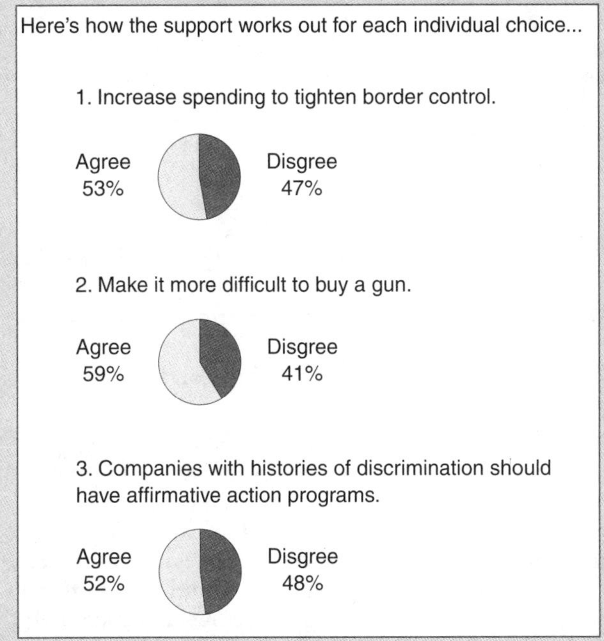

Here's how the support works out for each individual choice...

1. Increase spending to tighten border control.

Agree 53% Disgree 47%

2. Make it more difficult to buy a gun.

Agree 59%

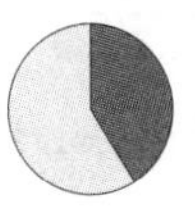

Disgree 41%

3. Companies with histories of discrimination should have affirmative action programs.

Agree 52%

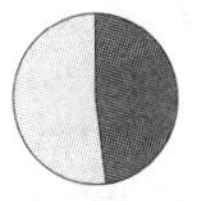

Disgree 48%

Figure 7-1
Interest Group Development

(All the data presented are based on national polls of adults carried out as part of the 2000 National Election Study, Survey Research Center, University of Michigan)

It is one thing to create an interest group around one issue, but it is much more difficult to find a set of issues on which a wide variety of Americans take the same position. Assume your group has already decided to back government policies to make it more difficult to buy a gun and you now want to take on a second issue.

Some of your members suggest affirmative action. In order to retain as much of the public as possible after taking a stand on two issues, which position would you have your organization take on affirmative action?

Choice 1
Requiring companies that have a history of discriminating against African Americans when making hiring decisions to have an affirmative action program.

Choice 2
Not requiring companies that have a history of discriminating against blacks when making hiring decisions to have an affirmative action program.

7-2 Rules of Interest Group Activity

Interest groups are not totally free to pursue their interests. From the founding of the Republic to the present day, policy makers have attempted to control interest group excesses while sustaining their important place in a democracy. Unlike political parties, interest groups continue to be viewed as private and voluntary groups rather than as quasi-public utilities (see Chapter 8). The American commitment to limit governmental intrusion into private affairs dampens the willingness to interfere in private group endeavors.

Answer to Time Out 7-1

Choice 1 for the second issue is the best you can do. An organization supporting stricter gun laws *and* affirmative action in businesses that discriminate would retain 39% of the public.

With Choice 2 for the second issue, you could do better. Only 23% of the public supports stricter gun laws *and* does not support affirmative action in businesses that discriminate. You would have retained 39% of the public by supporting affirmative action.

Figure 7-2A
Interest Group Positions Further Refined

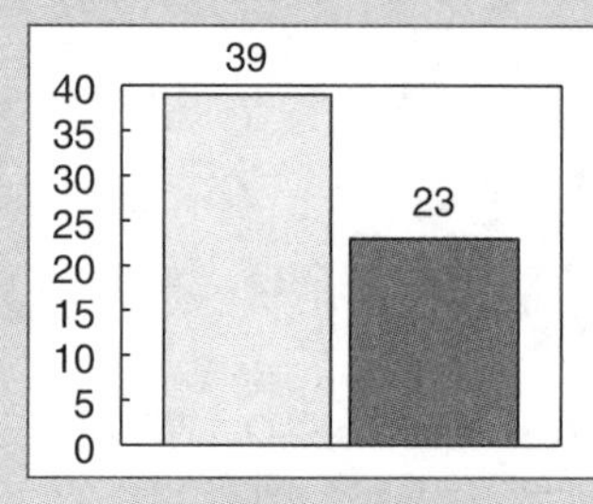

An organization supporting stricter gun laws *and* affirmative action in businesses that discriminate would retain 39% of the public, and only 23% of the public supports stricter gun laws and do not support affirmative action in businesses that discriminate.

Now let us add in a third issue, illegal immigration. Which of the following positions should your organization support?

1. Increase federal spending to tighten border security and prevent illegal immigration.
2. Do not increase federal spending to tighten border security and prevent illegal immigration.

If you said Choice 1 for the third issue, you've chosen the best you can do; 19% of the public supports the positions you have taken on the three issues. This shows how difficult it is to create an interest group that takes stands on a variety of issues, even if the majority of the population supports each individual stand you took. Single-issue groups that establish a "litmus test" position on one issue are much easier to design, since position-taking on a variety of issues inevitably will offend some of the group's original supporters. Remember, even if members of the public support your positions, there is no guarantee they will join your organization.

If your selection was Choice 2 for the third issue, it does not seem at first like you made a good choice. Only 13% of the public supports the positions you have taken on the three issues. Do not feel too badly. Even if you had chosen to increase federal spending on border security and maintained your other issue positions, you would have retained only 19% of the public's support.

Figure 7-2B
Interest Group Positions Further Refined

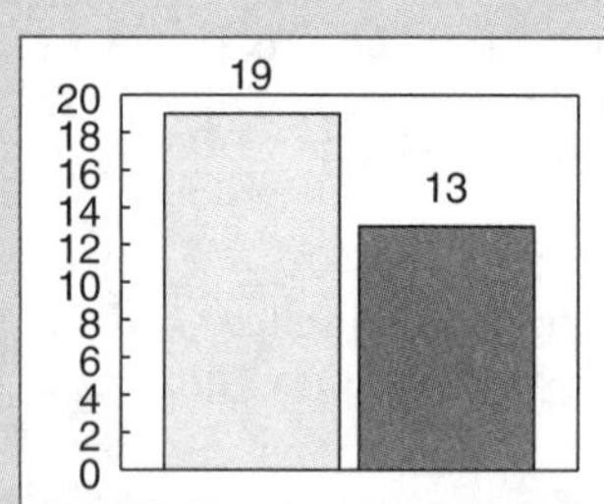

When you add in the third issue, you lose even more people. 19% of the public supports the positions you have taken on the three issues if you chose to increase spending for border security here, and 13% of the public supports the positions you have taken if you chose not to increase spending for border security.

This shows how difficult it is to create an interest group which takes stands on a variety of issues, even if the majority of the population supports each individual stand you took. Single-issue groups that establish a "litmus test" position on one issue are much easier to design, since position-taking on a variety of issues inevitably will offend some of the group's original supporters. Remember, even if members of the public support your positions, there is no guarantee they will join your organization.

7-2a Freedom of Association versus the "Mischief of Faction"

The Founders recognized that democracy was impossible unless citizens with legitimate interests had the right to associate freely and to "petition the Government for a redress of grievances" (from the 1st Amendment). Individuals and associations petition government every time they communicate their interests to an elected or appointed official. Free speech enables citizens to recognize the issues on which they have a common interest, and freedom to assemble allows them to identify the individuals with whom they share that interest. As you read in Chapter 6, like-minded individuals have found new ways by which to communicate. The right to petition provides a means by which they can attempt to put their preferences into action.

This process of joining together around common interests results in the development of competing groups. It was clear even during the earliest period of the Republic that religious, ethnic, economic, geographical, and philosophical interests would divide U.S. citizens. A great number of competing viewpoints on the proper role and policies of government was the certain result.

The Founders were practical politicians who recognized that narrow interests could influence policy makers to do their bidding at the expense of other less organized or less powerful individuals. In *Federalist* No. 10, James Madison eloquently warned against "the mischiefs of **faction,**" a term he used to represent any group—minority or majority—that was organized to influence government in ways "adverse to the rights of other citizens, or to the permanent and aggregate interests of the community." Modern political parties and interest groups both fit Madison's definition of a faction to the degree that their actions are unfavorable to the rights of others or to the national interest (see Box 7-1: Allowing Mischievous Factions" into the Game).

faction *A subgroup within a larger organization or society.*

The Founders did not tamper with the freedom of factions to organize. Rather, they attempted to control them by (1) having many points of **access,** and (2) creating political entities geographically large enough to include a number of competing interests. While the word *faction* is not used much any more, Madison's concerns—and the structure of government that resulted—set the stage for the role of contemporary interest groups. Interest groups must compete on a playing field that both respects the rights of those groups and recognizes their potential dangers. The Founders' fears about interest groups grew from their intimate experiences as group promoters. The Sons of Liberty, which fostered the American Revolution, was an early example of a well-organized interest group. Contemporary citizen militia groups see themselves as following in the footsteps of these patriots. Their fervent

access *The ability to get the attention of policy makers to present one's position.*

Box 7-1 *Allowing "Mischievous Factions" into the Game*

The essays gathered as *The Federalist* were designed to sell the new Constitution to the public by pointing out its advantages and outlining the dangers it would help to avoid. These essays are a comprehensive statement of the political philosophy of the Founders. In *Federalist* No. 10, James Madison wrote:

> Measures are too often decided, not according to the rules of justice and the rights of the minor party, but by the superior force of an interested and overbearing majority.
>
> There are two methods of curing the mischief of faction: the one, by removing its causes; the other, by controlling its effects. There are again two methods of removing the causes of faction: the one, by destroying the liberty that is essential to its existence; the other, by giving to every citizen the same opinions...The first remedy...is worse than the disease...The second expedient is as impracticable, as the first would be unwise.
>
> The *causes* of faction cannot be removed; and...relief is only to be sought in the means of controlling its *effects*.
>
> If a faction consists of less than a majority, relief is supplied by the republican principle, which enables the majority to defeat its sinister views by regular vote...When a majority is included in a faction, the form of popular government, on the other hand, enables it to sacrifice to its ruling passion or interest both the public good and the rights of other citizens.

Madison went on to point out that a republican form of government, like the one being proposed, allowed elected representatives to "refine and enlarge" the narrow views of citizens. He also asserted that the larger the number of citizens being governed, the less individual factions should be feared, since there would be so many competing groupings.

antigovernment rhetoric and their desire to bring the government down—as opposed to trying to influence it—separate the militias from most other interest groups.

While interests groups have long been part of U.S. politics, the real expansion did not begin until the 1960s. A look through the Washington, D.C., telephone book, or at the interest groups registered with the U.S. Congress, gives the impression that just about every possible interest has a Washington office, a staff of professional **lobbyists,** and an interested and active membership. It is not too difficult to determine what organizations such as the American Blind Lawyers Association, the National Turkey Federation, and the Wall and Ceiling Foundation Institute promote. The goals of organizations such as the United National Association of the USA and Public Citizen are not quite as clear from their names alone. More than six thousand national groups and the more than twenty-three thousand individual lobbyists register their intentions to lobby Congress annually. They only scratch the surface of the large number of interests that might draw individuals together. More than twenty-two thousand national nonprofit organizations show up in the *Encyclopedia of Associations*, and more than two hundred thousand different organizations are thought to be involved at the state and local levels.[5] An estimated eighty thousand full-time representatives of special interest groups work in Washington, D.C.[6] The fact that a group is listed or registered says little about the group's degree of formal structure or its available finances.

lobbyists *Individuals, often paid by an interest group, who communicate group interests to government officials. The term originates from the practice of waiting in the "lobby" of legislative chambers to attempt to persuade legislators before a vote.*

7-2b Rules Controlling Contemporary Interest Groups

The multiple levels of government in the federal system, along with the separation of powers doctrine that divides power among a number of institutions, limit the influence of interest groups. Interest groups are forced to deal with many power holders in a variety of arenas. Yet, as we have noted, the Constitution guarantees the right of interest groups to organize. In fact, American political theory and practice have made a virtue of the extensive competition among interest groups, an approach called pluralism (see Chapter 1). The recognition that interest groups provide a useful way for individual citizens to participate in the democratic process has created a political atmosphere in which groups have been allowed to organize with minimal control. In some cases, they receive active governmental support.

Does it seem not believable, and contrary to James Madison's antidemocratic warnings about factions, that the government would support organizations designed to influence its activities? Consider the following: the American Farm Bureau Federation, one of the most powerful agricultural interest groups, can thank the national government for its existence. Earlier in the century, the Department of Agriculture wished to create a group of well-informed farmers who would speak for agricultural—and presumably the Department of Agriculture's—interests.[7] The Department of Agriculture sent out county agents to educate farmers about new farming techniques and to organize them. Local farm bureaus soon began to see that putting their interests into words by writing letters and signing petitions allowed them to make demands on government and could give them a political advantage.

Such groups as the National Alliance of Business, the National Urban Coalition, and Planned Parenthood receive a significant portion of their budget from federal government sources.[8] Other organizations, such as the National Governors' Association and the U.S. Conference of Mayors, receive direct federal funding as well as indirect funding from the membership fees paid by governmental units. The government has also created thousands of advisory commissions and committees that meet with government employees to make suggestions on public policy. As described in Chapter 16, this gives some interest groups direct impact on the decision-making process.

Governmental rules dealing with interest groups focus on limiting the strategies that groups may use when gathering resources and participating in the political process. For example, union or professional group members cannot be forced to contribute campaign funds as a requirement for membership. Also, campaign-financing laws limit how much an individual can give. Other laws specifically restrict the amount that an interest group as a whole can give to a candidate and when it can be given. Tax laws allow groups to divide their activities into nontaxable charitable and educational efforts or into taxable commercial and strictly political endeavors. An individual can give a tax-deductible donation only to those charitable and educational organizations having a "501(c)(3) status" (referring to the specific rule in the Internal Revenue Code). Such legally exempted charitable and educational organizations also do not have to pay taxes themselves.

To a large degree, U.S. laws dealing with interest groups emphasize **disclosure** rather than control. Groups whose primary purpose is to affect public policy are required to register with the government and to report how they raise and spend certain types of funds. The assumption is that a watchful public and competing interests will enforce legal and proper behavior. **Bribery** is against the law. But definitions of bribery do not include general campaign contributions unless the participants are foolish enough to make an exchange of money for a specific vote.

disclosure laws *Legislation requiring groups or individuals to publicly report various aspects of their behavior, with the expectation that the fear of public embarrassment will stop illegal or undesirable actions.*

bribery *The direct exchange of items of value for a public official's vote or support.*

The protection of free speech, free association, and the right to petition government must be balanced with the fears of special interest politics. Overly strong interest groups can lead to the domination of one group and/or to policies that do not contribute to the national interest. This balancing act makes it difficult to control the potential negative aspects of interest groups without denying their positive contributions. Many view the present regulations as more loophole than law.

7-3 Organizing to Play the Interest Group Game: Who Gets Involved?

Many Americans view joining groups to influence government as both a sacred right and a preferred political strategy. This is especially true of middle- and upper-class citizens.[9]

7-3a Deciding to Play the Game

The existence of more than two hundred thousand organized political groups is impressive when the effort and resources required to establish a formal organization are considered. An identifiable interest group fails to exist until potential members

- perceive commonly shared interests,
- feel that organizing will help to achieve those interests, and
- show a willingness to expend some personal resources to establish an organization to pursue those interests.

Characteristics shared with others do not necessarily imply interests that could be pursued through the political process. Members of **categoric groups,** such as tall people, people with blond hair, or students doing poorly in American Government class, do not think much about their common interests, and they do not see them as having any relationship to the political process.[10]

categoric group *Individuals with common characteristics, but who see no way those characteristics are related to some interest that might be pursued in the political realm. See also* ***potential group*** *and* ***interest group.***

Individuals with common interests are often unaware of an interest they share with others until some significant event brings their attention to it. Categoric groups may possess **latent interests** that could be activated by an event or a challenge to the well-being of individuals sharing particular characteristics. American cigarette smokers seldom thought of themselves as having anything in common until government began to ban smoking in restaurants and other public places. Smokers began to view themselves as victims and tried to fight back. The tobacco industry encouraged and helped organize their opposition.

latent interests *Common outlooks and policy goals that could be activated and stimulate political involvement.*

New technologies such as targeted mail and computerized communications make it easier to make individuals aware of their latent interests. In 1994, when the federal government was discussing the installation of a code-breaking device (the "clipper chip") into all computers, to make it easier to trace illegal computer communications, computer

Box 7–2 Creating an Interest Group out of Thin Air

Since political advantage goes to groups and individuals who effectively tap the capabilities of new technology, it is not surprising that computerized bulletin boards and user lists would be used for political purposes. In 1994 the White House announced that it would support a National Security Agency (NSA) proposal to require that computers include a "clipper chip," which would allow government access to any data coded for security reasons. Such a chip would assure that government could investigate secret communications for reasons of national security or judicial proceedings. Almost instantaneously, the bulletin boards and user lists began to buzz with activity. Immediately, two entrepreneurial groups, Computer Professionals for Social Responsibility and the Electronic Frontier Foundation, sprang into action. Within six weeks, more than fifty-five thousand email messages opposing such a government "invasion of our privacy" had been collected and delivered to decision makers. Soon after, the proposed legislation was quietly dropped.[a]

A few months later, lobby reform legislation, with stricter reporting requirements for interest groups, was interpreted as having a chilling effect on grassroots lobbying. Activists used the Internet, fax machines, and talk shows to drum up opposition. In a barrage of frenzied criticism, the bill died in the Senate. As Ralph Reed of the Christian Coalition saw it:

> This vote demonstrates that grassroots citizens, using modern technology like fax machines, computerized bulletin boards and talk radio, now have more influence on Capitol Hill than powerful lobbyists wearing Armani suits and Gucci shoes.[b]

Recent experience seems to show that not only can citizens be activated by new technology, but also that they have become very protective about the right. Since younger individuals are more comfortable with the technology, one significant political activation wave of the future seems to be technology-driven.

a. Graeme Browning, "Zapping the Capitol," *National Journal*, October 22, 1994, 2449.
b. *Ibid.*, 2447.

bulletin boards were used to sound an alert. More than 50,000 individuals sent email to the White House to protest the proposed policy (see Box 7-2: Creating an Interest Group out of Thin Air).

The very existence of a latent interest that could be activated affects the policy process. Public officials often avoid certain issues because they anticipate the reactions of the latent group and want to let sleeping dogs lie. The existence of latent interests does, however, create the potential that the interests may activate those affected. For example, homeowners who receive significant tax benefits by being able to write off their mortgage interest costs have long been able to thwart any attempt to undermine that benefit, since politicians fear what their reaction might be.

potential group Individuals who recognize a common interest and have some awareness of who they share the interest with. See also ***categoric group*** and ***interest group.***

Once latent interests are activated and a set of separate individuals develop a "we" feeling, they become a **potential group** that is willing to become organized. When this awareness is combined with the realization that some governmental unit might be helpful in promoting their mutual interest, the result can be a fully organized political interest group. Organization requires the expenditure of resources, such as time and money. It also implies the selection of leaders, the development of communication channels, and often the hiring of a professional staff to keep the organization going.

group entrepreneur An individual who sensitizes potential group members to their interests and attempts to organize them. See also ***potential group*** and ***interest group.***

The shift from a category of separate individuals to a potential group recognizing its self-interest may be furthered by events or encouraged by a **group entrepreneur.** An individual who recognizes the benefits of making others aware of common interests may succeed in encouraging them to move toward formal organization (see Box 7-3: A Rose Is a Rose, But a Group May Not Always Be a Group).[11] Some entrepreneurs are driven by an unselfish commitment to the issue alone; others use the issue as a vehicle for status, power, and/or employment.

Box 7–3 A Rose Is a Rose, But a Group May Not Always Be a Group

As a categoric group students doing poorly in an American Government course might suffer alone and in embarrassed or bitter silence. Then one day the professor announces that, after separating the class's written essays into major and nonmajor piles for grading, two-thirds of students not majoring in political science are in danger of failing the course, whereas only 5% of the majors are in this category. If the professor had avoided making such an observation, he or she would have been dealing with a latent group. Once the announcement is made, however, it would probably not take long for nonmajors to recognize their common interest and to become a potential group. By evaluating the majors' and nonmajors' essays separately, the professor may have allowed bias to enter into the grading. If one of the nonmajor students steps forward as a group entrepreneur and suggests that they might enter a discrimination case against the professor or the department chair, the nonmajors might begin to act on their interests. If the group entrepreneur is successful in getting the others to come to an organizational meeting, to choose a spokesperson, and to develop a strategy, the group would be on its way to becoming an organized interest group attempting to influence the governance of the course.

Box 7–4 Why Join that Group?

Think of some groups or organizations you belong to. Did you join or maintain your membership for any of the reasons listed below?

1. Provides a chance to meet and enjoy the company of others
2. Promotes values or causes of great benefit to society
3. Keeps me better informed about topics in which I have an interest
4. Is important for my job or is protection for my future employment
5. Has special advantages or benefits not available to nonmembers

If you chose reason 2 as the motivation for maintaining membership in one of the organizations, you are motivated by a desire for **collective benefits.** All of the other responses represent **selective benefits** that are available only through membership in the organization. We specified both "joining" and "maintaining membership:" Motivations can vary over the course of a person's affiliation with a group or organization. Individuals may join a group for a reason that later becomes less relevant. Once in the group, they may find other reasons to maintain their membership. For example, a person may join a group to acquire new information or skills concerning a hobby or profession and later find that he or she is dependent on the group to satisfy social needs for friendship or support.

Groups are made up of individuals who must do a cost/benefit analysis of the advantages and disadvantages of joining the group. Group involvement may cost time and money but often does provide some clear benefits (see Box 7-4: Why Join that Group?).

collective benefits *Those goods, services, and rewards that cannot be limited to members of a particular group. See also* **selective benefits.**

7-3b Motivations for Joining

A few groups can coerce membership by making it impossible for a person to make a living without joining the organization. Examples are labor unions and professional associations responsible for licensing. Some states allow "closed shops," which means that a person must be a union member in order to work. Some states make membership in a professional organization a requirement to practice.

selective benefits *Those goods, services, and rewards that can be limited to members of a particular group. See also* **collective benefits.**

Most organizations in the United States, however, are voluntary. Individuals have different motivations for joining. Analyzing the reasons why individuals join a group is somewhat different from outlining the goal of the group itself. A public interest group such as Common Cause exists to provide benefits to society. An individual may "selfishly" join it to meet new friends or to feel good about promoting better government. On the other hand, a doctor may join the American Medical Association because it establishes professional standards for medicine and ignore its emphasis on enhancing the economic well-being of doctors.

Some individuals join the political game to secure collective benefits. Individuals motivated by collective benefits expect little in the way of specific personal rewards. They get involved for the good of the larger society. If organizations such as Save the Whales or the Women's Strike for Peace (to curb the spread of nuclear weapons) are successful in promoting their causes, their members will not get a larger share of the societal benefits than will nonmembers.

Another motivation behind joining political interest groups is the attraction of selective benefits. Interest groups often secure members by openly offering benefits that are available only through membership. Small, local groups provide a social outlet for individuals who want contact with others, but this benefit is gained only by those who attend meetings. Some national groups, such as MADD, the National Organization for Women (NOW), the Chamber of Commerce of the United States, and Common Cause, have extensive networks of local chapters that make membership a social benefit. Larger national groups provide their members with newsletters containing insider information, technical expertise, and special rates on insurance or travel. Many individuals join such groups as the American Automobile Association (AAA) for its emergency and travel services and have little awareness of the organization's lobbying efforts. Similarly, when most AARP members join, they have little idea about its political agenda and join to get special insurance and travel deals available to senior citizens. When selective benefits allow a group to turn a profit, its legitimacy as a political activist comes into question.

Both theory and evidence indicate that more individuals join groups on the basis of selective than of collective benefits.[12] Many individuals cannot see the logic in paying membership fees or attending meetings to support causes that will not, if successful, directly benefit them or from which they will get the benefit anyway. Many "free riders" support group goals but are unwilling to contribute their own resources to the group effort.

Apart from desiring certain personal benefits, such as discounts on health insurance, individuals are generally driven to organize more out of fear of losing something than out of hope of gain. When the benefits they have become accustomed to are challenged, individuals become aware of common interests they share with others. The threat to close a local school almost always generates a concerned parents committee fighting the change, but plans for a new school seldom generate such passion and commitment. Governments faced with the necessity of locating potentially undesirable facilities (toxic waste dumps, halfway houses for drug addicts, homeless shelters) in local communities can almost be assured of the emergence of an interest group opposing the location. Fearful of reduced property values or increased crime, local residents often support the basic program idea but argue that its location be "not in my backyard," or **NIMBY.** Such groups tend to be relatively temporary and disband when the threat is removed or the cause is lost. In 1995 the Supreme Court limited the ability of municipalities to use zoning laws to bar group homes for drug addicts and individuals with disabilities. This action may well spur more group activity.

NIMBY *The acronym for "not in my backyard," referring to the hesitancy of residents to accept relatively undesirable government facilities in their area.*

In the wake of the events of September 11, 2001, a number of groups of families and survivors of the terrorist attacks emerged. While interested in the collective benefit of thwarting future terrorist acts, most were more interested in the selective benefits associated with honoring the dead and guaranteeing government and insurance payments to the families of the survivors. Once the memorial to the victims at Ground Zero is finished and payouts are completed, it will be more difficult for the groups to maintain interest.

As part of their struggle for survival, most interest groups attempt to cover all the bases. They both appeal to potential members and assert that what they want is really also good for the broader society. Strong interest groups tend to have a mix of collective and selective benefits with which to entice membership.

7-4 The Uneven Interest Group Playing Field: Organizational Resources

Interest groups join the political game with widely varying resources. The most important of these are bodies, money, and power.

7-4a Membership and Financial Support

In a democracy, where votes count, the size of the membership is important. The number of group supporters is not fixed or easily determined. Outnumbered interest groups often attempt to make up for their competitive disadvantage either by expanding their formal membership or by claiming public support.[13] The larger the organization, however, the more likely it is to include individuals with varied interests. Large organizations tend to lose their singular purpose and to depend on a membership with more limited commitment. Yet groups whose membership is geographically dispersed have an advantage. Since legislators look toward their constituencies for guidance, each legislator is more likely to have some constituents among the members of a widely spread group. New communications technologies have expanded the type of people and range of issues around which interest groups form (see Box 7-5: Joining the Game by "Farming" the Interested Public). Physical proximity and frequent interaction among potential members reduce communication costs and strengthen commitment to the cause. Targeted mailing techniques have made it possible for large interest groups to expand their membership and to raise funds

Box 7–5 *Joining the Game by "Farming" the Interested Public*

In 1980 Douglas P. Wheeler, a former deputy assistant secretary in the Department of the Interior, read a Historical Agricultural Lands Study that sensitized him to an environmental cause that had no spokesperson. Soon thereafter, his attention was caught by an article about a family unable to pass down its farm to one of its children due to the high property taxes. Looking around, he found no group focusing on the protection of the family farm. With a small grant, he gathered an advisory board and marched into battle. Lacking staff and without a well-defined legislative agenda and supportive membership, Wheeler used his computer as a weapon. Armed with little more than an idea, Wheeler and a supportive volunteer board of directors proceeded to create an interest group—the American Farmland Trust (AFT).

AFT purchased and borrowed computerized mailing lists of existing conservation interest groups, such as Friends of the Earth, the Sierra Club, and the Nature Conservancy. AFT thought that members of those organizations might also share a commitment to protecting a natural resource such as the family farm.

AFT used a variety of letters that warned of the dangers of losing family farms to developers and large corporations. The group pre-tested both the form of the letter and the mailing lists by measuring return rates of its solicitations. The "mining" of the lists encouraged expanded mailings, including an opinion poll to individuals on some of the lists. The poll included such questions as "Would you like your children to be able to see farms in operation?" and "Do you see the family farm as one of America's natural resources?" The solicitation requested a $15 minimum contribution to join. The first wave of mailings had a low return rate, but contributions more than covered the investment. Within a year, more than twenty thousand people had joined an organization that until that time had done nothing but define an issue and expend all its resources to create a membership. Now, with money in the bank, the American Farmland Trust could begin to spend some of its net income to pursue the cause of the family farm.

Since that time the organization has amassed an impressive record of informing the public and encouraging state and federal legislation designed to keep family farms in the family. Remembering its roots, the organization continues to invest some of its resources in new computerized mailing lists and in refinements to its solicitation strategy. Through new technology, Doug Wheeler tapped a latent strain of support for the family farm, identified those willing to act on their feelings, and created a viable interest group.

through small contributions. As F. Christopher Arterton, professor at George Washington University, sees it:

> The evolving mix of communications media appears to be conducive to the development of stronger interest groups; they will be able to use these narrower, private links to mobilize their membership. . . . The capacity to communicate more readily with other citizens who share the same interest might result in strong groups that transcend geographical boundaries.[14]

Television and computer networks diminish some of the long-distance communications barriers to recognizing common interests. The growing popularity of email, computerized bulletin boards, and special-interest user lists provides a new technique for political activation. Individuals who use bulletin boards and subscribe to user lists are by definition members of a potential group, since they share the interests leading to the creation of the bulletin board or list. With minimal effort they log onto the bulletin board to see what is happening in an area related to their job or hobby. After joining a user list, members automatically receive email messages associated with specific topics. Most lists are interactive, allowing recipients to respond either to individuals or everyone on the list. The Internet and commercial services such as America Online and CompuServe have expanded access to such resources. Thousands of bulletin boards and user lists have been created on topics as broad as world peace and women's issues to narrow concerns such as Kentucky politics and the Transnational Radical Party.

slack resources *Political resources, such as time and money, that are left over after the basic necessities of life are taken care of.*

Since membership requires the expenditure of resources such as time and money, groups are more likely to draw membership from wealthier individuals with **slack resources,** such as free time. Those individual factors associated with political participation in general—higher socioeconomic status and trust in the value of participation (efficacy)—also help to predict the kinds of individuals who would be easiest to organize into interest groups. Groups representing individuals willing to contribute significant personal resources, such as time and money, can use those resources to expand their membership, plan more effective strategies, and hire professional staffs. The concrete resources of competing organizations often vary considerably. An organization such as the NRA, with a budget of more than $130 million, can outspend its primary interest group rival, Handgun Control (now the Brady Campaign), by a margin of more than eight to one.

Some interest groups parlay the appeal of their cause or the social status and respect for those individuals who make up their membership into an effective resource. Business groups love to repeat the phrase, "The business of America is business."[15] Groups that include religious leaders or entertainment figures among their membership imply that endorsement by such individuals legitimizes the organization's cause. A survey of Washington interest group leaders ranked a group's reputation for being credible and trustworthy over the more visible aspects of group strength, such as the size of the group's membership and its annual budget.[16]

Not all individuals or interests are equally represented in the interest group game. Lack of motivation, skills, and resources keeps many interests off the playing field and out of the policy discussion. Membership alone may not prove to be much of a resource. While representatives of a large organization can say, "our members think . . .," the implied threat has little force unless the membership is committed enough to take action on their thoughts. Large organizations often include such a widely divergent group of individuals that coordinated political action is impossible.

7-4b Lobbyists: The First Team Players

Few interest group members have the time, skill, or motivation to play the political game full time. The effectiveness of interest groups, especially at the national level, depends on their ability to hire knowledgeable lobbyists to research the issues, monitor the policy developmental process, and develop strategies of intervention (see Box 7-6: Some Lobbyist Player Profiles).

Effective lobbyists use information as a key resource in playing the political game. Lobbyists know who is making which decisions (staff members, congressional subcommittees, executive agencies) and the kinds of information that might affect the final res-

Box 7–6 *Some Lobbyist Player Profiles*

To many observers, the typical lobbyist is a sleazy and overly clever character who throws around big bills and twists the arms of legislators and bureaucrats in the hope of gaining illegitimate favors. Lobbyists, on the other hand, see themselves as professionals who use legal and well-established strategies for making the most positive cases possible in representing their clients. They feel they are providing decision makers with the information they need to make better decisions. Most lobbyists fall closer to the second rather than the first definition, and some are particularly interesting, as the following profiles indicate.

Clark Clifford would chafe at being called a mere lobbyist. As a close adviser and appointee to two Democratic presidents (White House Chief of Staff to Harry Truman and Secretary of Defense for Lyndon Johnson), Clifford views himself as a superlawyer whose contacts and knowledge of Washington politics allow him to give advice without getting his hands dirty in direct lobbying. He is described as someone "who has made a career out of knowing the score" in Washington.[a] His advice and efforts to influence policy do not come cheap:

> A Midwestern corporation general counsel . . . asked Clifford what his company should do concerning certain tax legislation. After several weeks, Clifford responded, "Nothing," and enclosed a bill for $20,000. Unaccustomed to the Clifford style, the general counsel testily wrote that for $20,000 he certainly was entitled to a more complete explanation. . . . "Because I said so," Clifford said in letter two and billed the corporation for another $5,000.[b]

For Tommy Boggs, learning politics was about as natural as learning to walk. He is the son of the late Democratic majority leader Hale Boggs and retired Representative Lindy Boggs (D-La.). Tommy Boggs has access, born of family friendship, to the old guard leadership in Washington and has built personal bonds with the new breed of leaders from his generation. Using his advantages, Tommy Boggs has become one of the superlobbyists, plying his trade for such corporations as Sony and Toyota and garnering himself a salary of more than $1 million as senior partner in the Washington law firm of Patton, Boggs, and Blow.

In moving in and out of government office, Joan Claybrook has become a fearsome consumer advocate. Her current position as president of Public Citizen, a consumer advocacy group founded by Ralph Nader, draws her into a wide variety of consumer issues, from health care and automobile safety to banking and campaign finance. A stint as an American Political Science Association Congressional Fellow facilitated her shift from a midlevel bureaucratic job with the Social Security Administration to being a full-time consumer activist. After several years of putting Ralph Nader's ideas into action, she was appointed head of the National Highway Traffic Safety Administration. Some of her former Nader associates saw her as the enemy who sold out on the purists' position on airbags.[c] With President Jimmy Carter's defeat, Claybrook's political job was given to a Reagan Republican, and she again crossed the street. She became a more effective lobbyist for having seen how the game is played from the inside. Other players argue that effectiveness is the name of the game for lobbyists, and Joan Claybrook is "very effective, very tough, very direct. She'll go to the end for whatever she believes in." (consumer advocate Esther Peterson) and "If you have just one person on your side, you would want it to be Joan" (Senator John Kerry, D-Mass.).[d]

---

a. Marjorie Williams, "Clark Clifford: The Rise of a Reputation," *Washington Post*, May 8, 1991, D1.

b. Ronald J. Hrebenar, *Interest Group Politics in America* (Armonk, NY: M. E. Sharpe, 1997), 94.

c. Judith Weintraub, "The Tiger in the Consumer's Tank," *Washington Post*, May 5, 1992, B1.

d. Weintraub, B1.

olution. Interest groups seek out professional lobbyists who know how the game is played and who have access to other key players. Many former members of Congress and top-level executive branch employees transfer their skills and contacts into lobbying careers. Under the current laws, former congresspersons must refrain for two years from lobbying on matters in which they were involved as legislators. Senior executive branch officials must wait a year before lobbying their former agencies.

The 1994 debate over health care reform unleashed one of the most expensive lobbying efforts ever. As one observer described the scene at the time in Washington, D.C.:

> The insiders' game began with a run on the PR and lobbying salons here. The hiring frenzy has produced a reunion of political alumni—ex-congressmen, top officials in past administrations, onetime staff directors of key health and taxing committees and former Democratic and Republican campaign operatives. They comfortably straddle the worlds of politics and money, veterans of that murky phase of legislating when tweaking an amendment or engineering a vote trade can shift the fortunes of clients.[17]

Effective lobbyists also know how to adapt to a new playing field. Box 7-7: A Primer for White House Lobbyists cites some strategies that lobbyists employed in dealing with the Clinton administration when President Bill Clinton was newly in office.

Box 7–7 A Primer for White House Lobbyists

While we generally think of lobbyists plying their trade in the halls of Congress, the power of the presidency draws some of the best lobbyists to White House and Cabinet departments. Early in the Clinton administration, some lobbyists worried about their effectiveness in an administration led by a president who vowed in speech after speech to "break the stranglehold the special interests have on our elections and the lobbyists have on our government."

It did not take the Clinton White House long to find out that lobbyists were important sources of information and political support. The lobbyists discovered four strategies that seemed to work:

1. Don't Call It Lobbying: If "lobbying" was a dirty word, they could use another. While the Clinton White House did not like lobbying, it did recognize "shareholders" and "stakeholders" desiring "empowerment" so that they can work in "partnership" with government.
2. Ante Up: Money is the concrete representation of a group's interest in seeing a particular administration succeed. Campaign contributions are the most obvious methods of getting the attention of politicians, but some groups prefer more subtle methods. The White House encouraged more than six hundred business groups to support the Democratic Business Leadership Forum, which offers contributors a retreat with key policy makers. A seemingly even less partisan opportunity was offered to groups and individuals interested in renovating the White House. Donors of gold drapes, bookcases, and a new Oval Office rug got credit for sprucing up the president's office and were invited to see the results of their efforts. It would not have been surprising if broad policy issues also came up during those viewings.
3. Find a Friend of Bill: Friendship and trust go a long way in Washington, where individuals are judged as much on the basis of who they are as on what they say. Individuals who knew Bill Clinton (or any other president for that matter) before he became president had a better understanding of how he and his advisers made decisions. At times old friends became "door-openers," allowing a particular point of view to be heard.
4. Use Others to Do Your Bidding: If the direct approach does not seem feasible, use an end run carried out by other elected officials such as governors or members of Congress. One White House staff member, who might show offense by being approached by a lobbyist, commented, "When a member of Congress says 'Jump,' we say 'How high?' " Other politicians not only "speak the language," but can threaten or cajole, using their vote in Congress or future electoral support as an "attention getter."

There is little indication that the basic rules changed during the George W. Bush presidency. The list of the president's friends and the groups with access are different, but the process remains the same. Lacking the capacity to respond to everyone, presidents and their staffs pay special attention to those they trust and those who have supported them in the past. The "friends of Bill," and the "friends of George" may represent widely different political outlooks, but they act in much the same way.

Source: Adapted using direct quotes from Sheila Kaplan, "Lobbying by Clinton's Rules," *Washington Post,* February 20, 1994, H1.

7-5 Playing the Interest Group Game for Keeps: Group Strategies

Interest group strategies vary considerably according to the type of issue, the decision makers involved, and the group's organizational resources (see Box 7-8: The Politics of Gun Control). Attempting to influence the technical aspects of tax legislation differs significantly from trying to affect the vote on a public and highly controversial issue such as gun control. Seeking to influence the decision of bureaucrats who administer a law bears little resemblance to lobbying efforts directed at elected officials in Congress or state legislatures. The strategies that a group chooses also depend on the nature of the group. The strategic options of groups with a large and dedicated membership differ from those of groups representing a few very wealthy clients.

Fifty years ago, interest groups typically began their efforts to influence policy *after* decision makers were chosen. The electoral arena was left largely to the candidates and political parties. The dominant interest group activity involved heated conversations in which lobbyists suggested the preferred course of action to elected or appointed officials. Such interchanges are still important, but the range of interest group strategies has broadened in recent decades.

7-5a Determining the Elected and Appointed Decision Makers

open games *Games that allow most interested individuals the ability to participate.*

Increasingly, interest groups have realized that an important way to affect the outcome of the game is to help determine the elected and appointed players. Modern interest groups,

Box 7–8 The Politics of Gun Control

Background

Gun control remains one of the most controversial issues in American politics. Politicians carefully craft their positions on this issue according to local traditions, shifting public opinion, and historical events, realizing that political careers are made and lost on this issue alone.

Gun control became a political football as Americans watched an increasing number of news reports about the shooting deaths of prominent individuals, drive-by shootings, and mass murders in public places. For many school systems, guns in schools have replaced concerns such as cheating or smoking on school grounds. In many communities teenagers are more likely to be killed with a gun than by disease or accident. Washington, D.C., has been called the "murder capital of the world," with guns the weapon of choice. Crimes involving guns in the United States far surpass those in almost any other country. Given the grim realities, public opinion increasingly supports stricter controls on guns, yet the outcome of the policy battle remains unclear.

Questions

As the proportion of guns used for sport and hunting decline in comparison to those used for criminal activity, a key question emerges: "Why has it been so difficult to pass strict gun control legislation?" In order to answer this question, we need to confront several related questions:

1. Who are the players in this game, and what are their relative advantages?
2. How can one justify opposing gun control?
3. What kind of a game does gun control represent, and how have the strategies and outcomes changed over time?

Analysis: The Players and Their Resources

The formal players have remained relatively constant. For decades, gun control was seen as one of the most uneven games in American politics. It matched the more than 3 million members of the National Rifle Association (NRA), with its large staff

continued

Box 7–8 The Politics of Gun Control

—Continued

and budget of more than $130 million, against the few hundred thousand members of Handgun Control Incorporated (HGCI), with its shoestring budget and handful of staff. While public opinion is increasingly on the side of stricter gun control, the commitment of gun control advocates seldom matches the fervor of its opponents.

It is always better to have one's players inside the arena rather than on the outside looking in. The NRA usually counts among its membership more than one hundred members of Congress, key politicians in other realms, and significant contingents within most congressional districts. For years the NRA dominated the playing field either by killing legislation or by watering it down.

The Justification of Opponents

For a large number of Americans, the freedom to own a gun is something akin to a sacred right. They read the 2nd Amendment of the Constitution as a blanket prohibition against any form of gun control. It is a classic case of competing values. Opponents of gun control emphasize freedom in society, while proponents place the higher value on social order.

Games, Strategies, and Outcomes

The battle over gun control clearly represents a continuous game. Victories by one side are never complete or permanent, and the competitors react to losses by redoubling their efforts and waiting for the right opportunity to strike back. The winners in turn attempt to solidify their gains and prepare for the next onslaught.

More than most realms, gun control is an **open game,** with players reacting to historical events, fluctuating public opinion, and players' changing commitments. Just as it seemed that the NRA was invincible, events began to overtake them.

The attempted assassination of Ronald Reagan and the wounding of his press secretary, James Brady, in 1981 eroded the NRA's domination of the playing field. Sarah Brady reacted to her husband's permanent disability by becoming chairperson of Handgun Control Incorporated (HGCI), bringing with her the visibility and energy that boosted its image and resources. In 1991 the Brady Bill defined the terrain of battle, requiring a seven-day waiting period for the purchase of a handgun. The NRA countered with a seductive and technologically sophisticated instant computer check that would take years to implement. HGCI met the NRA's typical aggressive lobbying with its own full-court press, including campaign contributions, lobbying, and mail generated from its membership. In many ways, Handgun Control "beat the National Rifle Association at its own game. Using a nationwide 900 telephone line it copied from the NRA, HGCI generated thousands of letters and telegrams to House members in the weeks before the vote."[a] The visible image of James Brady going from office to office in his wheelchair lobbying, coupled with the timely endorsement of longtime NRA member Ronald Reagan, tipped the balance.

As HGCI was becoming more aggressive in its strategies, the NRA faced setbacks. NRA membership dropped by 18 percent (more than three hundred thousand members) during 1990,[b] the incidence of gun-related violence expanded, public opinion polls showed increased support for gun control, and many public officials began to object to the intransigent position of the NRA. As NRA member and former opponent of gun control Representative Les AuCoin (D-Wa.) put it, "The gun lobby has overplayed its hand. Frankly, I'm sick of it, and I'm sick of gun violence. After too long at the table, I'm ready to do what I can to bust up the game."[c]

Congressman AuCoin was obviously not the only one. For the first time in history, the NRA clearly lost an up-and-down vote on gun control in the House of Representatives. Success for gun control proponents was more elusive in the Senate as a veto from President George H. Bush awaited. Democratic success in the 1992 election created a playing field with a number of new players in both Congress and the White House. The Brady Bill eventually passed in 1993 and was followed by an assault weapon ban in 1994. Recognizing that gun control politics is a continuous game, the NRA shifted its efforts to expanding its membership and securing a new group of congressional players in the 1994 elections.

Both strategies were effective. After aggressive recruitment, more than eight hundred and fifty thousand new NRA members were enrolled at a cost that far exceeded their membership fees.[d] In the 1994 election, some of the Democratic losers were hurt by their support of gun control. A number of winners in the Republican sweep owed a debt of gratitude to NRA efforts. While undoing existing legislation is more difficult than preventing new legislation, the NRA was back in the game.

Just as it seemed that the NRA was regaining the upper hand and could secure the congressional reversal of recently passed legislation, however, the game took another turn when the NRA faced a series of crippling blows. Some were self-inflicted. In their aggressive strategy of expanding membership and contributions, NRA solicitation letters referred to federal agents searching for guns as "jackbooted thugs." This was enough for some high-visibility members such as former president George Bush to publicly resign. Close on the heels of this bad publicity emerged news that expensive NRA recruiting and lobbying efforts had resulted in four years of deficit spending, putting the organization into a precarious financial position.[e] In the midst of this one-two punch, the Oklahoma City bombing confronted the NRA with an external challenge. While quickly condemning the violence, the NRA had to be careful not to undermine their support among the various right-wing militia and anti-gun control groups linked with the bombing. Testimony that the bombing had been subsidized through the sale of stolen guns through legitimate gun dealers convinced many in the public of the need for stricter gun control laws and enforcement.

The shootings in Columbine High School in Colorado and a series of other highly publicized gun incidents in schools forced the issue of gun control back on the public agenda. While the NRA struggled with a public relations disaster, opponents silently developed plans to capitalize on the events and cause the NRA more discomfort. As the dust settled, proponents of gun control attempted to use the NRA's bad publicity to their own advantage. The immediate reaction among congressional leaders was to delay any consideration of repealing the ban on assault weapons.

In the meantime, the "Million Mom March" for gun control in Washington had little result; the House and Senate were unable to agree on issues such as deadlines for gun purchase, background checks, and the definition of gun shows. As one congressional staff member argued, opponents were "just trying to run out the clock for the rest of the year."[f] While public support for stricter gun control remained, passing time led to diminished passion.

As an organization, the NRA battled back, with gun control opponents turning back to the NRA for support. NRA membership, which had dropped well below the 3 million it likes to have for "bragging rights," shot up to more than 3.4 million. Anti-gun control interests seemed to have waited out the storm. A year after Columbine, gun control had been pushed to the back burner again.

More recently, HGCI re-christened itself the "Brady Campaign" (www.bradycampaign.org) and formally combined with the Million Mom March organization. The 2001 terrorist attacks and a high visibility sniper spree during 2002 in Washington, D.C., pushed gun control to the fore once again, while Republican success in the 2002 elections with a great deal of credit claimed by the NRA promised to strengthen the hand of those opposed to gun control.

The 2004 election campaign resulted in a confrontation between pro gun control candidate John Kerry and anti gun control advocate George W. Bush. Issues such as renewal of the ban on assault weapons and shielding gun manufacturers from product liability claims hang in the balance.

The final score of the gun control game is still unknown, and the seesaw battle shows no sign of a once-and-for-all conclusion.

---

a. Michael Isikoff, "The Brady Bill Success and Growing Pains Fresh from House Victory, Handgun Control, Inc. Is Learning 'Tasteful Hardball,'" *Washington Post*, May 31, 1991, A17.

b. Jack Anderson and Dale Van Atta, "Membership Losses Riddle Gun Lobby," *Washington Post*, December 21, 1990, E5.

c. Les AuCoin, "Confessions of a Former NRA Supporter," *Washington Post*, March 18, 1991, A11.

d. Fox Butterfield, "Aggressive Strategy by N.R.A. has Left Its Finances Reeling," *New York Times*, June 26, 1995, A1.

e. *Ibid.*

f. Letitia Stein, "Gun Control Legislation Stagnating," *Houston Chronicle*, July 14, 2000, A6.

therefore, play a meaningful role throughout the entire political process. They help to select the policy makers and then help guide their behavior once in office. Interest groups with a large loyal membership often focus their efforts on the electoral arena, where numbers count. Organizations such as the NRA, AFL-CIO, and AARP have the membership resources to play effectively in the electoral arena, where they can change the personnel of government. When these organizations send out an alert that a candidate threatens gun ownership, undermines American workers, or endangers Social Security, many of their loyal members will vote on the basis of this single issue. The following are some of the largest membership organizations in the United States:[18]

American Automobile Association:	40 million
American Association of Retired Persons:	32 million
American Federation of Labor-Congress of Industrial Organizations:	13.3 million
National Committee to Preserve Social Security and Medicare:	5 million
National Rifle Association:	3.4 million
American Legion:	2.7 million
Handgun Control, Inc. (now the Brady Campaign):	400,000

Defining the Electoral Playing Field

The ability to determine the rules and conditions under which the electoral game is played has an important impact on the final outcome. Some interest groups jump into the state-level political fray. They become involved in drawing legislative district lines, determining voter eligibility, specifying the location and hours of poll operation, establishing campaign financing laws, and defining candidate eligibility. Not surprisingly, interest groups seek to have rules adopted that improve the chances of those candidates who support their cause. For example, interest groups that represent minorities who are concentrated by geographic area, such as African Americans and members of other ethnic groups, propose legislative redistricting plans that combine their areas of strength. Unions representing government workers won a major victory in 1993 by trimming **Hatch Act** restrictions on the rights of government employees to campaign and run for office (see Chapters 10 and 16).

Hatch Act *A law designed to limit the partisan political activities of government employees.*

Recruiting Candidates

Some interest groups encourage their own members to seek public office with the expectation that, once in office, the members will work for the group's interests. The U.S. Chamber of Commerce uses such an approach, offering an effective course on practical politics to employees of various businesses. Business owners are encouraged to give their management-level employees time off to attend in the hope that the course will spark an interest and give business-oriented individuals the tools to pursue political office. Other organizations use a more direct strategy, encouraging individual members to run for office and pressuring political party organizations to support them.

Providing Resources

According to Tom Korologos, a former White House lobbyist whose current firm lobbies for such groups as the major league baseball owners and the Black Entertainment Network, "Democracy is not a spectator sport . . . it's a hands-on sport to help those that help us."[19] Political campaigns require a variety of resources, and interest groups stand ready and willing to provide many of them (see Time Out 7-2: Playing the Game without Being Thrown Out by the Referee). Early in the campaign, candidates seek to be seen as legitimate contenders with broad-based support. Endorsements of a candidate by large and well-respected interest groups can scare off potential opponents and encourage voter or contributor support. The provision of volunteer campaign workers or **in-kind contributions**—such as computer time, telephone banks, and mailing lists—also give a favored candidate an important advantage.

in-kind contributions *The direct provision of goods and services, such as computer time, office supplies, and transportation, to a preferred candidate.*

Playing the Game without Being Thrown Out by the Referee

Time Out 7-2

Campaign finance laws allow one to attempt to walk a fine line between avoiding undue influence of individuals with money and supporting the First Amendment right to "petition government for the redress of grievances." The Supreme Court has ruled that campaign expenditures are a form of protected expression and that the limits are only acceptable under certain conditions.

Assume you are a political action committee (PAC) manager for an interest group and are asked to carry out the tasks that follow. For each task, your first determination should be whether the task is legal.

1. During the general election, your organization wants to give $3,000 from its PAC fund directly to a congressional candidate to whom you have not previously contributed.
   Legal? Illegal? It depends.
2. Your public relations director plans a $30,000 advertising campaign in support of a candidate.
   Legal? Illegal? It depends.
3. As a good employee, you keep a confidential notebook in your safe listing all the contributions you have made in order to prove your organization's political activity if anyone were to investigate you.
   Legal? Illegal? It depends.
4. You want to contribute $50,000 of your PAC funds to the Democratic Party to help underwrite a voter registration initiative and get-out-the-vote drive. You justify the large expenditure to your board by reminding them that the more Democrats who vote, the better the candidates you support will do in the election.
   Legal? Illegal? It depends.
5. In the next session of Congress, you anticipate an important vote affecting your organization. Your executive director wants to send a letter outlining your position and include a direct contribution of $4,000 to thirty members whom you have not supported before, thanking them in advance for "their support and cooperation."
   Legal? Illegal? It depends.
6. Your organization has reached its $5,000 limit in a number of key races that are in desperate need of direct hard money contributions. Your chief executive proposes drafting a memo telling key employees of the problem and urging them to consider contributing $3,000 of their own money directly to those campaigns.
   Legal? Illegal? It depends.
7. You want to send out a letter to all the members of your organization listing a half dozen key congressional races in which you are interested. To monitor contributions and increase their visibility to the candidates, you ask your members who have not yet contributed to those campaigns to send you checks of less than $2,000 made out to the candidate. You then promise to forward them to the appropriate campaign.
   Legal? Illegal? It depends.

Source: Stephen E. Frantzich and Steven E. Shier, *Congress: Games and Strategies* (Cincinnati, OH: Atomic Dog Publishing, 2003).

The most important resource that an interest group can provide to a campaign is money, since the candidate needs to purchase other resources, such as staff, office supplies, and advertising. The dramatic increase in the cost of campaigning and the importance of large contributions are directly related to the expanded uses of new technologies, such as computerized mailings and television, in electoral campaigns at all levels (see Chapter 11).

Abuses in campaign funding led to the passage of the **Federal Election Campaign Act (FECA)** and its amendments during the 1970s (see Chapters 8 and 11). The FECA

Federal Election Campaign Act (FECA) *Law passed in 1972 and amended in 1974, 1976, and 1979 establishing the rules for campaign financing of federal elections. The act establishes reporting requirements for the Federal Elections Commission for all federal races and provides for public financing of presidential races.*

Answer to Time Out 7-2

Designing campaign finance laws that promote democracy is difficult. The extreme importance of money in campaigns encourages candidates and interest groups to be creative in working within the laws. Purported infractions are investigated by the Federal Elections Commission, which has the right to impose fines. The primary vehicle for discouraging illegality is public disclosure. The potential of bad publicity for participating in illegal activities is usually enough to keep candidates and organizations honest. The media and opponents carefully scrutinize required Federal Elections Commission reports for potentially embarrassing activity.

Answers to Questions in Time Out 7-2

1. ***Legal.*** The contribution is legal, since your organization has not reached its $5,000 limit for that candidate. PACs can give direct contributions of $5,000 in the primary election and another $5,000 in the general election.
2. ***It depends.*** You need to look into this more. The legality of such a large expenditure would depend on whether it was coordinated with the candidate. If done without the candidate's (or candidate's staff's) knowledge, organizations can spend any amount they wish as an independent expenditure.
3. ***It depends.*** All direct contributions of candidates and indirect expenditures either supporting or opposing a candidate must be reported to the Federal Elections Commission. These records must be publicly available to the media and general public.
4. ***Illegal.*** Starting with the 2004 elections, such a contribution is illegal. Until the passage of the Bipartisan Campaign Reform Act in 2002, this would have been a legal example of "soft money." Individuals and organizations were able to give unlimited funds to political parties for their party-building activities, such as voter registration and promoting a slate of candidates.
5. ***Illegal.*** Offering contributions contingent on the future behavior of an elected official is illegal and considered bribery. It is one thing to work to get the "right" kind of people in office, but quite another to trade contributions for specific votes.
6. ***Illegal.*** You have a sharp eye for details, and in campaign finance, as the old saying goes, "the devil is in the details." The general idea of encouraging others to contribute is all right, but the specific proposal would get the employees into trouble. Individuals can only give $2,000 directly to a general election campaign (they could have given another $2,000 in the primary).
7. ***Legal.*** This is a legal example of "bundling." As long as the checks are not deposited in the organization's account and then paid out with the organization's check, it is legal for the organization to pass through any amount of such funds. The contributors are still limited to the $2,000 maximum per race. EMILY's List, a liberal organization that supports female candidates, has become one of the largest funding sources for campaigns in this way. Reflecting the importance of seed money in raising more money, EMILY is an acronym for Early Money Is Like Yeast.

Political Action Committee (PAC) *A group of citizens who voluntarily combine their individual campaign contributions and support favored candidates, often with the encouragement of organized interest groups or corporations.*

uncoordinated expenditures *Campaign advertising done without the knowledge and/or cooperation of the candidate. Such expenditures do not fall under the normal campaign contribution limitations.*

continued the prohibition against direct contributions from corporations and labor unions. It allowed these and other groups to establish independent **political action committees (PACs)** that could voluntarily solicit funds from their members and supporters and directly contribute a limited amount to campaigns ($5,000 for each election to each candidate) as long as they make a public disclosure. Interest groups can get around these limits by supporting or opposing candidates without their permission or knowledge (see Table 7-1). These **uncoordinated expenditures** are unlimited, since the Supreme Court (*Buckley v. Valeo*) equated them to the constitutional guarantee of freedom of expression.

Interest groups create PACs as a mechanism for handling contributions to election campaigns (see Figure 7-3). Over time, the number and variety of PACs have grown dramatically, as has the percentage of campaign funding emanating from PACs. Business and

Table 7-1 The Heavy Hitters in the PAC Game

Organizations with a large membership willing to contribute financially to campaigns can accumulate these funds by forming a Political Action Committee (PAC). They hope to elect those who support their policy goals and make them beholden to them. They may not, however, make their support contingent on a particular vote without crossing the line from support to bribery. PACs can contribute directly to candidates but are limited to $5000 per candidate. Some of the largest PACs use more funds for independent expenditures to support or oppose specific candidates. Among the most financially active PACs in the 1999–2000 election cycle were:

PAC	CONTRIBUTIONS[a] Millions of dollars (ranking)[b]	EXPENDITURES Millions of dollars (ranking)[b]
Realtors Political Action Committee	$3,432,411 (1)	$4,036,656 (16)
Association of Trial Lawyers of America PAC	$2,656,000 (2)	$6,082,160 (7)
American Federation of State, County and Municipal Employees	$2,590,074 (3)	$8,557,040 (4)
International Brotherhood of Electrical Workers	2,455,325 (6)	6,236,036 (5)
United Auto Workers PAC	$2,155,050 (8)	$3,671,024 (18)
National Education Association PAC	$1,734,693 (16)	$6,108,964 (6)
National Rifle Association Political Victory Fund	$1,583,304 (18)	$16,821,436 (1)

a. Direct contributions go directly to a candidate with the candidate being aware of the contribution and controlling its use. Overall expenditures include both direct candidate contributions and indirect expenditures controlled by the PAC and done without consulting the candidates. Source: Federal Elections Commission reported at www.fec.gov .

b. Rankings indicate the relative expenditures and contributions. PACs ranking high on only one of these categories are not included in this table. While some groups excel in providing direct contributions and making indirect expenditures, others specialize. For example, the National Rifle Association ranked number 18 in direct contributions but number one in overall expenditures.

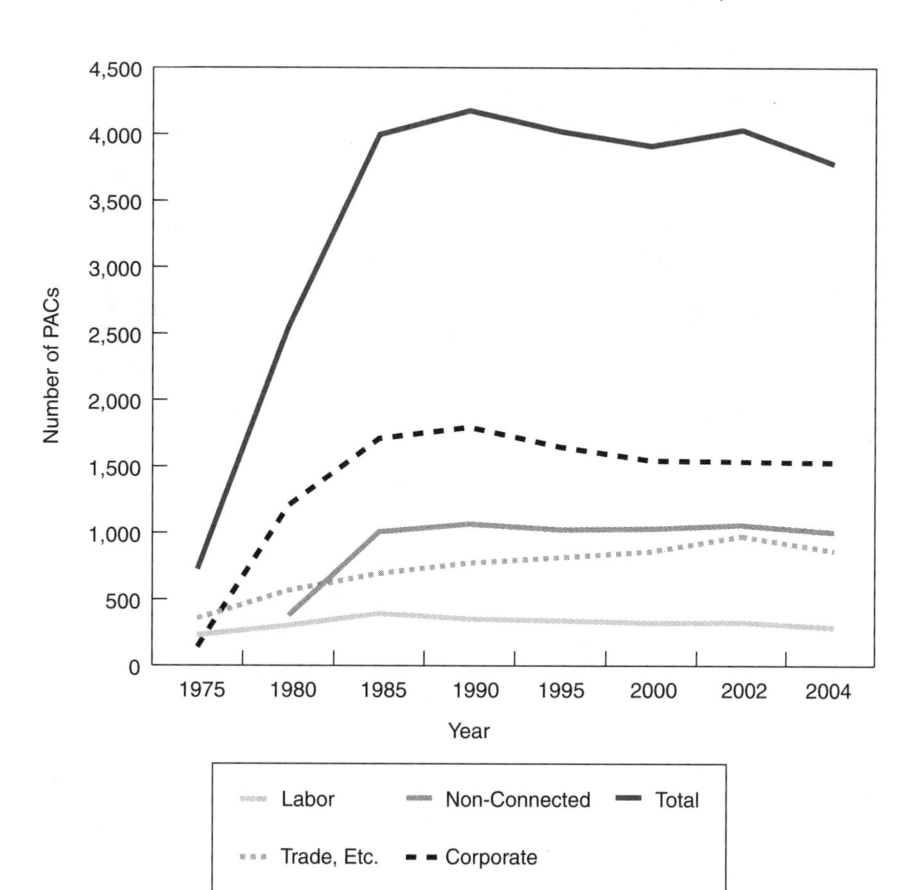

Figure 7-3
The Growth of Political Action Committees, 1975–2004

The number of political action committees has soared in recent years, with corporate PACs becoming the most numerous.

Source: Harold Stanley and Richard G. Niemi, *Vital Statistics on American Politics, 2003-2004,* Washington, D.C.: Congressional Quarterly, Inc., 2003, p. 102.

Figure 7-4
The Relative Importance of PAC Funding in House Campaigns

Democratic congressional candidates depend on PACs considerably more than do Republican congressional candidates, although the gap has narrowed as Republican control of the House has drawn PAC funding.

Source: Harold Stanley and Richard G. Niemi, *Vital Statistics on American Politics, 2003-2004* (Washington, D.C.: Congressional Quarterly, Inc., 2003), pp. 96–97.

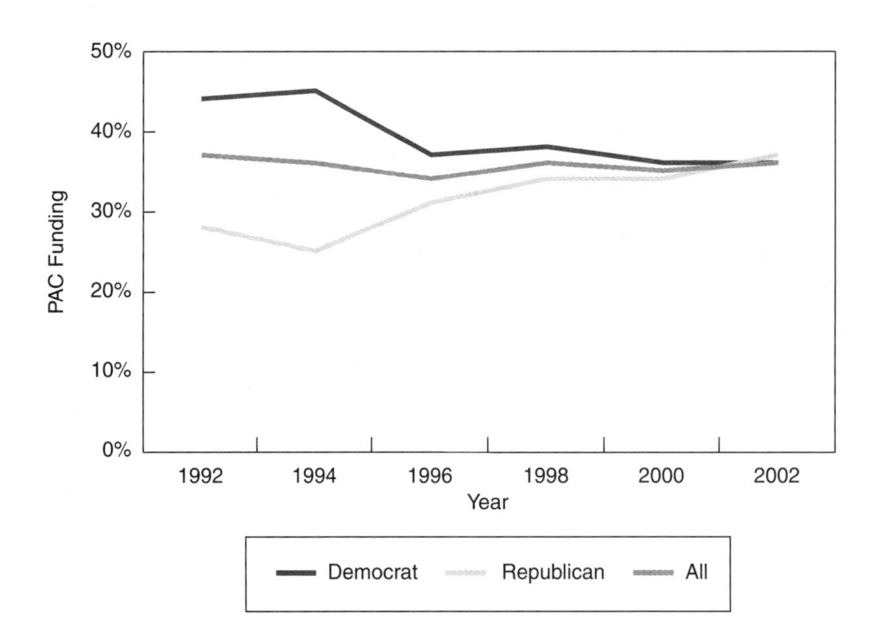

Figure 7-5
The Relative Importance of Total PAC Contributions to Federal Candidates by Type of PAC, 1999–2000 (in Millions of Dollars)

Different types of PACs employ varying strategies. Until 1992, all types of PACs favored the Democrats. After the Republicans became the congressional majority in 1995, all types of PACs except for labor favored the Republican office holders.

Source: Data from www.fec.gov, also reported in Harold W. Stanley and Richard G. Niemi, *Vital Statistics on American Politics, 2001-2002* (Washington, D.C.: Congressional Quarterly, Inc., 2001), p. 108.

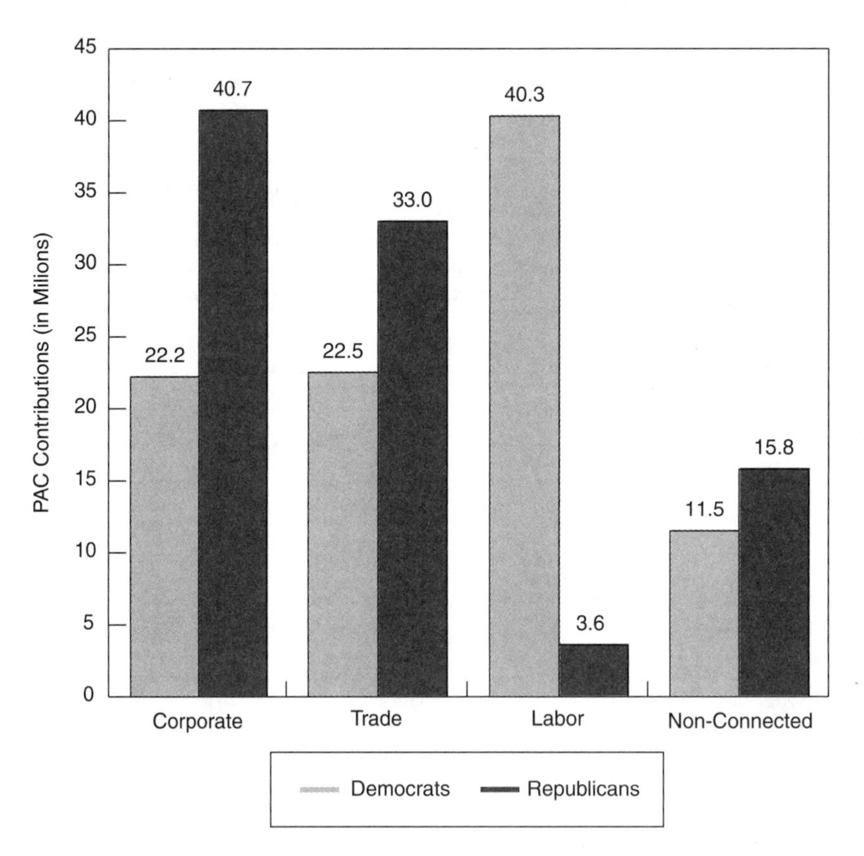

corporate PACs give the largest amount of funds, with most PACs following a strategy of supporting incumbents rather than challengers (see Figures 7-4, 7-5, and 7-6). The overwhelming majority of interest groups and PACs represent corporations and business interests and favor the issue positions taken by Republican candidates. Nevertheless, the desire to back winners pushed them for much of the 1960s to the 1990s toward Democrats, who then represented the majority of incumbents. The only place where the Republican advantage clearly showed up was in races with no incumbent. Since 1994, when the Republicans took over the majority in Congress, the partisan balance of contributions from PACs has shifted to the Republicans.

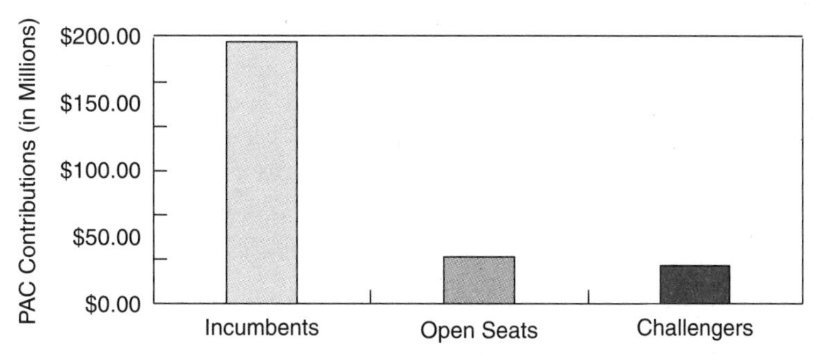

Figure 7-6
PAC Contributions to Federal Candidates by Type of Candidacy, 2000

PACs tend to use the bulk of their funds to support incumbent officeholders.

Source: Data from www.fec.gov.

In the 1994 election, the Republicans' conservative economic message and the public mood of blaming the Democrats struck a responsive chord with business PACs. In 1994 a record high of 35 percent of business PAC contributions—as opposed to 18 percent in 1992—went to nonincumbents, most of whom were Republicans.[20] With the Republicans taking over Congress after the 1994 elections, PACS began favoring this new group of incumbents. Republicans made it clear that they would take a dim view of business PACs that continued to support Democrats (who tend to vote against business interests). In the 2000 elections, PACS contributed $243 million in direct contributions in congressional accounting for 37 percent of House and 14 percent of Senate receipts. The majority party Republicans received more than the Democrats did in the Senate, but the Democrats received more direct PAC contributions in the House ($98.9 million versus $93.3 million), reflecting a significant attempt by some PACs to try to unseat House Republicans.[21]

Perhaps the most abiding characteristic of campaign finance laws is the creativity expended in getting around them. With limits on direct expenditures and the potential for not getting credit from the recipients of indirect expenditures, interest groups are always on the lookout for legal ways to increase their impact. For some groups **bundling** became the vehicle in the 2000 election cycle. Groups such as EMILY's List and the WISH List solicit individual checks from donors for specified races. They then "bundle" the checks without cashing them and send them to the favored candidate with a note saying, "Thought this might help in your race." The group is not bound by any legal limits on how much they can give, and the recipient feels a debt of gratitude for the donation. EMILY's List backed Democratic candidates who were pro-choice on the issue of abortion. After identifying viable candidates, they solicited checks for those candidates whose impact would be the largest. In the 2000 election cycle, EMILY's List distributed over $14.7 million to candidates, making it second only to the NRA ($16.8 million) in PAC disbursements. Their Republican counterpart, the WISH List ("Women in the Senate and House"), used similar bundling tactics but raised much less money.

bundling *A campaign fund-raising technique in which a group identifies worthy recipients and serves as a collection point for contributions and hands over a "bundle" of checks.*

Attempts at campaign finance reform have run into constant conflicts involving personal benefits, political philosophy, and partisan advantage. Incumbents generally do not want to undermine their advantages in fund raising. Conservatives are uncomfortable with the use of tax money to finance campaigns. Democrats, who traditionally have been more dependent on PACs and bundling, want to retain their advantage. Republicans, who can draw on large contributors more easily, do not want to hinder their financial base. Interest group leaders often complain that they are being "mugged" by candidates and parties, but they fear that withholding funds will put them at a political disadvantage. Because of such ongoing conflicts, campaign finance laws have either failed to emerge from Congress or have been subject to presidential veto.

The fact that Republicans won houses of Congress in 1994 and yet were less dependent than Democrats were on PACs—and especially the big-spending business PACs—caused Democrats concern. Many PACs switched their allegiances to the new Republican incumbents but did some hedging of their bets by also helping Democratic candidates, who could capture the majority again in the near future. Democrats had little expectation that the PAC bubble would burst. As one analyst put it, "Democrats made a horrible mistake not pushing through campaign finance reform when they had a chance."[22] It is interesting to note that campaign finance reform was not mentioned in the Republican Contract with America. Once in the majority and receiving the largesse from many PACs, many Republicans cooled their earlier ardor for limiting PAC activity. During the 2000 nomination battle, Republican Senator John McCain (R-Ariz.) found voters receptive to his strong stand against PACs, but he garnered little legislative or political support from his fellow Republican members of Congress.

Affecting Appointments

More government officials receive their positions through appointment than through election, and interest groups rigorously attempt to get people who are supportive of their causes into these offices. When a new president, governor, or mayor is elected, groups suggest names for specific positions and often have the informal right to veto potential nominees. For example, no president would name a secretary of Labor without attempting to clear the nominee with major labor organizations or propose a secretary of Commerce without seeking approval of the business community.

advice and consent *The constitutional right of the Senate to approve major presidential appointments, such as cabinet members, ambassadors, and Supreme Court nominees.*

Many presidential appointments require the **advice and consent** of the Senate. While advice and consent is often routine, it gives interest groups a second chance to affect the outcome. Some of the most vigorous interest group battles have occurred over Supreme Court nominees. Ronald Reagan's attempt to place outspoken conservative judge Robert H. Bork on the Supreme Court in 1987 precipitated an "interest group battle royal" and set the stage for "the major liberal-conservative conflict of the 1980s."[23] Groups on both sides spent millions, with liberal forces finally thwarting the nomination by convincing enough senators to deny Judge Bork's confirmation. Similar battles occur behind the scenes for other appointments.

To avoid such battles, President George H. Bush appointed Judge David H. Souter to the Supreme Court in 1990. Judge Souter's lack of a clearly documented ideological record outlined in writings and court decisions allowed his nomination to sail through the Senate. A similar fate did not face Judge Clarence Thomas's confirmation battle in 1991. A long and bitter set of hearings fueled by competing interest groups preceded the close vote that confirmed Justice Thomas. As one group representative lamented, "A nominee can appear before you and stonewall you and refuse to answer, be evasive, and yet be confirmed. . . . You may be dooming us to a similar game plan for all future nominees."[24] President Bill Clinton learned a lesson from recent Supreme Court battles and nominated moderate judges lacking extensive written records. Interest groups paid relatively little attention to the confirmation hearings of Ruth Bader Ginsburg and Stephen G. Breyer.

Cabinet and key executive branch appointees are often supported or opposed for their specific positions on controversial issues. In recent years, presidents have faced serious interest group opposition to the appointment of secretaries of Health and Human Services and surgeon generals because of the nominees' positions on abortion, drug use, and cigarette smoking. Groups representing tobacco interests did not want to have a surgeon general on a crusade against smoking, and each side of the abortion battle wanted an advocate in the highest levels of government.

Working to determine the players is the most effective strategy that an interest group can have. Once in a position, an individual favorable to a particular cause is more likely to grant access to the group's lobbyists (unless, of course, the individual is a judge). After an election or appointment, interest groups use a variety of strategies to sway the decisions of government officials.

7-5b Long-Term Lobbying: Building a Positive Image

Preparing for the next round is a good strategy in many games, and some interest groups have learned this lesson well. At the height of a legislative or nomination battle, interest groups that have an image of being irresponsible or overly self-centered may find their views discounted. Between crises, therefore, many of the most effective interest groups seek to build a reservoir of goodwill to draw on when the next battle begins.

The NRA, for example, sponsored a "We Are the NRA" campaign in television and press advertisements. In these ads, celebrities and everyday citizens explain NRA initiatives for the environment and gun safety. The Brady Campaign (formerly the HGCI), the NRA's major opponent, countered with statistical evidence of the dangers of handguns (see Box 7-9). Major corporations often run advertisements about the contributions they and their individual employees make to the community. Or they encourage us to favor items with a "Made in the USA" tag and to support policies favoring U.S. manufacturers. The International Ladies' Garment Workers' Union (ILGWU) reminds us to "Look for the Union Label" and attempts to implant a more positive image of unions. Dow Chemical downplays the dangers of chemicals and tries to engender support for chemical industry interests by informing us that "Dow lets you do great things." Such long-term strategies are not directed at one impending battle. They are launched in the hope that public and government officials will recognize the positive side of these groups rather than seeing them only as pleaders for special treatment.

7-5c Short-Term Lobbying: The Insider Strategy

Lobbyists typically are thought of as working in the legislative arena. Effective lobbyists recognize, however, that the development of public policy is a process with a number of distinct stages and involving a variety of arenas. Winning a series of legislative battles may end up meaning little: the bureaucrats who administer the new law may do it in a way that is antagonistic to the group's interests, or the courts could block the application of the law. Skillful interest groups recognize that the effectiveness of their lobbying strategies varies with the arena in question. What is an acceptable approach when dealing with members of Congress might not work when appealing to bureaucrats or judges. Legislators expect lobbyists to approach them directly, to remind them of past campaign support, and to make a pitch for their case. Such direct, face-to-face lobbying would not be appropriate when dealing with the courts. It might even be illegal.

Monitoring the Process

A significant portion of lobbyists' time is spent monitoring the policy process to determine when and in what arena significant decisions will be made. The constant need for information about impending events requires that lobbyists personally communicate with the other players. Increasingly, lobbyists must have knowledge of computer systems that monitor the progress of bills through legislatures, that publicize the docket of upcoming court cases, and that provide the schedule of bureaucratic meetings and rule-making proceedings (see Chapter 16). Interest groups that lack the skill or the resources to keep track of the many arenas may miss the opportunity to influence important decisions and, thus, effectively represent the interests of their membership.

Lobbying Elected Officials

Elected officials often complain about being constantly pressured by lobbyists. They recognize, nevertheless, that lobbyists provide important information about both the technical aspects of proposed laws and their potential political implications. Lobbyists justify their right to be heard and put their profession in the most positive light by arguing that, in the words of Robert M. McGlotten, Legislative Director of the AFL-CIO:

> This is not a game of winning and losing. . . . We are here to represent our members, to tell Congress what we believe is good for our members, which is good for their communities and which is good for this country.[25]

Securing Access

Campaign contributions often assure access to individual elected officials. They enable lobbyists to present the arguments of their interest groups. There is little evidence, though, that individual decisions are regularly bought. In the political arena, information is the key resource. Having access to a decision maker can be just as important in affecting an outcome as having direct control would be. The "Keating Five" case in the U.S. Senate hinged on the propriety of businessman Charles H. Keating giving large contributions to five senators in exchange for hearing his side of the controversy over regulation of savings and loan institutions (see Chapter 13 for further details about this case).

Presenting Information

Interest groups present their cases in a variety of ways. Government decision makers receive numerous written reports and analyses supporting interest group assertions. Lobbyists frequently show up on the list of witnesses asked to testify before legislative committees. At times, powerful committee members can stack the list of witnesses to leave the committee with a particular impression of an issue.

Organizations with large research, public relations, and/or legal staffs often focus their efforts on the decision-making process either in Congress or the courts. During the 1995 debate over the right to sue for personal injury from product liability, electric toolmakers used data about the normal life of their products to persuade lawmakers to strike five seemingly unimportant words from the existing law—"which is a capital good"—thus limiting *all* liability claims to 15 years from purchase. In fighting the legislation, Ralph Nader's Public Citizen used a more visual public relations strategy, inviting a badly scarred victim of product liability to greet wavering senators as they entered the chamber to vote. These groups would not have been effective in the electoral arena, but they can have a dramatic impact on decision-making bodies.

Most interest groups understand that the policy process is a continuous one rather than one in which victories are won once and for all. This encourages them to play the game in such a way that their future access to the playing field is protected. Whether lobbying directly to individual elected officials or in committee testimony, lobbyists know that a reputation for providing accurate information is very important. Everyone expects lobbyists to present the information most supportive of their case. Openly misleading elected officials with false or distorted information does more harm than good in the long run. In spite of the public image of sleaziness and shrewdness, it is credibility and reliability that help to ensure a lobbyist's long-term success.

Grassroots Lobbying

grassroots lobbying *Calling on group membership to take concrete actions, such as writing or calling decision makers, in support of an interest group policy.*

Elected officials who depend on votes to remain in the game react positively to groups representing a large number of voters. Many groups strive to impress elected officials with the level of their support or opposition to proposed legislation by rallying their supporters. Using **grassroots lobbying** techniques, groups can stimulate an outpouring of mail, telegrams, phone calls, or email to elected officials. Techniques include informing their membership of the issues by regular and electronic mail and providing them with suggested letters and appropriate addresses (see Box 7-9: The "Stuff the Mailbox" Game). As journalist Hedrick Smith described it:

> The old inside game of lobbying was upstaged by the new outside game of lobbying. Intensive private lobbying was often less potent than extensive mass lobbying. Lobby groups could no longer bank on some pricey Washington superlawyer to make their pitch in private; they had to generate grass-roots movements to pressure scores of legislators, turning increasingly to the techniques of . . . campaign organizers, pollsters and direct mail specialists.[26]

The 1994 debate on health care involved a wide range of lobbying tactics and strategies. Two participants in the process discussed the use of their groups' membership:

> This is the pre-game hour of lobbying, the time for positioning, for flaunting popular followings and big budgets. Organizations are being built and gathering momentum in the hope of getting attention. Now is the season of grass roots. (Gary Fendler of Aetna Insurance Company)

> You use the people back home to sensitize members of Congress and staff. . . . I get listened to on the Hill because they know I have 600,000 small businessmen behind me back home. The grass roots give me standing. (John Motley, lobbyist for the National Federation of Independent Businessmen). [27]

Box 7–9 The "Stuff the Mailbox" Game

After Congress passed President Ronald Reagan's proposal to withhold taxes on interest and dividends in 1982, the banking industry pulled out all the stops to get the plan repealed, fearing that keeping track of these taxes would cost the banks time and money. Newspaper ads, letters to depositors, and speakers' bureaus advertised the issue. Mail-back postcards to members of Congress were provided to customers at teller windows and in monthly bank statements. Customers received continuous encouragement to return the cards. The campaign resulted in an estimated 22 million letters and postcards flooding Capitol Hill. The mail was literally weighed, since there was too much to count. In a dramatic reversal of its previous decision, Congress repealed the law by a one-sided margin before it was ever enforced. Congressional supporters of the proposal called it "democracy in action," while opponents characterized it as "undemocratic" and a "freight train coming down the track."[a]

Communications with government officials are not limited to letters, postcards, and telegrams. One interest group got more than eight hundred thousand people to send their members of Congress pie plates imprinted with "Save School Lunches" during the 1983 budget debate. Another 40,000 sent nickels to the 83 members wavering about the creation of an agency for consumer protection, arguing that it would cost each citizen only five cents. An official of the congressional post office stated, "After what I have seen come through the mail, I don't think I could ever be surprised again. Organized mailings from oranges with messages on them to pieces of lumber, we have seen and delivered them all."[b]

The arrival of computerized electronic mail and the spread of fax machines increase both the volume and timeliness of interest group communications to members of Congress.

a. Quoted in Stephen Frantzich, *Write Your Congressman: Constituent Communications and Representation* (New York: Praeger), 1986, 67.
b. *Ibid.*, 104.

Increasingly, interest groups are using political advertising to change public opinion, which they hope will be translated into supportive communications to decision makers. This process takes grassroots lobbying a step further than simple activation into the creation of opinions. Despite being criticized as "astroturf" as opposed to true "grass roots," the efforts are effective. The "Harry and Louise" television ads criticizing President Bill Clinton's 1994 health care initiative cost $17 million and generated more than two hundred and fifty thousand calls and letters to Congress.[28] Similar strategies have now become standard for well-financed lobbying campaigns.

Protests and Demonstrations

Some interest groups attempt to gain public exposure and media attention through public demonstrations. By and large, such tactics are an admission that other approaches to making one's case have not been successful. Although many demonstrations are completely legal, the denial of permits by local officials forces some groups to break the law—at least in a technical sense.

At times it is necessary to challenge the laws more directly. The colonists' actions during the Boston Tea Party and the abolitionists' sheltering of fugitive slaves are examples of breaking laws that were viewed as unjust. During the 1960s, members of the civil rights movement broke the laws supporting segregation of public facilities and effectively made their stand known (see Chapter 20).

The nation's capital, Washington, D.C., has long been a magnet for demonstrations and protest. Over the last few decades, Vietnam War protestors, civil rights advocates, farmers, and numerous other groups have attempted to draw attention to their causes by shutting down the city. Amassing hundreds of protestors or parking a line of tractors on the bridges to the city effectively makes Washington, D.C., an island, unreachable by most government workers. Protestors feel that such forms of civil disobedience are justified because of the importance of making their issues public. The government workers who are kept away from their jobs and the taxpayers who are upset by the resulting inefficiency generally call for police intervention.

The difficulty in judging the legitimacy of a civil disobedience strategy hinges, of course, on the importance of the issue being pursued. Virtually everyone can conceive of a cause that is so important that law and order should be broken. When an issue is critical and when all peaceful strategies have failed, individuals willing to pay the consequences have the right to show their commitment by breaking the law.

The problem is that individuals often disagree about the importance of issues for which civil disobedience is used and about the willingness to choose this strategy while other options remain open. When farmers came to Washington in the 1970s to protest low crop prices and lack of government help, they used the time-honored strategy of blocking access to the city by having their tractors conveniently run out of gas on the bridges. When a conservative Midwestern farmer heard his tactics compared to those of Vietnam protestors, he took offense and said, "We are nothing like those long-haired hippies, draft dodgers, and bra burners." When asked to explain the difference, he simply said with great conviction, "Well, *our* cause is just."[29] In 2000, protestors clogged the streets of Seattle, Washington, and Washington, D.C., protesting the World Trade Organization (WTO) for everything from the fear of world government to a mistreatment of workers and damage to the environment. Justice is in the eye of the beholder, a fact that makes civil disobedience both necessary and newsworthy.

Recent attempts by anti-abortion groups such as Operation Rescue to bomb abortion clinics to publicize their cause clearly push the limit of legitimate civil disobedience for most Americans. Civilized society can tolerate a limited amount of civil disobedience as long as the perpetrators pay a price for their actions. Breaking the laws and expecting to get away with it, no matter how important the issue, both demeans the act of protest and smacks of terrorism. (The delicate balance between civil liberties is explored in Chapter 4.)

Building Coalitions

coalitions *Groups of individuals or organizations joining together to pool resources for a common outcome.*

Rather than relying on a single interest group to make the case for a particular decision, groups may form lobbying **coalitions.** Individual groups may differ on the basis of their position but can agree on general opposition to or support for a proposed policy. For example, the opposition to the B-1 bomber in the late 1970s brought together groups for peace, government efficiency, and the environment. During the 1990s, a variety of groups opposed to the Clinton health care package cooperated to attack it through advertising, letter writing campaigns, political contributions, and congressional testimony. Different segments of the health care industry took responsibility for each initiative. By working together, each group in the coalition can use its unique strengths and resources. Those groups with strong research staffs could prepare testimony. Those with effective public relations could work with the media. Since politics is a game of numbers, a coalition automatically expands the number of individuals with a perceived common interest. A united front presents the image that what the groups want not only represents good public policy but also has broad support among a wide range of citizens—who also happen to be voters.[30]

At times clever coalition managers find points where seemingly divergent interests coincide. A group pushing to replace the dollar bill with a coin inventively framed the issue to expand possible support. As one observer noted:

> The pro-coin forces know how to play the game. Their bill states, "The reverse side of the dollar shall have a design recognizing America's Veterans." And veterans, of course, are a large and powerful interest group.[31]

Although joined by the Dollar Coin Coalition backed by the vending machine interests keen on expanding sales with coins that are more reliable than dollar bills, the initiative still failed. The potential for change increased when the pro-coin forces compromised, proposing a dollar coin in addition to the retention of the paper version as opposed to a complete replacement. Expanding the coalition further, the proposal was redrawn to require a woman's likeness on the coin, a first since the ill-fated Susan B. Anthony coin, which never received wide acceptance. Bolstering support by backing a coin design featuring a member of an ethnic minority, the ultimate design featured Sacagawea, the young Indian woman who accompanied Lewis and Clark on their expedition whose exploits had recently been featured in a best-selling book and TV documentary.[32] Combining effective compromise, practical necessity, good timing, and the ability to honor a courageous woman who happened to be a member of a minority group helped the dollar coin sail through the policy process.[33]

Effectively lobbying Congress to pass legislation is one thing, while getting the public to accept the dollar coins is another. Widespread usage of the coin has been elusive.

Lobbying the Bureaucracy

Much public policy emanates not from elected officials but rather from the specialists who design the administrative regulations that direct the carrying out of public policies (see Chapter 16). Interest groups that can influence bureaucrats have an inside track for getting their legislative preferences enacted into law.

Many executive branch agencies view certain interest groups as representing the agencies' constituencies. For example, the Department of Agriculture looks to such groups as the American Farm Bureau Federation for guidance. The Department of Veterans' Affairs seeks input from such groups as the American Legion and the Veterans of Foreign Wars (VFW). The agencies expect that satisfying the needs of their interest group constituents will win support in the legislative and judicial arenas for their own continuation and growth.

Interest groups recognize that few laws are self-executing. Legislatures and executives approve legislation embodying general goals. They leave it to the bureaucracy to work out the details. Once legislation is passed and the action moves to the bureaucratic arena, lobbyists often find a less crowded playing field. The intense competition marking much of the initial passage of a law is often replaced by a one-sided contest, with one or more of the past participants missing. The most interested and aware lobbyists speak at administrative hearings designed to develop the specific regulations for administering the law. Some of the most outspoken get themselves appointed to permanent advisory committees and make individual contacts with program administrators. By recognizing that policymaking is continuous, wise groups remain vigorous at all stages either to protect past gains or to compensate for earlier losses.

Lists of witnesses to come before administrative hearings are almost always dominated by interest groups with narrow goals, while representatives of the broader public interest are often conspicuous by their absence. Hearings on agricultural crop subsidies, for example, are filled with agricultural organizations. They seldom receive input, however, from consumer groups or taxpayer organizations. Groups with broader interests, such as consumers and taxpayers, often have no representative organization or spokespersons rooting for them. Even if organized, these groups have difficulty keeping up with all the specific policy issues that might affect their membership.

Lobbyists in Court

As author Lee Epstein points out, strategies are not limited by ideology:

> Like their liberal counterparts conservatives have entered the judicial arena with increasing regularity. . . The courts are increasingly being asked to mediate competing group claims, rather than claims between two parties with narrow, personal interests.[34]

A game is not over until it is over, and in politics this means that even while some issues are being settled in one arena, new ones are emerging in another. A number of interest groups have scored significant victories in the courts shortly after being scorned by elected officials and bureaucrats.

Interest groups become involved in a case when it is appealed to a higher court to refine the meaning of public statutes. In the classic school desegregation case of *Brown v.*

The Board of Education of Topeka (1954), the NAACP was less interested in the fate of one individual than in the broader issue of segregation. As you may know, this case resulted in desegregation of the public schools. Most court cases do not go beyond determining an individual's innocence or guilt, but some cases raise broad issues of judicial procedure or constitutionality and establish new precedents for future cases. It is these cases that interest groups attempt to affect.

Lobbyists cannot legitimately approach judges in the same direct way that they approach other decision makers. Instead, they use more indirect strategies. For example, recognizing that the appeals process is expensive, interest groups often offer financial support for appeals cases that they hope will result in a judicial finding favorable to their cause. In some high-publicity cases, interest groups get involved in the initial trial. They might provide legal expertise and special supporting research, such as public opinion polling data or **jury profiling** information, to help the lawyers choose the most supportive jury.

jury profiling *An attempt to research the type of juror who would be most favorable to one's cause. Based on the right of lawyers to challenge the right of a certain number of potential jury members to sit on the jury.*

If the case goes to appeals court, interest groups file written **amicus curiae briefs** that outline the groups' arguments on the case. Cases such as *Roe v. Wade* (1973) and *Webster v. Reproductive Health Services* (1989), which defined a woman's right to an abortion, pitted a large number of competing interest groups against each other. The *Webster* case generated 78 briefs with more than 400 organizations as co-sponsors.[35]

amicus curiae brief *"Friend of the court" brief in which an outside party presents arguments on one side or another of a case being considered by the court.*

Interest groups continually watch for cases to appeal. They also help to organize **class action suits.** Such suits collect a large group of individuals, each with a limited stake in the outcome, who join together to make the effort of a judicial proceeding worthwhile. The courts are often favorable playing fields for interest groups that, because of their size, issue area, or type of resources, have less success in the legislative or bureaucratic arenas.[36]

class action suit *The joint action of similarly affected individuals in taking a case to court even though the individual impact of the situation may be minimal.*

7-6 Winners and Losers: The Interest Group Box Score

Identifying consistent interest group winners and losers is difficult. Politics in America is relatively noncumulative. Today's winners may be tomorrow's losers, and few games are permanently zero-sum, with one group winning completely at the expense of another. Compromise and a variety of policy arenas provide some victories and losses for almost all organized groups.

Interest groups vary in their chances of getting preferences enacted into law and administered in a desirable way, though organized interests clearly win more often than unorganized ones. Because unorganized categoric and potential groups are often invisible to decision makers, their interests are not taken into account. The economic "haves" in American society, who have the motivation, skill, and resources to organize and protect their interests, generally win more often than do the "have-nots."

Persistence also pays off. The group that wins at one stage in the policy process and then rests on its laurels often finds its fortunes reversed as the policy-making process moves to another arena. As author David Knoke notes, "Because the associations that are broad in scope play in several policy games, they are more likely to succeed in some arenas than are groups that put their entire effort into one game."[37] Groups recognizing that the policy process is a *continuous game* of constant compromise, with "no final victories,"[38] tend to be more successful than groups that draw a line in the sand. Groups with flexible demands and anticipations of staying in the game are taken more seriously by decision makers than are transitory participants unwilling to accommodate the needs of others.

Long-term and persistent participants become part of the complex of **issue networks,** made up of the members of the congressional subcommittee, the executive branch agency, and the interest group most concerned with a narrow policy area.[39] These individuals and organizations work together on a continuing basis. Policy making in certain realms—agricultural crop subsidies, military weapons procurement, the regulation of business—are commonly dominated by issue networks. Most of the players know each other from long interaction and have a basic agreement on goals.

issue networks *The natural and continuous interaction of government and private players with an interest in a specific policy area. These relationships involve members of federal agency bureaus, congressional committees, and interest groups who share an interest in a specific area of public policy. They are sometimes also called "iron triangles."*

In many cases, the existence of issue networks implies a closed game. The participants agree on most issues and deny outsiders access to the decision-making process. Although players may be classified as opponents at times, they need each other. The elected officials need the political support of the interest groups and the information and service from the bureaucracy. The bureaucrats need to be supported by the interest groups when they face the elected officials for policy guidance and funding. The interest groups need favorable legislation from the elected officials and favorable policy implementation from the bureaucrats.

Interest groups are generally most powerful where it matters least. On technical details of legislation and administration, narrow interest groups representing only one side of the issue often have the expertise and motivation to determine much of the outcome. Opposing groups will be more likely to organize, express their positions, and force the decision-making process out into the open the more important the issue is to society. Additional groups and public opinion can then have an impact. The stage is set for compromise and moderation rather than for domination by a single interest.

In spite of the apparent stability of the policy process and its participants, the tendency and the right of Americans to join together in political interest groups are key variables in the policy game. The successes of such groups as MADD and the various tax revolt groups around the country spell trouble for any political player who acts as if there is nothing new under the sun. Modern communications technology allows almost instant mobilizing of persons with new interests. Virtually any categoric group that can be urged to come out of the stands and onto the playing field can have some impact on the ultimate outcome. While there is a danger that many clashing voices could create immobility in the policy process, free and open access by interest groups is a trademark of modern democracy.

Conclusion

Interest groups were not mentioned in the Constitution and were held in low regard by many of the Founders. Nevertheless, interest groups have proven to be both durable and effective players in a wide variety of political arenas. Joining together in teams based on common interests increases the power of individuals and informs decision makers of those interests in a significant way. Interest groups also affect who plays the game in a number of arenas through both the elective and appointive process. Lobbyists continue to provide much of the information on which elected and appointed officials base their decisions.

The American pluralist system encourages the contributions of interest groups while avoiding what Madison called the "mischief of factions." The advantages and disadvantages of a relatively inclusive game between competing interests are a continuing issue in the larger game of American politics and government.

Key Terms

access
advice and consent
amicus curiae brief
bribery
bundling
categoric group
class action suit
coalitions
collective benefits
disclosure laws
faction
Federal Election Campaign Act (FECA)
grassroots lobbying
group entrepreneur
Hatch Act
in-kind contributions
interest group
issue networks
jury profiling
latent interests
lobbyists
NIMBY
open games
Political Action Committee (PAC)
potential group
private interest group
public interest group
selective benefits
slack resources
uncoordinated expenditures

Practice Quiz

1. An individual who works diligently to bring people with similar interests into a formal organization is know as an interest group _____
a. lobbyist.
b. factionalist.
c. entrepreneur.
d. protagonist.

2. What is the difference between political parties and interest groups?
a. Interest groups consist of people of lower socioeconomic status than do political parties.
b. Interest groups are more interested in policy, whereas parties are more interested in controlling elections.
c. Parties are more interested in policy, whereas interest groups are more interested in controlling elections.
d. There is really no difference in contemporary politics compared to the past.

3. What occurs when latent interests are activated and a set of disparate individuals organize around noneconomics issues?
a. Public interest groups are formed.
b. Private interest groups are formed.
c. Potential groups are formed.
d. Political action committees are formed.

4. What type of benefit is cleaner air?
a. A private benefit
b. A collective benefit
c. A selective benefit
d. A zero sum benefit

5. What type of benefits are farm subsidies?
a. Private benefits
b. Collective benefits
c. Selective benefits
d. Zero sum benefits

6. Why do many people not join public interest groups?
a. Because they will receive selective benefits regardless of whether they join
b. Because they will receive collective benefits regardless of whether they join
c. Because public interest groups are almost universally corrupt
d. Because the Hatch Act makes members legally liable for group actions

7. Which individuals will be more likely to organize into an interest group?
a. Those with high socioeconomic status
b. Those with low levels of efficacy and who are mad about government policy
c. Those in need of slack resources
d. Those with nothing to lose

8. What strategies can interest groups use in influencing the decision in a court case?
a. Contacting judges personally and providing information
b. Filing a "judicial action statement"
c. Making financial contributions to judges
d. Filing an *amicus curiae brief*

9. The largest number of political action committees represent _____ interests.
a. labor
b. agriculture
c. business
d. health.

10. Most effective interest groups play politics as if it were a _____ game.
a. discrete
b. closed
c. positive-sum
d. continuous

You can find the correct answers to these questions by taking the quiz and then submitting your answers in the Online Edition. The program will automatically score your submission. Where you miss a question, the program will provide the correct answer, a rationale for the answer, and the section number in the chapter where the topic is discussed.

Further Reading

Interest Group Politics in America by Ronald J. Hrebenar (Armonk, NY: M. E. Sharpe, 1997) is a very readable text on the development and operation of interest groups.

In *Organized Interests and American Democracy* (New York: Harper and Row, 1986), Kay L. Schlozman and John T. Tierney use an extensive survey of Washington lobbyists to profile the activities of lobbying organizations in the nation's capital.

Bruce Wolpe and Bertram Levine's *Lobbying Congress: How the System Works* (Washington, D.C.: Congressional Quarterly Press, 1996) combines short lists of effective strategies from a successful Washington lobbyist with a series of lobbying case studies.

Public interest groups that represent noneconomic interests are discussed in Jeffrey Berry's *Lobbying for the People: The Political Behavior of Public Interest Groups* (Princeton, NJ: Princeton University Press, 1977).

Endnotes

1. Katherine Griffin, "No Longer MADD," *San Francisco Chronicle*, August 7, 1994, 6/Z1. Glenda Winders, "Drowning Her Pain in Money?" *The Houston Post*, January 30, 1994, C1. For a more detailed discussion, see Stephen Frantzich, *Citizen Democracy: Political Activists in a Cynical Age* (Lanham, MD: Rowman and Littlefield, 1999).
2. Senator Robert Dole, *Congressional Record*, July 17, 1990, S-9824.
3. Kay Lehman Schlozman and John T. Tierney, *Organized Interests and American Democracy* (New York: Harper and Row, 1986), 31–32.
4. Kettering Foundation, *Citizens and Policymakers in Community Forums* (Dayton, OH: Kettering Foundation, 1991), 25.
5. Ronald J. Hrebenar, *Interest Group Politics in America* (Armonk, NY: M. E. Sharpe, 1997), 14–17.
6. Gary Lee, "Hearings to Review Lobby Disclosure Law," *Washington Post*, June 10, 1991, A9.
7. Schlozman and Tierney, *Organized Interests*, 122.
8. Schlozman and Tierney, *Organized Interests*, 93.
9. Hrebenar, 33–34.
10. The concept of a progression of types of groups differing in their consciousness about their self-interests and their potential for being organized was first discussed in Earl Latham's *The Group Basis of Politics* (Ithaca, NY: Cornell University Press, 1952) and refined in David Truman's *The Governmental Process* (New York: Knopf, 1971).
11. See Robert H. Salisbury, "An Exchange Theory of Interest Groups," *Midwest Journal of Political Science* 13 (1969): 11–15; and Norman Frolich, Joe A. Oppenheimer, and Oran R. Young, *Political Leadership and Collective Goods* (Princeton, NJ: Princeton University Press, 1971).
12. See Mancur Olson, *The Logic of Collective Action* (Cambridge, MA: Harvard University Press, 1965) for the distinction between "collective" and "selective" goods and services.
13. Schlozman and Tierney, *Organized Interests*, 122–31.
14. F. Christopher Arterton, *Teledemocracy: Can Technology Protect Democracy?* (Newbury Park, CA: Sage, 1987), 17, 188.
15. President Calvin Coolidge actually said, "The chief business of the American people is business" in an address before the American Society of Newspaper Editors in 1925, but this shortened version has been passed down since that time as a justification for giving business interests special consideration in the policy process. See Suzy Platt (ed.), *Respectfully Quoted* (Washington, D.C.: Library of Congress, 1989), 21.
16. Schlozman and Tierney, *Organized Interests*, 104.
17. Michael Weiskopf, "Lining Up Allies in the Health Care Debate," *Washington Post*, October 3, 1993, A4.
18. All figures from the *Encyclopedia of Associations* [2000] except NRA figures from *Los Angeles Times*, May 14, 2000, A1.
19. Quoted in Hedrick Smith, *The Power Game* (New York: McGraw-Hill, 1988), 216.
20. Peter Stone, "Republican Victors Pac-ing In Contributions," *Orlando Sentinel*, December 18, 1994, G1.
21. www.fec.gov.
22. Mary Beth Regan et. al, "PACs Cross the Street," *Business Week*, April 10, 1995, 94.
23. Hrebenar, 4.
24. Harriet Woods, President of the National Women's Political Caucus, as quoted in Ruth Marcus, "As Thomas Hearings Wrap Up, Democrats Question the Process," *Washington Post*, September 21, 1991, A7.
25. Quoted in Kirk Victor, "Labor Pains," *National Journal*, June 8, 1991, 1336.
26. Smith, *The Power Game*, 217–18.
27. "The Battle to Win Public Opinion: Let the Games Begin," American Political Network, Healthline, October 5, 1993, LEXIS-NEXIS database.
28. Eric Schine, "From the Folks Who Brought You Harry and Louise," *Business Week*, April 17, 1995, 37.
29. Quotations from author's interviews.
30. Bruce C. Wolpe, *Lobbying Congress: How the System Works* (Washington, D.C.: Congressional Quarterly, 1990), 37.
31. James Glassman, "Dollar Coin: It Makes Cents to Buck Tradition," November 5, 1993, D1.
32. Stephen Ambrose's best-selling account of the Lewis and Clark journey, *Undaunted Courage*, was on the public's "must read" list during the period of discussion. A companion film by Ken Burns expanded public awareness of Sacagawea.
33. Greg Hassell, "Sacagawea Guides America back to the Dollar Coin," *Houston Chronicle*, March 26, 2000, 1.
34. Lee Epstein, *Conservatives in Court* (Knoxville, TN: University of Tennessee Press, 1985), xii.
35. Susan Bheuniak-Long, "Friendly Fires: Amicus Curae and *Webster v. Reproductive Health Services*," *Judicature* 74 (February/March 1991), 261–63.
36. See Hrebenar, 297.
37. David Knoke, *Organizing for Collective Action: The Political Economies of Associations* (Hawthorne, NY: A. De Gruyter, 1990), 321.
38. The late Larry O'Brien, one of the twentieth century's most effective political organizers, popularized this phrase when he titled his autobiography *No Final Victories* (Garden City, NJ: Doubleday, 1974).
39. See Hugh Heclo, "Issue Networks and the Executive Establishment," in *The New American Political System*, ed. Anthony King (Washington, D.C.: American Enterprise Institute, 1978).

Political Parties: Organizing around Broad Themes

Key Points

- **The components of modern American political parties.**
- **The history of the two-party system and the factors working against third parties.**
- **How party candidates are chosen.**
- **Consequences of party strategies and resources.**
- **The impact of party identification on party members appointed or elected to office.**

Preview: Creating Permanent Political Teams

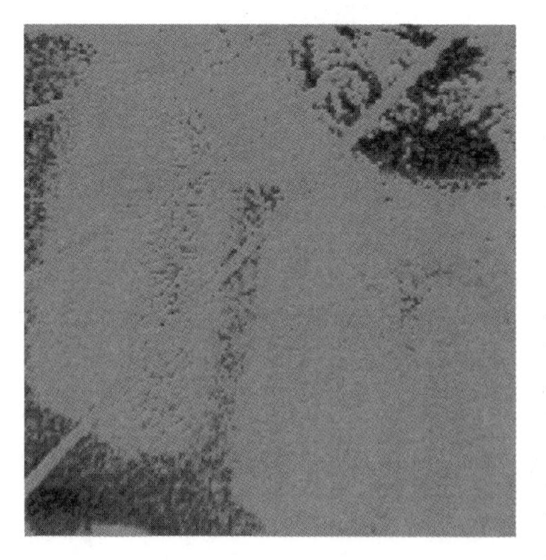

In his book Democracy in America *(1835), French writer Alexis de Tocqueville made a series of insightful comments about American political behavior, theory, and institutions. These were the result of his travels in 1831 to observe the United States firsthand. Should a modern-day de Tocqueville stop by the two national party headquarters, he, too, would immediately observe some interesting facts about physical and organizational differences. At one headquarters he would find a large staff, organized in a highly structured manner, typically making decisions in a top-down hierarchical manner. A glance at the titles on office doors would indicate a series of activities, such as finance, public relations, and research, which might be found in any large corporation attempting to sell a product. Just a few blocks away, also on Capitol Hill, at the other national headquarters, he would find a much newer and more flexible organization, designed to mediate between competing outlooks. This group, indeed, seems almost to reject organization-*

al structure. Here the nameplates on the doors indicate a series of organizations connected with groups such as women, labor, and state governors.

One might reasonably assume that the observer's first stop was at the Democratic Party, with its almost two hundred years of existence and its philosophical commitment to larger government and centralized control. Using similar logic, one might guess that the second stop was at the newer Republican Party, whose philosophy embraces more limited government and places decision making in the hands of those more directly affected. These conclusions would in fact be wrong. By the mid-1990s the Republican National Committee had adopted more corporate, task-oriented, and centralized organizational structure. The emphasis is now on order and efficiency. The Democratic National Committee, meanwhile, downplays the importance of organizational effectiveness in favor of internal democracy and freedom. One might be reminded of Will Rogers's famous quip of the 1930s: "I am not a member of any organized party—I am a Democrat."

The seeming inconsistency has some logical roots. The business backgrounds of many Republicans and the conservative commitment to order and efficiency make Republicans more comfortable with their clearly structured organization. The greater diversity within the Democratic Party and its liberal commitment to freedom makes it more difficult for Democrats to impose decisions. This is also a case where names do make a difference. The philosophical concept of republicanism, from which the party takes its name, implies indirect decision making by the more capable segments of society. The root of the term democracy, on the other hand, emphasizes equal participation by all.

The consequences of party structure can be dramatic. Over the years the Republican Party's efficiency in raising funds and training candidates allowed them to hold their own during periods when Democratic voters far outnumbered Republicans. The ability of the Republicans to get the vast majority of their 1994 candidates to sign

1848 Whig Party Banner for the Taylor-Fillmore Presidential Campaign

Library of Congress, Prints & Photographs Division [LC-USZC2-584]

its centrally created Contract with America—and really campaign on it—amazed most Democrats, who could not agree on any consistent election theme. At the announcement of the Contract, Republican leader Newt Gingrich (R-Ga.) boldly asserted: "Our government operates on the party system. We are a team. And we're offering you a contract on what our team will do."[1]

Thus our modern-day observer would find that contemporary Republicans rely on a centralized party structure in their attempt to decentralize government and reduce its involvement in our lives. He would see that the Democrats, on the other hand, seek to impose greater uniformity of laws and an active reliance on government through a party structure that is decentralized. To de Tocqueville's earlier inspired observations, he could add a description of this fascinating inconsistency in American politics.

political party *An organized group of individuals with similar ideologies, joined together to control the personnel and policies of government through elections.*

Political parties are relatively permanent organizations that join like-minded individuals together under a given label. Their aim is to control the personnel and policies of government through elections. Like interest groups, parties are institutions attempting to link citizens to government. Unlike interest groups, though, parties attempt to cover a wide range of issues and are more interested in electing the personnel of government than in affecting its policy. In this chapter we will look at the origin of American parties, the components of parties, the rules under which parties operate, and their impact on the political system.

8-1 Origin of the Parties: The Unwelcome Players

The seeds of political parties predate the Revolution. Political activists in colonial America disagreed about how to deal with England. They used the political process to build support for their preferred positions among their fellow citizens. It remains curious that James Madison and George Washington, winners in the factional battle that resulted in the founding of the American republic, would have negative feelings about political Parties, but they did:

> The goal is to secure the public good, and private rights, against the danger of . . . faction. . . . By a faction, understand a number of citizens . . . who are united and actuated by some common impulse of passion, or of interest, adverse to the rights of other citizens. . . . (James Madison, *Federalist* No. 10, 1787)

> Let me now . . . warn you in the most solemn manner against the baneful effects of the spirit of party. (George Washington, Farewell Address, September 17, 1796)

In reaction to the selfishness and divisiveness of the British political parties of their day, the Founders opposed permanent party divisions as "the last degradation of a free and moral agent" (Thomas Jefferson), "dangerous organizations" (James Madison), and "the curse of the country" (James Monroe).[2] For all the Founders' fears, it remains true that without these precursors of contemporary American political parties, the Republic never would have been formed.

During the colonial period, Tories (or Loyalists) supported British rule, while Whigs (or Patriots) chafed under British control and ultimately became supporters of the revolutionary movement. Starting in Massachusetts in 1772, the Whigs developed a network of groups throughout the colonies to protest British policies and, eventually, to drum up support for the independence movement. Fifteen years later, when the ratification of the Constitution required collective action, the Federalists and Anti-Federalists sought to control political outcome through organization and communication (see Chapter 2). Like modern parties, their organizations brought together individuals with common outlooks. They established means of communication and collective strategies for pursuing political goals. The major component that these early groups lacked was the permanent organization and electioneering activity that are associated with modern political parties.

National political players soon recognized both the divisions in the nation and the advantages of permanent political organization. When Alexander Hamilton, George Washington's secretary of the treasury, attempted to centralize national government power and to favor business interests, Thomas Jefferson left the cabinet for partisan reasons and became the first modern political organizer. He brought together more than three dozen state and local organizations committed to limiting the role of national government. The emerging party—the Jeffersonians—met to debate and endorse candidates in opposition to the policies of the Federalists. By 1794 they had developed a party **caucus** in Congress to nominate leaders both for the presidency and within the legislature.[3] Six years later the fruits of Jefferson's party-building efforts resulted in his election to the presidency and the eventual disappearance of the Federalists.

caucus *A meeting of party activists to select nominees, choose leaders, determine party policy, or plan strategy.*

For the next few decades, the parties split and came together again under a variety of different names as new issues and personalities joined the game. By the time of the Civil War, the stage was set for the modern two-party era. The Democratic Party had emerged as the remnant of the Jeffersonians, supporting more local democracy and the interests of less economically privileged voters, especially in the South and West. With the decline of the Federalists, the Whigs had emerged to represent business interests. During the 1850s, the Republican Party emerged as a third party that merged supporters of business and commerce with an array of antislavery parties.

As the right to vote was expanded, the political parties took on the task of organizing and motivating the mass of voters.[4] Parties helped voters to make sense out of politics by nominating **slates** of candidates committed to a general set of policy goals. **Nominations** were initially made by legislative caucuses and then by party conventions. (The opportunity for broad participation in the nomination stage did not arrive until the twentieth century.) Party organizations helped their candidates to gather resources for election campaigns and expected elected officials to remain loyal to party policy goals once in office.

slate *The group of candidates nominated by a party running as a team.*

nomination *The stage in the election process during which the official competing candidates are chosen.*

Even though the individual fortunes of the Republican and Democratic parties have varied from one historical period to the next, political parties per se were the dominant political teams until after World War II. Candidates and elected officials then began to act more independently. Most voters in the prewar period used the party label as a shorthand method of selecting candidates for which to vote. Few elected officials made it into office without the direct support of one of the parties, and party-based coalitions supported the organization and actions of officials once they were elected.

Unlike most countries, the United States has a party system that has historically involved competition between two relatively evenly matched teams, as opposed to single or multi-party systems. Events such as the Civil War and the Great Depression played a major role in realigning the strength of each partisan team. Periods of one-party domination have led to the resurgence of the opposing party or to the emergence of a new party to replace the faltering opposition. From the 1950s through the 1980s, the parties developed divergent institutional bases of strength on the national level. During that period, the Republicans dominated presidential elections and the Democrats controlled Congress. In 1992, however, the Democrats won the presidency. The campaign was marked by a strong third-party showing. In 1994, after forty years of Democratic control, the Republicans captured both houses of Congress.

In 1996, 1998, and 2000, Republicans lost seats in Congress but maintained razor-thin margins in both chambers. After the 2000 election, the 50-50 tie in the Senate allowed the Republicans to use Vice President Dick Cheney's tie-breaking voting power to maintain control. Less than five months into the session, Senator James Jeffords of Vermont returned majority control to the Democrats by renouncing his Republican label and becoming an independent. In 2002, George W. Bush and the Republican Party broke the pattern of incumbent president's parties losing seats in midterm elections. Small gains allowed them to strengthen their majority in the House and take back the Senate.

As we will see, the two-party system is bolstered by election laws, voter behavior, and party strategies.

8-2 Players in the American Party System

The term *political party* obscures the diverse aspects of parties. In an ancient Indian fable, a group of blind men gathered around an elephant were asked to describe it. With considerable conviction each proceeded to affirm his findings. The man touching the trunk proclaimed an elephant to be like a snake. The man with his arms around a leg was just as firmly convinced that an elephant was like a tree. The man holding the tail interrupted to complain that anyone with any sense would know that an elephant was really like a rope. And so it went, with each of the blind men using his grasp of a partial piece of reality to misunderstand the larger and more complex creature.

A similar problem has faced students of American political parties. Parties are complex creatures with a variety of different and seemingly separate parts. If sent out to find and describe a political party, one person might come back with a list of characteristics of an organization—offices, budgets, staff, and volunteers—while another person, seeing the party as a set of ideas and psychological affiliations, might describe the nature and number of people who call themselves Republicans, Democrats, Socialists, and the like. Still another intrepid investigator might focus on elected officials sharing a party label as they meet to plan strategy for making party ideas into law.

It is not that any of these observers is wrong, but that modern political parties are all of these things and more. At times, the separate components of political parties fail to work together. Like the elephant threatened with extinction, the parties have often been given up for dead by political observers, yet they continue to emerge as key players in the political game, sometimes with just a change of emphasis regarding different aspects of their complex nature.

In the next few pages, we will look at what parties do, party organization, party adherents in the electorate, party activities in campaigns, and the officials elected under the party label.

8-2a Political Party Functions

Political parties continue to exist because they perform important tasks for the American political system,[5] including:

- ***Socializing voters***: Parties transmit political values and encourage attitudes supporting political participation. Political parties emphasize learning the importance of political involvement. They attempt to develop among voters long-term ideological orientations through which they will choose policy alternatives.
- ***Managing and contributing conflict***: They suggest options, aggregate like-minded individuals, and simplify alternatives for voters. Parties are motivated to raise new issues, to assure that most election contests have at least two candidates, and to frame issues as a simple choice between party perspectives.
- ***Recruiting, training, and providing resources to candidates***: Parties encourage viable candidates and assure viable competition in most elections. They encourage the feasibility of political contests by directly funding campaigns and by indirectly offering training and advice to potential candidates.
- ***Monitoring the rules of the game***: Parties help to assure an even playing field and watch for infractions by the opposing team. They look out for their own interests and attempt to structure political processes that allow their candidates and policy initiatives to win.
- ***Encouraging political involvement and informing voters***: Parties help expand the electorate through registration and get-out-the-vote drives as well as through educating voter choices on issues and candidates. Party organizers realize that campaigns both among the electorate and within policy-making bodies are won by determining who participates and by convincing the participants of the value of the party position.
- ***Ameliorating the separation of powers***: Parties accumulate power and encourage officeholders in different institutions to cooperate. They establish a team outlook so

that party members in different political institutions recognize that their success is determined in part by their ability to work together.

The performance of these tasks varies both over time and between parties. Politics is largely a team sport, and parties represent the most constant set of teams in the political arena.

8-2b The Party Organization

The most visible aspect of a political party is its formal organization. Organization charts and lists of committees—precinct, county, state central, and the Republican and Democratic national committees—identify the players who keep the party organization going. Many party organizations operate with paid staffs, significant budgets, and well-equipped offices. The degree of organizational resources varies considerably, however, from one level and/or geographical area to the next.

From the Civil War to World War II, volunteer-run state and local party organizations dominated politics. During this period, local parties far surpassed the much more informal and transitory national parties in terms of organization, resources, and impact. Even today, wherever local party organizations remain active, it is the volunteer officers of state and county parties who meet regularly and do much of the day-to-day work of pursuing party interests. The national parties rarely meet as single entities, and their organizational presence is dominated by their permanent paid staff in Washington.

In many cities, **party "machines"**—so named for their efficiency and their emphasis on materialistic motivation for political involvement—dominated local politics during the late 1800s and early 1900s. Through their right to nominate candidates at caucuses and conventions, they controlled who ran for office. They also provided the resources necessary for election and determined who benefited from winning. Local party leaders attempted to balance party tickets with members of various geographic and ethnic backgrounds. For their part, voters accepted the slate of candidates presented by their parties and voted a straight party ticket. Strong party organizations sent active precinct volunteers door-to-door to spread the party word. It was an era of labor-intensive campaigns dominated by interpersonal communications.

> ***party machine*** *Sophisticated and carefully crafted organizations that controlled city politics by awarding favors (that is, patronage jobs or city licenses) in return for electoral support.*

The **political boss** running the party machine offered **patronage** jobs to party workers and made sure that party voters received favored treatment.[6] Political bosses gained power in the view of higher levels of the party by delivering votes from their local area. In exchange, they received a say in party politics and material rewards, such as government jobs and contracts to hand out to their supporters. Party machines flourished in the Northeast and in urban centers elsewhere, such as Chicago. Because they lacked education and other resources, new immigrants and poor residents often traded their votes for jobs, for help with legal problems, and for basic necessities (see Chapter 18).[7]

> ***political boss*** *An individual, who might or might not be an elected official, who headed a political machine and wielded strong influence in local government politics.*

> ***patronage*** *The practice of bestowing public-sector jobs as a reward for political support or personal loyalty.*

While not all machine politics was corrupt, politicians of this era often had employees on the public payroll who spent most of their time promoting party goals rather than providing public service. Buying votes was certainly not unheard of, and government contracts often personally benefited party activists.

Potential candidates accepted the rules of the game, which required them to work their way up through the party organization. Although Theodore Roosevelt is remembered as a swashbuckling national leader, he took his turn as a precinct worker in his local party organization (see Box 8-1: Teddy the Political Hack). Until the twentieth century, political candidates clearly needed the political party more than the political party needed the candidates.

A variety of legal and societal changes undermined party machines in the first decade of the twentieth century. The passage of **civil service** laws reduced the number of patronage jobs available, while the introduction of **nonpartisan elections** and the **primary election** as the dominant method of nomination undercut party control of candidate recruitment (see Chapter 11). Primary elections, in which voters chose among potential party nominees, fostered conflict within a party and undermined the ability of a party to reward members' efforts. The increased education levels of some members of

> ***civil service*** *A system for selecting government employees on the basis of merit rather than political connection or patronage.*

> ***nonpartisan elections*** *Electoral contests in which candidates do not campaign as party representatives; no party affiliations are listed on ballots.*

> ***primary election*** *A preelection selection process to determine the official nominees of a party when more than one candidate has filed.*

Box 8–1 *Teddy the Political Hack*

Resplendent in evening dress, [Teddy Roosevelt] would dash across Fifth Avenue, round the corner of Fifty-ninth Street, and up a shabby flight of stairs. Morton Hall, as the headquarters of the Twenty-first District Republican Association was grandly called, was a barn-sized chamber over a store. . . . Here the cheap lawyers, saloonkeepers, and horsecar conductors who ran Theodore's district—Irishmen, mostly—met together for political meetings once or twice a month. . . . He had been by no means welcome, for his side-whiskers and evening clothes made the "heelers" uncomfortable. But he came back again and again until he was eventually accepted for membership in the association. . . . He could, of course, have entered the government in the respectable way—by cultivating the society of men in leather armchairs, qualifying as a lawyer himself, and, in ten years or so, running for a seat in the United States Senate. But some instinct told him that if he desired raw political power . . . he must start on the shop floor, learn those greasy levers one by one. . . . By March he was taking a more active role in party politics, attending a series of primaries in addition to regular meetings, working his way into the executive committee of Young Republicans, and presuming to address the association on its new charter.

Theodore Roosevelt

Source: From Edmund Morris, *The Rise of Theodore Roosevelt* (New York: Coward, McCann and Geoghegan, Inc., 1979), 142–145.

the population and the advent of federal, government-run, social welfare programs reduced dependence on the local party organization for voter information and services. At the same time, the corruption found in some of the party organizations encouraged the passage of laws limiting the rights and operation of the parties.

Local parties are currently the "weakest link in the party organization chain."[8] The most extensive growth in party organization is on the national level.[9] State and national parties now actively recruit potential candidates, train candidates and campaign workers, and provide campaign resources in the form of direct financial *in-kind contributions*.

For a number of years the parties had allowed candidates to stray from the party to acquire modern campaign services from paid consultants. Following the lead of the national Republican Party, both parties now play the role of service vendors, creating television advertisements, conducting public opinion polls, registering voters, helping candidates to raise funds, and getting the party message out (see Figure 8-4 later in the chapter). The parties are fighting their way back into the game by attempting to provide candidates with high-tech campaigning at lower cost. Their offerings include more politically astute application of the principles of public relations and marketing to the political arena.

Potential candidates are given a shopping list of services that the party can perform. In some cases, the services are free; in others, they are provided at cut rates. All of the services that follow are provided to some degree by the national party organizations, while more and more state and local parties have developed competence in providing some of them, too. The most common services include:

- ***Training:*** Candidate schools that teach everything from strategy and scheduling to how to smile and shake hands effectively; campaign support staff schools for everyone from campaign managers and treasurers to children and spouses

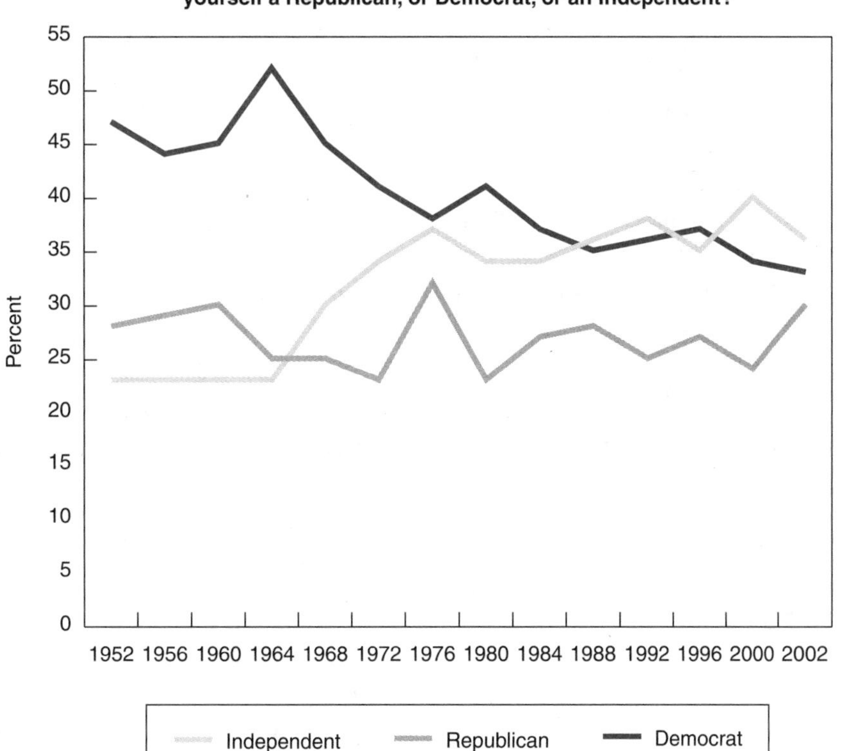

Figure 8-1

Party Identification: Joining a Party Team on the Psychological Level

Respondents who gave replies other than Democrat, Republican, or Independent are excluded.

Source: National Election Studies, reported in Harold W. Stanley and Richard G. Niemei, *Vital Statistics on American Politics, 2003–2004* (Washington, D.C.: Congressional Quarterly, Inc.), 2003.

- ***Demographic Analysis:*** Sophisticated precinct-by-precinct analysis of past election results, combined with census and polling data, to target potential contributors and supporters
- ***Opposition Research:*** Clipping files and computerized database searching of every documented statement of opponents
- ***Polling:*** Help in the design, application, and interpretation of sophisticated polling techniques
- ***Legal Services:*** Advice and counsel on how to get on the ballot, how to use the voting registration process to your advantage, and how not to run afoul of the complex campaign financing laws
- ***Fund-raising:*** The provision of mailing lists of potential contributors, help in designing effective direct-mail appeals, and suggestions for effective fund-raising events
- ***Advertising:*** The expertise of a virtual full-service advertising agency to design ads, write scripts, produce the final product, and purchase radio or television time
- ***Brokerage:*** Recommendations regarding campaign consultants with a proven track record to handle specialized services that the party organization cannot provide directly; help in negotiating favorable contracts with campaign consultants
- ***Public Relations:*** Offering a speaker's bureau of party notables to attend campaign events

8-2c The Party-in-the-Electorate

Political parties do not exist by organization charts alone. Less visible but just as important are psychological affiliations in the hearts and minds of voters. More than 60 percent of voters express a **party identification,** psychologically linking themselves to either the Republican or the Democratic party, and make up the **party-in-the-electorate** (see Figure 8-1). Recent years have seen significant gains in the percentage of voters calling themselves Independents. National polling data fail to identify that small percentage of voters aligning themselves with one of the minor parties.

party identification *The sense of affinity or feeling of belonging to one of the political parties.*

party-in-the-electorate *Those voters who psychologically identify with one of the parties and tend to vote for its nominees.*

Time Out 8-1

Joining a Partisan Team

1. In politics today, do you consider yourself a Democrat, a Republican, or an Independent?
   ____(Democrat) ____(Republican) ____(Independent)
2. Does your father consider himself a Republican, a Democrat, or an Independent?
   ____(Democrat) ____(Republican) ____(Independent) ____(Don't know or not applicable)
3. Does your mother consider herself a Republican, a Democrat, or an Independent?
   ____(Democrat) ____(Republican) ____(Independent) ____(Don't know or not applicable)

Go to the Answers to Time Out 8-1 box on page 238 for discussion of party identification.

Becoming a formal "card-carrying" member of a political party is far less common in the United States than in many of the European countries. Without officially joining, American partisans feel akin to party organizations to which they have no formal attachment (see Time Out 8-1: Joining a Partisan Team). They cheer on "their" partisan team and generally contribute their vote to its efforts. In a number of states, voters must register a party identification or classify themselves as independent. This encourages them to make a decision about the party to which they feel closest. During much of this century, more Americans considered themselves Democrats than Republicans. In recent years, the gap in party identification between Republicans and Democrats has almost disappeared, with a significant growth in the number of independents (see Figure 8-1).[10]

Party identification reflects more than a casual expression of support. Most individuals cast votes consistent with their party identification (see Figure 8-2). However, both the percentage of individuals expressing a party identification and the level of party-line voting have declined in recent years. Republicans show slightly more party loyalty. A higher percentage of Democrats usually engage in **ticket splitting.**

ticket splitting *The abandonment of a straight party-line vote in favor of picking and choosing among the candidates of different parties.*

The Origin of Party Identification

As much as Americans might like to think of themselves as independent thinkers, they are the products of their environment. They typically receive their introduction to the parties from their parents through the **socialization** process (see Chapter 5). When both parents have the same party identification, most often their children see themselves as supporters of that party.

socialization *The process by which political attitudes and outlooks of society are transmitted from one generation to the next through teaching or emulation.*

To accept the party identification of one's parents is not necessarily blind and unthinking support. Most children develop the same general values and ideology as their parents and find themselves in similar social and economic conditions. The party that looks out for the interests of the parents might do the best job of looking out for the interests of their children as they grow into adulthood and begin socializing their own children into the political game. To the degree that the parties present meaningful alternatives and their candidates live up to their commitments once in office, party labels provide a cue for voters. Parties are conveniences. They reduce the cost in terms of the time and effort that an individual would have to spend to make a considered voting choice. Republicans tend to have relatively more education, higher incomes, higher status jobs, and more traditional attitudes and ideology than do Democrats. Democrats have an edge among women, blacks, and Latinos. Geographically, Democrats are more numerous, with greater concentrations in urban areas and the East. Republicans tend to live in suburbs and small towns in the Midwest and West.

Shifting Party Loyalties

The South, which has been going through a dramatic transformation over the last fifty years, is an example of shifting party loyalties. In the 1850s the Republican Party chal-

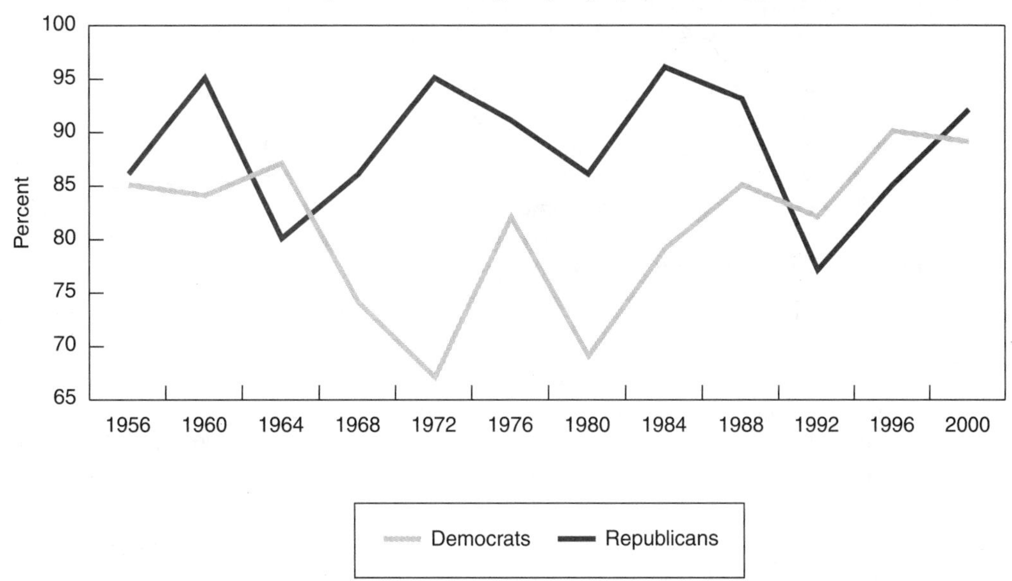

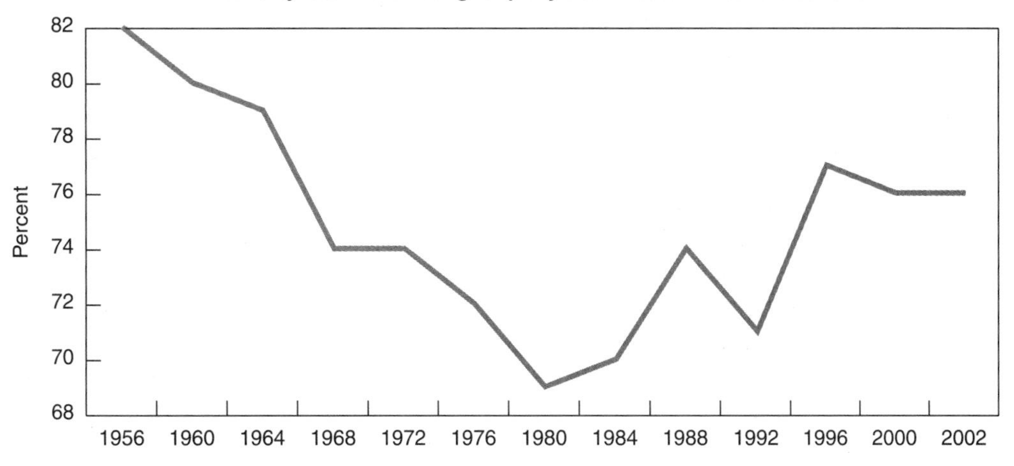

Figure 8-2
Party Identifiers Voting for a Party's Presidential Candidate

Source: Harold W. Stanley and Richard G. Niemi, *Vital Statistics on American Politics, 2003–2004* (Washington, D.C.: Congressional Quarterly, Inc., 2003), p. 138.

lenged slavery, which helped to precipitate the Civil War. Because the Republican Party controlled the national government during the war and its aftermath, southern hatred of the Republicans resulted. This led to almost a century of Democratic Party domination in the South. But during the middle part of the twentieth century, the growing liberalism of the national Democratic Party strained traditional party identifications among southerners. The "solid" Democratic South has been breaking apart in recent years over issues of race and economic policy. Contemporary white southerners now tend to vote for more conservative Republican presidential candidates, although they go back to their traditional Democratic Party loyalties for lower-level offices.[11] By the 1990s, voting Republican for other state and federal offices became more acceptable in the South. Many of the Republicans' gains in the 1994 election, in fact, came from their capturing Democratic seats in the South (see Figure 8-3).

Today, shifting party loyalties are not limited to the South. Nationally, Republicans have been encouraged that although younger voters are a bit more likely to vote as independents, when they do choose a party, they have been increasingly more likely to identify themselves as Republicans. With the aging of the Democratic voting bloc, supporters have worried that "time is most definitely not on their side."[12] Nonwhites, a fast-growing voting bloc, have become only slightly more Republican than they were in the past.

Answer to Time Out 8-1

Compare your party identification with that of your parents. Well over two-thirds of children whose parents agree on a political party (or where only one parent is partisan) choose to identify with that party (only about 10 percent switch to the opposing party, with the remainder becoming independents). When parents disagree on their party identifications, more than a third of the children become independents, with the remainder about equally likely to adopt the party identification of either parent. If your choice is not consistent with your parents' party identification, can you think of some of the factors pushing your political loyalties in another direction? You might consider the degree to which your educational level, lifestyle, and economic position match that of your parents.

Women are also somewhat less likely to become Republican than are men (see Table 8-1). Because of Republican gains in 1994 and their ability to sustain congressional majorities in 1996 and 1998, Democrats worried that the Clinton victories in 1992 and 1996 represented only a temporary reversal of Republican fortunes.

The 2000 presidential election became one for the history books due to its closeness and partisan maneuvering over vote counts and recounts, but most patterns from the past were sustained: Republicans supported George W. Bush at a higher rate than Democrats supported Al Gore, with third party candidate Ralph Nader drawing most of his votes from typical Democratic voters, just as Ross Perot drew most of his votes from probable Republican voters in 1992 and 1996. The gender gap remained, with Gore garnering the majority of votes from females and Bush those from males. Blacks maintained their over 90% support for the Democratic nominee, while the fast-growing Latino voting block gave only about two-thirds of their votes to Gore.

realignment A dramatic change in the balance between the political parties involving a shift in the way major social groups vote.

Partisan attachments are not permanently fixed. Dramatic historical events and changes in personal conditions can cause individuals to switch their party preference. Partisan **realignments**—dramatic shifts in the voting patterns of groups of individuals, with emergence of a new majority party—occur more rarely. Historically, such shifts have occurred every forty years or so. Some have argued that massive shifts in party loyalty are cyclical,[13] while others have pointed out the unique historical characteristics giving rise to the abandonment of one party for another (see Table 8-2). The last recognized shift was the result of the Great Depression, which caused African Americans and poorer whites to vote in large numbers for the Democratic Party because of its economic policies in 1932.

Figure 8-3
Republican Party Office Holding in the South, 1970–2004

Source: Calculated from Harold W. Stanley and Richard G. Niemi, *Vital Statistics on American Politics, 2003–2004* (Washington, D.C.: Congressional Quarterly, Inc., 2001).

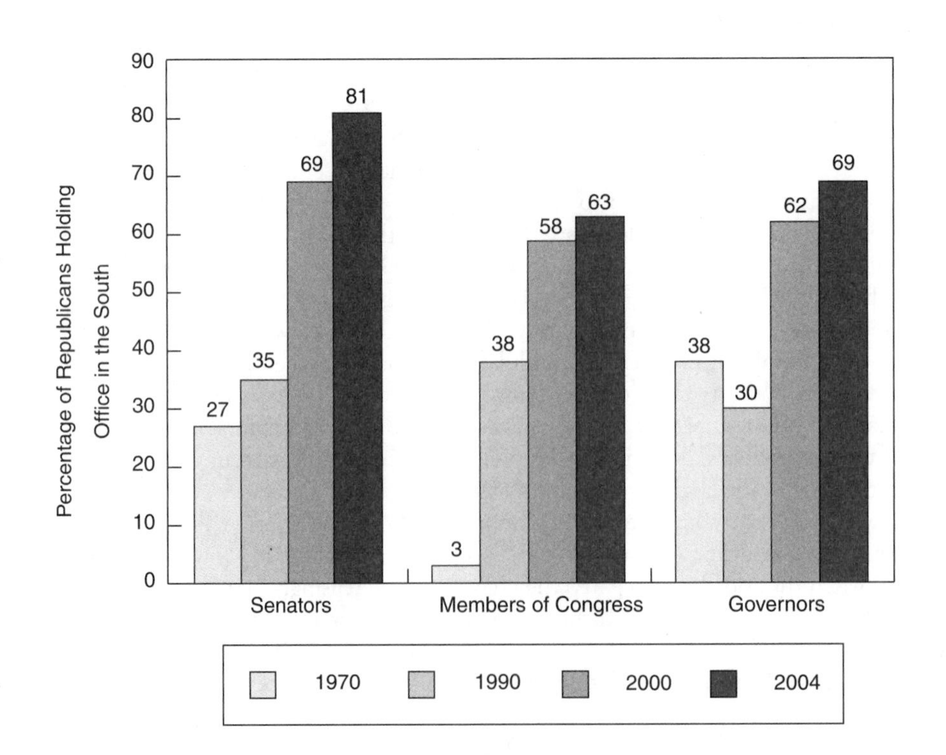

Table 8-1 The Shifting Social and Political Background Composition of Partisan Voting Teams, 1968 and 1998

	1968 Republican %	1998 Republican %	Republican shift**	1968 Democrat %	1998 Democrat %	Democratic shift**
Total*	27%	30%	+1%	46%	30%	–16%
Sex						
Male	28%	31%	+3%	44%	23%	–21%
Female	26%	26%	Even	48%	37%	–11%
Race						
White	29%	32%	+3%	43%	26%	–17%
African American	7%	8%	+1%	75%	58%	–17%
Age						
Under 30	22%	30%	+8%	38%	20%	–18%
30–49	24%	31%	+7%	36%	29%	–7%
50+	31%	23%	-8%	39%	48%	–9%
Region						
East	29%	28%	–1%	46%	29%	–17%
Midwest	30%	25%	–5%	42%	28%	–14%
South	17%	25%	+8%	52%	34%	–18%
West	33%	38%	+5%	42%	28%	–14%

*Self-identified party identification.

**Positive numbers indicate a shift toward the party and negative numbers a shift away from the party.

Note: Republicans have gained moderately and Democrats have lost significant numbers of party identifiers among almost all population groups. A large percentage of voters have moved from being partisan voters to being independents.

Source: The Gallup Poll, historical data from *The Gallup Poll, 1935–1971* (New York: Random House), 1972, 2136; February 1998 Gallup poll of 1,041 adults, LEXIS NEXIS database.

Previous patterns indicated that the United States was due for a partisan realignment during the 1970s, but none was evident. Contemporary signals are mixed. Republicans have dominated presidential elections, while Democrats have held onto Congress for most of the last three decades. The 1994 elections signaled increasing fluidity of voter choices more than a true realignment. With a larger group of self-proclaimed independents and a greater willingness of partisans to support some candidates from the other party, significant changes in election outcomes could occur without an underlying change in actual partisan identification.

Television and new computer-based campaign technologies have made a variety of divergent political messages more accessible to voters. Individual candidates can now go directly to the voters, bypassing the party. With such richness of information available, voters no longer need to choose between one of the two packaged sets of information and options transmitted by party workers.

Such diversity of information may well undermine the chances for a true realignment in the near future. Instead, the contemporary era reflects more of a dealignment, with self-identified independent voters less tied to any one party, partisan candidates downplaying their party labels, and shifting partisan voting patterns among a number of groups of voters.

Table 8-2 Realigning the Partisan Teams

Time Period	Causes	Results
1789–early 1800s	Proposed ratification of the Constitution Intra-party factionalism within the Federalists and emergence of the Jeffersonian Democrats	Emergence of the Federalists and Anti-Federalists
1820s	Factionalism within the dominant Jeffersonian Democrats opposed by a relatively unstable coalition of parties running as Whigs	Emergence of the Jacksonian Democrats
1850s–1860s	Rise of slavery becomes an issue and the resulting Civil War in opposition to slavery	Emergence of the Republican party in 1854 with the election of 1860 ushering in decades of Republican domination
1890s	Decline of Civil War sentiment Disenchantment with parties with emphasis on limited government	Continued Republican domination Antiparty legislation
1930s	Great Depression	Shift in voter sentiment toward the more activist Democratic Party
1970s–1992	Decline in party line voting Voter preference for Republican presidents and Democratic members of Congress	Era of "divided government"
1994–2000	Anti-incumbent mood Third parties draining votes from major parties	Divided government with Republican Congress and Democratic president
2000	Politically indecisive presidential election in which third-party votes determine outcome with virtually even split in Congress	Divided government followed by Republican president and marginally Republican House and Senate
2004	Decisive Republican victory but lacking the 60 votes to fully control the Senate	Unified government

8-2d The Party in Campaigns

Author Hedrick Smith wrote:

> The parties have been shoved into the shadows by the modern technology and techniques of politics. Television, not the party network, is now the main channel of communications between candidates and the electorate.[14]

Earlier in the twentieth century, the party *was* the campaign, providing virtually all the funding, securing campaign workers, and planning strategy. The parties organized armies of volunteers to go door-to-door, dropping off literature and discussing political issues with the voters. Candidates ran for office with a slate of fellow party members. Advertising was coordinated, and voters were encouraged to vote the straight party ticket (see Box 8-2: Harry Truman Rallies the Troops).

Parties controlled the route to the ballot by dominating the nomination process. During the early 1900s, however, both the nature and importance of the players in the electoral process began to change. One of the most important of the changes noted earlier in this chapter was the introduction of the *primary* nomination process. Ambitious candidates gained the right to compete for nominations directly. Working one's way up through the party ranks now became only one of the ways to gain political office.

Today, the parties are not the dominant players they once were. The party loyalty of voters declined after World War II, which forced candidates to find new ways of reaching them. The parties, uncomfortable with change and lacking resources, hesitated in capitalizing on new campaign technologies, such as television, polling, and targeted mailings. Candidates were forced to go elsewhere for support. Consultants willingly took on political accounts, but their services did not come cheaply. Increased costs required candidates to seek additional private funding from individuals and interest groups.

Box 8-2 Harry Truman Rallies the Troops

On the eve of the 1948 presidential election, Democratic President Harry S. Truman made the following pitch to the convention hall and radio audience:

> I only have one request of you, vote on election day. You don't have to vote for me. Vote in your own interests and then you can only vote one way. Vote for the welfare of the country. Vote for the welfare of the world, and vote in your own welfare by voting the Democratic ticket straight on election day.[a]

a. Republican National Committee videotape footage.

The day of the **candidate-centered campaign**[15]—run by the candidate rather than a party organization—arrived, and the parties have been playing catch-up ever since. The leaders of the national Republican Party were the first to realize that they would have to beat their competitors at their own game by providing candidate services in the election arena. By the mid-1970s, Republicans had developed a sophisticated computerized direct-mail fund-raising operation, state-of-the-art television facilities, and a pool of in-house political consultants. The national Democrats did not begin to offer similar campaign services until almost a decade later.

candidate-centered campaign *Campaigns dominated by the personal organization of the candidate, in which voters judge candidates more on their personal characteristics than on their party.*

Today the national and many local party organizations actively recruit candidates and provide the kind of professional expertise once only available from paid consultants. The parties provide advertising, polling, computerized mailing, and fund-raising support well beyond what most candidates could afford (see Box 8-3: From Labor-Intensive to Techno-Intensive). To supplement marketing and technical assistance, established party leaders from the president down spend the last few weeks of the campaign **stumping** for favored candidates in tight races.

stumping *Campaigning for a candidate. The term comes from the practice in old-time campaigns of standing on a stump to give a speech in order to be seen and heard.*

Obviously, providing campaign help to candidates running under the party label stems in part from the need to elect more Republicans or Democrats. But it also comes from the desire to maintain the parties as the significant players in the policy-making arena. Candidates who have won in candidate-centered campaigns are less motivated to promote party goals, especially if party leaders initially opposed their nomination. The parties work on the assumption that successful candidates who can give credit to the party's crucial role in their elections will feel more loyal to party principles and goals once in office. Thus, campaign help by the party may reap rewards for the party after the election.

During the 1994 campaign, the Republican Party, under the guidance of then House whip Newt Gingrich (R-Ga.), attempted to recapture some of the party's agenda-setting role. Three hundred candidates agreed to sign the *Contract with America*. While few voters had any idea of the specific reforms contained in the Contract, the Republicans gained media visibility and voter support by being perceived as the party with a plan. The Contract was seen by party leaders as more than a campaign document. Because they had publicly signed a contract, party leaders hoped that the elected candidates would feel committed to a clear agenda once in office. The Contract brought about record levels of party voting the first year, but subsequent elections have not seen the repetition of such detailed commitments.

8-2e The Party in Office

The rise of candidate-centered campaigns and a party's inability to screen candidates for ideological and partisan commitment do diminish the guarantee of party loyalty. Nevertheless, most elected officials have more in common with fellow party members than with members of another party. Party members often share similar attitudes on issues and come from districts with similar needs and political outlooks. Going to fellow party members for advice or for help in pursuing particular policies comes naturally.

Box 8–3 From Labor-Intensive to Techno-Intensive

In their heyday, local political parties capitalized on their large number of willing precinct workers to spread the party word face-to-face in personal communications. Partisan newspapers fed party workers the information they then relayed to friends and neighbors (see Chapter 6). With the decline of local party organizations and the development of a more objective press, the parties had to innovate or become extinct. Organizational innovation usually stems from failure rather than success: the loss of the presidency in 1976 and the continuing difficulty in capturing Congress motivated Republicans to look to new technology. The Democrats did not react to their loss of the presidency during the 1980s with technological innovation. They did become serious, however, after their loss of Congress in 1994. A look at some of the applications of technology by the parties gives a feel for their creativity.

Republicans[a]

- GOP-TV produces its own television show for more than two thousand cable systems and sends 15 minutes of partisan news to 750 stations.
- The National Republican Congressional Committee uses satellite technology to allow members to beam images of themselves back to local stations.
- The Republican National Committee sends a partisan weekly fax to more than four hundred talk-radio hosts and news departments in an attempt to focus the national agenda and discussion.
- The official Republican news magazine, *Rising Tide*, has a circulation of more than five hundred thousand.
- The party sends out email talking points to nearly twenty-two thousand members of the Republican Forum and encourages them to discuss issues online.
- One of former Speaker Newt Gingrich's first actions when he began as Speaker was to activate a World Wide Web page for Congress, which includes both descriptive and partisan material (www.loc.thomas.gov).
- The Republican National Committee creates the eGOP department with a $5 million budget for 2000 and launches GOPnet.com.
- The party offers a seminar on "Winning in a Web World," bringing together more than three hundred Republicans from 42 states.

Democrats[b]

- The Clinton White House posted all public presidential documents and transcripts of speeches on the Internet and commercial services (www.whitehouse.gov).
- Congressional video clips are sent to television stations via satellite.
- After the 1994 election, the Democratic congressional leadership instituted a twelve-line fax system to get out their message.
- The Democrats launched freeDem.com, providing free Internet access to subscribers.
- Democratic congressional leaders use the Internet to post partisan materials.
- Howard Dean energizes his primary supporters using Meetup.com to arrange face-to-face meetings of contributors and workers in his 2004 bid for the Democratic nomination. He also raised a record breaking $3.5 million in contributions on the Internet.[c]

Both Parties

- Both parties grant Pseudopolitics.com the rights for the first Internet TV coverage of the national conventions, allowing viewers to choose from multiple camera feeds and interact with politicians and journalists.[d]
- Both parties arrange for a selected group of weblog ("blog") creators to get credentials at their national conventions and provide online journals of their experiences.[e]
- Party workers using Palm Pilots and wireless connections collect public opinion data, carry out voter registration drives, and urge supporters to e-mail their neighbors.[f]

---

a. See Richard Wolf, "Fulfilling the Contract, GOP Turns to Selling It," *USA Today*, February 17, 1995, 4A; Ian Miller, "Parties Battle for Virtual Voter," *The Hill*, June 14, 2000.

b. Charlotte Grimes, "Democrats Launching Missives into Cyberspace," *St. Louis Post Dispatch*, February 23, 1995, 5B, and Ian Miller, op. cit.

c. http://press.meetup.com/ and http://www.usatoday.com/news/politicselections/2003-07-14-online-cover-usat_x.htm

d. PR Newswire, May 16, 2000

e. Brian Faler, "Parties to Allow Bloggers to Cover Conventions for the First Time," Washington Post, July 6, 2004, A4.

f. http://news.minnesota.publicradio.org/features/2004/08/17_scheckt_hitechcampaigns/

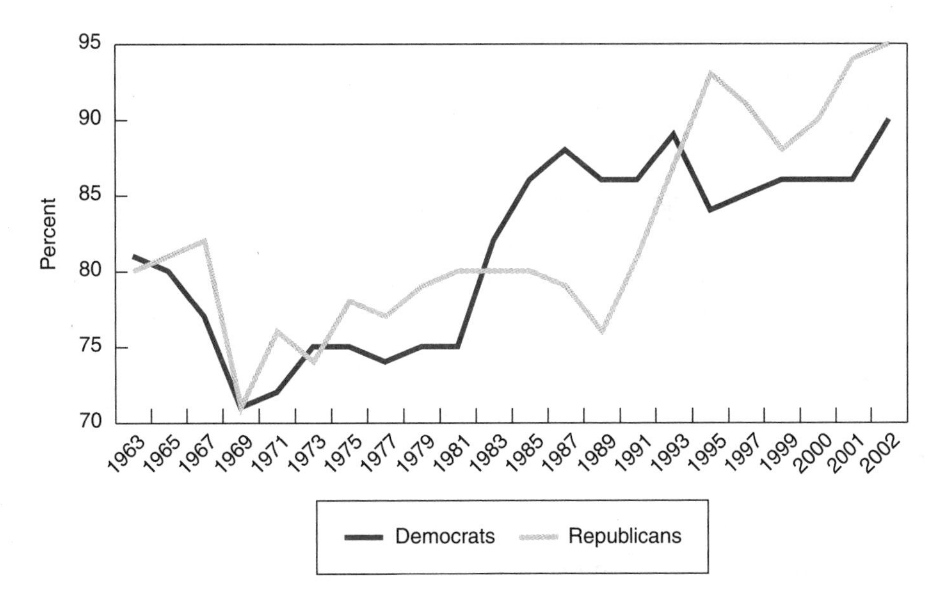

Figure 8-4

Party Cohesion in the House of Representatives—the Teams Close Ranks

Percentages of party members voting with the majority of their party on roll call votes in which a majority of Republicans opposed a majority of Democrats.

Source: Harold W. Stanley and Richard G. Niemi, *Vital Statistics on American Politics, 2003–2004* (Washington, D.C.: Congressional Quarterly, Inc., 2003), p. 217.

Collective decision-making bodies, such as Congress, state legislatures, and city councils, typically organize into opposing teams on the basis of party labels. The majority party caucus chooses the leadership of the chamber, often dominates the establishment of the policy agenda, and attempts to guide the outcome of formal decisions. Although American legislators are known for their independence in voting, party affiliation remains the best method of predicting how a member will vote. The data in Figure 8-4 indicates that voting in accordance with one's party in Congress has varied considerably in different eras. After reaching a low point during the 1970s, it has increased in recent years.

Parties are cohesive to the degree that their members in elected office tend to vote together on divisive issues. In some cases, the cohesiveness of party members' voting stems from active attempts by party leaders to establish a solid bloc of votes, but more often **bloc voting** results from the attitudes and values of party members with similar outlooks and political needs. Many of the early votes on the Republican *Contract with America* reveal almost complete Republican unanimity in favor of issues such as the Balanced Budget Amendment—and almost equal Democratic opposition. During the last years of the Clinton administration, Republicans and Democrats in Congress split over the president's impeachment, gun control, and the use of the budget surplus (Republicans favoring tax cuts and Democrats supporting new programs and debt reduction).

bloc voting *Highly unified voting by elected officials from one political party.*

Chief executives (presidents, governors, mayors) surround themselves with party members as advisers and use the party label as a criterion for appointment to executive or judicial positions, assuming that it provides a clue to the policy positions of potential appointees. The **spoils system,** and its rewarding of party label, became less important as civil service laws limited the number of appointments that elected officials could make. Still, it is rare for key White House, statehouse, or city hall staff members not to share the party label of their political benefactor.

spoils system *A comprehensive method of distributing jobs and government benefits to supporters of a particular party or candidate while discriminating against individuals who either remain neutral or support the opposition. During the 1800s, it became common to assert that, in politics, "to the victor belong the spoils of the enemy" (Senator William Marcy, 1832 Senate debate).*

Through their appointment power and the impact of their party affiliation, officials in the executive branch affect the other branches of government. Presidents and governors make many judicial appointments in which party identification and party activity are significant criteria. President George H. Bush did not have to ask David Souter, a potential appointee to the Supreme Court, his position on abortion or on the regulation of business. Bush felt comfortable in knowing that Souter, as an active Republican in a conservative state, would have views similar to his.

Other judges gain office through a partisan election process. Once a judge is in office, his or her party identification helps to predict judicial behavior, since it often implies a particular ideological outlook. The same ideological factors that draw a judge to a particular party often apply to issues of law. Also, Democratic judges are more likely to support the defense in criminal cases, the claimant in unemployment cases, the labor union in labor-management cases, and the private citizen who is confronting a corporation. They are also more likely to take a more expansive view of the basic freedoms of speech and assembly.[16] Judges make party-based decisions, as do legislators, not so much because of party pressure but because of the same personal background factors and opinions that caused them to join their party in the first place.

8-2f The Party as a Symbol

The political preferences of party supporters, the patterns of candidate recruitment, and the actions of elected officials sharing a party label combine to develop an image of the party and for what it stands. The goal of reformers to develop ideologically pure and politically unified political parties may fall short in the American context. The parties do, however, take on a consistent character in their public commitments and in the minds of voters (see Time Out 8-2: Knowing the Party Players without a Program).

Modern Republicans support more limited government, more restrained change in public policy, and a greater concern for national security and order as opposed to domestic programs and freedom (see Chapter 9, Section 9-1, Rules of Opinion Formation). Republicans tend to favor policies that help business interests and those individuals who have been most successful in the capitalist economic system. Many Republicans favor prayer in public schools and oppose abortion.

Modern Democrats generally take the opposite view on the issues of prayer in public schools and abortion and support the individual's freedom to make these choices. Democrats see government as a force to bring about change and especially to lessen economic and political inequality. Democrats prefer the use of tax dollars to help domestic programs rather than to increase defense projects. In 1992 Democrats found a way to end the Republican domination of the presidency and much of the national policy agenda. They put together a package of policy positions that would better help them to challenge the Republicans in the presidential contest. Bill Clinton emphasized the economy and moderated his stand on many traditional liberal Democratic issues in order to win. After the Republican victories in the 1994 election, a number of moderate Democrats blamed Clinton for what they viewed as his extreme activist positions on issues such as gay males and lesbians in the military and radical health care reform. In 1996 Bill Clinton neutralized traditional Republican issues by supporting initiatives such as balancing the budget and welfare reform, giving Republican Bob Dole little on which to run.

The 2000 presidential candidates split in expected ways on the issues. Al Gore supported a woman's right to choose an abortion, opposed school vouchers, guaranteed putting Social Security funds in a "lock box," emphasized new government programs, and proposed targeted tax cuts for middle and lower income citizens. George W. Bush opposed abortions,

Time Out 8-2

Knowing the Party Players without a Program

Pollsters have long asked voters which party they feel best handles specific societal problems. For each of the following problems, indicate the party in which you have the most confidence:

Which political party, Democratic or Republican, you trust to do a better job of . . .

Reducing crime?	Democrats	Republicans
Handling the economy?	Democrats	Republicans
Handling Social Security?	Democrats	Republicans
Making wise decisions about foreign policy?	Democrats	Republicans
Dealing with gun control?	Democrats	Republicans
Handling Medicare?	Democrats	Republicans
Handling education?	Democrats	Republicans
Handling taxes?	Democrats	Republicans
Handling the war on Terrorism?	Democrats	Republicans

Compare your responses with the responses in a recent public opinion poll in Answers to Time Out 8-2 on page 246.

supported school vouchers, favored allowing workers to divert some of their Social Security payments into investments, emphasized smaller government, and favored an across-the-board tax cut. Despite clear differences, assumptions about probable performance in office, character, and experience took center stage. Gore voters touted his experience, while Bush voters felt their candidate would return public respect to the presidency.

Images of the Republicans as the party of big business and of the Democrats as the supporters of the little guy are simplifications of the distinctions between the parties, but they do contain some truths. The images of the Republicans as the party of peace and of the Democrats as the party of prosperity stem back to the Depression (for which the Republicans were blamed) and World War II (the Democrats were blamed for the international dislocation that followed). These images are further fed by new realities, such as successful Republican foreign policy initiatives (for example, the Persian Gulf War), combined with economic downturns during Republican administrations.

Party images affect election outcomes. The recent presidential elections that were dominated by foreign affairs issues have favored Republican candidates, while those stressing domestic and economic issues have favored Democratic candidates (see Box 8-4: Issues

Box 8–4 *Issues and the Home-Field Advantage*

As the table that follows indicates, the candidates of a particular party tend to have an advantage when an election emphasizes the issues in which their party has a recognized competence. Republicans are better known for their handling of foreign affairs, while Democrats have more credibility on domestic issues.

Table 8-3 lists only elections resulting in a first term for a new president, since elections for a second term are dominated by a tendency not to change horses in midstream. Also, summarizing a campaign in terms of one or two issues, given the complexity of candidate programs and the bases on which voters make their decisions, can be dangerous. The identified issues do, however, dominate much of the discussion. The italicized issues in parentheses were generally seen as most important.

Table 8-3 Dominant Issues and the Election Results that Accompanied Them

Year	Dominant Issues	Election Result
1952	Ending the Korean War (*foreign policy*)	Republican victory (Eisenhower)
1960	Recession (*domestic policy*)	Democratic victory (Kennedy)
1964	Protecting Social Security and other domestic programs (*domestic policy*) and fear of nuclear war (*foreign policy*)	Democratic victory (Johnson)
1968	Ending the Vietnam War (*foreign policy*)	Republican victory (Nixon)
1976	"Misery Index"—high inflation and unemployment (*domestic policy*)	Democratic victory (Carter)
1980	Iran hostages, Soviet invasion of Afghanistan (*foreign policy*)	Republican victory (Reagan)
1988	Patriotism, crime (*defense, foreign policy*)	Republican victory (George H. Bush)
1992	Unemployment, deficit (*domestic policy*)	Democratic victory (Clinton)
1996	Continuation of booming economy (*domestic policy*)	Democratic victory (Clinton)
2000	Morality in government, general versus targeted tax cuts (*domestic policy and candidate characteristics*)	Republican victory in the Electoral College (Bush), Democrats win popular vote
2004	Protection from terrorism, evaluation of the war with Iraq (defense, foreign policy), moral issues (gay marriage) to the exclusion of domestic issues	Decisive Republican victory

Answers to Time Out 8-2

Despite variations associated with transitory events, public evaluation of the strengths and weaknesses of the parties is relatively consistent over time. Although public perceptions may be incorrect, they represent powerful beliefs on which many voters base their behavior.

Which political party, the Democrats or the Republicans, do you trust to do a better job of . . .	Democrats	Republicans
reducing crime	43%	57%
handling the economy	49%	51%
handling Social Security	57%	43%
making wise decisions about foreign policy	43%	57%
dealing with gun control	52%	48%
handling Medicare	58%	42%
handling education	51%	49%
handling taxes	47%	53%
handling the war on terrorism	34%	66%

You should have had little difficulty categorizing party strengths and weaknesses in concerns listed at the top and bottom of the lists, where the images and performances of the parties vary significantly. In the areas of concern listed in the middle of the list, neither party has much of an advantage. If your evaluations were considerably different from those of the general public, either your personal party loyalties affected your responses or you interpreted the questions differently.

Source: Princeton Survey Research Associates national polls of 1000-2000 adults conducted in September and October of 2002. LEXIS-NEXIS database. The figures include only those taking a stand (60-80% of respondents).

and the Home-Field Advantage). While both parties attempt to portray themselves as competent to deal with the full range of issues, each party's public image makes it more difficult to emphasize credibly some issues. When 1988 Democratic presidential nominee Michael Dukakis rode around in an Army tank and professed his strong support for national defense, it ran counter to decades of Democratic attempts to restrain defense spending and activities. Republican George H. Bush looked just as out of place campaigning in poor black neighborhoods and expressing support for such domestic programs as welfare, education, and environmental protection (which many Republicans have long sought to cut). In 1996 the Democrats focused the campaign on domestic issues in order to take credit for the economic successes during Bill Clinton's first term. The Republicans questioned the adequacy of the Democratic commitment to national defense, portrayed their own plan of cutbacks in domestic government activity as the route to long-term economic well-being and unsuccessfully attempted to make the election a referendum on President Clinton's character. In 2000, George W. Bush bucked the tide by focusing on traditionally Democratic ground when he based much of his campaign on domestic issues such as tax reform and education. Al Gore found himself hampered by his association with President Clinton and saw much of the campaign focusing on his character and performance as a candidate.

8-3 Rules of Party Politics

single-member district *A process of distributing seats so that each geographic district has one, and only one, elected official representing it.*

Political parties enter an election arena structured by specific election rules. Rules such as the **single-member district** system, which divides voters into geographic districts to be represented by one elected official, affect the parties as well as the overall political process. In such a system, each election becomes a winner-take-all contest in which the parties cannot share power. Many **parliamentary systems,** on the other hand, avoid single-member districts and use **proportional representation** voting, in which each party presents a list of candidates for districts entitled to several winners. Under such a system, each party receives the same percentage of winners as it receives votes and can thus share the victory. Minor parties have a better chance of winning seats under a proportional representation system than under a single-member district system, where there is only one winner.

A variety of other formal governmental rules are aimed more directly at the parties themselves. Until the late 1880s, American political parties were viewed as private organizations. Early laws treated parties as responsible to no one but their internal leaders and activist supporters. To a degree, the parties became victims of their own success. The increasing power of party organizations during the latter part of the nineteenth century forced reformers, such as the **Progressives** of the late 1800s, to take them on. This movement emphasized increased democratic participation and the application of science and specialized knowledge. It reached its climax with the nomination of Theodore Roosevelt for president in 1912. Although unsuccessful as a party, the Progressives left many legacies of their drive for good government, such as civil service reform, primary elections, and more professionalized public administration.

Reformers began to characterize parties as public utilities,[17] like the telephone or electric company: They play such a crucial role in the life of society that government must regulate their impact. Today, the United States has the world's strongest laws regulating parties.[18]

parliamentary system *A government system, common among democracies, in which voters select the legislature (parliament), which in turn elects the chief executive (prime minister) from its ranks.*

proportional representation *A system of electing representatives from lists nominated by the political parties in which more than one representative is selected from each district.*

Progressives *A political movement flourishing in America between 1890 and 1920 that promoted progress in government.*

8-3a Parties and Voting Rules

Ordinary procedures for casting ballots often have significant consequences. The earliest colonial elections required voters to appear before election officials and to express their candidate preferences orally. With friends, neighbors, and party leaders within earshot, whether or not a person supported a party was clearly evident, and the individual often felt pressured. When written ballots were introduced, the parties printed the ballots in distinctive colors so that party poll workers could still identify party supporters. Beginning in the late 1800s, the secret ballot, printed at government expense and cast in private, reduced the ability of parties to buy votes and to monitor party loyalty.

Although parties lost control of ballot distribution, which limited their ability to monitor or to intimidate voters, they were still concerned with the ballot format. Parties fought for **party-column ballots**, which make it easy for voters to follow the party column from the highest to the lowest office and to cast a straight party ticket. Two-thirds of the more than thirty states using the party-column ballot further simplify supporting a single party by providing a single box or lever that allows the voter to cast a ballot for the entire party ticket. States with weaker party organizations use **office-bloc ballots,** in which candidates are grouped by office rather than by party. Voters must then examine the entire list of candidates to make their choices. Office-bloc ballots facilitate ticket splitting.

Parties fought the antiparty reform efforts of the early 1900s to increase the number of offices contested through nonpartisan elections. Naturally, the parties preferred to have the ballot clearly indicate each candidate's party identification. Nonpartisan elections in the United States are limited to some local contests and to the election of judges. The short ballot movement advocated by the progressive reform movement attempted to limit the number of offices filled by election. It, too, found little support among the parties. Longer lists of voting choices gave the party organization greater control over the vote. The confused voter would nicely accept a party-picked slate of candidates.

party-column ballot *Arranging the names on the ballot by party to encourage party-line voting.*

office-bloc ballot *Arranging names on the ballot by office to encourage voting on the basis of the characteristics of specific candidates.*

8-3b Parties and Nominating Rules

Since parties were originally considered private organizations, they were given, without interference, the right to nominate candidates to run under their label. Parties defined their own rules for membership, established internal procedures, and held caucuses or

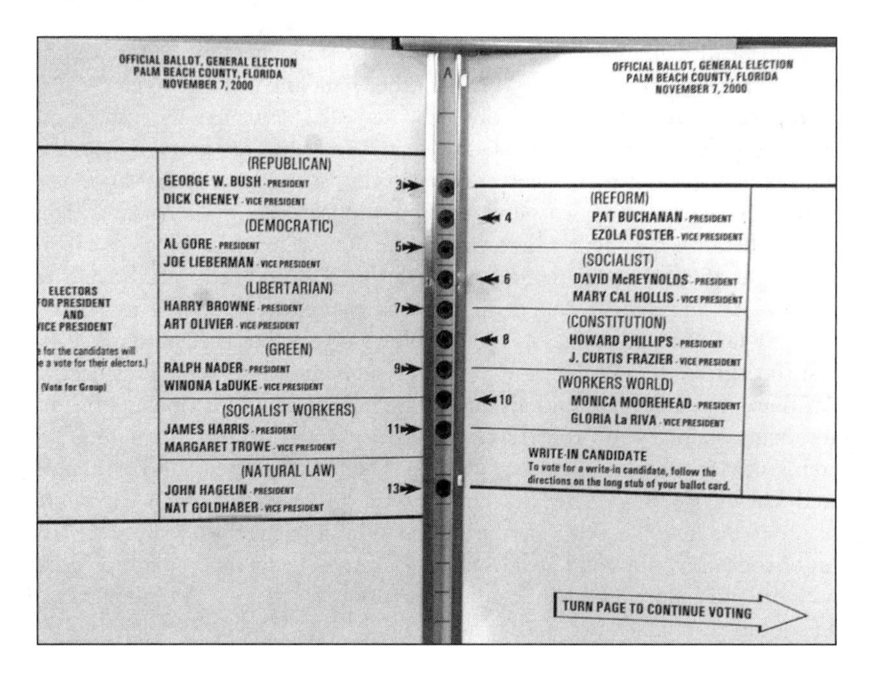

The highly questioned "butterfly" ballot used in some parts of Florida.

Photo courtesy of *Sun-Sentinel*.

balancing the ticket *Increasing the political appeal of a party's candidates by including candidates popular with different geographical, ethnic, social, and/or ideological groups.*

conventions to nominate their slate of candidates. Party leaders attempted to assure that all significant groups in the party were represented in the slate. **Balancing the ticket** rather than seeking the most qualified person for the job was emphasized. This was done to satisfy partisans from different geographical regions of the electoral district or politically important ethnic groups. State election laws guaranteed the established parties a place on the ballot, and party control over nominations gave the parties significant power over voters and potential candidates.

Expanded Use of Primaries

Public distrust of the political parties and the desire to broaden the base of citizens involved in the political process led to another type of reform in the early 1900s. Reformers railed against decisions made in smoke-filled rooms, where a small group of unrepresentative party bosses made deals and chose the nominees. They sought and won the creation of primary elections to nominate candidates. Primary laws redefined the players in party politics. They now included more than the activist members of the party organization. Parties were no longer a small group of official party members and workers. For the task of nomination, the party became defined as those voters in the electorate willing to identify themselves in partisan terms. The states adopted differing primary laws and required varying levels of party commitment for participation. The states with the strongest parties required voters to register officially as party supporters well before the election in order to participate in the party primary (see Chapter 11).

Lingering Conventions

Although their dominance over nominations has declined, party activists still meet in convention. Party conventions occur on the national, state, and local levels and provide the opportunity for the party to take collective action.

For the presidential nomination process, the national party conventions retain the legitimate right to nominate the party's standard-bearer, but recent conventions have largely endorsed the candidate who has emerged as a clear winner of the presidential primary season (see Chapter 11).

National conventions have shifted their focus and now perform a number of other functions. The conventions center public attention on the party and generate considerable press coverage. A successful national convention allows the party to turn from division to unity in front of the whole nation (see Box 8-5: Television and the Taming of

Box 8-5 Television and the Taming of National Conventions

The history of national party conventions includes legions of raucous intramural fights and divisive bickering over both policy and nominees. Party activists treated the convention as a family meeting and saw little difficulty patching up what went on out of sight of the American public. Most causes were given their say on the convention floor, numerous frivolous candidates were nominated, and sessions dragged on and on.

The 1924 Democratic Convention set a record of 103 ballots and lasted 17 days before John W. Davis received the nomination. Although the length of the 1924 convention was atypical, almost half of the conventions between 1856 and 1952 required more than one ballot to choose a nominee.

After 1900 the growth of primary elections for selecting convention delegates served to narrow the field of serious contenders before the convention. Candidates dropped out after each set of primaries, leaving the field to a few survivors.

The arrival of television cameras on the convention floor in 1952 caused a change in perspective. Party leaders began to realize that intrafamily squabbles were one thing, but washing the party's dirty linen in public was another. Recognizing the importance of the convention portraying the image of a unified team, party leaders sought to control conflict and to harness television's potential. Sessions were shortened, important speeches scheduled for prime time, and conflict reduced. Only one post-television convention (the 1952 Democratic convention) was not settled on the first ballot.

Modern conventions are made-for-television affairs. Entertainment figures sing the national anthem, "spontaneous" demonstrations use hired bands and are given time limits to avoid viewer boredom, and glossy filmed productions glorifying the party and its past are scheduled for optimal audiences. The sessions have been shortened and are paced to fit the immediacy of television.[a] Detailed scripts tell commentators what is going on. Deviations from the script not only become news items in and of themselves but may foretell of impending campaign problems. One example was George McGovern's allowing the platform conflict over Vietnam to delay his acceptance speech in 1972 until the middle of the night.

In 1984, for the first time since television arrived on the convention floor, the networks decided that they would no longer allow the parties to control the coverage. The traditional gavel-to-gavel coverage was dropped in favor of prime-time summary specials, with cutaways to live action only for important news events, such as key votes and speeches. Recent national conventions have been covered gavel-to-gavel by C-SPAN and public television. The 2000 convention became the first with live multicamera Internet feeds allowing viewers to be their own producers.

Television's involvement has clearly changed the goals of national conventions and the nature of the playing field. Both the parties and the rest of the media are attempting to adapt to its demands.

a. See Stephen Wayne, *The Road to the White House* (New York: St. Martin's Press, 1988), 141.

National Conventions). Internal party rules are debated, and policy goals and strategies become part of the **party platform** (see Table 8-4) Despite their generality, excessive rhetoric, and moderate tone, party platforms do establish a policy direction for the party and include significant commitments that elected officials do follow.[19]

party platform *The official statement of party policy goals and the means for reaching those goals.*

State and local parties also hold conventions to establish platforms and party rules. Many state laws allow party conventions to make nominations directly for some state offices or to endorse candidates in primaries for some offices. In the states that do not have presidential primaries, delegates to the national party conventions are chosen at state and local conventions.

8-3c Controlling Party Resources in the Election Game

When most campaigns depended on labor-intensive door-to-door campaigning and voters remained linked to their party, political parties played a significant role in campaigns. The increasing use of radio, television, and computerized mailings, however, allowed candidates

Table 8-4 **2004 National Party Platforms: The Policy Game Plan**

	Democrats	Republicans
Environment	We reject the false choice between a healthy economy and a healthy environment. We know instead that farming, fishing, tourism, and other industries require a healthy environment.	We reject the false choice between a healthy economy and a healthy environment. We know instead that farming, fishing, tourism, and other industries require a healthy environment.
Family and Marriage	We support full inclusion of gay and lesbian families in the life of our nation and seek equal responsibilities, benefits, and protections for these families. In our country, marriage has been defined at the state level for 200 years, and we believe it should continue to be defined there.	We support [the] call for a Constitutional amendment that fully protects marriage, and we believe that neither federal or state judges nor bureaucrats should force states to recognize other living arrangements as equivalent to marriage.
Equality	We will restore vigorous federal enforcement of our civil rights laws for all our people, from fair housing to equal employment opportunity, from Title IX to the Americans with Disabilities Act. We support affirmative action to redress discrimination and to achieve the diversity from which all Americans benefit.	Our nation is a land of opportunity for all. We support a reasonable approach to Title IX that seeks to expand opportunities for women without adversely affecting men's athletics . . . We reject preferences, quotas, and set-asides based on skin color, ethnicity or gender which perpetuate divisions and can lead people to questions the accomplishments of successful minorities and women.
Gun control	We will protect Americans' Second Amendment right to own firearms, and we will keep guns out of the hands of criminals and terrorists by fighting gun crime, reauthorizing the assault weapons ban, and closing the gun show loophole.	We believe the Second Amendment and all of the rights guaranteed by it should enable law-abiding citizens throughout the country to own firearms in their homes for self-defense.
Abortion	Because we believe in the privacy and equality of women, we stand proudly for a woman's right to choose, consistent with *Roe v. Wade*, and regardless of her ability to pay.	We say the unborn child has a fundamental individual right to life which cannot be infringed . . . Our purpose is to have legislative and judicial protection of that right against those who perform abortion. We oppose using public revenues for abortion.
Taxation	We want a tax code that rewards work and creates wealth for more people, not a tax code that hoards wealth for those who already have it.	We believe that good government is based on a system of limited taxes and spending . . . The taxation system should not be used to redistribute wealth.

Sources: http://www.democrats.org/platform/ and http://msnbcmedia.msn.com/i/msnbc/Sections/News/Politics/Conventions/RNC-2004platform.pdf

to bypass campaign workers, "giving candidates an independent route to the minds and pocketbooks of constituents."[20] The technological expertise required by the electronic revolution and the dramatic increases in campaign costs associated with them made traditional levels of party contributions insignificant.

Political parties directly contribute only a small portion of the funds that most candidates use in their campaigns (see Figure 8-5). However, money from the party organization is often provided early in the campaign, when it is most necessary. Direct party monetary contributions to the candidate are also supplemented by indirect expenditures on voter registration and get-out-the-vote drives, which help the candidate to define the electorate and to get them to the polls on Election Day.

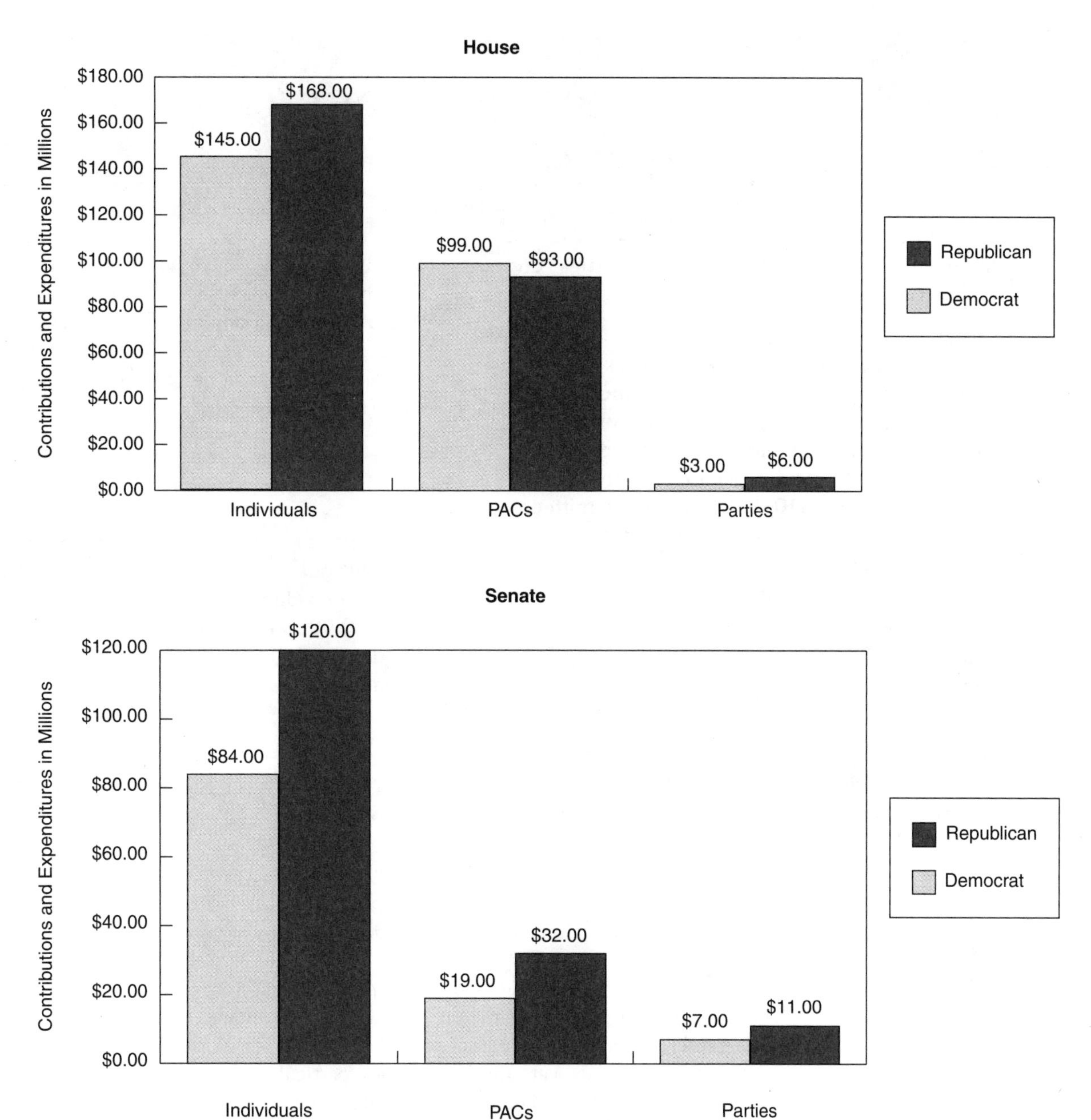

Figure 8-5

Parties as the Source of Candidate Funding, 2000 (in Millions of Dollars)

Source: Norman J. Ornstein, Thomas Mann and Michael Malbin, *Vital Statistics on Congress, 2001–2002* (Washington, D.C.: American Enterprise Institute, 2001), pp. 104–105.

Since the passage and revision of the Federal Election Campaign Act (FECA) in the 1970s, parties have been restricted in the amount and type of contributions that they can make to candidates for federal offices (see Box 8-6: Federal Rules for Party Resource Distribution). Campaign financing laws in the states vary considerably. Most have fewer restrictions than the national rules impose. Government financing of presidential election campaigns, which began in 1976, found most support among Democrats, since their party habitually has more difficulty raising funds for national races. Recurring battles over federal funding for congressional campaigns typically reveal much stronger support among Democrats than among Republicans for the same reason.

Above and beyond financial help, the parties are given almost free rein in helping candidates indirectly. The large staff of campaign experts employed by national and state parties shares their knowledge without a fee. With the goal of increasing citizen participation, the laws purposely allow state and local parties to spend any amount of resources on such activities as voter registration and get-out-the-vote drives. In recent presidential campaigns, presidential candidates have expended considerable effort raising this **soft money** in the hope that its expenditure would increase the numbers entering the voting booth. Such

soft money *Contributions and expenditures given by national parties to state parties to encourage voter participation through registration, party building, and get-out-the-vote drives.*

Box 8–6 Federal Rules for Party Resource Distribution (After the 2001 Bipartisan Campaign Reform Act)

Direct Contributions to National Parties and Limits on National Party Expenditures

Sources:

- *Individuals* can give up to $95,000 per two-year period to candidates, national party committees, and PACs. Up to $37,500 can be given directly to candidates out of that total. Up to $25,000 can be given to national party committees and $10,000 to state committees. Money given to PACs counts against the aggregate $95,000 limit.
- *Political action committees* can give up to $15,000 per year to each of the units of the national party (national committee, senatorial committee, and congressional committee), with state laws determining contributions at that level.

Expenditures:

- *National parties* can give $5,000 to the primary and $5,000 to the general election campaign of a House candidate and $17,500 to the primary and $17,500 to the general election campaigns of a Senate candidate.
- *State parties* can give $5,000 to the primary and $5,000 to the general election campaign of Senate and House candidates.

"Soft money" (encouragement of citizen involvement through registration and get-out-the-vote drives)

- *Soft money contributions to national parties are now illegal* (the major change in the 2001 law). Individuals and organizations are limited to $10,000 in contributions to state parties. Federal candidates cannot solicit soft money contributions.

For more details, see the Campaign Finance Institute website: www.cfinst.org/eguide

fund-raising is now illegal for the political parties with the passage of the Bipartisan Campaign Reform Act (BCRA) in 2001. Get-out-the-vote drives will have to be funded in other ways.

The most dramatic fund raising change in 2004 involved the 527 groups (named for the relevant section of the tax code) which are allowed to raise money from individuals and corporations and are not regulated by the Federal Elections Commission. They cannot directly advocate the election of a particular candidate, nor coordinate their efforts with a candidate, but can underwrite voter registration and get-out-the-vote drives. Democrats took an early lead in raising millions of dollars from large contributors until the Republicans saw their traditional fund raising advantage evaporate and geared up their supporters. The big change meant that these funds were not flowing through the parties.

Reforms in an area as crucial as campaign resources have led to monumental battles between the parties. Each side has attempted to protect its unique sources of funding while trying to undermine the resource advantages of the opposing party. Republicans have attacked political action committees (PACs). These interest-based organizations have had a record of following a safe strategy of backing incumbents (see Chapter 7), which historically benefited the Democrats. After Republicans took over each chamber of Congress, PAC money began flowing their direction.

Democrats talk about limiting overall contributions. They recognize that challengers generally need to outspend incumbents to have a chance at defeating them. While much of the rhetoric of party reformers favors creating a more even playing field, the typical intent is to tilt the field for one's own partisan advantage. After the 1994 elections, the fund-raising advantages of incumbents began to look more appealing to the Republicans with their majority in Congress.

A number of observers have come to the conclusion that the parties may have been held in check too much. They argue that strong political parties are key to competitive elections:

> The surest way to get more resources to underfinanced challengers is to increase the limits on what the two parties can give. . . . The political parties are the only organizations that have a built-in interest in unseating the other side's incumbents. In a political game that is ruthlessly stacked in the incumbent's favor, real reform lies in empowering the parties.[21]

8-3d Determining How Parties Play Their Internal Game

The existence of state laws specifying the operation of political parties implies that parties are more than just private organizations. State constitutions and supporting laws specify the composition and duties of state party committees that manage party affairs between elections. Some states outline in great detail the places, times, and decision-making procedures for official party meetings. Some of the most important rules relating to political parties specify procedures for selecting delegates to national party conventions. Until the 1970s, such procedures were almost exclusively based on intraparty rules and tradition. After a stormy national Democratic Convention in 1968, however, the party nomination process changed dramatically. Frustrated by the Vietnam conflict and cutbacks in social programs, antiwar, minority, youth, and women's groups protested their lack of representation and power during the 1968 Democratic Convention. Violent confrontations between the police and protesters made the Democratic Party look bad on television and hurt their electoral chances. This forced the creation of a reform commission to analyze procedures for delegate selection.

The next decade saw a series of five Democratic Party reform commissions specifying quotas and procedures for assuring adequate representation of women, minorities, and youth. Each took a slightly different approach. The Supreme Court (*Cousins v. Wigoda*, 1975) confirmed the power of national party rules over state party rules.[22] The easiest way to meet national Democratic Party guidelines was to select delegates in primaries. Numerous states shifted from state conventions to primaries.

The result was that after two decades of reform, the Democratic Convention was more representative of Democrats. This did not, however, automatically translate into success at the polls during presidential contests. The time and energy committed to giving top priority to expressive reforms (those focusing on the degree of democracy in party decision making) took time and energy away from emphasis on competitive reforms (those focusing on the party's capacity to win elections).

To a large degree, the national Republican Party reversed these two priorities.[23] However, it was also affected by the societal forces and laws resulting from the Democratic Party reforms. Republicans felt pressured to increase public participation in primaries and state conventions. And in those states changing their nominating procedures to include presidential primaries, the new laws passed by state legislatures applied to the Republicans as well as to the Democrats.

In the final analysis, the composition of national party players has changed significantly in the direction intended by the reformer (see Figure 8-6). National convention delegates still may not be a random sample of either the U.S. population or of party voters, but having new players in the national convention does lead to different types of nominees, who are more responsive to the newly represented groups. This is especially true in the Democratic Party. The growing importance of primaries has helped relatively obscure candidates, who have the resources and time to campaign, to demonstrate their support among the voters. Jimmy Carter (1976), Michael Dukakis (1988), and Bill Clinton (1992) probably would not have won their nominations without the increased number of primaries.

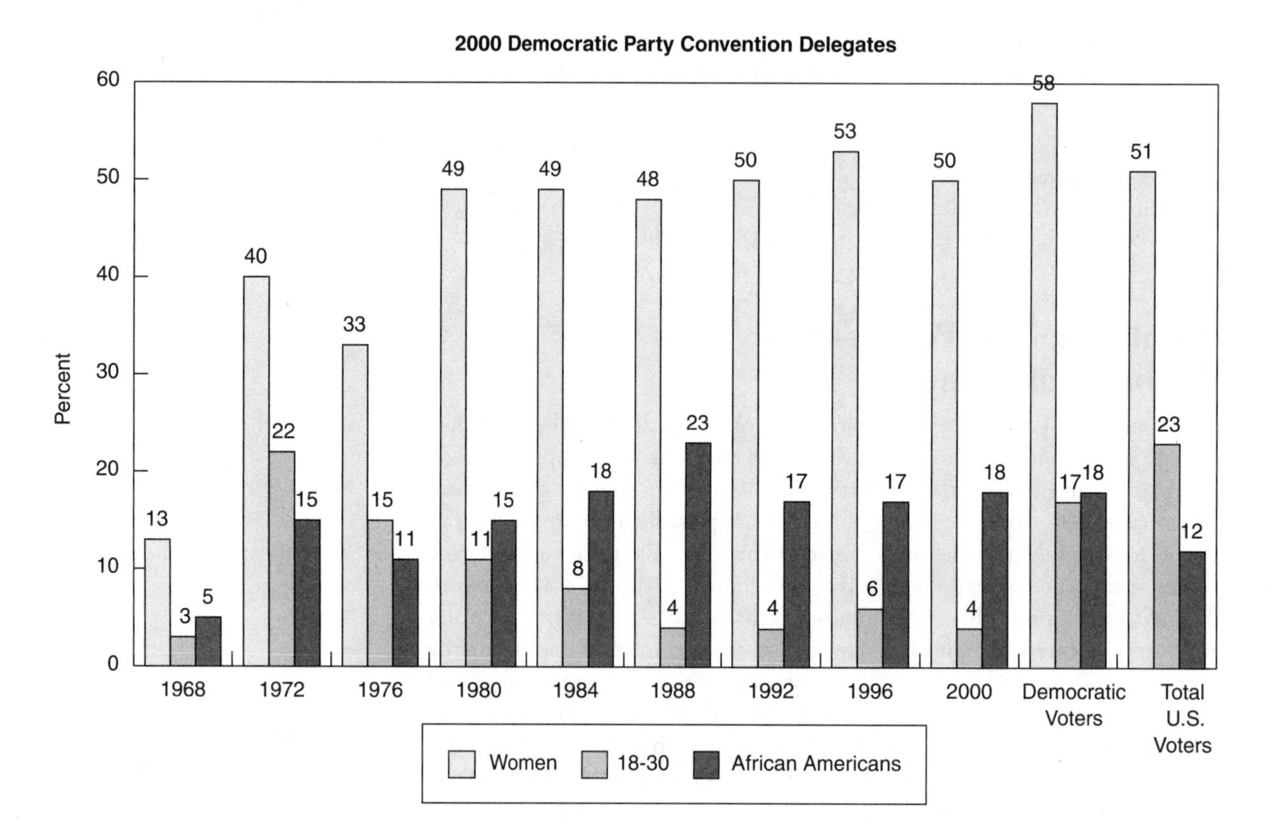

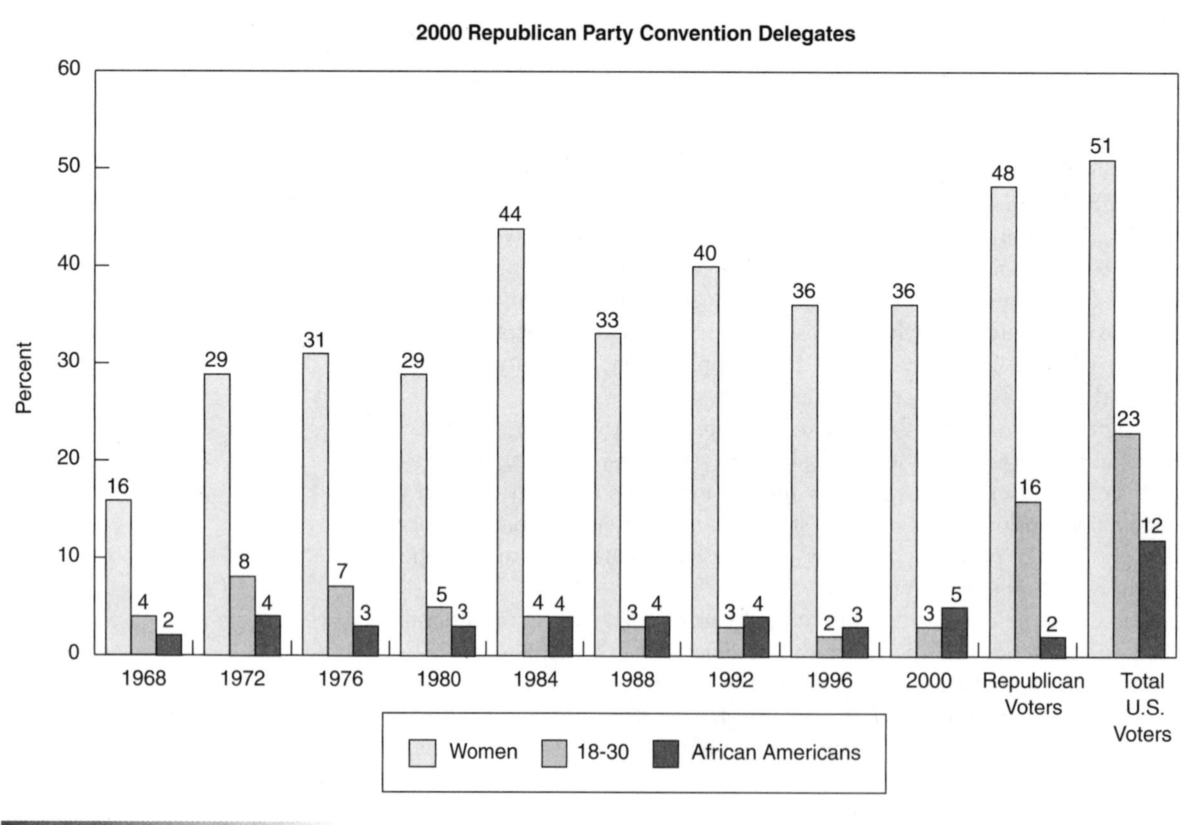

Figure 8-6
Changing the National Party Convention Players

Sources: Delegate Data from Harold Stanley and Richard Niemi, *Vital Statistics on American Politics*, Congressional Quarterly, Inc., 2002, p. 73; Associated Press survey of 2000 delegates (http://images.cnn.com/2000/ALLPOLITICS/stories/08/12/delegates.profile.ap/ and http://images.cnn.com/2000/ALLPOLITICS/stories/07/28/blacks.gop); Voter demographic data recalculated from Voter News Service exit poll of 13,049 voters reported in "Closer Look at the Voters," *Washington Post*, November 8, 2000, p. A38.

8-3e Party Rules Favoring a Game with Two Parties

The United States stands almost alone as a developed democracy with only two viable political parties. Most countries of the world have either a single- or multi-party system. A combination of tradition and social divisions, reinforced by electoral laws, bolsters the existing U.S. parties and undermines third-party attempts to siphon off the power held by the major parties.

Historical Precedents and Natural Divisions

Many major political battles in American politics have divided the country. There were Federalists versus Anti-Federalists, proslavery groups versus antislavery groups, and government intervention during the Great Depression versus a free market economy. In the first two cases, two competing parties were spawned. However, the concept of a **natural dualism** fails to capture much of the complexity of American parties.[24] Many issues have more than one side, and individuals agreeing on one issue may well disagree on other issues. At various points in history, great issues have realigned society and brought new people into each party. Party strategies, election laws, and personal voting traditions, however, have limited the readjustments. The two-party system remains intact.

natural dualism *The view that all major issues divide into two alternatives (liberal/conservative, "ins/outs," pro/con, and so on).*

Major Party Survival Strategies

Political parties must change to survive. Perhaps more than any other American political entity, parties view politics as a continuous game rather than a discrete game (see Chapter 1). When fighting policy or election battles, they do not seek all-out win-or-lose wars. Rather, parties strive to structure outcomes for survival, so that they can compete again another day.

Both American political parties have long been noted for **inclusiveness.** They welcome potential participants even if these players do not completely agree with the party's policies or ideology. The Republican and Democratic parties are **pragmatic** electoral coalitions, more interested in getting party members into office than in pursuing a narrow ideological policy agenda. Each party willingly accepts the resources of campaign contributors and the promised votes of potential voters while adjusting party policy positions to the interests of their campaign resource providers.[25]

inclusiveness *An organization's strategy of including, rather than excluding, potential supporters by making organization positions more appealing to them.*

pragmatism *A practical approach to politics in which slavish commitment to ideology or past loyalties is replaced with a more realistic acceptance of flexibility.*

The emphasis on pragmatism means that the differences between American parties are often narrower than the differences within them. The range of opinions held by candidates running under each party label is dramatic. The Democratic Party accepts conservative Democrats from the South, just as the Republican Party embraces liberal Republicans from the Northeast. Candidates are given significant leeway to pursue the ideological and policy positions that will be necessary to win election among residents of their districts. The parties attempt to downplay the differences that divide them internally and to emphasize ambiguous generalities, such as "helping out the little guy" (Democrats) and "improving the business climate" (Republicans), which bring the parties together.

Although the parties differ in their approaches to specific issues, the range of alternatives they pursue tends to be limited largely to moderate options rather than to wholesale changes in direction. When party control of the White House or Congress shifts, only marginal changes in policy result. In the past especially, potentially divisive issues, such as Social Security and health care, were removed from the debate quite early. As of the 1994 congressional election this pattern may be shifting. The Republican Contract with America directly confronted a number of controversial issues and proposed significant changes. The House of Representatives passed most of the key components on party-line votes, while the Senate proved to be more hesitant. Even the Contract avoided the divisive issues of abortion and Social Security.

Election Laws and Discrimination against New Teams

As the dominant players in the party arena, the Republican and Democratic parties have fought long and hard to maintain their positions. One of their most effective strategies stems from maintaining and strengthening the rules in favor of the major parties and against

Box 8-7 *Sideline Skirmishes and the Big Game Background*

For more than a century American presidential politics have been dominated by contests between only two viable teams. At times some voters have questioned those teams and their leaders, but when it was time to vote, most voters took the position "my party, right or wrong, but my party" and cast their ballots for their party's nominee. Aspiring politicians, who recognized voter tendencies and the rules of the game, joined one of the major teams in their quest for office. Sideline skirmishes involving third-party and independent candidates occasionally drew the attention of the spectators, but they usually turned out to be little more than interesting diversions from the big game on the field.

Questions

From a legal perspective, third-party and independent candidates have overcome the hurdles to become players in the game. Who are those players and why have they entered the game? More importantly, a fuller understanding of such candidates requires answering the question of what impact these players have on the way the major teams play the game.

Analysis

Understanding the diverse motivations of non-major-party presidential candidates requires knowledge of the specific candidates themselves. If asked who besides George H. Bush and Bill Clinton ran in 1992, most Americans are likely to mention only Ross Perot. In reality more than two hundred candidates registered with the Federal Elections Commission as presidential candidates. Many of these candidates, such as Billy Joe Clegg from the "Clegg Won't Pull Your Leg for President Committee" and Russell Munoz Baptiste Hirshon, supported by the "Put Russell Hirshon in the Big House Committee,"[a] are simply on a personal ego trip and/or suffer from delusions. Others such as the Prohibition Party support single-issue candidates, using the presidential contest as a method of drawing attention to a cause in which they deeply believe. Only a small proportion of the registered candidates believe they have any chance of winning or even affecting the outcome of the game.

The 1996 presidential campaign generated a great deal of interest focused on a wide range of potential third-party or independent candidates for whom a possible winning scenario could be framed. The memory of Ross Perot's impressive showing in 1992 allowed supporters to speculate that with the right candidate, a little luck, and adequate effort, a non-major-party candidate could provide a "wake-up call" to the major parties or even win the contest. Names such as Ross Perot, retired Chairman of the Joint Chiefs of Staff Colin Powell, civil rights activist Jesse Jackson, and conservative columnist Pat Buchanan were prominently mentioned.

The impact of third-party candidates depends on the tenor of the times, the effectiveness of the particular candidate, and the reactions of the major party candidates. Third-party and independent candidates have been able to refocus the issues in campaigns. In 1968 the appeal of former Alabama Governor George Wallace's conservative position on civil rights pushed both major party candidates to take more restrictive stands on these issues to avoid losing support. In 1992 Ross Perot forced both candidates to focus more heavily on the deficit than might have been the case without his presence.

In general, third-party candidates have been spoilers, drawing support disproportionately from one of the major parties and contributing to a win by the opposition team. Teddy Roosevelt's 1912 third-party run against his former Republican vice president, William Howard Taft, siphoned off enough Republican votes to guarantee the victory of Woodrow Wilson. Ross Perot's 1992 campaign garnered 19 percent of the vote and drew significantly more votes from among voters who would typically have supported George H. Bush. Both of the major party teams faced

third parties. Among the most important of these rules are the single-member district and electoral college systems of election, which create a multitude of winner-take-all situations (see Box 8-7: Sideline Skirmishes and the Big Game Background, and Chapters 2 and 11). Such zero-sum games have room for one winner and a prime competitor; there is little room for parties that would splinter the opposition. State election laws guarantee the major parties a position on the ballot and require new parties to conquer such hurdles as holding a convention or submitting petitions to place their candidates on the same ballot.

In presidential elections, federal financing of campaigns is largely limited to the two major parties. Strong third parties are given the less useful alternative of receiving a small proportion of major party funding *after* they prove themselves in the election.

the 1996 contest concerned that third-party or independent challenges would damage their core constituencies of voters. For the Republicans, both Ross Perot and Pat Buchanan represented a particular threat. If the Republican candidate was too moderate, Buchanan could capture many conservative voters who opposed abortion, affirmative action, and internationalism. If the Republicans nominated a more conservative candidate, Perot could snatch more moderate voters. Anticipating their entrance in the race, then House Speaker Newt Gingrich (R-Ga.) commented, "a third-party candidate is a total disaster and is the only way Bill Clinton will get re-elected."[b] On the Democratic side, Jesse Jackson could undermine typical party support among members of minorities and secure the votes of liberals who felt Bill Clinton had become too moderate. As it turned out, the one-sided nature of the outcome and Ross Perot's disappointing 9 percent of the vote had little effect on the outcome.

The 2000 presidential race began with a power struggle within Ross Perot's Reform Party in which the supporters of Minnesota governor Jesse Ventura took over the party organization. High-visibility candidates such as Pat Buchanan and businessman Donald Trump vied for the Reform Party nomination. Actor Warren Beatty caused a stir for a number of months when he considered running as a third-party candidate. Jesse Ventura eventually broke with the Reform Party. The Reform Party national convention brought no end to the conflict, with Pat Buchanan receiving the nomination of the primary faction and a rump (unofficial) convention endorsing John Hagelin.

Pat Buchanan eventually won the Reform Party nomination in a rancorous convention, and after a court battle he secured $12.5 million in federal funds guaranteed by Ross Perot's 1996 showing. His candidacy never caught on, garnering him an asterisk (less than 1%) in both the public opinion and voting polls. Showing that money isn't everything, Ralph Nader's run under the Green Party banner caught on in some states, but his less than 3% final showing was significantly less than the pre-election polls had indicated for the size of his following. That 3% turned out to be very important, however, when the closeness of the final election outcome and the distribution of his 2.8 million votes in key states denied Al Gore the presidency. Nader's backers saw the support Nader received as a wake-up call for the Democrats and hoped to lure them back to traditional liberal ideals.

In 2004, despite the entreaties of many Democrats, Ralph Nader decided to enter the race again as an independent, arguing that the Democratic Party could not satisfactorily address the issues or take the positions he felt were important. Democrats used the courts to deny Nader access to the ballot in a number of key states.

Party teams are clearly in flux. With declines in party identification and party-line voting, a larger percentage of voters are up for grabs than at any time in recent history. Members of Congress and local officials changed teams with seemingly few negative repercussions. It should be of little surprise that with such demonstrable actions the nature of the party team line-ups on the presidential level should be so uncertain.

---

a. These committees took the effort to register with the Federal Election Commission. Some actually raised funds and got their candidates on the ballot. Other more colorful committees supporting independent candidates in 1992 included the "Messiah for President of the U.S. Committee" (backing Fred Sitnick, who calls himself Messiah), the "If You've Had Enough Vote Hoff" for President Committee, and the "Tax-U-All Committee to Elect Paul Trent President."

b. Richard Berke, "The Specter of Perot Haunts Major Parties," *New York Times*, June 6, 1995, A20.

The federal system, with its differing election dates and large number of elected officials, insulates American parties from total defeat and dampens the potential for the emergence of new parties. A loss in the national presidential election is often balanced by a party's success in congressional, state, and/or local elections. Pockets of party support sustain party organizations until their next national victory.

Voter, Media, and Interest Group Support for the Major Party Players

Political parties need the votes of citizens, the attention of the media, and the resources of interest groups. All three groups of players accept the reality of the two-party system and give comparatively little attention or support to third parties that attempt to enter the game. Most voters continue to identify with one of the two major parties. Until relatively recently, splitting a ticket by voting for candidates of more than one party for different offices was relatively rare (see Chapter 11). In spite of an increase in self-defined independents and increased ticket splitting among the electorate, third parties generally have not benefited from voters' temporary dissatisfaction with one of the major parties. Ticket splitters by and large do not gravitate to third parties but rather cast their votes for the candidate of the other major party. Contemporary third-party presidential candidates, such as George C. Wallace (1968), John B. Anderson (1980), and H. Ross Perot (1992 and 1996), saw impressive early percentages dwindle closer to Election Day as more and more voters were convinced by the major parties not to waste their votes. In 2000, conservative Pat Buchanan's takeover of the Reform Party was the highlight of his success, with his candidacy drawing less than 1% of the final vote. Ralph Nader's run under the Green Party label looked as if it would reach the 5% threshold to gain millions in federal campaign funding, but as in the past many voters abandoned Nader at the last minute out of fear of wasting their votes and/or tipping the race toward George W. Bush.

Success of third-party and independent candidates increases somewhat at state and local levels, where personal ties and party identification mean even more. The 1990 gubernatorial elections in Alaska and Connecticut saw two former major-party officeholders (Walter Hickel and Lowell Weicker, respectively) use their personal reputations to win as independents. In 1998 Reform Party candidate and former professional wrestler Jesse Ventura won a surprising gubernatorial victory in Minnesota, beating out the Republican and Democratic candidates. Despite such highly publicized victories, the major parties still dominate the electoral game.

Third parties tend to emphasize issues and emerge when the major parties fail to face up to key conflicts in society. On the national level, the issues of third parties that capture public attention are absorbed, along with their ideas and potential supporters, by the two major parties. In the 1992 campaign, Ross Perot pushed both major-party candidates to take a more anti-Washington approach and to urge the rejection of politics as usual. Perot played the spoiler, taking more votes from Bush than from Clinton. His later attempt to influence the 1994 election with a series of bipartisan endorsements seemed to have limited effect. Most of Perot's 1992 voters ended up swelling the 1994 Republican tide, with 56 percent supporting Republican congressional candidates and only 25 percent supporting Democrats.[26]

Ross Perot's run in 1996 gained 8.5% of the vote but had no effect on the one-sided presidential outcome. The longer-term impact was that by maintaining 5% of the vote, he guaranteed his party a place on the ballot and over $12.5 million in funding for 2000. The third-party candidacies in 2000 might have been a footnote if the election had not been so close. The role of third-party candidates as spoilers was reinforced with a vengeance. Purported ballot confusion in some counties of Florida led to legal challenges as to whether a significant number of Gore voters punched their ballots for Buchanan instead. In a number of states, Ralph Nader's totals cost Gore victory, giving clear evidence that Nader drew much more heavily from probable Gore supporters. The election eventually came down to allocating the electoral votes of Florida. Assuming Nader voters would have turned out to support Al Gore, their 97,000 votes would have given Gore a clear victory without the torturous recount that resulted in a winning margin of less than 500 votes for George W. Bush. In 2004, Nader's campaign resulted in 1% of the vote and was not decisive in any key state.

The media, although often critical of party politics, pay more attention to the major party candidates. Given the limited attention span of most voters, the media use their limited access to the public's mind to focus on the key players. In the process, they support the current players to the detriment of potential replacements. Third-party efforts remain largely invisible to newspaper readers and television viewers. For example, third-party candidates are usually denied equal status with the major parties for televised candidate debates. They fight similar discrimination in the quantity and quality of general media attention that they receive. Ross Perot garnered significant media attention early in the 1992 campaign but saw his serious coverage dwindle as the final campaign round began. Unlike all other recent third-party candidates, Perot's ability to finance personally his campaign at a level commensurate with those of Bush and Clinton allowed him to purchase significant exposure. Under current electoral laws, Perot's success is likely to be the exception to the rule. Voters do show an increased interest in third parties, but there are still numerous obstacles to be overcome.

Because of the numerous factors supporting the two-party system, players from the two major parties are able to push almost all other competitors from the playing field. Although gaining elective office themselves lies beyond their grasp, third-party candidates can take some consolation in their ability to identify emerging issues and to encourage candidates of the major parties to pursue them.

8-4 The Partisan Profiles of Winners and Losers

The ambitions of one party are never completely fulfilled due to the significant and often distinctive powers of the opposing party. Although the Founders might be amazed at the staying power of the Republican and Democratic Parties, they would applaud their ability to encourage "ambition . . . to counteract ambition."[27] They would feel vindicated in their desire to protect the nation from too great a concentration of power.

Elections are never clean sweeps, with one party winning all offices. On the national level, postwar Democratic domination of Congress and Republican domination of the presidency created the kind of ambition-countering situation that the Founders would have relished. Similar splits occur regularly on the state and local levels.

American political parties have found it relatively easy to compensate for weaknesses in one realm with strengths in another. During the 1970s and 1980s, Republican Party shortcomings among the party-in-the-electorate led to increased emphasis on bolstering the resources and technological capabilities of the party organization. When the Democrats felt threatened by the Republican victories in the 1980s, they followed the lead of the Republicans and became a service-vendor operation providing campaign services. After losing both Congress and the presidency in 1992, the Republicans emphasized national agenda-setting. Their *Contract with America* was, among other things, a way to distinguish themselves from the Democrats. The parties clearly want to be players in the American political process for the long haul and are willing to innovate to do so (see Box 8-8: The Parties Enter the Information Highway).

Box 8-8 *The Parties Enter the Information Highway*

Political parties do not want to miss any opportunity to communicate with likely voters, and most have established a page on the World Wide Web. If you have access to the Internet, you might want to drop in and see what they have to offer.

Republicans	http://www.rnc.org/ (see also http://www.gop.gov/)
Democrats	http://www.democrats.org/ (see also http://www.freedom.com/)
Reform Party	http://www.reformparty.org/
Libertarian Party	http://www.lp.org/
Green Party	http://www.greens.org/
New Party	http://www.newparty.org/
Democratic Socialists of America	http://www.dsausa.org/
Constitution Party	http://www.ustaxpayers.org/
We the People Party	http://www.wtp.org/

8-5 The Party in Government

Party responsibilities do not end when the campaigns are over. Party teams ask for a mandate to govern and are judged on the basis of their performance.

8-5a The Ambiguity of Electoral Success and Control of Public Policy

divided government *When one coequal branch of government is controlled by one party and the other branch or branches is/are controlled by the opposing party.*

The initial test for each party comes on election night. Few election nights result in an unambiguous victory for one party and an inglorious defeat for the other; each party can usually take some solace in the results. Americans have become accustomed to **divided government,** the election of state or national chief executives from one party and of legislatures dominated by the opposing party. During the first century and a half of American constitutional history, single-party government was the norm 80 percent of the time.[28] In recent years, the pattern has reversed. Since World War II, the presidency has been held by one party 60 percent of the time while at least one house of Congress has been controlled by the other.

A number of factors contribute to divided government. For example, the Republican Party—at least until very recently—seems to have more difficulty recruiting good candidates for lower-level offices:

> The Democratic party is the party of government in the United States, the vehicle for those who grow up interested in government and politics and want to make a career of it. The Republican party is the vehicle for those who believe that government is a dirty business and that they demean themselves by taking part. . . . The dilemma that confronts Republican professionals whose job it is to recruit candidates for office [is] that they must persuade people who do not think very highly of government to drop what they are doing and spend months maneuvering for a chance to become part of it.[29]

Part of the 1994 Republican success resulted from recruiting better candidates. As far back as 1987, Newt Gingrich "had a vision: Raise millions of dollars and spend it to nurture a dynamic new generation of Republican politicians—a farm team that could some day march from the state houses to Congress."[30] Thirty-three of the 73 newly elected Republicans in 1994 came from that farm team.[31] There is a problem on the horizon, though. The fact that most newly elected Republicans in 1994 stuck with their Contract with America commitment to term limitations speaks well of their consistency. It could, however, result in undermining the ability of the Republican Party to build a permanent congressional majority.

Once they are in office, the advantages of incumbency traditionally protect members sitting in Congress and in state legislatures. Even in 1994, more than 90 percent of the House incumbents running for reelection won. Evidence indicates that during the 1980s some voters consciously attempted to divide power by supporting Republican presidents and Democratic legislators.[32] When the presidency was captured by the Democrats in 1992, the stage was set for increased Republican voting in the 1994 congressional elections. Americans seem to have made a virtue out of necessity, since a strong majority of those with an opinion believe that divided government is a good idea to prevent either Congress or the president from "going too far."[33] Similar divisions are common on the state and local levels.

While the Republicans prepared to glory in their victory, the Democrats revealed considerable confusion in terms of their reaction to the 1994 election results. After forty years in the majority, they were not clear on why they had been thrown out of the game. More importantly, they did not see an effective way to fight their way back in. Senator John B. Breaux (D-La.), representing the more conservative wing of the party, argued that the electorate was telling their party that they had stopped being mainstream and that the route to success lay in moving toward the center.[34] Former Senator Howard M. Metzenbaum (D-Ohio), a traditional liberal, argued just as forcefully, "If we try to walk like Republicans, talk like Republicans and act like Republicans, people will want the real thing and just vote Republican. We don't need two Republican Parties."[35] By the time the 104th Congress convened in 1995, Democrats had begun to coalesce around a strategy of actively opposing much of the Republican *Contract with America*. On many policies, Republicans needed Democratic votes, just as Democrats had needed Republican votes in the past. This created the possibility that the Democrats could provide the balance of power on some issues and thus be able to fight for more acceptable compromises.

After the 2000 election, Republicans faced the unfamiliar opportunity of controlling the presidency and both houses of Congress, albeit by razor thin majorities. It soon became clear that they would need some Democratic votes in Congress to pass legislation, since they could not count on all of their party members. Within a few months, former Republican Senator James Jeffords of Vermont, who already had a record of bucking the party, became an independent and the short period of unified government became history.

The 2002 election returned both houses of Congress to the Republicans, with a great deal of credit going to President George W. Bush, who campaigned extensively for party candidates. The outcome was a dual-edged sword, with the Republicans responsible for delivering the kind of government the public voted for. While the Democrats soothed their egos with the threat that the voters would now have a clear partisan target to turn on if the Republicans failed to perform, the Republicans tried to hide their glee with the recognition that in politics winning is always better than losing. With their decisive victory in 2004, the responsibility for government outcomes shifted even more directly on the Republicans.

No one party can control all of the governmental institutions that share power, especially with the narrow margins recent elections have resulted in. Compromise has become the political coin of the realm. The parties organize elected officials around broad themes but allow individual party members considerable leeway in terms of the degree of party loyalty expected. Policy victories on most levels of government are due to **bipartisan** compromises and coalitions rather than narrow partisan victories. The coalition that wins one policy contest often looks very different from the coalition that comes together for the next issue.

bipartisan *Support for a course of action not split exclusively along party lines.*

The Performance of Party Teams

Even the members of party teams at times work at cross-purposes. State legislators and members of Congress organize into party caucuses and choose party leaders for their chambers, but they feel little constraint when voting on legislation (see Chapter 13). While party voting in Congress has increased in recent years, fewer than two-thirds of the votes reveal the majority of one party opposing the majority of the other. While presidents can generally expect higher support from members of their own party, support is not guaranteed. Despite the authority of their offices, neither presidents nor party leaders control the electoral fortunes of other elected officials.

Political scientists and political reformers have long pursued the goal of the **responsible parties model,** in which voters choose among candidates taking clear party-based stands on the issues and elect partisan teams of officials who are committed to pursuing these party goals. While party positions guide many political decisions, they do not dictate them. Party teams are just one of the many bases of American political coalitions. They are often overwhelmed by ideological, regional, or other considerations, such as personal preferences or, simply, political survival.

responsible party model *An idealized party system marked by clearly differentiated parties, party-oriented voters, candidates committed to party goals, and cohesive support for the party by elected and appointed officials.*

Conclusion

Given the wide diversity of voter opinions, the changing issues, and the alternative ways in which proponents of particular positions can harness new communications technologies to activate voters, the staying power of the Republican and Democratic parties is impressive. The parties continually fight to remain important players in the game. They adjust to the legal environment, recruit candidates, provide alternatives to voters, subsidize the efforts of nominees, and organize elected officials. The parties draw together coalitions of individuals who agree on a broad set of concerns. The lack of unanimity and the level of internal conflict reveal the difficulty of this task. That much of American politics is explained in partisan terms is testimony to the effectiveness of parties' efforts. Innovative technologies that link voters directly to politicians and provide opportunities for virtual communities of individuals with common interests will challenge the parties in new ways. The need to simplify alternatives and forge enforceable compromises will remain. The political party is an essential part of democracy.

Key Terms

balancing the ticket
bipartisan
bloc voting
candidate-centered campaign
caucus
civil service
divided government
inclusiveness
natural dualism
nomination
nonpartisan elections
office-bloc ballot
parliamentary system
party-column ballot
party identification
party-in-the-electorate
party machine
party platform
patronage
political boss
political party
pragmatism
primary election
Progressives
proportional representation
realignment
responsible party model
single-member district
slate
socialization
soft money
spoils system
stumping
ticket splitting

Practice Quiz

1. How did the Founders generally feel about political parties?
- **a.** They protected their status in Article VI of the Constitution.
- **b.** They opposed permanent partisan divisions.
- **c.** They believed parties reduced the violence inherent in starting a new nation.
- **d.** They saw parties as inherently good.

2. What helped weaken the power of state and local party organizations?
- **a.** Patronage
- **b.** Political bosses
- **c.** Party machines
- **d.** Civil service laws

3. What percentage of the population expresses a party identification?
- **a.** Under 10%
- **b.** 20–30%
- **c.** 40–50%
- **d.** Over 60%

4. Which statement *best* describes the rules governing direct party contributions to congressional elections?
- **a.** As private organizations, parties can contribute any amount of money to a candidate.
- **b.** Parties cannot make direct campaign contributions to candidates.
- **c.** Parties are not limited in the amount of campaign contributions they can make.
- **d.** Parties can contribute a fixed amount of their income to candidates.

5. Parties generally prefer _____ ballots.
- **a.** party column
- **b.** office-bloc
- **c.** non-partisan
- **d.** punch card

6. The party platform is important because it
- **a.** determines who can attend the national convention.
- **b.** outlines the party position on key policy issues.
- **c.** serves as a legal contract between the party and elected officials.
- **d.** shows that politicians seldom live up to their promises.

7. Sophisticated and well-organized political parties are often likened to a
- **a.** long distance runner.
- **b.** game.
- **c.** machine.
- **d.** umbrella.

8. The Progressives are credited with promoting all of the following reforms except which one?
- **a.** Primary elections
- **b.** Single-member-districts
- **c.** Civil service hiring
- **d.** Professionalized public administration

9. Ticket splitting is more common among _____, while party loyalty is stronger among _____.
- **a.** Democrats, Republicans
- **b.** Republicans, Democrats
- **c.** Republicans, Independents
- **d.** Independents, Democrats

10. Contemporary American parties can be described by all of the following terms except which one?
- **a.** Ideological
- **b.** Pragmatic
- **c.** Inclusive
- **d.** Weak

You can find the correct answers to these questions by taking the quiz and then submitting your answers in the Online Edition. The program will automatically score your submission. Where you miss a question, the program will provide the correct answer, a rationale for the answer, and the section number in the chapter where the topic is discussed.

Further Reading

Political Parties in the Technological Age by Stephen Frantzich (New York: Longman, 1989) is a comprehensive text on American political parties that considers the impact of modern information technologies on the operation and fortunes of the parties. See also William Keefe, *Parties, Politics, and Public Policy in America* (Washington, D.C.: Congressional Quarterly Press, 1994).

L. Sandy Maisel has brought together a number of experts on political parties in *The Parties Respond: Changes in the American Party System* (Boulder, CO: Westview Press, 1990) to discuss contemporary changes in the parties.

For a look at the expanded role of the national party organizations, see Paul Herrnson's *Party Campaigning in the 1980s* (Cambridge, MA: Harvard University Press, 1988). A series of studies defined as the "Party Transformation Project" have been published by Cornelius P. Cotter, James Gibson, John Bibby, Robert Huckshorn, John P. Frenreis, and Laura Vertz and focus on state and local party organizations. The most comprehensive summary can be found in *Party Organization in American Politics* (New York: Praeger, 1984).

Endnotes

1. Quoted in David Broder, "GOP Offers More Tax Breaks for Rich," *Washington Post*, September 29, 1994, A15.
2. Gary Orren, "The Changing Styles of American Party Politics," in *The Future of American Political Parties*, ed. Joel Fleischman (Englewood Cliffs, NJ: Prentice-Hall, 1982), 4.
3. At various points in time, the Jeffersonians ran under the labels of "Republicans" and "Democratic-Republicans," names that are unnecessarily confused with the contemporary parties using those names.
4. Alan R. Gitelson, M. Margaret Conway, and Frank B. Feigert, *American Political Parties: Stability and Change* (Boston, MA: Houghton Mifflin, 1984), 31.
5. For a more complete discussion of party functions, see Stephen Frantzich, *Political Parties in the Technological Age* (New York: Longman, 1989), 10–12, and Paul Allen Beck, *Political Parties in America* (New York: Longman, 1997), 7–16.
6. For a classic study of party machines, see Martin and Susan Tolchin, *To the Victor: Political Patronage from the Clubhouse to the White House* (New York: Random House, 1971).
7. While political machines have long been credited with integrating new immigrants into American society, some recent research questions the effectiveness of this integration. See Stephen P. Erie, *Rainbow's End: Irish-Americans and the Dilemmas of Urban Machine Politics* (Berkeley, CA: University of California Press, 1988).
8. Xandra Kayden and Eddie Mahe, *The Party Goes On: The Persistence of the Two-Party System in the United States* (New York: Basic Books, 1985), 105.
9. See Paul Herrnson, *Party Campaigning in the 1980s* (Cambridge, MA: Harvard University Press, 1988); and Frantzich, *Political Parties*, 84–90.
10. Harold W. Stanley and Richard G. Niemi, *Vital Statistics on American Politics, 1999–2000* (Washington, D.C.: Congressional Quarterly Press, 2000), 114.
11. William Booth, "'Party Stuff Is Getting In the Way,' Young Tuned-Out Voters Tell Poll," *Washington Post*, November 6, 1994, A28.
12. Mark Shields, "Democrats: The Party's Almost Over," *Washington Post*, June 10, 1991, A11. (Shields is a prominent Democratic campaign consultant.)
13. Walter Dean Burnham, *Critical Elections and the Mainspring of American Politics* (New York: W. W. Norton, 1970).
14. Hedrick Smith, *The Power Game* (New York: Random House, 1988), 670–71. For similar sentiments, see Richard Hollander, *Video Democracy* (Mt. Airy, MD: Lomond Press, 1985), 93, and Alan Westin, "A Workable Government," in *The Constitution After 200 Years*, ed. Burke Marshall (New York: American Assembly, 1987), 191.

15. Barbara G. Salmore and Stephen A. Salmore, *Candidates, Parties and Campaigns* (Washington, D.C.: Congressional Quarterly Press, 1989), 20.
16. See Sheldon Goldman, "Voting Behavior of the U.S. Courts of Appeals Revisited," *American Political Science Review* 69 (June 1975), 496; Stephen Wasby, *The Supreme Court in the Federal System* (New York: Holt, Rinehart and Winston, 1988); and Stuart S. Nagel, "Political Party Affiliation and Judges' Decisions," *American Political Science Review* 55 (December 1961), 845.
17. Leon Epstein, *Political Parties in the American Mold* (Madison, WI: University of Wisconsin Press, 1986), 155.
18. Leon Epstein, *Political Parties in Western Democracies* (New Brunswick, NJ: Transaction Books, 1980), 44.
19. Gerald Pomper, *Election in America* (New York: Longman, 1980), 168–76.
20. Alan Westin, "A Workable Government," in *The Constitution After 200 Years*, ed. Burke Marshall (New York: American Assembly, 1987), 191.
21. David Broder, "Phony PAC Ban," *Washington Post*, April 7, 1991, D7.
22. *Cousins v. Wigoda*, 419 U.S. 477 (1975).
23. For a more detailed discussion, see Stephen Frantzich, *Political Parties in the Technological Age* (New York: Longman, 1989), 125–28. For an analysis of the Republican approach to rules changes, see John F. Bibby, *Political Parties and Elections in America* (Chicago, IL: Nelson-Hall, 1987), 178–80.
24. See Maurice Duverger, *Political Parties* (New York: Wiley, 1954).
25. See Thomas Ferguson and Joel Rogers, *Right Turn: The Decline of the Democrats and the Future of American Politics* (New York: Hill and Wang, 1986), which argues that the resources of more conservative contributors have moved both parties to the right.
26. November 10, 1994, national poll of 1,300 adults conducted by the Progress and Freedom Foundation.
27. James Madison, "*Federalist* No. 51," *The Federalist Papers* (New York: Mentor Books, 1962).
28. Hedrick Smith, *The Power Game* (New York: Random House, 1988), 653.
29. Alan Ehrenhalt, "The Rise of a Political Class," *Washington Post*, July 21, 1991, C3. [This is an excerpt from his book *The United States of Ambition: Politicians, Power and the Pursuit of Office* (New York: Times Books, 1991).]
30. Stephen Engelberg and Katharine Q. Seelye, "Gingrich: The Man in the Spotlight and Organization in Shadow," *New York Times*, December 18, 1994, 1.
31. *Ibid*, 32.
32. See Gary C. Jacobson, *The Electoral Origins of Divided Government* (Boulder, CO: Westview Press, 1990).
33. NBC News/ *Wall Street Journal* poll of 2,005 adults, 29 September 1998, LEXIS-NEXIS database.
34. Quoted in Lawrence M. O'Rourke, "Divided Democrats Bickering Over How to Make Comeback," *Sacramento Bee*, December 11, 1994, A3.
35. *Ibid.*

Public Opinion: From Political Culture to Political Impact

Key Points

- **The challenge of gauging public opinion accurately.**
- **Tools for becoming a sophisticated poll consumer.**
- **How attitudes and opinions change.**
- **The ideologies of liberals and conservatives compared.**
- **The strategic uses of public opinion in the political process.**

Preview: The Public Speaks Loudly

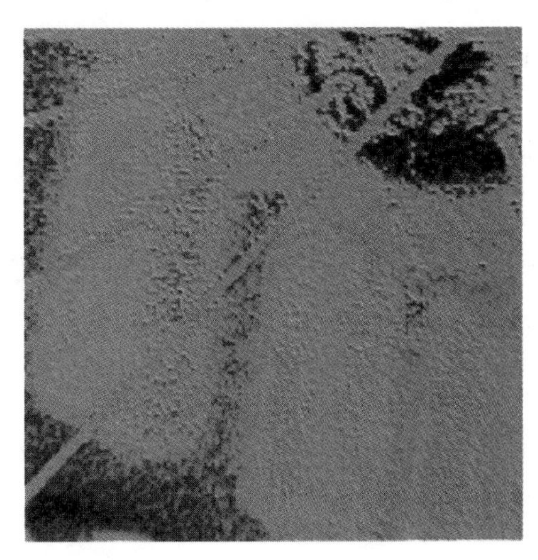

*A visibly tired and haggard man walked down the stairs toward the microphone. His eyes were puffy as though he had been crying and, his voice spent from overuse, he croaked out a few words of thanks. Most observers chalked up the obvious emotion to the relief of being home again in Plains, Georgia, after a long campaign. Few of those watching knew the full source of the emotion. Jimmy Carter had finally realized that he had just become one of the few presidents in history to be denied reelection. It would be hours before the polling places around the country would be closed, but he knew that his fate was sealed. One of his seatmates during the flight home had been presidential pollster Pat Caddell. Caddell's hour-by-hour **tracking polls** showed that the trend was going in Ronald Reagan's direction. Samples of voters around the country had been asked whom they favored in the election, and their responses were compared with the responses of a few hours earlier. The impact of fast-moving events such as the American hostage negotiations in Iran was clear. Long-term partisan attitudes were falling victim to the short-term opinion that Jimmy Carter was not up to the job.*

tracking polls A series of polls taken at short intervals that attempt to measure changes in opinion.

Across the country another politician began to fret about his fate. While long-term attitudes tend to protect incumbents by encouraging voters "not to change horses in midstream," Al Ullman, Democratic congressman and chairman of the powerful Ways and Means Committee, saw mounting dangers. His opponent had been able to establish concerns in voters' minds about being represented by a congressional leader who had lost touch with the district. Ullman knew the race had become close even though he did not have the resources for detailed tracking polls. He knew that the outcome would hinge on voter turnout.

Ullman's political future began to unravel when the network news ***exit polls*** *led to a projection that Jimmy Carter had been defeated. The official polling places would be open in Oregon for three more hours, but this new broadcasted information hit many Democratic voters hard. A few moments earlier, they had been committed to doing their public duty and voting for Carter and Ullman. Now many of them quickly developed the new opinion that their vote would not count. Thousands of usually Democratic voters didn't bother to show up, and both Carter and Ullman were thereby denied votes. On the other hand, supporters of Denny Smith, Ullman's Republican opponent, became even more strongly motivated. They could now join the political bandwagon by voting with the winner in the presidential race—even as they cast their congressional vote for a fellow Republican. Within a few hours both Jimmy Carter and Al Ullman had given their concession speeches. Both Pat Caddell's presidential polls and the network's exit polls turned out to be uncannily accurate. Ullman's less scientific hunches were also borne out.*

exit poll *Informal survey of voting patterns based on interviews of those who are exiting election sites.*

As is often the case in politics, the gathering of information and its political impact are intertwined. Public opinion polls both measure and create opinions.

At the heart of any definition of democracy is the idea that governmental policy decisions should reflect the views of the country's citizens.[1] Public opinion—a set of views or preferences held by a large segment of the population—defines the range of acceptable strategies and solutions. It is at the core of the political process, as Abraham Lincoln noted in his first debate with Stephen A. Douglas, in Ottawa, Illinois, on August 21, 1858: "Public sentiment is everything. With public sentiment, nothing can fail. Without it, nothing can succeed. Consequently, he who holds public sentiment goes deeper than he who enacts statutes or pronounces decisions."

Public opinion arises out of a political culture and is influenced by the mediating institutions described in later chapters of this book. The media provides the information on which opinions are based. Interest groups organize when strong public opinion exists—or can be stirred up—about an issue. Political parties both use public opinion to select viable candidates and to decide on issues, and they actively work to affect it. It is public opinion, or *attitudes* about issues, that pulls individuals into the voting booth or to other forms of political participation. Politicians expend considerable effort to sway the opinions of other players and of the general public.

Various new technologies have dramatically increased the ease with which opinions can be measured. Others facilitate the communication of those opinions. Public opinion polls allow citizens to communicate their wishes without having to take any action to do so. Traditional technologies, such as writing letters and using the telephone, have been augmented with tools such as email and computer-facilitated petitioning. Elected officials must sort through the expanded representations of public opinion, weighing relevance and legitimacy.

9-1 Rules of Opinion Formation

Private opinion creates public opinion. Public opinion overflows eventually into national behavior, and national behavior, as things are arranged at present, can make or mar the world. That is why private opinion, private behavior, and private conversation are so terrifyingly important.[2]

Few formal rules affect political opinion. The "freedom of expression" guarantees of the Constitution (found in the 1st Amendment) specifically prohibit encroachment on individuals' opinions—although taking action based on some opinions may be limited by the legal system. Americans can believe what they want, but when those beliefs turn into action that could harm others, government can step in. For example, although you are free to believe that the American government should be violently overthrown, the American government will punish you should you actively engage in the revolution.

In a broader sense, however, social rules determine how individuals develop the opinions that guide their behavior. In Chapter 5 we explored a system of shared values as a major component of American political culture. We differentiated between values, attitudes, and opinions. Participants in a political arena have entered it with a set of long-term predispositions (attitudes). Their short-term preferences (*opinions*) remain in flux. Both of these factors influence their political behavior.

Many attitudes and opinions reflect deeply held *values*—our visions of a good life and a perfect society—formed through the socialization process. Box 9-1: The Four Es of Socialization summarizes the process described in Chapter 5.

The dividing lines between values, attitudes, and opinions are not always clear. In general, however, values reflect permanent goals, while both attitudes and opinions focus on the means for reaching those goals. Attitudes are broader, more permanent, and more abstract than the short-term opinions they precede. For example, an individual who values security above all else is likely to develop the attitude that national defense is the government's primary task. That same individual could have the short-term opinion that specific cuts in social programs are preferable to alternative cuts in defense. Values, attitudes, and opinions guide the actions of participants and help observers to make sense of individual choices (see Time Out 9-1: Team or Individual Players).

9-1a Potential for Attitude Change

Basic political attitudes are pretty well fixed before individuals leave high school.[3] A subsequent accumulation of new life experiences has the potential for changing established attitudes, but the forces of change must compete vigorously against the well-ingrained attitudes acquired through socialization.

Box 9–1 *The Four Es of Socialization*

Four simultaneous and interrelated processes underlay the process of political socialization:

1. *Exposure:* The pattern of information outlooks and preferences that the individual is allowed to hear, see, or read about.

   Typical family scenarios [Parent talking to child]: "Turn off that program. It is too violent" or "Read that article on drugs. It makes good sense."

2. *Education:* Intentional attempts of family, friends, and organizations (schools, churches, social groups, and so on) to directly impart information, outlooks, and preferences.

   Typical family scenarios [Parent talking to child]: "Here are four good reasons why Bush is the best candidate" or "If the federal government were run like our family budget, we wouldn't have the big deficit."

3. *Emulation:* Patterning one's outlooks and preferences after those of another person out of respect or fear.

   Typical family scenarios [Child thinking to herself]: "Dad is generally right on most things—although I wouldn't admit it to him—so I guess his stand on abortion is probably right also." [Parent talking to child]: "You are a chip off the old block. You have learned to be very responsible with your allowance. I guess we will have to increase it."

4. *Experience:* Creating generalizations about the world from the events in one's individual life.

   Typical family scenarios [Child thinking to himself]: "Mom and Dad seem to be fair. I guess police officers are also" or "I never get treated fairly at home. I can't expect anything different from my teachers."

Time Out 9-1

As honestly as possible, indicate your attitudes, those of your mother and father, and those held by your best friend about the following statements. If you are not sure, make an educated guess.

1. "The recreational use of illegal drugs should be a matter of personal choice."

	Agree	Disagree
Your attitude	_____	_____
Your mother's attitude	_____	_____
Your father's attitude	_____	_____
Your best friend's attitude	_____	_____

2. "Human life begins at the moment of conception."

	Agree	Disagree
Your attitude	_____	_____
Your mother's attitude	_____	_____
Your father's attitude	_____	_____
Your best friend's attitude	_____	_____

3. "Government involvement in the lives of individuals has become too intrusive."

	Agree	Disagree
Your attitude	_____	_____
Your mother's attitude	_____	_____
Your father's attitude	_____	_____
Your best friend's attitude	_____	_____

4. "Life is better for people like me when there is a Democrat in the White House."

	Agree	Disagree
Your attitude	_____	_____
Your mother's attitude	_____	_____
Your father's attitude	_____	_____
Your best friend's attitude	_____	_____

A comparison of your answers with those of your mother, your father, and your friend will probably reveal substantial consistency. As much as we like to view ourselves as independent thinkers, most of us end up with attitudes similar to those of the people closest to us, the teams with whom we identify. This tends to reinforce our attitudes and to make them less subject to change.

Change comes most often at those times in life when the traditional social structure is upset (marriage, moving to a new social setting, taking a new job)—when we begin to view ourselves as members of new teams. Changing an attitude requires acknowledging, at least subconsciously, that we were wrong or misinformed. For many this is not an easy admission.

Life experiences and societal changes often confront us with choices for which our socialization leaves us unprepared. For example, many of today's parents grew up when violence in schools was less of a problem, when lesbians and gay men were largely "in the closet," and when it was relatively uncommon for couples to live together before marriage. They are often at a loss, therefore, in reacting to the contemporary situation. Socialization may tell them that they do not like the change, but it gives few guidelines on how to react. The lack of a firm expectation of the "proper" reaction allows some flexibility.

Dramatic historical events, such as wars and economic crises, often confront entire societies with life-changing experiences. Old attitudes stemming from earlier socialization serve as the basis for interpreting new events, but they may not stand up to conflicting evidence. Vietnam shook the confidence of many Americans, in both U.S. military capabilities and the country's political leadership. A series of White House and congressional scandals forced many Americans to reassess their trust in the honesty of public officials. The changes in Eastern Europe and the Soviet Union undermined long-term fears of a threatening, powerful, and unified Communist movement. The Persian Gulf War turned many skeptics of U.S. military involvement into at least reluctant cheerleaders. Police impropriety, captured on videotape during the arrest of Rodney King, set the stage for public skepticism of police neutrality when it came to the O. J. Simpson trial. Mass communications technologies allow millions of Americans to experience indirectly or participate in events simultaneously, and, in the process, open the potential for broad attitude change. The series of high school shootings epitomized by the Columbine tragedy forced many individuals to reassess their views of gun control.

9-1b Ideology: Patterns of Political Attitudes

Most individuals hold attitudes on a wide variety of topics, but these attitudes are not simply a set of unconnected orientations. The socialization process—and an individual's desire for consistency—leads to many individuals holding similar sets of attitudes. **Ideology** refers to an organized set of ideas defining social goals and the best governmental arrangements for achieving them. Ideologies, for example, often include judgments as to whether a social goal should be pursued by government or individual action, as well as which units of government are most capable of pursuing goals entrusted to the government.

ideology *A comprehensive set of beliefs about the proper nature of people and society.*

liberals *Supporters of a political ideology that trusts human nature, who see an active role for government, welcome change, emphasize freedom over order, and strive for complete equality in society.*

Content of Ideological Beliefs

Summarizing political attitudes is a complex and difficult task. Observers of American politics often outline a mainstream continuum of opinions, with **liberals** at one end and

Time Out 9-2

Please take the following poll, frankly representing your views and your perception of the views of others.
How do you stand on these controversial issues?

1. "The government should provide many more services, even if it means an increase in spending."	Agree	Disagree
2. "The government should greatly reduce defense spending."	Agree	Disagree
3. "It is better to have medical bills covered by a government insurance plan than by a private plan."	Agree	Disagree
4. "A company with a history of discrimination against blacks should be required to have an affirmative action program that gives blacks a preference in hiring."	Agree	Disagree
5. "The government should make every effort to improve the social and economic positions of blacks."	Agree	Disagree
6. "Women should have an equal role with men in running business, industry, and government."	Agree	Disagree
7. "By law, a woman should always be able to obtain an abortion as a matter of personal choice."	Agree	Disagree
8. "It is important to protect the environment, even if it costs some jobs or otherwise reduces our standard of living."	Agree	Disagree
9. "Homosexuals should be allowed to serve in the U.S. Armed Forces."	Agree	Disagree
10. "The Federal government should make it more difficult for people to buy a gun."	Agree	Disagree

Answer to Time Out 9-1

Count the number of statements you agreed with in Time Out 9-1 before reading the chart below. The issues presented are some of the most divisive in American politics and consistently separate liberals and conservatives. If you agreed with six or more of the previous statements, you have more liberal attitudes. If you agreed with three or fewer, you tend to take conservative positions.

Here are the answers of self-declared liberals and conservatives to these questions in a national public opinion poll:

% of Liberals who agree	% of Conservatives who agree	
82%	52%	1. "The government should provide many more services, even if it means an increase in spending."
37%	16%	2. "The government should greatly reduce defense spending."
73%	48%	3. "It is better to have medical bills covered by a government insurance plan than by a private plan."
61%	50%	4. "A company with a history of discrimination against blacks should be required to have an affirmative action program that gives blacks a preference in hiring."
30%	17%	5. "The government should make every effort to improve the social and economic positions of blacks."
93%	86%	6. "Women should have an equal role with men in running business, industry, and government."
60%	33%	7. "By law, a woman should always be able to obtain an abortion as a matter of personal choice."
76%	58%	8. "It is important to protect the environment, even if it costs some jobs or otherwise reduces our standard of living."
86%	69%	9. "Homosexuals should be allowed to serve in the U.S. Armed Forces."
71%	51%	10. The Federal government should make it more difficult for people to buy a gun."

Source: 2000 National Election Study, ICPSR data file, Survey Research Center, University of Michigan. Data include only those taking a stand on the issue.

conservatives *Supporters of a political ideology that distrusts human nature, who envision a limited role for government, require significant justification for change, emphasize order over freedom, and assume a natural hierarchy in society.*

moderates *Individuals whose views fall between those of liberals and conservatives. Moderates often hold their views less fervently than individuals with more extreme opinions.*

conservatives at the other. In the middle are **moderates,** who either do not have a strong commitment to either extreme or accept some views of both. Dividing political outlooks into these categories goes back to the earliest days of politics.[4] The specific content of attitudes associated with each view, however, has varied to some degree over time. While ideologies imply more consistency than really exists, distinctions between people who think of themselves as liberals and those who think of themselves as conservatives are relatively clear.

Contemporary liberals generally express optimism in the ability of government to improve society through innovative government programs. They see government's ultimate goal as ensuring as much equality of outcome and freedom as possible to all members of the society. They believe that progress both domestically and internationally comes through cooperation and a commitment to change. Liberals tend to emphasize domestic social programs and international cooperation and diplomacy in foreign affairs.

Conservatives generally distrust the nature of humans and the governments they create. They prefer to see government used for more limited purposes, such as protecting individuals and their property from their fellow human beings. They emphasize the differing motivations and abilities of individuals and recognize that this leads to both conflict and inequality. Making a virtue out of necessity, conservatives view competition as an invigorating force that motivates individuals by rewarding the most productive participants. Conservatives often doubt the utility of social programs. They emphasize support for police protection domestically and for a strong national defense to protect against international enemies (see Box 9-2: The Liberal and Conservative Checklist).[5]

The Republican Contract with America (see Box 9-3: A Conservative Contract) set the stage for a number of the ideological battles that followed. It included items over which liberals and conservatives disagreed.

The differences between liberals and conservatives came into focus during the 1995 debate over a national crime bill. Liberals wanted to maintain strict standards for the admissibility of evidence during trials, while conservatives were frustrated with criminals getting off on technicalities associated with faulty search warrants. Representative Henry J. Hyde (R-Ill.), the conservative chairman of the House Judiciary committee, argued, "It is a defining issue. They [the liberals] are very concerned about the rights of the accused, and we [the conservatives] are very concerned about the rights of society and the victim."[6] It was a classic case where the liberal priority for freedom from government conflicted with the conservative desire for more order.

During the 2000 presidential campaign, both Al Gore and George W. Bush focused on education. Al Gore emphasized providing more funding and giving schools the freedom to pursue better education. George W. Bush's "leave no child behind" program focused more on evaluating teachers and improving discipline, both attempts to create more order in the educational environment.

The 2004 presidential campaign pitted Senator John Kerry (D-MA), one of the most liberal members of the U.S. Senate, against George W. Bush's conservatism. The two men strongly disagreed on issues such as abortion, gun control, tax cuts, and affirmative action.

The beliefs of individuals calling themselves liberals or conservatives do not always fit into neat categories. Inconsistencies abound, and competing values often supersede ideological consistency. For example, many conservatives who generally oppose government involvement are willing to have the government stop abortions or limit access to books and movies. Liberals, who generally accept government involvement, want government to shy away from involvement in abortions and oppose any government censorship. Liberals who discount the "sanctity of human life" arguments of anti-abortion conservatives interject a similar rationale when they oppose capital punishment.

A clear distinction between liberals and conservatives really breaks down when we compare attitudes dealing with economic preferences and social issues. Economic liberals support higher minimum wages and considerable governmental control over business to help bring about equality of condition. Economic conservatives believe more in a free market economy without government intervention. Social liberals emphasize individual freedom in such areas as speech and a woman's right to receive an abortion. Social conservatives are more willing to use government to enforce societal standards and order. It is relatively common for a person to be an economic liberal and a social conservative, or vice versa. Despite the obvious limitations, the "liberal" and "conservative" labels still capture a number of important differences that help guide political behavior.

After studying the information content and internal logic of American ideological preferences, one scholar confirmed that

> Neither conservatives nor liberals are, in general, more sophisticated. . . . Most policy debates entail trade-offs between important values, such as equity and efficiency. When liberals and conservatives differ, it is usually because their priorities among those values are different, not because the facts and principles of the matter are so obvious as to lead the sophisticated mind to an inevitable conclusion.[7]

Box 9–2 The Liberal and Conservative Checklist

Party Perspectives		
The Nature of Human Beings	Conservatives are more likely to see human beings as inherently selfish and competitive, that is, as inevitably possessing negative traits. They see a need to protect individuals from themselves and from threats around the world.	Liberals tend to view human beings as basically "good," or at least perfectible. Liberals believe that, if given a chance, humans will generally do the right thing. They are not afraid of people making bad choices on issues such as free speech or abortion.
Ultimate Role of Government	Conservatives see protecting order as the ultimate task of government. Since selfishness and competitiveness are so inherent in the conservative view, government must step in to protect its citizens from each other and from foreign threats.	Liberals see protecting freedom as the ultimate task of government. They assume that good people will do good things and that freedom is no threat.
Striving for Equality	Conservatives argue that differences in motivation and effort will always ultimately result in unequal outcomes. They recognize the need to provide equality of opportunity in laws and government benefits but feel that even then the outcomes will differ widely.	Liberals tend to strive for equality of outcome. They see most inequalities in income or performances as based on unequal opportunities perpetuated by the biases and unfairness of society.
Economic Growth	Conservatives emphasize support for the purportedly more economically productive segments of the economy that supply jobs and investment capital. "Supply-side" economics calls for cuts in corporate taxes and other programs that will spur economic growth and allow benefits to "trickle down" to the average worker.	Liberals support programs that help those on the lowest levels of the economy (higher minimum wages, tax cuts for low-income individuals, etc.). "Demand-side" economics is asserted to help the entire economy by creating a demand for goods and services that will create more jobs and profits.
General Policy Priorities	Conservatives emphasize funding for police and national defense in their attempt to increase order in society. They are also more willing to limit some basic civil liberties (such as allowing military tribunals for foreign terrorists) as crucial to protecting order. Conservatives approach the issue of education with priorities of maintaining order in schools and measuring the quality of output.	Liberals emphasize programs such as the protection of civil liberties (freedom of speech, freedom of assembly, etc.), increased education funding, increased Social Security benefits, and a general emphasis on domestic social programs as ways of allowing people to be perfected and to equalize their status in life.
Support Base	Conservatives tend to be supported by those who have more to lose by equalizing income (those better off economically) and by individuals whose views and lifestyles are seldom questioned by society.	Liberals draw their support from individuals in society who have more to gain from equalizing income (minorities, low-income individuals, etc.) and from individuals who might be subject to having their freedom limited (gays and other minority groups).
Specific Policy Preferences: *Guns and Babies*	Gun control: Conservatives see gun ownership as a way of protecting the owner from the bad people in society. They are more likely to accept the argument that "If you outlaw guns, only the outlaws will have guns."	Gun control: Liberals see guns as decimating thousands of innocent victims and support limits on gun ownership. Lacking guns, they see good people settling conflicts peaceably.
	Abortion: Conservatives see abortion as undermining the moral order of society, allowing potentially bad people to make bad choices about terminating innocent life.	Abortion: Liberals take the freedom side of this issue, emphasizing the woman's right to protect her own body.

Source: Stephen E. Frantzich and Steven E. Shier, *Congress: Games and Strategies* (Cincinnati, OH: Atomic Dog Publishing, 2003).

Box 9–3 A Conservative Contract

Amid a flurry of publicity, more than three hundred Republican congressional candidates signed a *Contract with America* on the steps of the U.S. Capitol prior to the 1994 election. It served as a midterm party platform and was one of the clearest statements of the conservative agenda. Its signers were publicly committed to push for consideration of specific legislation, including the following:

Economic Conservatism

Fiscal Responsibility Act: Requiring government to live under the same constraints as families and businesses—by adopting a balanced budget amendment and allowing for a line-item veto.

American Dream Restoration Act: Adopting tax cuts for the middle class and facilitating savings.

Senior Citizens Fairness Act: Allowing Americans to keep more of what they have earned—by raising the Social Security earnings limits, repealing tax hikes on Social Security benefits, and providing tax incentives for private health insurance.

Common Sense Legal Reform Act: Placing limits on product liability for businesses and limiting punitive damages to discourage litigation.

Social Conservatism

Personal Responsibility Act: Increasing individual responsibility by cutting welfare programs—by putting a two-year limit on recipients, requiring recipients to work, and prohibiting increased welfare for additional children born to current welfare recipients.

Taking Back Our Streets Act: Providing secure neighborhoods and schools by enacting effective death penalty provisions, increasing spending for law enforcement personnel and prisons, requiring criminals to serve their full sentences, and loosening the requirements for legal police searches.

Family Reinforcement Act: Reinforcing the central role of families in American society by strengthening parents' rights in their children's education, enforcing stronger child pornography laws, and increasing tax incentives for adoption and elderly dependent care.[a]

While not all Republicans (or even the candidates who signed the Contract) agreed with every portion of it, the Contract with America served as a brave statement of philosophical principles. Although less than one-third of American voters could describe any specific components of the Contract, Republicans gained the benefit of being viewed as the party with a plan. With the dramatic Republican victories in 1994, the Contract became the agenda for the 104th Congress.

a. Adapted from the Republican *Contract with America*.

Ideological goals are among the most debated aspects of American politics. The liberal and conservative categories obviously do not cover all the possible options. We placed liberals and conservatives at opposite ends of the continuum, as the prime ideologies in the United States. To be accurate, we would have to extend the continuum. **Communism** never took much root in the United States, but it is still accepted as a viable approach in some parts of the world. And with the growing cynicism about government and politics came the **libertarian** ideology, which would limit government to provide little more than police and military protection.

communism *A political and economic ideology based on the elimination of private property, with goods owned in common and distributed on the basis of need.*

The Ideological Makeup of Americans

Although the ideological beliefs of Americans are not as clearly differentiated as those of citizens of many other countries, most Americans find it relatively easy to classify themselves ideologically. As Figures 9-1 and 9-2 reveal, the numbers of self-identified liberals have markedly declined over the last two decades, and conservative identification has increased slightly. Conservatism, with its acceptance of inequality in society, finds its support among those who have already "made it" economically and politically. Those who are less successful economically and who are largely excluded from the political game (see Box 9-4: Political Ideology, and Figures 9-3 to 9-5) tend not to embrace these ideas.

libertarians *Advocates of a political philosophy marked by a distrust of all government and a desire for maximum individual freedom and approval of those government actions that protect one individual or country from another.*

There has also developed an increasing gender gap in terms of ideology. Women take more liberal views on many contemporary issues (see Figure 9-6) than do men.

Figure 9-1
Ideological Self-Identification of Adults, 1978–2002

Source: General Social Survey, National Opinion Research Center, The University of Chicago.

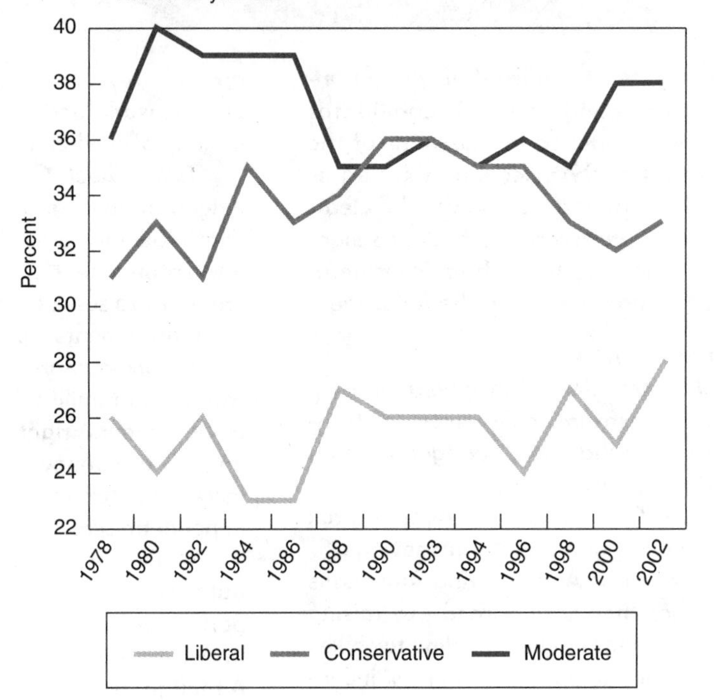

Figure 9-2
The Ideological Self-Identification of College Freshmen, 1978–2001

Source: Higher Education Research Institute, Alexander W. Astin, et al., *The American Freshman Twenty Year Trends: 1966–1985, 1987, 197; The American Freshman National Norms for Fall 1986–2001*. University of California, Los Angeles: American Council on Education.

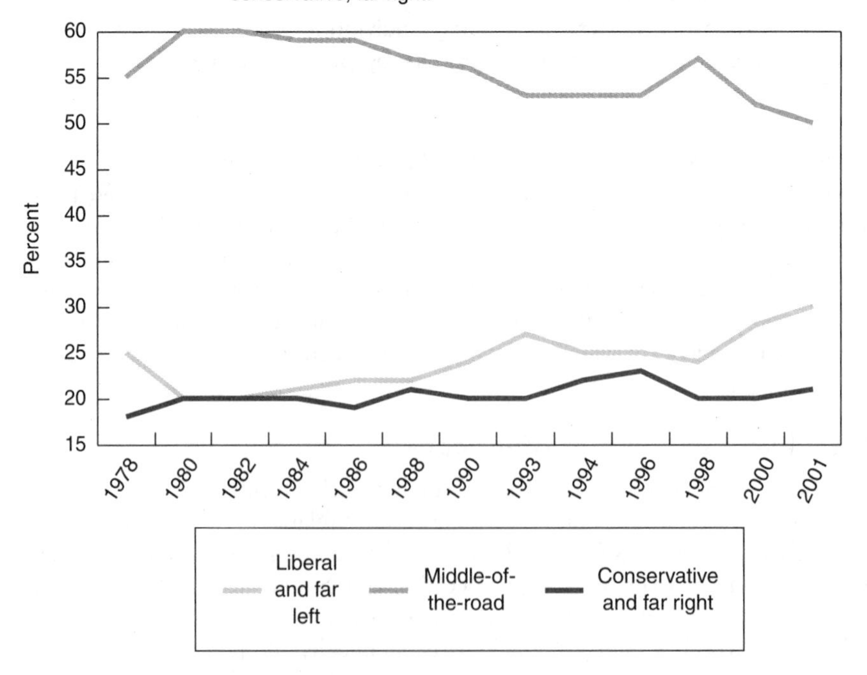

Box 9–4 Political Ideology: A Major Difference

An individual's ideology is not an isolated phenomenon relating solely to political issues. There tends to be some consistency between political ideology and other choices we make in life. Individuals who are politically conservative are somewhat more likely to live a conservative lifestyle—not spending money until they have it, not dressing in controversial clothes, and enjoying less radical music.

Even the choice of an academic major relates to personal ideology. What kinds of people tend to choose your academic major, or intended major? While considerable variation occurs, the following continuum ranks academic majors from those with most appeal for political liberals to those with most appeal for political conservatives.

More Liberal Majors	More Conservative Majors
Humanities	Business
Social sciences	Hard sciences

Why do you think people who deal with "things" (the hard scientists and business people) are more likely to be conservative than people who deal with people and their emotions (individuals in the social sciences and the humanities)?

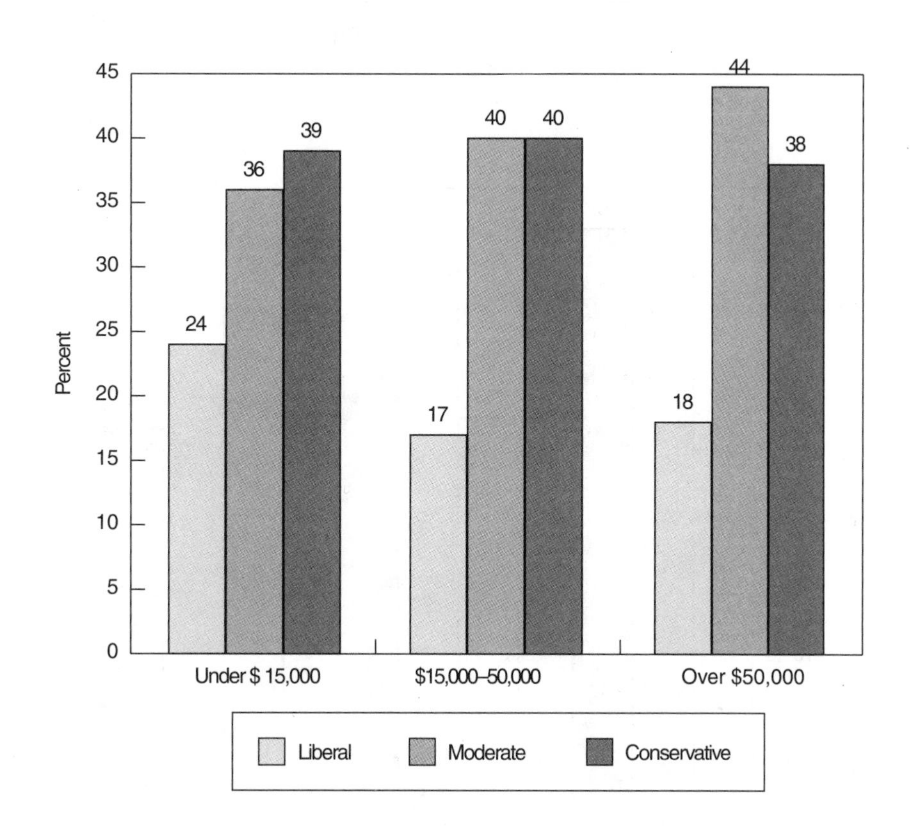

Figure 9-3
Ideology and Income

Source: Gallup poll of 1,031 adults, July 16, 1999, LEXIS-NEXIS database.

9-1c Attitudes, Opinions, and Personal Political Strategies

Politics gives individuals the opportunity to make decisions regarding alternative issues and candidates and to act on them. A political opinion is an expressed attitude on some political choice at a particular moment.[8] Thus, we have opinions (as opposed to long-term attitudes) on specific policy alternatives and about our preferences for certain candidates. Rather than forming each opinion entirely anew, we call upon our long-held attitudes to make sense of the available alternatives.

Figure 9-4
Ideology and Education

Source: Gallup poll of 1,031 adults, July 16, 1999, LEXIS-NEXIS database.

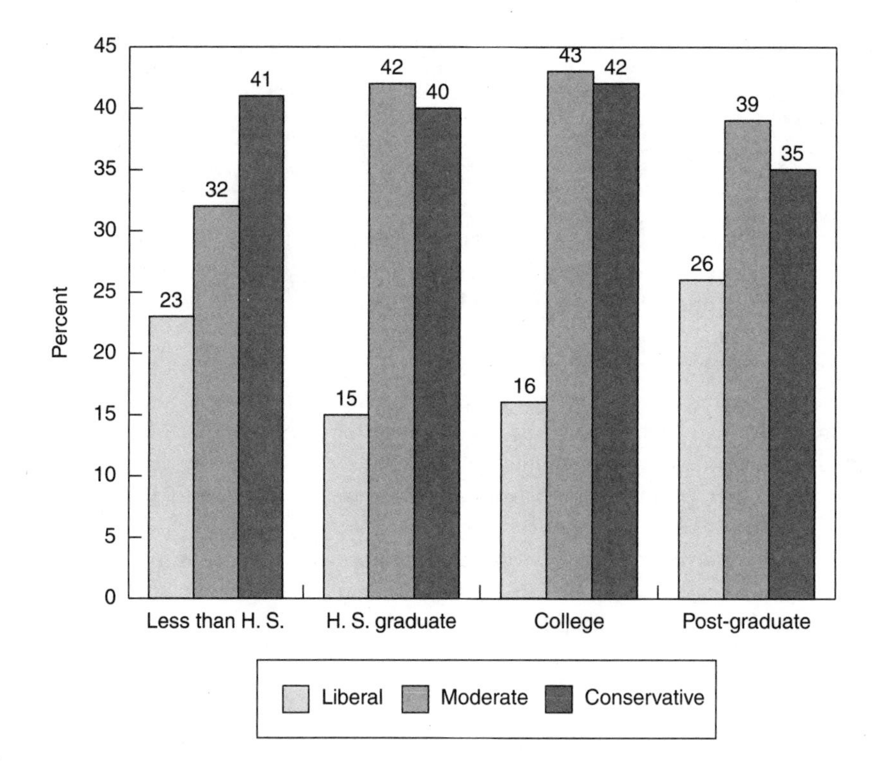

Figure 9-5
Ideology and Race

Source: Gallup poll of 1,031 adults, July 16, 1999, LEXIS-NEXIS database.

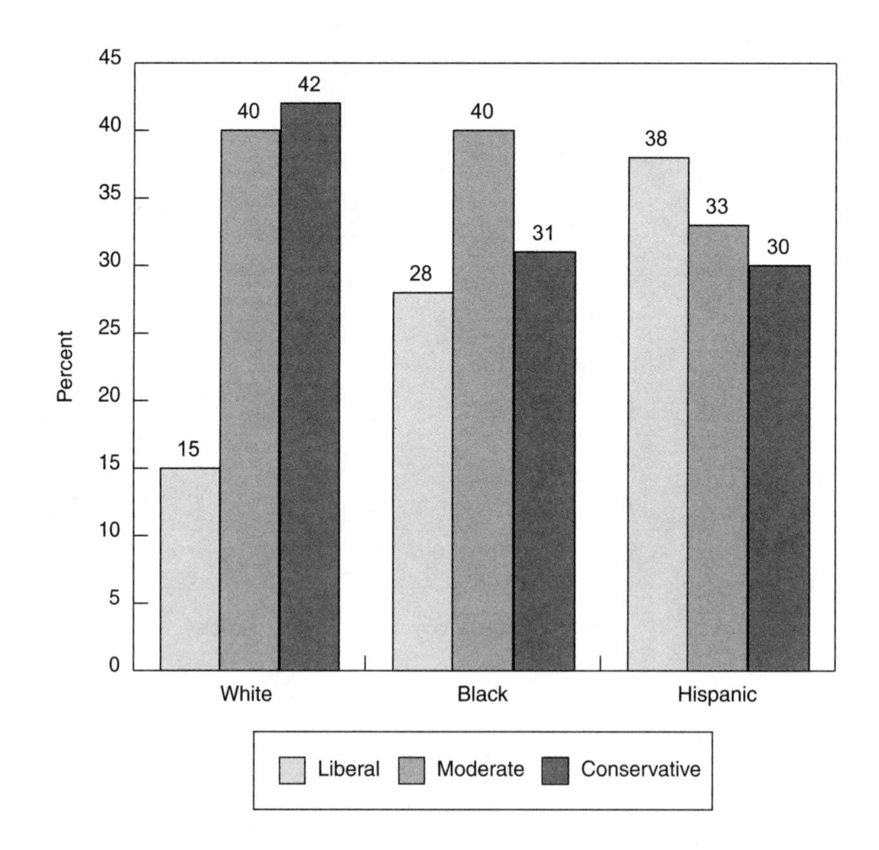

Attitudes remind us of the values and criteria we should consider in making decisions. The importance of attitudes is that they often ease political behavior. Not every opinion leads to action, but the behavior of those who do take political action is generally consistent with their ideologies. The more closely an opinion is linked to a long-term attitude, the more likely that consistent action will follow. Political decisions and the

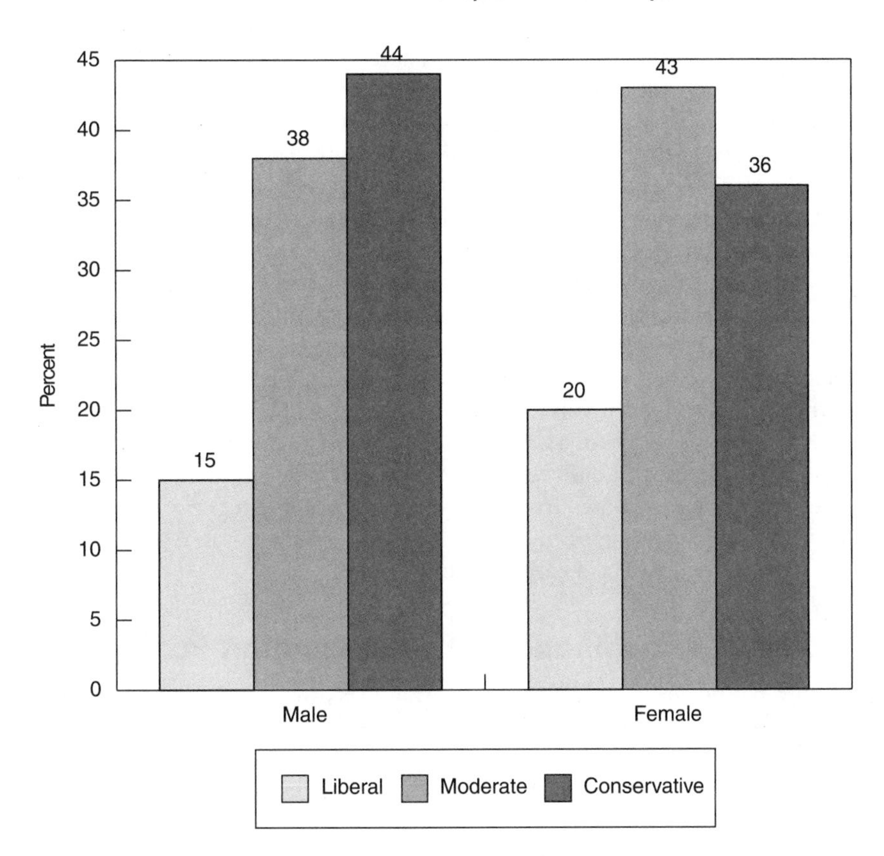

Figure 9-6
Ideology and Gender

Source: Gallup poll of 1,031 adults, July 16, 1999, LEXIS-NEXIS database.

opinions that precede them may involve potentially conflicting attitudes. In the face of conflict, some individuals **compartmentalize** their attitudes and refuse to recognize the conflict. For example, many opponents of extensive government expenditures firmly support a balanced budget. These same individuals support increased expenditures for national defense. Ignoring the inconsistencies is often impossible, however. In that case, individuals **rationalize** positions by creating distinctions that seem to explain the contradictions without altering the underlying attitudes. For example, individuals who are both abortion opponents and capital punishment defenders sometimes explain the apparent inconsistency by pointing out that innocent lives deserve more sanctity than tarnished ones.

When the available alternatives make conflict inevitable, individuals must **prioritize** and determine the attitudes of deepest interest. Democrats opposed to abortion rights must often choose between party loyalty and their beliefs, since Democratic presidential candidates in recent years have been pro-choice. Republicans favoring a constitutional amendment guaranteeing women's rights have faced similar conflicts as their presidential candidates have refused to back such an amendment. **Cross-pressured** individuals have competing demands pushing them in different directions.[9] If they can find no way to diminish the inconsistency, they may become paralyzed and be incapable of entering the political game.

compartmentalizing *Isolating attitudes, opinions, and/or behavior into categories (compartments) without recognizing the connection between them.*

rationalizing *Explaining away inconsistencies between attitudes, opinions, and/or behavior in an attempt to erase the apparent conflict.*

prioritizing *Choosing among competing attitudes to establish an opinion with the potential for action.*

cross-pressures *Conflicting attitudes that make it difficult to form an opinion or to take satisfying and consistent action on them.*

9-2 Using Public Opinion as a Political Strategy

In democratic systems, elected and appointed players are powerfully predisposed to respond to public opinion, since they realize that citizens are likely to act on their opinions. Players also have an important stake in measuring, interpreting, and attempting to influence public opinion. With prior knowledge and/or the ability to influence opinion, decision makers can plan responses that will gain them more political support.

Throughout history, politicians have attempted to measure public opinion both formally and informally. Public opinion polling first appeared less than sixty years ago, but attempts to assess and influence the opinions of citizens go back to the founding of the United States. The authors of *The Federalist* did not have a **Gallup Poll** to chronicle the change in public opinion that their efforts generated. They used whatever means were available to determine where the public stood on the issues of the day. Visits with constituents at town meetings and through informal encounters are attempts to see which way the political wind is blowing. Careful monitoring of news stories, letters to the editor, and talk-show commentary gives a politician an idea of what people are talking about. The analysis of election returns, incoming mail, and phone calls provides a more precise measure of those willing to take action on their opinions. The earliest polls were rather informal affairs involving a reporter asking people on the street what they thought or asking people to return a page from the newspaper. By the 1940s, the development of market research techniques established a model by which more scientific acquisition of data was possible. Through trial and error, sources of inaccuracy were discovered and corrected. Modern polling techniques simply have added precision, speed, and comparability to the measurements of early politicians.

Gallup Poll *A widely recognized national opinion polling company that asks standard questions on a regular basis.*

9-2a The Technique of Public Opinion Polling

Ideally, politicians would like to know what everyone thinks about every issue, but time and money limitations demand some shortcuts. Proper polling techniques allow the collection of information from a relatively few people (the **sample**) and the formation of generalizations about everyone in whom the pollsters are interested (the **population**). Doctors checking a hospital's blood bank, for instance, use the same premise when taking a small blood sampling to make judgments about the entire blood supply.

sample *A subset of individuals (or entities) that serves as the basis for making generalizations about a population.*

population *The individuals (or entities) about which one wishes to make generalizations in a public opinion poll.*

Randomness

The key factor in a good sample is **randomness.** All of the individuals that a pollster wants to describe—the population—must have an equal chance of being selected for the sample. Randomness assures that the sample is as representative of the population as possible. Depending on the purpose of the poll, the population might be all adults, likely voters, or registered Republicans. "Instant" polls, which allow people to call in their preferences or are based on calling a large number of people in a short amount of time, fall short of randomness. Individuals who call in on their own initiative are seldom similar to those unwilling to take such effort. Individuals who happen to be home the hour after a presidential speech or debate are different from those not available at that time. Without randomness, all the assumptions about a poll's accuracy lack validity.

randomness *A process for selecting a sample from a population in which every individual (or entity) has an equal chance of being selected.*

The size of a random sample determines the accuracy of the findings. National polls of 1,500 respondents are accurate to within 3 percentage points 95 percent of the time. In other words, if the poll concludes that 55 percent of voters plan to vote for one candidate, the candidate's support actually lies somewhere between 52 and 58 percent (3 percent in either direction of the finding) with less than a 5 percent chance that the findings are wrong. Larger samples reduce the error but also increase the cost.

Misleading Results

Random samples with an adequate number of respondents can still give misleading results if poor interviewing methods are used. Polls attempt to compare the responses of individuals who have experienced identical stimuli. The stimuli in a poll include the wording of the question, the method of questioning, the impression given by the interviewer, and the setting in which the questions are asked (see Box 9-5: The Power of Words). If any of these stimuli vary across respondents, comparisons of their responses may mean little. For example, if the questions are asked using different words or emphases, the variations in responses may result from real variations in opinions, or they may be caused simply by the differences in the questions. During the 1995 debates over the Balanced Budget Amendment, 80 percent of Americans agreed with the plan in the abstract.

Box 9–5 *The Power of Words*

Polls are based on the psychological concept of stimulus-response. The pollster stimulates or arouses each person being polled with a question and then compares the responses given by everyone questioned. If the stimulus changes, the responses are often affected. Asking a question in a slightly different way can produce widely differing responses and suggest different interpretations.

Public opinion poll ratings (approval ratings) of the president of the United States are important strategic information for political players. The two major pollsters providing these evaluations ask their questions in somewhat different ways. The Gallup Poll asks: "Do you approve or disapprove of the way [president's name] is handling his job as president?" By providing no middle position, pollsters force respondents to take a stand. The data indicate that mildly dissatisfied respondents are more likely to move to the positive position if given only two choices.

The Harris Poll, on the other hand, asks: "How would you rate the job that [president's name] is doing as president? Would you say he is doing an excellent, pretty good, only fair, or a poor job?" By providing two middle options, pollsters allow respondents to make finer distinctions about their level of approval.

Although the Harris Poll summarizes presidential approval by combining the "excellent" and "pretty good" categories to compare with Gallup's "approve" category, this underestimates approval. In a survey using questions from both polls, more than 50 percent of the respondents giving the president an "only fair" rating on the Harris Poll question indicated their "approval" of the president when asked the Gallup Poll question.[a] As the line graph shows, while the trend lines are similar, surveys taken on roughly the same date result in absolute percentages that often vary well beyond the statistical margin of error. The lesson for the user of such poll results is that one can legitimately compare polls only when they posed identical questions.

a. Barry Sussman, "The Jury Is Still Out on Carter: Distortion in Popularity Polls," *Washington Post*, February 12, 1978, A1.

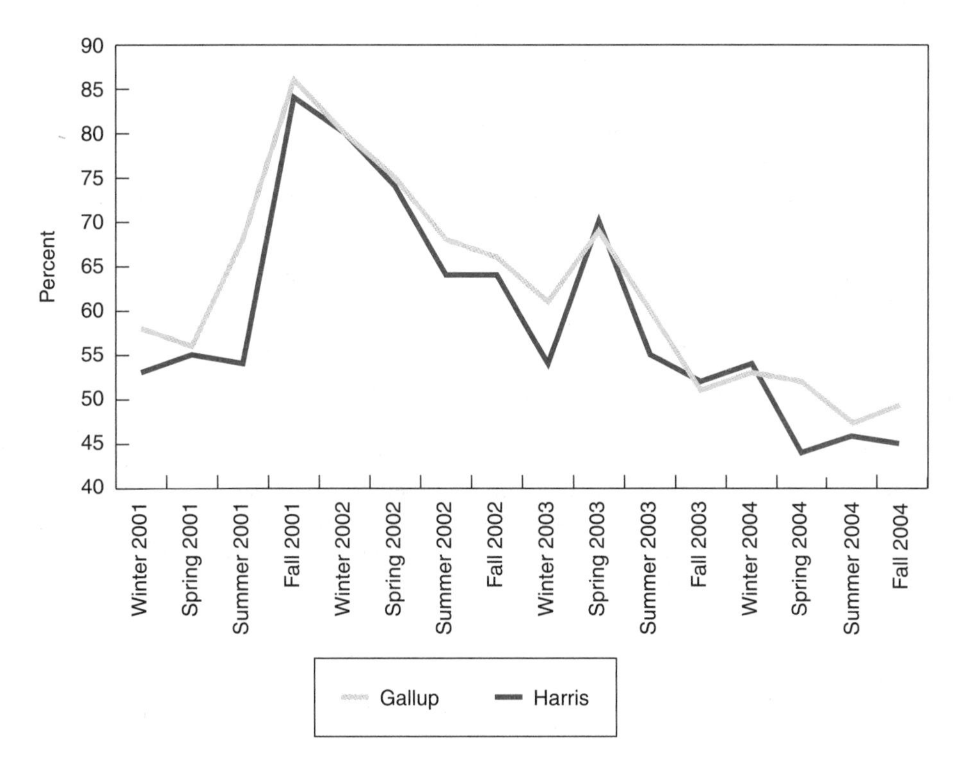

Figure 9-7
President Bush's Approval Ratings According to Two Polls

Harris Poll figures include those saying that the president is doing an "excellent" or a "pretty good" job, while Gallup results include those who say they "approve" of the way the president is doing his job.

Source: LEXIS-NEXIS database, 2004, and www.harrisinteractive.com/harris_poll/index.asp, www.gallup.com/poll/releases.pr021018.

When the question was rephrased to ask if they would support such a plan when it required cuts in Social Security, support dropped to less than 50 percent.[10] Shifts in measured opinion may also result from wording alone. Questions with very emotional words (for example, *revolutionary, Nazi, welfare mother*) may affect some respondents so deeply that the true meaning or intent of the question is overshadowed.

As a poll consumer in a world that is increasingly the subject of polls, it is important to understand their limitations and advantages (see Box 9-6: Becoming a Sophisticated Poll Watcher).

In responding to interview questions, individuals may give opinions on topics they have never thought much about. Such opinions contribute little to predicting behavior. The most useful polls screen out respondents with no opinion by giving them an unembarrassing way of admitting that they lack the information or interest to express a valid opinion.

Polls present a snapshot of a moving picture: They reveal what respondents are willing to say to an interviewer at a particular moment. There is little evidence that the respondents in public opinion polls lie, but individuals' opinions on some subjects vary significantly with time. Dramatic events force individuals to reassess even deeply held opinions. For example, support for cooperating with the former Soviet Union increased dramatically during the early 1990s as the Communist governments in Eastern Europe fell and the Soviet Union backed U.S. initiatives against Iraq.

Is the Effort Worth It?

Accurate national opinion polls using in-person interviews cost more than $50,000 each, but the overwhelming evidence indicates that, with proper methods, the results are extremely accurate. Since 1950 the results of the final preelection Gallup Polls on the presidential contest have varied from the actual election results by an average of fewer than 1.4 percentage points.

9-2b Strategies for Using Public Opinion

Public opinion is the summation of individual opinions. The term *public opinion* is, however, a misnomer insofar as it implies that the mass of citizens have given thought to, or have clear preferences concerning, every issue or candidate. In most cases, we must talk about **issue publics.** Subsets of citizens do have strong interests in various specific issues or candidates because they are directly affected by them.[11] Politicians have little interest in casual, offhand comments made to interviewers unless they feel that the individuals holding such casual opinions can be activated to support their cause (see Chapters 10 and 11). Politicians generally seek out individuals with strongly held opinions in the hope of motivating behavior and turning spectators into players in such realms as voting, organizing, and communicating.

issue publics *That portion of the population that has given serious consideration to an issue or a candidate and has a well-thought-out preference.*

At any given time, different segments of the population may have widely differing opinions on the same issue. When public policies affect different demographic groups in varying ways, opinions of those policies are likely to vary significantly (see Box 9-7: The Affirming Opinions of Different Players).

Separating the Serious Players from the Uninformed Spectators

A sophisticated analysis of the American public indicates that about 20 percent of the population pay little attention to politics and have few real opinions. On the other end of the continuum is a small group—seldom more than 5 percent of the population—who pay close attention to politics and act on their beliefs. The great majority lies between these two extremes and is composed of people who monitor the political process half-attentively. These individuals can be drawn into the political game "if fellow citizens sound the political alarm" that the issue is important enough to pay attention to.[12]

Interpreting Public Opinion

Public opinion has three identifiable aspects:

- Distribution
- Intensity
- Stability

Box 9–6 Becoming a Sophisticated Poll Watcher

Poll results fill our newspapers, magazines, and television screens. Simply accepting the reported results is like believing everything you hear or read. Polling "literacy" is an important skill for anyone desiring to use poll results effectively. Fortunately, reputable pollsters and newspapers increasingly provide their readers with some idea of the way in which the polls reported on their pages were conducted, thus alerting readers to potential limitations. Similar but briefer notices now accompany many reports of poll results on television. The following checklist of factors indicates some of the important things to look for.

Defining the population: Whose opinions are being sought?

Determine who is being sampled. Is the population appropriate to your interests? A sample of legally eligible voters will tell something about general opinions but may not tell much about likely voters—those who will probably go to the polls. This latter group would be of most interest to a candidate facing an election.

Randomness: Does everyone's opinion have an equal chance of being counted?

Be wary of samples selected from incomplete or selective listings. Telephone books miss individuals without phones, with cell phones, and with unlisted numbers. Registered voter lists do not cover individuals who might be encouraged to register. Standing on a street corner and asking questions misses those people unlikely to pass by that street corner.

Accuracy: How accurate should the poll be?

Assuming a random sample, accuracy is based on the fixed laws of statistics. Samples of the same size have the same potential for error. The 3 percent error for a sample of 1,500 increases to more than 6 percent for a sample of 300.

Watch for smaller subsets in a larger sample. A national poll of 1,500 people with a 3 percent error includes a potential error of 8 percent for the approximately 150 responses from African Americans, who make up about 10 percent of the national population and therefore should be 10 percent of the sample. Also, questions that many respondents refused to answer result in smaller samples and greater error.

Bias: How were the questions asked?

Look for the actual wording of the question, and check for obvious bias. For example, questions beginning with "Do you agree with most Americans that . . ." encourage support, while questions asking respondents to agree with views of unpopular groups or individuals discourage support.

Evaluate who conducted and who funded the poll. Polls funded by interest groups often use questionable methods or report only the most favorable results.

Consider the method of questioning. Mail questionnaires tend to have low and nonrandom response rates, since not all respondents return their questionnaires. Polling by telephone not only raises sampling problems but also limits the type and depth of questioning possible. Personal interviews are generally best, especially those conducted by reputable polling organizations. Care should be taken to make sure that interviewers do not affect the results by extraneous comments or by the way they look.

Timing: Who responded to what, when?

Look at the date of the poll and consider the major intervening events that might have altered opinions.

Consider the time it takes to do a good poll. Instant overnight analyses require major shortcuts, such as relying exclusively on the telephone and omitting people not at home. National polls taking hours rather than days should be viewed with skepticism, since methodological shortcuts were obviously necessary. On the other hand, the longer it takes to complete a poll, the more likely that intervening events could affect the results.

Legitimacy: Some so-called polls are not worth the paper on which they are written.

Do not be misled by straw polls based on filling out a ballot at the state fair, returning a preprinted form, or calling a toll telephone number. The only people whom such techniques allow you to generalize about are those willing to make the effort or to pay the cost to be included.

For more information on being an effective poll consumer, see the Suggestions for Further Reading at the end of the chapter.

Box 9–7 The Affirming Opinions of Different Players

Background

It is often said about elected and appointed players in the political process that "where one stands depends on where one sits." Individuals in different formal positions see the world in very different ways. The same is true of the citizen players. They carry with them perspectives molded by their experiences and tempered by their aspirations. As members of the public look at the rules that government will enforce, an often silent—but nonetheless very pertinent—question asked frequently is, "What's in it for me?" We cannot tap motivations of political players directly, but public opinion polls indicate player views related to their motivations.

Players have definite views about society's rules. The contemporary debate over affirmative action clearly points out how different players see the rules in very different ways. Affirmative action legislation provides educational admissions, hiring, and promotion benefits to groups (such as women and minorities) who have historically faced discrimination. The current debate revolves around questions such as whether or not affirmative action is still needed. Are we at a point where rules supporting an even playing field would now benefit both society and individuals from *all* groups?

Questions

The game analogy invites us to look at differences between players and at those whose preferences prevail. In this case, we would want to know:

- What players hold which preferences on affirmative action?
- Which players win by having their preferences prevail?
- Who are the losers, and how do they react?

To a large degree, and not surprisingly, members of groups who have benefited from preferences based on affirmative action hold much more positive opinions about such programs than do those groups denied favor by the rules. Once one gets beyond vague commitments to principles such as fairness and justice and into the specifics of rule-making and application, it is clear that different players have widely divergent opinions as to what is fair and just. The following poll results indicate who wants rule changes and who wants the status quo.

Question: *Do you agree with the following statement?*
Statement: *We should make every possible effort to improve the position of African Americans and other minorities, even if it means giving them preferential treatment.*

Percent Agreeing that We Should Improve the Position of Minorities

	(Percent agreeing)	
	Whites	**African Americans**
1987	18	64
1988	20	70
1990	17	68
1992	29	67
1994	25	62
1997	25	63
1999	26	62

Based on national polls reported in The Times Mirror Center for the People and the Press, "The New Political Landscape," October 1994. 1997–1999 data from Pew Research Center, LEXIS-NEXIS database. The Pew Center took over the polls of Times Mirror, using the same methodology.

Question: *Do you agree with the following statement?*
Statement: *We have gone too far in pushing equal rights in this country.*

Percent Agreeing that We Have Gone Too Far in Pushing Equal Rights

	(Percent agreeing)	
	Whites	**African Americans**
1987	46	16
1988	47	22
1990	45	25
1992	42	21
1994	51	26
1997	49	18
1999	51	21

Based on national polls reported in The Times Mirror Center for the People & the Press, "The New Political Landscape," October 1994. 1997–1999 data from Pew Research Center, LEXIS-NEXIS database. The Pew Center took over the polls of Times Mirror, using the same methodology.

Analysis

When opinions of different players vary significantly, it makes a great deal of difference who actually plays. Those with the skills and resources to act on their opinions are more likely to frame rules that put their goals into force.

In 1995 the Supreme Court gave a new set of answers to the questions of who wins and who loses by significantly constraining the role of affirmative action in the awarding of government contracts and in creating legislative districts. Since the decisions over affirmative action represent a continuous game, the final word has not been spoken. Minority politicians reacted to the Court decisions with alarm, attempting to change both public opinion and judicial reasoning. Some of the most vocal opponents of the decision concerning majority-minority legislative districts were minority members of Congress who feared losing their positions. Executives of minority-owned businesses, facing the loss of preferences and therefore income, protested that previous policy had significant social benefits. In 2004, the Supreme Court handed down a mixed decision on affirmative action in school admissions. It approved taking race into account but indicated that it must be considered as just one factor in a student's set of qualifications. With such high stakes and the lack of clear-cut guidelines, the game is likely to continue.

Not all opinions expressed by the public become factors in the political game, but public officials who want to play the game of politics effectively need to be concerned about all dimensions of public opinion.

Distribution

distribution *The way public preferences are arrayed across the various alternatives.*

The **distribution** of public opinions refers to the way opinions array themselves along the continuum of possible alternatives. The public may be in almost total agreement on an issue (see Figure 9-8, A and B), equally split between two or more alternatives (see Figure 9-8, C), or unequally split between alternatives (see Figure 9-8, D). Democratic theory and the necessities of political survival encourage politicians to follow the policy preferences of majorities (Figure 9-8, A, B, and D). President Gerald R. Ford, for example, overrode his own preferences and extended the amnesty program for Vietnam draft evaders when public opinion polls showed strong support. When issues clearly divide the public (Figure 9-8, C), politicians attempt to avoid the issue. Few politicians willingly take strong stands on such issues as abortion, gay rights, and the death penalty unless forced to by an opponent or as a strategy to satisfy a one-sided constituency.

Intensity

intensity *The depth to which opinions are held and the emotional tie that individuals have to those opinions.*

Some opinions mean little to the individuals who hold them. Other opinions reflect powerful emotional reactions, that is, **intensity**. Politicians assume that intensely held opinions are likely to influence political behavior, such as voting or contributing to campaigns. If the distribution of overall public opinion and the distribution of individuals holding intense preferences coincide (see Figure 9-9), the careful politician moves toward the position of the majority. The real art of political strategy is demonstrated when the distribution of the opinion of the general public and that of an intense minority differs (see Figure 9-10). In conditions where the intense minority wants a new prison while the majority of constituents oppose it, the astute politician might wisely support the building of a new prison. The politician assumes that a higher percentage of members of the intense minority vote for one candidate or the other because of this opinion. Contemporary issues such as abortion and gun control often fall into this category.

Political observers conclude that "given the choice between an apathetic majority and an intense minority, public officials are likely to be swayed by the intense minority."[13] Overall public opinion about the war in Vietnam remained positive long after an intense and active minority began protesting the war on the streets and through the ballot box. Many

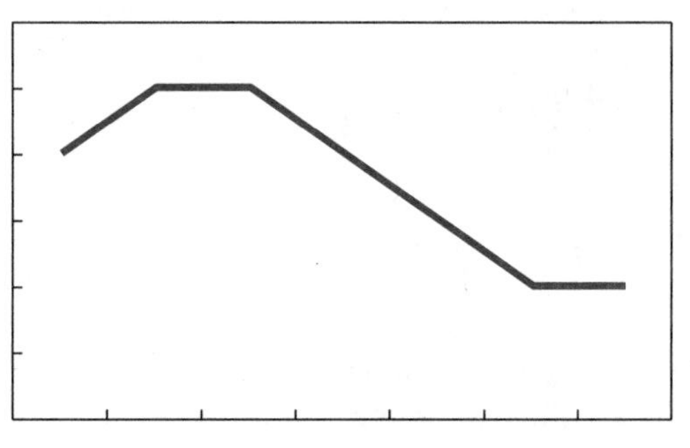

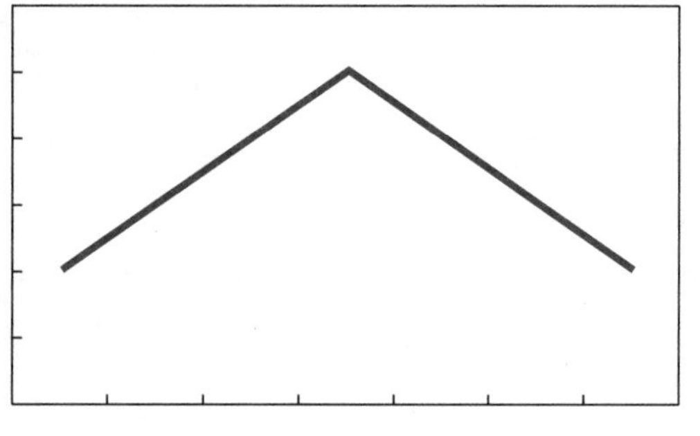

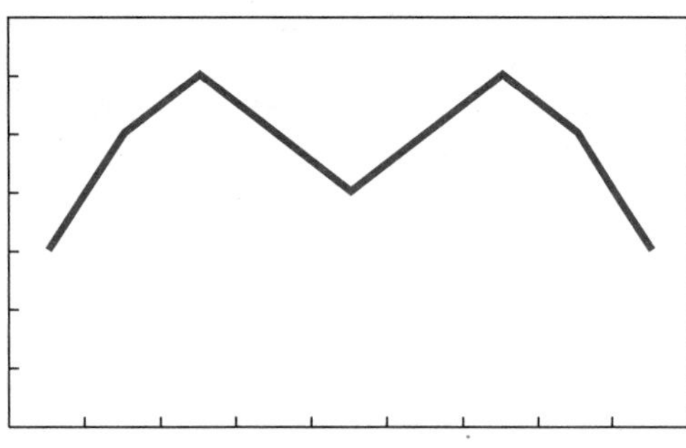

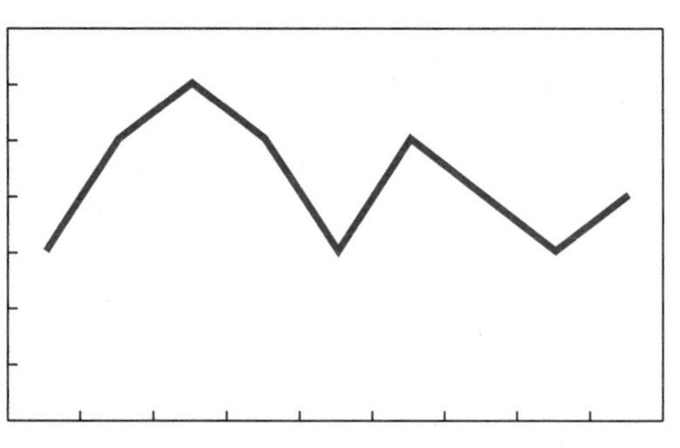

Figure 9-8
Hypothetical Patterns of Public Opinion Distribution about Building a New Prison

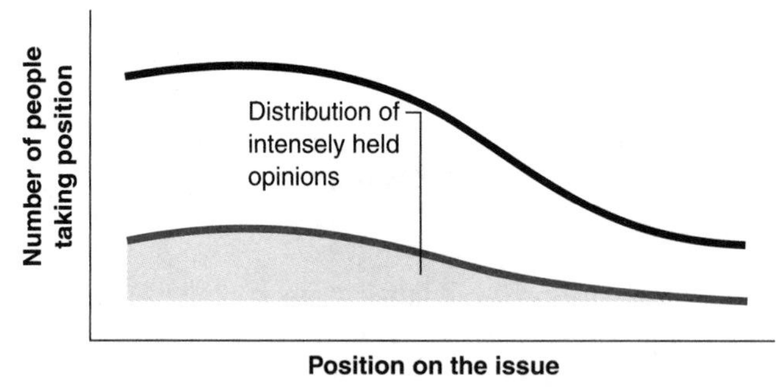

Figure 9-9
Consistency between General Public Opinion and Intensely Held Opinions

Source: Stephen E. Frantzich and Stephen L. Percy, *American Government: The Political Game* (Dubuque, IA: Brown & Benchmark, 1994), 154.

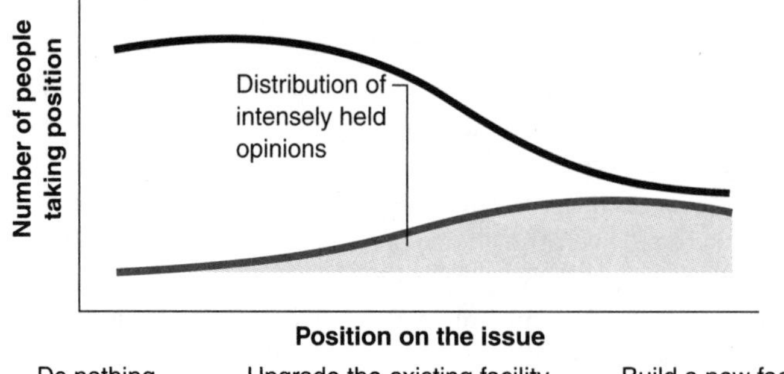

Figure 9-10
Inconsistency between General Public Opinion and Intensely Held Opinions

Source: Stephen E. Frantzich and Stephen L. Percy, *American Government: The Political Game* (Dubuque, IA: Brown & Benchmark, 1994), 154.

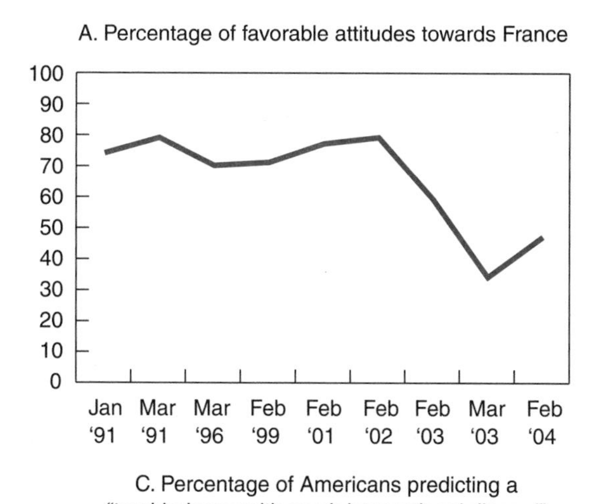

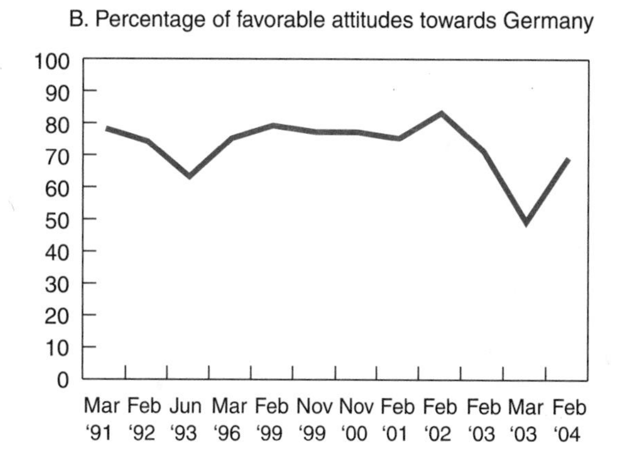

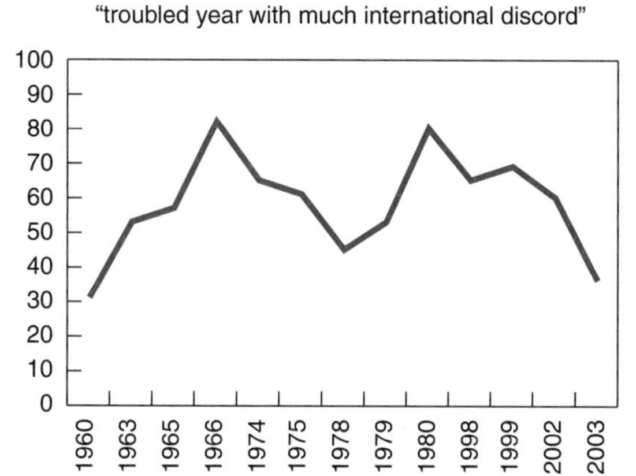

Figure 9-11

Stability of Attitudes toward Germany and France and the Possibility of Peace

Source: Gallup polls from the LEXIS-NEXIS database.

public officials, however, increasingly shifted their positions away from all-out support of the war for fear that the active minority would get its way at the polls.

Stability

Some opinions vary over time, while others retain **stability**. Opinions grounded in deeply held basic attitudes remain relatively immune to change, although dramatic events can undermine even the most deeply held opinions, as we saw with public reaction to the events in Eastern Europe during the late 1980s. Individuals revealed a more positive general attitude toward the former Soviet Union as it politically disintegrated. Optimism about a more peaceful future increased dramatically as Communism began to wane, but it dropped significantly after events such as the 1990 Gulf War. Opinions about the prospects for peace change dramatically with international events (see Figure 9-11).

stability (of public opinion) *The degree to which the distribution of public opinions remains consistent over time.*

Other issues show considerable stability over time. For more than two decades, support for abortion and stricter gun control laws has varied relatively little (see Figure 9-12). Opinions on emerging issues tend to vary considerably until the bulk of individuals have solidified their positions. Individual politicians, political parties, and organized interest groups seek to guide the development of opinions on emerging issues. Using the media, these players attempt to set the **agenda** of issues on which opinions need to be held and to portray their answers as the preferred ones (see Chapter 6). Despite the fact that many individuals in 1992 had only a vague idea about the state of the economy, Bill Clinton constantly reminded his staff that "It's the economy, stupid." Much of his campaign revolved around convincing voters that the economy was important and in trouble unless he was elected. In 1995, when former House Speaker Newt Gingrich (R-Ga.) suggested cutting federal funds for public radio, supporters of the Corporation for Public Broadcasting embarked on a public relations campaign designed to create supportive public opinion. They had to educate the public about the importance of the public subsidy and create in the public's mind a feeling that something important would be lost if these outlets with relatively small audiences were to disappear.

agenda *A set of problems a decision maker either chooses or is forced to take action on.*

Figure 9-12
Stability of Attitudes toward Basic Policy Issues

Sources: (top graph) Gallup polls reported in NEXIS-LEXIS database.
(bottom graph) Harold W. Stanley and Richard G. Niemi, *Vital Statistics on American Politics, 2003–2004* (Washington, D.C.: Congressional Quarterly, Inc., 2003), p. 163.

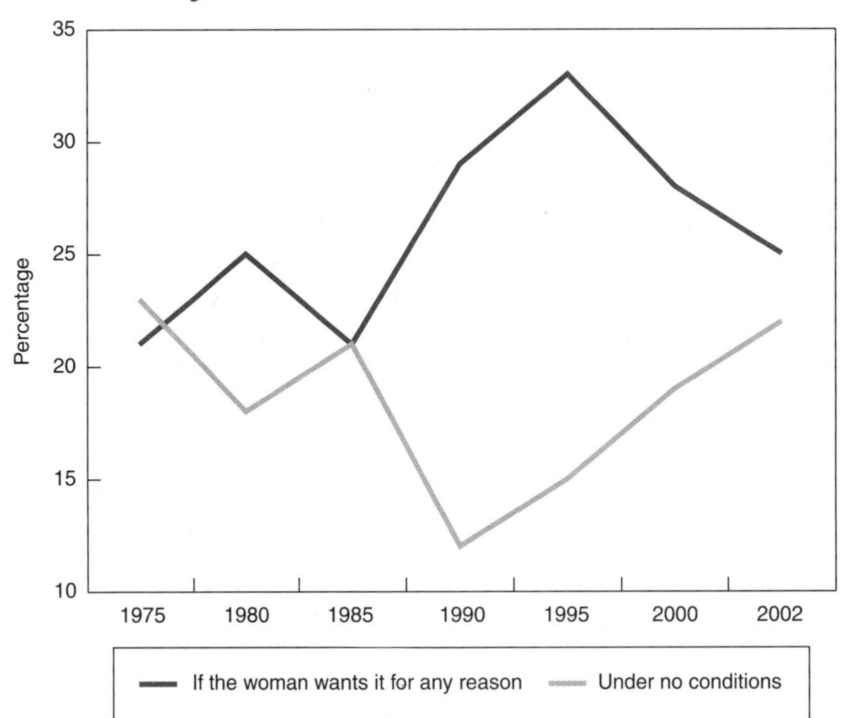

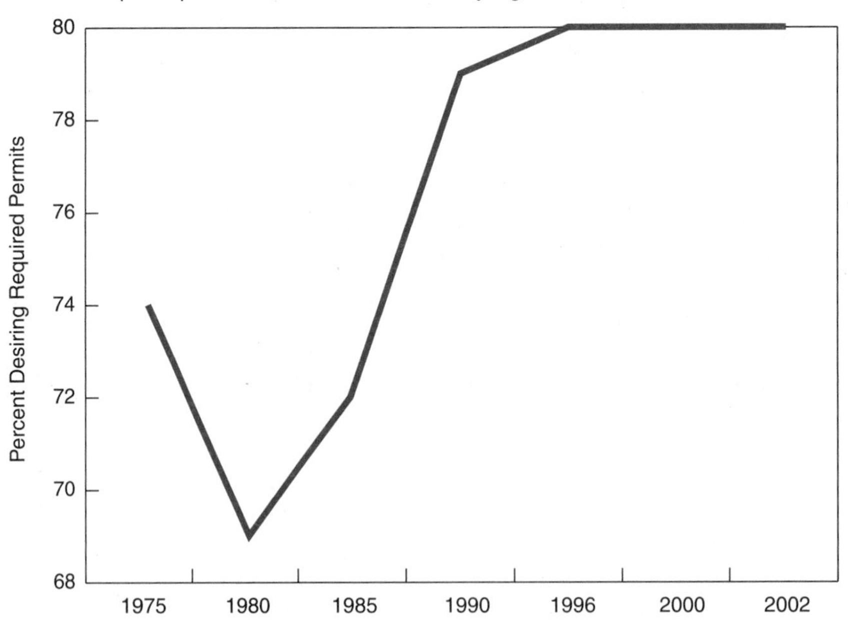

Not all issues can be managed. Politicians try to ignore the most volatile issues until they are no longer in a state of flux. In the early years of the AIDS crisis, politicians did not want to take a stand until they could predict whether the bulk of the population would view those with AIDS as unfortunate victims or as rightful recipients of retribution for a deviant lifestyle. Once the incidence of AIDS spread to the heterosexual community and the media picked up stories about innocent victims, compassion tended to win out over condemnation. Politicians were then willing to take a stand.

9-2c Acting on Public Opinion

Public opinion often serves as the basis for choosing a strategy in the political game. Players attempt to:

- Capitalize on supporting opinions,
- Counter opposing opinion, and
- Change opinion to benefit their career or cause.

Using Supporting Opinion

When public opinion supports their cause, players in the political game make sure that everyone else knows it. President Lyndon Johnson used to carry opinion polls on the Vietnam War in his coat pocket to influence others—at least until the polls began to undermine his position. Since Jimmy Carter, all presidents have retained the services of pollsters to chart opinion and provide political ammunition. Interest groups regularly commission polls and vigorously disseminate the results favorable to their cause (see Box 9-8: Taking Aim at Misinterpreting Poll Results, or Smoking out the Opposition). Congressional speeches and political rhetoric at all levels equate supportive poll results as the "voice of the people" to which a democratic society ought to respond.

plurality *The category (or set of categories) having the greatest number of responses—not necessarily more than one-half (a majority).*

Box 9–8 *Taking Aim at Misinterpreting Poll Results, or Smoking out the Opposition*

During the 1980s, the National Rifle Association (NRA) purchased a series of questions on a national poll conducted by the Gallup organization. As owners of the question results, the NRA could use the data as it liked. When the results showed that more than 50 percent felt that gun control was one of the top ten issues facing America and that more than 60 percent felt that guns should be controlled, the NRA chose to publicize the first finding and ignore the second. NRA press releases touted the high public interest in the gun control issue and followed up with a legal and philosophical discussion supporting the NRA position opposing gun control. The impression that the NRA intended to give was that all the people concerned about gun control were opposed to it. In reality, many of the respondents who highlighted the importance of gun control actually supported increased controls. Fearful that their reputation would be damaged by such a selective interpretation, the Gallup organization decided to change the wording of their contract. Subsequently they had a legal right to publicize portions of their polls purchased by others if the purchaser publicized the results in a nonobjective manner.

The Tobacco Institute used a similar tactic in reporting a poll that it had commissioned in 1991 to counter proposals to ban cigarette advertising and increase cigarette taxes. The poll indicated that 41 percent of the respondents favored a complete ban on advertising, 34 percent favored continuing the present ban on television and radio advertising, and 23 percent opposed any limitations. In press releases and newspaper advertisements, the Tobacco Institute referred to the poll and asserted, "A ban on cigarette advertising is not supported by a majority of Americans." While technically correct, simply adding together the 23 percent favoring no ban and the 34 percent approving the current rules fails to point out that a **plurality** of respondents did support a complete ban.

When it came to cigarette taxes, the most popular response (44 percent) was that taxes "should be significantly increased." The Tobacco Institute combined those supporting no change (38 percent) and those favoring a reduction (15 percent) and asserted that "a majority of Americans do not support an increase in cigarette taxes." A leading pollster argued that the "ad carefully distorts the results so that they could be easily misinterpreted. . . . It is a cleverly written misrepresentation of the findings."[a] Unfortunately, the public must grope their way through the smoke to determine the true findings.

---

a. Richard Morin, "Tobacco Institute Shaded Truth: Survey Summary Reveals Much Stronger Anti-smoking Sentiments," *Washington Post*, January 26, 1991, A19.

Countering Opposing Opinion

silent majority *A term used by politicians that refers to views held by a large number of individuals who fail to make their preference known through dramatic political action.*

Counteracting negative public opinion is often as important as publicizing positive results. President Richard M. Nixon popularized the concept of a **silent majority**, who, although not visibly protesting in the streets or forcefully expressing their opinions, were portrayed as standing firm for the values he was promoting. President Johnson, like many politicians, sought to counteract the appearance of opposing public opinion by selectively leaking positive private polls, which influenced the content of subsequent polls and affected poll reporting.[14] If no other approach works, candidates who are behind in a race simply attack the polling methodology and assert that "the only real poll is on election day."

Creating and Changing Public Opinion

Public opinion is not a fixed component of the political game, and political players do more than simply react to the existing distribution of opinions. At times, underlying attitudes and the opinions they spawn can be dramatically influenced by events, as has been seen in recent years on such issues as concern over terrorism. In most cases, however, the national distribution of attitudes and opinions are subject only to slow change.

The media have emerged as a potent force for chipping away at old perspectives and replacing them with new. The media both reflect and lead public opinion. Shifts in opinions on issues such as civil rights, women's rights, the importance of the environment, the shortcomings of the legal system, and the problems of urban violence would not have been possible without the media. By reporting dozens of similar individual stories from around the country, the media help create a more national set of issues and opinions.

Isolated incidents become representations of national trends, which must be dealt with (see Chapter 6). When a woman was awarded $3 million for spilling a hot cup of McDonald's coffee on herself, the news media portrayed it as another example of the courts acting in an irresponsible manner. The story created great interest, since a large segment of the population had developed negative attitudes toward outrageous awards by the courts. Within a few weeks a large percentage of the population had heard about this incident and had an opinion. Within a year, Congress reflected these opinions and passed legislation limiting awards in such liability cases.

A strategy more effective than attacking deeply held values lies in stimulating individuals to apply their attitudes in new ways. Civil rights leaders during the 1950s used the media and public demonstrations to confront the public with an apparent inconsistency. Most of the public expressed attitudes supporting equality, yet many of the existing laws that the public supported led to segregation and unequal treatment of African Americans. The public was forced to move from accepting equality in the abstract toward thinking of it in terms of specific concrete situations. The courageous fight and eventual death of young Ryan White helped to redefine the AIDS epidemic. Since he had contracted AIDS through a blood transfusion, he became the symbol of an innocent victim. No longer could AIDS be seen as exclusively the result of irresponsible (and, to much of the public, immoral) actions of gay men and lesbians. Rather it could now be seen as a human tragedy, with the potential of affecting any of us.

Interest groups have been as influential as the media. Drinking, and even drunk driving, was long seen as a sign of freedom from government intervention in private lives in American society until groups such as Mothers Against Drunk Drivers (MADD) revealed the level of human carnage involved and the inability of existing law enforcement to stem the tide. Even the thought of compromising one's privacy through drug testing was unthinkable a few years ago, until a series of drug-related public transportation accidents allowed attitudes about public safety to overcome fears about privacy. Long service in public office was held desirable until groups opposed to a permanent set of elected officials solidified opinion around term-limitation legislation.

opinion leaders *Individuals who command enough respect and/or knowledge that others use their opinions as models to follow.*

Political leaders from the national level down to local communities do more than redefine existing issues. They are **opinion leaders,** seeking to set the agenda of issues and alternatives on which the public forms opinions. They use their authority to help the public define what they should be thinking about. Political campaigns are fertile ground on which citizens develop opinions not only of candidates but also on policy issues.

President Jimmy Carter forced Americans to rethink the importance of human rights in foreign policy deliberations. President Ronald Reagan highlighted the negative image of extensive government activity and regulation. George H. Bush focused public interest on patriotism, taxes, and failures of the criminal justice system. Bill Clinton urged voters to think about America's economic problems, the rights of gay men and lesbians to serve in the military, the U.S. role as a peacekeeper and nation builder, and the need for universal health care.

Efforts to mold public opinion go well beyond the White House or elected officials. For more than twenty years, Ralph Nader has stimulated Americans to think of themselves as consumers and to consider safety every time they get in their cars. These opinions on safety not only encouraged car manufacturers to emphasize safety in car design; they encouraged public officials to mandate safer cars through legislation requiring airbags and safer bumpers. The group Common Cause keeps the issue of campaign financing on the minds of Americans. By their very choice of what to cover, the mass media selectively provide the public with issues, information, and alternatives on which public opinion depends. Environmental groups keep the fragility of natural resources in the public mind through such efforts as Earth Day and legislative initiatives. Women's groups have forced Americans to reconsider our definitions of personal freedom and to take stands on issues such as job opportunities, pay equity, and sexual harassment.

9-3 Winners and Losers in the Public Opinion Game

Political scientist W. Russell Neuman argues that:

> The paradox of mass politics is the gap between the expectation of an informed citizenry put forth by democratic theory and the discomforting reality revealed by systematic survey interviewing.[15]

Democracy means little without a meaningful role for public opinion. Observers disagree, however, on key aspects of measuring and using public opinion:

- How much should public opinion dominate the decision process?
- What is the quality of the opinions the public holds?
- How accurately is public opinion measured?

New technology facilitated the once difficult and expensive processing of public opinion data. Computers now draw samples, automatically dial telephone numbers, store data, and help to analyze the results. Public opinion measurement has become an industry, with many major television networks and newspapers having their own national polling capabilities. Local newspapers and television stations carry out low-cost telephone polls and person-on-the-street interviews to assess opinions. The investment in polling almost forces the media to recoup the investment by reporting the results. In sum, no shortage of public opinion measurements exists. Availability, however, does not answer the questions of when and how poll results should be used in the political game.

The more one trusts the quality of public opinion, the more one is willing to have public opinion determine public policy. But there is considerable evidence that the public lacks well-defined and well-informed opinions on many key issues. Even individuals who have opinions often cannot back them up with adequate information or logical justification.[16] This problem stems from public officials and the media (1) not providing all the options, (2) being able to manipulate the data, and (3) oversimplifying the possible choices. Policy makers must balance public opinion with other information and make decisions even when the public gives them no clear guidance.

Concern among the media and policy makers over public opinion has increased as polling of the public has become more frequent, pervasive, and precise. Many observers argue that polling increases citizen influence in the political game by providing decision makers with timely and accurate information on the opinions of all citizens. Through

Box 9–9 Technology and the Unlocking of Public Opinion

New technologies often have an "unlocking" effect, making once-difficult tasks easy. This is particularly true in the realm of public opinion polling.

The once extremely laborious tasks of choosing samples, finding telephone numbers, recording answers, and analyzing results are now facilitated by computers. The problem of unlisted telephone numbers is circumvented by having the computer perform random-digit dialing, in which both listed and unlisted numbers become available for selection. Telephone interviewers receive question prompts on their terminals and record responses directly into the computer, increasing efficiency and reducing the potential for clerical error. A few polling firms have begun using completely automated systems, in which the computer asks the question with its synthetic voice and computerized voice recognition programs interpret responses.

What technology gives, it can also take away. Cell phones and caller ID make it more difficult to choose a random sample. Cells phones are often not linked to a particular geographic area, and caller ID makes it easier to avoid calls from pollsters. Since cell phone owners and caller ID users are not a random subset of the population, their exclusion throws off the randomness of samples.

Despite current limitations of the technology and narrow public acceptance, technology-enhanced polling seems to be the wave of the future. Whatever the method of gathering responses, the results of major polls are almost invariably analyzed in multiple ways by computers. To some degree, by making once impossible tasks manageable, new technology has encouraged the expanded polling of the American public.

regular measurement and reporting of public opinion, spectators become influential—if somewhat indirect—players.

Not everyone agrees with this position. Some observers bemoan the fact that polls discourage individuals from taking part in the more demanding forms of political participation, such as voting, organizing, and communicating with decision makers. The narrative opening this chapter gives one scenario. It has been said that extensive dependence on polls reduces the ability to distinguish between levels of public intensity and opens the process to possible manipulation by decision makers.[17] Despite the fears, the modern technology of public opinion polling has reduced the cost, increased the precision, expanded the availability, and encouraged extended use of polling results in the policy process (see Box 9-9: Technology and the Unlocking of Public Opinion).[18]

Conclusion

Public opinion is an important component in the political game, especially in a political system that sees itself as a democracy. Concern for public opinion broadens the definition of players to include those who *think about* political issues, even if they take no other action.

Opinions stem from basic values and attitudes that define individual preferences for the goals that the political system should pursue and the mechanisms to be employed for reaching those goals. Opinions can justify the status quo or provide a powerful impetus for change.

Opinions are seldom random choices but result from socialization and specific life experiences. Individuals tend to hold a set of relatively unified opinions that can often be characterized in ideological terms as liberal or conservative. For individuals, attitudes and opinions are precursors to behavior and increase the predictability of their reaction to the world around them.

Supportive public opinion is a powerful resource for winning in the political game. Precise measurement of public opinion allows political players to anticipate the reaction of the interested public. Political leaders must conform to public opinion, attempt to change it, or justify contradicting it. They can seldom simply ignore it.

Key Terms

agenda
communism
compartmentalizing
conservatives
cross-pressures
distribution
exit poll
Gallup Poll
ideology
intensity
issue publics
liberals
libertarians
moderates
opinion leaders
plurality
population
prioritizing
randomness
rationalizing
sample
silent majority
stability (of public opinion)
tracking polls

Practice Quiz

1. To what does *public opinion* refer?
   a. Long-term predispositions held by a large segment of the population
   b. Political culture
   c. Short-term preferences held by a large segment of the population
   d. Visions of what is "good" in society

2. Ideology refers to
   a. public opinion.
   b. an organized set of ideas about societal goals.
   c. socialization.
   d. a disorganized set of ideas about how government should work.

3. Which statement best describes liberals and conservatives?
   a. Liberals tend to stress equality of outcome, while conservatives tend to stress equality of opportunity.
   b. Liberals tend to believe government is corrupt, while conservatives tend to trust government.
   c. Liberals tend to be suspicious of human nature, whereas conservatives tend to be optimistic.
   d. Liberals stress government's role in providing order, and conservatives stress its role in assuring freedom.

4. How do we tend to deal with attitudes that conflict?
   a. Emulation and compartmentalizing
   b. Compartmentalizing and rationalizing
   c. Emulation and rationalizing
   d. Socializing and rationalizing

5. Whose opinion would an astute politician typically follow?
   a. An apathetic majority
   b. A stable majority
   c. An intense minority
   d. A homogeneous minority

6. Which dimensions of public opinion do politicians most often consider?
   a. Diversity, homogeneity, and heterogeneity
   b. Distribution, diversity, and stability
   c. Distribution, intensity, and emulation
   d. Distribution, intensity, and stability

7. One concern about the heavy use of public opinion polling is that it
   a. may decrease other forms of citizen involvement in politics.
   b. increasingly generates inaccurate results.
   c. gives an advantage to liberals.
   d. often incorrectly predicts election results.

8. A random sample of 1,500 respondents assures that 95 times out of 100 the results will be within _____ percentage points of the actual population characteristics.
   a. plus or minus 1
   b. plus or minus 3
   c. plus or minus 5
   d. plus or minus 10

9. Not everyone has an opinion on every topic. Those individuals having strong views on a topic are called
   a. retrospective voters.
   b. respondents.
   c. liberals.
   d. issue publics.

10. The population of a public opinion poll is made up of
   a. everyone in the United States.
   b. all voters.
   c. the subset of people from whom the pollster collects data.
   d. those about whom one wants to generalize.

You can find the correct answers to these questions by taking the quiz and then submitting your answers in the Online Edition. The program will automatically score your submission. Where you miss a question, the program will provide the correct answer, a rationale for the answer, and the section number in the chapter where the topic is discussed.

Further Reading

To get a better feel for public opinion methodology and the criteria for evaluating polls, see Herbert Asher, *Polling and the Public: What Every Citizen Should Know* (Washington, D.C.: Congressional Quarterly, 1998); Albert H. Cantril, *The Opinion Connection* (Washington, D.C.: Congressional Quarterly, 1991); and Michael Traugott and Paul Lavrakas, *The Voter's Guide to Election Polls* (New York: Chatham House, 2000).

A comprehensive text on public opinion in the political process is Robert S. Erickson and Kent L. Tedin, *American Public Opinion: Its Origins, Content and Impact* (Boston, MA: Allyn & Bacon, 2000).

W. Russell Neuman's *The Paradox of Mass Politics* (Cambridge, MA: Harvard University Press, 1986) presents an interesting analysis of the link between public opinion and democracy.

For a critical look at the dangers resulting from emphasizing public opinion and public opinion polls, see Benjamin Ginsberg, *The Captive Public* (New York: Basic Books, 1986).

Finding the results of public opinion polls can often be frustrating. Many libraries carry the *Gallup Poll Tuesday Briefing* (formerly the *Gallup Poll Monthly*), which reports many of its national polls and makes a serious attempt to provide historical comparisons of poll results. Yearly summaries of poll results are often published in book form, such as *The Gallup Poll: Public Opinion 1989* (Wilmington, DE: Scholarly Resources, 1990). Poll data can be retrieved from the web at:

http://www.harrisinteractive.com
http://www.gallup.com/
http://www.policyattitudes.org/
http://www.pollingreport.com/
http://www.irss.unc.edu/data_archive/pollsearch.html

The major center for scholarly polling is the Inter-University Consortium for Political and Social Research (ICPSR) at the University of Michigan. The consortium is best known for its national election studies. Many schools are members of this consortium and have collections of codebooks that provide overall responses to the surveys. More detailed data sets for computer analysis can be ordered. A number of computerized databases (such as LEXIS-NEXIS) offer online searching for polls. Check with your college librarian to see what they have available for online searching.

Endnotes

1. See Robert S. Erickson and Kent L. Tedin, *American Public Opinion: Its Origins, Content and Impact* (New York: Longman, 1995), 2–5.
2. Jan Struther, "The Weather of the World" in *A Pocket Full of Pebbles* (New York: Harcourt Brace, 1946).
3. Erickson and Tedin, *American Public Opinion*, 145.
4. The term *ideology* first arose during the French Revolution to express a school of thought, separate from religion, about how a society should be organized. See Jay M. Shafritz, *The HarperCollins Dictionary of American Government and Politics* (New York: HarperCollins, 1993), 233.
5. The classic distinction between modern liberals and conservatives was outlined by Herbert McCloskey, "Conservatism and Personality," *American Political Science Review* 52 (March 1958): 27–45. See also Pamela Conover and Stanley Felman, "The Origins and Meaning of Liberal and Conservative Self-Identification," *American Journal of Political Science* 25 (1981), 617–45.
6. Quoted in Katharine Q. Seelye, "House Approaches Easing of Rules on U.S. Searches," *New York Times*, February 9, 1995, A1.
7. W. Russell Neuman, *The Paradox of Mass Politics* (Cambridge, MA: Harvard University Press, 1986), 32.
8. Jerry L. Yeric and John R. Todd, *Public Opinion: The Visible Politics* (Itasca, IL: F. E. Peacock, 1983), 30.
9. The first major work to emphasize the concept of cross-pressures was Bernard R. Berelson, Paul F. Lazarsfeld, and William N. McPhee, *Voting: A Study of Opinion Formation in a Presidential Campaign* (Chicago, IL: The University of Chicago Press, 1954).
10. David E. Rosenbaum, "In Loss, Republicans Find Seeds of Victory," *New York Times*, March 5, 1995, section 4, 16.
11. See Neuman, *The Paradox of Mass Politics*, 67–73.
12. Neuman, *The Paradox of Mass Politics*, 189.
13. Yeric and Todd, *Public Opinion*, 20.
14. Bruce E. Altschuler, "Lyndon Johnson and the Public Polls," *Public Opinion Quarterly* 50, no. 3 (Fall 1986), 285–99.
15. Neuman, *The Paradox of Mass Politics*, 189.
16. Cantril, *The Opinion Connection*, 136, and Erickson and Tedin, *American Public Opinion*, 59–65.
17. Benjamin Ginsberg, *The Captive Public: How Mass Opinion Promotes State Power*. (New York: Basic Books, 1986), 1984.
18. For a brief history of presidential use of polling results, see Michael Barone's "The Power of the President's Pollsters," in *American Government: Readings and Cases*, ed. Peter Woll (Glenview, IL: Scott, Foresman, 1990).

10

Political Participation: Who Plays the Game?

Key Points

- **The costs and benefits of political participation for both the individual and the political system.**
- **The impact of rules in determining participation.**
- **Encouraging and/or discouraging political participation as political strategy.**
- **The impact of new technology on political participation.**
- **Political participation and democracy.**

Preview: A Taxing Outpouring

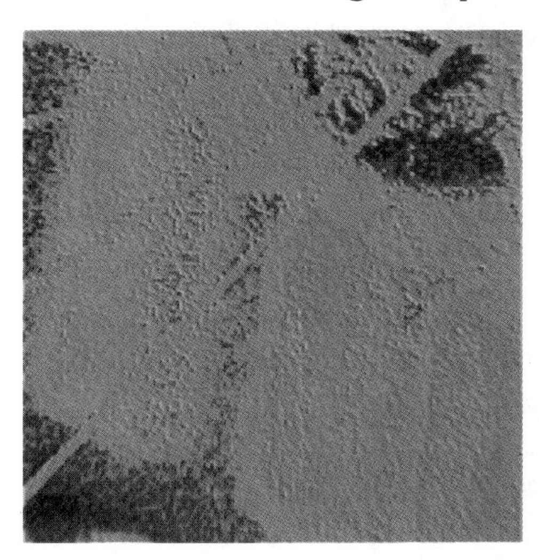

In the early 1980s, the Reagan administration became concerned about the number of individuals failing to report income from dividends and interest. Legislation was proposed to require banks and brokerage houses to withhold a portion of that income for tax purposes. Congress, feeling justified in expanding upon the withholding process used for income taxes, passed the legislation. (The House vote was 226 to 207, and the Senate vote was 53 to 47.) There was relatively little public awareness or commentary on the issue. Most participants felt that the public would simply sit back and allow the change to happen. They assumed that no one would really object to the withholding of owed taxes. They were wrong.

Individual members of the general public knew little about the issue, but banks and brokerage houses objected to the new administrative burden and activated a set of customers ripe for political participation. Information and mail-back postcards went into monthly statements. Advertising was directed at activating senior citizens, who often have no tax burden but significant investments. Speakers' bureaus were established to spread the word, and a spate of news items fanned the flames. Within a few weeks, congressional mail almost tripled, with the total mail volume reaching

ROCK
THE
VOTE®

Rock the Vote is dedicated to protecting freedom of expression and to helping young people realize and utilize their power to affect change in the civic and political lives of their communities.

Source: "Rock the Vote"

more than 20 million pieces. The congressional post office got to the point where it could no longer count the mail and resorted to counting boxes and bags.

Within a few months, Congress reversed itself through a repeal of the withholding provision by a one-sided margin (382 to 41 in the House and 91 to 5 in the Senate). On this issue, the public spoke loud and clear in hopes of protecting itself from unwanted government intervention, and Congress heard the message.[1]

A decade and a half later, despite evidence of public cynicism and growing disenchantment with government, another affected public again used their right to "petition government for the redress of grievances" (from the 1st Amendment of the Constitution). This time the tool of participation was the computer—which was also at the core of the dispute, over cyberspace pornography. After legislation was introduced to censor communication on the government-subsidized Internet, the information superhighway began to buzz with email messages. In the first week, more than 80,000 messages of opposition arrived in Congress, and an issue as down home as apple pie—promoting decency—erupted into a major battle over free expression and government involvement in our lives. The legislation, the Communication Decency Act, was eventually ruled unconstitutional by the Supreme Court in 1997. With public outcry on both sides, Congress passed the revised Child Online Pornography Act, only to have it ruled unconstitutional in 2004.[2]

The American public seldom stands ready and eager to participate fully in the political process. Once angered, however, citizens can act with relative unanimity and force. The goal of "government by the people" is both irregular and unsure, but under the right conditions it is real.

Do you stay up late on election night waiting for returns from places to which you have never been? Or do you go to bed at your regular time, assuming that the news of who won will still be there in the morning? If you remain glued to the television set into the night, you fall into the small group of fans of the game for whom politics remains a passion. Those who are interested in politics can find many different ways to participate at the local, state, and national levels (see Figure 10-1).

Chapter 9 looked at political opinions, the precursors of political activity. We now attempt to understand the options available for acting on those opinions. In this chapter, we explore various forms of political participation and the level of individual involvement in the political game. We begin with a discussion of the rules affecting participation

Figure 10-1
The Participation Pyramid

Sources: Data from Margaret Conway, *Political Participation in the United States* (Washington, D.C.: Congressional Quarterly Press, 2000), pp. 8–9; Steven Rosenstone and John Mark Hansen, *Mobilization, Participant and Democracy in America* (New York: Macmillan Publishing Co., 1993), pp. 42–43.

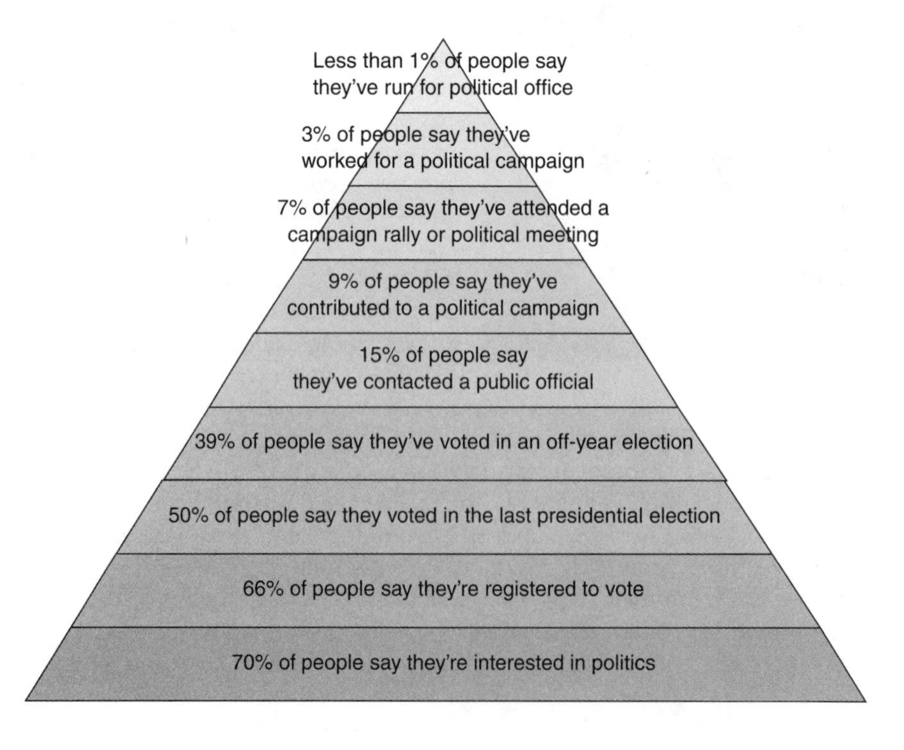
Less than 1% of people say they've run for political office
3% of people say they've worked for a political campaign
7% of people say they've attended a campaign rally or political meeting
9% of people say they've contributed to a political campaign
15% of people say they've contacted a public official
39% of people say they've voted in an off-year election
50% of people say they voted in the last presidential election
66% of people say they're registered to vote
70% of people say they're interested in politics

and outline the characteristics of those who actively play the game. The remainder of the chapter emphasizes that in a democracy, where numbers count, encouraging and discouraging participation becomes a potent strategy used to help determine who wins and who loses. Understanding the nature of political participation in the United States sets the stage for Chapter 11's discussion of elections, the most realistic game in which the public can play an active role.

10-1 Relating the Individual to the State

Individuals are linked to governmental institutions and processes in a number of ways. As we saw in earlier chapters, mediating institutions, such as interest groups and political parties, serve as vehicles for individuals to join together to have an impact. We will now focus on the linkages to government that remain largely within the control of the individual. In a number of cases, we will discover that individual initiative will be subject to formal rules and/or the receptivity of government officials with whom individuals wish to interact. Individuals are linked to the political game in a variety of ways. They function as

- complete citizens
- constituents
- clients and/or
- victims

Citizens include those individuals who live within a political unit and who have the legal right of involvement, but whose legal status indicates little about their actual participation. **Complete citizens** exhibit a continuing and intensive relationship to all stages of the political process. They inform themselves on issues, actively support causes and candidates, vote in elections, and communicate their concerns to elected and appointed officials on a regular basis. Some of these individuals virtually become full-time players, transforming their hobby into their work. For most of us, playing in the political arena is a part-time activity at best. Direct input from complete citizens depends not only on the willingness of government officials to accept such involvement[3] but also on the willingness of the citizens to exert the necessary effort.

complete citizens *Individuals who fully relate to the political process in a deep and continuing manner; they are more than simply legal residents of a political unit.*

Constituents, on the other hand, are more sporadically linked to a limited number of political institutions or processes. They play a periodic but more limited role in the game. We typically think of legislators as having constituents who select them in elections but who exhibit limited contact between elections. Various government agencies also have constituents upon whom they call for support during budget dealings or at times of crisis. The Department of Agriculture, for example, serves the needs of farmers and expects farmers to support the expansion of departmental activity and budgets through communications with policy makers.

constituents *Individuals who must be taken into account by public officials because they live in a particular electoral district or represent an identifiable political interest.*

Constituents periodically get called off the bench, especially during election campaigns, in the hopes of changing the outcome of the game. Elected and appointed officials view the interests of constituents as something that must be taken into account, since their support, even on an irregular basis, is necessary. Constituents have power. They are a valuable resource, since they can and do intervene in the political process. They both elect officials and reveal support for the programs promoted by appointed officials.

Individuals in a **client** relationship with government depend on a government institution for some services but often lack the skills, interest, and/or status to have any real say in the delivery of those services. Clients are like a team's fans. They depend on team performance for their satisfaction but have little to say about team operations. Bureaucratic agencies view clients as individuals to be taken care of, but neither the agencies nor the individuals expect any real consultation on the broader policy issues. When the public welfare recipient meets with the government social worker, the recipient typically does not try to change the welfare system or to forcefully present his or her grievances. At the same time, the social worker has little fear of what the recipient might do if not satisfied.

clients *Individuals taken care of by government but not expected to participate in the political process.*

victims *Individuals affected by government policies whose interests are not taken into account in the policy process.*

While government has a perception of clients' needs, **victims** of government action find themselves affected by governmental policies without the benefit of having been taken into account. Policies often result in unanticipated consequences or implications for groups and individuals who cannot be aware of the end result of government policy for themselves. For example, the imposition of a 55-mile-per-hour speed limit reduced gasoline use and cut the profits of many gasoline stations. To reduce costs, more stations became self-service operations and cut their staffs. Thousands of teenagers who might have found jobs at full-service stations became unexpected victims of the speed limit policy. When government uses its powers to acquire private property or to discontinue government programs, inadequate compensation or the loss of business can turn private citizens into unintentional victims (see Box 10-1: Military Base Cutbacks and the Public).

Box 10–1 Military Base Cutbacks and the Public

Background

During the last few decades, attempts to increase the efficiency of the Defense Department (also known as the Department of Defense, or DOD) have led to the closing of many military installations. The collapse of the Soviet Union as an abiding threat encouraged a further round of defense cutbacks as a "peace dividend." Closing military bases has a direct impact on military personnel stationed there and the civilian employees supporting their efforts. More broadly, such closures affect the local economy. Since the stakes are so high, such decisions engender a great deal of interest, and it has been difficult to satisfy all players.

Questions

To understand the process of base closing, a number of questions arise:

- Who are the players in this game?
- How do the players' perspectives differ?
- How has the game been changed to reduce the disruptions caused by some players?

Analysis

A typical base-closing decision involves several categories of individuals who approach the game with different perspectives and opportunities to play. These categories include:

Complete citizens: A few individuals may be drawn directly into the policy process. Either on their own or at the request of the DOD, individuals with long-term interests in the particular base may fully research the issue and its implications. Local businesspeople whose economic well-being depends on the continued existence of the base will emphasize the broader economic implications, while others may look into the national defense implications. These groups may present their findings to the DOD and Congress on the basis of their expertise. Their findings could point out unanticipated consequences or faulty assumptions built into the initial analysis. If their arguments persuade decision makers, they have been accepted as complete citizens.

Constituents: A wider group of individuals is likely to appeal the decision by threatening to withdraw political support if the base is closed. The local member of Congress invariably faces an angry set of individuals threatening to base their vote in the next election on the member's successful defeat of this initiative. Even the DOD may view some individuals, such as department employees or members of Congress on key defense committees, as constituents whose interests must be taken into account. If threats of rewards or sanctions alter the outlook of decision makers, the individuals have become constituents.

Clients: The DOD is likely to view most of its employees, especially those on the base to be closed, as clients. Through memos and meetings, the department assures the employees that they will be taken care of in the decision process. Other military organizations that are dependent on the base to train personnel or to provide services are told, "Don't worry. We have arranged a better alternative." If the individuals have no real say in the outcome but are not really hurt by it, they have been treated as clients.

The categories of citizens are not firm and fixed. Few, if any, individuals participate as complete citizens all the time. A victim of one policy arena may be a constituent in another. For example, individuals not taken into account by the bureaucracy often turn to members of Congress for help, since they know that they are more likely to be viewed as valued constituents in that arena. At any one point in time, only complete citizens and constituents are true participants in American politics, but statuses change. Clients and victims may rise up and demand that government pay attention to them, thereby moving themselves into one of the participatory categories. For example, families grieving over the death of a loved one at the hands of a drunk driver largely accepted their fates as victims until the creation of MADD (Mothers Against Drunk Drivers) in the 1970s (see Chapter 7). MADD members fought their way into the political arena, demanding

Victims: The closing of a military base affects the local economy, school population, and a variety of other indirect conditions not taken into account in the policy process. The local residents whose land values decline, the student whose local school is closed and who must now take the bus across town, and the civilian employee who does not get a new job become victims of the base closing.

Until recently, the game was dominated by constituents. The DOD would recommend suggested closures to Congress based on the contribution of each base to national defense. Members of Congress from the districts affected would immediately be inundated by pleas for help from their constituents. Much of the constituent concern is motivated and orchestrated by complete citizens with close ties to the member. The members would forcefully be informed that their political futures were on the line. The rationale of the DOD would be severely questioned, and those directly affected would passionately speak up for the interests of the victims, turning them into clients. Each closure decision would involve a specific play in the game with identifiable winners and losers. The broader goals of efficiency and cost savings would be lost in the individual skirmishes, and few base closure suggestions would ever make it out of Congress and to the president's desk.

It became clear that a game dominated by constituents would not work. During the late 1980s, an independent Base Closure and Realignment Commission was created. Members of this commission would consider recommendations from the DOD, pay special attention to the testimony of experts (complete citizens), and take into account the arguments of affected parties. But they would make their decisions without concern for personal political reprisal. The members of the commission are not in a constituent relationship with anyone. The clients of the commission are the public as a whole. Commission members do not have to take care of a specific group of individuals.

The package of closures suggested by the Base Closure and Realignment Commission must be approved or rejected as a package by the president. Rejected packages are reconsidered by the commission and sent back to the president. Once approved by the president, the package is sent to Congress. Members of Congress gain some political "cover" in supporting the package by being able to argue that "we all have to sacrifice a bit for the public good."

The 1995 commission recommendations raised a considerable number of objections, especially from California and Texas, which faced the loss of thousands of jobs. Facing a tough reelection battle in which California and Texas would play a key role, President Bill Clinton was very tempted to deal with California voters as constituents and reject the plan. In the end, the angry president called the recommendations "an outrage,"[a] but he accepted the plan out of fear that he would lose his credibility as a serious budget cutter. In an attempt to soften the blow for constituents, clients, and victims alike, the president pressured the DOD to guarantee that a large number of the lost jobs would remain in the area in the hands of private contractors.

---

a. Ann Devroy and Bradley Graham, "Angry Clinton Accepts List of Base Cutbacks," *Washington Post*, July 14, 1995, A1.

Time Out 10-1

Getting Drawn into the Game

Make a list of the various contacts you have had with government officials in the last twenty-four hours. Don't forget routine contacts, such as having your mail delivered, asking a government official for information, or slowing down when you see the police on the highway. Some of the contacts have been indirect. For example, was the food you ate or the elevator you rode in inspected by the government?

List each of your contacts and categorize it (by checking off its category), indicating the participatory role you were expected to play. Were you a complete citizen, constituent, client, or victim?

What does the categorization of one day's activities tell you about your typical participatory role in the game of politics?

Contact	Complete Citizen	Constituent	Client	Victim
1.				
2.				
3.				
4.				
5.				
6.				
7.				
8.				
9.				
10.				
11.				

to be viewed first as valued constituents and eventually as fully participating citizens. Through organization and research, MADD pressured Congress and state legislatures to raise drinking ages and to stiffen penalties for drunk driving.

The battle for recognition as a player is not always one-sided. Government agencies may offer their clients the status of constituent in exchange for increased support. In the early 1900s, the Department of Agriculture reacted to the shift away from an agricultural economy by organizing farmers and creating a series of advisory groups (see Chapter 7).[4] Being accepted as a rightful player facilitates and encourages further participation. The impact of government on our lives encourages involvement (see Time Out 10-1: Getting Drawn into the Game).

10-2 Rules and the Determination of the Players

Individuals have a variety of options in determining the political arenas in which they want to participate and how much they wish to undertake. The desire and opportunity to participate, however, is not evenly distributed throughout the population.

Most participation, such as informing oneself on political issues or joining political groups, is protected under constitutional guarantees of free speech and freedom of association. Formal rules and public laws inhibit only a few types of political participation. Certain classes of people face special limitations, however. The federal Hatch Act (and its state-level counterparts), which was enacted in 1939 and extended in 1940, denies government employees the right to participate in certain partisan activities. They may not run for partisan office, collect campaign contributions among subordinates, or use their offices to promote partisan causes. These limitations attempt to prevent the use of government employees to benefit the party in power (see Box 10-2: Redefining the Political Bench). Corporations with government contracts operate under rules that limit their political activity. Citizens of other countries cannot contribute to political campaigns in the United States.

Some forms of political participation are so central to a democratic society that they are directly regulated by government. These include voting and campaign contributions.

10-2a Rules of Voting

Many contemporary Americans seem casual about the right to vote. They take **enfranchisement** for granted and do not do justice to the sacrifices and tremendous battles fought by their predecessors to gain that right. Each expansion of the electorate involved groups of dedicated activists willing to press their claims.

enfranchisement *Having the legal right to vote.*

Voting Rights

The history of the American electoral system reflects a gradual broadening of the electorate (see Figure 10-2). While the Constitution originally left the determination of voter eligibility to the states (Article I, Section 4), state laws changed both from within and in

Box 10-2 *Redefining the Political Bench*

The Hatch Act grew out of the era of "spoils" (described in Chapter 8), when political activists were rewarded for their support of party candidates with jobs in the government. Once in office they were expected to continue their partisan activity in order to keep their party in office and to retain their jobs. The need for a more professional set of government employees—who would not be distracted by partisan politics—had become obvious by the 1930s. Restrictions against political activism were gradually placed on most government employees.

There was, however, discomfort with limiting citizen involvement in politics, and the number of people restricted continued to grow. Federal government employees numbered more than 3 million by the early 1990s. The Democratic Party recognized that the limitations were hobbling the involvement of many individuals who would normally support Democratic candidates. These factors led to pressure for reform, but many Republicans fought the changes. The following analogy was offered:

> Suppose we were at a baseball game and there were 60,000 fans supporting and cheering loudly for the home team. All of a sudden, all of the umpires join in the cheers. Would they be considered impartial? . . . Even if they called every ball and strike and every out perfectly the next game, every baseball fan would begin to doubt their impartiality.[a]

With a Democratic majority in Congress and a Democrat in the White House, the time for expanding the potential bench of players was ripe. The Hatch Act Revision was signed by Bill Clinton in 1993. Under the new law, government employees may take a more active role in partisan campaigns on their own time. They are still prohibited from running for office on a partisan ticket, raising funds, and coercing subordinates to support partisan causes.

---

a. William V. Roth, Jr. [R-Del.], *Congressional Record*, July 13, 1993, S-8603.

Figure 10-2
Expansion of the Electorate

*percentage of adults eligible to vote (the definition of adults was changed in 1971 when the voting age was lowered to 18)
**percentage of eligible voters actually voting
***percentage of total population voting

Source: Jerrold G. Rusk, *A Statistical History of the American Electorate* (Washington, D.C.: Congressional Quarterly, Inc., 2001), pp. 30–54.

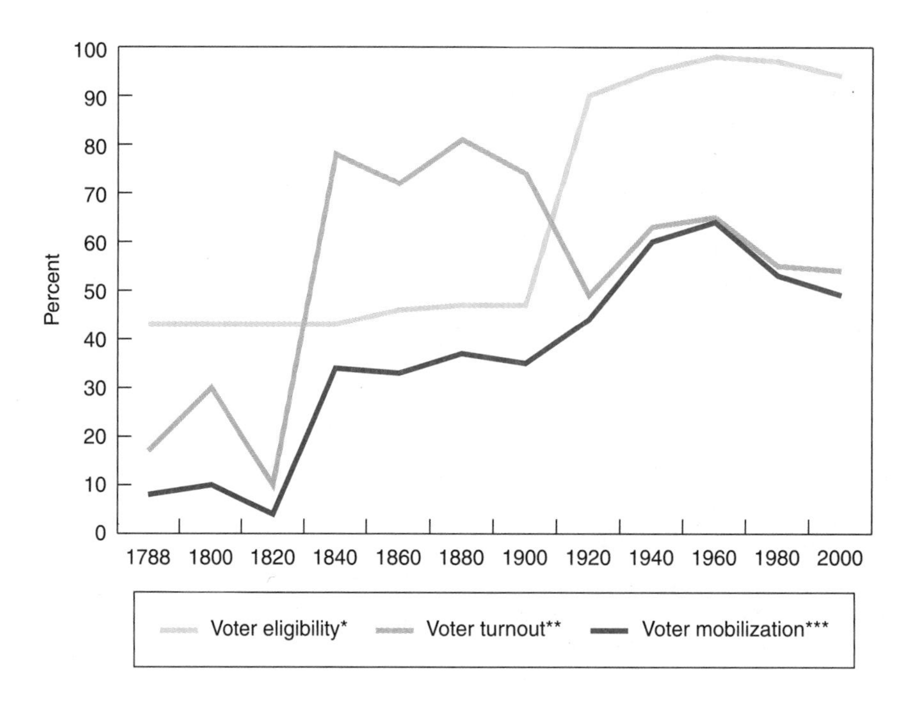

1800: State requirements on property holding loosened.
1870: Race outlawed as criterion for voting (15th Amendment)
1920: Women given the right to vote (19th Amendment)
1964: Poll tax outlawed (24th Amendment)
1971: 18- to 21-year-olds given the right to vote (26th Amendment)

suffrage *The legal right to vote.*

reaction to new national requirements (see Box 10-3: The Battle to Join the Game). **Suffrage,** the legal right to vote, initially resided in the hands of white male property owners. A succession of constitutional amendments extended voting rights to members of minorities, expanding the electorate to include nonwhites (1870), women (1920), and 18- to 21-year-olds (1971) (see Box 10-3).

The battles over expanding the number and nature of players were seldom fought on the basis of grand principles. The assertion made during the height of the Vietnam conflict—that if 18 was old enough to fight, it was old enough to vote—carried less weight among politicians than feelings about whose partisan interests would be helped. Active players in interest groups and political parties expended considerable effort attempting to determine whether the proposed changes would help or hurt their causes. Party leaders naturally advocated changes in player participation rules that increased their political power and opposed those changes that decreased it. The 18-year-old vote was promoted most wholeheartedly by Democrats, who assumed that younger voters would be more apt to support their candidates.

Despite constitutional guarantees, during the late 1800s and early 1900s a number of states and localities erected legal barriers to hold back the expansion of the electorate. The most significant barriers arose in the southern states to prevent voting by blacks and poor whites. Poll taxes, literacy tests, "whites only" primaries, and a variety of other tactics gained the force of law. Combined with intimidation and uneven application of the laws, these state laws dramatically reduced minority participation. Four national laws, numerous lawsuits, and vigorous federal enforcement were necessary to make the guarantees of the 15th Amendment (outlawing race as a criterion for voting) a reality.[5] The impact of efforts since the 1960s to open the political game has been rather dramatic, with the gap between white and black voter registration narrowing (see Figures 10-3 and 10-4). The 2000 election saw dramatic increases in black registration and voting.

The lowering of the voting age to 18 by the 26th Amendment in 1971 was also initially thwarted by local customs and procedures. Many newly enfranchised students were

Box 10–3 The Battle to Join the Game

Women's Suffrage

The denial of women's right to vote in early American history did not exist without protest. As early as 1647, Margaret Brent, a wealthy resident of Maryland, petitioned the colonial government for the right to vote. In 1787 Abigail Adams wrote to her husband, John, as he was helping to draft the Constitution to "remember the ladies." Both pleas were denied. During the 1800s, women began being granted the right to vote in some local elections, especially those for the school board. Active female involvement in the antislavery movement prior to the Civil War helped women to develop organizational skills and generated political leadership.

The formal beginning of the women's rights movement came at the Women's Rights Convention in 1841. Working on a state-by-state basis, the suffragists presented their argument for equity and slowly gained success in a number of states and territories. The active role of women in World War I—taking over the jobs of men in the military service—helped to redefine women's role in society. Southern political leaders, with a traditional patriarchal view of society, and political party bosses, fearing that women would support reforms of the political process that would weaken their power, were among those who fought the women's initiative.

By the time the 19th Amendment was proposed in 1919, twenty-six states already allowed women to vote. Although the amendment was ratified by the requisite thirty-six states in August 1920, several states refused to reopen their registration rolls to allow women to vote in that year's presidential election. Initial voting levels of women were quite low, with the gap between women and men disappearing only toward the end of the twentieth century.[a]

Suffrage Parade, New York City, 1912

Source: Library of Congress, Prints & Photographs Division [LC-USZC4-5585]

a. For a more detailed discussion, see M. Margaret Conway, *Political Participation in the United States* (Washington, D.C.: Congressional Quarterly, Inc., 2000), 108–111.

barred from local elections during the 1970s when some college towns, fearful of the student vote, refused to recognize dormitory living as meeting residency requirements. In the end, younger voters participated at relatively low levels and voted in ways differing little from the general population.

Residency and Registration Requirements

While state and federal laws provide for universal adult suffrage, the level of voter participation in the United States remains considerably lower than in most countries in the world. Much of the explanation for low participation stems from voter registration requirements.[6] The desire to reduce election fraud led to the development of strict registration laws. The fact that the laws are administered by local government officials stems from the American commitment to local control of the administration of elections. Individuals earn their right to vote through their legal residency in a state and local political jurisdiction. With rare exceptions (such as military personnel temporarily stationed away from their legal residence), potential voters must meet the local registration laws to vote.

Figure 10-3
Voter Turnout, 1888 to 2004

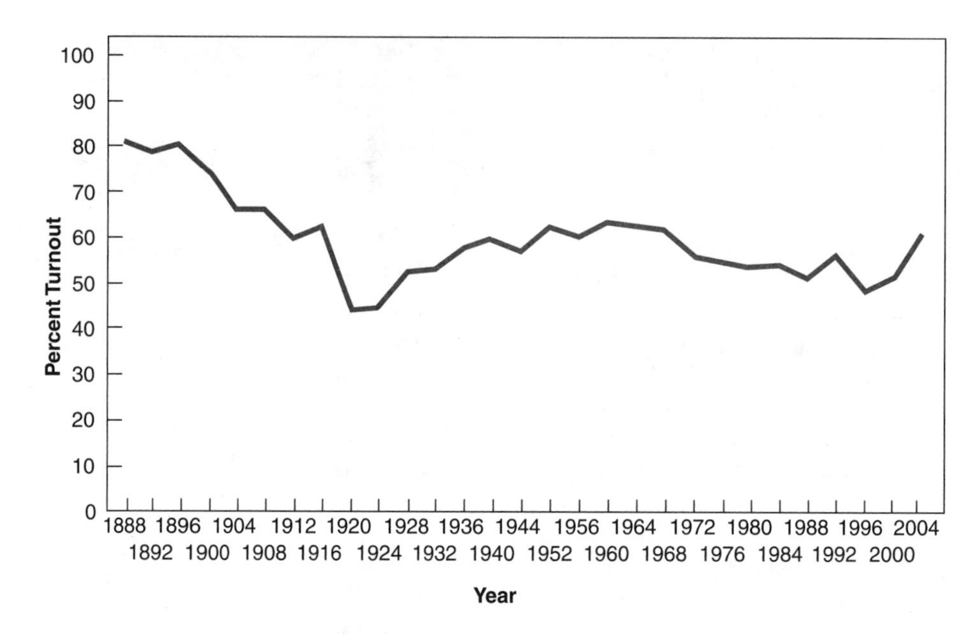

Turnout declined sharply from 1896 to 1920, increased until 1960, and then began another uneven decline. In 1992, 55% of the eligible electorate voted. In 1996, however, turnout dropped again, to 49%, then edged up to 51% in 2000, and spurted to 61% in 2004.

Sources: Source for turnout through 1996: *America Votes 22: A Handbook of Contemporary American Election Statistics,* ed. Richard M. Scammon, Alice V. McGillivray, and Rhodes Cook. Washington, D.C.: Congressional Quarterly 2000: "Report: Gore Won Popular Vote by 539,897," *Washington Post,* 21 December 2000, p. A9; Brian Faler "Election Turnout in 2004 Was Highest Since 1968," *Washington Post,* January 15, 2005, Page A05.

Figure 10-4
Reported Voter Registration by Race (Percentage of Eligible Voters Reporting They Had Registered)

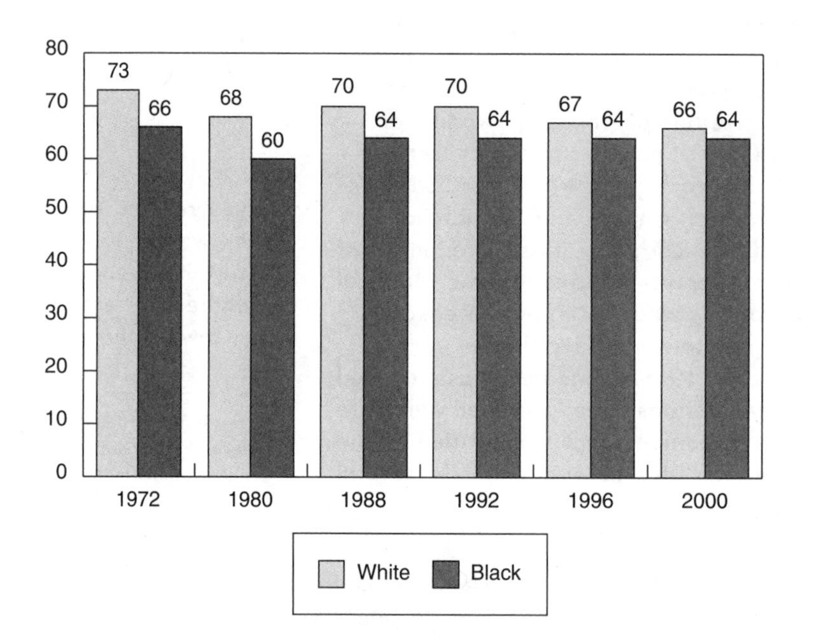

"Reported" registration and voting data is based on surveys and tends to overestimate actual registration and voting.

Sources: U.S. Bureau of the Census, Statistical Abstract of the United States; U.S. Bureau of the Census, Voting and Registration in the Election of November, 2002, Series P-25, 2003, table Y19, pp. 20-21; Harold W. Stanley and Richard G. Niemi, *Vital Statistics on American Politics, 2001–2002* (Washington, D.C.: Congressional Quarterly, Inc., 2002).

Individuals choose not to register for a number of reasons. A survey of unregistered eligible voters revealed that 40 percent of them claimed they were too busy to get around to registering. A significant portion of the unregistered individuals (33 percent) expressed cynicism toward politics and politicians. They felt that "there aren't many candidates worth voting for." The remaining unregistered eligible voters reported physical impairment or illiteracy as their reason for not registering.[7]

In recent years, many states have reduced the time period required for establishing residency, discontinued the requirement to periodically register, established easier mail-in procedures, and/or allowed Election Day registration. States with less demanding registration procedures exhibit greater voter participation. Election laws often get entwined with partisan politics. Democrats traditionally find it harder to get their supporters to the polls. In 1993 they were finally able to pass a national motor-voter registration law requiring states to allow voters to register when they get a driver's license or register for other public services.[8]

In arguing for a national procedure to make registration easier, Senator Wendell H. Ford (D-Ky.) asserted:

> Lack of interest is the major reason for not voting. The problem with our present system is that if a person's interest is not aroused until close to the end of the race, that person may not vote if not already registered. We are all familiar with the scenario of how people who generally show little interest in sporting events will be taken up with the excitement of a World Series or Super Bowl. Interest in political races also peaks as Election Day approaches, but unlike the Super Bowl or World Series, only those registered in advance can take part. This bill would assure that almost everyone who is qualified will have a ticket for the championship game on Election Day.[9]

Easy voting access laws have not done much to stem the tide of decreasing political participation. Prospects for future increases look bleak when one considers the decline in political interest among younger citizens and the increasing gap in political interest between generations of voters (see Figure 10-5). There is little evidence that the current generation of disinterested voters will somehow magically become dramatically more interested as they age.

Not much can be done to directly increase citizen interest. Registration laws remain the most significant formal voting hurdle. Individuals who have the motivation to register will more than likely take the initiative to vote. While 50 to 55 percent of eligible voters cast ballots in recent presidential elections, more than 80 percent of registered voters participated.[10]

Election Day Laws

The easier it is to vote, the more people will turn out. Long open hours for the polls, convenient and numerous polling places, and efficient administration all encourage participation. Absentee ballots allow voters unable to appear at their polling places on Election Day to cast their ballots by mail in advance of the election. States vary considerably on absentee ballot rules. Some states require complex application procedures, while others have flexible features that, for example, allow party workers to take ballots to shut-ins.

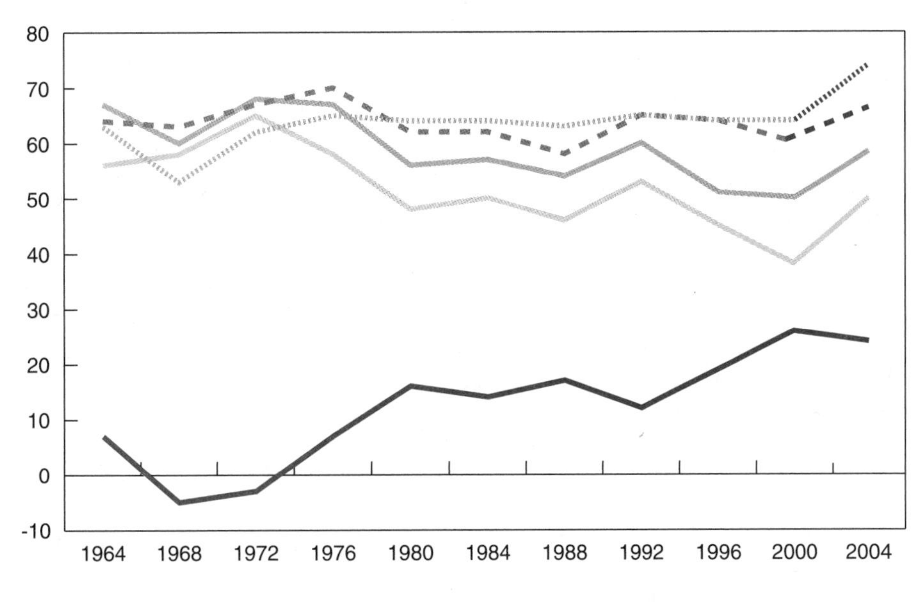

Figure 10-5
General Interest in Public Affairs by Age, 1964–2004

Entries indicate average interest level of respondents in each group when responses are recorded as follows: "hardly at all" = 0; "only now and then" = 33; "some of the time" = 66; and "most of the time" = 100.

**Positive numbers indicate older citizens being more interested in politics than are younger citizens.

Source: National Election Studies, reported in Martin P. Wattenberg, *Where Have All the Voters Gone?* (Cambridge, MA: Harvard University Press, 2002), p. 89.

In recent years, candidates and parties have attempted to change the nature of participation on Election Day by selectively facilitating absentee voting by their supporters. Although both parties now make some effort to capitalize on the absentee ballots, a greater percentage of absentee voters tend to be Republican than voters casting their ballots in person. Using computerized lists of individuals likely to vote by absentee ballot (traveling salespersons, nursing home residents, military personnel, and so on), the party or campaign organization contacts those voters favorable to their cause, provides information supporting their candidate, and offers them help in casting their ballots. In a number of states, the parties can be designated auxiliary registrars and directly provide application forms. The general trend has been toward easing the regulations on absentee ballots and moving toward "no fault" rules in which the registrant is not required to present an excuse for not voting in person.

This strategy was first used effectively on a massive scale in 1982 by the California Republicans. In spite of losing the gubernatorial vote in the regular balloting, the expanded number of absentee voters (from 4.4 percent to 6.5 percent) supported the Republican candidate with 61 percent of their votes and granted him the election.[11] By 1990, 1.4 million California voters (18.4 percent) cast their ballots using absentee procedures. In that year Republican gubernatorial candidate Pete Wilson received 48 percent of the ballots cast in person and 57 percent of the absentee ballots, which turned his razor-thin margin in direct votes into a comfortable 4 percent margin. The attorney general candidate, who lost among direct votes, gained victory due to the one-sided nature of the absentee ballots.[12] In recent elections, a number of races were determined by the absentee ballots. The close vote and large number of absentee ballots in Florida during the 2000 election revealed the critical role they could play. It seems that physically getting to the arena is no longer necessary for affecting the outcome of the game.

Rules about Contributing to Campaigns

Political candidates prove their support and amass the resources needed to mount a campaign by seeking campaign contributions. Until the 1970s, individuals, groups, and corporations were largely free to contribute any amount they wished to political candidates. Revelations of million-dollar contributors gaining ambassadorial posts or preferential access eventually made "fat cats" a target of the Federal Election Campaign Act (FECA). (See also Chapters 8 and 9.) First passed in 1971, this legislation sought to encourage small contributions and required public disclosure of campaign finance activity.

Initial attempts to establish laws limiting the size of individual contributions faced a challenge in the Supreme Court. In *Buckley v. Valeo* (1976), the Court asserted that contributing money was directly related to free expression and was protected by the 1st Amendment to the Constitution. It allowed for federal financing and financial monitoring of presidential campaigns. Revisions of the law made a distinction between contributions given directly to a campaign and those made independent of a campaign organization. Individuals were originally allowed to give $1,000 directly to a candidate but could spend any amount they wished to otherwise support that candidate, as long as the efforts were separate from those of the campaign organization. Individuals use this provision allowing **independent expenditures** to buy newspaper and television ads in support of their preferred candidate. Individual campaign contribution limits under the original Federal Election Campaign Act and the current limits are as follows:

independent expenditures *The purchase of goods or services in support of a candidate without any consultation or coordination with the candidate or the campaign staff.*

- Candidate or candidate's authorized committee: $1,000 per election (now $2000),[13]
- National party committee: $20,000 per year (now $25,000),
- Any other committee: $5,000 per committee; total per year: $25,000 (now $95,000 per election cycle; the per-committee amount remained the same).

Shortly after Congress convened in 2001, Congress passed the McCain-Feingold bill, which increased contribution limits for individuals to $2000 and made it illegal to contribute "soft money" to political parties for their use in party-building activities. The limit on total contributions was increased to $95,000 for the two-year election cycle. The legislation was largely opposed by Republicans, who feared undermining their success in raising funds from organized groups. With the reality of campaign finance reform passing, even the Democrats in the House began to have pause and the progress of the bill slowed.

In recent election years, approximately 10 percent of adults have given direct campaign contributions to parties or candidates, and 5 percent have given contributions to political action committees (PACs), which pool individual contributions to increase their impact (see Chapter 7).[14] Only a minuscule proportion of the population take advantage of their right to make independent contributions.

While election and campaign finance laws affect the opportunity to participate, a stronger influence is individual motivation. Motivation remains the most significant factor determining the level of participation in the political game.

10-3 Varieties of Participation

> About one-third of the American adult population can be characterized as politically apathetic or passive; in most cases, they are unaware, literally, of the political part of the world around them. About 60 percent play largely spectator roles in the political process; they watch, they cheer, they vote but they do not do battle. In the purest sense of the word, probably only one or two percent could be called gladiators.[15]

The American political process provides numerous opportunities for individuals to participate in their own governance. The pattern of participation resembles a pyramid. At the top is the small percentage of individuals who devote large amounts of time and effort to political activities. Individuals on each of the less demanding levels take part not only in the activity at that particular level but generally also in most of the even less demanding activities at the levels below (see Figure 10-1).[16] For example, if you take the initiative to work in a campaign or to contribute funds, your motivation to pay attention to politics and to vote is high. On the other end of the scale, simply informing yourself about political issues does not necessarily motivate you to vote or to work in a campaign.

10-3a Feelings about Participation

Some individuals drag themselves to the voting booth out of habit or a sense of civic duty, but most people make a judgment as to whether or not the various types of participation are an efficient use of their time and resources. As we know from Chapter 5, political efficacy is the feeling that political involvement is worth it. Over the last twenty-five years, Americans' belief that their efforts will influence governmental decisions has declined. A recent intensive study of voters indicated that

> Americans . . . do feel *impotent* when it comes to politics. They still care, yet they feel "pushed out" of virtually every area of the political process. Citizens no longer see that they have a role in politics.[17]

Such attitudes depress the willingness to get involved. Individuals with the greatest sense of efficacy translate these attitudes into higher levels of participation, while those convinced of their impotency stay on the sidelines.[18]

10-3b Costs and Benefits of Participation

Participants in politics incur a number of costs, and not everyone has the same ability to pay:

- Time is the most universal cost. Becoming informed about political issues through the media and acting on them takes time, and time spent on politics means less time for earning income or enjoying leisure. Individuals with competing demands for their time are at a disadvantage.

- Participation in politics also may involve the expenditure of money, a particularly unevenly distributed resource in American society.
- Taking stands on issues and selecting among candidates may involve social and psychological costs. Some individuals shun politics for fear of offending friends, relatives, or coworkers. The dictum to "never discuss religion or politics" tempers the ardor of potential participants. From a psychological perspective, supporting a cause or a candidate expands an individual's vulnerability, since victory or defeat in the political realm engenders a sense of personal success or failure. Some individuals avoid acting on political commitments to avoid the psychological agony of defeat.[19]

What are the benefits or rewards of political participation? Some individuals enter a political arena with specific policy goals in mind. Helping to elect candidates with policy preferences similar to their own—and communicating their policy desires to the candidates—may influence the policies pursued by government.

Frustration and fear motivate more participants than satisfaction or hope do. Individuals are often drawn into the game to protect benefits to which they have become accustomed. The threat of a specific new tax or the closing of the neighborhood school are more potent activators than are vague hopes for a better tax system or abstract issues such as school reorganization (see Box 10-4: Exit, Loyalty, or Voice). A constant motivating issue in American politics is the Social Security system. Any perceived tampering with its distribution formula or financial security is met with a loud public outcry from both individuals and organized groups. Membership in organizations such as the American Association of Retired People (AARP) increases dramatically when benefits to senior citizens seem to be in jeopardy. Another example is Speaker of the House Newt Gingrich's 1995 attempt to zero out the federal financial support for public television. That resulted in an avalanche of calls and letters to congressional offices. Public television performers as well as individual listeners felt threatened by attempts to harm "their" stations. Fear of new gun control laws motivated National Rifle Association supporters to almost double their contributions to the NRA's PAC in the month after the 1999 shooting in Columbine High School. The $567,000 contributed that month allowed the NRA to spend more than $1.5 million to successfully oppose the legislation proposed in response to the shootings.[20]

To affect the course of public policy represents only one reason for participating. Many voters pursue political activity without a specific policy goal in mind. Through the socialization process described in Chapters 5 and 9, many Americans develop a strong sense of **civic duty.** More than 90 percent of adults believe that good citizens should vote in elections, although a much lower number follow through.[21] The accompanying cartoons (Box 10-5: Cartoons on the Obligation to Participate) from high school social studies texts make the point that those not participating lose the right to complain.

civic duty *The sense of obligation to participate in the political process.*

For some individuals, joining political groups or working in campaigns is a social outlet. Rather than getting involved in religious or sports groups, these people work in political campaigns or for political causes to meet new friends.

Throughout American history, immigrant and minority groups have fought for legal citizenship and used politics as a way of increasing their social status and gaining political power. The American political game tends to be inclusive, welcoming the participation of new mainstream groups with a broad base of followers and individuals whose views are not too extreme. Nontraditional and more extreme groups, such as, skinheads, proponents of child pornography, anarchists, Nazis, and the Ku Klux Klan, have more difficulty breaking into the political game.

10-3c Spectator and Occasional Player Activities

Fewer than one third of American adults are truly indifferent to politics, ignoring and often unaware of what is occurring in the political arenas. Most citizens watch the political game and occasionally come off the benches and into the voting booths to express their support for one team or another.

Box 10–4 *Exit, Loyalty, or Voice*

No American is forced to participate in the political game. Each individual must make some basic choices about the type and level of involvement desired. Faced with dissatisfaction or a threat against cherished values, individuals in a political game have three possible choices: exit, loyalty, or voice.[a]

Assume that you are a smoker and local officials have just passed a law banning smoking in all public places. You would have three options:

1. Exit

The most extreme option is to "take one's ball and go home," exiting the game for good. It is possible to physically leave the game by moving out of the country or to another locality where smoking is allowed. But the costs are generally so great that such a form of protest is rare. If the politicians from your party back the ban, you may want to disassociate yourself from them. Exiting from a political team, such as a political party or an interest group, is more feasible, but the former participant then loses the ability to affect the course chosen by the remaining participants. Being "on the outside looking in" provides little leverage for influence during the next round.

Former senator Lowell Weicker (R-Conn.) and former Republican governor of Alaska and Secretary of the Interior Wally Hickel abandoned the Republican Party to successfully run for governor of their states as independents in the early 1990s. Their victories were largely personal and short-lived, since neither of their hand-picked independent successors was able to get elected. Senator James Jeffords, elected as a Republican, quit the Republican party and became an independent in 2001, shifting party control of the Senate to the Democrats. As long as the Democrats remained in the majority he was rewarded. With the return to Republican control of the Senate after the 2002 election, he became politically marginalized.

2. Loyalty

Some individuals stick with the political system or organization and go through the motions of involvement out of loyalty, in the hope that the situation will improve. The smoker may simply abide by the new rules and accept the fact that the legitimate authorities have spoken. Loyalists retain their position as someone "on the inside looking out" and indirectly support the game by not challenging its very legitimacy. In the extreme case, loyalty is expressed as "my country (or party), right or wrong, but my country."[b] Loyalty is a way station, where the individual sits out a round in the game, awaiting evidence that "someone will act or something will happen to improve matters."[c]

3. Voice

Some individuals directly involve themselves in the political game, voicing their dissatisfaction and attempting to set the game back on the right track. The smoker taking this approach would actively express his or her opposition and try to drum up support for a reversal of the decision. The American system provides numerous opportunities for such participation—from the relatively timid and anonymous voicing of preferences in the voting booth, to more bold and public outcries, such as writing letters or publicly protesting. Voicing dissatisfaction implies general support for continuing the game, but now the participant becomes the "someone" who directly attempts to change the outcome.

---

a. The basis for this discussion lies in Albert O. Hirschman's insightful book, *Exit, Voice and Loyalty: Responses to Decline in Firms, Organizations and States* (Cambridge, MA: Harvard University Press, 1970).

b. The quote originated with Stephen Decatur's 1816 toast, "Our country! In her intercourse with foreign nations, may she always be in the right; but our country, right or wrong." Quoted in *Respectfully Quoted* (Washington, D.C.: Library of Congress, 1989), 70.

c. Hirschman, *Exit, Voice and Loyalty,* 710.

Developing an Interest and Becoming Informed

Americans express some interest in public affairs, especially on the national level. In this age of easy access to newsmagazines, newspapers, news online, talk radio, and televised news programming, not to be exposed to political information and opinion requires serious avoidance strategies. About 43 percent of adults reported having watched each presidential debate during the 1992 presidential campaign, but only 29 percent did so in

Box 10–5 *Cartoons on the Obligation to Participate*

The cartoons that follow come from two of the best-selling high school civics textbooks. They represent the subtle goal of civics texts to encourage participation and to counteract apathy.

© Jack Bender. Courtesy of the *Waterloo Courier.*

© Frank Cammuso

1996. Over 50% of voters claimed to have watched the debates in 2004. About 40 percent of American adults claimed to have paid "quite a bit" of attention to television news about presidential campaigns. About one quarter of American adults report paying attention to public affairs "much of the time."[22] Less than one third report discussing politics with family and friends more than twice a week.[23] A number of states, such as Maryland and Ohio, have attempted to encourage intelligent citizenship by requiring students to pass a citizenship proficiency test before they can graduate from high school.

Deciding to Vote

Voting remains the top civic activity, although there has been a general decline in voting levels during the last few decades (see Figure 10-6). Levels of voting vary significantly across the national, state, and local political arenas. National elections draw more voters to the polls than do congressional midterm, state, or local elections. The growing domination of the national news media (see Chapter 6) and the higher stakes in presidential elections increase the excitement and allow easy access to information that, in turn, encourages higher voting levels in presidential contests. In nonpresidential elections, voters are often faced with more one-sided races and must work harder to gather the information necessary to make choices.

socioeconomic status (SES) A *composite measure of one's level of education, income, and occupational status. These three variables are highly, but not perfectly, correlated.*

The likelihood that a person will vote varies according to a set of social factors. An individual's **socioeconomic status (SES)** consistently shows a relationship to voting (see Box 10-6: Who Are the Public Players?). The higher one's income, education, and occu-

Box 10-6 Who Are the Public Players?

A key defining characteristic of democracy is extensive public participation. If too few people bother to play, we question the right of a political system to call itself democratic. If those who do participate are considerably different from those who do not, the democratic character of the game comes under further questioning.

In recent presidential elections, only about half the eligible voters actually cast ballots. The following graphs indicate that when we ask people if they voted, more than half the public *claim* they voted. Such responses probably reflect the public expectation that good citizens should participate through voting. We also find that the older, more educationally qualified and economically secure citizens vote. Some observers see this as quite positive, while others express concern about the degree to which other groups of citizens can have a say in the game.

There is no absolute answer as to whether enough people—or the right people—are playing the game. Politicians whose supporters tend to participate are more accepting of current levels of participation than those who tend to lose out because of nonparticipatory partisans. As long as nonparticipants have the opportunity to get involved and voluntarily decide not to, most commentators would accept the fact that democracy prevails. When electoral laws as well as inadequate skills and knowledge keep identifiable groups out of the game, it is time to evaluate the degree to which the political process has a level playing field.

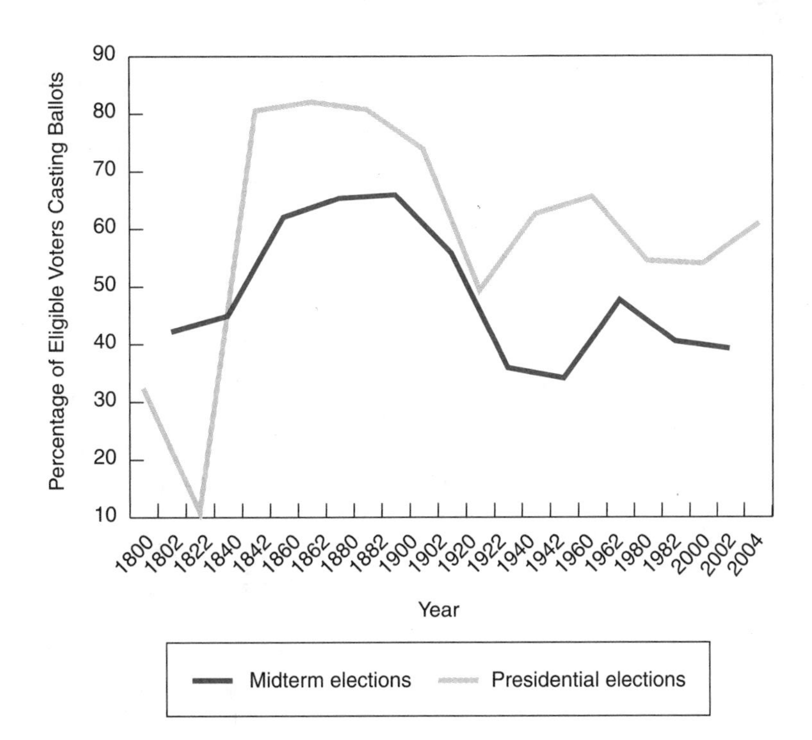

Figure 10-6
Voting Participation

Source: Harold W. Stanley and Richard G. Niemi, *Vital Statistics on American Politics, 2001–2002* (Washington, D.C., Congressional Quarterly, Inc., 2001), pp. 12–13, and LEXIS-NEXIS database, 2002. Brian Faler "Election Turnout in 2004 Was Highest Since 1968," *Washington Post,* January 15, 2005, Page A05

pation, the more likely one is to vote. The life experiences of such individuals encourage higher levels of efficacy and resources for participation. SES factors provide them with the skills and resources for participation and increase their perceived stake in the process.

Individuals who express a commitment to a political party vote more often than those who classify themselves as independents. Republicans, with their higher average SES, can generally be counted on to go to the polls much more regularly than Democrats. This is especially true in nonpresidential election years.

The general decline in voter participation worries many observers and practitioners. According to then senator Herbert Kohl (D-Wis.): "Politics may be a fun game, but the fans are leaving the stands—they are not watching any more."[24] Democracy is in peril if citizens fail to express themselves at the ballot box. In spite of increases in the socioeconomic status of many Americans, voter participation diminished in recent years. Apart from declining efficacy and voter registration hurdles, reductions in partisanship help to explain the decline in voting.[25] Many eligible voters lack a personal party label to help them simplify their voting choice. The changing demographics of the U.S. population also play a role in declining participation. Senior citizens, who often find it difficult to participate due to physical infirmities, and less participatory groups, such as Latinos, are now a larger percentage of the population than they were in the past.

Some groups in society, however, have bucked this trend of declining participation. Women once participated at a much lower level than men, but current gender differences in voter participation are insignificant. African Americans participate as much or more than they did two decades ago. This reflects a combination of changes in the rules, active registration efforts by such leaders as the Reverend Jesse Jackson, and an increased awareness of the utility of political participation. Voter participation historically has been higher among whites than African Americans, but the difference between the rate of white and African-American voter turnout began to narrow in the mid-1970s. It is not clear whether the increased turnout in 2004 was a reversal of recent trends, or the anomaly of a highly visible campaign during a time of war. In any case, turnout seems to have increased for all groups in the population relatively evenly retaining the gaps in participation rates between demographic groups (see Figure 10-6). By 1994, African-American turnout rates surpassed that of whites when demographic characteristics are controlled for (see Figures 10-7 and 10-8).

New communications technologies exhibit a mixed impact on voter participation. On the one hand, reducing the burden, or cost in time, of gathering information about candidates makes the voting choice easier. On the other, the increasing nationalization of the news media (especially television) may discourage voters from paying attention to local political concerns. The speed of communications, combined with computerized vote counting and computer-analyzed Election Day polling, has reduced the uncertainty about election outcomes (see Box 10-7: Time, Technology, and Calling the Game before It's Over).

Figure 10-7
The Voting Participation Gap between Blacks, Whites, and Latinos, 1980–2000

*Latino figures are limited to citizens. Voting participation of all Latinos is considerably lower (for example, 27.5% versus 45% in 2000).

**Reported turnout is somewhat higher than actual turnout.

Source: U.S. Bureau of the Census, *Statistical Abstract of the U.S.*; Harold W. Stanley and Richard G. Niemi, *Vital Statistics on American Politics, 2001-2002,* Washington, D.C.: Congressional Quarterly Inc., 2001, p. 17; and M. Margaret Conway, *Political Participation in the United States* (Washington, D.C.: Congressional Quarterly, Inc., 2000), p. 33. Recent data available at http://www.census.gov/prod/2002pubs/p20-542.pdf.

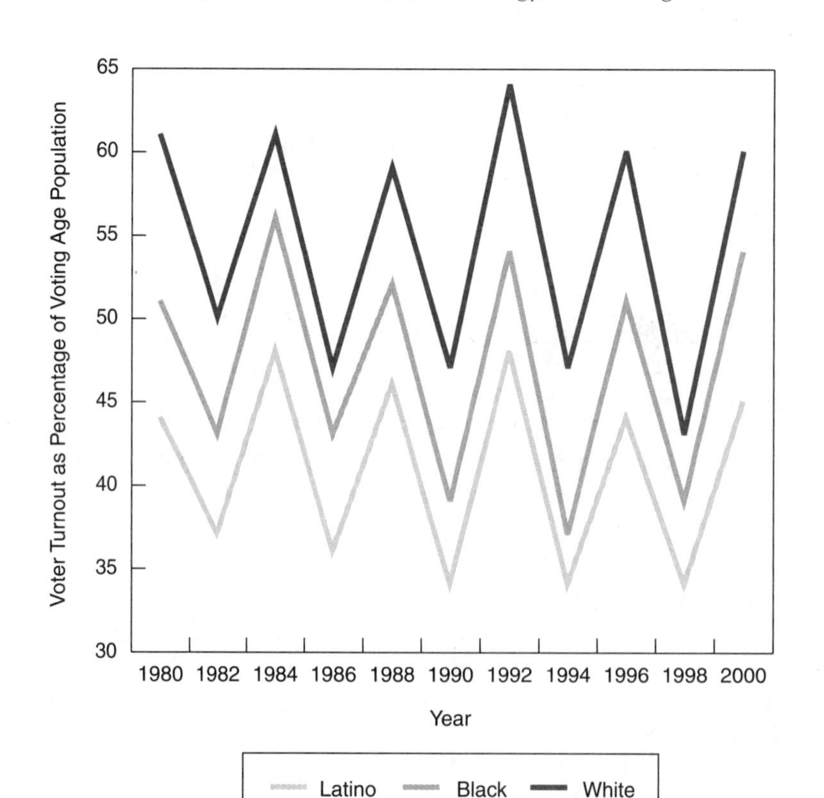

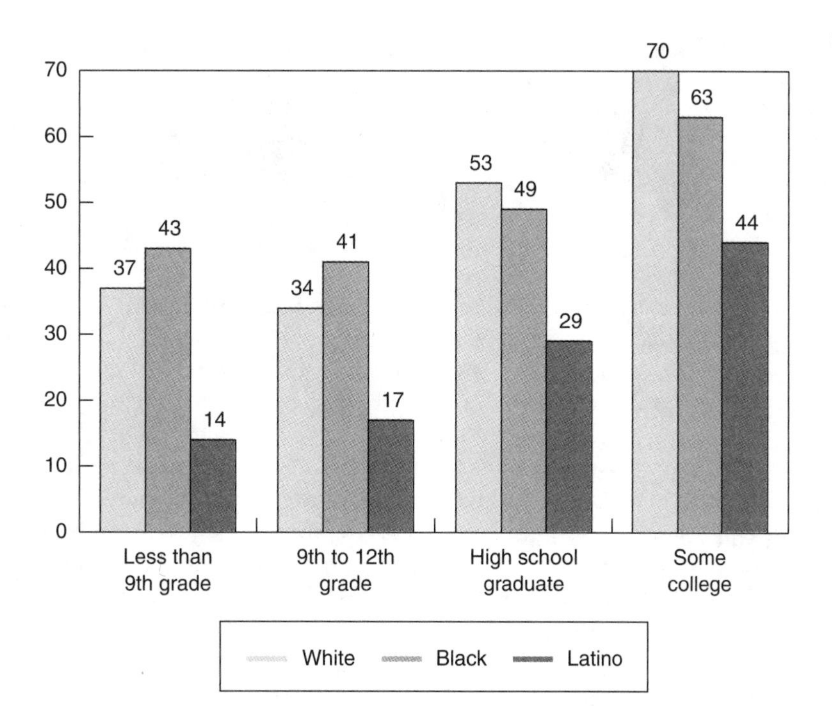

Figure 10-8
Reported Voting Participation by Race and Education, 2000 Election

Source: U.S. Census Bureau, Current Population Report 20-542; www.census.gov.

Box 10-7 *Time, Technology, and Calling the Game before It's Over*

Determining the winner of the presidential election once took a matter of days or weeks. The development of a national electronic media, the availability of Election Day exit polls, and the utilization of computerized projection models turned election night into a contest between the television networks. "Who can project the winner the earliest?" is the name of that game. The networks established a computerized News Election Service (NES) in 1964. It receives telephone reports from thousands of precincts around the nation and gives results much more quickly than election officials can. Each network also conducts polls of voters in selected precincts as they leave the polling place. The result of feeding all of this data into a computer is that networks can usually predict winners and losers well before all the votes are in.

In response to the concern, the networks did agree not to project the winner in any state using exit polls until that state's polls had closed.[a] In 1992 the networks showed self-restraint by not projecting a winner until after the polls on the West Coast had closed, but competition led to lowering the level of restraint in subsequent elections.

The 2000 and 2002 elections seriously brought such predictions into question. With the 2000 election seeming to hinge on Florida, the networks were quick to use exit polls to call the state for Gore a few minutes before the polls closed in most of Florida and over an hour before they closed in the western part of the state. With the closeness of the race, no one will ever know the degree to which some Florida voters were discouraged from voting. Later in the evening the networks reversed themselves two more times.

After reversing themselves twice about the winner of the 2000 presidential election, NBC anchor Tom Brokaw declared, "We don't just have egg on our face—we have an omelet."[b]

The best word for network election night coverage in 2004 was "timid," with news anchors failing to declare state-by-state winners even when the results were in.

In 2004, anomalies in the NES computers led to an intentional shutdown of the system, leaving the network news anchors scrambling for something to say.

The issue goes beyond one of valid predictions, since projections of a winner in one race may affect voter turnout and the outcome of other races. Given time zone differences, presidential races have often been called well before the polls on the West Coast

continued

Box 10-7 *Time, Technology, and Calling the Game before It's Over*

—Continued

were closed (see the Preview in Chapter 9). A number of defeated West Coast politicians have protested, claiming the prediction discouraged voters who might have supported the losing presidential candidate and members of his party; these citizens lost the desire to vote when the presidential results (using early exit polls) were announced. The years with clearly one-sided presidential elections do result in lower voting participation in the West.[c] Failure to vote is assumed to cost the party that loses the presidency votes for state and local offices too, but the evidence is not clear.

After each presidential election, a congressional discussion ensues concerning legislative remedies such as uniform national polling hours or prohibitions against media projections. Although the impact of such projections is not absolutely clear, a variety of solutions have been proposed. Changing the opening and closing times for the polls in different regions would solve the problem, but keeping the East Coast polls open late and closing the West Coast polls early would be a hardship for voters. Washington State passed a law prohibiting exit polls in its precincts, but the law was declared invalid by the courts.

While the debate as to the actual effect of projections continues, the communications, videographics, polling, and analysis technologies march on. Quicker, more accurate, and more visually powerful images of election results are available each year—even though many of the voters have not yet "spoken."

a. For a fuller discussion, see Stephen J. Wayne, *The Road to the White House* (New York: St. Martin's Press, 1992), 250–55.
b. *Washington Post,* November 9, 2000, p. A1.
c. *Ibid.*

Considerable evidence indicates that eligible voters are most likely to vote in close races in which the outcome is unknown. Election Day projections appear to discourage voting among a small but significant proportion of the electorate.[26] While the decline in turnout due to projections does not affect the presidential contest, it may well determine both the turnout and the outcome of congressional and local races being held at the same time.

10-3d Serious Player Activities

As political scientists see it, "the realities of the political arena require more for de facto democracy than merely going to the polls occasionally."[27] A wide variety of other political duties make up the full range of participation options available to U.S. citizens.

Contributing and Contacting

About 10 percent of Americans put their money where their mouths are by helping to finance candidates or parties. Contributors tend to be more interested in politics, better educated, and wealthier.[28] Contemporary fund-raising techniques, using computerized mailing lists (see Chapter 11), expand the base of individuals who contribute small amounts to candidates and to interest groups especially.

The dictum "write your congressperson" exemplifies the American commitment to a government that is open and responsive to the public interest.[29] Less than 20 percent of Americans have ever entered the political game by directly contacting any government official. Individuals contact political officials for two basic reasons: to express opinions on policy issues or to secure help with a personal problem they are having with the government (see Box 10-8: The Automated Pen Pal). As Congress and the nation become more "wired," the options for two-way communication have increased through email and teleconferencing.

Government officials refer to requests for help with personal problems as casework. Casework includes everything from finding a missing Social Security check to fixing a pothole. Individuals from lower economic groups, who need government assistance most, are

Box 10-8 The Automated Pen Pal

Congressional offices receive thousands of letters each week and have turned to technology to deal with them. All incoming mail is logged in on a computerized mail-handling system for tracking and adding the writer's name and interests to the member's mailing list that is used to send targeted communications about issues. The information is also often shared with the campaign committee for use in the next election cycle. Incoming letters are coded in terms of what the person wrote about and any personal or political information that can be gleaned.

Incoming mail is sorted by staff into two piles. **Casework** mail, dealing with requests for intervention in the bureaucracy or help with such things as tickets for tours of the White House, are handled by a special staff of caseworkers. Most offices only respond to mail from their state or district. Letters from outside the district are bucked to the office of the relevant congressman or senator.

Mail relating to pending policy issues is forwarded to legislative assistants for evaluation and response. Most offices keep weekly mail counts on hot issues. They report constituents' views to members of Congress, indicating whether the communication was a telegram, petition, form letter, or personal letter. Most offices pay more attention to "cold sweat" letters. These are detailed personal communications in which constituents clearly identify the issue at hand and explain how they think particular legislative initiatives will affect themselves. Members and their staffs assume that constituents willing to write such detailed personal letters have more concern about the issue, which will affect the writers' voting decisions at the next election.

While virtually all congressional offices use email and have websites, incoming email correspondence is seldom viewed as requiring enough effort to be taken very seriously. To find your congressperson's website, go to www.house.gov or www.senate.gov.

Most communications are responded to with a stock set of computerized paragraphs. The member's position is outlined, along with the areas of agreement with the writer. There is usually a promise to keep the letter writer's views in mind when the final vote on the legislation occurs.

It is unreasonable to expect that most letters will change a member's mind on an issue, but there is plenty of evidence that on receiving a large number of letters on one side of an issue, most members will think through the position advocated.

Participation through writing a member of Congress seldom stops with one interchange of letters. Members and their staffs recognize that those who are interested enough to correspond need to be cultivated. Members send out newsletters as well as targeted letters to those who have taken the first step to make themselves heard.

only slightly more likely than others to contact officials with their personal casework problems. The mismatch between need and behavior stems from the knowledge, confidence, and skills possessed by individuals with higher SES; they understand how to make casework contacts on behalf of their personal needs.[30] Those writing on issues (rather than casework) tend to be better educated and have a fuller grasp of the information surrounding the issues.[31] This clearly follows the typical pattern of government that overrepresents individuals with high SES and extensive knowledge about the political process.

casework *The individualized services done by elected and appointed officials to help solve the problems of constituents.*

10-4 Nontraditional and Emerging Activities

Especially on the local level, Americans have come to expect an open decision-making process. Some city and county council meetings draw large and often vocal audiences of local residents. An increasing number of public bodies, from city councils and courts to the U.S. Congress, have opened their sessions to television cameras. This has expanded the public gallery and provided more opportunities for serious spectators to monitor the game. The availability of such information allows a small but well-informed segment of the population to intervene and play the game in those arenas.

While American political history from the Revolution onward has been marked by both peaceful and violent protests, the frequency and potency of such strategies increased during the latter half of the twentieth century. During the 1960s, public demonstrations and **civil disobedience** were participation strategies for such causes as civil rights and the opposition to the conflict in Vietnam. This willful breaking of the law became a useful strategy for drawing public attention to public policy that was based on questionable morality or legitimacy. More recently, such strategies have been brought to bear on both sides of such issues as abortion, the environment, nuclear power, and lower taxes. Civil disobedience is neither a liberal nor a conservative strategy. It is simply an outlet for frustration when other strategies fail.

civil disobedience *Acts of lawbreaking (such as refusing to pay taxes or demonstrating without a permit) designed to draw attention to laws or public policy of questionable morality, legitimacy, or constitutionality.*

New mass communication technologies have expanded the power of public protest. Vocal and/or violent action draws television cameras much more readily than detailed and reasoned analysis. Protests in one isolated community become part of the national consciousness through the electronic media.

Traditionally, political activity has resulted from people using face-to-face communication to discover their common interest and plan strategy. The Internet offers the interesting potential of creating "virtual communities" unbound by geographic constraints. Individuals from around the country—or around the world—can now find each other on the Net, share ideas, and use the technology to communicate with government officials. Although some examples of successful activation on the Net exist, it is not yet clear whether virtual communities will have the staying power supporting long-term political involvement, and the degree to which elected officials will take email communications seriously remains to be seen.

Political participation is normally considered a voluntary activity, but this is not always the case. Some individuals are required to participate in governmental programs either as a legal duty or as a condition for receiving some other benefit. Serving on a jury, answering the call for military service, or compulsory "volunteering" for a civic program are all forms of participation (see Box 10-9: A Different Kind of Public Service).

In recent years, some observers have bemoaned the lack of civic-mindedness of Americans and the tendency toward serving one's more selfish personal interests. But according to one source:

> Americans have not turned their backs on civic duty. Citizens do engage in specific areas of public life—mostly in their neighborhoods and communities—but only when they believe they can make a difference and bring about change.[32]

Contemporary citizens have shown a new interest in reestablishing a commitment to the community and retaking some responsibility for public services. They have created recycling centers, opened volunteer homeless shelters and soup kitchens, and developed neighborhood crime-watch programs. Volunteer groups such as Habitat for Humanity depend on direct civic action to help solve homelessness and other problems. Rather than relying on government entirely, these Americans have undertaken such **coproduction** activities to assist public agencies and their community.[33] The massive outpouring of volunteer efforts and contributions after devastating hurricanes, floods in the Midwest and fires in California, and disasters abroad indicate that volunteerism is not dead.

coproduction *Residents taking on activities often performed only by government, if at all, to enhance the level and quality of community services.*

10-5 Intensive Player Activities: Joining Political Groups and Participating in Campaigns

Here are the words of two past presidents on the subject of acting directly in the political arena:

> It is not the critic who counts; not the man who points out how the strong man stumbles, or where the doer of good deeds could have done better. The credit belongs to the man who is actually in the arena . . . who at best knows in the end the triumph of high achievement, and who at worst, if he fails, at least fails while daring greatly, so that his place shall never be with those cold and timid souls who know neither victory nor defeat. (Theodore Roosevelt)[34]

Box 10–9 A Different Kind of Public Service

Young Americans have been called on in the past to give public service to the nation. During the first half of the 1960s, when a strong national spirit of idealism swept the country, many youths voluntarily joined the Peace Corps to help people in developing countries or VISTA (Volunteers in Service to America) to aid poor and disadvantaged individuals within the United States.

The outbreak and escalation of armed conflict in Vietnam caused the government to reintroduce a mandatory form of public service for young males: the military draft. In the early 1970s, the draft was replaced with an all-volunteer military. Thirty-one percent of adults favor a program requiring all 18-year-olds to perform two years of mandatory service such as enlisting in the military or working at limited pay for a community organization.[a] Not surprisingly, the support for mandatory service is lowest among those most affected, the 18- to 24-year-olds.

Some school districts require community service as a condition for graduation, while other programs have suggested making community service a necessity for eligibility for higher education grants and loans. The popularity of such plans has actually waned since their first public discussion in the 1970s, when 87 percent of adults approved. By 1996, only 66 percent of adults favored such a plan, with most support coming from women (76 percent), well-educated individuals (77 percent), Democrats (71 percent), and middle-aged adults (72 percent).[b]

The habit of volunteerism is more deeply imbedded in young college students than are traditional forms of political participation. While only 32 percent reported they had registered to vote, nearly two-thirds had recently volunteered in a community service activity and 89 percent had done so in high school.[c]

---

a. Rasmussen Research poll of 1,000 adults, 1996, LEXIS-NEXIS database; The Gallup Poll, "National Service: Voluntary Service Favored; Support of Mandatory Service Wanes," The Gallup Report, December 1987, 20–21.

b. Gallup Poll of 1,539 adults in April 1978 and Gallup poll of 1,329 adults in May 1996, LEXIS- NEXIS database.

c. *A National Survey of College Undergraduates*, Harvard University, Institute of Politics, October 2002, available at www.iop, harvard/2002survey.pdf

> What is your responsibility? It's to join me in the arena—not in the peanut gallery—in the arena—and fight, and roll up your sleeves, and be willing to make a mistake now and then, be willing to put your shoulder to the wheel, be willing to engage. (Bill Clinton)[35]

Only a small proportion of the U.S. population stays in the political arena out of continuing and intensive commitment. Americans are group-oriented (see Chapter 7), but definitions of political groups are elusive. Organizations themselves move in and out of the political arena. Many organizations—primarily religious, educational, or social—on occasion expend some of their efforts to influence politics. It is much easier to organize groups representing the interests of better-educated and wealthier individuals than those appealing to the interests of lower SES segments of the population.

Only highly motivated individuals work in political campaigns. Most campaign organizations welcome volunteers with open arms, although new campaign technologies, especially at the national level, reduce the need for such traditional volunteer activities as addressing envelopes and contacting voters. Campaign workers tend to be drawn into politics because of intensive commitment to the issues or ideology, but many stay in the process because of the social outlet it provides.

Individual motivation remains the key factor in determining who will play the political game and how intensively they will participate. Few formal rules either deny or guarantee access to the playing field. Lack of education may result in individuals not having the knowledge and attitudes conducive to participation. Limited time, skills, or finances may discourage individuals from political participation but do not automatically deal them out of the opportunity to participate.

The rosters of participants and nonparticipants are not etched in stone. Since democratic politics involves amassing supporters, changes in the mix of players affect how the political game is played. The increasing political involvement of gay males and lesbians, women, anti-abortion activists, and individuals against current tax policy has changed the issues with which elected and appointed officials must deal.

10-6 Political Participation as a Strategy

The focus of most political attention tends to be on outcomes such as election results or the passage of legislation. We often attempt to explain the outcomes by looking at preceding events. What we tend to forget is that the outcomes of many political games are rigged rather early by the nature of the competing players.

Changing the Pool of Voters

Recognizing the importance of controlling who plays the game, interested groups and individuals attempt to capitalize on the rules and motivations that affect participation. Each American political party is intensely interested in increasing the number of voters who will support its team. Since the individuals most likely to vote Democratic are also those who are less likely to register and vote, the Democratic Party, not surprisingly, pushes for rules that ease registration requirements and facilitate voting, such as mail-in and motor-voter registration, more polling places, and longer voting hours.

Two opposing strategies are used to activate potential voters. Until very recently, the majority of voters with a party affiliation thought of themselves as Democrats rather than Republicans (see Chapter 8). Politicians worked under the assumption that Democrats would win most elections if equal numbers of self-identified Democrats and self-identified Republicans bothered to vote. Democrats assumed that increasing registration and voter participation would help Democratic candidates. They thus tended to emphasize broad-pattern shotgun strategies of voter activation, making a general pitch at all individuals about the importance of voting.

Republicans, on the other hand, saw the advantages of a more targeted approach. Likely Republican voters were identified through polls or door-to-door solicitation, and then Republican organizers attempted to activate their party supporters—without encouraging Democratic participation. Democratic candidates expend a higher proportion of their campaign resources on Election Day get-out-the-vote drives than their Republican counterparts do. Republican candidates realize that most Republican voters belong to the socioeconomic groups that will vote anyway[36] (see Figure 10-9).

Absentee ballots traditionally come from traveling business persons, military personnel, and senior citizens, resulting in a significant Republican advantage. The closeness of the 2000 presidential race in Florida drew detailed attention to absentee voter activation strategies. Extensive and seemingly effective Republican strategies to contact and activate absentee voters drew a court challenge, while Democratic election officials' patterns of rejecting absentee ballots in some Florida counties led to Republican complaints.

With large expenditures for new voting equipment, redesign of ballots, and more careful attention to procedures, the 2004 voting was carried out with little controversy. No systematic disenfranchisement emerged.

2004 brought a new twist, with an increasing number of states loosening requirements for absentee balloting and allowing early voting. In order to reduce the disenfranchisement of voters because of clerical errors or their confusion as to where to vote, Congress mandated provisional ballots which could be checked for eligibility before being counted. With the outcome hinging on Ohio and its over 150,000 provisional ballots, John Kerry did not concede to George W. Bush until over 12 hours after the regular ballots had been counted.

10-6a Changing the Sources of Campaign Contributions

The policy battles over campaign finance rules reflect partisan considerations as to who should be encouraged to participate. Republicans, who find it easier to raise money from individuals and corporations, seek to retain the right to raise as much money as possible

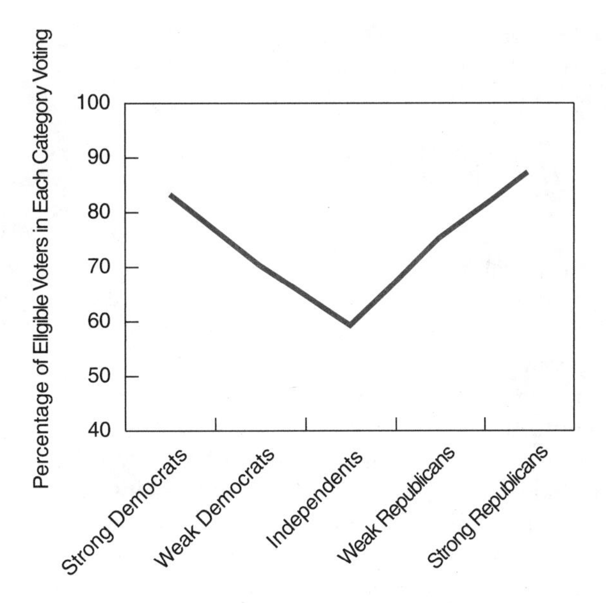

Figure 10-9
Partisan Differences in Voter Turnout (2000 Presidential Election)

With Republicans narrowing the party identification gap with Democrats, we may see the two parties revising their voter activation strategies. In any case, Democrats will have to work even harder to get their supporters to the polls if they hope to remain competitive.

Source: William Flanigan and Nancy Zingale, *Political Behavior of the American Electorate* (Washington, D.C.: Congressional Quarterly, Inc., 2002), p. 82.

from these sources. Democrats have depended on PAC contributions to a greater degree because of the tendency of PACs to support incumbents. Therefore, Democrats have fought to either retain PAC funding or to exchange limitations on PACs for public financing of campaigns with low expenditure limits. As the PACs began to favor the new Republican majorities in the House and Senate, Republicans warmed to the desirability of PACs. Financing campaigns from the public treasury would relieve Democrats of the burden of fund-raising. Keeping the limits low is seen as a way of protecting the large number of Democratic incumbents. Republicans argue that—at least in the congressional arena—Democratic proposals for public funding would close the political game to Republican challengers. Historically, Republicans needed to spend more money to compete with better-known incumbents. Again, since the Republicans currently have more incumbents, their views may well change.

10-6b Expanding Participation in the Policy Process

Encouraging participation goes well beyond the campaign arena or the voting booth. Individuals are asked to attend city council meetings, to sign petitions, or to contact government officials. These activities raise the officials' awareness of issues and give them the basis for estimating public support. Shifts in public support, especially among active political participants, often precede policy changes (as shown in the opening of the chapter). Active and vocal groups often gain influence that is out of proportion to their numbers. For example, public support for the war in Vietnam waned more slowly than it did in Congress. Members of Congress reacted to that small group of antiwar individuals who were willing to take action on their beliefs. Officials work on the assumption that individuals who write letters, join groups, and take part in the more demanding forms of participation around an issue will certainly use that issue as a basis for their vote.

Teledemocracy: Harnessing New Technology to Expand Participation

By the early 1980s, political scientists foresaw the development of cyberdemocracy (see Chapter 1). It was argued that "with the help of teledemocratic processes, public opinion will become the law of the land."[37]

Since the founding of the Republic, proponents of broader public participation have been stopped by the logistical problems of actively involving the millions of people in America. The New England town meeting, with its opportunity for everyone to have an equal say in local decisions, stood until recently as an unreachable goal for anything but

Box 10–10 *Democracy*

The Video or Computer Game

The technology of two-way citizen involvement in the political game is probably the least of the problems in initiating teledemocracy. Television sets could easily be outfitted with simple voting terminals to transmit voting preferences by telephone lines to a central computer. In France, the government provided more than five million free computer terminals and screens to support its Minitel Network, allowing French citizens to gather information, shop, and communicate with more than 12,000 services from their homes.[a] By 1990, close to 40 percent of American homes already had Nintendo units, which have the capability of adaptation for two-way communication via telephone lines.[b]

The television networks could be required to carry policy debates before the voting terminals are opened for a policy decision. At their discretion, viewers could order background analyses and further information for presentation on their television screen. Secret identification numbers or even electronic fingerprint verification could assure that only eligible voters participate and that each person votes only once. Costs might simply be passed on to advertisers and to companies that wish to use the system for advertising or home shopping.

In the age of the Internet, a computer-based discussion of issues and automated voting is clearly feasible from a technological perspective, but it may be problematic in other ways. Almost two-thirds of Americans are connected to the Internet from home or the office,[c] but even at such a high percentage, the pool of potential participants would not mirror the U.S. population, since technology tends to be in the hands of those who are better educated and who can afford it. Access codes could be used to identify legitimate voters, but the opportunities for rigging decisions would be considerable. Perhaps most importantly, "the new technology is fast, and democratic deliberation at its best is slow and thoughtful . . . [it] is about defending your views in front of a group, not registering your biases from home."[d]

The national "town meeting," with everyone able to participate from their living rooms, is clearly a technological possibility. The real question is whether it is politically possible or socially desirable.

a. Mimi Tompkins, "A Second French Revolution," *U.S. News & World Report*, May 7, 1990, 56.
b. "Nintendo: Wham! Zap! You Just Made a Million," *Economist*, August 18, 1990, 60.
c. Jonathan Alter, "The Couch Potato Vote," *Newsweek*, February 27, 1995, 34. See also *The America Online/Roper Starch Worldwide Adult 2000 Cyberstudy* and "America's Online Pursuits," December 2003, at http://www.pewinternet.org.
d. Alter.

the most local decisions. The technologies now exist for national town meetings and direct citizen involvement (see Box 10-10: Democracy). For example, periodic televised debates on the key issues could be followed by direct voting by telephone or by an inexpensive voting keyboard attached to television sets.[38] Ross Perot, a pioneer in the computer industry, interjected the idea of teledemocracy into the 1992 campaign when he suggested that he would "give the government back to the people" by making some decisions through the results of the process of national electronic town meetings.

Technology holds both promise and pitfalls for democracy. Carry out the task in Time Out 10-2: A Technology-Determined Playing Field to help you understand the issues.[39]

The Meaning of Participation Levels

Participation means little in isolation. If the general level of participation falls too low, it could signal that the mass of individuals have lost confidence in the political game. The future of American democracy would be threatened. On the other hand, moderate or even very low levels of participation could indicate that most people feel that things are going pretty well.[40] The most obvious signal is when events lead to dramatic swings in the traditional levels of voter participation. A rapid drop in participation levels indi-

Time Out 10-2

A Technology-Determined Playing Field

Assume that the technological problems could be worked out for a national system of teledemocracy. Twice a month, a two-hour television debate or a computer-mediated discussion would be held on a controversial issue. Citizens would be asked to vote by telephone or through the Internet. A majority vote would determine the policy adopted.

Even the technologically possible may not be politically desirable. Before looking at the Answer to Time Out 10-2, make two lists. One should outline the advantages and the disadvantages of teledemocracy.

cates that something has reduced citizens' trust in the system or in the candidates, while a rapid increase signals that voters are turning to politics for an answer to an important problem.

10-7 Winners and Losers in the Participation Game

> If voting makes elites attend to citizens' opinions, its fundamental value to democracy is firmly established. A ballot may be . . . a very blunt instrument for tying elites' behavior to ordinary people's wishes. But just as the proverbial Missouri mule's attention could be captured by applying a two-by-four to his forehead, so also have elections occasionally been successful in refocusing public officials' attention.[41]

Political participation has implications well beyond determining who is elected and what policies are pursued by government. The most straightforward conclusion is that participants generally tend to win and nonparticipants generally tend to lose in the American political process. Both elected and appointed officials most often respond to those groups and individuals making their wishes known through the ballot box and by the other means already discussed.

In politics we often say, "the squeaky wheel gets the grease." In this day and age of preventive maintenance, that phrase has less practical meaning. We tend to grease all the wheels on our car regularly even before they begin to squeak. In the early days of wagon travel, however, grease was too expensive to administer before an obvious need. The alert driver would listen for the sounds from each wheel that signaled a potential problem and then grease that wheel alone.

Politics in America often follows this more old-fashioned maintenance pattern. Political leaders tend to react more than they act. If no one complains about a problem, it is assumed that no problem exists. Active participation on an issue alerts decision makers that something needs to be done. Stacks of letters, the formation of new interest groups, public demonstrations, and other forms of participation represent the "squeaks" that must be greased. "Squeaking" is, thus, a very powerful political strategy in a democracy.

The American Revolution was fought over **representation.** The word *representation* means more if we think of its semantic roots. It involves the process of "re-presenting" (presenting for a second time) the interests of individuals. Before the American Revolution, British political leaders argued that this process occurred indirectly, through the process of **virtual representation.** Leaders looked out for the interests of the colonists even if the colonists could not send direct representatives to the British Parliament. British politicians viewed the colonists as clients rather than as constituents or citizens. The colonists rightly rejected the principle of virtual representation. They recognized that without the potential for stepping directly into the political game to choose leaders and to make their wishes known their interests could be forgotten. The colonists' experiences continually remind us that participation is a necessary condition for self-government.

representation *The process of taking into account the interests of others (often constituents) and of fighting for those interests.*

virtual representation *The view that a government official can look out for the interests of a specified group of individuals even though the individuals have no control over the official's actions.*

Answer to Time Out 10-2

Experts on teledemocracy have indicated these possible consequences.

Advantages	Disadvantages
• Increased participation • More direct representation • Broad range of citizens involved • Increased citizen satisfaction • Reduced power of politicians	• Superficial responses (less time for reflection) • Power goes to those setting the agenda of issues to vote on • Potential for voter manipulation through biased presentation of issues • Little room for compromise (ideas not tested and tempered in the crucible of face-to-face discussion) • Danger of excluding the views of those who lack the technology

Conclusion

No political system will ever engender total participation. Discriminatory rules and, most importantly, differing levels of motivation and interest reduce overall participation in the political game. Participants have characteristics and outlooks different from those of nonparticipants. Some current elected and appointed players—and the policies they promote—would be in considerable trouble if the number and nature of public players changed.

The relatively unlimited potential that individuals have for participation forces decision makers to be responsive. Politicians recognize that opponents can win the next political game by activating a previously uninvolved group of individuals. Elections tend to be more important for what happens *because* of them than for what happens *at* them. Knowing that dissatisfied voters could rise up on Election Day or afterward to show their displeasure keeps officials more mindful of public desires.

In the next chapter we will look at elections, a key arena for public participation. Our emphasis will be on the emergence of candidates and the strategies they use to channel political participation and choice in ways designed to give them electoral victory.

Key Terms

casework
civic duty
civil disobedience
clients
complete citizens
constituents
coproduction
enfranchisement
independent expenditures
representation
socioeconomic status (SES)
suffrage
victims
virtual representation

Practice Quiz

1. What term describes people who are occasionally linked to political institutions and who play a limited role in the political game?
a. Citizens
b. Constituents
c. Clients
d. Victims

2. What prevents an Internal Revenue Service clerk from serving as the campaign chairman for a Democratic candidate for Congress?
a. Personal ideology
b. The FECA
c. The Hatch Act
d. Nothing, except for personal time and interest

3. What increases the likelihood that someone will vote?
a. High socioeconomic status
b. Low socioeconomic status
c. Low efficacy barriers
d. Unemployment and the need for government services

4. Casework refers to
a. the collection of political favors by candidates seeking to pass a bill.
b. efforts by political officials and their staffs to handle constituent problems related to government.
c. efforts to increase voter turnout.
d. decisions of federal judges concerning constitutional issues.

5. The proportion of the population that contributes financially to political campaigns is
a. about 10%.
b. about 20%.
c. about 40%.
d. over 50%.

6. Women in the United States were given the vote in national elections in
a. 1789.
b. 1830.
c. 1885.
d. 1920.

7. Political efficacy refers to feelings that
a. a two-party system is efficient for America.
b. political involvement is worth the effort.
c. politics is often corrupt.
d. political action is ineffectual.

8. Individuals are allowed to give _____ directly to a candidate in each stage (primary and general) of a federal election.
a. $50
b. $1000
c. $2000
d. any amount they wish

9. Which of the following has NOT been used to limit voting participation?
a. Residency requirements
b. Literacy tests
c. Poll taxes
d. Intelligence tests

10. Approximately _____ percent of eligible voters cast ballots in American presidential elections.
a. 50
b. 60
c. 70
d. 80

You can find the correct answers to these questions by taking the quiz and then submitting your answers in the Online Edition. The program will automatically score your submission. Where you miss a question, the program will provide the correct answer, a rationale for the answer, and the section number in the chapter where the topic is discussed.

Further Reading

For a comprehensive text on political participation, see M. Margaret Conway, *Political Participation in the United States* (Washington, D.C: Congressional Quarterly, Inc., 2000).

For a regularly updated text emphasizing election behavior and participation, read William H. Flanigan and Nancy H. Zingale, *Political Behavior of the American Electorate* (Washington, D.C.: Congressional Quarterly, Inc., 1999).

The classic study comparing participation between elections with voting behavior is Sidney Verba and Norman Nie, *Participation in America: Political Democracy and Social Equality* (New York: Harper and Row, 1972).

Martin P. Wattenberg's *Where Have All the Voters Gone?* (Cambridge, MA: Harvard University Press, 2002) and Thomas Patterson's *The Vanishing Voter* (New York: Knopf, 2002) analyze the roots of declining participation in elections. Robert Putnam's *Bowling Alone* (New York: Simon and Schuster, 2000), looks at the broad decline in "social capital" in America. *Cyberage Politics 101: Mobility, Technology and Democracy* (Stephen Frantzich, Lanham, MD: Rowman and Littlefield, 2002) uses the 2000 election data to test the impact of modern social trends and technology on political involvement.

Endnotes

1. Karyn Barker, "Hill's Paper Tiger Has a Voracious Appetite," *Washington Post*, May 8, 1983, A1.
2. John Schwartz, "On-Line Obscenity Bills Gains in Senate," *Washington Post*, March 24, 1995, A24 and http://www.cnn.com/2004/LAW/06/29/scotus.online.porn.ap/.
3. See Eugene Lewis, *American Politics in a Bureaucratic Age: Citizens, Constituents, Clients and Victims* (Lanham, MD.: University Press of America, 1988).
4. Kay Lehman Schlozman and John T. Tierney, *Organized Interests and American Democracy* (New York: Harper and Row, 1986), 122.
5. M. Margaret Conway, *Political Participation in the United States* (Washington, D.C.: Congressional Quarterly Press, 2000), 111.
6. Conway, *Political Participation*, 115.
7. "On the Political Sidelines: The Non-electorate," *Washington Post*, November 4, 1990, A1.
8. Conway, *Political Participation*, 120. For a discussion of the battle to secure motor-voter registration, see Stephen Frantzich, *Citizen Democracy: Political Activists in a Cynical Age* (Lanham, MD: Rowman and Littlefield, 1999).
9. *Congressional Record*, 28 September 1990, S-14233.
10. Conway, *Political Participation*, 117.
11. F. Christopher Arterton, *Communications, Technology, and Political Campaigns in 1982: Assessing the Implications* (Washington, D.C.: Roosevelt Center, 1983).

12. Mark DiCamillo, "Absentee Voters Are Reshaping Politics in California," *Public Affairs Report* 32, no. 3 (May), 1.
13. Primary, special, and general elections are considered separate elections under the law, and individuals can contribute $1,000 to each.
14. William H. Flanigan and Nancy H. Zingale, *Political Behavior of the American Electorate* (Boston, MA: Allyn and Bacon, 1994), 13.
15. Lester Milbrath quoted in W. Russell Neuman, *The Paradox of Mass Politics* (Cambridge, MA: Harvard University Press, 1986), 510.
16. See Sidney Verba and Norman H. Nie, *Participation in America: Political Democracy and Social Equality* (New York: Harper and Row, 1972), 27–110. Verba and Nie point out that levels of participation are not totally cumulative. Some individuals specialize in more difficult modes of participation without bothering to involve themselves in the less demanding modes.
17. Kettering Foundation, *Citizens and Politics: A View from Main Street America* (Dayton, OH: Kettering Foundation, 1990).
18. Flanigan and Zingale, 47.
19. See F. Christopher Arterton, *Teledemocracy: Can Technology Protect Democracy?* (Newbury Park, CA.: Sage, 1987), 51.
20. David Hawpe, "The Changing Politics of Guns," *The Courier-Journal*, September 12, 1999, 3d; "House does NRA Bidding on Guns," editorial, *Seattle Post-Intelligencer*, June 20, 1999, C2.
21. Flanigan and Zingale, 38.
22. Princeton Survey Research Associates poll of 985 adults, September 1999 LEXIS-NEXIS database; Charles Prysby and Carmine Scavo, *Voting Behavior: The 1992 Election* (Washington, D.C.: The American Political Science Association, 1993), 59.
23. Conway, *Political Participation*, 87; Prysby and Scavo, *Voting Behavior*, 60.
24. Herbert Kohl, *Congressional Record*, June 13, 1991, S-77010.
25. See Paul R. Abramson and John H. Aldrich, "The Decline of Electoral Participation in America," *American Political Science Review* 76 (1982), 502–21.
26. Conway, *Political Participation*, 95.
27. Robert Struble, Jr., and Z. W. Jahre, "Rotation in Office," *PS: Political Science and Politics*, March 1991, 35.
28. Frank J. Sorauf, *Money in American Elections* (Glenview, IL: Scott, Foresman/Little, Brown, 1988), 47–410.
29. See Stephen Frantzich, *Write Your Congressman: Constituent Communications and Representation* (New York: Praeger, 1986).
30. See Elaine B. Sharp, *Urban Politics and Administration* (New York: Longman, 1990), 84–85.
31. See Verba and Nie, *Participation in America*, 118; and Diana E. Yiannakis, "The Grateful Electorate: Casework and Congressional Elections," *American Journal of Political Science* 25 (August 1979), 574–75.
32. Kettering Foundation, *Citizens and Politics*, 6.
33. See Stephen Percy, "Citizen Participation in the Coproduction of Urban Services," *Urban Affairs Quarterly* 19, no. 4 (June 1984): 431–46; and Charles Levine, "Citizenship and Service Delivery: The Promise of Coproduction," *Public Administration Review* 44 (March 1984), 178–86.
34. Theodore Roosevelt, "Citizenship in a Republic," in *The Strenuous Life*, vol. 13 of *The Works of Theodore Roosevelt* (New York: Charles Scribner's Sons, 1926), 510.
35. Bill Clinton, LEXIS-NEXIS transcript from the Democratic Leadership Council Gala, 6 December 1994.
36. Stephen A. Salmore and Barbara G. Salmore, *Candidates, Parties, and Campaigns: Electoral Politics in America* (Washington, D.C.: Congressional Quarterly Press, 1985), 190.
37. Political scientist Theodore Becker quoted in Michael Malbin, "Teledemocracy and Its Discontents," *Public Opinion* 5 (June/July 1982), 510.
38. See F. Christopher Arterton, *Teledemocracy* (Newbury Park, CA: Sage, 1987); Benjamin Barber, *Strong Democracy: Participatory Politics for a New Age* (Berkeley, CA: University of California Press, 1984); and Ted Becker, "Teledemocracy: Bringing Power Back to People," *The Futurist* (December 1981), 6–9.
39. For discussions of the advantages and disadvantages of teledemocracy and cyberdemocracy see Michael Malbin, "Teledemocracy and Its Discontents," *Public Opinion* 5 (June/July 1982): 57–58; Ted Becker, "Teledemocracy: Bringing Power Back to the People," *The Futurist* (December 1981): 6–9; Jeffrey Abramson et al., *The Electronic Commonwealth: The Impact of the New Media Technologies on Democratic Politics* (New York: Basic Books, 1988); and Jonathan Alter, "The Couch Potato Vote," *Newsweek*, February 27, 1995, 34.
40. See Conway, *Political Participation* 2; and Bernard L. Berelson, Paul F. Lazarsfeld, and William N. McPhee, *Voting: A Study of Opinion Formation in a Presidential Campaign* (Chicago, IL: The University of Chicago Press, 1954), Chapter 14.
41. Stephen Earl Bennett and David Resnick, "The Implications of Nonvoting for Democracy in the United States," *American Journal of Political Science*, vol. 34 (August 1990): 771-802.

11

Campaigns and Elections: Determining the Individual Winners and Losers

Key Points

- **Legal factors affecting the strategies and outcomes of elections.**
- **The nature and impact of the primary election process.**
- **The rise of candidate-centered campaigns.**
- **Differing motivations and strategic options of the campaign process.**
- **How new technologies have changed campaigns.**
- **Causes and implications of electoral success.**

Preview: Hitting the Electoral Bull's Eye

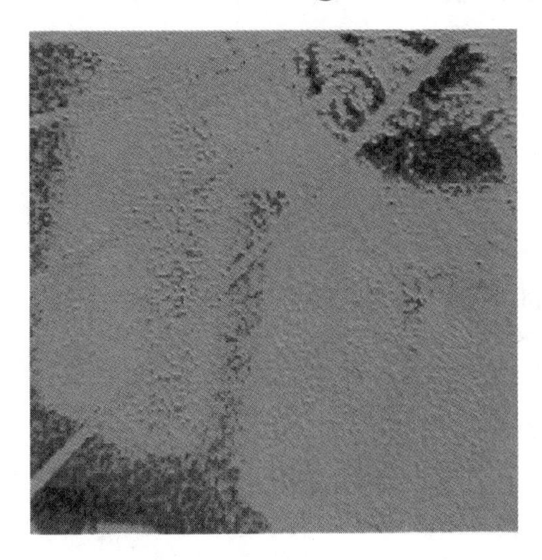

Congressman Peter Smith (R-Vt.) had seemingly done all the right things in office. He had acted as a moderate representative of his relatively conservative Vermont constituency. He was, however, blindsided by an unlikely candidate, a hot issue, and the influx of a large amount of money.

In 1988, supported by the National Rifle Association, he had gone on to oppose most gun control. His tolerance was tested, though, when it came to a vote on banning assault weapons, which he felt had nothing to do with the interests of law-abiding citizens and hunters.

Waiting in the wings was the self-proclaimed socialist mayor of Burlington, Vermont, Bernie Sanders. Bypassing Sanders' liberal views on social issues—which contradict the more conservative views *of most NRA members—the NRA fixated on the single issue of Sanders' opposition to gun control. The NRA proceeded to give Sanders the maximum direct contribution of $10,000 from its political action committee. They then took advantage of the campaign contribution law and independently waged an ad campaign costing more than $15,000 to defeat Smith. In a small state such as Vermont—and especially in an era of limited party loyalty—the NRA effort was very effective. The well-known Sanders went on to become the only independent in the 102nd and 103rd Congresses. He chalked up an almost perfect liberal voting record—except for his opposition to gun control.*

In the game of politics, where today's friend can become tomorrow's enemy, the story does not end there. When a ban on assault weapons was voted on during the 103rd Congress, Sanders supported it. In the 1994 election the NRA tried to repeat its strategy of four years earlier. The group urged voters to again ignore party identification and the advantages of retaining an incumbent in office. Voters were encouraged to switch to a newcomer who could be trusted on the single issue of gun control. The NRA poured thousands of dollars into the campaign to help the Republican leader of the state senate, John Carroll, upset incumbent Bernie Sanders. Capitalizing on a hot local issue, a well-known challenger, and the influx of money, the NRA again hoped to use the election process to change the players in Congress. This time Bernie Sanders withstood the Republican tide and became one of the few NRA targets to win reelection. With the advantages of incumbency, Sanders solidified his political base and had little trouble gaining reelection in subsequent elections.

legitimacy *Public perception that an individual is the rightful occupant of a position of power and/or the feeling that the political process deserves public respect.*

Few American political games result in clearer winners and losers than do elections. The rules of the selection game determine acceptable strategies for choosing legitimate players. Formal elections are the mechanism for leadership selection and for granting **legitimacy** to the winners in all systems that have democratic aspirations. Electoral systems vary, however, in how they reflect the democratic ideals of full and informed citizen participation in free and open contests.

In this chapter we outline the rules under which American campaigns are conducted. We then look at the perspectives and behavior of both the institutional and individual players as they participate in the electoral process. Building on our previous discussions of the creation and operations of mediating institutions, we will look in detail at how they behave in the electoral arena. Considerable attention will be paid to the strategies of the electoral game and to the factors that determine winners and losers.

11-1 The Electoral Rules

It is difficult to generalize about election laws in America because, as we have seen, the Founders left the determination of most election procedures to the states (see Chapter 2). The Constitution contains few general guidelines for elections other than those establishing the unique presidential selection system. Although procedures still vary considerably among the states, decades of practice and accommodation have narrowed the differences.

11-1a Some Structural Givens

While election outcomes generally are explained in terms of issues and candidates that are specific to one campaign, a number of the key factors are fixed. Structural factors such as the following define the playing field and often determine the outcome:

- regularly timed elections
- single-member districts
- the boundaries of electoral districts
- the electoral college

Candidate George W. Bush campaigns for reelection.
White House photo

Regularly Timed Elections

No active political observer in the United States would have difficulty telling a foreign visitor the date of an upcoming presidential election. Most foreign visitors, however, would not understand the American pattern of predetermining election dates and limiting elected officials to fixed terms in office. In **parliamentary systems,** which dominate the international political landscape, prime ministers *call* elections—either when their popularity is high or when they have lost the confidence of the legislative branch that selected them. While parliamentary systems do impose an overall limit on the amount of time in which a government can rule, strategic considerations result in irregular terms of office.

parliamentary system *A government system in which voters select the legislature (parliament), which in turn elects the chief executive (prime minister) from its ranks. Most democratic systems in the world use a parliamentary system rather than its chief alternative, the presidential system.*

The British version of a parliamentary system is fairly typical. The parties run candidates in each district, with the national party having considerable control over who can run under the party label. The party winning a majority of seats chooses its leader as prime minister; he or she then forms a government. Once elected, a government has five years in which it can rule before being required to call an election. In most cases, elections are called earlier, either when the party in power is quite popular or when they have lost the support of their majority in Parliament on a key vote. Margaret Thatcher, for example, called a new election in 1982 after the popular Falkland Islands War, and her party won a stunning victory. On the other hand, prime ministers losing an important vote are said to have suffered a "vote of no confidence" and are forced to call new elections. In 1992 Prime Minister John Major, faced with the impending five-year limit and a severe recession, called a new election before the economy could get worse. His surprise victory gained him credit for his sense of timing. In parliamentary systems, good or bad policy choices can lead to a particular electoral schedule. The Conservative Party under John Major was not so fortunate in 1997 when the Labor Party gained the majority and Tony Blair became prime minister.

In preset, or fixed, elections, such as we have in the United States, the electoral calendar tends to lead to somewhat predictable policy choices. That is, politicians take the electoral calendar into account when planning policy. Tax cuts and increases in popular government programs are regular features of election years.[1] Unpopular policy choices, such as tax increases and program cutbacks, occur just as regularly in nonelection years. During the 1988 presidential campaign, candidate George H. Bush made a commitment of "read my lips, no new taxes." By 1990, it was clear that new taxes were necessary, and President George H. Bush reluctantly changed his mind. The president struck a deal with

Democratic leaders to consider increased taxes only if they stood by him to shoulder the blame and to neutralize the partisan advantage. In the long run, President George H. Bush's reelection chances were dampened in 1992 when he was attacked for not living up to his tax-cut pledge. Candidates from both parties began discussing tax cuts and the popular theme of more limited government early in both the 1996 and 2000 election campaigns. In the 2000 contest, it was not an issue of whether there would be a tax cut, but rather its size and who would get it. In 2004, George W. Bush promised to continue his general tax cuts, while John Kerry promised to rescind tax cuts for wealthier Americans, but maintain them for those with less income.

Regularly timed elections level the playing field because they allow all opponents to establish campaign strategies years in advance. Ronald Reagan began preparing for 1980 almost immediately after his defeat by Gerald Ford in the 1976 Republican nomination battle. Neither George H. Bush nor Bill Clinton needed to wonder about the date of the 1992 election when planning their strategies. And soon after the Republican congressional sweep in 1994, numerous Republican candidates began to position themselves for the presidential election that they knew would occur in 1996. The 2000 presidential election campaign began almost before the 1998 congressional campaigns were underway.

Single-Member Districts

A pervasive characteristic of the American system of representative government is the desire to link elected officials legally and politically to a set of voters in a specific geographic constituency. Most U.S. elections allow voters to choose only one representative to each political body (see Chapter 8). This single-member district system makes the representative feel responsible to the citizens he or she represents. It also encourages the citizens to monitor their representative's actions. Each American voter chooses only one representative in the House of Representatives and generally selects only one state legislator, one county council member, and one member of the school board. The process of drawing district lines has become one of the major battles in establishing power (see Time Out 11-1: Marking the Lines).

Drawing the Lines

Electoral contests begin well before the first lawn sign is pounded in and before the first television ad is run. Pre-election strategies often determine the outcome. The importance of redistricting is reflected in the following comments from political analysts:

> Redistricting is the political equivalent of moving the left-field fence for a right-handed hitter. By changing the boundaries, redistricting helps some, hurts others—and leaves just about everyone else scrambling.[2]

> [Redistricting] combines musical chairs with a hangman's noose. Unlike the children's version of these games, the losers in this redistricting-spawned contest will face grievous consequences: the loss of their seats in Congress.[3]

> Redistricting in the 1990s will not be just a donkey vs. elephant game of partisan checkers. It will be an intricate contest of multidimensional political chess in which party interests are by no means paramount.[4]

reapportionment *The allocation of legislative seats to each state after a census.*

redistricting *The process of redrawing constituency boundaries for electoral districts.*

Candidates run *for* office by running *in* a specific district. This is seen most clearly in elections for the U.S House of Representatives. Every ten years, after the national census of the population is calculated, Congress applies a **reapportionment** formula based on the new population figures to determine the number of seats assigned to each state. State legislatures then create **redistricting** legislation to define the actual district lines and send it to their governors for approval. The political party in control of a state legislature often proposes plans that give its party the most favorable districts.

Until the middle of the twentieth century, the number of members in the House of Representatives continued to increase in order to reflect new states and a growing population. When states added districts, they often showed relatively little concern for the equality of population in the new districts. When the size of the House was permanently set by legislation for the 1912 elections, reapportionment became a zero-sum game. A seat gained by one state (because of population growth) had to be taken from another state.

Time Out 11-1

Marking the Lines

Assume that you are a state legislator striving to benefit your party as much as possible by redistricting your state into three districts. The courts will expect your districts to be equal in population, compact, and contiguous (that is, all segments of the district must be attached to each other). Draw three plans for the hypothetical simplified state that follows. One districting plan should benefit Republicans, one should benefit Democrats, and one should be the fairest plan possible.

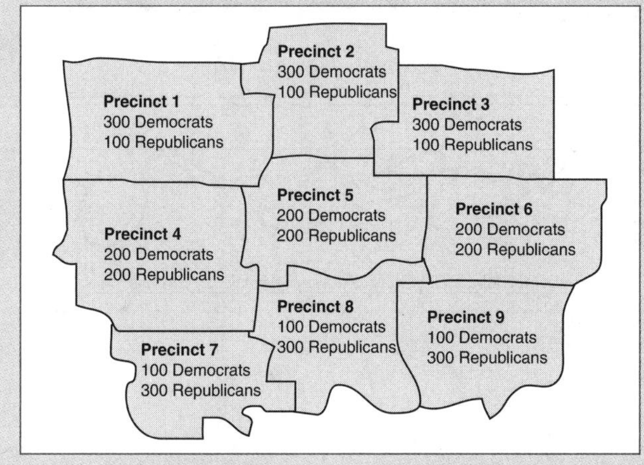

Figure 1A
The Nine Precincts and the Partisan Division Among all Eligible Voters in Each Precinct

Each new district must include three touching precincts (that is, precincts with shared geographical boundaries).

Source: Stephen E. Frantzich and Steven E. Shier, *Congress: Games and Strategies* (Cincinnati, OH: Atomic Dog Publishing, 2003), 44–46.

Increased pressure to treat all voters fairly emerged during the 1960s, when a series of court cases, beginning with ***Baker v. Carr,*** asserted that wide disparities in district populations denied voters in the large population districts "equal protection of the laws." Individual voters from large population districts argued that their votes were worth less than those of individuals from small population districts.

These **one-person, one-vote** decisions spawned extensive redistricting activity for all elective bodies as states were required to create districts of equal population. Rural areas lost representation to urban areas and particularly to the burgeoning suburbs. Striving for equal population in congressional districts required cutting across other social and political boundaries, thus creating districts with increasingly heterogeneous populations. Political parties and legislatures in many states now use sophisticated computer programs to draw alternative plans that provide population equality and varying types of political advantages.

Despite requirements for population equality, **gerrymandering** is still quite common (see Figure 11-1a). In 1986 the Supreme Court ruled in *Davis v. Bandemer* that partisan gerrymandering is unconstitutional, but it did not provide clear guidelines as to when "the electoral system is arranged in such a manner that will consistently degrade a voter's or a group of voters' influence on the political system as a whole."[5]

Redistricting is a very political process that is full of conflict. New players enter the redistricting game when state legislatures and governors fail to come to a decision. In some states blue-ribbon commissions are called in. More often, the courts serve as referees drawing the new plans. After years of Republican control of the presidency and, therefore, the right to appoint federal judges, Republican plans did quite well when the courts intervened.

The very act of redistricting can have an indirect impact on elections. The anticipation of having to campaign in a newly drawn district was partially responsible for the record number of retirements from the House of Representatives in 1992. A number of other districts became more competitive, encouraging higher-quality candidates from the party or group that once had little likelihood of success.

Redistricting subsequent to the 1990 U.S. Census took a new twist, which is difficult to call anything but intentional gerrymandering. The revision of the Voting Rights Act (see Chapter 4) required states to look out for the interests of racial minorities by providing them with winnable districts whenever possible. This led to a rather strange coalition of the Republican Party and minority groups both supporting plans that concentrated

Baker v. Carr *A 1962 Supreme Court case affirming the Court's jurisdiction over redistricting and affirming the lack of one-man, one-vote as a violation of the equal protection clause of the 14th Amendment.*

one-person, one-vote *The attempt to make all citizens' votes count the same by creating districts of roughly equal population size.*

gerrymandering *The process of designing political districts for partisan or group advantage. The term derives from an elongated set of districts created by Governor Elbridge Gerry of Massachusetts, which eighteenth-century political cartoonist Elkanah Tinsdale drew as a salamander and dubbed a "Gerrymander."*

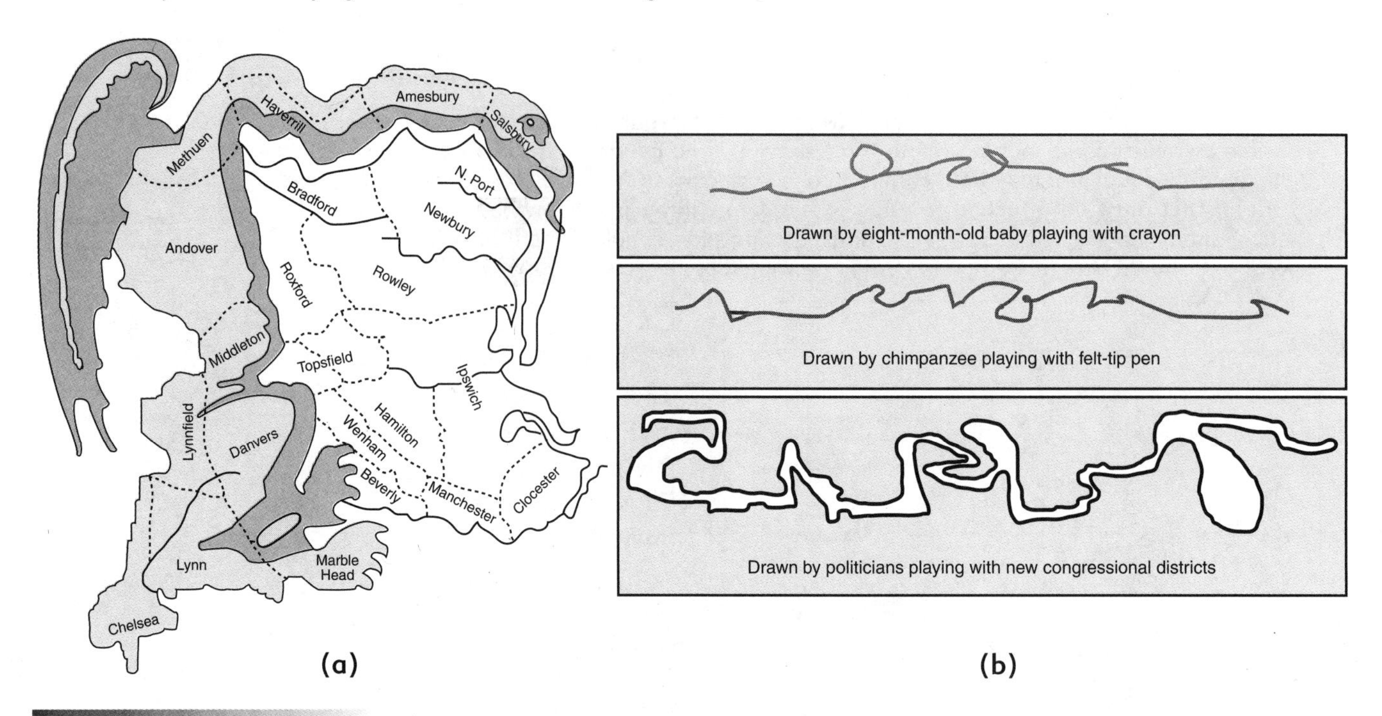

Figure 11-1
Gerrymandering

Redistricting has often drawn the attention of cartoonists.
(a) The original Tinsdale cartoon of an early partisan drawing of the lines in Massachusetts under the guidance of Governor Elbridge Gerry led to dubbing such partisan maneuvering "gerrymandering."
(b) Contemporary cartoonist's view of gerrymandering.

Sources: (a) Stephen E. Frantzich and Steven E. Shier, *Congress: Games and Strategies* (Cincinnati, OH: Atomic Dog Publishing, 2003), 47. (b) Copyright Don Wright, *The Palm Beach Post*. Reprinted with permission.

majority-minority district *An electoral district designed so that an ethnic minority has a numerical majority.*

minorities—making the racial minority a numerical majority in those districts. The minorities favored concentration to improve their chances of winning districts. The Republicans saw the advantage of concentrating minorities, who generally vote for Democrats, thereby giving Republicans a better chance of winning the remaining districts.

A number of these **majority-minority districts** resulted in the election of minority members of Congress in 1992 and 1994. All seventeen African Americans elected to Congress from southern states in 1994 came from majority-black districts. In the 1994 election, Republicans did particularly well in the southern districts surrounding the majority-minority districts. They capitalized on the weakening of Democratic strength in those areas. Observers estimate that due to redistricting the Democrats lost as many as ten southern seats in 1994 on top of the five seats that they felt were lost in 1992. High-quality Republican candidates, who had been discouraged in the past by the Democratic advantage, came out in large numbers to contest the more competitive districts.[6]

The battle over majority-minority districts shifted to the courts when white voters in the South challenged the constitutionality of the odd-shaped districts and their racial basis. In 1993 the Supreme Court sent the case back to the lower courts, questioning districts based on race (*Reno v. Shaw*). The 1994 election was conducted before the cases had been reheard. In late 1994 the Supreme Court agreed to hear *U.S. v. Hays*, a broad ruling by a three-judge panel in Louisiana that outlaws "race-conscious decision-making" in the drawing of district lines. The case pitted a number of longtime political allies against one another. Local Democrats who brought the case decried the impact of majority-minority districts on Democratic Party chances and the contribution of such districts to racial polarization. The Clinton administration and many civil rights groups supporting majority-minority districts argued that such districts give minorities "a realistic opportunity to elect a candidate of their choice," and that a negative ruling would "roll back just about all the progress that has been made since 1965 in electing more blacks."[7] In 1995, by a vote of 5 to 4, the Supreme Court made its first ruling on majority-minority districts. While the issue is far from closed (see Chapter 17), the Court asserted that race could not be the "predominant factor" when establishing congressional district lines. Refinements and specific applications of this ruling will keep the courts and state legislatures busy for years. Most of the minority members initially winning in majority-minority districts weathered redistricting plans that placed them in districts without a minority racial majority. The combination of incumbent advantages and moderating racial prejudice has led to a more diverse racial composition of American elected officials. In 2004, the redistricting battle in Texas became so filled with conflict that Democratic legislators left the state in an attempt to block a redistricting plan that favored the Republicans.

Answer to Time Out 11-1

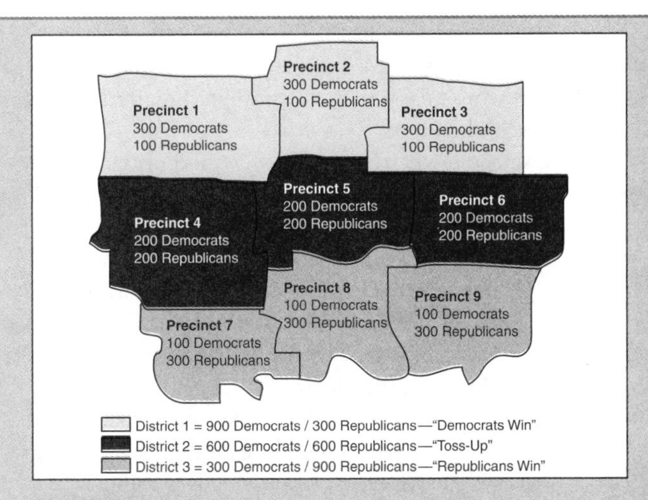

Figure 1B

Plan 1: "A Competitive Plan"

Assuming that everyone voted, Plan 1 would lead to one strong Republican district, one strong Democratic district, and a toss-up district. This would not be bad for the Republicans, but they could do better.

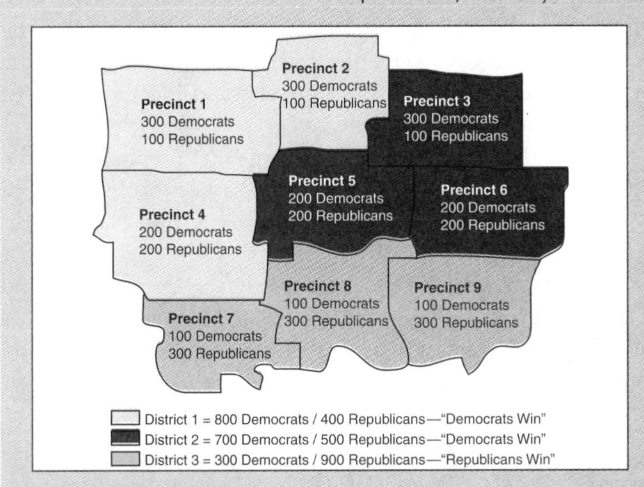

Figure 1C

Plan 2: "A Democratic Party Plan"

Assuming that everyone voted, Plan 2 would be most beneficial to the Democrats, leading to two strong Democratic districts and one strong Republican district. This is not a good Republican plan.

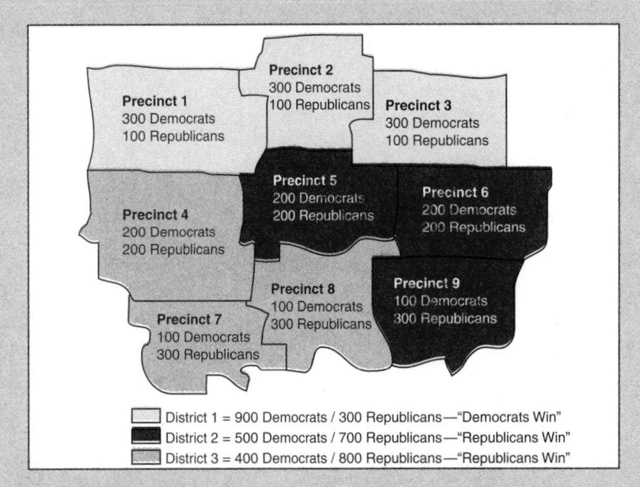

Figure 1D

Plan 3: "A Republican Party Plan"

Assuming that everyone voted, Plan 3 would be the most beneficial to Republicans, leading to two strong Republican districts and one strong Democratic district. If your plan looks like this one, you are ready to sign on as a Republican strategist.

Source: Stephen E. Frantzich and Steven E. Shier, *Congress: Games and Strategies* (Cincinnati, OH: Atomic Dog Publishing, 2003), 44–46.

The Electoral College

Unique and confusing rules underlie the election of the U.S. president. While Americans watch the election returns on election night and focus on the total votes for each candidate, the official results of the presidential election are based on votes cast by relatively anonymous electors.

Each state is assigned a number of electors in the electoral college that is equal to the number of members of the House of Representatives from that state plus the state's two senators (see Chapters 2 and 8). Each presidential candidate nominates a slate of electors from among the party faithful. The candidate who receives the most votes in a state generally wins the entire slate of electors from that state. This winner-take-all rule means that voters whose candidate fails to win a majority in the state have no representatives in the electoral college.

The selected electors are morally and politically (but not legally) bound to vote for the candidate to whom they are pledged. The Founders initially assumed that the electors would come from the more responsible segments of the population and would use independent judgment in voting for a presidential candidate. Although there are occasionally **faithless electors,** the vast majority report to their state capitals in December and cast their votes for the candidate whose slate they represented. Tallies from each state are then forwarded to Congress by the state governor and officially counted in January. If no one has a majority in the electoral college, the House of Representatives selects a president, but this has happened only three times (in 1800, 1824, and 1876).

faithless elector *A member of the electoral college who is selected as a supporter of one candidate but who votes for another.*

Criticism of the electoral college emerges from a number of quarters. On the surface, the system is blatantly undemocratic. It is possible to win the popular vote for president and lose in the electoral college (winning many states by very small margins and losing others by large margins). Nevertheless, since 1888 no one has been elected president without a majority of the two-party popular vote until 2000. Faithless electors could swing the election, but historically they have not been numerous enough to do so. The lack of a realistic threat that might lead to an undemocratic outcome dampens any reform, although the anticipated success of third-party candidate Governor George Wallace of Alabama in 1968 fostered a temporary flurry of reform efforts. The hesitancy to carry out significant reform was evident after the 2000 election. Even with Vice President Al Gore winning the popular vote but losing to George W. Bush in the Electoral College there was not widespread movement for change. By returning to the normal pattern of the same candidate winning both the popular and Electoral College vote in 2004, any remaining pressure for reform was released.

Players have learned to live with the current electoral system and to capitalize on the advantages it provides for specific strategies. The winner-take-all aspect of the electoral college strengthens the two major parties by making the victory of a third-party candidate highly unlikely.

The Electoral College system affects where presidential candidates decide to expend their campaign effort. Since the winner-take-all rule applies, strategically wise candidates write off states they are sure to win and those they are sure to lose and concentrate instead on those states where campaigning might make a difference (see Box 11-1: The Bigger They Are, the Harder They Are Fought For).

11-1b Rules for Getting on the Ballot

The election process involves two stages: the selection of candidates (*nominations*) and making the final choice among the nominees. Until the turn of the century, political par-

Box 11–1 The Bigger They Are, the Harder They Are Fought For

From a policy perspective, the Electoral College system encourages candidates to pay special attention to the highly populated, industrial, and politically competitive states whose large number of electoral votes are in doubt. The system thus tends to make presidential candidates more sensitive to the interests of urban areas, with their concentrations of minorities, and to suburban areas, with their large concentrations of voters. The outmoded Electoral College system remains because of an odd coalition of conservatives who say, "If it ain't broke, don't fix it," and liberals who appreciate the special attention that presidential candidates pay to urban and minority problems because of the potential for it causing them to profit from candidates trying to garner necessary votes.

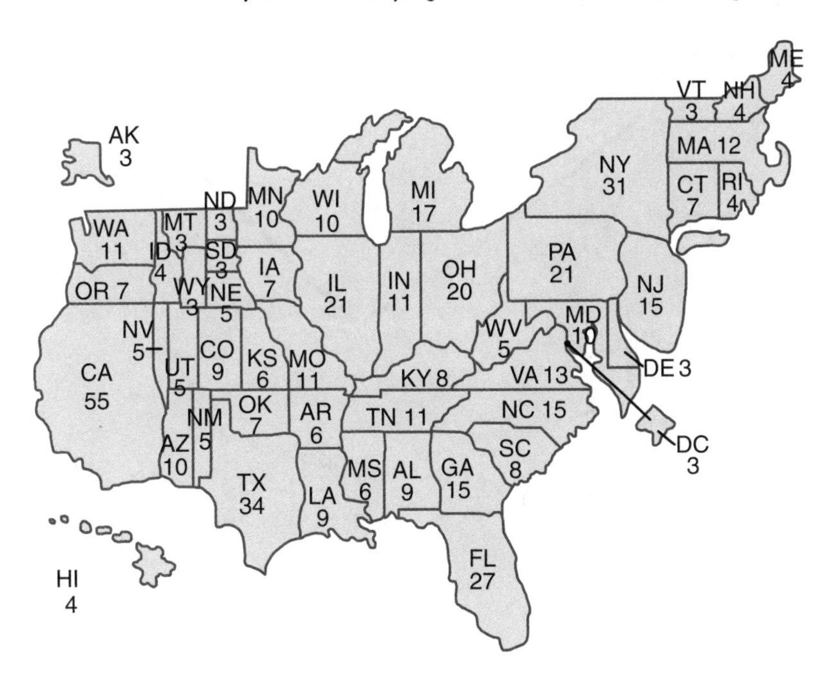

Figure 11-2
Electoral Votes per State for the 2004 Election

This map of the United States demonstrates the relative importance of large-population states such as California and New York in the Electoral College.

Source: Peverill Squire, et al., *Dynamics of Democracy* (Cincinnati, OH: Atomic Dog Publishing, 2001), 430.

ties controlled access to the ballot through the nomination of candidates at party meetings (caucuses or conventions). Rules for getting on the ballot clearly worked against third-party and independent candidates (see Chapter 8).

Dissatisfaction with party corruption and control led to the spread of primary elections for most offices and a broadening of participation in the nomination process. As explained in Chapter 8, a primary is a pre-election selection process in which voters determine the official nominees of the party. Primaries are necessary if more than one candidate files for a particular office. We must distinguish between primaries that determine the nominee and the presidential nominating process, in which the primary is only one step.

"Garden-Variety" Primaries and Alternative Routes to the Ballot

Potential nominees for most elective offices in the United States file for the primary election of their party and conduct a campaign among the primary electorate. In most states, primaries are considered intramural contests among voters with a commitment to a particular party rather than part of the state election process.

The thirty-eight states with **closed primaries** require voters to register publicly their party affiliation prior to voting in a primary. Thus, only those registered as Republicans can vote in the Republican primary and only those registered as Democrats can vote in the Democratic primary. Individuals registering as independents in these states forego the right to help select party nominees. Closed primaries generally have low turnout and tend to draw the most active and best-educated partisans[8] (see Figure 11-3).

closed primary *Nomination elections involving only affiliates of the party.*

Nine states (Hawaii, Idaho, Michigan, Minnesota, Montana, North Dakota, Utah, Vermont, and Wisconsin) hold pure **open primaries.** Unencumbered by party registration, voters simply show up on primary day and vote in either their own party's primary or in another one. (Independents can vote in either primary.) While turnout for most of these open primaries is light, a more politically varied group of voters may be drawn to a particularly exciting open primary contest. In another ten states (Alabama, Arkansas, Georgia, Illinois, Indiana, Mississippi, Ohio, South Carolina, Tennessee, Texas, and Virginia), primary voters do not have to declare their party until they pick up a ballot on Election Day.

open primary *Nomination elections allowing voters to choose on Election Day in which party's nomination process they wish to participate.*

Twenty-five states use a closed primary in which voters must register by party and can only vote in that party's primary. In about half of those states, Independents are allowed to vote in the primary of the party of their choice.

The remaining four states (Alaska, California, Louisiana, and Washington) have **blanket primaries,** in which voters have the right to skip back and forth between the parties when voting for nominees. These primaries encourage strategies that emphasize

blanket primary *Nomination elections in some states that allow voters to shift among parties for different offices.*

Figure 11-3
Primary Turnout and Voter Partisanship

Source: Flanigan and Zingale, *Political Behavior of the American Electorate*, Congressional Quarterly, Inc., 10th ed., 2002, p. 82.

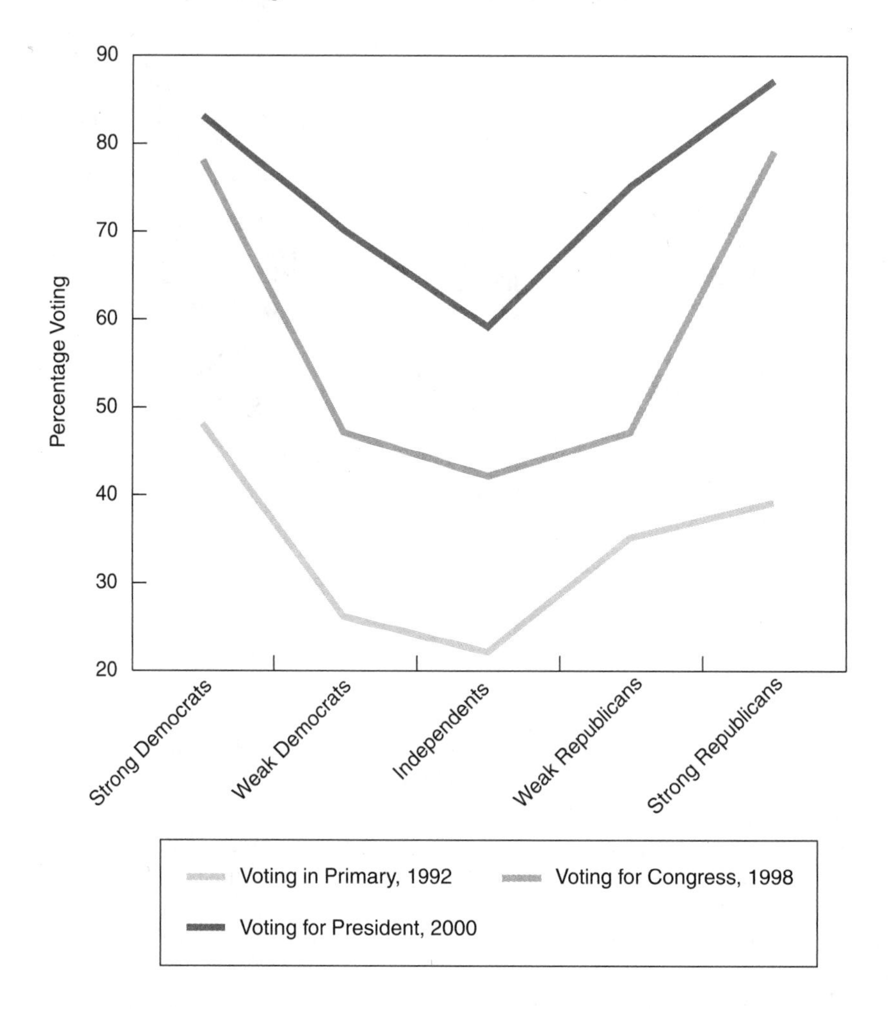

crossing party lines and focusing on candidates' personal characteristics. In 2003, the 9th Federal Circuit Court of Appeals declared the Washington state blanket primary unconstitutional and the Supreme Court refused to review the decision, signaling that blanket primaries would be outlawed in any state. In 2004 Washington state voters approved a new version of the blanket primary setting the stage for future court battles.

For the most recent information on state voting laws, go to: http://www.fec.gov/votregis/primaryvoting.htm.

Twelve states allow or require the use of party conventions as an alternative method of making nominations for some state offices[9] (see Table 11-1). Convention delegates are generally chosen in a succession of party caucuses that begin at the local level and move up through the congressional district and eventually to the state level. Typically, state and local party conventions include only the most active and generally ideologically extreme partisans.

Organization and concerted effort by like-minded groups of players pay off more directly in conventions than in primaries. In recent years, "new right" anti-abortion and pro-family groups have found it relatively easy to dominate Republican caucuses and conventions. More extreme liberal groups, who are pro-choice on abortion, favor women's rights, and support the causes of lesbians and gay males, have focused their efforts on Democratic gatherings. This domination of party conventions by single-issue groups often hampers the party nominee in the general election, when a broader political appeal is necessary.

Since nomination contests involve divisiveness and the expenditure of resources, parties often discourage some potential candidates from entering the race. In some states, the parties use conventions for preprimary endorsements to narrow the field. More informally, potential candidates may be asked to step aside or be encouraged to run for some other office. In such cases, party organizations must exhibit great care not to put too

Table 11-1

Nomination Procedures for State Officials

All Statewide Candidates Selected by Primary	Some Statewide Candidates Selected by Convention	Statewide Candidates Selected by Convention
Alaska	Indiana	Alabama*
Arizona	Iowa**	Colorado*
California	Michigan	Connecticut**
Delaware	South Dakota	Georgia
Florida		New York
Hawaii		South Carolina
Idaho		Utah
Illinois		Virginia
Kansas		
Kentucky		
Louisiana		
Maine		
Maryland		
Massachusetts		
Minnesota		
Mississippi		
Missouri		
Montana		
Nebraska		
New Hampshire		
New Jersey		
New Mexico		
North Carolina		
North Dakota		
Ohio		
Oklahoma		
Oregon		
Pennsylvania		
Rhode Island		
Tennessee		
Texas		
Vermont		
Washington		
Wisconsin		
Wyoming		

*Party committee can opt for using a state convention. **Convention used unless there is a challenger receiving a specified percentage of the convention vote (15–35 percent).

Source: Book of the States, 1998–99 (Lexington, KY: Council of State Governments, 1998), 159–60.

much pressure on a candidate for fear that, if he or she does win the nomination, hard feelings will follow.

The Special Case of Presidential Nominations

Presidential nomination procedures are unique among American electoral contests and different from the selection of chief executive candidates in other democracies:

> Most presidential primary seasons have unfolded in three phases: the winnowing, when a large field becomes a small field; the showdown, when the nomination is effectively won in head-to-head battles in the large states; and the end game, when voters close ranks or register belated second thoughts about their party's likely nominee.[10]

Table 11-2

Candidate Nominations

Year	Event
1824	"King Caucus" in which presidential candidates were chosen by party caucuses in Congress is replaced by nominations by state legislatures.
1831	The first national party conventions are held by the Anti-Mason and the National Republican parties in Baltimore, but both end up losing the 1832 election.
1832	The Democrats hold their first national party convention and nominate the eventual winner, Andrew Jackson.
1856	Democrat Franklin Pierce becomes the only elected president denied renomination by his own party after alienating fellow northerners over slavery.
1901	The first presidential primary law is passed, in Florida.
1904	Wisconsin governor Robert La Follette, offended by not having his followers seated at the Republican convention, starts a movement for electing delegates to national elections in primaries.
1944	The Supreme Court outlaws white primaries (*Smith v. Allwright*), rejecting the view that parties are private organizations.
1962	The Supreme Court decides a number of cases (beginning with *Baker v. Carr*) asserting that political districts with wide population variations denied equal protection of the laws.

For more details see the *Congressional Quarterly Guide to U.S. Elections* (Washington, D.C.: Congressional Quarterly, Inc.), 14–20.

Each party's official presidential nominee emerges from the party's national convention, which is held during the summer of the election year. At one time, conventions were controlled by state party bosses, who managed handpicked delegations of party loyalists. Party conventions now serve as the often anticlimactic result of a long series of state-by-state delegate selections. The use of primary elections to choose convention delegates emerged slowly at the beginning of the twentieth century (see Table 11-2). In recent years this trend increased dramatically as the parties reacted to charges of undemocratic procedures and unrepresentative conventions. The process by which presidential candidates are selected in primaries is described in Chapter 14.

The national party conventions, which once served as highly charged arenas for selecting presidential nominees, now tend only to give a final and public nod to unstoppable delegate majorities accumulated by the leading candidate. Conventions are now more important instead for establishing party rules, energizing the party activists, developing **party platforms** (the formal statement of party policy ideals), and publicizing the party, its leaders, and its platforms to a national audience.

11-1c Financing Campaigns

Modern campaigns cost a great deal of money in large part because of the high cost of new technologies that use television and computers. Candidates prove their appeal by raising funds from individuals and organizations. Most financing laws emphasize publicly disclosing fund-raising activity rather than limiting contributions or expenditures. For federal offices (the presidency and Congress), the Federal Elections Commission maintains a computerized record of each campaign's financial activity and makes this record available to the press and the public.

The major exception to private financing of campaigns occurs in presidential contests. During the primary period, in many states those candidates who are able to raise money through small contributions from a large citizen base receive dollar-for-dollar matching contributions from the federal government up to an established limit. Once nominated, presidential candidates receive a one-time federal payment (which totaled over $70 million in 2004) to run their campaigns, and they can use no other funds.

Human creativity and the desire to gain political advantage encourage candidates to sometimes circumvent the good intentions of these laws. In recent presidential elections, candidates have helped to raise millions of dollars of so-called soft money designed to build state and local parties and to get out the vote. While this money is not directly used in a presidential candidate's campaign, it does help to support his or her efforts. Soft money contributions to parties were outlawed beginning after the 2002 election.

A few states provide public financing for nonfederal offices, and public financing for congressional races is under consideration. Individuals nevertheless remain the major source of campaign funds for nonpresidential campaigns.

A major area of contention concerning campaign financing involves the role of political action committees (PACs), discussed in Chapter 7. A PAC may be composed of employees or stockholders of a particular company, members of an interest group, or individuals with a common ideological outlook. According to current campaign finance laws, PACs can contribute up to $5,000 to each campaign or can make independent expenditures promoting a candidate. Working under the assumption that in unity there is strength, PAC advocates argue that combining the contributions of many individual supporters into one relatively significant amount enhances the impact of like-minded citizens. Opponents assert that the growing number of PACs, their imbalance toward specialized interests, and candidates' increasing dependence on them serve to threaten democracy by electing candidates beholden to large monied interests.

11-1d Rules of Campaigning

American political campaigns reward creativity and rely more on the voters' sense of acceptable strategies than on established rules to control candidate behavior. Some of the standard rules against libel (written untruth) and slander (oral untruth) are almost impossible to apply to candidates.

The specific rules underlying the nomination, financing, and campaign processes are important. The numerous deadlines to file as a candidate and to report campaign expenditures force candidates to use legal and accounting experts to help them avoid running afoul of the rules. More important, however, is that candidates and their managers know how to use the existing rules for their benefit—and how to avoid the embarrassment and potential legal liability for transgressing them.

11-2 The Players

The way players are chosen to do combat in the electoral arena has changed significantly over the years. Not all players approach the election game from the same perspective. The changing mix of players affects both how the political game is played and the nature of winners and losers.

11-2a Political Parties

As chronicled in Chapter 8, early party domination gave way to more candidate-centered procedures in the twentieth century. In recent years the parties have attempted to get back in the game, but they must now compete with a wider range of players.

Unwilling to accept a ticket to oblivion, the political parties have begun to fight their way back into the campaign game. Especially on the national level, the parties have become service vendor organizations, providing candidates with up-to-date technical services (polling, advertising, and fund-raising) at reduced prices in the hope of affecting the nature of elected officials and making candidates feel more beholden to the party.[11]

In 1994 the Republican minority in Congress attempted to insert a greater national party role into the election. Their highly publicized *Contract with America* was designed to nationalize the campaign around a series of specific campaign promises. This midterm party platform, originating from the top, was derided by much of the media, the Democrats, and even some Republicans as a meaningless gimmick. For its originator, Newt Gingrich (R-Ga.), and the more than three hundred candidates who pledged their support, it had more meaning. With the massive Republican victory, the Contract was credited by many for providing the electorate with a plan for which to vote and for giving the newly elected members of Congress a **mandate.** Newly elected Speaker Gingrich clearly challenged voters to use the *Contract* as a yardstick against which to measure the Republicans' success. In selecting committee members and party officials, the new Republican leadership used support of the *Contract* as one key factor. The experiment with non-presidential-year party platforms such as the *Contract* did not become an established pattern and was not renewed in subsequent off-year elections.

mandate *The message implied in an election result endorsing a particular set of public policy choices.*

11-2b Candidate-Centered Campaigns

The emergence of radio and television provided candidates with methods of bypassing the parties and bringing their individual messages directly to the voters. Later, computerized mailings and satellite communications refined candidates' ability to target particular messages to specific audiences. (See the discussion of campaign strategy in Section 11-4.) The decline of straight party voting encouraged candidate-centered campaigns. The inability of most party organizations to play a significant role in the nomination stage led candidates to seek professional campaign advisers, staff, and volunteers whose loyalties lay with the candidates, not with the party.

The importance of harnessing the new media technologies encouraged candidates to seek expert advice. A new profession of campaign consultants emerged to help candidate organizations raise funds, conduct public opinion polls, and design effective television advertisements. Eventually, these consultants completely took over the management of many campaigns.[12] As two prominent consultants put it,

> Political consulting filled the hole created by the collapse of these other institutions that buttressed political leadership, essentially the party, but also the weakening of unions, urban machines, ethnicity, unions, and church membership. (Bill Clinton's pollster, Stan Greenberg)[13]

> I think that what has happened is that in many ways the political consultants have replaced political parties and political leaders. (Republican consultant Robert Stone)[14]

During the 1960s and 1970s professionalized candidate-centered campaigns were most obvious in races for the presidency, Congress, and state governorships, but similar developments spread throughout the entire campaign process. Volunteers, who once dominated campaign staffs, became less useful because at that time most of them lacked the necessary technical skills.

In spite of the efforts of the parties, the candidate-centered campaign continues to dominate. Presidential campaigns run by independent organizations, with little or no coordination with the national party committees, are no longer uncommon. Richard Nixon's "Committee to Re-elect the President," Ronald Reagan's "Reagan-Bush Committee," Michael Dukakis's "Dukakis/Bentsen Committee, Inc.," George H. Bush's "Bush-Quayle, '92," Bill Clinton's "Clinton-Gore Committee," George W. Bush's "Bush-Cheney 2000," Al Gore's "Gore-Lieberman 2000," John Kerry's "Kerry/Edwards," and George Bush's "Bush/Cheney 04" were typical in their personal rather than party emphasis. Long-term political party loyalty is no longer an absolute requirement for playing the game. National elected leaders reveal mixed partisan backgrounds (both Republican presidents Eisenhower and Reagan were Democrats at one time), while some leaders are able to switch parties and still retain their offices (Senators Strom Thurmond [R-S.C.], Donald W. Riegle, Jr. [D-Mich.], Phil Gramm [R-Tex.], Richard C. Shelby [R-Ala.], and Ben Nighthorse Campbell [R-Colo.] each switched parties while in an office that was won under the opposing party label). In 2001, Senator James Jeffords of Vermont began the process of testing the validity of candidate-centered politics by dropping out of the Republican Party to become an independent only a few months after being elected under the party label. Despite outcries from national and state party officials, few observers felt this ultimate act of party disloyalty would threaten his reelection chances.

11-2c Competing Player Perspectives

The desire to win supports the actions of all the players in the campaign and election games, but the definitions of winning and losing vary. The following survey differentiates player perspectives.

Candidates

Candidates enter the campaign with short and limited perspectives. Few candidates in competitive races can see much beyond Election Day. Despite public pronouncements of doing "what's good for the party" or "what's good for the country," they cannot imagine much good coming out of an election result that does not include their victory. Some candidates may enter a race to expand public awareness of an issue or to increase their visibility for a future race. For most, politics is a zero-sum game, in which anything but winning is defined as defeat.

Throughout much of American history, viable candidates were drawn from a relatively narrow demographic base (see Table 11-3). As the types of people running for office changed, so did their motivations and the types of issues they pursued.

Parties

Party officials see candidates as vehicles for promoting party policies and the party organization. Parties take a long-term view and see the electoral process as a continuous game. There is little hesitation about withdrawing party support from an unlikely winner or an embarrassing candidate if that results in a long-term organizational benefit. Many

Table 11-3 **Candidate Emergence**

1870	The first African Americans are elected to Congress; Hiram Revels of Mississippi serves a partial term. Mississippi Republican Blanche K. Bruce is elected in 1874 to the first full term.
1876	Romualdo Pacheco, a California Republican, becomes the first Latino elected to Congress.
1916	Jeannette Rankin, a Montana Republican, is elected to Congress four years before women were allowed to vote. She became the only member of Congress to vote against both World Wars.
1924	The first women governors, both Democrats, were elected to succeed their husbands: Miriam "Ma" Ferguson in Texas and Nellie Tayloe Ross in Wyoming.
1931	Arkansas Democrat Hattie W. Caraway becomes the first woman elected to the U.S. Senate. Earlier, Rebecca L. Felton, a Democrat from Georgia, had been symbolically appointed to the Senate and served one day.
1949	Margaret Chase Smith, Republican of Maine, begins her career as the first woman to serve in both the House and the Senate, a career that lasted until 1973.
1958	Hiram Fong, a Hawaii Republican, is elected as senator, becoming the first Asian-American member of Congress.
1966	Edward Brook (R-Mass) becomes the first African American to serve in the Senate since reconstruction.
1968	Shirley Chisholm, Democrat from New York, becomes the first black woman elected to the House. She would later become the first black and the first woman to mount a serous presidential bid.
1984	Democratic House member Geraldine Ferraro becomes the first woman nominated on a national party ticket.
1984	Illinois elects the first black female to the Senate, Democrat Carol Mosely-Braun.
1987	Motorcycle-riding Ben Nighthorse Campbell begins his career in the House, leading to his 1992 election as the only Native American in the chamber. Elected originally as a Democrat, he served as a Republican.
2004	Mel Martinez (R-Fla) becomes the first Cuban-American to serve in the Senate. Barack Obama (D-Il), a young African American state senator capitalized on his galvanizing speech to the Democratic National Convention to become the first male African American Democrat in the Senate in modern times.

For more details see the *Congressional Quarterly Guide to U.S. Elections* (Washington, D.C.: Congressional Quarterly Inc.), 14–20.

Republican Party officials in 1964 and Democratic Party officials in 1972 intentionally paid limited attention to the candidacies of Barry Goldwater and George McGovern, respectively. They believed that these candidates' chances were doomed from the start and that the image of these candidates as extremists threatened to hurt the party in the long run. Many Democratic state party officials withdrew resources from the presidential race in 1988 when the Dukakis candidacy began to falter. Some components of the Democratic Party began disassociating themselves from Bill Clinton in 1994 when his popularity began to slide. The 1994 off-year elections were interpreted as a significant judgment against Clinton and his presidency, which hurt his ability to rally Democrats to support his policies. On the other hand, Republican victories in 2002 which allowed them to maintain their control of the House and gain control of the Senate were credited to George W. Bush, enhancing the desire of Republican office holders to support his legislative initiatives.

Loss of control over nominations in the candidate-centered era places American political parties in a vulnerable position. During the 1980s, in spite of legitimately winning the nominations of their parties, a Ku Klux Klan official in California and representatives of extremist Lyndon LaRouche in Illinois were disavowed by Democratic Party leaders because the candidates were seen as embarrassments to the party's national image.

The Consultants

A successful political consultant, anguishing over the worth of the profession, lamented:

> What we do makes politics a game, it makes voters think this is a game between consultants and strategists. . . . You end up with various campaigns that don't have anything to do with life. Politics deteriorates not even into a game, it's war.[15]

Although most political consultants have some individual policy preferences and will work only for candidates from a particular party, business considerations rank very high. The prime selling point for consultants is their "batting average": How many of their candidate customers have won, and how many have lost? Few consultants take on candidates with slim chances of victory. As the campaign gets down to the wire, candidates often find themselves pushed into uncomfortable strategies by consultants desiring to achieve one more victory. As one consultant put it:

> We'll use whatever the press will let us get away with. In the marketplace, the standard is winning, and my sense is that the standards get lower and lower all the time. . . . Consultants get judged on their won-lost records, not on the character of their campaigns.[16]

After election day, the consultant packs up and departs, leaving the candidate to deal with the consequences of the campaign tactics. Unlike the political parties, who remain responsible for the actions of their candidates, consultants who can walk away are less hesitant to use questionable strategies just to win.

Media

The media tend to view electoral campaigns as a horse race, emphasizing who is ahead and who is behind rather than focusing on the issues. As one insider described an upcoming race:

> This is going to be one of the great campaigns, bruising contest, two groups of guys on a hill in the mud, wrestling in the rain for control of the ball. An inch-by-inch battle, and every week the observers will be saying, "This team is winning," and then the next week, "That team is winning."[17]

Only rarely do the media analyze candidate capabilities and policy positions in depth. Stories about the candidates' personal peculiarities and the internal workings of their campaigns are seen as having greater viewer or readership interest.

Workers and Volunteers

Individuals participate in election campaigns for many reasons. They may work for a candidate on the basis of personal loyalty, because they deeply dislike the current officeholder, or to support a particular issue position. Some volunteers have little interest in the candidate or the issues; they use the campaign as a way of interacting with people and adding some excitement to their lives. Campaigns that can afford paid workers draw most of them from the ranks of individuals who hope to catch a rising star. If they are effective workers and their candidate wins, a new and exciting job in the elected official's office may be waiting. Incumbent officials often find ways for their current staffs to help with their campaigns (usually not while on the government payroll). They know that these people will be highly motivated out of interest in retaining their jobs.

Resource Providers

Individuals and organizations contributing to political campaigns reveal a number of motivations. Candidates for lower-level offices must make significant financial contributions to their own campaigns in order to launch their political careers. Individual contributors, still the dominant financial source for most campaigns, give to personal friends or to candidates promoting preferred policies. The use of computers to create targeted mailing lists of likely supporters increases a candidate's efficiency in discovering potential contributors (see Box 11-2: Targeting Contributors through "Merging and Purging").

Political parties have recently expanded their resources through direct-mail fundraising. Although relatively insignificant in terms of total contributions, parties often provide candidates with the important early money to get campaigns started.

Giving through PACs is a strategy to provide access to decision makers who will assumedly promote the policy preferences of the interest group sponsoring the PAC. PACs support old friends and seek out new candidates whose electoral prospects look good. In competitive races that have candidates favorable to their position on both sides, some PACs hedge their bets and contribute to both. PACs generally contribute most heavily to incumbents, the idea being that since they are likely to win anyway, it makes little sense to offend them.

Voters

Voters react to campaigns for political offices in different ways. They tend to be more willing to break away from their party orientations in high-visibility races (for president, senator, or governor), where issue information other than party labels is more readily available. In local races, personal knowledge of the candidates and local issues hold sway. Voters still use party labels for races where issue information is more difficult to obtain (congressional, state legislative, and state constitutional office races).

Voters view campaigns with a mixture of annoyance, amusement, frustration, entertainment, and hope. The less interested they are in the outcome, the less voters pay attention. It then becomes more likely that only the entertainment components (such as personal scandals) and the horse race aspects (who's ahead? who's behind?) dominate.

The increase in independent voters who lack a party identification makes the information generated by the campaign more important as a voting cue. Voters with the most interest in the campaign are the easiest to reach using mass media, but they are the most likely to make up their minds early.[18] Once voters make up their minds, they selectively gather campaign information to justify the choices they have already made. The bottom line is that the voters most amenable to changing their minds because of a campaign's efforts are often the least likely to be paying attention.

The American voter is a moving target, going into and out of the electoral game. The size and composition of the electorate depend on the office being contested and the level of competition (see Table 11-4). Electorates for noncompetitive state and local races tend to be small and made up of strong partisans who vote along party lines. A larger and more diverse set of voters usually goes to the polls for hotly contested races for national office.

Voters fall into one of two categories. **Dependent voters** approach the voting booth with an abiding and predetermined yardstick by which to judge candidates.[19] Strong partisans vote for every candidate with their party label, saying to themselves, "I support her because she is a Republican." Members of ethnic or religious groups often use these labels to tell contenders apart.

dependent voters *Voters using a relatively fixed set of criteria, such as party identification or ethnic background, to differentiate candidates.*

Box 11–2 *Targeting Contributors through "Merging and Purging"*

Mail solicitation of potential campaign contributors is expensive and relatively ineffective unless the candidate can concentrate on individuals with a high likelihood of contributing. Candidates buy or borrow mailing lists from government agencies, publications, and organizations. Computers are used to merge two or more lists and exclude (purge) individuals with specified characteristics. The remaining list has no duplicates and is made up of a more homogeneous group of potential contributors. A candidate wishing to target wealthy Republicans might use the following strategy:

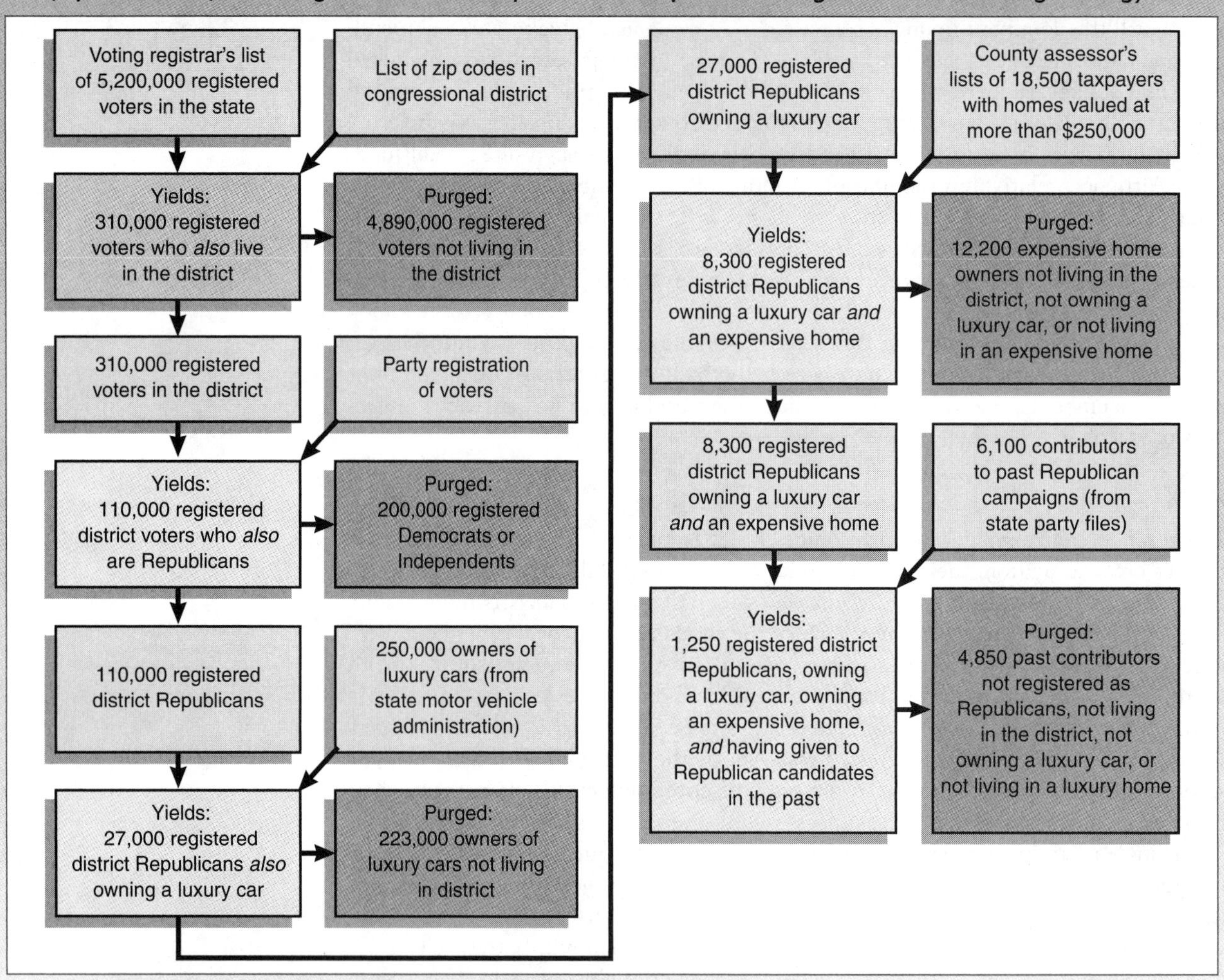

Source: Stephen E. Frantzich and Stephen L. Percy, *American Government: The Political Game* (Dubuque, IA: Brown & Benchmark, 1994), 296.

The remaining list of 1,250 wealthy Republican voters from the district might then be sent a letter encouraging them to contribute to the campaign of a "good Republican who strongly favors lower property taxes and opposes special taxation of luxury cars." The creation of this targeted mailing list would be impossible by hand but takes only a few minutes of computer time.

responsive voters *Voters amenable to having their voting decision affected by campaign communications.*

Responsive voters approach each campaign with more flexibility than do dependent voters, and they are more open to issue appeals. They look at a candidate and say, "I support him because of his stand on gun control." The last few decades have been marked by an increase in responsive voting.

Fewer and fewer voters simply follow the party line, although there has been some recovery of party-line voting in the most recent elections. Ticket splitting—a key indication of more responsive voting—has become common (see Figure 11-4). More voters

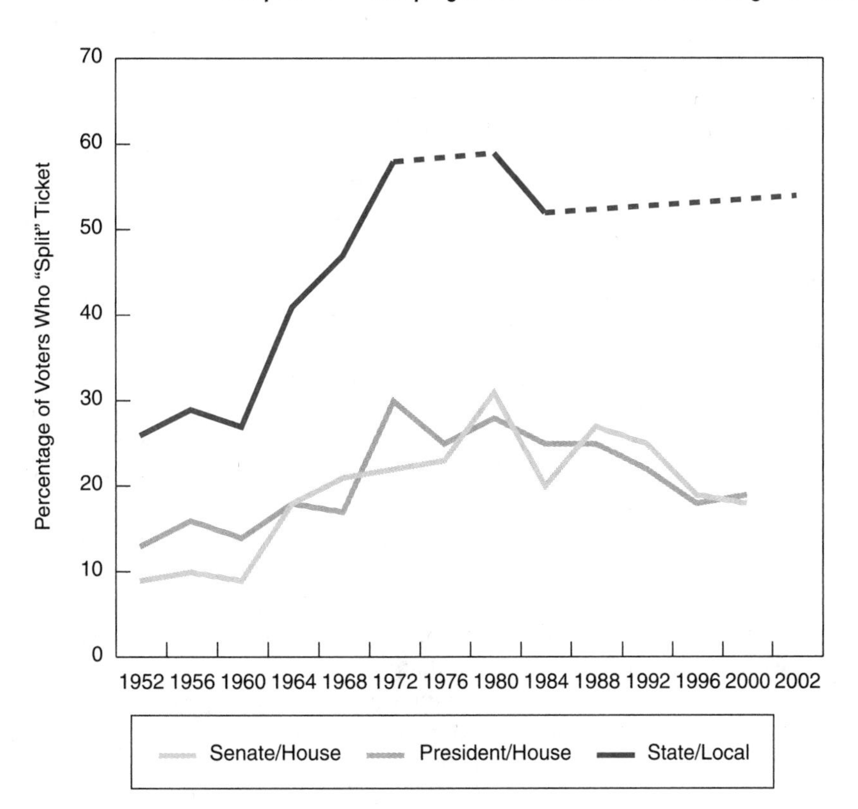

Figure 11-4
Ticket Splitting

State/local figures not available for 1976 and 1988–2000.

Source: Harold W. Stanley and Richard G. Niemi, *Vital Statistics on American Politics, 2001-2002* (Washington, D.C.: Congressional Quarterly, Inc., 2002), p. 27. Data from Richard Morin, "Unconventional Wisdom," *Washington Post*, December 1, 2002, p. B5.

Table 11-4 **Voting and Campaign Appeals**

1787	States given the right to establish voter qualifications. No serious thought given to allowing women or slaves to vote, although both are counted toward apportionment (slaves at three-fifths rate).
1870	The 15th Amendment allows free blacks to vote, although state laws and procedures often thwart such efforts.
1874	Cartoons by Thomas Nast lead to the emergence of the donkey and elephant as symbols of the Democratic and Republican parties. The symbols become helpful for semi-literate voters.
1892	The first mechanical voting machines are used in Lockport, New York.
1913	Direct election of senators replaces election by state legislatures in all states after the passage of the 17th amendment.
1961	Ratification of the 23rd Amendment gives residents of Washington, D.C., the right to vote in presidential elections, even though they still have no voting member of Congress.
1964	The 24th Amendment abolishes the poll tax, which had been used to disenfranchise economically disadvantaged African Americans.
1965	The Voting Rights Act provides the federal government with the power to assure the right to vote.
1971	The 26th Amendment lowers the voting age to 18 nationally.
1980s	A number of states developed majority-minority districts, concentrating ethnic minorities to increase their potential for electing candidates they preferred. Later court decisions indicated that race could not be the dominant factor in determining the district in which individuals cast their ballots.
2000	Oregon becomes the first state to conduct its entire presidential vote by mail.
2000	Problems with punch card voting and the counting of absentee ballots in Florida cast attention on voting procedures.
2002	Congress passes the Helping Americans Vote Act (HAVA), appropriating $3.8 billion to the states to improve registration procedures and to replace punch-card and lever voting machines.
2004	Relaxed absentee ballot and early voting procedures allow up to 70% of voters to vote early, often with no requirement to provide an excuse. Many voters take advantage of the opportunity.

(For more details see the *Congressional Quarterly Guide to U.S. Elections* (Washington, D.C.: Congressional Quarterly, Inc.), 14–20)] are "in play," susceptible to candidate appeals. Candidate-centered campaigns, the mass media's role in campaigning, and new campaign technologies have all resulted from and contributed to the decrease in party-line voting.

instrumental voting *A voting choice motivated by the match between the voter's policy goals and the candidate's promises.*

Responsive voting can be based on a number of criteria. The democratic ideal encourages **instrumental voting,** in which the voter compares his or her policy preferences with the issue positions presented by the candidates. Instrumental voters must recognize their own policy preferences and then determine the relative likelihood of each candidate being able to satisfy them.[20]

social needs *A voting choice based on the influence of friends or relatives.*

Not all voters live up to this ideal. As social beings, voters receive input from relatives and friends. A variety of **social needs** influences voting decisions. Voters attempt to affirm their bond with associates by going along with their preferences. Husbands and wives often vote the same way, one of the partners taking the lead in political decisions, and the other going along out of respect or admiration. Until recently men more often than women set the tone for a family's voting. That distinction has largely disappeared today.

psychological needs voting *A voting choice based on the attempt to use one's vote as a verification of one's self-image.*

The vote can also satisfy **psychological needs.** Individuals carry around with them a set of images of themselves that includes an association with various political symbols. There is considerable personal pressure to act consistently with one's self-image. For example, voters who see themselves in ideological terms can be swayed to support a particular candidate by the argument that "This is what a *good* liberal (or conservative) would do." Jimmy Carter did much better than most recent Democratic presidential candidates among southern voters by capitalizing on his southern heritage and asserting that good southerners should support a fellow southerner. As the first southerner to win the presidency on his own since the Civil War, Carter's victory gave many southerners satisfaction that their days of second-class citizenship were over. If a voter consistently responds to a partisan or other type of symbol without thinking, he or she has become a dependent voter. If the voter has to think through his or her vote each time, she or he has become a responsive voter, responding to specific symbols of that campaign.

Men and women increasingly perceive political choices in different ways. For decades women have been more liberal on key issues and have voted more for Democratic candidates. Typically about 4 percent more women than men support Democratic candidates in contemporary congressional elections. This figure doubled from the 1994 election onward. Gender-related voting patterns tend to be more volatile in presidential elections, with evidence of a gender gap initially coming to the forefront during the Reagan years (see Figure 11-5). On key issues such as abortion and women's rights, many women see the Democratic Party as more of an ally.

11-3 Deciding to Play the Game: Candidate Emergence

> The game of politics allows one to draw upon your abilities and background. It is different than team sports. It's like individual sports. It's like a boxing match. (Senator and 1992 presidential contender Tom Harkin, D-Iowa)[21]

Elections are more than academic exercises involving potential participants. The emergence of real candidates who attempt to motivate real voters creates the environment for the ultimate electoral contest. A candidate's decision to run for office is typically based on a combination of motivation, opportunity, and resources.

11-3a Motivation

Although the American political tradition discourages candidates who seem too eager, few are dragged kicking and screaming into the political arena. Even candidates who have been recruited by parties or other political activists have generally harbored some desire to gain electoral office. Most of them have placed themselves in positions where they would be noticed. The motivation of most candidates is to win, although some will run in hopeless races simply to gain name recognition for a future race, to highlight a par-

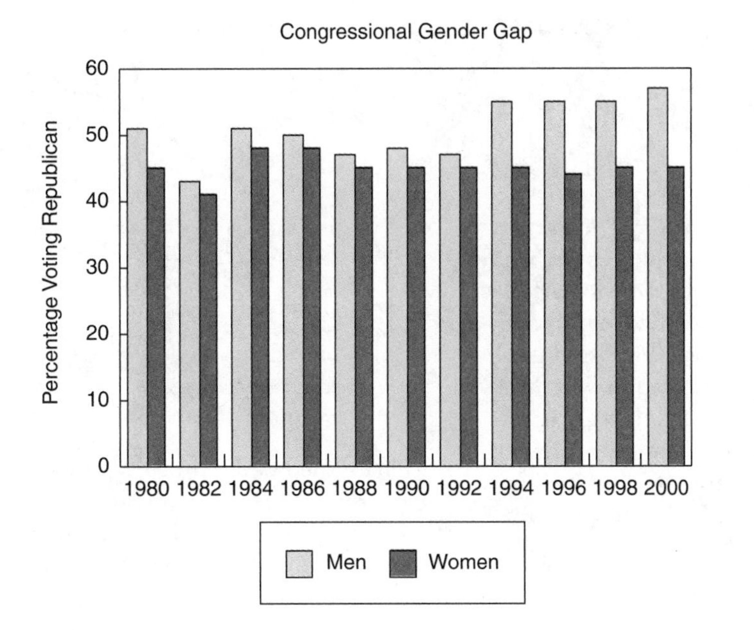

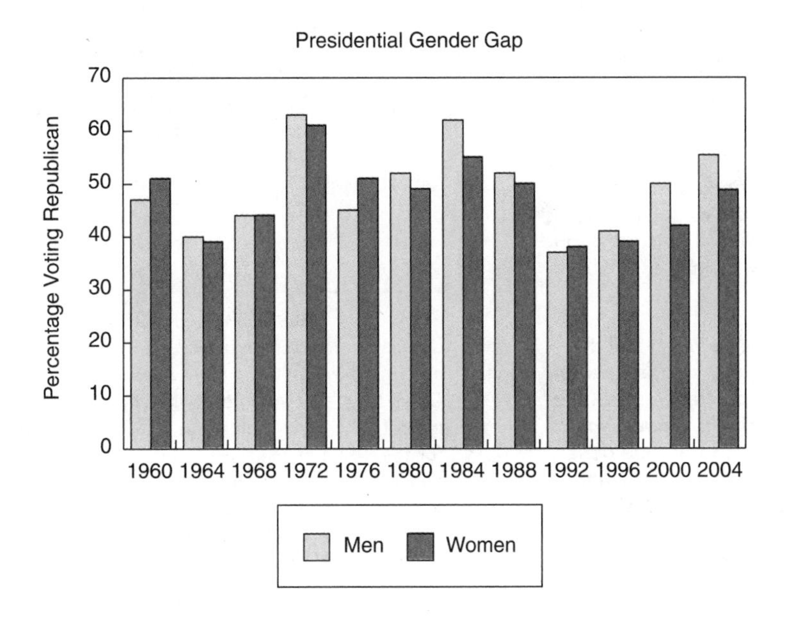

Figure 11-5

The Gender Gap in Voting

Sources: New York Times, November 13, 1994, A15, based on *New York Times*-CBS polls; Gallup polls reported in Harold W. Stanley and Richard G. Niemi, *Vital Statistics on American Politics,* 2001–2002 (Washington, D.C.: Congressional Quarterly, Inc., 2001), p. 120. 1992 and 1996 figures are misleading due to the Perot candidacy, which siphoned off a large number of male votes. Twenty-two percent of men and sixteen percent of women reported having voted for Perot in 1992, and 11 percent of the men and 7 percent of the women reported supporting him in 1996. 2000 and 2004 figures from The Center for American Women and Politics http://www.cawp.rutgers.edu/.

ticular issue, or to prove their loyalty to the party organization. The desire to win political office also serves a number of deeper motivations. These range from a commitment to a particular issue position to a sense of public service to pure personal ambition. Many candidates during the 1980s and 1990s have been drawn into the political process by single issues such as abortion, gun control, or the environment (see Box 11-3: The Motivation for Throwing One's Hat into the Ring).

11-3b Opportunity

Multiple factors determine a candidate's opportunity to run. The existence of an incumbent from one's own party daunts all but the most motivated candidates. Facing an incumbent in the opposing party gives challengers at least pause. Open seats, where there is no incumbent, draw the largest number of contenders.

Potential candidates must pass a number of legal hurdles for eligibility other than the age and citizenship requirements set by the Constitution. Certain classes of individuals give up their rights to run for many offices. Federal government employees, for example, are limited by the Hatch Act to running for nonpartisan offices only. The opportunity to

Box 11–3 The Motivation for Throwing One's Hat into the Ring

The term "throw your hat into the ring" comes from the tradition of pick-up boxing matches where anyone willing to take on all comers doffed his hat and threw it into the ring. Contemporary presidential campaigns are perhaps a bit less bruising, but they confront potential challengers with the real possibility of psychological injury to their egos and their favored policy positions. The motivations for making such a commitment vary. With no incumbent president running in 2000, a large number of candidates emerged, with a variety of justifications for running:

> *I was born into America's service. . . . It wasn't until I was deprived of her company that I fell in love with America. . . . It is because I owe America more than she has ever owed me that I am a candidate for president of the United States.*—Senator John McCain (R-Ariz.)[a]

> *This year, I believe, is our last chance to save our republic before she disappears into a godless world order. Our vaulted two-party system has become a snare and a delusion, a fraud upon the nation.*—Reform Party nominee Patrick Buchanan[b]

> *If you entrust me with the presidency, I will marshal its authority, its resources, and its moral leadership to fight for America's families. . . . We have closed our budget deficit. But today find a deficit of even greater danger. . . the time deficit in family life; the decency deficit in our common culture; [and] the care deficit for our little ones and our elderly parents. . . . You deserve a leader who has been tested.*—Vice President Al Gore[c]

> *I will give our country a fresh start after a season of cynicism. . . . [I] trust local people to make the right decision for schools, cities, and counties. [I] understand that capitalism is the backbone of our free enterprise system . . . [and] always put America and American workers first. [I] understand the importance of family and the need for personal responsibility.*—Governor George W. Bush[d]

With the need to raise significant funds and the long primary season, candidates these days throw their hat in earlier and earlier. Almost two years before the 2004 election, Senator John Kerry (D-MA) unofficially entered the race by creating an "exploratory committee" when he said:

> *I come to this campaign with a set of experiences that are directly relevant to the times that we are in . . . This race is about the country and the anxiety and aspirations of the American people. . . . This is not a debate about left and right. This is a debate about basic issues.*—Senator John Kerry [D-Ma][e]

---

a. "McCain Makes Candidacy Official," Associated Press state and local wire, September 28, 1999.
b. Chris Burritt, "Campaign 2000: Buchanan Launches Reform Candidacy," *The Atlanta Constitution*, October 26, 1999, X.
c. Scott Shepard, "Campaign 2000: Gore announces 'moral' bid for the White House," *The Atlanta Constitution*, June 17, 1999, and *The Tennessean*, June 17, 1999.
d. *Los Angeles Times*, June 14, 1999.
e. Quoted in Adam Nagourney, "Antiwar Veteran Eager for Battle," *The New York Times*, December 8, 2002, A24.

run may also be stifled by professional or personal commitments. For many years, public school teachers and members of the clergy were expected to be politically neutral. Doctors with heavy time commitments, young mothers raising children, and blue-collar workers dependent on overtime pay represent people with the kinds of commitments that often make political involvement impossible. With the increased scrutiny by the media of candidates' personal lives, some potential candidates are discouraged by fear of exposing past mistakes.

gatekeeper *An individual or organization controlling access to a desired resource such as publicity or a nomination for public office.*

Political **gatekeepers** such as party leaders and the media often impose their own criteria in evaluating candidates. Due to unfounded assumptions, women and minorities were long thought to be unlikely winners. Recent experience and research indicate that minorities can win in non-majority-minority districts and that women are just as likely to win as men, particularly when incumbency is not a factor.[22] In 1994 incumbent female state legislators won 95 percent of their races as compared to 94 percent for their male counterparts. In open-seat state legislative races, men won 53 percent of the time and women followed closely behind at 52 percent.[23] The slow increase in the number of minority and female

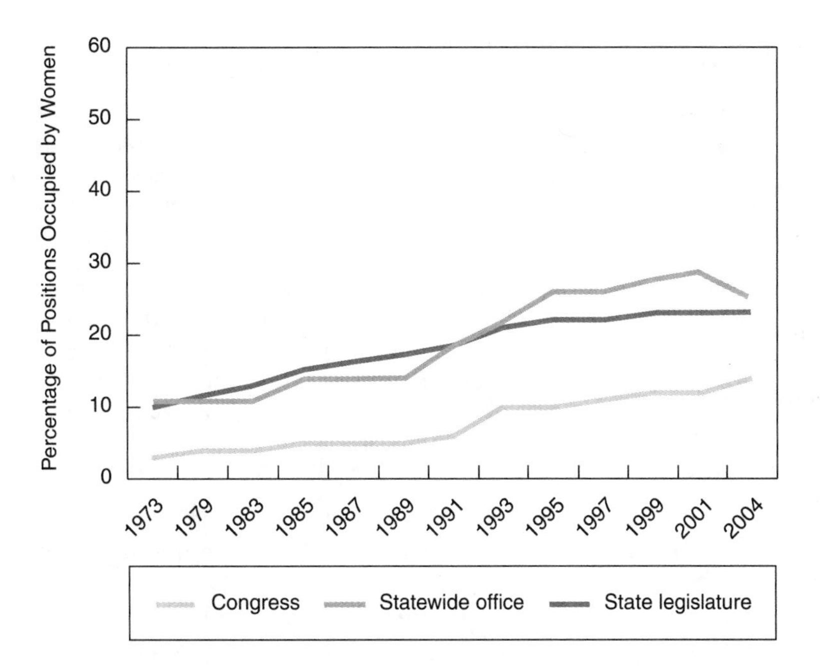

Figure 11-6
The Changing Gender Farm Teams

Source: Rutgers University, Center for American Women and Politics, fact sheets (www.cawp.rutgers.edu).

candidates is based primarily on the vast number of male and nonminority incumbents, who are so difficult to unseat. Hesitancy among women to run for elective office is fading. The bench of minority and female candidates in lower-level elective offices is growing dramatically and will eventually filter into the higher-level offices (see Figure 11-6).

11-3c Resources

Viable candidates require a variety of resources to mount an effective campaign. Personal financial resources allow potential candidates to leave their jobs during the campaign and to cover the start-up costs. Jobs with flexible schedules obviously facilitate having time when it is needed. The self-employed lawyer starts out with an advantage over the assembly-line worker who must work a specified shift. Personal skills in communicating and in organizing others are useful in all campaigns; the abilities to use television effectively and to harness computers are increasingly important. With the decline of party-line voting, personal name-recognition becomes significant. Individuals who have made a name for themselves through local community activity, participation in sports, or involvement in the entertainment industry need to spend less effort getting themselves known. In the 1990s, elections elevated entertainers such as musician Sonny Bono (R-Calif.) and actor Fred Thompson (R-Tenn.) to Congress and put actor Clint Eastwood in office as mayor. In 2003, actor Arnold Schwarzenegger translated his name identification and popularity into a successful run for governor of California. Outside of the entertainment world, Hillary Clinton (D-N.Y.) transitioned from the White House to the Senate, beating a lesser-known member of Congress who had closer personal ties to New York.

Working up from lower-level offices to more significant offices with larger constituencies remains the most likely political career path. The political career in America is not really a ladder, with one step predictably following the one before; it is more like a playground jungle gym. There are a number of entry points where candidates can prove their abilities and become known. The higher one reaches, the more limited are the previous offices from which one can rise. For example, state legislators may have previously served in a wide variety of offices, but U.S. senators emerge mainly from the House of Representatives. Modern presidential candidates usually emerge from the U.S. Senate, the vice presidency, or state governorships. Individuals with high name-recognition can often bypass some of the lower levels on the political jungle gym. Former astronaut John Glenn (D-Ohio) and former basketball player Bill Bradley (D-N.J.) both have had the exceptional experience of becoming U.S. senators on their first run for elective office.

Time Out 11-2

Entering the Electoral Game

Relatively few individuals pursue the opportunity to run for office. Assume it is ten years from now and you have followed your current career plan. Answer the nine questions that follow by relating them to the congressional district in which you currently have your permanent residence (where you would register to vote). Alternatively, answer the questions using the characteristics of an older friend or family member.

The scenario makes you ten years older for two reasons. First, it will ensure that you meet the legal requirements of being twenty-five years old to run for the House. Second, few candidates compete for political office without finishing their education and working in their career for a number of years.

The geographic component recognizes that members of Congress run for office by running from geographically defined districts. Voters expect candidates to have and retain a tie to their district.

1. I would like to have a political career. (Yes or No)
2. The majority of people in my district belong to the same party I do. (Yes or No)
3. I work for the federal government. (Yes or No)
4. I am a doctor, dentist, or sole proprietor of a business. (Yes or No)
5. I enjoy meeting people and feel at ease meeting strangers. (Yes or No)
6. How many clubs or organizations do you now actively belong to as an officer? (choose a number between 0 and 4)
7. I have a law degree. (Yes or No)
8. I was born in this district, went to school in this district, or have worked in this district since leaving school. (Yes or No)
9. Are you male or female?

Source: Stephen E. Frantzich and Steven E. Shier, *Congress: Games and Strategies* (Cincinnati, OH: Atomic Dog Publishing, 2003), 58–59.

11-4 Campaign Strategy

Campaign strategy involves gathering the necessary resources, creating the most favorable electorate, and attempting to motivate a majority of the voters to cast their ballots in your behalf. A candidate seeks admission to a specific playing field. The nature of the field as well as the personality of the player dictate strategies. Especially because voters are activated and motivated by different factors, candidates must utilize a complex combination of campaign strategies, approaching each type of voter in a different way. With the decline in party management of individual campaigns, candidate-centered campaigns face the task of building an able organization and gathering the resources to play the election game.

11-4a Gathering the Necessary Resources

"To get in the ballpark, you have to pay the ticket,"[24] remarked Congressman Wayne T. Gilchrest (R-Md.), referring to the high cost of campaigning. Entering the election game requires bringing together significant human and material resources. The candidate who puts a competent staff in place and raises significant early money is ready for the competition ahead. Those two accomplishments may also scare away potential challengers.

The amount of resources necessary to launch a campaign varies with the office sought and the nature of the contest. Winning a House race now typically requires over $800,000 and a seat in the Senate over $7 million. Senate races vary more in cost because of the varying size of states. Incumbents harbor a double advantage. They need less money to make themselves known, and they find it easier to raise funds. Republicans generally find it easier to raise money than do Democrats. In 2002, incumbent Republican

House candidates spent an average of $797,000, while Democratic incumbents spent $746,000. Challengers in those races spent an average of less than $65,000. In open seat races, the average Republican candidates spent $1,128,000, while Democratic candidates in such races spent $961,000.[25]

11-4b Creating a Favorable Electorate

> Divide your county into small districts and appoint in each a committee. Make a perfect list of the voters and ascertain with certainty for whom they will vote. Keep a constant watch on the doubtful voters and have them talked to by those in whom they have the most confidence. On election day see that every Whig is brought to the polls. (Abraham Lincoln's advice to his party in 1840, as a member of a five-man Whig Party campaign committee in Illinois.)

In many ways things have not changed much in politics in the more than 150 years since Lincoln gave this advice. Many elections are won or lost before the first campaign commercial goes on the air or the first speech is given. Before a campaign is noticeably under way, candidates and political parties are busy developing an uneven playing field that works to their advantage. As we have seen, candidates and parties involve themselves in a long-term strategy of determining potential voters through active involvement in the redistricting process. Careful drawing of district lines almost assures victory.

In the shorter term, candidates sometimes conduct extensive voter registration drives to make sure that their supporters meet voter eligibility requirements. In 1984 Jesse Jackson expanded the electorate dramatically in key primary states by registering millions of African Americans and promoting a **Rainbow Coalition.** Although Jackson did not win the nomination, the new voters registered by Jackson changed the playing field for other candidates. The passage of a national motor-voter registration law in 1993 was designed to make it easier for people to register. As earlier noted, Democratic politicians were particularly supportive of such an approach, since the majority of unregistered voters would typically vote Democratic.

Rainbow Coalition *An organization that attempts to weave together peoples of all races and genders into a viable political force for progressive policies.*

Closer to Election Day, candidates expend a considerable portion of their resources getting voters to the polls. Since Democrats are less likely to vote than Republicans, get-out-the-vote drives involving telephone calls to potential supporters and rides to the polls have become a staple for Democratic campaigns. Using the capabilities of computerized mailings, Republicans have led the way in targeting voters who might be away from home on Election Day and need absentee ballots.

11-4c Motivating Voters

Given the variable nature of voter motivations, candidates employ different strategies to reach dependent or responsive voters. New technologies provide campaigns with more effective methods of reaching both kinds of voters and are changing the playing field.

Activating Dependent Voters

Only those who vote affect the bottom line of an election, determining who wins and who loses:

> Participation is like being a fan who votes favorably for media products by purchasing them. . . . [V]oting is consuming, and consistent voting is product or brand loyalty.[26]

In spite of the decline in party-line voting, party loyalists still are an important base of candidate support. Candidates battle mightily to show that they deserve support as the inheritor of all for which the party stands. In states with registration by party, computerized lists of party loyalists have replaced card files as the basis for party-oriented mailings, telephone calls, and door-to-door solicitation. Since the Democratic Party dominates in terms of party registration, Democrats highlight their party affiliation in the campaign. Republicans, hoping to attract some Democrats, urge voters to support the person, not the party.

Activating Responsive Voters

Changing voters' minds is far more difficult than getting them to act on established attitudes. Responsive voters want a candidate to prove that a vote for him or her will satisfy

Answer to Time Out 11-2

Your Likelihood of a Political Career

Determine your likelihood of a political career by scoring the survey questions in Time Out 11-2 as follows:

1. Yes: 2; No: 0
2. Yes: 3; No: 0
3. Yes: –20; No: 0
4. Yes: –5; No: 0
5. Yes: 2; No: –2
6. Number of clubs and organizations
7. Yes: 3; No: 0
8. Yes: 2; No: 0
9. No points either way

If your total is 9 or more, you are a budding politician. Start on your announcement speech. You have an inside track. If your total is 0 to 8, you are a box seat spectator.

You will probably stay on the sidelines unless a unique opportunity or a change in your life comes along. If your score is less than 0, you are a bleacher's fan at best. Change your career plans, change districts, or forget a political career.

Explaining the Career-Shaping Factors

The point values assigned to the various characteristics are not absolutes, but rather rough estimates of the degree of impact each has on the feasibility of a political career.

Here is each factor and the points associated with it:

1. I would like to have a political career. ("Yes" adds 2 points to your total. Political involvement takes a great deal of motivation.)
2. The majority of people in my district belong to the same party I do. ("Yes" adds 3 points to your total. Although voters are less tied to their parties today, party-based voting is still quite common in low information congressional races.)
3. I work for the federal government. (A "yes" answer here largely knocks you out of the competition. Federal government employees have their political participation regulated under the Hatch Act, making it illegal for them to run as a partisan candidate for office.)
4. I am a doctor, dentist, or sole proprietor of a business. (A "yes" to this question reduces your availability by 5 points, since you would have to close your business and give up your career to serve in Congress.)
5. I enjoy meeting people and feel at ease meeting strangers. (A "yes" adds 2 points to your total and a "no" reduces it by 2 points, since politicians need strong interpersonal skills.)
6. How many clubs or organizations do you now actively belong to as an officer? (Social connections help build political networks. Individuals with a strong record of community involvement are clearly advantaged in politics. Each organization of which you are a part adds 1 point to your total.)
7. I have a law degree. (Although the percentage of lawyers in Congress is declining, law is still the most common route to political involvement. A law degree adds 3 points to your total.)
8. I was born in this district (the district I plan to run from), went to school in this district, or have worked in this district since leaving school. (Voters prefer candidates with close ties to the district. Answering "yes" to this question increases your chances of being a viable candidate by 2 points.)
9. Are you male or female? (As late as a decade ago, women were less viable candidates. They found it harder to establish political ties and to raise money. They also found that voters were less willing to support them. Today, disadvantages for women running for office have largely disappeared. The answer to this question does not affect your viability as a candidate.)

some significant personal need. After moving away from dependence on the party organizations and party labels, candidates initially sent vague impersonalized messages by way of the mass media. Increasingly, contemporary candidates attempt to personalize use of the news media by sending the right messages to the right people in the right way.

Sending the Right Messages

Campaigns fashion different messages to different sets of voters. To appeal to **instrumental voters**, candidates focus on issue stands. On issues where the constituency shows considerable consistency, the candidate boldly affirms his or her support for the most popular position. If 80 percent of the constituency oppose gun control, only the foolhardy politician reveals his or her support for such legislation. On issues that stir up considerable conflict, the candidate either avoids the issue or takes a vague stand with which few would disagree. Neither Richard Nixon nor George McGovern faced up to the energy issue in 1972, since both alternatives—higher fuel costs and a lower standard of living resulting from limiting consumption—were unpopular. Although George H. Bush and Bill Clinton differed on the issue of abortion in 1992, both sought to give the impression to those on the opposite side of the issue that they could be flexible. In 1996 President Clinton pre-empted the key Republican issues of a balanced budget and welfare reform, leaving Bob Dole with little on which to campaign. Recent congressional and presidential campaigns have maintained support of Medicare and Social Security as sacrosanct.

instrumental voting *A voting choice motivated by the match between the voter's policy goals and the candidate's promises. See also social needs and psychological needs voting.*

During the 2000 campaign, both Al Gore and George W. Bush expressed support for the popular issue of tax cuts. Reflecting his philosophical bent and the electoral base of the Republican Party, Bush proposed across-the-board cuts. Predictably, Al Gore showed little enthusiasm for overall cuts, preferring to target lower income tax payers and protect as much of the budget surplus as possible for maintaining and expanding government programs, a position more in tune with the philosophy and interest of likely Democratic voters. Above and beyond the specifics, each man wanted to be viewed as the tax cut candidate.

In the 2002 off-year elections the Republicans steered clear of focusing on the weakened economy and emphasized the foreign policy challenges of terrorism and maintaining tax cuts. The Democrats were never able to find their "voice" and present a coherent message.

Most voters have little difficulty with candidates who extol their own virtues. They may cry foul, however, when the candidates use **negative advertising** and criticize their opponents. As much as we might like campaigns to focus on the positive, however, it has become clearer and clearer in recent years that negative advertising does work. Voters react to campaign spots that point out the inconsistencies and shortcomings of opponents (see Box 11-4: The Willie Horton Ad). With increased anger among the voters, negative ads seem to be particularly effective. In evaluating the 1994 campaign, one political consultant concluded:

negative advertising *Campaign ads that directly question the behavior and/or consistency of one's opponent as opposed to touting one's own virtues.*

> Polls show there's nothing good about politicians that people will believe, and nothing bad they won't believe. The big question this year is whose negative campaign is better. If it's negative, it works. If it's positive, save it for your tombstone.[27]

Modern methods of opinion assessment allow candidates to monitor more carefully voter reactions to issues and to determine where politicians can lead and where they must follow. Very little is done by chance anymore, as candidates attempt to anticipate voter reactions. As one journalist described the process in 1988:

> It was dial-a-president night at the Holiday Inn here. . . . Some 85 earnest Iowans participated in an exercise in instant democracy that was as fascinating as it was frightening. As the seven Democratic presidential hopefuls answered questions in a Houston auditorium, the Iowans—likely participants in next February's first-in-the-nation caucus—watched a big-screen television picture of the candidates. Each of the spectators held a hand-sized dial, numbered from one to seven, connected by wire to a nearby computer. As the candidates came on the screen, . . . each Iowan rotated the pointer in his palm to indicate the degree of comfort or discomfort he felt with what he was seeing. . . . Out of sight, their individual responses were merged by the computer every three seconds and plotted on a line on a graph, overlaid on the telecast of the debate. . . . It was instant, summary judgment—as final as the thumbs up-thumbs down of the Roman emperors viewing the gladiatorial combats.[28]

Box 11–4 The Willie Horton Ad

Television, with its large audience and visual impact, has changed the way candidates communicate with voters. It has encouraged advertisements that simplify issues and influence voters through the use of powerful visual images. Willie Horton became an instant part of American political history in 1988 when George H. Bush's campaign managers decided to use him to symbolize what was wrong with presidential candidate Michael Dukakis's position on crime. Willie Horton was an African-American convict who had committed a murder while on a Massachusetts furlough program that was supported by Governor Dukakis. The original Willie Horton television ad showed the convict's mug shot and was initially used by an independent conservative group and disavowed by the Bush campaign as being too extreme.[a]

Once this ad had created a national discussion, the Bush campaign created its own furlough ad, using a revolving door outside a prison to imply the insecurity of the program without mentioning Willie Horton or using his picture. Despite generating cries of unfairness by the Dukakis campaign and racism by others, these ads solidified in many voters' minds the opinion that George H. Bush was tougher on the crime issue.

The original Willie Horton ad used a rather menacing mug shot of the convicted murderer. George H. Bush's "revolving door" ad more subtly made the point that the criminal justice system fails to protect us against crime by allowing criminals out too easily.

a. Martin Schram, "The Making of Willie Horton," *The New Republic* 3932 (May 28, 1990): 17.

"bandwagon" effect *Encouraging socially motivated voting by implying that everyone else is jumping on the bandwagon and that the voter should not be left behind.*

VIDEO

The Swift Boat Veterans for Truth challenged John Kerry's military record.

Charges about John Kerry flip-flopping on issues were dramatized using a digitally modified set of pictures.

Voters motivated by social needs prove difficult to reach through the formal campaign. Prestige endorsements from popular political or entertainment leaders encourage some voters. Public opinion polls showing a candidate's strong support help to create a **"bandwagon" effect.** Buttons, bumper stickers, and lawn signs all provide evidence of whom one's friends and neighbors find acceptable.

Psychologically motivated voters respond to symbols and labels. Candidates attempt to appropriate the most popular symbols of a society. Use of the American flag is supposed to convince voters that voting for a particular candidate is the patriotic thing to do. Pictures of candidates playing with their children, holding their dog, or talking with farmers are intended to give an overall positive impression of the candidates. They suggest that supporters of the family, or of animals, or of farmers would be remiss if they fail to support this candidate.

The use of symbols, however, does not always work. When Michael Dukakis's 1988 campaign managers had him photographed riding in a tank to prove his patriotism, the pictures and the press reaction to them emphasized the silliness of the stunt. The George H. Bush campaign capitalized on this gaffe by producing a campaign spot using the same pictures and challenging Dukakis's support of national defense. Likewise, attempts to associate Al Gore with the future and technology in 2000 backfired when his statements about "inventing" the Internet undermined his credibility.

Communicating with the Right People

Getting the message across to those who count is essential. Chicago mayor Richard M. Daly, commenting on the strategy of his father, Richard J. Daly, a former Chicago mayor and the last of the great political bosses, said this about gathering voters:

> My dad knew one thing. He wanted everyone for him on election day. Politics is a game of addition, not subtraction.[29]

Much campaign rhetoric and advertising is wasted. Messages to nonvoters fail to advance the candidate's cause. Effective campaigns seek to target their messages and to build a majority-voter coalition one block at a time. For example, a liberal candidate might buy lists of registered voters and merge them with mailing lists for liberal causes or magazines to create lists of likely supporters for fund-raising and activism. A conservative would work in a similar manner.

Buying advertising time on television programs that are watched by particular segments of the population is useful. So is utilizing computerized lists of voters with certain characteristics that increase the likelihood of getting the message heard by the right people. Ronald Reagan promoted his campaign using midday radio programs on easy-listening stations. His media handlers knew that their audiences included a large proportion of relatively conservative senior citizens. In 1992 Bill Clinton appeared on MTV to appeal to younger voters and followed other television audiences by appearing on talk shows such as "Arsenio Hall" and "Donahue." George H. Bush, on the other hand, avoided such avenues—in a misguided attempt to remain presidential—until his campaign became desperate. By 1996, all presidential candidates were vying for time on cable channels and programs appealing to voters unlikely to pay much attention to the major network news programming. In 2000, both George W. Bush and Al Gore had learned the lesson of following the audience and appeared on "Oprah" and "David Letterman," venues that would have been seen as "below" presidential candidates in the not so distant past. As the 2004 election cycle began, both Senator John McCain (waiting in the wings for George W. Bush to finish his time in office) and Senator John Kerry (D-MA) a willing challenger to Bush in 2004, both hosted "Saturday Night Live," not previously the typical outlet for national candidates.

VIDEO

George W. Bush appeals to the growing U.S. Hispanic population by campaigning in Spanish.

Few voters actively seek out political information. Political programs that are sponsored by candidates or party organizations appeal to small audiences made up of people already supportive of the cause. Short **spot advertising** has become the basic approach for national and statewide campaigns, since it avoids the selective attention that voters pay to political programming (see Chapter 6). We often remember presidential campaigns by the 30- or 60-second spots summarizing the issues in a dramatic visual form. During the 1992 campaign, the most memorable ads were George H. Bush's spots, which questioned Bill Clinton's character, and Ross Perot's half-hour **infomercials** filled with charts and graphs. Although much advertising simplifies issues and can be misleading, research indicates that voters receive as much or more issue information from political ads as from news programs.[30] In a new twist, much of the presidential campaigns since 1992 have been fought on talk shows, such as "Larry King Live."[31]

spot advertising *A short—usually 30- or 60-second—promotion for candidates or causes on radio or television.*

infomercial *An advertisement designed to look like an information program.*

During the 2000 campaign, both George W. Bush and Al Gore targeted their travel and focused their campaigns on a small number of "battleground" states that were still seen as being in play (see Tables 11-5 and 11-6). With the expanded numbers of Latino

Table 11-5 **Battleground States for Candidate Visits During the Last Month of the 2000 Campaign**

States in Order of the Most Candidate Visits					
Bush			Gore		
State	Electoral Votes	Vote Percentage	State	Electoral Votes	Vote Percentage
Florida	25	49%	Florida	25	49%
Michigan	18	46%	Michigan	18	51%
Wisconsin	11	48%	Pennsylvania	23	51%
Missouri	11	50%	Missouri	11	50%
Iowa	7	48%	Iowa	7	49%
Pennsylvania	23	46%	New York	33	60%
Illinois	22	43%	Wisconsin	11	48%

Table 11-6 Battleground States for Spot Advertising in the 2000 Campaign

States in Order of the Most Campaign Ads Aired					
Bush			Gore		
State	Electoral Votes	Vote Percentage	State	Electoral Votes	Vote Percentage
Florida	25	49%	Pennsylvania	23	51%
Ohio	21	50%	Ohio	21	46%
Pennsylvania	23	46%	Michigan	18	51%
Michigan	18	46%	Florida	25	49%
California	54	42%	Wisconsin	11	48%

voters in key states, both candidates aired numerous Spanish commercials in targeted markets, using their own proficiency with the language as a signal of their responsiveness to Latino interests.

Success in politics often involves using new technology to gain a strategic advantage. In 1992 George H. Bush carried out a 1980-style campaign. He focused on the major television networks, seemingly unaware that more than half of the prime-time audience had shifted to cable programs. Bill Clinton unabashedly looked to these new channels and went where the audience was.

Candidates cannot go everywhere and do everything to promote their campaigns, so geographic targeting of efforts is a necessity. Campaign consultants suggest that, when hunting for votes, candidates should go where the ducks are. Seeking support in areas of current strength is likely to have a better payoff than cavorting with the opposition. Increasing support from 70 to 75 percent is easier than increasing it from 20 to 25 percent. Voters who are surrounded by a candidate's supporters find themselves under social pressures to conform.

Communicating in the Right Way

Getting the message across on the best media is essential, as noted by Senator Fritz Hollings (D-S.C.):

> Television advertising is the name of the game in modern American politics. In warfare, if you control the air, you control the battlefield. In politics, if you control the airwaves, you control the tenor and focus of the campaign.[32]

The mechanics of political communication vary with the type of office sought (the playing field), the resources available, the technological environment, and the goals pursued. Local campaigns often can still get by with door-to-door distribution of brochures and a few lawn signs. Flooding the district with bumper stickers, billboards, and buttons may be enough if name recognition is the primary goal.

National campaigns have long used extensive television advertising and sophisticated computer-based targeted mailing. Until recently, such approaches were beyond the capabilities and resources of many more local campaigns. The arrival of low-cost microcomputer campaign software, the increased flexibility of moderately priced video equipment, and the expanded use of low-cost cable television advertising have led campaigns at all levels to look more similar.

New technologies are revolutionizing the ways in which candidates can interact with voters (see Box 11-3). The ability to personalize communications and to react quickly to the advertising efforts of one's opponent make modern campaigns frenetic enterprises. Those candidates able to harness appropriate technologies to their advantage often emerge the victors.

Effective politicians go to the voters using the established information-gathering patterns to their own political benefit. When voters used to sit around the cracker barrel in the general store, successful politicians went from town to town to join the conversation. When voters began to use the radio for information gathering, effective politicians mastered the new medium. With the arrival of television as the major mode of communication, smart politicians adapted their strategies and hoped they were video-friendly.

By the early 1990s, the information superhighway grew quickly into an effective means of information exchange. The arrival of the Internet and commercial services such as America Online, Prodigy, and CompuServe linked millions of Americans by email, computer bulletin boards, and targeted computerized mailing lists. Originally the Internet was limited to transmitting only words, but the World Wide Web allows the transmission of photographs and moving video. Unlike traditional campaign communications, these new technologies are personalized and interactive; users can select to receive only the information in which they are interested, and they can often either talk back to the sender or become part of a dialogue with other users.

In 1992, the Clinton presidential campaign began transmitting all of the candidate's speeches and position papers electronically, a practice that was expanded when Bill Clinton reached the White House. Each of the commercial services developed its own political "chat forums." In 1994, political activists in a number of states developed computerized political forums. Using the Minnesota E-Democracy system, gubernatorial and senatorial candidates participated in electronic debates through email. By 2000, all the candidates had active web pages for fund-raising and communicating their messages. One candidate commented on its general utility and potential for equalizing the campaign process:

> As more and more people cruise the superhighway, the Internet will become a crucial platform of the political debate...On the Internet, it doesn't matter whether Lincoln is taller than Douglas...[Y]ou can only judge our words and our ideas.[33]

Numerous initiatives, such as Project Vote Smart (http://www.vote-smart.org) and Democracy Net (http://www.dnet.org/), provide voters with nonpartisan candidate information for both local and national campaigns. Campaign consultants are telling their candidates to get ready to participate in the electronic forums or face becoming road kill on the information superhighway. Savvy citizens use all tools at their disposal to monitor the political process (see Box 11-5: Monitoring Politics in Cyberspace).

Some observers are predicting that as electronic shopping and email replace going to the mall and the visit by the mail carrier, the concept of showing up at the polling place

Box 11–5 *Monitoring Politics in Cyberspace*

If you want to explore the electronic superhighway for political information, the following addresses should be useful. Since many of the political forums are run by volunteers, quality varies and systems come and go. Do not get discouraged if the information you want is not available or the address is no longer operational. Remember, just by tapping in you have become a pioneer in the electronic democracy domain.

The following addresses will lead you to a main menu and submenus that guide you to detailed information. Once you get into one of these menus, you will often be automatically led to a variety of other computerized information sites.

American Political Science Association:
http://www.apsanet.org/
House: http://www.house.gov/
Senate: http://www.senate.gov/
C-SPAN: http://www.c-span.org/

to cast a ballot may become irrelevant. Voting from home, after selectively gathering candidate information, and then tapping into the vote count in real time is technologically possible.[34] One of the political questions of the future is whether such high-tech democracy is politically desirable.

11-5 Winning and Losing in the Electoral Arena

Winning and losing are seldom ambiguous in electoral contests:

> Elections are the big game in politics. Election night is one of the few times in politics when it is absolutely clear who knows how to play the game and who does not. Little kids used to reach for the brass ring on the merry-go-round; grown up political kids replace the brass ring with a campaign victory.[35]

All elections involve a winner and most a loser. The nature and implications of winning and losing vary, depending on the type of election involved.

11-5a Some Patterns of Success

A number of factors lead to an uneven playing field in elections. Incumbents tend to beat challengers. Candidates with more resources and a party label consistent with their district generally have an enhanced chance of success. Sometimes, however, tides of public sentiment can upset typical patterns.

The Power of Incumbency

If you want a good idea of what the next Congress or state legislature will look like, take a close look at the last one. As one member of the House put it:

> I would rather not run against another incumbent. They have financial advantages and a greater ability to play the political game. (Congressman Joe Barton, R-Tex., facing redistricting)[36]

More than 90 percent of House of Representatives members and more than 75 percent of Senate members running for reelection in recent decades won. Overwhelming reelection rates for incumbents at other levels are the rule rather than the exception. Although three of the last five incumbent presidents (Ford, Carter, and Bush) failed in their reelection bids, the overall reelection record of incumbent presidents remains high.

Compared with challengers, incumbents are better known, raise more money, and can reap the benefits of holding office. Incumbents can use their government-paid staffs in indirect ways to support their candidacy. Legitimate government services, such as the **franking privilege,** which eliminates some postal expenses, helps incumbent officeholders to keep their names and accomplishments before the eyes of voters.

franking privilege *The right of legislators to send out official mail at no cost.*

Even in an election year such as 1990, when frustration over the budget process and a series of scandals rocked Congress, the result was not massive defeats of incumbents. There was only a modest decline in their electoral margins. Anti-incumbent fever reached a new high in 1992, helping to contribute to a record number of incumbent retirements and some significant defeats. However, even in a year where "throw the rascals out" became a battle cry, the vast majority of incumbents running for reelection were successful.

In 1994 voters were selective about punishing incumbents. Not one incumbent Republican lost. Even though a set of high-profile Democrats, such as Speaker of the House Thomas S. Foley (D-Wash.) and former Ways and Means Committee Chairman Dan Rostenkowski (D-Ill.), were turned out of office, the overall incumbency success rate in the House was more than 90 percent. In 1994 Republicans actually gained significantly from 1992, while Democratic incumbents continued to lose ground. In the elections of 1996 and 1998, the 90 percent reelection rate was maintained for the Senate and increased to 98 percent for the House. Incumbent senators were somewhat more vulnerable in 2000, revealing only a 79% re-election rate, while House incumbents maintained a success rate in the upper 90% range. In 2002, 98% of House members and 85% of Senators wishing reelection were successful, despite significant redistricting after the 2000 census.

The very existence of an incumbent often scares away many potential candidates from the presidential election arena. In recent years, few incumbent presidents have faced significant challenges from within their own parties. Furthermore, they have often been able to keep the opposition challengers to a set of second-string players. As the deadlines for organizing nomination campaigns for 1992 approached, few major Democratic contenders showed much willingness to give up secure positions to challenge President George H. Bush, who enjoyed high public approval ratings following the Persian Gulf War victory. As his ratings declined, candidate interest increased, but by that time the Democratic nomination was almost locked up by Bill Clinton. Sensing public dissatisfaction with both candidates, Ross Perot, a wealthy entrepreneur, saw an opening for an independent campaign, despite the existence of an incumbent. In the end, his 19 percent of the vote—much of it garnered from probable Bush voters—made him a spoiler, damaging the incumbent president's chances for reelection. As the 1996 campaign approached, President Bill Clinton's variable popularity encouraged significant activity by potential Republican opponents almost two years prior to the election, but Republican nominee Bob Dole was unable to overcome the strong economy for which President Clinton readily accepted credit. As the first presidential election since 1988 without an incumbent, the 2000 presidential campaign attracted a large group of contenders from both parties.

Occasionally incumbents face electoral defeat by losing touch with their constituency or by involvement in a scandal, but the primary source of turnover comes from voluntary retirements. The pattern in Congress is instructive. Between 1992 and 2000, an average of over forty House members and eight Senators chose to voluntarily leave office each year. In 2004, 18 House members and 8 senators decided not to run for re-election. These numbers far overshadow primary or general election defeats. More than two-thirds of new House and Senate members in recent years won in races with no incumbent running for the seat.

The Vestiges of Partisanship

In spite of the decline in party-line voting, aspiring politicians would be well advised to find constituencies dominated by their party. Independent and third-party candidates seldom have seriously challenged candidates from the major parties at any level of American politics (see Chapter 8).

The party label greatly helps define the playing field. In 1990 less than 8 percent of congressional seats changed parties.[37] Consistency across elective offices has declined somewhat in recent years. During the early part of the twentieth century, less than 5 percent of congressional districts supported a president from one party and a member of Congress from another. This figure increased to more than 30 percent during the 1960s and 1970s, with some recovery of party-line voting in recent years (see Figure 11-7).

The fact that until very recently a clear plurality of Americans (more than 40 percent) thought of themselves as Democrats rather than as Republicans (closer to 30 percent) suggests that national elections should normally have been won by the Democratic candidate. When registered voters vote predominantly for candidates of their majority party (as Democrats did in 1960, 1976, 1992, and 1996), it is called a **maintaining election.** When a minority-party candidate, say a Republican, is able to hold onto self-identified Republicans and to capture a significant number of Democrats (as was the case in 1980, 1984, and 1988), it represents a **deviating election.** In those rare cases when not only voting but also individual party identifications shift significantly in the direction of one party (as was the case in 1932), it is called a **realigning election**[38] (see Chapter 8).

The utility of the above classifications may be waning; from the 1950s through the 1980s, Republican success on the presidential level led to an almost "permanent Republican presidency"[39] without an underlying realignment. The Democratic victory in

maintaining election *An election in which the candidate of the majority party in the electorate wins.*

deviating election *An election in which the candidate of the minority party wins by gaining enough votes from voters identifying with the majority party.*

realigning election *Election in which individual party identification shifts toward one party.*

Figure 11-7
Split-Party Ticket Voting for Presidential and Congressional Votes, 1900–2000

In 1996, for example, the 25.3 percent of House districts were carried by a presidential candidate of one party and a congressional candidate of another party.

Source: Norman J. Ornstein et al., *Vital Statistics on Congress, 2001-2002* (Washington, D.C.: American Enterprise Institute, 2001), p. 78.

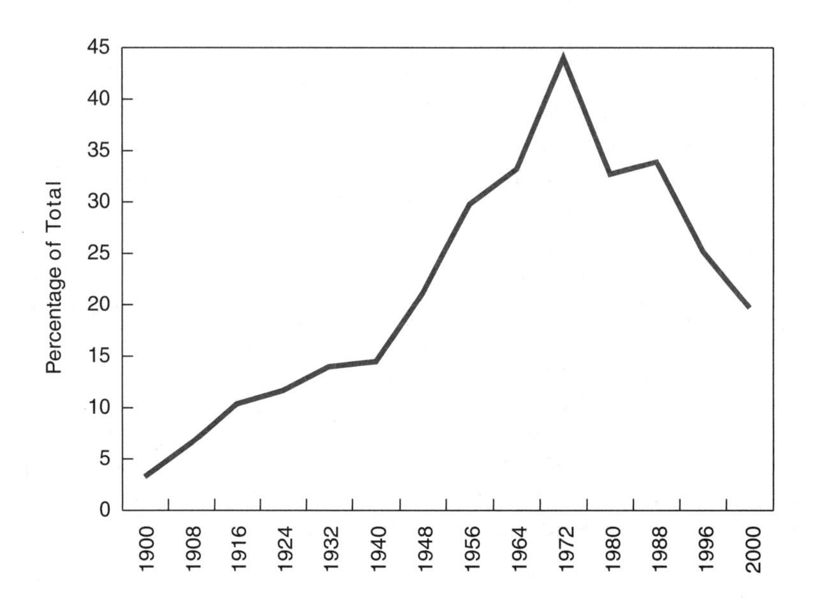

1992 and its reinforcement in 1996 resembled a maintaining election more than any clear realignment. With party identification being almost equal between the parties and with a significant number of independents and split-ticket voters, many observers see the contemporary period as one of **dealignment.** The Republican success at all electoral levels in 1994 was seen by some as a sign of a new realignment of party fortunes, but their more mixed results in subsequent elections brought this conclusion into question.

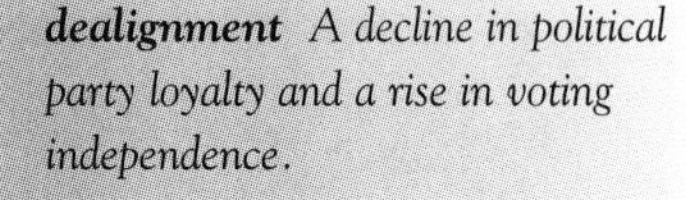

dealignment *A decline in political party loyalty and a rise in voting independence.*

The Availability of Resources

Funding does not necessarily win elections, but lack of it dooms many campaigns to failure. The candidate who spends the most does not necessarily win, but without a certain minimum to purchase key resources, the campaign quickly falters. Money available early in the campaign is more useful than money arriving so late that effective spending strategies cannot be used. Once enough money is raised to get the candidate's message out, factors other than money determine the outcome.

The Political Spillover Effect

coattail effect *The ability of candidates on the top of the party ticket to affect races at lower levels, either by changing the composition of the electorate or by directly encouraging voters.*

The growth of candidate-centered campaigns, the legacy of party identification, and the strength of incumbency insulate many campaigns from general public opinion on issues and governmental performance. But campaigns are not run in isolation. Popular presidential candidates activate enough supporters to make a difference in some lower-level races, although the degree of this **coattail effect** is not as dramatic as it once was. Since 1972, winning presidential candidates have picked up an average of twelve House seats and one Senate seat for their party. Midterm elections see a decline in the number of actual voters and a return to a more normal distribution of voter preferences.[40] Incumbent presidents lose an average of nineteen House seats and three Senate seats from their party during midterm elections. Some might interpret the shifting of congressional seats as measurements of presidential success. Actually, such interpretation only makes sense if a president's party performs significantly better or worse than the historical averages. The 1994 Republican sweep was hard to interpret in any way except as a negative judgment on both President Bill Clinton and the 40 years of Democratic control of the House (see Box 11-6: The Power of Incumbency and the Continuing Players).

The nature of political campaigns and elections is that they follow regular patterns, with unique electoral outcomes serving as the exceptions that prove the rule (see Table 11-6). Despite the success of incumbents, elected officials do change. Sporadic incumbent defeats and an increasing number of incumbents choosing not to run create room for an influx of new players. While partisan differences are significant, the social and

Box 11-6 The Power of Incumbency and the Continuing Players

Background

Social or political institutions clearly mirror the populations from which they are drawn in terms of the social background characteristics of their members. The steps involved in securing and maintaining a position in a political institution favor some individuals and hamper others. Elections represent a clear example. By winning an election, an individual is guaranteed a position in the game. The motivations, skills, and resources that allow an individual to join a game in the first place increase the chances that he or she will be able to participate effectively in subsequent rounds. To a large degree, knowing who is playing today will tell you a lot about who will be likely to play tomorrow. If the previous players fail to make the electoral cut, they tend to be replaced by individuals with similar backgrounds and orientations.

Questions

A key question to face in this realm is "Who are the players who succeed in the electoral game?" This general question suggests two more specific questions:

- To what degree are successful players able to repeat their victories?
- To what degree do new players resemble the players they replace?

Analysis

The power of incumbency is dramatic at all levels of American politics. As the graphs indicate, yesterday's players are likely to be today's players as well. Few past winners are dramatically ejected from the game against their will, although some players choose not to risk defeat and retire instead when faced with an electoral challenge. The pattern in the House of Representatives is particularly clear. More than 90 percent of House incumbents running for reelection have been successful in recent years. That level was even maintained in an election year that was filled with dramatic change: 1994. Success rates for governors and senators are somewhat lower and more variable but still quite high. Clearly, the skills, resources, and motivations that allow for victory carry over from one round to the next.

political characteristics of the new players are relatively similar to both those they replaced and those with whom they will interact in the political arena. The 1994 election was hailed as a revolution in Congress, but as Table 11-7 indicates, the new players share many characteristics with the old and are similar to those first elected in 2000.

Elections without Candidates

Not all American elections involve choosing personnel. About half the states allow proposed laws to be directly voted on through an **initiative** procedure. Proposition 13 in California reduced taxes and resulted in a decline in government services. In 1994 public frustration with the pressure that illegal aliens put on state programs erupted. A cry arose for making illegal aliens ineligible for state services in California. Proposition 187 won handily, but it was found to be unconstitutional by the courts. Voters in other states have held initiative votes to cap auto insurance, allow gambling casinos, decriminalize physician-assisted suicide, limit government efforts to protect gay men and lesbians, and limit the terms of officeholders.

initiative *A procedure allowing voters to propose and vote directly on legislation.*

Most states and localities either allow or require submission of certain types of decisions to the voters in a **referendum.** Wisconsin and other states have legalized horse racing and dog racing in this way. Most referenda involve amendments to state constitutions and local government charters. Referenda often involve issues such as changing the manner of election for public officials and revising governmental taxing and spending powers.

referendum *An election in which state or local officials submit a proposed legislative or constitutional change to the public for a vote.*

A number of states allow voters to present a petition and then to hold a recall election to reconsider specific officeholders before their term expires. Former San Francisco mayor Dianne Feinstein (now a U.S. senator) survived a **recall** election. The former governor of Arizona and a number of judges have been less successful. These specialized elections tend to draw only a small number of voters, since communicating the complexities of the options is so difficult.

recall *The procedure by which voters may submit a petition and vote as to whether an elected official should be removed from office.*

Figures 11-8A, B, C
Percentage of House/ Senate Members/ Governors Running for Reelection and Winning

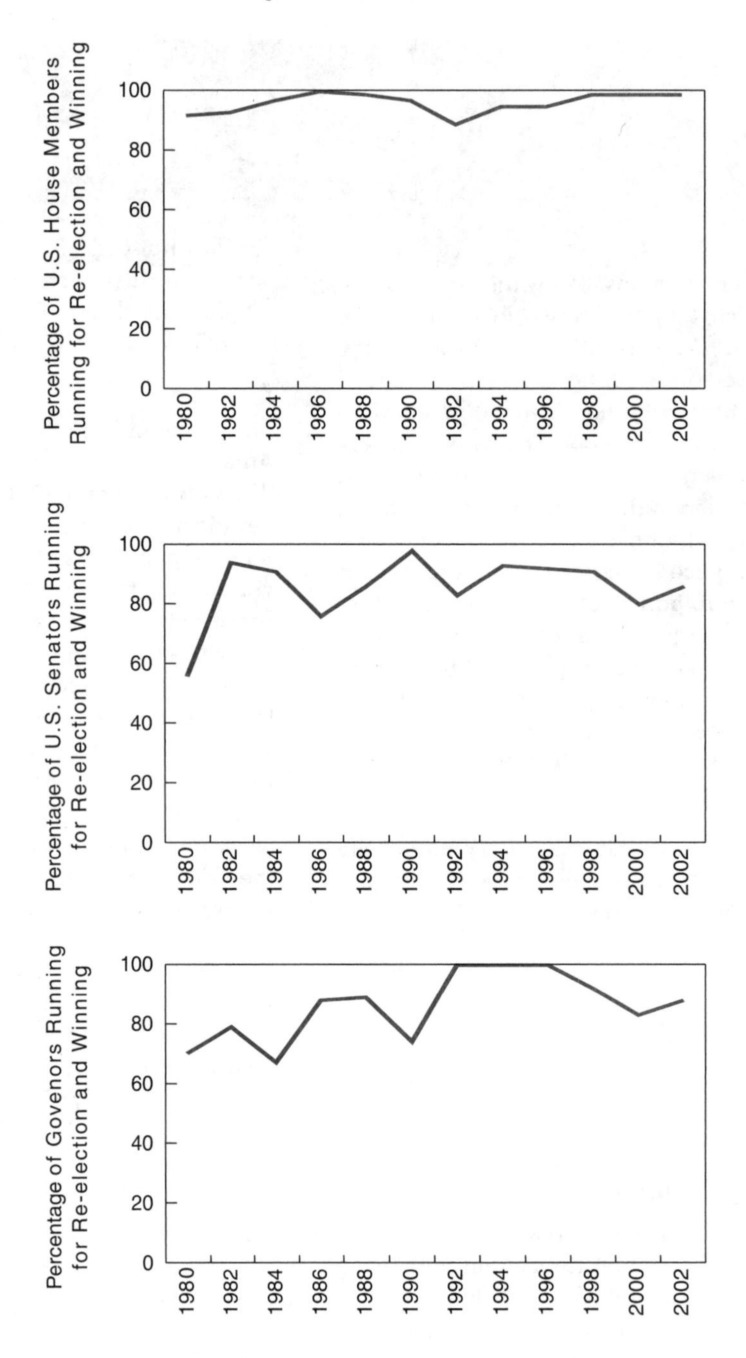

11-6 Broader Implications of Winning and Losing the Election Game

Electoral victories have implications above and beyond the personal ambitions of the candidates. Each election highlights the policy preferences of voters and affects the mix of public officials.

Policy Mandates

The intentions of voters come into focus only dimly through the electoral process. The variety of voter motivations and the vagueness of candidate commitments make clear policy mandates the exception rather than the rule. Ronald Reagan claimed a mandate for scaled-down government and fiscal conservatism after the 1980 election. However, an equally convincing case could be made that many voters simply expressed their dissatisfaction with Jimmy Carter, not their endorsement of the Reagan policy program. George

Table 11-7 Characteristics of Incumbents

	House Incumbents First Elected Prior to 1994 (as of 1994)	House Members First Elected in 1994	House Members First Elected in 2000
Similarities			
Male	90%	86%	83%
Held Previous Political Office	70%	63%	74%
Protestant[a]	52%	67%	62%
Differences			
Under age 45	21%	58%	74%
Lawyers	40%	34%	31%
Business Persons	32%	44%	45%
Republicans	45%	85%	69%

The new members elected in 1994 and in 2000 differed from their predecessors in some specifics. They were younger, more likely to be Republican, and more likely to have had business backgrounds. In other realms such as gender, political experience, religious preference, and occupation they are quite similar to the typical profile of members of Congress. In comparison to the population as a whole, winners of the congressional electoral game are older, better educated, and wealthier, and they include a greater percentage of males. The players in Congress are clearly the "haves" of our society. The numbers of non-college-educated, blue-collar workers, younger citizens, and women are clearly below the national figures.

[a] Based on those who expressed a religious preference.
Sources: Reelection rates: Harold W. Stanley and Richard G. Niemi, *Vital Statistics on American Politics* (Washington, D.C.: Congressional Quarterly Press, Inc., 1994), 128–129; Demographics: Center for the American Woman and Politics press release, March 15, 1995; *Black Elected Officials* (Washington, D.C.: Joint Center for Political and Economic Studies Press, 1993), xvi; Norman J. Ornstein, Thomas E. Mann, Michael J. Malbin, *Vital Statistics on Congress, 1999–2000* (Washington, D.C.: Congressional Quarterly Press, Inc., 1994), 22–42; and LEXIS-NEXIS database. 2000 Demographics calculated from *Congressional Quarterly Weekly Report,* November 11, 2000.

H. Bush emphasized the importance of his no-new-taxes pledge in the 1988 campaign, even though public opinion polls showed Americans almost evenly split in their willingness to support some new taxes to reduce the deficit.[41] As noted, President George H. Bush's commitment on taxes gave way to economic reality relatively early in his term.

In 1992 Bill Clinton campaigned on the theme of change and stressed refocusing American efforts inward on economic problems. While many voters used their vote to show displeasure with the Bush domestic record, President Clinton claimed a mandate for government efforts to reduce unemployment and to shift the tax burden to wealthier Americans. The idea of a mandate took on new meaning in 1994 when a large number of Republican congressional candidates signed their Contract with America as a midterm platform of specific government initiatives. The new Republican majority in Congress acted as if they had a clear mandate despite the fact that less than a third of the voters had heard of the Contract. Of those with knowledge of its content, only about half supported it in full.[42] Clear mandates most often exist only in the minds of elected officials who seek direction and legitimacy for their actions. They are rarely distinct blueprints emanating from the actions of voters. Despite the questions over the results of the 2000 election, President George W. Bush interpreted his victory to be a mandate for lowering taxes. He maintained that commitment even in the face of budget pressure for defense and homeland security after the events of September 11th.

Personnel Impacts

Elections, of course, determine the key personnel of government. The election of one particular individual or even marginal changes in the makeup of a collective body can

Table 11-8 Election Outcome Anomalies

1800	Thomas Jefferson and Aaron Burr tie in electoral votes, throwing the election into the House, where Jefferson is elected.
1824	Andrew Jackson wins the popular vote but fails to get a majority in the Electoral College, again throwing the election into the House. John Quincy Adams is elected by the House, even though he placed second in both the electoral and popular vote.
1840	Martin Van Buren and Richard M. Johnson become the first sitting president and vice president to be defeated for re-election.
1888	Benjamin Harrison becomes the third president elected without winning the popular vote.
1954	Strom Thurmond of South Carolina becomes the only senator ever elected by a write-in vote.
1960	John Kennedy and Richard Nixon participate in the first presidential debate, which is widely regarded to have turned the tide for Kennedy, who became the first Catholic president.
1994	Congressional Republicans propose a "Contract with America," gaining the image of the "party with a plan." The Republicans become the majority in both the House and Senate.
2000	For the first time, the Supreme Court settles a disputed election, voting 5–4 to end Al Gore's challenge of the narrow popular vote in Florida. George W. Bush is elected by the electoral college despite narrowly losing the popular vote.

For more details see the *Congressional Quarterly Guide to U.S. Elections* (Washington, D.C.: Congressional Quarterly Inc.), 14–20.

have a significant effect. In 1980 the victory of Ronald Reagan set the stage for the implementation of policies very different from those that would have stemmed from the reelection of Jimmy Carter. The twelve new Republican senators elected in 1980 turned Senate control over to the Republicans and made a significant portion of the Reagan agenda a reality. Bill Clinton's victory in 1992, after twelve years of Republican domination of the presidency, signaled the public desire for change and set in motion forces that altered both the personnel and policies of government. The 1994 Republican takeover of Congress not only brought in new Republican members but also changed all committee chairmanships and the staffs associated with them. Not one of the House Republicans elected in 1994 had ever served in a House with a Republican majority. The new majority proceeded quickly to change House operating procedures, which they had criticized for years as members of the minority. Their initiatives in restructuring committees and placing limits on how long party and committee leaders could serve changed the power bases of many members as they were required to seek other leadership positions.

accountability *The process by which voters are given the opportunity to judge the actions of government officials and affect the officials' power and career.*

Conclusion

Campaigns and elections increasingly involve large expenditures of time and money, especially with the growing competition in the use of effective campaign technologies. The existing and emerging rules and strategies determine the success and failure of different sets of players. The electoral playing field remains relatively uneven, favoring the major parties over other teams and individuals and favoring players with significant resources over those who lack them.

Incumbent politicians see elections as a continuous game in which they hope to remain players. The existence of regularly scheduled elections may well be more important than the election results themselves. The **accountability** of elected officials to the voters breathes life into the concept of democracy. Knowing that they will have to regularly face the electorate, politicians may act in a more responsible and representative manner than officials insulated against regular review. The fact that the spectators from time to time enter the game in significant numbers stimulates the full-time players.

The election game is one in which the winners and losers are easily discerned. The results determine players and affect the policy of government. Perhaps even more importantly, public perceptions of how the game is played determine to a large degree the legitimacy with which the entire political system is viewed.

Key Terms

accountability
Baker v. Carr
bandwagon effect
blanket primary
closed primary
coattail effect
dealignment
dependent voters
deviating election
faithless elector
franking privilege
gatekeeper
gerrymandering
infomercial
initiative
instrumental voting
legitimacy
maintaining election
majority-minority district
mandate
negative advertising
one-person, one-vote
open primary
parliamentary system
psychological needs voting
Rainbow Coalition
realigning election
reapportionment
recall
redistricting
referendum
responsive voters
social needs
spot advertising

Practice Quiz

1. How are elections determined in a parliamentary system?
a. They are called by the prime minister.
b. They occur every two years.
c. They occur every four years.
d. They are called by judicial officials when conflict threatens to harm national interests.

2. What do fixed elections cause?
a. Fraud
b. A two-party system
c. Policy choices that are made with the electoral calendar taken into account
d. Policy choices that are made for long-term interests.

3. What is the process by which state legislatures define congressional constituency lines to reflect changes in population?
a. Gerrymandering
b. Proportional representation
c. Redistricting
d. Reapportionment

4. What is gerrymandering?
a. Designing election districts based on population
b. Designing election districts that give an advantage to a party or group
c. Designing election districts by population, income, or occupational status
d. Any of the above

5. Which of the following has stimulated intentional gerrymandering in recent years?
a. The one-person, one-vote decision of the Supreme Court
b. The principle of contiguity
c. Large-scale immigration in western states
d. The desire to create minority districts

6. Today, most states use which method to select delegates to national nominating conventions?
a. Caucuses
b. Primaries
c. State party conventions
d. The electoral college

7. The decline of straight party voting has encouraged which of the following?
a. Candidate-centered campaigns
b. Presidential primaries
c. The resurgence of partisanship by elected officials
d. All of the above

8. In *Baker v. Carr*, the Supreme Court affirmed the doctrine of
a. campaign contributions as a form of expression.
b. refusing to allow political candidates to sue for slander.
c. outlawing gerrymandering.
d. one-person, one-vote.

9. Voters have the most freedom in which of the following types of primaries?
a. Closed
b. Open
c. Presidential
d. Blanket

10. The "bandwagon" effect has the greatest impact on _____ voters.
a. psychological
b. instrumental
c. primary
d. social

You can find the correct answers to these questions by taking the quiz and then submitting your answers in the Online Edition. The program will automatically score your submission. Where you miss a question, the program will provide the correct answer, a rationale for the answer, and the section number in the chapter where the topic is discussed.

Further Reading

The key monthly journal of modern campaign technology and strategy is *Campaigns and Elections*, published in Washington, D.C.

For a comprehensive look at contemporary political parties and their role in election strategy, see Stephen E. Frantzich, *Political Parties in the Technological Age* (New York: Longman, 1989).

For a collection of essays placing the 1992 presidential election in context, see William Crotty (ed.), *America's Choice: The Election of 1992* (Guilford, CT: Dushkin Publishing Group, 1993). For interpretations of the 1996 and 1998 elections, see Paul Abramson, John Aldrich and David Rohde, *Change and Continuity in the 1996 and 1998 Elections* (Washington, D.C.: Congressional Quarterly Press, 1999).

The classic study on the rise of political action committees is Larry J. Sabato, *PAC Power* (New York: W. W. Norton, 1985).

For a detailed look at campaign financing law and strategy, see Frank Sorauf, *Money in American Elections* (Glenview, IL: Scott, Foresman/Little, Brown, 1988).

Theodore White wrote books on each presidential election from 1960 to 1972 under the general title *The Making of the President*. This series gives an excellent behind-the-scenes view of American politics of the era.

The oddity of the 2000 election led to a spate of books analyzing both campaign strategy and electoral law. For example, see Steven E. Schier, *You Call This an Election?: America's Peculiar Democracy* (Washington, D.C.: Georgetown University Press, 2003) and Gerald Pomper (ed), *The Election of 2000: Reports and Interpretations* (Washington, D.C.: Congressional Quarterly Press, 2001).

Endnotes

1. See Edward R. Tufte, *Political Control of the Economy* (Princeton, NJ: Princeton University Press, 1978).
2. Jack Quinn, Donald J. Simon, and Jonathan B. Sallet, "Redrawing Political Maps: An America of Groups," *Washington Post*, March 24, 1991, C1.
3. Richard Cohen, "Redistricting Memo," *National Journal*, April 20, 1991, 934–35.
4. Phil Duncan, "Partisan Remapping Not Cut and Dried," *Congressional Quarterly Weekly Report*, (November 17, 1990): 3902.
5. *Davis v. Bandemer*, 92 L. Ed. 2d 85 (1986).
6. Steven Holmes, "The 1994 Election: Voters," *New York Times*, November 13, 1994, sec. 1, 32; and Steven Holmes, "Experts Say Redistricting Added to the G.O.P. Surge," *New York Times*, November 13, 1994, A16.
7. Clinton administration and American Civil Liberties Union spokespersons quoted in Aaron Epstein, "Jurists to Hear Vote Rights Case," *Houston Chronicle*, December 10, 1994, A15.
8. William H. Flanigan and Nancy H. Zingale, *Political Behavior of the American Electorate* (New York: Allyn and Bacon, 1994), 38.
9. Advisory Commission on Intergovernmental Relations, *The Transformation in American Politics: Implications for Federalism* (Washington, D.C.: ACIR, 1986), 146.
10. Paul Taylor, "California's Early Primary," *Washington Post*, February 27, 1990, A11.
11. See Stephen Frantzich, *Political Parties in the Technological Age* (New York: Longman, 1989), 89; and Paul Herrnson, *Party Campaigning in the 1980s* (Cambridge, MA: Harvard University Press, 1988).
12. Larry Sabato, *The Rise of Political Consultants* (New York: Basic Books, 1981).
13. Thomas Edsall, "Kingmakers for Hire," *Washington Post*, December 5, 1993, A11.
14. *Ibid.*
15. *Ibid.*
16. Democratic pollster Geoff Garin quoted in David S. Broder, "Politicians, Advisors Agonize Over Negative Campaigning," *Washington Post*, January 19, 1989, A1.
17. Peggy Noonan, "Red Meat and Astroturf: Decoding the Convention," *Washington Post*, August 8, 1992, C1.
18. Flanigan and Zingale, *Political Behavior*, 163.
19. Gerald Pomper, *Voter's Choice* (New York: Harper and Row, 1975), 5–9.
20. See W. Russell Neuman, *The Paradox of Mass Politics* (Cambridge, MA: Harvard University Press, 1986), 125–26.
21. Lloyd Grove, "Dueling for Third, Harkin and Kerry," *Washington Post*, February 10, 1992, B1.
22. Based on research by the National Women's Political Caucus, Joanne Connor Green and Christine Wolbrecht, quoted in David Broder, 1994, "Key to Women's Political Parity: Running," *Washington Post*, September 8, 1994, A17.
23. James Driscoll, "Caucus Helps Women Run and Win," *Sun Sentinel* (Ft. Lauderdale, FL), February 19, 1995, 7G.
24. Quoted in Howard Schneider, "Challenger Tries to Pull Rank on Dyson," *Washington Post*, October 30, 1990, B5.
25. Norman J. Ornstein et al, *Vital Statistics on Congress*, 2001–2002, (Washington, D.C.: American Enterprise Institute, 2002).
26. Timothy W. Luke, *Screens of Power* (Urbana and Chicago, IL: University of Illinois Press, 1989).
27. Melinda Henneberger, "As Political Ads Slither into Negativity, the Real Venom Is Not Found on TV," *New York Times*, October 30, 1994, 45.
28. David Broder, "The Amazing New High-Speed Dial-a-President Machine," *Washington Post*, July 8, 1987, A19.
29. Quoted in Bill Peterson, "In His Father's Shadow No More," *Washington Post*, January 20, 1989, A3.
30. Thomas E. Patterson and Robert D. McClure, *The Unseeing Eye* (New York: Putnam, 1976).
31. See Larry King and Mark Stencel, *On the Line: The New Road to the White House* (New York: Harcourt Brace and Co., 1994).
32. *Congressional Record*, July 31, 1990, S11188.
33. Will Sletterly, Grassroots Party candidate quoted in Peter H. Lewis, "Electronic Tie for Citizens and Seekers of Office," *New York Times*, November 11, 1994, A15.
34. Bob Herbst, "Interactive Democracy," *Campaigns and Elections*, April 1994, 53.
35. Author's interview with local campaign activist.
36. Quoted in Richard E. Cohen, "How a Texan Might Be Unhorsed in '92," *National Journal* 23, no. 7 (February 16, 1991): 403.
37. Norman Ornstein et al., *Vital Statistics on Congress, 1999–2000* (Washington, D.C.: Congressional Quarterly Press, Inc., 2000), 55.
38. See Philip E. Converse, "The Concept of a Normal Vote," in *Elections and the Political Order*, ed. Angus Campbell et al. (New York: John Wiley & Sons, 1966), 9–39; and Gerald Pomper, *Elections in America* (New York: Dodd, Mead, 1974), 104–11.
39. Michael M. Gant and Norman R. Luttbeg, *American Electoral Behavior* (Itasca, IL: F. E. Peacock, 1991).
40. Angus Campbell, "A Comparison of Presidential and Midterm Elections" (Paper presented at the 1985 Annual Meeting of the American Political Science Association, New Orleans).
41. By early 1990, the Yankelovich telephone poll of five hundred American adults indicated that 47 percent of the respondents approved of a tax increase and almost 75 percent believed that there would be an increase.
42. CBS News poll of 1,120 adults, November 1994, LEXIS-NEXIS database.

12

Congress: The Election and Survival Games

Key Points

- **The changes in Congress over the last two hundred years.**
- **The unique character of congressional elections and their impact on Congress.**
- **How members of Congress define their jobs and organize for action.**
- **The team character of Congress.**
- **Techniques for playing the congressional survival game.**

Preview: Drawing the Line

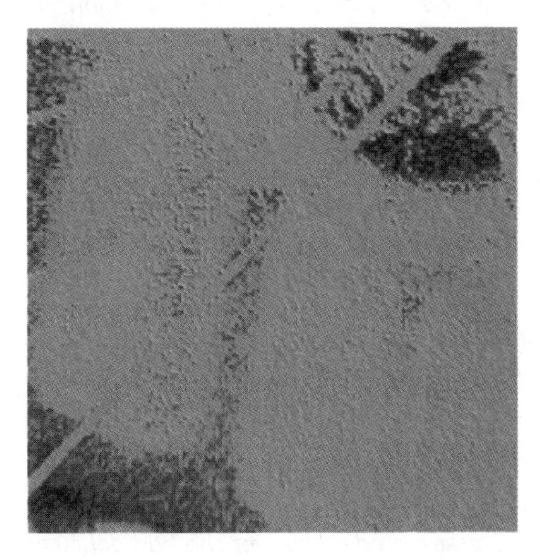

Texas state senator Eddie Bernice Johnson pondered over the detailed maps of Texas and recognized the tremendous importance of her decisions. As chair of the Senate Subcommittee on Redistricting, it was Senator Johnson's job to design the political playing field for the next decade. The U.S. Constitution requires reapportioning congressional seats to the states after each census, and population growth had earned Texas three additional seats. While adding seats is less painful politically than cutting back, the job was filled with challenges. At a minimum, the courts would require districts of equal population. Sitting members of Congress expressed considerable concern over the dismantling of their current districts. Party leaders on both sides wanted districts that would maximize party fortunes. Since the last redistricting, after the 1980 census, a new requirement had entered into the redistricting battle. The Justice Department had interpreted the 1982 amendments to the 1965 Voting Rights Act as

The Chamber of the House of Representatives.

supporting, wherever feasible, majority-minority districts, in which ethnic minorities would have an opportunity to win elections. As an African-American female, Senator Johnson felt a great deal of enthusiasm for achieving that goal.

Since redistricting is fraught with so much political conflict, it was not particularly surprising that a relatively junior second-term senator would be saddled with the task. One of her greatest challenges came from incumbent African-American congressman Martin Frost. He did not like the way she was drawing the new black-majority district in Dallas because it reduced his personal political base. In designing the new thirtieth district in Dallas, Senator Johnson had one additional goal above and beyond those imposed by the law and by pressures from her party allies. She was ever conscious that this was to be the district in which she lived—and from which she hoped to run for U.S. Congress. When the dust settled, her plan won approval of both the state legislature and the governor, as well as preclearance by the Justice Department. In 1992 Eddie Bernice Johnson went on to win a seat in Congress from the district she had created. She entered the 103rd Congress as a Democrat in January 1993. Despite an anti-Democratic mood in 1994, Representative Johnson had little trouble winning once again in her carefully created district.

While politics has long been a process of "seeing one's opportunities and taking them," Representative Johnson was far from an inexperienced nobody who selfishly took advantage of a political fluke. At age fifty-six, she was somewhat older than her average House colleagues. She had paid her political dues.

Elected to the Texas state House of Representatives in 1972, she was the first African-American woman to represent Dallas. During her second term in office, she became the first woman in the history of the state to chair a major House committee. During the Carter administration, she took time out from elected office to serve as regional director of the Department of Health, Education, and Welfare. In 1986 she became the first woman and the first African American to represent Dallas in the state senate since Reconstruction. In the private sector, Representative Johnson was a successful businessperson and served on numerous corporate boards of directors.

It is true that the lucky creation of a tailored majority-minority district opened the door for Eddie Bernice Johnson to enter the House of Representatives. Representative Johnson entered the political game with impressive credentials, yet she had difficulty in achieving success in the big league of the congressional arena until the rules were changed. She is one of the many success stories of the move for majority-minority districts. Recent court rulings may now make that route more difficult (see Chapter 8 and Box 12-4: Ruling for the Minority*). In future rounds, minority candidates from around the country may not get an "assist" from the rules.*

Shortly after emerging from the Constitutional Convention, Benjamin Franklin was asked, "Well, Doctor, what have we got—a Republic or a Monarchy?" Franklin replied simply, "A republic, if you can keep it."[1] Franklin's words contained a description and a warning. In describing the new government as **republican**—with a small *r* (not to be confused with the Republican Party)—Franklin and his fellow delegates were acknowledging that the new nation's land area and population were too large for everyone to participate directly in government. Under the new Constitution, members of Congress were assigned an intermediary role between the citizens and the new national government. The primary task of the members of Congress was, and is, to make the laws of the land and thus to represent the views and interests of the citizens who send them to Washington.

republicanism *Democratic political game in which groups of citizens are constituents who choose others (elected representatives) to look after their interests in government decision making.*

Should a member of Congress from those early years return to either chamber today, he (the first woman was not elected to Congress until 1916) would find some rules and strategies familiar. Undoubtedly he would be surprised, however, at the way Congress has adapted to changes in society, technology, and the nature of its membership. The historical visitor would be amazed at the complexity of modern policy issues, the increased size and importance of congressional staffs, and the extensive use of modern information technology. New campaigning techniques and requirements have altered the nature of congressional membership. They have paved the way for a more diverse set of candidates than the relatively similar group who attended the Continental Congress and the Constitutional Convention.

In today's Congress, several games are played at the same time. Members seek office via the electoral game. Once elected, players position themselves to exercise power. They then become embroiled in the survival game as they attempt to retain their offices. In the policy game, members of Congress tackle public problems and determine public policy. In a system based on a "separation of powers," Congress is forced to protect its authority by playing the institutional balance of power game. Each game involves different players, rules, strategies, winners, and losers. This chapter focuses on the initial two games, which determine who plays in the congressional arena. It also describes the organization of the elected players into teams. Chapter 13 examines the other two games and explores the strategies involved in the functions and responsibilities of Congress as an institution.

12-1 Historical Perspectives

Congress has gone through numerous changes since the days of the Founders. A full understanding of Congress today—both in terms of the selection of players and the players' roles—requires an understanding of its beginnings. We start by looking at the first Congress and at some of the Congresses in later centuries.

12-1a The First Congress

The first members of Congress gathered in New York in 1789. The seat of government then shifted to Philadelphia in 1790 and eventually settled in Washington, D.C., in 1800. The impermanence of the meeting location reflected the lack of structure and procedures confronting the new members. The young nation's basic rule book, the Constitution, did not cover the internal rules of each chamber. The fifty-nine House members themselves established rules and procedures—the most significant of which was the centralization of power in the Speaker. The smaller Senate, with its twenty-two members, settled upon a more flexible and leisurely working style. From the beginning, Congress played an important public policy role in passing legislation, but in both the House and Senate, members seldom introduced their own bills. Instead, problems were brought to the chamber by members, and **ad hoc committees** were established to propose and draft legislation. After passage of a particular bill, the committee responsible for it was dissolved.

ad hoc committee *A body such as an investigating committee formed to serve a specific purpose only.*

The Senate, whose members were elected by state legislatures, was initially overshadowed by the popularly elected House of Representatives in terms of power, legislative activity, and prestige.[2] The early Senate met behind closed doors and saw its primary role as that of adviser to the president. The first Senate spent numerous hours debating such topics of protocol as the appropriate title of address for the president. The Senate often adjourned so that its members could wander over to the open sessions of the House and listen to the more vigorous and meaningful debates there.

Despite the fears of the Founders that members of Congress would become entrenched in power, reelection rates to the early Congresses were low. During the first decade of the new nation, over one-third of the senators resigned before completing their terms. Bored by the lack of significant action, they went on to pursue their personal business interests. Similarly, many House members served only a term or two.[3]

12-1b The Thirtieth Congress

When Abraham Lincoln entered the Thirtieth Congress in 1848, he knew that after one term in the House he would be back in Springfield, Illinois. Lincoln's victory was due more to the strength of the Whig Party in his district than to his personal appeal or any extensive campaigning on his part. At a time when the active electorate in the average district numbered just over ten thousand voters, his campaign had cost him 75 cents for a few handbills.

Following the party dictate of share and share alike, Lincoln heeded the norm and passed the nomination on to another party member from a different county after two years.[4] More than half of his fellow representatives were also serving their first term.[5] Lincoln entered an institution that was more important than the presidency and whose internal power structure was more "top down" than democratic. Key issues of the day—such as slavery—were decided by Congress with little presidential input. Committees were largely temporary ad hoc groupings of members whose general knowledge was thought to be sufficient to deal with the limited number of policy concerns handled at the national level. Serving in Congress was a part-time job. Members spent only a few months each year in Washington, where they established temporary residence in boardinghouses and managed their legislative affairs with the help of only a handful of clerks.

12-1c The Mid-Twentieth-Century Congresses

A century later, during the 1950s and 1960s, five future presidents (Kennedy, Johnson, Nixon, Ford, and Bush) served in a Congress both more and less powerful than in Lincoln's day. While expansion of the federal government's policy-making role had increased the absolute scope of congressional responsibilities, Congress's power in relation to the executive branch had eroded. The long-term erosion of congressional power compared with that of the executive branch was due to several factors:

- the mass media's tendency to focus on the president rather than on Congress;
- the president's inherent capacity to make timely individual decisions in a crisis; and
- the public's confidence in presidential leadership in policy making.

The membership of Congress also had changed by the 1950s. The passage of the 17th Amendment in 1913 provided for the direct election of senators, replacing the previous process of election by state legislators. This subjected members of the Senate to the same electoral pressures experienced by House members. The increased popularity of the primary at the turn of the century, as a means of nominating candidates to both houses, changed the entrance rules and weakened party control over the nomination process (see Chapters 9 and 11) House districts grew in size to about two hundred thousand eligible voters. Since equalized redistricting was not required until the 1960s, districts varied greatly in population.[6]

seniority *The process of choosing congressional committee chairs on the basis of their length of service on the committee.*

The selection of legislative leaders was governed by new rules, both informal and formal. Criteria based on **seniority** (length of service), for example, became the norm, encouraging members to make a career of congressional service. Incumbents routinely gained reelection.

Other changes within Congress weakened the power of the parties over the legislative process. Abuses by the party leadership a half century earlier led to stripping them of much of their power. Congressional leadership now resided with the committee chairs, who, at times, acted independently of their parties. As a result, the success of party leaders was now based on personal skills rather than on formal authority alone. Even so, lining up one's fellow party members remained the logical first step in successfully building a coalition within Congress to support any individual piece of legislation.

12-1d Recent Congresses

Congress, like most social institutions changes over time:

> The Washington power game has been altered by many factors: new congressional assertiveness against the presidency, the revolt within Congress against the seniority system, television, the merchandising of candidates, the explosion of special interest politics. . . . Altogether, it's a new ball game, with new sets of rules, new ways of getting power leverage, new types of players, new game plans and new tactics that affect winning and losing.[7]

A comparison of the Congresses of the 1990s with those of the 1950s reveals both change and continuity. Party-line voting patterns within Congress and executive domination of the policy process gave way to a reawakened and more individualistic Congress during the 1970s and 1980s, returning to a more partisan era as the century ended. Although Congress's basic role as a representational body remains intact, and the decision-making rules have been altered only slightly, much else about Congress has changed.

Today, congressmen and congresswomen (there have been more than fifty female representatives and more than a dozen female senators in recent Congresses) more often than not have achieved their position with only limited help from their party. They rely instead on their own organization and support from interest groups. Increasingly, the successful candidates are those who make the best use of modern campaign technologies, such as television and highly targeted direct-mail campaigns. With the weakening of party control over nominations, the halls of Congress are populated by a more varied group of members who better reflect the diversity of American society. Contemporary constituents expect more than oratory or party loyalty from their elected representatives. They also demand a member who does not blindly follow party dictates and who provides a high level of personal service.

Members of Congress of late have expanded their staffs to help them handle casework (constituents' demands) and to cope with the intricacies of increasingly complex legislation. Congressional sessions run throughout the year, and most members live in the Washington area rather than in their districts. (They of course make frequent visits to their home states.) By the 1980s enhanced internal democracy and the sharing of power within Congress had replaced the period of almost absolute control by often **autocratic** committee chairs.

autocratic *Rule by one having complete and unlimited power.*

Often outmaneuvered by the president as the initiator of new policy, Congress began to monitor aggressively the executive branch through such dramatic activities as the Watergate, Iran-Contra, Whitewater, and Clinton impeachment hearings. Through its appropriating and authorizing powers (see Chapter 13), Congress affirmed its power to amend budgets and policy proposals.

12-1e The 104th Congress and Beyond

After forty years of Democratic control of the House and a general pattern of Democratic control of the Senate, the Republicans gained solid majorities in both chambers after the 1994 elections. While many Republican senators had experienced majority status before, not one Republican member of the 104th session (1995–1996) of the House of Representatives had served in a House controlled by Republicans. After decades of criticizing Democratic policy and guardianship of the chamber, Republicans now had the chance to mold Congress to their own image. The potential for significant institutional change was dramatic.

Unlike recent candidate-centered elections, most of the Republican winners had signed the Contract with America, a midterm party platform (mentioned in Chapters 2, 7, and 8, and discussed in Chapter 9). It included ten specific policy recommendations, which became the agenda for the first one hundred days of the new Congress. The influx of a strongly committed Republican majority in the House made it quite simple to pass the items in the Contract through that chamber. In every case, except for term limits, the Republicans were able to pass Contract items without needing any Democratic votes. (Since changing term limits would necessitate a constitutional amendment, a two-thirds vote was required in each chamber, so this issue was not so easily pushed through by Republican members.) The Senate expressed more hesitation on Contract items. The **line-item veto** for the president was passed into law in hopes of curbing Congress's proclivity to spend but was later ruled unconstitutional by the courts. The balanced budget amendment and term limitations for members of Congress failed to receive adequate support in 1995 (see Box 12-1: The Contract with America), but a strong economy and voluntary spending cuts led to a balanced budget by the late 1990s.

line-item veto *The power given a governor or president to disapprove specific sections of legislation otherwise approved.*

Internally, Republicans, who had long complained about wasteful and inefficient procedures in Congress, attempted to redesign the House. At the outset, the leadership trimmed congressional staffs and cut some committees. The position of the party leadership was strengthened both by rule changes and revised procedures. Incoming speaker Newt Gingrich (R-Ga.) violated the norm of seniority to select committee chairs more in step with his agenda. He opened the policy process to more public scrutiny by allowing television cameras to cover his morning briefings and by making it more difficult to bar cameras from committee meetings. Similar but subtler changes occurred under the leadership of Majority Leader Robert Dole (R-Kans.) in the Senate.

Above and beyond procedural changes, the election of 1994 brought to power a group of Republican leaders, especially in the House, who exhibited an aggressive commitment to a conservative agenda of cutting back government. Although partisan voting had increased since the 1980s, the new Congress was poised for conflict. Many of the initial votes (see Box 12-1) revealed a cohesive Republican Party who were joined by a few Democrats to pass key elements of the Contract. Many of the moderates from both parties had retired or been defeated. The assertiveness of the House leadership led by Speaker Newt Gingrich tended to overshadow the more accommodating style of Senate Majority Leader Bob Dole. The election of 1994 was interpreted as a mandate for Republican policies, or at least a rejection of President Bill Clinton's agenda and of the Democratic stewardship of Congress.

Congressional partisanship reached new levels with an ethics investigation of Speaker Gingrich and the House impeachment and Senate trial of President Clinton. Bob Dole was superceded by Trent Lott (R-Miss.) as Senate majority leader during the 1996 presidential campaign. After Speaker Gingirch resigned in the wake of Republican election reversals in 1998, the House Republicans chose Dennis Hastert (R-Ill.), a more low-key insider operator, as Speaker in hopes of avoiding the experience of another speaker serving as a partisan lightning rod.

The 1998 and 2000 elections maintained fragile Republican majorities in both chambers. Senator James Jeffords of Vermont, frustrated with lack of Republican support for his education initiatives, threw the Senate back into Democratic control by becoming an independent after the 2000 election. Republicans did well in both the 2002 and 2004 congressional elections, retaining control of both chambers. The 109th Congress (2005–2006) gave Republicans a 232 to 201 margin in the House and a 55 to 44 majority in the Senate.

12-2 The Electoral Game

In Congress, where at least four games are played at any given time, it is the electoral game that determines the players in the other games. To most citizens, congressional elections are the most visible of the many congressional games. They make up the arena in which the average citizen is most likely to become directly involved through the act of voting. Each member of the House of Representatives and one-third of the members of the Senate are elected to office every other year. Along with the weakening of party control over

Box 12–1 The Contract with America

The Republican Contract with America initially included ten basic principles. In going through the legislative process, some principles were combined and others were divided into separate pieces of legislation. During the first one hundred days of the 104th Congress, the House took twenty-one final votes specifically on contract proposals. While some of the votes were overwhelming, those on which there was disagreement tended to be divided between the two parties.

	Vote	Republican Vote	Republican Votes as a Percent of Total
Congressional Process			
Require Congress to end its exemptions on eleven workplace laws	429–0	224–0	52%
Changes in House rules to cut committee staffs, impose term limits on chairs, end proxy voting, and require a three-fifths majority for tax votes	416–12	224–0	54%
Budgeting			
Balanced budget amendments[a]	300–132	228–2	76%
Line item veto for the president	294–134	223–4	76%
Crime			
Create bloc grants to give communities flexibility in spending anticrime funds	238–192	220–9	92%
Increase grants for prison construction	265–156	206–20	78%
Speed the deportation of criminal aliens	380–20	216–1	55%
Require victim restitution	431–0	228–0	53%
Modify the exclusionary rule to make it easier to use evidence	289–142	220–7	76%
Welfare			
Tighten welfare	234–199	225–5	96%
Families			
Require parental consent for children participating in surveys	418–7	225–0	53%
Increase penalties for sex crimes against children	417–0	225–0	54%
National Security			
Prohibit use of U.S. troops in UN missions under foreign command; prohibit defense cuts to finance social programs; develop a missile defense system	241–181	223–4	93%
Taxes			
Institute middle-class tax cut; reduce "marriage penalty"; cut capital gains tax; reduce taxes on Social Security income	246–188	219–211	89%
Government Regulations			
Reduce unfunded mandates	360–174	230–0	64%
Reduce federal paperwork	277–141	219–8	78%
Civil Law			
Limit product liability damages	265–161	220–6	83%
Limit investors' suits against companies	325–99	226–0	70%
Apply "loser pays" rule to some federal cases	232–193	216–11	93%
Term Limits			
Send to the states a constitutional amendment limiting congressional terms[b]	227–204	189–40	83%

a. Defeated in the Senate.

b. Failed to receive the two-thirds vote necessary

nominations and the rise of candidate-centered elections came the era of the continuous campaign. The electoral game never stops.

12-2a The Players

The most obvious players in the electoral game are the 100 senators and 435 members of the House of Representatives. The legal requirements to run for office (see Box 12-2: Meeting the Legal Requirements to Run for Congress) are less stringent than are the barriers associated with motivation and political resources (see Box 12-3: Creating the Congressional FARM Team). This group of decision makers is relatively small when compared to the hundreds of candidates who fail to pass the electoral test and to the thousands of paid campaign staff members and volunteers whose support makes a candidate's election possible. Numbers alone, however, fail to tell the whole story. If we understand who the candidates for Congress and their staffs are, we possess significant clues as to how they will act once in office.

Unlike most individuals wishing to develop a career, members of Congress cannot simply work their way up through a single and well-defined career path. No specific educational or occupational experience is required. To have previously held elective office at the state or local level might help a person gain election to Congress, but many members arrive with no such experience. Despite the number of ways by which one may become a member, there are still several fairly well-worn paths to Congress. Members of the House of Representatives, for example, frequently have served as state legislators, while the House of Representatives itself serves as a primary training ground for future candidates for the Senate.

Some candidates are actively recruited by the political parties and/or civic leaders. Many other candidates work hard to develop a positive reputation for public service and enter the game on their own. To decide to run for Congress involves a combination of personal motivation and availability (see Chapter 11). To aspire to a position in Congress (or any political office) requires enough motivation to overcome the detriments of a heavy time commitment, extensive public exposure, and a disruption of one's career and family life. Availability encompasses a number of factors, such as meeting the legal requirements for election and having access to the resources necessary to wage a competitive campaign.

12-2b Rules of the Electoral Game

After meeting the legal requirements to run for office, potential candidates must look at the nature of the constituency for which they plan to run. Members of Congress run *for* office by running *from* a geographic constituency.

The single-member district system, in which each elected representative is responsible to the residents of one specific geographic area, creates the expectation among vot-

Box 12-2 Meeting the Legal Requirements to Run for Congress

Requirements to Run for the House

- 25 years of age (when taking office)
- Citizen of the United States for seven years
- Resident of the state (not necessarily the district) from which he or she is elected. (District residency is a political, not legal requirement.)

Requirements to Run for the Senate

- 30 years of age (when taking office)
- Citizen of the United States for nine years
- Resident of the state from which he or she is elected

Source: U.S. Constitution, Article 1

Box 12–3 *Creating the Congressional FARM Team*

Viable congressional candidates rank high on the following "FARM" team criteria:

Feasibility: Does the candidate come from a district where no incumbent is running? Since over 95% of incumbents win in most congressional elections, stepping into the race with an incumbent is usually a waste of time.

Availability: Running for office takes time and effort. Individuals with fixed and long work schedules or significant family commitments are generally not available to run for office.

Resources: Political campaigns are expensive, so they tend to draw candidates with personal wealth or access to the wealth of others. On the personal level, the public expects verbal skills and campaigns are facilitated by organizational skills. Name recognition from a previous political office or public success gives a candidate an advantage over an unknown competitor.

Motivation: Temporally preceding the other factors is the desire to run for office. Few candidates are dragged kicking and screaming into the electoral arena. Wanting to serve helps ameliorate the sacrifices involved.

ers that the representative will look out for the interests of that district. Senate districts (entire states) have always been relatively diverse in their political interests. With the growth in population of House districts, most members of the House of Representatives now face many of the same difficulties that senators do. Today members of the House must represent districts that are made up of people with varying characteristics and interests. By law, the average House member today represents over six hundred thousand constituents (with the apportionment of seats after the 2000 census). Since being responsive to such a large and diverse group is virtually impossible, most members listen to the smaller sets of citizens. These are the individuals who take the time and make the effort to participate in government decision making and to communicate their wishes to legislators.

Congressional elections are seldom played out on an even playing field. The tendency to gerrymander congressional districts (see Chapter 11 and the opening to this chapter) to favor particular parties, groups, or candidates gives an advantage to some contenders beginning the campaign. The nature of the district and its voters deeply affects the strategies a candidate must use to win. In the mid 1990s, the legitimacy of intentional gerrymandering to guarantee congressional seats to racial minorities was embroiled in extensive testing of the rules by the courts (see Box 12-4: Ruling for the Minority).

12-2c Campaign Strategies

Winning congressional office requires organizing the necessary resources and using them effectively. Financial resources, name recognition, and party membership generally distinguish the winners from the losers.

Resources for Success

Modern political campaigns are expensive. Television advertising, the polling of voters, and computerized mailing strategies have significantly increased campaigning costs. Incumbent officeholders generally find it easier to raise and spend more campaign funds than do challengers, and the gap has widened in recent years. Congressional candidates, unlike candidates for the presidency, receive no federal campaign funds, which helps established incumbents more than challengers.

That the majority of winners in congressional campaigns outspend their rivals leads some critics to assert that Americans have "the best Congress money can buy."[8]

Box 12-4 Ruling for the Minority

Background

As an institution charged with representation, Congress has long lacked representativeness. The halls of Congress include far fewer members of ethnic and racial minorities than does the population as a whole. Numerous reasons help explain the situation. Electoral success for any group in society depends on at least two factors, the emergence of viable candidates and the ability to build a solid base of voter support. Ethnic minorities have come up short on both counts. Good candidates were hard to find, and political players involved in the nomination process through the party organization were hesitant to give minorities the right to play. Recognizing the limited likelihood of winning, many potential minority candidates refused to get involved. Even when they did run, members of minority groups often lacked the financial resources to run viable campaigns.

When it came to building a base of support, minority politicians recognized that they would have to start with members of their own ethnic group. Until relatively recently, voters from the ethnic majority were hesitant to support minority candidates. The political behavior of ethnic minorities also often placed minority politicians on shaky ground. Historically, minority voters were discriminated against in the application of voting laws and tended not to vote. Even when the legal right to vote was enforced, members of minority groups—consistent with their lower average socioeconomic status—voted at lower levels. This made it more difficult for minority politicians to establish a powerful voting bloc. Politically, African Americans and Latinos tend to support Democratic candidates, and Democratic Party politicians hesitated to upset the pattern of spreading minority voters to help create coalitions to elect white Democrats to office.

Questions

The goal of increasing the opportunities for minority candidates raises a number of questions:

1. What methods can be used to grant members of ethnic minorities a greater chance of achieving political office?
2. What are the political repercussions of changing the opportunities for minorities?
3. What competing values emerge to challenge attempts to increase minority representation?

Analysis

Most methods of leveling the playing field are either unacceptable or impossible. Financially undergirding political campaigns of minority candidates would be unfair to nonminority candidates. Changing voter attitudes and participation levels is a long-term solution at best. In the late 1980s the unique political situation of Republican control of the executive branch and growing restiveness among many African-American and Latino political leaders led to an interesting initiative. A series of court cases plus the Justice Department's interpretation of the 1992 amendments to the 1965 Voting Rights Act established a

Exceptions to the general rule that money wins elections abound, however. More than 80 percent of the thirty-two Democratic House incumbents who lost in 1994 significantly outspent their winning Republican challengers. In 2000, House incumbents who eventually lost (six) spent an average of $2.59 million, while the winning challengers in those races spent an average of $1.98 million. The average House incumbent in 2000 was able to raise and spend more than $815,000, while the average challenger spent $370,000. Winners in open seat House races spent over $1.3 million, while losers in open seat races were "only" able to expend an average of $1 million.[9]

In the broad picture, the financial advantage of winners may simply show that projected victors receive the most money because they are expected to win. For example, an increasing percentage of congressional campaign funds come from political action committees (PACs), who primarily donate to the campaigns of the candidates most likely to win (see Chapter 7 and Table 12-1). Thus, the lion's share of congressional campaign financing tends to go to already advantaged incumbents, further increasing their advantage. Incumbents and favored open-seat candidates also tend to get "early" money, which new mandate to, wherever feasible, create districts in which a minority group enjoys majority status. Such intentional concentration of minority voters had the support of many minority politicians, who foresaw the creation of winnable districts for their own ethnic groups. Republican leaders saw this as a way of siphoning off Democratic voters from nearby districts, which they would then have a better chance of winning while gaining the credit for supporting greater political opportunity. Democratic Party leaders were left in a quandary, not wanting to upset their political allies but recognizing the potential political costs.

The results of creating more than fifty majority-minority districts after the 1990 census were dramatic. Most of them elected Democratic members from the ethnic majority of the district, increasing the number of minority members in Congress. Surrounding districts, stripped of their minority strongholds, were more likely to go Republican. Some argued that Republican gains in these adjacent districts in 1992 and 1994 were responsible for the Republican takeover of the House in 1995. There were some obvious downsides above and beyond partisan concerns. A number of prominent white Democrats were removed from office when their districts' ethnic composition changed. Many of the newly created districts were oddly shaped as they wiggled across the countryside to pick up ethnic concentrations.

The story did not end there. White voters went to court. In the first case reaching the Supreme Court, the justices ruled, in a close vote, that race cannot be the "predominant factor" in drawing districts but that it could be one of the factors. The majority opinion asserted that the Constitution does not allow segregation by race whatever the purpose, and that the Justice Department's pressure to create majority-minority districts involved the "worst forms of discrimination [and] to demand the very racial stereotyping the 14th Amendment forbids."[a] Dissenters on the Court saw it differently, arguing that the decision "makes racial minorities the only group not allowed to have their group interests taken into account in reapportionment matters."[b] In 2003, the Court reaffirmed that race could only be one of the factors in designing districts, allowing state legislatures to move away from majority-minority districts as the only way to assure minority representation.[c] As is often the case in judicial decision making, the Court has not had its final say on this issue. Related cases will be decided before the final contours of the right to establish majority-minority districts are decided once and for all.

---

a. See Linda Greenhouse, "Justices, in 5–4 Vote, Reject Districts Drawn with Race the Predominant Factor," *New York Times*, June 30, 1995, A1.

b. See "Supreme Court's Final Day: Gutting the Voting Rights Act," *New York Times*, June 30, 1995, A20.

c. Jeffrey McMurray, "Supreme Court Orders More Consideration of Georgia Political Map," Associated Press, LEXIS-NEXIS database, June 26, 2003.

they can use to raise additional funds and to plan their entire campaign. Clearly, all candidates—whether incumbents or challengers—would like to have more money rather than less, since money is one of the most flexible campaign resources.

While individual contributions still serve as the dominant source of campaign funding, incumbents depend more on PACs, while challengers must underwrite more of their own campaigns, especially for the Senate, as Table 12-1 shows.

Name recognition and a favorable public image are also important resources in congressional elections. These assets may be acquired through long years of public service, accomplishments in sports or entertainment, or simply by being a member of a well-known and highly regarded family. Members of the Kennedy, Jesse Jackson, and Rockefeller families, for example, have had considerable success securing nominations and gaining seats in Congress. Members of Congress have included former sports stars, such as Senator Bill Bradley (D-N.J.), a former New York Knicks basketball star, and former Oklahoma Sooner star quarterback Representative J. C. Watts, Jr. (R-Okla.). Entertainers-turned-congressmen include Representative Sonny Bono (R-Calif.), who

Table 12-1

Sources of Congressional Campaign Funds (in Percent) by Party and Incumbency Status (2000)

	Incumbent		Challenger*	
	Repub.	Dem.	Repub.	Dem.
House				
Individual Contributors	54%	48%	56%	57%
Political Action Committees	39%	45%	13%	17%
Political Parties	1%	1%	14%	2%
Candidate (to self)	1%	0%	23%*	19%*
Senate				
Individual Contributors	60%	56%	70%	43%
Political Action Committees	27%	20%	8%	8%
Political Parties	5%	6%	8%	1%
Candidate (to self)	2%	12%	3%	41%*

*The figures from individual contributions are dramatically skewed by a few races where candidates contributed huge amounts to their own race.

Source: Norman J. Ornstein, Thomas E. Mann, and Michael J. Malbin, *Vital Statistics on Congress, 2001–2002* (Washington, D.C.: American Enterprise Institute, 2002), 104–105.

made a name for himself during the 1970s with his partner Cher (and whose wife took over his seat after his death), and Senator Fred Thompson (R-Tenn.), best known for his roles as an admiral in *The Hunt for Red October* and an air traffic controller chief in *Die Hard 2.*[10] Congress lost of some its star quality when both Watts and Thompson decided not to run in 2002.

Meeting the legal requirements, raising adequate money, and being widely known are necessary to seeking a seat in Congress, but alone they are seldom sufficient for success. Prospective candidates must also recognize and fulfill the expectations of voters and political activists. Members of Congress are generally expected to have and maintain strong local roots—either by birth or by long, continuous residence—back in their districts. Local voters and party activists assume that such roots assure that members of Congress will keep the interests of their constituency in mind at all times. The lack of credible roots in one's district invites charges of **carpetbagging.** This scornful term for political opportunists originated with northerners who moved hastily into the South immediately after the Civil War in pursuit of political office and economic gain. They often carried all their possessions in a flimsy suitcase made from a piece of carpet. Relatively new residents, and those who have spent long periods away from the district, must overcome serious disadvantages to win election.

carpetbagging *A derisive term used to describe opportunist politicians moving into a new electoral district and running for office.*

Effective communication skills, a superior campaign organization, and personal motivation may be sufficient to offset a candidate's initial lack of financial resources or name recognition. Some candidates with limited resources have for years successfully run for office by literally walking—going door-to-door in an intensive but relatively inexpensive effort to show their commitment and increase their public visibility (see Box 12-5: Running for Office by Taking the Bus).

Better-financed candidates, however, hire consultants to help them target potential supporters and to communicate with them through personalized computer-generated direct-mail campaigns. As we have seen, new technologies have changed the nature of the skills most useful in seeking political office. This is nowhere truer than in congressional elections. The spellbinding stump orator who stirred his listeners to a frenzy has largely been replaced by the "blow-dried" candidate, who communicates a message in short bites of thirty to sixty seconds on television (see Chapter 11).

Box 12–5 *Running for Office by Taking the Bus*

Voters have become accustomed to high-technology campaigns utilizing slick television advertising and a candidate flitting from stop to stop in a private plane or helicopter. The image of the well-financed and efficient campaign is supposed to imply an effective and competent candidate.

Powerful symbols are often very important in political campaigns. Nowhere was this more important than in the 1990 senatorial campaign in Minnesota. Facing a seemingly well-entrenched incumbent (Republican Rudy Boschwitz) with a six-million-dollar campaign treasury, Paul Wellstone, an underfinanced and uncompromising liberal college professor, took to crisscrossing the state in an old green school bus. It was a year of severe voter dissatisfaction with "the mess in Washington" and a series of scandals affecting other Minnesota politicians. By exploiting the unfairness of inequities in campaign finances, Wellstone turned the campaign into a David-versus-Goliath contest, encouraging voters to root for the little guy. The school bus and Wellstone's low-budget television advertisements provided a fresh populist image. While Wellstone hammered away at the politics of big contributors and out-of-touch politicians, Boschwitz was stuck in Washington for the protracted budget debate.

Despite being outspent almost 6 to 1, Wellstone became the only challenger to unseat an incumbent senator in 1990. Realizing the importance of his symbol, Wellstone drove to Washington in his faithful green school bus to take up his senatorial duties. While the outsider image worked well in the campaign, Senator Wellstone's combative approach led to an awkward initial period in the Senate.

In a fight for his political life during the 2002 campaign, Senator Wellstone's plane went down in a snow storm. A last-minute replacement, former vice president Walter Mondale, was not able to retain the seat in the face of an aggressive Republican challenger, Norm Coleman.

VIDEO

Campaign Ads

Kentucky Republican senatorial candidate Jim Bunning.

Wisconsin Democratic senatorial candidate Russ Feingold.

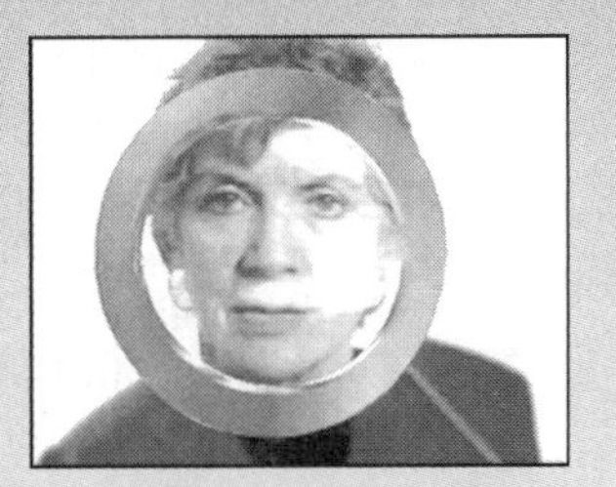

Colorado Republican Senator Ben Nighthorse Campbell's "flip/flop" ad.

Democrat Pat Leahy of Vermont.

Republican Senator John McCain.

Oklahoma Republican Congressman J.C. Watts.

Value of Party Labels

Political partisanship structures campaign strategy and underlies voter decisions:.

> Each candidate is engaged in the delicate task of consolidating his base while making enough inroads in the other's to win. . . . "The name of the game is turnout."[11]

Winning a seat in Congress once involved joining the dominant political party in your district and working your way up through the organization. The latter half of the twentieth century has not been kind to political parties. As described in Chapter 8, the growing expense of campaigns and the availability of costly campaign technologies have forced candidates to look beyond party support for the resources to run their campaigns.

As outlined in Chapter 11, the increasing popularity of primary elections for nominating party candidates and the decline in party-line voting have forced candidates to campaign more as individuals than as party representatives.

Despite the party's declining role in funding and managing congressional campaigns, party labels still play a significant role in those campaigns—larger than in campaigns for other offices. Voters depend on party labels when choosing between candidates, and congressional candidates are comfortable presenting themselves as partisans. Most political activists develop a psychological identification with one of the political parties quite early in life. They choose a party that comfortably coincides with their basic ideological and policy views, and defections are rare. It was news when, after the 1994 election, two Democratic senators and one Democratic House member switched to the Republican Party, indicating that it now better represented their political views. In 2001, Senator James Jeffords of Vermont, uncomfortable with the policy positions of the party under which he was elected, switched from being a Republican to being an Independent. His seemingly personal redefinition switched control of the Senate from the Republicans to the Democrats. Although American parties are quite broad in their composition and do not require a **litmus test** of political views for casual membership, individuals too far out of the mainstream of their party seldom achieve leadership roles.

litmus test *Borrowed from a test in chemistry, a stand on a specific political issue that defines a person or group.*

The congressional election process itself forces members to associate themselves with a political party. Candidates must win their party primary to be placed on the ballot. At that point they usually accept willingly any help the party might give to their campaign. Candidates recognize that party loyalists in their district serve as the backbone of their political support, which they must maintain.

The only thing that many voters know for sure about congressional candidates is the candidate's party affiliation. This situation increases the likelihood of voters supporting their party's candidate. In fact, many voters stray from their party in voting for the presidency and local offices only to cast a penance vote. Feeling guilty about supporting a presidential or local candidate of the other party, they go back to their traditional party when voting for Congress. Over the last two decades Democrats have generally gained seats in Congress when they engendered more loyalty from their partisan ranks than Republicans did and won a majority of the independents' votes. The key to Republican successes in 1980 and especially 1994 lay in increases in Republican voter loyalty and dramatic swings of independents toward Republican candidates (see Figure 12-1).

Figure 12-1 Partisan Voting in Congressional Elections, 1956–2002

Note: Party-line voters supported their party in House or Senate elections.

Source: Harold Stanley and Richard G. Niemi, *Vital Statistics on American Politics, 2003–2004* (Washington, D.C.: Congressional Quarterly, Inc., 2003), p. 138.

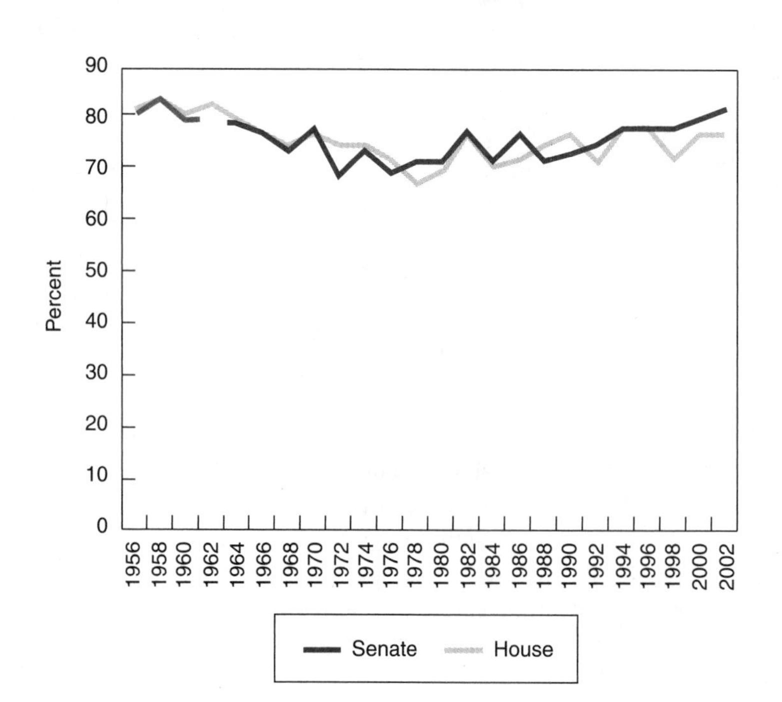

The growing number of independents and ticket splitters is another factor that encourages candidates to run candidate-centered campaigns. Perhaps as a result of all these developments, party-based voting in Congress declined significantly in the 1970s. The Republicans' daring 1994 strategy of binding more than 300 candidates to a specific policy platform (the Contract with America) was a bold attempt to reassert the party's role in defining the political agenda. Although it was derided at the time as a gimmick, in the glow of the Republican landslide it began to be viewed as a stroke of political genius. While party-line voting has increased, the strategy of midterm party platforms did not extend beyond the 1994 victory in a significant way.

12-2d The Winners: Describing the Elected Players

Representation is the process by which elected officials take into account the interests of those who have selected them, *re-presenting* (presenting a second time) and working to achieve the desired goals of those whom they represent (see Chapter 8). While virtually anyone can, in theory, represent another's interests, it is easier to fight for causes that you understand and in which you believe. **Representativeness** assesses the degree to which the individuals involved in the process of representing are similar to those for whom they are asked to speak. It is assumed that individuals from identifiable groups in society will do a better job of speaking for their interests.

representativeness *The degree to which the personal characteristics of the members of an institution match the characteristics of the general population that the institution represents.*

Representativeness (or Unrepresentativeness) of Congress

One way to determine whether a legislative body is representative is by examining the degree to which its total membership mirrors the characteristics of the population as a whole. The assumption here is that legislators who are similar to their constituents will better understand and share their constituents' goals and thus will be more likely to represent their constituents' interests effectively.

At first blush, the U.S. Congress fails the representative test (see Table 12-2). Members of Congress are considerably older, better educated, and far more likely to have pursued a relatively high-status occupation—such as the law—than are members of the population as a whole. The most obvious signs of the lack of representativeness are race and gender—there is a much higher proportion of whites and males than in the general population. In the 108th Congress (2003–2004), only fifty-nine women served in the House and thirteen in the Senate. Since more than 50 percent of the U.S. population is female, strict representativeness would have required over two hundred female House members and more than fifty female senators. The thirty-seven African Americans in the House and zero African Americans in the Senate in the 108th Congress fell far below the fifty-plus House members and twelve senators that their percentage of the population (12 percent) would suggest. Other ethnic groups such as Latinos and Asian Americans are even more underrepresented. Latinos, who make up more than 12 percent of the population, should have more than fifty members in the House, and Asian Americans should have approximately fifteen House members, as opposed to three.

As Table 12-2 shows, neither the House nor the Senate mirrors the U.S. population in basic demographic characteristics.

Although existing players in Congress recognize that the playing field is not level when it comes to facilitating the election of women and minorities, they have little motivation to change the outcome. As Senator Joseph R. Biden, Jr. (D-Del.), expressed it:

> When you are a challenger . . . if you are a woman, if you are a black, if you are somebody who does not come from an institutional constituency, you have a hard time getting in the game. . . . We do not want other people in the game. . . . People in this body think we own this place; we do not.[12]

While no formal rules dictate this unrepresentative outcome, individuals from the groups most common in Congress—summarized as older white high-status males—begin with three advantages. First, the motivation to play in the high-stakes game of competing for public office is not randomly distributed. Groups such as women and minorities

Table 12-2

The Social Background Characteristics of the 109th Congress (2005–2006) and the U.S. Population (in Percent)

	House	Senate	U.S. Population
Gender			
Male	85%	86%	49%
Race			
White[a]	83%	95%	80%
Age			
Average age	55 years	60 years	73% of Americans are under 50
Occupation			
Law	36	58	less than 1
Business (managers, owners)	37	30	10
Education			
College graduate	over 90	97%	21
Religion			
Protestant[b]	44	46	20
Catholic	28	24	22
Jewish	6	11	2
Other/none	20	19	56

[a]Blacks, some Latinos, and Asians are defined as nonwhite

[b]Protestant figures are limited to Baptists, Episcopalians, Lutherans, Methodists, and Presbyterians. Sixty-one percent of Americans claim a religious affiliation.

Sources: Congressional data from Mildred Amer, "Membership of the 109th Congress: A Profile," Congressional Research Service Report RS22007, December 20, 2004: www.catholicnews.com, and www.congresslink.org. General population characteristics from John W. Wright, *The Universal Almanac*, (Kansas City, MO: Andrews and McMeel 1999), 253–264.

are still less socialized to feel that running for office is either possible or desirable. Second, educational and occupational accomplishments reflect skills, abilities, and financial resources that are helpful in an election campaign. This puts at a disadvantage groups that lack these resources. Third, voters respect individuals with particular characteristics. The common citizen seldom really wants a common person as a representative.

All of this results in a relatively homogeneous set of decision makers who are demographically atypical of the population as a whole. The representativeness of Congress improves somewhat when you compare members of Congress with those citizens who have chosen to play in the congressional selection game by registering and voting. The overall picture has also improved over time. Congress is more representative today than at any time in the past.

The problems that Congress is expected to solve are complex and the legislative process intricate. In view of this, some argue that it would not make sense simply to take a random sample of citizens off the street in order to carry out the nation's business. Our best hope, these people say, would be for a concentration of better-educated and more skilled representatives. Recognition of the possible undesirability of pure representativeness does not justify a selection process that discriminates. Large blocks of capable individuals should not be denied entrances to the winner's circle solely because they happen to fall into categories such as minorities or women.

The Incumbency Factor

Holding office is of great benefit when one wants to stay in office:.

> The current power game has given incumbents, especially those in the House of Representatives, enormous advantage. Once they are in Congress, they have a high-technology arsenal that ensures that all but a tiny handful will survive any challenge.[13]

Most members of Congress prefer to stay in office. Not surprisingly, Congress as a body has encouraged rules and practices that put challengers at a disadvantage and solidify the position of current players. For example, state laws that forbid an individual to run for more than one office at a time protect members of the Senate from wholesale challenges by current members of their states' House of Representatives delegations. The challengers back home would have to give up their seats just to run for the opportunity of moving to Washington. These laws also discourage senators up for reelection from simultaneously pursuing the presidency (see Chapter 14). It should be noted that under pressure from then-senator Lyndon Johnson, the Texas law was changed to allow running for more than one office simultaneously. This allowed Senator Johnson to pursue the presidency with little risk. In 1988 Senator Lloyd Bentsen (D-Tex.) ran for vice president with Michael Dukakis and also for senator. When the Dukakis-Bentsen ticket was defeated, Senator Bentsen retained his Senate seat. In the 2000 campaign, there was some concern that if the Gore-Lieberman ticket won, Senator Joe Lieberman would be replaced with a Republican by the Republican governor of Connecticut. Senator Lieberman refused to submit to pressure from party leaders to withdraw as a Senate candidate to protect the seat. The nomination of two senators (Kerry and Edwards) by the Democrats in 2004 did not raise that issue, since neither was up for reelection.

Despite the wild card of redistricting, which often provides the potential for upsetting the security of incumbents, over 98 percent of House members running for reelection won in the 2002 and 2004 elections. In the Senate the figure was 85 percent in 2002 and 97 percent in 2004.

Members of Congress have provided themselves with numerous opportunities to keep their names in the public eye, including:

- government-funded newsletters, distributed under the rationale of increasing incumbents' name identification (see Box 12-6: You Might Not Know the Players without a Program) and informing the public of congressional activities,
- the facilitation of media visibility by chamber-provided cameras and press galleries,
- the right to announce government grants awarded to their districts,
- the franking privilege (the right to mail newsletters and other communications to their constituents at no charge),
- frequent trips (using monetary allowances) back to the district, which help to enhance their name-recognition among their constituents, and
- official office staffs, paid for with government funds, who are skilled at helping constituents with problems.

A major task in most congressional offices lies in advertising the member's accomplishments.[14] These activities and privileges also enhance a congressperson's reelection prospects.

12-3 Defining the Congressional Job

No one hands new representatives or senators a job description that tells them how to use effectively their most important but scarce resources: time, attention, and effort. The use of these resources is based on the members' own personal views of their jobs and input from outside sources, such as constituents, fellow members, interest groups, and the White House. Balancing competing demands consumes a great deal of most members'

Box 12–6 You Might Not Know the Players without a Program

Can you name your current member of the House of Representatives, your two senators, your House member's challenger in the last election, and the losing Senate candidate in the last election?

Don't be too upset if you don't know the names of all of these people. Recent national surveys reveal that only 56 voters could name the senatorial challenger in their state *during the campaign,* while only 75 percent could name the incumbent. The level of knowledge is even lower for House members and during nonelection periods.[a]

To find out the name of the incumbents who represent you, go to one of the following websites, which allow you to input your state and or zip code to get their names and backgrounds:

http://www.dnet.org
(under officeholders)
http://capwiz.com/c-span/dbq/officials/

Congressional rules and strategies function amazingly well for the incumbents. Even in the most volatile years, more than 90 percent of incumbent members of Congress and more than 80 percent of incumbent senators who run for reelection are successful. In 1994 a number of highly visible incumbents, such as Speaker Thomas S. Foley (D-Wash.), lost, but the overall numbers were consistent with past elections. The key difference was that all 32 incumbent House members who lost were Democrats. In recent elections, 98 percent of incumbents running won reelection to the House.

Often, the "incumbency lock" discourages potential challengers as well as the potential contributors who might support them. In recent years, the most common method of replacing members of Congress has become voluntary retirement rather than electoral defeat. During this same period, the pressures associated with holding congressional office have increased the number of voluntary resignations. The game has been opened to a larger group of new players. Once in office, these new members quickly latch onto the numerous benefits available to help them stay there.[b]

Public frustration with both incumbents and their electoral advantages—and with government institutions in general—has led to a variety of attempts to even the playing field. Proposals for federal financing of congressional elections and for discontinuing the franking privilege would make it easier for challengers. Term limits for members of Congress are supported by a large majority of Americans, and term-limit initiatives passed in more than twenty states. These were, however, ruled invalid by the Supreme Court in June 1995. Given current Supreme Court opinion, the only route to congressional term limits would be a constitutional amendment. The likelihood of such limits was diminished in 1995 when House Republicans failed to garner the two-thirds vote necessary to propose such an amendment to the states. The term-limitation movement is not dead but has fallen victim to significant reversals.

The goals of term limit proponents remain the same. Competitive open-seat elections at regular intervals would lead to an increased and regularized influx of new members, which would affect the composition of Congress, its internal operations, and policy outputs.

---

a. Kim Fridkin Kahn and Patrick Kenney, "How Negative Campaigning Enhances Knowledge of Senate Elections," in James Thurber et al. (eds.), *Crowded Airwaves* (Washington, D.C.: Brookings Institution Press, 2000), 78.
b. *Ibid.*

time and is closely linked to their personal goals, which in most cases include reelection. The Founders viewed Congress as the most important branch of government and expected that it would perform a variety of tasks. Congress was designed to develop legislation and to provide for the gathering and distribution of government funds. It was also expected to keep an eye on the operation of government and to investigate wrongdoing. In performing all of these tasks, members of Congress were to be guided by concern for the interests of the local constituencies, which had sent them to Washington. Because this range of expected tasks is too large and complex for any one member to master fully, members must make some choices. Members work on the assumption that voters look more favorably on representatives and senators who serve and satisfy constituent needs.

In reality, however, constituents send mixed signals. Recent national polls found that 71 percent of the public expressed dismay that members "are more interested in what's best for their district, and not what's best for the country" while 67 percent felt that "each member of Congress should think about the whole country's interests," rather than "what is best for his or her district." On the other hand, poll respondents indicated by substantial margins that *their* members should try to "direct more government spending" to their congressional district (58 percent), "bring federal projects" to their district (73 percent), and "help create jobs" in their district (90 percent).[15]

Members of Congress allocate their time and energy to many different tasks:

- crafting legislation,
- overseeing the bureaucracy,
- representing constituents,
- providing information, and
- acting as an intermediary between citizens and the federal bureaucracy.

Although members cannot completely ignore any one of these roles, they differ dramatically in where they place their emphasis (see Box 12-7: A Day in the Life of a Member of Congress). Senior members with strong electoral margins often view legislating and overseeing as their primary roles. They spend much of their time in committee meetings, refining legislative proposals and listening to bureaucratic officials justify their actions.

Less politically secure members engage in more communication with and problem solving for their constituents. They may well choose to return to the district to speak to the local Rotary Club instead of staying in Washington to work out the details of a complex piece of legislation. The member of Congress whose last margin of victory was one hundred votes is much more likely to be seen back home than is the colleague who faced no opposition.

Congress works through a number of subarenas—its committees and subcommittees—that gather individuals with expertise and interest in working in particular areas of public policy. Most politically insecure members of Congress work to improve their chances for survival by seeking out committee assignments related to constituency interests. More secure members have the freedom to follow their own policy interests and to aspire to powerful committees, such as Appropriations (program funding) and Ways and Means (taxes), which make more general policy.

Large organizations such as Congress require some members to rise above their more narrow interests and to take on the tasks of leadership. Politically secure members of Congress most often seek out party and chamber leadership positions, while their less secure colleagues avoid positions that consume a great deal of time but do not contribute directly to enhancing constituent support. Chapter 13 offers a more detailed discussion of committees and leaders in action. In Section 12-4, we look at how party connections organize the players.

12-4 Organizing for Power and Survival

Few members of Congress are willing to place their political future in the hands of fate. They do all they can to associate themselves with the most favorable political teams, develop their own staff support teams, and develop strategies for securing long tenure in office.

12-4a Party Teams

The party label, often a useful element of campaign strategy, carries over to direct new members of Congress to "one side of the aisle"—to a political team. The more members of Congress feel beholden to their party, the more they use it as the main vehicle for congressional involvement and as a significant influence on decision making.

Box 12–7 A Day in the Life of a Member of Congress

Unlike many jobs, there is really no "typical" day for a member of Congress. Much of the official actions of Congress (committee meetings, floor debates, votes, etc.) occur from Tuesday to Thursday, allowing many members to return to their constituencies for meetings. While in Washington, members have multiple responsibilities, often having to choose between a number of meetings happening at the same time. The following is a composite day of a middle seniority member while in Washington. In between the officially scheduled events, the member talked with House colleagues, fielded staff questions, and informally chatted with three lobbyists outside the House chamber.

6:30 Up to read the papers and scan the schedule for the day

8:00 Breakfast meeting with visiting mayors

8:45 Quick "on the fly" briefing by staff director about upcoming legislation

9:00 Staff meeting: Discussion of new office equipment, upcoming legislation, and redistricting concerns

9:30 Haircut in House barbershop (cancelled since staff meeting ran long)

10:00 House goes into session

10:10 Give a one-minute speech on the House floor

10:00 Railroad subcommittee hearing

10:00 House Administration subcommittee meeting (sent staff member to monitor)

10:45 (unscheduled) Called to House floor for a vote

11:00 Back to subcommittee for remainder of the Railroad subcommittee hearing

11:20 (unscheduled) Called back to floor for quorum call and vote

12:00 Interview with a writer from a local paper

12:30 Working lunch briefing by party leaders on Social Security reform

1:45 Met with local community service organization delegation for photo on House steps

2:15 Met with Cellular Telecommunications and Internet Association lobbyists to discuss privacy and federal excise tax repeal

2:45 (unscheduled) Fielded two calls from local supporters concerned about upcoming votes

3:30 Speech at local law school (arrived late and had to apologize for not allowing more than 5 minutes for questions)

4:30 State delegation meeting on redistricting prospects

5:30 Picture on Capitol steps with district school group

5:45 Met with Lymphoma Research Foundation representatives, led by a constituent, asking for increased research funding

6:30 League of Conservation Voters Reception (had pictures taken, schmoozed a bit, and made brief comments)

7:30 Fund raiser for House colleague trying to reduce his campaign debt (arrived late, but made an appearance)

7:30 Embassy reception (sent regrets)

10:00 Home, to read papers and review tomorrow's schedule

Electing Team Captains: Choosing the Party Leadership

The House and Senate are organized around political parties:

> The process [of choosing party leaders is] described by one Democratic aide as an "inside, inside game" involving multiple promises, commitments and arrangements reached in private conversations. . . . Voting is by secret ballot, so no one can be sure which promises will be kept.[16]

Few new members arrive in Congress owing their election solely to the support of the party organization, but most have received assistance and encouragement from both the local and national offices of their chosen political party. Shortly after each election, each party invites all members who ran and won under its banner to Washington for a **legislative caucus.** At these meetings, the party chooses its leaders and provides training for new members. It also recommends a slate of candidates for committee assignments and leadership positions and establishes policy objectives.

legislative caucus *The meeting of party members in a legislature to choose leadership and set policy direction.*

The leadership of Congress is generally drawn from among the most senior and experienced members. Each party chooses a leader, who becomes either the **majority** or **minority leader** for that house. Party caucuses in the House nominate a candidate for **Speaker** for election by the entire House. Since members vote along party lines, the candidate of the majority party always wins. When the Republicans won a majority of House seats in 1994, Newt Gingrich (R-Ga.) became the first Republican Speaker since 1954, the last time the Republicans had a majority. Speaker Gingrich resigned from Congress in 1998 after a disappointing showing for his party in that year's elections. He was eventually replaced by Dennis Hastert (R-Ill.). In the Senate, Robert Dole (R-Kans.) took over the top party leadership position as majority leader, a post he previously held in 1986 when the Republicans last had a majority in the Senate. As a dramatic indication of his commitment to the 1996 presidential race, Senator Dole resigned from the Senate to campaign full time and was replaced by Senator Trent Lott (R-Miss.). The 107th Congress began with no change in party leadership and with particularly tenuous party control in the Senate, given the 50-50 tie between Republicans and Democrats. Majority leader Lott initially cut a deal with the Democrats providing for an even partisan split on committees. With the defection of Senator James Jeffords from the Republican Party, the Democrats became the majority in June 2001. Tom Daschle (D-S. Dak.) became the new majority leader, and the committee chairmanships shifted to the Democrats. In 2004, Daschle, Senate Minority Leader since the Republicans regained the majority in 2002, went down to defeat after an expensive race which saw the Senate Majority Leader, Bill Frist (D-TN) uncharacteristically campaign against his Democratic counterpart.

majority leader *The head of the majority party in each house of Congress.*

minority leader *The head of the minority party in each house of Congress.*

speaker *The presiding officer in the House of Representatives.*

After the 2002 election, House minority leader Dick Gephardt (D-Mo.) relinquished his leadership position after presiding over a disappointing set of election results that kept the Democrats in the minority. Democrats decided to both present a clear ideological image and send a message on inclusiveness by electing Nancy Pelosi, a liberal from California. Republicans filled their open majority leader position with an equally avowed conservative, Tom DeLay (R-Tex.). The continuation of Senate leadership for the 108th Congress with the Republicans back in the majority garnered little attention, until incoming Senate majority leader Lott got in trouble for praising outgoing Senator Strom Thurmond (R-S.C.) and for raising questions about his commitment to racial equality. After a series of apologies, Lott eventually resigned and Senator Bill Frist (R-Tenn.) was chosen as majority leader as a representative of the "new South." Since the Lott story broke at the beginning of the holiday season, there was little other news to keep it off the front page. The Republicans took advantage of technology in a hastily orchestrated conference call to nip the negative story and replace it with their own story of leadership selection.

Each party also chooses a chair for each internal party committee (such as the policy and campaign committees) and a majority or minority party **whip,** who advises members on upcoming votes and tries to convince them to vote the party line (see Box 12-8: Whipping Members into Shape). In some legislatures, both within the states and in foreign countries, party caucuses adopt positions on upcoming policy issues that are binding on all party members, but caucuses in the U.S. Congress have relatively few disciplinary powers over their members and thus educate and encourage more than coerce.

whip *A party official with the responsibilities of assessing member preferences, presenting the party position, and getting supporters of the party position to the floor for voting.*

Traditionally, party leadership positions have gone to members who have proven their loyalty through previous service and who get along with a broad range of party members. Senate majority leader Bob Dole clearly fits this pattern. He even refused to attend lunches sponsored by the ideological groups in his Republican Party in order to maintain his role as an honest broker and source of compromise.[17]

Former House Speaker Newt Gingrich was more clearly associated with one wing of his party than has been the case for most recent congressional leaders. During the 1980s, as the key leader of the Conservative Opportunity Society, Gingrich used the televised coverage of Congress to attack the liberal Democratic leadership. He was described as a

Box 12–8 Whipping Members into Shape

The term *whip* arises out of fox hunting, where a "whipper-in" is assigned to keep fox-sniffing dogs from straying by whipping them back into the pack.[a] Using more subtle tactics, majority and minority whips contact the members of Congress assigned to them by party leaders to ascertain their likely vote on upcoming measures, to encourage those who support the party's position to be there for the vote, and to suggest to those who do not to take a walk.

Taking a walk can be either a group or an individual action in which the choice is to opt out of a key decision. On President Bill Clinton's first budget proposal in 1993, for example, the Republicans as a group chose not to participate. They symbolically took a walk at the negotiating stage. A number of conservative Democrats, who hoped to avoid the extreme pressure from the White House, and who also did not want to offend the president by voting against his proposal, literally absented themselves from the floor and did not vote on key proposals.

After designating a majority or minority whip, each party then divides the chamber into several geographically based zones and assigns an assistant whip to each zone. On important votes, assistant whips are expected to know the whereabouts of their assigned members and to get them onto the chamber floor. Serving as an assistant whip is often the first stage in moving up the party leadership ladder.

Whips also try to solicit "pocket votes"—initial opponents willing to support a particular position only if their vote would make a crucial difference.

Many of the agreements brokered by the whips are based on an understanding of secrecy, to avoid the public impression of making a deal. At times, though, the agreements do come out in the open. The closer the vote, the more likely the whips will consider urging an opponent to consider other options if it is clear that they will not simply change their mind and support the leadership outright. For example, Senator Nancy Kassebaum (R-Kans.) opposed George H. Bush's nomination of John Tower as Secretary of Defense but agreed not to vote or even support the nomination if her vote would mean victory or defeat. As it turned out, the vote was one-sided enough that she could vote the way she had intended.

---

a. Jay M. Shafritz, *The Dorsey Dictionary of American Government and Politics* (Chicago, IL: Dorsey Press, 1988), 588.

"conservative rebel [who] harassed the House."[18] Gingrich positioned himself for the speakership in 1989 by winning a race for the number two position, party whip, by two votes. He garnered the votes of conservatives and of some Republican moderates who were frustrated with the way they were treated by both the House Democrats and the Bush administration.[19] Despite his responsibilities as whip to line up Republican votes, he orchestrated the opposition to the 1990 budget deal that President George H. Bush had worked out with the Democrats. From that point on, the White House "never regarded him as a trustworthy team player."[20]

In spite of what many refer to as his "bomb-throwing rhetoric," Gingrich continued to build alliances with more moderate Republicans as he moved up the leadership ladder. In view of Robert H. Michel's (R-Ill.) retirement as Republican leader and Gingrich's successful strategy with the Contract with America, there was no question that he would become Republican leader. He set the tone for his tenure in his first speech after the 1994 election by saying, "I am prepared to cooperate. . . . I am not prepared to compromise . . . on those things which are at the core of our philosophy."[21] Dennis Hastert, who replaced Gingrich, has proven to be a more low-key coalition builder willing to compromise to get things done. Current House majority leader Tom DeLay (R-Tex) has taken up the role of conservative ideological leader.

Party Leaders in Action

In the House, the majority leader is primarily responsible for party-related efforts. The Speaker plays the dual role of party spokesperson and presiding officer, chairing House sessions. Prior to the opening of a new session of Congress, the Speaker is responsible for coordinating the organization of the chamber. He helps choose other leaders and makes sure that committee rosters are filled out. Leadership in the smaller Senate is more informal and collegial. The Senate majority leader manages majority-party strategy and establishes the legislative agenda in cooperation with the minority leader. The more routine chamber proceedings are handled by the relatively nonpartisan presiding officer, the **president pro tempore,** who is chosen from the majority party. According to the Constitution, the vice president serves as the presiding officer of the Senate. (In reality, vice presidents take on this role only during important debates, particularly when their power to vote in the case of a tie might be exercised. During day-to-day debate, the president pro tempore or a designee presides over debate.)

president pro tempore *The presiding officer in the Senate when the vice president is not in attendance.*

Party Rules

The parties have developed rules for dealing with such items as the choice of leaders and assignments to committees. The limited role of the parties in the election of most individual members, however, makes forced adherence to party rules or positions relatively difficult. Attempts to impose sanctions on party members for failing to support party policy positions are rare. In one of the better-known exceptions, the Democratic caucus in the House attempted to punish Congressman Phil Gramm (then D-Tex.), who had worked against party interests by becoming a chief spokesperson for Republican president Ronald Reagan's tax and budget policies. When the Democrats stripped Gramm of his committee position, he resigned and successfully ran as a Republican in the next election. Several years later, he added insult to injury by winning election to the Senate as a Republican.

The general tendency not to punish party colleagues was again borne out in 1995. Senator Mark O. Hatfield (R-Oreg.), chair of the Senate Appropriations Committee, held the crucial vote on the balanced budget amendment. He refused to cave in to pressure. A short-lived challenge to his chairmanship and his access to party campaign support ensued, but it was quickly dropped.

Party Strategies

Both parties attempt to further their objectives by maintaining internal unity and encouraging disloyalty among members of the opposing party. Loyal party members—those who regularly vote in line with party positions—are rewarded. They receive party assistance in passing their legislation, through caucus endorsements and assignment of the legislation to favorable committees.

The majority party's ability to influence the outcome of specific legislative decisions is enhanced by its control over key committee leadership positions and floor proceedings. Outnumbered both in committee and on the floor, the minority party's greatest bargaining power lies in its ability to delay and obstruct passage of legislation that it opposes. Members of that party may propose amendments or use parliamentary maneuvers, such as asking for recorded votes or requesting an interpretation of the rules.

12-4b Special-Interest Caucuses and Coalition Teams

Because winning at the policy game requires gaining the support of others, members of Congress have found it an advantage to create teams composed of those players who share one or more interests. In the contemporary Congress, an increasing number of these teams or caucuses are based on geography, ideology, or policy goals.

The most visible and established of the geographic groups are the **state delegations,** which meet regularly to discuss the implications of legislation for their state. There are also a number of regional groups, such as the Northeast-Midwest Congressional (or Senatorial) Coalition, formed to ensure that an uneven share of the benefits that accrue from federal government programs does not go to the Sun Belt states of the South and West at the expense of states in the Rust Belt areas of the Midwest and Northeast.

state delegation *The members of Congress from a particular state. Some delegations meet on a bipartisan basis, while members from other states meet separately as Republicans or Democrats.*

The largest ideological organization in Congress is the Democratic Study Group, an organization of more than 150 liberals who meet to study issues and to obtain policy guidance. Paralleling this group are several conservative groups, such as the Conservative Opportunity Society. By voting as a bloc and coordinating floor debate, these groups can affect both the policy process and the types of legislation produced (see Box 12-9: "As the Hill Turns").

Finally, a growing number of specialized policy groups in Congress have been organized to push particular policy agendas. These groups include a range of organizations, such as the Black Caucus, Women's Caucus, Arts Caucus, Footwear Caucus (attempting to protect the shoe industry), and Military Reform Caucus. One of the first reforms after the 1994 election involved dropping public funding for internal caucuses. While the caucuses remain free to meet, they no longer receive office space or staff from Congress.

12-4c Congressional Staffs: The Other Players

The insiders pay their respects to the person with the title and then work the serious issues with the less-celebrated staff people who actually draft policy. The wise game player always paves the way to higher-ups through the staffperson.[22]

Each member of Congress arrives in office with a relatively large entourage of secretaries, clerks, and aides. Many staff members come from the campaign staff, while others are hired from among the contingent of professional congressional staff in Washington. These players depend on the member for their jobs but are also crucial to the member's goal of keeping his or her elected position. Walking through the corridors of the U.S. Capitol or of the various congressional office buildings, you see few members of Congress. You are more likely to see some of the more than twenty thousand staff

Box 12-9 "As the Hill Turns"

Live, gavel-to-gavel coverage of House of Representatives proceedings began in 1979. By the early 1980s, members of the Republican "Conservative Opportunity Society" became frustrated with the limits of being in the congressional minority. They recognized the power of television to spread their message and counteract the power of the Democrats, who controlled the chamber. Using the "special orders period," which allows members to sign up to give speeches at the end of each day's session, Conservative Opportunity Society members made speeches promoting conservative positions and castigating the Democrats. At first, the Democrats ignored the speeches made to a virtually empty chamber. But when constituents watched the speeches on C-SPAN (the cable television network covering all congressional floor proceedings) and began to recognize conservative spokesmen, such as Newt Gingrich (R-Ga.) and Robert Walker (R-Pa.), and to comment favorably on their assertions, the Democrats became nervous.

In 1984 Speaker Thomas "Tip" O'Neill had had enough. As Speaker, he controlled the House staff who ran the cameras, and he decided to surprise and embarrass the conservatives by panning the chamber to show that all the rhetoric was falling on an empty chamber. In the dispute that followed, Speaker O'Neill lost his temper and became the subject of a mild rebuke from the chamber for his comments (his words were stricken from the *Congressional Record*).

The conservatives' strategy worked. They had challenged O'Neill and the Democratic majority, and they had won. Recognizing the visibility of the conservative position afforded by televised coverage, the Democrats belatedly organized their own members to take advantage of the special orders period.

For Representative Gingrich, the success was even more direct (see the opening of Chapter 6). A few years later, he parlayed his visibility into a major asset when he fought for and won the position of minority whip, beating a colleague with considerably more experience. In the long run, the strategy of capitalizing on new technology looks even better. Newt Gingrich, often called "Son of C-SPAN," aides, who outnumber their employers—the elected members—more than 50 to 1. In the post-World War II era, congressional staffs became the fastest-growing bureaucracy in Washington. Until a few decades ago, members of Congress functioned with a modest number of clerks and secretaries. Today, elected members' personal staffs (an average of seventeen for House members and forty-one for senators) function like small bureaucracies.[23] They analyze and track legislation for their employers, represent them in meetings, and plan and carry out extensive public relations activities designed to enhance their boss's image.

Other congressional staffers are employed by congressional committees and the congressional research agencies: the Congressional Research Service (747 staff members), the Congressional Budget Office (232 staff members), and the General Accounting Office (3,375 staff members). Reacting to congressional requests, these agencies identify emerging problems, research policy options, and monitor the execution of the laws that Congress passes.

Because they are responsible for analyzing issues and suggesting legislative remedies, congressional staffers are often more knowledgeable about the details and mechanics of legislation than anyone else on Capitol Hill. As a result, they themselves have significant power in the legislative game. One scholar characterized them as the "unelected representatives,"[24] while another set of authors called them the "invisible force."[25]

The majority party controls much of the staff that is not assigned to members' personal offices and uses many of these positions as *patronage* appointments. During decades as the minority party, Republicans, especially those in the House, complained about the advantages that Democrats had because of staff support. After the 1994 election, the leaders of

Newt Gingrich
[www.newt.org]

became the first party leader of the C-SPAN generation. He readily admitted that he would not have become Speaker without C-SPAN.[a] When the Republicans gained a majority in the House after the 1994 elections, he became the first Republican Speaker in forty years.

Speaker Gingrich became a "hot commodity" in more ways than one. His confrontational style garnered media attention, but in a classic case of "live by the camera, die by the camera," Gingrich became a liability to his party. An attempt by the Democrats to remove him for ethical lapses and an abortive coup within his own party failed but became the fodder for extensive media coverage. After publicly laying down the gauntlet and putting his leadership on the line in the 1998 midterm elections, Gingrich eventually resigned his seat and the speakership, turning it over to Dennis Hastert (R-Ill.), a low-key insider chosen intentionally because he lacked the media flair of his predecessor.

a. See Stephen Frantzich and John Sullivan, *The C-SPAN Revolution* (Norman, OK: University of Oklahoma Press, 1996), 274–75.

the new Republican majority cut congressional committee staffs by one-third both to save money and to represent a new era of leaner and meaner government. Significantly, the cuts targeted committees, interest group caucuses, and support agency staff, as opposed to the more politically crucial personal staffs.

Congressional staffers tend to be relatively young and well educated. Traditionally, they came from the districts represented by their boss, but today, increased professionalism has led to the development of a cadre of staff who move from one congressional office to the next as their skills are needed.

As political appointees, congressional staffs traditionally were not covered by federal laws dealing with equity, sexual harassment, and discrimination. As these issues gained greater national attention and the public became aware that laws applied to the rest of the country did not apply to Congress, pressure built for change. One of the first steps made by the Republicans in the 104th Congress was to reverse this anachronism and treat congressional employees like those everywhere.

Despite making employment rules more normal, congressional staffs still play a unique role. In a highly political institution like Congress, they exist to promote the causes and careers of their partisan and political bosses. Inevitably, staff effort and skills are often focused on helping incumbents play the survival game.

12-4d Survival Rules

A number of chamber rules limit what members of Congress and their staffs can and cannot do to assure electoral survival. For example, staff members cannot raise funds or directly solicit electoral support for their bosses while on the government payroll. All members of Congress, however, involve their staff in a range of activities focused on improving the member's image—in effect, selling the member to his or her constituents. These efforts are considered perfectly acceptable. The preparation and mailing of newsletters to constituents, responding to letters from constituents, and writing speeches are all considered part of a congressperson's official functions and thus a legitimate use of staff.

On the personal front, members of Congress who accept payment in direct return for their vote on a given piece of legislation are subject to bribery charges. However, members are not prohibited from being supportive or sympathetic to the position taken by an interest group that has contributed to their campaigns. Similarly, members of Congress cannot use televised tapes of chamber proceedings in a campaign commercial. The timing and content of televised floor speeches are, just the same, often arranged so that they will be picked up by the local media and will enhance a member's standing with his or her constituents. Franked mail cannot be used for birthday or Christmas cards but is used extensively for informational mailings of several types, such as newsletters and press releases that promote the member. In general, the rules discourage the use of government funds for the most obvious campaign-related activities, but they do provide numerous opportunities to use the resources of being in power.

12-4e Survival Strategies

For many members of Congress, retaining their seat is a preoccupation and influences their policy decisions and daily schedules. They must play the survival game if they wish to retain their seats. The basic rule of the game is simple: Find as many ways as possible to make yourself look good in the eyes of your constituents. This requires more than personal effort, and the key to survival lies in putting together a supportive team. Staying in office is more a matter of skill than luck. Members of Congress develop behavior patterns and utilize resources to help assure reelection.

A prime survival strategy is marshaling the resources of the congressional office. The bulk of staff time is spent dealing with constituency interests. Capitol Hill offices look like a series of small businesses with one product to sell—the member. Handling the mail dominates the staff effort, especially in offices of less politically secure members.

The average House member receives more than six hundred pieces of mail per week and the average senator more than twelve hundred.[26] With the arrival of fax machines and email, both the volume and timeliness of incoming communications have increased. The typical congressional strategy is to respond to all incoming mail, especially that from constituents, in a polite and nonoffensive manner. Anyone likely to write is also likely to vote and expects their elected representative to respond.

Approximately 45 percent of the incoming mail involves casework, that is, constituent requests for help with individual problems.[27] Casework is a legitimate activity that also happens to have electoral payoffs. Large bureaucracies like the federal government make mistakes, and individuals need help in getting their difficulties straightened out. Congressional offices go to bat for constituents to make sure that the bureaucracy treats them fairly. Letters from constituents whose Social Security checks never arrived regularly appear in a member's mailbag and are attended to by the member's personal staff. This provides the member with an opportunity to remind the constituents involved of his or her helpfulness when the next election comes around.

Congressional offices do more than simply respond to constituent mail. Extensive outreach programs, now greatly facilitated by computers, result in the mailing of millions of individually targeted letters and newsletters annually to keep the names of members in the public mind (see Box 12-10: Hitting the Target with a Letter). Increasingly, members of Congress choose to locate a significant portion of their staffs in district offices, rather than in Washington, to keep in closer contact with constituents. In 1972, only 22.5 percent of

Box 12–10 *Hitting the Target with a Letter*

Many members of Congress realize that general newsletters fail to excite most constituents. Few issues are of importance to the entire range of potential voters within the member's district. Because of this, many congressional offices now use computers to send personalized messages to targeted lists of constituents to whom the message is most likely to appeal.

If you have ever written your representative, your name is undoubtedly on a computerized mailing list that can be categorized in a variety of ways. At a minimum, your name, the area of the district in which you reside, and the issue that prompted you to write become part of the data file. Any comments in your letter that might further identify you—for example, as a member of a minority group or a student—are filed with your name.

Even if you have never written to your members of Congress, they can both easily and legally obtain your name as part of a list they purchase or rent through a commercial list broker. Invariably, these lists, compiled from commercial or government sources, contain additional information that can be used to determine what to say to you. You may be, for example, identified and addressed as a subscriber to a particular magazine, as the owner of a particular make and year of car, as a member of a particular group, and so on. Furthermore, a number of firms specialize in breaking down mailing lists available from other sources by electoral district.

Congressional offices do not wait for you to write. They identify groups with whom they want to communicate, devise a message that they think members of those groups might want to hear, create hundreds or even thousands of personalized letters via computer, and use an automatic pen to affix a personalized signature.

If you are tempted to write to your representative about an issue of importance to you or to get background material for a paper that you are writing, you can use the following addresses:

Congressman/Congresswoman ______
House Office Building
Washington, DC 20515

or

Senator ______
Senate Office Building
Washington, DC 20510

Most congressional offices have websites and accept email. See Box 13-12: Congress: Policy and Power, in Chapter 13 for addresses. Remember that given the perceived low effort of email, congressional offices tend to pay less attention to it than to a well-crafted personal letter.

Box 12-11 Transportation Technology Facilitating the "Fast Break"

When asked about the most important technological change affecting Congress, former senator Russell Long (D-La.) reflected on his life on the Hill as the son of a senator and as a long-time elected official. He did not mention radio, television, or computers. His quick answer was "the jet airplane." He explained himself by saying:

> In the old days, coming to Washington was like going to camp. Members came for the duration. We worked together all week and got together on the weekend to golf and play cards. We knew every other Member. Today it is hard to get to know your colleagues. They rush from meeting to meeting during the week, and now even a Member from the most remote location can grab a jet and go home at will.[a]

National Airport in Washington, D.C., is a dramatic symbol of how the needs of members of Congress are served. Designed for an era of propeller airplanes, National has few of the requirements of a modern and safe facility, but it has an advantageous location. Members of Congress can leave their offices and board an airplane in 15 minutes. Special parking lots, plane schedules, and check-in procedures all facilitate trips back to the district. Planes arriving and departing from National Airport, however, must thread their way through a maze of high-rise office and apartment buildings. While airports in most parts of the nation are being moved farther out into the country to provide more safety and parking, National Airport had little trouble getting significant funds for extensive renovation from its primary passengers—members of Congress.

a. Author's interview.

House staff members worked in district offices. By 1999 that figure had almost doubled to 42 percent. The comparable shift in the Senate for that period was from 12.5 percent to 31 percent.[28]

Time is one of the scarcest resources for a member of Congress. The average member's day includes numerous time conflicts between committee meetings and appointments with constituents and representatives of various interests. It also includes the need to make numerous decisions on a variety of legislative proposals (all of which must be read, understood, and analyzed) and requests for his or her time back in the district. In addition, daily sessions of the entire chamber require the member's attendance, at the very least for **quorum** calls and **roll call votes.**

quorum *The necessary number of individuals to legally carry out business in a legislature or other meeting.*

roll call vote *A legislative vote in which the position of each member of Congress is recorded.*

The conflicting demands upon its members has led Congress to attempt to accommodate their needs (see Box 12-11: Transportation Technology Facilitating the "Fast Break"). Most important business occurs on Tuesday, Wednesday, and Thursday, which allows extended weekend trips back to the district. The chamber and party organizations provide subsidized support for the production of radio and television spots to help members keep in touch with constituents.

Direct subsidies for staffs, mailings, and district trips are substantial. Office expenses for each House member total more than $1,000,000, or about $1.50 for each person in the House member's district. Senate allowances vary with the size of the state and average about three times those of House members.

Congress has designed a set of rules and benefits that dramatically increase the chances of political survival for its members. The existence of such an uneven playing field makes dramatic reversals for incumbents truly significant events. One should not assume that the current state of affairs is permanent, however. Changes in member motivations, political technology, formal rules, and public expectations each have the potential for affecting the survival game.

Conclusion

The congressional arena has changed considerably over the last two centuries, but a significant part of the game still involves the selection and retention of players. The winners in the election and survival games are those members of Congress—and their staffs—who are able to gain office, join the appropriate teams, define their job in a suitable way, marshal the official resources, and stay in office. On the positive side, long tenure and limited turnover in Congress contribute to continuity and the development of expertise. On the negative side, secure members may lose touch with their districts, and the effort spent by all members on retaining their positions limits time available to perfect legislation or to monitor the other branches of government.

The congressional game is about more than getting into the arena. Few members see winning and retaining office as complete ends in and of themselves. Electoral victory and increasing political security serve as vehicles for affecting public policy and for taking care of the legitimate needs of one's constituency. The nature of the members of Congress recruited and retained through the election and survival games affects the more broadly important policy game, which is discussed in the next chapter.

Key Terms

ad hoc committee
autocratic
carpetbagging
legislative caucus
line-item veto
litmus test
majority leader
minority leader
president pro tempore
quorum
representativeness
republicanism
roll call vote
seniority
speaker
state delegation
whip

Practice Quiz

1. What is an expectation that voters have of congressional candidates?
a. Carpetbagging
b. Strong local roots
c. Personal financial resources
d. Not having been tainted by prior political experience

2. Which of the following is NOT a legitimate official use of congressional staff members?
a. Drafting legislation
b. Doing casework favors for constituents
c. Improving a member's image
d. Raising campaign funds

3. Those who run for Congress without a substantial personal history in the district have been termed
a. log rollers.
b. carpetbaggers.
c. cajolers.
d. one-termers.

4. The "franking" privilege refers to
a. free use of the U.S. mail.
b. voting when not personally present.
c. trading campaign pledges for contributions.
d. vote trading among members of Congress.

5. Candidates for the U.S. Senate must be _____ and a citizen for _____years.
a. 35 years of age; 5
b. 30 years of age; 9
c. 21 years of age; 10
d. 40 years of age; all of those

6. A republican form of government implies that the
a. Republican party receives an advantage when presenting its candidates for the presidency.
b. American system was modeled almost exactly after the Roman republic.
c. American voters would have their interests represented by elected officials they chose.
d. power would be divided between the branches of government.

7. Which of the following is not a legal requirement to be a member of the House of Representatives?
a. Being 25 years of age
b. Being a resident of the district
c. Being an eligible voter
d. Being a citizen of the U.S. for 7 years

8. The U.S. Congress directly employs approximately _____ staff members.
a. 5,000
b. 20,000
c. 30,000
d. 34,000

9. Which of the following is NOT a support agency of the U.S. Congress?
a. Congressional Research Service
b. Congressional Budget Office
c. Office of Management and Budget
d. General Accounting Office

10. The average member of the House of Representative serves a district with a population of approximately _____people.
a. 50,000
b. 150,000
c. 330,000
d. 600,000

You can find the correct answers to these questions by taking the quiz and then submitting your answers in the Online Edition. The program will automatically score your submission. Where you miss a question, the program will provide the correct answer, a rationale for the answer, and the section number in the chapter where the topic is discussed.

Further Reading

For up-to-date, comprehensive, and highly readable textbooks on Congress, see *Congress and Its Members* by Roger H. Davidson and Walter J. Oleszek (Washington, D.C.: Congressional Quarterly Press, Inc.); or Stephen Frantzich and Steven Schier, *Congress: Games and Strategies* (available on-line and in hard copy from Atomic Dog Publishers, 2002).

The trade magazine of Congress is the privately published *Congressional Quarterly Weekly Report*. Extensively used by both congressional insiders and outside observers, this weekly periodical contains member profiles, analyses of significant policy battles, voting statistics, and a chronicle of each week's key happenings.

Two roughly comparable almanacs of Congress—*Politics in America* (Washington, D.C.: Congressional Quarterly Press, Inc.) and *The Almanac of American Politics* (Washington, D.C.: National Journal)—provide an in-depth look at each member of Congress and his or her district. Both contain election statistics, information on campaign contributions, demographic profiles of each member's district, voting patterns in Congress, and a political profile of each member. Both are published every other year.

The Congressional Directory (Washington, D.C.: U.S. Government Printing Office), published every two years, is the official guide to Congress. It provides biographies supplied by the members as well as committee listings.

The Dictionary of American Government and Politics by Jay M. Shafritz (New York: HarperCollins, 1993) is a useful guide to key political concepts and terms. The entries span the entire range of American politics, and the book explains legislative terms particularly well.

For a quantitative, historical look at the nature of Congress and its Members, see *Vital Statistics on Congress* by Norman J. Ornstein, Thomas E. Mann, and Michael J. Malbin (Washington, D.C.: Congressional Quarterly Press, Inc.). Issued every two years, this volume summarizes overall election statistics, the congressional workload, and voting patterns. It includes data going back to the First Congress on many items.

Endnotes

1. Jay M. Shafritz, *The Dorsey Dictionary of American Politics and Government* (Chicago, IL: Dorsey Press, 1988), 473.
2. Congressional Quarterly, *Origins and Development of Congress* (Washington, D.C.: Congressional Quarterly Press, Inc., 1976), 174.
3. Congressional Quarterly Press, Inc., *Origins and Development*, 182.
4. Carl Sandburg, *Abraham Lincoln: The Prairie Years and the War Years* (Pleasantville, NY: Readers Digest Association, 1970), 83, 97.
5. Roger H. Davidson and Walter J. Oleszek, *Congress and Its Members* (Washington, D.C.: Congressional Quarterly Press, Inc., 1990), 36.
6. Total average district populations were close to four hundred thousand, with about 50 percent of the voters participating in congressional elections. See Davidson and Oleszek, *Congress and Its Members*, 26.
7. Hedrick Smith, *The Power Game* (New York: Ballantine Books, 1996), xvi.
8. See Philip M. Stern, *The Best Congress Money Can Buy* (New York: Pantheon Books, 1991).
9. Norman Ornstein, Thomas Mann, and Michael Malbin, *Vital Statistics on Congress, 2001–2002* (Washington, D.C.: Congressional Quarterly Press, Inc., 2002), 87–92.
10. See David T. Canon, *Actors, Athletes and Astronauts: Political Amateurs in the United States Congress* (Chicago, IL: The University of Chicago Press, 1990).
11. James R. Dickinson, "House Rivals Tread Fine Line in Race-Conscious Mississippi," *Washington Post*, October 29, 1986, A1.
12. Senator Joseph Biden (D-Del.), *Congressional Record*, May 27, 1993, S-6681.
13. Smith, *The Power Game*, 122–23.
14. See David Mayhew, *Congress: The Electoral Connection* (New Haven, CT: Yale University Press, 1974).
15. See Richard Morin, "You Think Congress Is Out of Touch? Look in the Mirror, Voters, The Trouble Starts With You," *Washington Post*, October 16, 1994, C1; and 1999 polls of 1,204 adults by the Center on Policy Attitudes reported in the LEXIS-NEXIS database.
16. Edward Walsh, "Hill Picking Leaders in Air of Faint Suspense Except for House Majority Whip," *Washington Post*, December 8, 1986, A4.
17. Helen Dewar, "In Fractious GOP, Dole Learns Tough Guys Don't Take Sides," *Washington Post*, July 9, 1994, A1.
18. Dan Balz and Charles Babcock, "Gingrich Allies Made Waves and Impression," *Washington Post*, December 20, 1994, A14.
19. Dan Balz and Serge Kovaleski, "Gingrich Divided GOP, Conquered Agenda," *Washington Post*, December 21, 1994, A18.
20. Ibid.
21. *New York Times*, November 12, 1994, A2.
22. Smith, *The Power Game*, 88.
23. All staff figures come from Norman Ornstein, Thomas Mann, and Michael Malbin, *Vital Statistics on Congress, 1999–2000*, Washington, D.C.: Congressional Quarterly, 129.
24. Michael J. Malbin, *Unelected Representatives: Congressional Staff and the Future of Representative Government* (New York: Basic Books, 1980).
25. Harrison W. Fox and Susan Webb Hammond, *Congressional Staffs: The Invisible Force in American Lawmaking* (New York: The Free Press, 1977).
26. Stephen Frantzich, *Write Your Congressman: Constituent Communications and Representation* (New York: Praeger, 1986), 10.
27. Frantzich, *Write Your Congressman*, 13.
28. Ornstein et al., 129.

13

Congress: The Policy and Power Games

Key Points

- **How a bill becomes a law.**
- **Formal rules, informal rules, and strategies of the congressional policy game.**
- **Coalition building as a primary legislative activity.**
- **The correlates of winning and losing the congressional policy game.**
- **The factions that determine who wins and who loses the congressional policy game.**

Preview: "Dance with Them that Brung You"

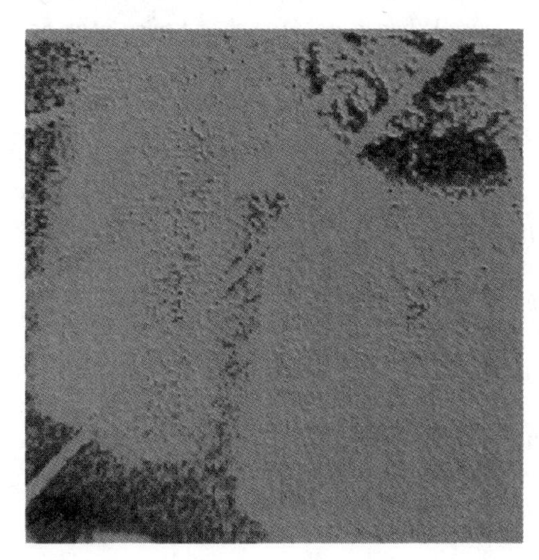

To hunt for votes in Congress would seem to be a pretty simple process. You look for your old friends and prevail on them for support. Ted Strickland looked like just such a good bet as Bill Clinton set out to create a winning congressional coalition to support his crime bill. The bill was filled with things that Democrats like to support: education initiatives and youth programs to keep kids off the streets. The bill included the popular "three strikes and you're out" provision to be tougher on career criminals. Many local officials particularly liked the federal funding for new police officers.

Freshman Democrat Ted Strickland, an ordained United Methodist minister and social worker, found a lot in the bill to like. Strickland had endorsed Clinton while winning his Ohio district in 1992, and he had already supported the president on key battles such as the Family Leave Bill and the president's economic package. His 93 percent support of the Democratic Party on partisan votes and his 75 percent support for presidential initiatives in 1993 all indicated Strickland would support the crime bill. As an adviser to the president's health care task force, Strickland had considerable contact with the president, the First Lady, and their staffs. Despite such a record, Strickland had other ideas.

In the House, the ongoing vote totals and individual votes are publicly displayed during the fifteen minutes of voting.

In the end, Ted Strickland joined fifty-seven other Democrats who crossed Democratic president Bill Clinton and forced him to negotiate with the Republicans for enough votes to get the bill passed. A momentary lapse in political judgment? A mistake? A case of being paid off? Not really. Congressman Strickland was just following a time-honored strategy.

The gun ban in the crime bill became one of those hot-button issues for his constituents, who expected him to be a pure representative. So, in the spirit of a mother's advice about being loyal to one's date at the prom by "dancing with the one that brung you," Congressman Strickland knew that there would be no next dance for anyone from his heavily Republican and pro-gun district who supported gun control. The dominant opinion in his district was that the assault weapon ban in the bill was just a first step in the slippery slide toward more extensive gun control.

It is true that the National Rifle Association had given him the maximum allowable contribution of $5,000, but that accounts for only about 3 percent of the PAC money he had raised—clearly not enough to buy his vote. More importantly, having been elected in a district that had been in Republican hands for over thirty years, Democrat Strickland did not want to strike out on a principle not shared by most of his constituents and thus return the district to Republican hands.

While such public thwarting of a president of your party might seem likely to lead to a counter blow, none was forthcoming. The president did not visit Ted Strickland's district in 1994—but not because he was unwilling. Strickland and his managers felt that he would do better to separate himself from a president who was not that popular in his district. Tipper Gore, with her more conservative views on family issues, served as the primary star attraction for the campaign.

The story of Ted Strickland reveals much about the freedom of contemporary members of Congress to tailor their behavior to their district as opposed to slavishly following the party line or the president's wishes. When the votes were counted, Ted Strickland's gamble almost worked. In spite of the Republican tide that should have overwhelmed him in such a heavily Republican district, he lost by only a few thousand votes. His vote on the crime bill helped keep the margin razor thin. It is both a strength and a weakness of contemporary congressional government that the wishes of members' constituents prevail in most cases. While it assures that policy making will be less efficient and predictable, such congressional independence reflects Americans' desire to guarantee that their local voice will be heard in Washington.[1]

With a well-known name, an experienced campaign organization and the ability to tout his congressional experience, Strickland came back in 1996 to reclaim his seat by a similar razor-thin margin that sent him back to the benches in 1994. His victory with that of other Democrats in 1996 began the erosion of the Republican majority from twenty-six seats in the 104th Congress, to twenty seats in the 105th Congress and to a less than ten-seat margin during the 106th Congress. Strickland sailed to victory with over 58% of the vote on 2000, while the Republican majority in the House slipped to a five seat margin in the 107th Congress. In the wake of the 2002 election, where the Republicans gained seats in the House, the now relatively senior Strickland bucked the Republican trend by increasing his margin to 59%, becoming one of the 98% of incumbents winning. In 2004, Strickland gets a free ride without a challenger and becomes one of the 99% of House incumbents running successfully for reelection.

Although members of Congress spend much time and energy getting into office and staying there, their primary motivation is usually to be players in the policy game. This game is complex, multilayered, and often confusing, with no clear beginning or end. It is an ongoing process in which Congress is but one of several major institutional arenas. The complexity of the policy game means that it can be completely mastered by no one, and even the most skillful of players must expect to lose on occasion. Winning or losing in the policy arena can affect the electoral game, but more importantly, it determines the laws governing the nation.

As components of a collective decision-making body engaged in making choices among policy alternatives, the 100 Senators and 435 House members must be organized for concerted action. Although individuals can and do make a difference, the complexity of Congress's tasks and the principle of majority rule encourage individual members to work together. In the process, some groups and individuals win and others lose. Like players in many games, members of Congress seek to improve their chances of winning by joining with other like-minded players to form teams.

Chapter 12 described the selection and initial organization of congressional players. New members of Congress arrive having already been a member of one team—their political party—which continues to be an influence on their behavior in the policy game. Most join several other teams in Congress. The most important are the various congressional caucuses and special interest groupings. While some members choose to expend considerable effort on maintaining their political bases back home, none can completely avoid committee work, floor deliberations, and voting on legislation.

Recognizing the breadth of the congressional task and the need to specialize, members seek out committee assignments that will allow them to work intensively on policy areas of special interest. This chapter looks at the goals, rules, and strategies that players seek to follow in committees and on the floor. Recognizing that Congress is only one player, the chapter concludes with an examination of the relationships between Congress and the other branches of government.

13-1 Stakes in the Policy Game

As played in Congress, the policy game has a straightforward objective—to influence **public policy** through the passage of legislation. Most legislation can be categorized as distributive, redistributive, or regulatory. Each type of policy presents Congress with a somewhat different challenge. Recognizing the political benefits, members of Congress prefer to distribute benefits. But in order to accomplish this, they must often tackle the trickier task of redistributing resources. In other realms, Congress is called on to regulate the behavior of individuals and organizations.

public policy *Outcomes of political games that distribute benefits or sanctions to players and others. Generally characterized as regulatory, distributive, or redistributive.*

Distributive legislation requires government to provide goods or services (which would otherwise be unavailable) to large segments of the population. Building a federal highway, establishing a military to provide national defense, and funding cancer research are all examples of distributive policies. Recognizing that resources are not sufficient to fully fund every possible program, members of Congress choose which goods and services will be provided.

distributive policy *Public policies that distribute goods and services widely among the population with no significant bias toward particular groups.*

Although governments are not required to fund only those programs they can pay for with current revenues, borrowing from future revenues and thereby creating a deficit has become a major concern in Congress and the United States. Reducing the deficit and creating a **balanced budget** can be accomplished only by decreasing spending or increasing revenues. In the current era of budget cutting, Congress increasingly faces a zero-sum game, in which increasing one program means decreasing another. Under different economic and political conditions, increasing taxes allows increases in a variety of government programs without comparable cuts in other programs.

balanced budget *A state of national income and expenses in which government receipts equal or exceed outlays.*

Unlike the business world, where the customer pays only for goods or services rendered, few governmental policies involve a one-for-one exchange. Governments take resources in the form of taxes and fees from some members of the population and **redistribute** them to purchase goods and services either for everyone (such as indivisible services like national defense or protection of the environment) or for individuals with special needs (such as welfare programs for persons with disabilities who have no means of supporting themselves). Recipients of redistributive policies do not necessarily pay for the services they receive but must meet a **needs test.** Congress plays a key role in determining who gives resources and who receives goods and services (by establishing criteria of needs before redistribution).

redistributive policy *Public policies that transfer wealth, rights, duties, responsibilities, or other values from one group to another.*

needs test *A provision in legislation specifying the minimum eligibility requirements for receiving government funds based on personal needs.*

The Constitution grants the House of Representatives, as the legislative body closest to the people, special powers as the originator of all tax legislation. Tax legislation passed by Congress has generally favored a *progressive tax* approach. Taxes that are paid for in greater proportion by wealthier citizens have traditionally been used to pay for goods and services for the less-well-off segments of the population. Tax policies of the 1980s emphasized this goal of the progressive tax less than in previous years. Contemporary proponents of a **flat tax,** which would tax everyone at the same rate, are in favor of lowering the tax percentage for wealthier individuals. They promote the flat tax as a way to encourage initiative and expand economic activity. A flat tax would be easier to administer, but it could put a greater burden on those with lower incomes.

flat tax *A taxation method in which everyone who earns enough to be taxed pays the same percentage of their income in tax.*

regulatory policy *Public policies that place government limits on or establish guidelines for the behavior of individuals, groups, and organizations within the political system.*

A significant portion of legislation in Congress regulates the actions of groups and individuals. Congress has determined such **regulatory** items as the amount of pollution that your car can emit, the rates that stockbrokers can charge, and the barriers that must be removed from buildings to provide access for individuals with disabilities. In recent years, considerable pressure has built to limit government regulation and to transfer jurisdiction to the states. In 1995 Congress repealed the national speed limit for cars, asserting that states better understand regional conditions and can thus set more appropriate limits. Significant realms once carefully regulated by the federal government, such as airline fares and radio and television licensing, have been deregulated.

In some cases, the Constitution gives Congress the specific right to regulate. In other cases, Congress has used its other powers creatively. For example, the Constitution says nothing about speed limits. In 1974, when Congress wanted to control them nationally, to conserve energy, it linked the payment of funds for building highways to the passage of specified state laws on speed limits. Congress later rescinded the 55-mile-per-hour restraint, again allowing states to set their own speed limits on most highways. Using the "carrot" of distribution of goods and services, Congress created the equivalent of the "stick" of regulation. There has been considerable opposition from the private sector and/or other levels of government when Congress has mandated new regulations without providing the necessary funding for administration or enforcement. President Bill Clinton's health care plan angered business owners who would have had to pay for the newly mandated coverage. A number of states dragged their feet on implementing new motor-voter registration regulations (see Chapter 11) when the federal government failed to accompany the regulation with funding. One of the first actions of the 104th Congress in 1995 was to pass legislation against unfunded mandates. Now if the federal government wants to regulate, it must either enforce the regulations itself or provide the states with the necessary funding. (Chapters 3 and 8 explore changing federal-state relationships.)

Although deliberating on and passing legislation are the premier activities of the policy game, Congress also serves as an incubator of ideas until the ideas are ready to be enacted into law.[2] It also investigates government performance and possible wrongdoing. The process of policy discussion can affect policy even if new legislation fails to emerge. The congressional debates on affirmative action are a good example. Government agencies and other political players often anticipate congressional reaction and change their behavior simply because a policy is under consideration. President Clinton began to redefine his position on affirmative action and agencies began to look carefully at their hiring practices even before any legislation had been proposed (see Chapter 20).

Only members of Congress have the right to introduce legislation formally, but the ideas for legislation come from many sources. Although members and their staffs originate legislative initiatives at times, more often interested players outside of Congress suggest problems in need of solution and even specific solutions. The White House, bureaucrats, and interest groups find it easy to convince members to introduce the legislation on their behalf. The legislative process is clearly a continuous game with many rounds. Box 13-1: Steps in the Legislative Process outlines the key official stages in the process. While the key steps are important, passing from one step to the next involves complex strategies and a detailed understanding of the rules. A piece of legislation starts its arduous movement through the legislative process by being assigned to a committee.

Box 13–1 Steps in the Legislative Process

Anyone may draft a bill; however, only members of Congress can introduce legislation, and by doing so become the sponsor(s). There are four basic types of legislation: bills, joint resolutions, concurrent resolutions, and simple resolutions. The official legislative process begins when a bill or resolution is numbered (H.R. signifies a House bill and S. a Senate bill), referred to a committee, and printed by the Government Printing Office.

The following are the steps of legislative procedure:

1. Referral Committee: With few exceptions, bills are referred to standing committees in the House or Senate according to carefully delineated rules of procedure.
2. Committee Action: When a bill reaches a committee it is placed on the committee's calendar. A bill can be referred to a subcommittee or considered by the committee as a whole. It is at this point that a bill is examined carefully and its chances for passage are determined. If the committee does not act on a bill, it is the equivalent of killing it.
3. Subcommittee Review: Often, bills are referred to a subcommittee for study and hearings. Hearings provide the opportunity to put on the record the views of the executive branch, experts, other public officials, supporters, and opponents of the legislation.
4. Mark Up: When the hearings are completed, the subcommittee may meet to "mark up" the bill, that is, make changes and amendments prior to recommending the bill to the full committee. If a subcommittee votes not to report legislation to the full committee, the bill dies.
5. Committee Action to Report a Bill: After receiving a subcommittee's report on a bill, the full committee can conduct further study and hearings, or it can vote on the subcommittee's recommendations and any proposed amendments. The full committee then votes on its recommendation to the House or Senate. This procedure is called "ordering a bill reported."
6. Publication of a Written Report: After a committee votes to have a bill reported, the committee chairman instructs staff to prepare a

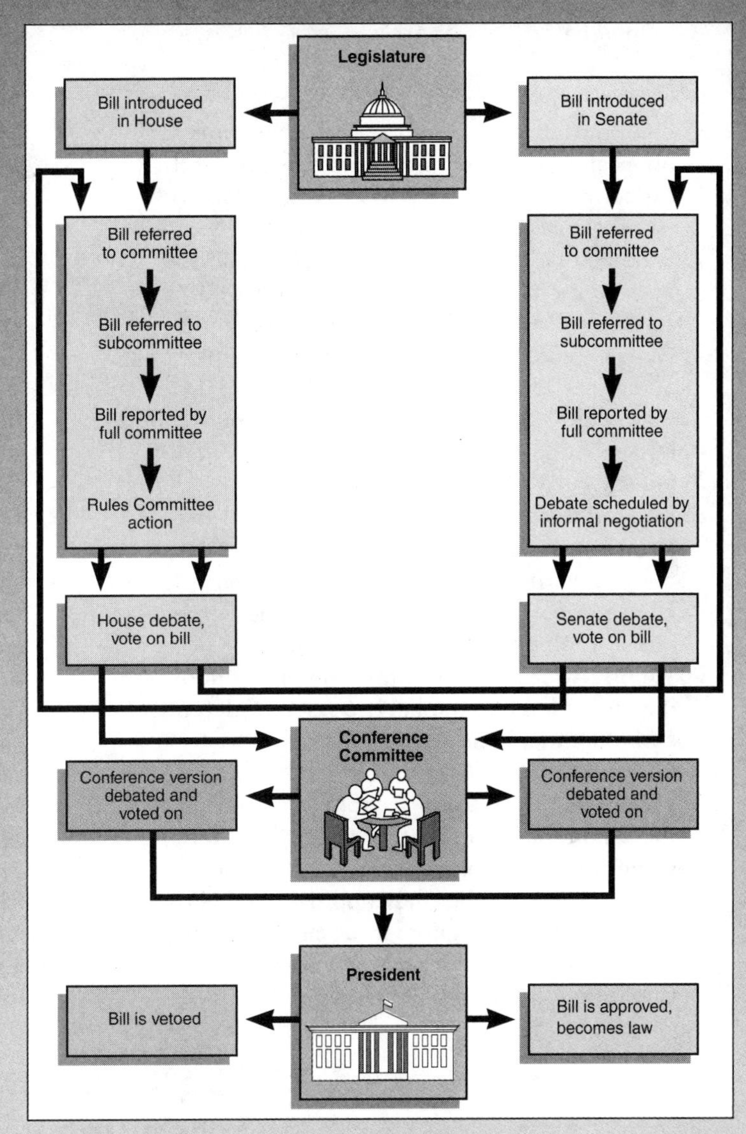

How a Bill Becomes a Law

A bill must overcome many obstacles before it is signed into law. Most bills never make it out of committee.

Source: William F. Hildenbrand and Robert B. Dove, "Enactment of a Law: Procedural Steps in the Legislative Process," (Washington, D.C.: GPO, 1982), p. 233.

continued

Box 13–1 Steps in the Legislative Process

—*Continued*

written report on the bill. This report describes the intent and scope of the legislation, impact on existing laws and programs, position of the executive branch, and views of dissenting members of the committee.

7. Schedule Floor Action: After a bill is reported back to the chamber where it originated, it is scheduled for floor action. Scheduling in the House is proposed by the Rules Committee and agreed to by the entire membership. In the Senate, scheduling is based on a more informal agreement worked out by the majority leader.
8. Debate: When a bill reaches the floor of the House or Senate, there are rules and procedures governing the debate on legislation. House rules are very formal, while the Senate has a tradition of more open debate.
9. Voting: After the debate and the approval of any amendments, the bill is passed or defeated by the members voting.
10. Referral to Other Chamber: When a bill is passed by the House or Senate it is referred to the other chamber, where it usually follows the same route through committee and floor action. This chamber may approve the bill as received, reject it, ignore it, or change it. For important legislation, both chambers work on similar legislation simultaneously.
11. Conference Committee Action: If only minor changes are made to a bill by the other chamber, it is common for one chamber to assent to the other's preferences and the legislation goes directly to the president for signature. However, when the actions of the other chamber significantly alter the bill, a conference committee is formed to reconcile the differences between the House and Senate versions. If the conferees are unable to reach agreement, the legislation dies. If agreement is reached, a conference report is prepared describing the committee members' recommendations for changes. Both the House and Senate must approve the conference report.
12. Final Action: After a bill has been approved by both the House and Senate in identical form, it is sent to the president. If the president approves of the legislation, he or she signs it and it becomes law. Or, the president can take no action for ten days, while Congress is in session, and it automatically becomes law. If the president opposes the bill, it can be vetoed, or if the president takes no action after the Congress has adjourned its second session, it is a "pocket veto" and the legislation dies.
13. Overriding a Veto: If the President vetoes a bill, Congress may attempt to "override the veto." This requires a two-thirds roll call vote in each chamber of the members who are present in sufficient numbers for a quorum.

13-2 The Committee Arena: Screening and Refining

When most people think of Congress, they imagine the full House or Senate assembled to consider a major issue, or perhaps the two houses meeting in joint session to hear the president's State of the Union Address. Such sessions, however, are relatively rare. For the most part, the work of Congress is conducted in smaller, more intimate, and less visible arenas. Chief among these is the committee arena.

Over the years, the following three types of relatively permanent committees have emerged:

standing committee *A permanent committee of one house of Congress assigned the responsibility of dealing with bills in a particular policy area.*

select committee *A congressional committee established to deal with a temporary task or emerging problem. Sometimes called a special committee.*

- Most of the work occurs in permanent **standing committees.** For example, each chamber has committees on agriculture, foreign affairs, and appropriations.
- **Select committees** (or special committees) are established for a limited period of time to deal with a specific problem. Examples are the Select Committee to Investigate Covert Arms Transactions with Iran or the Select Intelligence Committee.

- At times, both houses of Congress agree to create a **joint committee** to deal with common problems (the Joint Committee on the Library or the Joint Committee on Printing) or to help bring about compromise on complex and ongoing issues (the Joint Budget Committee or the Joint Committee on Taxation).

joint committees *Permanent committees made up of both House and Senate members.*

Most committees are too large and too diverse to work efficiently. Smaller **subcommittees** are established and report back to the full committee on their work.

subcommittee *A specialized unit of a full congressional committee that deals with the details of legislation before passing it on to the full committee for its approval.*

More than a century ago, congressional scholar and future president Woodrow Wilson observed that "Congress in its committee rooms is Congress at work."[3] In 2000, there were nineteen standing committees, eighty-five subcommittees, and one permanent select committee in the House, and seventeen standing committees, sixty-eight subcommittees, and four select committees in the Senate. All are organized around categories of policy that Congress deals with (see Table 13-1). It is in these committees and subcommittees where most of the work of Congress is carried out and where the outcome of the policy game is often decided.

Table 13-1 **The Committees of the 108th Congress**

HOUSE STANDING COMMITTEES

- Committee on Agriculture
- Committee on Appropriations
- Committee on Armed Services
- Committee on the Budget
- Committee on Education and the Workforce
- Committee on Energy and Commerce
- Committee on Financial Services
- Committee on Government Reform
- Committee on House Administration
- Committee on International Relations
- Committee on the Judiciary
- Committee on Resources
- Committee on Rules
- Committee on Science
- Committee on Small Business
- Committee on Standards of Official Conduct
- Committee on Transportation and Infrastructure
- Committee on Veterans Affairs
- Committee on Ways and Means

HOUSE SPECIAL AND SELECT COMMITTEES

- House Permanent Select Committee on Intelligence
- Select Committee on Homeland Security

JOINT COMMITTEES

- Joint Economic Committee
- Joint Committee on Printing
- Joint Committee on Taxation
- Joint Committee on the Library

SENATE STANDING COMMITTEES

- Agriculture, Nutrition, and Forestry Committee
- Appropriations Committee
- Armed Services Committee
- Banking, Housing, and Urban Affairs Committee
- Budget Committee
- Commerce, Science, and Transportation Committee
- Energy and Natural Resources Committee
- Environment and Public Works Committee
- Finance Committee
- Foreign Relations Committee
- Governmental Affairs Committee
- Judiciary Committee
- Health, Education, Labor and Pensions Committee
- Rules and Administration Committee
- Small Business and Entrepreneurship Committee
- Veterans' Affairs Committee

SENATE SPECIAL AND SELECT COMMITTEES

- Senate Select Committee on Intelligence (JOINT)
- Senate Select Committee on Ethics
- Indian Affairs Committee
- Senate Special Committee on Aging

13-2a Choosing the Committee Players

Members of Congress seek seats on those committees responsible for the policies of most interest to their constituents. If they fail to get the desired committees as a freshman, they attempt to move to those committees during subsequent Congresses. A member from a corn-growing area, for example, will often seek a seat on the Agriculture Committee and on its corn subcommittee. More senior members, who are often more politically secure, seek assignments on prestigious and powerful committees with responsibility for broad issues, such as the Appropriations and Budget committees. Most members of Congress, and especially senators, serve on so many committees and subcommittees that meeting conflicts are inevitable. One result is that many members rely heavily on their personal staff to attend meetings in their place. In today's Congress, the work of the people's elected representatives is often delegated to the unelected players—the staffers—whose role in the policy game is increasingly significant.

13-2b Committee Rules: Formal and Informal

During the early part of the twentieth century, the informal practice of appointing the committee member with the longest continuous service on the committee as the chair became an established procedure with the force of a formal rule. With the rise of the seniority system, committee chairs came to dominate their committees through their power to set agendas, direct the committee staff, schedule sessions, and preside over meetings. The seniority system was challenged during the 1970s, which led to a modification of the selection process and limitations on chairs' power. Currently, chairs are determined not by seniority alone but by majority vote in the party caucuses. In choosing committee chairs for the 104th Congress, Republicans violated the seniority norm several times to seek more activist and supportive members. The Republicans have also committed themselves to the rotation of committee chairs. Formal committee bills of rights now ensure that committee majorities can control such things as dates of meetings, committee agendas, staff allocation among the majority and minority members, and meeting procedures. Modern committee chairs preside with more openness and fairness than did their predecessors. They remain influential players, however, on their respective committees or subcommittees. The informal rules in the committee arena differ by type of committee. Richard Fenno found that congressional committees fall into at least three distinct categories, each with a distinctive membership and an informal set of norms and rules:[4]

- policy-oriented committees,
- re-election committees, and
- power committees.

Members of more policy-oriented committees, such as International Relations, Economic and Educational Opportunities, and Banking and Financial Services, are drawn to these committees by a deep concern for legislative issues. Because individuals with passionate commitments to policy outcomes often become involved in considerable conflict, the politics of these committees is marked by divisiveness. They are typified by numerous close showdown votes and a lack of unanimous committee reports. Committees dealing with programs that distribute goods and services helpful for reelection, such as Public Works and Veterans' Affairs, attract members with an interest in mutual cooperation. These committees bend over backward to ensure that all members get what they need to maintain their elected position.

Senior members and those interested in a leadership role within Congress are found on the power committees, such as Appropriations, Ways and Means (which deals with taxes), and the House Rules Committees. These committees pride themselves on working out their differences in private, presenting a unified front in dealings with the full chamber, and intimidating potential opponents along the way. Thus, each distinctive type of committee draws certain types of members and operates under different norms.

13-2c Committees as Players

Few bills pass Congress without acquiring committee approval. First, an individual member of Congress formally introduces a bill into the legislative process. Most of the discussion and revision of bills takes place in subcommittee **hearings.** Committee staffs often develop studies prior to the hearing and suggest questions for the experts. Subcommittees report back to the full committee and, if the full committee approves, the legislation is recommended for floor action. To become a law, a proposal must successfully pass each stage. It takes only one failure to kill a bill (see Box 13-1).

hearing *A committee meeting in which experts are brought in to testify about proposed legislative action.*

A common and often effective strategy for killing a bill is to defeat or revise it in the committee arena. Only about 20 percent of introduced legislation passes the committee hurdle. Many bills never receive a hearing, while others emerge from committee deliberations in forms vastly different from those first proposed.

Because most committees forward proposed legislation to the appropriate subcommittees specializing in the policy area involved, subcommittees, by and large, determine what bills will be considered by the full committee. Members of Congress recognize the advantages of specialization, and to a great extent committees defer to the judgment of the subcommittees. The entire chamber in turn accepts the recommendations of the full committees as to the appropriate content of a particular piece of legislation.

There is considerable continuity among the congressional players involved in most policy areas. A federal agency spokesperson or interest group representative concerned with a specific policy area is likely to interact with the same members year after year in committee hearings and informal discussions. Bureaucratic agencies charged with carrying out policy also interact continually with the same committees to get their programs authorized and their funding appropriated. Hearings of the Armed Services committees, for example, often look like gatherings of old friends, as Defense Department officials, representatives of weapons manufacturers, and members of Congress with large military bases or concentrations of defense contractors in their districts sit down for another round of informal discussions.

This overlap of players involved in a series of rounds gives rise in many policy areas to a cozy and closed policy game played by members of what are sometimes known as **iron triangles** or *issue networks* (see Chapter 7). These sets of players are made up of the committee or subcommittee members, the bureaucrats that they oversee, and representatives of the affected interest groups. The term *issue networks* implies the natural and regularized interaction between players involved in a narrow policy realm. For example, during the debate over health care, it was natural for members of health-related committees, employees of the Department of Health and Human Services, and lobbyists for health care providers to interact on a regular basis. As long as the process is relatively open, few eyebrows are raised. At times the policy process becomes more of a closed game. The characterization as an iron triangle emphasizes that this interaction often develops into a relationship forged among players who become completely insulated from outside scrutiny.[5] Unless something occurs to draw broader congressional or public attention to one of these closed games, the players involved are tempted to pursue only the interests of the narrow set of participants with whom they interact regularly rather than the broader public interest (see Box 13-2: Issue Network Teams from a Player's Perspective).

iron triangles *Enduring relationships among members of federal agency bureaus, congressional committees, and interest groups who share an interest in a specific area of public policy. Participants generally discourage outsiders from joining their closed game.*

13-3 The Floor Arena: The Rules of Legislative Politics

> I've learned the rules. I know how to play the game. I can go to the mat.[6] (Senator Barbara A. Mikulski, D-Md.)

> Knowing the rules of the game makes it more interesting to watch. . . . It's like a game of chess. To get good at it you have to watch it played. . . . It's exciting when you see a move and can say, "Oh, I know what the counter move to that should be!"[7] (Congressional rules expert, Ilona Nickels)

Box 13–2 Issue Network Teams from a Player's Perspective

John W. Gardner, former cabinet secretary and founder of the interest group Common Cause, described the workings of issue networks during congressional testimony by saying:

> As everyone in this room knows but few outside Washington understand, questions of public policy . . . are often decided by a trinity consisting of (1) representatives of an outside body, (2) middle-level bureaucrats, and (3) [selected members of Congress]. . . . In a given field, these people may have collaborated for years. They have a durable alliance that cranks out legislation and appropriations on behalf of their special interests. Participants in such durable alliances do not want the department secretary strengthened. The outside special interests are particularly resistant to such change. It took them years to dig their particular tunnel into the public vault, and they don't want the vaults removed.[a]

[a] Quoted in Jay M. Shafritz, *The Dorsey Dictionary of American Government and Politics* (Chicago: Dorsey Press, 1988), 148–9.

floor *Referring to the main level of a legislative chamber, the arena for voting and other formal business.*

proxy voting *Allowing one individual to cast the vote of another.*

After passing the committee hurdle, legislation goes to the **floor** of each chamber. There, more diverse groups of players operate under different sets of rules and strategies. When legislation reaches the floor of each chamber, the only official players are the 100 senators and the 435 members of the House of Representatives. Staff may advise and other interested parties may attempt to influence, but voting is done by members of Congress alone. There is no **proxy voting;** members must be physically present to cast a ballot.

Two sets of rules control Congress. The first is the formal set of rules embodied in the Constitution and in the rules of each chamber. A second and more informal set of individual social *norms* guides members' behavior, especially in their dealings with one another.

13-3a The Formal Powers of Congress

The Founders saw the legislative branch as the "chief repository of governmental powers" and the "keystone of energetic government."[8] The decision to establish a two-chamber (bicameral) legislature not only provided two bases for representation but also ensured a legislative game with built-in conflict and competition. Each chamber has an absolute veto over most actions of the other and also retains unique independent powers.

The House, with its shorter term of office and direct election, was felt to be closer to the people. It therefore received the right to:

impeachment *The formal bringing of charges against a government official that could lead to the official's dismissal.*

- initiate bills dealing with the sensitive issue of taxation, and
- initiate charges of misconduct in **impeachment** proceedings.

The Senate, the more deliberative body with longer terms of office, was assigned the responsibility to:

- "advise and consent" on most presidential appointments and treaties, and
- try impeachment cases of federal officials.

Each chamber independently retains the power to judge the election qualifications of its members, determine its own internal rules and procedures, punish members for misbehavior (see Box 13-3: Congress and the 800-Pound Gorillas), and publish a record of its actions.[9]

The two chambers play different roles in the removal of government officials. The House brings charges of impeachment (comparable to a grand jury charging someone with a crime in a judicial proceeding), while the Senate tries the individual on the charge

Box 13–3 Congress and the 800-Pound Gorillas

Background

Ethical standards in politics are often unclear, and charges of misconduct are often intertwined with political considerations. Uncomfortable with the idea of trusting outsiders to evaluate actions of their members, both houses of Congress established ethics committees to enforce moral standards. While few members want to pass judgment on their colleagues, they would rather do it themselves than delegate such power to the courts or to the executive branch.

Two recent cases provided significant ethics challenges to the Senate. When it became public that Arizona entrepreneur Charles H. Keating had funneled over $1.5 million to five senators and had repeatedly encouraged the senators to intervene with government regulators investigating his Lincoln Savings and Loan, pressure built for an ethics inquiry.

When a number of former staff members and political acquaintances of Bob Packwood (R-Oreg.) charged him with making improper sexual advances, the issues of sexual harassment and the misuse of power came to the forefront.

Questions

The manner in which Congress handles ethics charges raises several questions:

- What ethical standards should apply to members of Congress?
- Who are the players in ethics cases?
- What are the rules for trying ethics cases?
- Who wins and who loses in ethics cases?
- Why is it so difficult for Congress to decide on ethics cases?

Analysis: The Standards

The Keating and Packwood cases involve different realms of potential ethical misconduct. Charles Keating, a multimillionaire banker, attempted to have five senators intervene on his behalf to save his failing Lincoln Savings and Loan. While direct bribery is a crime, intervention on behalf of a constituent to determine the status of administrative actions has long been a major activity of members of Congress. However, Special Counsel Robert S. Bennett argued that campaign contributions from Charles Keating and the extra effort of these senators reflected anything but routine constituent service. In his view, large campaign contributors were buying services not available to others. He also believed that some senators had initiated the exchange. According to Bennett, senators have significant power far beyond routine status inquiries, since they control the budgets of agencies whose actions may be in question. Bennett asserted:

> If I'm sitting on a park bench, and an 800-pound gorilla comes along and says, "Excuse me, I'm just making a status inquiry if there are any seats available," you say, "You're damn right, there's a seat available." And there's a lot of 800-pound gorillas around this place.[a]

Above and beyond the formal rules, Special Counsel Bennett argued that senators live under an "appearance standard" that makes actions reflecting disrepute on the Senate subject to disciplinary action.

The charges against Bob Packwood were more personal. Sexual harassment of subordinates is unacceptable behavior, and it has now come out into the open. The case of a U.S. Senator forcing himself on female staff and associates has opened the door for applying this standard of behavior to all members of Congress, who have often been immune to many of the rules they have passed.

The Players

The key players in each of these cases included those making the charges, those charged, those investigating the charges, and the Senate Ethics Committee. In both cases the charges came from the outside. The public interest group Common Cause identified senators who became known as the Keating Five—Alan Cranston (D-Calif.), Dennis DeConcini (D-Ariz.), John Glenn (D-Ohio), John McCain (R-Ariz.), and Donald W. Riegle, Jr. (D-Mich.). A victim of Senator Packwood's alleged sexual harassment initially brought that issue to public light, and she was soon joined by many additional alleged victims. Recognizing the difficulty of evaluating colleagues with whom they must work on a day-to-day basis, the Senate Ethics Committee brought in special counsels to gather evidence and make recommendations.

The Rules

Unlike a courtroom, there were no formal charges against the Keating Five senators. The special counsel was charged with finding the facts, and the committee had the right to exonerate, criticize, or suggest removal of the senators. Each senator was allowed a lawyer to defend his interests and could make his own case against the allegations.

The key rules battle in the Packwood case involved whether the hearings would be open to the public. After acrimonious and partisan debate, the

continued

Box 13–3 Congress and the 800-Pound Gorillas

—Continued

Senate voted 53 to 48 to keep the hearings closed while publishing the testimony.

The Strategies

The Senate Ethics Committee, with its partisan balance of members, attempts to maintain an image of nonpartisanship. In the Keating Five case, Special Counsel Bennett took the active role of making allegations. When he suggested dismissing allegations against Senator Glenn and lone Republican Senator McCain prior to the 1990 elections, the committee split along partisan lines.

All of the Keating Five denied any wrongdoing and argued that their actions were simply routine constituent service. They suggested that they had done nothing different from their colleagues. As it became clear that both Special Counsel Bennett and members of the Senate Ethics Committee would deal with each case separately, the game became one of each man for himself, as each accused senator only explained the ethical basis for his own actions.

The Packwood case was very partisan from the outset. The initial charges came just before the 1992 election and were dismissed by many as partisan politics. After the Republicans gained the majority in 1994, Senator Packwood became chair of the powerful Finance Committee, lessening some senators' willingness to take him on. Members of the Ethics Committee battled publicly over both substance and procedures. Senator Packwood first denied the allegations, then claimed impaired judgment as a result of alcohol. He attempted to release his diary selectively and to challenge some of the charges. The Packwood case dragged on for over three years. Senator Packwood's expressed interest in getting the case behind him was tempered by the realization that delay could reduce public interest.

The Winners and Losers

The Senate Ethics Committee divided the Keating Five into three groups. Senator Cranston received the harshest judgment when the committee asserted that he had "violated the Senate's general standard against improper behavior" by initiating fundraising activities in exchange for intervention. During the investigation, Cranston announced that he would not be running for reelection; he was, however, reprimanded by the entire Senate.

Senators DeConcini and Riegle were singled out for using poor judgment and for giving the appearance of improper action by initiating meetings with Keating and aggressively pursuing his interests after receiving campaign contributions. Senators Glenn and McCain were chided only for using poor judgment in their intervention. Since none of these four broke specific Senate rules, the committee closed their cases.[b] Senator McCain's run for the 2000 presidential nomination was not hindered by the ruling.

The Packwood case finally went to the Senate Ethics Committee in the fall of 1995. After the committee found him guilty of sexual misconduct, Senator Packwood resigned in the face of probable expulsion by the full Senate.

The Senate as an institution was one of the losers in this case. Evidence of ethical misconduct of its members and the Senate's slow reaction to it tarnished the Senate's image.

The eventual disposition of these cases may improve the general ethical behavior of Congress. While the Keating Five decision did not give an absolutely clear definition of ethical behavior in politics, elected officials will hesitate to use their status as 800-pound gorillas with executive agencies on behalf of other 800-pound gorilla contributors. This case encouraged some senators to push for stricter campaign contribution legislation. The high visibility of a sexual harassment case against a powerful U.S. Senator such as Bob Packwood (and his subsequent departure from office) undoubtedly tempered the relationships that senators have established with their staff and campaign workers.

The Next Round

The Keating Five and Packwood cases were not the end of the Congress's ethics challenges. In recent years the House has faced its own set of ethics scandals involving Speakers of both parties and improper use of the House bank. Members of Congress are fallible human beings in a profession with many temptations and many gray areas concerning ethical standards. Members of Congress do not relish passing judgment on a colleague, since they may well need the support of that colleague in subsequent political battles. While no one supports reducing the standards, the danger of partisan politics dominating the ethics process tempers Congress's ability to deal effectively with legitimate cases. There will undoubtedly be plenty for the ethics committees to do in future rounds.

---

a. Quoted in John R. Cranford, "Keating Five Asks Exoneration as Panel's Hearings End," *Congressional Quarterly Weekly Report 49*, no. 3 (January 19, 1991): 169.

b. John R. Cranford, Janet Hook, and Phil Kuntz, "Decision in Keating Five Case Settles Little for Senate," *Congressional Quarterly Weekly Report 49*, no. 9 (March 2, 1991): 517–527.

brought by the House. Federal officials are removed from office after being impeached by the House and convicted by the Senate. The full process has never run its course and forced the removal of a president (see Chapter 14), and only a handful of judges have been impeached and convicted.

If the independent powers of each chamber look impressive, the joint powers of Congress are even more so. No federal funds can be expended without congressional approval, and without funds, there can be no federal program. This **power of the purse** allows Congress to play a role in the initiation of new programs and to oversee the actual expenditure of the funds appropriated. Presidents propose a budget to Congress, and members of Congress must approve the budget before funds can be expended. In recent years, Congress has spent much of its time and energy considering and revising the president's budget. After funds are approved, Congress uses its power of **oversight** to monitor the executive branch's administration of legislation.

power of the purse *The prerogative of Congress to appropriate public funds.*

oversight *Congress' formal review of the expenditures and performance of the executive branch.*

The rules allowing Congress to oversee the executive branch have in recent years led to such highly visible congressional activities as the 1974 Watergate investigation, the 1987 Iran-Contra hearings, and the 1999 Bill Clinton impeachment hearings. In each of these cases, high-ranking government officials were required to come before congressional committees and to justify their behavior in a highly public forum. Congress also investigated President and Mrs. Clinton's financial involvement in the Whitewater land deal in Arkansas. Less visible and ongoing attempts to oversee the bureaucracy occur daily in congressional hearings and committee meetings.

All rules need interpretation and, at times, refinement. The roles of Congress and the president have changed over time, necessitating rule changes. For example, the Constitution grants Congress the power to declare war, but this power was substantially eroded by a series of presidential decisions to commit troops without requesting a declaration of war. By the 1970s, Congress felt frustrated by its inability to limit the scope of military actions by nonbinding resolutions and attempts to limit funds. The **War Powers Resolution** was passed in 1973 in the wake of the ten-year Vietnam conflict, a costly and undeclared war conducted vigorously by a succession of presidents against growing congressional opposition. The War Powers Resolution requires the President "in every possible instance" to consult with Congress before committing troops, to report to Congress concerning any such actions within forty-eight hours, and to terminate the use of troops within sixty days unless Congress approves their continued use or issues a declaration of war. Since its enactment, presidents and Congress have quibbled over definitions of hostilities, the timing of informing Congress, and even the constitutional basis for the act. To buy some leeway, the George H. Bush administration did not start the time clock for the War Powers Act during the initial stages of the Persian Gulf War. This resolution is a good example of the general principle that *the* importance of a rule is reflected in the degree to which the affected parties fight over it, both at the creation and implementation stages. (See Chapter 15 for more discussion of the War Powers Resolution.)

War Powers Resolution *The 1973 act of Congress designed to limit presidentially initiated military actions by requiring consultation with Congress and congressional approval.*

In recent years, Congress has tended to react to presidential initiatives and to the application of laws rather than to act independently. A significant change occurred after the 1994 elections. The Republican takeover of the House and Senate, combined with the specific proposals in the Republican Contract with America, allowed Congress to set the agenda for the initial months of the 104th Congress. President Bill Clinton was forced to fight his way back into the agenda-setting game. After recapturing the Senate in the Spring of 2001, Democrats became more aggressive in pursuing their agenda on issues such as health care, forcing President George W. Bush to react to their priorities. Divided government with different institutions controlled by different parties tends to set the stage for broader and more conflictual policy initiation. The 2002 election returned both houses of Congress to Republican control. Despite a slim margin in the Senate, experience with one-party control enabled President George W. Bush to pursue his legislative agenda. With small increased majorities in the House and Senate after the 2004 election, President Bush's potential legislative fortune increased, but the need for extraordinary majorities in many cases still threaten to thwart his efforts.

13-3b Rules for Passing Legislation

Floor action reveals the extensive influence of rules on the final outcome of legislation. The NAFTA debate, discussed in Chapter 1, was deeply affected by the decision to consider it under a fast track procedure. Members agreed ahead of time to set a deadline for consideration and to disallow any amendments. In the normal course of events, House rules impose more structure on the deliberation process than do those of the smaller Senate. The House Rules Committee plays a special role, determining the agenda and the conditions (rules) under which House debate is conducted. Rules proposed by the Rules Committee have the short-term purpose of defining the conditions of debate on a specific bill. The proposed rules included such factors as the length of debate and whether the bill can be amended (an open rule) or whether it must be accepted or rejected as proposed by the initiating committee (a closed rule). Rules must be accepted by a majority vote in the chamber. Approved rules outline the length of debate and whether amendments will be allowed. This committee not only plays the role of traffic cop, coordinating chamber proceedings, but also has the power to block or facilitate legislation based on a bill's content. During floor consideration, House floor managers for each side parcel out time to speakers supporting their position. When amendments are allowed, House rules require that they be relevant to the issue under debate. Although limited delaying tactics are allowed, voting occurs pretty much on the schedule established by the Rules Committee.

Floor procedures in the Senate reflect its more manageable size and deeply held desire to be the "world's greatest deliberative body" (see Box 13-4: "Gee, I Wish I Had Said That"). Senate rules allow unlimited debate without any requirement that it be to the point. The rules also allow senators the unique right to **filibuster,** a debating tactic in which one or more senators speak continuously and refuse to give up the floor. This enables a group of senators who may not be able to muster a majority on behalf of their position to delay almost indefinitely a decision on the issue involved. As part of his opposition in 1995 to President Bill Clinton's nomination of Dr. Vincent Foster as surgeon general due to his record of having performed abortions, Senator Phil Gramm (R-Tex.) threatened a filibuster. The threat crystallized opposition, and the nomination was eventually defeated. Filibusters end when the senators conducting them either win what they want or give up, or when three-fifths of the Senate membership supports **cloture,** a motion establishing a time to end debate.

filibuster *A delaying tactic used by a legislative minority to control floor proceedings until a compromise is reached. Allowed in the U.S. Senate only.*

cloture *Cutting off debate during a filibuster by acquiring a three-fifths vote of those present and voting (used in the Senate only).*

Differences in the size, membership, responsibilities, and rules of the House and the Senate lead to different strategies and outcomes (see Table 13-2). While it may be convenient to talk about "the Congress," not all generalizations apply to both chambers.

Voting on the floor of Congress represents the final act of legitimating policy, although most of the key decisions have already been made in committee. Voting can either be done orally or by a formal roll call vote, in which each member's individual vote is recorded. Initial **voice votes** are often challenged and require follow-up roll call votes, which result in a public record of each member's position. House roll calls are generally done electronically; senators must announce their vote when their name is called. Congressional players often protect each other by using oral votes for conflictual issues on which few members want to take a public stand. Control over the voting process can often determine the outcome (see Box 13-5: Controlling the Game by Controlling the Technology).

voice vote *A method of voting in Congress in which members orally answer yes or no to a proposal.*

If both chambers pass the same bill in identical form, it goes directly to the president. More commonly, there are differences in wording or substance (or both) in the bills passed by each chamber. When this occurs, the two versions of the bill are assigned to a **conference committee.** These temporary committees, usually made up of senior members of the relevant committee from each house, are responsible for ironing out differences in the two versions of the bill so that a compromise piece of legislation can successfully be returned to each chamber for passage before being sent to the president for signature or disapproval (**veto**).

conference committee *A joint House and Senate committee established to reconcile differences between two different versions of the same legislation.*

veto *The president's (or governor's) formal refusal to approve a piece of legislation, requiring it to go back to Congress (or the state legislature) for reconsideration.*

If vetoed by the president, the legislation dies unless supporters can muster enough votes to override the veto with another vote. Unlike many state governors, the president traditionally has not had the right to a line-item veto but must either accept or reject a

Box 13–4 "Gee, I Wish I Had Said That"

VIDEO

The rules of Congress allow members to "revise and extend" the remarks they made during debate. Most often, these revisions involve correcting grammar or minor misstatements of fact, though at times, the revisions completely change the content or flavor of the debate.

During a heated budget debate in 1992, Senator Alfonse D'Amato (R-N.Y.) and Senator Robert Byrd (D-W. Va.) got into a shouting match. The official printed record of the debate fails to completely record what happened, as the following excerpts indicate.

The Spoken Record
Video courtesy of C-SPAN.

The Official Record

Mr. D'AMATO. But let me refer to the Standing Rules of the Senate, page 18, Senate Manual, October:

No Senator in debate shall, directly or indirectly, by any form of word, impute to another Senator, or to any other Senators any conduct or motive unworthy or unbecoming of a Senator.

I am simply going to make a point that this is out of order, and that we are not doing this body any good by this.

Mr. BYRD. Mr. President, I ask for the regular order. I know enough about—

Mr. D'AMATO. I raise a point of order—

Mr. BYRD. I know enough about the Senate Rules that

I have not violated rule XIX.

Mr. D'AMATO. I ask the—

Mr. BYRD. The Senator can just—

The Spoken Record (with variations italicized)

Mr. D'AMATO. But let me refer to the Standing Rules of the Senate, page *19*, (page number changed) Senate Manual, *October* (not said)—

OK (said, but not put in the record):

It is clear, No Senator in debate shall, directly or indirectly, by any form of word, impute to another Senator, or to any other Senators any conduct or motive unworthy or unbecoming of a Senator.

I am *just* simply going to make a point that this is out of order, and that we are not doing this body any good by this.

Mr. BYRD. Mr. President, I ask for the regular order. I know enough about—

Mr. D'AMATO. I raise a point of order—

Mr. BYRD. I know enough about the Senate Rules *to know* that I have not violated rule XIX.

Mr. D'AMATO. I ask the—

Mr. BYRD. The Senator can just—*Would the Senator just shut his own mouth and let the chair rule?*

Sources: Formal record, *Congressional Record,* June 26, 1992, S-9043; Actual words, Tape of floor debate, C-SPAN.

Table 13-2 Different Games and Players: The House and Senate Compared

	House	Senate
Membership Characteristics (109th Congress 2005–2006)		
Occupation (percentage of lawyers)	37%	58%
Average age	55	60
Average number of years in office	9	11
Women	16%	13%
Structure		
Size (members)	435	100
Term of office (in years)	2	6
Number of standing committees	19	16
Number of subcommittees	86	69
Unique powers	Originates revenue (tax bills)	"Advise and consent" on treaties and appointments
	Brings impeachment charges	Tries impeachment cases
Operation	Formal debates with fixed schedules	Less structured debates
	Discussion must be relevant (germane)	No rule of germaneness
	Debates limited	Debates unlimited (filibuster possible)
Orientation	Short term; responsive to election	Long term; deliberative; emphasis on traditional results; sees itself as "the people's house"

Source: Norman J. Ornstein, Thomas E. Mann and Michael J. Malbin, *Vital Statistics on Congress, 1999–2000* (Washington, D.C.: *Congressional Quarterly, 2000)*, 1–32; http://oncongress.cq.com

Box 13–5 Controlling the Game by Controlling the Technology

Once a vote is called for, House rules allow 15 minutes for members to get to the floor, insert their plastic ID cards, and vote. The Speaker makes the final decision on closing the vote, a power that can sometimes make a difference, as the following scene involving a vote on welfare reform indicates. The Republican minority wanted a budget plan that included welfare reform, while the Democratic leadership opposed tying welfare reform to the budget.

When the 15 minutes allowed for the roll call vote had elapsed, the vote stood at 205 to 206 against final passage. This was a major embarrassment for the Speaker [a Democrat], so he held the vote open, came down from the chair, and began working the floor—trying to find one Democrat who would switch from no to yes. After about 10 minutes no one had switched. . . . He returned to the chair, picked up the gavel, and announced that the time had expired. Just then, freshman Democrat Jim Chapman from Texas was brought back on the floor by one of the Speaker's aides. Chapman indicated that he was changing his vote. The Speaker immediately brought down his gavel and announced that the bill had passed, 206-205.[a]

a. Richard B. Cheney, "What's Wrong about Wright," *Washington Post*, April 9, 1989, B2.

bill in its entirety. Recent presidents and many Republican legislators have pushed for legislation allowing such a veto. Legislation allowing the president to select items to veto passed in 1996 and was used a few times by President Bill Clinton before being ruled unconstitutional in 1998.

Congressional rules and their application are not without their critics. Members of the minority party regularly complain about mistreatment by the majority party. Former representative Dick Cheney (R-Wyo.) voiced a common concern among House Republicans (then in the minority) when he stated:

> To people outside Congress, the rules produce big yawns. . . . The contemporary dispute turns on whether the majority's desire to act should be allowed to run roughshod over debate and accountability. . . . In the United States majority control over the rules is used not to enhance partisan accountability but to screen members from being accountable. . . . The minority would be willing to accept restrictive rules as long as they are fair. . . . If we do not win, so be it. We are willing to take our chances on a level playing field. The question is whether the other side is willing to play.[10]

Newt Gingrich (R-Ga.), then minority party whip, was even more forceful when he argued:

> It is very important for people around America to start studying the Committee on Rules and study the procedures of the House, because one cannot really appreciate exactly how power is used in Washington until they watch the way in which the game is rigged.[11]

After years of frustration as the minority, the Republicans began to even out the playing field when they took control of the House following the 1994 elections. While not giving up the advantages of being in the majority, they made it easier for members to enter into debate and to amend legislation on the floor.

Party leaders are torn between two competing goals—acting on their legislative agendas and promoting internal democracy. While a congressional majority of either party does not justify unfairness per se, it usually asserts that aggressive use of the rules is part and parcel of effective legislating. As in any game, those who know the intricacies of the rules gain an advantage over those with little more than casual awareness of what is possible. For example, House leaders recognize that it is difficult to maintain a quorum on the floor, so they use a legal fiction—the Committee of the Whole. Rather than having to get a normal quorum of half the membership plus one (218), business in the Committee of the Whole can be conducted by any one hundred members wishing to stay around for debate and amendment. After the Committee of the Whole passes a piece of legislation, it goes to the full chamber, with its expanded quorum, for final approval.

Each chamber maintains its own set of formal internal rules and precedents, and considerable power goes to those who master their use. Chamber rules are intended to force compromise, to protect minority positions, and to prevent hasty decisions. Complaints that congressional procedures are slow, redundant, and inefficient miss the point. That is what they were and are intended to be. Getting a bill through Congress requires a series of decisions in different arenas. This assures that most of the underlying issues have been brought out and taken into account. The goal of the rules is to develop better legislation by providing all sides with numerous opportunities to affect the outcome, not to facilitate rapid decisions.

13-3c Informal Rules: Social Rules and Norms

Congress, like all social organizations, has developed norms or social expectations that are imposed on its members. Individuals unwilling to abide by these expectations are labeled "uncooperative" and can expect to lose the respect of colleagues. Widespread acceptance of these norms smoothes interpersonal relationships by bringing some predictability and civility to interactions among members. In recent years, increased internal democracy, the influx of new members, and the general loosening of norms in society as a whole have weakened or effectively repealed some well-established congressional norms. For example, the long-term expectation that new members serve an apprenticeship

Box 13-6 Bagging a Leadership Position

New technologies demand—or at least invite—new strategies. The arrival of television cameras in the House of Representatives in 1979 and in the Senate in 1986 encouraged members to capitalize on the highly visual character of television. Typically dull and detailed discussions of complex legislation were enlivened by rhetorical flourishes and visual aids. Members increasingly brought to the floor maps, charts, and representative objects to make their points. Junior members were generally more comfortable using a technology they had grown up with. Newt Gingrich (R-Ga.), Robert Walker (R-Pa.), and other junior members took to the floor in the 1980s to make speeches questioning Democratic leadership in the House and liberal policy alternatives. Their obvious affront to the apprenticeship and institutional loyalty norms clearly rankled more senior colleagues. Nevertheless, their ability to get their message out effectively engendered as much admiration as contempt.

Perhaps the clearest example of a member of Congress bypassing traditional apprenticeship expectations is Jim Nussle (R-Iowa). Only a few months after entering the House in 1991, he became the first member of Congress to address the chamber with a paper bag over his head. A few decades before, a new member would think twice about making any speech on the floor during his or her first year. This stunt, expressing embarrassment over the House check-bouncing scandal, captured the imagination of the media and caught the attention of Republican whip Newt Gingrich. After the Republicans captured the House majority in 1994, the Speaker-elect bypassed many senior members to appoint Nussle to guide the transition from the minority to the majority. Jim Nussle put a paper bag over his head to express his embarrassment over the Democratic leadership. Jim Nussle's highly visual bag gave him considerable control over the rules of the new Congress and guaranteed him major party leadership in his fifth year in the House.

period, during which they look and listen rather than take an active legislative role, no longer describes the behavior of junior members (see Box 13-6: Bagging a Leadership Position). The traditional expectation that members specialize in a small set of legislative topics is more likely to be observed in the House than in the Senate. Members are still expected to display a certain amount of institutional loyalty toward their own chamber by defending its actions and its members. Growing cynicism toward government in general and Congress in particular has, however, encouraged many members to run *for* Congress by running *against* Congress.[12] Institutional loyalty today is more a question of House or Senate members supporting their own chamber rather than loyalty to Congress as a whole.

Other norms remain more influential. Reciprocity—the willingness to exchange favors—underlies the bargaining and compromise so vital to getting things done in Congress. Personal courtesy, particularly the prohibition on personally criticizing fellow members and other Washington players in public and the practice of referring to them by title on the floor ("The Senior Senator from Minnesota" or "My esteemed colleague, the Representative from the First District of Florida"), takes some of the sting out of intense policy conflicts and facilitates future coalition building (see Box 13-7: Different Games, Oceans Apart). Not all members abide by the norms. When Representative Robert K. Dornan (R-Calif.) questioned the patriotism of President Bill Clinton during the early days of the 104th Congress, his colleagues had his words removed from the *Congressional Record* and attempted to enforce the norm by banning him from floor debate for a day. Carrie Meeks (D-Fla.) was also chastised by the chamber for her attacks on Speaker Newt Gingrich's ethics a few weeks later. Success in the committee arena and on the floor requires the observance and mastery of both the formal and informal rules of the game.

The internal characteristics of Congress and its members set the stage for the heart of the policy game—the passage of legislation. In the final analysis, members of Congress are individual players when it comes to casting their votes. Their actions are influenced by others, but the aggregate vote of Congress is based on the combination of individual voting decisions.

Box 13–7 *Different Games, Oceans Apart*

VIDEO

The U.S. House and Senate share the designation of "legislature" with the British House of Commons, but their members act in quite different ways. U.S. legislators almost invariably treat each other with at least superficial respect and respond to presidential speeches with, at worst, polite applause. Speeches in the House of Commons, on the other hand, are regularly interrupted with hoots, hollers, and catcalls from other members. When the prime minister fields oral questions from the members twice a week, there is a fair amount of largely good-natured but often sharp bantering directed at England's chief executive.

If you have access to C-SPAN, compare the norms of legislative chambers. C-SPAN covers House and Senate sessions during the week and the British House of Commons at 9 P.M. (eastern time) Sunday evenings. You will find the tenor of the debate and the tolerance for noise and interruptions significantly different.

President Bush delivers his annual State of the Union Message to Congress.

British Prime Minister Tony Blair faces his parliamentary colleagues during the weekly "Question Time."
Video courtesy of the House of Commons.

13-4 Legislative Strategies of the Policy Game

Both members of Congress and media observers recognize the strategic complexity of passing legislation:

> Legislation all too often is like a sophisticated pro football game. The plays look very complicated, but when you go back to the instant replays, you see it was very simple. It was about blocking and tackling, it was about running the prescribed routes or not running the prescribed routes by a receiver, about throwing the ball on target. Legislation is the same. It is about writing, it is about calling legislators, it is about expressing your desires.[13] (Representative George Miller, R-Calif.)

> [On] the Senate floor . . . the name of the game is to make no public commitments until after the votes are counted.[14]

In an average year, members of the House participate in over six hundred recorded votes and hundreds of additional voice votes on the floor, with Senators called on to vote on record about half that many times. Members also are involved in thousands of decisions in committee. The number of issues involved far exceeds the number that any single individual can be expected to master, so members use a number of strategies to simplify their process for making decisions on proposed laws.

Deciding Which Policy Goals to Pursue

One strategy for making a large number of decisions involves categorizing them. For decisions involving proposals similar to ones considered in the past, the easiest strategy is often to follow past precedent and do whatever seemed to lead to positive results for the member in the past. Representing such a strategy would be a member who said:

> This program increases defense spending. I voted for expanded defense capabilities eight times last year and did not get criticized by my constituents. This vote is pretty much like previous votes on defense. Therefore, I should vote for it.[15]

For new issues or those that lie outside the member's previous range of experience, members often seek out and rely on the advice of trusted colleagues. This often means someone from their party, a member representing a similar constituency, or a colleague with a similar ideological outlook. The party caucuses and other informal groups serve as primary mechanisms for transmitting such advice.[16] While most issues generate little constituent mail, congressional offices generally do mail counts for those that do. Numbers alone do not determine the amount of weight given to the opinions expressed. Congressional offices assume that the more effort that constituents take to communicate a preference, the more their guidance should be taken into account when voting on legislation. Thus, ten well-argued personal letters supporting one side of an issue may well have more impact on the member's final decision than 100 preprinted postcards supporting the other side. Members assume that many of the individuals who tear out a preprinted postcard from their interest group magazine and simply send it in are not as interested in the issue as the person who writes his or her own letter.

Even when constituents do not make direct contact, astute members of Congress keep their finger on the public pulse by paying attention to polling data and public expressions in the media (see Box 13-8: Talk Show Politics). Other external influences, such as direct contacts by interest group lobbyists or the White House, are effective in the absence of an expressed constituency interest.

Members of Congress struggle when deciding how much attention to give constituents (Time Out 13-1). They are well aware that those who write or call are generally not representative of all constituents. On many issues, the general public simply does not have the expertise to fully understand the implications of specific policy alternatives.

Time Out 13-1

Representing Others

Representation is the process of transmitting the interests of others to relevant decision makers. It is the link between the public and the policymakers. Assume that you are frustrated with the number and variety of courses offered in your major department (or have some other complaint about the academic program). Your experience and a few random comments from classmates lead you to believe that there are some major problems. You want to go to the department chair to express your concerns and those of your classmates. Before going, which two of the following would you do?

Choose two:

1. **Do research on other departments and find out how they handle similar situations.**
2. **Analyze your own experience and knowledge about the issue and develop a proposal to bring forward.**
3. **Call a meeting of your classmates to solicit their ideas, which you will consider incorporating into your proposal.**
4. **Survey your classmates or call a meeting where a formal vote is taken to develop the demands you will make.**
5. **Call a meeting to present your perspective and seek the support of your classmates for your proposal.**

Source: Stephen E. Frantzich and Steven E. Shier, *Congress: Games and Strategies* (Cincinnati, OH: Atomic Dog Publishing, 2003), 98.

Box 13-8 Talk Show Politics

As the 103rd Congress was winding down in 1994, one of the key pieces of legislation awaiting action was lobby reform. While the label "reform" made it appealing to most Americans, the secret details were known by few. After failing to pass health care reform, legislators of both parties wanted to come to some agreement so they could enter the election period with credit for accomplishing reform.

The bill would have banned gifts from lobbyists and expanded registration requirements for lobbyists. In a previous form, the bill had passed the Senate with little difficulty and sailed through the House. Just prior to the final vote in the Senate, the bill, which seemed to face easy passage, was done in by a combination of new technologies. House Republican whip Newt Gingrich (R-Ga.) sent faxes to several conservative talk-show hosts and organizations. The statements argued that the registration requirements would inhibit grassroots lobbying efforts because they required organizations to disclose the names of citizens doing volunteer work for civic and political groups. Those in favor of the bill argued with this interpretation and asserted that there was no intention to stifle citizen activity. The wording was vague enough, however, to engender debate. Conservative talk-show host Rush Limbaugh picked up the cause. According to his reading of the prospective bill, "such volunteers could face fines of up to $200,000 for failing to register as lobbyists . . . [and] this is anti-American and unconstitutional."[a] The activist Christian Coalition mobilized its own grassroots campaign against the bill "with calls to 250,000 people in all fifty states through a state-of-the-art network of computers, telephone trees, and fax machines." [b]

Capitol Hill was immediately flooded with letters, calls, and faxes that gave several senators cold feet. A piece of legislation that might have slipped by with little outside awareness in the waning hours of the session was side-tracked in the new age of technology-supported, "real-time" politics. In the end, Senate Democrats could not muster the sixty votes needed to break the Republican filibuster. With proven political activists upset, and a highly contested election in the offing, many senators concluded that no bill was better than a controversial one.

The broader lesson may well be that new technology speeds up public response time and gives well-organized causes that have access to the public mind the ability to redirect the policy debate. From the perspective of senators, the new technologies reduce their time for contemplation and subject them to more public pressure. Thomas Jefferson supposedly said, "We pour legislation into the senatorial saucer to cool it." He would probably find the contemporary turn of events—in which senators are excessively affected by a policy process heated up by new technologies—disturbing.

a. Christopher Drew, "Religious Right Phone Banks Put Lobby Reform on Hold," *Chicago Tribune*, October 7, 1994, 1.
b. Ibid.

Members tend to pay more attention to constituents who act on their preferences and are a key part of that member's political base. Member goals and experiences determine the degree to which they pay careful attention to public expressions or use their own personal judgment in making decisions. At a minimum, all members attempt to take positions that they can at least explain to the voters.

Because of the competing pressures on members, the two chambers of Congress have devised a variety of strategies for protecting members from embarrassment in the wake of controversial decisions. Unless demanded by an insistent minority, recorded roll call votes are avoided on the most controversial and potentially embarrassing issues, such as abortion and raising the pay of members. Such measures are commonly dealt with as part of **omnibus legislation,** a piece of legislation dealing simultaneously with a number of topics. This tactic allows a member to argue that "on balance, the legislation is good, and I had to take the bad with the good," thus deflecting criticism. Take, for example, a member who is generally opposed to increased defense funding. He or she might support a piece of legislation protecting the environment that also included an amendment increasing some defense expenditures.

omnibus legislation *A wide variety of often unrelated legislation included within a single and very complex bill.*

Answer to Time Out 13-1

Scoring: **Total the points for your two choices: If you chose number 3, give yourself 1 point; if you chose number 4, give yourself 3 points; if you chose numbers 1, 2, or 5, give yourself 0 points.**

If your score is 1 or less, you tend to approach the process of representation as a trustee. A trustee looks out for the interests of those he or she represents but does not necessarily draw them into the decision-making process. Trustees work on the assumption that their superior interest and experience help determine what is best for others. Trustees may look for input from others but would trust their own knowledge and intuition over the whims and wishes of individuals who have not thought deeply about the issue. A delegate, on the other hand, follows the wishes of others, even if it does not follow his or her personal preferences.

If your score is 2 or more, you tend to approach the process of representation as a delegate. A delegate transmits the wishes of others, even if they are not exactly the personal desires of the delegate. A delegate may try to structure the options but would follow the will of the majority. Trustees, on the other hand, assume that their knowledge and interest are greater, giving them the responsibility to follow their own judgment as the best way to protect the interests of those they represent.

trustee *A style of representation in which the person uses his or her individual judgment in looking out for the interests of others.*

delegate *A style of representation in which the person represents the views of others, no matter what he or she might prefer.*

There is no shortage of other tactics designed to avoid the heat associated with controversial decisions. In a bicameral legislature, with relatively decentralized power in committees and subcommittees, members have plenty of others to blame for congressional action or inaction. Like many other players in the political game, members of Congress try to claim credit without absorbing the blame.

13-4a Strategies for Achieving Policy Goals

Successful policy emerges less from the excellence of its content than from the strategies of its supporters and opponents:

> Congress is the principal policy arena of battle, round by round, vote by vote. People there compete, take sides, form teams, and when one action is finished, the teams dissolve, and members form new sides for the next issues.[17]

Legislation is the primary product of congressional activity. In each two-year session, members of Congress introduce over seven thousand bills, of which less than 10 percent are eventually passed by both chambers combined. After deleting the duplicates, this results in about four hundred new pieces of legislation per session. Because most are stalled somewhere in the process, and because steps that a bill must pass through are complex and time-consuming, players adopt strategies to enhance the prospects for passage of their legislation.

Timing is critical in an institution like Congress that reacts to outside pressure from constituents, interest groups, and the president. Issues perceived as crises take precedence over other concerns, and Congress can move relatively quickly in crisis situations. For example, Congress acted in a matter of hours to support President Jimmy Carter's boycott of the Moscow Olympics, President Bush's actions against General Noriega of Panama, and disaster aid following numerous natural disasters. President George W. Bush pushed for legislative support for a strong stand against Iraq in 2002 just before the critical congressional elections. In the wake of his party's electoral success, he pushed for his version of a homeland security bill right after the elections, attempting to use the mandate he believed the election gave him.

For more typical legislation, drafting the bill so that it will be assigned to a supportive committee or lining up numerous and powerful cosponsors increases the likelihood of passage. Finally, bill sponsors often encourage outside involvement in the form of presidential support, helpful media stories, constituent letter-writing campaigns, and active lobbying by interest groups.

The most important strategy for passing legislation is building a coalition, a group of players willing to support a particular piece of legislation, often for highly different reasons. Such alliances are temporary, although they may recur in similar form over time as similar legislative proposals come up for consideration. The typical congressional supportive coalition includes two types of players:

- **Natural coalition** members favor the proposed legislation on its merits; their support requires no further inducement.
- **Bought coalition** members are willing to trade their support for a piece of legislation to receive a specific payoff. (There also can be natural and bought coalition members who oppose the proposed legislation.) The process of "buying" a majority in Congress through bargaining is often referred to as **logrolling.** For example, farm bills have often been "bi-partisan vote-trading marathons linking rural Democrats and Republicans in protection of commodity prices [and] urban Democrats swapping votes to protect the food stamps program."[18]

natural coalition *A group of individuals agreeing to support a particular position without any additional inducement.*

bought coalition *A group of individuals agreeing to support a position only after a change in the substance of the legislation or in exchange for some other benefit.*

logrolling *The cooperation among politicians as they attempt to build a coalition by trading favors. The term is derived from the necessary cooperation among lumberjacks when they attempt to move logs on the water.*

Natural coalitions develop around similarities in constituent interests, party affiliations, and ideological preferences. For example, legislators from farming districts almost automatically support proposals for increased agricultural research. Party members normally back their party's candidates for chamber leadership positions. Conservative members favor increased defense expenditures more readily than do liberal members. The task of the natural coalition builder lies in connecting the specific proposal with the constituent needs, partisan preferences, and/or ideologies of as many members as possible. Omnibus legislation that covers many topics increases the chances of pleasing a larger number of members and of having them join the coalition.[19]

A natural coalition often needs to be broadened through the addition of new members whose support is bought either by coalition managers within Congress or by the White House. The support of potential coalition members who have difficulty with the substance of the legislation can sometimes be bought by compromise on the legislation's content or the inclusion of desirable provisions. A well-timed amendment or the elimination of a particular provision may bring in a number of new supporters. For example, a member opposing a new program to aid small businesses might be supportive if an amendment to help the kinds of businesses in his or her district is included. In 1993 President Bill Clinton secured the passage of his economic program by dropping an increase in gasoline tax and thereby securing the support of several members of Congress from western states. Similarly the North American Free Trade Agreement (NAFTA) gained passage in 1993 after special arrangements were made for agricultural commodities of special importance to some members.

A more specific form of compromise involves adding benefits that most closely fit everyone's interests and thereby broaden the base of support. Such so-called **pork barrel** bills provide benefits such as highway funds, job training programs, or defense contracts. Members whose districts benefit find such legislation very appealing. Coalition managers, though, must be aware that coalition-building strategies may not be cumulative. The compromise that encourages some members to join may simultaneously offend some existing coalition members and force their departure.

pork barrel *Legislation favoring the districts of particular members of Congress by guaranteeing them public works projects, defense contracts, and other government programs.*

A variety of **side payments,** unrelated to the substance of the bill, may be offered to obtain the support of potential coalition members. For example, a coalition manager might endorse a member's campaign for a committee post or might support a public works project, such as a highway or postal facility, to be located in the member's district. Sometimes, the mere expectation of the coalition manager's future goodwill—the opportunity to say, "Remember when I helped you out? Well, now I need some help from you"—may well suffice. Bargaining for side payments may involve an explicit deal or a very vague agreement.

side payments *Benefits having nothing to do with the issue at hand but that are given to an individual joining a coalition.*

Box 13-9 Speedy Success in Assembling a Winning Coalition

During the 1974 oil shortage, Congress passed legislation mandating a fifty-five-mile-per-hour speed limit on all federal highways in the interest of energy conservation. As the energy crisis dissipated, opposition to the lower speed limit grew. By 1987, Congress was ready to reassess the situation, and legislation rescinding the fifty-five-mile-per-hour speed limit was included in the highway bill.

Two natural coalitions emerged. Members of western states joined with conservatives to support increasing the speed limit and giving drivers more latitude in choosing their speed. Westerners were motivated by the inconvenience and cost of travel between their distant population centers, while conservatives objected to federal regulation of what they felt should be a state or local matter. Opponents to an increased speed limit accepted the argument that slower speeds (as opposed to better highways, stiffer drunk-driving laws, reduced driving distances, better cars, and other factors) were the primary reason why highway deaths had decreased since 1974.

Members were bought into the coalitions through a variety of means. One set of compromises involved the types of highways that were to be allowed to have a higher speed limit. For example, members from congested urban areas wanted their highways to have the fifty-five-mile-per-hour speed limit. In addition, there were a series of side payments in the form of specific public works projects slated for a large number of congressional districts. The final bills passed overwhelmingly in each chamber.

This was not the end of the story, however. President Ronald Reagan, philosophically attuned to returning the power to set speed limits to the states, nevertheless vetoed the bill, citing the "budget-busting pork barrel projects." He attempted to lure budget-conscious members into a coalition to uphold the veto, relying on their ideological commitment to reducing the deficit. In the House, Democratic Speaker Jim Wright (D-Tex.) favored the override and threatened denial of future side payments when he reminded his colleagues that he had a long memory and would not forget members' votes on this issue.

In spite of considerable pressure, only one House Democrat switched to the president's side. Among House Republicans, only fifty-five members came to the president's aid and reversed their votes, while more than one hundred Republicans rejected his request and voted for the override. Even Republican minority leader Robert Michel (R-Ill.), lured by the completion of a highway in his district, refused to forfeit this side payment and support President Reagan's cause.

President Reagan needed a minimum of 34 votes in the Senate to sustain his veto. With the help of thirty-three Republicans and two Democrats, the initial 65 to 35 vote looked like a victory for the president. Using a parliamentary maneuver, however, Majority Leader Robert Byrd (D-W. Va.) switched his vote during the final moments to the prevailing side in order to retain the right to call for reconsideration. The Democrats began to work on freshman senator Terry Sanford (D-N.C.), the lone Democratic dissenter. After assuring him that the existing bill provided more highway funds for North Carolina than he had been led to believe, the Democrats successfully convinced him to switch his vote.

President Reagan and his supporters then went to work to convince at least one of the thirteen Republicans supporting the veto override to switch sides. Word went out that "Whatever you want, just tell us, and you can have it"—about as good a definition of side payments as can be imagined.[a] In spite of a rare personal vote-hunting trip to Capitol Hill by President Reagan, the dissenting Republicans stood firm, and the veto was overridden with a minimum winning coalition vote of 67 to 33.

Few congressional votes end up as the kind of cliffhanger discussed here, but the extreme cases of coalition building, where every vote counts, offer the best picture of coalition strategies. The next time you drive down the highway (legally) at 65 miles per hour, enjoy the thrill of speed but also remember that you are experiencing the fruits of coalition building.

---

a. Paul Starobin, "Highway Bill Veto Overridden after Close Call in the Senate," *Congressional Quarterly Weekly Report* 45, no. 14 (April 4, 1987): 606.

Since bargaining is an "expensive" strategy in the sense that it takes time and requires the expenditure of scarce bargaining chips, coalition managers tend to stop bargaining when they have assembled a **minimum winning coalition.**[20] As one Senate insider put it, "It's a rule of this game that, when you got the votes, vote; and when you don't, delay."[21] Box 13-9: Speedy Success in Assembling a Winning Coalition discusses a case of coalition building that illustrates many of the points discussed here.

13-5 Winning and Losing in the Congressional Policy Game

The ultimate consequence of conflict over policy is that some groups and individuals reach their objectives, while other groups and individuals are less successful. Winning and losing in the policy process are seldom random; there are relatively fixed patterns of consistent winners and losers, and identifiable groups of players win more often. Being a member of the majority party in Congress, holding a formal leadership position, and/or actively demanding policy provisions increase one's chances of policy victory.

minimum winning coalition *The minimum number of coalition members required to achieve a particular policy goal. The number involved, usually a simple majority, varies from case to case but as a general rule represents the maximum size of managed or bought coalitions.*

13-5a Partisanship

Although **party discipline** is much weaker in the U.S. Congress than in many state legislatures or other nations' parliaments, partisanship pervades much of congressional decision-making. In recent years, party discipline has increased dramatically based on aggressive party leadership, the recruitment of more ideological members, and the existence of "divided government," with one party holding the presidency and another the Congress. When in doubt or when deciding issues of little perceived importance, members of Congress tend to support positions backed by their party. At times, party leaders try to sway votes directly, but more often members of the same party vote alike, since they come from similar districts or have common outlooks (see Box 13-10: The Unendangered Leadership).

party discipline *The willingness of members of a legislative party to follow the wishes of the majority of their party when voting.*

The rules of Congress give many advantages to the majority party and expand the strategies available to them. For much of the last forty years, the Democrats controlled both houses of Congress and tended to get their way on legislation. General frustration with Democratic stewardship of national policy making resulted in a reversal of their fortunes in 1994 and shifted the policy advantage to the new Republican majority. The Republicans were quick to capitalize on their new power position and to push their legislative agenda.

13-5b Power Fiefdoms

A number of players within Congress have established realms in which they can control the consideration of bills either by setting the agenda or by affecting the outcome of decisions. Senior members—especially those holding committee leadership positions—retain considerable control over policy issues under the authority of their committees. Increased democratization of Congress and the emergence of issues crossing the jurisdictional boundaries of many committees have paved the way for a new breed of **policy entrepreneurs.**[22] Through their "willingness to invest their resources—time, reputation, energy, and sometimes money—in the hopes of a future return," individuals are able to wield influence in a particular policy area.[23] Policy entrepreneurs may come from either within or outside of government. Members of Congress are, however, particularly well placed to have an impact.

policy entrepreneur *Individual or group among decision makers who devotes time and energy to promoting a policy or set of policies.*

13-5c Activism

Congressional policy makers tend to respond to those who demand response. A silent majority generally loses out to a vocal minority. Members of Congress use the level of constituent involvement as a measure of citizen concern about a problem. Congress *reacts* to expressions of concern more than it *acts* in anticipation of problems. Representative government places a heavy responsibility on those desiring representation, and nowhere is that more evident than in Congress. Silent spectators are assumed to approve of the way the game is being played.

13-5d Causes That Prevail

The essential nature of policy proposals affects their likelihood of passage. Congress is most comfortable dealing with **incremental** changes and with policies that provide benefits to individual members' districts.

incrementalism *Breaking large problems into small segments and taking limited actions designed to correct the most troublesome aspects.*

Box 13–10 The Unendangered Leadership

For years it has been fashionable to talk about the dispersion of power in Congress and the severe limits on leadership. The arrival of the 104th Congress, especially in the House of Representatives, may have signaled a reversal of this trend. Incoming Speaker Newt Gingrich was credited by many as a visionary who guided the new Republican majority into acceptance of a comprehensive agenda encompassed in the Contract with America.

Speaker Gingrich's plans were marked by sweeping changes in the nature, activity, and cost of government. A key component was budget cutting. While one measure of Gingrich's motivation and leadership skills was reflected in keeping these broad issues on track, a more specific example reveals the human side of leadership.

As the Speaker was closeted with key supporters planning budget strategy involving billions of dollars in cuts, Mark Neumann, a junior Republican from Wisconsin, felt that he was doing his part by suggesting a cut of $800,000 in funding for foreign aid to help in the preservation of tigers, elephants, and rhinoceroses. The dollar figure was little more than a rounding error on the entire package of cuts, but it hit a responsive chord with Speaker Gingrich.

The House was in the mood to make dramatic cuts, not knowing that Gingrich had a personal interest in the issue of animal preservation. He rushed to the floor, explained that he had a "particular affection for rhinos," and asked his colleagues to "join together in sending a signal to these poor countries... that this is a project they ought to have courage to stay with."[a] Within moments, the mood on the floor had changed, and a sure budget cut had been defeated by a healthy 289 to 132 vote.

With the Republican's loss of seats in both 1996 and 1998 and Newt Gingrich's resignation as Speaker over the losses, the less confrontational Dennis Hastert (R-Ill.) was elected Speaker. With a razor thin majority of only six seats during the 106th Congress, the maneuvering room for the Speaker was more limited. After the 2000 election for the 107th Congress, the Republican majority in the House shrank even more, with the balance of power in the hands of a few swing votes from both parties. Talk of a Republican (or Democratic) agenda in the House enforced by party discipline became more rhetoric than reality.

The Republican gains in 2002 and 2004 again gave the Republican Party leadership a bit more breathing room to create winning coalitions as long as they could keep their troops in line.

a. See Francis X. Clines, "Gingrich: Speaker, Author—But King of the Jungle?" *New York Times*, July 14, 1995, A17.

Incrementalism

Much congressional policy is incremental. Rather than attacking major problems with wholly new or complete solutions, Congress tends to break large problems into small parts and then adopts limited corrective measures for the most difficult aspects of the problem. If these measures prove successful, additional steps in the same direction may follow.

Parochialism

parochialism *The tendency to look out for the narrow interests of one political group or geographic area.*

The tendency to look out for the narrow interests of one political group or geographic area, or **parochialism,** abounds in Congress. When asked whose interests they look out for, members of Congress often respond that, as we have said before, they believe in the wisdom of "dancing with the one that brung you." Most members openly assert that their first responsibility is to represent their particular set of constituents. Laws passed by Congress often provide special considerations for constituents of the most influential members. Senator Robert C. Byrd (D-W.Va.), former Senate majority leader and former chairman of the Appropriations Committee, has been called the "King of Pork" for his success in bringing government funds to his state of West Virginia.

One of the significant challenges in the post-cold war era involved closing military bases as the need for defense facilities declined. Military bases and research facilities provide jobs and other economic benefits to a large number of congressional districts. Congress found that parochial interests turned the process into a political nightmare and therefore created an independent base closure and realignment commission. After studying Department of Defense recommendations and local arguments, the commission was assigned the job of recommending to the president and Congress a list of closures, which must be accepted or rejected in its entirety. This procedure was designed to avoid having members of Congress vote to maintain bases in their own districts while willingly cutting those in other areas. Under the current procedure, members of Congress play an important role in presenting arguments in support of local bases to the commission. If the commission rules against them, they have some political cover in the process, since congressional votes are not taken on specific individual closures. During the 1995 round of closures, President Bill Clinton was tempted to reject the recommendations, since they made major cuts in Texas and California—two crucial states in the 1996 election process. In the end, he accepted the recommendations after assurances that privatization of military activities would retain many of the jobs in the affected areas.

Concern has been expressed both inside and outside of Congress that campaign contributions lead members to favor the more narrow policy positions of the contributors. While special condemnation is reserved for contributions made by political action committees (PACs), most members accept the contributions and argue that interested parties can assist their friends in Congress as part of the right of free expression. Building on his success in the presidential primaries, Senator John McCain (R-Ariz.) found his proposal to ban soft money (uncontrolled contributions to the parties) reinvigorated. Although extensive campaign finance reform backed by senators McCain and Feingold (D-Wisc.) passed in the Senate with strong Democratic Party support, it bogged down in the House as the potential implications of actually reforming a system with which many members had become comfortable began to look like a reality. Members were quick to point out that their vote in Congress is not for sale and that contributors are, at best, assured that their point of view will be heard. With numerous voices attempting to get members' attention, however, access guarantees some groups and individuals a more meaningful role in the game. The bill that eventually prevailed in 2002 represented a significant change in the rules governing funding of political parties with soft money (not directly spent by the candidate's campaign), but its blow was softened by increasing the amount individuals could give directly to candidates. It is of course those candidates, not political parties, who get elected and vote on legislation.

Parochialism also pervades congressional preferences concerning the way distributive programs will be organized. Proposals drafted in a way that makes it easy to highlight the benefits to each member's constituency are more likely to pass than those whose benefits are distributed in a less predictable and visible manner. Members of Congress prefer government programs featuring project grants or block grants (for which their constituents might apply) above overall formula grants (available to any individual or organization meeting the criteria involved). (Chapter 3 details the fiscal aspects of federalism.) The Model Cities Program, for example, was designed to promote a few large showcase examples involving urban renewal, drug rehabilitation, and job retraining. It was dramatically expanded to include a large number of smaller projects in order to spread the benefits around.

The application process for block grants and pilot projects gives members a legitimate way of claiming credit for their efforts. Constituents feel indebted to the member—a feeling the congressperson hopes will continue until Election Day. **Entitlement programs,** such as Social Security, Medicare, and veterans' benefits, on the other hand, are based on rigid formulas defining eligibility and benefits. If an entitlement program is the only feasible alternative for distributing or redistributing goods and services, members of Congress attempt to win points by establishing eligibility requirements beneficial to the types of constituents they represent.

entitlement programs *Programs in which persons automatically qualify to enroll and receive benefits if they satisfy established eligibility criteria.*

13-6 The Institutional Balance-of-Power Game

Congress as an institution finds itself in a political battle with the other branches and levels of government. If Congress is unwilling or unable to deal with an issue, other political institutions will find ways to do so. The primary usurper of legislative prerogatives during the twentieth century was the executive branch. Presidents, with the help of the executive branch, have access to information and the ability to move in a relatively quick and decisive manner. At times, presidents simply provide visibility and claim credit for ideas that Congress has been working on. Typically, presidential campaigns and speeches are used to introduce new issues into the political game that Congress must then consider.

Backing up the president is the extended executive branch. Its size, its day-to-day experience in implementing programs, and its geographic spread make it a premier information-gathering organization. Congress, on the other hand, has a comparatively small information-gathering staff and tends to speak with many voices. Congress has reacted to these challenges with a number of strategies.

13-6a Expanding Congressional Information Resources

Information processing is the "core technology" of Congress, and access to information is a significant power resource:

> Word purveying isn't the only game in town, but it is surely Washington's major industry . . . in the same way that in Detroit people make cars and in New York people buy and sell stocks and in Los Angeles people wait tables and dream of being a movie star. Words are what we make.[24]

Succeeding in a game based on words gives an advantage to those with the best and most timely information. Realizing that information is the lifeblood of the political process, Congress has attempted to make itself less dependent on, and more competitive with, the executive branch for information. Among the measures taken have been the expansion of congressional staff and the automation of information resources. Congressional support agencies, such as the Congressional Budget Office, the Congressional Research Service, the General Accounting Office (GAO), and the (former) Office of Technology Assessment, provide expertise and information independent of the executive branch (see Box 13-11: Supporting Congress's Voracious Appetite for Information). The contemporary U.S. Congress is a model for legislatures around the world in the use of computers to track legislation, manage communications, and analyze policy alternatives. Although such steps in no way reduce the complexity of making decisions involving difficult value choices, they help to clarify alternatives and to assess potential consequences. Technology has made Congress a more meaningful player in the policy game.

13-6b Increasing Public Exposure

The decision to allow television cameras into the House and eventually the Senate chambers stemmed from a desire to make the public more aware of Congress's activities in the hope that familiarity would breed support. Currently, over 70 million households have access to live gavel-to-gavel coverage of Congress on C-SPAN. The actual viewing audience is much smaller, but it is composed of some of the most politically active and vocal American citizens.[25] Direct access to the floor of each chamber turned the debate on the Persian Gulf War into a virtual town meeting, with large audiences watching the policy game up close and personal. Congress is slowly but surely entering the information superhighway, making much of its information available on the Internet and working on the premise that "to know us is to love us" (see Box 13-12: The On-Ramp to Congress's Information Superhighway).

13-6c Pressing Its Prerogative

There is no legal reason why Congress cannot attempt to dominate the policy agenda. After initial skepticism, the media developed a fascination with the 1994 Republican Contract with America, shifting the typical imbalance of attention away from the presidency. The first 100 days of the Republican 104th Congress were portrayed as a new beginning, an honor usually reserved for the beginning of a new presidential administration. After the House delivered on much of the Contract and skillfully won the public relations skirmish, President Bill Clinton was forced to go on national television with the

Box 13–11 Supporting Congress's Voracious Appetite for Information

Aside from its large personal and committee staffs, Congress has created three major research agencies to do its bidding. Even though each agency has 535 partisan bosses (the members of Congress), considerable effort is made to produce objective and thoughtful analysis.

The Congressional Research Service (CRS) developed from a limited bibliographic reference service into Congress's in-house general research agency. The staff members emphasize quick and confidential analysis for members and their personal staffs. Many of the over 800,000 requests per year are for a particular quote or statistic and can be handled over the phone. More detailed inquiries result in printed "Issue Briefs" that bring members up to speed on the current issues facing Congress.

The General Accounting Office (GAO) began as a set of government auditors dispatched by Congress to make sure that legislative intent was being followed in the expenditure of funds. Currently, its staff members include not only auditors but also scientists, economists, political scientists, and other professionals, who analyze the administration in great detail and the impact of public policies at the request of individual representatives and congressional committees.

Until 1995, the Office of Technology Assessment (OTA) prepared long-range studies focusing on the impact of new technologies on society. The studies alerted Congress to emerging technology-based issues and provided alternative solutions. The OTA fell victim to budget cutting in 1995 and was eliminated.

The Congressional Budget Office (CBO) was created to place Congress on a more even footing with the executive branch when it comes to budget preparation and planning. The CBO analyzes budget alternatives and assesses their impact on the broader economy.

All final reports of the GAO are publicly available through the U.S. Government Printing Office (GPO). The GPO regularly publishes catalogs that are available in most libraries. The GPO website (http://www.access.gpo.gov) provides access to many reports. Some of the CRS reports are publicly available on committee websites (see http://www.house.gov/rules and http://www.senate.gov/~dpc/crs/index.html). Most reports can be obtained by contacting your member of the House or Senate, while some remain the confidential property of the member or committee requesting the information.

Box 13–12 The On-Ramp to Congress's Information Superhighway

For those with Internet access and the ability to tap the World Wide Web, a large number of congressional documents are free for the asking. Everything from member and committee lists to bill status information and the full text of bills is available. The C-SPAN site offers an archive of video clips of congressionally related programming.

House and Senate websites:

House http://www.house.gov/

Senate http://www.senate.gov/

Library of Congress http://thomas.loc.gov/

Related Congressional websites:

C-SPAN http://www.c-span.org/

A comprehensive guide to Congress and its members http://congress.org/

The Dirksen Center's guide to learning about Congress http://www.congresslink.org/

plaintive assertion that the president is still a relevant player. Congress's new role as an agenda setter was a short-term phenomenon, with the media turning its attention back to the presidency within a few months.

13-6d Changing the Legal Playing Field

impoundment *A president's refusal to spend money appropriated by Congress.*

Congress attacked specific abuses of power by the executive branch by changing the rules in ways that increase Congress's ability to oversee the conduct of presidents and bureaucrats. In reaction to the Nixon administration's practice of killing programs by refusing to spend funds appropriated by Congress (**impoundment**), Congress passed the Budget and Impoundment Control Act in 1974. This legislation established new procedures for Congress's handling of the president's budget. It also severely limited the president's right to refuse to spend funds for programs approved and funded by Congress. With a Democratic president and a Democratic Congress, the president's ability to refuse to expend funds was loosened a bit in 1993. The line-item veto passed by the 104th Congress allowed the president to delete specific portions of appropriations bills, expanding his ability to not spend funds. The grant of power was short-lived, however, as the Supreme Court ruled it unconstitutional.

In the foreign policy realm, the 1973 War Powers Resolution was an attempt to regain some congressional power. As explained earlier in this chapter, it requires the president to consult with Congress in advance of committing troops to hostile action and to secure congressional approval of such actions within 60 days. President George W. Bush was careful to get congressional official approval before challenging Iraq on its weapons of mass destruction. In the aftermath of sending troops and defeating Saddam Hussein, the failure to clearly discover weapons of mass destruction led some in Congress to argue they had been intentionally or unintentionally misled by the White House.

Congress has also employed its power of the purse to curb the executive branch's conduct of foreign policy. The Boland Amendment, for example, made it illegal for the Reagan administration to furnish aid to the Nicaraguan Contras for uses above and beyond that specifically authorized by Congress. Much of the controversy over the Iran-Contra affair hinged on the interpretation, practicality, and constitutionality of this amendment.

In recent decades, the Senate has used its power of advice and consent of presidential appointments more aggressively. A number of key presidential appointments have been challenged and, in some cases, withdrawn by the White House. More rarely, senators opposing the personal characteristics and/or the policies of the potential appointees have been able to defeat presidential nominees to the executive branch or to the Supreme Court. Two of President Bill Clinton's attorney general nominees were forced to withdraw in 1993 when it was revealed that they had broken regulations of the Immigration and Naturalization Service (an agency they would have been supervising). The confirmation process itself has forced some nominees to rethink previous actions and to make commitments about what they would do in the future. The highly publicized debate over Supreme Court nominee Clarence Thomas highlighted the issue of sexual harassment in the workplace, even though Justice Thomas's confirmation was eventually approved.

By asserting itself in these and other ways, Congress seeks to maintain its standing as the most powerful independent legislature in the world. Some observers decry Congress's interference and lack of cooperation with the executive branch, but a powerful and independent Congress is exactly what the Founders intended when they designed a governmental system based on separation of powers. A weak and spineless Congress might facilitate efficiency in the sense of quick decisions by the president, but it would not, in James Madison's terms, allow ambition "to counteract ambition."[26]

To some degree, Congress deals from relative weakness when it attempts to improve its power position. The public and many other players see Congress as a relatively inefficient organization filled with self-serving and parochial decision makers. Congress's lack of attention to the then-impending savings and loan crisis in the mid 1980s and such scandals as the Keating Five ethics case (see Box 13-3), the House banking problem (in which many members bounced checks in their in-house credit union), the ill-fated and partisan impeachment confrontation with President Bill Clinton, and a series of internal

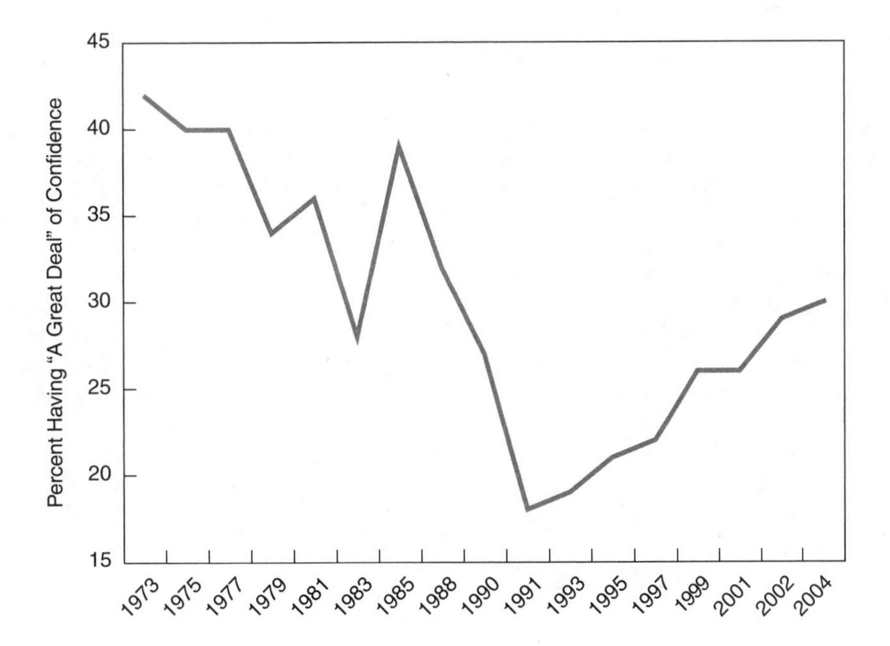

Figure 13-1
Public Confidence in Congress 1973–2004

Question: Please tell me how much confidence you, yourself, have in Congress—"a great deal, quite a lot, some, or very little."

Source: National Gallup Polls of adults, LEXIS-NEXIS database. For years with multiple polls, percentages indicate averages.

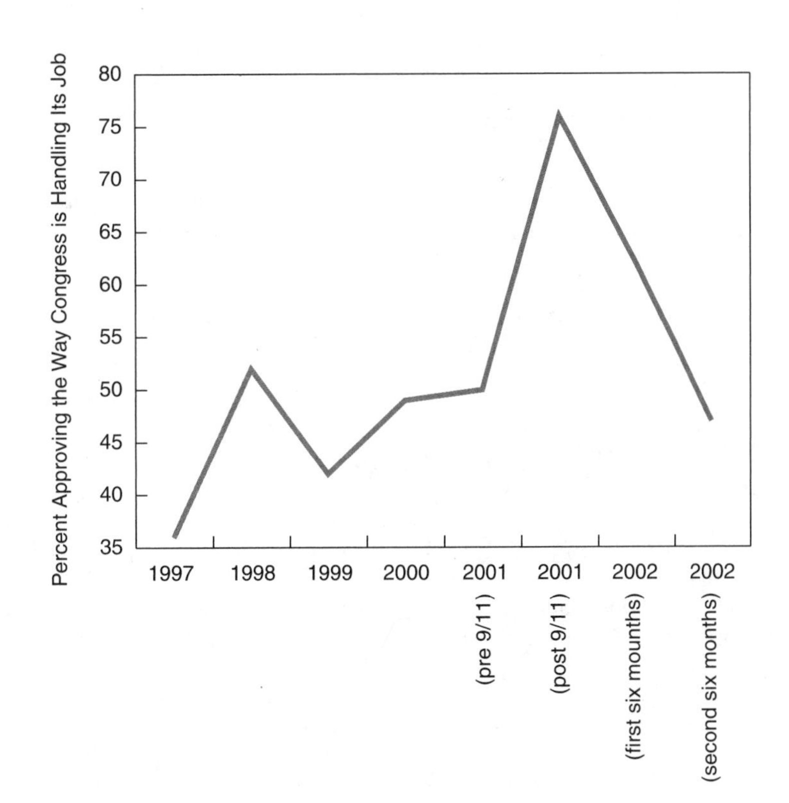

Figure 13-2
Congress and the 9/11 "Bump" in Approval

Do you approve or disapprove of the way Congress is handling its job?

Source: CNN/USA Today/Gallup polls of adults asking, "Do you approve or disapprove of the way Congress is handling its job?" Available at http://www.pollingreport.com/job.htm and through LEXIS-NEXIS.

leadership battles that have toppled many of the recent congressional leaders did little to engender confidence in Congress. The long-term trend has been a declining trust in Congress, although dramatic events such as the 2001 terrorist attacks can lead to temporary improvement (see Figures 13-1 and 13-2). Members of Congress themselves often do their own institution little good by waging a pitched battle against the institution in which they serve while on the campaign trail. In addition, the degree to which interest groups bankroll congressional campaigns through PACs leaves the negative impression that Americans have the "best Congress money can buy."[27] The task of rebuilding public confidence in Congress is awesome, with the success of democratic government probably hanging in the balance.

Conclusion

Congress's ongoing battle with the other branches and levels of government would hearten the Founders, for it is exactly what they intended. The Founders would be surprised at the breadth of congressional activity and the dominant role played by committees, but they would stand back and cheer on the multiple levels of conflict.

The growth of presidential involvement in legislating during much of the twentieth century is the primary change in modern politics that the Founders might least have expected. Although they might be wary of the development, they would recognize that Congress's primacy in initiating, revising, and legitimizing public laws is not the only measure of its viability. Even if Congress were to surrender its initiative in lawmaking to the other branches of government, its powers of oversight would ensure a continuing and significant role in the policy game. Congress's more recent ability to dramatically reinsert itself into the policy game reflects its resiliency. Despite considerable changes in the political arena, the U.S. Congress remains the strongest independent legislature in the world.

The adaptability of Congress over the last two centuries implies that it is not simply going to fold its tents and go home. Congress must continue to adapt if it is to remain a vital force in American politics, and these changes will undoubtedly have an impact not only on the rules and strategies of future policy games but on who wins and who loses.

Key Terms

balanced budget
bought coalition
cloture
conference committee
delegate
distributive policy
entitlement programs
filibuster
flat tax
floor
hearing
impeachment
impoundment
incrementalism
iron triangles
joint committees
logrolling
minimum winning coalition
natural coalition
needs test
omnibus legislation
oversight
parochialism
party discipline
policy entrepreneur
pork barrel
power of the purse
proxy voting
public policy
redistributive policy
regulatory policy
select committee
side payments
standing committee
subcommittee
trustee
veto
voice vote
War Powers Resolution

Practice Quiz

1. Who are the players in issue networks or iron triangles?
   a. The president, committee chairs, and the Speaker
   b. Committee or sub-committee members, the bureaucrats they oversee, and the representatives of affected interest groups
   c. The "big three" interest groups in each policy realm
   d. Committees, caucuses, and interest groups

2. Who can vote on legislation?
   a. Members of Congress only
   b. Elected members and staff members carrying a member's proxy
   c. Elected members and party leaders carrying a member's proxy
   d. Members and staff members in the member's absence

3. Omnibus legislation
   a. deals with public transportation.
   b. is a single complex piece of information dealing with a number of issues.
   c. involves detailed revisions of minor aspects of major legislation.
   d. makes members accountable by requiring sequential votes on each section.

4. Which of the following is true of standing congressional committees?
   a. They have members in both chambers of Congress.
   b. They are permanent and deal with specific areas of legislation.
   c. They "stand" as long as an issue is important and then are disbanded immediately.
   d. Their chair is appointed by the president pro tem.

5. _____ policy provides goods and/or services to all, or to a relatively large segment, of the population.
   a. Redistributive
   b. Regulatory
   c. Distributive
   d. Entitlement

6. Members of _____committees deal with temporary issues or emerging problems.
   a. select
   b. joint
   c. standing
   d. conference

7. Members of _____committees are most clearly motivated by issues.
a. reelection
b. power
c. regulatory
d. policy

8. The House Rules Committee does all of the following EXCEPT:
a. proposes the scheduling of legislation.
b. modifies the content of legislation.
c. proposes the conditions for debate.
d. negotiates compromises with the Senate.

9. Bargaining in Congress is most clearly facilitated by the norm of
a. reciprocity.
b. courtesy.
c. apprenticeship.
d. specialization.

10. Individual legislators who support a policy without any additional inducement are best characterized as members of a _____coalition.
a. bought
b. broadened
c. natural
d. minimum-winning

You can find the correct answers to these questions by taking the quiz and then submitting your answers in the Online Edition. The program will automatically score your submission. Where you miss a question, the program will provide the correct answer, a rationale for the answer, and the section number in the chapter where the topic is discussed.

Further Reading

See the Suggestions for Further Reading in Chapter 12 for sources presenting a general overview of Congress.

Some of the most insightful and classic writings about Congress are those by Richard Fenno. His *Congressmen in Committees* (Boston, MA: Little, Brown, 1973) provides a keen understanding of what motivates members on different committees, while his *Home Style* (Boston, MA: Little, Brown, 1978) assesses how members of Congress play the survival game in their home districts.

Hedrick Smith's *The Power Game: How Washington Works* (New York: Random House, 1988) offers a journalist's view of American politics as a series of games with a significant emphasis on Congress.

Shaping Legislative Strategy by Edward V. Schneier and Bertram Gross (New York: St. Martin's Press, 1993) provides a rich source of detail on the machinations of legislative strategy.

Endnotes

1. See Kevin Merida, "By Defying the President, He Pleased the Constituents," *Washington Post,* August 23, 1994, A1; National Public Radio, "All Things Considered," LEXIS-NEXIS transcript, September 6, 1994.
2. Norman Ornstein alerted the authors to this important function.
3. Woodrow Wilson, *Congressional Government* (1885; reprint, Boston, MA: Houghton Mifflin, 1981), 69.
4. Richard Fenno, *Congressmen in Committees* (Boston, MA: Little, Brown, 1973), Chapter 1.
5. See Roger H. Davidson, "Breaking Up Those Cozy Triangles: An Impossible Dream," in *Legislative Reform and Public Policy,* eds. Susan Welch and John G. Peters (New York: Praeger, 1977); and Hugh Heclo, "Issue Networks and the Executive Establishment," in *The New American Political System,* ed. Anthony King (Washington, D.C.: American Enterprise Institute, 1978).
6. Sandra Sugawara, "Mikulski: A Trailblazer and Irritant," *Washington Post,* August 29, 1986, A1.
7. Harold Rosemary, "Deciphering the Rules," C-SPAN Update, May 9, 1984, 11.
8. Roger H. Davidson and Walter J. Oleszek, *Congress and Its Members* (Washington, D.C.: Congressional Quarterly Press, 1990), 18.
9. See Section 5 of Article I of Congressional Quarterly, Origins and Development of Congress (Washington, D.C.: Congressional Quarterly Press, 1976), 44.
10. Richard B. Cheney, "An Unruly House: A Republican View," *Public Opinion* 11, no. 5 (January/February 1989): 41–44.
11. Newt Gingrich, *Congressional Record,* September 24, 1990, H-7986.
12. For the classic study of Senate norms, see Donald R. Matthews, U.S. Senators and Their World (Chapel Hill, NC: University of North Carolina Press, 1960); and for House norms, see Herbert B. Asher, "The Learning of Legislative Norms," *American Political Science Review* 69 (June 1973): 119–46.
13. David Broder, "Moynihan Shakes White House With Stance on Health Reform," *Washington Post,* January 12, 1994, A12.
14. Edward Walsh, *Washington Post,* December 7, 1987, 6.
15. See Aage Clausen, *How Congressmen Decide: A Policy Focus* (New York: St. Martin's Press, 1973).
16. John W. Kingdon, *Congressmen's Voting Decisions* (Ann Arbor: University of Michigan Press, 1989).
17. *Congressional Record,* September 24, 1991, H-6792.
18. There also, of course, can be natural and bought coalition members who oppose the proposed legislation.
19. See Davidson and Oleszek, *Congress and Its Members,* 354–59, and Stephen Frantzich and Steven Schier, *Congress: Games and Strategies* (Madison, WI: Brown and Benchmark, 1994), 196–197
20. See William H. Riker, *The Theory of Political Coalitions* (New Haven, CT.: Yale University Press, 1962).
21. Quoted in Ann Devroy, "Path to Confirmation Became a 'Slippery Slope,'" *Washington Post,* October 9, 1991, A6.
22. David Price, *Who Makes the Laws?* (Cambridge, MA: Schenkman Publishing, 1972), 297. Professor Price not only studied lawmakers, he became one himself by serving in Congress from 1986 to 1994, representing North Carolina.

23. John W. Kingdon, *Agendas, Alternatives, and Public Policies* (Boston, MA: Little, Brown, 1984), 129.
24. Joel Achenbach, "The Land of Desk Potatoes," *Washington Post*, January 17, 1993, F1.
25. National polling figures indicate that over 70 percent of regular C-SPAN viewers vote and that they are much more likely to work in campaigns, contribute to campaigns, and communicate with their elected representatives than are members of the population as a whole. See Stephen Frantzich and John Sullivan, *The C-SPAN Revolution* (Norman, OK: The University of Oklahoma Press, 1996), Chapter 6.
26. James Madison, *Federalist* No. 51
27. The title of Philip M. Stern's book *The Best Congress Money Can Buy* (New York: Pantheon Books, 1988) engendered many smiles among both players and observers, with few if any of them disagreeing with its thrust. Four years later, Stern came out with *Still the Best Congress Money Can Buy* (Washington, D.C.: Regnery Gateway, 1992), indicating how little had changed.

14

The Presidency: Election and Structure

Key Points

- **The legal and political requirements for becoming a viable presidential candidate.**
- **The presidential nomination process.**
- **The nature and impact of the institutionalized presidency.**
- **The roles of the cabinet, the executive office of the president, and the White House staff.**
- **The selection and role of the vice president.**
- **How presidential personality affects behavior.**

Preview: Character Check

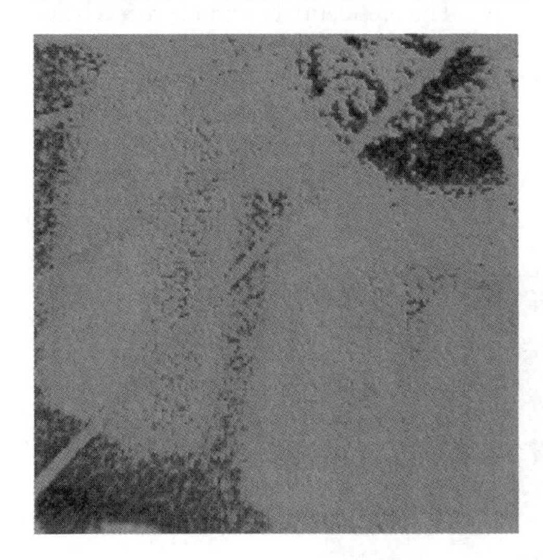

He was young, good-looking, and intelligent, and he had extensive political experience. A former southern governor, he entered the White House after a lively election where no one had received an absolute majority. After twelve years of control of the presidency by the opposition party, the new president had defeated a one-term former vice president. One of the key issues in the campaign was the large deficit, which was mainly due to military expenditures. A major theme of the campaign was reducing the power of the wealthy and of commercial interests and returning power to the common citizen. Unlike his rivals, he was greatly influenced by the experience of having lived overseas and having seen America through the eyes of others.[1] In spite of having gained the presidency, however, he was dogged by rumors concerning his personal character, especially when it came to women.[2] His party had won control of both houses of Congress as well as the presidency. History would nevertheless show that this did not guarantee smooth sailing for his policy alternatives.

The new president immediately struck out to cut back the military, return to a less activist national government, and demonstrate an abiding willingness to defer to congressional will. Did we say less activist and willing to defer to Congress? Does this fit the image of Bill Clinton? He is a liberal with great faith in expanded national government programs in areas such as health care and education. He exhibits a willingness to use the full range of powers of his office. The description above does not completely fit President Clinton because we are not talking about William Jefferson Clinton but rather another Jefferson—Thomas Jefferson, to be precise.

Even though they are separated by almost 200 years, the parallels between Bill Clinton and Thomas Jefferson point out some of the enduring consistencies in presidential selection. Presidential elections are often reactions against excesses of the past. Personal characteristics of candidates have always been part of the presidential selection process. The lessons go beyond those involving elections. Controlling both houses of Congress does not guarantee total cooperation between presidents and the Congress.

The presidential selection process is the most visible game in American politics. It receives a great deal of media attention and draws a large number of players. Each electoral contest is, furthermore, part of a larger, continuous game. As soon as one presidential election process is over, players almost immediately begin jockeying for the next round, preparing strategies and gathering resources. Presidential election is also a prime example of a zero-sum game: winning the presidency results in a victory that does not have to be shared with competing players.

Americans elect an individual as president, but in reality they get a team of participants chosen by the president—a group that the president must then organize, motivate, and control.[3] This team provides daily top management of executive branch activities. The success of modern presidencies hinges as much on the skills and performance of the presidential team as on the actions of the president as an individual. The president is the star player on the White House team, receiving the most attention and guiding much of the play. Yet presidents lack the power to make their preferred plays unilaterally. They must coordinate their administrations and work with players in other arenas.

Winning elections and serving as president are not unrelated activities. The presidential election process determines not only *who* will serve as president; it also defines much of *how* the president and his staff will serve. The presidential election process helps determine the agenda of issues and the political alliances with which the newly elected president must deal. In this chapter we will begin by analyzing the way in which presidents get nominated and elected. Our attention will next turn to the ways in which presidents choose and manage their staffs. In evaluating the role of the president as an individual, the chapter ends with a discussion of how presidents define their role in the political process.

George W. Bush Is Sworn In
White House Photo

14-1 Selecting the President

The process of winning the presidency involves a number of stages. It begins with a series of caucuses, state conventions, and primaries in which a series of contenders attempt to line up political support. After gaining the nomination, the official party candidates must compete in the general election.

14-1a Seeking and Gaining the Party Nomination: Legal and Political Requirements

Before a presidential candidate can get on the ballot, he or she must get the party nomination, the importance of which is a relatively recent development:

> The rules of the game have changed so much, with the increase in the primaries . . . allowing a candidate to virtually lock up the nomination [very early].[4]

The route to the White House is long and arduous, and candidates must be both willing and able to embark on it. The constitutional requirements of being at least thirty-five years of age, a fourteen-year resident of the United States, and a **natural-born citizen** say little about the actual pool of serious contenders. Extralegal criteria place further limits on potential candidates waiting on the bench for their turn to play. Historically, voters and party activists have hesitated to nominate anyone other than white Protestant males with northern European heritages. The only Catholic prior to John F. Kennedy (1960) and John Kerry (2004) ever nominated for the presidency was Al Smith in (1928), and the only non-northern European candidate was Michael Dukakis (1988), who is of Greek ancestry.[5] Although many individuals remain as potential players after making these legal and political "cuts," achievement, motivation, and skill reduce the likely contenders even more (see Box 14-1: Determining the Potential Players on the Presidential Bench).

natural-born citizens *Individuals born in the United States or children born abroad of U.S. citizens. The presidency is the only elective office that specifies that candidates be natural-born citizens.*

Box 14–1 Determining the Potential Players on the Presidential Bench

No one ever claimed that life is fair. Despite the American commitment to equality, the presidential selection process takes place on an uneven playing field. The rules historically have eliminated many more potential players than they have included. Party leaders and voters have relatively stringent criteria about the social and political background characteristics of potential presidents.

The constitutional criteria are legally established, and there is no apparent interest in amending their content. While the extralegal criteria are not absolutely fixed, they change slowly, at best. The combined criteria may summarily disqualify a number of potentially excellent presidents. The steps making the cut have been described as:

1. Begin with all U.S. citizens.
2. Apply the constitutional requirements and discard everyone
   - under 35 years of age.
   - who is a naturalized rather than a natural-born citizen.
   - who has not been a U.S. resident for fourteen years.
3. Check potential players' personal characteristics and drop *all*
   - women.
   - people of color.
   - ethnic minorities.
   - non-Christians.
   - noncollege graduates.
   - bachelors and nonfamily men.
4. Consider the political necessities and ignore most
   - individuals with no experience in politics or public service.
   - residents of small states.

continued

Box 14–1 Determining the Potential Players on the Presidential Bench

—Continued

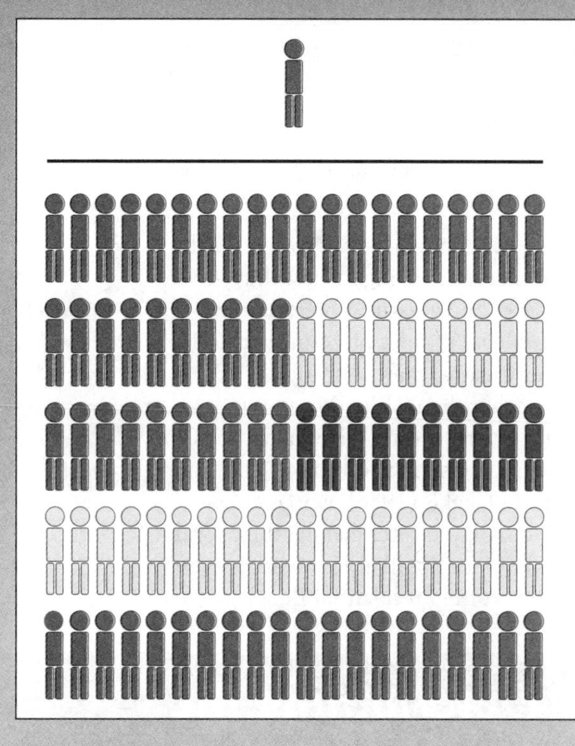

Once you take into consideration all of the constitutional requirements and the factors typically required by votes, there aren't many of us who can realistically hope to become president. In fact, out of the entire U.S. population, less than 1% have reasonable odds of becoming the Chief Executive.

Determining the Players

- nonveterans.
- individuals without some claim to competency in international affairs.

5. Discourage most
   - individuals not of northern European stock.
   - people under 45 or over 65 years of age.
   - individuals who are conspicuously rich or conspicuously poor.
   - intellectuals.
   - individuals without roots in small-town America.
   - people who are overweight or bald or who have other extraordinary physical characteristics.

Although most of the standards of viability have been maintained over the entire history of the United States, some have shifted from absolute disqualifications to simple detriments. John F. Kennedy broke the barrier and became the first successful Catholic nominee, while Ronald Reagan was the first divorced president. By 2004 little was made of the fact that John Kerry was both divorced and Catholic. In 1992 Bill Clinton weathered criticism for avoiding the draft during Vietnam and questions about the stability of his marriage. In 1996 Senator Bob Dole challenged the age limitations, asserting that on inauguration day at age 73 he would have both the stamina and experience to do the job. The 2000 election cycle revealed no significant challenges to the general assumptions about viable candidates. Al Gore hailed from a small state, and George W. Bush had little international experience, but each fit the other criteria.

The legal and political criteria leave a political bench of no more than a few hundred individuals who realistically might be mentioned as presidential hopefuls (see Time Out 14-1: Playing the Presidential Game Yourself). Moving from the bench to the presidential playing field still requires personal motivation, performance that attracts the media spotlight, and luck at being the right person, in the right place, at the right time.

Source: Adapted from Clinton Rossiter, *The American Presidency*, (New York: Harcourt Brace, 1960), 201–2.

Playing the Presidential Game Yourself **Time Out 14-1**

American society prides itself on providing equality of opportunity and projecting the image that anyone can aspire to the presidency. Compare your personal characteristics with the criteria expected of presidents in Box 14-1.

What are your chances of meeting these criteria right now? Which of these characteristics might you be able to achieve in the future? Are you eliminated from the pool of potential presidents by criteria that you see as inappropriate? Can you think of people who might be excellent presidents but who cannot meet the requirements?

Consider why these criteria might have entered the presidential selection process. What is the value of a political mythology proclaiming equal opportunity when so few people can realistically aspire to the presidency?

Establishing a national reputation through highly visible activity, particularly in the political arena, is helpful. This increases an individual's likelihood of being mentioned by the press and accepted by political activists as a possible presidential candidate. All twentieth-century presidents except Dwight Eisenhower launched their campaigns with significant experience in elected office. The Senate seems to breed the ambition necessary to run for the presidency, but it has not proven to be a very effective platform from which to win. Almost half of the presidents elected since 1921 arrived in the White House without any significant *Washington* political experience. Given the decline in public respect for political institutions and derision for the inside-the-Washington beltway mind-set, many contemporary presidential candidates approached the campaign as outsiders. Jimmy Carter, Ronald Reagan, and Bill Clinton all criticized politics as usual and promised a different perspective.

Candidates and their supporters recognize that the voters want it both ways. They want someone who is not tainted by Washington, but they also desire someone with enough experience to be an effective participant in the Washington game. An early supporter of General Colin Powell, former head of the Joint Chiefs of Staff, for the 1996 nomination pointed out:

> I'm very impressed by Colin Powell. I think he's a first-rate American. He's also, however, a politician. He's not altogether an outsider. He knows how to play the game; he's played it very well.[6]

Former Tennessee governor Lamar Alexander downplayed his position as a member of President George H. Bush's cabinet when he announced his bid for the 1996 Republican nomination. He underlined his outsider perspective by making public appearances in a flannel shirt as opposed to the more Washington-like jacket and tie. In 2000, former senator Bill Bradley attempted to position himself as an outsider whose four years out of office helped erase the taint of Washington, and Texas governor George W. Bush portrayed his lack of Washington experience as a badge of honor.

Despite the strategy of campaigning as an outsider, the best place to start a campaign for the presidency is from the inside. Incumbent presidents are almost always guaranteed renomination if they decide to seek reelection. Sitting vice presidents, governors, and senators start from an advantageous position for a presidential bid, although in recent years, vice presidents and senators have had a difficult time winning election to the presidency.

With regard to party affiliation, in spite of arduous efforts by third-party candidates such as George C. Wallace (1968), John B. Anderson (1980), H. Ross Perot (1992, 1996), and Pat Buchanan and Ralph Nader (2000), contemporary presidential politics has largely been a closed game reserved for players from the major parties. Numerous Republicans smelled victory after the 1994 Republican off-year landslide and announced their plans to run in 1996. President Bill Clinton took the unprecedented step of announcing his reelection intention two years before the 1996 race in order to solidify his Democratic base and to thwart challenges from within his own party.

Third-party candidates lack a solid base of party supporters, receive more limited media attention, often find it difficult to raise sufficient funding, and run into the voter's desire not to waste a vote on a slim chance. Nevertheless, discontent with the political status quo and an emergent populism might serve as the seeds for change. The media feed on change and were quick to highlight the possible trend of a viable third party in 1996 by giving the idea considerable attention. Ross Perot's unique ability to finance his own campaign with more than $50 million and his achievement of having received 19 percent of the vote in 1992 are inspirations to some. These acccomplishments were sufficient to whet the appetites of voters who desire an alternative to the major parties and of candidates who perceive more political opportunities. As early as 1994, former Democratic primary contender Paul Tsongas began pushing for a major third-party initiative in 1996 with a candidate such as General Colin Powell. Perot was unable to pull off a reprise of his 1992 success, garnering less than 9 percent of the vote in 1996 and losing control of his Reform Party by the 2000 election-year cycle. After a bitter split over control of the party organization and the federal campaign funding Ross Perot earned based on his 1996 showing, the Reform Party emerged as a shadow of its former self in 2000. Nominee Pat Buchanan garnered less than 1% of the national vote. As the Green Party nominee, Ralph Nader received 2.8% of the national vote, serving as a spoiler by taking votes from Al Gore in key states. Many Democrats attempted to discourage Ralph Nader from running in 2004, while a few prominent Republicans helped him get on the ballot.

Motivations, Skills, and Tactics

It is a long and arduous road to capture a presidential nomination:

> Presidential politics, like stock market investing, is rapidly becoming a game only professionals can play. Presidential campaigning has become almost continuous.[7]

Only a few of all the potentially viable candidates for president seek the nomination. An unwillingness to endure intensive public scrutiny, to disrupt family life, and to spend a year or more raising funds dissuades all but the most motivated. Despite being regularly mentioned as possible nominees, both former vice president Dan Quayle and Jack Kemp, former secretary of the Housing and Urban Development Department, decided to withdraw early in the 1996 nomination process. The long odds of success make the risks of giving up safe congressional seats unacceptable for most House members and many senators up for reelection, since all states except Texas forbid candidates to run for more than one office at a time. In the 2000 contest, Elizabeth Dole received a great deal of early attention but dropped out over a year before the election when her ability to secure adequate funding faltered. The 2004 quest for the Democratic nomination began with a large number of contenders who dropped out one by one as their funding and popular support in the caucuses and primaries faltered.

The modern presidential nomination process requires candidates to succeed in several political arenas before the formal nomination decision is made at the **national party convention.** About one-fourth of convention delegates are selected in state-level conventions, which favor candidates with large and effective campaign organizations. Some individuals are named as "super delegates" to the Democratic convention, since they hold offices such as governor or member of Congress. The remainder of the delegates emerge from presidential primary elections. Currently, two-thirds of the states use presidential primaries to choose more than three-fourths of the delegates to nominating conventions.

national party convention *The quadrennial (every fourth year) meeting of party members to choose the party's presidential nominee, establish policy goals, and decide on party rules.*

Potential presidential nominees spend months, even years, going from state to state, attempting to amass national convention delegates in conventions and primaries. Victories in these contests are often more important for proving the credibility of one's candidacy than for acquiring delegates (see Figure 14-1). Winning several primaries or conventions (especially early in the process) provides momentum, encourages campaign contributions, stimulates volunteers, and increases media coverage. The Iowa caucuses and the New Hampshire primary, which come early in the selection process, have developed reputations for making or breaking potential candidates. Winning or losing in these

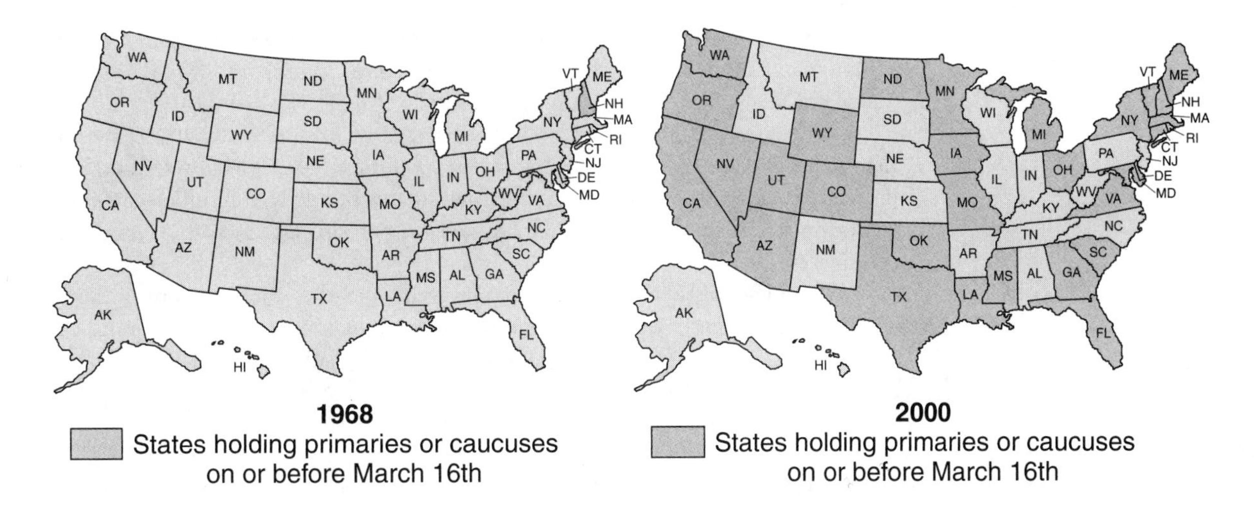

Figure 14-1
Frontloading the Presidential Nomination Process

Most states now hold their primaries or caucuses by mid-March. This development, called frontloading, means candidates must start campaigning very early to stand a chance of winning their party's nomination.

Source: Michael L. Goldstein, *Guide to the 2000 Presidential Election*, (Washington, D.C.: Congressional Quarterly, 2000), pp. 32–35.

states depends less on the absolute number of votes than on exceeding expectations created by the press and the candidates. Candidates who win early primaries and caucuses receive important media recognition and momentum.[8]

In recent years, the primary process has become "front-loaded," as more and more states attempt to increase their influence by holding their primaries *before* a candidate has locked up enough votes to win the nomination. In 1988, ten states joined together to hold their primaries on a "super Tuesday" early in March. In 1996, five New England states agreed to hold simultaneous primaries on "junior Tuesday," a week before super Tuesday.[9] As one candidate put it, the 1996 GOP primary was "a 50-yard dash,"[10] dependent on raising money early and capturing a significant number of votes in the increasingly early primaries. In 2000 and 2004 the primaries were even more compressed, with a majority of the delegates locked up by the end of March. Presumptive 2004 Democratic nominee Senator John Kerry (D-Mass.) had four months to campaign after locking up the nomination before getting the official party nomination at the Democratic National Convention in July.

Primaries have played a significant role in recent presidential nomination battles. In 1988 Senator Robert Dole (R-Kans.) almost derailed George H. Bush's candidacy by unexpectedly beating him in the multicandidate Iowa caucuses. Dole rode into the New Hampshire primary a few weeks later as the heavy favorite, but Bush's narrow victory in this state tipped Dole's campaign onto the long slide into oblivion. In 1992 a relatively unknown Bill Clinton used the primary process to bump off a series of better-known challengers. With George H. Bush's popularity at great heights after Operation Desert Storm in the Mideast, many of the Democratic heavy hitters decided to sit out 1992. Although he did not often win the early primaries, Clinton presented a strong showing—despite a series of personal scandals "that would have destroyed a lesser candidate"[11] and did better than expected. As one academic observer put it, "In electoral politics, the game is always to minimize expectations for your candidate so that a limited success will be seen as evidence of great strength."[12]

The 2000 campaign began early. The fact that Bill Clinton could not run for reelection, having served two terms, and Vice President Al Gore's reputation as a lackluster candidate encouraged both a challenge from within the Democratic Party and a great deal of activity on the Republican side. Al Gore fought off a vigorous challenge from former Senator Bill Bradley (D-N.J.). On the Republican side, Texas Governor George W. Bush beat out Arizona Senator John McCain in the primary process.

With the decision in late 2002 by former vice president Al Gore not to run in 2004, the battle for the Democratic Party nomination began in earnest almost two years before voters would be going to the polls. Since only one incumbent president has been denied renomination by his party, the Republicans faced no primary battle coalescing around

George W. Bush. The Democrats had a rousing battle for the nomination, with former Vermont governor Howard Dean and North Carolina senator John Edwards the final viable challengers to Senator John Kerry's bid.

Candidates with the resources and skills necessary to be effective in television advertising and mass media campaigning gain an advantage in the primary system. By winning primary and state convention contests, candidates not only secure delegates committed to voting for them at the national convention but also enhance their images as viable candidates.

Since clear winners have usually emerged from the state convention and primary arenas, national party conventions now typically resemble coronations more than decision-making bodies. Presidential nominees formally submit potential vice-presidential nominees to the convention, although they have come to expect automatic approval. They usually attempt to **balance the ticket** by choosing someone from a different geographical region, interest group, or ideological wing of the party (see Box 14-2: Balancing the Team: The Politics of Choosing Vice-Presidential Nominees). In 1992 Arkansas governor Bill Clinton decided not to balance his ticket geographically when he chose fellow southerner Albert Gore from Tennessee. Clinton did balance his own inexperience in foreign affairs with a senator who had dealt with those issues. In the 2000 battle, George W. Bush attempted to strengthen the experience quotient of his ticket with the selection of former congressman, White House aide, and secretary of Defense Dick Cheney of Wyoming. In order to blunt the criticism of his being too close to President Clinton's moral failings, Al Gore chose widely respected senator Joseph Lieberman of Connecticut, the first Orthodox Jew on a national ticket and an outspoken defender of morality in the White House. In 2004, John Kerry chose one of his key challengers in the Democratic primaries, Senator John Edwards (D-N.C.), a relatively young and energetic campaigner whose southern ties were anticipated to help Democratic party slippage in that region.

balance the ticket *Increasing the political appeal of a party's candidates by including candidates popular with different geographical, ethnic, social, and/or ideological groups.*

14-1b The Presidential Campaign

Presidential campaigns are serious business for anyone interested in American politics:

> In politics, like football, "winning isn't everything, it's the only thing." To that end, each party has prepared is team depth charts and each candidate his game plan—one of which will probably be right.[13]

Successful candidates must gather the necessary resources, develop an effective message, and communicate it to the voters.

Gathering Campaign Resources

Presidential candidates used to rely on the financial and manpower resources of their parties to carry out their campaigns. The growing cost of campaigns and the development of alternative methods of political communication have increasingly meant that party resources and campaign techniques are no longer adequate. New applications of campaign technology, especially television, allow candidates to bypass the party and appeal directly to the voters.

The *Federal Election Campaign Act (FECA)* of 1972 provided federal government financing of presidential campaigns in an attempt to even the playing field for the nominees of the two major parties. Prior to this time, Democratic leaders had argued that the Republicans had an advantage in raising funds from private donors. Richard Nixon, himself the recipient of large contributions, refused to sign any public funding bill that would affect the 1972 election, in which he was a candidate. The proposed bill was changed so it would not fully go into effect until the 1976 election. The public disclosure aspects of the 1972 law played a major role in uncovering the source of the funds used to finance the break-in at the Democratic Party headquarters in the Watergate complex.

Once nominated, the major party candidates receive a check to fully cover their campaign expenses (approximately $70 million in 2000) in exchange for not directly solicit-

Box 14-2 Balancing the Team: The Politics of Choosing Vice-Presidential Nominees

While presidential nominees always justify their vice-presidential choices as "the best person for the job," balancing the ticket is often a primary consideration in the decision process, as shown in the table that follows.

Presidential Nominee (Year)	Vice-presidential Nominee	Characteristics of the Vice-presidential Nominee
John F. Kennedy (1960)	Lyndon Johnson	Johnson represented the old guard and the South as opposed to Kennedy's youth and northeastern residence.
Richard Nixon (1968)	Spiro Agnew	As former governor of Maryland, Agnew bolstered Nixon's appeal to southern voters.
Jimmy Carter (1976)	Walter Mondale	An establishment midwesterner, Mondale offset Carter's outsider and southern political base.
Ronald Reagan (1980, 1984)	George H. Bush	Bush was an experienced Washington insider with ties to both New England and Texas.
Walter Mondale (1984)	Geraldine Ferraro	Ferraro's nomination was an attempt to appeal to women.
George H. Bush (1988)	Dan Quayle	Quayle's youth was intended to appeal to the new generation of voters.
Bill Clinton (1992, 1996)	Al Gore	Senator Gore provided Clinton with a Washington connection to help him deal with Congress.
Bob Dole (1996)	Jack Kemp	Kemp was a relatively young former House member with ties to New York.
Al Gore (2000)	Joseph Lieberman	As the first Democratic senator to question Bill Clinton's moral shortcomings, Lieberman helped Gore immunize himself from implying approval of Clinton's personal behavior.
George W. Bush (2000)	Dick Cheney	An experienced occupant of numerous top appointed and elected positions, Dick Cheney helped compensate for some of Bush's lack of national political experience.
John Kerry (2004)	John Edwards	A proven and energetic campaigner chosen to balance Kerry's more reserved personality, Edwards was also a southerner and was expected to bolster falling Democratic support in that region.

ing or accepting any privately raised funds. As Box 14-3: There Are Hard Rules and Then There Are Soft Rules outlines, there are exceptions to this rule. Third-party nominees have access to **public funding** only *after* they acquire at least 5 percent of the vote in the subsequent election. Major-party candidates, who, it is assumed, will reach the 5 percent threshold, have the money to spend *during* the campaign, while third-party candidates have only a promise of future money. Candidates such as Ross Perot in 1992, who offered

public funding *Government provision of funds for the running of a political campaign.*

Box 14–3 There Are Hard Rules and Then There Are Soft Rules

The flat assertion that presidential candidates are prohibited from raising campaign funds after gaining the nomination is not borne out. Presidential candidates engage in extensive fund-raising efforts during their campaigns. The drafters of the Federal Elections Campaign Act (FECA) wanted to limit the influence of campaign money on elected officials. They did not, however, want to hinder voter mobilization and party-building activity. The act placed activities such as voter registration drives, get-out-the-vote initiatives, and advertising for the party ticket outside the fund-raising limitations and reporting requirements. The money raised for these purposes outside of the FECA regulations is known as soft money.

The activities funded through soft-money contributions obviously have an indirect effect on presidential campaigns, and candidates know it. Presidential candidates take an active role in assuring that their party has as much of this money as possible. For the 1988 campaign, George H. Bush raised approximately $22 million and Michael Dukakis raised $23 million in soft money.[a] Both candidates Bush and Bill Clinton expended considerable effort in raising soft money for the 1992 campaign. Once in office, President Clinton, like his Republican predecessor, used his position to chalk up the soft-money receipts effectively. During his first two years in office, Bill Clinton helped raise more than $21 million,[b] encouraging Fred Wertheimer, president of Common Cause, to comment: "During the 1980s, President Bush was king of the corrupt soft-money system, but the crown and scepter now belong to President Clinton, the new soft-money king."[c]

With the shift of Congress back into Republican hands, soft-money contributors diversified and the Republicans were able to fill their coffers. Between 1995 and 1998, Republicans raised $270 million in soft money while the Democrats raised $216 million.[d] Campaign finance laws have often been described as "more loophole than law," and the soft-money strategies contribute to this view.

The Bipartisan Campaign Reform Act, which covers the 2004 presidential campaign, changed the rules again, making contributions of soft money to parties illegal. Candidates and parties have had to adapt to a new set of rules and find alternate ways to gain advantage.

---

a. See Frank J. Sorauf, *Inside Campaign Finance* (New Haven, CT: Yale University Press, 1992), 148.
b. Bill Lambrecht, "Watchdogs Bark at Donations for Democrats," *St. Louis Post-Dispatch*, June 22, 1994, 5B.
c. Quoted in Buddy Nevins, "Political Notes," *Sun Sentinel* (Fort Lauderdale, FL), July 3, 1994, 4b.
d. Harold W. Stanley and Richard G. Niemi, *Vital Statistics on American Politics, 1999–2000* (Washington, D.C.: Congressional Quarterly, Inc.), 97.

to take no public funds, can accept private contributions and are unlimited in the amount of funds they can personally contribute to their campaign.

Targeting the Most Appropriate Voters

popular vote *The actual number of votes cast for a candidate.*

electors *The individuals chosen to serve in the electoral college and to cast votes electing a president.*

The electoral college system of counting votes, in which the candidate winning the majority of the **popular vote** in a state wins all the **electors,** encourages presidential candidates to focus their campaign efforts on the politically competitive states with the largest number of electoral votes. Advertising campaigns and candidate visits emphasize major urban areas of large-population states, where the candidate can efficiently see a lot of voters and capture the attention of both local and national media. The winner-take-all nature of the electoral college encourages candidates to ignore both the voters and issues of those states they have little chance of either losing or winning. (See Chapter 11 for a more detailed discussion of elections.)

Communicating in the Right Way

Modern presidential campaigns rely heavily on television and other mass media to convey their message (see Box 14-4: A Day in the Life of a High-Tech Media Candidate). This leads to repetitive emphasis on a few simplified messages differentiating the candidates.

Box 14–4 A Day in the Life of a High-Tech Media Candidate

The primary task presidential candidates face today is not building a coalition of organized interests, or developing alliances with other candidates or politicians in their party, or even winning over the voters whose hands they shake. If candidates have their modern priorities straight, they are first and foremost seekers of favorable notice from the journalists who can make or break their progress.[a]

The era of the candidate who campaigned from his front porch, such as William McKinley,[b] or the candidate who traveled around the country to meet with party leaders and voters face-to-face is gone. The schedules and content of national campaigns are largely determined by the needs of television. Campaign events are chosen and timed more for their visual appeal to a wider audience than for their impact on the audience attending the event.

Advance men—a term taken from the public relations promoters who arrived in town a few days before the circus to put up posters—precede presidential candidates. They build a crowd and prepare the site so that it will look good on television. Camera angles emphasizing American flags, large crowds of beautiful people, or natural wonders such as rivers and mountains are sought for their symbolic message. Candidate schedules reflect the deadlines of the electronic media.

Candidates often spend more time preparing for media events, such as debates, than participating in them. The goal is to get free media coverage on regional and national news that will complement the themes and images emphasized in the candidate's purchased campaign commercials. A fictional, but typical, day for a presidential candidate (a man in this scenario) at the height of the campaign might look something like this:

7:00 A.M. (Los Angeles) Breakfast with labor leaders: Photo opportunity for local news stations and labor press.

7:45 A.M. (Los Angeles) Visit to Latino day care center: The event allows the candidate to talk about the need for day care and to recognize the importance of the Latino community. The candidate fingerpaints with children and greets them in Spanish in front of a specially invited Spanish-speaking television station crew.

8:15 A.M.–12:00 P.M. Travel to Chicago and time zone change: Working session with staff on campaign strategy includes the candidate making a few spirit-lifting calls to state campaign coordinators. After reviewing the speech prepared for today's noon rally, the candidate gives two of the television networks twenty-minute personal interviews for the candidate profiles they are preparing.

12:00–12:20 P.M. Police-escorted motorcade to downtown Chicago: The candidate cools his heels for a few minutes at the edge of downtown so that the news media buses can get ahead of him and record his triumphant entry. He uses the time to reread the efforts of his speechwriters one more time.

12:30–1:30 P.M. Downtown motorcade ride down State Street at the height of the lunchtime crowd: This is the primary media event of the day, designed to get the candidate on the evening news. The large and enthusiastic audience, made up of noontime gawkers and the party faithful trooped out by the advance men, cheer (with a little encouragement) at the concise one-liners that the candidate hopes to get on the evening news. Leaving the platform, the candidate refrains from answering a media question about his personal finances for fear that his answer will dominate the evening news.

2:00–4:00 P.M. (Chicago Hotel) Mock debate: Presidential candidate studies briefing books on issues and prepares for the upcoming debate by participating in a pretend debate, with a staff member standing in as the opponent. The candidate and his staff review videotapes of the debate to create "spontaneous" throw-away lines that the media might pick up for the news.

4:00–5:00 P.M. Participation in online email chat room, allowing average citizens to question the candidate. Given the heavy media coverage, the candidate actually types in the responses rather than expressing them verbally to a staff member for input as he has in the past.

5:00–7:00 P.M. Motorcade to the airport and a trip to New York: The candidate puts his feet up for a few minutes of rest but is interrupted by three phone calls and a visit from the speechwriter, who has just finished the candidate's address for that evening.

7:00–7:30 P.M. Motorcade to Madison Square Garden: During the ride, the candidate calls a popular local call-in show and gets right on the air to dispel charges that he opposes urban development programs.

7:30–8:30 P.M. Live call-in program with Larry King: The candidate fields questions from the radio and television audience from a temporary studio.

8:30–9:00 P.M. Interview: While waiting to go on stage at the Veterans' Convention, the candidate gives a long-promised interview to ABC's *Nightline*, which will show the interview a few hours later as if it were live.

9:00–10:00 P.M. Speech to the Veterans' Convention: Hoping to get a photograph in the major morning

continued

Box 14–4 A Day in the Life of a High-Tech Media Candidate

—*Continued*

newspapers and a story on the morning news programs, the candidate revs up the crowd with his standard stump speech and adds the new segments that his speechwriter just gave him about the plight of veterans.

10:00–11:00 P.M. Reception with major supporters: After an hour of schmoozing with the mayor and key backers, the candidate begs off more socializing and goes to his room.

11:00 P.M.–1:00 A.M. Strategy session with staff: The candidate and his staff review the tapes of the evening news programs and conclude that future speeches need to be shorter so that the media will have less from which to choose. A full-text computer search of newspapers shows that coverage of the campaign in the west is slipping. The pollsters indicate that the most recent results show that voters support the candidate's issue positions but feel he is not human enough. The campaign team looks at the schedule for the next week, decides to add two more stops out west, and determines to have the candidate tell more homey stories to reveal his human side. By 1:30 A.M., they are all asleep, knowing that five hours later the whole process will start again.

---

a. James David Barber, *The Pulse of Politics: Electing Presidents in the Media Age* (New York: W. W. Norton, 1980), 9.

b. William McKinley's successful 1896 campaign against William Jennings Bryan has often been viewed as the last of the traditional party-oriented campaigns featuring an unwilling candidate who is uncomfortable about interacting with the voters. In one sense, though, McKinley carried out the first technological campaign. Beside him on the porch was a relatively new invention, the telephone, which he used assiduously to manage his campaign operatives around the country. See Richard Armstrong, *The Next Hurrah: The Communications Revolution in American Politics* (New York: Beech Tree Books, 1988), 139–140.

Symbolic issues, such as patriotism, concern for the common person, fear of crime, fairness in taxation, and support for national defense, are outlined in general terms with few specifics.

Debates between the major-party nominees have become critical arenas in contemporary presidential campaigns. Determination of the winner of the debate depends more on media and public reaction to how the candidates looked and how they reacted on camera and less on their statements about the issues. Candidates and their supporters attempt to put the most positive *spin* on the debate performance. Instant polls of voters taken by telephone immediately after the debates and the conclusions of media commentators help to develop the conventional wisdom, or accepted view, of who won or lost. The label of "debate winner" gives a presidential campaign momentum; the perceived loser spends time trying to undo the harm.

Richard M. Nixon's unflattering face makeup during the televised 1960 debate with John F. Kennedy and George H. Bush's seemingly bored glance at his watch during the 1992 debate have become legendary in the history of damaging performances. So has Gerald Ford's slip of the tongue that there was no Soviet domination of Eastern Europe. Michael Dukakis's unemotional response to a hypothetical question of how he would react to a rape of his wife did not help him. Ronald Reagan's bold challenge of Jimmy Carter—in asking the debate audience whether they were really "better off today than they were four years ago"—worked for him in 1980. John F. Kennedy's photogenic and conversational approach and Bill Clinton's ability to interact with the audience convinced observers that televised debates can, under some conditions, dramatically improve a candidate's chances. A campaign can be turned around by a debate. In 1992 Bill Clinton came out on top by looking presidential and by not being overwhelmed by President Bush. Ross Perot made a name for himself by challenging the front-runners on the issues. The 1992 vice-presidential debate turned nasty, and James Stockdale, Ross Perot's running mate, was unable to match the rhetorical skill of his fellow vice-presidential candidates.

While marked by no one particular mistake, the expectations game helped determine the winner of the 2000 presidential debates. High expectations of Vice President Al Gore's knowledge and experience ran counter to his erratic performance, which vacillated from aggressive rudeness to forced politeness. The low expectations of Texas governor George W. Bush's debating skill were challenged when he held his own across all three debates. While the media pundits still gave the cumulative nod to Gore, the debates helped Bush more than Gore among the undecided voters. For voters with a presidential preference before debates, the evaluation of the outcome is deeply colored by the desire to have their candidate come out on top. A candidate's supporters almost always see that candidate as the winner. In 2000, Gore supporters saw his combativeness in the first debate as a sign of aggressive leadership, while Bush supporters saw it as condescending rudeness. Bush supporters saw his lack of smoothness as representing the antithesis of the slick Washington-insider politician, while Gore supporters saw it as a reflection on his purported inadequate intelligence and capacity to govern. Benchmarks for evaluating political events are often in the eyes of the beholder.

Debates are high-stakes games with the potential for either a big win or a big loss.[14] With the decline in party identification as a basis for presidential voting, debates often provide cues that voters consciously or unconsciously seek. Since debates and the general media place emphasis on the personal characteristics of the candidates, voters' "personal evaluations of the candidates play an increasingly important role in their voting decision."[15]

14-1c Winning and Losing

As we saw in Chapter 11, a variety of factors go into winning an election. Presidential elections follow many of the patterns found in other lower-level elections. Historically, presidential incumbents have generally won, although the second-term campaigns of Gerald Ford, Jimmy Carter, and George H. Bush indicate that this trend may be changing.

Incumbent presidents can often manipulate economic conditions and the policy agenda so that the most favorable results occur in presidential election years. Stimulating economic growth or engaging in military operations often make the voters more supportive of the incumbent. The reputations of the two parties help define their favored issues. Republican presidential candidates usually do better when the campaign focuses on foreign policy and defense issues, while Democratic candidates gain an advantage when voter attention is drawn toward economic and domestic issues. Voters are more willing to abandon their traditional party loyalties in presidential campaigns than in elections for other offices.

Many voters use the presidential campaign as a simulation of how the candidate will perform under pressure. Misstatements, inappropriate public reactions, and campaign staff improprieties all foster a negative image. Recent campaigns have largely been won by the candidate making the fewest mistakes. (Box 14-5: The Presidential Scorecard, a handicapping scorecard, will help you choose your "winner.") In 1992 George H. Bush was very late in recognizing public concern about the economy, and his increasingly negative campaign was viewed by many as being both unpresidential and a sign of desperation. Bill Clinton, on the other hand, ran an almost flawless campaign, focusing on public dissatisfaction and the hope for change. The strength of the economy in 2000 was seen as a major advantage for Vice President Al Gore, but the voters gave him little credit for its success and focused on other factors, especially his personal performance as a candidate. George W. Bush made fewer mistakes during the campaign and was able to neutralize issues such as education and portray himself as an untainted Washington outsider with a plan for cutting taxes.

Newly elected presidents interpret their victory as a *mandate* for the policy goals they emphasized during the campaign, but such an interpretation may not always be legitimate. Many voters do not cast their ballots on the basis of issues, and candidates often remain vague about their issue stands. Some presidents win because voters voted *against* the opponent. In 1992 almost one-quarter of the Clinton voters and almost one-third of the George H. Bush voters reported that they had voted against the other candidates rather than actually supporting the candidate for whom they had voted. In the 2000 race, almost 30% of George W. Bush voters indicated their vote represented a rejection of Al Gore.[16] Other presidents have found that once they attempt to design specific policies to implement campaign proposals, former supporters begin to find fault.

Box 14–5 The Presidential Scorecard

> The sport of kings [horse racing] has so much in common with the political sport of the people. In the race for the [presidential] nomination, the starters are out of the gate and nearing the clubhouse turn.[a] (political commentator William Safire)

Predicting the outcome of presidential elections is a popular activity among journalists as well as among the public at large. Presidential elections are so complex that such predictions are more of an art than a science. That does not mean there are no clear signposts. The ability to predict depends a great deal on factors surrounding a particular contest and the stage in the election cycle. It is obviously easier to predict the outcome late in the process when the number of candidates has been winnowed down and dominant factors have emerged. The media often likens presidential contests to horse races. In the world of horse racing, experts betting on races use rules of thumb to establish handicaps for particular horses and thus improve their chances of winning. Although the handicapping information is not perfect, it helps sort likely winners from probable losers. By working through the following scorecard with its handicapping suggestions, you should be able to hone your political predictions.

Factor 1: Is there an incumbent president in the race? (If not, skip to Factor 2.)

Throughout much of American history, incumbent presidents have won reelection with little difficulty. Since 1976, success has been more elusive; Gerald Ford, Jimmy Carter, and George H. Bush lost their bids. Factors helping to predict the vulnerability of a sitting president include:

Did the incumbent president face a serious challenge for his party's nomination? Politicians are hesitant to challenge members of their own party. An intraparty challenge is clear evidence that the incumbent is in trouble.

How large, aggressive, and impressive was the field of candidates from the opposing party during the primary season? A large number of early, well-known opponents signals the political judgment of a vulnerable incumbent. Politicians do not like to enter races in which they have little chance of winning. They are especially hesitant to run if they must give up their present office. House members and senators whose terms are up cannot run for two offices at the same time.

> *Handicapping Hint:* Check out the electoral status of the k\ey contenders. Determine how many of them would be out of office if they ran for the presidency and lost. The more serious the risk takers are, the more trouble there will be for the incumbent.

How is the economy doing? Americans tend to vote their pocketbooks. Incumbent presidents are blamed for economic difficulties. If the economic news is bad at election time, the incumbent is in political trouble.

> *Handicapping Hint:* Look at the various economic indicators reported by the government. Particularly helpful is the percentage change in real disposable income per capita. At 2 percent or below, the incumbent president or party is in trouble (Jimmy Carter in 1980 was saddled with negative growth, and George H. Bush in 1992 presided over a 2 percent change rate). When the figure is more than 3 percent, the incumbent president or party should win. Between those two figures, the race will be tight (for example, Ford's narrow loss in 1976, when the figure was at 2.5 percent, and George H. Bush's narrow win in 1988 at the same percentage).[b]

How popular is the incumbent president? Regular measurements of how good a job the public feels a president is doing provide a good sign of his potential for winning reelection.

> *Handicapping Hint:* Remember that public evaluations vary from month to month and tend to decline over time. Measurements after dramatic presidential action tend to be more positive than during times of relative inactivity. A president does not need an approval rating greater than 50 percent approval to win, but his chances decrease the more the percentage drops below that figure. Presidential popularity figures are regularly published in major newspapers.

Factor 2: Who is seen by the public, the media, and organized interest groups as the likely winner? Numerous measures of a candidate's support can be used at various stages in the presidential campaign.

Who is ahead in fund-raising? Campaign contributors tend to be pragmatic rather than idealistic—individuals and PACs give to candidates who are likely to win. Money is crucial, especially in the primary stage. Early money is more useful than money that comes later. Leaders in the fund-raising game have the double advantage of appearing as likely winners and having the resources to communicate their messages. Once the nomination stage is complete, federal funds finance the direct costs of major party candidates, but this does not halt the fund-raising process. Presidential candidates are expected to help raise party-building funds (the so-called soft money, discussed in Chapter 8). Candidates who excel at raising such funds not only reveal their popularity but also have the resources to build indebtedness among state and local party leaders.

Handicapping Hint: The Federal Elections Commission is charged with gathering and recording campaign funding information. They publish reports at various stages in the campaign, and many of these find their way into the media. (To get your own free copy of the most recent report, call 1 (800) 424-9530. You will need to specify which candidate(s) you are interested in. You can also find fund-raising data on the commission's website: http://www.fec.gov/.)

Which candidate is receiving the most media coverage? The horse race orientation of the media and their limited resources encourage them to cover only likely winners.

Handicapping Hint: The winner of a primary or general election almost always receives more media attention before the election than do unsuccessful candidates(s). You can test this assertion by measuring the relative length of news stories about each candidate for a week or so prior to the election. You might simply count the number of column inches allotted each candidate in the newspaper or time spent on the stories on the evening news.

What do public opinion polls tell you? Public opinion polls have proven themselves to be good measures of how people actually vote. The closer to the election a poll is taken, the more precise it is likely to be. For the last four decades, the last Gallup Poll before the presidential election has missed the actual outcome by less than 2 percent.

Handicapping Hint: Remember that polls are only as accurate as their methods. Review the criteria for good polls in Chapter 9. Poll results relate to a particular population. During the primary season, the polls to watch are polls of likely voters from the party and state in which the primary is being held. The media regularly report such polls.

Who has joined the candidate's team of supporters? Top political consultants worry about their batting averages and sign on with candidates they believe to have the best chance of winning. Since politicians tend to have long memories of past support, candidates who are perceived to have little chance of winning have difficulty lining up endorsements from interest groups and established politicians. A presidential candidate who is well behind in the polls may even have difficulty finding a vice-presidential running mate.

Handicapping Hint: Look at who has associated with each candidate. Does the candidate need them more than they need the candidate? Strong candidates almost have to fight off potential supporters, while weak candidates must be happy with what they can get. If top-flight staff and consultants are giving up secure jobs to join a campaign, it is a very good sign. A presidential nominee turned down by his top choices for a running mate has little likelihood of winning. The media tend to cover such information as they analyze the internal aspects of campaigns.

Factor 3: Who has made the fewest mistakes? Modern campaigns have been marked as much by mortal mistakes as by significant successes. The potential missteps range from a poor choice of running mate to ineffective handling of personal revelations or the publication of unguarded words. Many voters look for reasons to vote *against* candidates, and such errors prove that they have found a solid reason.

Which candidate presents himself most effectively to the public? Candidates have plenty of opportunities to make misstatements or react poorly to personal charges. The candidate whose image is not permanently tarnished is most likely to win.

Handicapping Hint: All candidates make mistakes. Focus on those mistakes that remain in the news a long time or that become labeled as character flaws. Often a candidate's *reaction* to a mistake is more important than the mistake itself. For example, Michael Dukakis's unemotional response to a question about a hypothetical rape of his wife marked him as inflexible and uncaring. The image

continued

Box 14–5 The Presidential Scorecard

—*Continued*

was solidified when he failed to refine his answer. Bill Clinton defused charges of alleged marital infidelity by directly facing the issue with his wife at his side. Al Gore had a hard time presenting a convincing and consistent image in 2000, vacillating between extraordinarily bland stiffness and forced aggressiveness. George W. Bush largely diffused an earlier drunk driving charge by admitting his mistake.

Which campaign uses the most effective strategy? Effective strategies allow candidates to communicate the right message, to the right people, in the right way (see Chapter 11). Weakness in any of these realms decreases a candidate's chance of winning.

> *Handicapping Hint:* The electoral college system defines the "right" voters as those who reside in the large electoral college toss-up states. A candidate spending too much time in states he is assured of winning or losing has chosen an ineffective strategy. In general, candidates should focus on undecided voters as opposed to talking to firm supporters or unchangeable detractors. Meeting voters on their preferred ground rather than relying on voters to seek out the candidate is a good sign of an effective campaign. As more and more Americans turned to cable television and talk radio, Bill Clinton was wise to communicate through those outlets.

Factor 4: What is the mood of the country, and what are the unique factors in this particular election? Each election has its own set of unique circumstances. The art of political prediction lies in determining which of these unique factors will play a role.

Is the mood of the country positive and optimistic or negative and cynical? During periods of optimism, voters tend to stick with current established leaders. As cynicism grows, they look for national leaders not tarnished by Washington experience and/or who represent a new generation of politicians.

> *Handicapping Hint:* The growing discussion and activity of third-party and independent candidates is an expression of frustration with politics as usual. The system is clearly stacked against third parties (see Chapter 8), but they can help set the agenda and play a spoiler role. Candidates who fail to react effectively to agenda items pushed by third-party candidates do so at their peril. Third-party candidates seldom affect major-party candidates equally. In 1992 Ross Perot not only highlighted George H. Bush's ineffective dealing with economic issues, but he also drew a significant number of voters who would have supported Bush in a two-way race. Under current conditions, the key question about third-party candidates is: Which major-party candidate will they hurt most?

---

a. William Safire, "Of Horses and Candidates," *New York Times*, June 4, 1995, A25.

b. Political scientist Edward Tufte is the prime proponent of this measure.

Bill Clinton's administration got off to a rocky start when his campaign promises concerning civil rights for gay men and lesbians resulted in a commitment to allow them to serve in the military. A number of Democratic congressional leaders who had supported his presidential bid immediately became his adversaries. Clinton was led to fritter away much of his mandate on something most Americans did not view as the most pressing problem facing the country. Rather than securing office with a publicly accepted game plan and a set of loyal fans, presidents soon realize that public support waxes and wanes, depending on the specific actions taken by their administration. The delayed and mixed results in 2000, with George W. Bush depending on a controversial decision by the Supreme Court to stop recounts and his failure to win the popular vote, robbed him of a clear mandate. Despite the outcome, he began his presidency as if the mandate was robust.

The transition from the electoral arena to governing the country can be difficult. There may be "a mismatch between the talents needed for campaigning and the skills necessary for governing."[17] The primary system, with its emphasis on gaining public support and attention, "rewards anti-Washington showmanship more than it does a proven capacity to forge the coalitions necessary to govern."[18] Jimmy Carter, for example, ran for the presidency as an outsider challenging the traditional way of doing things in Washington. Once in office he found that this approach had confused and angered many of the people he would have to work with as president. Relatively soon after the 1992 election, some observers remarked that Bill Clinton was a much better candidate than he was a president.[19] Newly elected presidents have little time to revel in electoral success. They must prepare for the next round of challenges by creating a staff and defining their approach to the job at hand.

14-2 The President in Office: Organizing the Players for Action

Shifting gears from the campaign mode to the governing mode can be difficult. New responsibilities, opportunities, and constraints emerge, and the skills of the campaign trail may not transfer to the White House. Candidates think in terms of rewarding loyal campaign workers, while presidents must consider the broader task of governing. Some of Bill Clinton's senior staff bemoaned the fact that they did not study White House operations and staff needs, so they could have hit the ground running. As one senior aide put it:

> We knew more about FEMA (Federal Emergency Management Agency) and the Tuna Commission than we did about the White House. We arrived not knowing what was here, and never worked together, and never worked in these positions.[20]

Modern presidents administer a dual set of bureaucracies: the Executive Office of the President and the federal bureaucracy. The **Executive Office of the President (EOP)** numbers more than 1,600 employees and is composed of a set of personal advisers (special assistants to the president—the White House Staff) and advisory agencies with their own staffs (such as the National Security Council, the Office of Management and Budget, the Domestic Policy Staff, and the Council of Economic Advisers). The EOP advises the president on policy matters. Its top leaders serve at the pleasure of the president, and the EOP staff can be dismissed if the **chief executive** so wishes. Their primary role is to advise the president on policy alternatives.

Executive Office of the President (EOP) *Set of agencies and advisers created to provide advice and assistance to the office of the president as the president directs and manages the executive branch.*

chief executive *The president's role as the administrator of the federal government.*

Few presidential decisions are implemented automatically. Presidents must rely on the federal bureaucracy to carry out their wishes. The federal bureaucracy today numbers more than two million civilian employees. Ninety-nine percent are permanent civil servants, with only the top layer responsible directly to the president through the cabinet secretaries, who are appointed by the president. The roles of executive appointees and the supportive work of the federal bureaucracy are explored in depth in Chapter 16. Here we briefly survey how the White House team is organized to support the president.

14-2a Staffing the White House Team: The Institutionalized Presidency

Staffing and managing the Executive Office of the President and the key officers of the departments take up much of the president's time and effort. Each task has grown in recent years as the size and functions of government expanded and became more interrelated. The pressure of time on presidents is tremendous. Highly involved presidents such as Bill Clinton often face the danger of spreading themselves too thin. After a rocky start, he brought in a time management expert to help him plan his schedule in order to spend more time on major policy issues rather than on the details of administration.

The Executive Office of the President

Earlier in the history of the United States, presidents managed the White House with a small circle of support. In 1933 Franklin Roosevelt began to attack the Great Depression and run the country with fifty clerks and secretaries inherited from the outgoing Hoover administration and a dozen or so personal assistants. It soon became clear that the president "needs help."[21]

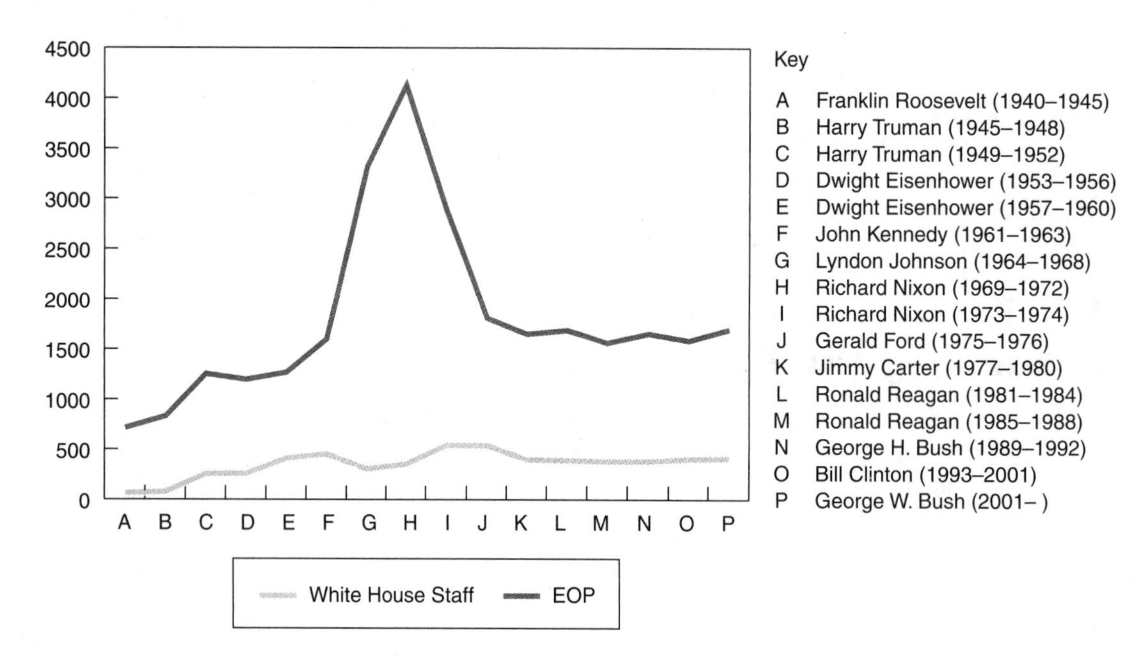

Figure 14-2
The Expanding Presidential Team from Franklin Roosevelt to George W. Bush

Source: Harold W. Stanley and Richard G. Niemi, *Vital Statistics on American Politics, 2001–2002*, Washington, D.C.: Congressional Quarterly, Inc., 2001, pp. 250–251. Figures are taken from the first year of each president's term except for Franklin Roosevelt, where the earliest figures are from 1943.

The growth of presidential responsibilities and initiatives spawned a greatly expanded presidential staff loyal to the president (see Figures 14-2 and 14-3). Reacting to required staff cuts in the rest of government, the Clinton administration promised to cut its staff by 25 percent. The task proved to be both difficult and, in many observers' minds, misguided. As one expert on presidential staffing put it, such reductions "undercut the president's ability to do what he needs to do."[22] In the long run, the cuts were much less dramatic than initially planned. As some Clinton aides put it, the promise to cut staff became a "quintessential Washington game." Candidate Clinton made an unrealistic pledge, only to find it unwise once he got into the White House. The pledge became a symbol, and the White House Staff had to scramble to make the numbers look as good as possible for fear of negative political ramifications.[23]

Staff size is only one factor to take into consideration. The nature and importance of the presidential staff have also changed. Structural changes such as the limiting of purely political appointments not only weakened the political parties but also reduced presidential influence over officials. Fragmented power in Congress, resulting from expanded use of subcommittees and more independent elected members, reduced a president's control over legislative agendas and outcomes. Such changes reduced a president's ability to rely on external players to carry out his or her wishes. More tasks had to be assumed by the internal White House staff. The technological diversity and expansion of modern mass communications also required the president to establish extensive personal public relations operations within the White House.[24]

Entourage Politics

Presidents today gather information and communicate their wishes with the help of a team of advisers and aides expected to show personal loyalty to them and their policies. Most key presidential staff members are team players, having signed on early with the presidential campaign and demonstrated their ability and commitment to the president: "They bring to their jobs an understanding of the president, loyalty, and . . . a set of skills that are transferable from the campaign—such as press relations and scheduling."[25] In selecting a personal staff, the president must balance the need for loyalty with the need for advisers with adequate experience in national government. Even those appointees selected for their expertise must accept the administration's larger goals. As one former science adviser to the president put it:

> The crucial thing is that the other members of the inner circle recognize you as a team player, recognize that you understand you're not a special pleader for some outside constituency.[26]

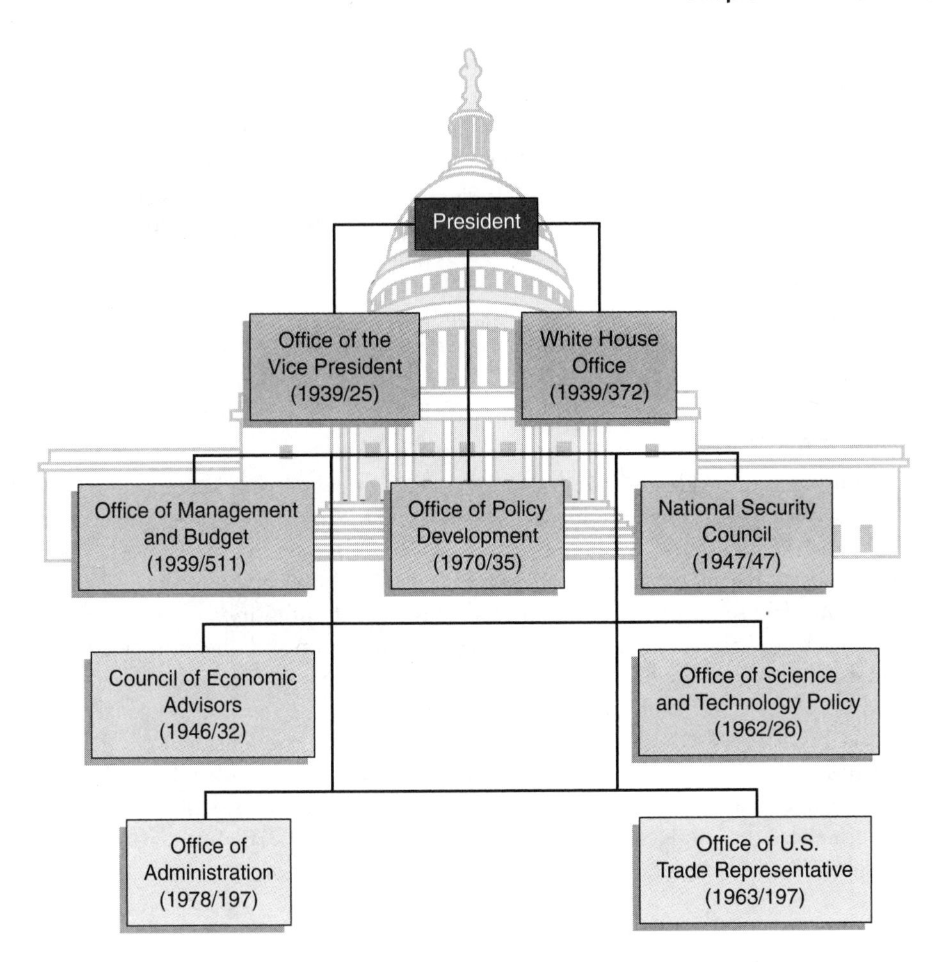

Figure 14-3
The White House Team: The Executive Office of the President

Numbers in parentheses indicate year of creation and the number of full-time staff in 2002, except for the Council of Environmental Quality (1992), the Office of the Vice President (1992), and the Office of National Drug Control Policy (1992).

Source: Data from Dana Priest, "White House Review Mired in Hill Panel Squabbling," *Washington Post*, April 10, 1992, p. A25; Harold W. Stanley and Richard G. Niemi, *Vital Statistics on American Politics, 2001–2002* (Washington, D.C.: Congressional Quarterly, Inc., 2003), p. 251.

After each change of administration, the new president and his aides sweep into office bent on "doing it better this time." Entourage politics,[27] involving family members, aides, and supporters, expands the presidential reach for information and control over other players. Controlling the entourage itself takes time and considerable effort. Close advisers provide absolutely necessary support but can also provide embarrassment. Presidents are judged by the people around them. When President Bill Clinton's surgeon general Joycelyn Elders's public comments about drugs and masturbation caused embarrassment, her resignation was requested.

Members of the president's entourage are expected to make the president look good, and inability to perform that task is a quick ticket to departure. President Clinton struggled with defining an acceptable role for his wife. Traditionally, first ladies have presided over ceremonial events and taken on sponsorship of widely accepted causes, such as highway beautification (Lady Bird Johnson), substance abuse (Betty Ford and Nancy Reagan), and literacy (Barbara Bush). Hillary Rodham Clinton, a competent lawyer and experienced political activist, was viewed by segments of the American public and the Washington establishment as having strayed too far from traditional ceremonial duties. When she was appointed to head the president's task force on health care reform, Mrs. Clinton became a lightning rod for opponents who wished to attack the plan. Adequate health care and quality of life for children remained special interests; in the course of 1995 her political activities focused more on the next presidential campaign. Hillary Rodham Clinton's successful run for the Senate from New York in the 2000 election frustrated her critics, who saw the act as another example of inappropriate behavior, and energized her supporters, who viewed it as verifying the right of women to have an independent career.

The future role of first ladies may well be presaged by their increasing role in the presidential election process. In 1996 one of the most memorable portions of the Republican convention was Libby Dole's speech profiling her husband Bob Dole, the eventual nominee. In 2000 and 2004, major-party candidates were introduced to the conventions by their wives, and the potential first ladies took an active role in the fall campaigns.

Presidential staffs are often labeled by their dominant characteristics. John F. Kennedy's "Harvard Brain Trust" was much different from Richard Nixon's "University of Southern California Crowd," Jimmy Carter's "Georgia Good Ole Boys," or Bill Clinton's "Arkansas FOBs (Friends of Bill)." It is natural to surround yourself with people with whom you feel comfortable. However, a similar group of advisers may not provide the breadth of advice that a president needs.

Managing the EOP

Presidents possess considerable freedom to organize their administrative team and distribute its responsibilities. Some presidents, such as Lyndon Johnson and Jimmy Carter, preferred involving themselves in administrative details. Others, such as Dwight Eisenhower, Richard Nixon, Ronald Reagan, and George H. Bush, established more formal **bureaucratic** White House structures, delegating a great deal of authority to subordinates. Bill Clinton took an activist role in the day-to-day administration and direction of the White House staff, running from meeting to meeting—often unable to keep to his schedule.

bureaucratic *A method of organization marked by formal rules, hierarchical structure, and delegation of authority.*

Although the basic units of the EOP have remained relatively consistent (see Figure 14-2 and Box 14-6: Key Offices in the Executive Office of the President (EOP)), each president's management style and personal ties with each adviser color the way staff and advisory agencies are used. As a general pattern, the longer a president is in office, the more formalized the presidential staff becomes. The president's **chief of staff** often plays a critical role, screening information and visitors and often serving as the president's closest adviser.

chief of staff *The top presidential aide, charged with controlling access to the president and managing the White House staff.*

Advisory agencies, such as the National Security Council, the Office of Management and Budget, and the Council of Economic Advisers, are intended to support presidential decision making with relevant information. If faced with a hostile and/or slow bureaucracy, presidents are often tempted to increase responsiveness by bringing the day-to-day administration of policy into the White House. There, they and their loyal staffs can maintain more direct control. The line between the pure staff functions of advising or encouraging policy coordination and taking on the operational responsibility of carrying out policy often becomes blurred. This is true especially when White House staff members and the president have deep commitments to policy goals.

The Iran-Contra affair was such a case. Lieutenant Colonel Oliver North, a staff member of the National Security Council, bypassed the departments of State and Defense to carry out covert operations in support of the Nicaraguan Contras from within the White House. Although it was never proven that he was working under explicit orders from President Ronald Reagan, his status as a member of the White House staff facilitated his ability to raise funds from private donors, sell arms to Iran, and transfer funds to the Contras. Congress had, however, explicitly opposed Contra aid.

The American system is based on the idea that each branch will have the information and power to control unacceptable behavior on the part of the other branches. Congress traditionally controls the presidency through the appropriation of funds, the approval of legislation, and the investigation of executive branch activities (*oversight*). White House reliance on staff advisers to carry out policy covertly can undermine the accountability built into the separation of powers system, making it impossible for Congress to have a meaningful say in policy implementation.

Modern presidents have found it necessary to appoint powerful chiefs of staff to coordinate the burgeoning White House bureaucracy. Chiefs of staff commonly move to the White House from key positions in the presidential campaigns, where they build a sense of trust in the president they serve. Individuals such as Hamilton Jordan (Carter), Donald Regan and James Baker (Reagan), John Sununu and Samuel Skinner (George H. Bush),

Box 14–6 Key Offices in the Executive Office of the President (EOP)

Office of Management and Budget (OMB) (created in 1970, played a more limited role as the Bureau of the Budget from 1921 to 1970).

Controls the development and administration of the federal budget while routinely providing the president with recommendations regarding the budget implications of legislative enactments. In its post-1970 expanded role, the OMB formulates and coordinates management procedures and program objectives within and among federal departments and agencies. The OMB employs several hundred permanent budget examiners and staff and is administered by a presidentially appointed director.

Council of Economic Advisers (created in 1946).

Analyzes the national economy and its segments, advises the president on economic developments, appraises the economic program and policies of the federal government, and recommends to the president policies for economic growth and stability. The council includes three professional economists and a small staff.

National Security Council (NSC) (created in 1947).

Advises the president concerning the integration of domestic, foreign, and military policies related to national security. Officially, the Council comprises only four members: the president, vice president, and secretaries of State and Defense. It is supported by a small National Security Council staff of advisers, headed by the assistant to the president for National Security Affairs.

National Economic Council (NEC) (created in 1993).

Advises the president on the coordination of all economic policy decisions and monitors the execution of those policies. Its creation signaled President Bill Clinton's desire to emphasize economics over foreign policy. It is modeled after the NSC, with the relevant cabinet members and a small staff.

Office of Policy Development (created in 1970).

Incurs name changes with most new administrations; formerly called the Domestic Council and the Domestic Policy Staff.

Advises the president in the formulation, evaluation, and coordination of long-range domestic and economic policy.

Office of the U.S. Trade Representative (created in 1963).

Charged with setting and administering overall U.S. trade policy. The U.S. trade representative is the chief representative of the nation in most trade discussions and negotiations with foreign nations.

White House Office on Environmental Quality (created in 1969 as the Council on Environmental Quality and renamed in 1993).

Develops and recommends to the president national policies that further environmental quality. The small council staff conducts research relating to ecological systems, the environmental impact of federal programs, and trends in environmental quality.

Office of Science and Technology Policy (created in 1962).

Serves as a source of scientific, engineering, and technical analysis and judgment for the president. The director of this office is supported by a small staff of scientists.

Office of National Drug Control Policy (created in 1989).

Coordinates federal, state, and local efforts to control illegal drug transactions and devises national strategies to assure that antidrug policies are effected. The director of this office is popularly called the *drug czar.*

and Thomas F. McLarty III, Leon Panetta, and John Podesta (Clinton) have wielded behind-the-scenes power that surpassed that of many of the more visible players. They often determine whom the president will see, the information included in the president's briefing booklets, and the presidential directives transmitted to other players. (The chief of staff's importance is proven by the complaints of other players regarding the extraconstitutional role of "assistant president.") President Bill Clinton followed a typical pattern.

He began his presidency with a low-key old friend (Mack McLarty) as chief of staff, but he later switched to a more aggressive Washington insider (former congressman and Office of Management and Budget director Leon Panetta) who could tighten up the organization and more aggressively look out for the president's interests. John Podesta, a long-time Clinton loyalist and former deputy chief of staff, took over just in time to handle the White House response to the impeachment proceedings.

Presidents rely heavily on their aides and advisory groups, and they can shift some blame to their assistants, but ultimately, in Harry Truman's words, "The buck stops here." Politically, if not always legally, presidents are held responsible for both their own decisions and those made by their staffs.

The Changing Cabinet

Members of the president's cabinet have two major functions. As individuals, they administer their departments and attempt to make sure that the president's preferences are carried out. As a group, they are an advisory body to the president (see Table 14-1).

Although cabinet secretaries are not officially sanctioned—or even mentioned—in the Constitution, few observers were surprised when early presidents began meeting with their appointed department heads for advice. This collective group became known as the **cabinet.** As administrators of their departments, **cabinet secretaries** offered an intimate knowledge of programs and, because of their own close ties, an access to congressional leaders. Controversial issues "were often thrashed out at cabinet meetings . . . [and] strong cabinets and weak Presidents characterized executive advisory relationships during most of the nineteenth century."[28]

cabinet *A body of advisers to the president who are appointed by the president.*

cabinet secretaries *Presidential appointees chosen to administer the major departments of government, who together report to and advise the chief executive.*

In spite of the power of the cabinet, the seeds of its contemporary decline as a decision-making body were evident in a number of early presidencies. In announcing the Emancipation Proclamation to the cabinet, Abraham Lincoln asserted, "I have gathered you together to hear what I have written down. I do not wish your advice on the main matter. I have determined that for myself."[29] Woodrow Wilson refused to involve the cabinet in major decisions, especially involvement in World War I.[30]

Appointments to the contemporary cabinet involve a combination of presidential needs and politics. Presidents often seek out experts to compensate for their own understood information gaps, or they look for widely recognized administrators who can bring a department into line. Some cabinet departments—such as the departments of Labor or Veterans Affairs—have clear political constituencies, and presidents may reward political supporters within that constituency with significant input in the appointment decision.

Recent presidents have attempted to make sure that their cabinets include women and minorities. Cabinet appointments are limited by the Senate's power of "advise and consent." Such appointments need approval by the Senate, which has become more aggressive in recent years in opposing nominees based on their partisanship, policy outlooks, and personal records.

Modern presidents have used the cabinet less as a decision-making body than as a sounding board for ideas and a forum for coordinating policies crossing different departments. With the expansion of national governmental activity, many cabinet secretaries found themselves caught between the pressure to speak *for* the president's policies within their departments and to advocate departmental positions *to* the president for action. Presidents want cabinet secretaries to show full commitment to the presidential team, while each secretary also has a departmental team of his or her own for whom to look out. The demands of each team often conflict (Chapter 16). The need to serve two masters puts considerable pressure on cabinet secretaries. Cabinet meetings thus have often become confrontational arenas of departmental advocates, with too many participants and perspectives to create a consensus.[31]

Some presidents have refused to call cabinet meetings and have encouraged one-on-one sessions with those department heads dealing with the most pressing policy issues. Other presidents have created either temporary (Kennedy) or permanent (Nixon, Reagan, George H. Bush, Clinton) subgroups. Variously called executive committees, cabi-

Table 14-1 Members of President George W. Bush's Cabinet

Current Position (as of 2005)	Previous Position(s)
Attorney General (Justice Department) Alberto Gonzales	Texas Supreme Court, White House Counsel
Secretary of Agriculture Mike Johannes	Governor of Iowa
Secretary of Commerce Donald L. Evans	Businessman; Bush campaign chair
Secretary of Defense Donald L. Rumsfeld	Secretary of Defense, White House chief of staff, and member of the House
Secretary of Education Margaret Spellings	Assistant to the President for Domestic Policy
Secretary of Energy Samuel Bodman	Businessman, Deputy Secretary of the Treasury
Secretary of Health and Human Services Michael Leavitt	Governor of Utah
Secretary of Homeland Security Tom Ridge	House member and governor (Pennsylvania)
Secretary of Housing and Urban Development Alphonso Jackson	Deputy secretary of HUD, president of American Electric Power-Texas
Secretary of the Interior Gale Norton	Colorado attorney general
Secretary of Labor Elaine Chao	Lawyer; Orange County, Florida, board chair
Secretary of State Condoleezza Rice	National Security Council; Provost, Stanford University
Secretary of Transportation Norman Y. Mineta	Democratic member of Congress; secretary of commerce (Clinton administration)
Secretary of the Treasury John W. Snow	Chairman, CSX (transportation conglomerate)
Secretary of Veteran's Affairs Jim Nicholson	Ambassador to the Vatican; Republican National Party Chair
ADDITONAL OFFICES GIVEN CABINET STATUS	
Chief of Staff Andrew Card	Assistant to the president in the first Bush administration, government-business relations officer in private sector
Director, Office of Management and Budget, Joshua Bolton	Executive director of Goldman Sachs International
Office of National Drug Control Policy Director John Walters	Staff aide, director of the Philanthropy Roundtable and president of the New Citizenship Project
U.S. Trade Representative Robert Zoellick	Undersecretary of state, White House deputy chief of staff (George H. Bush administration)

Note: Traditionally the president's cabinet is composed of the top administrators of key government departments. Increasingly, however, presidents have granted cabinet status to various other high-ranking officials; www.whitehouse.gov.

net councils, or task forces, they include cabinet secretaries, among others, and deal with specific policy areas. In general, though, the decline of the cabinet has left a void that has been quickly filled by centralizing power in the White House.

The cabinet and the president's personal staff often experience a conflict in perspectives. The staff takes its direction directly from the president and wants action on policies. Cabinet secretaries, deeply involved in the day-to-day administration of their departments, understand the realities of implementation and try to protect their departments. Recognizing their inability to control cabinet secretaries, modern presidents tend to use their personal staffs to oversee, stimulate, and coordinate cabinet departments and thus retain control of policy.

Even a president's staff develops areas of disagreement. Personal preferences and task assignments lead to competition for the president's time and support. An important part of a president's job involves serving as a referee between his or her aides.

14-2b The Human Side of Presidential Players

With all the pomp and circumstance surrounding the presidency, we tend to lose track of the fact that presidents are relatively normal human beings, subject to the same virtues and foibles as other citizens. Understanding presidents as human beings with psychological needs and desires is helpful in predicting their behavior in office.

Personality is the pattern of behavior developed since childhood to satisfy personal psychological needs. Political scientist James David Barber argues that two aspects of personality—*orientation toward power* and the *enjoyment of politics*—categorize potential behavior patterns.[32] Some individuals actively invest their personal energy to change their environment, while others passively accept things as they find them. According to Barber's theory, presidents who had happy and productive childhoods enjoy the challenge of politics and join the political game for the positive goal of accomplishing broad public policy. Barber believes that presidents who were denied adequate love and affection view the political game negatively and use political involvement as a means to satisfy their more personal needs for status and affection. Each personality type thus approaches the tasks of the presidency with a different orientation. Using the orientation toward power and enjoyment of politics, Barber presents four categories of presidents and identifies the dominant personality characteristics of modern occupants of the White House:

- *Active-Positive:* Self-confident but does not take oneself too seriously; flexible; creates opportunities for action; attempts to rationally master one's environment. Presidents such as Franklin Roosevelt, Harry Truman, John F. Kennedy, Gerald Ford, Jimmy Carter, and George H. Bush fall into this category. Categorizing recent presidents is difficult, since we know too much about them and the broad lessons of their presidencies have not yet become clear. Most observers would, however, place Bill Clinton in the active-positive category.
- *Active-Negative:* Compulsive; expends great effort but derives little enjoyment from it; low self-esteem; takes every success or failure personally; pessimistic about the future; rigid. Woodrow Wilson, Herbert Hoover, Lyndon Johnson, and Richard Nixon are the clearest examples of this category.
- *Passive-Positive:* Compliant; low self-esteem overcome by developing an ingratiating personality; reacts rather than initiates; superficially optimistic. William Howard Taft, Warren Harding, and Ronald Reagan represent presidents with a passive-positive approach.
- *Passive-Negative:* Politics seen as a duty rather than as a pleasure; responds rather than initiates; compensates for low self-esteem by serving others. Calvin Coolidge and Dwight Eisenhower are best described as passive-negative.

It is too early to reliably categorize George W. Bush. He does seem to enjoy being president and wielding power but is also willing to delegate considerable power, especially to his vice president, Dick Cheney. As you observe George W. Bush in office, think about the above categories and see if you can decide which applies to him most clearly.

Personality traits carry over into how presidents play the political game. The demands of the modern presidency have forced most presidents to take an active role in accomplishing their tasks. In Barber's terms, both Richard Nixon and Lyndon Johnson were active-negative presidents. Their desire for status and respect made it difficult for them to admit mistakes. Both fell victim to attempts to cover up bad policy decisions and mislead the American public. Criticism of either, within or outside the White House, was viewed as disloyalty, with Richard Nixon going so far as to create an "enemies list." According to Barber, Franklin D. Roosevelt and John F. Kennedy represent active-positive presidents, whose drive to succeed and enjoyment of politics allowed them to learn from their mistakes and to accept criticism as part of the game.

The more we know about the complexity of a president's life, the more difficult it is to make such a broad classification of personality and behavior. Classifying Ronald Reagan as a passive-positive helped to predict his nonvindictive approach to policy conflict. Nevertheless, it failed to point out how active his presidency would be in such areas as budget cutting and tax reform. George H. Bush's performance and background made him an active-positive president. Bill Clinton's love for politics and commitment to an active presidency suggests an active-positive approach. After analyzing his background and observing Clinton's first years as president, Barber concluded:

> With his tough early life, he could have been a Richard Nixon and become angry at the world. But that didn't happen because he's interested in results. And when he gets troubled, he doesn't give up; he knows that in the end, it's results the people are interested in, too.[33]

Barber asserts that active-positive presidents are least likely to fall victim to personality-based errors—such as rigidity and the inability to learn from their mistakes. Barber's analysis is relatively controversial, speculative, and difficult to test with solid evidence. Nevertheless, it does provide some useful insights into one of the key factors shaping how a president plays the game.

14-2c The Vice President: Team Captain in Waiting

Vice-presidential candidates are more often selected for their ability to strengthen the election ticket than for their qualifications to be second-in-command at the White House. It is therefore no surprise that, once elected, many vice presidents are ignored. The Constitution gives the vice president two tasks: presiding over the Senate with the right to vote in case of a tie and assuming the presidency in case of the death, resignation, or incapacity of the president. Vice presidents preside over the Senate only during the most controversial debates and cast a deciding vote less than once a year.[34]

Explicit attempts to prepare the vice president to take over the presidency have been irregular and sketchy. The selection process fails to guarantee that the president and vice president will either have close personal relationships or agree on major policy options. During the early years of American history (1789–1804, before the ratification of the 12th Amendment), there was no assurance that the president and vice president would come from the same party. Even today, when a president and vice president disagree on policy or have a cool personal relationship, the hope for a significant role evaporates, since the vice president depends on assignments from the president.

For much of American history, vice presidents were perceived as ineligible for executive branch functions. Even though they spend little time in their official role of presiding over the Senate, they have been seen as legislative arena players.[35] Modern presidents use vice presidents with close congressional ties to sell their legislative programs on Capitol Hill. Vice presidents also represent the United States on goodwill trips and on a number of boards and commissions.

Contemporary presidents tout attempts to use their vice presidents effectively. Jimmy Carter involved Vice President Walter Mondale regularly as a personal adviser and participant in policy-making groups. Ronald Reagan provided George H. Bush with similar, if more limited, access and duties. The stream of criticism for George H. Bush's selection of Dan Quayle as vice president dampened the ardor of Bush and his staff to give Dan Quayle a visible role in key decisions. Vice presidents have few real duties, which makes it difficult for them to change first impressions. President Bill Clinton made Albert Gore, Jr,. a full partner in his administration, giving him specific responsibility for the "Reinventing Government" initiative. As we saw in Chapter 1, Gore became an effective spokesman in the battle over NAFTA. He served as the key proponent of the government's role in promoting the Information Superhighway. Grasping the key backup-player function of the vice presidency, Al Gore was able to fill "the gaps aggravated by Mr. Clinton's uneven management, especially in foreign policy . . . [reaching] selectively into important areas of foreign and domestic affairs." George W. Bush chose Dick Cheney because of his extensive experience and has relied on his vice president more than have many presidents. Vice President Cheney's heart problems early in the administration shook the confidence of many Bush supporters who relied on

Box 14–7 *Rules for Changing Team Captains*

Background

The words "the president is about to begin his concession speech," or "the president is being rushed to the hospital after an attempt on his life," have been heard more frequently in recent years. Only two of the ten presidents since World War II served the two terms established by George Washington and formalized by the 22nd Amendment. Three were defeated outright in their bids for reelection, and three left office before serving two full terms without running for reelection. The remaining two died in office.

Even if the incumbent remains in office, there is no assurance that a sitting president will have the physical stamina or mental ability to remain an effective leader. Presidents are human beings, subject to sickness and accident. At least two of the post World War II presidents suffered physical problems serious enough to force them to relinquish significant portions of their duties. Since the presidency is such a demanding position, it is important to assure that it is filled by someone with the ability and legitimacy to perform at adequate levels.

In order to play any game, one must be accepted as a legitimate player. In politics a set of formal and informal rules determine who is allowed to play. Most attention is usually focused on the rules for entering the game. Just as important, however, are those rules that determine when someone is no longer allowed on the playing field. Unlike countries where chief executives have refused to relinquish power at the end of their terms or when incapacitated, U.S. presidents give up their positions when defeated, when they choose not to run, or when they complete the two-term limit.

Incapacity has proven to be a more difficult problem. Woodrow Wilson refused to give up power even though a stroke had disabled him for much of his last year in office. Dwight Eisenhower suffered a heart attack and a stroke and had major surgery while in office. In addition to his hospitalization after an assassination attempt, Ronald Reagan faced surgery. Both Eisenhower and Reagan relinquished the presidency briefly to their vice presidents but returned to their duties full-time.

Questions

The need to assure continuity in office suggests the necessity of paying attention to issues of presidential succession. Several questions immediately come to mind.

What is the general nature of the rules of presidential succession, and how have they changed?

What happens when a president is impeached, dies, or is defeated?

What rules apply to a president who suffers physical incapacitation?

Analysis: The General Rules

The Founders established a set of formal rules for replacing presidential players. The Constitution (Article II, Section 1) states that "in case of removal of the president from office, or of his death, resignation, or inability to discharge the powers and duties of said office, the same shall devolve on the vice president." This clause provided clear guidance for retired, defeated, impeached, or deceased presidents.

As in most games, experience in playing reveals areas where the rules are too vague or unworkable. When games first develop, the rules tend to be simple. Over the years, the rule book becomes more complicated, attempting to account for every possible contingency. Many games and sports have national or international bodies that establish and enforce official rules. In recent years they have had

Cheney's expertise to compensate for Bush's perceived weaknesses. While vice-presidential power is tenuous and variable, nearly one-third of America's vice presidents have succeeded to the presidency. Nine took over directly upon the death or resignation of the president, and five won election on their own (see Box 14-7: Rules for Changing Team Captains).

to deal not only with infractions on the field of play, which could get a player removed, but also with off-the-field behavior such as drug use, commercial endorsements, interference with competitors, and betting on the game's outcome.

Many of the same considerations are true for the political game. Rules must be specified and the nature of acceptable behavior and performance defined. Through the constitutional amendment process, our basic rule book can be adapted to solve perceived problems. The 25th Amendment, ratified in 1967, was an attempt to define the process of changing presidential players. As is often the case in games, the impetus for change was a crisis followed by a series of "What if?" questions. The 1963 assassination of President John F. Kennedy raised the question, "What if he had lived but was mentally impaired?" It became clear that neither the Constitution nor historical precedent was very specific in the guidance offered.

Impeachment, Death, Resignation, or Defeat

In case of removal of the president by impeachment (see Chapter 15), death, or resignation, the vice president becomes the president. He or she legally inherits all the rights of any presidential player.

Tradition dictates that a defeated president gracefully—at least in public—relinquish powers and facilitate the transition to the winner. No president has ever attempted to thwart the inauguration of his successor. The cultural norm of graciously winning—and graciously losing—remains deeply ingrained in the presidential succession process, as it does in most American games.

Incapacity

The constitutional language on presidential incapacity does not make it clear whether the vice president is to become the "official" president or merely the "acting" president in such cases. More important, how a president would be declared unable to "discharge the powers and duties" of the office was never clearly spelled out. Presidents Garfield, Wilson, Eisenhower, and Reagan all had serious medical problems that interfered with their ability to serve yet were not officially replaced. Under the 25th Amendment an incapacitated president can declare his or her own inability to discharge the duties and the vice president then becomes acting president. Ronald Reagan voluntarily turned over power to Vice President George H. Bush for the period he was under anesthesia during surgery. The vice president and a majority of cabinet members can also declare the president incapacitated, in which case the vice president then becomes acting president until the president requests a return to power. If the president disagrees with the vice president and the majority of the cabinet on his or her ability to carry out the duties, Congress serves as the umpire. To avoid a partisan or political removal of the president, a two-thirds vote of both the House and the Senate is required to continue the declaration of the president's incapacity.

Not all of the ambiguities have been cleared up. The accurate judging of the mental incapacity of a president is beyond written rules and subject to political manipulation.

By attempting to establish a clear set of rules for when and how a president stays in the game, it is hoped that conflict will be avoided. No rule book, however, is infallible, nor can it anticipate every contingency. The current procedures will prevail until an unanticipated situation or unfortunate outcome surfaces. The pressure will then build to revise and clarify the rules for removing this key player.

Conclusion

The presidential selection process determines the incoming leader and shapes the nature of the presidency and of the team that accompanies the president into the White House. Constitutional requirements and public preferences limit the bench of potential players to a relatively restricted set of contenders. The electoral college system of voting and the domination of new campaign technologies determine the strategies most effective for winning the presidential sweepstakes. The limited role of issues and the typical lack of distinctiveness of candidates' stands often make it difficult to determine what the electorate is trying to say. For the elected president, the legacy of campaign choices and the perception of the reasons for victory determine the commitments and priorities with which the winner enters the White House.

Presidents are human beings who bring with them a series of past behavior patterns and personal goals that affect the ways in which they view and carry out their duties. Presidents set the tone of their administrations and establish key policy priorities.

The modern presidency is more of a team effort than an individual performance. Presidents surround themselves with appointed advisers and departmental administrators whose loyalty and agreement on the issues increase presidential control of policy initiation and implementation. Presidents depend heavily on their teams to provide them with advice, information, and a presence in the wide variety of arenas in which presidents must become involved. Vice presidents, although often nominated for electoral reasons, take on tasks assigned by the president and stand ready to take over in case of presidential incapacity.

Filling the presidency through election and appointment represents an important set of games in American politics, but it is only the precursor to the more significant games of presidential policy making and administration, to which we turn in the next chapter.

Key Terms

balance the ticket
bureaucratic
cabinet
cabinet secretaries
chief executive
chief of staff
electors
Executive Office of the President (EOP)
national party convention
natural-born citizens
popular vote
public funding

Practice Quiz

1. Where is the formal nomination for president made?
a. In party primaries
b. At state conventions
c. In open primaries
d. At a national convention

2. Who chooses candidates for vice president?
a. State party conventions
b. Party leaders in legislative caucuses
c. Presidential nominees
d. Delegates to the Electoral College Convention

3. When a newly elected president claims he has a "mandate" for change, we can assume
a. the president will be able to carry his policy agenda through Congress.
b. the president will maintain his popularity throughout his term.
c. that voters support the platform of the winner.
d. very little, since many interpretations of mandates may be illegitimate.

4. Which is generally true of presidential cabinets?
a. They are often used more as sounding boards than as decision-making bodies.
b. They play a key role in all important policy decisions.
c. Their affirmative vote is required for most major policy change.
d. They seldom meet, and when they do there is seldom any consensus.

5. National party conventions have the power to do everything EXCEPT
a. choose the party's presidential candidate.
b. change party rules.
c. fine party candidates for campaign finance infractions (in primaries).
d. establish party policy goals.

6. _____ serve(s) as chief administrator(s) of the major departments of government.
a. Special assistant to the president
b. Members of the Senior Executive Service
c. Cabinet secretaries
d. The staff of the Executive Office of the President

7. The president's _____ is charged with coordinating presidential information gathering and initiative development.
- **a.** chief of staff
- **b.** vice president
- **c.** president pro tempore
- **d.** press secretary

8. In 2000, each major party presidential candidate received approximately $ _____ from the government to run their campaign.
- **a.** 20 million
- **b.** 40 million
- **c.** 60 million
- **d.** 20 million in direct funds and $70 million in services

9. Which president was most associated with creating the institutionalized presidency with its increased staff and activity?
- **a.** Theodore Roosevelt
- **b.** Franklin Roosevelt
- **c.** Dwight Eisenhower
- **d.** Ronald Reagan

10. Presidents with active-negative personalities are particularly likely to be
- **a.** nonvindictive.
- **b.** willing to learn from mistakes.
- **c.** ingratiating.
- **d.** rigid.

You can find the correct answers to these questions by taking the quiz and then submitting your answers in the Online Edition. The program will automatically score your submission. Where you miss a question, the program will provide the correct answer, a rationale for the answer, and the section number in the chapter where the topic is discussed.

Further Reading

James David Barber's *Presidential Character: Predicting Performance in the White House* (Englewood Cliffs, NJ: Prentice-Hall, 1985) popularized the personality approach for studying presidents. Barber applies his theory to the leading candidates of each election cycle.

Three excellent contemporary textbooks on the presidency provide comprehensive coverage, with each taking a slightly different focus. James W. Davis's *The American Presidency: A New Perspective* (New York: Praeger, 1995) emphasizes presidential roles. The nature of leadership underlies much of the discussion in George C. Edwards and Stephen Wayne's text *Presidential Leadership: Politics and Policy Making* (New York: St. Martin's, 1994). Steve Schier's *Big Risk and High Ambition: The Presidency of George W. Bush* (Pittsburgh, PA: University of Pittsburgh Press, 2004) is a first cut at comprehensively analyzing the early Bush presidency.

Students either doing presidential research or evaluating the research of others will find an extensive analysis of research methods applicable to the presidency in *Studying the Presidency* (Knoxville, TN: University of Tennessee Press, 1983) by George C. Edwards and Stephen J. Wayne. *Vital Statistics on the Presidency* by Lyn Ragsdale (Washington, D.C.: Congressional Quarterly Press, 1998) brings together a plethora of empirical data on both the historical and modern presidency.

Two journals focus on the presidency. The *National Journal* (Washington, D.C.: National Journal) is published weekly and analyzes contemporary happenings in the White House and the executive branch. It complements the coverage that the *Congressional Quarterly Weekly Report* (see Chapter 13) gives to Congress. *Presidential Studies Quarterly* (New York: Center for the Study of the Presidency) presents articles by academics and practitioners.

Endnotes

1. John McCaughry, 1993, "Clinton's Jeffersonian Mantle," *Washington Times*, January 20, 1993, E4 (election conditions, Jefferson's policy positions, deference to Congress).
2. Sarah Booth Conroy, "Yes, Even Jefferson," *Washington Post*, April 4, 1994, B3 (Jefferson's "scandals" included admitting that he made improper advances toward the wife of John Walker).
3. See James P. Pfiffner, ed., *The Managerial Presidency* (Pacific Grove, CA.: Brooks/Cole, 1991).
4. Erwin Hargrove quoted in Dom Bonafede, "Echoes of the Past," *National Journal*, December 12, 1987, 3147.
5. See George C. Edwards III and Stephen J. Wayne, *Presidential Leadership: Politics and Policy Making* (New York: St. Martin's Press, 1994), 45–46.
6. John McLaughlin's "One on One," December 20, 1994, Federal News Service Transcript, LEXIS-NEXIS database.
7. Dennis Farney, "Only the Bland Survive," *Wall Street Journal*, December 4, 1987, 34d.
8. George C. Edwards III and Stephen J. Wayne, *Presidential Leadership* (New York: St. Martin's Press, 1990), 39.
9. Laurie Kellman, "Upcoming Tests Crucial to the Front-Runner," *Washington Post*, March 4, 1996, A1.
10. Robert Dornan (R-Calif.), "Presidential Announcement Speech," Federal Document Clearing House, July 5, 1995, LEXIS-NEXIS database.
11. Ross Baker, "Sorting Out and Suiting Up: The Presidential Nominations," in Gerald M. Pomper, ed., *The Election of 1992* (Chatham, NJ: Chatham House, 1993) 68.
12. Jack Germond and Jules Witcover, "Bush and the Gulf Expectations Game," *National Journal* 23, no. 4 (January 26, 1991): 234.
13. James David Barber, "Campaign Game Plans," *National Journal*, November 14, 1987, 2842–50.
14. For a detailed analysis of debate history and strategy, see Myles Martel, *Political Campaign Debates: Images, Strategies and Tactics* (New York: Longman, 1983).
15. Edwards and Wayne, *Presidential Leadership*, 85.
16. President George W. Bush's support in the 2000 election was also not completely an endorsement of him personally, since almost 30 percent of his voters indicated they were voting against Al Gore.

Reasons for supporting particular candidates based on Princeton Survey Research Associates pre-election polls of national adult samples of registered voters with a clear voting intention, November 5, 1992, and November 2, 2000. LEXIS-NEXIS database.
17. Hedrick Smith, *The Power Game* (New York: Random House, 1988), 648.
18. Smith, *The Power Game*, 648.
19. See Dan Balz, "For the Candidate and the President, Then and Now Are the Same," *Washington Post*, May 16, 1993, A4.
20. Quoted in Jack Nelson and Robert J. Donovan, "The Education of a President," *Los Angeles Times*, August 1, 1993, 12.
21. *President's Commission on Administrative Management* (The Brownlow Commission) (Washington, D.C.: U.S. Government Printing Office, 1937).
22. Kathy Lews, "White House Critics Differ on Staff Cuts' Significance," *Dallas Morning News*, October 2, 1993, 6A.
23. Burt Soloman, "Scrimping on White House Staff Could Damage Clinton's Fortunes," *National Journal*, August 14, 1993, 2046.
24. Samuel Kernell, "The Evolution of the White House Staff," in *The Managerial Presidency*, ed. James P. Pfiffner (Pacific Grove, CA: Brooks/Cole, 1991), 48–50.
25. Stephen Hess, *Organizing the Presidency* (Washington, D.C.: The Brookings Institution, 1976), 16–17.
26. Graeme Browning, "Unwanted Advice," *National Journal*, May 18, 1991, 1172.
27. See Matthew Holden, Jr., "Why Entourage Politics Is Volatile," in *The Managerial Presidency*, ed. James P. Pfiffner (Pacific Grove, CA: Brooks/Cole, 1991).
28. Edwards and Wayne, *Presidential Leadership*, 171.
29. Cited in Robert DiClerico, *The American President* (Englewood Cliffs, NJ: Prentice-Hall, 1995), 198.
30. DiClerico, *The American President*, 198.
31. Edwards and Wayne, *Presidential Leadership*, 163–75.
32. James David Barber, *The Presidential Character: Predicting Performance in the White House* (Englewood Cliffs, NJ: Prentice-Hall, 1985).
33. Quoted in Nelson and Donovan, 12.
34. Thomas Cronin, *The State of the Presidency* (Boston, MA: Little, Brown, 1975), 213.
35. DiClerico, *The American President*, 374.

15

The Presidency: From Priorities to Action

Key Points

- **Constitutional and extra-constitutional roles for the president.**
- **The historical growth of presidential power and the functioning of restraints.**
- **The president as national agenda setter.**
- **Strategies used in different types of presidencies.**
- **The White House as central arena for interrelated policy games.**

Preview: Executive Expansion

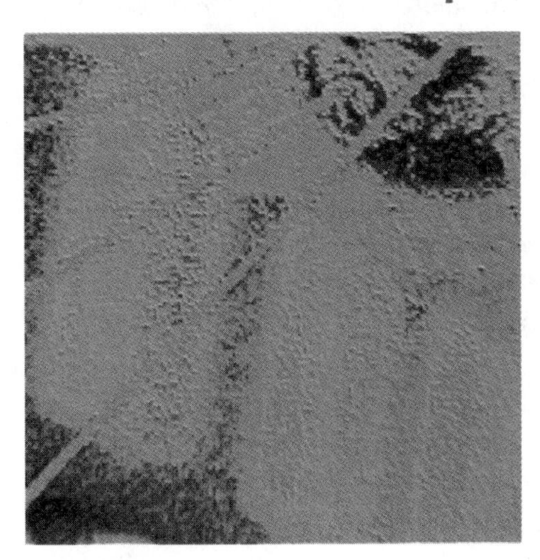

The president's media adviser stopped by early in the morning to discuss public opinion and how the president might attempt to influence it. In a meeting a short time later with his congressional liaison adviser, the president established priorities for his legislative agenda. The president's personnel chief submitted a list of appointments that needed to be made, and the president's political adviser discussed the importance of taking into account the impact of appointments on the party organization. A few minutes later, the president's foreign policy adviser broke in to alert the president to an emerging foreign policy crisis. By the time the president's domestic policy adviser had weighed in on his concerns of the day, the president's keeper of the calendar pointed out that the president was already running twenty minutes behind schedule. It sounds like a typical day at the White House: the large, well-oiled White House bureaucracy anticipating problems, providing information, advising the

President George W. Bush at the Department of Defense Service of Remembrance for those Killed at the Pentagon on September 11, 2001.
White House photo by Paul Morse.

president, and seeing that his decisions are carried out. Thus it has been for more than two hundred years.

But wait! A time traveler would see one important difference. During most of our history, the same two or three people would be floating in and out of the Oval Office, putting on different hats and shifting their perspectives. The president's domestic adviser might also be his political adviser and his press agent. Until the 1930s all of the above tasks would have been done by a handful of people. Franklin Roosevelt created the first formal White House Office with six professional staff advisers. James Rowe, one of these first six, reflected that, by the time Harry Truman took over, they had "nine people doing what I used to do" and speculated that by the mid-1980s "they must have 300 or 400 [people] doing what I used to do."[1]

Today each of the advisers described above would be separate individuals with their own entourage of assistants, advisers, and support staff. They would often bring conflicting advice based on their particular positions in the organization chart, personal proclivities, and their staffs' experience. Gone is the clubby atmosphere of a few long-term personal advisers with general and overlapping job assignments designed to make the president's job easier. In its stead is a set of bureaucracies within a bureaucracy. The president, however, still wears two hats as manager and referee as he attempts to forge compromise and accommodation within his White House staff.

American presidents are key players in the public policy process; other players tend to look first to the president for guidance. The issues pursued by presidents and the effectiveness of their strategies have implications for both this country and the wider world. Chapter 14 discussed presidential selection and how the executive team is organized for action. In this chapter we look at how the president establishes priorities and attempts to carry them out. The president plays in a variety of political arenas, each having different rules and requiring different strategies and skills. A combination of aggressive presidents and public expectations has expanded presidential roles. Societal and technological changes have required granting presidents significant new power.

15-1 Formal Rules and Informal Roles in the Presidential Arena

Newly elected presidents receive no explicit job description but are called upon to play a number of different roles, or positions, in the political game. Each role involves a different set of skills. The Founders described presidential powers and responsibilities in the broadest of terms. The more specific duties evolved through time. The roles performed by modern presidents have various origins. For instance,

- they reflect their personal policy agendas,
- they emanate directly from the Constitution,
- they have a constitutional basis but represent significant expansion from the intentions of the Founders, or
- they have developed over time and are based on presidential initiative and external demands.

15-1a Personal Policy Agendas

To some degree, presidents can define their own agenda, but often they must react to problems and issues not of their own making. Presidents fill their working days attempting to satisfy expectations coming from other political players and the public, as well as their own preferences. The emphasis that a president gives to a particular task or area of public policy varies according to personal interests and the nature and immediacy of contemporary social problems. Richard Nixon largely ignored domestic issues in favor of foreign policy, which he enjoyed. Lyndon Johnson and Jimmy Carter were more comfortable with domestic politics but were forced by world events—armed conflict in Southeast Asia and the taking of hostages in Iran, respectively—to spend most of their efforts on foreign policy. Ronald Reagan enjoyed setting broad ideological goals while delegating most of the responsibility for administering policy. George H. Bush campaigned to become the "education president" and the stimulus for a "kinder, gentler nation" while requiring "no new taxes." Once in office he reluctantly endorsed both new taxes and cutbacks of federal social programs, because of the realities of outside events. Bill Clinton focused his campaign around his first theme, the informal "It's the Economy, Stupid," and he wanted to make health care his second priority. Instead he was embroiled in foreign policy crises in Somalia, Haiti, and Bosnia from his first days in office. When he did have his choice of agenda items, many felt that President Clinton started out on the wrong foot by emphasizing gay rights. He then moved to an emphasis on health care and other domestic issues, such as family leave. George W. Bush initially focused on his tax cut pledge from the 2000 campaign to the exclusion of other concerns, but he was forced by political realities to deal with foreign policy after the downing of a U.S. plane in China and the terrorists attacks of September 11, 2001. A closer look at the ways presidents prioritize their agendas will come later in this chapter.

15-1b Roles That Are Constitutional Imperatives

The Constitution outlines a series of presidential responsibilities. These include fulfilling the roles of chief executive, commander-in-chief, and chief diplomat.

Chief Executive

As *chief executive* (Article II, Section 1), the president oversees the executive branch; the oath of office requires the president to "faithfully execute" the laws enacted by Congress. The president appoints the top level (approximately 1 percent) of federal officials as cabinet secretaries and their assistants to manage the departments and agencies. Recognition of the key policy role of top appointees and divided government has led at times to a drawn-out confirmation process delaying senatorial approval. Both presidents Bill Clinton and George W. Bush had hundreds of appointments still to be approved over six months into their terms. The remainder of federal government employees are part of a career civil service core appointed on a nonpolitical basis (see Chapter 16). Unlike top executives in the corporate world, the president lacks a number of important administrative powers, such as the ability to hire and fire much of the bureaucracy that he or she must administer. Many presidents arrive with little administrative experience and often lack an interest in the details of administration. The size of the executive branch and the breadth of its functions are each sufficient cause to force presidents to delegate substantial authority. Cabinet secretaries are usually given the power to appoint much of their high-level staff and to decide how policy will be administered, with minimal White House involvement. In addition, the independent powers of other players (Congress and the courts) to set funding levels and to oversee the administration of policy thwart the president's administrative control.

Commander-in-chief

Commander-in-Chief *The president's role as manager of the U.S. armed services.*

The role of **Commander-in-Chief** (Article II, Section 2) is the basis for much of the expanded power of the modern presidency. The president's control over the U.S. military may in modern times have become a factor far beyond the Founders' expectations. A world of instant communications and sophisticated weaponry requires speedy military reaction. Because obtaining a formal congressional declaration of war is a slow process, the stage is set for more one-sided presidential initiatives in this area.

Congress's increasing frustration with being called upon only after the fact for financial and policy support during the Vietnam conflict led to a redefining of the rules. As discussed Chapter 13, the War Powers Resolution (1973) recognized the necessity of unilateral presidential action in time of crisis, but it encouraged presidents to consult with Congress "in every possible instance" before committing troops. The resolution also required immediate congressional consultation after any troop commitments and limited the commitment of troops into hostilities to 60 days (plus an additional 30 days for troop withdrawal) unless authorized by Congress.

In spite of its goal of limiting presidential power, the War Powers Resolution may well have *expanded* it by making independent presidential action legal. Once troops are already committed, Congress will almost always support those troops in the field, at least in the beginning. Although there was a highly divided vote just a few days earlier, Congress gave President George H. Bush almost unanimous support for troop involvement once the troops had been formally committed in the Persian Gulf.

Every president since Richard Nixon has questioned both the wisdom and the constitutionality of the War Powers Resolution and has complied with its intentions only in the most limited fashion. In recent U.S. military actions, such as in Grenada, Panama, the Persian Gulf, Bosnia, and Haiti, the White House agreed to the act's consultation requirements without accepting the full implications of the resolution. Although he did not seek a formal declaration of war, George H. Bush did seek a formal resolution of support for the Persian Gulf War. President Clinton argued that it was not legally mandated that he obtain congressional approval for the 1995 invasion of Haiti, because it involved a U.S.-created coalition of U.N. troops. At the height of the invasion, more than 20,000 troops from the United States and 2,000 from other nations were involved. The courts have refused to intervene in the power game between Congress and the president in the war-making realm. Legislation has been introduced to repeal the War Powers Resolution. Proponents claim that it does not work and has the potential for hampering presidential actions that are clearly in the national interest.

In 2002, President George W. Bush sought and received broad and flexible authority to seek regime change by military force in Iraq. Seventy-seven of the 100 senators and 296 or the 435 House members voted for the resolution. Partisanship played a role in the grant of authority as most of the opponents were Democrats.

Chief Diplomat

The Founders recognized the importance of the nation speaking with one voice in foreign policy, yet they believed that the president "should be the Senate's agent . . . [and] at the most, the president should be a joint participant in the field of foreign affairs, but not an equal one."[2] As **chief diplomat,** the president was given the formal power to make treaties, to receive ambassadors from foreign nations, and to appoint U.S. ambassadors (Article II, Section 2). These powers gave the president (1) the consequent right to recognize specific foreign governments officially as legitimate players, and (2) the duty to represent the nation abroad.

chief diplomat *The president's role as manager of U.S. relations with other countries.*

Despite the Founders' goals, for "most of our history the president has been the 'sole organ' of foreign relations."[3] The Senate's power of "advice and consent" over treaties and appointments, however, requires presidents to take its wishes into account. Battles for Senate approval of treaties—such as Woodrow Wilson's attempt to secure U.S. involvement in the League of Nations, Jimmy Carter's attempt to return control of the Panama Canal to the Panamanians, and Bill Clinton's efforts in securing NAFTA—required those presidents to negotiate with Congress. In foreign policy, the president remains in the driver's seat, but "the Congress [is] the rear wheels, indispensable and usually obliged to follow, but not without substantial braking power."[4] (Chapter 21 examines the making of foreign policy.)

15-1c Roles Based on Constitutional Duties

Another set of roles, only indirectly mentioned in the Constitution, trace their origin and importance largely to forces outside of the Constitution itself. The presidential system combines two roles that are separated in many governmental systems. The president is not only the functional head of government, responsible for managing government operations, but is also the *symbol* of government, national unity, and the nation's heritage.

Chief of State

As **chief of state,** the president functions to "receive Ambassadors and other public Ministers" (Article II, Section 3). Like the British monarchy, the president symbolically represents the country at state funerals and serves as a spokesperson for national aspirations and ideals. Presidents are often known by the grand goals they express for the nation. John F. Kennedy's "New Frontier"; Lyndon Johnson's "Great Society"; George H. Bush's "Kinder, Gentler Nation," "A Thousand Points of Light," and "New World Order"; and Bill Clinton's "New Covenant," and George W. Bush's "Compassionate Conservatism" are a few recent examples. Presidents may ask their vice presidents to take on some of these tasks, but they cannot delegate the symbolic aspect of being chief of state. Television has dramatically expanded the powers of symbolic leadership as Americans increasingly see the president and/or the First Lady greet foreign dignitaries, light the national Christmas tree, throw out the first baseball at the World Series, and honor the Super Bowl or Olympic victors.

chief of state *The role of the president as the symbolic leader of the country, representing the United States at official events and embodying national goals and aspirations.*

At times of national crisis, the president's symbolic leadership is very important for diminishing fears and fostering healing. Shortly after the 1995 bombing of a federal building in Oklahoma City, President Bill Clinton was on television to assure the American public that this was an isolated incident. A few days later, he represented the grief of the nation by attending a prayer meeting for the victims.

The president's domination of the media as a national symbol is not complete. The media came under dual pressure when the decision on the civil case in the O. J. Simpson murder trial came in the middle of President Clinton's State of the Union Message. The lure of breaking news associated with a media superstar as opposed to a political speech revealed the penchant of modern media for drama and timeliness. ABC ran a large-print on-screen message about the verdict, while CNN and MSNBC chose covering the verdict over airing the president's speech.

The president's image as a unifying symbol has political benefits for the occupants of the White House. Presidents "frequently relish the practice of cloaking blatantly political goals in the magisterial robes of the Chief of State."[5] President Clinton used the Oklahoma bombing to express concern about the divisive impact of talk radio and paramilitary militias on American society. Although the link between talk radio, militias, and the bombing was hazy, President Clinton had become the favorite whipping boy for some of the most popular talk-radio hosts and the symbol of despised government for many members of the militias.

President George W. Bush forcefully expressed the grief of the nation after the terrorist attacks on the World Trade Center and the Pentagon and became the "mourner-in-chief." He used his heightened popularity to promote his anti-terrorism agenda.

Chief Legislator

chief legislator *The extra constitutional role of the president in defining problems worthy of legislative action and suggesting the preferred legislative solution.*

presidential program *The package of policy initiatives proposed by a president for legislative or administrative action.*

State of the Union Message *The annual message to Congress in which the president lays out the presidential legislative agenda. Nineteenth-century presidents sent a written message, while modern presidents personally promote their policy goals.*

While the Constitution indicates that the president "shall from time to time give the Congress information on the State of the Union, and recommend to their Consideration such Measures as he shall judge necessary and expedient" (Article II, Section 3), the Founders did not intend the president to be the **chief legislator.** Presidents were expected to execute policies largely conceived and passed by Congress; yet they were to play only a limited role in the legislative arena.

Contemporary presidents, however, find themselves in the thick of the legislative game. The differing perspectives among members of Congress mean that their policy agendas often lack focus and coherence. The success of the Republican Congress's Contract with America in focusing the national agenda attracted significant attention because it was unique. The **presidential program** ordinarily provides the more integrated set of legislative proposals, designed to solve America's problems as the president sees them.

The president's constitutionally mandated **State of the Union Message**—delivered to Congress and televised to the nation each January—outlines where the nation stands and where the president feels it should be going. This general statement is followed by a more detailed yearly budget proposal and other policy statements. A president attempts to set much of the agenda for Congress and is judged by the ability to do so and see it passed. The right to veto legislation passed by Congress was initially designed primarily to protect the president from congressional threats to the office.[6] Now it allows the president to play a significant role. Even at the beginning of the legislative game, the threat of a veto can be used to thwart unwanted legislation, but more often it is used as a bargaining tool. Given the difficulty of overriding a veto (a two-thirds vote in both houses is needed), Congress is generally willing to compromise with the president.

President George W. Bush placed tax cuts on the public agenda during the 2000 campaign and made them an integral part of his State of the Union message. It is not surprising that, with the Republican majority in both houses, tax cuts were his first legislative victory. The President's re-election and Republican gains in both houses of Congress in 2004 solidified his ability to define the issues the national government would emphasize.

15-1d Extraconstitutional Roles: Going Beyond the Rule Book

party leader *The president's informal status as the spokesperson and agenda setter for his or her political party.*

As the only nationally elected official and the most visible representative of his or her party, the president is the **party leader**. Even though the president holds no formal party office and often lacks the resources to control the actions of other party members, this is a presidential role. Presidents usually determine the national party chairpersons but have little say over state and local leaders. The increasing nationalization of the parties could expand the president's power by building a party team on whom the president can depend (see Chapter 8). The president exerts little influence over the choice of congressional party leaders, but those leaders generally become presidential policy spokespersons. Presidents generally have more success with Congress shortly after their election, losing some of their advantage as their term continues. Presidents find it easier to influence the votes of fellow party members in Congress (see Figures 15-1 and 15-2) because "Members of the president's party know that if they make him look bad, they also make themselves and their party look bad."[7] Congressional party leaders traditionally serve as the president's advocates in Congress in spite of their personal preferences. As one leader put it, "I do my arguing in the huddle, but when the signals are called [by the president], the argument ends. My only idea is to get the ball over the line."[8]

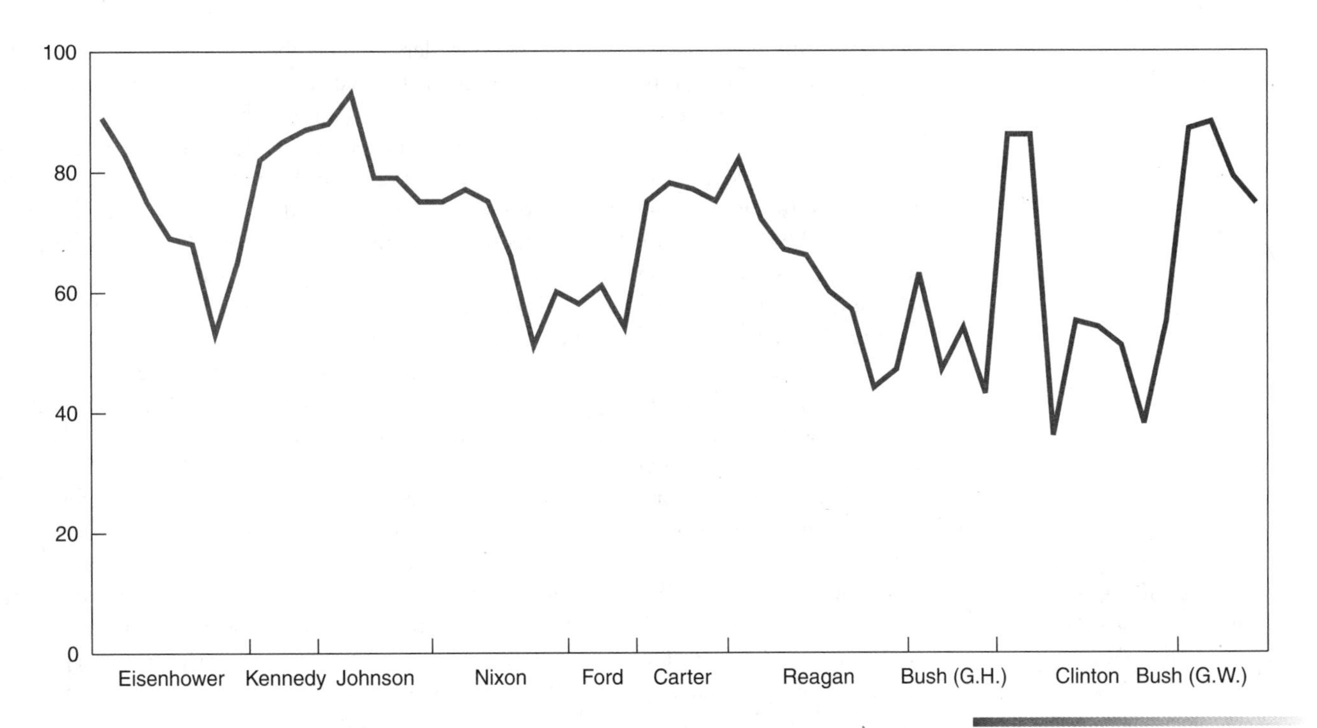

Figure 15-1
The Long-term Pattern of Presidential Support from Congress

Source: Congressional Quarterly Almanac (Washington, D.C.: Congressional Quarterly, Inc., 2002), p. B-6.

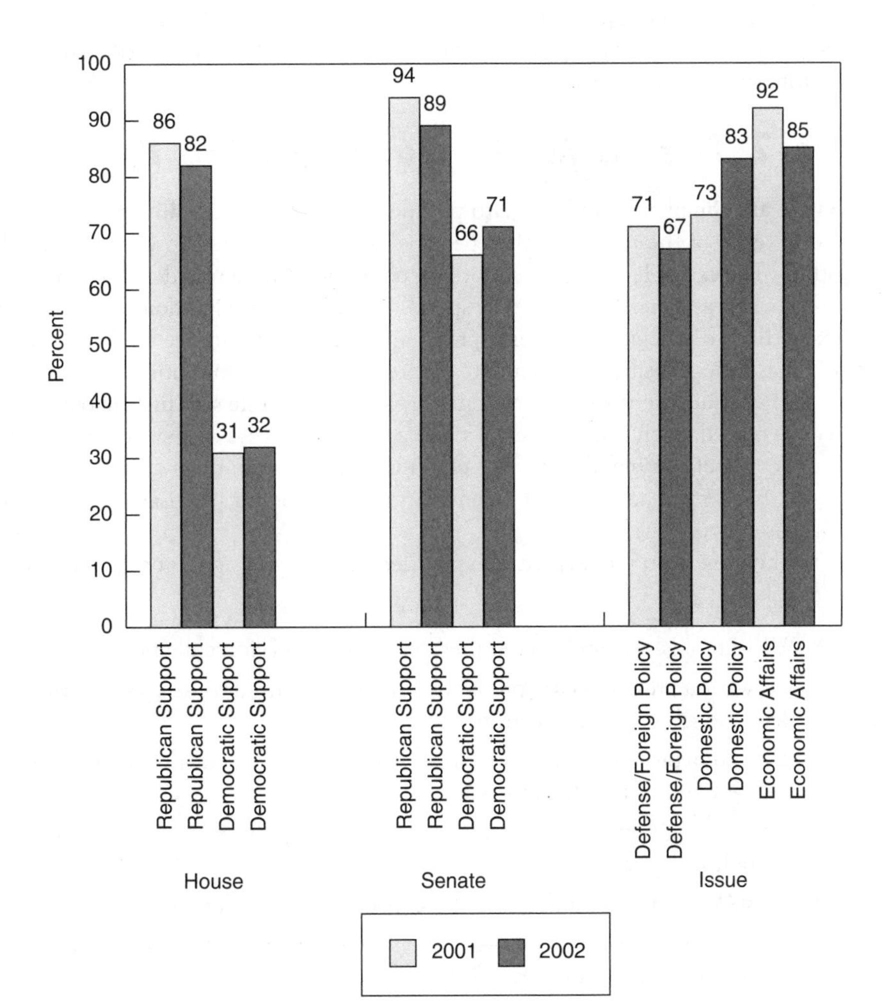

Figure 15-2
The Demographics of President Bush's Support in Congress

Source: Congressional Quarterly Almanac (Washington, D.C.: Congressional Quarterly, Inc., 2002), p. B-14.

The willingness of congressional party leaders and members to follow the president's initiative blindly has waned in recent years. In the battle over the 1991 budget, then-House Republican whip Newt Gingrich (R-Ga.) was (through his party position) given the task of lining up Republican votes for President George H. Bush's budget plan. However, he boldly asserted that "the whip's office is closed on this vote,"[9] and he joined the majority of Republicans in opposing the plan. Despite presidential displeasure, Gingrich maintained his party position, and defecting Republicans felt no presidential payback. In a seeming reprise in 1993, House Democratic whip David E. Bonior (D-Mich.) and House majority leader Richard A. Gephardt (D-Mo.) broke with President Bill Clinton on the North American Free Trade Agreement without any lasting effect.

The president remains the key partisan coalition builder, even in an age of declining partisanship. Presidents retain a number of concrete rewards that they can promise wavering supporters. Few members of Congress are willing to subject themselves to potential presidential sanctions unless absolutely necessary.

Presidential coalition building extends beyond American shores. During the post-World War II division of the world into communist and noncommunist sectors, the American role in world economy and political order made the president the **leader of the free world.** With the collapse of communism in Eastern Europe and the rise of state-sponsored terrorism, the U.S. president retained the role of international spokesperson on foreign policy and leader of Western alliances such as NATO (North Atlantic Treaty Organization). World leaders accepted President George H. Bush's leadership of the coalition opposing Iraq's 1990 invasion of Kuwait. President Clinton followed this course, attempting to create international coalitions to solve the problems in Somalia and Bosnia. George W. Bush sought to create a coalition behind his attempt to reduce the threat of weapons of mass destruction and change the regime in Iraq, recognizing that going it alone was not popular with the public or consistent with American traditions. His "coalition of the willing" was a pale comparison to his father's broader coalition, reducing the legitimacy of his Iraqi initiative.

leader of the free world *The president's position as spokesperson and coordinator of joint efforts by the noncommunist nations.*

15-2 The Game of Coordinating Roles

There are complexity and range to presidential tasks. Historically, presidents have varied in terms of the roles that they personally emphasize and those that they delegate to others. For example, some relish foreign policy roles (commander-in-chief, chief diplomat), whereas others would rather spend their time satisfying domestic demands (chief executive, chief legislator). Some presidents take full advantage of their power sources, whereas others hesitate to dominate all areas of government action.

The requirement that a president play a particular role says little about *how* that role will be played. Each role can be played in a number of ways. For example, a president can use the role of commander-in-chief either to bully other nations or as the basis for diplomacy. As party leader, the president can either promote partisan advantage or make bipartisan cooperation easier.

The American public gives the president conflicting signals on how to play the various roles:

- We want a gentle and decent president who is also forceful and decisive.
- We want a programmatic president who is committed to issues but who is also practical enough to make necessary compromises.
- We want a president who will lead us with new ideas, yet who will also listen to what we want and not push us too far.
- We want a statesmanlike president who is above politics but who can also succeed in the political game.
- We seek out a "common man" and expect an uncommon performance.
- We reward ambiguity on issues and public relations skill by presidential candidates, but we expect directness in office.

- We need a president who will pull us together as a society, yet who will make tough decisions on priorities.[10]

These paradoxical demands probably frustrate presidents, but they also allow them the freedom of knowing that they can't please everyone.

Just as the real stars in many games can play a number of positions well, so must successful presidents move from one role to the next with ease. Presidents who can play only one role well, by either ignoring or stumbling in other roles, set themselves up for broader failure. *The public expects competency across the board.* Presidential success requires blending and coordination among the various roles. Strength in playing one role may well increase success in another area, while an obvious weakness in the performance of one presidential responsibility threatens to undermine other areas.

Jimmy Carter's success as chief diplomat in getting the Camp David Accords (between Egypt and Israel) signed broke the logjam in Congress for some of his domestic policy and helped him to play the chief legislator role. His later failures—as chief diplomat and commander-in-chief—to secure the return of the hostages in Iran crippled his role as party chief and eventually contributed to his defeat for reelection.

Ronald Reagan achieved a number of early policy victories by focusing his efforts on limited aspects of the presidential job such as budget and tax concerns. Other realms were delegated or ignored. When his staff admitted that they did not even wake him to participate in a potentially dangerous confrontation with Libya, President Reagan was forced to engage himself in a greater range of policy. As competing demands—particularly in the international realm—intruded, he was compelled to spread himself more thinly.

President George H. Bush experienced early problems with Congress and the public, but once the Persian Gulf War began, his success as commander-in-chief enhanced his image as party leader and his success as chief legislator. The success was not permanent. As public attention shifted to more domestic concerns, Bush's almost single-minded emphasis on foreign policy turned into a detriment, and his public support dropped precipitously.

Bill Clinton struggled to reach his stride in the presidency. Demands for action covered a variety of policy areas. He experienced some impressive legislative success with his budget, NAFTA, and narrow issues such as liberalized family leave policy, federal funding for abortion, and a national motor-voter registration law. Other broader initiatives, such as his economic stimulus package and health care reform, had tougher sledding. As foreign policy crises began to overshadow Clinton's domestic agenda, his popularity plummeted and the public feared he had lost direction. The 1994 Republican sweep of Congress was widely interpreted as a negative midterm report card on the Clinton presidency. Clinton expressed frustration with the demands and public expectations of the job:

> The primary difference between this job and the job I had when I was governor is that sometimes . . . feel that I get behind the eight ball and I can't get out from under it . . . It's not easy to reach out directly to the people and cut through the cacophony of noise and rhetoric . . . It's always frustrating to feel that you're misunderstood. That people have an impression of who you are, what you believe, or what you're trying to do that is not quite accurate.[11]

The Clinton presidency rallied a bit with the passage of welfare reform and the presentation of a series of budgets with enough surpluses to begin paying down the national debt. Despite severe partisan disagreement over impeachment, a semblance of cooperation developed over some issues.

George W. Bush's ascension to the presidency after a contested election and the near even partisan split in Congress threatened to cripple his presidency, but he marched forward successfully, claiming a mandate for tax cuts. Moderate Republicans and later the unprecedented shift of partisan control of the Senate to the Democrats required him to emphasize compromise on issues such as health care and campaign finance reform. With the return of Republican control of both Houses of Congress after the 2002 election, President Bush's potential for success with Congress increased. The results of the 2004 election emboldened his claim to a mandate (see Box 15-1).

Box 15–1 A Bird in the Hand

In his first public reaction to his 2004 election victory, President George W. Bush was not shy about claiming a mandate for his plans to reform Social Security, simplify the tax code, fight the war of terror, curb lawsuits, and continue with the reconstruction of Iraq. His words were clear:

> I earned capital in this campaign, political capital, and now I intend to spend it. . . .When you win, there is . . . a feeling the people have spoken and embraced your point of view. . . . I really didn't come here to hold the office, just to say 'Gosh, it was fun to serve.' I came here to get some things done.[a]

a. Quoted in Marc Sandalow, "Bush Claims Mandate, Sets 2nd Term Goals," *San Francisco Chronicle*, November 5, 2004.

15-3 Presidential Power: Growth and Specification

The twentieth century has been called the "age of executive ascendancy." The increased number of crises requiring decisive governmental action has contributed to increased presidential power. A shortening of reaction time to crises and other developments, due to new communications technologies, has fueled this tendency. The focus of public attention is on the federal government as the primary arena for action. Most modern presidents take an expansive view of the presidential role (see Box 15-2: Presidents Describe Their Role in the Political Game). Other institutions of government, especially Congress and the federal courts, have granted presidents expanded legal rights, staff resources, and powers. Nevertheless, the other two branches have also attempted to define more specifically what the president can and cannot do.

15-3a Expanding the President's Role in the Game

A number of milestones mark the expansion of the president's role at the center of the political game. Crisis periods had always provided presidents with the rationale for expanding their powers. Abraham Lincoln was a president who bypassed Congress and used **executive orders** to carry out some of his wishes. Later presidents continued to use this power.

executive order *A rule or regulation issued by the president without the formal approval of Congress but having the force of law.*

Woodrow Wilson took an active role in foreign policy making during World War I. He unsuccessfully challenged the Senate to approve his concept of the League of Nations (the forerunner of the United Nations). In the process, he established the president as the nation's primary spokesperson on international events.

Control over federal expenditures is a crucial tool for affecting government. Prior to 1921, each department of government independently sent its budget request to the appropriate congressional committee. No one took responsibility for an integrated national budget, which made it difficult to choose among priorities. The Budget Act of 1921 created the centralized presidential budgeting process and made the president the key player in the distribution of public resources. It required each department to clear its proposals with the White House and allowed the president to present Congress a budget for the total government. The **Office of Management and Budget (OMB)** (originally called the Bureau of the Budget) was created to help the president with the task of budget development and coordination.

Office of Management and Budget (OMB) *The agency of the Executive Office of the President supporting the development of the president's budget.*

The Great Depression, beginning in 1929, revealed the need for an activist federal government. Franklin Roosevelt ran on the promise of reversing Herbert Hoover's policy of letting the economy correct itself. Roosevelt's election was seen as a mandate for presidential leadership. He set the stage for public expectations of modern presidents as unrivaled national leaders.

Box 15–2 *Presidents Describe Their Role in the Political Game*

Perspectives of contemporary presidents can be traced to outlooks expressed by their predecessors. Most modern presidents would agree more with Abraham Lincoln and Theodore Roosevelt than with William Howard Taft.

The President's Prerogative to Take Extreme Action to Preserve the Game

> My oath to preserve the Constitution. . . imposed upon me the duty of preserving, by every indispensable means, that government . . . measures otherwise unconstitutional might become lawful to the preservation of the Constitution through the preservation of the nation. (Abraham Lincoln, letter to A. G. Hodges, 1864)

The Restricted President: Deferring to the Rule Book

> The president can exercise no power which cannot be fairly and reasonably traced to some specific grant of power.[b]

The President as a Powerful Steward: Seeking to Control the Game on Behalf of the Spectators

> Every executive officer in a high position was a steward of the people bound actively and affirmatively to do all he could for the people . . . My belief was that it was not only his [the president's] right but his duty to do anything that the needs of the Nation demanded unless such action was forbidden by the Constitution or the laws.[a]

a. President Theodore Roosevelt, *The Autobiography of Theodore Roosevelt* (New York: Scribner's, 1924), 197, 357.
b. President William Howard Taft, *Our Chief Magistrate and His Powers* (New York: Columbia University Press, 1916), 138.

Roosevelt could not carry out his expanded tasks without help. The creation of the Executive Office of the President (EOP) in 1939 dramatically increased the advisers and aides available to monitor and manage the agencies of the federal government. New federal programs required an expanded federal bureaucracy to administer them. The ensuing bureaucracy is studied in Chapter 16.

The spread of national news coverage and the arrival of the electronic media (radio and television) made the presidency "the most visible national office...always in the news."[12] Visibility and access to the public's mind made the president a more serious force with which to reckon.

John Kennedy, and especially Lyndon Johnson, expanded the role of the presidency as the domestic agenda setter. Johnson's *Great Society* program outlined the key domestic policies of the 1960s. Much of Johnson's time and energy was spent, however, on the conflict in Vietnam. His deep involvement in day-to-day tactical decisions (such as personally picking bombing sites) and his willingness to bypass Congress created concerns about the proper role of each branch of government in the control of military initiatives.

Richard Nixon centralized policy making and policy implementation in the White House, often bypassing executive agencies that might place obstacles in the way. President Nixon also renewed the presidential practice of selectively not spending funds appropriated by Congress (see Chapter 13 for a discussion of this strategy).

Changing the Rules to Restrain Presidents

Presidential power did not grow without criticism or attempts to check it. Republican reaction to the domination of politics by four-term Democratic president Franklin Roosevelt led to the 22nd Amendment, which limits presidents to two terms in office. Frustration with the gradual enhancement of presidential powers that allowed presidential initiatives such as making war led to charges of an "imperial presidency."[13]

The Watergate scandal, involving use of presidential authority to cover up interference with the 1972 elections, reinforced the image that presidents and their staffs sometimes view themselves as above the law, and pressure grew to remove President Richard Nixon from office. All games include basic rules that, if transgressed, make the individual ineligible for further play; the potential for ejection by a referee or other participants keeps most players in line. Most elected and appointed officials in the United States do, however, either serve fixed terms in office or remain until they decide to retire. The inability to eject officials at will protects all officials from being punished for making unpopular decisions—but it can also protect individuals who have transgressed the rules.

impeachment *The formal bringing of charges against a government official that could lead to that official's removal from office.*

Impeachment is a quasi-legal procedure for removing public officials from office. Presidents, vice presidents, federal judges, and all civil officials can be removed from office if found guilty of an impeachable offense. In the strict use of the word, impeachment only means the bringing of charges, not the actual removal of someone from office. For federal officials in the executive and judicial branches, the House of Representatives brings the charges and the Senate then sits as a court and decides on innocence or guilt. A two-thirds vote in each house of Congress is then required to remove the individual from office. Richard Nixon was eventually charged with impeachable offenses by the House but resigned before being tried by the Senate (see Box 15-3: Throwing Players Out of the Game). President Bill Clinton's reckless personal life and his willingness to lie about it led to impeachment charges by the House, but he avoided conviction in the Senate.

Congress reacted to the image of an unrestrained president with a new set of rules designed to restrain presidential power. In addition to the War Powers Resolution of 1973, the Congressional Budget and Impoundment Act of 1974 created the Congressional Budget Office to analyze the president's budget. The new budget procedure also

Box 15-3 *Throwing Players Out of the Game*

Impeachment is not designed to remove political opponents from the game but rather to punish individuals for treason, bribery, and other high crimes and misdemeanors committed while in office. Considerable disagreement arises over the definition of impeachable offenses, and the actions of some House and Senate members may be politically motivated.

Ten federal judges, three presidents, and one cabinet member have been formally charged with impeachable offenses by the House, with only four convictions (all judges) by the Senate. Only three presidents have faced a serious impeachment challenge. In 1868 President Andrew Johnson, the unpopular administrator of post-Civil War Reconstruction policies, challenged the Tenure in Office Act, which required congressional approval to remove appointees subject to the advice-and-consent procedure. Political opponents in the House charged him with "high crimes and misdemeanors," but after 11 weeks of deliberation, the Senate came up one vote short of the two-thirds needed for conviction.

In 1974, the House Committee on the Judiciary charged President Richard Nixon with the impeachable offense of obstructing justice by attempting to cover up illegal activities. This was in the wake of a break-in at the Democratic Party headquarters in the Watergate office building by employees of Nixon's reelection committee. Republican Richard Nixon had made a career out of being a tough partisan. Not surprisingly, he had generated harsh feelings among many Democrats, who disliked him as an individual as well as disliking his policies. The offenses were blatant enough that other Democrats and some Republicans felt that Nixon clearly deserved impeachment. When tapes of private White House conversations indicated obstruction of justice, many more of Nixon's fellow Republicans abandoned him. Facing almost certain impeachment by the Democrat-controlled House and probable conviction by the Senate, Richard Nixon resigned the presidency.

After it became clear that President Bill Clinton had engaged in inappropriate intimate activities in the White House with a young intern and then misled others about it, the House voted in 1998 largely along partisan lines to impeach President Clinton for lying about his personal relations with a White House intern. The trial in the Senate ended with a majority of senators voting largely along party lines supporting conviction, but the results were far from the two-thirds vote necessary for conviction.

revised the timetable for the budget process, allowing Congress earlier input. It also limited the president's right to refuse to spend funds appropriated by Congress.

With growing budget deficits, some participants believe that the president's tools for limiting spending have been curtailed too severely. Republicans have long argued for a line-item veto provision, which would allow the president to cancel specific expenditures in an approved budget. In passing that provision in 1995, Congress again strengthened the hand of the president. The shift turned out to be temporary when the Supreme Court struck down the line-item veto as unconstitutional. With a Democrat in the White House able to use it to promote his policy preferences, the Republicans in control of Congress lost much of their motivation to find a way to reinstate the line-item veto.

The Gramm-Rudman-Hollings Act (1985) attempted to limit both congressional and presidential authority by mandating a regular lowering of the deficit until a balanced budget would result in 1991. If target dates along the way were not met, procedures were in place for automatically making budget cuts. The act's limited success led to efforts to pass a balanced budget amendment to the Constitution in 1995, which would require the federal government to spend no more than it receives. The amendment passed the House but failed in the Senate. Republicans promised to attempt passage again.

Additionally, an increasingly aggressive Congress has used existing rules to thwart presidential action. The advice-and-consent role has been activated more frequently in recent years to withhold approval of Supreme Court nominees and other key presidential appointees. President Reagan had trouble gaining approval of his nominees to the highest court. President George H. Bush was rebuffed when he nominated John Tower as Secretary of Defense. A number of President Clinton's initial cabinet and sub-cabinet nominees also had to be withdrawn due to senatorial opposition. George W. Bush expended considerable political capital in the drawn-out battles to get his openly conservative attorney general (John Ashcroft) and secretary of the interior (Gale Norton) confirmed. He also was forced to withdraw his nomination for secretary of labor due to senatorial opposition.

Legislation has also been passed either to force presidents to take actions that they would not have taken on their own or to limit certain White House actions by making them illegal. For example, in its attempt to limit presidential support for the Nicaraguan Contras, Congress passed specific legislation designed to restrain the White House (see Box 15-4: The Iran-Contra Affair and the Limits of Rules).

Under the separation of powers doctrine, Congress stands watch over the actions of the executive branch. It requires regular reports (see Figure 15-3) and at times launches full-scale investigations of executive branch activities. The possibility of a congressional investigation dampens but does not eliminate presidential temptation to bend or break the rules.

Box 15–4 *The Iran-Contra Affair and the Limits of Rules*

The Reagan administration's desire to financially support the anti-communist resistance movement in Nicaragua (the "Contras") was not shared by many members of Congress. Beginning in 1982, Representative Edward Boland (D-Mass.) received congressional support for a series of amendments intended to prevent covert executive branch support of the Contras. Congress felt that the rules were made clear by those amendments, but a number of White House staff members—primarily National Security Council staff member Lieutenant Colonel Oliver North—redefined these rules to meet their own goals. They proceeded to use their official positions to encourage private contributions to the Contras and to sell arms to the Iranians, giving the profits to the Contras. Furthermore, they lied about these actions to Congress and the American public. The congressional investigations and court cases on these actions revealed a contempt for congressional rules by many in the White House and indicated the difficulty of assigning blame for illegal actions.

Figure 15-3
The Growth of Department Reports Required by Congress

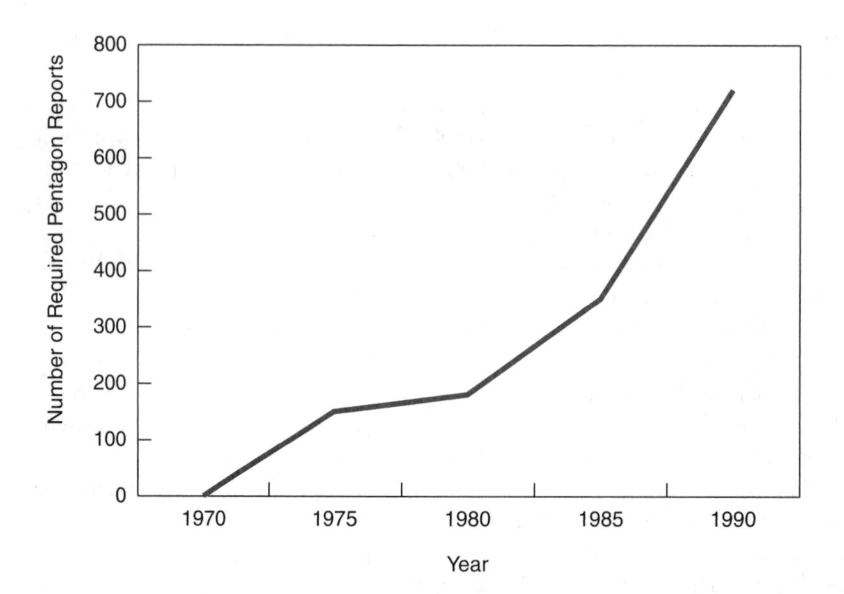

15-4 Presidential Policy Strategies

Presidents dominate the policy process by setting the agenda, controlling information, and capitalizing on their political resources. Effective presidents use their power resources strategically, pick their battles carefully, and keep an eye on their public support.

15-4a Setting the National Agenda

At any one point in time, hundreds of issues vie for governmental attention:

> Of the big games, the first for any president is the agenda game...The effectiveness of the presidency and the capacity of any president to lead depends on focusing the nation's political attention and its energies on two or three top priorities.[14]

By using their access to the media, presidents can place issues and problems before the public. Their strategy is obvious: by choosing the terrain of battle, they increase the likelihood that their policy priorities will win. Theoretically, and historically, the White House team is much more unified than Congress, which has multiple leaders and competing chambers. By taking the president's lead and presenting a unified set of priorities, the White House usually presents an image of strength and well-thought-out policy positions. After the 1994 elections, however, the Republicans in Congress presented their own agenda (the Contract with America), and they forced President Bill Clinton to react to it. Polls indicated that voters began to look to Congress to take the lead in solving the nation's problems. The enhanced expectation of Congress was maintained through the Clinton and George W. Bush presidencies, helping to share some of the blame for inaction.[15]

15-4b Controlling Information

Information is the raw material of the policy process and the basis of considerable power. The American president, as the leader of the federal bureaucracy, controls the largest and most effective information-gathering mechanism in the world. Executive branch agencies generate an almost endless stream of studies, policy analyses, and data on program performance and technological developments—both as part of their legal mandate and at the request of the White House. Presidents use their information advantage to persuade other political players to follow their lead.

__executive privilege__ A president's right to withhold information from the other branches of government in order to guarantee receiving candid advice from presidential advisers or to protect national security.

Through the tradition of **executive privilege,** presidents have long claimed the right to acquire confidential information from their staffs and to control sensitive national security secrets. Presidents often deny Congress and the public access to certain of the information on which they base decisions. Confidential discussions with foreign leaders, the results of covert intelligence gathering, and frank assessments of political advisers shape presidential decisions but are seldom made public. The courts have upheld a president's right to executive privilege but have maintained that it is not absolute. Executive privilege must be balanced against such concerns as the right of Congress and the courts to evidence of criminal activity[16] (see Box 15-5: New Technology and the Undoing of White House Information Control).

Box 15-5 New Technology and the Undoing of White House Information Control

New technology is sometimes responsible for a loss of White House control over information, as the following incidents demonstrate.

The Taped Record

Richard Nixon installed a tape-recording system in the Oval Office to capture his presidency for history. When a staff member let it slip to the congressional committee staff investigating the Watergate break-in that tapes of White House meetings existed, the revelation unleashed demands for access to these tapes. After an appeal to the Supreme Court, the tapes (minus a crucial 18-min. section "mistakenly" erased) were the basis for some of the impeachment charges brought by the House of Representatives. Without such taped evidence, Richard Nixon probably would not have had to resign the presidency.

The Computer's Memory

By the 1980s, paper shredders were customary equipment in many government offices. After an internal investigation had begun into possible illegal activities associated with aiding the Contras and exchanging arms for hostages, Lieutenant Colonel Oliver North spent many hours in his National Security Council office in the White House shredding sensitive papers. They could have linked him and other White House staff to the Iran-Contra affair. The independent White House investigation team (the Tower Commission) thought that it had reached a dead end until someone discovered that North's computerized word processing system had backup file copies for many of the shredded documents. As one writer noted, "Computers have an unnerving habit of remembering what you wrote even after you tell them to forget it."[a] The supposedly deleted but simultaneously backed-up records were used by the Tower Commission, Congress, and the courts to assign much of the guilt. Another writer cautioned:

> [The lesson from this] is not that the country can rely on computerized records of this and future administrations; the lesson is that those being investigated were too technologically illiterate to cover their tracks by purging their files. No one can count on future officials being that dumb.[b]

The Open Mikes

We have come to expect presidents to be seasoned performers in public. Public events are carefully scripted and presented to create the most positive image, but some of the same technologies that allow presidents to expand their public relations reach can also be their undoing. While testing his mike for a radio broadcast, Ronald Reagan joked, "My fellow Americans, I'm pleased to tell you today that I've signed legislation that will outlaw Russia forever. We begin bombing in five minutes." The public furor over joking about nuclear war resulted in a negative image of Reagan both in the United States and among foreign leaders.[c]

George H. Bush also was tripped up by an open mike. For a number of months, he used the new teleconferencing facility in the White House to hold press conferences with specialized audiences. The image of a freewheeling question-and-answer period implied presidential competence and openness. That the sessions involved planted questions and scripted answers came to light when Bush complained into an open mike after a session, "We lost everything! . . . We've got to get this sorted out." Through the mike, an aide was also heard to say, "They flip-flopped the questions."[d] From that point on, some of the positive impact of these events was diminished.

George W. Bush seemingly failed to learn from his father about open mikes. During the campaign, he made a snide and crude side comment about a top *New York Times* reporter that was picked up by the C-SPAN microphones and became a lead story the next day.[e]

---

a. Alan Paller, "Deleting Those Embarrassing Files...Completely," *Government Executive*, February 1991, 50.

b. "Memories," *Government Computer News* 16 (April 24, 1987): 30.

c. Charles Press and Kenneth Verberg, *American Politicians and Journalists* (Glenview, IL: Scott, Foresman/Little, Brown, 1988), 128.

d. John E. Yang, "Bush's Unintended Postscript: Open Mike Reveals Group Q & A Sessions Are Far from Spontaneous," *Washington Post*, November 27, 1991, A4.

e. http://www.snopes.com/politics/bush/bushcuss.asp

Box 15-6 The President's Plane Is Leaving

Ronald Reagan's press handlers did an outstanding job of making full use of symbolic presidential events. Virtually every Friday afternoon, the press was trooped out to the edge of the White House Rose Garden to observe the president's departure for Camp David. The media, who were often getting their first glimpses of the president that day, felt considerable pressure to get some footage for the evening news. The stage was set for a perfect media event.

The presidential helicopter stands with its engines running, awaiting the chief executive. On cue and dressed for the part, Ronald Reagan steps out of the White House for the 100-yard walk. In cowboy boots, riding pants, and a Pendleton shirt, the president exudes youth and vigor, dispelling any thoughts of his advanced age. Immediately, the media begin yelling questions, but Reagan's deafness, the distance at which the media are kept, and the hum of the helicopter limit press aides' fear that Reagan will spoil the scene by making an impromptu statement.

The other members of the entourage also play their parts well. Aides in three-piece suits and carrying briefcases silently indicate that this is a working weekend and that Americans will be getting their money's worth out of the president. Nancy Reagan, dressed in her finest, arrives with the dog, sending the message that "anyone who loves dogs can't be all bad."

The short trip to the helicopter involves a serious pantomime. The president cups his ear, straining to hear a reporter's question but then points to his watch and then to the helicopter, indicating that he does not have the time to answer for fear that the helicopter will take off without him. Of course, the helicopter is completely under his command, and its crew would wait for even the longest interchange with the media. A jaunty wave from the steps of the helicopter completes the desired image of a young-acting and vigorous president, willing to be accessible to the media but under tremendous time pressure to carry out the important business of the country, even on Friday evening, when most Americans are preparing for a relaxing weekend.

news leaks *A government official's deliberate disclosure of secret information to embarrass others or to promote a particular policy.*

The prestige and authority connected to the idea that the president knows something they don't know encourages other decision makers to defer to the president's wishes, especially with regard to national security and foreign policy. **News leaks** of supposedly unauthorized information from the White House are often used as trial balloons to test public reaction to possible alternatives. If the press and/or public reaction is negative, the president can disavow the information without risking a tarnished reputation. As President George H. Bush's director of the Office of Management and Budget put it:

> If you have diversity of views in the policy debate, you're going to have winners and losers. Winners leak out of pride in what they have done. Losers leak to try to change policies.[17]

An extensive staff of press aides labors to make the president look good in the media and to stifle negative coverage. Daily press briefings provide the White House interpretation of events and attempt to put a positive spin on stories. Information about the president is carefully managed, with direct media access to the president allowed only in controlled settings (see Box 15-6: The President's Plane Is Leaving). Arrival and departure ceremonies for world leaders, speeches, press conferences, and other formal events in which the president looks "presidential" are the staple of presidential coverage and enhance the aura of the presidency. New technology, especially television, has expanded the ability of presidents to communicate directly with the public.

Presidents have long seen technology as a way of expanding their power and influence by adapting relatively new technologies to political purposes. While seldom among the earliest adopters of technology, the White House has generally been more forward-looking than the other branches of government. Recognizing that information is a power resource, presidents have turned to new technology for both expanding their incoming

President Clinton took a page out of Ronald Reagan's media book. Each of his early morning jogging sessions had an agenda well beyond his physical fitness. The media was allowed to record the events and was often given the opportunity to ask a few questions, thus dispelling criticisms of an inaccessible president. On most mornings the president was accompanied by political and social activists whose support he needed for policy initiatives. The public got the impression of a president always working. With all the concern for security in an era of terrorism, a president jogging in public presents the image that he is not afraid and will not be held captive in the White House by a few crazy individuals. The very act of jogging reinforced the energy and youthfulness of President Clinton.

Both presidents Reagan and Clinton learned that simple functional events such as a presidential departure or a jog through the park can have public relations benefits. In the political game, no potential advantage can be overlooked.

President and Mrs. Reagan Waving from the Helicopter (Marine 1) on the White House Lawn
Courtesy Ronald Reagan Library

information resources and improving their ability to communicate with the public more effectively (see Table 15-1 and Box 15-7: Accessing the Electronic Presidency).

15-4c The "Nonpolitical" Politician

While public unease with politics leads to a desire for political leaders to be "above" politics, such a goal is unrealistic:

> Whatever else his qualities, the president needs to be a working politician who can work with or otherwise win over the Washington community.[18]

Presidents must be much more than good administrators who let the facts speak for themselves. They must pursue a variety of goals—whose correctness often cannot be proven by facts alone—through budgets, specific laws, and the authority to commit troops. Furthermore, presidents can only rarely use unilateral command decisions in which their wishes are carried out automatically. Most often, presidents must strike bargains and persuade other political players that what the president is asking them to do is what they really want to do.[19] One of President George H. Bush's key successes involved building a coalition of countries to oppose Iraq's invasion of Kuwait. President Reagan succeeded in overseeing the passage of his initial budget plan by reaching out to southern conservatives who joined ranks with his Republican supporters. The presidency is inherently a political office whose occupant must be a politician in the best sense of the word. Effective presidents build supportive coalitions through political strategies.

As bargainers, presidents have an advantage: "When the president says it is a deal, then it is a deal, while at the other end of Pennsylvania Avenue [Congress], it is very difficult for the leadership to deliver their part of the deal."[20] On key issues the White House

Table 15-1 Milestones in the High-Tech Presidency

1866	Andrew Jackson installs the White House's first telegraph
1879	Rutherford B. Hayes installs the first telephone in the White House
1924	Calvin Coolidge makes the first national presidential radio speech
1933	Franklin Roosevelt inaugurates his regular "fireside chats" on the radio
1939	Franklin Roosevelt makes the first presidential television appearance at the New York World's Fair
1945	Harry Truman allows audio recording of press conferences for later radio broadcast
1953	Dwight Eisenhower allows video recording of press conferences for later television broadcast
1958	NBC first broadcasts President Eisenhower in color
1960	Richard Nixon and John Kennedy participate in the first televised presidential campaign debates (black and white)
1961	John Kennedy initiates live televised news conferences
1965	Lyndon Johnson installs three television sets in the Oval Office to monitor the three networks
1977	Jimmy Carter attempts to recreate Roosevelt's fireside chats on television
1981	Ronald Reagan returns to using radio as a major method of communicating with the public by giving weekly radio addresses
1981	White House email system installed
1991	George H. Bush becomes the first president with a computer terminal in his office but shows little sign of using it
1993	Bill Clinton publishes his email address, and White House documents are made available on the Internet through a gopher server
1994	The Clinton White House establishes a home page on the web, allowing the transmission of text, sound, pictures, and video
2001	The George W. Bush White House launches a children's site, www.whitehousekids.gov
2004	Hackers attack the White House website

Source: Much of the information comes from Phil Patton, "Disk-Drive Democrats," *New York Times,* November 28, 1993, 7. Specific radio and television innovations are described in John Tebbel and Sarah Miles Watts, *The Press and the Presidency* (New York: Oxford University Press, 1985).

Box 15-7 *Accessing the Electronic Presidency*

Communication is the first step toward public acceptance of a president and his policies. Contemporary presidents have made this information and offices accessible via the Web, recognizing it as one more effective tool for communicating with the public.

Email address: President@Whitehouse.gov

Web: http://www.whitehouse.gov/

speaks with one voice, while it is often difficult to determine who speaks for Congress. House and Senate leaders, even when they come from the same party, often have different priorities and preferences. The White House can often deal with members of Congress one at a time and undermine any position taken by the congressional leadership.

Good politicians protect their power bases by monitoring their opponents and supporters and determining how particular actions will affect their support. Compromise between reasonable people holding diverging views is a practical necessity among politicians. The basis for effective compromise and bargaining begins with an understanding of the personal and political needs of opponents. Politicians solidify their support by rewarding supporters and either ignoring or punishing opponents. Wise politicians seldom close the door completely on today's opponents, since their support might be needed in the future.

In building a coalition to support a policy, presidents must often use their entire stock of power resources to prevail. These resources vary in terms of their method of application and cost to the president. The least expensive resources require little effort and are not depleted in the process of application. For example, if a congressperson or bureaucrat supports a presidential action on the basis of presidential authority, to gain that support may require only that the president remind the person of the constitutional or legislative basis of that authority. Personal trust in the president, based on the wisdom of past decisions, shared beliefs, and interpersonal skills, establishes the president's personal *leadership*. Creating trusting followers, however, requires considerable effort. Information advantages allow the president to understand the motivations of other players better and to present those bits of information that might persuade an individual to join the coalition.

Explicit rewards or sanctions—support or opposition to a policy position, or promises to do something *for* or *to* another player—are direct motivations. Rewards or sanctions are the most costly method of encouraging support because they are limited and, once used, often cannot be replaced. As wise politicians, presidents usually rely on the least costly power resources first and move to the more costly ones only when others fail (see Box 15-8: The Panama Canal Treaty: Textbook Coalition Building and Box 15-9: Presidential Power and Iraq).

Box 15-8 The Panama Canal Treaty: Textbook Coalition Building

In 1977 President Jimmy Carter signed a treaty with the Republic of Panama to transfer ownership of the Panama Canal, which had been under American control for seven decades, to Panama. The advice-and-consent provision of the Constitution required Carter to build a supporting coalition of at least two-thirds of the Senate. Carter began by asserting his authority as chief spokesperson for U.S. foreign policy but was still far short of the necessary votes. A number of meetings between the new president and senators were scheduled so that Carter could impress upon his guests his personal charm, skill, and resolve in the hope of building the trust needed for leadership.

Through speeches and personal meetings, the president began the process of persuasion. He played to the biases of liberal senators by pointing out that it was alien to American principles of freedom, liberty, and human rights to retain Panama as a virtual colony. To conservatives, he asserted that absolute American control was not vital to American defense interests. Still lacking sufficient votes, Carter began intensive bargaining, using a set of implied sanctions and explicit rewards. Senators were reminded that the White House would remember their unwillingness to support the president on this key issue. This reminder signaled to reluctant senators that the president might fail to support or might even block the legislator's policy plans in future rounds of the policy-making game. Also, the president could threaten to withhold support for the senator's next election effort.

One example illustrates the subtle use of presidential rewards. After holding out, Senator Dennis DeConcini (D-Ariz.) received two rewards: an amendment to the treaty that allowed military intervention to keep the canal open[a] and a private commitment by the federal government to purchase Arizona copper.[b] There is always a danger that, when rewards become public, other legislators will want something for themselves. Because reward concessions such as those given to Senator DeConcini came late in the process, when most senators were already publicly committed, the floodgates of additional demands were not opened, at least until the next time. In the end, President Carter's strategy of moving from cheap to expensive power resources worked, as the Senate approved the treaty by a small margin.

---

a. David Maxfield, "Senate Backs Turning Canal to Panama," *Congressional Quarterly Weekly Report* 16 (April 22, 1978): 951–52.

b. Donnie Radcliffe, "The Panama Gadfly," *Washington Post*, April 14, 1978, B1.

Box 15-9 Presidential Power and Iraq

Saddam Hussein's invasion of Kuwait in 1990 thrust America into a newly defined world leadership position and reinforced President George H. Bush's role as the leader of the free world. Despite America's claim that it won Desert Storm in 1991, Saddam Hussein stayed in power and according to many experts supported terrorism and stockpiled weapons of mass destruction. George W. Bush became convinced after the terrorist attacks in 2001 that Saddam Hussein remained a threat to the United States and attempted to build support for regime change through diplomatic pressure or military action.

The president attempted to exercise his power over this decision and secure approval for military intervention. In each of the following possible actions, what power strategy did the president use, authority, leadership, persuasion, or rewards/sanctions?

- The president rejects the necessity of having a formal declaration of war and asserts his right to commit troops.
- The president points out that the longer the United States waits, the more prepared the Iraqi military will be.
- The president indicates that he "has a long memory" and will be closely watching the voting by members of Congress.
- The president meets with members of Congress to show his resolve and to assure them of the seriousness with which he views the action and his commitment to it.
- The president points out that disunity at home sends a powerful signal to Iraq that America lacks commitment.

One of the president's most abiding tasks lies in building coalitions within Congress to support presidential legislative initiatives. Wise presidents begin with a natural coalition of supporters and then add to it through bargaining (see Box 15-10: You Have to Know When to Hold Them and Know When to Fold Them and Chapter 13 for discussions of coalition-building strategies). President Bill Clinton faced a coalition-building challenge with NAFTA (see Chapter 1). There was no clearly partisan natural coalition because the Democrats, who held a congressional majority, were split on the issue. President Clinton had to reach out to the Republicans and a number of wavering Democrats. He broadened the coalition by making a number of commitments of rewards directly related to the issue at hand. He offered Republican supporters some political cover by promising to encourage anti-NAFTA challengers not to use NAFTA support as a campaign issue in 1994 congressional races. He also revised the trade agreement to provide more favorable provisions for agricultural crops in districts of wavering supporters. Once success was assured, the bargaining stopped, and NAFTA won by a narrow margin.

Presidents walk a fine line in flexing their political muscles and advertising their political cleverness. Given the negative image of being a mere politician, presidents expend great effort downplaying the political aspects of their job. Symbolic events, such as greeting dignitaries in the White House Rose Garden and transmitting holiday messages, are designed to portray the president as above politics.

Too much of nonpolitical emphasis, however, hurts the president when the game calls for political astuteness. Presidents who are unable to get legislation through Congress or who are stymied by a resistant bureaucracy may not be using their political power effectively. They may be ignoring the political process or failing to use its time-honored strategies. Of course, not all failures rest on a president's shoulders. Some factors are beyond presidential control. Other players' actions, such as renewed congressional assertiveness, increased bureaucratic independence, and the expanded role of the media, can all reduce a president's potential for success.

15-4d Establishing Priorities

The range of government activities is so broad that no presidential administration can affect every detail of policy development and administration. Presidents must choose

Box 15–10 You Have to Know When to Hold Them and Know When to Fold Them

Background

Coalition building is a key strategy of the political game, especially for a president attempting to deal with a collective decision-making body such as Congress. The definition of winning in Congress is usually a matter of securing a majority of the votes in support of your position on a piece of legislation. Clever presidential players begin by determining whether a natural majority already exists for their policy initiative. Lacking a majority at that point, the next step is to win blocs of players to the president's side before engaging in the more labor- and resource-intensive one-on-one stage of the game. If successful in building a majority coalition with blocs of supporters, the president's team will urge an immediate vote. Lacking a majority, a president hopes for a delay in the game while lining up needed support.

Questions

Coalition building is a general strategy in politics. In the process of building a supporting coalition, a number of operational sub-strategies are used. In order to understand the process, we need to know the following:

- What are the various strategies of the coalition-building game?
- What are the most effective ways of using one's strategic resources?
- Who are the important players associated with each sub-strategy?
- How do players view the results of coalitions in different ways?

Analysis

In 1993 President Bill Clinton was faced with a number of different coalition-building tasks early in his presidency. In each case, both the president and members of Congress were the players. A primary battle was over Clinton's economic-stimulus plan. President Clinton, using the five coalition-building resources we have discussed, attempted to use the authority of his office, unleashed his personal leadership, and tried to persuade potential supporters that his position was right. He refrained from using rewards and sanctions until later.

The targets of his initial efforts were any members of Congress who would listen. If any one or a combination of these strategies had secured a majority, the president would have won this round of the game without wasting other strategic resources. However, after the first round, President Clinton still lacked the necessary congressional votes for his economic package, which faced two natural coalitions—most Democratic players favored the legislation and all Republicans opposed it. Clinton's next step was to solidify the Democrats as a bloc, but Democratic defectors denied him victory.

The president was the key player in this coalition-building game. The unresponsive Republicans had dealt themselves out, and President Clinton relegated them to the sidelines, limiting his bargaining to rewards for Democrats. Early supporters required little presidential attention; therefore his efforts involved focusing on wavering Democratic defectors. The president approached them one-on-one. This is a labor-intensive game with players targeted very carefully. After days of meetings, the White House knew the vote would be close. The outcome of the congressional game came down to the final moments. Just as the vote total in the House was deadlocked at 210–210, President Clinton focused his attention on freshman representative Marjorie Margolies-Mezvinsky (D-Pa.). Coming from a Republican constituency and having won her seat by the slimmest of margins, she had already announced her intention to vote against the proposal. As a freshman member, though, she also wanted to stay on the right side of the president—who was from her party—in fear of being targeted for sanctions. The pressure was intense. President Clinton eventually convinced Representative Margolies-Mezvinsky to change her vote in exchange for a side payment: the offer to hold an entitlement-spending conference in her district. When the final votes were counted, the president's economic proposal won with a minimum winning coalition. The economic stimulus round was over, but reverberations for other rounds at both the national and local levels would continue as a reminder of the price paid.

The results of this coalition differed depending on where one sat. For President Clinton, the victory was sweet. By winning a hot contest early in his presidency—especially without any Republican votes—he established himself as an effective player. As a numerical minority, the Republicans had to reassess

continued

Box 15-10 You Have to Know When to Hold Them and Know When to Fold Them

—Continued

their strategy. If the president could regularly win without their votes, they were effectively dealt out of the game. In future contests, President Clinton honed the bargaining lessons he had learned, and the Republicans decided to join the game.

The economic stimulus package victory was sweeter for President Clinton than for Representative Margolies-Mezvinsky. It turned out that supporting one's president can have its negative consequences. She immediately became the symbol of a member selling out her principles and constituents to a manipulative president. Although the president delivered on his commitment to hold a policy conference in her district, it was not enough. Office seekers clamored to oppose her in the next election, and Representative Margolies-Mezvinsky was dealt out of the congressional game after one term in the 1994 election.

The 1994 election dramatically changed the playing field for coalitions. Holding a majority in both chambers, the Republicans took a page from President Clinton's coalition playbook. They attempted to deal the president and his party out of the game by lining up winning coalitions without Democratic votes. On a number of the issues in the Republican Contract with America, this worked well, especially in the House. President Clinton then attempted to fight his way back in the game by attempting to build bipartisan coalitions.

their battles. The narrower the agenda, the more probable it is that a president will be able to marshal the resources needed to achieve his or her goals. In comparing President Clinton to President Reagan, two respected observers pointed out:

> Part of Clinton's problem with the Congress may be that, after citing the gamebook of President Reagan's first legislative victories as his strategic plan, the new president ignored three of its major elements: a single-minded attention to one subject, an intensive early effort to build a bipartisan coalition, and massive, unrelenting public salesmanship.[21]

Attempts by presidents to deal with issues in order of priority often fall victim to political reality and world events. The balance of power at opposite ends of Pennsylvania Avenue, which separates the White House from the Capitol Building, does tip at times. Congress may attempt to claim the initiative.

As mentioned earlier, most presidents find that much of their own personal agenda involves reacting to problems and issues not of their own making. President Carter did not *choose* to deal with the taking of hostages in Iran or with the Soviet invasion of Afghanistan. President George H. Bush was forced to react to Iraq's invasion of Kuwait and to the massive costs associated with the failed savings and loan organizations. President Clinton wanted to focus on domestic issues such as health care and the reinventing of government but had to spend much of his time on crises abroad. Early in his term, President George W. Bush was forced to expend considerable effort on recovering a U.S. crew and airplane forced down in China, taking time away from other policy initiatives. The September 11th, 2001 terrorist attacks pushed everything off of President Bush's immediate agenda and consumed much of the White House attention for months. Not all distractions from the president's agenda involve foreign policy. Domestic crises such as natural disasters or emerging problems obviously demand immediate presidential attention.

15-4e Presidential Power and Maintaining Spectator Support

Public support is an essential political resource for modern presidents. Popular presidents find that other political players are ready and willing to take the president's lead. On the other hand, presidents lacking public support are fair game for challenges from Congress, the bureaucracy, and the courts. The growth in public opinion polling technology means that presidents—and the public officials they hope to influence—have frequent and in-depth measures of citizen satisfaction with the incumbent president.

Most presidents enter office with a clean slate and a hopeful and supportive national constituency. Presidents are often granted a honeymoon period early in their terms. Criticism by the public and the media is muted at this point out of respect and anticipation. Within a few months, though, high expectations often give way to increased frustration as presidents deal with tough issues in which some citizens are winners and others are losers. Wise presidents recognize their impending popularity decline and attempt to make their biggest plays early in the game.

The public expects an almost superhuman president to act decisively to solve problems, while they simultaneously desire a leader with whom they can identify. National crises focus media attention on the president and provide an opportunity to reap public support through action. Foreign policy crises initially benefit presidents as citizens "rally around the flag."[22] President George H. Bush's public support declined following his budget battles with Congress, but it increased dramatically in 1991 with the onset of Operation Desert Storm. Public support again declined significantly after the peace treaty was signed. After that, the president was viewed as oblivious to the problems facing everyday Americans. On the other hand, the "political leverage deriving from this visibility is offset by the danger of becoming the scapegoat for national woes."[23] President Clinton's dramatic drop in popularity resulted from a variety of factors, one of which was overexposure. During his initial years in office, television cameras were allowed to follow a sweaty president into McDonald's for a Big Mac and to cover his admission to an MTV audience that he preferred briefs to boxer shorts.

> Clinton's biggest problem may be that he squandered the moral authority of the office he holds...People want a certain dignity and majesty in the presidency...[Clinton] has been so much with us that...when he's on television, people in airports don't even stop to see what he has to say...As a result of his stripping away the aura of the office, Clinton has often been out there without the trappings of the presidency to protect him.[24]

After the Oklahoma City bombing in 1995, the comforting public presence of President Clinton and the quick action by the FBI in identifying a suspect garnered immediate results. The president's ratings among the public increased significantly. President Clinton played a similar role after the shooting at Columbine High School, expressing national concern and grief.

Recognizing his less than brilliant ability to perform on television, George W. Bush took considerable efforts to "go to the people" with his tax cut plan and other initiatives. He used of mix of strategies to "look presidential" and at the same time appear human. Pictures of the president playing t-ball on the White House lawn were designed to soften his image.

Presidential popularity is affected by obvious examples of societal well being, such as economic indicators, and by clear measures of policy failures, such as battlefield deaths. Evaluations of presidential popularity indicate that the public is concerned less about *what* the president does than that he does *something*. Specific, dramatic presidential challenges and initiatives, whether they ultimately prove to be wise or foolish, help a president recover from a general decline in popularity, but the turnaround is seldom permanent (see Figure 15-4. President George W. Bush's widely hailed efforts in the days immediately following the terrorist attacks in 2001 boosted him to record levels of support which dissipated slowly as competing demands and expectations emerged (see Figure 15-5).

Presidents actively woo public support through press conferences, speeches, television addresses to the nation, and extensive public relations efforts. A key White House strategy lies in distancing the president from bad news. Typically, "the president announces good news, and others—preferably other agencies—handle the bad news."[25] The president's skill in portraying himself as the only national leader with significant popular support has the potential for either making or breaking a presidency.

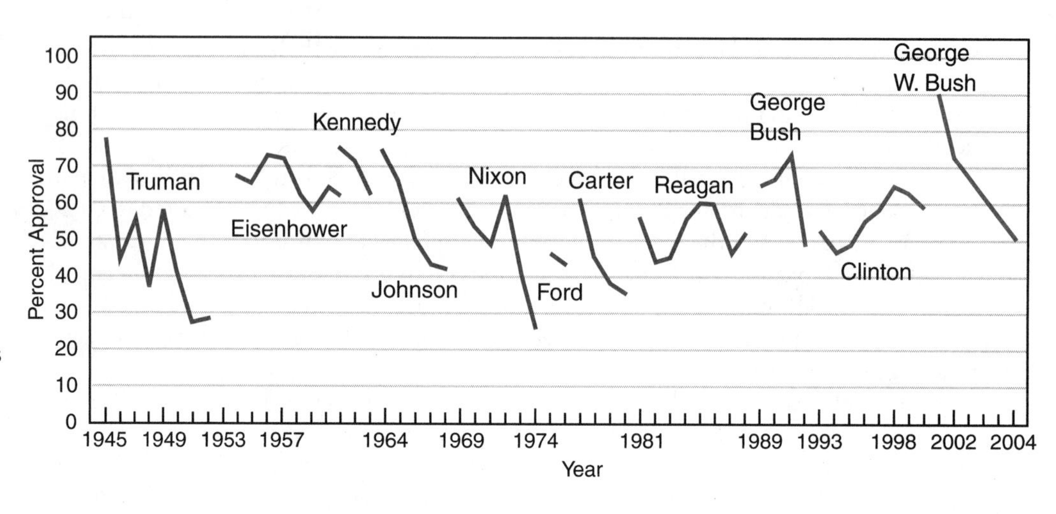

Figure 15-4
The Long-Term Picture of Presidential Popularity

Most presidents experience declining levels of public approval over the course of their term due to artificially high initial levels of support and high public expectations that most presidents fail to fulfill. This gives presidents an incentive to accomplish their goals early in their terms.

Source: Adapted from *Public Opinion,* February/March 1986, 37–38, and updated from successive volumes of *Gallup Poll Monthly.* Reprinted with the permission of the American Enterprise Institute for Public Policy Research, Washington, D.C.

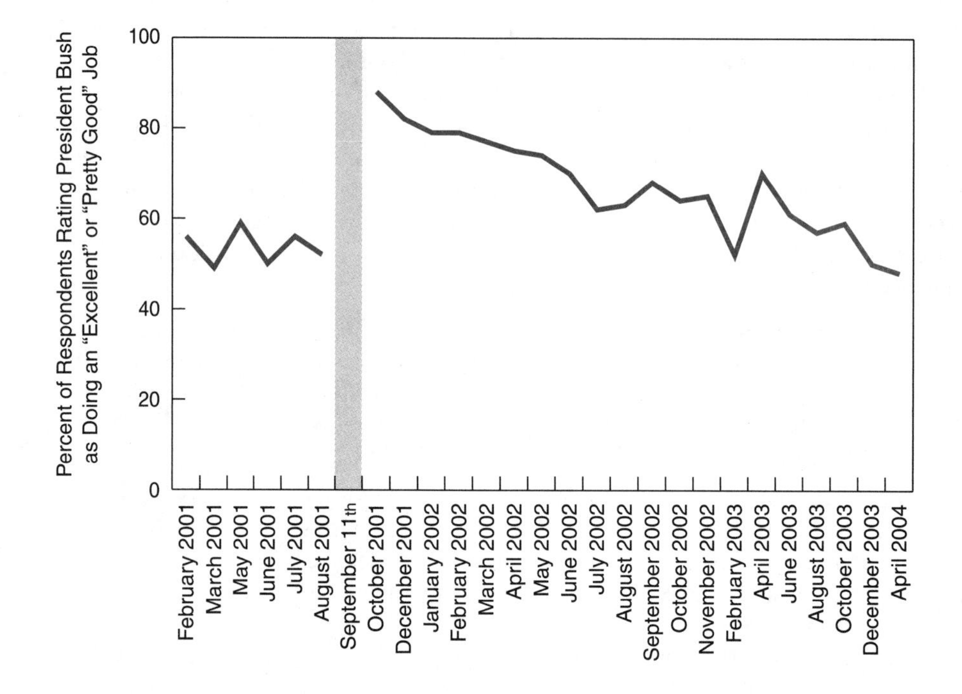

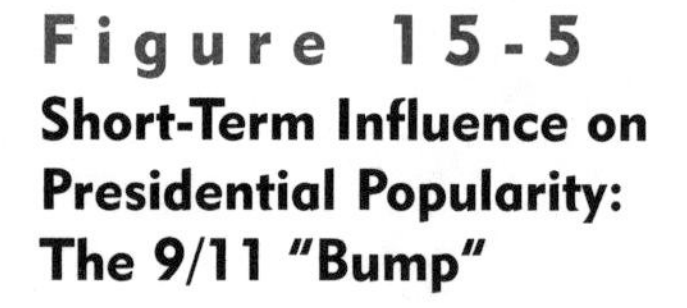

Figure 15-5
Short-Term Influence on Presidential Popularity: The 9/11 "Bump"

Source: Harris Poll national adult surveys of 1000+ respondents asking respondents, "How would you rate the job President George W. Bush is doing as a president?" LEXIS-NEXIS database.

15-5 Winners and Losers in the White House

At the conclusion of White House discussions of a complex foreign policy question, President John F. Kennedy stated:

> I hope this plan works. If it does, it will be another White House success. If it doesn't, it will be another State Department failure.[26]

The success or failure of a presidential administration is difficult to measure definitively. Popularity might be relatively easy to measure, but it has less significance than the president's legacy of policy adoption and administration. However, popular presidents are usually more successful in leading the other branches of government.

In the short run, the separation of powers doctrine means that the president's prime adversary in achieving policy objectives is the Congress. From a longer perspective, the course of policy also depends on the president's ability to guide the bureaucracy and to affect the courts. Many presidents get legislation passed, only to forget that a policy's real impact emerges from the way in which the policy is administered.

Several factors determine the likelihood of presidents achieving their objectives. Most of these factors are related either to the nature of the issue or to the character of the opposing teams.

15-5a The Nature of the Issue

Narrow issues, involving *incremental* changes, generally reap more presidential success than do broader policy changes, which are more likely to offend other players. President Clinton's comprehensive health care program was to be his primary policy initiative during his first two years in office. Its success was doomed, however, because it challenged so many groups in society and involved the jurisdictions of so many congressional committees that it became impossible to forge an acceptable compromise. Clinton was more successful in bringing about changes in more limited policies such as fetal tissue research, rules on political activity of federal employees, and voter registration laws.

Congress and the public generally give presidents considerably more leeway in foreign policy issues than in domestic issues (see Chapter 13). In fact, Congress typically has allowed the president to reign in foreign policy, although a more aggressive Congress in the wake of Vietnam has found numerous ways to challenge presidential initiatives. The War Powers Act was designed to guarantee consultation with Congress. Congressional threats to cut funds or put limitations on foreign policy initiatives have become more common. At a minimum, Congress wants to participate in the game. As one key congressional staff member put it:

> For years Congress has been asked to help clean up the crash sites of presidential foreign policy failures. Increasingly members of the House and Senate want to be in on the take-offs to have some say about the initial direction.[27]

The public and Congress look to the president for guidance and leadership on foreign policy decisions. Issues of party loyalty tend to play less of a role in foreign policy. President Clinton enjoyed considerable success on issues such as NAFTA and the General Agreement on Tariffs and Trade (GATT) despite widespread opposition within his own party. As Republican representative Henry Bonilla (R-Tex.) pointed out:

> We just had an excellent bipartisan meeting with the president. You know, he's our quarterback in this NAFTA game, and he's demonstrating to people on both sides...that his heart's in the game.[28]

15-5b The Key Opposing Team: Congress and the President—An Invitation to Struggle

Wise presidents realize that they are playing in a continuous game with multiple rounds and a variety of opposing players. Success at one stage, or in relation to a particular player, may not stick for a future round, whereas failure in one round can often be overcome in another.

Through the checks and balances system, Congress and the president were designed to be opposing teams, prone to more conflict and struggle than compromise.[29] Constitutional ambiguities over the separation of powers keep each institution wary of infringements by the other. Differing terms of office and constituencies make Congress and the president responsive to differing political forces.[30] Congress and the presidency have been described as "tandem" institutions that must work together to accomplish anything:

> The word *tandem*...generally includes in its meaning the placement of one member behind the other, as on a tandem bicycle...The president may sit at the "front" of the process, providing direction by influencing the policy agenda—using devices such as the State of the Union Address—but the choice of direction lacks significance without a synchronized response from the "rear."[31]

Political parties once bridged much of the gap between Congress and the president, because presidents could generally depend on members of their political parties to support them in the legislative arena. Much of the modern era, however, has been marked by *divided government*, with different parties controlling the White House and Congress

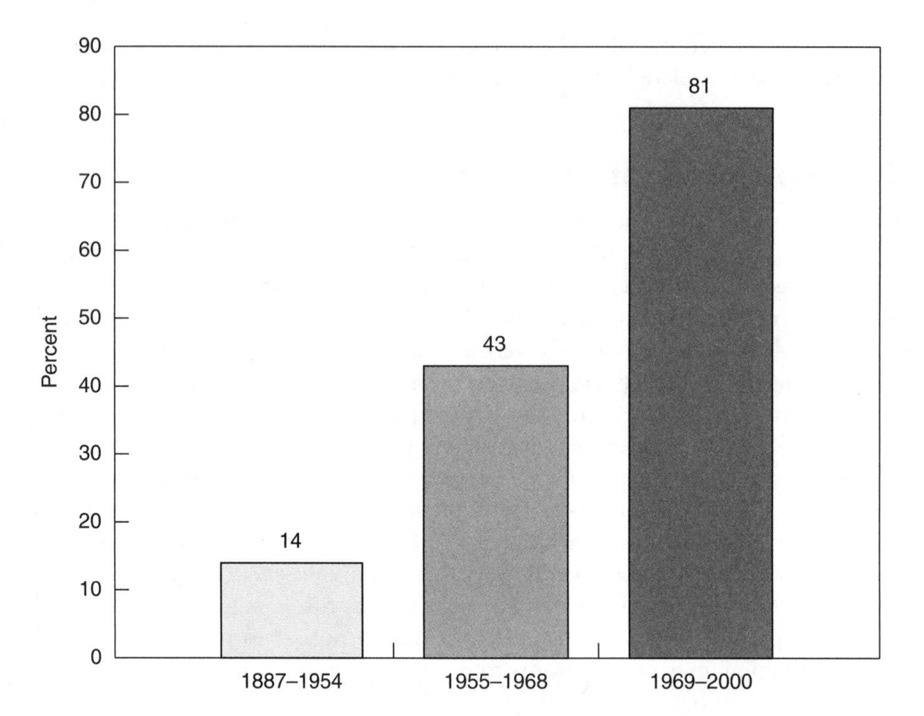

Figure 15-6
Divided Government: Built-in Conflict among the Teams (Percentage of Time Opposing Parties Have Controlled the Presidency and One or Both Houses of Congress)

Source: Data from James A. Thurber, *Divided Democracy* (Washington, D.C.: Congressional Quarterly, Inc.), p. 5; and Harold W. Stanley and Richard G. Niemi, *Vital Statistics on American Politics, 2001–2002* (Washington, D.C.: Congressional Quarterly, Inc., 2001), pp. 36–39.

(see Figure 15-6). Presidential success in gaining approval for proposed legislation is more closely associated with the partisan and ideological balance in Congress than with the quality of the legislation or the president's skill.[32] Congress often gets its way through its ability to obstruct and amend. The need for presidents to compromise with Congress assures that presidential victories will seldom be clear-cut.

After winning re-election and strengthening Republican majorities in both Houses in 2004, President George W. Bush commented frankly on his position of power as a president with unified government acknowledging that Americans expected:

> bipartisan government . . . [but] my goal is to work on the ideal, and to reach out to continue to work and find common ground . . . On the other hand, I've wisened to the ways of Washington. I'm not blaming one party or the other, it's just the reality of Washington, D.C.[33]

More often than not, the president succeeds in seeing much of the presidential legislation through the congressional process (see Figure 15-7). Until the Clinton administration, success tended to be more likely on votes dealing with foreign policy and national security as opposed to those concerned with domestic issues. After initial legislative action, the presidential power to disapprove congressional decisions through the veto assures that presidential wishes will win unless two-thirds of each house overrides the veto. From the founding of the nation until now, Congress has only overridden the presidential veto about 7% of the time.[34] The threat of a veto often forces Congress to the bargaining table, responsive to the idea of compromise.

15-5c Opposing Teams with the Power to Act: Presidents and the Bureaucracy—Responsibility with Limited Authority

When General Dwight Eisenhower won the presidency, President Harry Truman made the following prediction:

> He'll sit here, and he'll say, "Do this! Do that!" and nothing will happen. Poor Ike—it won't be a bit like the Army. He'll find it very frustrating."[35]

To a significant degree, the president's role as chief executive reflects presidential desire and public expectation more than reality. The focus on presidential success and

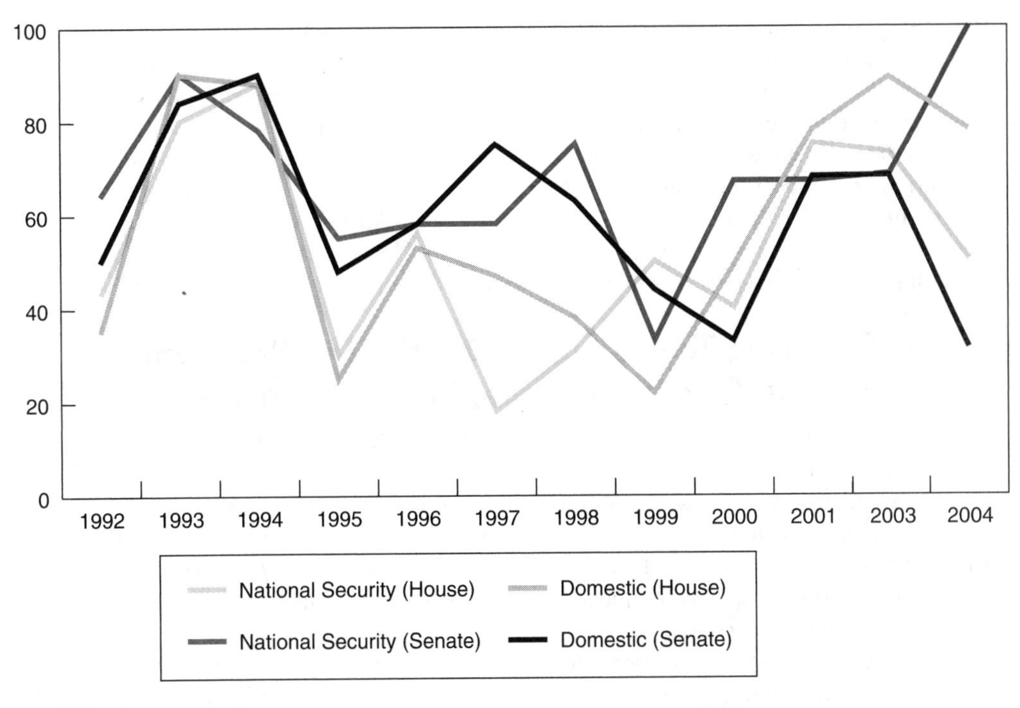

Figure 15-7
Presidential Success in Congress

Source: Data from *Congressional Quarterly Almanac,* 1992–2002. Beginning in 1999, "national security votes" were renamed "defense/foreign policy," and economic affairs votes were taken out of the domestic policy calculations.

failure in the public battle over policy ignores the fact that the real impact of policy decisions occurs in the less visible bureaucracy. Few presidential decisions are self-executing. In most cases, action must be taken by a string of political appointees and permanent bureaucrats, whose understanding of the instructions may be unclear or whose preferences may vary from that of the president. The crisis nature of the White House and the tendency of most presidents to ignore details have lead many presidents to emphasize creating policy more than carrying it out.[36] White House inattention and the **discretion** built into most public laws allow bureaucrats significant flexibility.

discretion *The legal ability of federal officials to employ experience and personal judgment in executing public policies. Restrained and limited by statutes and administrative rules.*

Most bureaucrats go about their jobs invisible to the occupant of the White House and affected only by very general presidential guidelines. Under normal conditions, their commitment is to their bureaucratic team rather than to a temporary administration in the White House. As two observers put it:

> A president can tell a Secretary of State to go to another country and deliver a policy pronouncement to its prime minister, with little concern that his message will not be accurately transmitted. But he cannot have the same confidence about messages aimed at caseworkers in a social security office or soldiers in the field.[37]

Presidential control of particular bureaucrats succeeds most often when the president takes a direct, personal interest and communicates with the decision maker, and when the commands are clear and consistent.

To increase their control, presidents are often tempted to bring the administration of crucial programs into the White House, where presidential power over the staff is greater. Officially, White House advisers assist only in policy development, delegating the day-to-day administration of policy initiatives to the permanent bureaucracy (Chapter 16). The bureaucracy often has its own ideas of how things should be done based on personal experience, agency traditions, and/or pressure from constituents. These bureaucratic orientations can thwart or dull presidential initiatives, encouraging the president to have the presidential staff actually carry out policy. Under such conditions, White House staff members attempt to deal directly with foreign countries or put pressure on private entities such as corporations. As White House scandals such as Watergate and Iran-Contra prove, bypassing a department may also bypass potentially important error-correcting criticism from departmental officials. It becomes more difficult to "remove the president's fingerprints from a policy disaster."[38]

In the long run, neither the president nor the president's staff has the time or resources to control the entire bureaucracy. The White House must rely on the goodwill and skill of career civil servants to implement most of the president's policy initiatives.

15-5d Opposing Teams on the Bench: The President and the Courts—Winning for the Long Term

The policy game does not stop at policy enactment or implementation. In cases brought before them, the federal courts compare the impact of public policy and the actions of executives with the courts' interpretation of constitutional dictates (see Chapter 17). Such determinations affect the political game longer than do most presidential, congressional, or bureaucratic decisions. Presidents wishing to leave a more lasting legacy often turn to their powers of appointing judges to the federal courts; this helps determine the government's position in court cases.

Supreme Court justices, who serve for life, usually remain in office well beyond the term of the president who appointed them. Presidents pay a great deal of attention to the general approach and specific policy outlooks that potential Supreme Court nominees bring with them. Two political commentators reacted to President George H. Bush's nomination of Judge Clarence Thomas, a conservative, to the Supreme Court by saying:

> The conservatives have the ability to really put the game on ice. They can get control of the Supreme Court right into the next century. (Pat Buchanan)
>
> It's like a game, right now, a game in the ninth inning and you have a one-run lead. Do you go for an insurance run or do you just coast and accept what you have? You obviously go for the insurance run. (Fred Barnes)[39]

In recent years, the Senate, charged with providing "advice and consent" for appointments to the Supreme Court, has become more vigilant in screening presidential appointees on ideological grounds. The 18% Senate rejection rate for Supreme Court nominees is the highest rate for any category of presidential nomination. The place of *ideology* in the Senate is best revealed by the fact that almost 60% of the rejections occurred when the presidency and the Senate were controlled by different parties.[40]

Although presidents cannot anticipate every possible position of their Supreme Court nominees, approximately 75% of Supreme Court justices' decisions are consistent with the positions held by the presidents who appointed them.[41] The real presidential winners in the judicial branch are those who are allowed to make a significant number of appointments (see Table 15-2). The ideological ghosts of many long-departed presidents haunt the judicial arena.

Groups or individuals defeated in the congressional or bureaucratic arena often question presidential actions in the courts. Most often, the questioning involves the nature of a president's power to do such things as send troops into battle, deny access to information, or seize private property.

When the president becomes a defendant in the courts because of a policy, the chief executive usually wins, especially when the issue involves foreign policy. The courts have generally sided with expanding rather than restricting presidential power,[42] although presidents do not always prevail. Richard Nixon was required to provide Congress with tapes of his White House conversations[43] and ordered to spend funds appropriated by Congress.[44] President Truman's seizure of private steel mills to avoid an interruption of

Table 15-2

Presidential Opportunities to Determine Supreme Court Players

President	Number of Years in Office	Number of Appointees
Franklin Roosevelt	13	9
Harry Truman	8	4
Dwight Eisenhower	8	5
John F. Kennedy	3	2
Lyndon Johnson	7	2
Richard Nixon	6	4
Gerald Ford	4	1
Jimmy Carter	4	0
Ronald Reagan	8	4
George H. Bush	4	2
Bill Clinton	8	2
George W. Bush	4	0 (as of 2005)

Source: Data from Henry J. Abraham, *The Judiciary*, 8th ed. (Dubuque, IA: Wm. C. Brown Communications, Inc., 1991), 216–17; and Harold W. Stanley and Richard G. Niemi, *Vital Statistics on American Politics, 1999–2000* (Washington, D.C.: Congressional Quarterly, Inc., 2000), 273.

the Korean War effort was also declared unconstitutional.[45] Despite some significant presidential defeats, of the 403 court cases involving presidential power between 1949 and 1984, the courts ruled in the president's favor over 70% of the time.[46]

Through the appointed **solicitor general,** the president and the White House staff can determine whether the executive branch will appeal cases in the federal courts or let them drop. Presidents also determine the official government position on cases in which the government is not a direct participant. At the president's direction, the solicitor general often files *amicus curiae* (friend of the court) briefs arguing for a particular outcome (see Chapter 17).

Solicitor General The chief attorney representing the United States in cases before the Supreme Court in which the national government is a party.

When the presidency changes hands, so do judicial strategies and positions. For example, the George H. Bush administration successfully defended the rights of abortion clinic protesters. The subsequent Clinton administration argued that federal racketeering laws should be applied to abortion protesters (*NOW v. Scheidler*) and that a buffer zone to shelter staff and clients from protesters should be established (*Madison v. Women's Health Center*). Another reversal involved compensation in sexual harassment cases. The Bush administration argued that sexual harassment cases in the judicial pipeline before the 1991 Civil Rights Act became law could not use that act to secure compensation, whereas the Clinton administration urged the justices to extend the law to cover pending cases (*Landgraf v. USI Film Products*). In both realms, the ideological orientations of the presidents and their solicitors general were clear. The political importance lies in the fact that when presidents weigh in on a judicial case through their solicitors general, they are often successful.[47]

Modern presidents are key players in a variety of political arenas involving all branches of government. Success in one realm can lead to success in another. Losing in one arena may encourage a president to expend more effort in another and increase the likelihood of success. As such a key player, the president has more options than any other participant.

Conclusion

The modern American political game is hard to imagine without the president at the center. The presidential selection process and the post-election media coverage focus the attention of players and spectators alike on the president as an individual. Behind the scenes, an extensive and growing set of aides provides the president with the information and policy alternatives necessary to maintain the image of a one-person team. Presidents attempt to control the game by setting the agenda, utilizing their superior information resources, selecting battles carefully, and capitalizing on national public support.

The separation of powers system requires presidents to participate continuously in several political arenas if they wish to succeed in achieving political and policy objectives. Presidential success in influencing Congress, managing the bureaucracy, or redirecting the courts comes at the price of considerable effort and the expenditure of resources. In the end, the president is a politician playing in a political game. Success or failure is marked to a large degree by the president's skill and willingness to go beyond the strict constitutional definition of the president as an administrator and to enter the political fray.

Key Terms

chief diplomat
chief legislator
chief of state
Commander-in-Chief
discretion
executive order
executive privilege
leader of the free world
news leaks
Office of Management and Budget (OMB)
party leader
presidential program
Solicitor General
State of the Union Message

Practice Quiz

1. Which role of the president is NOT established by the Constitution?
a. Party leader
b. Commander-in-Chief
c. Chief diplomat
d. Chief executive

2. As chief executive, what is the president's responsibility?
a. To control the military
b. To oversee the executive branch
c. To make treaties and appoint ambassadors
d. To initiate legislation

3. Which of the following activities are included in the president's role as chief of state?
a. Negotiating with Congress
b. Appointing ambassadors and guiding the State Department
c. Declaring war
d. Serving as the symbolic representative of the country

4. What role does the Office of Management and Budget play?
a. Assisting Congress with budget formulation
b. Assisting the president in the formulation of the budget
c. Seeing that the bills for U.S. indebtedness are paid
d. Serving as an independent watchdog of the president and Congress on budget issues.

5. To enhance its power with regard to the federal budgeting process, Congress created the
a. Congressional Budget Office.
b. General Accounting Office.
c. Office of Management and Budget.
d. Inspector General's Office.

6. The president's role as commander-in-chief is
a. extra-constitutional and a matter or tradition.
b. clearly specified in the Constitution.
c. unclear in the main body of the Constitution, but clarified by the 15th Amendment.
d. challenged constitutionally by conservatives but not by liberals.

7. Which president had the most restrictive view of presidential rights and responsibilities?
a. Abraham Lincoln
b. Teddy Roosevelt
c. Ronald Reagan
d. William Howard Taft

8. Executive privilege
a. requires members of the executive branch to share information with Congress.
b. allows presidents to acquire confidential information from their staffs.
c. assures that the president's legislative proposals will be considered first.
d. refers to the almost monarchical ceremonies associated with the president.

9. A president's assertion of a constitutional right to take a particular action is relying on _____ as his or her power resource.
a. persuasion
b. sanctions
c. authority
d. leadership

10. Presidential success in Congress tends to
a. be greater for domestic issues than for national security issues.
b. be greater for national security issues than for domestic issues.
c. increase over a president's term.
d. Both a and c

You can find the correct answers to these questions by taking the quiz and then submitting your answers in the Online Edition. The program will automatically score your submission. Where you miss a question, the program will provide the correct answer, a rationale for the answer, and the section number in the chapter where the topic is discussed.

Further Reading

See the Suggestions for Further Reading in Chapter 14 for sources presenting a general overview of the presidency.

Presidential Power and the Modern Presidents: The Politics of Leadership from Roosevelt to Reagan (New York: Free Press, 1990) is Richard E. Neustadt's current edition of his 1960 path-breaking study of the nature of presidential power. His work moved students of the presidency beyond the formal constitutional powers to emphasize such informal powers as persuasion.

In *Divided Democracy*, edited by James A. Thurber (Washington, D.C.: Congressional Quarterly, Inc., 1991), a variety of authors discuss the origins and consequences of the contemporary pattern of a president from one party and a Congress dominated by the other. *Divided Government*, edited by Peter F. Galderisa (Lanham, MD: Rowman and Littlefield, 1996), looks at the issue from various perspectives.

For a discussion of presidential relations with Congress, see John R. Bond and Richard Fleisher, *The President in the Legislative Arena* (Chicago, IL: University of Chicago Press, 1991).

Elizabeth Drew provides a good look at the first years of the Clinton presidency in *On the Edge: The Clinton Presidency* (New York: Simon and Schuster, 1995).

Presidential War Power by Louis Fisher (Lawrence, KS: University Press of Kansas, 1995) systematically examines the president's role in making war from the beginning of this nation to the present day.

Andrew Rudavige's, *Managing the President's Program: Presidential Leadership and Legislative Policy Formulation* (Princeton, NJ: Princeton University Press, 2002) provides an inside look at presidential strategies for dealing with Congress.

Endnotes

1. Quoted in Katie Louchein (ed). *The Making of the New Deal: The Insiders Speak* (Cambridge, MA: Harvard University Press, 1983), 285.
2. Leonard W. Levy, *Original Intent and the Framers' Constitution* (New York: MacMillan, 1968), 30.
3. James W. Davis, *The American Presidency: A New Perspective* (New York: Harper & Row, 1987), 207.
4. Louis Henkin, *Foreign Affairs and the Constitution* (Mineola, NY: The Foundation Press, 1972), 123.
5. Davis, *The American Presidency*, 293.
6. *The Federalist*, no. 73.
7. Paul Beck and Frank Sorauf, *Party Politics in America* (Glenview, IL: Scott, Foresman/Little, Brown, 1992), 411.
8. Former Republican leader Charles Halleck, quoted in the *New York Times*, March 4, 1986, I24.
9. C-SPAN (Cable-Satellite Public Affairs Network) live coverage of Newt Gingrich meeting with the press, November 26, 1991.
10. Adapted from Thomas E. Cronin, "The Presidency and Its Paradoxes," in *The Presidency Reappraised*, ed. Thomas E. Cronin and Rexford Tugwell (New York: Praeger, 1977), 69–85.
11. Jack Nelson and Robert J. Donovan, "The Education of a President," *Los Angeles Times*, August 1, 1993, 12.
12. George C. Edwards and Stephen J. Wayne, *Presidential Leadership* (New York: St. Martin's Press, 1994), 10.
13. This term was popularized by Arthur Schlesinger, *The Imperial Presidency* (Boston, MA: Houghton Mifflin, 1973).
14. Hedrick Smith, *The Power Game* (New York: Random House, 1988), 333.
15. According to a Times-Mirror poll of 1,511 adults in December 1994, 43 percent of the respondents felt that Congress should take the lead in solving the nation's problems and 39 percent gave the task to President Clinton. A similar split was evident through much of Clinton's term. LEXIS-NEXIS database.
16. See Supreme Court case *United States v. Nixon*, 418 U.S. 683 (1974).
17. Richard Darman, quoted in Smith, *The Power Game*, 440.
18. Fred I. Greenstein, quoted in David Broder, "Leadership in the Modern Presidency," *Washington Post*, March 17, 1988, A19.
19. The classic discussion of this point can be found in Richard E. Neustadt, *Presidential Power and the Modern Presidents: The Politics of Leadership from Roosevelt to Reagan* (New York: Free Press, 1990).
20. James Miller III, former OMB director, quoted by Timothy Clark, "Budget Lessons from the Director," *Government Executive*, February 1988, 22.
21. Ann Devroy and David Broder, "Missteps Mired Clinton Package," *Washington Post*, April 11, 1993, A1.
22. John Mueller, *War, Presidents and Public Opinion* (New York: John Wiley and Sons, 1973).
23. Broder, "Leadership," A19.
24. Elizabeth Drew, "Why Clinton Hit the Skids," *USA Today*, November 2, 1994, 11A.
25. Smith, *The Power Game*, 430.
26. Quoted in Harlan Cleveland, *The Future Executive* (New York: Harper & Row, 1972), 95–6.
27. Author's interview.
28. Federal News Service transcript, October 1, 1993, LEXIS-NEXIS database.
29. See Cecil V. Crabb, Jr., and Pat M. Holt, *Invitation to Struggle: Congress, the President and Foreign Policy* (Washington, D.C.: Congressional Quarterly, Inc., 1989).
30. See James A. Thurber (ed.), *Divided Democracy: Cooperation and Conflict Between the President and Congress* (Washington, D.C.: Congressional Quarterly, Inc., 1991), 2–4.
31. Mark A. Peterson, *Legislating Together: The White House and Capitol Hill from Eisenhower to Reagan* (Cambridge, MA: Harvard University Press, 1990), 9.
32. James Pfiffner, *The Managerial Presidency* (Pacific Grove, CA: Brooks/Cole, 1991), xxi.
33. Quoted in Marc Sandalow, "Bush Claims Mandate, Sets 2nd-Term Goals," *San Francisco Chronicle*, November 5, 2004. [online]
34. Thurber, *Divided Democracy*, 1991, 2.
35. Quoted in Neustadt, *Presidential Power*, 10.
36. Edwards and Wayne, *Presidential Leadership*, 260–61.
37. Edwards and Wayne, *Presidential Leadership*, 262–63.
38. Francis Rourke, "Presidentializing the Bureaucracy: From Kennedy to Reagan," in *The Managerial Presidency*, editor James P. Pfiffner (Pacific Grove, CA: Brooks/Cole, 1991), 133.
39. *The McLaughlin Group*, June 29, 1991 (transcript from Federal News Service).
40. P. S. Ruckman, Jr., "The Supreme Court, Critical Nominations and the Senate Confirmation Process," *Journal of Politics*, 55, August 1993: 794.
41. Robert Scigliano, *The Supreme Court and the President* (New York: Free Press, 1971), 146.
42. Davis, *The American Presidency*, 304–5.
43. *United States v. Nixon*, 418 U.S. 683 (1974).
44. *American Federation of Government Employees v. Phillips*, 358 F Sup 60 (1963).
45. *Youngstown Sheet and Tube Company v. Sawyer*, 34 U.S. 579 (1952).
46. Craig R. Ducat and Robert L. Dudley, "Presidential Power in Federal Courts During the Post-War Era." Paper presented at the September 1985 meeting of the American Political Science Association, New Orleans.
47. See Lincoln Caplan, *The Tenth Justice* (New York: Vintage Books, 1987), 257–58.

16

Federal Bureaucracy: The Politics of Administration

Key Points

- **The function of cabinet departments, independent executive and regulatory agencies, and public corporations.**
- **The nature of players in the executive branch: short-term political appointees and career civil servants selected on the basis of merit.**
- **How the civil service system is designed to avoid the abuses of corruption and patronage.**
- **How important policy making takes place within agencies of the executive branch and the process of administrative rule making.**
- **The dynamics of political games that take place between presidents and their political appointees, between appointees and civil servants, and between the bureaucracy and Congress.**

Preview: Administration and the Fine-Tuning Laws

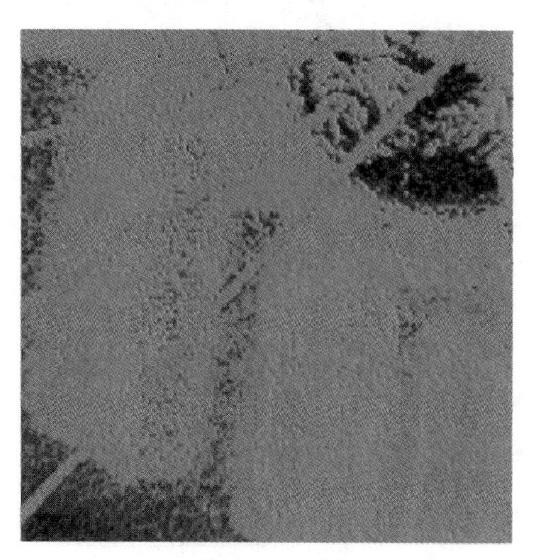

The tall distinguished African American raised his hand to take the oath of congressional office, while his white predecessor closed the last of the boxes containing the accumulation of 12 distinguished years in the House of Representatives. The change in representatives stemmed from one phrase in a piece of legislation: one of the individuals had been instrumental in inserting a few words that would affect his life in unforeseen ways. The phrase was not "equal opportunity" or "one person, one vote." The story is more complicated; it cannot be summed up by slogans, and it involves players who had no idea where their decisions would lead.

When Congress approved the War on Poverty sections of President Lyndon Johnson's Great Society programs in the mid-1960s, Representative Jeffrey Cohelan from Berkeley, California, a Democrat and a liberal, felt strongly that local citizens should have some say in the distribution of federal funds in their areas. He supported key legislation that would include the phrase "maximum feasible citizen participation," and, like most supporters, he emphasized the word feasible. After passage, the legislation moved out of the congressional arena and into the bureaucracy for implementation. In creating the Community Action Boards (CABs) called for by the legislation, bureaucrats in the Office of Economic Opportunity (OEO), who were largely out of the sight of Congress, chose to emphasize the word maximum. They encouraged the development of vibrant CABs made up of minority citizens and gave them plenty of resources and clout.

Ron Dellums, a young African American social worker, saw his chance, and he was not alone. Dozens of other local activists used the CABs as alternative routes to power and public office. With the encouragement of his bureaucratic overseers, Dellums used the CAB elections and distribution of political resources to build a political base much like partisan political machines of earlier years. He was able to provide many of the services such as jobs and federally funded programs normally reserved for higher political officials such as members of Congress. Based on the bureaucratic interpretation of the phrase "maximum feasible citizen participation," Ron Dellums was handed the political resources to defeat Jeffrey Cohelan, one of the key authors of that phrase.

While the results of free bureaucratic choice in the application of laws are often not this obvious, key players recognize that the meaning of a legislative decision often isn't revealed until a law is applied by the bureaucracy. Ron Dellums, former chairman of the House Armed Services Committee, was in the late 1990s one of the most senior African Americans in politics, overseeing our largest bureaucracy, the Department of Defense. He was expected to be particularly vigilant in monitoring legislative phrases that could give the bureaucracy the power to change key aspects of American politics.[1]

When Americans picture the national government to themselves, it is likely that they imagine the president in the White House, congressional leaders in floor debates, and Supreme Court justices sitting on the bench. Less often, probably, do they think about the officials who work in executive branch agencies, but these are the people who manage the national government's daily operations.

In spite of their low visibility, these public officials perform crucial functions. Without their efforts, Social Security checks would not be issued, the mail would not be delivered, and the safety of food and drugs would not be monitored. In addition, violators of federal laws would not be prosecuted, space shuttles would not be launched, currency would not be printed, and air traffic would not be directed. America would not be protected from foreign invasion, and foreign relations would not be managed. And the list goes on. These federal government employees have daily responsibility for executing a wide assortment of public laws that have been enacted by Congress.

The federal bureaucracy has sometimes been termed the fourth branch of government, supplementing the executive, legislative, and judicial branches. This designation arises from the large number of federal agencies and their relative separation from the president, who serves as the chief executive. The departments and agencies of the U.S. federal government today contain over 2 million civilian employees, who work not only in the nation's capital but also in regional field offices across the country.

The departments and agencies of the executive branch represent important arenas in which two types of players, **political executives** and **civil servants,** influence the formation and implementation of policies. Political executives are political players appointed by the president and confirmed by the Senate. They arrive expecting to pursue the political goals of the president who appointed them and are an important link between the chief executive and the multitude of departments and agencies that together make up the executive branch.

political executives *Officials appointed by the president to manage federal government agencies; they include cabinet secretaries and about 600 officials who hold top positions in federal agencies.*

civil servants *Public-sector employees selected for their jobs through a civil service system, usually involving a process of competitive examination or competitive evaluation of applications.*

The other set of players are federal civil servants, who are hired on the basis of competence and training rather than on political affiliation or policy preferences. Civil servants have job protection, which is intended to prevent presidents and others from overpoliticizing the operations of the federal government.

It is seldom recognized that agencies of the federal government regularly formulate public policy—a function normally associated with the legislative branch. Given the extensive technical knowledge, expertise, and experience of agency officials, Congress, when enacting laws, has increasingly given agencies some flexibility in designing policies and regulations to guide implementation.

The executive branch has come under extensive scrutiny in recent years, with both Republicans and Democrats calling for major reorganization. Some have called for even more drastic changes aimed at reducing the size and functions of the national government to a large extent. Some politicians, both inside and outside of Congress, have called for the elimination of agencies such as the Department of Education, the Department of Commerce, and the Department of Housing and Urban Development. Others have advocated plans to privatize some governmental functions, such as turning operation of the Amtrak passenger rail service and federal air traffic controllers over to private companies. Other reforms have focused on reforming management practices and using new technologies to improve overall governmental efficiency and performance. The organizational structure of the federal government bureaucracy and the impact of advocated reforms on agency structure and operations are key themes to be explored in this chapter.

16-1 Underlying Rules of the Executive Branch

When designing the rules for the executive functions of the national government, the Founders directed most of their attention to the president, in whom the executive power shall be vested (Article II of the Constitution). Their principal objective was to empower the president to execute laws enacted by Congress. They also instituted checks on presidential power to prevent the rise of executive tyranny. Although the Founders recognized the necessity of creating executive agencies to conduct the daily business of government, they did not extensively treat the issue within the Constitution.

16-1a Constitutional Foundations

Beyond rules about the presidency, the Constitution empowers Congress to create, abolish, or revise agencies and departments in the executive branch. Congress also grants these agencies and departments specific powers and responsibilities. The earliest cabinet departments—State, War, and Treasury—were created in 1789 to handle pressing national needs to conduct foreign relations, to prepare for national defense, and to coin money and to cope with the debt built up during the Revolutionary War.

Since then, the federal government bureaucracy has steadily grown in complexity. The day has long since passed when the president and a small group of assistants could oversee operation of the executive branch. Modern presidents are assisted by a large group of advisers and assistants, many of whom are clustered into the Executive Office of the President (see Chapter 14). The executive branch is composed of cabinet departments such as the departments of State, Defense, Justice, Transportation, and Treasury; independent executive agencies; independent regulatory agencies; and public corporations charged with specialized functions.

16-1b Cabinet Departments

There are currently 15 cabinet departments (see Figure 16-1), each charged with broad functional responsibilities. The largest departments in terms of employees and budgets are the departments of Defense, charged with national defense and defending American

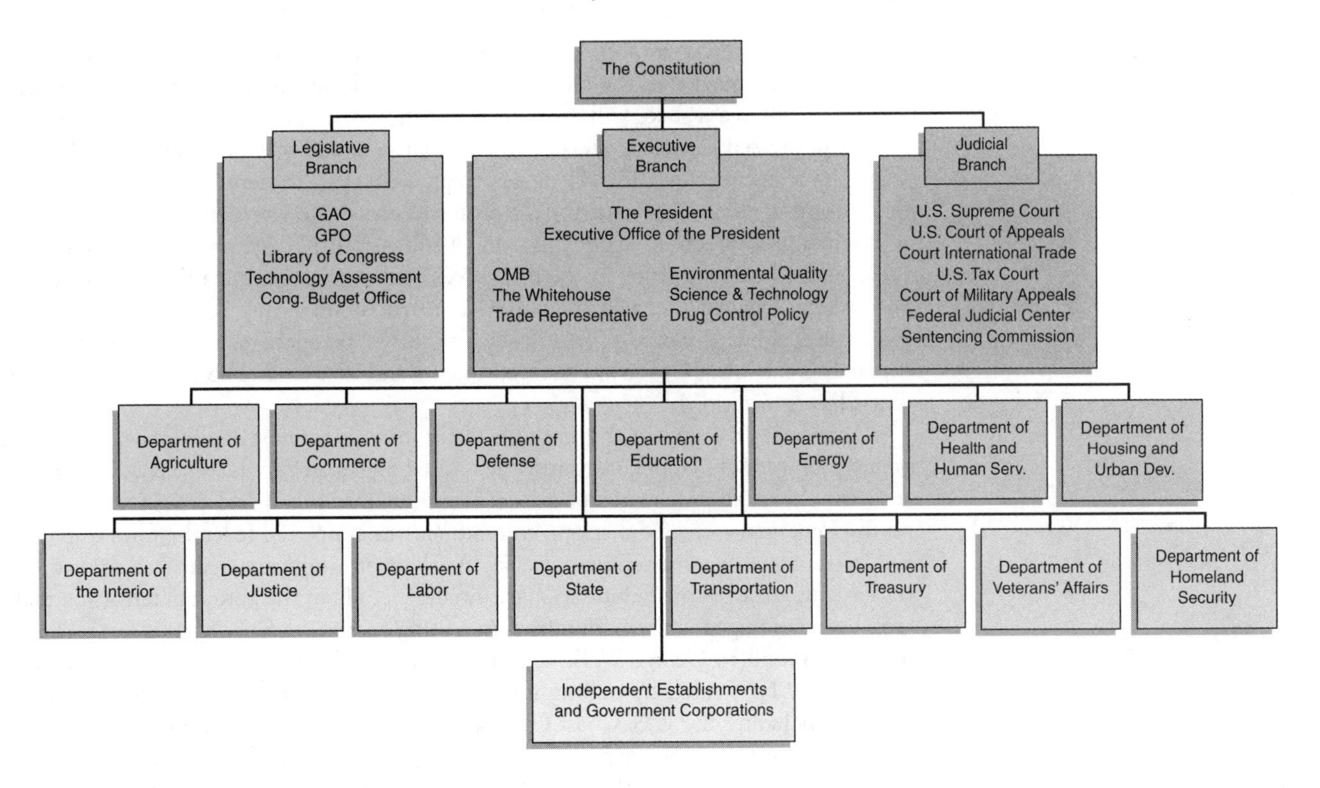

Figure 16-1
Organization Chart of the U.S. Government

interests abroad; Veterans' Affairs, which oversees medical and other programs for military veterans; Health and Human Services, which administers Social Security and important health programs; and Treasury, charged with collecting taxes and issuing money. The Department of State oversees the nation's political relations with other countries, and the Department of Justice, headed by the attorney general, investigates and prosecutes violations of federal law.

Creation of Cabinet Departments

New cabinet departments are created by Congress in response to widespread public concerns about some problem or issue facing the nation. The Department of Housing and Urban Development (HUD) was created in 1965 as the nation turned its attention to the problem of insufficient housing for poor Americans. Congress created the Department of Energy in 1977 soon after the United States suffered its first energy shortage as the result of an oil embargo by Middle Eastern nations.

Presidents have sometimes taken the lead in calling for the creation of new cabinet departments. Pressure has been put on Congress to expand the executive branch by reassigning offices from existing departments and adding new resources in order to create a new department. President Jimmy Carter, for example, lobbied Congress in 1979 to create a separate Department of Education by carving out educational offices from the Department of Health, Education, and Welfare. Through this reorganization, which created the Department of Education and the Department of Health and Human Services, the president and Congress signaled greater federal commitment to elementary, secondary, and college education.

Presidents are not always strong supporters of new cabinet departments. The politics of executive reorganization were evident during the early 1980s when the Reagan administration sought to eliminate the Department of Education. President Ronald Reagan did not share his predecessor's strong belief in a greater federal role in public education. Reagan and other conservatives viewed education as the appropriate responsibility of state and local governments. Congress, however, ignored Reagan's plea to have the Department of Education dismantled.

Organized interest groups also participate in political games to create new federal agencies. They expect that the creation of a cabinet department responsible for policies in which they have a stake will assist their constituents. For example, American veterans' groups pressed for many years to have policies related to veterans organized into a cabinet-level agency. In 1988, Congress created the Department of Veterans' Affairs. After assuming office, President Bill Clinton was pressed to ask Congress to elevate the Environmental Protection Agency to cabinet status. With budget cutting and reduction of regulations being so strong in the mid-1990s, calls for instituting a Department of the Environment have not been acted upon. Other structural reforms were considered in the 1990s as Republicans vowed to shrink the size and scope of the federal bureaucracy (see Box 16-1: Comparing Government Departments and Box 16-2: The Politics of Governmental Reorganization).

A national crisis led to the creation of the newest cabinet department, Homeland Security. The attacks launched against the United States on September 11, 2001—by terrorists who hijacked passenger jets and crashed them into the World Trade Center towers and the Pentagon—created a strong commitment to concerted federal efforts to protect the United States against terrorist attacks. Analysis of intelligence gathered prior to the attacks demonstrated that failures to share intelligence about the potential terrorist attacks across agencies impeded the nation from mounting a strong defense against terrorism. As a response, President George W. Bush proposed in 2002 that a new Department of Homeland Security be created by pulling intelligence units out of 22 existing governmental agencies (including the U.S. Coast Guard, the Immigration and Naturalization Service, the Border Patrol, and the Secret Service) and organizing them into the new department.

One immediate sign of this new agency is the Transportation Security Administration, a component agency in the Department of Homeland Security. Air travelers will see this administration in action when personnel who wear "TSA" badges scrutinize them and their baggage as part of the check-in process for airline travel.

Organization of Cabinet Departments

Each cabinet department is headed by a secretary appointed by the president and confirmed by the Senate. Departments are divided into a set of administrative units. These units are generically referred to as **bureaus,** although they carry such names as *office* (e.g., the Office of Civil Rights), *administration* (e.g., the Food and Drug Administration), *division* (the Antitrust Division), and *service* (the U.S. Marshals Service). Each bureau has responsibility for specific programs and a top official who oversees it and manages its employees.

bureau *Generic term used to describe organization units within agencies; may also carry such names as Office, Administration, or Division.*

The organization of one cabinet department, the Department of Transportation (DOT), is shown in Figure 16-2 (see Box 16-3: The U.S. Government Manual for a comprehensive resource on federal government structure). The bureaus listed in this organization chart indicate the variety of DOT functions, including the regulation of airports and air transit (Federal Aviation Administration), railroads (Federal Railroad Administration), highway safety (National Highway Traffic Safety Administration), mass transportation including subways and buses (Urban Mass Transportation Administration), and the interstate highway system (Federal Highway Administration). DOT also contains the U.S. Coast Guard and the St. Lawrence Seaway Development Corporation.

16-1c Independent Executive Agencies

In addition to cabinet departments, the executive branch includes other independent agencies whose heads are appointed and can be dismissed by the president (see Box 16-4: Independent Regulatory Agencies in the Federal Government. Among these are the National Aeronautics and Space Administration (which oversees space exploration), the Central Intelligence Agency, and the Selective Service Commission. Although these agencies have not been granted cabinet department status (partially because of their specialized responsibilities), they perform important functions related to national security and scientific exploration.

Box 16–1 Comparing Government Departments

Cabinet Departments by Date of Creation

Treasury	1789
State	1789
War	1789*
Interior	1849
Justice	1870
Agriculture	1889
Commerce	1913
Labor	1913
Defense	1947
Health, Education and Welfare	1953**
Housing and Urban Development	1965
Transportation,	1966
Education	1979
Health and Human Services	1979
Veterans' Affairs	1989
Homeland Security	2003

*A separate Department of the Navy was created in1798. All the armed forces were combined into the Department of Defense in 1947.

**This department was separated into the Department of Health and Human Services and the Department of Education in 1979.

Where the Money Goes: Departmental Budgets, 2003

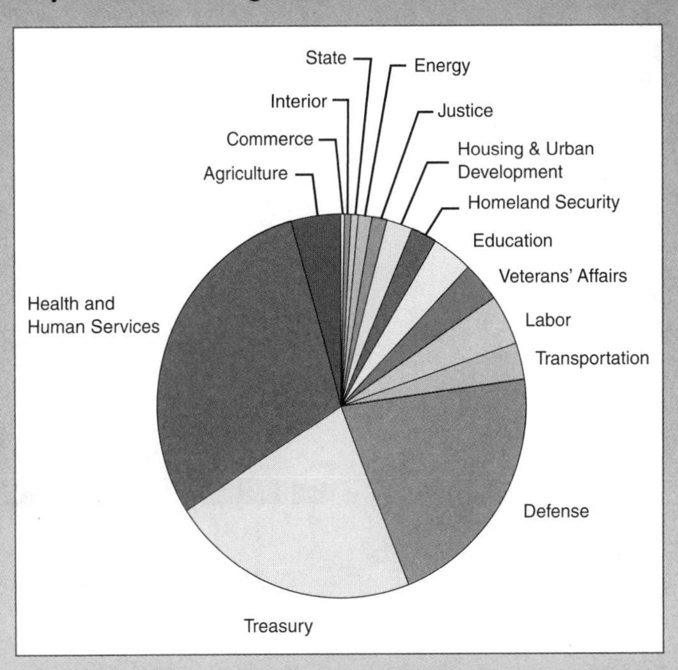

Source: U.S. Bureau of the Census, *Statistical Abstract of the United States*, Table 473 (Washington, D.C.), GPO, 2003; www.census.gov/statab/www/ and www.whitehouse.gov/homeland

Where the Money Goes: Off-Budget and Special Programs, 2003

Not all expenditures are allocated to departments. Among the larger budgets and special programs are:

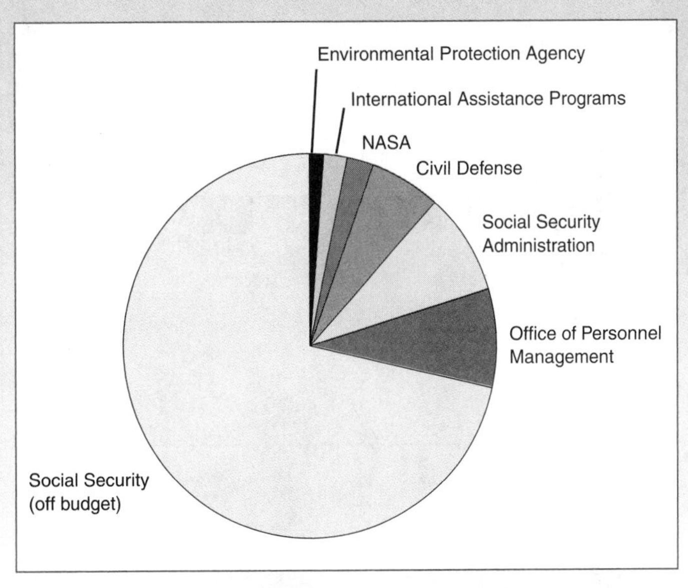

Source: U.S. Bureau of the Census, *Statistical Abstract of the United States*, Table 478 (Washington, D.C.), GPO, 2003; www.census.gov/statab/www/

continued

Box 16–1 Comparing Government Departments

—Continued

Where the Money Goes: Civilian Employees, 2002

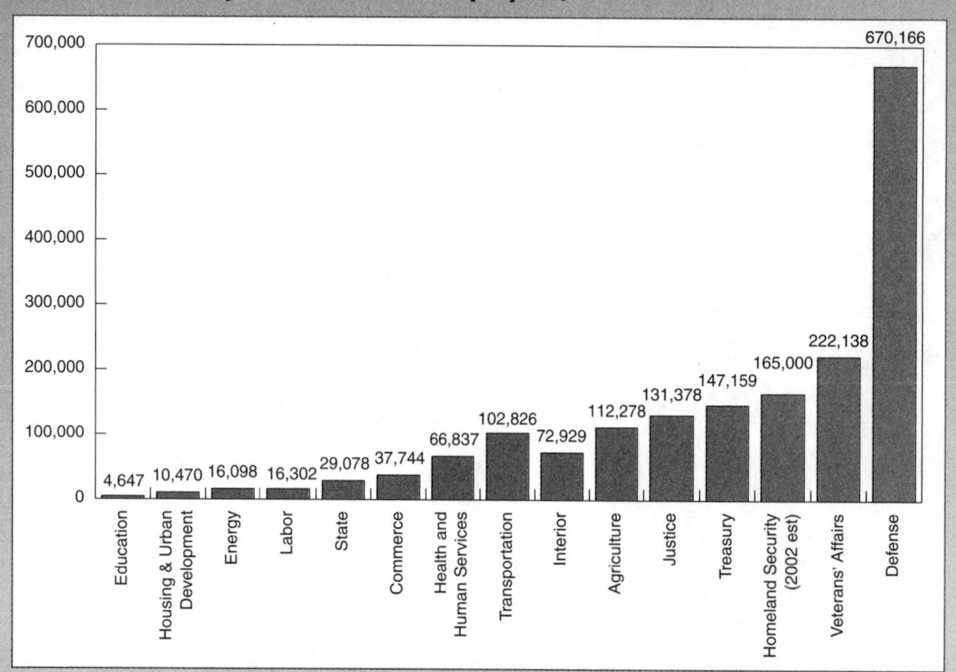

Source: U.S. Bureau of the Census, *Statistical Abstract of the United States*, Table 500 (Washington, D.C.), GPO, 2003; www.census.gov/statab/www/ and www.foxnews.com/story10,2933,70974.html

Departmental Winners and Losers: Gains and Losses in Civilian Employees, 1990–2002

Although the number of employees is only one measure, changes in employees indicate changing societal priorities.

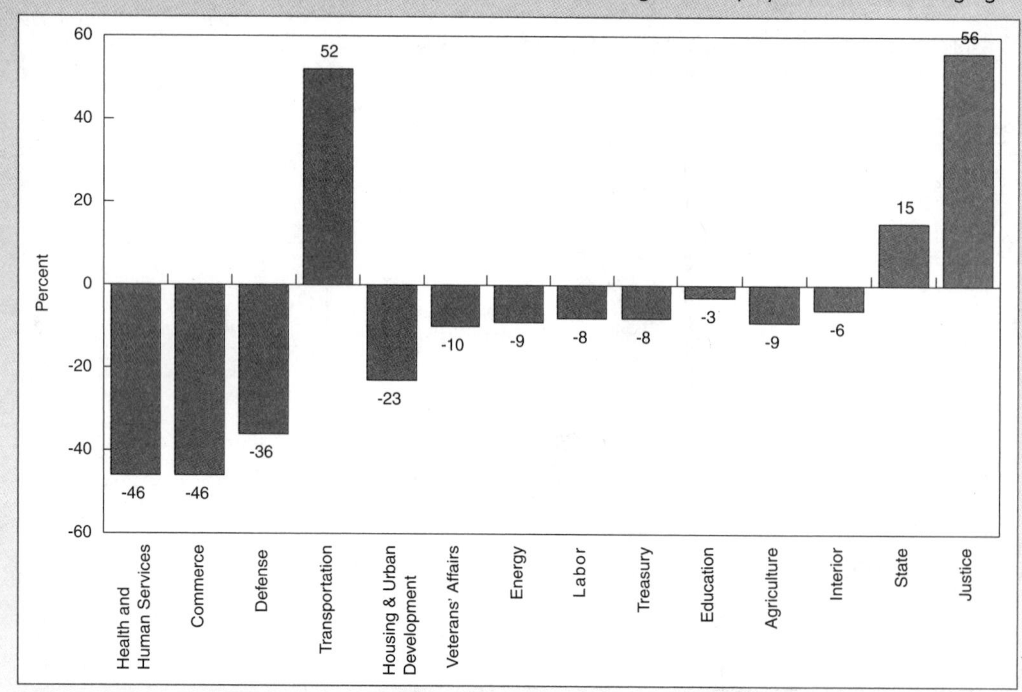

Source: U.S. Bureau of the Census, *Statistical Abstract of the United States*, Table 478 (Washington, D.C.), GPO, 2003; www.census.gov/statab/www/

Who Is Winning the Battle for Resources? Changes in Federal Outlays, 1990–2003

Changing budgets are one measure of a society's priorities

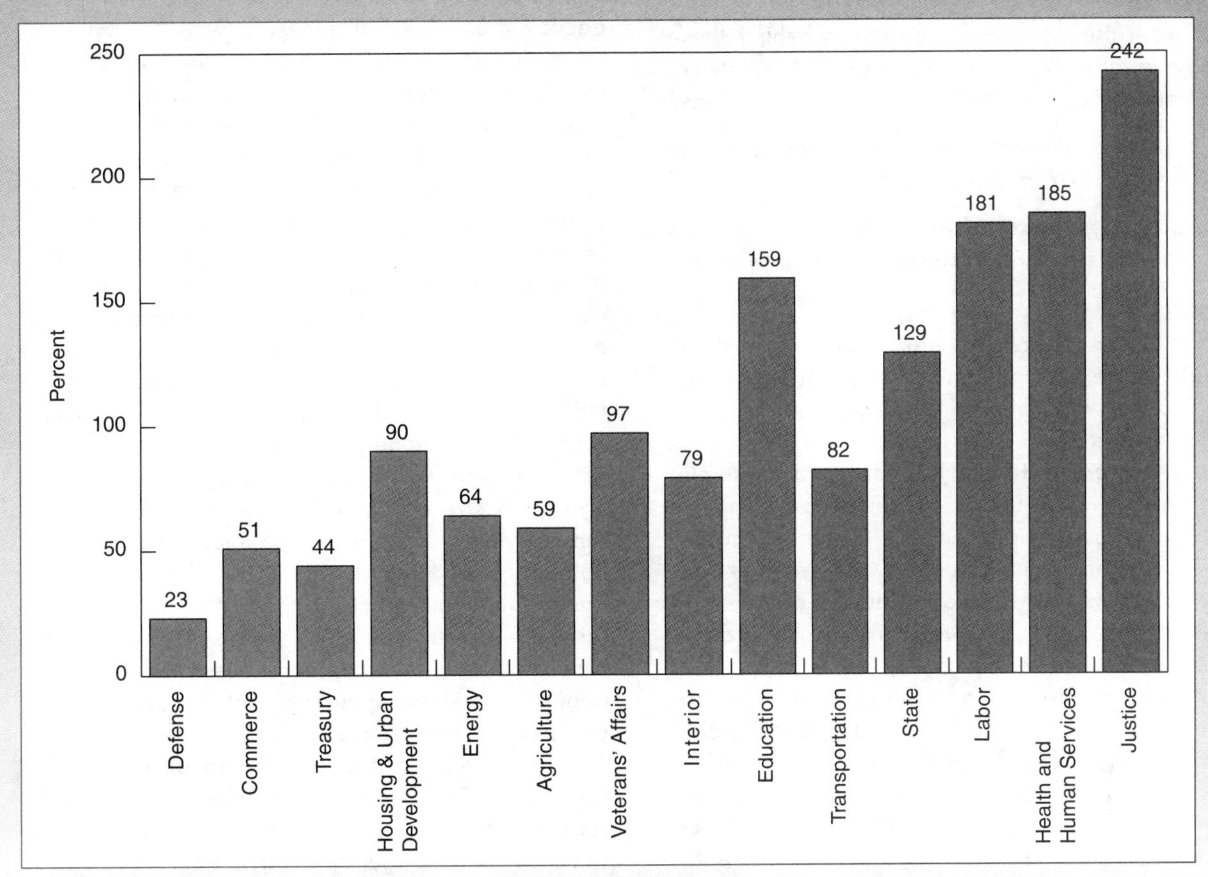

Source: U.S. Bureau of the Census, *Statistical Abstract of the United States*, Table 478 (Washington, D.C.), GPO, 2003; www.census.gov/statab/www/

Box 16–2 The Politics of Governmental Reorganization

Background

Proposals for reforming the federal government often advocate major restructuring of federal agencies. They have called for such changes as creating new agencies, combining existing agencies, streamlining agency operations, and even abolishing several agencies. Some plans have called for privatization, by turning agencies over to private-sector companies. Some specific proposals included the following:

- Combining the Departments of Education and Labor and the Equal Employment Opportunity Commission into a new Department of Education and Employment;
- Eliminating government funding of the Public Broadcast System (PBS);
- Eliminating the National Endowment for the Arts (NEA); and
- Substantially reducing the funding and operations of the Environmental Protection Agency (EPA).

continued

Box 16–2 The Politics of Governmental Reorganization

—Continued

Questions

What were the underlying motivations behind these governmental restructuring proposals? What political values are associated with these reorganization plans?

Which players will benefit from the reforms if they are implemented? Which players will lose?

What obstacles are reformers likely to encounter as they move to enact restructuring reform proposals?

Analysis

Several different political motivations and values underlie these governmental reorganization proposals. Two motivations were efficiency and cost savings. Restructuring departments was seen as a strategy to reduce federal spending. For example, illustrating the savings that might be achieved through reorganization, the U.S. General Accounting Office estimated that a new Department of Education and Employment would save $1.65 billion in administrative costs and would result in the elimination of 4,200 federal jobs.

Another motivation for reform was to make program operations more effective. Perceived breakdowns in the federal government's capacity to effectively use and act on intelligence information—notably surrounding the September 11, 2001, terrorist attacks on the World Trade Center and Pentagon—led President George W. Bush to propose and the Congress to approve creation of the new cabinet department of Homeland Security.

Some reformers supported reorganization for ideological reasons. Conservatives in Congress have long been concerned about the growth in size and power of the federal bureaucracy, which they see as the federal government overpowering the states. Because they prefer less government to more and want reduced federal government power overall, conservatives support reducing and eliminating agencies as a means of scaling back the size and scope of the federal government. Privatization of governmental operations, such as the air traffic control system, meshes nicely with the laissez-faire and free enterprise ideas that conservatives hold so dear.

Yet another argument for governmental reorganization concerned congressional displeasure with the purposes and activities of federal agencies. Sometimes ideological views also played a role here. Republicans in both houses of Congress have suggested that federal funding for the National Endowment for the Arts be axed. Their opposition to this agency arose from displeasure with the types of projects that the endowment was funding, some of which were seen as antithetical to traditional family values. They questioned, too, the need for governmental support for artistic expression.

Governmental reorganization can create many winners, but also many losers. Agencies can grow or shrink in responsibilities and employees, and those who receive benefits from modified or eliminated programs are affected. For example, in discussing the NEA, artists who had received funding through the arts endowment would be losers if the NEA was eliminated. Winners under this reorganization plan would be conservatives, who would have achieved their objective of reducing the federal government's size and its influence in the federal system. Similarly, logging companies and industrial polluters would be winners should the monitoring and enforcement offices of the EPA be eliminated or reduced. Other winners of governmental reform proposals could be taxpayers across the nation, who might see federal spending and deficits reduced, and perhaps even taxes cut.

Reformers faced opposition to all reorganization plans. The heads of agencies, threatened by reform proposals, took every opportunity to press the case for their agency being spared. Actress Jane Alexander, head of the National Endowment of the Arts, used her fame and influence in the mid-1990s to press Congress to sustain funding for the arts. She made the point that many communities have a stake in the funding fight, although few realize it, saying, "I don't think people make the connection between [the endowment] and their community arts center or their local little museum." Others also stressed that most NEA grants go to programs and institutions that bring arts to areas where they would not otherwise exist—to more than two thousand communities over the last 10 years—covering everything from museums to theater and dance groups to arts education programs.

Source: Federal Reorganization: Congressional Proposal to Merge Education, Labor, and EEOC. Report GAO/HEHS-95-140 (Washington, D.C.: U.S. Government Printing Office, 1995). Quoted in *USA Today,* February 20, 1995, 4D.

Box 16-3 The U.S. Government Manual

Visit the website below to access the *U.S. Government Manual*:

http://www.access.gpo.gov/gmanual/index.html

This manual is the official U.S. government description of the national government, including a full description of all U.S. departments, agencies, commissions, and other organizations. To learn about this useful information source, visit this site and look for all the information you can find on the U.S. Department of Transportation.

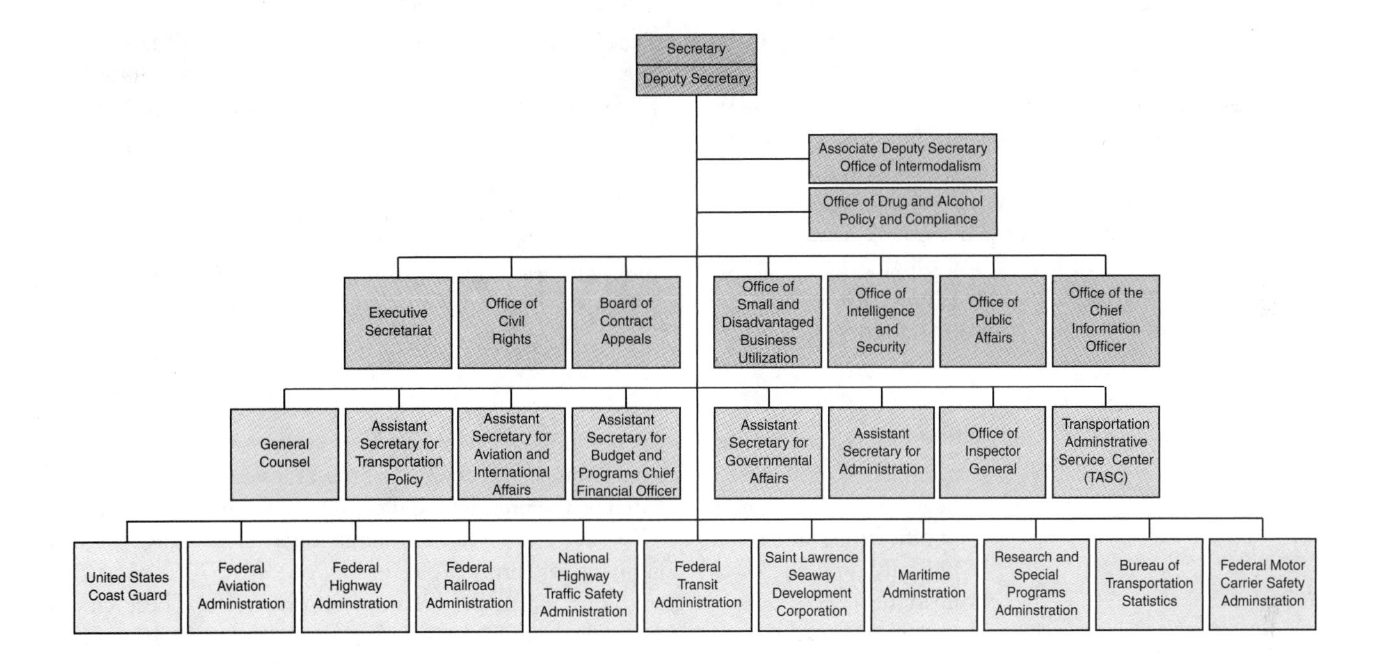

Figure 16-2
Organization Chart for U.S. Department of Transportation

Source: United States Department of Transportation

16-1d Independent Regulatory Commissions

Certain actions and transactions in the private sector can exert significant and possibly negative impacts on citizens. To limit the potential for harm to citizens, **independent regulatory commissions** have been created. They monitor and control activities as diverse as interstate trucking, unfair advertising practices, sales of stocks and bonds, environmental pollution, broadcasts of television signals, and consumer product safety. Some of the most important federal regulatory commissions are described in Box 16-4.

independent regulatory commissions *Federal agencies charged with regulation for private-sector activities that directly affect the public; designed to be partially insulated from political forces.*

Rules to Isolate Regulatory Agencies from Politics

Because regulatory commissions exercise focused regulatory power over specific industries, Congress designed them to be more isolated from daily politics than other federal agencies. Commissions are relatively independent of presidential direction. Regulatory commissions are directed by a governing board composed of multiple members instead of a single cabinet secretary. This arrangement broadens governing authority and dilutes the power of any single commissioner. Political isolation helps to ensure that the regulatory decisions of these commissions are based on broad public interest and scientific knowledge rather than on narrow political or economic factors. (As we will see, however, total isolation from politics is not possible.)

Box 16–4 *Independent Regulatory Agencies in the Federal Government*

Interstate Commerce Commission (ICC; 1887): Regulates specific areas of interstate trade: Responsibilities include setting rates for and prohibiting actions by railroads, trucking companies, bus lines, freight carriers, and overnight delivery services, as well as oil pipelines.

Federal Trade Commission (FTC; 1914): Created to regulate fair trade practices and foster competition. Works to prevent and uncover price fixing, deceptive advertising, and product mislabeling, and to promote product safety.

Federal Communications Commission (FCC; 1934): Regulates and manages television and radio communications as well as the electronic media in the United States. Grants and reviews the awarding of operating licenses for television and radio stations as well as of frequencies for these media and other users of radio communications. Also approves rates for interstate telephone and telegraph communications.

Securities and Exchange Commission (SEC; 1934): Protects investors and maintains the integrity of the securities markets.

Consumer Product Safety Commission (CPSC; 1972): Protects consumers from unreasonable risks of injury associated with consumer products. Investigates such products and issues warnings about those that pose risks to personal safety.

Federal Elections Commission (FEC; 1975): Oversees and manages the provisions of the Federal Election Campaign Act of 1971. Monitors campaign contributions and provides partial funding for presidential candidates.

Federal Energy Regulatory Commission (FERC; 1978): Fixes rates and controls natural gas companies, electric utilities, and interstate oil pipelines

The selection of regulatory commissioners and the design of terms of office are also intended to provide some separation from day-to-day politics and safeguards for the public. Commissioners are nominated by the president and confirmed by the Senate for terms of office that range from 4 to 7 years. The terms of commissioners are usually staggered; typically only one or two commissioner terms expire in any one year. Also, most commissioners serve terms longer than a single presidential term of office. These circumstances reduce the power of individual presidents to select the full membership of independent regulatory commissions. In addition, since commissioners can be removed only for violation of their oath of office, presidents cannot fire them. The laws creating these independent commissions also generally stipulate that members cannot all be selected from one political party.

The Move toward Deregulation

A move toward deregulation began in the Carter administration and expanded during Ronald Reagan's term of office. As a result, the mandates of some independent regulatory agencies were reduced.[2] For example, the Federal Aviation Administration ceased the practice of setting airline fares, which opened the door to more competition and possible variations in ticket fares. Similarly, the Federal Communications Commission no longer requires radio and television stations to give equal time to all political views. This allows audience reaction to be the prime factor in maintaining fairness in media broadcasts (see Chapter 6).

In spite of significant moves to reduce some forms of federal regulation, the independent regulatory agencies still oversee a wide variety of private-sector activities. Many regulatory mandates including those concerning civil rights, product safety, worker safety, and environmental protection remain in force. Problems arising from deregulation can result in a renewed push to tighten regulations. Most notable here is the widespread failure of savings and thrift institutions in the late 1980s and early 1990s. Many analysts claim that these failures were the result of a trend in the 1980s toward reducing restrictions on the lending activities of financial institutions. These bank failures and the federal (and ultimately public) responsibility for covering most depositor losses have generated calls for renewed regulatory control and oversight of the financial industry.

The question of deregulation of state and local governments became a major political issue in 1994 as Congress debated legislation that would, in most cases, prohibit the federal government from creating new regulatory mandates on states and localities. Prior to this legislation, governors, mayors, state legislatures, and city councils had been pleading for fewer federal mandates in areas such as environmental protection, consumer safety, and accessibility for physically disabled people.

Congress finally responded to the cries from states and localities by passing a law in 1994 that aimed at eliminating the creation of new unfunded regulatory mandates. Under this legislation, Congress promised to estimate compliance costs of any new regulations and to pay those costs unless there was a separate vote to suspend the principle of compensation. (Regulatory mandates created prior to 1995 were not be affected by this legislation.)

16-1e Public Corporations

A final set of agencies located within the executive branch are organized as public corporations. In structure they resemble business corporations. Like the regulatory commissions, public corporations are managed by a governing board of appointed officials. In creating these corporations, Congress intended that private-sector management skills and practices be applied to increase efficiency and service quality.

A prime example of a public corporation is the U.S. Postal Service, whose roots date back to America's earliest days. The postal service functioned as a cabinet department until 1970, when it was reorganized as a public corporation. The intent of the reorganization was to insulate the postal service from political pressures (especially patronage) and to focus attention on efficiency, service quality, and improved management.

Within the executive branch are other examples of public corporations. The Corporation for Public Broadcasting coordinates and channels public funds into public radio and television programming. The Federal Deposit Insurance Corporation and the Federal Savings and Loan Insurance Corporation are charged with protecting the savings deposits of citizens in financial institutions. Another prominent public government corporation is the Tennessee Valley Authority, which has constructed dams and operates power-generating plants in Tennessee and surrounding states.

Some of the public corporations have come under heavy scrutiny. Some members of Congress, mostly in the Republican Party, have called for the federal government to eliminate them and to turn over their function to the private sector. Examples include proposals introduced in Congress (but not enacted) to end federal government funding of the Corporation for Public Broadcasting (which in turn funds Public Broadcasting Stations [PBS]) and for Amtrak, the public corporation providing passenger rail service on routes across the nation.

16-2 Executive Branch Players

There are two kinds of players in the bureaucracy. They are differentiated by the ways in which they came onto the playing field.

16-2a Political Executives: Short-Term Bureaucratic Players

An important set of players in the executive branch are the political executives who hold top administrative positions in federal government agencies. These players are appointed by the president, and most must be confirmed by the Senate.

The political executive must be a game player. Game playing is the nature of the job. Moreover, political executives may have little choice concerning which games they play, with what objectives, or even with what intensity.

Cabinet Secretaries: The President's Team

The secretaries of cabinet departments, the vice president, and members of a few other agencies form the presidential cabinet. This group meets at the request of the president to discuss problems facing the nation (see Chapter 15). Cabinet members—the president's team—also provide counsel on political issues facing the presidential administration. Cabinet meetings are an opportunity for cabinet secretaries and other agency leaders to relay to the president information regarding issues and perspectives from the agencies they represent.

As the heads of governmental agencies, cabinet secretaries perform many key roles. They are responsible for overall agency management and accomplishment of the responsibilities given to the agency by Congress. Cabinet secretaries serve as spokespersons for their agencies in many forums, including testimony given in committee hearings held by the Senate and House of Representatives.

Other Short-Term Players

Under the cabinet secretaries are layers of other political appointees who perform top-level administrative roles within federal agencies. These officials, currently numbering about six hundred, together with cabinet secretaries, manage the daily operations of the federal government.[3] They perform several leadership functions, including advising cabinet secretaries, devising public policies, overseeing administrative activities, and implementing agency directives.[4] Titles for these players include undersecretary, assistant secretary, and deputy secretary. Nominated by the president and confirmed by the Senate, these officials, as political scientist Hugh Heclo noted, "commonly move in and out of government positions, returning to private corporations or law firms when they leave government service. This relatively short-term tenure in top executive branch positions contrasts markedly with professional civil servants, who spend decades, if not full careers, within the federal bureaucracy."[5]

The Nomination Game: Selecting Political Appointees

The power to appoint cabinet secretaries and other political executives provides the president with an opportunity to fashion a management team and a political agenda for operation of the federal government. The process by which political executives are selected is an important political game.

The Constitution requires that presidential nominations be reviewed and confirmed by the Senate, which typically defers to the president and confirms nominations. Occasionally confirmation is granted only after grueling nomination hearings, during which nominees are carefully scrutinized and extensively questioned. This type of scrutiny was evidenced in confirmation hearings on the appointment of Condoleezza Rice as Secretary of State in 2005. On rare occasions, the Senate has refused to approve presidential nominations.

The process for selecting cabinet secretaries recognizes the importance of a political linkage between the president and the departments of the executive branch. As stated earlier, presidents typically select individuals who share their political belief and ideologies. Not surprisingly, most appointees belong to the same party as the president. Recent presidents have come under pressure to appoint a more diverse group of individuals, including women and people of color, to top federal government positions. The cabinet appointed by President George W. Bush in 2001 included four women (Gale Norton, Secretary of Interior; Elaine Chou, Secretary of Labor; Christine Whitman, Administrator, Environmental Protection Agency; Ann Veneman, Secretary of Agriculture), two African Americans (Colin Powell, Secretary of State; Ron Paige, Secretary of Education), an Asian American (Elaine Chou), and a Latino American (Mel Martinez, Secretary of Housing and Urban Development).

Presidents can remove political executives whenever they so choose without approval by Congress. Generally, when presidents are dissatisfied with a cabinet secretary, they quietly let the individual know that they would like his or her resignation. The individual usually complies immediately. A refusal to resign may result in the official being fired. Sometimes, the secretary leaving office is given some other post as a means of sav-

Time Out 16-1

How Big Is the Federal Government?

The federal bureaucracy has been pictured as a huge network of different agencies filled with countless government employees. While the federal government could be thought of as a large agency, it is useful to put it in perspective. Consider the following questions and write down a brief answer to each.

- **Excluding the military, about how many federal employees are there?**
- **Has the number of federal employees been growing or shrinking in the past decade or two?**
- **How does the number of federal employees stack up against the number of government employees at the state and local levels?**

ing face. Thus, when Ronald Reagan wished to replace Margaret Heckler as his Secretary of Health and Human Services, he appointed her Ambassador to Ireland.

16-2b Civil Servants: Permanent Bureaucratic Players

The other set of primary players in the federal government are civil servants, who seek employment within the executive branch as a long-term career. Both the rules and procedures for selecting individuals for federal government employment have changed since America's founding.

The Spoils System: A Political Game of Power and Control

At one time, federal government jobs were distributed as political favors to presidential supporters and confidants. Selecting persons for federal government jobs had become a central part of party politics by the time Andrew Jackson assumed the presidency in 1828. Following a practice originated by his predecessors, the newly elected Jackson fired officials appointed by earlier presidents. In their place, he nominated individuals who were personal acquaintances or supporters of his political party, the Democrat-Republicans. Patronage, the award of government jobs to personal friends and party supporters, was also known as the *spoils system*. Under this practice, government jobs became a political resource that presidents (and governors and mayors at state and local levels) could use to reward supporters.

The spoils system developed from the efforts of political parties to control governmental operations and to reward party workers (see Chapter 8). Its fundamental drawback was that it did not place the most competent and skilled persons in federal government jobs. It also caused frequent turnover of personnel, making it difficult for federal agencies to develop a body of experienced workers. Inefficiency and incompetence in the administration of the federal government followed. The spoils system also led to rampant corruption in government during the administrations of Ulysses S. Grant and subsequent presidents. Governmental decisions regarding the awarding of construction contracts and the regulation of public utilities such as railroads were made on the basis of political connections, favoritism, and bribery instead of public interest.

By the last decades of the 19th century, popular opinion began to run against the spoils system, specifically, and governmental corruption more broadly. As part of a broad-scale effort to clean up and reorganize governmental practices, reformers in the Progressive Movement pressed for elimination of patronage as a means of allocating federal government jobs. Their plan for reform gathered steam in 1881, when newly elected President James A. Garfield was assassinated by a political supporter who had been angered about not receiving an ambassadorial position. This event served as a catalyst to reformers, whose efforts led to the passage of the Civil Service Reform Act of 1883. This important legislation, also known as the Pendleton Act, fundamentally restructured the process for awarding federal government jobs.

Not all federal government employees work in the nation's capital. Large states have more need for federal employees to operate federal programs within their borders. Other states draw federal employees because of their proximity to Washington D.C. or long established federal programs. It is not simply a matter that the large population

Answer to Time Out 16-1

In 2000, the federal government included 2.7 million employees, down from 3.1 million in 1990.

In spite of the prominence of the federal government in the media and widespread misperceptions about the magnitude of the federal government, the federal civilian workforce shrinks in comparison to the combined state and local government workforce, as shown below for 1999:

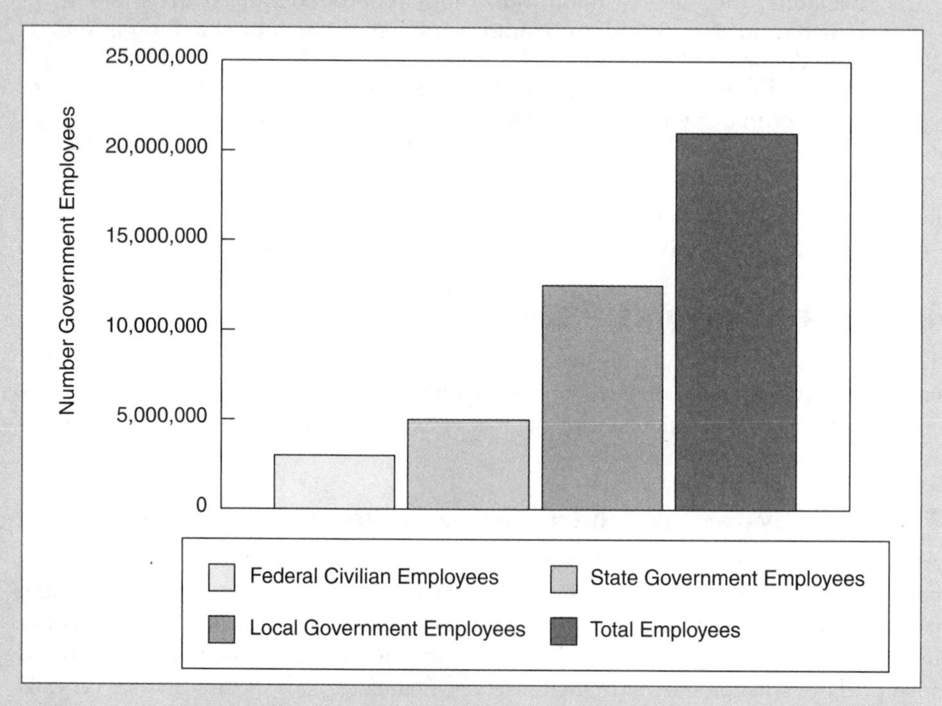

[a]U.S. Department of Commerce, *Statistical Abstract of the United States, 2001*, Table 449, page, 294

These numbers, however, underestimate the magnitude of the federal government influence. Some state and local government employees work in programs that are largely funded with federal dollars. One reason for the substantial growth in state and local government has been the hiring of state and local employees to implement federal programs and enforce federal regulatory mandates.

states receive the lion's share of the benefits. Strong lobbying and natural characteristics also affect the distribution, as Tables 16-1 and 16-2 make clear.

The Civil Service System

merit principle *Belief that jobs should be awarded on the basis of education and job skill (merit) as opposed to political connection or favoritism.*

The rationale of a civil service system is to replace patronage and the spoils system with a process that uses neutral competence as the principle in awarding government jobs. Under the current federal civil service system, employee selection is intended to be neutral, or free from political interference. Based solely on the competence, expertise, and experience of office seekers, this approach is sometimes known as the **merit principle.**

competitive examination *The civil service system practice of measuring the competence of job applicants through a standardized test designed to assess information and talents relevant to job performance; most common in lower-level and specialized job functions.*

Traditionally, the merit system used by the federal government has relied on two related practices. The first is the **competitive examination,** a test of skills and information relevant to the job in question. Under civil service laws, agency administrators may only consider those individuals with the highest scores for job openings.

Competitive examinations came under fire during the 1980s, when there were claims that they contained cultural bias in that their content and format worked to the disadvantage of ethnic and minority groups. Analysts also challenged that the broad-scale competitive examinations were poor indicators of job performance. Given this controversy, the federal government replaced many broad-scale competitive examinations with specialized examinations for particular fields.

Table 16-1 How Does your State Stack Up in Terms of Federal Employment?

States compete over the location of federal installations, since federal employment brings money into the state. States without the presence of large defense installations fight to locate and expand the presence of other federal programs in their states.

	Number of Federal Employees	Percent of Federal Employees in Defense		Number of Federal Employees	Percent of Federal Employees in Defense
Alabama	48,000	42%	Montana	11,000	10%
Alaska	14,000	31%	Nebraska	15,000	21%
Arizona	43,000	18%	Nevada	13,000	15%
Arkansas	20,000	18%	New Hampshire	8,000	12%
California	248,000	24%	New Jersey	62,000	22%
Colorado	51,000	20%	New Mexico	15,000	26%
Connecticut	21,000	12%	New York	134,000	39%
Delaware	5,000	25%	North Carolina	57,000	29%
Florida	113,000	23%	North Dakota	8,000	21%
Georgia	89,000	35%	Ohio	84,000	27%
Hawaii	23,000	70%	Oklahoma	43,000	49%
Idaho	11,000	13%	Oregon	29,000	10%
Illinois	94,000	13%	Pennsylvania	107,000	24%
Indiana	37,000	24%	Rhode Island	10,000	40%
Iowa	18,000	8%	South Carolina	26,000	35%
Kansas	25,000	21%	South Dakota	9,000	12%
Kentucky	30,000	22%	Tennessee	50,000	14%
Louisiana	33,000	23%	Texas	162,000	23%
Maine	113,000	42%	Utah	30,000	46%
Maryland	130,000	24%	Vermont	6,000	9%
Massachusetts	53,000	13%	Virginia	145,000	55%
Michigan	58,000	13%	Washington	62,000	35%
Minnesota	34,000	7%	West Virginia	18,000	9%
Mississippi	24,000	38%	Wisconsin	30,000	10%
Missouri	54,000	17%	Wyoming	6,000	15%

Source: U.S. Department of Commerce, *Statistical Abstract of the United States, 2002,* Table 474, p. 320.

The second merit system practice, **competitive evaluation,** invites persons interested in federal job openings to submit formal applications that describe their relevant training, job skills, education, and work experience. Jobs must be offered to the applicants rated highest by a panel of reviewers. The competitive evaluation process is most often used for middle- and upper-level management positions in federal agencies, whereas competitive examinations are utilized in specialized job functions, such as health care, law enforcement, and engineering.

competitive evaluation *The civil service system practice of measuring the competence of job applicants through a process in which applications and resumes are competitively rated by a review team to identify the most qualified applicants; most common in midlevel managerial job positions.*

Once appointed to a federal civil service position, individuals can be dismissed only on the basis of gross negligence of duty or formal elimination of their position. Like initial

Table 16-2

Top Ten States: Population vs. Federal Civilian Employment

Top 10 States in Population	Top Ten States in Federal Civilian Employment
1. California	1. California
2. Texas	2. Texas
3. New York	3. New York
4. Florida	4. Virginia
5. Illinois	5. Maryland
6. Pennsylvania	6. Florida
7. Ohio	7. Pennsylvania
8. Michigan	8. Illinois
9. New Jersey	9. Georgia
10. Georgia	10. Ohio

Source: U.S. Department of Commerce, *Statistical Abstract of the United States, 2002,* Table 474, p. 320.

job recruitment, promotion within the federal workforce is based on merit criteria. Civil servants are protected from being dismissed or overlooked for advancement on political grounds. Without such protections, a spoils system might quickly re-emerge.

veteran's preference *Practice within the civil service system that adds points to competitive examinations and evaluations for all applicants who are military veterans.*

Congress has chosen to include a **veteran's preference** as part of merit determination. Veterans are rewarded for their military service to the nation by being given a slight advantage in the allocation of federal government jobs. Receiving a few extra points on competitive exams and evaluations, veterans are the only group of citizens to have a favored status in the federal personnel system.

The Senior Executive Service

Senior Executive Service (SES) *Program created in the late 1970s to develop top-quality managers within the executive branch and to discourage them from leaving the public sector for better-paying jobs in the private sector.*

An important innovation in the federal personnel system is the **Senior Executive Service (SES)**, created as part of the Civil Service Reform Act of 1978. It is designed to attract and retain top-level managers who might be tempted to leave public service for private-sector jobs. The key incentive offered by the SES is higher salaries and substantial cash bonuses. These enticements help build a dependable group of top executives who can move easily across agencies to handle important management tasks. The federal government currently has about seven thousand jobs designated as SES positions.

16-3 Bureaucratic Reform and Reinventing Government

At various times in the nation's history, dissatisfaction with the structures and functions of government has led to calls for reform and restructuring of the federal bureaucracy. As noted above, one such time was the Progressive Era, when widespread recognition of the evils of the spoils system led to the creation of the civil service and other mechanisms to reduce the political influences on the administration of government. During the New Deal, President Franklin D. Roosevelt and Democratic majorities in both houses of Congress created many new agencies to stimulate the depressed economy and regulate the banking and securities industries.

Since the beginning of the New Deal, a variety of task forces, study commissions, and other initiatives have been undertaken for the purpose of analyzing the organization and operation of the federal bureaucracy. Each issued a report and made recommendations for reorganization and reform. As a result of the Committee on Administrative Management (the Brownlow Commission) appointed by President Roosevelt, the Executive Office of the President was created. Two commissions headed by former president Herbert Hoover—one appointed by Harry Truman and the other by Dwight Eisenhower—made recommendations that stimulated reforms. Two of these were the merger of all military forces into a single Department of Defense and changes in the federal budget-making process.

Box 16–5 *So You Want a Job with the Government: Will the Testing Ever End?*

And you thought you would be done with testing when you finished high school. Not if you want to work for the government. The Civil Service system was designed to base hiring and promotion for government jobs on merit. For a large number of such jobs a key component in hiring is one's performance on a competitive civil service examination. The content of examinations varies depending on the type of job one seeks. To get a feel for what is covered and the implications, read on.

Try Your Hand at Questions on the Civil Service Exam

Most civil service examinations evaluate verbal ability, focusing on word meanings, grammar, spelling, and reading comprehension.

Clerical positions require speed and accuracy, so assessments geared toward these positions are the most carefully timed portions of the examinations. Here are three examples of actual questions from a civil service examination that you can try your hand at:

1. RESEARCH is related to FINDINGS as TRAINING is related to
   a. skill.
   b. tests.
   c. supervision.
   d. teaching
2. Indicate the correct spelling
   a. sequance
   b. sequence
   c. sequense
   d. none of the above
3. Precedent most nearly means
   a. law.
   b. example.
   c. theory.
   d. conformity.

Specialized Tests

Particular jobs require special knowledge and abilities. For example, police officers are tested on their memory and observation skills. Individuals desiring to join the Foreign Service (State Department) are expected to have a broad knowledge of American history, political institutions, culture, and economics.

What Happens After the Examination?

Applicants meeting the minimum education and experience for a particular job are then ranked based on their civil service examination score. As openings occur, individuals at the top of the list are usually called in for interviews. Hiring officers are expected to choose from among those on the top of the list. If not chosen for a particular job, opening applicants are kept on the top of the list for future openings.

Answers

1. a. (The desired result of research is findings, while the desired result of training is the development of a skill.)
2. b.
3. b.

Presidents have often launched reform efforts intended to change the number, position, and functions of federal agencies. President Richard Nixon proposed the creation of four "super" cabinet departments and the elimination of the departments of Agriculture, Commerce, Labor, and Transportation. These reforms were not adopted by Congress (the body with ultimate power to create, reform, or abolish departments and agencies in the executive branch). President Jimmy Carter was more successful in achieving his reform objectives: enhancing the position of federal education programs, creating a new Department of Energy, and reforming the federal civil service system.

16-3a Reinventing Government: The National Performance Review

Throughout the 1980s, conservatives raised the cry for cutting back government, reducing waste, and eliminating some federal programs and agencies. These calls intensified as public dissatisfaction with government performance, taxes, and concerns about the persistent federal budget deficit became major political issues. In response, many types of reforms were proposed. One approach to reform that took root in the early 1990s focused on the idea of reinventing government and adapted the entrepreneurial spirit of business to the operation of government. Reflecting this approach is the book *Reinventing Government*, whose authors argued:

> Today's environment demands institutions that are extremely flexible and adaptable. It demands institutions that deliver high-quality goods and services, squeezing more bang out of every buck. It demands institutions that are responsive to their customers, offering choices of nonstandardized services; that lead by persuasion and incentives rather than commands; that give their employees a sense of meaning and control, even ownership. It demands institutions that empower citizens rather than simply serving them.[6]

The reinventing government theme was seized by the Clinton administration as it took office in 1993. Vice President Al Gore was appointed to head the National Performance Review (NPR). In announcing the formation of this performance review task force, President Bill Clinton stated:

> Our goal is to make the entire federal government less expensive and more efficient, and to change the culture of our national bureaucracy away from complacency and entitlement toward initiative and empowerment. We intend to redesign, to reinvent, to reinvigorate the entire national government.[7]

After several months of work, the National Performance Review issued a series of reports containing strategies and specific recommendations. Overall, the reform recommendations focused on cutting red tape and bureaucratic inefficiency, putting citizens—as customers—first, ahead of bureaucratic norms or standardized procedures, decentralizing authority to empower employees to get better results, and getting government back to the basics by eliminating program duplication and special interest privileges.[8] For more information on the recommendations of the National Performance Review, see Box 16-6: Findings and Recommendations of the National Performance Review.

Many of the themes and strategies outlined in the National Performance Review were drawn from similar organizational reforms with such names as *Total Quality Management* or *Strategic Planning* being debated and implemented in the private sector. Dominant themes in both the public and private sectors include an emphasis on efficiency. Box 16-7: Using Technological Innovation to Enhance Government Performance examines emerging techniques for enhancing efficiency.

16-3b Assessing the National Performance Review

A report on the status of the National Performance Review issued a year after its origin documented individual success stories in governmental reform.[9] It stated that 90 percent of its recommendations were under way and noted that over one hundred agencies were publishing customer service standards. About the same time, the General Accounting Office (GAO), the investigative arm of Congress, reported that, while some progress had been made in implementing recommendations, few had been fully implemented and many would take years to completely execute. The GAO also argued, "We believe that government 'reinvention' requires the executive branch and Congress to shift the focus of government management and accountability from an emphasis on inputs, outputs, and processes to an emphasis on outcomes and results."[10] In other words, the GAO saw a need for less attention to processes of government and more focus on achieving the intended reform results.

Another examination of the National Performance Review, one conducted by analysts outside of government, recognized some achievements but noted two fundamental implementation problems. First, the study found that reform had been preoccupied with achieving immediate savings rather than with developing longer-term strategies for performance improvement. Seeking short-term savings, it is argued, can undermine long-term attempts to increase the performance of agencies and employees. Second, there was no clear strategy for involving the legislative branch in executive branch reform. This analysis concluded that the National Performance Review, in its first year, accomplished far more than cynics suggested might be possible. Nevertheless, and this is the NPR's critical problem, the short-term accommodations it made to get the movement going weakened its chances for long-term success."[11]

Box 16–6 Findings and Recommendations of the National Performance Review

The purpose of the 6-month National Performance Review, headed by Vice President Al Gore, was to reexamine the federal government with the twin purposes of making government work better and cost less. The National Performance Review issued a report on improving the structure and performance of each agency of the federal government along with an overview report that laid out major themes to guide reform. The major themes stressed in the overview report on the National Performance Review are quoted here:

Cutting Red Tape: The Federal Government does at least one thing well: It generates *red tape*. But not one inch of that red tape appears by accident. In fact, the government creates it all with the best of intentions. It is time now to put aside our reverence for those intentions and examine what they have created: a system that makes it hard for our civil servants to do what we pay for, and frustrates taxpayers who rightfully expect their money's worth.

Implementation Strategies: (1) Streamline the budget process with the president setting broad priorities at the start of the process and Congress instituting a biennial (2-year) budget process; (2) decentralize the departments' and agencies' primary responsibility for recruitment and retention of employees from the current centralization of these functions in the Office of Personnel Management; (3) streamline the procurement process through which the federal government purchases goods and services; (4) eliminate regulatory overkill, that is, the creation of more and more federal regulations; and (5) empower state and local governments by reducing federal regulatory mandates whose implementation is not funded with federal monies and by consolidating rigidly defined federal categorical grants into broad flexible grants where states and localities have more discretion in operating programs.

Empowering Employees to Get Results: Now we must create a culture of public entrepreneurship of people willing to innovate. We must discover what the private sector has already embraced: that more isn't always better, but better is better. We must pursue a new goal: quality. And we must organize around it.

Implementation Strategies: (1) Decentralize decision making to lower levels within federal agencies; (2) hold federal employees accountable for results; (3) increase employee training, install good management information systems, and use modern information technologies; (4) enhance the quality of work life within federal agencies; and (5) form labor-management partnerships.

Cutting Back to Basics: Is government still doing things it no longer needs to do? Are we paying for obsolete programs? Are we paying for programs that weren't needed in the first place? Are we spending public money to benefit special interest groups? Are we doing all we can to stop fraud? Are we doing all we can to deny benefits to people who aren't eligible for them? When we start acting on the answers to the questions, we will begin to have a more effective government.

Implementation Strategies: (1) Grant the president the power to eliminate wasteful spending; (2) consolidate field offices in some agencies; (3) eliminate duplication among agencies; (4) collect more revenues through debt collection, user fees, and eliminating fraud; (5) invest in great productivity; and (6) use modern technology to reengineer programs to cut costs.

Conclusion of the National Performance Review: The National Performance Review will not end with this report. We have identified what we need to do. Now, we will do it. We will change the environment in government from one that resists change to one that fosters it; from one that stifles innovation to one that encourages it; from one that creates horror stories to one that creates successes. We will cut red tape, serve our customers, empower our employees, and cut back to basics.

Source: From Red Tape to Results: Creating a Government That Works Better and Costs Less. Report of the National Performance Review (Washington, D.C.: U.S. Government Printing Office), 1993.

Box 16–7 Using Technological Innovation to Enhance Government Performance

Not only does technology influence the conduct of politics, it can also influence the operation of government. As it tried to scout out new ways to enhance federal government performance, the National Performance Review team explored a variety of information technology innovations. These innovations were expected to make government operations more efficient and responsive to the needs of citizens. Some of them increase citizen knowledge of government, allowing them to be more effective players in political games.[a]

The National Performance Review recommended that the following technological reforms be implemented:

A Nationwide Integrated Electronic Benefit Transfer

The problem: Millions of Americans each year receive benefits in the form of Social Security checks, food stamps, disability insurance benefits, and many others. Provision of benefits relies upon paper-based systems that are costly, not always customer-friendly, and sometimes prone to fraud and abuse.

The idea: Create a nationwide system linking the government to banks so that benefits can be directly deposited into recipient accounts without the issuance of checks, coupons, and other printed materials. Recipients could draw upon these benefits through a single plastic access card, similar to a credit card.

An Integrated Electronic Access to Government Information and Services

The problem: Access to government services is often cumbersome, particularly if more than one agency is involved. The use of telephone access points and toll-free numbers was a first step in easing the access of consumers (i.e., American citizens) to governmental services and information. The Internal Revenue Service, for example, now handles 70 percent of taxpayer contacts by telephone. This is only the beginning, however, of using advanced technology to increase citizen contact with government.

The idea: Implement a single integrated 800 number to connect callers with a trained operator who can route them to whatever government agency or service they need. Also, create a single, integrated electronic bulletin board so that computer-users can access government agencies more easily.

Intergovernmental Tax Filing, Reporting, and Payments Processing

The problem: Enormous administrative costs are associated with processing the paperwork associated with filing taxes, reporting tax withholding, and processing tax returns. These actions are multiplied by each level of government.

The idea: Provide an intergovernmental tax filing, reporting, and processing system whereby citizens could receive their federal, state, and local tax bills through one national system (the revenues, of course, would be distributed to the appropriate government). Citizens could also pay tax bills by calling a toll-free number and using a credit card.

A Government-Wide Electronic Mail System

The problem: Email provides a quick and effective means of communication between workers in federal agencies and between agency workers and the public, but currently agencies are not systematically organized; some agencies have no email system.

The idea: Create an integrated email system where federal workers can easily make contact with counterparts in any federal government agency or office within Congress. Enhanced communication is expected to substantially increase the efficiency of government operations.

---

a. *Source: From Red Tape to Results: Creating a Government That Works Better and Costs Less.* Report of the National Performance Review (Washington, D.C.: U.S. Government Printing Office, 1993).

Overall, these assessments of the National Performance Review suggest that a fundamental reform process has begun. Analysts and managers have begun to reexamine existing governmental programs, structures, and operations, generally with an eye toward efficiency, customer satisfaction, and downsizing. Such changes from within, however, do not come easily. The reforms made were the simplest and easiest to accomplish. For a true governmental reinvention to take place, diligent work will be required as difficult issues of policy changes, technological innovations, personnel reward systems, and other features of the federal bureaucracy are restructured and new forms of federal-state-local partnerships are explored.

16-4 The Administrative Rulemaking Game

American government has increasingly become a 'bureaucratic democracy'; that is, democratic decision making takes place more and more in bureaucratic settings.

Under the Constitution, members of Congress, as elected representatives of the people, are granted legislative power to enact laws governing the nation. However, the functions of the federal government now include such diverse areas as space exploration, mental health, highway construction and safety, occupational health and safety, and pollution control. As government has expanded, the topics covered in public laws have also grown and become more technical (consider for yourself a technical decision situation in Time Out 16-2: The Challenge of Making Administrative Decisions). The extent of government expansion makes it impossible for twentieth-century lawmakers to be experts in all areas of federal lawmaking.

The Challenge of Making Administrative Decisions

Time Out 16-2

Introduction

Assume that you are a financial aid officer at a public university. As part of your job, you administer a federal government student aid program that provides fellowships to college students. In this role, you are participating in the implementation of a federal government program, even though you are an employee of the university.

Imagine that you have been given $5,000 to distribute in fellowship aid, with the following federal stipulations:

1. Awards can be made in any amount, from $1,000 to $5,000.
2. You may not discriminate on the basis of race or gender.
3. You may consider financial need and academic performance in making awards.
4. Students whose income is greater than $4,000 per year are ineligible.

Given these criteria, read the profiles that follow of the individuals who are applying for financial aid.

Student Profiles

Joe: An African-American student in his sophomore year with a 3.23 grade point average (GPA). His application indicates that he has earned $5,000 in the last 12 months; he intends to continue working but only part-time, which will reduce his earnings. Joe requests $3,500 in fellowship support for the next academic year.

Susan: A white cheerleader with a GPA of 3.7. She does not work, and her parents provide financial support for her college education. She requests $2,500 in fellowship support for the next college year.

Juan: A Latino engineering student in his third year. He has an overall GPA of 2.1, although his GPA for his sophomore year was 3.5. His overall GPA was hurt because of very poor grades in his freshman year, when he was unsure about his major and less interested in his studies. Juan's parents provide some of his college expenses but cannot cover them all. Juan requests $3,500 for the next academic year.

Joanne: An African-American senior biology major with a GPA of 3.1. Joanne studied during her first 2 years of college at a local junior college and transferred to your university in her junior year. Her GPA at the junior college was 3.85. Joanne cannot afford to attend college without some financial support. The lab requirements for her major are sufficiently demanding that she cannot take an outside job. She is requesting $5,000 in fellowship support.

Your Task

With these student profiles and federal government guidelines in mind, decide how you would allocate the $5,000 in fellowship monies. You are free to allocate the funds in any way you see fit as long as you adhere to the government guidelines. Make sure you can justify your choices.

Answer to Time Out 16-2

If you chose Joe, you have violated federal guidelines, unless you interpreted the prohibition against earning more than $4,000 as applying to NEXT year.

If you chose Susan, you were probably impressed with her GPA. It would be a piece of hard data with which you could justify your choice.

If you chose Juan, you may have been impressed with his academic improvement. If you gave him an advantage because of his Latino background, you would have violated the nondiscrimination rule.

If you chose Joanne, you indicated your sensitivity to her special needs, but if you chose her on the basis of race, you would have violated the nondiscrimination rule.

There are no right or wrong answers in this exercise. The government guidelines provide you with substantial discretionary decision-making power and do not stipulate an automatic formula for determining fellowship allocations. What is required here, and in many government decisions, is the exercise of judgment, given factual information about cases and guidelines for policy implementation.

One tricky component of your decision making may have concerned the issue of grade point averages (GPAs). The guidelines only stipulate that GPAs may be considered. They do not indicate how much this criterion should be weighed against others (e.g., financial need) or what GPA level is considered satisfactory. This is your responsibility and, as you probably recognized, such choices are not easy to make.

Again, there are no right or wrong answers here. The point of this example has been to demonstrate the application of discretionary decision making.

16-4a The Delegation Doctrine

Members of Congress have come to rely upon the political executives and civil servants within federal agencies for technical information and advice from federal agencies during the process of drafting and enacting laws. Congress frequently decides to set only broad policy directions when designing statutes, leaving the specifics of policy implementation to be worked out by designated federal agencies. This process is formally known as the **delegation doctrine.**

delegation doctrine *Process whereby Congress enacts laws that give general policy directions and instruction, leaving specific policy execution to designated federal agencies.*

statutory intent *The goals and objectives of Congress outlined in public laws, which are intended as instructions to the federal agencies that engage in policy implementation.*

The delegation doctrine does not mean that Congress gives up total policy-making authority to the executive branch. What Congress does in public statutes is to set out goals, general methods, and policy expectations. After specifying this **statutory intent,** Congress delegates to specified federal agencies the responsibility of refining the policies outlined in the statute, so that detailed plans for policy implementation can be formulated. The delegation doctrine means that policy making has become a shared responsibility between Congress and federal agencies. Congress is the dominant player on this team, but substantial policy power also resides with federal bureaucrats.

Legislative delegation has been defended on several grounds. First, delegation enhances the efficiency of lawmaking. Members of Congress cannot study every statute in detail or write long and comprehensive legislation for every federal government activity. Congress does not have the time, for example, to draft laws covering every dimension of such complex issues as public health, education of elementary and secondary school students, and occupational safety of workers.

Second, legislative delegation provides for flexibility in the execution of federal laws. The discretion given to federal bureaucrats through delegation allows them to apply general principles creatively to specific situations, some of which might not have been anticipated by Congress.

Third, legislative delegation recognizes the expertise of public officials in the executive branch. For example, a thorough understanding of environmental protection requires scientific knowledge about pollutants, their source and spread, and their impact on human beings and the environment. Officials in the Environmental Protection Agency (EPA) are hired on the basis of specialized knowledge regarding ecology. Their formal training provides them with the information and expertise that members of Congress lack.

Fourth, legislative delegation allows Congress to draw upon the extensive experience of civil servants in the executive branch, most of whom are pursuing a lifetime career in public service. Through their daily experience, federal bureaucrats have firsthand knowledge about strategies used to implement specific public policies. They know which strategies have worked and which have been ineffective. They also may have ideas about how existing programs might be improved. (See Time Out 16-3: Legislative Controls on Discretion to learn more about how Congress can constrain administrative discretion).

16-4b The Dangers of Delegation

In spite of its advantages, some dangers are associated with the delegating of policy-making authority by Congress to the executive branch. One concern is that the delegation principle places federal bureaucrats in the middle between the president (as chief executive) and Congress (as lawmakers). The president is charged with faithfully overseeing the laws enacted by Congress. Congress has this expectation but also desires to delegate some policy decisions to bureaucrats who have relevant policy expertise and experience. Federal bureaucrats are thus caught between the influence of the president and presidential staffers on the one side and lawmakers and their staffs on the other.

Probably the foremost concern is the violation of the separation of powers doctrine. If Congress delegates too much policy-making authority to federal agencies, then the executive branch becomes a legislative body. Appointed officials, instead of legislators elected directly by citizens, would be the primary policy makers. The system of checks and balances cannot work if the individual branches lose their separateness and become fused.

Citing the separation of powers principle, challenges have been made in the federal courts, typically by parties who dislike the regulations that agencies have created through delegated powers. Generally, the Supreme Court has upheld the delegation doctrine as long as Congress provides some guidelines for policy execution in authorizing statutes.[12]

Legislative Controls on Discretion

Time Out 16-3

Reconsider for a moment the awarding of student fellowships that was examined in Time Out 16-2. Suppose now that Congress has carefully studied the fellowship program at several universities and is dissatisfied with what it finds. One major concern is that fellowships are not being awarded consistently: students with similar circumstances but who attend different colleges are not being treated alike. Members of Congress also feel that too little of the fellowship support is being given to the students with the greatest financial need.

What might Congress do to (1) improve consistency in program implementation, and (2) more carefully target funds to disadvantaged students? Think about this for a moment before reading on.

The usual means of exerting greater control over the fellowship program is to refine the guidelines given to program administrators. Congress could change these guidelines by revising them and placing them in public laws. Or it could give the responsibility for fine-tuning award guidelines to the federal agency that oversees fellowship support. To enhance consistency, the guidelines need more clarity, particularly concerning how student income should be counted, how grade point averages should be weighed, and how student financial aid should be determined. Greater detail in directives would likely reduce that discretion.

Similarly, the guidelines could be revised to more carefully target fellowship monies to the most needy students, if, indeed, that is the intent of Congress. To achieve this objective, grade point average might be counted less while student financial need and income might be highlighted. The guidelines would have to require that financial aid officers give top priority to the students with the least financial resources to support their college education.

The Court has also looked more favorably on delegation when it can be shown that federal agencies follow procedural safeguards as they design administrative regulations. (Such safeguards include the processes of administrative rulemaking,[13] described in the next section.) The Supreme Court retains the power to assess whether legislative delegation is too broad, thus violating the doctrine of separation of powers. In a few cases, it has judged excessive delegation to be unconstitutional.[14]

16-4c The Administrative Procedure Act

During the first half of the 20th century, members of Congress became increasingly concerned about the delegation doctrine. While recognizing the tendency of the Supreme Court to uphold it, and Congress's need to rely upon the experience and talents of federal bureaucrats, lawmakers remained anxious about giving up substantial policy-making power to the executive branch. In particular, they worried about accountability, given that elected representatives of the people were transferring some policy-making power to nonelected political executives and civil servants.[15]

Immediately after World War II, Congress decided that it was time to formalize and structure the procedures used by federal agencies to devise policies to implement federal laws. This was accomplished through the Administrative Procedure Act of 1946 (APA).[16] This important legislation requires federal agencies to follow one of two processes when designing **administrative rules** (regulations and guidelines that outline how public laws are to be executed by public officials).

administrative rules *The guidelines and procedures (also known as administrative regulations) designed by agencies of the executive branch to implement public laws; agencies rely upon the statutes enacted by Congress when designing administrative rules.*

One process, known as **adjudication,** is required when the federal government makes decisions that directly affect the operations of one or only a few industries or parties. Included here would be regulations concerning freight and passenger rates for railroads or the licensing of new drugs. In cases such as these, federal government decisions can have a profound impact on the economic livelihood of the companies affected.

adjudication *A quasi-judicial process used to make rules that have a major impact on a limited number of parties.*

Adjudication is a quasi-judicial process. The federal officials designing the administrative rules and the parties to be regulated by them meet in a structured hearing that resembles a court trial. An administrative judge presides as both sides present evidence and question and cross-examine witnesses. The APA stipulates that final decisions about formal rules be based on the evidence presented at the hearing.

A more common process than adjudication is **informal rulemaking,** a series of actions to be followed by agencies when designing rules for executing policies with broad impact. The APA stipulates a three-stage process for informal rulemaking. First, agencies engaged in rulemaking must publish in the *Federal Register* a draft copy of proposed administrative rules that includes references to the law that grants the agency relevant policy responsibility. (The *Federal Register* is published each day by the federal government; it contains notices about the rulemaking activities of federal agencies. See Box 16-8: The *Federal Register*.)

informal rulemaking *A process to devise administrative rules with broad application; proposed rules must be published in the Federal Register and public comments solicited before issuing rules in final form.*

Second, the agency invites the public, including those who will be most affected, to comment on the rules. This provides an opportunity for external criticism and for suggestions regarding rule changes. Some agencies hold public hearings to obtain ideas and to gauge public reactions to proposed rules.

Box 16-8 *The Federal Register*

Visit the following website to access the *Federal Register*:

http://fr.cos.com

To get a glimpse of the organization and contents of the *Federal Register*, pick any weekday this past year—your birthday, yesterday, any day you please—and visit the website. On the main page, select the "Browse through back issues of the Federal Register" link, identify the date you selected, and learn what business the federal government announced on the date you selected.

Finally, at the close of the comment period, the agency examines the public input, considers rule changes, and then publishes the final rule in the *Federal Register*. This process opens agency rulemaking to public scrutiny and input. While the APA does not require the rulemaking agency to change proposed rules in light of public comments, agency officials typically examine these comments carefully and consider whether they justify rule changes.

16-4d Rulemaking and Players in the Political Game

Agency officials engaged in rulemaking often find themselves at the center of conflicting pressures for policy implementation. In designing regulations, they must first comply with the legislative intent and instructions included in statutes enacted by Congress. As they craft implementation strategies, they typically receive extensive input and pressure from interest groups, who actively submit comments on proposed rules and otherwise seek to influence agency decision making.

An example of the games associated with administrative rulemaking is presented in Box 16-9: Rulemaking Games Regarding Transportation Policy for Persons with Disabilities. In this case, the Department of Transportation became embroiled in a political struggle between groups representing people with disabilities on one side and public transit providers on the other. Through several years of controversy, transportation policies for people with disabilities changed direction several times. Members of Congress, the federal courts, and interest groups all took actions that led to the revision of administrative rules.

Interest Groups and Other Players in Rulemaking

Interest groups have learned that legislative enactments by Congress no longer represent the last step in policy development. Because important policy decisions are made during rulemaking, the parties affected by those policies are interested in the content of both proposed and final rules.

Interest groups are active players in games concerning administrative rulemaking. Regulatory policies involving environmental protection are a case in point. Groups representing polluters (often private companies but sometimes local governments) struggle to convince rulemakers to grant greater flexibility in achieving compliance. They want rules that provide them with latitude in satisfying pollution control mandates while at the same time minimizing the costs of compliance. These players also seek to defer compliance deadlines. On the other side are environmental interest groups that seek aggressive enforcement, clear guidelines with limited flexibility, and quick compliance deadlines.

The companies and organizations that these interest groups represent may be thought of as the clientele of the public agencies that regulate them. This clientele network has a direct stake in government decisions; their interests, often including profits, are immediately affected by government policies.[17] For this reason, clientele groups lobby hard and seek to establish cordial relations with the agency that regulates them. Agencies often appreciate good relationships with their clients. On the one hand, they value the specialized information that the clientele members possess. They also value the political support that the clientele may offer when Congress reviews the agency and considers its funding.

Federal agencies are sometimes criticized for having too-close relationships with companies and organizations that they are monitoring and regulating. This charge is called **co-optation** and holds that agency decision making is too heavily influenced by the clientele groups.[18] Although the short-term response of agencies to charges of cooptation is to distance themselves from their clientele members, these two sets of players continue to have much in common. For this reason, clientele groups remain important players in agency decision making and implementation.

co-optation *Development of close ties between an agency and the organizations and companies it is intended to regulate; may interfere with enforcement of the agency's regulatory responsibilities.*

In rulemaking games, it is not clear that all types of players are able to participate equally in the rulemaking game. Interest groups that are well organized and staffed with professional lobbyists (see Chapter 7) are more likely than others to have an impact on the rulemaking decisions of federal bureaucrats. These groups, sometimes formed together

Box 16–9 Rulemaking Games Regarding Transportation Policy for Persons with Disabilities

Background

Congress enacted section 504 of the Rehabilitation Act of 1973, prohibiting recipients of federal funds (including state and most local governments) from discriminating on the basis of handicaps. This law provided little explanation of statutory intent and few guidelines for policy implementation.

Round 1: Full Accessibility Rules

The Department of Transportation (DOT) initiated rulemaking to devise implementation strategies for section 504. Following a mandate to make public transit facilities fully accessible to persons with disabilities, DOT designed administrative rules that required that public mass transportation stations be accessible to persons with disabilities. These regulations also required that buses purchased with federal funds be accessible to wheelchairs.

Groups representing persons with disabilities applauded what they saw as a powerful and positive move to enhance accessibility; the reaction from transit systems was negative. Led by the American Public Transit Association (APTA), local public transit providers submitted comments, complaints, data reports, and threats of bankruptcy to DOT during rulemaking. DOT largely lent a deaf ear to these complaints.

Round 2: Full Accessibility Rules Are Challenged and Invalidated

APTA fought the full accessibility rules in the federal courts, charging that DOT regulations exceeded the intent of Congress in enacting section 504. APTA argued that the brief language of section 504 did not justify the strong accessibility policy designed by DOT. The federal circuit court agreed, and, accepting the court decision, DOT suspended the full accessibility regulations.

Round 3: Special Efforts Rules

With the full accessibility rules repealed, DOT issued temporary rules requiring transit providers to make special efforts to enhance the access of people with disabilities to public transportation. These rules were weaker than the full accessibility ones and did not clearly state what types of efforts were required.

Round 4: Persons with Disabilities Fight Back

Groups representing disabled Americans, dissatisfied with the weak special efforts rules, convinced Congress in 1982 to stipulate that transportation services to persons with disabilities must be the same as or comparable to those provided to other users. This stimulated DOT to issue new administrative rules describing how transit providers should make services to riders with disabilities comparable to those given to other transit users. These regulations contained a cost cap whereby transit providers would be in compliance if they spent a specified dollar amount in a given year toward achieving comparability.

Round 5: Challenging the Rulemaking

Groups representing citizens with disabilities challenged the cost cap provision on the grounds that it violated statutory intent. They argued that the law requiring comparable services did not include any language indicating that cost was a legitimate issue in deferring compliance. As the case moved through the courts, federal judges sided with the groups representing persons with disabilities.

Round 6: Legislators Get the Ball

The seesaw struggle between opposing groups was pre-empted by the passage of the Americans with Disabilities Act (ADA) of 1990. In enacting this law, Congress moved the political struggle out of the administrative process and back into the legislative arena. Included within the ADA are requirements that public transit authorities make all new buses, trains, and subway cars accessible to people in wheelchairs. The ADA required yet another round of rulemaking by DOT to guide implementation of its transportation provisions.[a]

---

a. Stephen L. Percy, *Disability, Civil Rights, and Public Policy: The Politics of Implementation* (Tuscaloosa, AL: University of Alabama Press), 1989.

into issue networks, have permanent staffs that carefully monitor agency rulemaking efforts and stimulate group participation when rules of interest to the group are being devised. The National Rifle Association, for example, pays just as much attention to regulations issued by federal agencies concerning the manufacture and sale of guns as it does to the lawmaking by Congress.

Not always adequately represented during rulemaking are poor and disadvantaged citizens.[19] These people have traditionally not been organized into groups that represented their interests in the political process. The growth of public interest lobbies (groups that lobby for the interests of the general public rather than specific groups or organizations), however, has changed this situation somewhat. These lobbies, which represent broad groups of citizens in contrast to narrow political and economic interests, have increased participation.[20] Public interest groups such as Common Cause (citizens working to end special-interest politics and reform government ethics) and Nader's Raiders (citizens investigating corruption throughout government) are examples of prominent public interest lobbies that have had considerable success in the administrative arena.

Rulemaking and Responses in Other Arenas

The issuance of final administrative rules does not end the policy game. Dissatisfied players, including members of the public, may turn to other political arenas with the intent of overturning the rules and regulations issued by agencies. For example, interest groups displeased with certain rules may turn to the federal courts. Interest groups may argue that rulemakers have violated statutory intent; that is, created policies that are contrary to or that go beyond what Congress intended in relevant public laws. Or they may argue that agency officials did not properly follow the procedures for adjudication or informal rulemaking. If the courts agree with the challengers, the administrative rules may be invalidated. This action returns the matter to federal agencies, which then conduct further rounds of rulemaking.

Congress, too, pays attention to rulemaking in federal agencies. If members of Congress disapprove of administrative rules created by federal agencies, they may voice their displeasure to agency leaders. Republican members of Congress, for example, in 1995 sent repeated messages to the EPA that they were concerned about environmental policies implemented by the agency and the stringency of their enforcement. These Republicans, often with strong support from private-sector companies involved in logging, energy production, and other industries, sought to weaken the enforcement of environmental protection policies that restrict business operations and require expenditures for pollution reduction.

Sometimes federal agencies defer to congressional sentiments and revise the rules. If the agency does not respond, Congress has the power to modify the original statute that underlies the rules in such a way as to invalidate administrative policies or the strategies contained in them. Congress may also threaten to withhold funding from agencies with whom it is displeased. This kind of congressional action can force agencies to revise administrative rules to be consistent with statutes and legislator intentions.

16-5 Right Politics, Strategies, and Bureaucratic Games

Throughout much of the nineteenth century, when political machines were dominant, there was little separation of everyday politics from the administration of the government bureaucracy (see Chapter 8). As noted, in the reforms of the Progressive Era most notably, initiation of the civil service system was intended to separate politics from the administration of government. Political scientist, and later president, Woodrow Wilson was among those who advocated efforts to separate politics and administration.[21] Whereas some reforms have reduced the daily interference of politicians in the administrative actions of federal bureaucrats, isolating bureaucracies from the political process is not only impossible but probably undesirable.

Several types of political games are played within and around the executive branch of the federal government. One series of games centers on the relationships between cabinet secretaries and other political executives with the president who appointed them. Other recurring games involve the ongoing associations between political executives and career civil servants. Still other games concern interactions between federal agencies on one side and Congress and the courts on the other.

16-5a Games between Presidents and Their Appointees

The president, as chief executive, cannot order an agency to terminate a program or drastically revise the formulas used for spending federal funds. This would violate the intent of Congress which enacted laws creating agencies and specifying their responsibilities as well as the presidential oath of office to execute faithfully the laws enacted by Congress. Still, presidents desire to have some control over the federal bureaucracy. They may seek to have some impact on the operation of the federal government by influencing the discretionary action of agencies. A president, for example, may wish to have input into environmental regulations being formulated by the Environmental Protection Agency or regulations on cable television formulated by the Federal Communications Commission.

To enhance their influence over the operation of the federal government, presidents rely heavily on their connections to political executives, specifically, the cabinet secretaries they appointed to office. These executives are expected to share the president's political ideology and to understand the need to join ranks with the president concerning policy debates. Presidents, however, often find themselves worrying about political executives adopting the perspective of and loyalty to the agency they manage.

Political executives are often caught in the middle between the president and the White House staff on one side and members of the career civil service on the other. Publicly, they must support the president's position; contradicting or criticizing the president would likely lead to political isolation or removal from office. Privately, however, within the citadels of their own offices, cabinet secretaries have to make decisions that reflect both presidential and agency perspectives. Political analyst Hugh Heclo noted a tendency for many political appointees to change teams over time:

> Even the most presidentially minded political executive will discover that his own agency provides the one relatively secure reference point amid all the other uncertainties of Washington. In their own agencies, appointees usually have at least some knowledge of each other and a common identity with particular programs. Outside the agency it is more like life in the big city among large numbers of anonymous people who have unknown lineages.[22]

For their part, presidents may seek leverage within federal agencies by reminding political executives about their responsibilities to the White House. Also, recent presidents have increasingly called upon the Office of Management and Budget, located within the Executive Office of the President (see Chapter 14) to monitor the activities of individual agencies. Although only Congress can appropriate funds, presidents have their own ways of financially controlling agency rulemaking activities. Presidents submit proposed budgets to Congress each year with detailed appropriation requests for each individual agency. Dissatisfaction with actions of agency officials may be reflected in reduced budget requests. Congress may or may not restore budgetary cutbacks. In these ways, the White House may seek to intervene in agency decision making. On rare occasions, presidents may fire or reassign political executives with whom they are displeased. This type of extreme response typically generates extensive media attention. For this reason, presidents seldom exercise the ultimate pink slip weapon when dealing with political appointees.

Beginning with President Gerald Ford, presidents have sought to increase supervision of the administrative rulemaking efforts undertaken by individual federal agencies. Worried about economic conditions in the nation, Ford ordered federal agencies engaged in rulemaking to identify possible inflationary consequences of proposed rules. Following this initiative, President Jimmy Carter created the Regulatory Analysis Review Group

(RARG) to apply cost-benefit principles during rulemaking. According to these principles, new regulations should be created only if their benefits exceed the costs of implementation. President Ronald Reagan elevated the status of RARG, based within the Office of Management and Budget, giving it responsibility for coordinating and scrutinizing rulemaking efforts throughout the federal government. Reagan used RARG as the lead agency in an initiative to reduce regulatory burdens imposed by federal mandates on business and state and local governments.

Following the Reagan approach, President George H. Bush established the White House Council on Competitiveness and named Vice President Dan Quayle as its head. The council was given responsibility for reviewing the costs that private businesses would incur because of proposed federal regulations. The Council on Competitiveness came under fire from Congress several times during the Bush administration for its efforts to weaken or eliminate proposed regulations. Regulations concerning environmental protection represented substantial costs to many business interests. Upon assuming office in 1993, Vice President Al Gore announced the abolition of the Council on Competitiveness, declaring that the Clinton administration would use a more open process to evaluate regulations proposed by federal agencies. The Clinton administration did review proposed regulations using White House staff and other presidential advisers.

16-5b Games between Political Executives and Civil Servants

Political appointees assume their leadership posts in federal agencies with enthusiasm, a sense of purpose, and a mandate for action from the president. At least at the outset, they are loyal to the president who selected them for office. They recognize that their tenure in the top agency leadership will probably be only several years, meaning that they must move quickly to leave their mark on the agency. Political executives arrive in their agencies as outsiders, lacking experience with the policies being administered by the agency. Most come to realize quickly that they will have to rely on the career civil servants to learn about agency operations and administrative routines.

The perspective of civil servants is quite different. These players have selected careers in the federal government, and many have spent decades working within the same agency. Civil servants typically accept a bureaucratic ideology that pervades the agency: a belief in the agency's role in improving society.[23] This ideology is enduring and reflects a shared commitment to existing goals and strategies to achieve policy objectives.

Given the different perspectives of political executives and civil servants, tensions between these two groups are not uncommon. Expertise and experience are important resources for civil servants when they become involved in political games with political appointees. Lacking extensive experience and policy-relevant knowledge, appointed officials may defer to the wisdom and guidance of career civil servants.

Political executives wishing to have maximum impact in their agency may pursue a strategy of reorganization. By shifting responsibilities and personnel within the agency, leaders may be able to recast routines and increase their influence over agency operations. This strategy, however, takes time and energy, and the disruptions caused by reorganization may harm morale and organizational performance.

Career civil servants who disagree with agency leaders may adopt different strategies, using their expertise and experience to persuade agency leaders to change their position. If this is unsuccessful, civil servants may resort to stalling and try to wait out the current leader, whose tenure may last only a year or two. Or these bureaucrats may seek to go around the political executive, seeking support and policy changes from friends in Congress.

16-5c Games between the Bureaucracy and Congress

Members of Congress often have a keen interest in federal agency activities because they want to ensure that their wishes, as expressed in public laws, are being faithfully and effectively carried out. Members also seek to monitor how federal agencies are using the policy-making authority delegated by Congress to guide the execution of public policies. Congress has several means at its disposal to monitor agency operations and the exercise of delegated rulemaking.[24] We now consider each of these.

Oversight

If they are concerned about agency actions, appropriate congressional committees or subcommittees may schedule oversight hearings. Federal officials are summoned to these hearings to testify and/or provide details about the operation of federal programs. Through the questioning of officials and statements made during the hearings, members of Congress can signal their concerns. Agency leaders generally take these signals seriously, especially if the signals come from committees responsible for the agency's budget.

If Congress wants independent information on program implementation, it may request that the General Accounting Office (GAO), its own investigative unit, undertake a study of the federal programs in question (see Chapter 13). The information obtained through GAO studies may prompt Congress to conduct further hearings on program operations or to consider changes in existing laws.

The power of congressional oversight over federal agencies was demonstrated throughout hearings held in August 1995 about the federal government's role in the 1993 tragedy outside Waco, Texas. These hearings were scheduled by the House of Representatives subcommittees of the Governmental Reform and Oversight Committee and were focused on the Federal Bureau of Investigation's (FBI) actions in storming the armed compound of religious zealot David Koresh. The FBI's move was designed to end the standoff between Koresh and his Branch Davidian sect, which had refused to cooperate with authorities and had engaged in armed conflict in an earlier confrontation with officers of the U.S. Bureau of Alcohol, Tobacco, and Firearms (ATF). This bureau was investigating reports of the purchase and storage of arms by the sect. After the FBI began its attack, repeatedly spraying tear gas into the armed complex, a fire was set off (presumably by sect members themselves) that led to total destruction of the compound. Eighty people—including many children, most of Koresh's followers, as well as several ATF agents—died in the fire. These deaths led many to question the appropriateness of the FBI's attack on the complex to resolve the standoff with Koresh. At the hearings, Attorney General Janet Reno took responsibility for the FBI's actions, mourned the tragic outcome, yet placed ultimate blame for the deaths on David Koresh.

Statutory Revision

Another congressional check on federal bureaucrats is the creation of new public laws or revision of existing ones. If the executive branch persists in taking actions of which Congress disapproves, lawmakers may enact legislation that prohibits specific implementation practices. Or Congress may require federal agencies to adopt new strategies or directions for program implementation. Thus, Congress can override the executive branch by changing the statutory authority for operating federal programs.

Nominations

Congress can also use the nomination game as a means of signaling displeasure with current program operations and expectations about future improvements. For example, during Senate hearings on George H. Bush's nomination of Jack Kemp for Secretary of HUD, senators voiced concerns about alleged scandal in awarding agency contracts. They made it clear to Kemp that they expected serious review and revision of HUD policies for awarding contracts to providers of public housing.

Spending Power

The power of the purse is another congressional check on the discretion of federal bureaucrats. Federal agencies cannot operate without funds appropriated by Congress. If dissatisfied with the operation of a specific federal program or the discretionary actions of bureaucrats, Congress has the option of cutting off funds or reducing appropriations.

Although such cutoffs are infrequent, members of Congress may use threats about funding reductions to pressure for changes in program operations.

Freedom of Information and Sunshine Laws

Congress has designed two provisions to increase public access to the decisions and records of federal agencies. Information from these sources is expected to provide Congress, the media, and the public with greater ability to scrutinize executive branch activities.

The Freedom of Information Act allows individuals to request in writing copies of records maintained by federal agencies. Agencies are required to provide the records unless they can demonstrate that a legal exemption applies. These exemptions include records pertaining to national security and individual privacy.[25]

Sunshine laws require some federal agencies (including the Securities and Exchange Commission, Interstate Commerce Commission, and Federal Trade Commission, among others) to give advance notice of meetings of top officials and to open the meetings to the public unless the officials vote to close the meeting. Sunshine laws specify the circumstances under which meetings can be legally closed to the public; these include discussions about national security, personnel matters, and individual privacy.

Legislative Veto

A final strategy to enforce legislative control over the actions of federal officials has been the **legislative veto.** These vetoes, included in many laws enacted by Congress, require that federal agencies receive the approval of Congress before taking certain specified types of actions.[26] In 1983, however, the Supreme Court ruled that most legislative vetoes are unconstitutional because they represent unwarranted legislative involvement in the execution of federal laws.[27] The Court construed legislative vetoes as intrusions into policy execution and as an inappropriate mixing of legislative and executive functions.

legislative veto *Federal law that requires congressional approval of actions before the actions can be taken by federal agencies; ruled unconstitutional by the Supreme Court in 1983.*

Since the Court's ruling, the status of legislative vetoes has remained unclear. While Congress has stepped back from introducing new legislative vetoes and has shown little interest in enforcing existing ones, congressional leadership has not totally abandoned vetoes as a means of legislative control of executive branch actions. The creation of a full legislative veto was supported by President Bill Clinton in his State of the Union address in 1994. It was supported at the same time by many Republican leaders in Congress who had long sought to give the president a weapon to combat specialized budget appropriations aimed at aiding specialized interest groups or pet projects for individual members of Congress.

16-5d Games between the Bureaucracy and the Courts

The federal courts comprise an arena in which the actions of bureaucrats can be challenged. As we have seen, individuals and groups can challenge the administrative rules adopted by federal agencies in court on the grounds that they violate either statutory intent or the procedural guidelines for rulemaking. Other actions of public officials can be legally questioned on the grounds that they are unconstitutional, are based on factual error, or violate individual rights to due process or equal protection under the law (see Chapter 4).[28] If the courts find in favor of the challengers, the administrative actions may be overturned.

Historically, bureaucrats had total **immunity:** they could not be held personally responsible for specific actions. This legal doctrine has its roots in an English tradition that held that the king and his ministers can do no wrong.[29] In recent years, the federal courts have begun to allow officials to be sued for certain actions, including those that violate a citizen's constitutional rights.[30]

immunity *Doctrine that public officials cannot be held personally accountable or sued for official actions and decisions; recent court decisions allow limited immunity.*

16-5e Restrictions on the Political Activities of Bureaucratic Players

While public-sector jobs offer many benefits, not the least of which is job security, they also restrict political activities. Most bureaucratic players are prohibited from participating in some political games and may perform only limited roles in others.

Federal employees may engage in passive political activities, such as contributing to campaigns, attending political rallies, and contacting congressional representatives. They may also vote. The federal Hatch Act, however, prohibits direct participation in party politics or political campaigns as either a partisan candidate or as a campaign worker. This means that federal employees cannot run for political office as party candidates or distribute campaign materials for party candidates.

The intent of the Hatch Act (and comparable state and local laws) is to insulate public-sector workers from the political process. When federal employees were not so isolated, corruption was rampant and government jobs were highly politicized. It was not uncommon for presidents to expect federal workers to provide large contributions to their electoral campaigns. In some cases, federal workers actually performed activities in support of presidential campaigns while supposedly performing their government jobs.

Some federal workers object to Hatch Act restrictions, claiming that their freedom of expression as outlined in the First Amendment to the Constitution is violated. The Supreme Court, however, has upheld provisions of the Hatch Act as constitutional, recognizing the dangers of politicizing the federal workforce.[31] See Time Out 16-4: "Hatching" Federal Employees to learn more about the provisions of the Hatch Act.

16-6 The Public and the Federal Bureaucracy

The American public has ambivalent feelings about the bureaucrats who staff and manage agencies of the federal government. While knowing little about the daily responsibilities of federal employees, the public sometimes expresses perceptions of slow action and red tape, unresponsiveness to individual problems and needs, unprecedented job security and benefits, and inefficiency. Although these attitudes are based more on common stereotypes than personal experiences, they have persisted for several decades. News stories about failing air traffic control systems, the botched attack on the Branch Davidian complex in Waco, and persistent budget deficits did nothing to dispel negative public images about the federal bureaucracy.

Time Out 16-4

"Hatching" Federal Employees

The growth of the federal bureaucracy and the fear that government employees involved in partisan politics could create a conflict of interest led to the passage of the Hatch Act in 1939. The Hatch Act only applies to national government employees, with state laws limiting political activity of state employees. In 1993, the Hatch Act limitations were loosened, but the act still limits many activities most citizens can participate in.

Assume you are a federal government employee with deep political interests but also the desire to keep out of trouble. Indicate which of the following you think are legal or illegal under the current Hatch Act.

1. **Joining and becoming active in a political party or club**
2. **Attending political fund-raising activities**
3. **Soliciting or collecting political contributions from a subordinate employee**
4. **Holding office in a political club or party**
5. **Engaging in political activity in your government office**
6. **Running for office in a partisan election**
7. **Running for office in a nonpartisan election**
8. **Displaying political buttons or posters on a government vehicle or while in uniform**
9. **Displaying a partisan bumper sticker on your personal vehicle**
10. **Campaigning for or against a candidate in a partisan election**

While federal bureaucrats have a moderately high level of job satisfaction,[32] they often feel unappreciated and unfairly maligned by the general public, who tend not to understand the constraints and problems that bureaucrats face in performing their jobs. Evidence of the frustration of federal government employees was documented in a study of senior federal officials in which 57 percent of the 3,900 respondents said that they would not recommend that young people start their career in public service.[33]

One area of frustration is the federal government's pay scale, which is generally seen as lagging behind compensation in comparable private-sector jobs. The General Accounting Office, for example, has reported that the pay gap between comparable public- and private-sector employees grew from around 10 percent in 1979 to over 25 percent in 1995.[34] Pay levels below those of the private sector are seen as discouraging individuals from seeking federal government jobs. Box 16-10: A Portrait of the Federal Government Workforce presents an overview of government employees.

Negative public perceptions about federal employees have harmed the federal government's ability to recruit and retain talented personnel and managers, yet all statistics demonstrate that federal employees are indeed representative of the public at large. The National Commission on the Public Service, chaired by Paul Volcker, spoke directly to the dual problems of recruitment and retention in 1989:

> There is evidence on all sides of an erosion of performance and morale across government in America. Too many of our most talented public servants, those with skills and dedication that are the hallmarks of an effective public service, are ready to leave. Too few of our brightest young people, those with the imagination and energy that are essential for the future, are willing to join.[35]

Box 16–10 A Portrait of the Federal Government Workforce

On Labor Day, 2000, the Secretary of Labor, Alexis M. Herman, took the occasion to describe the federal government's work force, noting that every federal worker can take pride not only in the advances of the past, but in the new age of innovation and change that lies ahead.[a]

Average Age: 45.9 years

Gender Composition of the Federal Workforce

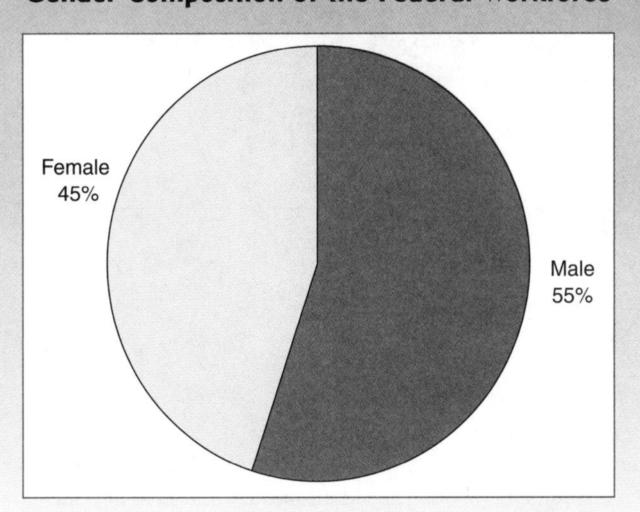

Education of the Federal Workforce

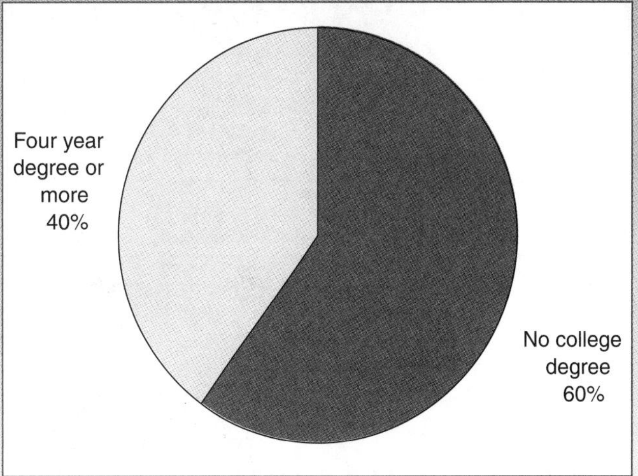

continued

Box 16–10 A Portrait of the Federal Government Workforce

—Continued

Average Pay of the Federal Workforce

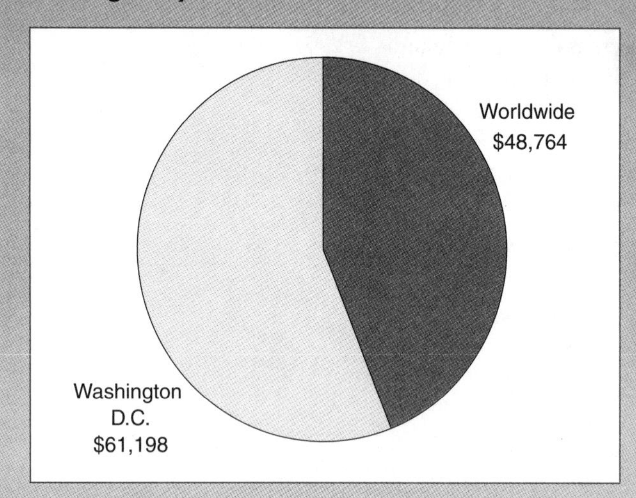

Union Representation of the Federal Workforce

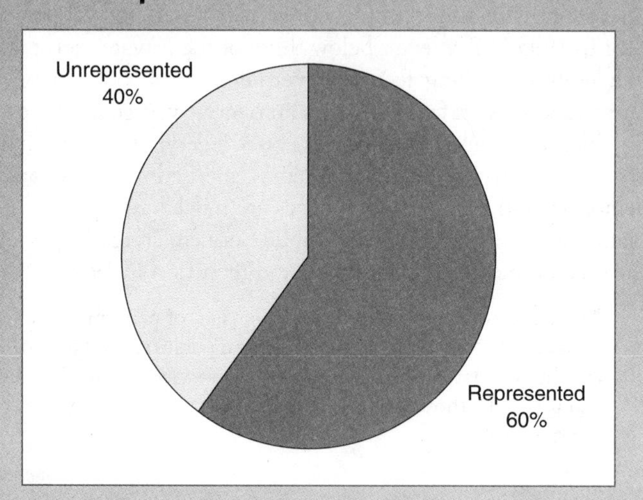

Racial/Ethnic Composition of the Federal Workforce

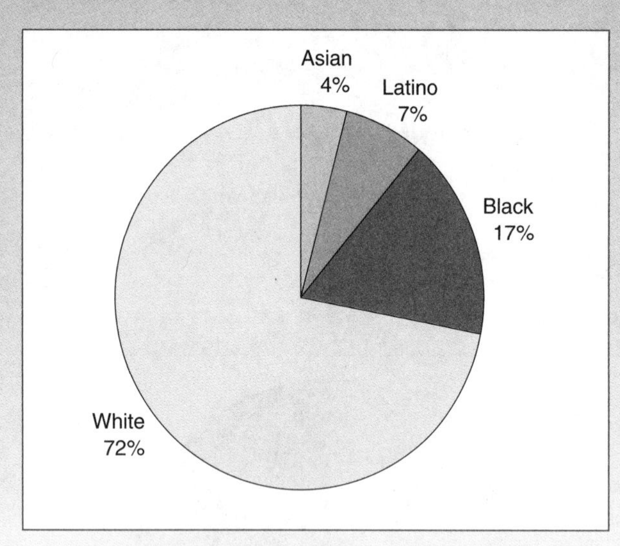

Position Divisions of the Federal Workforce

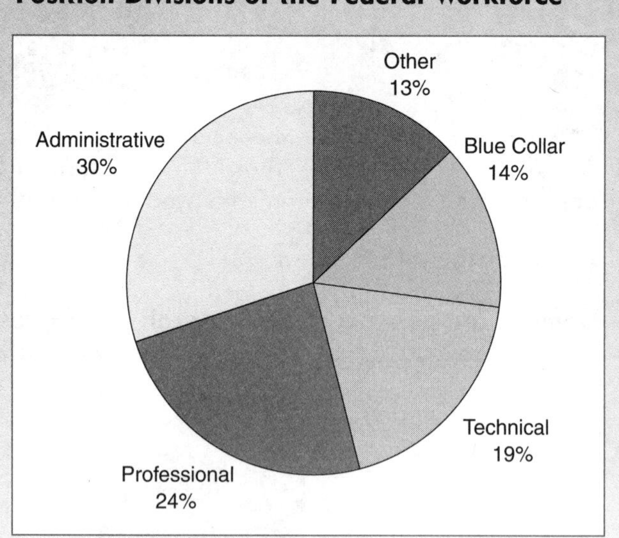

[a]Alexis M. Herman, "Under the Hood," *The Washington Post* (September 4, 2000), A23.

Following this assessment, the Volcker Commission recommended enhancing public service by, among other things, increasing the training, education, and salaries of federal employees. The commission also urged both the president and Congress to publicly commend the necessary and honorable role performed by public sector employees in the federal government.

Answers to Time Out 16-4

Here are the answers to Time Out 16-4. Are you surprised by any of them?

1. Joining and becoming active in a political party or club is legal: Even as a federal employee you have this basic right of freedom of association.
2. Attending political fund-raising activities is also legal: Since campaign contributions are viewed as a mode of expression, you are free to do this.
3. Soliciting or collecting political contributions from a subordinate employee is illegal: This could be viewed as using one's government position to coerce the subordinate.
4. Holding office in a political club or party is legal: This is one of the restrictions loosened in 1993 with the argument that political organizations in some areas were starved for leadership if all government employees were prohibited from participating.
5. Engaging in political activity in your government office is illegal: This is forbidden based on the argument that it would involve using government resources (heat and light if nothing else) to promote a political cause.
6. Running for office in a partisan election is also illegal: The law makes a distinction between partisan and nonpartisan offices, with federal employees forbidden to run for partisan (but not nonpartisan) office.
7. Running for office in a nonpartisan election is legal: The law makes a distinction between partisan and nonpartisan offices, with federal employees forbidden to run for partisan (but not nonpartisan) office.
8. Displaying political buttons or posters on a government bulletin board or vehicle or while in uniform is illegal: Since one would be posting material on government property, it would be illegal.
9. Displaying a partisan bumper sticker on your personal vehicle is legal: Since one would be posting material on one's own property, it would be legal.
10. Personally campaigning for or against a candidate in a partisan election is legal: All citizens (including federal employees) have this right, with federal employees denied the right to use the resources of their offices in such campaigning.

Some analysts contend that public concerns about and mistrust of governmental bureaucracies are overstated. In a thorough study of public perceptions of government bureaucracies, political scientist Charles T. Goodsell argued:

> Direct reports from citizens on their experiences with bureaucracy as distinct from generalized conventional wisdom on the subject indicate that they perceive far more good than bad in their daily interactions with it. Client polls, public opinion surveys, exit interviews, and mailed questionnaires all repeat the basic finding that the majority of encounters are perceived as satisfactory.[36]

At least in terms of individual encounters with government officials, citizens' views of bureaucracy tend to be more positive than negative.

Conclusion

The structure of the executive branch has emerged gradually as Congress has created and reorganized agencies. The emergence of agencies as cabinet departments signifies recognition that various issues or problems facing the nation deserve substantial attention by the national government.

The main players are of two different types. Political executives are selected by an appointment process that involves two branches of government: the president and the Senate. The political nature of these appointments is expected to produce accountability of top agency officials.

A civil service system stressing neutral competence and merit provides the remainder of the personnel. The apolitical nature of the system replaced the spoils system, with its extensive use of political patronage. Efforts to reform the civil service system focus on trying to make the current system work more effectively through such initiatives as merit pay and the Senior Executive Service. No system will be perfect, and it may be that protecting a few inefficient workers is the price that must be paid to prevent the return of widespread political corruption in the federal workforce.

Important policy-making activity takes place in the agencies of the executive branch. Congress has found it necessary to delegate important policy-making responsibilities to federal agencies, which have more expertise and experience in these matters. Administrative rulemaking regularizes the process by which agencies develop policies for implementation and also increases public input into policy development. In addition, Congress can check the discretionary power of federal agencies through other means, including oversight, budget allocations, and sunshine laws. The discretion wielded by bureaucrats continues to worry some analysts who see important policies being made not by elected officials but instead by appointed officials and civil servants, who are not directly accountable to the people.

The size and structure of the executive branch remain key issues as the president and members of Congress debate how to eliminate the federal budget deficit, shrink and streamline agency responsibilities and operation, and reconsider the relative roles of the federal and state governments in operating major programs. The National Performance Review recommended a wide-ranging set of reform proposals intended to enhance the performance of executive branch agencies. More radical proposals have been offered by members of Congress, including Republicans who have proposed the wholesale elimination of certain agencies, many of which have operated for decades. It is clear that the structure of the executive branch, and the responsibilities of federal agencies, will remain a key focal point of debate concerning a reformulation of the federal government.

Key Terms

adjudication
administrative rules
bureau
civil servants
competitive evaluation
competitive examination
co-optation
delegation doctrine
immunity
independent regulatory commissions
informal rulemaking
legislative veto
merit principle
political executives
Senior Executive Service (SES)
statutory intent
veteran's preference

Practice Quiz

1. What does the U.S. Constitution say about creating agencies and departments in the national government?
- **a.** The Constitution itself creates agencies and departments; new agencies and departments are created by constitutional amendment.
- **b.** The president is empowered to create agencies and departments.
- **c.** The Congress is empowered to create agencies and departments.
- **d.** The federal courts are empowered to create agencies and departments.

2. The newest cabinet-level department is
- **a.** Veterans' Affairs.
- **b.** Health and Human Services.
- **c.** the Environmental Protection Agency.
- **d.** the Department of Homeland Security.

3. An example of a public corporation is the
- **a.** U.S. Postal Service.
- **b.** Environmental Protection Agency.
- **c.** Department of Energy.
- **d.** Nuclear Regulatory Commission.

4. How do cabinet secretaries assume office?
- **a.** Nomination by the Supreme Court; confirmation by Congress
- **b.** Nomination by the president; confirmation by the House of Representatives
- **c.** Nomination by the president; confirmation by the Senate
- **d.** Nomination by Congress; confirmation by the president

5. Factors that typically motivate efforts to reform the government bureaucracy include
- **a.** a desire for efficiency/cost savings.
- **b.** a desire to enhance effectiveness in achieving national government goals.
- **c.** recognition of national issues or challenges that need high-level national government attention.
- **d.** All of the above.

6. The delegation doctrine refers to a recognition that
- **a.** Congress allows the president to enact budgets for cabinet departments.
- **b.** Congress allows executive branch agencies and departments to create rules to guide laws and policies enacted by Congress.
- **c.** Congress confirms the nominations of Supreme Court justices.
- **d.** All of the above.

7. The civil service system is based on the idea that national government jobs should be awarded on the basis of
- **a.** seniority.
- **b.** political connections.
- **c.** party affiliation.
- **d.** merit.

8. A danger of the practice of delegation is that
   a. agencies and departments may create rules that go beyond the intent of Congress.
   b. the Supreme Court may declare laws enacted by Congress to be unconstitutional.
   c. the veteran's preference may be abused.
   d. political appointments will replace civil service as a means to select most federal government employees.

9. Presidents typically nominate what types of people to be cabinet directors?
   a. People who share similar beliefs about policy issues
   b. People who have challenged them in election primaries
   c. People who are first confirmed by the U.S. Supreme Court
   d. Both a and c

10. How does oversight provide a check and balance over the powers and action of the executive branch?
   a. It is a process whereby the U.S. Supreme Court judges the constitutionality of laws implemented by the executive branch.
   b. It is the process whereby the president nominates cabinet secretaries with confirmation of the U.S. Senate.
   c. It is the authority of the U.S. Congress to conduct hearings, investigations, and budget reviews of actions by the executive branch.
   d. Both a and b

11. Immunity refers to
   a. the legal doctrine that government officials are free from prosecution for their governmental actions.
   b. prohibitions against performing campaign activity while on duty as a public official.
   c. the rights of states to share governing powers with the national government.
   d. the authority of federal agencies to make rules to guide implementation of laws enacted by Congress.

12. The "spoils system" is associated with
   a. creation of the Environmental Protection Agency.
   b. the award of jobs based upon patronage.
   c. the control of politics by political bosses.
   d. Both b and c

You can find the correct answers to these questions by taking the quiz and then submitting your answers in the Online Edition. The program will automatically score your submission. Where you miss a question, the program will provide the correct answer, a rationale for the answer, and the section number in the chapter where the topic is discussed.

Further Reading

Detailed information on the organization of the federal government is provided in the *U.S. Government Manual*, published annually by the Office of the Federal Register, National Archives and Records Administration, and printed by the U.S. Government Printing Office. This volume, which should be available in most college and university libraries, outlines each agency and office in the executive branch of the federal government. It also names top administrators of each agency and office.

Frederick C. Mosher discusses the evolution of public service within the federal government in his book *Democracy and the Public Service*, 2nd ed. (New York: Oxford University Press, 1982).

Federal Administrative Agencies: Essays on Power and Politics, edited by Howard Ball (Englewood Cliffs, NJ: Prentice-Hall, 1984) contains essays related to many aspects of federal agencies, including agency powers, the regulation of politics, congressional oversight, judicial review, and executive control.

A conservative perspective on possible reforms in the operations of the federal government is presented in Charles L. Heatherly and Burton Yale Pines, eds., *Mandate for Leadership III: Policy Strategies for the 1990s* (Washington, D.C.: Heritage Foundation, 1989). This ambitious volume suggests policy initiatives and reforms for specific government agencies.

The politics of bureaucracy is a topic explored by the Congressional Quarterly in *Cabinets and Counselors: The President and Executive Branch* (Congressional Quarterly Press, 1997), B. Guy Peters, *The Politics of Bureaucracy*, 3rd ed. (White Plains, NY: Longman, 1989), and Kenneth J. Meier, *Politics and the Bureaucracy: Policymaking in the Fourth Branch of Government* (Pacific Grove, CA: Brooks/Cole, 1993).

Among the treatments of presidential and congressional control of the federal bureaucracy are William T. Gormley, Jr., *Taming the Bureaucracy: Muscles, Prayers, and Other Strategies* (Princeton, NJ: Princeton University Press, 1989) and Bernard Rosen, *Holding Government Bureaucracies Accountable*, 2nd ed. (New York: Praeger, 1989).

Students who wish to learn more about administrative rulemaking should consult Cornelius M. Kerwin, *Rulemaking: How Government Agencies Write Law and Make Policy* (Washington, D.C.: Congressional Quarterly, 1998) and Ernest Gellhorn and Barry B. Boyer, *Administrative Law and Process in a Nutshell* (St. Paul, MN: West, 1981).

Readers who would like to know more about how to get a job with the federal government should see Dennis V. Damp and Samuel Concialdi, *The Book of U.S. Government Jobs: Where They Are, What's Available, and How to Get One* (Ashland, OH: Bookhaven Press, 2000).

For an interesting discussion of the role of ethics in executive branch management, see Terry L. Cooper, *The Responsible Administrator: An Approach to the Ethics for the Administrative Role* (Hoboken, NJ: Jossey-Bass, 1998).

Several books that describe the evolution of specific federal policies give extensive attention to the role of administrative rulemaking. Two of these, studies of disability policy, are Stephen L. Percy, *Disability, Civil Rights, and Public Policy: The Politics of Implementation* (Tuscaloosa, AL: University of Alabama Press, 1989) and Robert Katzmann, *Institutional Disability: The Saga of Transportation Policy for the Disabled* (Washington, D.C.: The Brookings Institution, 1986).

An important work in the current round of governmental reform aimed at reinventing government is David Osborne and Ted Gaebler,

Reinventing Government: How the Entrepreneurial Spirit Is Transforming the Public Sector (Reading, MA: Addison-Wesley, 1992).

The initial findings and recommendations of the National Performance Review, headed by Vice President Al Gore, are presented in a series of reports under the general title of *From Red Tape to Results: Creating a Government That Works Better & Costs Less* (with an overview published under the same title; Washington, D.C.: U.S. Government Printing Office, 1993). There are reports for each federal agency and other reports dealing with regulation, leadership, and intergovernmental relations; each report presents analysis and recommendations.

Assessments of the preliminary implementation of the recommendations of the National Performance Review are provided in two sources: Donald F. Kettl, *Reinventing Government?: Appraising the National Performance Review* (Washington, D.C.: The Brookings Institution, 1994) and *Management Reform: Implementation of the National Performance Review's Recommendations* (Washington, D.C.: U.S. Government Accounting Office, 1994), Report GAO/OCG-95-1. A practical guide to governmental reform is presented by David Osborne and Peter Plastrik, *The Reinventor's Handbook: Tools for Transforming Your Government* (Hoboken, NJ: Jossey-Bass, 2000).

Endnotes

1. Source material includes Carl M. Cannon, "How a Radical Joined the Establishment," *Sacramento Bee* May 23, 1993, p. F01, and Rochelle L. Stanfield, "Earning Their Stripes in the War on Poverty," *National Journal*, Vol. 11 (March 3, 1979), p. 345.
2. Thorough treatments of deregulation are presented in Susan Tolchin, *Dismantling America: The Rush to Deregulate* (New York: Oxford University Press, 1983); Larry N. Gerston, Cynthia Fraleigh, and Robert Schwab, *The Deregulated Society* (Pacific Grove, CA: Brooks/Cole, 1988); and Martha Derthick and Paul J. Quirk, *The Politics of Deregulation* (Washington, D.C.: The Brookings Institution, 1977).
3. Hugh Heclo, *A Government of Strangers: Executive Politics in Washington* (Washington, D.C.: The Brookings Institution, 1977).
4 George C. Edwards III and Stephen J. Wayne, *Presidential Leadership: Politics and Policy Making* (New York: St. Martin's Press, 1985).
5. Hugh Heclo, *Government of Strangers*, 103.
6. David Osborne and Ted Gaebler, *Reinventing Government: How the Entrepreneurial Spirit is Transforming the Public Sector* (Reading, MA: Addison-Wesley, 1992), 15.
7. Remarks of President Bill Clinton in announcing the creation of the National Performance Review, Washington, D.C., March 3, 1993.
8. *From Red Tape to Results: Creating a Government That Works Better & Costs Less: Executive Summary* (Washington, D.C.: National Performance Review, September 7, 1993).
9. *Ibid.*
10. *Management Reform: Implementation of the National Performance Review's Recommendations* (Washington, D.C.: U.S. General Accounting Office, December 5, 1994), 2.
11. Donald F. Kettl, *Reinventing Government? Appraising the National Performance Review* (Washington, D.C.: The Brookings Institution, 1994), vii.
12. *Field v. Clark*, 143 U.S. 649, 692 (1891); *Hampton & Company v. United States*, 276 U.S. 394, 406 (1928).
13. William F. West has argued in *Administrative Rulemaking: Politics and Process* (Westport, CT: Greenwood Press, 1985) that "The issue of the constitutionality of delegated authority has never been resolved by the courts; it has become mute" because of the "judiciary's willingness to accept delegated authority in practically any form" (p. 23).
14. *Panama Refining Company v. Ryan*, 293 U.S. 388 (1935) and *Schechter Corporation v. United States*, 295 U.S. 495 (1935).
15. A. Lee Fritschler, *Smoking and Politics: Policymaking and the Federal Bureaucracy*, 3d ed. (Engelwood Cliffs, NJ: Prentice-Hall, 1983), 12.
16. 5 *United States Code Annotated*, Section 551.
17. Grant McConnell, *Private Power and American Democracy* (New York: Knopf, 1966); Eugene Lewis, *The Urban Political System* (Hinsdale, CA: Dryden Press, 1973), 160–75.
18. Philip Selznick, *TVA and the Grass Roots* (Berkeley, CA: University of California Press, 1949); Susan Rose-Ackerman, "Cooperative Federalism and Cooptation," *Yale Law Journal* 92, no. 7 (1983): 1344–8.
19. Arthur E. Bonfield, "Representation for the Poor in Federal Rulemaking," *Michigan Law Review* 67 (January 1969): 511–68.
20. Jeffrey M. Berry, *Lobbying for the People: The Political Behavior of Public Interest Groups* (Princeton, NJ: Princeton University Press, 1977).
21. Woodrow Wilson, "The Study of Administration," *Political Science Quarterly* 2 (June 1887); 197–222.
22. Hugh Heclo, *A Government of Strangers: Executive Politics in Washington* (Washington, D.C.: The Brookings Institution, 1977), 111.
23. Anthony Downs, *Inside Bureaucracy* (Boston, MA: Little, Brown, 1967).
24. Edgar G. Crane, *Legislative Review of Government Programs* (New York: Praeger, 1977); Marcus Ethridge, *Legislative Participation in Implementation: Policy Through Politics* (New York: Praeger, 1985).
25. Samuel Archibald, "The Freedom of Information Act Revisited," *Public Administration Review* 39 (July/August 1979): 311–7; *Attorney General's Memorandum on the 1986 Amendments to the Freedom of Information Act* (Washington, D.C.: U.S. Department of Justice, December 1987).
26. John R. Bolton, *The Legislative Veto* (Washington, D.C.: American Enterprise Institute, 1979).
27. *Immigration and Naturalization Service v. Chadha*, 462 U.S. 919 (1983).
28. Bernard Rosen, *Holding Government Bureaucracies Accountable*, 2nd ed. (New York: Praeger, 1989), 113.
29. Bernard Rosen, *Holding Government Bureaucracies Accountable*, 123.
30. *Biven v. Six Unknown Agents of Federal Bureau of Narcotics*, 408 U.S. 388 (1971).
31. *Civil Service Commission v. National Association of Letter Carriers, AFL-CIO*, 413 U.S. 548 (1973).
32. U.S. Merit Systems Protection Board, *Working for the Federal Government: Job Satisfaction and Federal Employees* (Washington, D.C.: Merit Systems Protection Board, October 1987).
33. Timothy B. Clark and Marjorie Wachtel, "The Quiet Crisis Goes Public," *Governmental Executive* (June 1988).
34. *Federal Personnel: Federal/Private Sector Pay Comparisons* (Washington D.C.: U.S. General Accounting Office, 1994).
35. National Commission on the Public Service, *Leadership for America: Rebuilding the Public Service* (Washington D.C.: The Volcker Commission, 1989), 1.
36. Charles T. Goodsell, *The Case for Bureaucracy: A Public Administration Polemic*, 3rd ed. (Chatham, NJ: Chatham House, 1994).

17

The Judiciary: Refereeing the Rules and Outcomes

Key Points

- The courts as an important arena within the game of American politics.
- The impact of judicial review power on public policy.
- The formal and informal rules that guide Supreme Court decision making.
- The role of the solicitor general, interest groups, and the public in judicial decision making.
- The responsibilities of courts at each level in the federal judiciary.
- The processes and political games that surround the selection of judicial players.

Preview: The Supreme Court at Work

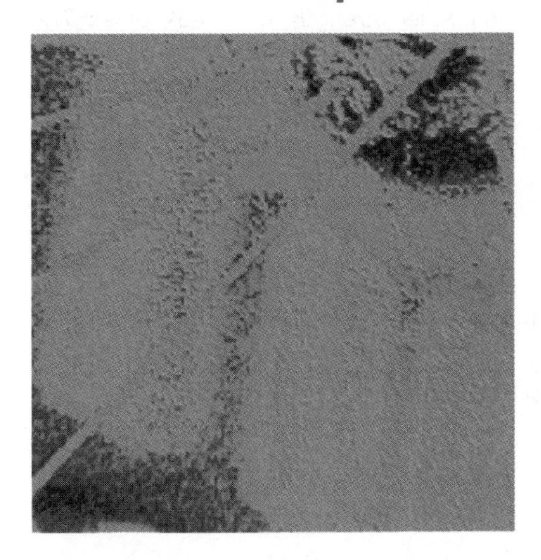

During the first weeks of October 1970, Harry Blackmun felt like the new kid on the Supreme Court team. His eight colleagues had been through the routine before. He read legal briefs, listened to complex oral arguments from competing attorneys, and oversaw the work of his law clerks as they did his research. As a former judge on the federal circuit court of appeals, he found these tasks familiar, although the importance of the decisions was far greater than that of earlier cases. The major unknown quantity was the Friday conferences when all nine justices would meet alone in absolute secrecy to argue their positions on pending cases. It was an awesome responsibility in an awesome setting. The high ceilings, thick carpets, and imposing wood furniture of the conference room added drama and the feeling that something

The Supreme Court, Washington, D.C.

important was going to happen. When the door was closed that first day, Justice Blackmun, sitting in the junior member's place at the end of the table, listened to the clack of the lock with both anticipation and a bit of fear.

As the arguments proceeded on the first case, Justice Blackmun began to feel more comfortable being entombed with his colleagues. A rap on the door suddenly startled him. Who could be breaking into this most private of meetings? The timid hand passing a note through the door to the chief justice only added to the suspense. The frown on the chief justice's face after opening the note conjured up the expectation of a disaster. Had the Russians attacked? Had the president been assassinated? As the note progressed down the table, the mystery deepened, since some of the justices were actually smiling at its contents. As last in seniority, Justice Blackmun had to wait. Unfolding the note, Blackmun was relieved to see that it was the first inning score of the World Series.

The experience revealed a great lesson to the newest justice. Despite the impressive setting, the long tradition of the Court, and the black robes, justice in America ultimately depends on human beings and on all their strengths and weaknesses. The human preferences, commitments, and biases developed over many years make individual justices fans of different teams in sports and in other arenas. Some justices seem to continually root for the liberal teams in society and others for the conservatives. Personal experiences and preferences become the lenses through which they interpret the Constitution and decide on particular cases. The humanness of the Supreme Court is a key defining characteristic.

The federal courts generally occupy a revered position in American politics. As the author of a basic text on the judicial system put it:

> Respect for the law is one of the select group of principles that we have come to regard as essential to the effective and equitable operation of popular government. As a democratic principle it is recognized as binding on both the governed and those who govern.[1]

The Supreme Court and the two tiers of lower federal courts are composed of individuals who are selected to perform the following important judicial tasks:

- interpreting the meaning of public laws and the Constitution,
- resolving disputes that arise from the application of federal laws, and
- mediating controversies that arise among individuals and organizations.

Legal controversies are also considered by a series of state courts; these courts and their role in the judicial process are described in Chapter 18.

Americans sometimes view the federal courts as being above politics as tribunals or forums where impartial judgments, based on the lofty ideas of the Constitution and public laws, are rendered on difficult legal questions. In some ways, the courts are isolated from the hectic daily life of politics. For example, federal judges are appointed to office for indefinite terms and therefore do not depend on popular elections for their positions.

Despite their relative isolation from everyday political events, federal judges—including those who sit on America's highest court, the Supreme Court—are players in American politics. Judges on the federal courts are representatives of important political institutions. They have an interest in protecting the legitimacy of the courts and the authority of federal judges in rendering decisions. They also have, as human beings, personal political ideologies and values that affect their opinions about current issues. Judicial players carefully consider legal principles and past decisions, but they cannot avoid making decisions that also reflect their personal perspectives. Members of the federal bench, therefore, have both their personal values and, like representatives of other political institutions, a stake in defending their institutional power.

This chapter begins with an overview of the several levels of the judiciary. It explores the judicial powers of the federal courts and focuses especially on the important process of judicial review, the role of the courts in interpreting the meaning of the Constitution. It then reviews the organization of the federal judiciary and how and when cases are heard in federal courts. Concluding the chapter is consideration of the process by which judicial players are selected for the federal courts and the impact of this selection on judicial decision making.

17-1 The Judicial Arena: An Overview

The judiciary is an important political arena in American government. The decisions made in federal courts influence public policy, including the services rendered, the assistance given, and the regulations created by the federal government. The political position of the courts arises primarily from their interpretive powers as they assess the meaning and constitutionality of laws enacted by Congress and the regulations issued by the executive branch.

The federal judiciary today is composed of a three-tiered system (see Figure 17-1) and a series of specialized courts (see Box 17-1: Special Federal Courts). The U.S. district courts, created in 1789, serve as the lowest tier. The United States and its territories are divided into 94 district courts.

The U.S. Courts of Appeals, established in 1891, hold an intermediate position between the Supreme Court and the district courts. The 50 states and U.S. territories are

Figure 17-1
The Federal Court System

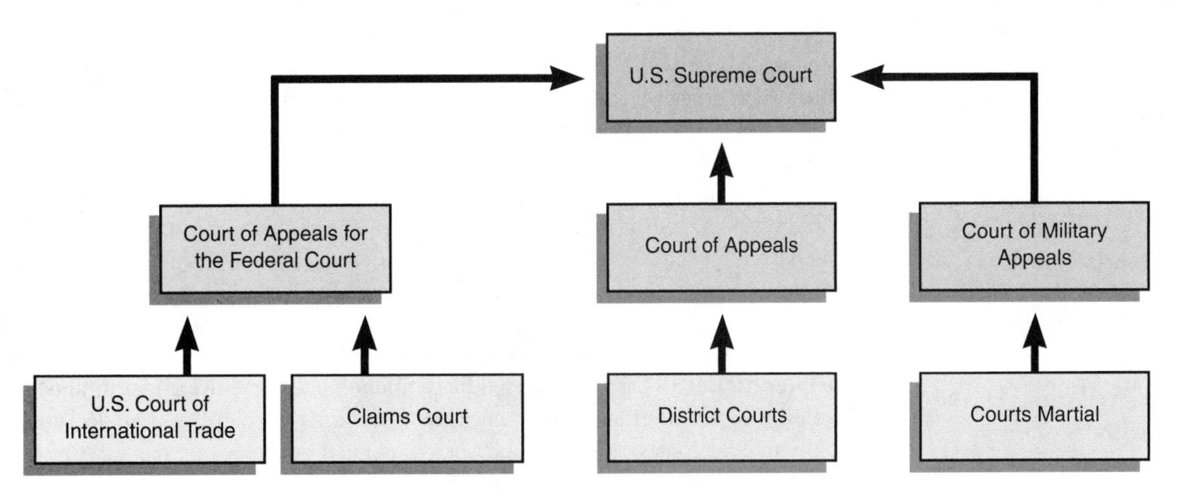

Box 17–1 Special Federal Courts

The Supreme Court, courts of appeals, and district courts are known as constitutional courts. They were created through Article III of the Constitution, which established a Supreme Court and empowered Congress to create courts that were inferior to the top court. Congress has also created other courts that are responsible for considering cases concerning specific functions of the federal government. These courts are generally known as legislative courts. Their basis lies not in Article III but in Article I, Section 8, of the Constitution, which empowers Congress to constitute tribunals inferior to the Supreme Court.

In creating these special federal courts, Congress sought to relieve workloads in the constitutional courts. Legislators also saw that specialized courts were needed to deal with complex and technical areas of federal law, including taxation and foreign trade. The special courts and their functions are as follows:

- The U.S. Claims Court hears cases involving disputes about contracts between federal agencies and private companies. It also considers cases involving claims about damages caused by the federal government.
- The U.S. Court of International Trade handles legal disputes about rulings made by customs collectors. For example, if a company that imports electronic goods feels that the duties levied by customs collectors are unfair, the company may seek redress in this court.
- The U.S. Tax Court has jurisdiction over cases involving taxpayer challenges to rulings of the Internal Revenue Service (IRS). This court, once contained within the IRS, was given separate status by Congress in 1969.
- The U.S. Court of Military Appeals, composed of three civilian judges, reviews appeals of decisions made in military courts, including court-martials.
- The Court of Veterans' Appeals hears appeals concerning disputes about benefits provided to military veterans.
- The Court of Appeals for the Federal Circuit was created by Congress in 1982 by merging two existing special courts. This court hears appeals from other special courts, including those related to patents, claims against the federal government, and disputes about customs duties.

geographically organized into 13 federal judicial circuits (see Figure 17-2). The principal function of these courts is to hear cases appealed from the district courts. They also review decisions of the federal regulatory agencies.

Most Americans hear little about the decisions reached in the lower federal courts. Nonetheless, the district courts and the courts of appeals are the real workhorses of the judicial system. These courts hear most of the cases that involve challenges to the constitutionality of federal and state laws.

Operating at the top of the federal judiciary is the nine-member Supreme Court, composed of one chief justice and eight associate justices. All justices on the Supreme Court, including the chief justice, are nominated by the president and confirmed by the Senate. Table 17-1 lists all persons who have held the position of Chief Justice of the U.S. Supreme Court.

jurisdiction *The types of matters that a given court is empowered to consider.*

original jurisdiction *The power of a court to be the first judicial tribunal in which a case is considered.*

appellate jurisdiction *The power to consider court cases that are being appealed from lower courts.*

Article III of the Constitution describes the **jurisdiction** of the Supreme Court, that is, the types of cases it may properly consider. The Supreme Court has both original and appellate jurisdiction. **Original jurisdiction** defines the cases that may receive the first hearing (i.e., go to actual trial). The Supreme Court has original jurisdiction in only two types of cases: (1) those affecting ambassadors and public ministers, and (2) those involving a dispute among two or more states (or the United States and a state). These cases are rare. Almost all cases considered by the Supreme Court arise under its **appellate jurisdiction,** the jurisdiction with which most Americans are familiar. The decisions reached by the federal courts of appeals may be challenged by the losing party, who seek further consideration of the case by the nation's highest court.

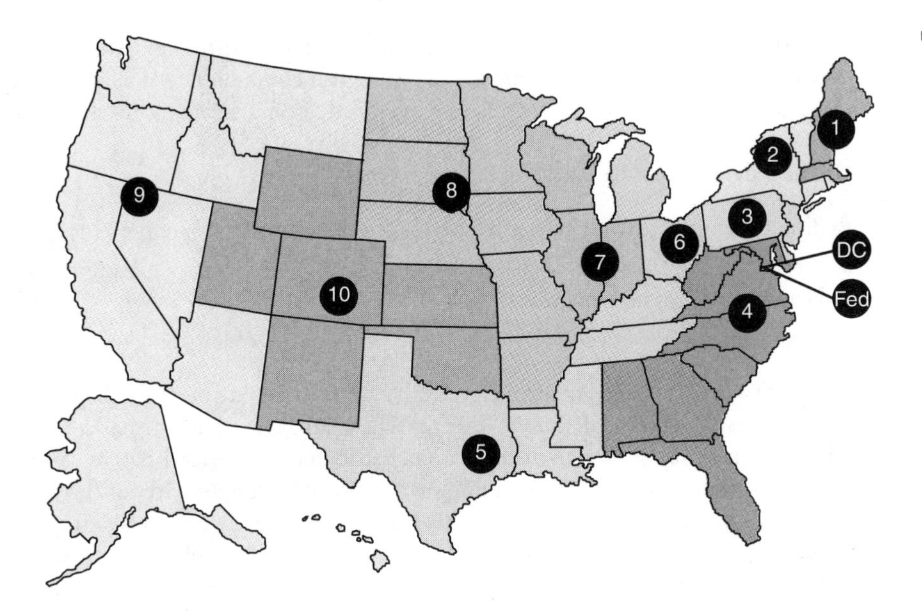

Figure 17-2
The Circuit Courts

Table 17-1
Chief Justices of the U.S. Supreme Court

Chief Justice	Year Assumed Office	Appointed by President
John Jay	1789	George Washington
John Rutledge	1795	George Washington
Oliver Ellsworth	1796	George Washington
John Marshall	1801	John Adams
Roger Brooke Taney	1836	Andrew Jackson
Salmon Portland Chase	1864	Abraham Lincoln
Morrison Remick Waite	1874	Ulysses S. Grant
Melville Weston Fuller	1888	Grover Cleveland
Edward Douglass White	1910	William Howard Taft
William Howard Taft*	1921	Warren Harding
Charles Evans Hughes	1930	Herbert Hoover
Harlan Fiske Stone	1941	Franklin D. Roosevelt
Frederick Moore Vinson	1946	Harry S. Truman
Earl Warren	1953	Dwight D. Eisenhower
Warren Earl Burger	1969	Richard Nixon
William H. Rehnquist	1986	Ronald Reagan

* William Howard Taft has the distinction of being the only former president to serve on the Supreme Court. As president, Taft nominated Edward Douglass White for chief justice to the Supreme Court. Upon Justice White's death, President Warren Harding nominated Taft as the next chief justice.

17-2 The Courts as Arenas for Resolving Disputes

Although it normally does not receive as much media attention as the other branches of the national government, the federal judiciary represents a vital component of the American political system. The Supreme Court and the lower-level federal courts serve as arenas where laws and their application can be challenged by individuals or groups who are dissatisfied with them.

statutory law *Written laws enacted by legislative bodies such as Congress, state legislatures, and city councils.*

common law *A cumulative body of law that evolved in England over several centuries and that is based primarily on judicial decisions and precedent rather than laws written by legislative bodies.*

Most laws that govern Americans are **statutory laws** written and enacted by a legislative body. Many of these laws are based on English **common law,** a body of legal principles dating to the 12th century and evolving mostly from custom rather than from written laws.

The federal courts hear several different types of cases:

- disputes among private parties where no criminal violations are present,
- the prosecution of individuals or corporations charged with violating the criminal laws created by the Congress, and
- disagreements about the meaning or constitutionality of laws enacted by Congress.

One example of a legal controversy decided in the federal courts is a dispute between camera giants Kodak and Polaroid. In the 1980s, Polaroid claimed that a new line of Kodak cameras used a design that Polaroid had patented. Federal patent laws protect inventors by preventing others from imitating innovated designs without the permission (and often compensation) of the inventor. Polaroid challenged Kodak in the federal courts on the grounds that Polaroid's licensed patent had been violated. After a long trial, the courts ruled in favor of Polaroid and required Kodak to pay hundreds of millions of dollars in compensation. This legal dispute is an example of a **civil case,** in which individuals or organizations seek to resolve their disagreement in the courts.

civil case *A dispute between private parties, not involving a governmental body.*

The federal courts also hear cases in which the federal government (generally through the U.S. Department of Justice) is seeking to prosecute individuals or organizations accused of violating federal laws. In these criminal cases, the federal courts consider the innocence or guilt of the parties being prosecuted on the basis of evidence presented by both sides. For example, the federal government prosecuted several prominent Wall Street investment brokers in the 1980s on the grounds that they had engaged in insider trading and other illegal practices. Several of these individuals were convicted and punished with fines and/or prison terms. Federal prosecution of the terrorists accused of bombing the federal building in Oklahoma City in 1995 is another type of criminal case considered in federal courts.

Cases heard in federal courts also may involve disputes among individuals and governments. Individuals, or groups representing them, can challenge the application of federal laws, their meaning, or, more fundamentally, their constitutional basis.

standing *The right to initiate legal action based on direct involvement in controversy and injury sustained from the controversy.*

They must first establish legal **standing,** that is, direct involvement in and harm by the policy or legal issue being challenged.

When disputing the application of a federal law, individuals are not contesting the law's validity. Instead, they are disputing the law's enforcement in their own circumstance. For example, a citizen might claim that he or she was unfairly charged with tax evasion or insider trading in stock purchases. In such cases, citizens are challenging the factual basis of their prosecution and seeking to have the courts help them resolve their dispute with federal authorities.

Some disputes between citizens and government center on the meaning of laws enacted by Congress. When government agencies take actions such as providing services or regulating business activities, they do so under authority granted by Congress in public statutes. Sometimes citizens or corporations believe that the actions taken by federal officials violate or exceed the authority as specified in federal law. In such circumstances, citizens or corporations can challenge the government's actions. The federal courts are then called upon to interpret the meaning of federal laws and the powers granted to government agencies in those laws. The courts may conclude that government actions are not consistent with the legitimate powers granted to them. Such was the case in the late 1970s, when the American Public Transit Association (APTA) challenged requirements issued by the Department of Transportation (DOT). DOT had decreed that all buses purchased by public transit providers with federal funds be accessible to citizens with disabilities. APTA, a large interest group representing local transit authorities, argued that

DOT's requirements exceeded the statutory authority provided by Congress. The federal courts agreed with APTA and struck down the DOT rules.[2]

Another controversy centered on regulations created by the Department of Interior to enforce the Endangered Species Act of 1973. Did they exceed congressional mandates to protect threatened animal species? During the 1990s, business and timber interests challenged Interior Department regulations that prohibit modifying habitats on federal and private lands when such action would impair endangered species. These regulations substantially hampered the timber industry's logging of forests inhabited by threatened species such as the Northern spotted owl. Commercial interests claimed that the Endangered Species Act was not meant to restrict activities like logging that might indirectly contribute to harming such species. In 1995, the Supreme Court upheld the authority of the Interior Department to regulate the alteration of natural habitats of endangered species. The Court held that the language of the act itself, and its broad objective of preventing extinction of species, justified the regulations.[3] (See Chapter 19 for more discussion of environmental policy and law.)

Still other cases heard in the federal courts challenge the fundamental legality and purpose of federal laws and policies. Here, challengers ask the courts to determine whether federal laws or policies are consistent with the Constitution. This is probably the most significant and controversial function of the federal courts. It is known as **judicial review.** The courts, particularly the Supreme Court, have the power to review laws enacted by Congress and state legislatures (and actions taken by federal officials) to determine whether they conform to the fundamental rule book of American government, the Constitution. In the late 1980s, free speech advocates disputed convictions, under state and federal laws, of persons who had burned the American flag as a means of political protest. Their cases were intended to test directly the constitutionality of federal and state laws that prohibited flag burning. In decisions rendered in these cases, the Supreme Court held that flag burning was constitutional when undertaken as a form of political protest.[4] (See Chapter 4.) See Time Out 17-1: How Unlimited Is the Power of the Federal Courts for an analysis of the limits of judicial power in the federal courts.

judicial review *The authority of the federal courts to consider the constitutionality of laws enacted by Congress and the actions taken by officials in the executive branch.*

Time Out 17-1

How Unlimited Is the Power of the Federal Courts?

Throughout the history of the nation, some critics of the federal courts have worried about the power of the federal judiciary. Greatest concern has surrounded the judicial review power, the ability of the courts to assess the meaning and constitutionality of federal laws. When the Supreme Court renders a decision in an important case (such as the *Brown v. Board of Education of Topeka* involving segregation), the implications for public policy and for the political system can be great and far-reaching. Some worry that once they have made a decision the federal courts are relatively unchecked.

Stop and think about this. What can political players do if they are unhappy with decisions reached in the federal courts, especially the Supreme Court? Do they have opportunities to challenge court decisions? Are there strategies that can be used to circumvent the courts or change future judicial decision making?

As you think about answers to these questions, you should consider the following: Can the Constitution, the fundamental rule book guiding judicial review decisions, be changed to influence court decisions? If so, how can this change be accomplished, and what players would be involved?

Or, using a different strategy, how might the process for choosing federal judges be used to affect court decisions? How might the nomination of judges and their confirmation by the U.S. Senate influence the decisions made in federal courts? Is the selection process one area where players may seek to influence future court decision making? We will enter that arena later in this chapter.

17-3 Judicial Review: The Courts in the Policy Game

Under judicial review, if the federal courts rule that a public statute or an executive action is unconstitutional, then the law or action is invalidated. Similarly, if the courts uphold the constitutionality of laws or actions, then those laws or actions are given firmer status in the political system. Political and citizen players may not like a decision, but they respect the referee at least in the present round of the game. In future rounds, through actions such as activating the amendment process, players may seek to challenge judicial rulings. Box 17-2: Judicial Review Illustrated shows how one citizen and his family brought action that led to closer examination of the Constitution.

17-3a The Foundations of Judicial Review

Given the importance of the judicial review power, one would expect that it would be prominently featured in the Constitution. This, however, is not the case. The Constitution says nothing directly about who should interpret the Constitution. Although Article III of the Constitution defines the jurisdiction of the nation's highest court, its language does not describe any role for the Supreme Court regarding constitutional interpretation. Over time, as the result of political practice, the power of judicial review has grown more extensive, and the federal courts, the Supreme Court, and lower courts have been recognized as the appropriate place for judicial review to be undertaken.

Constitutional scholars have long debated the origins and basis of judicial review power. Most scholars believe that the Founders were aware of the judicial review issue. Some of them argue that the Founders' intent was for this power to be placed in the federal judiciary.

The concept of judicial review is considered in *The Federalist,* most notably in *Federalist* No. 78, written by Alexander Hamilton. He sought to calm those who feared the power of the proposed national government generally and the legislative power of Congress more specifically. Hamilton argued that constitutional provisions have a higher status than public laws. He claimed that the courts would resolve conflicts between the Constitution and public laws through judicial review. In his words:

> A constitution is, in fact, and must be regarded by judges, as a fundamental law. It therefore belongs to them to ascertain its meaning, as well as the meaning of any particular act proceeding from the legislative body. If there be an irreconcilable variance between the two, the Constitution ought to be preferred to the statute.

Judicial review became an issue early in the history of the new nation. Within a decade after the Constitution's ratification, the Supreme Court had begun to consider the idea of judicial review. In one case, it upheld the constitutionality of a law enacted by Congress. In others, it toyed with the notion of ruling some legal provisions unconstitutional.[5]

Marbury v. Madison *Supreme Court decision in 1803 that established the Supreme Court's prerogative to perform judicial review of laws enacted by Congress and of actions taken by federal officials.*

In the landmark case of ***Marbury v. Madison,*** the Supreme Court in 1803 asserted its intention to engage in judicial review.[6] This legal case was based on strong partisan wrangling between the Federalists, led by outgoing president John Adams, and the Jeffersonian Republicans (see Chapter 8). Upon assuming office, President Thomas Jefferson learned of a series of judicial appointments made by Adams at the very end of his term and that the commissions for these appointments had not yet been delivered. Jefferson ordered his secretary of state, James Madison, not to deliver the commissions that formally appointed the new judges. One of those whose commission was held back was William Marbury, who was to serve as the justice of the peace in the District of Columbia.

Marbury, using a provision of the Judiciary Act of 1789, sued to force Madison to deliver his commission. After considering the case, the Supreme Court, under the lead of Chief Justice John Marshall, dismissed Marbury's case. The Court argued that the section of the Judiciary Act under which Marbury sought to coerce delivery of his commission was unconstitutional. Chief Justice Marshall argued that it was within the Supreme Court's authority to review statutes enacted by Congress to determine their consistency with constitutional provisions. In his words, "It is emphatically the province and duty of the judicial department to say what the law is."[7]

Box 17-2 Judicial Review Illustrated: The Case of Drug Testing in Schools

Judicial review, the power of the federal courts to determine the constitutionality of laws and policies, was demonstrated in a Supreme Court case involving the right of schools to conduct random drug testing of student athletes.

In the 1980s and 1990s, following the passage of certain laws, drug testing was instituted in a variety of settings as a means of deterring drug use. Such laws balanced the traditional expectations of the right to privacy that are part of our political culture with the need for government to respond to the growing drug problem. Drugs harm society in many ways, ranging from reduced productivity of workers to increased violent crime and severe health problems of citizens.

Laws and policies concerning mandatory drug testing have often been challenged in the federal courts. The courts have tended to uphold laws or policies for mandatory drug testing of certain sets of federal employees. For example, the Supreme Court in 1989, in two separate cases, upheld federal regulations. One required blood and urine tests for railroad employees following major train accidents.[a] The other required of the U.S. Customs Service that persons having a direct involvement in drug interdiction be required to submit to random drug checks.[b]

In 1995 the federal courts considered the issue of mandatory drug testing in another context: student athletes in public schools. The case involved the policy of a small school system in Vernonia, Oregon, which required unannounced urine tests of student athletes to determine whether they were using drugs.[c] The school system created the policy to cope with what it saw as growing drug and discipline problems among student athletes.

The policy was challenged by the parents of a seventh-grader, James Acton, who had tried out for football but was not allowed to join the team because he and his parents refused to sign a form giving their consent to random drug testing. There was no suspicion that James was using drugs. For the Actons, the school drug policy violated their son's constitutional rights under the 4th Amendment, which prohibits unreasonable searches and seizures by the government. In order to defend their son's rights, the family filed suit in federal courts in 1991. The federal appeals court that heard the case ruled in favor of the Actons, holding that the drug policy was unreasonable. Officials, the ruling explained, should not invade the student's privacy without a basis for suspecting the individual of any wrongdoing.

The Supreme Court disagreed and overturned the appeals court ruling in a 6–3 decision. The majority opinion, authored by Justice Antonin Scalia, argued that the school's policy was reasonable and hence constitutional, for three reasons. First, students have low expectation of privacy in locker room situations and restrooms where urine tests would be conducted. Second, the testing program was designed so that students could produce their samples in relative privacy. And third, the policy advanced the school district's important interest in combating drug abuse among the student body. Justice Scalia called athletes important role models in the war against drugs.

For the Actons, and for the American Civil Liberties Union, the case was a disappointment. From a broader perspective, the Supreme Court's decision clarified the limits of 4th Amendment protections and the right of public agencies to institute drug testing under specified circumstances. In this way, the Acton case set a legal precedent that will guide future cases involving drug testing by public schools. Furthermore, the Court's interpretation of the 4th Amendment could have implications for other types of cases.

a. *Skinner v. Railway Labor Executive's Association v. U.S.*, 489 U.S. 602 (1989).

b. *National Treasury Employees Union v. Von Raab*, 489 U.S. 656 (1989).

c. *Vernonia School District v. Acton*, No. 94-590.

The concept of judicial review has become an accepted working principle of American government. Its real power lies in the willingness of political players to accept the constitutional interpretations of federal judges. The judiciary has few tools to coerce compliance with its decisions. In *Federalist* No. 78, Hamilton called the federal judiciary the least dangerous branch. By this he meant that the courts have no police force or military power to enforce decisions, nor any power of the purse with which to force compliance. Persuasion and reason are the courts' primary means to engender compliance. Judicial review works because political players (including presidents, members of Congress, and lower courts) recognize the courts' primary role in constitutional interpretation and agree to abide by it.

17-3b Judicial Review and Public Policy

precedent *The decision or guideline established in a case that will be used by the courts in determining future decisions.*

Judicial review can have great impact on American society. Through an interpretation or a reinterpretation of constitutional principles, the federal courts establish **precedents** that may lead the way in crafting new policies and practices and/or in eliminating existing ones. Precedents are formed through written explanations of the reasoning rendered in a particular case. These explanations are called *opinions*. Through judicial decisions and the precedents they create, the courts can signal Congress that existing practices conflict with constitutional provisions. They can thereby invalidate laws enacted by the people's representatives. Similarly, they can send a message to the president and other executive branch officials that certain of their actions are unconstitutional.

The power of judicial review is evident in the area of racial segregation. Relying upon the equal protection clause of the 14th Amendment, the Supreme Court in *Plessy v. Ferguson* (1896) upheld the practice of separate public facilities for African Americans and whites.[8] For half a century, this decision worked to uphold the practice of requiring separation of the races, particularly in schools and other public facilities. The ruling in *Plessy v. Ferguson* became a precedent whereby courts upheld segregation practices. In 1954, the Court changed its interpretation and declared that segregation in public facilities violated the equal protection clause, since separate facilities were inherently unequal.[9] The new constitutional precedent set in ***Brown v. Board of Education of Topeka*** signaled that the 14th Amendment and its equal protection clause could no longer be used to justify segregation. The Constitution itself did not change. What did change was the interpretation of the meaning of the Constitution. A fundamental change in governmental policy resulted from action not by Congress or the executive branch but from judicial decision making.

Brown v. Board of Education of Topeka *Landmark Supreme Court case that ruled that segregated public schools were unconstitutional under the equal protection clause of the Constitution.*

Judicial review represents a check on the powers of Congress and of the executive branch. If Congress (or state legislatures) enacts a law that violates the Constitution, or if federal bureaucrats create policies or take actions that run counter to constitutional provisions, the courts can invalidate them. The Supreme Court, however, will not rule on constitutionality until a case involving a constitutional question is brought before it. The Court long ago decided that it would not issue advisory opinions or make determinations of constitutionality prior to legislative enactment and policy implementation.

17-4 Judicial Power: Do the Referees Control the Game?

The power of federal judges, particularly their exercise of judicial review powers, has ignited substantial debate in recent years. Some critics have challenged what they see as excessive judicial power in the American political system. True to the spirit and the reality of the American political system, control and persuasion are sometimes used to counteract judicial power.

17-4a Sources of Judicial Power

As noted, judicial review applies not only to laws enacted by Congress but also to those created by state legislatures. Through the process of selective incorporation (see Chapter 4), the civil rights and liberties granted by the Constitution are now guaranteed not only at the federal level but also at state and local levels. State and local legislatures, like Congress, sometimes are frustrated by Supreme Court rulings that render laws they have enacted unconstitutional.

Laws do not have to be struck down to be affected by judicial decisions. Another consequential power of the courts is their ability to interpret the meaning of laws enacted by Congress. Where congressional statutes are vague or imprecise, judicial interpretation can substantially influence the meaning and application of federal laws.

Still another power of the judiciary is the ability of federal judges to participate in the execution of judicial orders. For example, the federal courts, in a series of cases, found many urban public school systems to have intolerable segregation.[10] Ruling that such segregation was unconstitutional, federal judges ordered that school systems take action to integrate their schools. A frequent means to achieve this end became court-ordered busing. In this context, federal judges not only rendered decisions but also directed actions to redress the unconstitutional practices.

Another area in which the courts have actively intervened is the administration of federal prisons. The courts have upheld claims that severe overcrowding in federal prisons may represent cruel and unusual punishment, which violates the 8th Amendment. In some cases, federal judges have played a supervisory role in setting maximum prisoner levels and requiring that overcrowded prisons reduce the number of persons incarcerated. In response to court mandates, some prisons have been forced to speed up the release of prisoners to prevent overcrowding.

17-4b Activism or Restraint?

While the principle of judicial review is widely accepted, its application in particular cases often generates controversy. Jurists, scholars, and public officials have varying views about constitutional interpretation, what can be termed *judicial philosophy*. At one extreme are those who hold a **strict constructionist view.** These individuals believe that constitutional interpretation should be based exclusively on the language expressed in the Constitution. According to this perspective, all powers not expressly granted in the Constitution are reserved to the states and to the people. Strict constructionists believe that a literal interpretation of the Constitution is a check on the exercise of federal government powers.

strict constructionist view *A judicial philosophy that holds that constitutional interpretation should be limited to the language of the Constitution and to the interpretation of the Founders' intentions.*

At the other end of the spectrum are persons who take a **broad constructionist view** of constitutional interpretation. Adherents of this position are willing to go beyond expressly granted powers when they examine the constitutionality of laws and executive branch policies. Broad constructionists believe that the national government may undertake many types of actions beyond those expressly listed in the Constitution. Many broad constructionists believe that the Constitution must be viewed as a living document. They feel that considering wide-ranging issues of social justice and civil rights is appropriate when interpreting the Constitution. In short, broad constructionists hold that the intent of the Founders must be creatively interpreted in order to be applicable to contemporary issues and problems.

broad constructionist view *A judicial philosophy that holds that constitutional interpretation should be based not only upon constitutional language and an appreciation for the intent of the Founders in designing its provisions, but also upon evolutionary ideas about civil rights and social justice.*

How are these two viewpoints reflected in debates about specific constitutional questions? In issues such as abortion policy, strict constructionists hold that strong federal action is not warranted. They reason that the Constitution includes no direct language about abortion. This group therefore sees abortion policy as the appropriate domain for state rather than for federal policy. In their view, state policy makers should decide whether or not, and in what ways, abortion should be regulated by the state government. Broad constructionists, on the other hand, recognize the Bill of Rights as collectively conveying a right of privacy that can be extended to cover the right to have an abortion. As documented daily in both the local and national media, the abortion issue continues to divide Americans. Apart from the issue of its morality, there is the political issue. Does the Constitution entitle the federal government to regulate abortion policies?

The accumulation of judicial powers, some analysts suggest, could lead to federal judges assuming unwarranted policy-making roles in the political process. They argue that, through broad constructionist interpretations of constitutional questions, the federal courts are increasingly *making policy* a prerogative supposedly centered in Congress. These critics are concerned that what has been termed **judicial activism** is expanding the role of the judiciary. Critics see this development as a possible violation of the principle of separation of powers.

judicial activism *Using powers of judicial review and statutory interpretation to expand the role of the judiciary in defining public policy.*

Judicial activism has been apparent for many years in the context of school desegregation. Citing the *Brown v. Board of Education of Topeka* decision, citizens and organizations in many cities sued their school districts in an effort to force racial integration in their schools. Federal judges often ruled that the school systems were guilty of discrimination and sometimes became directly involved in achieving racial integration of public schools. When judges refused to resolve the dispute until extensive busing of students was put into effect, they played a key role in crafting a remedy to discrimination and in overseeing implementation of the remedy.

judicial restraint *Belief in a limited role for the federal courts in defining public policy.*

Those who are uncomfortable with judicial activism call instead for **judicial restraint.** An early advocate of judicial restraint was Supreme Court Justice Marshall Harlan (the elder), who made the following argument as part of a court opinion in 1895:

> Is the judiciary to supervise the action of the legislative branch of government upon questions of public policy? Are they to override the will of the people as expressed by their chosen servants, because, in their judgment, the particular means employed by Congress in executing of the powers conferred by the Constitution are not the best that could have been devised?[11]

Harlan goes on to argue that, although Congress may abuse its legislative powers or enact improper laws, the remedy for such abuses is to be found at the ballot box, and in a wholesome public opinion which the representatives of the people will not long, if at all, disregard.[12]

Proponents of judicial activism have responded to the calls for judicial restraint by arguing that courts need to take an active role in constitutional and statutory interpretation. The courts, they believe, must go beyond the strict wording of the Constitution when applying it to modern problems and issues. They also see a need for the courts to be vigilant in defending the civil rights and liberties protected by the Constitution.

17-4c Countervailing Forces

While the debate over judicial philosophy continues in American politics, there are factors at work that place some limits on judicial power. First of all, the Supreme Court cannot enact laws as Congress does. The Court plays a role in policy making only through judicial roles related to interpretation and specific court orders.

Congress can respond if it disagrees with a court's interpretation of public statutes. For example, Congress can enact a law and be pleased with executive branch efforts to implement it, only to have those actions challenged in the courts. Apart from striking down laws enacted by representatives of the people, the courts have sometimes struck down existing administrative practices because they viewed them as inconsistent with the intent of the law. The federal courts' interpretation of what the members of Congress meant in creating public laws may represent a direct challenge to the legislative branch. Congress may respond by modifying the law in order to clarify its intent about public policies and their execution. In taking such action, Congress is engaging in a dialogue with the courts, instructing them more specifically about the meaning and intent of public laws.

An example of such dialogue is found in the civil rights case *Grove City College v. Bell.*[13] Included within several civil rights laws is a provision for the termination of federal funds for programs that have been found to discriminate on the basis of race, gender, religion, ethnicity, or disability. From 1964 through the mid-1980s, this provision was interpreted within the executive branch to mean that if a recipient of federal funds discriminated in any of its operations, then all funds would be terminated. During the mid-1980s, the Supreme Court decided a case that upheld a different practice: withholding federal funds not from entire programs but only from those parts that have been judged to discriminate.

The case involved private Grove City College, which received federal funds for student financial aid. Because it was ruled that the school's athletic program discriminated against women, the Department of Education (DOE) moved to cut off all federal funds for the college. The college sued DOE, claiming that the law required only that funds to the athletic program be terminated. In a decision that surprised many, the Court agreed with the college. This angered many in Congress, which responded by changing civil rights laws in order to specify that any form of discrimination required cutoff of all funds to the institution involved. The revised statute was a clear statement of congressional intention and reinstated the previous administrative practice.

Short of amending the Constitution, Congress has little recourse when its members disagree with Supreme Court interpretations of the Constitution. For example, if the Supreme Court upholds a practice on the basis that prohibition would violate a basic freedom, Congress usually accepts the Court's view on constitutionality.

If sufficiently dissatisfied with Supreme Court decisions, Congress could act to change the Constitution itself. It could either propose a constitutional amendment and pass it on to the states for ratification, or it could respond to a request from two-thirds of the states to hold a constitutional convention (see Chapter 2). However, members of Congress have seldom initiated amendments to the Constitution in direct response to Court rulings. Presidents and members of Congress alike have been reluctant to call for a constitutional convention, given the uncertainties about the changes that might be proposed.

One exception, where a ruling by the Supreme Court did stimulate a constitutional amendment, concerned the national income tax. In the last decade of the 19th century, Congress enacted a provision that amounted to a 2% tax on incomes from all sources in excess of $4,000. This provision was challenged on the grounds that it violated the constitutional provision that direct taxes be levied among the states according to population. In other words, such a tax could not be collected directly by the federal government from citizens of the nation. Furthermore, the fact that the tax was levied only on those earning more than $4,000 was claimed to violate the constitutional stipulation that taxes be uniform across the United States.[14] The national government's need for a more direct revenue source could not be denied. Recognizing the Court's view of the constitutionality of income taxes, Congress proposed a constitutional amendment that would specifically allow the collection of a national income tax. Enough state legislatures approved the measure, and the 16th Amendment was added to the Constitution in 1913.

The case of abortion demonstrates the tensions that can exist between the federal courts and the state legislatures. The *Roe v. Wade* decision upheld the right of pregnant women to have an abortion in the early months of pregnancy, striking down the laws of many states that prohibited abortion. That decision was based on the constitutional right to privacy. Since *Roe*, the Supreme Court has rendered decisions in other abortion cases that indicate that it will uphold state laws that place some restrictions on abortions. State legislatures and abortion foes have monitored Court decisions with interest, seeking to ascertain what latitude they might have to restrict abortions. Pro-choice advocates monitor this situation as well, worried that Supreme Court decisions will weaken a woman's right to an abortion and encourage states to enact laws making it difficult to obtain an abortion.

Debate surrounding judicial activism versus judicial restraint has grown more strident in recent years, as the courts deal with such controversial issues as abortion, gay marriage, and flag burning. There is no simple solution here, no arena in which the issue can be answered unequivocally. Probably the most enduring impact on this debate is the appointment of judges to the federal courts. Because of the appointments made by presidents Reagan and Bush, conservative perspectives will likely prevail for some time in the federal courts. We will consider the rules and strategies behind influencing judicial decision making later in this chapter as we examine the selection of judicial players.

17-5 Judicial Review in Practice

In any given era, the Supreme Court is characterized both in terms of the prevailing ideologies of justices and the Court's perspective on judicial activism. The decisions reached in the Court often result from coalitions of justices who share similar or at least compatible views on judicial interpretation and political ideology. Sometimes the coalitions are strong and dominant; at other times they are shifting and transitory.

17-5a Shifting Patterns of Judicial Interpretation

The presiding chief justice often lends his or her name to a particular era of Supreme Court history. Traditionally the term of office of a chief justice is sufficiently lengthy to allow this classification. For example, the Warren Court (the Supreme Court during the period that Earl Warren was chief justice, 1953–1969) is recognized as a liberal court, which used a broad interpretation of the Constitution to expand civil rights and liberties. It was this court that struck down the legal principle of segregation as unconstitutional. This decision led to a sustained period in which segregation was challenged and outlawed. At the same time, new policies to protect and expand the rights of women and of minorities were created (see Chapter 19). Critics, often conservatives, railed against the Warren Court for what they saw as judicial activism gone wild.

The Warren Court gave way to a more conservative one during the years that Warren Burger served as chief justice (1969–1986). This Court shifted to a more conservative position, largely in response to the appointment of conservatives such as Burger, William Rehnquist, and other justices by presidents Nixon and Ford. The Burger Court, however, did not substantially change the Supreme Court precedents that were set by the Warren Court. The tendency during the Burger Court was to uphold major Supreme Court precedents while narrowing some interpretations in a conservative direction.

The Supreme Court under Chief Justice William Rehnquist, beginning in 1986, is still leaving its mark on judicial interpretation. This Court has become more conservative than the Burger Court, which by today's standards seems more moderate than conservative. The shift to the political right by the Rehnquist Court reflects the appointment of several conservative jurists by presidents Reagan and Bush; these include Sandra Day O'Connor, Antonin Scalia, and Clarence Thomas.

Some decisions in the last fifteen years reflect a strict constructionist view of Constitutional interpretation. In one important case, the Court was asked to determine the constitutionality of federal laws that banned the carrying of a gun within 1,000 feet of a school.[15] Given the conservative ideology of several judges, one might have expected the court to take a law-and-order stance and support the federal law. This was not the case. For the first time in 60 years, and demonstrating a renewed tendency for judicial restraint, the Supreme Court made a federal law invalid on the basis that it went beyond constitutionally specified powers.

The Court has also taken a more conservative view of federal programs designed to compensate for discrimination and to enhance the rights of women and minorities. In a key case concerning affirmative action, the Court did not strike down federal government policies that set aside a percentage of contracts to minority firms. The Court did declare, however, that henceforth it would use a stricter standard when assessing the constitutionality of affirmative action programs.[16] In a separate ruling, the Court struck down the use of race as the primary factor in drawing congressional district boundaries. Following mandates of the Voting Rights Act of 1965 and its 1992 amendments, and using data from the 1990 census, the Justice Department pushed states to redraw congressional district boundaries to create districts with large, even majority, representation by African Americans (see Chapter 11 and Chapter 12 for a discussion of such majority-minority districts). This move increased the representation of African Americans in Congress. In a case involving Georgia's 11th Congressional District, the Court ruled that using race as the primary criteria for drawing district boundaries violated the equal protection clause of the 14th Amendment.[17] From the Court's perspective, race can be one of the criteria, but not the primary criterion, upon which Congressional districts can be drawn.

Support for government regulation intended to support law-and-order policies was evident in other decisions reached by the Court. In one case (see Box 17-2) the Court upheld random drug testing of student athletes in public schools, leaving open the question of whether other students might be tested.[18] Other decisions made it more difficult for inmates to bring constitutional lawsuits to challenge actions by prison officials[19] and allowed for reasonable exceptions to the requirement that police knock and announce their presence before entering a home to execute a search warrant.[20]

In another ruling the Court rendered a decision that affirmed the power of federal government against encroachment by the states. Throughout the 1990s, several states had enacted laws setting limits on the number of terms of office that representatives and senators from the state could serve in Congress. These laws were challenged in the federal courts on the grounds that these offices were created and defined at the national level through the Constitution. The Supreme Court upheld this challenge and ruled that states alone did not have the authority to change the office of national legislators through imposition of term limits.[21] Such limits would only be constitutional if they were created through amendment of the Constitution.

17-5b Shifting Coalitions on the Bench

Coalitions of justices are needed to achieve a majority vote on a case. When the same coalition is successful in many decisions, it may have a major impact on Supreme Court decisions over one or more terms. Such a coalition is prominent in recent times as conservative coalition with a preference for judicial restraint rather than judicial activism came to hold power on the Court. At the heart of this conservative coalition were three players: justices Rehnquist, Scalia, and Thomas. The commonality of this coalition is demonstrated by the fact that justices Scalia and Thomas voted together in 83% of the signed decisions. These three were frequently joined by two others, O'Connor and Kennedy. Whenever these five came to agreement, they achieved a five-vote majority.

On the other side was a group of four justices who formed a coalition of their own. This coalition, made up of justices Stevens, Souter, Ginsburg, and Breyer, is typically characterized as moderate. There is, as of 2004, no liberal bloc on the Court such as there was when justices William O. Douglas and Thurgood Marshall sat on the nation's highest bench. The moderate coalition today generally tends to uphold existing Supreme Court precedents, but it is not generally sympathetic to a strong judicial activist position. Unlike previous Supreme Court eras, there is little evidence today of any central position between the two competing coalitions.

Coalitions in the Supreme Court, as in other political arenas, change as members change. With the current close split between conservatives and moderates, future appointments to the Court will be closely watched. Such appointments will undoubtedly have substantial impact on future Supreme Court decisions and could shift the relative power positions of the existing coalitions. For this reason, the right to make appointments to the Supreme Court has been among the important stakes in recent presidential campaigns. See Table 17-2 for an analysis of agreements among Supreme Court justices in cases before the Court.

Table 17-2

"Batting Average"

Justices vary in terms of agreement with their colleagues. On each case they have the option of signing the majority opinion, signing a dissenting opinion, or writing an individual opinion. As the court changes, the nature of the majority also changes. Some justices spend much of their time disagreeing with colleagues, while others are usually in the majority.

Following is the percentage of times the justice joined the majority as opposed to joining a dissenting opinion during his or her time on the Court:*

Anthony Kennedy	91%
Sandra Day O'Connor	86%
David Souter	83%
William Rehnquist	82%
Antonin Scalia	81%
Clarence Thomas	79%
Ruth Bader Ginsburg	79%
Stephen Breyer	78%
John Paul Stevens	71%

*As of 2003 and reported in the online Congressional Quarterly Electronic Library, "Supreme Court Collection."

17-6 Other Players in the Judicial Arena

Because the decisions of the federal courts influence public policy, the courts are subject to political pressure. As noted, some features of the courts, notably the permanent appointment of judges who face no elections, protect the courts from some political activities. Nevertheless, the courts remain a political arena within the American political system. Judges are not the only active players. The national government, including the president, has an interest in court decisions. So do interest groups, whose members are often directly affected by judicial decisions. For this reason, these players have developed strategies designed to increase their participation in judicial decision making. These parties are aided by attorneys and legal specialists who represent them in court.

17-6a The Role of the Solicitor General

The interests of the national government, and particularly of the president and the executive branch, are represented within the federal courts by the solicitor general, a high-ranking official in the Department of Justice serving under the attorney general, who heads the entire department.[22] The solicitor general determines what policy position the national government will take in cases being heard in the federal courts. In cases in which the national government is itself a party (when it is suing or being sued in federal court), this official determines when the government should appeal lower court rulings and what position the government will take in the briefs it submits in appeals.

Representing both the interests of President George H. Bush and a majority of Congress, former solicitor general Kenneth Starr vehemently argued in 1990 that the Supreme Court should uphold the law enacted by Congress to prohibit flag burning. Starr sought to argue that there are strong legal grounds for upholding this statute. An inside look at Starr's presentation to the Court is included in Box 17-3: Does Television Belong in the High Court? In the end, however, the Supreme Court struck down the law as unconstitutional on the grounds that flag burning was protected as a free speech right of citizens (see Chapter 4). As discussed earlier in this chapter, the ball then returned to Congress's court, where members of Congress initiated action to amend the Constitution in order to specifically outlaw flag burning.

There are cases in which, although the national government is not a party, the presidential administration nevertheless has some interest in the precedent that the case may create. Here, the solicitor general decides if an *amicus curiae brief,* which presents views on relevant legal and constitutional arguments surrounding the case, will be filed in the federal courts on behalf of the government. In some cases the Supreme Court asks the solicitor general to appear before it in order to determine the government's position on a policy issue involved in a case to be heard.

The solicitor general is a political player as well as a legal specialist facing many different political expectations. As a presidential appointee, the solicitor general is expected to represent presidential policy interests in legal cases, especially in those where important precedents will be set. As a representative of the executive branch, the solicitor general is also presumed to uphold the interests of the federal bureaucracy, which implements federal laws. And as a representative of the national government, the solicitor general is expected generally to defend it in controversies with states and localities.

17-6b Interest Groups and Their Strategies

While it is not publicly recognized, interest groups seek to play a role in the decision making of the federal courts (see Chapter 7). Because judicial decisions can influence public policy, interest groups engage in strategies to influence court decisions just as they do in such other arenas as Congress and the executive branch. To be effective players in the judicial arena, many interest groups have created legal departments to represent them in the courts.

Interest groups may use the judicial arena to achieve specific objectives. Environmental groups are among those that have sued both private industry and government concerning actions, such as logging in national forests and the development of off-shore oil operations.

Box 17–3 Does Television Belong in the High Court?

To date, the Supreme Court has refused to allow television cameras into its chamber, fearing that the cameras would disturb and interfere with judicial proceedings. Noted columnist James J. Kilpatrick disagrees with this stance and argues that television cameras should be allowed into the nation's highest court:

It didn't rank with Daniel Webster's oratory in the Dartmouth College case of 1819, and it was less dramatic than Thurgood Marshall's impassioned plea in the school segregation case of 1954, but Monday's oral argument in the Supreme Court over desecration of the flag was a beauty. Sorry you couldn't be there.

The nine justices were there. Opposing counsel were there. A couple of hundred privileged spectators had first-class tickets. Huddled behind the grillwork, riding in coach, were 100 reporters straining to hear the argument. But no television cameras were there. The whole business is absurd. Given today's inconspicuous TV technology, the high court's adamant, blockheaded refusal to permit TV coverage of oral argument is inexcusable. Who do these nine eminences think they are? Gods? Immortals?

The trouble is, that is exactly what the justices think they are. Former chief justice Warren Earl Burger is authority for the proposition that to permit television coverage would be to destroy the mystique of the high court. If the people once discovered that human beings were beneath the black robes of judicial office, the game would be up. During his tenure as chief justice, Burger often swore that TV cameras would enter the courtroom only over his dead body. I have great affection and respect for the gentleman, but on this question his attitude is intolerable.

The two companion cases that were argued Monday morning provided a superb opportunity to educate the American people not only in the function of the high court but also in the meaning of the First Amendment. There was no valid reason to deny the people the surrogate services of TV. The court, after all, belongs to the people who pay the justices' salaries. What is wrong with letting the people see what is going on?

Forty-two of the 50 states permit television coverage of appellate proceedings. Have their walls of judicial prestige come tumbling down? Have jurists and lawyers hammed it up? No convincing evidence supports the notion that these state courts have suffered from letting the people in.

The argument began at 10:28 A.M. with presentation of the government's case by Solicitor General Kenneth W. Starr. He is a mild-mannered fellow, orderly, almost prim. He had his argument so well-organized that we could hear the Roman numerals as he spoke. He contended (I) that Congress had carefully considered the anti-desecration act of 1989; (II) that the act was narrowly drawn; (III) that the act of flag-burning in itself, carried no particular message; and (IV) that the law implicated intangible values of the highest order.

Starr had a tough case to argue. When the flag bill was before Congress last year, Assistant Attorney General William Barr said a mouthful: It cannot be seriously maintained that a statute aimed at protecting the flag would be constitutional. But here was Starr doing his serious best to maintain precisely that.

His best was not quite enough for Justice Antonin Scalia, a former law professor who dearly loves to challenge counsel. Hunched forward over the bench, the volatile Scalia peppered Starr with tough questions. Surely, he thought, the defendants in the two cases had meant to say something: they were saying I hate the United States. Besides, Scalia persisted, the very verbs in the act contradicted the notion that the act is content-neutral. Scalia ticked them off: mutilate, deface, defile, burn, trample. "If I get a spot on my tie," Scalia mused, "I don't say, 'Gee, I've defiled my tie.'"

Starr stayed gamely on his feet for 27 minutes, contending stubbornly that the act does nothing to inhibit robust debate on the concerns that provoked the defendants to action. Justice Anthony Kennedy gave him no help. He asked if flag-burning is not universally recognized as a form of protest. Starr had no particular answer.

William M. Kunstler did better in his half-hour. He is a shaggy, craggy man, with the face of an eccentric English peer. His hair fits him like an untrimmed wig. His glasses get shoved to the top of his head. In a raucous voice, roughened by years of rousing the rabble, Kunstler argued effectively that flag-burning is indeed a form of free speech just as a divided court had ruled in the Texas case a year ago. Scalia gave him a hard time, too.

So it went for a fascinating hour, as keen minds on the bench and at the bar explored the first of our great freedoms. I wish you could have been there. One day you will be.

Source: From *A Conservative View* by James J. Kilpatrick. Copyright 1990. Universal Press Syndicate.

In other cases, an interest group can sponsor a case on behalf of an individual or organization. Interest groups serve as sponsors for cases that raise issues or question government policies that are of concern to group members. Such was the case when the National Association for the Advancement of Colored People (NAACP) sponsored the case of Linda Brown, an African American who was refused admission to a segregated white elementary school in Topeka, Kansas. The NAACP saw this case as an opportunity to retest the constitutionality of school segregation laws. The decision in this case (*Brown v. Board of Education of Topeka*) ultimately struck down segregation practices throughout the nation. When interest groups serve as sponsors, they either provide legal counsel or pay for private counsel. They also may work to organize legal arguments and shepherd the case through the courts.

Another strategy of interest groups is to encourage class action suits, where a few plaintiffs can sue in court on behalf of a much larger group of persons with a stake in the case. Anti-tobacco groups have encouraged class action suits against major tobacco companies on the grounds that their products caused serious health problems for smokers. Interest groups may sponsor class action suits in the same way that they can sponsor individuals and organizations in private lawsuits, again with the intention of influencing case outcomes that are favorable to the group.

An interest group may file an amicus curiae brief in a case where important precedents will be made and/or where the decision will have impact on other members of the group. Through such briefs, an interest group states its position in the legal controversy and provides legal reasoning to support it. The filing of amicus briefs to influence the outcomes of federal court cases is roughly analogous to lobbying efforts by interest groups to convince members of Congress to make decisions that support their group.

Researchers have begun to explore the impact of interest groups' use of amicus curiae briefs in judicial decision making. The findings to date suggest that filing briefs may make it more likely that higher courts will agree to hear cases appealed from lower courts.[23] The research does not find, however, that amicus curiae briefs have a substantial impact on the judicial decisions.[24]

17-6c The Courts and Public Opinion

Judicial analysts have studied the extent to which the ideological position of the federal courts reflects the broad ideological mood of the public (see Chapter 9). Because judges are not directly elected by the people, the public has little direct influence over judicial decisions. Yet if the ideological position of the courts substantially differs from the ideological mood of the nation, the legitimacy of the courts might be threatened and the political position of the courts would be weakened.

Political scientists have begun to use public opinion polls to study the correlation between the ideological positions of the courts and of the public. Research findings suggest that there is a two-way relationship between public opinion and judicial decisions. The courts both respond to public opinion and, at the same time, can serve to promote or reinforce legitimate changes in public opinion.[25] Debate continues: Are the courts responsive to public opinion because justices themselves consciously consider such opinion? Or does public opinion influence the elections of presidents and members of the Senate, who appoint and confirm new judges, who in turn reflect current public opinion? Either way, the general public has an indirect influence on the judicial decisions reached in the federal courts.

17-7 The Judicial Arena: Organization and Rules

The constitutional basis of the federal judiciary is outlined in Article III, which states that "the judicial power of the national government is vested in one Supreme Court, and in such inferior Courts as the Congress may from time to time ordain and establish." With these words, the Founders created a hierarchical judicial system, with a permanent Supreme Court at the top, accompanied by lower courts as created by Congress.

17-7a Organization of Federal Courts

Through the Judiciary Act of 1789, Congress created the initial structure of the federal judiciary. This law designated that the Supreme Court should consist of six members: one chief justice and five associate justices. This number has subsequently been changed on several occasions by Congress. The Supreme Court today is composed of a chief justice and eight associate justices.

This act also established 13 district courts (with one district judge assigned to each) and 3 circuit courts to hear appeals from district courts. Originally, a district judge and two Supreme Court justices traveled to the circuit courts to hear appeals cases. This traveling, known as "riding the circuit," placed a heavy burden on the justices. Today, the nation is divided into 94 district courts. Every state has at least one district court; more populous states have as many as four. Each district court has several judges, each of whom hears cases filed in the court. There are 13 federal courts of appeals at the present time. The number of judges in these courts ranges from 3 to 23, depending on population size and caseload in the court's jurisdiction. Normally, these judges hear cases in panels of three.

17-7b The Supreme Court

The Supreme Court operates at the pinnacle of the nation's judicial system according to a variety of rules. Some are stipulated in the Constitution, and others have been developed by the Court as practiced over time.

Rules for Selecting Cases

Most of the cases before the Supreme Court arrive through its appellate jurisdiction. Each year, several thousand cases are appealed to the nation's highest court. The justices review these cases and agree to hear only about 150 appeals a year. In selecting cases, the Court uses a **rule of four:** If four or more justices vote to hear an appeal, then the Court certifies a **writ of certiorari** (a Latin phrase meaning "to make more certain"), signaling that it will consider the case. This selection method provides the Supreme Court with almost total control over the cases that it will hear. Congress enacted legislation in 1988 that enhanced the power of the Supreme Court to determine which cases it will hear on appeal. Currently, federal laws require that the Court hear appeals only in cases where (1) a state or federal court has declared a law unconstitutional, or (2) a state court has upheld a state law that has been challenged on the basis that it contradicts federal laws. Most often, the justices choose cases that involve substantial legal disputes about the constitutionality of federal laws or practices.

rule of four *Rule used by the Supreme Court stipulating that a minimum of four judges must vote to consider an appeals case before it can be selected for consideration and placed on the Court's schedule.*

writ of certiorari *An order from a higher court demanding that a lower court send up the record of a specified case for review. This signals that the Supreme Court will hear a case appealed from lower federal courts.*

Rules about Hearing Cases

After a writ of certiorari is issued, the Supreme Court schedules a date for the case to be heard. Lawyers on both sides are invited to submit written arguments, or briefs, in advance of their appearance before the Court. At the discretion of the Court, outside groups are allowed to file amicus curiae briefs that support one side or the other.

The Court specifies the length of oral arguments to be presented before it; each side is normally given 30 minutes. The justices may interrupt the attorneys making arguments to ask clarifying questions or to raise any point they wish.

The Supreme Court generally is in session from the first Monday in October through the following June, although sessions sometimes have extended further into the summer months. Oral arguments usually are presented from 10:00 A.M. to noon and from 1:00 to 3:00 P.M., three days a week. These sessions are open to the public, although to date, no cameras or television crews have been admitted into the courtroom. See Box 17-4: Learning More about the Supreme Court for the Court's website.

Decision Making

At some point after oral arguments are completed, the justices meet to consider the case at a **judicial conference.** These conferences, usually held on Wednesday afternoons or

judicial conference *Closed meeting in which members of the Supreme Court discuss cases and make decisions about them.*

Box 17–4 Learning More about the Supreme Court

For more information on the Supreme Court, visit their website at http://www.supremecourtus.gov/ At this site you can learn more about the history and operations of the Supreme Court. Visit the site and find the biographies of the justices to learn more about their background.

Fridays, are private sessions behind closed doors; no reporter or political analyst has ever witnessed these proceedings. Even law clerks and other Supreme Court staff are excluded from these meetings. This privacy allows the justices to openly discuss cases, frankly present ideas, and debate the merits of each case. As a general rule, discussions begin with arguments by the chief justice, followed by comments from other justices in order of seniority. When the discussion is ended, the justices vote. A majority vote (five justices or more if all participate) decides whether the lower court decision is upheld or overturned. On most occasions, all nine judges participate in decisions about every case. However, a judge may disqualify himself or herself on the basis of conflict of interest. Also, fewer than nine may participate if illness or resignation depletes the bench of full membership.

Opinions

majority opinion *The written rationale explaining the views of the justices who were in the majority when voting on an individual case.*

concurring opinion *Opinion by one or more justices who agree with the majority decision in a case but disagree with the legal reasoning of the majority.*

dissenting opinion *Opinion by one or more justices who voted with the minority (against the majority) on a given case.*

We have seen that for most cases heard before the Supreme Court, the Court issues an opinion that explains the reasoning behind the decision rendered in the case. When a majority of the judges agree on the legal basis of the decision, their written decision and its justification is known as the **majority opinion.** If a member of the Court agrees with the majority decision but not with the reasoning behind it, the justice may write a separate **concurring opinion.** The arguments presented specify the Court's current thinking about constitutional issues. In this way, opinions establish precedents, which, as described earlier, serve as legal guidelines for lower courts considering similar cases. (Several legal precedents related to constitutional rights and civil liberties were described in Chapter 4.)

The Court has internal rules to determine who is assigned to write case opinions. If the chief justice votes with the majority, then he determines which of the justices will write the majority opinion. Chief justices may also decide to write the majority opinion themselves. If the chief justice is in the minority, then the senior justice in the majority assigns the responsibility for preparation of the majority opinion.

Justices who vote with the minority in a given case are entitled to write **dissenting opinions,** in which they explain their views about the case. Dissenting opinions show the divisions and differences of attitude that exist among justices about constitutional issues. They also may present openings for lawyers to use in another round in future cases heard before the Supreme Court. On some occasions, the Supreme Court has overturned its own past decisions and used the language from earlier dissenting opinions to establish a new majority position.

The votes of justices are not final until the decision is formally announced by the Court. The coalition-building process is fluid, and justices may change their votes while opinions are being written. A persuasive opinion may lead a justice to reconsider and change his or her vote on the case. Sometimes, the author of an opinion will take into account the objections or concerns of one or more other justices in order to keep them in the coalition.

Lesser-known but significant players in the Supreme Court are the law clerks assigned to each justice. These clerks, young lawyers individually selected by the justices, perform legal research and analysis. They also often write initial drafts of opinions, as instructed by the justices for whom they work. Chief Justice William Rehnquist and Associate Justice John Paul Stevens served as law clerks on the Court in the early days of their legal careers.

17-7c State and Local Courts

The American judiciary contains many state and local courts in addition to the federal courts. (These are described in more detail in Chapter 18). The structure and organization of these courts are based on state constitutions and laws that vary across the states and localities. In some states, judges are nominated by governors and then approved by state legislative bodies. Other states use judicial elections to select judges for the state bench. In those states, voters have the opportunity to select among competing players when selecting justices.

At the local level, many types of specialized courts have been created to handle particular types of legal disputes, such as small claims, traffic violations, and the probate (determining the validity and the administering) of wills and estates. Localities also have municipal and county courts, which hear criminal and major civil cases.

The state judicial system resembles the federal court structure, in that it typically has both lower state courts and a state supreme court. The lower state courts hear civil and criminal cases based on state law. State supreme courts hear appeals from lower state courts and play an important role in interpreting the meaning of state constitutions.

17-8 Games to Select Judicial Players

The selection of federal jurists, both lower court judges and Supreme Court justices, is an important political game that determines which judicial philosophies will prevail. The opportunity to appoint Supreme Court justices occurs infrequently only after the death or resignation of one of the Court's current nine members. New appointments are more common at the lower court levels because of the larger number of district and appellate court judges. Some rules by which the judicial selection game is played are laid out in the Constitution; other rules and norms have developed and become institutionalized through political practice.

17-8a The Constitutional Rules

The Constitution specifies a two-stage process for selecting federal court judges. It includes participation by both the executive and legislative branches. Article III stipulates that federal judges must first be nominated by the president and then confirmed by the Senate. Once selected for the federal bench, judges serve no specific term of office. Instead, they remain on the bench for a period of good behavior. Unless a judge violates oath of office and is therefore removed through impeachment and conviction, the judge himself/herself decides how long to remain on the federal bench.

While the Constitution places age and some residency requirements on players in the executive and legislative branches, no such stipulations are placed on those who serve on the federal judiciary. Federal judges are not required to be lawyers or to have law degrees. In practice, however, most judges have law degrees. Many have served first as judges in local or state courts prior to their appointment to the federal judiciary.

Because they feared legislative interference with the courts, the Founders included a provision in the Constitution stating that the compensation given to judges cannot be diminished during their term of office. This was intended to prevent Congress from using reductions in judges' salaries as a means of influencing court decisions or of forcing judges to leave the bench.

17-8b Nominating Lower Court Judges

While the constitutionally defined process of presidential nomination and senatorial confirmation pertains to all federal judges, the selection process for lower court judges is different from that for nominees to the Supreme Court. Presidents have not always taken an active role in selecting judges for district courts and courts of appeals. Sometimes, they have relied on recommendations from members of Congress or had Justice Department officials screen candidates and recommend nominees. Recent presidents, however, have taken a greater interest in the nomination of lower court judges. Today presidents typically scrutinize nominees and direct staff to identify candidates whose political values and judicial outlooks are consistent with their own.

senatorial courtesy *A practice whereby presidents consult with senators from a state when considering the nomination of federal judges to positions in that state. Also, members of the Senate tend to defer to their colleagues from the state in which the appointment is being made.*

An informal but often-followed rule of **senatorial courtesy** applies to the selection of lower court judges. Presidents consult with the senators of the state in which a judicial vacancy has occurred, especially if they are from the same political party as the president. Once the nomination is made, members of the Senate generally defer to the wishes of the senator of that state during the confirmation process.

Judgeships, particularly for the lower federal courts, may be used as a reward for prior political support or personal loyalty.[26] Presidents have been known to nominate individuals who have previously supported their electoral campaign or served in their administration. Senators may seek to convince presidents to select individuals who have given them political or other support in the past.

Presidents commonly appoint members of their own party to federal judgeships. The party label implies a particular ideological outlook and helps presidents to predict how judges may decide future cases. A Republican president, for example, expects that appointing Republicans to the federal bench will increase the likelihood that conservative values will be considered in federal court cases.[27] Over 85% of Ronald Reagan's and George H. Bush's appointments to the district courts and courts of appeal were Republican, whereas Bill Clinton's appointments were overwhelmingly Democrats. President George W. Bush's appointments to the federal courts have generally been conservatives. (See Time Out 17-2 for further discussion of the politics of presidential appointment of federal judges.)

Another player in the nomination game for lower court judges is the American Bar Association (ABA). This professional organization of lawyers created a Committee on Federal Judiciary in 1946 to assess the legal qualifications of persons nominated to the federal bench. The ratings given by this committee receive attention from both the president and the Senate. A nominee with a weak rating from the ABA committee is likely to face intense scrutiny and at least some opposition during the confirmation process.

17-8c Nominating Supreme Court Justices

Given the importance of Supreme Court decisions in interpreting the Constitution, presidents become personally involved in selecting Supreme Court nominees. As with lower

Time Out 17-2

Presidents and the Nomination of Federal Judges

Imagine, for a moment, that you are the president of the United States and that you have just been informed that a justice on the Supreme Court has resigned for health reasons. You realize that you will soon be expected to select and announce a nomination for a replacement to the highest court in the land.

List the qualities that you, as president, would look for when selecting a new Supreme Court justice. What type of person would you think would make a good Supreme Court justice? Is judicial experience a relevant standard to consider? What about political ideology? What qualities would lead you automatically to exclude an individual from further consideration?

In Section 17-8c we will look at the bases that presidents have used in selecting Supreme Court justices. These presidential judgments are based on political practice and personal viewpoints, not on constitutional or statutory provisions. As you read the discussion of the selection of judges, compare your answer to the questions posed at the opening of this box with the practices generally used by modern presidents.

court judges, presidents consider prior judicial experience an important standard in selecting justices to the nation's highest court. Not surprisingly, about 40% of presidential nominees to the Supreme Court were judges in either lower federal or state courts at the time of their nomination.[28] Another 20 percent were attorneys in private practice or law school professors at the time of their appointment.

In addition to legal experience, Supreme Court nominations are influenced by the agreement between the judicial philosophies of presidents and nominees, policy positions, moral conduct, and representativeness.

Agreement of Judicial Philosophy

Presidents today closely examine the ideology and judicial philosophies of potential Supreme Court nominees as part of the screening process. However, because direct questioning of potential nominees is generally considered inappropriate, presidents rely on indirect cues about judicial behavior. These include past experience on the bench and party identification.

If the nominee has had prior experience as a judge, the president and advisers look over the nominee's judicial decisions and written opinions carefully to learn about the candidate's judicial philosophy. From these, they try to predict how the nominee might vote in future Supreme Court cases. Presidents seek to identify and nominate a candidate who shares a similar judicial philosophy and outlook on the role of the judiciary in American politics.

Policy Positions

The position of a potential Supreme Court nominee on specific policy issues may grant him or her access to the nation's most important judicial arena. Presidents seek nominees who have policy preferences similar to their own. Box 17-5: Court Packing describes President Franklin D. Roosevelt's frustration with a Supreme Court that initially ruled many of his New Deal programs invalid. In his later Supreme Court nominations, Roosevelt made certain that his nominees were sympathetic to the mission of the New Deal.

When George H. Bush was called upon to nominate a replacement for retiring Supreme Court justice William Brennan in 1990, he was pressed by pro-life groups to select a jurist who opposed abortion because the Court was almost evenly divided on the issue. While sympathetic to the aims of pro-life organizations, Bush did not feel it appropriate to focus the nomination entirely on a candidate's stand on any single policy. In his words, he refused to create any one-policy litmus test to screen potential candidates. Given the past judicial decisions made by his eventual nominee David Souter, Bush was confident that he was appointing a fellow conservative to the bench.

Ethical or Moral Conduct

Federal judges generally, and Supreme Court justices especially, are expected to exemplify strong moral conduct and ethical standards. While these concepts have no clear definitions, evidence of legal or moral problems can severely harm an individual's chances for nomination and confirmation.

The ethical issue arose in the case of Douglas Ginsburg, nominated for the Supreme Court by Ronald Reagan in 1987. Reagan nominated Ginsburg after a review of his record indicated that he had a conservative judicial philosophy that was compatible with Reagan's. Following the nomination, however, there were rumors that Ginsburg had smoked marijuana as a college student and during his tenure as a law professor. The use of an illegal drug was quite troublesome to both Reagan and his conservative followers. Soon after the controversy began, pressure from conservatives led Ginsburg to withdraw his nomination.

The issue of moral conduct was raised dramatically in 1991 during the confirmation hearings for Clarence Thomas, a federal judge and former director of the Equal Employment Opportunity Commission (EEOC). During the initial hearings, Thomas was grilled by

Box 17–5 Court Packing—A Political Game about Numbers

The close connection between politics and the federal courts was demonstrated earlier in the 20th century when President Franklin D. Roosevelt contemplated a bold move to increase the number of Supreme Court justices. As the Democratic Party nominee, Roosevelt was elected to office in 1932, during the early years of the Great Depression. To combat the Depression, Roosevelt and his advisers devised the New Deal, a broad plan to use new government agencies and policies to stimulate and regulate the economy. Congress (both houses were controlled by Democrats) rallied around the New Deal initiatives, creating such agencies as the Works Progress Administration, Federal Emergency Relief Administration, and National Recovery Administration.

Not all political players approved of the New Deal. Many conservatives were alarmed at the rapid expansion of federal government involvement in the economy and at the regulation of the private sector. Far outnumbered in Congress, New Deal opponents were unable to stop the enactment of laws implementing the Roosevelt plan. Selecting a different strategy, opponents challenged the constitutionality of the new federal agencies and programs in the courts. Following a relatively narrow interpretation of the Constitution, the Supreme Court invalidated several New Deal programs as going beyond the powers granted to the national government. These Court decisions threatened to stifle the New Deal response to the Depression.

Roosevelt claimed that the Supreme Court decisions about New Deal programs returned the Constitution to horse-and-buggy days and represented a constitutional crisis. As a means of circumventing this roadblock to the New Deal, Roosevelt in 1937 proposed a plan whereby Congress would increase the number of seats on the Supreme Court by one for each justice over the age of 70. The public rationale for this reform was that it would ease the demands on individual justices and increase the efficiency of Court operations. Clearly, however, the real motivation behind the reform was a quest for political power, not judicial efficiency. By placing on the bench judges with judicial philosophies that were favorable to the New Deal mission, Roosevelt hoped to overcome judicial objection to his policy initiatives. Opponents cried foul and charged Roosevelt was trying to pack the Court in his political favor. The plan proved unpopular in many quarters and was not seriously considered by Congress. As a tactical ploy, however, the plan may have had an impact, since some justices softened their opposition to New Deal programs. In subsequent cases, the Supreme Court upheld several components of the New Deal, and the push for increasing court membership subsided.

The court-packing episode represented a direct challenge to the authority of the Supreme Court and highlights the political role of the federal courts in American government. Roosevelt simply felt that the Court's objections to the New Deal were unacceptable and outmoded. His court-packing plan, while not executed, was intended to politicize the Supreme Court in a direction favorable to the New Deal.

As an interesting historical aside, during his 13 years as president Roosevelt ultimately had the opportunity to appoint eight justices to the Supreme Court.

members of the Senate Judiciary Committee, especially Democrats, about his judicial philosophy and tenure as administrative head of the EEOC. During the process of Senate consideration of confirmation, Anita Hill, a law school professor and former administrator at the EEOC, charged that, in the early 1980s, Clarence Thomas had sexually harassed her when they both worked as federal officials in Washington. In televised hearings that received extensive public attention, Professor Hill made allegations of sexual harassment, and Judge Thomas vehemently denied the charges. Other witnesses testified about the characters of these two individuals, but no conclusive evidence to prove or rebut the charge of sexual harassment was presented. Ultimately, the Senate, by a slim margin that largely followed party lines, confirmed the nomination of Clarence Thomas as associate justice.

In the wake of the confirmation hearings, Americans continued to discuss and debate the extent and seriousness of sexual harassment in the workplace. Substantial

Box 17-6 The Backgrounds of Supreme Court Justices

Throughout America's history, 108 individuals have been appointed to the Supreme Court.[a] The social, political, and occupational backgrounds of these candidates indicate a nonrandom selection of justices.

Occupation at Time of Appointment

About one-fifth of nominees were public officials in the executive branch when they were nominated to the Supreme Court, another fifth were lower federal court judges, about a fifth were judges in state courts, and still another fifth were attorneys in private practice. The remaining nominees were members of Congress, state governors, or professors of law.

Religion

At the time of appointment, about a quarter of Supreme Court justices were Episcopalians, another quarter were unspecified Protestants, and about a fifth were Presbyterian. A smaller proportion of justices acknowledged other religions, including the Roman Catholic, Unitarian, Baptist, Jewish, and Methodist faiths.

Political Affiliation

When nominating Supreme Court justices, presidents tend to select those from their own political party. Of the justices nominated to date, 49 have been Democrats and 46 have been Republicans. The remainder (earlier appointees) were Federalists or Whigs.

Race and Gender

As of 2004, only two African Americans (Thurgood Marshall and Clarence Thomas) and two women (Sandra Day O'Connor and Ruth Bader Ginsburg) had been appointed to the Supreme Court.

a. Three individuals, Edward D. White, Harlan Fiske Stone, and William H. Rehnquist, were associate justices who were later appointed to serve as chief justice. They are not counted twice in this number.

debate also centered on the behavior of senators who had questioned witnesses during the confirmation hearings and on the appropriateness of televised hearings to examine the charges of sexual harassment.

Representativeness

Representativeness also influences presidential decision making concerning judicial nominations (see Box 17-6: The Backgrounds of Supreme Court Justices). At various times, presidents have felt pressured to nominate justices who would diversify the geographic areas and social groupings represented by Supreme Court members.[29] In the 19th century, many presidents sought to make Supreme Court nominations that maintained a regional balance in the Court.

Earlier in the 20th century, religious representation was seen as important by several presidents, who made a point of nominating members of the Roman Catholic and Jewish faiths to the Court. At various times, analysts described positions on the Court as the Catholic seat or the Jewish seat.

More recently, questions about representativeness have shifted toward issues of race, ethnicity, and gender. Lyndon Johnson's nomination of Thurgood Marshall to the Supreme Court in 1967 placed the first African American in the highest federal court at a time when the issue of civil rights was hotly debated in the nation. Responding to persistent pressure to nominate a woman to the Court, Ronald Reagan nominated Sandra Day O'Connor in 1981. Antonin Scalia, nominated by Reagan in 1988, was the first individual of Italian American descent to be appointed to the Supreme Court. Ruth Bader Ginsburg, nominated by Bill Clinton, is the second woman to sit on the nation's highest court.

When Thurgood Marshall retired from the Supreme Court in 1991, President George H. Bush was faced with the question of how to replace the first African American incumbent, a jurist with a decided liberal perspective on constitutional issues. There was no question that Bush would appoint as Marshall's successor a jurist with a conservative judicial philosophy. What was unknown was whether Bush would maintain the notion of a black seat on the bench.

Bush faced somewhat conflicting pressures on this question. Throughout his presidency, he had consistently argued against the wisdom of using quotas reserving jobs for members of minority groups as a means to reduce discrimination on the job. He did not now want to acknowledge publicly that he perceived that there was a black seat on the Court. At the same time, Bush and his advisers were political realists. They recognized that many citizens saw diversity on the Court as an advantage.

Reacting to both pressures, Bush nominated Clarence Thomas, an African American, to replace Marshall. Thomas was a vocal opponent of racial quotas. In announcing the appointment, Bush described Thomas as the best candidate for the job and denied that race had been the main motivation in the appointment. As noted earlier, Thomas was ultimately confirmed by the Senate. Table 17-3 is a scorecard on some of the most recent Supreme Court nominations and their confirmations, and Table 17-4 describes several background characteristics of the current members of the Court.

17-8d Appointments as Legacies

Presidents recognize that the judges they nominate for the federal bench represent a legacy, since judges often remain on the bench for many years beyond the term of the president who appointed them. Ronald Reagan left a substantial judicial legacy through his appointments of federal judges who shared his narrow view of constitutional interpretation. During his two terms as president, Reagan appointed three new Supreme Court justices (Sandra Day O'Connor, Antonin Scalia, and Anthony M. Kennedy) and nominated a seated justice to the position of chief justice (William Rehnquist). In addition, he appointed 292 judges to the federal district courts and 83 judges to the courts of appeals; the total number of new appointments represented about half of all federal judges.[30] In the words of one scholar, "In the final analysis, the Reagan judicial legacy will be with us well into the next century."[31] During his term as president, George H. Bush continued the nominating of conservative jurists to serve on the federal bench.[32] The combined effect of the judicial appointments by these two presidents is expected to have the long-term impact of moving the federal courts in a conservative direction. Although the judicial nominations of Bill Clinton generally reflected a more liberal position, those of George W. Bush, once again, are more conservative.

Not all presidents have the opportunity to leave an extensive judicial appointment legacy. President Jimmy Carter never had the chance to appoint any Supreme Court justice during his 4-year presidency. However, Carter was able to nominate many judges to the lower federal courts and, through these appointments, increased the number of women and minorities in the federal judiciary.

The resignation of Justice Byron White in 1993 gave Bill Clinton an opportunity early in his presidential term to nominate a justice to the nation's highest court. He selected a judge on the U.S. courts of appeals, Ruth Bader Ginsburg, as his first appointment. Clinton received a second opportunity to nominate a member of the Supreme Court when Harry Blackmun announced his retirement. Clinton nominated Judge Stephen Breyer for the Court's open position in 1993. The Senate confirmed the presidential nominations of both Ginsburg and Breyer.

Given the aging of the Supreme Court Justices at the start of the new century, it was widely expected that President George W. Bush, first elected in 2000, would have the opportunity to appoint one or more Justices to replace those retiring. Such was not the case in his first term since no Justice retired. However, given the fact that the Chief Justice, William Rehnquist, experienced serious illness in 2004 and the overall aging of the court's members, it is very likely that President Bush will have the opportunity to nominate new members to the court in his second term in office.

17-8e The Senate and the Confirmation Game

The second half of the judicial nomination game is played by members of the Senate, who wield the power of confirmation. Section 2 of Article II of the Constitution empowers the

Table 17-3 Recent Appointees to the Supreme Court: A Scorecard on Several Rounds of the Nomination Game

Game	Year	Vacancy	Nominee	Outcome
Reagan Appointments				
1	1981	Potter Stewart	Sandra Day O'Connor[a]	Confirmed by Senate, 99–0
2	1986	Warren Burger	William Rehnquist[b]	Confirmed by Senate, 74–3
3	1986	William Rehnquist	Antonin Scalia[c]	Confirmed by Senate, 98–0
4	1987	Lewis Powell	Robert Bork[d]	Rejected by Senate, 42–58
5			Douglas Ginsburg[e]	Nominee withdrew
6			Anthony Kennedy[f]	Confirmed by Senate, 97–0
Bush Appointments				
1	1990	William Brennan	David Souter[g]	Confirmed by Senate, 90–9
	1991	Thurgood Marshall	Clarence Thomas[h]	Confirmed by Senate, 52–48
Clinton Appointments				
1	1993	Byron White	Ruth Bader Ginsburg[i]	Confirmed by Senate, 96–3
2	1993	Harry Blackmun	Steven Breyer[j]	Confirmed by Senate, 87–9

a. Through the nomination of O'Connor, Reagan fulfilled his campaign pledge to appoint a woman and a conservative to the Supreme Court.
b. Rehnquist, already an associate justice, was nominated by Reagan to replace Chief Justice Warren Burger, who was retiring. Rehnquist, originally appointed by Nixon, had demonstrated a judicial philosophy that was compatible with Reagan's.
c. The shift of Rehnquist to the chief justice slot opened a new position on the Court. Reagan nominated Antonin Scalia, a conservative judge, for this opening.
d. Bork had a staunchly conservative judicial philosophy and a belief in judicial restraint. His views were articulated in scholarly writing and decisions rendered from the bench. Many senators worried about replacing the moderate Powell with the so-called extremist Bork. In the end, the Senate rejected the nomination.
e. A conservative jurist, Ginsburg withdrew from the nomination after concerns about conflict of interest during his time in the Justice Department and media reports of his use of marijuana as a professor at law school.
f. Both Reagan and the Senate were worn down by political fights about two previous nominees for the Powell vacancy. While conservative, Kennedy demonstrated a more moderate judicial stance than did Bork. The Senate unanimously voted to confirm, ending a 3-round struggle to replace Lewis Powell.
g. Compared to other recent Supreme Court nominees, Souter did not have an extensive body of writings or judicial decisions upon which his judicial views could readily be determined. Bush was convinced, however, that Souter was a judicial conservative. Souter made a candid and effective appearance at the nomination hearings and was approved by a strong margin.
h. Judge Thomas not only served on the federal bench but also was the director of the Equal Employment Opportunity Commission (EEOC) during the Reagan administration. At the EEOC, Thomas made it clear that he opposed many types of affirmative action policies. Groups representing African Americans split over the nomination; some supported Thomas's nomination, while others opposed it, primarily on the grounds of his position on affirmative action. During confirmation hearings, former colleague and law professor Anita Hill charged Thomas with sexual harassment. These charges became the subject of hearings televised across the nation.
i. Seeking to avoid a difficult confirmation battle with the Senate at a time when important economic legislation was being considered in Congress, Clinton nominated a judge from the U.S. Courts of Appeals with a record of being both liberal and willing to work collaboratively with other justices in reaching judicial decisions.
j. Breyer was considered by Clinton as a nominee for the first court vacancy of his administration, created by the retirement of Byron White. In that round, however, Clinton chose instead to nominate Ruth Bader Ginsburg. With his second choice, Clinton sought a respected jurist who would be confirmed without substantial opposition, ultimately nominating Breyer.

president to nominate federal judges with the advice and consent of the Senate. The fundamental rulebook says nothing, however, about what criteria senators should use in their advice and consent role. The appropriateness of various criteria remains a controversial issue.

The Senate gives the selection of Supreme Court justices close scrutiny. After a president forwards the name of a Supreme Court nominee to the Senate, the Senate Judiciary Committee schedules a confirmation hearing on the appointment and invites the nominee and other interested parties to testify. After the hearing, which may take several days, Judiciary Committee members vote to approve or disapprove the presidential nomination. The committee vote is reported to the full Senate, which votes to confirm or reject the nominee.

Table 17-4 The Supreme Court Lineup

Members of the Supreme Court are far from being a random sample of the population. The following lists show some of the experiences and traits they have in common.

LAW SCHOOL

Harvard
- Stephen Breyer
- David Souter
- Anthony Kennedy
- Antonin Scalia

Columbia
- Ruth Bader Ginsburg

Yale
- Clarence Thomas

Stanford
- Sandra Day O'Connor
- William Rehnquist

Northwestern
- John Paul Stevens

JUDICIAL EXPERIENCE

U.S. Court of Appeals
- Stephen Breyer
- Ruth Bader Ginsburg
- Clarence Thomas
- David Souter
- Anthony Kennedy
- Antonin Scalia
- Paul Stevens

State Court of Appeals
- Sandra Day O'Connor

No Previous Experience as a Judge
- William Rehnquist

RELIGION

Catholic
- Clarence Thomas
- Anthony Kennedy
- Antonin Scalia

Jewish
- Ruth Bader Ginsburg
- Stephen Breyer

Protestant
- Sandra Day O'Connor
- John Paul Stevens
- William Rehnquist
- David Souter

PARTISAN POLITICAL ACTIVITY

Democratic Congressional Staff
- Stephen Breyer

Republican Congressional Staff
- John Paul Stevens

Republican White House Staff
- Antonin Scalia

Republican State Official Staff
- Clarence Thomas

Republican State Elected Office
- Sandra Day O'Connor

State Republican Activist
- Anthony Kennedy
- William Rehnquist
- David Souter

PRESIDENT MAKING THE APPOINTMENT

Richard Nixon
- William Rehnquist

Gerald Ford
- John Paul Stevens

Ronald Reagan
- Sandra Day O'Connor
- Antonin Scalia
- Anthony Kennedy

George H. Bush
- David Souter
- Clarence Thomas

Bill Clinton
- Ruth Bader Ginsburg
- Stephen Breyer

AGE (Age as of 2003)

Less than 60
- Clarence Thomas (55)

60–70
- David Souter (64)
- Stephen Breyer (65)
- Anthony Kennedy (67)
- Antonin Scalia (67)
- Ruth Bader Ginsburg (70)

more than 70
- Sandra Day O'Connor (73)
- William Rehnquist (79)
- John Paul Stevens (83)

AGE AT APPOINTMENT

50 or less
- Clarence Thomas (43)
- William Rehnquist (47)
- Antonin Scalia

51–60
- Sandra Day O'Connor (51)
- David Souter (51)
- Anthony Kennedy (51)
- John Paul Stevens (55)
- Stephen Breyer (56)
- Ruth Bader Ginsburg (60)

MILITARY EXPERIENCE

Navy
- John Paul Stevens (1942–45)

Army
- William Rehnquist (1943–46)

National Guard
- Anthony Kennedy (1961)

None
- Sandra Day O'Connor
- Stephen Breyer
- Ruth Bader Ginsburg
- Clarence Thomas
- David Souter
- Antonin Scalia

FOR MORE INFORMATION

For more information on the justices, go to http://oyez.org

For more information on the justices, go to http://oyez.org.

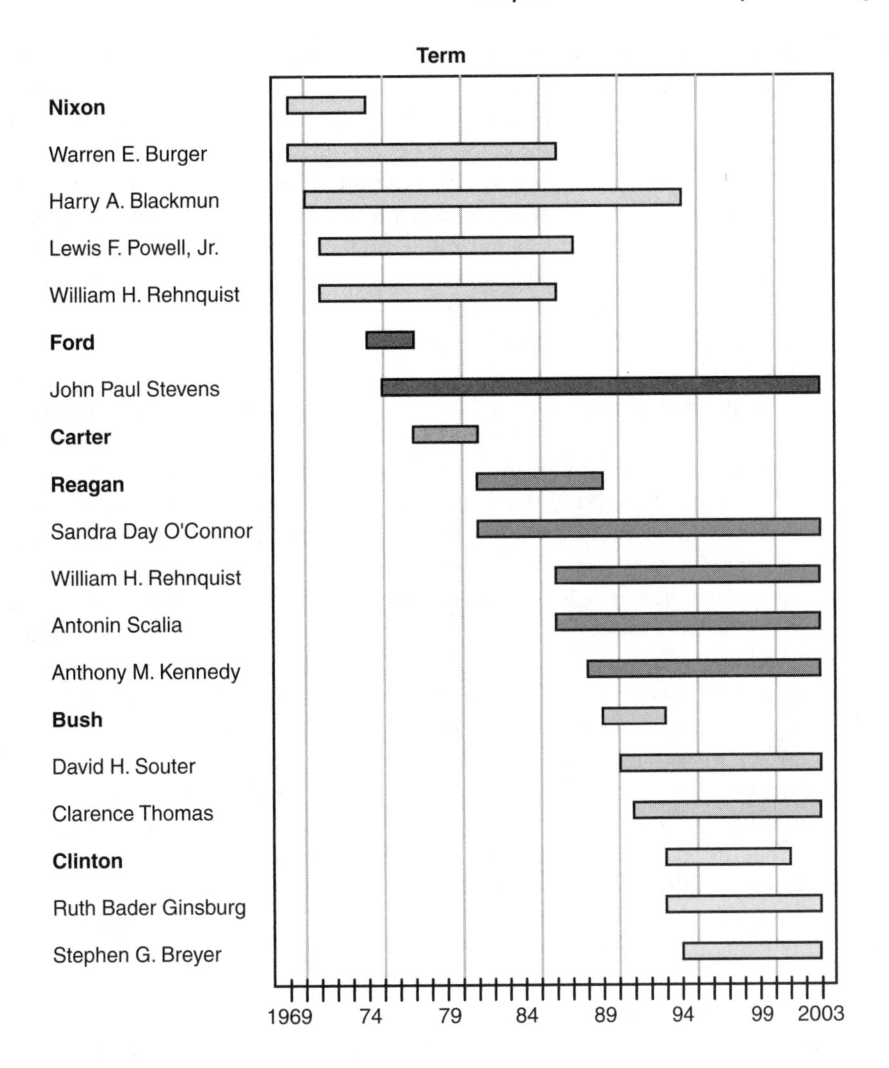

Figure 17-3
Presidential Legacies on the Supreme Court 2001

Presidents can influence Supreme Court decision making long after they have left the Oval Office.

Source: Peverill Squire, et al., *Dynamics of Democracy* (Cincinnati, OH: Atomic Dog Publishing, 2001), 508.

On the confirmation of Stephen Breyer as associate justice, a telling comment was made at the Senate Judiciary Committee hearing:

> A continuing aspect of the game in these Supreme Court nominations is the committee's efforts to learn or try to learn a nominee's position on one legal issue or another, countered by the nominee's effort to avoid disclosing where he or she stands on specific issues. This is our ritual.

Senators have articulated and used various criteria when engaged in their advice and consent role. One criterion focuses on merit (i.e., the nominee's legal qualifications and experience). Some argue that senators should concern themselves primarily with assessing a nominee's professional qualifications. Most senators share with presidents a concern about a nominee's ethical standards and moral conduct. Violation of legal standards or perceived immoral actions can harm nominated candidates.

Senators also may have a keen interest in the policy preferences of nominees. During their confirmation hearings in 1990 and 1991, David Souter and Clarence Thomas were asked several times about their stances on public laws that forbid abortion. Souter deftly sidestepped these questions, including his views on the *Roe v. Wade* decision, indicating that it would be inappropriate for him to take a stand on the abortion issue prior to joining the Supreme Court. Thomas also refused to take a position on the abortion issue, claiming (to the amazement of many on the Judiciary Committee) that he had never discussed the abortion issue prior to the confirmation hearings.

Another factor of concern to some senators is perceived extremism in judicial philosophy. Proponents of this standard argue that individuals who have views that run counter to most legal precedents should be rejected from appointment to the bench. These senators are more comfortable with candidates whose judicial philosophies tend toward mainstream rather than extreme positions. The anti-extremism argument was evident in 1987, when the Senate considered Ronald Reagan's nomination of Robert Bork to the Supreme Court. Both as a judge and as a legal scholar, Bork had written extensively on his preference for a literal interpretation of the Constitution. In his writings, Bork opposed many judicial precedents that were based on broad interpretations of constitutional principles. Partially because many senators saw Bork's views as too extreme and too far outside the judicial mainstream, the Senate rejected Bork's nomination.

A related but distinct factor is balance. At certain times in the Supreme Court's history, the Court's members have been fairly evenly divided on liberal versus conservative perspectives. At other times, the balance on the Court has tipped in one ideological direction or the other. As noted earlier, the Warren Court was a relatively liberal Court, which used a broad interpretation of the Constitution to expand civil rights and liberties. The Burger Court, by comparison, was more conservative.

By the middle of the Reagan presidency, the Court was roughly split between liberal and conservative justices. Justice Lewis Powell was often identified as a swing member because his vote appeared to determine many of the close votes decided by the Court. When Powell announced his resignation during Reagan's second term, many in the Senate worried about replacing this moderate and pivotal justice.

When Reagan nominated Robert Bork, a jurist with well-known conservative views, as a replacement for Powell, many senators expressed concern about disrupting the Court's liberal-conservative balance. Bork's defeat at the confirmation stage resulted not only from his relatively extreme views but also from the sense that he would markedly tip the balance of the Court in a more conservative direction.

Overall, the Senate has generally taken a deferential stance in confirmations of presidential appointments to the Supreme Court. Only 29 of 146 Supreme Court nominations have failed to achieve confirmation.[33] Twelve of these nominees were rejected by Senate vote; the remainder failed because the nomination was withdrawn (usually due to political pressures) or the confirmation vote was indefinitely postponed.

Conclusion

The Constitution and laws enacted by Congress together have created a three-tiered federal judiciary, with the Supreme Court serving as the highest judicial tribunal in the United States. Through the practice of judicial review, the federal judiciary plays an important role in American politics. The federal courts make decisions that substantially influence policy and that become precedents for future legal cases.

Controversy continues about the appropriate role of the federal judiciary in the broader political process. Judicial activists support an energetic role for the courts in defining public policy, particularly in the areas of social justice and civil rights. Others disagree, arguing for judicial restraint and limited court involvement in defining public policy.

Recognizing the importance of judicial review power, presidents play a personal role in determining nominees to the Supreme Court; they also closely supervise the selection of judges to the lower federal courts. Through nominations to the federal bench, presidents hope to influence judicial decision making. A formal partner in the judicial selection game, the Senate generally defers to presidential wishes and confirms appointments, though sometimes only after spirited hearings. In reviewing nominees, the Senate, like the president, considers judicial philosophy, merit, ethical conduct, and ideological balance.

The real power of the federal courts, and particularly of the Supreme Court, rests in public acceptance of the courts as the interpreters of public laws and the Constitution. The courts have little power to coerce compliance with its decisions and can only rely upon the willingness of citizens and other government players to comply with its judicial decisions.

Key Terms

appellate jurisdiction
broad constructionist view
Brown v. Board of Education of Topeka
civil case
common law
concurring opinion
dissenting opinion
judicial activism
judicial conference
judicial restraint
judicial review
jurisdiction
majority opinion
Marbury v. Madison
original jurisdiction
precedent
rule of four
senatorial courtesy
standing
statutory law
strict constructionist view
writ of certiorari

Practice Quiz

1. Which of the following statements is true of the U.S. Courts of Appeals?
  a. The courts are organized into 13 federal circuits.
  b. There are 91 of these courts.
  c. The Chief Justice presides over sessions of these courts.
  d. These courts were eliminated during the Civil War.

2. Original jurisdiction defines
  a. the right to interpret laws enacted by Congress.
  b. Common Law practice.
  c. cases that receive first hearing in a specific court.
  d. the right to receive legal counsel.

3. What does the U.S. Constitution say about judicial review—the power of U.S. courts to ascertain the constitutionality of laws enacted by Congress?
  a. Nothing
  b. Outlines boundaries of judicial review in *Marbury v. Madison*
  c. Limits this power to the Supreme Court
  d. Devolves this power to state courts

4. *Brown v. School Board of Topeka* is a landmark case that focused upon
  a. the secession of southern states from the Union.
  b. the legality of abortion.
  c. segregation in public schools.
  d. creating election boundaries for House of Representative districts.

5. The Supreme Court's pattern of judicial interpretation is considered to be more liberal under Chief Justice _____ and more conservative under Chief Justice _____.
  a. Hamilton; Rehnquist
  b. Warren; Rehnquist
  c. Warren; O'Connor
  d. Rehnquist; Warren

6. One, if not the most, significant decision of the Supreme Court during the tenure of Chief Justice Earl Warren was
  a. *Marbury v. Madison*.
  b. *Grove City College v. Bell*.
  c. *Roe v. Wade*.
  d. *Brown v. School Board of Topeka*.

7. The "rule of four" refers to the
  a. rule used to decide Supreme Court cases.
  b. right of the President to nominate four Supreme Court Justices.
  c. rule used to decide if the Supreme Court will hear a case.
  d. membership of individual U.S. Courts of Appeals.

8. The _____ nominates individuals to become Supreme Court justices, and the _____ confirms these nominations.
  a. U.S. Senate; U.S. House of Representatives
  b. president; U.S. Senate
  c. chief justice; U.S Senate
  d. president; U.S. House of Representatives

9. Sandra Day O'Connor is the first
  a. woman to serve on the Supreme Court.
  b. woman to serve as chief justice of the Supreme Court.
  c. senator to become a Supreme Court justice.
  d. Republican to serve as a Supreme Court justice.

10. The majority opinion in a Supreme Court case outlines
  a. reasons the case was selected for hearing before the court.
  b. reasons that a majority of justices reached a common decision in a case.
  c. the means used to select justices to hear the case.
  d. All of the above

11. How long do Supreme Court justices serve in office?
  a. For the remainder of life until they die, retire, or are removed by impeachment and conviction
  b. Three five-year terms
  c. Two four-year terms
  d. Until they reach age 75

12. Provisions concerning the U.S. Supreme Court are outlined where in the U.S. Constitution?
  a. Article I
  b. Article II
  c. Article III
  d. Bill of Rights

You can find the correct answers to these questions by taking the quiz and then submitting your answers in the Online Edition. The program will automatically score your submission. Where you miss a question, the program will provide the correct answer, a rationale for the answer, and the section number in the chapter where the topic is discussed.

Further Reading

Basic texts that describe the fundamental elements of the federal judiciary include Henry J. Abraham, *The Judiciary: The Supreme Court in the Governmental Process* (Dubuque: IA: Wm. C. Brown Publishers, 1996) and Lawrence Balm, *American Courts: Process & Policy*, 2nd ed. (Boston, MA: Houghton Mifflin, 1990).

A detailed study of the relationships between presidents and Supreme Court justices, including presidential nomination of justices, is provided by Henry J. Abraham in *Justices and Presidents: A Political History of Appointments to the Supreme Court*, 3rd ed. (New York: Oxford University Press, 1992).

A classic and thorough text concerning the role of judges in the American judicial system is *The Nature of the Judicial Process* (New Haven, CT: Yale University Press, 1921) by Benjamin N. Cardozo.

Several books explore the operation of the Supreme Court and its role within the American political system. These include: William H. Rehnquist, *The Supreme Court* (New York: Knopf Publishers, 2001) and Tinsley E. Yarbrough, *The Rehnquist Court and the Constitution* (New York: Oxford University Press, 2000).

David M. O'Brien analyzes the role of the Supreme Court within the operation of American politics in *Storm Center*, 2nd ed. (New York: Norton, 1990). Gary L. McDowell explores the question of judicial activism and the means by which the judicial power of the federal courts might be curbed in *Curbing the Courts: The Constitution and the Limits of Judicial Power* (Baton Rouge, LA: Louisiana University Press, 1988).

For a work that discusses some key Supreme Court cases in American history, see Jerry Goldman, *The Supreme Court's Greatest Hits* (Evanston, IL: Northwestern University Press, 1999).

A recently published behind-the-scenes look at the Supreme Court is James F. Simon's *The Center Holds: The Power Struggle Inside the Rehnquist Court* (New York: Simon & Schuster, 1995). Although it does not take into account the shift toward conservative dominance, it is useful because it examines justices' papers to reveal personal reasoning behind Court deliberations and decisions.

To explore how the U.S court system compares to that of other nations, see Tim Koopmans, *Courts and Political Institutions: A Comparative View* (New York: Oxford University Press, 2003.

Endnotes

1. Henry J. Abraham, *The Judicial Process*, 5th ed. (New York: Oxford University Press, 1986), 3.
2. *APTA v. Lewis*, 655 Fd 2d 1272 and 12 (D.C. Cir. 1981).
3. *Babbitt v. Sweet Home Chapter of Community for a Greater Oregon*, No. 94-859.
4. The Supreme Court overturned anti-flag-burning state laws in *Texas v. Johnson*, 491 U.S. 397 (1989). The Flag Protection Act of 1989 prohibiting flag burning was overturned in *United States v. Eichman, Blalock and Tyler*, 110 S. Ct. 2404 (1990).
5. Louis Fisher, *Constitutional Structures: Separated Powers and Federalism, Volume I of American Constitutional Law* (New York: McGraw-Hill, 1990), 41–58.
6. *Marbury v. Madison*, 5 U.S. (1 Cr.) 137 (1803).
7. *Marbury v. Madison*, 5 U.S. (1 Cr.) 137 (1803).
8. *Plessy v. Ferguson*, 163 U.S. 537 (1896).
9. *Brown v. Board of Education of Topeka*, 347 U.S. 483 (1954).
10. See, for example, Richard A. Pride and J. David Woodward, *The Burden of Busing: The Politics of Desegregation in Nashville, Tennessee* (Knoxville, TN: University of Tennessee Press, 1985) and Judith F. Buncher, ed., *The School Busing Controversy, 1969–75* (New York: Facts on File, 1975).
11. *Pollock v. Farmers' Loan & Trust Company*, 158 U.S. 601 at 679-680 (1895).
12. *Pollock v. Farmers' Loan & Trust Company*, 158 U.S. 601 at 679-680 (1895).
13. *Grove City College v. Bell*, 104 S. Ct 1211 (1984).
14. See Alfred H. Kelly, Winfred A. Harbison, and Herman Belz, *The American Constitution: Its Origins and Development*, 6th ed. (New York: W.W. Norton, 1983), 411–414.
15. *United States v. Lopez*, No. 93-1260.
16. *Adarand Constructors v. Pena*, No. 93-1841.
17. *Miller v. Johnson*, No. 94-631.
18. *Veronia School District v. Acton*, No. 94-590.
19. *Sandin v. Connor*, No. 93-1911.
20. *Wilson v. Arkansas*, No. 94-5707.
21. *U.S. Term Limits v. Thornton*, No. 93-1456.
22. See Rebecca Mae Salokar, *The Solicitor General: The Politics of Law* (Philadelphia, PA: Temple University Press, 1992).
23. See, for example, Kevin T. McGuire and Gregory A. Caldeira, "Lawyers, Organized Interests, and the Law of Obscenity: Agenda Setting in the Supreme Court," *American Political Science Review* 87, September 1993, 717–726, and Gregory Caldeira, "Organized Interests and Agenda Setting in the U.S. Supreme Court," *American Political Science Review* 82 December 1989, 1109–1127.
24. See, for example, Lee Epstein and C. K. Rowland, "Debunking the Myth of Interest Group Invincibility in the Court," *American Political Science Review* 85, March 1991, 205–217, and Donald R. Songer and Reginald Sheehan, "Interest Group Success in the Courts: Amicus Participation in the Supreme Court," *Political Research Quarterly* 46, 1993, 339–354.
25. William Mishler and Reginald S. Sheehan, "The Supreme Court as a Countermajoritarian Institution: The Impact of Public Opinion on Supreme Court Decisions," *American Political Science Review* 87, March 1993, 87–101.
26. Lawrence Baum, *American Courts: Process and Policy*, 2nd ed. (Boston, MA: Houghton Mifflin, 1990), 117.
27. Stephen E. Frantzich, *Political Parties in the Technological Age* (New York: Longman, 1989), 258.
28. Henry J. Abraham, *Justices and Presidents: A Political History of Appointments to the Supreme Court*, 2nd ed. (New York: Oxford University Press, 1985), 61.
29. Henry J. Abraham, *The Judiciary: The Supreme Court in the Governmental Process*, 8th ed. (Dubuque, IA: Wm. C. Brown Publishers, 1991), 54.
30. Joan Biskupic, "Bush Boasts Bench Strength of Conservative Judges," *Congressional Quarterly Weekly Report* 19 (January 1991), 171–74.
31. Sheldon Goldman, "Reagan's Judicial Legacy: Completing the Puzzle and Summing Up," *Judicature* 72 (April/May 1989): 318.
32. Neil A. Lewis, "Selection of Conservative Judges Guards Part of Bush's Legacy," *New York Times*, July 1, 1992, A9.
33. Harold W. Stanley and Richard G. Niemi, *Vital Statistics on American Politics*, 2nd ed. (Washington, D.C.: Congressional Quarterly Press, 1990), 269.

18

State and Local Governments: The Other Playing Fields

Key Points

- **How demographic diversity and political cultures affect government in the American states.**
- **The basic organization and functions of state governments, including state constitutions, governors, state legislators, and state courts.**
- **Key issues of state-local relations and evolving patterns of state-local cooperation.**
- **The different types of local governments in U.S. metropolitan areas and their respective functions.**
- **The evolution of urban governance and the urban reform movement.**
- **The changing state and local government responsibilities associated with devolution of federal government power and programs.**

Preview: The State of States' Rights

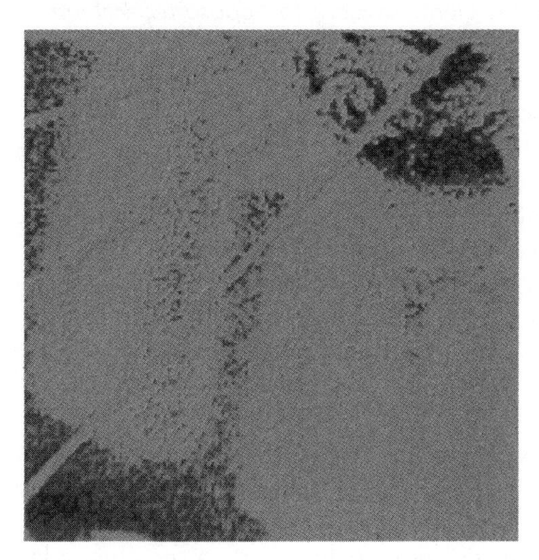

The organizers were excited about the conference they were planning. They were concerned about the ever-growing power of the central governing authority and the weakening political power of the states. The meeting was billed as a kind of town meeting for state officials to discuss ways of restoring a balance of power between the states and the central government.

Does this sound like a call for the Constitutional Convention that met in 1787? This proposed meeting of the states was actually planned for 1995.[1] The idea for this Conference of the States was proposed by Republican governor Mike Leavitt of Utah and Democratic governor Ben Nelson of Nebraska. The underlying purpose of the conference would be to search for the missing amend-

Wisconsin's Capitol Building in Madison

ment to the Constitution—the 10th—which reserves to the States, respectively, or to the people all powers not delegated to the United States by the Constitution. In essence, the idea would be to reconsider the governing power of states and to enhance that power through a revised understanding of federal-state relations. Conference organizers wanted to start a dialogue on the issue of states' rights in the 1990s. They did not intend that any plans to revise the Constitution itself would emerge from the meeting.

To obtain legitimacy for the conference, organizers decided that the event would take place only if 26 states passed official resolutions in favor of it. This number had no constitutional significance but would simply demonstrate that a majority of states favored a meeting to discuss the power of states within the federal system.

Organizers expected opposition from one set of political players: liberals. Liberal politicians have typically favored a strong role for the federal government in pursuing national objectives, such as integration of schools, civil rights, and fighting poverty. But ultimately, it was not this group of players who scuttled the conference. It was a very different set of players: right-wing activists.

A group of conservatives were worried about the proposed Conference of the States. They feared that it would open up into a full constitutional convention, where plans would be laid to change the fundamental rulebook itself. The leader of the opposition to the meeting was state senator Charlie Duke of Colorado. He argued that the Constitution already gives the states plenty of clout to oppose federal intrusion into state sovereignty. Some right-wing extremists even saw the conference as a secret plan to increase the power of government under the guise of states' rights. Duke and his supporters used modern communications strategies to send out their anti-conference message. They flooded state legislators across the nation with faxes, phone calls, letters, and lobbyist visits, all arguing that the conference actually represented a threat to states' rights. The strategy worked. It raised substantial concerns within state legislatures about the ultimate purpose and likely outcome of a Conference of the States. By mid-1995, organizers put the conference on hold when only 14 states (12 short of the required 26) had enacted resolutions supporting the conference. Instead, organizers planned to develop their own political strategy to convince legislatures across the nation of the wisdom of having such a conference.

The games of American politics are played in many arenas. The national news media focus attention on government leaders in Washington, D.C., but important decisions are made daily in state and local governments across the United States. In many ways, the decisions of state and local players affect Americans more directly than those made by national leaders.

Chapter 3 described the American system of federalism, whereby the national government was designed to share governing powers with the states. Later, as cities grew across the nation, they, too, became players in the game of federalism. This chapter explores the structure, operation, and functions of first state and then local governments in America. It examines the executive, legislative, and judicial branches of states and localities. It also explores the ongoing and sometimes tense political games that take place between cities and states. The winners and losers in conflicts between levels of government have changed as the rules and play of these political games have changed.

It is more important than ever to recognize that governance in America occurs at multiple levels. In the 1990s the American people witnessed profound alterations of the political landscape. The governing roles of states, in particular, began to change substantially as the national government acted to cut federal spending and to shift programs and decisions about their operation to the states. For the first time in decades the Republican Party controlled both houses of Congress. Given this new power position, the Republicans moved to enact their conservative agenda. This agenda included broad public policy initiatives to balance the federal budget deficit and to reduce federal regulation of the private sector and of the environment. One goal was to increase state involvement in the operation of programs that were previously controlled by federal funding, federal standards, and federal rules of operation. This **devolution** of programs and powers meant a stronger governing role for the states. With it came more responsibility for funding and operating programs. State governments did and do have the option, however, of passing some of their new powers to localities (counties and cities), which may serve as partners in redesigning programs that were once dominated by the federal government.

***devolution** The transference of authority and control by a national government to local governments (including states).*

18-1 State Playing Fields: American Diversity

In many senses, the states that comprise the nation of the United States are more different from one another than they are similar. An understanding of politics and government in the American states must start with recognition of states' social, economic, and political diversity. When we consider the principles and processes of state government, it is important to recognize that characteristics of the individual states influence the practices, priorities, and politics of their governments.

18-1a Population

The statistics of population size, rate of growth, and composition are significant differences to consider among the states (see Table 18-1). According to the 2000 U.S. census, the states with the largest populations were, in order, California, Texas, New York, Florida, Illinois, Pennsylvania, and Ohio.

The rate of population growth in the states between 1990 and 2000 varied. Population increases ranged from less than one percent in North Dakota to more than 25 percent in Arizona, Colorado, Georgia, Idaho, and Nevada. Additional population pushes concerns such as funding new schools or increased welfare payments to the front burner. Population gains translated into greater representation in Congress for several states: Arizona, Florida, Georgia, and Texas each gained two seats in the U.S. House of Representatives (see Table 18-2). Four other states gained one seat. Because the size of the U.S. House of Representatives is fixed at 435, the redistribution of House seats every 10 years is a zero-sum game. Allocations of new seats to states with population gains must be offset by reductions in seats to other states. As a result of the 2000 census count, New York and Pennsylvania each lost 2 House seats and eight states each lost one seat.

Changes like these have repercussions throughout the political system. Each state has a vote in the Electoral College equal to the number of its representatives plus two. Therefore, changes in the number of House seats also influence the size of a state's electoral vote and may affect the way candidates view states when deciding to enter primaries or run electoral campaigns (see Chapters 11 and 14).

Table 18-1

Demographic Characteristics of the American States in 2000

State	2000 Population (in Thousands)	Population Rank	Population Change 1990–2000(%) The average state gained 13%
Northeast			
Maine	1,275	40	3.8
New Hampshire	1,236	41	11.4
Vermont	609	49	8.2
Massachusetts	6,349	13	5.5
Rhode Island	1,048	43	4.5
Connecticut	3,406	29	3.6
New York	18,976	3	5.5
New Jersey	8,414	9	8.9
Pennsylvania	12,281	6	3.4
Midwest			
Ohio	11,353	7	4.7
Indiana	6,080	14	9.7
Illinois	12,419	5	8.6
Michigan	9,938	8	6.9
Wisconsin	5,364	18	9.6
Minnesota	4,919	21	12.4
Iowa	2,926	30	5.4
Missouri	5,595	17	9.3
North Dakota	642	47	0.5
South Dakota	755	46	8.5
Nebraska	1,711	38	8.4
Kansas	2,688	32	8.5
South			
Delaware	784	45	17.6
Maryland	5,296	19	10.8
Virginia	7,078	12	14.4
West Virginia	1,808	37	0.8
North Carolina	8,049	10	21.4
South Carolina	4,012	26	15.1
Georgia	8,186	10	26.4
Florida	15,982	4	23.5
Kentucky	4,042	25	9.7
Tennessee	5,689	16	16.7
Alabama	4,447	23	10.1
Mississippi	2,845	31	10.5
Arkansas	2,673	33	13.7
Louisiana	4,469	22	5.9
Oklahoma	3,450	27	9.7
Texas	20,851	2	22.8
West			
Montana	902	44	12.9
Idaho	1,293	39	28.5
Wyoming	494	50	8.9
Colorado	4,301	24	30.6
New Mexico	1,819	36	20.1
Arizona	5,130	20	40.0
Utah	2,233	34	29.6
Nevada	1,998	35	66.3
Washington	5,894	15	21.1
Oregon	3,421	28	20.4
California	33,871	1	13.8
Alaska	627	48	14.0
Hawaii	1,212	42	9.3

Source: U.S. Bureau of the Census, 2000 Census of the Population.

Table 18-2 Congressional Representation in 2000 and Changes since 1990, by State

State	Apportionment Population	Number of Apportioned Representatives Based on the 2000 Census	Change from the 1990 Census Apportionment
Alabama	4,461,130	7	0
Alaska	628,933	1	0
Arizona	5,140,683	8	+2
Arkansas	2,679,733	4	0
California	33,930,798	53	+1
Colorado	4,311,882	7	+1
Connecticut	3,409,535	5	-1
Delaware	785,068	1	0
Florida	16,028,890	25	+2
Georgia	8,206,975	13	+2
Hawaii	1,216,642	2	0
Idaho	1,297,274	2	0
Illinois	12,439,042	19	-1
Indiana	6,090,782	9	-1
Iowa	2,931,923	5	0
Kansas	2,693,824	4	0
Kentucky	4,049,431	6	0
Louisiana	4,480,271	7	0
Maine	1,277,731	2	0
Maryland	5,307,886	8	0
Massachusetts	6,355,568	10	0
Michigan	9,955,829	15	-1
Minnesota	4,925,670	8	0
Mississippi	2,852,927	4	-1
Missouri	5,606,260	9	0
Montana	905,316	1	0
Nebraska	1,715,369	3	0
Nevada	2,002,032	3	+1
New Hampshire	1,238,415	2	0
New Jersey	8,424,354	13	0
New Mexico	1,823,821	3	0
New York	19,004,973	29	-2
North Carolina	8,067,673	13	+1
North Dakota	643,756	1	0
Ohio	11,374,540	18	-1
Oklahoma	3,458,819	5	-1
Oregon	3,428,543	5	0
Pennsylvania	12,300,670	19	-2
Rhode Island	1,049,662	2	0
South Carolina	4,025,061	6	0
South Dakota	756,874	1	0
Tennessee	5,700,037	9	0
Texas	20,903,994	32	+2
Utah	2,236,714	3	0
Vermont	609,890	1	0
Virginia	7,100,702	11	0
Washington	5,908,684	9	0
West Virginia	1,813,077	3	0
Wisconsin	5,371,210	8	-1
Wyoming	495,304	1	0
Total Apportionment Population[a]	281,424,177	435	

a. Includes the resident population for the 50 states, as ascertained by the Twenty-Second Decennial Census under Title 13, United States Code, and counts of overseas U.S. military and federal civilian employees (and their dependents living with them) allocated to their home state, as reported by the employing federal agencies. The apportionment population excludes the population of the District of Columbia.

Note: As required by the January 1999 U.S. Supreme Court ruling (*Department of Commerce v. House of Representatives*, 525 U.S. 316, 119 S. Ct. 765 (1999)), the apportionment population counts do not reflect the use of statistical sampling to correct for overcounting or undercounting.

Source: U.S. Department of Commerce, U.S. Bureau of the Census, 2000 Census of the Population.

population density *The number of people per square mile of a geographic territory (for example, city, county, or state).*

The land area of the states also varies dramatically, ranging from Rhode Island's 1,214 square miles to Alaska's whopping 570,833 square miles. Demographic analysis shows that **population density** varies from a low of one person per square mile in Alaska to more than a thousand per square mile in New Jersey. States with high population densities typically have large urban concentrations that require extensive transportation systems, law enforcement activities, and other urban services. Those with low population densities have their own priorities, such as support for higher speed limits.

18-1b Social Characteristics

States differ in terms of the race and ethnic heritage of their residents (see Table 18-3). States with the highest proportion of African Americans include Mississippi, Louisiana, South Carolina, Georgia, and Alabama. Latinos are most highly concentrated in California, New Mexico, and Texas. Persons of Asian descent are most populous in Hawaii, California, Washington, and New York.

The data of Table 18-3 show the relative size of minority and ethnic concentrations across the states. Studying the figures one can find documentation of immigration patterns, with people of Asian and Latin American origin concentrated in coastal or border states and the largest urban areas and all ports of entry.

The social composition of a state may influence both the nature of political games and the types of policy debates that occur in that state. Racial and ethnic groups have developed ties with specific political parties, thereby enhancing their political clout. Areas with large African-American concentrations, for example, have been typically more Democratic than Republican in voting patterns. Cuban Americans in Florida, on the other hand, have developed strong ties with the Republican Party. Some policy debates in individual states are influenced by the racial and ethnic makeup of the state. Policy questions about the appropriateness of bilingual education, for example, have arisen in states in the Southwest and the West, where large concentrations of Spanish-speaking people reside.

18-1c Political Culture

Political culture includes beliefs about the appropriate role of government. Remember, though, that it is difficult to generalize about American society. As we saw in Chapter 3, regional development has led to somewhat differing value systems within the United States. Political scientist Daniel Elazar identified three dominant political cultures in the American states: *individualistic*, *moralistic*, and *traditionalistic*.[2] The pattern known as individualistic is the belief that government exists primarily to distribute rewards to government supporters and to regulate the economic marketplace so that individuals can pursue their own opportunities. Having a moralistic culture means that people believe in government acting in the public interest. They favor an active government and encourage citizen participation. The third type of political culture, traditionalistic, features the beliefs that government should operate to preserve social order and to protect property rights. Citizen participation is not strongly valued within this political culture. In the mid-1980s, Elazar classified the political culture of each American state. He used a variety of measures and allowed states to adopt more than one cultural pattern.

According to Elazar, the more traditionalistic states tend to be located in the South, whereas the moralistic ones are in the upper Midwest and the Far West. Individualistic states include the Great Lakes states of Illinois, Indiana, and Ohio, as well as Pennsylvania, Maryland, and Connecticut.

American states differ not only in terms of political culture but also in their ideologies, that is, the mix of liberal and conservative views in the states' populations (see Chapter 9). Extensive research has shown that the most liberal states—those whose residents are willing to have government take an active role in tackling public problems—include New York, Massachusetts, New Jersey, California, Oregon, and Wisconsin.[3] The most conservative states—those whose residents are cautious about government intervention—are typically located in the South and West. These include Mississippi, North

Table 18-3 **Racial and Ethnic Composition of the American States in 2000**

	Percent of State Population in Racial/Ethnic Groups				
State	White (%)	Black (%)	American Indian(%)	Asian/Pacific Islander (%)	Latino[a] (%)
U.S. TOTAL	75.1	12.3	0.9	3.7	12.5
Northeast					
Maine	96.9	0.5	0.6	0.7	0.7
New Hampshire	96.0	0.7	0.2	1.3	1.7
Vermont	96.8	0.5	0.4	0.9	0.9
Massachusetts	84.5	5.4	0.2	3.8	6.8
Rhode Island	85.0	4.5	0.5	2.4	8.7
Connecticut	81.6	9.1	0.3	2.4	9.4
New York	67.9	15.9	0.4	5.5	15.1
New Jersey	72.6	13.6	0.2	5.7	13.3
Pennsylvania	85.4	10.0	0.1	1.8	3.2
Midwest					
Ohio	85.0	11.5	0.2	1.2	1.9
Indiana	87.5	8.4	0.3	1.0	3.5
Illinois	73.5	15.1	0.2	3.4	12.3
Michigan	80.2	14.2	0.6	1.8	3.3
Wisconsin	88.9	5.7	0.9	1.7	3.6
Minnesota	89.4	3.5	1.1	2.9	2.9
Iowa	93.9	2.1	0.3	1.3	2.8
Missouri	84.9	11.2	0.4	1.2	2.1
North Dakota	92.4	0.6	4.9	0.6	1.2
South Dakota	88.7	0.6	8.3	0.6	1.4
Nebraska	89.6	4.0	0.9	1.3	5.5
Kansas	86.1	5.7	0.9	1.7	7.0
South					
Delaware	74.6	19.2	0.3	2.1	4.8
Maryland	64.0	27.9	0.3	4.0	4.3
Virginia	72.3	19.6	0.3	3.8	4.7
West Virginia	95.0	3.2	0.2	0.5	0.7
North Carolina	72.1	21.6	1.2	1.4	4.7
South Carolina	67.2	29.5	0.3	0.9	2.4
Georgia	65.1	28.7	0.3	2.2	5.3
Florida	78.0	14.6	0.3	1.8	16.8
Kentucky	90.1	7.3	0.2	0.7	1.5
Tennessee	80.2	16.4	0.3	1.0	2.2
Alabama	71.1	26.0	0.5	0.7	1.7
Mississippi	61.4	36.3	0.4	0.7	1.4
Arkansas	80.0	15.7	0.7	0.8	3.2
Louisiana	63.9	32.5	0.6	1.2	2.4
Oklahoma	76.2	7.6	7.9	1.5	5.2
Texas	71.0	11.5	0.6	2.8	32.0
West					
Montana	90.6	0.3	6.2	0.6	2.0
Idaho	91.0	0.4	1.4	1.0	7.9
Wyoming	92.1	0.8	2.3	0.7	6.4
Colorado	82.8	3.8	1.0	2.3	17.1
New Mexico	66.8	1.9	9.5	1.2	42.1
Arizona	75.5	3.1	5.0	1.9	25.3
Utah	89.2	0.8	1.3	2.4	9.0
Nevada	75.2	6.8	1.3	4.9	19.7
Washington	81.8	3.2	1.6	5.9	7.5
Oregon	86.6	1.6	1.3	3.2	8.0
California	59.5	6.7	1.0	11.2	32.4
Alaska	69.3	3.5	15.6	4.5	4.1
Hawaii	24.3	1.8	0.3	51.0	7.2

a. Persons classified as Latino may be of any race.
Source: U.S. Bureau of the Census, 2000 Census of the Population.

Time Out 18-1

What Is the Political Culture of Your State?

Growing up, you may have had the opportunity to hear what people in your state thought about government. Even if you did not actively study state government, you may have had some idea about the major political issues in the state and how people thought government should respond to these issues.

Given your experience, how would you classify your state according to Daniel Elazar's political culture categories? Allow for some overlap if you think that more than one category describes your state. Try to cite one or two examples of government action that illustrate your classification. Write down your ideas on a separate sheet of paper.

Compare your speculation about your state's political culture with Professor Elazar's findings.

Carolina, South Carolina, Texas, Alabama, Arizona, and Georgia. (See Time Out 18-1: What Is the Political Culture of Your State?)

Both political culture and ideology influence the political games played in states. They also have an impact on the types of public policies created by state governments. States with a moralistic political culture and more liberal residents are more likely than other states to actively regulate businesses and consumers in order to protect the environment (e.g., to implement mandatory recycling). Traditionalistic and individualistic states and states with more conservative residents are less likely to have governments that engage actively in environmental protection and other regulatory policies.

18-2 Governing the American States: Rules and Players

Political games in the American states are based on fundamental rules specified in state constitutions and take place as a variety of players inside and outside of government seek to shape state government laws and policies. Although few of us are familiar with the constitution of our home state, its rules direct action that has great significance for each of us. An author analyzing changes in states' power put it this way:

> For more than two hundred years, the states have been the chief architects, by conscious and sometimes unconscious action or inaction, of the welter of serving, financial, institutional, and jurisdictional arrangements that form our fifty state-local systems. Moreover, they have provided the means by which most of domestic U.S. governance is conducted and nearly all domestic policies are implemented.[4]

18-2a State Constitutions: 50 Variations on a Theme

Each state has its own fundamental rulebook, a state constitution that spells out the legitimate powers of the state government, the selection of government players, and the rules by which government decisions are made. The average state constitution has about 26,000 words in contrast to the national Constitution, with only 8,700.[5] This is because state constitutions go into greater detail about government operation. Some analysts contend that shorter and more general state constitutions, with the details of government operation left to state legislatures, would be better. The greater the detail in the state constitution, the less governing power is granted to the legislature.

Although the U.S. Constitution has never been comprehensively reconsidered or extensively amended, many state constitutions have been completely revised. Since the nation's founding, state constitutions have been rewritten on over 95 occasions.[6] Such overhauls tend to expand the governing powers and to clarify the structure and organization of a state government. Many more revisions will undoubtedly be required as the trend toward devolution continues and gives states added responsibilities.

State constitutional revisions typically follow a two-step process: changes are first approved by the legislature and then submitted by referendum to the public for approval.

18-2b State Legislatures

The 50 state legislatures, often known as general assemblies, resemble the structure of the U.S. Congress. All state legislatures, except in Nebraska, are *bicameral*, or composed of two houses. Each upper house is known as a Senate, while the lower house may be termed House of Representatives, Assembly, House of Delegates, or General Assembly.

The number of legislators in state senates ranges from 20 in Alaska to 67 in Minnesota. Like the U.S. Congress, states typically have designed state senate membership to be smaller than that of the lower house, where the number of members ranges from 40, again in Alaska, to 400 in New Hampshire. The representation of women in state legislatures increased during the 20th century; by 2002, slightly more than 23% of legislators at the state level were women (see Box 18-1: Women in State Legislatures, 1895–2002).

Box 18-1 Women in State Legislatures, 1895–2002

The progress of female representation in state legislatures began in the last years of the 19th century in western states. The progress of women in obtaining elected office in state legislatures is shown in the following timeline.

1894: Colorado elected the first women legislators to the Colorado State House of Representatives: Carrie Clyde Holly of Pueblo and Clara Cressingham and Frances S. Klock of Denver. Because U.S. senators were elected by state legislatures prior to 1913, these pioneers were the first women to vote for a senator. These women legislators initiated successful legislation giving mothers equal rights with fathers to their children and creating a home for delinquent girls.

1896: Utah elected the first woman state senator in the nation, Dr. Martha Hughes Cannon of Salt Lake City. Cannon, a practicing physician and mother, won on a Democratic slate by defeating a Republican slate of candidates that included her husband.

1899: Idaho elected Mary A. Wright, a teacher; Hattie F. Noble, a businesswoman; and Clara Permilia Campbell to the Idaho House. Wright became the first woman to serve as a minority leader and to be nominated for Speaker of the House.

1900: As the 19th century ended, 16 women had served in state legislatures, all in the western states of Colorado, Utah, and Idaho.

1920: In the year that the U.S. Constitution was amended to grant women the right to vote, 69 women in 12 states had already served as state legislators.

1995: As the 20th century approached its end, women represented 21% of the 7,424 state legislators in the nation. Women constituted 22% of all Democratic legislators and 19% of all GOP legislators. The state with the most nearly equal representation was Washington, with 40% women legislators. Other states with high percentages of women lawmakers were Nevada, Colorado, Arizona, New Hampshire, Vermont, Maryland, Idaho, Maine, and Kansas. Alabama had the lowest female representation, with only 4% of legislators being women, followed by Kentucky, Louisiana, Oklahoma, Virginia, Pennsylvania, Mississippi, New Jersey, and South Carolina. Female representation in state legislatures was higher than in Congress, where women held 8 seats (8%) in the Senate and 47 seats (11%) in the House of Representatives.

2002: The progress of female representation continued to increase from 1995 levels, growing to 23%.

Sources: Elizabeth M. Cox, *The Three Who Came First, State Legislatures* (November 1994), 12–19; and Dianna Gordon, *Republican Women Make Gains,* State Legislatures (February 1995), 17; Center for American Women and Politics, http://www.cawp.rutgers.edu.

In most states, members of the lower house are elected for 2-year terms; members of the senate are elected for either 2- or 4-year terms. Some states have begun to limit the number of years that an individual can serve in the state legislature. More than a dozen states have enacted term limits on state legislators. Iowa, for example, adopted legislation limiting the term of state legislators to a maximum tenure of 12 years.

States differ on the length of the legislative session, that is, the amount of time the legislature meets in formal session. Unlike the U.S. Congress, which is generally in session year-round except during times of scheduled breaks, some state legislatures meet for only a few weeks, usually at the beginning of the year. In fact, a few state legislatures meet only once every two years. In these states, serving as a state legislator is considered a part-time position. When state business needs to be conducted outside of formal legislative sessions, special sessions can be called, either by the governor or by legislative leaders.

In some states (mostly smaller ones), legislators receive no base salary but are provided with living expenses during the session. Other states have long legislative sessions and pay $35,000 or more in salary per year. While no state legislator will get rich from his or her salary, the level of pay may influence the extent to which individuals are willing to participate as players in state legislative bodies.

State legislatures perform many of the same roles as the U.S. Congress does. They enact laws to govern the people of the state, with approval required in both houses. They monitor and oversee the execution of state laws by the agencies of state government. For example, state legislators may review policies related to the construction and repair of state highways, the operation of welfare programs and prisons, and pollution control programs. In addition, these legislatures levy taxes to support the operation of state government. Also, like members of the U.S. Congress, state legislators perform casework, aiding their constituents in dealings with state government agencies.

In the last two decades, state legislatures have become more professionalized to increase the efficiency of their operation. Increasingly, states have provided legislators with staff to help perform their duties during and between legislative sessions. These staffs can gather and organize policy information, commence investigations on policy questions under consideration, and advise legislators. State legislators have also created organizations known as legislative reference bureaus to assist in drafting state laws. Some states have legislative audit bureaus that, like the U.S. General Accounting Office, investigate administrative agencies at the request of legislators. These agencies provide legislators with an independent source of information on the operation of state government. State legislatures have also moved to take advantage of computerized systems in order to track laws and legislative votes and to provide citizens with up-to-date information on legislative activities and decisions (see Box 18-2: State Legislatures Enter Cyberspace).

18-2c Executives in State Government

The governor, the chief executive of state government, is empowered to direct the execution of state laws. In all but two states, governors serve 4-year terms of office. Over half of the states limit the governor to no more than two consecutive terms in office. Some southern states do not allow sitting governors to run for reelection beyond their current term. The governorship is an important position because of its visibility in the state and the nation.[7] Many presidents, including Jimmy Carter, Ronald Reagan, Bill Clinton, and George W. Bush, served terms as governor prior to entering the White House.

Governors as Key Players

Governors and their staffs perform a variety of important functions related to both the creation and execution of state laws. Like presidents, governors take a leading role in advocating new or modified public policies to cope with contemporary issues and problems. Some governors have gained places in the national spotlight for innovative and often controversial programs. In 2001, President George W. Bush—formerly the governor of Texas—turned to innovative governors when forming his cabinet. Among those

Box 18–2 State Legislatures Enter Cyberspace: Increasing Connections with Constituents

State legislatures across the nation are joining other public and private institutions by entering cyberspace—that is, creating linkages to constituents through electronic communications systems. Using a personal computer, citizens in many states can now access information systems that provide data on activities and decisions in state legislatures. Some systems also allow constituents to send messages to legislators. A few states are even further out on the cutting edge of technology. Maryland, for example, has been installing a fiber-optic network to put virtually the entire conduct of state government online.

Providing information on legislative activities to the public is not new—this information has long been available in printed form. What is new is the immediacy of the access to such information. Distant locations can be connected efficiently to legislative databases through electronic communications and the Internet.

The legislature in Hawaii was the first in the nation to create a data system accessible through the Internet. In 1991, the legislature created the Hawaii FYI system, which provides information on the text of bills and resolutions, the status of bills being considered by the legislature, and notices on committee hearings. The system is available free of charge and helps residents on the state's chain of islands become greater participants in government.

Other states have followed suit, using communications technology to increase the ability of constituents to obtain information on legislative activities. Assemblywoman Debra Brown sponsored a bill in California that required the legislative counsel to make information on the legislative calendar available electronically. This includes the text and status of pending bills and the voting records of legislators.

Demonstrating the connection between technology and politics, Brown publicized her pending bill electronically, through computer bulletin boards. Over 1,300 pieces of electronic mail supporting the legislation were received. In the first eight months of operation, the system received over 200,000 queries for information from users all over the world.

Most state legislatures have joined the venture into cyberspace. Utah, Minnesota, and North Carolina have created electronic systems to provide many types of information on legislative operations, while Colorado, Georgia, Maryland, Michigan, Texas, and Vermont have more limited systems that make selected legislative information available. The Internet offers substantial potential to improve the democratic process. Whereas citizens previously had to rely on newspaper reports or request public documents to get detailed information on legislative decision making, such information can now be obtained easily in a few moments at the convenience of the user. Although creating, maintaining, and updating information systems require expenditure of state funds, most analysts agree that such costs are far outweighed by the benefits of a more informed citizenry.

Source: Jo Anne Bourquard, "Legislatures Hit Cyberspace," *State Legislatures* (August 1994), 31–33.

he tapped were Tommy G. Thompson—for Secretary of Health and Human Services—and Christine Todd Whitman—for Administrator of the Environmental Protection Agency.

In most states, governors prepare a budget package for legislative review. They also appoint the heads of state agencies and seek to coordinate the execution of state laws throughout state government agencies.

Most governors have the power to veto the laws passed by their state legislature, which, in turn, has the power to override gubernatorial vetoes. Some governors have a line-item veto, which allows them to disapprove of specific portions of bills instead of vetoing whole legislative packages. With line-item vetoes, governors can direct attention to and disapprove of specific legislative provisions that legislators may have tried to bury within long, comprehensive laws. Legislators, for example, may insert funds for projects in their districts within long and complex appropriations bills. Through the line-item veto, the governor can disapprove of funding for these pork barrel projects. By calling public attention to them, he or she can potentially embarrass the legislators who sponsored specific projects for their own districts.

Governors today are strong players in state and often national politics (see Box 18-3: Governors as Active Players in National Politics). As chief executives, governors have special access to information on state programs and enjoy media visibility. Media attention often extends far beyond state borders. A governor's power to declare states of emergency (to qualify for federal assistance in case of earthquakes, floods, hurricanes, etc.), to reverse death sentences, or to deal with nationwide problems such as welfare reform are all newsworthy. This information and visibility coupled with their powers of budget preparation, political appointment, and legislative vetoes enable most governors to have a dominant position in policy making. State legislatures often have difficulty obtaining the initiative in proposing public policy. This is particularly true in states with short legislative sessions, since legislators are infrequently in the state capital, where the governor exercises day-to-day responsibilities and enjoys media exposure throughout the year.

Still another reason for the enhanced political status of governors has resulted from the recognition that states have become important laboratories for policy experiments. In the case of welfare, for example, states across the nation have received waivers from the federal government to experiment with reforms and innovations in the AFDC program.

Box 18–3 *Governors as Active Players in National Politics*

Historically governors played limited roles in national politics, instead exercising most power and influence at the state level. Some governors attained national attention that aided their campaigns for national office in Congress or the White House. The power of these players in the national arena, however, largely began when they won national office.

Today, however, governors are enjoying a greater visibility at the national level and far more attention than usual from both Congress and the White House. Governors are frequently being called to Washington to meet with the president or to testify before Congress. Meetings of the National Governors' Association receive prominent press attention, and major national political figures attend the conferences to confer with state chief executives.

There are a number of reasons for the growing influence of governors in national politics. First, Republican-controlled Congresses have favored cutting back federal programs and devolving many programs to the states. A prime example was welfare, with Republicans in both the House and Senate pushing for elimination of the Aid to Families with Dependent Children program. Welfare would be replaced by block grants that would allow states to operate welfare programs of their own design. Republicans, distrusting nationally designed programs to deal with problems like poverty, preferred to give more power to the states. In planning for devolution, members of Congress sought the advice and counsel of governors.

A second reason for the growing prominence of governors reflects the efforts of these players to influence decision making in Washington. Governors across the nation recognized that the devolution of federal authority represented both an opportunity and a threat. They welcomed the discretion to redesign programs but worried about possible new federal requirements and reduced funding. The Medicaid program that subsidizes the health care of poor persons and families is a relevant example here. While governors and states were generally enthusiastic about the opportunity to redesign the Medicaid program in their states, they had two major concerns. Overall reductions in federal spending on the program would force them to find additional funds or cut back services. Debates continue between the federal and state governments about the funding of Medicaid and controlling the ever-growing costs of the program.

These experiments, which include stronger requirements that welfare recipients obtain work or job training, provide important information to legislators in Congress as they seek to overhaul the nation's welfare program.

Governors today are ready and willing to use their enhanced visibility and power to influence national politics. They are no longer willing to sit back and wait for Congress to enact laws without input from the states. As Congress ponders proposals to reduce federal spending in many federal-state programs and to give states more authority to operate programs, governors are among those at the forefront pressing their views forward for consideration.

Other State Executives

Forty-two states have created the position of lieutenant governor. The person holding this office, which is roughly equivalent to the U.S. vice president, is the successor to the governor if he or she leaves office, becomes disabled, or temporarily leaves the state. Also, like the vice president, the lieutenant governors in 28 states preside over the state senate and in most cases can cast a vote to break ties.

Another important office in the state executive branch is that of the attorney general, often an elected rather than appointed position (in contrast to the U.S. attorney general, who is appointed by the president and confirmed by the U.S. Senate). This official is responsible for law enforcement, criminal prosecution, and enforcement of regulations of the private sector. Attorney generals also provide guidance about the interpretation of state constitutions and laws. The offices of lieutenant governor and attorney general are both seen as stepping stones to the governor's office.

States have other executive offices that are filled by election rather than by appointment. These typically include the secretary of state (who oversees elections in the state), treasurer, auditor, and members of state boards of education.

18-2d State Courts

State courts perform many of the same roles as the federal courts (see Chapter 17). They consider cases involving violations of criminal law, including felonies (serious crimes) and misdemeanors (less serious offenses). State courts also serve as a forum for civil cases that involve disputes among two or more parties. Through civil suits, individuals can challenge the legality of actions taken by other parties, including the state government itself. These courts also interpret the meaning and application of state constitutions.

State judicial systems are hierarchies of courts (see Figure 18-1). At the top is what is generally termed the supreme court, which interprets the state constitution and hears

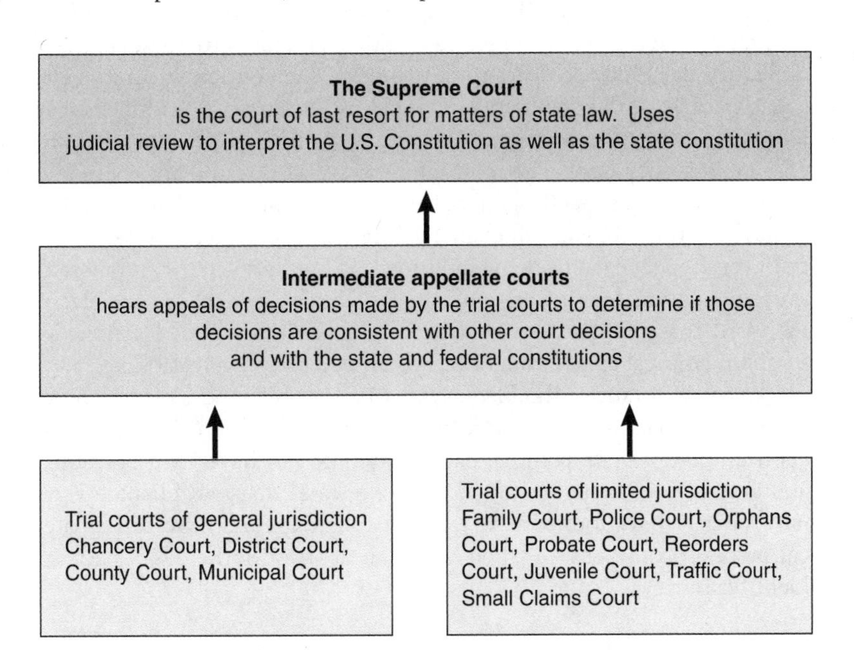

The Supreme Court
is the court of last resort for matters of state law. Uses
judicial review to interpret the U.S. Constitution as well as the state constitution
Intermediate appellate courts
hears appeals of decisions made by the trial courts to determine if those
decisions are consistent with other court decisions
and with the state and federal constitutions
Trial courts of general jurisdiction
Chancery Court, District Court,
County Court, Municipal Court
Trial courts of limited jurisdiction
Family Court, Police Court, Orphans
Court, Probate Court, Reorders
Court, Juvenile Court, Traffic Court,
Small Claims Court

Figure 18-1
Judicial Arenas: Organization of State Courts

appeals from the appellate courts. The intermediate appellate courts hear appeals from lower courts, which usually are organized into trial courts of general jurisdiction and limited jurisdiction. Courts of general jurisdiction are organized around existing units of state and local government (for example, municipal courts or county courts); these tribunals hear serious civil and criminal cases. Many states also have trial courts of limited jurisdiction. These are organized for specific purposes, such as handling traffic violations, juvenile offenses, and small claims.

States use a variety of methods to select state court judges. Unlike federal judges, who are appointed, some state judges obtain office through popular election. Some judicial elections are nonpartisan, that is, candidates do not campaign on a party ticket; in other states, the judicial candidates campaign directly as representatives of political parties. Other state judges are appointed, either by the governor or the state legislature. A third approach is known as the merit plan, whereby a commission composed of citizens, standing judges, and the state bar association recommends a pool of candidates to the governor, who then makes appointments from this pool. In some cases, after this initial appointment, these appointees may be required to run for election subsequently, at which time voters decide whether judges should retain their positions.

18-2e Political Parties as Competing Teams

In most states, political parties are alive and well and influential.[8] Indeed, as political scientist John Bibby has noted, in the face of a changing and often unfriendly environment, political parties in the American states have demonstrated adaptability and resiliency.[9] Parties influence the selection of elected officials including the governor, state legislators, and, in many states, judges through their role in the nomination process. Most states hold partisan primaries, in which candidates for state office run on one or more party tickets. In a few states, party caucuses (gatherings of party members) are used in place of primary elections to designate party nominees for the general elections.

Historically, in states outside of the South, politics has involved continual competition between the Republican and Democratic parties. Some states have additional parties; in New York, for example, the Republican and Democratic parties are supplemented by Liberal, Conservative, and Right-to-Life parties. In Minnesota, the Democrats are identified as the Democratic Farm Labor Party, and the Republicans are officially called the Independent Republican Party.

The key focus of state party competition is the state legislature where, as in the U.S. Congress, the majority party determines key leadership positions. During periods of legislative redistricting (see Chapter 11), the party composition of the state legislature is critical, for the majority party has the upper hand in designing the boundaries of legislative districts for the U.S. House of Representatives and for both houses of the state legislature.

Until the 1980s, the pattern of two-party competition was not relevant in southern states, because of the dominance of the Democratic Party. Within these states, most residents identified themselves as Democrats even though they differed on how liberal or conservative they were. The most important elections in many southern states were the primaries, not the general election, because the Democratic Party's nominee was unlikely to have a serious Republican challenger in the general election. Beginning in the 1980s, however, Republicans made many inroads in southern states and more and more local, state, and national politicians with the Republican label have been elected. This change increased the competitiveness of parties in many southern elections and transformed southern political games from one-party to two-party competitions.

In some instances, the ideology and policy preferences of state residents can influence policy-making games more than party competition does. Such is the case with abortion policy. State political parties often do not have clear positions with regard to abortion. In fact, many are afraid to take a stand that may alienate voters. In this vacuum, citizens have formed separate political groups and have participated in the political process on the basis of their views on abortion rather than because of their party identification.

18-2f Interest Groups as Other Player Teams

Much as on the national level, state politics includes an active role by interest groups that represent the business sector, labor unions, professions, occupations, and other policy interests within the state. In fact, the number of interest groups operating at the state level has grown substantially in the past thirty-five years. Many of these groups are state chapters affiliated with national organizations. Others represent interests and concerns more specific to the state. The primary weapons of these interest groups are information and persuasion coupled with campaign contributions and threats to support electoral opponents.

The growth in interest groups and lobbying activity at the state level has several roots. States have moved into new fields and have become active in consumer affairs, the environment, the workplace, and other areas dealing with social issues.[10] In addition, the devolution of federal power to the states has meant that states are more active in creating regulatory policies that are of interest and concern to interest groups. Because of the growth in state regulatory policy making, new groups have sprung up to articulate and protect the interests of those regulated by the state policies.

18-3 Funding and Governing State Programs

States receive revenues from a variety of sources to fund the operation of state programs and agencies. State spending, which varies substantially on a per capita (or per individual person) basis across the states, is concentrated on several key areas. These include, but are not limited to, public education, welfare, and health care.

18-3a State Government Revenues and Expenditures

States collect tax revenues from multiple sources. In all but five states (Alaska, Delaware, Montana, New Hampshire, and Oregon), a **sales tax** generates substantial revenues. The sales tax is a flat tax levied on the sale of most goods. Many states also rely on income taxes levied on individuals and corporations to provide revenues for the state treasury. Forty-three states have imposed an income tax on individuals, and 45 have a corporate income tax. Most income tax systems are progressive; that is, individuals with higher incomes are taxed at a greater rate than those with lower incomes. States also derive revenues from license fees, including those on automobile registrations and hunting and fishing permits.

sales tax *A tax using one rate and applied to the sale of most consumer goods; housing and food are often exempt.*

More than three quarters of states across the nation have turned to gaming in the form of public lotteries as another revenue-generating strategy. These lotteries use scratch-off tickets and games in which players pick numbers, which are then compared with numbers that are drawn daily or weekly by lottery officials. Across all the states, lotteries raised over $42 billion in annual revenues in 2002, with Florida, California, and New York leading the pack.

Another important category of state government revenue is federal financial aid. The amount varies according to population size, ranging in 2004 from $958 million for Delaware to over $42 billion for California.

An examination of expenditures highlights state governments' primary functions (see Figure 18-2). The largest spending category in practically all states is public education, where the states provide local school districts with funds to support elementary and secondary schools. Public welfare is the second largest state expenditure category, followed by spending for highways, hospitals, and health care services. States also spend substantial amounts on natural resources, jails and correctional services, law enforcement, and governmental administration.

In the early 1990s, when a slowdown in the nation's economy and in consumer spending reduced sales and income tax revenues, many states faced dire economic circumstances. States encountered budget deficits as tax revenues failed to keep pace with expenditures approved by legislatures. In response, states enacted mid-year budget cuts

Figure 18-2
State Government: Expenditures by Function, All States, 2003

Source: U.S. Bureau of the Census, Statistical Abstract of the United States, (Washington, D.C., GPO, 2003), Table 443, p. 286.

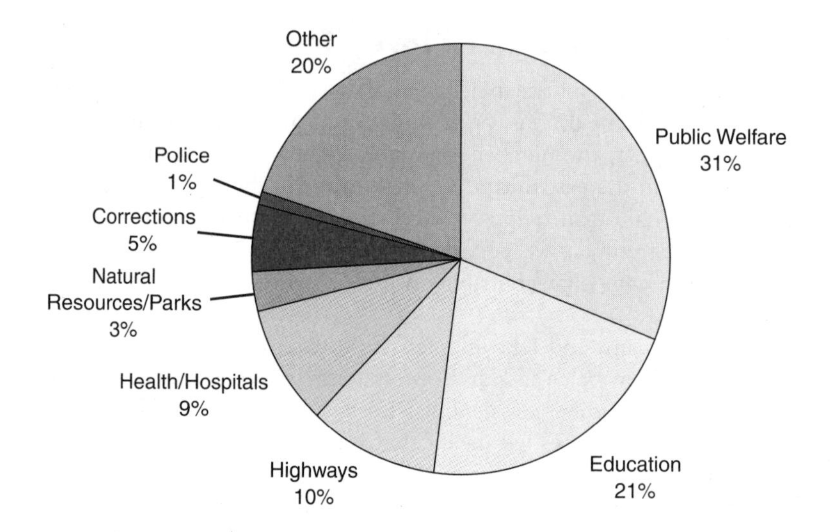

as well as longer-term reductions in many state programs. By the late-1990s, this budget crunch eased a bit, as a stronger economy helped to generate higher than expected state tax revenues. In addition, the previous explosive growth in state expenditures for welfare and health care was moderated somewhat as the result of program reforms.[11] This budgetary breathing space offered little relief, however, as states faced new program responsibilities and budgetary needs following the federal devolution of responsibilities for operating welfare, health care, and other social programs. The states with growing populations, especially of elderly and minorities, faced some of the most serious problems.

By 2002, states faced a new and critical challenge. Declining state revenues—caused by the September 11th, 2001 terrorist attack on the United States and the growing economic recession—made it very difficult for states to balance their budgets. In response to this fiscal crisis, state governments, by 2003, were making drastic reductions in state spending and employment of state workers. By 2005, with economic recovery underway, the fiscal crisis abated.

18-3b State-Federal Relations: Changing Roles

Relationships between the federal government and the states took a dramatic turn beginning in the mid-1990s. As discussed in Chapter 3, intergovernmental relations evolved into an expanding governing role for states. As the Republican-controlled Congress sought to shrink federal government, reduce its spending, and cope with the national budget deficit, it considered various means of giving the states a greater role in many policy areas.

One reform strategy was to replace federal categorical grants to states (that contain strict requirements about program operation) with block grants (that give states far more latitude in designing and operating programs). A shift to block grants was proposed in several policy areas, most notably in welfare programs like the Aid to Families with Dependent Children (AFDC). Although they provide states with more discretion in operating programs, block grants often mean that less federal money will be available to support the programs, which places a fiscal strain on the states.

Other reforms were reducing regulatory requirements on states and localities and preventing the creation of future federal regulatory mandates without funds to support their compliance. For example, Congress considered legislation to weaken those environmental protection mandates that would require states and localities to reduce air and water pollution.

The states have welcomed the new opportunity to become more active players in designing and operating programs, even though this new responsibility represented a substantial challenge to state officials. State officials across the nation believe that it is time for the states to have a chance to design programs to deal with important problems like poverty and health care. They believe that turning responsibility over to the states will encourage creativity and efficiency in program operations.

Some analysts worry about whether state governments are up to the challenge of operating several new programs on their own without substantial direction from the nation's capital. Giving states more authority to design and operate programs will require that states become more active in policy development and administration. Some states, particularly conservative ones in the South, have pursued little social policy outside of federal programs and, therefore, have little experience in policy development. Some who supported giving states more power, including former senator Robert Packwood (R-OR), conceded that some states may not be successful, at least initially, in operating programs.[12] They argued, nonetheless, that it is worth the risk because federal government programs have failed so badly to achieve their objectives.

In order to be successful in their new responsibilities, states will be required to cultivate administrative talent for policy development and execution. In addition, because some reforms call for federal cuts in spending on many programs, state governments will have to increase spending to make up for cutbacks. And they will have to find ways to operate programs more effectively. They may also need to develop new collaborative relationships with city governments that operate many social programs for the states. In fact, local governments, by definition in closer touch with citizens, have shown initiative in program development. One kind of relatively low-cost social service experiment is described in Box 18-4: An Ounce Makes All the Difference.

Box 18–4 An Ounce Makes All the Difference

You probably know about Head Start, a 30-year-old federal program aimed at boosting preschoolers' skills. One city is attempting to enhance the chances of the urban poor even earlier, at the prenatal level. Its success could serve as a model for states and localities forced to become program designers and operators.

On the basis of a demonstration project done in 1989, the city of Baltimore, Maryland, was given federal funds in 1992 to establish a program called Healthy Start to combat infant mortality. Directors of the new program felt that it was vital to operate out of the targeted community itself, not import professionals from outside. Eighty percent of the staff lives in the neighborhood, and local women—many employed for the first time in their lives—have been hired to go door-to-door and locate pregnant women. These expectant mothers are given information, encouragement, and assistance to help them give birth to healthy babies.

Among early results are women who were able to quit smoking and taking illegal drugs, and women who gave birth to live babies with birth weights higher by all-important ounces than those of children of women living in similar circumstances but without benefit of Healthy Start. Some women gave birth and later found jobs and even got off welfare, and an impressive number of young men discovered how to become nurturing fathers. Perhaps most heartening of all, citizens discovered that they, indeed, have a choice and felt empowered to plan their lives and potentially to become more active players in political games.

Source: Sara Engram, "Social Services Done Right," *Baltimore Sun*, (August 13, 1995), 3F.

18-4 State and Local Government Relations: Intergovernmental Games

The basic rulebook of American government, the U.S. Constitution, makes no reference to cities or urban government. As described in Chapters 2 and 3, the Constitution represents a plan for a formal sharing of powers by the national and state governments. Most powers not delegated to the national government are reserved to the states.

18-4a Legal Standing of Cities: Dillon's Rule

Dillon's Rule *Legal interpretation that state governments have full powers over city governments.*

As cities grew in population and political importance, questions arose about their legal standing. Proponents of one view held that cities were units of government on par with state governments. Over time the courts rejected this view, and **Dillon's Rule** was accepted. According to this judicial interpretation, first articulated by Judge John Dillon in 1911, cities operate as creatures of the state government. States have the legal power to create, control, and regulate city governments as part of their overall responsibility to govern within state boundaries.

The practical meaning of Dillon's Rule is that the organization, operation, and service delivery of cities must conform to the rules outlined in the state constitutions. Cities must act in compliance with laws that specify how urban areas may legally incorporate in order to obtain legal corporate status as a **municipality** or a **special district.** States also regulate the services that local communities may deliver as well as the means, expenditures, taxation, and borrowing to pay for them.

municipality *General-purpose local government that provides an array of public services to residents of the jurisdiction; requires population concentration and incorporation under state laws and constitutions.*

special district *Single-purpose unit of local government that provides one basic service or function.*

18-4b Home Rule: Changing the Rules of the Intergovernmental Game

Not surprisingly, past players in city politics often resented regulation by state government. To undertake new functions or activities, levy taxes, or change the structure of city government, city leaders had to petition the state legislature to enact new laws granting them permission to make changes. Local resentment about state involvement and interference in city affairs spawned the movement for **home rule.** The purpose of this movement was to press state governments to provide cities with broader governing powers. Given the growing size of cities and their increased representation in state legislative bodies, state legislatures eventually responded to the request for greater home rule powers.

home rule *Powers of self-government granted to municipalities; the extent of the powers is often determined by the size and classification of the city.*

Most states today specify the general governing (home rule) powers granted to cities as part of the process of legal **incorporation.** Generally, states categorize incorporated cities into classes based on population, with the largest cities receiving the most governing powers and the smallest cities the least. At the point of incorporation, states may allow cities to select specific governing arrangements, such as the council-manager or strong mayor plan (as described in Section 18-6b).

incorporate *To obtain the legal corporate status of municipality through procedures specified in state laws and constitutions.*

The provision of home rule powers has alleviated much but not all of the tension surrounding state regulation of local government. In spite of these powers, cities seeking to create a new taxing source or to provide a new service may find that they are not legally empowered to take these steps without the state legislature's formal permission.

18-4c Patterns of City-State Cooperation

Although home rule suggests an ongoing tension in intergovernmental relations between states and localities, substantial cooperation between these government units also exists in many areas. States, for example, have assumed a prominent role in helping cities to provide public education, highways, public welfare, and hospitals. In 2003, states typically targeted from about 20 to almost 50 percent of their expenditures to assist local governments in providing services. During the 1990s, as the federal government, in response to its budget deficit, reduced its spending on programs that provided funds to local governments, some states increased state aid to localities.

18-4d New Tensions: Regulatory Mandates

A recent tension in state and local relations concerns state regulatory mandates. Like the federal government, states have enacted within the last thirty years a variety of requirements in the areas of environmental protection, health care, and public safety. These laws have forced cities to undertake new activities even when the state has not provided funding to cover the costs.

For example, some states now require cities and counties to create formal recycling operations as part of their waste collection services. The intent of these mandates is to reduce the amount of waste deposited in landfills. While cities may applaud the purpose of recycling efforts, they often feel squeezed to fund regulatory mandates along with all the other community services they offer. Local government players are increasingly pressing state-level players to provide the funding for the regulatory mandates that they impose.

Taking an even more aggressive stance, communities in some states are coming together to press for either a constitutional amendment or a state law that prohibits state legislatures from creating new unfunded regulatory mandates.

18-5 Urban America: Patterns of Diversity

Politics arises out of conflicts, and it consists of the activities (e.g., reasonable discussion, impassioned oratory, balloting, and street fighting) by which conflict is carried out. In the foreground of a study of city politics belong the issues in dispute, the cleavages which give rise to them and nourish them, the forces tending toward consensus, and the laws, institutions, habits, and traditions that regulate conflict.

Cities in the United States contain the best and worst of American life. American cities are places of amazing opportunity, with breathtaking skyscrapers, the finest museums, dazzling shopping complexes, convention centers, cultural facilities, and sports arenas. The headquarters of corporate America, as well as the largest array of job opportunities, are traditionally found in cities.

While cities offer some of the best features of American life, they also contain some of the gravest problems. U.S. cities include areas with high crime, extensive poverty, serious drug abuse, disease, homelessness, and despair. Urban blight, run-down housing, vacant lots, abandoned buildings, and vandalized property can be found in pockets of every large city.

An important trend in urban life has been the emergence of suburban communities which operate with small governmental operations and serve smaller populations. Suburbs, with a first major burst of activity in the 1920s and 1930s, grew during the 20th century, as residents of large cities across the nation sought to create new communities near big cities but without city problems. The advent of the automobile, interstate highways, and mass transit systems hastened the development of suburbs, which typically are residential environments dominated by single-family homes. Suburbanization has resulted in population declines in most large American cities for more than a half century. Suburban residents, however, have not totally deserted the big central cities. They may continue to work in the business district, shop in downtown stores, and enjoy cultural and sports events all in the big city while living in a single-family home in the suburbs.

This section surveys the characteristics of the urban playing field. We will thereafter look at how American cities emerged.

18-5a Units of Local Government

Most Americans are unaware of the full set of governments that function in the local areas where they live and work. Units of local governments vary in size and function and include counties, cities and villages (known more formally as municipalities), townships, and special districts. All of them are legal subdivisions of state government.

county *Unit of local government originally designed as an administrative subunit of state government; provides state-designated and other local services.*

One important local government is the **county,** found in all states but two: Connecticut and Rhode Island. Contemporary counties in urban areas provide many types of services to residents in their jurisdiction, from social welfare programs to highway maintenance. County sheriffs provide the law enforcement services that in cities are delivered by city police departments.

Municipalities are units of local government that provide a full range of urban services, including police and fire, garbage collection, and public works. Both big cities and suburban communities are municipalities.

township *Unit of local government found in some states and based on geographic territory rather than population concentration.*

In contrast to municipalities, which were created under state law by citizens seeking to receive urban services, **townships** (also known as towns) were established to serve populations without regard to population concentrations. Township governments are found in 20 states, primarily in the Northeast and the Midwest. In some states, counties are subdivided into townships; in this case, townships serve as units of local government. While townships today provide various limited services, their role typically has diminished in areas where larger municipal governments have arisen.

Special districts are units of government that provide only one or a very small set of services. One prominent example is the school district, which operates primary and secondary schools in many states. Special districts also include water districts, airport authorities, soil conservation districts, and many others.

In 2002, the U.S. Census Bureau counted over 87,525 units of local government, including 19,429 municipalities and 3,034 county governments (see Table 18-4). (The U.S. Census Bureau surveys and counts the units of local government every 5 years, in years ending with 2 and 7.) The most numerous form of local government is the special district (excluding school districts); these have been proliferating since the 1970s. These districts, which often overlay the boundaries of municipalities, are being used as a means to solve problems that have a larger scope than an individual community.

While special districts have generally been growing in number across the nation, school districts have decreased in number, primarily as the result of consolidation. Small school districts have merged with larger ones so that schools have more resources to provide specialized educational and athletic programs.

Urban analysts have recently recognized the importance of other local entities that in some ways resemble and act like local governments. These entities are residential community associations (RCAs), private organizations created through stipulations attached to deeds for private property (meaning that if you purchase property with these stipulations, you automatically become an RCA member).[13] RCAs can be apartment buildings or complexes, apartment cooperatives (co-ops), or subdivisions of single-family

Table 18-4

Government Units in Urban America

Type of Government Unit	Number of Units 1942	2002	Percent Change, 1942–1997
Municipality	16,620	19,429	17%
Township	18,919	16,504	–14%
School District	108,579	13,506	–88%
Special Districts[a]	8,299	35,052	428%
County	3,050	3,034	–1%

a. Includes, in order of frequency, natural resources, fire protection, housing and community development, water supply, cemeteries, sewage, parks and recreation, libraries, hospitals, school building authorities, highways, health, and airports.

Note: These data document the variety of local governmental units that operate in urban areas across the United States. Special districts have been proliferating as a means to tackle problems such as water provision and soil erosion, while the number of school districts has been declining as the result of school district consolidations.

Source: Data from U.S. Bureau of the Census, Census of Governments, 2002.

homes. RCAs perform a quasi-governmental role through the provision of services to residents, most notably landscaping, garbage pickup, water and sewer services, and street maintenance. Services are paid for through mandatory fees levied on RCA members. In spite of their private status, the over 150,000 RCAs in the United States contribute to the overall level of services provided in urban areas.

18-5b Measuring Urbanism and Metropolitan Growth

Urbanism is a somewhat ambiguous term. It generally conveys the idea of large concentrations of people living and working in an area. Sometimes the term *urban* is used to mean an individual city, but it also is used more broadly to refer to a whole set of communities in a metropolitan area.

During the 20th century, with advances in transportation technology, especially the automobile, many people moved outside of city boundaries to establish quieter residential neighborhoods. Today, people are mobile within urban areas; they may live in one suburb, shop in a second, participate in a sports or cultural activity within a third, and work in the central city. In many cities, the reverse pattern is becoming common. In these cases, people live within central cities and commute to work at corporate parks located in the suburbs. Social activities and economic transactions in modern urban America are no longer limited to the political boundaries of municipalities. Neither are radio and television communications, which transcend the metropolitan region.

Struggling to identify and describe the full urban area that includes and surrounds central cities, the U.S. Census Bureau developed the concept of the **Metropolitan Statistical Area (MSA).** To be classified as an MSA, an urban area must have at least one city of 50,000 or more inhabitants. When this criterion is met, the central city and its surrounding county form the core of the MSA. Adjoining counties and their populations may be added to the MSA if they have sufficient economic interaction with the core county. Economic interaction is defined as persons commuting back and forth to work between the core and the adjacent counties. Obtaining MSA status can have important implications for urban areas, since several federal programs target funds to cities and counties located within MSAs. MSA status, therefore, allows cities to obtain a greater share of federal grants.

Metropolitan Statistical Area (MSA) *The U.S. Census Bureau designation of a central city with a population of 50,000 or more and its surrounding county, plus other counties economically tied to the core county.*

As of 2000, the U.S. Census Bureau had designated 258 MSAs across the United States. Three-quarters of the U.S. population reside in an MSA, demonstrating the extent to which the United States has become an urban nation. Of this MSA population, more live in suburbs than in central cities.

In some parts of the United States, MSAs are tightly concentrated, indicating a vast, urban complex that demographers call a *megalopolis*. Megalopolis areas, which often cross state lines, tend to be clustered on the two coasts and include the Boston-New York-Washington, D.C., corridor and the Los Angeles area.

18-6 Evolution of Local Governance

Unlike national and state governments, which adopted similar models of government structure in the early years of the nation's history, city governments grew haphazardly, with no accepted structural model. At the beginning of the 1800s, the United States had few large cities beyond Baltimore, Boston, New York, and Philadelphia.

18-6a Emergence of American Cities

Several factors combined to stimulate urban growth in the first half of the nineteenth century. First, the industrial revolution encouraged the growth of large manufacturing firms requiring substantial numbers of employees. Economic and industrial growth served to pull workers from farms and rural areas to the cities. At the same time, improvements in agriculture allowed farms to produce more with fewer workers. No longer were whole families required to operate farms. Technological improvements pushed some agricultural workers into the cities in search of new job opportunities.

A second stimulus to urban growth was the immigration of millions of Europeans to the United States. First from northern Europe, and then from its central and southern regions, emigrants flooded into America in search of new social and economic opportunities. Many of these emigrants settled in American cities, usually in the northern half of the nation. More recently, emigrants from Mexico and Latin America and Asians from Southeast Asia have streamed into urban America.

Third, American cities grew rapidly as the result of the migration of African Americans to cities in the North. At the start of the 20th century, only about one-fourth of African Americans lived in cities; the majority lived in the South and earned their living from agriculture. Throughout the century, African Americans migrated from southern rural areas to northern cities in search of better job opportunities. By the 1980s, over 80% of African Americans lived in cities, predominantly in the North.

18-6b Development of Urban Government

Early American cities provided few services beyond keeping public order on at least a basic level. Periods of disorder and violent labor strikes were common. As cities grew in population and became more crowded, a variety of problems emerged. Roads and streets were poor in quality and prone to congestion. Crime rose dramatically as small towns of well-acquainted neighbors were transformed into large collections of unrelated strangers. Density meant that crowded, wood-frame buildings, once ignited, too often became the scenes of large-scale fires. Public sanitation was minimal, and health problems and disease increased with urban crowding. Urban residents turned to local governments to handle these problems.

Early City Governments

During the early 1800s, city governments grew as they took on new responsibilities for police and fire services, road and bridge building, traffic regulation, construction of water utilities and sewers, and street lighting. To manage these services, many new departments were created and given responsibility for delivering specific services.

City governments were highly political in the 1800s, as public officials, candidates for office, ethnic groups, and political parties recognized the possible opportunities for power. The construction of **infrastructure**—public works in the form of streets, bridges, sewers, street lighting, and utilities—meant large-scale government expenditures. Those in charge of local government controlled these expenditures and also managed the allocation of city government jobs, which increased dramatically as cities began providing education, public safety, and garbage collection services.

infrastructure *The buildings, utilities, power and water lines, and other constructed features of urban areas.*

During this period of city growth, party machines emerged (see Chapter 9). Machine organizations worked on the principle of **brokerage politics,** games of politics in which public officials dispensed jobs, building contracts, and other favors in return for electoral support. The private benefits provided by government became more important than what was best for the city overall.[14] While most Americans today would find this type of raw politics repugnant, it was widely accepted during most of the 1800s.

brokerage politics *Form of politics whereby elected officials obtain support by providing tangible benefits to constituents, who return the favor by providing votes for elected officials.*

The machines were headed by political bosses. They made key decisions in local government, including the award of city jobs and construction contracts to friends and supporters. In this environment, political corruption prospered. Bosses amassed large personal fortunes through their control of city government. **Kickbacks** and other favors by contractors were common. Decisions about awarding contracts and business licenses were made on the basis of connections with political leaders.

kickback *Payoff made to a public official from a company or individual who received favorable treatment as the result of intervention by the official.*

Party machines developed extensive organizational networks in the city, generally based on electoral areas. Most cities of the time were divided into **wards** (sometimes called precincts), geographic areas from which one or more city council members were elected. Party machines placed a representative—the ward leader in each ward. This person served as an intermediary between the machine and residents of the ward. Following the practice of brokerage politics, ward leaders dispensed jobs, obtained licenses, and sometimes provided financial assistance to ward residents. In return, ward leaders expected support for their machine candidates in the next election.

ward *Electoral unit within city boundaries where residents are entitled to elect representatives to the city council.*

Party machines needed votes to retain political power. For this reason, a key task of ward leaders and their subordinates (called *ward heelers*) at the precinct level was to ensure high voting support for machine-designated candidates. One strategy in this regard was to meet newly arrived immigrants as they entered the city; the immigrants were encouraged to trade their votes for help from the machine as ward leaders assisted them in settling into a new life in urban America.

Most cities during this time had a **strong mayor** form of government, where the elected mayor possessed extensive powers, including the ability to appoint large numbers of city employees. Mayors were often either themselves political bosses or were controlled by bosses in political parties.

strong mayor *A plan of local government in which the city council operates as the local legislature and the elected mayor serves as the local chief executive to residents.*

Urban Reform

The corruption and inefficiency of local government generated a backlash by the end of the 19th century in the form of the **urban reform movement.** This movement called for:

urban reform movement *A reform initiative, dating from the late 1800s, in which reformers sought to change, modernize, and professionalize local government and to reduce corruption and the power of political machines.*

- Efficiency: Governments should operate to achieve as much as possible with taxpayers' money.
- Scientific management: City services should not be provided on the basis of political influence. They should instead be organized and delivered on the basis of modern principles of management similar to those used in business corporations.
- Merit appointment of city officials: City employees should be selected on the basis of competence and education rather than political favors.
- Fair award of contracts: The award of city contracts should be based on fair bidding practices, with contracts given to the lowest competent bidder.
- End to corruption: Corrupt practices should be eliminated and replaced with fair, professionally managed government.

These principles, championed by progressive reformers, had strong appeal to urban citizens who had grown weary of corruption and powerful bosses. The reformers, often including local business leaders and civil organizations interested in clean government, eventually achieved political support for a widespread restructuring of local governments across the nation. The principal objectives of reform plans were to reduce or eliminate the power of party machines and to replace the machines with officials who would manage city government on the basis of fair and efficient management practices.

As part of the reform, many cities moved from a strong mayor system to the **council-manager plan.** Under this arrangement, the daily administration of city government is given to a **city manager,** a trained professional working for the city as a paid employee. Managers are selected by the city council (whose members are elected by community residents). The council enacts local laws and provides the manager with general instructions. City managers are selected on the basis of education, management skills, and experience; they are expected to concentrate their energy on administration of the city's business. This plan of city government reduces the power of mayors and political machines and infuses greater management expertise into city government. Mayors in cities with the council-manager plan represent the city as the symbolic leader but do not exercise the power or influence of strong mayors.

council-manager plan *A plan of local government whereby the city council is responsible for major policy decisions, and daily administration is managed by a professionally trained executive hired by the council.*

city manager *A professionally trained executive hired by a municipality to oversee the daily administration of local government.*

When the council-manager form of government was originally adopted, the reformers expected the administration of city government to be separated from local politics.[15] A famous phrase of the time was "There is no Republican or Democratic way to collect the garbage." Refuse collection, it was argued, should be managed from the basis of efficiency and scientific principles, not partisan politics. The reformers believed that the responsibility for administration should be given to a city manager and that political decisions should be made by the city council. The manager's role was simply to translate the will of the city council into administrative action.

The initial conception, however, has proven too simple and unworkable. Given their central role in administration, city managers cannot help but be pivotal political players in some circumstances. As head of the large bureaucracies that comprise city government, city managers have access to important information about service delivery information that is a political resource. City councils often expect some political leadership from the city manager, who has experience, professional training, and familiarity with the day-to-day management of city affairs. Sometimes, the city manager serves as a broker, or facilitator, seeking to fashion a compromise among disputing members of the city council.[16] Generally, however, city managers seek to play their political roles from behind the scenes, without widespread public or media attention, to avoid taking the spotlight from the council members who hired them.

In addition to the council-manager plan, other reforms were similarly intended to reduce the electoral power of political bosses and their machines. Some cities adopted a plan for nonpartisan elections, which weakened the role of parties in the political process. Another reform was the creation of **at-large elections,** where candidates run for election throughout the entire city. This reform was intended to weaken machines by attacking their power to organize and deliver votes at the ward level. It was also expected that candidates running for election on a citywide basis would campaign on issues related to improving the entire city and not on narrow ward interests (see Box 18-5: How Rules Affect the Winners).

at-large elections *Elections in which candidates run for office on a citywide basis rather than from wards or electoral districts within cities.*

As a response to political patronage, where city jobs were given out by political bosses to machine supporters, many (but not all) cities adopted a civil service system. Under this system, employees are hired and promoted on the basis of qualifications, not political connections. Merit is typically determined by a competitive examination intended to measure job-related knowledge (see Chapter 16).

Many cities also adopted **competitive bidding** arrangements to fight the corruption typically found in the awarding of contracts. In this process, cities advertise their need to find a contractor to construct a facility or to provide a service and potential contractors are invited to submit a closed bid. The contract is generally awarded to the firm with the lowest bid. In order to comply with federal affirmative action policies, certain exceptions have been made to give advantage to businesses owned by minorities or women (see Chapter 19).

competitive bidding *Process whereby local governments award contracts. Bidders are required to submit closed bids prior to a specified date, at which time the bids are opened and the contract is generally awarded to the lowest bidder thought to be capable of fulfilling contract requirements.*

18-6c Governing Counties

Unlike cities, where mayors or city managers serve as the single chief executive, counties traditionally have been governed by an elected board of supervisors or commissioners. Here, executive and legislative powers are intermingled, clearly different from the separation of executive and legislative authority at the state and national levels. Governing authority in the county is also vested in specific elected officials, including the sheriff, treasurer, coroner, tax assessor, and, sometimes, the superintendent of county schools.

As administrative units of the state, counties receive state funds and manage programs authorized by the state legislature, including welfare, social services, highway construction, administration of justice, and schools. The primary county revenue sources are state aid, sales taxes, and **property taxes.**

property tax *A tax levied by a local government on the owners of private property in the jurisdiction according to the value of the property.*

Traditionally, counties had a low profile, lacked clear executive leadership, and served principally as the provider of state-determined services. They had not been viewed as important players in local government until recently.[17] Their low-profile image has been changing, particularly in metropolitan areas. Increasingly, urban area counties have become major service providers, delivering such essentials as welfare services, jails, child protective services, and hospitals for the poor. Recognizing the substantial growth in county-provided services, many urban counties have moved to create the office of county executive, responsible for daily administration. Some counties have copied the council-manager plan by empowering the county board to hire a professional manager, who serves at the board's pleasure. Others have created an arrangement whereby the county executive is popularly elected; these executives resemble strong mayors.

Governing Townships and Special Districts

Similar to counties, both townships and special districts are typically governed by a board that also oversees policy execution. Town boards are generally elected by residents and

Box 18-5 *How Rules Affect the Winners*

The Case of At-Large Elections

Background

During the growth of American cities in the 1800s, political machines rose to power in many cities. These machines, headed by powerful bosses, built a firm base of political power by controlling the award of city government jobs and contracts. The heart of the machine operation was the ward electoral units within cities. Under the machines, each ward had its ward boss, who worked to keep the machine humming by drumming up votes for machine-backed candidates.

As part of the Urban Reform Movement in the late 1800s, at-large elections were proposed and adopted in many cities. Under the at-large system, wards were abandoned as the unit from which members of city councils were elected. Instead, council candidates ran for office on a citywide basis. Reformers saw the at-large election system as a means of reducing the power machines. They also expected that at-large elections would force city council candidates to campaign on issues of citywide concern rather than on narrow issues within the ward. Many cities accepted the reformers' arguments and transformed all or some of their city council seats into at-large positions. In the 1990s, the at-large electoral system came under attack and has been repeatedly challenged in court cases around the nation.

Questions

A system of at-large elections poses at least two groups of questions, one concerning the players and the other about the courts' response.

What players might be harmed by a system of at-large elections, where candidates are elected on a city-wide basis rather than by residents of a legislative district within the city? How would an at-large system harm these players politically?

On what legal grounds might at-large elections be challenged in the courts? How might the federal courts respond to these challenges?

Analysis

At-large elections have been challenged in the courts on the grounds that they discriminate against minority groups. To illustrate, imagine a city with a population that is 30% African American. If voters tend to vote for candidates of their own race (and evidence indicates that this occurs in many cities), then African Americans in this hypothetical city might not be able to elect any council members. Even if all of them vote for one African American candidate, the candidate is unlikely to win a majority. Critics of the at-large system argue that minority populations would have a better chance of electing candidates to the city council if cities returned to ward or district elections.

Court cases brought by groups representing minorities have challenged at-large elections in both state and federal judiciaries. The courts have frequently ruled at-large systems to be unconstitutional because they deny minorities the opportunity to obtain adequate political representation. To win in the courts, parties challenging at-large electoral systems must demonstrate that minorities have little or no potential to elect minority representatives under the system. Where sufficient evidence has been provided to back this claim, the courts have struck down at-large elections. In response, cities have returned to the system of dividing the city into districts and electing city council members from these districts.

work like a city council or county board of supervisors. The governing boards for special districts may be appointed or elected.

The most visible special districts—public school districts—are governed by a board of education, composed of elected members. The members of governing boards for other special districts, however, are often appointed by local officials, judges, or governors. Some critics are concerned that such boards have limited accountability to the public because of their low visibility and nonelected nature.

18-7 The Game of Urban Politics

Urban politics involves multiple political games and a diverse group of players. The focus of most urban political games is on the type, level, and delivery frequency of urban services.

18-7a Two Ways to Play the Game: Partisan and Nonpartisan Politics

In the largest cities, strong mayor plans are most common. Politics is heavily partisan, with political parties actively involved in nominating, electing, and influencing city officials. In cities that have adopted nonpartisan elections, parties are much less able to influence government decisions and the selection of public officials. This gives rise to participation by a broader set of players. The requirement of nonpartisanship means that elections focus on specific issues and personalities rather than on parties. Issues are most salient when the city faces a major problem or crisis, such as a financial emergency, a substantial rise in crime, or an economic decline. When the city is facing no major problems or crises, elections tend to focus on the experience, talents, and charisma of individual electoral candidates.

In medium-sized cities, where residents share many values regarding their community, the council-manager form of government is most prominent. Often, these cities use nonpartisan elections. City politics is most pronounced during elections for city council. Members of the council are often elected on the basis of recognition within the community rather than on political positions. City managers are generally expected to remain outside of politics even though their actions have significant impact on city affairs.

18-7b Urban Issues

Two prominent local issues are taxation and service delivery. Citizens pay substantial attention to local taxes, particularly property taxes, levied on the basis of property value. The value of property is determined through a process known as assessment, which is designed to measure the current market values of all property in the community, including private homes and businesses. Communities undertake assessment on a regular basis either through their own government employees or through a contractual arrangement with private assessing companies. Property taxes are paid in a lump sum once or twice a year and are keenly felt by property owners, who in recent years have placed substantial political pressure on city (and sometimes state) officials to hold the line on tax increases. With such pressures placed on property taxes, city officials have been forced to find different sources of tax revenue. Some cities have increased sales taxes and **user fees** (charges on the consumption of specific services). Examples of user fees include entry fees at local parks, charges for the use of public swimming pools or golf courses or the town dump, and parking charges.

user fees *Charges made by local government on individuals or businesses that consume specific city services, including fees to use recreational and other city-provided services.*

Urban residents also are concerned about the services they receive for their tax dollars. They care about what services are delivered, when and how fast they are delivered, whether there is a charge, and the quality of services. When citizens become dissatisfied with the quantity and quality of services received, whether it is the quality of local public schools, the frequency of trash collection, or the number of police officers assigned to patrol, they are more likely to enter the game of local politics. Multiple strategies are available to dissatisfied residents. They can choose to run for the city council, create citizen organizations to press local governments to change service delivery policies, or express their complaints to elected officials.

Figure 18-3 lists the primary urban services provided by city governments. The most costly services include police and fire protection, education, sanitation and waste removal, and highways services that are labor-intensive (requiring extensive personnel to deliver). City governments also pay substantial monies each year to cover the interest on and repayment of borrowed funds.

Contemporary city leaders are hard-pressed to finance the ever-growing costs of service delivery, particularly those related to social welfare programs. In an effort to reduce costs and enhance service quality, some cities have commenced the practice of **privatization.** Under this arrangement, cities finance services but contract with a private company or nonprofit agency to provide the service in the community. The services most commonly privatized in American cities include road and building construction, legal services, food services in public buildings, janitorial services, solid waste collection, security services, parking garages, and automobile towing. The privatization of education has also become a controversial issue in recent years (see Box 18-6: An Experiment in Privatization).

privatization *Shifting the management of government programs to private-sector firms and nonprofit organizations.*

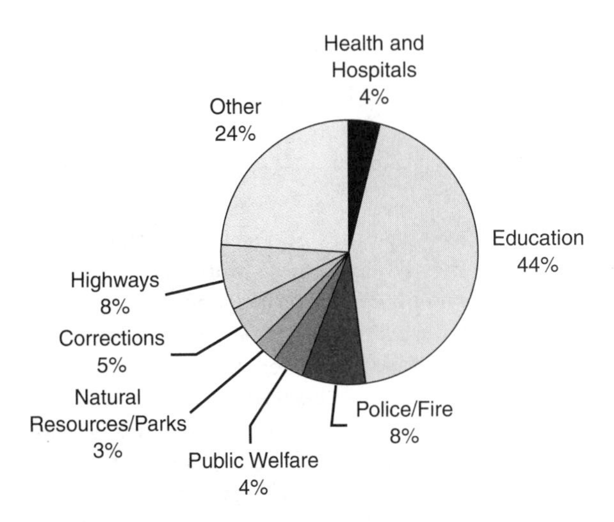

Figure 18-3
Direct Expenditures by Local Governments by Category, 2000 (Total = $996.3 billion)

Source: U.S. Bureau of the Census, Statistical Abstract of the United States, (Washington, D.C., GPO, 2003), Table 443, p. 286.

Box 18–6 An Experiment in Privatization

The Case of Public Schools

Local governments across the nation have been experimenting with privatization of many types of programs and services. Perhaps the most controversial area of privatization has been that of public education. Traditionally, responsibility for most elementary and secondary school education has rested with state and local governments. States have provided substantial funding of public education and have set standards for school operations and curriculum. Local school systems under the direction of school boards elected by area residents hire teachers and build and operate schools.

The provision of education has generally been viewed as a public-sector responsibility. The importance of public education is demonstrated by the large amounts of state and local budgets spent on schools, the sustained interest of parents in the education of their children, and state policies that make school attendance compulsory through at least the early teen years. The system of public education has been supplemented by private and parochial schools where students typically pay tuition to attend a school outside the public school system.

Privatization Strategy 1: School Choice

Beginning in the 1990s, a variety of experiments were proposed that would move the education of elementary and secondary students in the direction of more private schools. One set of experiments has developed under the label of *school choice*. Under this plan, the local school system provides parents of school-age children with a certificate or voucher that parents can use to pay the tuition of private schools in which they enroll their children. The state of Wisconsin has been a leader in the school choice movement. For several years, poor families in Milwaukee have been allowed to enroll their children in private (but not religious) schools with the state and local system picking up the tab. In 1995 the state expanded the school choice program to allow students from poor families in Milwaukee to attend religious schools. This program was the first in the nation to include parochial schools under a school choice plan.

Proponents of school choice argue that public school systems in large cities have become too large and bureaucratized to be effective. They point to major problems in school attendance, student achievement, and graduate rates as evidence that the traditional public schools are not working. Opponents see many problems with school choice. They worry that good students will be siphoned off into private schools, leaving public schools to deal with the most disadvantaged students and those with behavior problems. Opponents also worry that privatization will lead to increased racial segregation. In the case of the Wisconsin plan, opponents argue that allowing students to use vouchers provided by the local school system to attend parochial schools violates the separation of church and state provision of the First Amendment. Immediately after Governor Tommy Thompson signed the Wisconsin school choice plan into law, opponents sued in federal court to stop implementation of the plan on

continued

Box 18-6 An Experiment in Privatization

—Continued

the grounds that it would violate the First Amendment by providing public sector support of religious education. Ultimately the federal courts ruled on this issue, ending, at least for the current time, debates about the constitutionality of school choice programs. In 2002, the U.S. Supreme Court ruled that the school choice program in Cleveland, which provided vouchers that parents could use to enroll their children in private and parochial schools, was constitutional (see *Zelman et al. v. Simmons-Harris et al.*, U.S. Supreme Court No. 00-1751).

Privatization Strategy 2: Private Companies Operating Public Schools

Another form of privatization of public schools involves the creation of private companies that contract with a local school system to operate all or some of the system's schools. Two major private players in this area are Educational Alternatives, Inc. (EAI) and the Edison Project. Both companies promise to invest in the schools they operate, to redesign and enhance their operation, and to improve student achievement. One of the largest tests of this reform strategy is being conducted in Baltimore, Maryland, where Educational Alternatives has been operating nine elementary schools since 1992 (the company is also operating other programs in Arizona, Connecticut, Florida, and Minnesota). Upon assuming responsibility for running the schools, the company bought new computing equipment, fixed up battered school buildings, and trained teachers in new teaching methods—all intended to convert the existing schools into community sanctuaries that will deliver world-class education.

As with school choice, the private operation of schools has both supporters and opponents. Supporters include individuals and groups that have become fed up with the inability of large public school systems to cope with declining educational achievement, even in the face of ever-increasing costs for operating schools. Opponents include teachers' organizations and unions that feel that privatization threatens their jobs and parents who are concerned about outsiders taking control of local schools.

The results are not yet in on the capacity of private companies like EAI to take over public schools, transform them, and substantially increase student performance. Preliminary results from the Baltimore experiment suggest that significantly improving student achievement scores is a daunting task. Dissatisfied with the level of achievement obtained by EAI, the mayor of Baltimore, facing a tough reelection battle against a strong opponent of privatized schools, threatened to end the program unless an independent evaluation showed the program to be achieving significant results.

18-7c Minority Politics: Expanding the Roster of Players

An important development in urban politics has been the increased role of African Americans, Latinos, and other minorities in city politics and government. In some cities, African American citizens represent a majority or large minority and have been able to translate this population strength into power at the ballot box. Several of the largest cities had African-American mayors in 2004 (including Atlanta, Detroit, Newark, Philadelphia, and Washington, D.C.), and the political power and organization of African Americans has continued to grow in major urban communities[18] Latinos, too, have moved into important positions in city government, particularly in cities of the South and the Southwest. Urban politics, a game once played predominantly by white males, now includes significantly more female, ethnic, and other minority players.

Urban politics has long been a training ground for new immigrants and other ethnic and racial groups seeking to join the political game. Irish and Italian immigrants in the last century earned positions in state and national politics through initial political successes at the local level.

18-7d Opposing Forces: Decentralization and Centralization

In the past quarter century, large American cities have faced two conflicting pressures. On the one hand, some urban residents have argued that cities have become too big and too unresponsive to citizen needs. These individuals have sought a greater role for neighborhood organizations and citizen participation in local government, arguing that cities should decentralize governing power by sharing it with neighborhood organizations that are closer to citizen needs and interests.

Opposing this idea has been a pressure for even greater centralization of governing power at the metropolitan level. Critics of existing urban governance have argued that citizens need a government unit that includes all of the citizens within the metropolitan area. The strongest proponents have extolled consolidation or merger of city governments with surrounding suburban communities and special districts. They contend that consolidation would make government more efficient and responsive to citizen needs by simplifying government structure and by using economies of scale. One consolidated city government would replace what has been seen as a tangled and disorganized web of central city and suburban governments.

Thus far, proponents of metropolitan governments nor of neighborhood governments have scored a few victories. When given the chance to create metropolitan governments through merger of central cities and suburbs, voters have generally defeated these plans. Their primary fears have been that consolidated governments will be too remote to meet their needs and that taxes will be increased. And while city officials have been reluctant to sponsor decentralization of power to neighborhood organizations, they have agreed to fund some of these organizations, so that they can provide limited services to neighborhood areas.

Conclusion

Responsibility for governance in the United States is dispersed throughout the federal system and includes decisions made by state and local governments. States have three government branches and, with one exception, have bicameral legislative bodies. City governments, however, show much more variety. They were designed and later reformed not on the basis of a standard model but instead as the result of political experience.

Within states and cities, chief executives (governors and mayors) often play pivotal roles in political games through their central position. Unlike the U.S. Congress, state and local legislative bodies usually do not meet on a full-time basis, providing a vacuum in which executive power is enhanced. Political parties and interest groups are important political players, particularly at the state level. In the local government arena, citizen groups organized around specific neighborhoods or policy issues are often regular participants in government decision making.

Relations between cities and states can be characterized as alternatively competitive and cooperative games. City efforts to obtain home rule powers were the subject of long and heated battles with state legislatures. Eventually, this zero-sum game resulted in extensive home rule powers being granted to cities in most states. States and cities today work together to provide a wide array of important services, not the least of which is public education. Recent state-versus-local tensions have focused on state regulatory mandates imposed on cities without the provision of funds to finance compliance.

States and cities face new challenges as the system of intergovernmental relations is being transformed in the last decade of the 20th century. The federal government has begun the process of restricting its own powers and of giving states and localities more authority to operate programs that were formerly dominated by federal government regulations and standards. Programs must be designed and modified to meet the unique state and local circumstances. Reduced federal authority has also meant reduced federal funding. Thus states and cities must determine not only how to redesign programs but how to operate them with less money. The devolution of federal government power will, therefore, rejuvenate the political status of states and localities, but it will also foist upon them substantial challenges in designing, operating, and funding social programs.

Key Terms

at-large elections
brokerage politics
city manager
competitive bidding
council-manager plan
county
devolution
Dillon's Rule
home rule
incorporate
infrastructure
kickback
Metropolitan Statistical Area (MSA)
municipality
population density
privatization
property tax
sales tax
special district
strong mayor
township
urban reform movement
user fees
ward

Practice Quiz

1. In the past three decades, in what region of the United States has population grown the most?
   a. Northeast
   b. Pacific Northwest
   c. Upper Midwest
   d. South and Southwest
2. As a state gains proportionally more population than others, over time the state's
   a. legislatures will grow in size.
   b. number of U.S. senators will increase.
   c. number of U.S. representatives will increase.
   d. number of U.S. representatives and U.S. senators will increase.
3. A traditionalist political culture focuses on
   a. social equity.
   b. political order and property rights.
   c. governing from a public interest perspective.
   d. political reform and social welfare.
4. What is true of most state legislatures?
   a. They are bicameral, that is, composed of two houses.
   b. They are unicameral, that is, composed of one house.
   c. They are usually composed of 100 members.
   d. Both b and c
5. A sales tax is a tax that is levied upon
   a. income.
   b. property value.
   c. purchase of goods or services.
   d. inheritance.
6. The judicial rule known as Dillon's Law focuses on the
   a. legal standing of localities within states.
   b. apportionment of state legislators.
   c. states' rights to enact an income tax.
   d. hiring of state employees on the basis of merit.
7. Which of the following statements is true of special districts of local government?
   a. They govern one or a limited number of services.
   b. They are organized as profit-making entities.
   c. They represent a merger of two municipalities.
   d. They use income tax revenues as the primary funding source.
8. The U.S. Census Bureau created the Metropolitan Statistical Area (MSA) as a measure of
   a. a city's population.
   b. a county's population.
   c. a major city and the urban region around it.
   d. the population of special districts.
9. Brokerage politics refers to early urban governments characterized by
   a. kickbacks.
   b. patronage.
   c. civil service.
   d. Both a and b
10. Under the city manager form of government, the day-to-day operation of local government is directed by
    a. a paid professional administrator.
    b. the mayor.
    c. the city council president.
    d. All of the above
11. What is true of at-large elections?
    a. They are always held on even-numbered years.
    b. They involve races for citywide office rather than representation of individuals in districts or wards within cities.
    c. They do not use party labels.
    d. All of the above
12. Which of the following is true of local politics today?
    a. Civil service systems are being replaced by patronage.
    b. People of color are playing a more prominent role.
    c. State governments are eliminating units of government frequently.
    d. Local government reliance on income taxes is growing significantly.

You can find the correct answers to these questions by taking the quiz and then submitting your answers in the Online Edition. The program will automatically score your submission. Where you miss a question, the program will provide the correct answer, a rationale for the answer, and the section number in the chapter where the topic is discussed.

Further Reading

Several textbooks on state and local politics provide greater detail on topics included in this chapter. These include Ann O'M. Bowman, *State and Local Government* (Boston, MA: Houghton Mifflin, 2001), James MacGregor Burns et al., *Government by the People: State and Local Politics*, 11th ed. (Old Tappan, NJ: Prentice Hall, 2003), and Robert S. Lorch, *State and Local Politics: The Great Entanglement*, 6th ed. (Old Tappan, NJ: Prentice Hall, 2000). For a discussion of satellite cities, see Sin Soracco, *Edge City* (New York: Dutton, 1992).

An interesting treatment of the social growth and development of cities is presented in James L. Spates and John J. Macionis, *The Sociology of Cities*, 2nd ed. (Belmont, CA: Wadsworth, 1987).

Students interested in state or local government should be aware of some important sources that provide many types of data on these units of government. *The Book of States*, published annually by the Council of State Governments (Lexington, KY), provides many types of data on the organization and operation of state governments across the nation. *The Municipal Yearbook*, published annually by the International City Management Association (Washington, D.C.), contains data on the operations and officers of local governments in the United States. In addition, the U.S. Bureau of the Census conducts a census of governments (as opposed to its census of the population) every 5 years, in years ending in 2 or 7. The census of governments reports provide extremely detailed information on both state and local governments. Current issues of all of these sources should be available in the reference section of your college or university library.

Students interested in party machines may find these books interesting: One, written when party machines were at their zenith, is *The Struggle for Self-Government* by Lincoln Steffens (New York: McClure, Phillips, 1906). For studies of the Chicago party machine, perhaps the last of its breed, see *Boss: Richard J. Daley of Chicago* by Mike Royko (New York: Dutton, 1988) and *Don't Make No Waves, Can't Back No Losers* by Milton Rakove (Bloomington, IN: Indiana University Press, 1975).

For information on county government see Frank J. Coppa, *County Government: A Guide to Efficient and Accountable Government* (Westport, CT: Praeger Publishers, 2000). A good introduction to urban politics is presented in Dennis Judd and Paul Kantor, *The Politics of Urban America* (Boston, MA: Allyn & Bacon, 1998).

An interesting book that contains chapters on many dimensions of state government and politics is Virginia Gray, Russell L. Hansen, and Herbert Jacob, eds., *Politics in the American States: A Comparative Analysis* (Washington, D.C.: Congressional Quarterly Press, 1999). See also Virginia Gray and Peter Eisenger, *American States and Cities* (Lebanon, IN: Addison-Wesley Publishing Company, 1997).

Stephen Goldsmith examines the future of American cities and prospects for revitalization in *The Twenty-First Century American City: Resurrecting Urban America* (Lanham, MD: University Press of America, 1999). See also Paul S. Grogan and Tony Proscio, *Comeback Cities: A Blueprint for Urban Neighborhood Revival* (Boulder, CO: Westview Press, 2000).

Among the books that explore the role of political parties in state politics are Malcolm E. Jewell and David M. Olson, *Political Parties and Elections in American States* (Chicago, IL: Dorsey Press, 1988), and L. Sandy Maisel, *The Parties Respond: Changes in American Parties and Campaigns*, 2nd ed. (Boulder, CO: Westview Press, 1994). A contemporary treatment of lobbyists and interest groups in state politics is Alan Rosenthal, *The Third House: Lobbyists and Lobbying in the States* (Washington, D.C.: Congressional Quarterly Press, 1992).

Sources on the growing number of residential community associations in the United States include Stephen E. Barton and Carol J. Silverman, eds., *Common Interest Communities: Private Governments and Public Interest* (Berkeley, CA: Institute of Government Studies Press, 1994), and U.S. *Advisory Commission on Intergovernmental Relations, Residential Community Associations: Private Governments in the Intergovernmental System?* (Washington, D.C.: Advisory Commission on Intergovernmental Relations, 1989).

Practical guides on running for local elections are presented in Lawrence Greg and Judge Lawrence Greg, *How to Win a Local Election: A Complete Step by Step Guide* (Lanham, MD: National Book Network, 1999), and Robert J. Thomas and Doug Gowen, eds., *How to Run for Local Office: A Complete, Step by Step Guide that Will Take You Through The Entire Process of Running and Winning a Local Election* (R&T Enterprises, 1999).

Endnotes

1. The primary sources for this chapter opener are Jonathan Walters, "The Phantom Conference of the States," *Governing* (June 1995), 15, and Dirk Johnson, "Conspiracy Theories' Impact Reverberates in Legislatures," *New York Times* (July 6, 1995), A1.
2. See Daniel J. Elazar, *American Federalism: A View from the States* (New York: Harper & Row, 1984).
3. Thomas Holbrook-Provow and Steven C. Poe, "Measuring State Political Ideology," *American Politics Quarterly* 15 (July 1987): 399–416.
4. Jahn Harrigan, *Politics and Policy in States and Communities*, 4th ed. (Glenview, IL: Scott, Foresman, 1991), 15.
5. *Ibid.*
6. Harrigan, *Politics and Policy*, 21.
7. Thad Beyle, "Governors," in *Politics in the American States*, Virginia Gray, Herbert Jacob, and Robert Albritton, eds. (Glenview, IL: Scott, Foresman, 1990). See also Larry J. Sabato, *Goodbye to Good Time Charlie: The American Governor Transformed* (Washington, D.C.: Congressional Quarterly Press, 1983).
8. John Bibby, Cornelius Cotter, James Gibson, and Robert Huckshorn, "Parties in State Politics," in *Politics in the American States*, Virginia Gray, Herbert Jacob, and Robert Albritton, eds. (Glenview, IL: Scott, Foresman, 1990).
9. John Bibby, "State Party Organizations: Coping and Adapting," in *The Parties Respond: Changed in American Parties and Campaigns*, 2nd ed., L. Sandy Maisel, ed. (Boulder, CO: Westview Press, 1994), 21–44.
10. Alan Rosenthal, *The Third House: Lobbyists and Lobbying in the States* (Washington, D.C.: Congressional Quarterly Press, 1993), 3.
11. "Blotting Out the Red Ink," *Governing* (August 1994), 37–9.
12. Cited in Eliza Newlin Carney, "Taking Over," *National Journal* (June 10, 1995), 1382.
13. See, for example, Stephen E. Barton and Carol J. Silverman, eds., *Common Interest Communities: Private Governments and Public Interest* (Berkeley, CA: Institute of Government Studies Press, 1994), and U.S. Advisory Commission on Intergovernmental Relations, *Residential Community Associations: Private Governments in the Intergovernmental System?* (Washington, D.C.: Advisory Commission on Intergovernmental Relations, 1989).
14. See, for example, Raymond E. Wolfinger, "Why Political Machines Have Not Withered Away and Other Revisionist Thoughts," *Journal of Politics* 34 (May 1972): 365–98, and Samuel P. Hays, "The Politics of Reform in Municipal government in the Progressive Era," *Pacific Northwest Quarterly* 55 (October 1964): 157–89.
15. This nonpolitical role of city managers was espoused by Richard Childs, the principal creator and advocate of the council-manager plan. To learn about Childs's view of the council-manager plan and the evolution of the city manager function, see Richard S. Childs, *The First 50 Years of the Council-Manager Plan of Municipal Government* (New York: National Municipal League, 1965).
16. Alan Ehrenhalt, "The New City Manager Is: (1) Invisible, (2) Anonymous, (3) Non-Political, (4) None of the Above," *Governing* 3, no. 12 (September 1990), 41–6.
17. See, for example, H.S. Gilbertson, *The County: The Dark Continent of American Politics* (New York: National Short Ballot Organization, 1917); Vincent L. Marando and Robert D. Thomas, *The Forgotten Governments* (Gainesville, FL: University Presses of Florida, 1977); and Mark Schneider and Kee Ok Park, "Metropolitan Counties as Service Delivery Agents: The Still Forgotten Governments," *Public Administration Review* 49 (July/August 1989): 345–52.
18. Rob Gurwitt, "A Younger Generation of Black Politicians Challenges Its Elders," *Governing* 3, no. 5 (February 1990): 28–33.

19

Domestic Policy: Social Programs and Regulatory Policy

Key Points

- **The process through which public policies are formulated, enacted, and revised in American politics.**
- **Criteria that can be used to evaluate public policies and programs.**
- **The evolution and operation of key social welfare programs that provide income assistance, health care, and education.**
- **The fundamental purposes of regulatory policies.**
- **The evolution and operation of key regulatory programs including financial and monetary systems, environmental protection, and safety protections.**

Preview: Who Benefits from Domestic Programs?

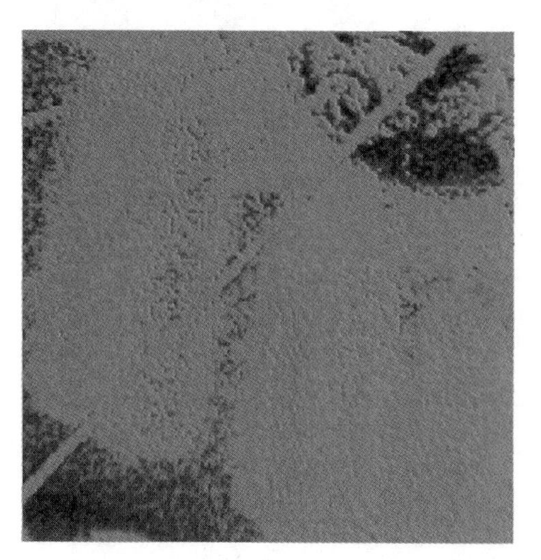

Individuals and the media often look very carefully at government expenditures, particularly around tax time. Recently, lawmakers have scrutinized federal spending to find ways to eliminate the budget deficit. The media is quick to point out that average Americans will work from January until "Tax Freedom Day" in early May just to earn enough money to pay their taxes. Particular derision is reserved for entitlement programs that provide benefits for specific groups in society. The public generally accepts the need for government programs such as highways and national defense that provide benefits to practically all taxpayers; however, when it comes to benefits for specified groups, it is common to hear the lament, "Can you believe what government is giving them? I am tired of all the handouts."

The residents of public housing in Chicago's South Side work on a community vegetable garden as part of a USDA urban revitalization program.
USDA Photo by Ken Hammond

Without question, some of the benefits of federal government programs are targeted at low-income individuals and families. These benefits are distributed through such programs as food stamps, welfare, public housing, and unemployment benefits. The costs of these programs have been rising, and thus such programs have lately received public derision due to their contribution to the federal deficit.

In hard fact, however, we should remember that the "them" is often us. It is hard to imagine anyone who does not have a friend or relative getting government "handouts." In fact, a majority—not some small segment—of American families receive some sort of benefit payment from the federal government.[1] Federal programs such as ***Social Security,*** *health care for senior citizens (Medicare), retirement benefits for governmental employees, and benefits for veterans are far bigger in dollar terms and are distributed to more households than are social welfare programs. They also have been traditionally distributed without regard to the income or wealth of beneficiaries, meaning that many affluent Americans receive government benefits. Couple these benefits with tax deductions for such things as the interest on home mortgages and it is easy to see that most Americans receive some type of federal government benefit. Cutting back government spending and operations, therefore, means that large segments of American society will be feeling the pinch.*

Social Security *A federal program that provides retirement benefits to senior citizens. Workers and employers pay payroll taxes to support the program.*

The decisions made by government and the actions taken to enforce those decisions are the heart of American political games. *Public policies* refer to government decisions to operate federal programs that provide benefits, regulate the actions of individuals and corporations, levy taxes, supply national defense, conduct relations with foreign nations, and protect the environment, as well as provide other services. Public policies result from the laws enacted by Congress, the regulations created and actions taken by executive branch personnel, and the rulings and orders issued by the federal courts.

Public policy choices—the outcomes of political action—are what people care most about in terms of government and politics; they are the stakes in political games.

Earlier chapters in this text have examined public policy from the vantage point of selected sets of players, such as interest groups (Chapter 7) and political parties (Chapter 8). Policy has been discussed in the context of individual arenas: the enactment of public laws by Congress (Chapter 13), the role of the president in formulating public policies (Chapter 15), the structure and functions of the executive branch (Chapter 16), and the role of the courts in determining the constitutionality of public policies and implementation practices (Chapters 4 and 17). The public policy process also can be viewed from a broad level that transcends individual government arenas.

This chapter examines public policy in the United States. It looks at the public policy process itself by exploring the successive games of policy making and execution that together constitute the broad game of American politics. This chapter also explores social welfare, health, and education policies that are an inherent part of American life. It also examines regulatory policies intended to manage the American economy, protect the environment, and enhance law enforcement. Finally, American foreign policy and the interdependence of American political and economic interests with those of other nations are considered in Chapter 21.

19-1 The Range of Public Policy Games

Policies are decisions that precede and underlie laws and executive orders. They are plans, guidelines, approaches to goals; they are ways of addressing problems. Some of the problems that a democratic government tries to resolve pervade society and concern protecting rights. Others have to do with more tangible benefits.

Both as individuals and as members of groups with shared interests, people prefer government policies that directly provide them with benefits. Teachers and parents want educational policies that expand school resources; environmentalists want more dollars spent on pollution control. Welfare recipients prefer more benefits; truck drivers and transportation companies want better highways; veterans want better-quality health care facilities. In all of these cases, governmental policies are aimed at providing benefits sometimes to all citizens and sometimes to targeted groups of citizens.

In addition to providing benefits, government policies also distribute sanctions (i.e., penalties for taking actions that violate public laws and regulations). Some government regulations set restrictions on behavior (e.g., the EPA dictates that reformulated gasoline be sold in areas with major air pollution). Others specify that certain actions must be performed (e.g., local laws requiring that sidewalks be cleared of snow or state requirements that municipal waste collection systems provide for the recycling of household waste).

Government policies may also offer incentives such as benefit payments or tax credits to induce behavioral changes by individuals and corporations. For example, federal tax credits have been offered to individuals who install heating insulation in their homes and to companies that modernize their production facilities.

Still other public policies concern negotiated contracts between the government and private companies. Relevant examples here include federal contracts with companies for the production of military hardware and for the provision of health care services.

In order to fund programs, services, and their administration, governments tax citizens and companies. In other words, there are financial policies that make other types of policies possible. The federal government relies on income taxes (personal and corporate); excise taxes on the sale of alcohol, tobacco, and gasoline; taxes on estates and gifts; and customs duties on imported goods as means to raise revenues. Such taxes, as any taxpayer knows, are mandatory. The types and levels of taxation—often controversial political issues—are determined through appropriations laws enacted by Congress.

American public policies, whether they provide benefits or sanctions, regulate behaviors, or levy taxes, develop in stages (see Figure 19-1).[2] These stages range from the earliest recognition of a problem in society, to the creation of a public policy, to the implementation of the enacted policy, and, eventually, to an evaluation of the effect of the policy. Each stage is an individual political game, and when taken together, these stages form a long and continuous public policy game. We will consider each in turn.

Stages	Activities	Key Players
Problem recognition	Efforts to increase recognition of some problem in society as substantial and meriting public sector intervention.	Media, policy entrepreneurs
Agenda setting	Actions to convince policymakers that identified problem requires immediate attention.	Policy entrepreneurs, legislative leaders, President, media
Policy formulation	The framing of public policies designed to respond to identified problem.	President, cabinet members, congressional subcommitees, interest groups
Policy enactment	Formal approval of public policies.	Congress (public laws), executive agencies (administrative rules)
Policy implementation	Execution of public policies.	Administrative agencies, state and local governments
Policy impact	The effect of public policies on problem that motivated the policies.	Persons and organizations affected by public policy
Evaluation	Assessment of the performance of public policies and their value in combating problem.	Interest groups, political parties, members of Congress, media, policy analysts in administrative agencies.

Figure 19-1
Stages in the Public Policy Process

Source: Stephen E. Frantzich and Stephen L. Percy, *The Political Game* (Dubuque, IA: Brown & Benchmark, 1994), 503.

19-2 Problem Recognition Games

The first stage in the public policy process centers on problem recognition—widespread understanding that some condition or event is important and requires government intervention. In some cases, recognition of the seriousness of the problem and of the need for government response is almost immediate. For example, when the Soviet Union launched the *Sputnik* satellite in the late 1950s, government leaders and the American public realized immediately that a Soviet lead in the space race was a threat to national security. In response, the federal government allocated more money for the design of rockets and satellites and created policies to increase educational training in the fields of mathematics and science. Similarly, when Iraq invaded Kuwait in 1990 and threatened principles of international law, national sovereignty, and worldwide access to Middle Eastern oil supplies, the United States and other countries immediately recognized a problem. Even more recently, in 2001, the terrorist attacks on the World Trade Center and Pentagon jolted the nation and raised fears about homeland security. The crisis nature of these problems required rapid policy solutions, sometimes known as acute innovations.[3]

Other types of problems are slower to receive widespread public attention. Environmentalists have faced this situation. Despite scientific evidence and research predictions, both policy makers and citizens have been slow to embrace such problems as acid rain and global warming as important policy issues. It is difficult for all but experts to understand the technologies used to measure and assess environmental dangers and the underlying causes of environmental damage. Higher gas prices at the pump (caused by a Middle East crisis) or long-delayed flights (arising from breakdowns in air traffic control systems) are readily perceived—they hit home. Global warming and other environmental problems, in contrast, are not captured in bold headlines or feature stories on national news programs. They are more abstract. Policy strategies to deal with problems such as the environment or education may generate incubated innovations.[4] These are slowly emerging strategies

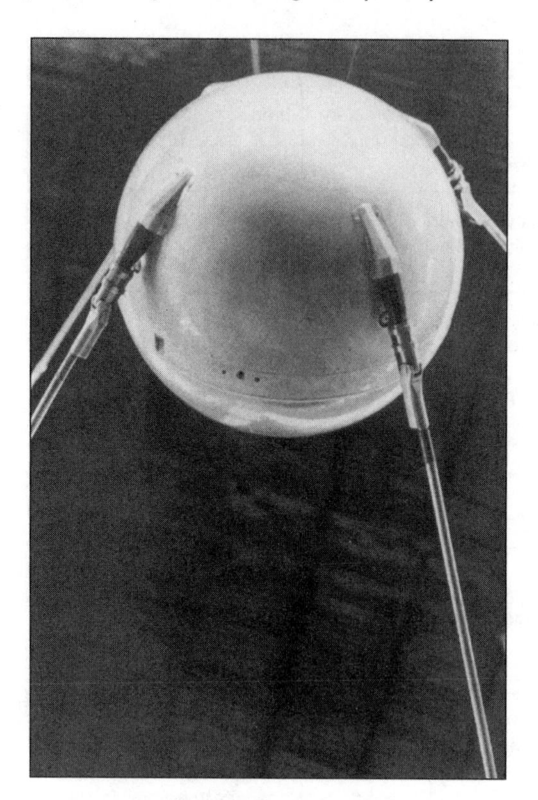

The 1957 launching of *Sputnik*, a pioneer Soviet earth satellite, jolted U.S. leaders, who feared the United States was falling behind in the race to outer space.
NASA

that result from publicizing the problem and convincing policy makers that the problem justifies government action. As another recent example, it took a long time before the public realized that the national budget had reached crisis proportions.

19-2a Policy Priorities: What the Public Wants

Though the public often lacks a detailed understanding of public policy, they do have preferences about the problems facing society. At times dramatic events trigger public concern about an issue, forcing it to the forefront of public consciousness. At other times long-festering concerns move to the top. Public preferences help shape the policy agenda as politicians react to public desires over which problems government should attempt to solve.

The numbers in parentheses in Figure 19-2 indicate the percentage of people who identify the issues as the "most important problem facing the country today." Notice that in some years there was a strong consensus, while in other periods preferences were quite split.

One important player in the problem recognition stage is the policy entrepreneur, a person or an organization willing to invest time, energy, and resources in attracting public attention to the problem and pressing for a government response.[5] Ralph Nader, for example, fought a long and often lonely battle to point out the problems of auto safety; this battle eventually led to better car bumpers and the availability of air bags (see Chapters 7 and 13).

When policy entrepreneurs are able to create a base of political support, their success in pushing policy initiatives onto the decision-making agenda is enhanced. The battle against drunk drivers, for example, was far more successful after MADD (Mothers Against Drunk Drivers) was created and the group forcefully pushed state after state to toughen penalties for alcohol-related traffic violations (see Chapter 7). In much the same way, government initiatives to cope with the AIDS epidemic were few until the deaths of some prominent figures and promotion of the cause by noted celebrities.

Policy entrepreneurs recognize that publicizing a problem is the first step in generating a public policy to deal with it. To achieve this objective, policy entrepreneurs often turn to the media. If they are able to convince the media to investigate and report on an area of concern, then public recognition of the problem likely will grow.

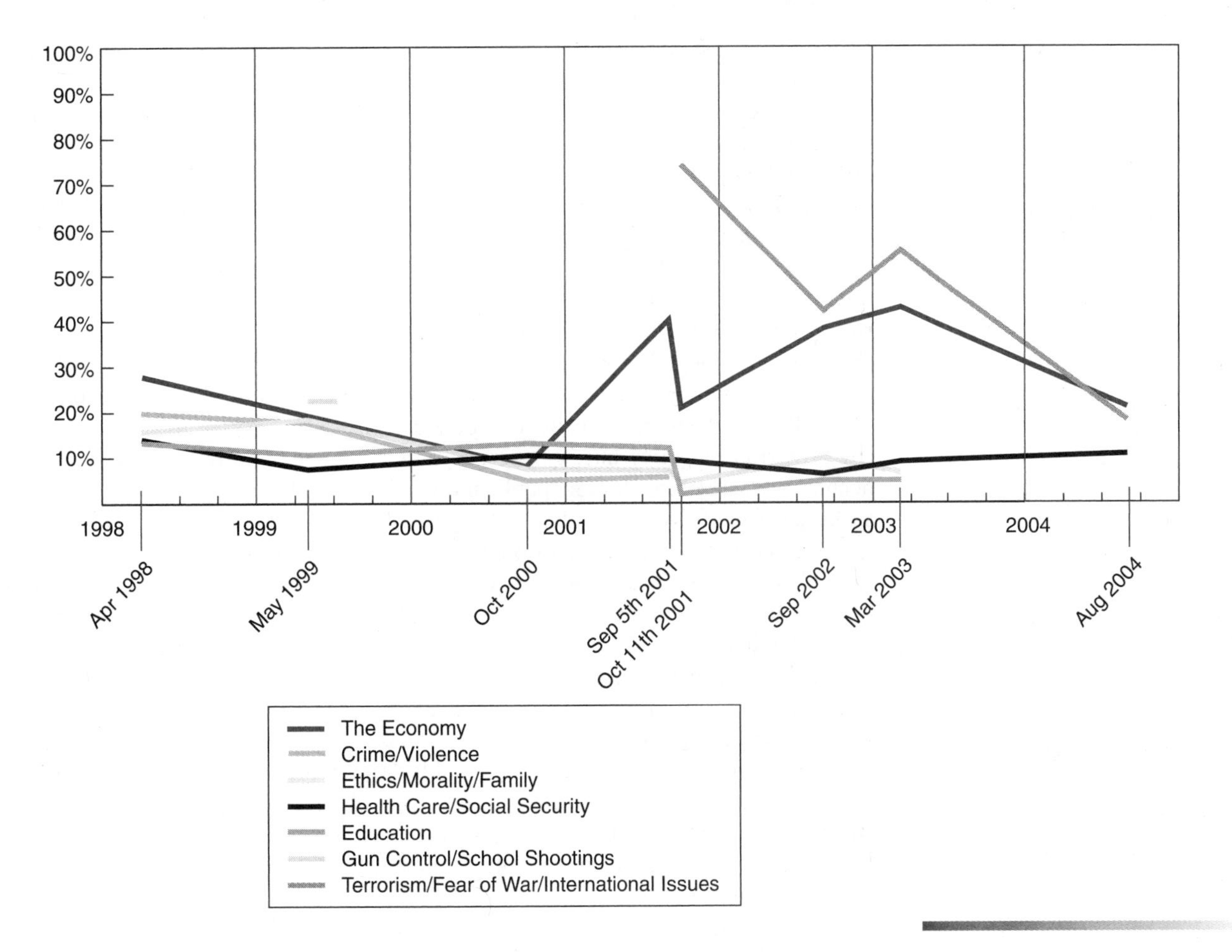

Figure 19-2
Policy Priorities: What Concerns the Public

Source: Gallup Poll of approximately 1000 adults. The poll closest to September of each year was included, except as noted. Lexis-Nexis database.

19-3 Agenda-Setting Games

In the next stage of the policy process, efforts focus on moving publicly recognized problems onto the active agendas of policy makers who can formulate strategies to cope with them. At any point in time, policy makers (including presidents, governors, state legislators, local government officials, and members of Congress) can consider only a few policy issues, which means that the agenda-setting game is zero-sum in nature. Policy entrepreneurs often play a primary role in this stage. They use the strategy of persuasion to convince policy makers to focus some of their limited attention on creating a specific policy.

Most issues have relatively narrow *policy windows*,[6] that is, special opportunities when policy makers will consider problems and possibly take action to resolve them. Policy windows may open because of regular political events, such as the change of presidential administrations or the shift in the party base of Congress after legislative elections.

Political crises, such as Watergate and the Iran-Contra affair, represent other, less predictable, opportunities for policy innovation. These particular crises caused public skepticism about the honesty and integrity of national leaders and stimulated calls for policies to prevent such situations from happening again. One result of concern about the abuse of presidential power during the Nixon administration was the War Powers Act (see Chapters 13 and 15). This legislation was intended to limit presidential powers to commit U.S. troops to military actions abroad.

Natural disasters that have harmful consequences, such as epidemics, hurricanes, and earthquakes, also focus government attention on new problems and strategies to cope with them. In 2004, Florida experienced multiple hurricanes in the same year, causing widespread devastation. The magnitude of the damage made it difficult for disaster relief personnel to respond effectively to help all needy persons. This experience led to renewed attention to emergency preparedness and plans for activating disaster relief. The tsunami tidal waves that struck several South Asia nations in late 2004 shocked the world and stimulated unprecedented disaster relief efforts and calls for new emergency warning systems.

Another factor that can open policy windows is a substantial change in the nature of intergovernmental relations. When the federal government decided to use its resources and spending powers to launch the Great Society (discussed in Section 19-11c) in the mid-1960s, an opportunity for many types of policy experiments was created. The Head Start program, for example, was designed by Congress to provide children from disadvantaged homes across the nation with preschool education. Other programs were created to improve the health care of senior citizens and poor people. Federal government devolution of policy authority to the states is opening up policy windows in state capitals across the nation. Through block grants, for example, state legislatures have the opportunity to redesign existing social welfare programs to meet state-based needs (see Chapter 18).

Policy windows are typically not open for long. Other competing problems may grab the attention of policy makers, especially if other policy entrepreneurs with separate agendas are active. In addition, public interest in particular policy problems is often transitory, particularly as more and more people realize how difficult and how costly to themselves a solution to the problem would be.[7] The case of the AIDS epidemic is instructive here. Policy makers and the general public at first were slow to recognize the magnitude of the AIDS problem and its probable impact on the health of Americans. After some widely publicized cases, including the death of actor Rock Hudson from the disease, national policy makers awoke to the problem in the mid-1980s. They created a presidential commission to study the societal and medical problems of AIDS, funded scientific research, and inaugurated several public information campaigns. Interest in the problem has since waned, however, because the public still identifies the disease primarily as the problem of homosexuals and drug users. In spite of warnings from health officials across the nation about the continued dangers of the disease, primarily to young people, by the late 1990s the AIDS problem had largely moved off the policy agenda.

The transitory nature of policy windows also has been clearly evident in the case of a national energy policy. When the flow of oil from the Middle East is cut off or slowed as the result of political turmoil, gasoline prices in the United States skyrocket, as does public concern. During these times, some entrepreneurs press for new public policies aimed at reducing energy consumption and preventing dependence on foreign oil. The actual crises prompt support from both the American public and policy makers for these policies. However, public interest quickly fades when adequate oil supplies resume, gasoline prices drop, and the costs of new energy policies are calculated. The challenge for the policy entrepreneur lies in seeking prompt government action before the policy window closes. Given the complex nature of legislative politics and the number of players who have a stake in most policies, obtaining quick action is generally difficult.

Finally, it should be noted that political players sometimes have a stake in keeping policy proposals *off* the political agenda. These players have a stake in the status quo and figure that they will lose by the creation of new programs. For this reason, business groups have fought against many types of environmental protection laws that require them to install expensive antipollution equipment. Similarly, groups that are satisfied with current programs have an incentive to protect them against policy changes that will modify or reduce program benefits. In this vein, groups representing senior citizens have worked diligently to prevent reductions in Social Security benefits coming on to the policy agenda.

19-4 Policy Formulation Games

Policy formulation involves designing specific solutions (laws, administrative rules, bureaucratic procedures) to resolve or lessen identified problems that face the nation. For example, the Americans with Disabilities Act (ADA) expanded civil rights for persons with mental or physical impairments in private-sector employment, public transportation, and public accommodations. The ADA emerged after two years of legislative consideration, during which time groups representing Americans with disabilities, professional and business associations, and state and local governments made policy proposals. After extensive debate and compromise, the ADA was enacted in 1990.

The pattern is much the same for other policies: Once a policy window opens, proposals are made and debated and compromises are reached. Not all policy proposals are enacted, however. Programs proposed to provide national health insurance have long been proposed and debated starting as far back as the administration of Harry Truman, without substantial consensus emerging about how such policy should be created and implemented. In spite of a substantial initiative by the Clinton administration in 1993 and 1994 to develop a plan to provide for a national health care system, no policy was enacted by Congress. The complexity of the plan, unknown but feared costs, and opposition by many interest groups caused sufficient debate and delay so that no action was taken before the policy window closed.

Players and player groups possessing the most knowledge about a problem and those who are most affected by it typically formulate possible solutions. Interest groups with clear stakes in specific policy outcomes often go so far as to prepare draft legislation that they hope legislators will introduce in Congress and in state legislatures. It is not uncommon to see lobbyists working on legislative drafts on laptop computers outside of congressional committee rooms, anticipating the next opportunity to participate in the political game.

Members of Congress themselves frequently propose policies to help constituents back home. For example, when districts face the loss of military bases as part of a national effort to scale back the military establishment, members of Congress typically become active opponents of base closings. They use their political clout to convince policy makers (in this case, the Military Base Closure Committee, the Defense Department, and the president) that their base should be spared and that bases in other districts should be closed instead. Members attempt to take credit for solving politically popular problems in their home territories in the hope of enhancing their reputations.[8] They also seek to have **appropriations** bills include projects designated for their home states; such pork-barrel activity allows the legislator to claim that he or she has brought federal dollars to the state or district. Members of Congress from many southern states, for example, have worked diligently to maintain subsidies for tobacco farmers in their districts and states, while some of their counterparts in northern states have taken similar action to support federal aid to dairy farmers. These actions are all part of the survival game discussed in Chapter 12.

appropriations *The monies approved by Congress from the public treasury for funding federal agencies and operating federal programs.*

Changes in communications technologies may assist the players involved in policy making. Citizens typically have relied upon their own elected representatives (and sometimes specialized interest groups) to represent their needs and interests in the policy formation process. Electronic communication through the Internet, however, is enhancing the opportunities of individuals to converse with policy makers. These communications also allow people with similar interests to talk with each other and to develop collective strategies to press for what they wish to see in public policies.

When responding to identified problems, policy makers formulate one of three types of policies: regulatory, distributive, or redistributive. These concepts were introduced in Chapter 13's discussion of the congressional role in policy making.

Governmental limits on, or guidelines for, the behavior of individuals, groups, or organizations are established through **regulatory policies**. When you observe the speed limit, take your vehicle in for a required emissions test, or stop at a red traffic light, you are responding to government regulations. Similarly, when auto companies design cars to meet federal emissions standards and when other companies create products that comply with federal safety standards, they are responding to federal regulatory policies.

regulatory policies *Public policies that place government limits on or establish guidelines for the behavior of individuals, groups, and organizations within the political system.*

The building of schools, paving of roads, and construction of mass transit systems by the government are examples of *distributive policies*. Distributive policies allocate goods and services that are broadly valued but that are unlikely to be made available without government action. The development of water resources and the interstate highway system are other examples of distributive policies.

The transfer of wealth, property rights, or other values from one group in society to another is accomplished through *redistributive policies*. The federal income tax system, for example, was designed to be progressive (i.e., to take a larger proportion of the incomes of high-income individuals in taxes than that of poorer persons). Disabled Vietnam veterans who receive free treatment at a Veterans Hospital and whose incomes are so low

Table 19-1

Recognizing Types of Public Policy

Establishing the allowable fat content in foods labeled "healthy"	[regulatory]
Cutting taxes	[redistributive]
Expanding a military base	[distributive]
Creating procedures for declaring bankruptcy	[regulatory]
Providing hot lunches to low-income children	[redistributive]
Making abortions illegal under certain conditions	[regulatory]
Providing grants for school constructions	[distributive]
Establishing caps on product liability awards	[regulatory]
Providing educational loans based on student need	[redistributive]

that they pay no taxes are benefiting from a redistributive public policy. When public policies are distributed so that the value of the governmental goods and services received by a group is either greater or less than the value of their original contribution, the policy involved is redistributive.

Redistributive policies come in many forms. One is *entitlement*, a policy that distributes benefits to all eligible persons automatically without regard to the overall costs of the program. Food stamps work this way. Food stamps are distributed to all persons who meet income and other eligibility requirements. Another variant is what has been called *regulated redistribution*.[9] In these policies, the distribution of entitlement benefits is linked to required actions on the part of beneficiaries. For example, many states operate workfare programs as part of their overall welfare program. Under these workfare programs, those welfare recipients who are able-bodied and not taking care of small children are required either to seek work actively or to enroll in job training programs. Individuals who do neither can have their welfare benefits terminated.

Public policies come in a variety of forms to serve a number of purposes. Table 19-1 presents a sampling of policy types.

19-5 Budgetary Implications: A Constraint on Policy Formulation

In the contemporary political environment, policy makers must consider the budget implications of policy proposals along with strategies to cope with identified problems. Practically all new policies require that new budget dollars be found to fund policy implementation. When tax revenues keep pace with growing federal budget—something that seldom occurs—the issue of finding monies to support new programs is not difficult. For three and a half decades, the federal government operated under deficit conditions, making it much more difficult to find monies to support new programs and the expansion of existing ones. After a period of substantial economic growth (and growing tax revenues) the federal budget operated with a surplus from 1998 through 2001. As a result of a lagging economy, and the costs of homeland security and the war in Iraq, the federal budget again returned to operating at a deficit beginning in 2002, reaching over $300 billion in red ink by 2003.

19-5a Budget Deficits: The Magnitude of the Problem

The concept of budget deficit is quite simple. For many years, the U.S. government has spent more than it has collected in taxes and other revenues (see Figure 19-3). It has been able to offset this net loss through continuous borrowing of funds from Americans and other investors throughout the world. Most borrowing takes the form of Treasury Certificates and other government securities, which are sold to investors. These securities,

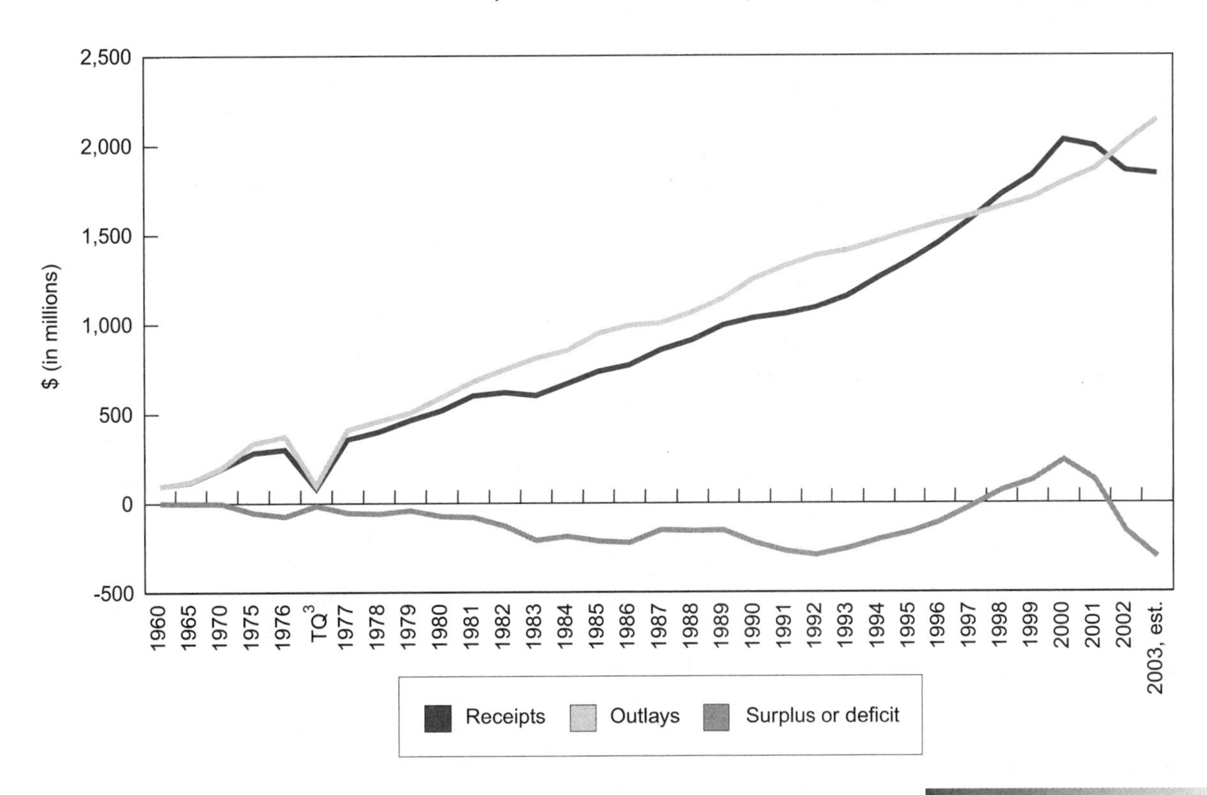

Figure 19-3
Federal Government Income ("Receipts"), Spending ("Outlays"), and Surplus or Deficit, 1945–2003 (est.)

Source: U.S. Bureau of the Census, *Statistical Abstract of the United States* Washington, D.C., GPO, 2001, Table 475, p. 322.

backed by the full faith and credit of the United States government, are generally viewed as a safe investment. To sell these securities effectively, the government must offer them at competitive rates.

19-5b Reasons for Budget Deficits

The reasons for the continued federal budget deficit throughout much of the past 40 years are many, but a few major culprits can be identified. First of all, federal spending has increased dramatically. Entitlement programs like Medicare, Social Security, and Medicaid (with their cost-of-living increases) have seen steady growth in participation and therefore in cost, totaling more than $1 trillion by the year 2004. The beneficiaries of some entitlement programs are primarily disadvantaged persons or families. Such is the case with Medicaid, food stamps, welfare, and family support programs. It should be noted, however, contrary to common public perceptions, that the beneficiaries of some programs are not primarily disadvantaged persons. Recipients of unemployment compensation, federal employee retirement benefits (both civilian and military), and veterans' benefits, for example, represent people from many different income levels.

Another form of federal government benefit comes in the form of tax breaks given to individuals and corporations. These breaks, known more formally as **tax expenditures,** represent tax revenues that the federal government gives up collecting in order to achieve some social or economic objective. The most prominent tax break given to individuals and families is the ability to deduct interest payments on home mortgages from personal income taxes. This break, intended to stimulate home ownership for Americans, represented $68 billion in tax revenues in 2004. Other examples of tax expenditures include the government's decision not to tax employee health benefits and to allow individuals to deduct state and local taxes from their federal income tax payments.

__tax expenditures__ Tax breaks given to individuals, families and corporation that represent forgone tax revenues that would be otherwise collected. Tax breaks are given to achieve social and economic objectives.

Other reasons for recurring budget deficits relate to strong political pressure to hold the line on tax increases that might be used to increase federal government revenues and reduce budget deficits. Beginning in the 1970s and reaching a peak with the Proposition 13 Initiative in California (which substantially cut property taxes in that state), Americans have signaled their elected officials that they are tired of and angry about tax increases. Such increases, which would reduce or eliminate deficits by increasing federal government revenues, are politically unpopular with a broad base of the American electorate. Recognizing this antitax fever, members of Congress have been slow to raise taxes, particularly visible ones, like personal income taxes.

19-6 Policy Enactment Games

Policy enactment, the formal process of establishing policies, is governed by specific rules, including several that are laid out in the federal and state constitutions. Proposed laws must be approved by both houses of the U.S. Congress or a state legislature. The president and the governors are empowered to veto these laws, an action subject to override or reversal by an extraordinary (normally two-thirds) vote in both houses (as opposed to the majority vote rule used to enact the laws in the first place). Of course, public policies require both the passage of statutes authorizing government action and the appropriation of funds to finance such action. Finally, executive agencies develop detailed administrative rules regarding the implementation of statutes (see Chapter 16).

Formal enactment does not mean that public policies are permanent and cannot be changed. On the contrary, Congress and other legislative bodies can, and often do, change both statutory authority and program funding for enacted policies. After initial creation of the food stamp program in 1965, for example, Congress expanded the program and increased its funding over several years. Then, in 1995, as part of a broad effort to reduce the federal budget, Congress considered program revisions that would reduce eligibility and federal spending. Executive agencies, too, can change public policies through the revision of administrative rules and regulations. The Department of Agriculture, responsible for implementing the food stamp program, has revised administrative rules to reflect the policy changes made by Congress.

Legislative enactments are not zero-sum games in the sense that there is no limit on the number of government policies that can be created. In actuality, it is limits on the amount of money available that turn legislative politics into a zero-sum game. Programs must compete with each other for attention, staffing, and financial support.

In recent times, as Congress has sought to reduce the role of the national government, federal spending, and the budget deficit, policy enactment has taken on a negative-sum character. Each set of players loses something. Monies needed for any new or expanded programs typically must come from reductions in other programs. The character of politics under the situation of negative-sum games creates substantial competition and friction among players who try to protect their own interests, positions, or constituents.

19-7 Policy Implementation Games

Policy implementation is the process of executing public laws enacted by the legislature. Executive branch agencies and personnel have primary responsibility for implementation, even to the point of having some policy-making authority (see Chapter 16). Implementation is sometimes incorrectly viewed as simply the application of scientific principles, standard operating procedures, and technology without regard to political issues or struggles. Implementation really represents one stage in the complex process by which policies are made and executed. It is a strategic point at which interested players seek to influence government decision making and action.

19-7a The Intergovernmental Connection

Many federal policies are implemented through the intergovernmental system, with state and local officials serving as primary actors. As discussed in Chapter 18, the trend toward devolution, the transfer of responsibility to the states, has recently added program design and management to the traditional implementation role. Although the workers who deliver mail and administer the Social Security program are employees of the federal government, federal programs are usually carried out by employees of state and local governments.

As the federal government created social welfare programs, such as Aid to Families with Dependent Children (AFDC), Medicaid, Medicare, and many others, it designed a team relationship for implementation. Guidelines for program implementation were established and forwarded, along with substantial federal funding, to state and local governments. These subnational governments bear primary responsibility for the ongoing activities related to achieving federal program objectives.

The nature of the intergovernmental team partnership has come under close scrutiny in recent years, primarily in the context of cutbacks in federal programs and spending. Since the 1970s, the federal government has shifted several programs toward block grants, reduced federal spending commitments, and increased state involvement in program planning and operation. All these factors lead to an expanded state and local role not only in the operation but also in the funding of several programs previously dominated by the federal government (see Chapter 18).

19-7b The Public-Private Connection

The implementation of some federal programs includes private-sector players. The Department of Defense, for example, contracts with a large number of organizations that manufacture military hardware. The federal government hires other private individuals and companies to provide services, conduct research, and evaluate federal programs. In addition, the federal government contracts for supplies and equipment, construction, data processing, the transport of military and civilian employees, and space for federal offices.

Governments at all levels are considering many types of new relationships with private companies as a strategy to reduce governmental bureaucracy and spending and to increase program performance. These new relationships are being pursued more actively at the state and local levels, which have smaller jurisdictions and have direct connection to private businesses. One strategy is privatization—shifting responsibility for operating programs from the public to the private sector (see Chapter 16). One prominent example at the state level has been transferring responsibility for constructing and operating prisons to private-sector companies. At the local level, communities are increasingly using businesses to perform such services as collecting trash and maintaining city streets. Some are even thinking about privatizing public schools (see Box 18-6 in Chapter 18).

Another type of new connection between governments and businesses are **public-private partnerships**, where government and business work together to solve problems or achieve important objectives. In these partnerships, both teams typically participate in program design, contribute funding, and participate in policy implementation. These partnerships have become quite significant for such objectives as building convention facilities, sports arenas, museums, and entertainment complexes. These initiatives are both costly and complex; the participation of both public and private partners is required to achieve the objective. For example, a complex partnership involving a state, county, and city government, as well as the local baseball team, was required in Milwaukee to build a modern new baseball stadium (see Box 19-1). The new stadium was expected to increase team profits and to stimulate the local economy, providing both sides with an incentive to join the partnership.

public-private partnerships
Partnerships of governments and businesses to design and operate programs with broad benefits.

19-7c Implementation and Complexity

At one level the implementation process surrounding any policy mandate can be usefully construed as the playing out of numerous political and bureaucratic games.[10] Policy implementation is characterized by the complexity of joint action.[11] This means that policy implementation requires the actions of many different political players. In federal programs these players range from cabinet secretaries in Washington, D.C., to officials in regional federal offices, to state and local officials. Each set of players may influence the overall effectiveness of policy implementation by the speed, energy, and diligence with which they seek to execute public laws. The actions of players in the implementation

Box 19–1 A Public-Private Partnership to Build a Baseball Stadium in Milwaukee

Beginning in the late 1980s, Milwaukee faced a challenge: constructing a new stadium for its baseball team, the Brewers. The economics of baseball made the new stadium essential; the old county-owned stadium lacked the seating and premium sky boxes that would generate funds to support the team. The team threatened to move to another community if the new facility was not constructed.

For almost a decade, team owners and state and local policy makers debated a new baseball stadium that would require not only a new sports facility but also extensive modification to area highways, streets, and parking lots. After years of negotiations between a variety of players (including the Brewers, the governor and his aides, state legislative leaders, the mayor, the county executive, and business leaders in the community), an unprecedented public-private partnership to build a new 42,500-seat stadium with a retractable dome was announced in 1995.

Under the agreement all of the players would participate in a complex financial plan. The team itself contributed $90 million toward construction of the $250 million stadium complex. A new quasi-public entity, known as the Wisconsin Professional Baseball District, issued tax-exempt bonds that would pay $160 million toward stadium construction. To help finance bond repayment, the state legislature approved a small increase in the local sales tax and in the hotel-motel room tax in Milwaukee County and adjacent counties. In addition, the city and county would each contribute $18 million to pay for highway and road construction improvements at the stadium site.

Milwaukee's Miller Park
Linda Lucas

The plan was hailed as a victory for stadium supporters. Creating the game plan took a long time. The scale of funds to be raised, the variety of plans for stadium design, and the number of public- and private-sector leaders who had to agree to the plan required a great many complex interactions. Although some opposition to the stadium plan arose, primarily from those opposed to tax increases to support the new stadium, the public-private agreement seemed acceptable to most players (both on and off the team), who saw keeping the Brewers in Milwaukee as essential to the city's image and the local economy. After several years of construction, the stadium—named *Miller Park* after receiving support from the Miller Brewing Company headquartered in Milwaukee—opened in the spring of 2001.

game are interdependent: Unless all players perform their assigned roles in program execution, objectives are not likely to be achieved.

The complexity of federal programs and the interdependence of players are evident in the highly publicized war against drugs. If the importation, manufacture, and sale of illegal drugs are to be combated effectively, law enforcement officials throughout the United States must join together as a team and communicate well on the playing field. Implementation strategies for drug enforcement must be acceptable to as many players as possible. If some officials are diligent while others are disinterested, or if some are better organized to combat the drug problem than others, then the net impact may simply be to move drug sellers from one location to another. In that case, the drug problem would not be reduced, only relocated.

Policy implementation is made even more complex by the multiple objectives of individual public policies themselves. The objectives of urban renewal programs, for example, were sometimes to remove blight and deteriorated housing, to create new and better housing, and to stimulate economic development and growth. These objectives were not always consistent, especially in the short run, where some objectives took priority over others. Evidence suggests that the objectives of removing blight and rebuilding commercial areas were pursued with more energy than the construction of new low-income housing.

Other complications are the interrelationships between the problems that public policies seek to address. Policies designed to address only one of a set of interrelated problems are seldom effective. This difficult lesson was learned in the field of public housing. In the 1930s and 1940s, the federal government began providing funds for the construction of public housing for low-income families. The primary implementation strategy was to construct high-rise buildings that provided modest apartments at subsidized rates.

The hope that such buildings would substantially improve the quality of life for low-income families was dashed as the buildings became centers of vandalism, crime, delinquency, and drug use.[12] Many families initially benefited from the provision of new homes, but they soon found themselves facing major problems. What the housing planners had failed to recognize was that the problems of crime, poverty, disease, and delinquency are interconnected. Public housing projects dealt only with the physical environment of low-income families without responding to other social problems associated with poverty.[13] These related problems frustrated federal efforts to provide good-quality, affordable housing to low-income families.

All of this complexity in policy implementation has led analysts to ask, Who is managing the system? In most cases, there is no single manager or arena involved in executing public policies. Implementation emerges from the actions and decisions of a large number of players, who generally are neither located in close proximity to each other nor interconnected in a clear chain of command.

19-8 Policy Impact: The Results of Implementation Games

The actual results of implementing public policies are referred to as policy impacts. The purpose of all public policies is to generate some pre-identified and positive impact that enhances the lives of citizens. Often, however, public policies fall short of their objectives. As noted earlier, the complexity and interrelatedness of human problems make their effective solution difficult. At best, public policies are able to reduce the problem to some degree. Seldom, however, is the problem completely eliminated through policy interventions. To complicate matters, the solution to one problem sometimes causes new and different problems.

Governments constantly deal with **unanticipated consequences**, the results of policy implementation that were not predicted when the policy was developed and first executed. Sometimes the consequences are positive, such as the many practical technological and medical advancements that originated from space exploration. Unfortunately, unanticipated consequences may also be negative and create other problems for governments to handle. Many urban analysts have cited federal funding of highway construction as harmful to the vitality of central cities. The beltways that surround major cities, which were designed to ease the flow of traffic in urban areas, also enabled central city residents to move to outlying areas and commute to work. This movement to the suburbs contributed to central city population decline, a reduction in city property tax revenues, and a change in central cities' economic and racial composition. These consequences of highway construction were neither planned nor intended. In the process of solving one problem, policy makers created a new set of problems for central city governments.

unanticipated consequences
The unplanned results of government policies. These consequences may stimulate policy changes.

Time Out 19-1

Policy implementation has consequences that serve as the basis for evaluation. Imagine for a moment that you are the police chief in a small community and that one of your responsibilities is to make the assignments for patrol officers. Your community is divided into the six beat areas shown on the map below with areas differing in the extent of criminal activity. For the day shift, you have six patrol officers to assign to the beat areas shown on the map.

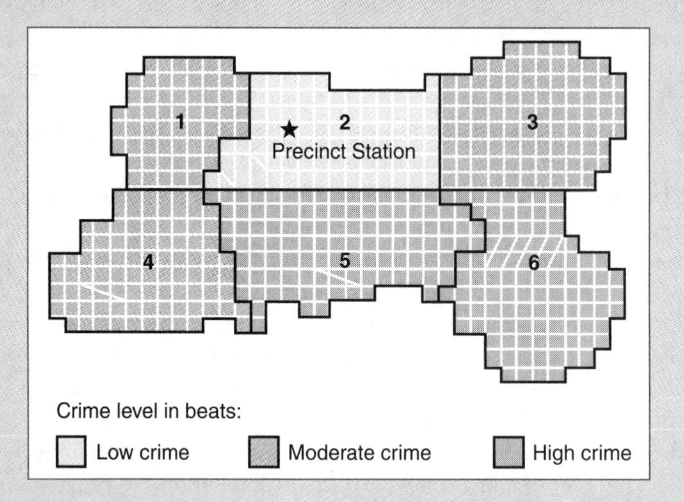

As the police chief, you feel that:

- Aggressive crime fighting is a critical goal of your department.
- Citizens in your community deserve fair and equal treatment in law enforcement and public safety.
- Dollar resources are precious, meaning that the department should actively seek ways to lower the cost of operations.
- Complaints from the residents of beat 3, who claim that police response time to calls for assistance is too slow, are a concern.

Where will you assign your six officers?

A. One to each beat
B. Two to beats 5 and 6 and two rotating between beats 1, 3, and 4
C. Two to beats 2, 5, and 6
D. Two to beat 3 and one to beats 1, 4, 5, and 6

Source: Stephen E. Frantzich and Stephen L. Percy, *The Political Game* (Dubuque, IA: Brown & Benchmark, 1994), 50.

19-9 Policy Evaluation Games

Policy evaluation refers to the assessment of the impacts and consequences of policy implementation. One form of policy evaluation is citizens' expressed perceptions of the quality of government services. If citizens are dissatisfied with government performance, they probably will use their voting and organizational power to join the political game, with the intention of forcing policy change or replacing government officials.

In the last few decades, all levels of government and especially the federal government have begun to view policy evaluation as an important component of the policy process. Increasingly, public policies require formal, systematic evaluations of policy implementation and its consequences. Federal laws have often required that the state and local officials who operate programs with federal funds provide regular quarterly reports and evaluation studies. Such reports and studies supply information about program operations and achievement of objectives. Feedback information can also be obtained through periodic performance audits, program reviews, and on-site visits by federal officials.

Individuals who receive government services also can provide feedback in the form of complaints or praise to elected representatives or to service-providing agencies. Sometimes, agencies actively seek to gather citizen feedback through surveys. Some programs require that service providers gather feedback from the citizens served by the program and then use that information to improve program operations. This is true of many community development programs where relevant federal agencies require that governments and organizations that receive funding involve community residents in program planning and evaluation.

Formal tools and methods of policy analysis must be applied in an objective manner to determine what, if any, impact public policies are having. Public policies may be assessed according to many types of **evaluative criteria**, which relate to basic elements of U.S. political culture. These criteria include efficiency, effectiveness, equity, and responsiveness.

One commonly used criterion is **efficiency.** The most efficient policy alternative is a program that provides the most benefit for the least cost. The quest for efficiency in the public sector mirrors the drive for profit maximization in the private sector.

Effectiveness is another criterion often considered during policy evaluation. Policies that achieve the highest level of planned goals are considered the most effective. Effectiveness can be measured only if public policy goals are specified in advance of policy implementation.

The values of fairness and equality, which are pervasive in the U.S. political culture, are represented in a system of **equity.** Equity directs attention to the fairness in distribution of a governmentally produced good or service. Analysts and political advocates have discovered that equity can mean different things to different people. One notion of equity refers to *equality of opportunity*, a belief that all Americans should have access to benefits and services of government and other opportunities in American society. Another version of equity, with quite different implications, is *equality of outcome*. When pursuing an equality-of-outcome approach, public policies seek to redistribute wealth and opportunities so as to equalize social, economic, and political status.

Finally, **responsiveness** concerns the extent to which public policies take into account and satisfy the needs and desires of citizens. The most responsive policy is the one that best satisfies the preferences of citizens. Table 19-2 summarizes the evaluative criteria used for public policies.

evaluative criteria *Standards used to measure and assess the impacts that result from public policy implementation.*

efficiency *An evaluative criterion that compares the costs of public policies with the benefits that result from the implementation of those policies.*

effectiveness *An evaluative criterion that compares the goals of public policies with the impacts that result from the implementation of those policies.*

equity *An evaluation criterion that considers the extent to which the impacts of public policy are equally distributed.*

responsiveness *An evaluative criterion that compares the policy preferences of citizens with the nature and impact of public policies implemented by governments.*

Table 19-2 Evaluative Criteria That Can Be Used to Evaluate Public Policy and Understand Policy Impacts

Criterion	Definition	What is Studied
Efficiency	Comparison of the costs and benefits of public programs; the most efficient program is the one that provides the greatest benefit at the least cost to the government	The costs and benefits of public programs, measured in common unit of valuation
Effectiveness	Comparison of program accomplishments with the original program goals; the program that achieves the highest level of goal attainment is the most effective	Program goals and the measurable achievements of the program
Equity 1: Opportunity	Equal access to the benefits of programs offered by government	The distribution of access to government services and programs
Equity 2: Outcome	Moving toward equalization of social, economic, and political positions of citizens	The distribution of government benefits as they impact social, economic, and political positions of citizens
Responsiveness	Comparison of public programs with citizen preferences about public programs and government operations	Citizen preferences for government programs; citizen ratings of government services and programs

Answers to Time Out 19-1

As with many of the exercises in this text, there is no single correct answer. The information in Time Out 19-1 presented broad goals and objectives that are not easily balanced nor capable of complete fulfillment. Each of the answers indicates the priority of a different criterion for evaluation.

If you chose A, assigning one officer to each beat, then you were probably following a norm of equity. This type of assignment distributes police resources evenly among the neighborhoods.

If you chose B, assigning more officers to the high-crime beats, you were reflecting an effectiveness norm. You were probably thinking that the best way to fight crime aggressively (one of your objectives as police chief) is to concentrate resources where the crime problem is the greatest.

If you chose C, assigning several officers close to the precinct station (in beat 2), so that they would have to travel less distance, you could save fuel costs. Your assignment pattern reflects a concern for efficiency.

If you chose D, assigning more officers to beat 3 because of the vocal citizen concerns about police response time, then your assignments reflect a norm of responsiveness. As the police chief, you probably were seeking to lessen citizen discontent.

As this exercise demonstrates, satisfying all evaluative criteria at the same time is almost always impossible. Generally, decisions about the allocation of scarce public resources reflect trade-offs among the different criteria. If one criterion is emphasized, another has to be minimized.

Public policies are often judged using the evaluation standards listed in Table 19-2. Poverty programs, for example, are meant to reduce the nation's level of poverty and malnutrition. Everyone can agree about this broad programmatic objective, but in evaluations of federal poverty programs, by what standard should success or failure be measured? Is a 5% reduction in the number of families living below the poverty level a success? Could more have been achieved with federal dollars? If poverty is reduced in some states and not in others, does this denote program failure? What impact do poverty programs have on spending and budget deficits? Answers to questions like these are difficult. Without a clear picture of federal policies, both of their objectives and the means and standards appropriately used to judge them, an understanding of what federal programs achieve and how they can be improved is difficult.

It is almost impossible for any single policy to be rated highly on all evaluative criteria at the same time. An otherwise effective policy may not work well in the distribution of policy resources. Or a policy that is highly effective in combating a public problem may be extremely expensive and inefficient to operate. The reality is that policy makers often face a trade-off situation; aggressively pursuing one evaluative criterion may mean reducing attention to other criteria.

19-10 Feedback: Stimulating a New Round of Play

The policy process, as illustrated in Figure 19-1, is circular in operation. Existing solutions result in new problems emerging on the policy agenda. The results of policy implementation, both policy impacts and the information gained through policy evaluation, flow back to decision makers as feedback, which may then initiate another round in the policy game. If policy impacts are positive, there will likely be a move to increase the magnitude of program operations and to encourage similar programs. If the impacts suggest policy failure, then legislators or administrators may move to eliminate or revise the program. Most often, public policies generate both positive and negative impacts. The challenge to policy makers lies in using information derived from feedback to modify public policies in order to increase positive results and minimize negative ones.

19-11 The Evolution of Public Welfare: Philosophy and Practice

Millions of Americans receive financial assistance, food, shelter, employment training, subsidies, and tax benefits because of domestic social policies established in the United States. Many, but by no means all, social policies are intended to aid disadvantaged individuals and families. Social programs have become such a prominent part of daily life that it is difficult to remember that the entry of the federal government into social welfare only began in the 1930s, largely as a result of the Depression. A second major wave of social programs was inaugurated during the Great Society program during the administration of President Lyndon B. Johnson (1963–1969). These developments are not peculiarly American. Western European and Scandinavian countries were models of **welfare states** long before the United States began its first program.

welfare state *A political system in which it is public policy that government strives to provide a broad set of health and social programs to all citizens—generally in exchange for high public sector taxes.*

Social programs today provide billions of dollars to Americans. Poor families receive income assistance, food stamps, and subsidized health care. Elderly persons receive health care benefits, and most also receive Social Security checks. Unemployed people may be eligible for federally funded job training programs. Farmers receive subsidies to boost the price of cash crops and sustain family farms. Many children in schools receive lunches whose cost is subsidized by the federal government. In all these cases, federal government programs—often implemented with state and local help—provide benefits intended to enhance the lives and opportunities of Americans.

The benefits of social programs are awarded in a number of forms. Welfare checks are issued to poor families and Social Security checks sent to retirees. Government-issued **vouchers** can be redeemed for specific purposes like purchasing food products for the family. Sometimes benefits are distributed more broadly than to single individuals or families. The federal government, for example, buys up surplus agricultural products, like milk and cheese, to keep dairy prices from falling. Dairy farmers who receive a higher price for products sold than they would in the open market without government involvement are the beneficiaries. Tax credits, which lower income taxes that must be paid, are another form of benefit provided by the federal government (such as tax credits given to working families with low incomes).

vouchers *Certificates provided by the government that allow recipients to purchase specific items. Food stamps are an example.*

The object of many domestic social policies is redistribution—the provision of governmental benefits to poor families to improve their lives, health, and standards of living. These benefits are financed largely by a federal income tax system that takes a higher proportion of tax revenues from middle-class and wealthy individuals and profitable corporations. Redistribution is the fundamental purpose of health care programs for the poor and elderly, income assistance to disadvantaged families and retirees, and tax credits for the working poor. Not all social policies, however, have a directly redistributive objective. One of the largest beneficiaries of federal programs is the American homeowner, who is able to deduct mortgage interest costs when calculating federal income taxes. This tax incentive, another form of governmental benefit, is intended to increase the capacity of American families to purchase their own home.

Despite the fact that these domestic programs have aided generations of Americans, they continue to be the subject of bipartisan debate. Several programs have been substantially revised by Congress. Let us explore further by outlining the creation and evolution of major federal government social policies that provide benefits to Americans. After examination of the contemporary debate over the U.S. welfare system, we will explore Social Security, housing, health care, and education, and will examine the reasons that many social programs were substantially reformed in the mid-1990s.

19-11a Early Programs: Charity and Local Relief

The earliest welfare assistance provided in the United States to poor and otherwise disadvantaged people—dating back to the colonial period—was almost exclusively private in nature and came in the form of assistance from private charitable and religious organizations. During the 1800s, both private and public forms of charity were created to provide limited assistance to the poor, particularly the "worthy" poor—individuals who were poor because of circumstances beyond their control (e.g., illness, industrial accidents, or mental impairment).

Charity assistance during the 19th century had two forms.[14] "Indoor relief" was the name for assistance provided through institutions like poorhouses, where indigent persons were housed and fed. "Outdoor relief" was aid given to needy people outside of institutions. Often it was home-based assistance and sometimes included the provision of public-sector jobs. The system of indoor and outdoor aid, covering a small population (compared with contemporary welfare systems), was provided by private charities, religious organizations, and local governments. Most of this aid was based in cities. There was no federal involvement at this time, and the level of benefits available to poor people varied substantially across communities.

Throughout the 1800s, even while municipal and private charity organizations were growing, a substantial debate arose about providing assistance to the poor, and the causes of poverty were at the heart of the controversy. The rhetoric of this debate sounds strikingly similar to the welfare reform arguments today. For many reformers, poverty demonstrated individual failure. In the American political culture—where individualism and appreciation for the free market tradition are highly valued (see Chapter 5)—poverty was "deserved" by individuals who were too lazy to find a job and take care of themselves. Only illness, incapacitation, or motherhood exempted a poor person from scorn.

Critics feared that the provision of benefits to the poor might actually *encourage* poverty. Welfare reformers wanted to avoid that. They associated poverty with the "demoralization of the poor through the erosion of independence and self-respect; the spread of idleness and the loss of the will to work; the promotion of immorality in all its ugly forms; and the increase in public costs through the growth of poorhouses and jails."[15] Given these arguments, many communities reduced or eliminated outdoor relief programs, leaving charity to private and religious organizations that operated poorhouses, orphanages, homes for mentally ill persons, and other institutions.

Not surprisingly, employment was seen as the primary remedy for able-bodied individuals. Public-sector jobs provided by local communities to the poor were an early manifestation of that view. Employment and self-sufficiency fit nicely with the American political culture that values free enterprise and individualism. The connection between poverty and employment is a theme, as we shall see, that continues to pervade arguments about welfare reform.

19-11b New Deal Programs

In the 20th century, all levels of the public sector, including the federal government, adopted a far more active role in providing assistance to disadvantaged people. Reform initiatives aimed at aiding and saving children stimulated states (40 of them by 1920) to give small pensions to widows with children.[16]

The calamitous Depression, which began in 1929 and continued through the 1930s, further focused attention on a public role in assisting poor people. The collapse of the private market during the worldwide economic crisis caused unemployment and poverty across a vast segment of the American population. It became clear at this point that unemployment and poverty could result from a failure of the market rather than the laziness of workers. This change in perspectives on poverty stimulated major initiatives—this time at the federal level—to deal with the problems of poverty and unemployment.

Many types of federal programs were created to get America working again. Cumulatively these are known as the *New Deal* initiatives, which were proposed by President Franklin D. Roosevelt and enacted by the Democratic-controlled Congress. Some projects were relatively short-term solutions to the Depression. One prominent example was the Works Projects Administration (WPA); for about a decade, unemployed workers were hired directly by the federal government to build scenic highways, public parks, and other recreational areas.

WPA supervisor instructing Spanish-American woman in weaving of rag rug in Costilla, New Mexico.
Library of Congress, Prints & Photographs Division (LC-USZ62-31799)

Other social programs of the Depression era have had much longer duration and function as integral components of today's welfare system. In what was seen by many as a bold move, Congress enacted the Social Security Act of 1935, thereby creating a variety of income-support programs. Though the hallmark of this act is the Social Security retirement program, the act provides assistance to a range of disadvantaged persons. For example, Social Security Disability Insurance (SSDI) provides monthly payments to disabled workers between the ages of 50 and 64. Supplemental Security Income (SSI), created through an amendment of the Social Security Act, gives payments to equalize within the nation benefits provided to needy, aged, blind, or disabled persons.

Through the Social Security Act, the federal government operates a cooperative program with state governments to provide unemployment compensation. All states have their own unemployment insurance laws whereby employers, but not employees, contribute to unemployment trust funds. Under state laws, benefits whose amounts are based on the individual's past earnings are paid to unemployed eligible workers. State laws vary concerning the length of time benefits are paid and their amount. The typical pattern is for states to pay benefits for 26 weeks (6 months). During periods of extended high unemployment, extended benefits beyond 26 weeks are payable under a federal-state program to those who have exhausted their regular state benefits. Today, about 97% of American workers are covered by unemployment insurance.

The Social Security Act also created the largest federal program to assist poor families: **Aid to Families with Dependent Children (AFDC)**. This federal program provided grants to state governments to provide cash payments to low-income families with dependent children. This was one of the largest federal antipoverty programs in terms of expenditures ($17.8 billion in 1992) and recipients (13.7 million). It also is the program most Americans think of as "welfare." This program was dissolved in 1995 as Congress transformed it into block grants to be given to states so that they can operate their own programs with few federal restrictions (as described later in the chapter).

Aid to Families with Dependent Children (AFDC) *A federal program that provides income support payments to poor families with children.*

In these welfare programs, poverty alone is not enough to trigger benefits. Recipients must be poor *and* fall into a category of persons recognized under law as appropriate to receive federal government assistance, including mothers with dependent children or persons with disabilities. (See Figure 19-4 for a description of poverty in the United States today.)

Figure 19-4
Poverty in the United States, 1975–1999

Source: U.S. Bureau of the Census, *Statistical Abstract of the United States*, (Washington, D.C.: GPO, 2003), Table 697, p. 463.

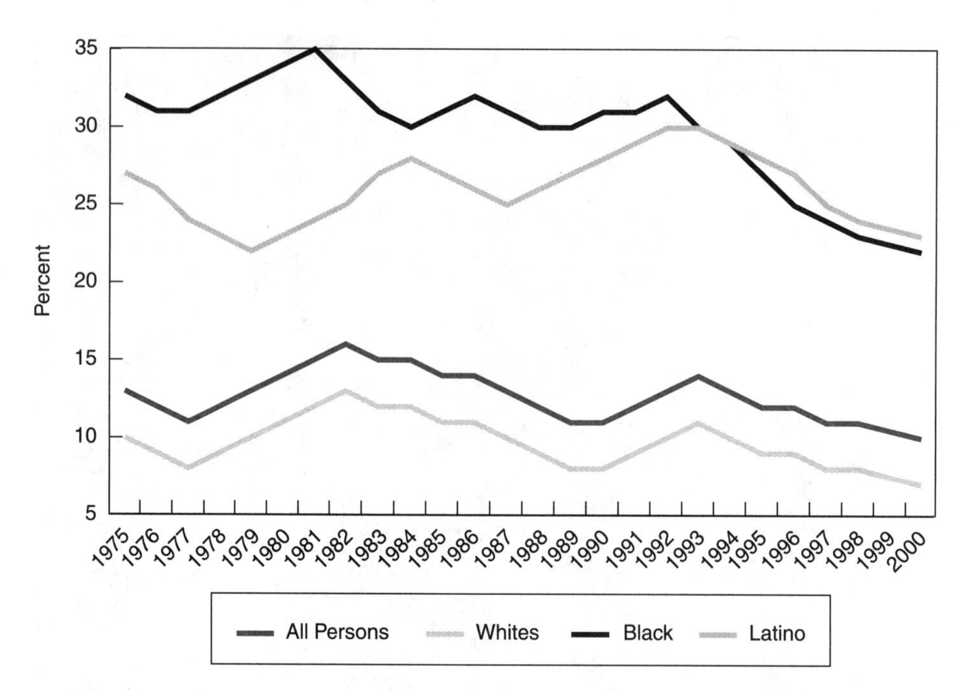

The incidence of poverty is substantially greater for African Americans and Latino Americans, as shown in this figure. Given the current level of prices, the federal government each year calculates a poverty index to consumption needs of families of different sizes. The index reflects only income and does not reflect non-cash benefits received such as food stamps, Medicaid, and public housing. The index is updated each year to reflect changes in the Consumer Price Index (CPI), which measures the level of changes in the prices consumers pay for goods and services. (Thus, the CPI is a measure of inflation in the economy.) The percentages of persons in the United States classified at below the poverty level for all persons and for Whites, African Americans, and Latinos for the years 1975-1999 are shown.

World War II stimulated American industry to full capacity, thus ending the Great Depression. As the health of the American economy improved, some Depression-era programs intended to stimulate employment, like the WPA, were abandoned. The major social programs—like AFDC—were retained to provide a more permanent safety net for classes of poor citizens in the nation. These programs have in recent decades come under scrutiny as reformers argue that new approaches to social welfare programs should be explored.

19-11c Great Society Programs

The next burst of energy in the social welfare field came during the Johnson administration. Under the banner of what he called the Great Society, Democratic president Lyndon Johnson called on the Democratic-controlled Congress to wage a **War on Poverty** by enacting bold new programs in the areas of social welfare and civil rights. The Great Society emerged at an interesting juncture in the nation's history. As the result of World War II, the United States had become one of two dominant world powers and the recognized leader of the free world. The American economy boomed during the postwar period as American industry both supplied Americans with new consumer goods and helped to rebuild the economies of nations devastated by the war. Given its world prominence and healthy economy, Americans became embarrassed when faced with the nation's social problems. Media presentations of poverty in two prominent places—rural areas and inner cities—disconcerted citizens in the world's richest nation, opening a policy window for social policies to be considered and enacted. Americans recognized that the American dream remained only a dream to some Americans who experienced poverty, malnutrition, discrimination, and hopelessness.

> **War on Poverty** *Set of programs including food stamps and urban redevelopment designed by the administration of President Lyndon Johnson and enacted by Congress in the mid-1960s.*

With great fanfare, President Lyndon Johnson announced a series of social programs intended to cope with these problems. One of the hallmarks of the Great Society was the food stamp program, initiated in 1964. This program provides food stamps (paper or electronic vouchers) to persons eligible for the program because of low incomes. Monthly allotments are based on income and family size. The stamps may be used to buy food and nutritional items. More than 20 million Americans received food stamp benefits in 2002. Federal expenditures for the program grew from $12.6 billion in 1985 to $24 billion in 2002.

The food stamp program was seen as promoting two important social goals. First, the program would enhance the nutrition of poor families, thereby enhancing their health and vitality. Second, the program was seen as a boon to American farmers interested in sustaining a strong consumer demand for agricultural products. The program was therefore supported in Congress by two diverse player teams: antipoverty reformers and agricultural interest groups.

Other important initiatives of the Great Society program were tied to health care, an important issue for poor Americans with insufficient money to obtain access to doctors and hospitals. **Medicare** was created to provide federal subsidy of health care services for senior citizens. **Medicaid** was designed with a shared role with the states to provide federal monies to subsidize the health care costs of poor persons. (These two programs are discussed in more detail later in this chapter.)

Medicare *A federal program created in 1965 that subsidizes the health care costs of senior citizens; consists of separate parts covering (a) some of the cost of hospital care for retired and disabled people covered by social security and (b) the costs of physicians' fees for persons 65 or over and disabled social security beneficiaries (who pay the premiums).*

Medicaid *Created in 1965, this program provides funds to subsidize the medical and hospital care of poor persons served though state health programs.*

Another set of social policy initiatives grew out of the Economic Opportunity Act (EOA) of 1964, another component of the Great Society program. Unlike programs that relied upon cash payments, the initiatives of this act stressed bringing people into the workforce and teaching them to help themselves. The basic philosophy of the program is exemplified in its motto: "A hand, not a handout." Among the components of this act were the Job Corps program, designed to provide job training skills to youth, and the Neighborhood Youth Corps, where youth are given part-time jobs and encouraged to remain in school through high school graduation. Still another hallmark of the Economic Opportunity Act was the Head Start program, which provided federal funding for preschool education of children from poor households with the goal of improving educational performance in elementary and secondary schools. Four decades later the program's ability to reach and sustain student enhancement continues to be studied. Still another EOA program was Upward Bound, a program created to help bright but underachieving children from poor families to get into college.

Perhaps the most innovative—and ultimately most controversial—component of the Economic Opportunity Act of 1964 was the Community Action Program (CAP), which provided funds to local community action agencies in poverty-stricken areas around the nation. The fundamental purpose of the CAP was to increase citizen-level involvement in antipoverty programs by increasing citizen participation in program formulation and implementation.

Together, the Great Society programs (food stamps, Medicare and Medicaid, and the equal opportunity initiatives) coupled with those of the New Deal (including AFDC and Social Security) form the heart of America's welfare system. Though these programs are supplemented by some state and local welfare programs, these federally based programs provide the largest proportion of public sector funding to assist disadvantaged persons.

19-11d Policy Mechanisms for Welfare Programs

To understand contemporary welfare policy in the United States and advocate welfare reforms, it is necessary to recognize some important mechanisms used to deliver welfare assistance and services. These include needs tests, entitlement status, and cost-of-living adjustments.

Eligibility and Needs Tests

The purpose of social welfare programs is to help persons with low incomes and those disadvantaged by age or disability. Persons seeking social program benefits are screened for eligibility requirements to determine whether their condition warrants entry into the program. Most social programs have created *needs tests* of economic, age, medical, and other conditions that must be established before individuals are eligible for program benefits. For example, to be eligible for food stamps, an individual cannot have an income or other financial assets that exceed preestablished levels set by the Department of Agriculture.

Establishing that individuals have satisfied needs tests at the point of application requires an extensive bureaucratic organization of workers who study documents and interview potential beneficiaries. These case workers must also monitor those already receiving benefits to ensure that their situation has not so improved that they should move out of assistance programs. Typically, these case workers are employees of local governments, and their salaries are paid by a combination of federal and state government funds. Sometimes, they are employees of nonprofit organizations that have received government contracts to provide welfare services.

Benefits as Entitlements

Most federal social welfare programs—including AFDC and food stamps—operate as *entitlement programs* in which all persons and families who meet the eligibility requirements are entitled under the law to receive benefits. Entitlement programs are favored by disadvantaged people because they can rely on them: If their resources (e.g., income, savings) fall below a certain level, they can count on being able to receive social program benefits. Entitlements are a challenge to administer, however. Neither Congress nor executive branch agencies can precisely predict the number of persons who will satisfy needs tests and qualify for program benefits in a given year. If economic conditions worsen and unemployment rises, then the number of persons seeking to enroll in social programs increases. The opposite happens during periods of strong economic performance.

The true challenge of entitlement programs is being able to provide the budgetary resources to cover program expenditures. Because these social programs operate as entitlements, Congress cannot easily reduce budgetary resources, as it can in nonentitlement programs. The only way to phase back entitlement programs is to remove their entitlement status—that is, by not making benefits automatically available to persons who demonstrate eligibility—or to make eligibility requirements stiffer. Several states, facing budget deficits and heavily mounting social program costs, opted in the early 1990s to tighten eligibility requirements so as to reduce social welfare expenditures.

Cost-of-Living Adjustments

cost-of-living adjustments (COLAs) *Automatic adjustments made to social programs that annually increase benefits according to the Consumer Price Index in order compensate for inflation.*

The financial pinch of entitlement programs is made greater by the automatic provision in some programs for **cost-of-living adjustments**, also known as COLAs. A COLA works by automatically indexing program benefits to keep pace with inflation. COLAs were created in the 1970s, when high inflation eroded the buying power of program benefits that were not raised often enough by Congress to match the inflation rate. COLAs compensate for inflationary effects automatically. COLAs share a problem with entitlements in general: Legal provisions allow program costs to grow automatically, requiring Congress to appropriate more and more funds to cover program expenditures.

19-11e Overhauling the Welfare System: Elements of the Debate

From their inception and through the mid-1990s, the welfare programs of the New Deal and the Great Society continued operation and grew in scope and budgetary expenditures. Increasingly through this period, questions were raised and criticisms were hurled at the set of social welfare programs that had become the "welfare system." Public views about welfare programs also grew more negative, although substantial support remained for truly disadvantaged persons. These questions and criticisms underscore important issues related to values and operational strategies and set the backdrop for the substantial overhaul of the welfare system in the mid-1990s.

As discussed earlier, one important issue surrounding welfare policy in the United States concerns equity. The norm of equity—making things more equal—underlies American social welfare programs. Americans, however, have mixed and sometimes conflicting views about equity. Most Americans accept the norm of equality of opportunity in social policy—the idea that all citizens should have the same chance to enjoy the basic opportunities available in American society, including those provided through social welfare programs. (Chapter 20 explores the history and controversy of affirmative action policies, which have similar goals.)

Americans are more divided about the extent to which government social programs should seek equality of outcome as their ultimate objective. True equality of outcome would mean that government programs would ultimately make all Americans equal in terms of their economic and social circumstances. This type of equity could only be achieved by taking substantial amounts of resources from the wealthier segments of society and distributing them among poorer persons and families.

Redistribution—moving resources from better-off individuals to less fortunate persons—lies at the heart of social programs. Resources are redistributed in a two-part fashion: Wealthier persons and corporations pay more in taxes, which are subsequently used to fund financial payments, health services, and other benefits that are available primarily to poorer individuals. Although most Americans favor some amount of redistribution to help needy persons and families, there is little consensus on just how far redistribution should go. Clearly, there is no agreement that full equality of outcome is warranted. In general, U.S. social policy has taken a "bring the bottom up" approach that does not imply "bringing the top down." Social programs are designed to boost the incomes, food supply, and health care of poorer persons to some minimum standard set by the federal government through laws or regulations issued by administrative agencies.

One criticism that became particularly strong in the mid-1990s was that welfare programs created a system whereby individuals and families become permanent recipients, with little motivation or ability to become self-sufficient. The initial goal of helping people through short personal economic crises has, at least according to critics, turned into a form of permanent financial support. Public welfare, according to this perspective, created dependency; instead of helping people through difficult financial periods, it created a group of welfare recipients who became permanently dependent on program benefits.

19-11f Redesigning the Welfare System

Responding to the long-standing concerns about America's public welfare system, Congress in 1996 took bold action to substantially redesign the nation's welfare program. As enacted by the Congress and signed into law by President Bill Clinton, the welfare overhaul bill eliminated the AFDC program. The new program would no longer provide indefinite support payments to low-income mothers and children. Instead, the federal government would provide each state with a lump sum payment (a block grant) that states can use to design their own state-based welfare programs. States are allowed to use these payments to provide short-term financial support to women and children in poverty. However, those receiving these benefits must begin working within 2 years of receiving aid; those not finding work will no longer receive benefits.

This change in the nation's public welfare system—eliminating AFDC and replacing it with Temporary Assistance for Need Families (TANF)—was a major change in federal policy, the type of change that happens infrequently. Often policy changes occur because of a crisis like a depression or major disaster. Here, however, policy changed because of a growing public dissatisfaction with the AFDC program, a dissatisfaction that was recognized by lawmakers who sensed the public mood and took strong action to reform welfare policy. The long-term impact of welfare reform is now being studied. There is clear evidence that the number of families receiving assistance has decreased significantly. While some see this as a sign of program success, others worry about the plight of families that once received AFDC and are not out of the system. Are these people working? Have they relocated to other areas? Are they successfully working and supporting their families? Answers to these questions will be needed to determine the real policy impact of welfare reform. (See Time Out 19-2: Where Do You Stand on Reforming Welfare Policy? to determine your own views on the issue of welfare reform.)

Besides AFDC, Congress also examined other types of reform in social programs for disadvantaged individuals and families. One target was the food stamp program. Some reformers sought to transform the federal food stamp program, operating as an entitlement, into

Time Out 19-2

Where Do You Stand on Reforming Welfare Policy?

Much discussion of welfare reform involves the desire to move people from being on welfare into participating in the job market. Decide which response to the following question best reflects your view of government's role in this process, and you can then read on to the Answers to Time Out 19-2 to see who among the public tends to agree and disagree with you.

> Some people feel the government in Washington should see to it that every person has a job and a good standard of living. Others think the government should just let each person get ahead on their own. Which is closer to the way you feel?
>
> Government should see to it that people have jobs.
>
> Government should let person get ahead on their own.

Figure 19-5
Private Charity Giving in the United States

Source: U.S. Bureau of the Census, *Statistical Abstract of the United States* Washington, D.C., GPO, 2000, Table 639, p. 397.

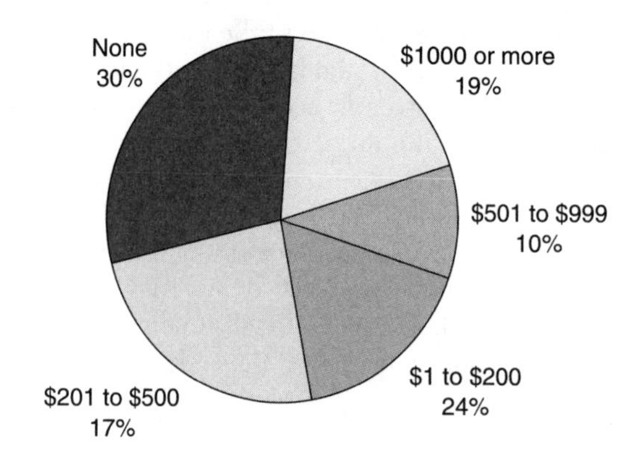

another block grant to states—similar in nature to the reformed welfare program. This more radical plan was abandoned under political pressure. Instead, Congress decided to give states more flexibility in program operations and to cut future spending on food stamps.

Overhauling the nation's social welfare system proved to be a very ambitious task. This overhaul was stimulated both by fiscal pressures and by the desire to change the system to encourage more employment, job training, and self-sufficiency among the individuals and families that had been receiving welfare assistance. Strategies for reform included transforming categorical entitlement programs into block grants to states, limiting benefits, making eligibility more strict, and significantly reducing federal spending commitments (see Time Out 19-3: Where Do You Stand? Post-Reform Opinion on Welfare Spending). Conservatives took the lead in introducing policy reforms, with key legislators serving as policy entrepreneurs working to push reforms through policy formulation and enactment.

Cumulatively, these reforms have fundamentally changed the delivery of welfare services in America. States now have a larger role in designing and implementing programs as the result of the transformation of categorical grant into block grants (as with AFDC) and the granting of more flexibility for operating federal entitlement programs (as with food stamps). The American welfare system will become more decentralized and more diverse, as standard federal requirements and formulas are replaced by state-based programs and operating procedures. The size of government expenditures on welfare programs will also drop, meaning reduced benefits and fewer beneficiaries. With cutbacks in public spending on welfare programs, it is likely that private charities, religious and nonprofit, may play a larger role in aiding people in poverty (see Figure 19-5 for a description of charity giving by American households).

Time Out 19-3

Where Do You Stand? Post-Reform Opinion on Welfare Spending

Choose the response to the following question that best reflects your view, and you will have a chance to see who among the public tends to agree and disagree with you in Answers to Time Out 19-3.

> **If you had a say in making up the federal budget this year, would you say that federal spending on welfare programs should be increased, decreased, or kept about the same?**
>
> **-Increased**
>
> **-Kept the same**
>
> **-Decreased**

19-12 Social Security and Retirement Benefits

A major social program in the United States is Social Security, a program that provides retirement benefits to Americans. This retirement system, sometimes known as *social insurance*, was set up as part of the Social Security Act of 1935.[17] The bank failures that occurred during the Great Depression of the 1930s had brought to public attention another problem facing many Americans: insufficient funds for retirement. Although some workers—particularly those represented by labor unions—received private pensions through their employers, many others had to rely on personal savings or investments to make ends meet after retirement. The Depression wiped out the savings of innumerable senior citizens, throwing many of them into poverty.

A system of social insurance had been advocated for some time prior to the Depression, but there was insufficient public support for a governmental system of retirement benefits. The economic crisis enabled Congress to take bold action in creating the Social Security program. The basic philosophy of the program was borrowed from other nations, including Germany, where social insurance provided protection against wage loss due to injury and disability, as well as distributing retirement benefits based on past earnings. The 1935 Social Security Act created a nationwide, federally administered, compulsory system where all but a few exempt workers contribute money into the system and then draw retirement benefits from it upon retirement.

The 1935 act created the Old Age, Survivors and Disabled Insurance (OASDI) program—what people generally refer to as Social Security. The program provides monthly cash payments to retired and disabled workers, to their spouses and children, and to survivors of insured persons. OASDI covers 93% of the U.S. workforce. In the Social Security system, both workers and employers make contributions that are deposited in the Social Security Trust Fund. In 2004 the contributions by employees and employers represented 6.2% of the first $87,900 of earnings. Workers who have worked a sufficient amount of time during their lifetimes, as well as their spouses and dependents, are eligible to draw benefits any time after they reach the age of 62. An amendment to the act in 1972 established an automatic annual cost-of-living adjustment so that benefits increase each year to keep pace with inflation.

Social Security today represents one of the federal government's largest social programs in terms of expenditures. In 2003, over 192 million Americans were enrolled in Social Security and over 29 million retired workers received Social Security payments.

Answers to Time Out 19-2

If you agreed that the government should see to it that people have jobs, you're among the minority. Based on the 2000 National Election Study, 29% of the respondents supported government job provision. The types of people most likely to agree with your support of government job provision were:

	(percent **supporting** government job provision)
Democrats	45%
Liberals	43%
People under 30 years of age	37%
Females	33%
People 30–49 years of age	30%
Independents	30%
NATIONAL AVERAGE	29%

If you feel that the government should let each person get ahead on their own, you have lots of company. Based on the National Election Study for the 2000 election, 72% of the respondents opposed government job provision. The types of people most likely to agree with your lack of support of government job provision were:

	(percent **opposing** government job provision)
Republicans	90%
Conservatives	87%
Moderates	80%
Males	76%
People over 50 years of age	75%
NATIONAL AVERAGE	72%

Maintaining the flow of revenues into the trust fund adequately enough to cover payout to beneficiaries has been a persistent problem for the Social Security system. Private pension plans typically invest employee and employer contributions in pension funds that yield returns that can be used to cover benefit payout. The Social Security Trust Fund works differently. The fund takes in current employee and employer contributions and uses them to cover the Social Security checks sent each month to residents. Sometimes the fund runs a surplus, however, as the baby boomer generation moves into retirement, the system will again face substantial strain, as it has during other periods in the past.

Social Security has become a major component of the income of most retired Americans. Given its importance, these players work diligently to protect Social Security from budget cuts that might reduce benefits or reduce the anticipated level of annual benefit increases. The American Association of Retired Persons (AARP) is among the active interest groups (see Chapter 7) fighting diligently to protect the Social Security system from any reforms that might reduce benefits. The effectiveness of interest groups like AARP is enhanced by the fact that senior citizens are often active voters, which means they wield political clout in Congress.

Financing Social Security remains a perplexing problem. The primary difficulty is that Social Security was designed as a consumption-based rather than a savings-based program. In private retirement programs, individuals contribute moneys (oftentimes with accompanying contributions from employers) into funds that are invested. At retirement, people can draw upon their investment plus the interest that has accrued upon it. Social Security in the United States does not work this way, and many Americans do not understand this. Currently, Social Security works by each generation of workers paying taxes into a fund to support the previous generation that is retired under the promise that the next generation will then support it.[18]

This system only works so long as there are consistent generations of about the same size contributing to the Social Security fund. Today, there are about 3.2 workers paying Social Security taxes for each retired person. In earlier times this ratio was much higher. An upcoming problem is the baby boomer generation—a large demographic group that

Answers to Time Out 19-3

If you said increased or kept the same, you share the majority opinion. Based on the 2000 National Election Study, 62% of the respondents supported welfare spending by indicating that spending should be increased (17%) or kept the same (45%). Remember that prior to reform almost two-thirds of Americans felt we were spending too much. The types of people most likely to agree with your support of welfare spending were:

	(percent **supporting** maintaining or increasing welfare spending)
Liberals	85%
Democrats	71%
People over 50 years of age	66%
Females	64%
People under 30 years of age	63%
Independents	63%
Moderates	63%
NATIONAL AVERAGE	62%

If you said decreased, you share the minority opinion. Based on the National Election Study for the 2000 election, 38% of the respondents supported cuts in welfare spending. Remember that prior to the 1995 reforms, almost two-thirds of Americans felt spending should be cut. The types of people most likely to agree with your lack of support of welfare spending were:

	(percent **supporting** welfare spending cuts)
Conservatives	54%
Republicans	51%
People 30–49 years of age	43%
Males	40%
NATIONAL AVERAGE	38%

will upset the balance of generational payments into the Social Security system. When baby boomers retire, there will be fewer than 3 contributors per retiree. It is estimated that without reforms, by the midpoint of the 21st century, Social Security will begin running a deficit; within 18 years after that, the system will be bankrupt.

There is widespread agreement that a financial crisis in Social Security looms in the future. At the same time, that future is a bit far off, allowing policy makers some time to find a solution to the problem. The solution is not likely to be easy, however. Seniors are politically active and have great financial stakes in sustaining the program without benefit cuts. And, the proportion of the population that is over age 65 continues to grow, enhancing the political clout of seniors. Given more immediate concerns about eliminating the budget deficit, reformulating the welfare system, and overhauling health care in the U.S., Social Security is not on the immediate policy agenda of reformers. What this means is that significant reform of the Social Security system remains a topic for future political games.

19-13 Health Care Policy

Health care is another area of social policy that underwent substantial evolution in the 20th century. Public sector involvement has moved from a very limited role at the start of the century to a very substantial one today. Americans have one of the finest health care systems in the world, but that system is in substantial crisis.

19-13a Health Care: Promise and Crisis

The good news is that the United States has a quality health care system that has the amazing capacity to increase life expectancy and the quality of life of Americans. The bad news is that, by practically all accounts, the American health care system is on the critical list.

The crisis arises primarily from cost. In the past two decades, health care costs began to rise far more rapidly than the rate of inflation. Workers and others with health insurance find their premiums rising each year and their coverage being reduced. The problem is obviously even more severe for the millions of Americans who have *no* health insurance to cover the costs of medical care. To understand the contemporary crisis, one needs to follow the evolution of health care policy.

19-13b The Evolution of Federal Involvement in Health Care

In the early days of the nation's history, Americans relied upon themselves for health care. As medical science and practice advanced, people became more reliant upon doctors and hospitals for their care and upon pharmacies for their medicines. Often Americans paid for services and medicines out of their own pockets. Recognizing the importance of appropriate health care, reformers at the beginning of the century began arguing for public sector financing of health care costs under the banner of national health insurance. Although major programs like Social Security and AFDC were created, President Roosevelt and the New Dealers stayed away from proposing a national health care system. In part, they feared the reaction of doctors and their primary representative organization, the American Medical Association,[19] whose opposition might stop not simply the new health care system but also other New Deal initiatives.

The health reform idea did not wither, however. President Harry Truman proposed a national health insurance plan as part of his 1948 election campaign. Unfortunately, his plan ran into ideological problems. Opponents linked national health insurance to socialism and communism; the phrase *socialized medicine* was frequently used. The political doctrines of socialism and communism were feared and despised by Americans in the late 1940s, dooming action on Truman's plan

19-13c Medicare and Medicaid

The time for a substantial federal government role in financing health care came during the 1960s as part of the Great Society program. While there was still little support for a system of national health insurance covering all Americans, there was sufficient support to create two important new health programs targeted at two classes of Americans: senior citizens and poor people.

The Medicare program, which originated during the Johnson administration, subsidizes the health care costs of the elderly. Medicare consists of two parts. Through Part A of the program, the federal government pays for part of the cost of hospital care for retired and disabled people covered by Social Security. Like Social Security, employers and employees pay payroll taxes to support the program (1.45% of earnings). Part B is a voluntary system of medical insurance that covers the costs of physician fees for persons 65 or over and disabled Social Security beneficiaries who pay the premiums.

Medicare has become a significant program for senior citizens, who work to guard this program almost as fiercely as they do Social Security. In 2001, over 40 million Americans received Medicare benefits that accounted for more than $240 billion in federal expenditures. The importance of Medicare to the nation was demonstrated in a national public opinion poll that showed that Americans followed news stories about possible reductions in Medicare spending more often than they followed other news stories about the health of the economy, the civil war in Bosnia, budget reduction resolutions in Congress, and the O.J. Simpson trial.[20]

A second major federal health insurance program is Medicaid, also created in 1965. This program provides federal funds to help pay for the medical and hospital care of poor persons served though state health programs. The percentage of state program expenditures that are covered by the federal government varies according to a formula based on a state's per capita income. The federal share ranges from 50% for wealthier states like New York to over 75% in Mississippi, West Virginia, and Utah.

Along with TANF and food stamps, the Medicaid program is one of the major federal programs that provide assistance to poor individuals and families. In 2003, the Medicaid program spent more than $256 billion on the health care of over 41 million low-income women, children, elderly, blind, and disabled Americans.[21] Medicaid coverage extends from newborn children in poor families to nursing home care for elderly people who have exhausted their personal savings.

19-13d Growing Pressures for Health Care Reform

Medicare and Medicaid have substantially increased the access of senior citizens, poor people, and disabled Americans to American health care. They did not, however, ensure that all Americans can afford health care. From the Great Society years through the early 1990s, several realities about American health care became apparent. First, medical and technological innovations continued, resulting in an enhanced capability to save lives and improve the overall health of Americans. Second, and more prominently, however, health care is more expensive each year, which threatens to reduce access to health care. From 1965 to the 1990s, Americans paid more for health care than did the citizens of other advanced industrial nations. The percentage of the national economy devoted to health continues to increase and outpace the rate of inflation. Health care costs loom as a major political issue in the United States, one that received significant attention in the 2004 presidential campaign.

Rising health care costs put many types of pressure on the health care system, pressures that sent shock waves through the political world. Increased federal expenditures on Medicare and Medicaid contributed to escalating federal government spending and budget deficits. Cost pressures were also felt by individual Americans. Those with private health insurance, mostly obtained through employment-based programs, saw their required contributions leap upward at the same time that insurance benefits were being restricted by companies seeking to pass along costs to employees. Americans without any health insurance often face even more dire circumstances, with rapidly increasing costs reducing their potential to receive health care. In 2001, just under 15% of the U.S. population (41.2 million Americans) had no health insurance. (See Time Out 19-4: Where Do You Stand on Health Care Costs? to assess your views on health insurance.)

Concerns about health care costs and access to the health care system operated as major stimulants for governmental action. Pressure was put on the federal government to find a solution to what was commonly termed the "health care crisis." Employers wanted relief from ever-escalating costs of health insurance benefits; employees with insurance wanted an end to ever-growing premium payments. The federal, state, and

Where Do You Stand on Health Care Costs?

Time Out 19-4

Choose the response to the following question that best reflects your view, and you will have a chance to see who among the public tends to agree and disagree with you as you read on to the Answers to Time Out 19-4.

There is much concern about the rapid rise in medical and hospital costs. Some people feel that all medical costs should be paid by individuals through private insurance. Others feel there should be a government insurance plan that would cover all medical and hospital expenses for everyone. Which is closer to the way you feel?

-There should be a government insurance plan.

-Individuals should pay through private insurance.

Answers to Time Out 19-4

If you said you are in favor of governmental insurance, you're in the minority. Based on the 2000 National Election Study, 37% of the respondents supported government medical insurance. The types of people most likely to agree with your support of government medical insurance were:

	(percent **supporting** government medical insurance)
Liberals	49%
Democrats	46%
Independents	41%
Moderates	39%
People under 30 years of age	38%
People over 50 years of age	38%
Females	38%
NATIONAL AVERAGE	37%

If you said you are in favor of self-insurance through private companies, you're part of the majority. Based on the National Election Study for the 2000 election, 62% of the respondents opposed government medical insurance. The types of people most likely to agree with your lack of support of government medical insurance were:

	(percent **opposing** government medical insurance)
Republicans	82%
Conservatives	80%
People 30–49 years of age	64%
Males	65%
NATIONAL AVERAGE	62%

local governments wanted to hold the line on public-sector expenditures on health care for poor and other disadvantaged Americans.

The Clinton Health Care Plan

As the 1992 Democratic presidential candidate, Bill Clinton pledged to bring about health care reform. Such a pledge seemed to make sense, given repeated public opinion polls that showed Americans favored some form of government-funded national health insurance program.[22] Clinton followed through on his campaign pledge very early in his administration by creating a Task Force on National Health Care Reform. Perhaps signaling the importance of this task force, Clinton named his wife, Hillary Rodham Clinton, as its head.

Throughout 1994, the Congress debated health care reform. Given the breadth of proposed change, the bill was considered in multiple Congressional committees, including three in the House of Representatives and two in the Senate. Although there was substantial support for the general idea of change and reform in the American health care system, consensus quickly disappeared about the appropriate means to implement reform. Several factors account for the collapse of health care reform that was a strong blow to the Clinton presidency. First, the change embraced in the Clinton welfare reform package was substantial and the complexity of the arrangements for the new system was immense. Except in times of dire emergency, American public policy is often incremental in nature. Policy change is usually relatively small, and policy innovations normally represent relatively minor changes from past policies. Despite public perceptions about a health care crisis, the proposed plan was too sweeping and complicated to obtain support either from the public or from relevant interest groups. None of the affected players could be sure how they would fare under the reform, but they could see the possibility of being substantially worse off. Ultimately, the "devil was in the details."

19-13e Health Care Reform: A Perennial Issue

Public concerns about health care and pressures for legislative and political action are unquestionably part of American politics as we enter the 21st century. After health care cost increases were slowed during the 1990s, they began to show significant increases by 2000. New and expensive technologies and increasing access to health care are driving up costs faster than the rate of inflation. This puts pressures on private and public employers to raise the premiums they pay for their share of total medical insurance costs, thus putting direct financial pressure on American families. This pressure will create new political pressure for the government to either control health care costs or increase public sector expenditures to cover those costs. One hopeful sign in health care cost reduction is the use of technology to make operations more efficient and to track and reduce fraud.

19-14 The Federal Government and Education

Education has historically been of great importance to Americans. Education can be viewed as a type of social policy because it contributes to equality of opportunity in America. It allows people to achieve personal goals, economic independence, and occupational preferences. It allows people to find employment, become self-sufficient, and avoid participation in social welfare programs.

Given consistent public support of education and the magnitude of federal government involvement in many areas of social policy, it often surprises Americans to learn that the federal government's role in education policy is relatively limited. By custom and tradition, education is largely a state and local matter (see Chapter 18). Public and elementary schools are governed by school boards that operate as special-purpose units of government; currently there are over 14,500 school districts across the 50 states. These boards are responsible for hiring teachers and principals, building and maintaining schools, and developing policies to manage the schools. School districts raise funds to support public schools primarily through property taxes levied on residents of the district. Over time, state governments have assumed a large role in public education by providing substantial amounts of state aid to support schools. Often this aid is allocated by a formula that provides greater state assistance to poorer school districts, thereby working toward equalizing per-pupil spending for public education. Most states also mandate a variety of measures concerning public education, most notably setting state standards and guidelines for the curriculum of each year of elementary and secondary education. States have played a large role in post-high school education by providing a set of higher education institutions. These include community colleges that offer 2-year degrees, baccalaureate schools with 4-year degrees, and major state universities that offer both undergraduate and graduate degrees. The states subsidize the costs of college education by contributing state revenues toward the operations of colleges and universities. In recent years, facing large budgetary pressures, many states have reduced the level of subsidy, thereby causing colleges and universities to raise tuition to cover expenses.

Federal government involvement in education has grown and is focused on particular areas of education and on particular groups of students. Federal aid to education can be traced back to the Civil War and the Morrill Act of 1862. Through this act Congress provided a generous grant of public lands to the states for support of education, stimulating the creation of land-grant colleges as part of state universities. Land-grant colleges pledged to perform certain services, initially including military training. In 1887 Congress passed legislation to give federal monies to land-grant universities to support agricultural experimental stations. Land-grant colleges—such as Purdue University in Indiana and the University of Wisconsin—today continue to provide substantial training and research in many fields including a continued focus on agriculture and farming.

During the 1960s, the federal government created a variety of new education programs, representing the most prominent federal move into public education. These initiatives were intended to enhance educational opportunities for disadvantaged students and fight racial and other forms of discrimination. Major federal laws concerning education include:

- *Head Start*, created as part of the Great Society, provided federal funding to support the education of preschool children from disadvantaged backgrounds. Early education was seen as a means to enhance the achievement of these children as they move through elementary and secondary education.
- *The Civil Rights Act of 1964* prohibited the federal government from giving financial aid to school districts that are segregated and that have not adopted effective plans to become integrated.
- *The Elementary and Secondary Education Act of 1965* provided school districts with monies to help poor children prepare for entering school and receive extra help in the classroom after they have enrolled.
- *The Education of All Handicapped Children Act of 1975* requires that school districts receiving federal funds provide all children with physical or mental disabilities with a "free and appropriate" education, including education instruction targeted to their individual needs.

Together, these programs provide local school districts with resources to operate specialized programs to aid disadvantaged children. They supplement the full range of educational programming provided in schools and financed by state and local governments.

Concerns about the performance of children in America's public schools created a policy window through which substantial reform of the national government was first debated in Congress and then enacted into law in 2001. The reform is embodied in the "No Child Left Behind Act," legislation strongly supported by President George W. Bush, and represents the strongest effort to date by the national government to assume a powerful role in elementary and secondary education—a policy area long seen as primarily a state and local government function. The No Child Left Behind Act received bipartisan support in Congress as lawmakers recognized that the educational achievement of American youth was lagging behind that of other nations, despite billions of dollars in federal support for schools.

The No Child Left Behind Act focuses on four policy strategies intended to improve the educational achievement and graduation rates of America's children. These include: (1) stronger accountability of schools for the performance of their students; (2) more flexibility for states and school districts in spending national government funds, (3) more choices about schools for parents of disadvantaged children, and (4) placing of stronger emphasis on teacher methods that have been demonstrated to work in educating students. State and local school districts are working to interpret these new policies and formulate strategies and programs to implement them. Substantial attention will be placed by federal, state, and local officials on the impact of this policy reform on the educational achievement of elementary and secondary students in the United States.

Box 19–2 No Child Left Behind

The U.S. Department of Education has created a web-based "desktop reference" for the No Child Left Behind program at www.ed.gov/offices/OESE/reference.html. Through this website you can learn about all of the features in this comprehensive piece of legislation, including plans for 21st century schools.

19-15 The Federal Government and Regulation

Federal government policies do more than provide benefits, services, and assistance to targeted groups of people and businesses. As described earlier, the federal government also regulates the behaviors of people, corporations, and government itself. Regulation is pursued through two basic strategies:

- prescribing actions that must be performed (for example, paying taxes or providing occupational safety in the workplace), and
- prohibiting or restricting behaviors or actions (for example, prohibiting the use of DDT as a pesticide or banning the sale of unsafe products or spoiled meat).

We will now examine key federal regulatory policies, beginning with an exploration of the many federal government roles in the economy. These roles are wide-ranging and include the regulation of the banking and securities industries. The federal government also engages in broad-based strategies to encourage economic growth and curb factors harmful to prosperity and a sound economy.

As we have seen, notably in the discussion of American cultural values in Chapter 5, the political system and the economic system are intertwined. Respect for private property rights—and an extension of these into free enterprise and **capitalism**—are values that underlie government and politics in the United States. The lion's share of federal regulatory policies focus on economic matters or on areas where the free marketplace has failed to properly balance business interests with the public good, health, and safety. Government regulations, as we shall see, help to achieve such objectives as promoting competition over monopoly power, sustaining economic growth without large increases in prices, and protecting consumer safety.

capitalism *An economic system based on the widespread private ownership of the means of production and trade, combined with an unrestricted marketplace for goods and services.*

Environmental policy is another important regulatory area. These policies—intended to reduce air pollution, clean up rivers and lakes, and protect natural beauty for future generations—are relatively new to the game of American politics. Policies for environmental protection have often generated substantial political debate during policy formation and implementation because they can severely limit the actions of individuals and firms. These policies can also require substantial monies to achieve compliance with environmental mandates. For these reasons, environmental policies have been recently a primary target of conservatives who seek to scale back the regulatory power of the federal government.

19-16 Regulatory Strategies and Players

The regulatory policies formulated by Congress and enforced by agencies within the executive branch of the federal government have been designed with multiple strategies. At a minimum, effective regulatory policies require the following:

- formulation of clear and workable regulatory standards that outline what actions are prohibited and/or what activities are required, as well as achievement levels where applicable,
- continuous monitoring of the behaviors of regulated people and organizations to identify noncompliance, and
- enforcement via the imposition of sanctions or incentives (and sometimes warnings for first offenses) when regulatory rules and standards are violated.

Many types of players have a stake in the creation and enforcement of the federal government's regulatory policies. While they can be classified in several ways, most fall within two important categories: regulated beneficiaries and regulated parties. Each of these two sets of players has its advocates, in terms of lobbyists, special interest groups, and governmental policy makers and regulation enforcers.

The individuals or organizations that directly benefit from the enforcement of regulatory requirements are known as *regulated beneficiaries*.[23] Sometimes, the beneficiaries are a relatively small group of people; some regulatory policies, for example, are designed to regulate hazardous materials that are used only in a limited number of research facilities. More often, the beneficiaries of regulatory policies are widespread and may even include future generations. The beneficiaries of occupational safety requirements are workers across the nation in industrial firms. The beneficiaries of restrictions on offshore drilling include coastal residents and others who enjoy the recreational opportunities of the nation's coastline. The beneficiaries of governmental regulations can be expected to take action to protect, or even expand, the policies from which they benefit.

Another set of players are those who are actually regulated by the government—that is, the persons and organizations whose behavior is restricted or directed by the government. These players are called the *regulated parties*. Sometimes regulated parties are individuals and families; this is the case with mandatory household recycling required by state or local governments across the nation as the result of federal solid waste management policies.

A frequent target of federal government regulations are business corporations. The federal government, for example, issues restrictions on logging in national forests, allocates broadcasting frequencies to radio and television stations, and makes stipulations about the disposal of industrial wastes. Businesses are often displeased with federal government regulation that limits the activities they can undertake in pursuit of corporate profits. Complying with regulations often entails substantial costs. The battle cry of the private sector in recent years has been for *regulatory relief*, the relaxation or elimination of federal regulations on business and industry. Businesses and other regulated parties—often represented by national associations and lobbying groups—often work through the political process to achieve regulatory relief.

Another set of regulated parties are governments themselves. For example, Congress has mandated regulatory requirements on agencies of the federal government that, for example, require safe workplaces and affirmative action to employ women, minorities, and people with disabilities (see Chapter 16). Congress has also created a series of mandates for state and local governments—mandates often enforced with the threat of reductions in federal funds (see Chapters 3 and 18). For example, state and local governments are required by the Americans with Disabilities Act to provide facilities and transit systems that are accessible to people with mental or physical disabilities.

19-17 Economic Policy

The federal government influences the nation's economic health through a variety of players, agencies, and policies. The economic policy activities of the federal government include federal spending, setting monetary policy, and regulation of the banking and securities industries.

19-17a The Politics and Realities of Economic Performance

gross domestic product (GDP) *The monetary value of all goods and services produced in a nation in a given year. Important indicator of economic performance.*

inflation *The rate at which the costs of goods and services increase or an economic period where prices are rising relatively, rapidly eroding purchasing power.*

Perhaps the most widely regarded measure of economic performance and growth in the United States is the **gross domestic product (GDP)**, a statistic reported quarterly and annually by the U.S. Department of Commerce. The GDP is the monetary value of all goods and services produced within the nation. Changes in the GDP indicate the level of growth or decline in the national economy (see Figure 19-6).

Americans commonly hold the president and Congress responsible for the nation's economic performance. Indeed, public opinion about the president's performance is closely linked to the nation's economic health. If unemployment swells, or prices rise rapidly (**inflation**), or economic downturn threatens jobs or earnings, Americans become unhappy. Often, they direct their dissatisfaction at the politicians in Washington, who are expected to take steps to improve economic conditions. President George H. Bush was defeated in his bid for reelection in 1992 partly because of voter dissatisfaction with the performance of the American economy.

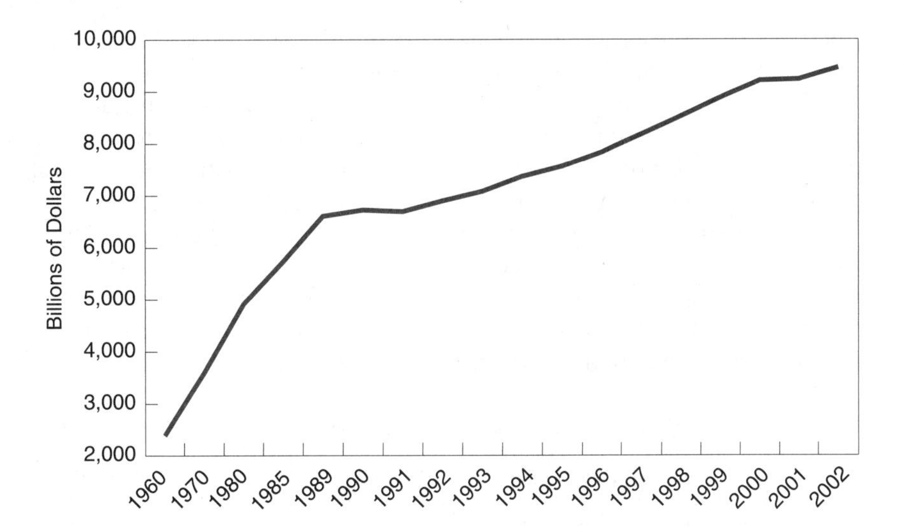

Figure 19-6
U.S. Gross Domestic Product, 1960–2002

The Gross Domestic Product (GDP), reflecting overall growth in the American economy, increases each year as the result of real growth and price increases. The figure shows GDP for the period 1960–2002, controlling for the impact of inflation by expressing figures converted into constant 1996 dollars.

Source: U.S. Bureau of the Census, *Statistical Abstract of the United States* (Washington, D.C.: GPO, 2003), Table 659, p. 438.

In reality, the ability of political players to direct the economy is limited. The American economy, based on a mixture of capitalism and government regulation, arises from the decisions of millions of economic players. Individual consumers influence the economy through their decisions about spending and saving, while corporations influence economic vitality through their decisions about hiring workers, purchasing raw materials, and setting production levels. Banks and financial institutions make lending decisions that allow businesses to expand and consumers to purchase on credit. In addition, decisions made outside of the United States, including those of foreign investors and of foreign companies seeking to export their products to the United States, also contribute to the overall health of the national economy. Therefore, the overall vitality of the economy depends upon the whole set of decisions made by a wide variety of economic players—it is not under the complete control of government leaders or any other small set of players. The federal government represents only one set of players who seek to influence the American economy. Efforts to regulate the economic life of the nation have evolved over centuries, with the public sector playing an increasingly important role.

19-17b From Laissez-Faire to Economic Regulation: Historic Overview

For roughly the first century of American history, the nation's economy operated primarily according to the doctrine of **laissez-faire**. This doctrine, articulated by English economist Adam Smith in the late 18th century, holds that private companies and firms should be "left alone" (free from government intervention) to make decisions about investment, production, and distribution of produced goods.[24] The laissez-faire doctrine fit nicely with traditional American values of individualism, private property, and limited government.

laissez-faire *The economic doctrine, often associated with economist Adam Smith, that holds that individuals and companies should be free to make decisions about investment, production, and distribution without government interference.*

Antitrust and Restraint of Trade

Unrestrained capitalism over time has caused several economic and political problems that the market was unable itself to rectify. Beginning in the late 1800s, the federal government took its first substantial step to regulate a portion of the American economy through enactment of the Sherman Antitrust Act (1890). This important legislation sought to prevent private companies from engaging in restraint of trade. **Antitrust policies** were aimed at breaking up monopolies and oligopolies (industries where production is controlled by one or a few major producers). Monopolies and oligopolies threaten economic efficiency through their ability to control prices and generate excessive profits.[25] After passage of the Sherman Antritrust Act, large monopolies were broken up into smaller, separate companies

antitrust policies *Federal government policies that seek to sustain competition in the economy by breaking up or regulating monopolistic industries.*

(for example, the Standard Oil Company was divided into such well-known companies as ARCO, Amoco, Sohio, Boron, and several others).

Today, the federal government—and particularly the Federal Trade Commission (FTC) and Department of Justice—continue to monitor monopoly power and restraint of trade. It monitors proposed mergers of companies and sometimes refuses to allow companies to combine when their merger would substantially harm competition. The government-imposed breakup of the mammoth American Telephone and Telegraph Company (AT&T) into a series of regional "baby bell" companies is the one prominent example of antitrust policy in action in the past 30 years.[26] Another example is the antitrust lawsuit filed against Microsoft concerning its control over operating software affecting a large proportion of personal and business computers.

Financial Institutions Become Regulated

The largest economic upheaval in the United States, the Great Depression, which began in 1929 and lasted almost a decade, stimulated a stronger federal role in managing the economy. The dual objectives of this federal involvement, championed by President Franklin D. Roosevelt, were to stimulate the economy and to regulate banking and security practices. It was clear at the time that unwise banking practices and uncontrolled sales of stocks and bonds contributed to the massive decline of the American stock market, which sparked the depression that followed.

During the early 1930s, Congress, at the request of President Roosevelt, created agencies to regulate the activities of banks and other financial institutions that broker stocks, bonds, and other securities. The Federal Deposit Insurance Corporation (FDIC) and the Federal Savings and Loan Insurance Corporation (FSLIC) were created in 1933 to protect savings deposited with financial institutions. Both the FDIC and FSLIC were called upon to provide funds to protect the savings of depositors in failed banks and thrift institutions during the late 1980s and early 1990s. These separate government agencies, which once maintained huge surpluses, faced the prospect of running out of funds during the height of the financial crisis and had to be provided with additional federal funds.

The Securities and Exchange Commission (SEC) was created in 1934 to oversee and regulate the advertisement, sale, and distribution of stocks, bonds, and other securities. This agency was designed to prevent abuses in the sale of stocks and bonds that contributed to the stock market crash of 1929.

19-17c Monetary Policy: Credit, Money Supply, and Interest Rates

Since the Depression, when the laissez-faire doctrine was largely abandoned in favor of a stronger government role in the economy, the federal government has used multiple strategies to enhance the nation's economic performance. When the nation faces economic downturns, the federal government seeks ways to speed up the economy and increase employment. When the economy becomes "overheated"—plagued by high levels of inflation—the federal government seeks to slow spiraling price increases. Inflation harms consumers by requiring that they pay more for goods and services. If their paychecks do not increase at the rate of price increases, then spending power is reduced.

Remember that federal policy makers do not have total control over the economy. They do have, however, two basic strategies to influence economic performance: monetary policy and fiscal policy. The logic behind **monetary policy** is that economic growth and stability are significantly influenced by:

monetary policies *Federal government policies designed to maintain economic growth and stability through control of the money supply, interest rates, and credit.*

- the amount of money in circulation,
- interest rates, and
- the functioning of credit markets and the banking system.

Economists have observed that when there is more money in circulation, consumers will spend more. This spending tends to drive up the prices of goods and services and to increase their production. When there is less money in circulation, consumers spend less and production tends to decline. Having the proper amount of money circulating in the economy is what monetary policy is all about.

Monetary policy also includes influences on credit—the ability to borrow money. Consumers rely on credit when they borrow money to buy a new home or car. Businesses use credit to build new factories, expand production facilities, or install modern production equipment—developments that generally increase private sector employment. The cost of obtaining credit—known generally as interest rates—influences the amount of credit that consumers and businesses can afford. When interest rates are low, the costs of borrowing are low, and people and firms are more likely to use credit. When the opposite is true—where interest rates are high—borrowing declines, consumers purchase less, and businesses defer production expansion. For these reasons, lower interest rates work to stimulate the economy and higher interest rates slow the economy down. Therefore, by influencing interest rates, the federal government uses monetary policy to influence economic performance.

The primary vehicle for orchestrating federal monetary policies is the Federal Reserve System, which is managed by the Federal Reserve Board (often referred to as "the Fed"). In response to fears of a repetition of a financial panic that occurred in 1907, it was created in 1913 to regulate the supply of money and credit in the United States. The Federal Reserve System is composed of 12 Federal Reserve Banks located across the United States. All national and many state banks are members of the Federal Reserve Bank in their district. The 12 banks keep deposits for member banks, supply currency and coins, and operate check clearinghouses.

The Federal Reserve Board is an independent agency managed by a board of governors—7 members who are selected for nonrenewable 14-year terms. The president appoints the governors, who must receive Senate confirmation. From among the 7 governors, the President also appoints a chair and a vice chair, who serve 4-year terms and may be reappointed. The Senate must confirm the appointments to these 2 leadership positions. The chair of the Federal Reserve Board is regarded as a prominent figure in national politics and frequently is called upon to report on economic conditions and the status of federal monetary policies.

The Fed regulates (but does not completely control) the money supply, the interest rates charged by banks and financial institutions, and the banking industry through the sale of government securities, financial reserves banks are required to maintain, and the rate at which member banks can borrow from Federal Reserve Banks to cover their cash needs. Discount rates influence the rates that banks charge their borrowers, thereby raising or lowering the interest rates that banks charge their customers.

The coordination of these 3 policies influences the availability of money and credit, which, in turn, influences economic growth. When the economy is in **recession**—characterized by negative economic growth and increased unemployment—the Fed uses its control over monetary policy to encourage growth by lowering discount rates and reserve requirements. These actions make it easier for individuals and corporations to borrow for spending or business development, activities that stimulate the economy.

recession *An economic period characterized by negative economic growth and unemployment.*

The opposite monetary approach is appropriate when coping with inflation; in this situation, the Fed is likely to raise discount rates and reserve requirements. These actions raise interest rates and the cost of borrowing money, making it more expensive to borrow. This makes borrowing funds less attractive to consumers and businesses, which slows the economy and, the Federal Reserve Board hopes, the rate of price increases.

Because of the Fed's critical role in managing the economy, its decisions receive extensive scrutiny from the media, financial analysts, and the general public. The statements of Fed chairs are carefully watched by financial analysts in search of wisdom on future Fed decisions about interest rates and other matters. Recent Fed chairs, like Alan Greenspan, are consulted by presidents and testify with some frequency before committees of Congress.

Often, the Fed finds itself in the middle of conflicting tensions and pressures, especially given that citizens and corporations may have different interests in economic issues. Some persons may be calling for the Fed to stimulate the economy so as to create new jobs, while, at the same time, others want it to raise interest rates so as to slow inflation. Operating within these pressures, the board of governors must make tough decisions.

19-17d Fiscal Policy: Government Taxing and Spending

fiscal policy *Policy designed to maintain economic growth and stability through government finance policies related to taxing and spending.*

Another set of strategies that the federal government can employ to influence the economy focuses on government spending, taxing, and borrowing. **Fiscal policy** refers to those policies that promote economic growth by raising or lowering taxes or by federal spending. The fiscal strategy used depends on the specific economic climate.

In an economic downturn, the federal government can lower taxes (providing consumers with more spendable income) and increase spending. Both activities put more money into the economy to stimulate economic growth. In an economic overdrive, where too much growth causes shortages of goods and spiraling price increases, the federal government can withdraw money from the economy through tax increases (which decrease the spendable income of consumers) and spending cuts.

Fiscal policy was a primary strategy of Franklin D. Roosevelt's New Deal program to fight the Depression and restart the economy. As discussed, the New Deal included programs like the Works Project Administration (WPA), through which the federal government spent money to hire unemployed people to build public works projects like school buildings, parks, and other facilities. These projects pumped public sector dollars into the economy for the purpose of stimulating economic recovery. Though the New Deal projects had some positive impact, the American economy returned to full health only after another form of public sector spending was undertaken: construction of weapons and ammunitions for the government's use in waging World War II.

income tax *A tax levied on the incomes of individuals, families, and corporations. Usually, a progressive tax; that is, tax rates increase with income.*

Although spending can stimulate the economy, government taxation can slow the pace of economic expansion by diverting dollars out of the economy and into the U.S. treasury. This strategy can be pursued through increases in the federal **income tax** on individuals and corporations—a form of taxation that began after ratification of the 16th Amendment to the Constitution in 1913. (As noted in Chapter 18, many states and a few cities also levy separate income taxes.) In the mid-1990s, about 45% of federal government revenues were derived from the individual income taxes and slightly more than 9% from income taxes on corporations. The federal income tax system is designed to be *progressive*—that is, the system is supposed to tax wealthier people at higher rates. The true progressivity of the tax is often questioned, however, because of the many specialized tax breaks and credits (often termed "loopholes") that have been created in the tax laws.

Given the complexity of tax law and the bureaucracy needed to process tax returns, some politicians in the 1990s called for a dramatic overhaul of the income tax system. Championed primarily by conservatives, one tax reform called for replacement of the current income tax system (based upon graduated rates for higher income levels) with a *flat tax*—one set rate that would be applied to all individuals. Supporters contend that the flat tax will make the tax system more fair by eliminating complex tax loopholes and simplifying the process for filing tax returns. Opponents decry what they see as abandonment of the principle of a progressive tax where wealthier people pay a higher rate of taxes—thereby enabling the federal government to redistribute resources from the more affluent to the less affluent in American society. The push for the flat tax did gain some steam in the mid-1990s, but there was insufficient political will to completely revamp the well-established federal income tax program.

The use of taxing and spending to pursue fiscal policy designed to fine-tune economic performance has its limits. First, governments create programs and spend money to achieve public policy objectives. Tinkering with budget levels to pursue fiscal policy is likely to interfere with long-term efforts to achieve public policy goals. Second, polls show that beneficiaries of public policies do not take kindly to cutbacks in their favored programs, even if taken for the purpose of managing the nation's economy. These beneficiaries and their lobbyists fight politically to protect those benefits from cutbacks. Third, fiscal policy requires a government to spend heavily during times of economic slowdown. However, if the government already has a substantial debt or budget deficits, then increased spending and further borrowing of funds may be difficult and unwise. For all of these reasons, fiscal policy is often a less feasible option than monetary policy in overall federal government efforts to sustain a healthy American economy.

19-18 Environmental Policy

In addition to its efforts to regulate the sale of stocks and bonds, monitor and regulate banking institutions, and sustain a healthy economy, the federal government also regulates other areas of American life to enhance public welfare. Environmental protection is another of the important areas of federal regulatory policy. Awareness of the environment and the often negative impact of human development on ecological systems is relatively new in America. Through much of world history, humans have viewed their progress and development as separate from the natural environment.[27] At the same time, progress was often achieved by exploiting the environment. Manufacturing and construction required the consumption of natural resources such as lumber, minerals, gas and oil, and water—resources that were taken from the earth typically without consideration of environmental impacts. Some of these natural resources are not replaceable, and others are being consumed on a worldwide basis faster than they can be replaced. In other cases, such as off-shore drilling in California and the Alaskan pipeline, extraction of natural resources spoils natural beauty and threatens major environmental damage should industrial accidents occur.

19-18a The Evolution of Public Awareness about the Importance of the Environment

Today, most Americans appreciate the importance of the environment and its relationship to human society. This awareness dates back only about 30 to 40 years, however. Prior to this time, environmental damage and pollution were largely unrecognized. One pioneer in the environmental movement, Rachel Carson, called attention to ever-escalating environmental problems in her influential book, *Silent Spring*, published in 1962. This book catalogued environmental dangers facing the planet—especially of the pesticide DDT—and called for new actions to protect the environment.

The move of the nation to enact environmental protection legislation began during the 1960s, even though public attention focused more on the social reforms of the Great Society and the expanding war in Vietnam. In 1963 Congress enacted the first Clean Air Act, which encouraged research and interstate cooperation in reducing air pollution. This was followed in 1964 with the Wilderness Act, intended to preserve substantial areas within the nation in wild condition unharmed by human development. Shifting from the wilderness to major transportation corridors, Congress enacted the Highway Beautification Act in 1965. This legislation—championed by the first lady, Lady Bird Johnson—provided federal funds to clean up junkyards and remove billboards along highways supported with federal funds.

Congressional passage of the National Environmental Policy Act in 1969 further demonstrated growing awareness of the need for protecting the earth's environment. This act required that federal agencies prepare an **environmental impact statement** each time they become involved in a project with potential consequences for the environment. These statements provide interest groups the opportunity to obtain environmental information on pending projects. Using environmental impact information to publicize the harmful effects of federally sponsored projects is one strategy used by lobbying groups to fight projects expected to harm the environment.

environmental impact statement *Reports that federal agencies must prepare for any project expected to have some impact on the environment. These reports, required by the National Environmental Policy Act, describe how projects will affect the environment.*

The continued awakening of the nation to environmental issues was demonstrated by the creation of "Earth Day" in 1970. The purpose of this event—actually multiple events held in cities across the nation—was to increase Americans' awareness of environmental problems and to enhance support for environmental protection. The credit for Earth Day is given Senator Gaylord Nelson (D-Wis.), who conceived the idea shortly after a major oil rig blowout in the Santa Barbara Channel off the California coast. As a result of this explosion, thousands of gallons of oil leaked into the ocean and drifted onto nearby beaches. The extent of the damage and the lack of preparedness of authorities to handle this type of environmental disaster crystallized attention to environmental issues and opened the policy window for new environmental protection policies. On his way to the University of California at Berkeley, Nelson read an article about how protests and teach-ins were being used as a political strategy by opponents of the war in Vietnam. Nelson had the idea of using the teach-in strategy in the context of another war—a war to protect the environment. Earth Day has been held each year since.

In many ways, the 1970s was the decade of the environment (see Table 19-3 for a listing and description of major federal environmental laws). Bipartisan support for creating environmental policies was evident during this period, as was growing public support for federal environmental protection policy.[28] Sweeping legislation to clean up the nation's air and water were enacted during this decade, along with new laws to protect

Table 19-3 Major Laws to Protect the Environment

For an easy reference to major U.S. environmental laws, see the following section of the U.S. Environmental Protection Agency website: www.epa.gov/epahome/laws.htm.

Beginning in 1963, Congress enacted a series of laws designed to protect wilderness areas, clean up air and water, regulate the disposal of hazardous wastes, protect endangered species, and manage off-shore oil drilling. A time line for the passage of environmental protection laws is depicted below.

Year	Law	Purpose
1963	Clean Air Act	Strengthened the national program to control air pollution by encouraging interstate cooperation as well as research and training on air pollution. Provided federal matching funds to local, state, and interstate air pollution control agencies and commissioned a study to evaluate the development of fuels and automobile devices to prevent auto exhaust pollution.
1964	Wilderness Act	Created a national wilderness preservation system to preserve substantial areas of the nation in wild, unspoiled condition.
1965	Highway Beautification Act	Authorized use of federal funds for beautifying the nation's federal-aid highways through removal of billboards and junkyards and the landscaping of areas adjacent to highways.
1965	Water Quality Act	Created the Federal Water Pollution Control Administration and required states to develop water quality standards for interstate waters.
1967	Air Quality Act	Strengthened the powers of local, state, and federal authorities to regulate air pollution. Funded efforts to study pollution levels and to assist states in developing air quality standards.
1968	Wild and Scenic Rivers Act	Preserved stretches of wild and scenic rivers in their natural state.
1969	National Environmental Policy Act	Required federal government agencies to prepare an environmental impact statement every time they undertake a policy or project that is potentially disruptive to the environment.
1970	Clean Air Amendments	Authorized the Environmental Protection Agency (EPA) to set emissions standards for all dangerous pollutants from motor vehicles, required automobile engines to comply with standards lowering emission of specified pollutants by 1975 or 1976 (depending on the pollutant), created a new office of Noise Abatement and Control, and allowed emission standard violators to be sued in federal court for failure to comply with air control mandates.
1970	Water Quality Improvement Act	Made it U.S. policy that no oil should be discharged into navigable rivers or adjoining shorelines, required federal agencies to comply with water quality standards, and provided for a National Contingency Plan for removal of oil or other pollution hazards in the event of a maritime disaster.
1972	Federal Water Pollution Control Act	Sought to reduce the dumping of raw industrial sewage into rivers and streams by regulating the discharge of pollutants and overflow from sewers. Provided grants to communities to build sewage treatment plants.
1972	Marine Mammal Protection Act	Designed to prevent the extinction of marine animals and to return threatened marine species to healthy populations.
1972	Coastal Zone Management Act	Declared it national policy to preserve, protect, develop, and, whenever possible, restore the nation's costal zone resources and authorized federal grants to support this policy.
1972	Federal Environmental Pesticide Control Act	Required that all pesticides in the United States be registered with the EPA and required the agency to set standards for certifying pesticide applicators. The law authorized the EPA to suspend registration of pesticides that present an immediate hazard to health or the environment.
1972	Noise Control Act	Declared a national policy to protect public health and welfare from detrimental noise and required that the federal government set noise emission standards for commercial products.
1973	Endangered Species Act	Made it illegal to kill, injure, trap, harass or otherwise "take" any animal or plant that is endangered or threatened. Created process to designate endangered species.

Year	Law	Purpose
1974	Safe Drinking Water Act	Created to protect the nation's supply of drinking water including its sources: rivers, lakes, reservoirs, springs, and groundwater wells.
1976	Resource Conservation and Recovery Act	Amended the 1965 Solid Waste Disposal Act, expanding the federal solid waste program by authorizing new funds to support solid waste disposal policies.
1976	Toxic Substances Control Act	Set a national policy that adequate data on the health and environmental effects of chemicals and toxins should be developed and required EPA testing of chemicals and toxins to ascertain health impacts.
1976	Fishery Conservation and Management Act	Created to halt overfishing by foreign fleets and to bolster the domestic fishing industry.
1977	Clean Air Act Amendments	Delayed standards for auto emissions for 2 years, set new standards to protect clean-air areas, extended deadlines for cities to meet national air quality standards, and gave most industrial polluters up to 3 more years to comply with federal standards before facing heavy fines.
1977	Clean Water Act	Expanded and specified the EPA's mandate to control the release of toxic pollutants into sewers and surface waters.
1977	Surface Mining Control and Reclamation Act	Found that strip mining harms the environment by destroying land use, creating polluted water, and destroying the natural landscape. The law called on states to regulate strip mining and gave federal funds to assist states in creating mining institutes to study the strip mining problem and its solution.
1978	Outer Continental Shelf Lands Act Amendments	Designed to foster competition for offshore oil and gas leasing, the law also restricted drilling and production to protect the environment.
1980	Comprehensive Environmental Response, Compensation and Liability Act	Required polluters to pay to clean up the worst hazardous waste sites or reimburse the EPA for cleanup costs. Law created a "superfund," based on a tax on oil and chemical manufacturing and environmental tax on companies, to finance the cleanup of hazardous wastes.
1980	Alaska National Interest Lands	Expanded 3 existing national parks and created 10 new parks in Alaska as well as creating Conservation Act wildlife refuges and wilderness protection areas.
1984	Hazardous and Solid Waste Amendments	Banned the disposal of non-containerized liquid solid waste in landfills, required the EPA to develop standards for regulating hazardous waste, and strengthened the 1980 superfund law for the cleanup of abandoned toxic waste sites.
1986	Safe Drinking Water Amendments	Toughened requirements for the testing and monitoring of contaminants and created new provisions to protect groundwater supplies.
1986	Superfund Amendments and Reauthorization Act	Reauthorized the superfund, expanding funding five-fold. The law set strict standards for cleaning up toxic waste sites.
1987	Water Quality Act	Adopted new programs to address polluted runoff from farms, factories, and city streets. Created new programs to clean up the Great Lakes, the Chesapeake Bay, and seriously impaired estuaries around the nation.
1988	Endangered Species Act Reauthorization	Reauthorized federal laws to protect endangered species by continuing the ban of their sale or exportation. Also required that federal projects, like new dams, do not threaten endangered species or their habitats.
1990	Clean Air Act Amendments	Tightened control on automobiles and gasoline, required automakers to install new pollution control devices to reduce emissions, set deadlines on communities with high ozone levels to meet federal air control standards, required industrial plants to cut pollutant emissions, and developed the method of "pollution allowances" designed as an incentive to reduce the emissions of coal-burning utilities that cause acid rain.
1990	Oil Pollution Prevention, Response, Liability, and Compensation Act	Increased the liability of spillers and imposed stiffer civil and criminal penalties. Required spillers to pay for cleaning up oil spills and compensate parties economically injured by them.
1992	Energy Policy Act	Restructured the electric industry to promote more competition, encouraged energy conservation, and promoted renewable energy and cars that run on nongasoline fuels.
1993	Colorado Wilderness Protection Act	Designated over 600,000 acres as wilderness and set aside other acreage in a less-protective management area.
1994	California Desert Protection Act	Created the largest wilderness area outside Alaska with two new national parks in California and a new national wildlife preserve in the Mojave Desert.
1996	Food Quality Protection Act	Altered the way the EPA regulates pesticides in food products.

wilderness areas, improve the safety of drinking water, and control the release of toxic substances. Federal efforts expanded beyond provision of financial support to include the creation of regulatory requirements concerning air and water quality standards. Support for the environment continued throughout the decade, although the Arab oil embargo in the 1970s shifted national attention toward energy supplies and away from conservation.

Throughout the 1980s and early 1990s, existing environmental policies were expanded and some air and water quality standards were toughened. In 1980 Congress enacted legislation to create a superfund—a special pool of federal monies dedicated to the cleanup of major hazardous waste sites across the nation. In 1990 Congress enacted revisions to the Clean Air Act, signed into law by President George H. Bush, that substantially expanded federal mandates designed to enhance air quality, particularly in smog-plagued cities across the nation.

One measure of the scope of federal government involvement in environmental protection is the amount of resources annually spent on projects to enhance the environment and sustain natural resources. By the end of the 1990s, the federal government was spending more than $22 billion on natural resource and environmental programs. The largest shares of these funds were allocated for pollution control and abatement, management of water resources, and conservation and land management.

The environmental protection movement is at an important crossroads in 2005. Substantial progress has been made in reducing air and water pollution, but other environmental problems persist. At the same time, questions about the utility of ongoing environmental protection and the negative impact of environmental regulation on businesses and state and local governments continues. The tradeoff between environmental protection and development of the earth's resources remains an ongoing issue in the American political games.

19-19 Other Federal Regulatory Policies

In addition to policies designed to influence the economy and protect the environment, the federal government has created a large number of other regulatory policies with purposes such as protecting workers, ensuring the safety of food, allocating the nation's radio and television broadcast frequencies, and controlling the sale of nuclear materials. Several of these policies have come under attack as part of the regulatory relief movement pursued by Republicans in the 104th Congress.

19-19a Ensuring Safe Food, Drugs, and Products

Several federal agencies have been created with regulatory powers intended to broadly protect Americans from products that can cause illness or injury. The Food and Drug Administration (FDA), for example, was created in by Congress in 1931. The agency's activities are directed toward protecting the health of the nation against impure and unsafe foods, drugs, and cosmetics, and other related hazards. The FDA must approve all prescription drugs before they can be offered for sale on the market. This agency has faced some controversy during the 1990s as AIDS activists pushed the FDA to approve experimental drugs to cope with AIDS and HIV infection. The FDA was caught between seeking solid, and often time-consuming, research on the health effects of experimental AIDS drugs on the one hand, and making drugs with any potential for effectively combating HIV infection available to AIDS patients as rapidly as possible.

The federal government's regulation of drugs came to the forefront in 2004 when a manufacturer of a popular drug used to treat arthritis removed the drug from the market after research showed links to heart problems. Questions were raised about whether the FDA had sufficiently reviewed the drug's safety prior to approving it for use.

The FDA also regulates the sale of tobacco products. For over four decades, health officials have voiced concerns about the harmful health effects of smoking and have amassed solid and conclusive evidence to support their point. Despite the warnings and evidence, however, smoking continues to be a major health hazard—to adults and children alike. The Centers for Disease Control and Prevention, for example, has collected data showing that 3,000 teenagers become regular smokers every day and that almost 1,000 of them will eventually die of diseases caused by smoking.

Since 1965, the federal government and FDA have developed a voluntary advertising code that restricts advertising of tobacco products. The federal government has also required that cigarette packages contain health warnings. In the most far-reaching move to regulate this industry—a move running counter to regulatory relief efforts being pursued in Congress—President Bill Clinton announced in 1995 that the FDA would henceforth consider nicotine (a key element in cigarette smoke) to be a drug. This designation would allow the FDA substantially more power to regulate the sale of tobacco products. The move was immediately challenged in the courts by the tobacco industry on the grounds that such a designation exceeds the power granted to the FDA through laws enacted by Congress.

The tobacco industry challenged the FDA rule in the federal courts. In 2000, the U.S. Supreme Court ruled that Congress had not expressly given the Food and Drug Administration authority power to regulate tobacco and, therefore, the agency had exceeded its powers in doing so (see *Food and Drug Administration, et al. v. Brown and Williamson Tobacco Corporation, et al.*, U.S. Supreme Court No 98-1152, 2000). To date, Congress has not enacted legislation to empower the FDA to regulate tobacco, thus nicotine is not currently being regulated as a drug.

Besides the FDA, other federal agencies have been created to enhance public safety. To protect consumers from harm and injury from products they buy in the nation's marketplace, Congress created the Consumer Production Safety Commission (CPSC) in 1972. This commission establishes mandatory product safety standards and bans sales of products that do not comply. The CPSC also requires manufacturers to report defects in products, collects information on consumer product-related injuries, conducts research on product hazards, and, when needed, formulates product safety standards.

The Federal Trade Commission (FTC) was created in 1914 to administer antitrust laws. Today, the FTC promotes competition in commerce by preventing price-fixing, illegal combinations of competitors, and other unfair methods of competition. The agency safeguards the public by preventing the dissemination of false or deceptive advertising of commercial products. This agency also regulates packaging and the labeling of specified commodities.

19-19b Occupational Health and Safety

Workplaces are not always safe, and accidents in the workplace are a serious problem in many businesses and industries. Workers' compensation plans created by states across the nation were a policy innovation intended to compensate victims of workplace accidents and provide income assistance during periods of rehabilitation. In 1970, Congress created the Occupational Safety and Health Administration (known most commonly as OSHA) as part of an effort to create a comprehensive federal industrial safety program. Congress granted OSHA responsibility for developing and enforcing worker safety and heath regulations and for conducting inspections to ensure compliance with regulatory standards.

In addition to workplace safety, the federal government has created other policies designed to expand the rights and protect the health of workers. The Fair Labor Standards Act of 1938, for example, set a maximum work week of 40 hours for all employers engaged in interstate commerce or the production of goods for interstate delivery. Through this law, the federal government also sets the minimum wage. This same act prohibits child labor (employment under the age of 16, or under 18 in hazardous occupations).

Occupational safety has been one of the areas targeted for regulatory relief. Businesses have asked for a lessening of requirements regarding the work activities and work conditions of teenagers. They have also sought to reduce strict safety regulations in the workplace.

19-19c Protecting Unions and Labor

As part of the New Deal, Congress enacted the National Labor Relations Act of 1935, also known as the Wagner Act. This law protects the right to pursue unionizing activities. Without this protection, many unions found it very difficult to pursue unionizing in plants and factories hostile to their labor organizing movement. The Wagner Act declares that workers affecting interstate commerce should have the right to organize and bargain collectively. It also bans employers from engaging in a variety of unfair practices, including interfering with workers seeking to organize unions, discriminating against union members, firing employees for engaging in union activities, and refusing to bargain with union representatives. Responsibility for implementing these mandates was given by Congress to the National Labor Relations Board.

The Wagner Act was influential in strengthening the power of unions within business and industry. Not surprisingly, groups representing the nation's industries were displeased with federal policies that expanded union power, especially in the process of **collective bargaining** through which employers determine salaries, wages, and fringe benefits for workers. Some instances of abuse of power by unions and some major industrial strikes prompted Congress to revisit the issue of protecting labor unions. In 1947 Congress enacted the Labor-Management Relations Act, more generally named after its chef sponsors as the Taft-Hartley Act. While maintaining many union rights, this legislation weakened some union powers. For example, it prohibits **closed shops** (a company that requires all employees to be union members in good standing) and allows **union shops** (companies that require new employees to join a union within a specified time) only under limited conditions. Taft-Hartley also allows states to outlaw union shops. Following the outline of Taft-Hartley, several states have enacted **right-to-work laws** that make it illegal for unions to include provisions calling for compulsory union membership in collective bargaining agreements.

collective bargaining *The process by which workers in plants or industries come together, usually through labor unions, to negotiate pay, benefits, and working conditions.*

closed shop *Requirements that all employees of a company are union members in good standing.*

union shop *Requirement that all employees that join a company be required to join a union within a specified time period.*

right-to-work laws *State laws that prohibit unions from including provisions for compulsory union membership in collective bargaining agreements.*

19-19d Regulating Communications

The nation's airwaves have traditionally been viewed as a national resource. In order to manage the use of radio, and then television, airwaves, Congress created the Federal Communications Commission (FCC) in 1934. Today, the FCC licenses civilian radio and television communications and regulates interstate and foreign communications by radio, television, wire, satellite, and cable. Through its regulatory responsibilities over the private sector, the FCC is responsible for the orderly development and operation of broadcasting sources and the provision of efficient long distance telephone service.

At the start of the 21st century, key regulatory issues concern the new electronic communications—email, the Internet, cell phones, and expanding cable and satellite services. Policy makers are studying these new communications and pondering possible regulation concerning such issues as transmission of pornography on the Internet, the security of financial information used to make Internet purchases, and the accessibility of electronic communications to poorer people and families who are unable to purchase a computer and Internet access.

Conclusion

Politics in the United States is about public policies that determine who will win and who will lose as government benefits, sanctions, regulations, and contracts are distributed to citizens, corporations, and associations. This is particularly true of domestic policies that provide social benefits, income assistance, regulatory protections, and monetary policy. American public policy develops in stages, during which problems are recognized, policy solutions are devised and enacted, public programs are implemented, and policy outcomes are evaluated.

Social policy in the United States largely developed through three watershed periods. During two of the periods—the New Deal of the 1930s and the Great Society of the 1960s—public sentiments were open to recognizing the plight of poor and elderly Americans as well as persons with disabilities. In the first period the economic chaos of the Great Depression served to open the policy window for social welfare and retirement programs. The second wave of policy reform came during the Great Society of the 1960s when a robust economy and media portrayals of poverty in America created strong political will to expand new social programs. These programs focused on food and nutrition, health care, and civil rights.

The third, more recent, period of policy reform has moved social policy in the opposite direction, emphasizing policy reform and constraining the breadth of benefits distributed. By the end of the 20th century, social policy was competing with other national priorities on the policy agenda: natural security, protection from terrorism, criminal justice, and economic development.

First during the Great Depression, and with greater ardor during the 1960s and 1970s, the federal government expanded regulation of the private sector, as well as state and local governments, to achieve national objectives related to securing the nation's banking and financial systems, environmental protection, and consumer safety. Implementation of regulatory policy spawned the growth of new regulatory agencies, including the Environmental Protection Agency, Securities and Exchange Commission, Federal Reserve Board, and Federal Trade Commission. American politics in the first years of the 21st century focus on how strong regulatory mandates should be and how much the private sector should be regulated for the benefit of the greater public.

Key Terms

appropriations
Aid to Families with Dependent Children (AFDC)
antitrust policies
capitalism
closed shop
collective bargaining
cost-of-living adjustments (COLAs)
effectiveness
efficiency
equity
environmental impact statement
evaluative criteria
fiscal policy
gross domestic product (GDP)
income tax
inflation
laissez-faire
Medicare
Medicaid
monetary policies
public-private partnerships
recession
regulatory policies
responsiveness
right-to-work laws
Social Security
tax expenditures
unanticipated consequences
union shop
vouchers
War on Poverty
welfare state

Practice Quiz

1. Policy windows refers to
a. efforts to reform the Social Security system.
b. fallout from the Iran Contra affair.
c. timely opportunities for policy issues to come to the forefront of attention.
d. times when the federal government is operating under a budget deficit.

2. Redistributive policies focus on policies that
a. transfer wealth, rights, or opportunities from one group of individuals to another group.
b. are broadly of value to citizens like public works and highways.
c. place limits on governmental spending.
d. regulate the activities of businesses and organizations.

3. An "entitlement program" is one in which the
a. federal and state governments share costs.
b. funding is based on revenues received.
c. funding is available to all persons who meet eligibility requirements.
d. funding is transferred to private sector businesses.

4. Tax expenditures refer to the
a. state government share of joint federal-state programs like Medicare.
b. cost of running federal government agencies.
c. funds raised through federal income taxes.
d. funds that the federal government does not collect when it creates tax breaks.

5. An example of an unintended consequence of public policy would be
a. tax cuts that stimulate the economy.
b. federal highway programs that enhanced interstate commence and stimulated the flight of people to the suburbs.
c. environmental protection programs that reduce air and water pollution.
d. federal programs that tax wealthier citizens to pay for programs for poorer citizens.

6. The evaluative criteria of efficiency refers to the extent to which
a. policies achieve maximum outcome at the lowest cost.
b. policies meet their established goals.
c. policies create a balanced budget.
d. tax expenditures are used to assist corporations.

7. The New Deal is associated with which American president?
a. Lyndon Johnson
b. Abraham Lincoln
c. Ronald Reagan
d. Franklin Roosevelt

8. What federal program is designed to give senior Americans access to health care?
a. Medicaid
b. Social Security
c. Medicare
d. AFDC

9. The federal government's Social Security program was created during
a. World War I.
b. the Great Depression of the 1930s.
c. the Great Society.
d. the period of New Federalism.

10. Which of the following has stimulated pressure for reform of health care programs in the last decade?
a. Rising health care costs to consumers
b. Rising health care costs to employers
c. Concern about uninsured citizens, mostly poor or senior citizens
d. All of the above

11. Categorical grants made by the federal government most resemble
a. a contract to provide specific services using federal funding.
b. a broad grant of dollars where states and localities have discretion to spend.
c. income tax structures.
d. All of the above.

12. A key federal government agency charged with enforcing competitive practices in U.S. business is the
a. Environmental Protection Agency.
b. Federal Trade Commission.
c. Office of Management and Budget.
d. Department of State.

13. What is true of the federal income tax system?
   a. It was created in the early twentieth century.
   b. It has higher tax rates for taxpayers with higher income levels
   c. It is administered by the Internal Revenue Service.
   d. All of the above

14. Which of the following statements is true about environmental policy in the United States?
   a. Substantial national government action to protect the environment dates back to the 1960s.
   b. The Environmental Protection Agency is the key national regulatory body for environmental regulation.
   c. The national government has enacted major policies to promote cleaner air and water in the United States.
   d. All of the above

15. Right to work laws prohibit
   a. companies from employing individuals who are not citizens.
   b. companies from employing individuals who are not legal representatives.
   c. unions form establishing dues
   d. unions from including compulsory membership as part of collective bargaining.

16. The national government agency most responsible for regulating the media is the
   a. Federal Communications Commission.
   b. National Broadcasting Company.
   c. Federal Regulatory Commission.
   d. National Public Radio.

17. The "laissez-faire" doctrine is most associated with what individual?
   a. Adam Smith
   b. Thomas Hobbes
   c. Charles Greenspan
   d. Karl Marx

You can find the correct answers to these questions by taking the quiz and then submitting your answers in the Online Edition. The program will automatically score your submission. Where you miss a question, the program will provide the correct answer, a rationale for the answer, and the section number in the chapter where the topic is discussed.

Further Reading

For a thorough treatment of the stages of the public policy process, see Charles O. Jones, *An Introduction to the Study of Public Policy*, 2nd ed. (North Scituate, MA: Duxbury, 1977), and B. Guy Peters, *American Public Policy: Promise and Performance*, 3rd ed. (Chatham, NJ: Chatham House, 1993). For an application of the policy process to the urban government context, see Bryan D. Jones, *Governing Urban America* (Boston, MA: Little, Brown, 1984).

Several useful books have been written on public policy implementation. The early study that launched many others was that of economic development in Oakland, California, by Jeffrey L. Pressman and Aaron Wildavsky entitled *Implementation*, 3rd ed. (Berkeley, CA: University of California Press, 1984). Other useful texts on policy implementation include those by Dennis J. Palumbo and Donald J. Calista, eds., *Implementation and the Policy Process: Opening Up the Black Box* (New York: Greenwood Press, 1990); Malcolm L. Goggin et al., *Implementation Theory and Practice* (Glenview, IL: Scott, Foresman/Little, Brown, 1990); Eugene Bardach, *The Implementation Game: What Happens after a Bill Becomes a Law* (Cambridge, MA: MIT Press, 1977).

For a treatment that explores the public policy process and the evolution of public policy in multiple policy arenas, see Thomas R. Dye, *Understanding Public Policy*, 9th ed. (Englewood Cliffs, NJ: Prentice Hall, 1997).

An interesting work on public policy analysis is Eugene Bardach, *A Practical Guide to Policy Analysis: The Eightfold Path to More Effective Problem Solving* (Washington, D.C.: CQ Press, 2000).

Models and perspectives for public policy analysis and policy evaluation include: George M. Guess and Paul G. Farnham, *Cases in Public Policy Analysis* (Washington, D.C.: Georgetown University Press, 2000); Gary Henry, George Jules, and Melvin Mark, *Evaluation: An Integrated Framework for Understanding, Guiding, and Improving Policies and Programs* (Hoboken, NJ: John Wiley & Sons, 2000); Joseph S. Wholey, ed., *Handbook of Practical Program Evaluation* (Hoboken, NJ: Jossey-Bass, 1994); and David L. Weimer and Aidan R. Vining, *Policy Analysis: Concepts and Practice*, 3rd ed. (Upper Saddle River, NJ: Prentice Hall, 1998).

An interesting book that explores unintended consequences of public policy is Steven M. Gillon, *That's Not What We Meant to Do: Reform and Its Unintended Consequences in Twentieth Century America* (New York: W.W. Norton & Company, 2000).

A troubling view of America's social programs, especially about their potential for creating incentives for dependency, is presented in Charles Murray, *Losing Ground* (New York: Basic Books, 1984). A more positive perspective on American social programs and their consequences is presented in John E. Schwarz, *America's Hidden Success: A Reassessment of Public Policy from Kennedy to Reagan*, rev. ed. (New York: W.W. Norton, 1988).

Michael B. Katz has written extensively on the history and evolution of U.S. welfare policy. Among his books on this subject are: *In the Shadow of the Poorhouse: A Social History of Welfare in the United States* (New York: Basic Books, 1986), *The Undeserving Poor: From the War on Poverty to the War on Welfare* (New York: Pantheon Books, 1989), and *Improving Poor People: The Welfare State, the "Underclass" and Urban Schools History* (Princeton, NJ: Princeton University Press, 1995). An historical examination of the evolution of liberal philosophies and the New Deal is presented in Alan Brinkly, *The End of Reform: New Deal Liberalism in Recession and War* (New York: Alfred A. Knopf, 1995).

Recent books on welfare reform include Neil Gilbert and Paul Terrell, *Dimensions of Social Welfare Policy* (Allyn & Bacon, 1997) and R. Kent Weaver and Michael H. Armacost, *Ending Welfare as We Know It* (Washington, D.C.: Brookings Institution, 2000).

Examples of welfare reforms being instituted within the states are presented in Donald F. Norris and Lyke Thompson, eds., *The Politics of Welfare Reform* (Thousand Oaks, CA: Sage Publications, 1995). Other sources on welfare reform include: Joel F. Handler and Yeheshel Hasenfeld, *The Moral Construction of Poverty: Welfare Reform in America* (Newbury Park, CA: Sage Publications, 1991) and *Welfare Reform* (Washington, D.C.: Congressional Quarterly, 1992).

Among books that examine health care in America, and ideas for health care reform, are Ian Morris, *Health Care in the New Millennium* (Hoboken, NJ: Jossey-Bass, 2000), Regina E. Herzlinger, *Market-Driven Health Care: Who Wins, Who Loses in the Transformation of America's Largest Service?* (Boulder, CO: Perseus Press, 1999); Stephen M. Shortell, Robin R. Gilllies, and David A. Anderson, eds., *Remaking Health Care Policy in America* (Hoboken, NJ: Jossey Bass, 2000); Joseph A. Califano, Jr., *America's Health Care Revolution: Who Lives? Who Dies? Who Pays?* (New York: Random House, 1986).

A description of the American health care system and its components is provided in Milton I. Roemer, *An Introduction to the U.S. Health Care System*, 2d ed. (New York: Springer Publishing Company, 1986). The politics of health care policy from 1980 to 1994 is described in Vincente Navarro, *The Politics of Health Policy: The U.S. Reforms 1980–1994*.

Two useful sources regarding Social Security are Faustin F. Jehle, *The Complete and Easy Guide to Social Security, Health Care Rights, and Government Benefits* (New York: Williamson Publishing, 2000); Dean

Baker and Mark Weisbrot, *Social Security: The Phony Crisis* (Chicago, IL: University of Chicago Press, 1999).

For a thorough discussion of the political origins and activities surrounding the passage of the Education of All Handicapped Children Act of 1975, see Erwin L. Levine and Elizabeth M. Wexler, *PL94-142: An Act of Congress* (New York: McMillan Publishing Company, 1981).

For an overview of current issues in educational policy, see Diane Ravitch, ed., *Brookings Papers on Education Policy: 2000* (Washington, DC: Brookings Institution, 2000).

A useful primer on U.S. economic policy-making is Carl Lieberman, *Making Economic Policy* (New York: Prentice-Hall, 1991). A cogent discussion of America's social welfare programs is presented by Sar A. Levitan in *Programs in Aid of the Poor*, 6th ed. (Baltimore, MD: Johns Hopkins University Press, 1990). Donald Kettl provides a useful overview of federal government budgeting and the problems of deficit spending in *Deficit Politics: Public Budgeting in Its Institutional and Historical Context* (New York: Macmillan, 1992).

Among the books that examine the politics of federal budget making, see Allen Schick and Felix Lostracco, *The Federal Budget: Politics, Policy, Process* (Washington, D.C.: Brookings Institution, 2000), Hobart Rowan *Self-Inflicted Wounds: From LBJ's Guns and Butter to Reagan's Voodoo Economics* (New York: Times Books, 1995).

Several books present critical assessments of contemporary environmental practices and policies and warnings about the future, including Jean-Francois Rischard, *High Noon 20 Global Problems: 20 Years to Solve Them* (New York: Basic Books, 2003), Paul R. Portney and Robert N. Stavins, *Public Policies for Environmental Protection* (Washington, D.C.: Resources for the Future, 2000), and G. Tyler, Miller, *Living in the Environment: Principles, Connections, and Solutions* (Florence, KY: Brooks/Cole Publishing Company, 1999).

Among the sources on federal clean air policy are U.S. Environmental Protection Agency, *The Plain English Guide to the Clean Air Act* (Washington, D.C.: U.S. Government Printing Office, 1993); and Gary C. Bryner, *Blue Skies, Green Politics: The Clean Air Act of 1990* (Washington, D.C.: Congressional Quarterly, 1993).

Other books that examine the environment focus on governmental policies and their potential for improving the environment. These works include James Gustave Speth, *Red Sky at Morning: America and the Crisis of the Global Environment* (New Haven, CT: Yale University Press, 2004); Norman A. Vig and Michael E. Kraft, *Environmental Policy: New Directions for the Twenty-First Century* (Washington, D.C. CQ Press, 2002; Charles O. Jones, *Clean Air: The Policies and Politics of Pollution Control* (Pittsburgh, PA: University of Pittsburgh Press, 1975); Lynton K. Caldwell, *Environment as a Focus for Public Policy* (College Station, TX: Texas A&M University Press, 1995); T. Nejat Veziroglu, *Environmental Problems and Solutions: Greenhouse Effect, Acid Rain, Pollution* (New York: Hemisphere Publishing Company, 1990); and James P. Lester (ed.), *Environmental Politics and Policy* (Durham, NC: Duke University Press, 1994).

An environmental science textbook with valuable information on ecology, pollution, and environmental management is presented in Daniel B. Botkin and Edward A. Keller, *Environmental Science: Earth as a Living Planet* (New York: John Wiley & Sons, 2003).

Among thorough treatments of governmental regulations are: James Q. Wilson, *The Politics of Regulation* (New York: Basic Books, 1980; James F. Gatti, ed., *The Limits of Government Regulation* (New York: Academic Press, 1981). See also Malcolm K. Sparrow, *The Regulatory Craft: Controlling Risks, Solving Problems*, and *Managing Compliance* (Washington, D.C.: Brookings Institution, 2000).

For an interesting discussion of public policy issues related to the Internet and e-commerce, see Nicholas Imparato, *Public Policy and the Internet* (Stanford, CA: Hoover Institution Press, 2000) and Robert E. Litan and William A. Niskanen, *Going Digital: A Guide to Policy in the Digital Age* (Washington, D.C.: Brookings Institution, 1998).

Endnotes

1. Congressional Research Service, reported in Robert J. Samuelson, "Sewing More Cynicism," *Washington Post*, October 19, 1994, A23.
2. The scholarly works that have explored the stages of the public policy process include Charles O. Jones, *An Introduction to the Study of Public Policy*, 2nd ed. (North Scituate, MA: Duxbury, 1977), and Bryan D. Jones, *Governing Urban America* (Boston, MA: Little, Brown, 1983).
3. Nelson W. Polsby, *Political Innovation in America: The Politics of Policy Innovation* (New Haven, CT: Yale University Press, 1984), 150.
4. Polsby, *Political Innovation in America*, 153.
5. John W. Kingdon, *Agendas, Alternatives, and Public Policies* (Boston, MA: Little, Brown, 1984), 6.
6. Kingdon, *Agendas, Alternatives, and Public Policies*, 6.
7. Anthony Downs, "Up and Down with Ecology—-the 'Issue Attention Cycle,'" *The Public Interest* 28 (Summer 1972), 40.
8. In a classic study, one political scientist found that members of Congress spend more of their effort claiming credit and advertising their accomplishments than accomplishing substantive tasks. See David Mayhew, *Congress: The Electoral Connection* (New Haven, CT: Yale University Press, 1974).
9. Marcus E. Ethridge and Stephen L. Percy, "A New Kind of Public Policy Encounters Disappointing Results: The Case of Learnfare in Wisconsin." *Public Administration Review* 53 (July/August 1993), 340–347.
10. Eugene Bardach, *The Implementation Game* (Cambridge, MA: MIT Press, 1977), 9.
11. Jeffrey L. Pressman and Aaron Wildavsky, *Implementation*, 3rd ed. (Berkeley, CA: University of California Press, 1984), 87–124.
12. Robert L. Greene, *The Urban Challenge: Poverty and Race* (Chicago, IL: Follett, 1977).
13. Lee Rainwater, *Behind Ghetto Walls* (Chicago, IL: Aldine, 1977).
14. See Michael B. Katz, *In the Shadow of the Poorhouse: A Social History of Welfare in America* (New York: Basic Books, 1986).
15. Katz, *In the Shadow of the Poorhouse*, 40.
16. Joel F. Handler and Yeheskel Hasenfeld, *The Moral Construction of Poverty: Welfare Reform in America* (Newbury Park, CA: Sage Publications, 1991), 67.
17. For historical background on the Social Security program, see Robert M. Ball, "The Original Understanding on Social Security: Implications for Later Developments," In Theodore M. Marmor and Jerry L. Mashaw, eds., *Social Security: Beyond the Rhetoric of Crisis* (Princeton, NJ: Princeton University Press, 1988), 17–39.
18. Bob Kerry and Alan K. Simpson, "How to Save Social Security," *New York Times* (May 23, 1995), A17.
19. Theodore Marmor, Understanding Health Care Reform (New Haven, CT: Yale University Press, 1994), 6.
20. Poll data from a national poll conducted by the Times Mirror Center for the People & the Press, "The GOP Pays the Price: Medicare Debate Gets More Attention than Bosnia, Dole on Hollywood, and Even OJ" (Washington, D.C.: Times Mirror Center for the People & The Press, June 14, 1995).
21 *Medicaid: Spending Pressures Drive States toward Program Reinvention* (Washington, D.C.: U.S. General Accounting Office, 1995), 2.
22. Vincente Navarro, *The Politics of Health Policy: The U.S. Reforms, 1980-1994* (Cambridge, Massachusetts: Blackwell, 1994), 185.
23. Stephen L. Percy, *Disability, Civil Rights and Public Policy: The Politics of Implementation* (Tuscaloosa, AL: University of Alabama Press, 1992), 25–26.
24. See Adam Smith, *The Wealth of Nations*, 1776. Key components of Smith's work may be found in George J. Stigler, ed., *Selections from the Wealth of Nations* (Arlington Heights, IL: Harlan Davidson, 1986).
25. This law initially covered labor unions; however, unions were exempted from provisions of the Sherman Antitrust Act through passage of the Clayton Act in 1914.
26. Although AT&T survived the breakup, it gave up its ownership of regional telephone companies. It retained long distance service and marketing of communications products.
27. A. M. Manion and S. R. Bowlby, "Introduction," in Manion and Bowlby, eds., Environmental Issues in the 1990s (New York: John Wiley & Sons, 1992).
28. Riley E. Dunlap, "Public Opinion and Environmental Policy," in James P. Lester, ed., *Environmental Policy and Politics*, 2nd ed. (Durham, NC: Duke University Press, 1995), 63–114.

20

Civil Rights: Protecting the Players and Nonplayers

Key Points

- **Segregation and prejudice based on race, ethnicity, national origin, disability, sexual orientation, and gender as historical forces.**
- **The political strategies of the civil rights movement.**
- **The impact of the civil rights movement on the formation and implementation of public policies designed to end discrimination.**
- **The major civil rights laws that today provide legal protections against discrimination.**
- **The struggle of women to achieve equal rights in society and the workplace.**
- **Current debates about affirmative action policies and their appropriateness today as strategies for overcoming discrimination.**

Preview: The Long Road to Civil Rights

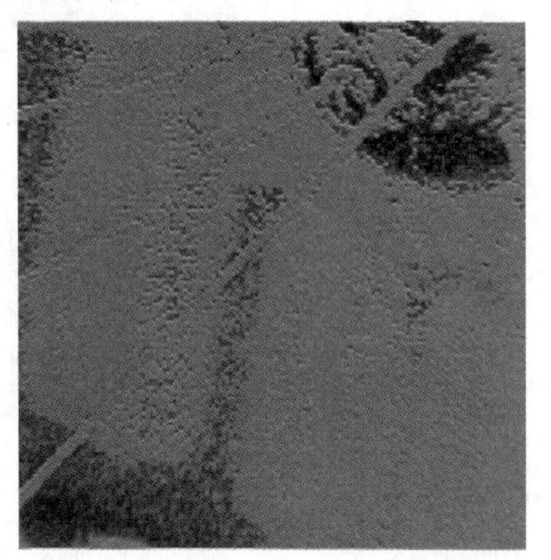

It was hot that day in 1930, and all the two boys could think about was dashing across the sand and into the water. They could not imagine walking the extra two miles to the beach they normally used. Instead, they turned onto the path to the beach closer to town. It was so hot that they simply ignored the signs saying the people of their background could not use that beach. Of course they were not allowed in, and the two little Catholic boys were dejected. They were not alone, for the sign said, "No Blacks, No Jews, No Catholics and No Mediterraneans." Lest you think that such behavior was accepted only in the deep South, this sign stood on Beverly Beach in Annapolis, Maryland, a border state that sided with the North in the Civil War.

Civil Rights March in Washington, D.C.
National Archives and Records Administration

It would be over 20 years before civil rights legislation and changing attitudes would erase such blatant discrimination. The breadth of groups discriminated against and their increasing political activism made change more likely. Initially the public beaches were forced to provide equal access to all; eventually the private beaches either closed or accommodated the times. The story might have ended there, but many of the private beaches closed their gates and sold off their land. In their place now stand upscale condominium developments with security walls and guards. The new source of discrimination is not so much on the basis of one's ethnic or religious background, but rather on the size of one's bank account. The two little boys might well be turned away today because their families don't own a piece of the beach.

To some, the term *civil rights movement* is identified with efforts of African Americans, especially in the 1960s, to strike down segregation and end discrimination in America. While these Americans have strived for decades to achieve a more equal position in U.S. society, they are not the only groups who have experienced discrimination and engaged in civil rights activities. Latinos, Asian Americans, Native Americans, gays and lesbians, and people with disabilities all have become players in long-range political games to end discrimination. Individuals in these groups have experienced persistent prejudice and discrimination, forces that have prevented their full enjoyment of citizenship and opportunities in American life. Over the course of American history, discrimination has denied some people the rights given to others, has reduced job opportunities, and has prohibited access to public facilities.

Through diligence, tenacity, and calculated political strategies, player groups representing women and minorities have won political battles and made substantial progress in obtaining the same rights that others take for granted. Many are now protected by public laws designed to guard their rights and privileges as American citizens and players in the political game. Other groups are still pressing for strong legal protections against discrimination. For this reason, civil rights remains a volatile area of American politics. Groups—or at least their representatives—continue to pursue varied strategies in several different institutional arenas with the intention of eliminating discrimination and, hopefully someday, prejudice itself. But of one point there can be no question: the civil rights efforts of groups in American society have led policy makers at all levels of government to strike down some policies, particularly segregation, and to enact a variety of others intended to end discrimination and provide equal opportunities to all Americans.

Portions of this chapter will explore a variety of groups of Americans who have battled for civil rights. An effort will be made to describe the evolution of these groups in American history, the political issues of most concern to them, and political strategies they have used in battles to enhance civil rights. It is important to recognize, at the outset, that none of these groups is completely homogenous. Every group to be examined is composed of unique and diverse people who may share some experiences and interests but who also have interests and policy concerns besides those customarily associated with their group. African Americans today, for example, include professionals in top positions in business and industry, middle-class families residing in suburbs, and poorer citizens living in decaying areas of central cities. Although all African Americans may share some sense of identity and some common experiences, they may also differ in their political outlooks and in what they would like government to achieve. The same is true of all other groups to be explored.

20-1 African Americans and the Civil Rights Movement

> There is nothing more dangerous than to build a society with a large segment of people in that society who feel that they have no stake in it, who feel that they have nothing to lose.
>
> —*Dr. Martin Luther King*

The gaining or upholding of civil rights concerning African Americans dates back to the first efforts to eliminate slavery. While arguments for eliminating the institution of slavery preceded the formation of the nation, the Founders sidestepped the issue in drafting the Constitution (see Chapter 2). Slavery was among the most prominent issues to divide the nation throughout the early decades of the new nation's history and was a key catalyst for the Civil War. Through the Emancipation Proclamation, Abraham Lincoln announced that all slaves living in states under control of the southern confederacy would be freed once the states came under control of the Union. Through the 13th Amendment, ratified in 1865, the practice of slavery was outlawed in the nation.

In a further effort to protect the rights of former slaves, the 14th Amendment was added to the Constitution. This amendment, which required equal protection under the law for all individuals, was intended to extend full citizenship rights to all African Americans (see Chapter 3). The purpose of the 14th Amendment, ratified immediately after the Civil War, was to force southern states to apply state laws equally to African Americans and whites. During the **Reconstruction** period, when southern states were under the control of northern officials, African Americans were elected to public offices, including the House of Representatives. As Reconstruction ended and federal troops departed, control of state government reverted to southern officials. Soon after, African American elected officials in the South were defeated in their bids for reelection.

reconstruction *The period immediately following the Civil War when the politics of southern states were dominated by politicians from the North.*

20-1a Segregation and a Separate but Equal Doctrine

A pattern of segregation evolved in the South that reduced the rights of African Americans and their participation in the political game. Prominent in this regard were **Jim Crow laws,** which prohibited African Americans from using the same public facilities as whites—from water fountains to seats in the front of the bus. Segregation was also rampant in public education, from elementary schools to colleges and universities. The persistent discrimination enforced through segregation laws reduced social and economic opportunities for African Americans.

Jim Crow laws *State and local laws that established segregation in public facilities and public schools. Initially upheld under "separate but equal" doctrine.*

Segregation laws were challenged in the federal courts on the basis that they violated the 14th Amendment's requirement that states provide equal protection under the law. In 1896, in ***Plessy v. Ferguson,*** the Supreme Court held that separate facilities for African Americans and whites did not violate the equal protection clause as long as the facilities were equal.[1] In fact, however, segregated facilities for African Americans were almost always inferior. Schools for African American children had fewer teachers and textbooks than did schools for whites. Other public facilities reserved for African Americans were consistently of poorer quality. The separate-but-equal doctrine established in Plessy clearly worked to uphold segregation, discrimination, and inequality.

Plessy v. Ferguson *Supreme Court case in 1898 that upheld segregated facilities if facilities were "equal." Legitimized "separate but equal doctrine." Overturned in* Brown v. School Board of Topeka *in 1954.*

By the 1930s, the tide had begun to turn against segregation. At this time, the Supreme Court required that universities and law schools either admit qualified African American applicants or else provide truly equal higher educational institutions. The cost of creating separate universities was too great, forcing states to begin admitting African Americans to these institutions. From the 1930s to the mid-1950s, the separate-but-equal doctrine was increasingly challenged on the basis that it fostered inequality rather than equal protection. (A time line of key events in the civil rights movement is presented in Table 20-1.)

In a move with major political repercussions, the Supreme Court struck down the practice of segregation. In the landmark case of *Brown v. Board of Education of Topeka*, the Supreme Court in 1954 rendered compulsory segregation in public schools unconstitutional on the grounds that it violated the equal protection clause of the 14th Amendment (see Chapter 17).[2] This judicial decision enervated the civil rights movement and indicated that all types of segregation in public facilities, not just schools, would henceforth be considered unconstitutional.

Table 20-1 Key Events in the Civil Rights Movement

The movement to enhance the civil rights of Americans—including racial and ethnic minorities, women, gays and lesbians, and people with disabilities—is notable for many different events and policy successes. A brief time line describing key events in the fight for civil rights follows.

1954: The Supreme Court rules in the *Brown v. Board of Education of Topeka* that segregated public schools are unconstitutional. Decision overrules the *Plessy v. Ferguson* decision of 1896 that upheld the constitutionality of separate but equal facilities.

1957: Governor Orval Faubus of Arkansas orders the National Guard to prevent African American students from enrolling in public high school in Little Rock. President Dwight D. Eisenhower counters by ordering paratroopers to escort students to school.

1963: Dr. Martin Luther King, Jr., gives his *I Have A Dream* speech at the March on Washington rally. The speech outlines a vision of society where race makes no difference.

1963: Congress passes the Equal Pay Act, designed to require men and women performing the same job to receive equivalent pay.

1964: The Civil Rights Act is approved by Congress. The law prohibits discrimination on the basis of race, color, religion, national origin, or gender. The law also creates the Equal Employment Opportunity Commission.

The 24th Amendment is ratified banning the use of poll taxes to prevent citizens from voting in primary and general elections.

1965: The Voting Rights Act is enacted by Congress. The act bans the use of literacy tests as part of voter registration and allows the federal government to register voters in counties where fewer than 50% of minority residents are registered.

1968: Congress passes a new Civil Rights Act that prohibits discrimination in housing and protects the rights of minorities to buy and sell property wherever they want.

1971: The 26th Amendment to the Constitution is ratified, giving citizens from 18 to 21 years of age the right to vote.

1972: Through Section 504 of the Rehabilitation Act, Congress prohibits recipients of federal funds from discriminating against persons with disabilities.

Congress approves the Equal Rights Amendment to the Constitution—prohibiting discrimination on the basis of gender—and sends the measure on to the states for ratification.

1978: In the case *Bakke v. California*, the Supreme Court rules that colleges and universities cannot establish firm quotas for admitting a certain percentage of students as part of affirmative action policies.

1982: The push to ratify the Equal Rights Amendment finally is declared dead, with an insufficient number of states ratifying the measure.

1990: Congress enacts the Americans with Disabilities Act prohibiting discrimination against persons with mental and physical disabilities and requiring that accommodations be made in employment and private sector accommodations to increase the access of disabled Americans to societal opportunities.

1991: In another round of civil rights legislation, Congress strengthens some civil rights protections and policies.

2003: U.S. Supreme Court hears key cases on gay rights and affirmative action. The Supreme Court reversed its own 1986 ruling and struck down state laws that make it criminal for individuals of the same gender to engage in sexual relations.

Martin Luther King, Jr.
Library of Congress

20-1b The Civil Rights Movement

Potent political protest was a strategy used by many African American and civil rights groups to fight discrimination and enable African Americans to become equal players in the game of American politics. The initiative to remove discrimination and increase the civil rights of black Americans focused not only on the federal courts but also on public protest and demonstration. In 1955 Rosa Parks, an African-American resident of Montgomery, Alabama, refused to give up her seat on the bus to a white man. She was arrested under the city's bus segregation law. Responding to Parks's arrest, the African-American community in Montgomery united around the leadership of Dr. Martin Luther King, Jr., a local minister, and engaged in a peaceful protest of segregation in the local busing system. For over a year, blacks boycotted the buses, placing economic pressure on the bus company. With the bus company near bankruptcy, downtown merchants decrying a loss in business, and a federal court ruling bus segregation illegal, the city of Montgomery finally eliminated the segregation laws concerning African Americans in public transportation.

The civil rights movement continued in the early 1960s with protests and marches focused in southern cities that continued to practice segregation. The Congress of Racial Equality, an interracial group founded in 1942, organized a freedom ride, involving buses of protesters who planned to ride from Washington, D.C., to New Orleans to protest segregation of waiting rooms, public restrooms, and restaurants across the South. When they reached Anniston, Alabama, the freedom riders were stopped by Ku Klux Klan members who stoned a bus and set it afire. The freedom riders barely escaped before the bus exploded. Other riders were severely beaten when they reached Birmingham. The governor of Alabama, John Patterson, refused to intervene and protect what he termed a bunch of rabble rousers. These events were captured in media pictures and television broadcasts that communicated the extent of racial hatred in some southern communities.

The Montgomery protest had made Reverend Martin Luther King, Jr., a national leader in the African-American civil rights movement. King and other African-American leaders organized and directed visible and symbolic protests against segregation and discrimination in cities across America. In one dramatic event, broadcast across the nation on the then-new technology of television, Dr. King led a march in 1963 to protest segregation policies in Birmingham, Alabama. With the nation watching, local police attacked the peaceful marchers and used clubs and fire hoses to force them to disperse.

In the summer of the same year, Dr. King and other civil rights leaders led a march of a quarter of a million people to the nation's capital. One of the largest protests in the nation's history, this march provided evidence of the growing political organization of African Americans and their determination to overcome discrimination. Addressing the assembled marchers in 1963, Dr. King gave his famous *I Have a Dream* speech, in which he described his dream of having his four children judged "not by the color of their skin but by the content of their character." (Box 20-1: Thirty Years Beyond *I Have a Dream* assesses American views about racial discrimination 30 years after that famous speech.)

civil disobedience *The political protest strategy of purposefully disregarding laws and failing to comply with them in order to show opposition to them. Usually involves peaceful protest.*

In addition to demonstrations and marches, some civil rights protesters adopted the strategy of **civil disobedience,** peacefully violating segregation laws to send a signal to public authorities that segregation practices would not be tolerated. In doing so, they followed the lead set by Rosa Parks. Box 20-2: The Protest Game examines the constitutionality of civil disobedience as a political strategy.

President John F. Kennedy became, somewhat reluctantly, a prominent figure in the civil rights movement in 1963 when he promised to uphold major civil rights. Kennedy recognized that African Americans had given him substantial support in his 1960 election and knew that the Democratic party platform in those elections called for new civil rights laws. He was slow, however, to move forward with civil rights legislation in the early 1960s, fearing strong opposition from southern Democrats in his party. However, when the city commissioner of Birmingham used snarling dogs, cattle prods, and high-pressure fire hoses to break up a crowd of civil rights demonstrators—all captured on television—the public reaction was strong and Kennedy realized that he would have to

Box 20–1 Thirty Years Beyond I Have a Dream: American Views on Race and Civil Rights

In 1993—three decades after the Reverend Martin Luther King, Jr., proclaimed his dream of racial equality—the Gallup Poll conducted a survey of American attitudes about race and civil rights. The results of this poll illustrate how racial issues remain important ones in American politics.

Those surveyed by the poll were asked the following question: *In general, do you think blacks have as good a chance as white people in your community to get any kind of job for which they are qualified, or don't you think they have as good a chance?* Their answers, compared with responses to a similar survey question asked in 1963, are as follows:

	Total	Whites	African Americans
As good a chance			
1993	65%	70%	30%
1963	43%	46%	24%
Not as good a chance			
1993	31%	27%	66%
1963	48%	44%	74%

In both time periods, whites were far more likely than African Americans to perceive that African Americans and whites have an equal chance to obtain jobs for which they are qualified.

The same 1993 poll asked respondents whether they thought new civil rights laws are needed to reduce racial discrimination, whether the civil rights movement is still having a major impact on American society, and whether, over the past 30 years, the civil rights movement has been mostly successful or mostly unsuccessful in achieving its goals. The following survey responses were obtained for these questions from the nationwide sample:

	Percent Saying Yes		
	% All Respondents	% White	% African American
Do you think new civil rights laws are needed to reduce discrimination against blacks?	38%	33%	70%
Do you think the civil rights movement is still having a major impact on American society?	65%	66%	57%
Over the past 30 years, do you think the civil rights movement has been successful?	76%	77%	68%

Whites and African Americans have very different views on the need for new civil rights laws to reduce racial discrimination. Seventy percent of African Americans favor such laws, whereas only 33% of whites favor them. The two groups are closer in their views about the impact of the civil rights movement. Majorities of both groups believe that the civil rights movement is still having a major impact on American society and that the civil rights movement has been mostly successful. Whites, however, were somewhat more likely than African Americans to recognize the achievements of the civil rights movement on American life.

Source: C. Gray Wheeler, *30 Years Beyond I Have a Dream*, Gallup Poll Monthly (October 1993), 2-4.

finally take a position. In a speech televised to the nation in the summer of 1963, Kennedy stated:

> We are confronted primarily with a moral issue. It is as old as the scriptures and is as clear as the American Constitution. If an American, because his skin is dark, cannot eat in a restaurant open to the public, if he cannot send his children to the best public school available, and if he cannot vote for the public officials who represent him, if, in short, he cannot enjoy the full and free life which all of us want, then who among us would be content to have the color of his skin changed and stand in his place?

Box 20-2 The Protest Game: Is Civil Disobedience Unconstitutional?

Civil disobedience involves a purposeful violation of laws, without the use of threat or hostility, to protest public laws or policies. Such was the case in the South when African Americans refused to follow segregation policies and move to the rear of the bus when told to do so by the driver. Often, the police were called in such cases and protesters were arrested.

An interesting question concerns whether the strategy of civil disobedience is constitutional. Through a series of cases, the Supreme Court has held that individuals can disobey laws that are obviously unconstitutional as written. However, individuals may not freely or legally disobey laws that are constitutional as written but that are inappropriately applied in their case. Here, they must rely upon the judicial process to register their complaint and seek redress.

In June of 1963 Kennedy moved civil rights legislation to the top of the agenda and proposed a broad civil rights package that included legislation to guarantee African Americans access to public accommodations. It also allowed the government to file lawsuits to desegregate schools and allowed federal-aid programs to be cut off in programs that discriminated on the basis of race. The public accommodation section was symbolically the most important part of the law, for it sought to strike down the exclusion that African Americans had long experienced at lunch counters, restaurants, theaters, hotels, and other public facilities.

20-1c Major Civil Rights Legislation

The assassination of John F. Kennedy in 1963 could have threatened the push for civil rights. President Lyndon Johnson, however, immediately took up the cause and turned enactment of civil rights legislation into a memorial for Kennedy. Speaking to Congress only five days after the Kennedy's assassination, Johnson said that no eulogy to the slain president could be more eloquent than passage of a major civil rights act. He repeated his call to action in his 1964 State of the Union address. The House of Representatives proceeded first to consider civil rights legislation. Both the House Rules Committee and the Judiciary Committee reviewed the legislation that had been introduced in 1963 and passed the bill along for consideration by the full House of Representatives. After nine days of debate the House approved the bill by a vote of 290 to 130. Strongest opposition came from southern Democrats, who voted overwhelmingly against the civil rights bill.

Political games for civil rights next moved to the Senate, which had decided to await a House-enacted bill before proceeding to consider civil rights legislation. In a procedural move the Senate voted to place the House bill directly on the Senate calendar without moving it through the Senate Judiciary Committee. This unusual and strategic move was intended to prevent the legislation from becoming bottled up in the Senate Judiciary Committee, headed by a conservative southern Democrat, James O. Eastland of Mississippi.

From the start it was expected that opponents of civil rights legislation—concentrated among southern Democrats—would resort to the filibuster as a strategy to obstruct legislative passage. Starting on March 26, 1964, southern Democrats engaged in a filibuster that lasted 57 days. A key leader of the southern opponents was Senator Richard B. Russell, a Democrat from Georgia. He was joined by Senator Robert C. Byrd (D-WV), who set the record for the longest speech of the filibuster, speaking for 14 hours and 13 minutes. House Republican leaders stated they would reject the civil rights legislation if its key provisions were gutted by the Senate. For their part, civil rights groups warned that they would take protest to the streets if the Senate did not approve a strong civil rights measure.

Under substantial public scrutiny, the Senate continued its debate on civil rights legislation in the spring of 1964. Bill supporters like Senator Majority Leader Michael Mansfield (D-MT) and Majority Whip Hubert H. Humphrey (D-MN) worried that the filibuster might be effective in stopping the legislation, given that no past filibuster on civil rights proposals had been previously ended by cloture. Yet on a key vote on June 10, with all members present, the Senate voted 71-29 for cloture, closing off debate. What then followed was vote after vote on amendments to the House legislation. Many of the amendments were proposed by southern Senators who, after being unable to hold up the bill through filibuster, moved to delete or weaken key legislative features. While some changes were made on the margins, key provisions of the act—including those related to public accommodations—remained in the legislation. Finally, on June 19, almost a year after President Kennedy had introduced the legislation, the Senate passed the civil rights bill by a vote of 73–27.

Civil Rights Act of 1964
Important legislation that prohibits discrimination in public accommodations and employment on the basis of race, national origin, religion or sex.

The **Civil Rights Act of 1964,** as enacted by Congress, contains wide-ranging anti-discrimination provisions. While the Constitution provides that governments cannot discriminate on the basis of race, color, religion, or gender, it does not directly prohibit such practices within the private sector. The 1964 Civil Rights Act overcomes this limitation by prohibiting discrimination based on race, religion, national origin, or sex in public accommodations and employment. By moving into such areas as hotel accommodations and jobs offered by private sector operations, this civil rights act greatly extended protections against discrimination to women and minorities.

The act also calls for the use of federal spending power as a means of combating discrimination. It thus requires federal officials to withhold funds from any institution that engages in racial discrimination. The act also created the Equal Employment Opportunity Commission to protect individuals from unfair and discriminatory employment practices.

The United States has continued since the mid-1960s to develop and implement new policies to eliminate discrimination. The Civil Rights Act of 1968 expanded the protections contained in the original act by prohibiting discrimination in housing and creating penalties for the obstruction of rights through violence or intimidation. The law, for example, prohibits practices in advertising and renting properties that would discriminate on the basis of race or color.

The struggle to advance civil rights through legislative action has continued to recent times. A two-year struggle within Congress—and between Congress and the president—finally resulted in the Civil Rights Act of 1991. This legislation refines and clarifies procedures regarding enforcement of nondiscrimination provisions of earlier civil rights laws. In large measure, this law was prompted by dissatisfaction with a series of Supreme Court rulings that made it more difficult to sue in job discrimination cases.

While both the White House and congressional leadership said that some response to the Supreme Court decisions was necessary, they disagreed about just how the enforcement of nondiscrimination provisions of civil rights should be redirected in light of the Court's ruling. Conservatives, led by Republican President George H. Bush, criticized early versions of the legislation that became the Civil Rights Act of 1991. Bush and others called the early legislation "quota bills" that, they argued, would require employers and others to set aside positions to be exclusively filled by minorities or women. Proponents of the bill in Congress, including both Republicans and Democrats, disagreed with Bush's contention that the bill would establish any form of quotas. They charged that Bush used the quota issue as a means of sidetracking the civil rights legislation.

One provision of the Civil Rights Act of 1991 concerned hiring and promotion practices (including tests) that are apparently fair but that, when applied, have a disparate impact. In other words, they actually do discriminate. This includes any tests used during the hiring process that appear to be fair but that result in hiring more African-American than white job applicants. According to the act, when an employment practice can be shown to have disparate impact, then the burden to justify the practice shifts to the employer, who must demonstrate that the practice is required by business necessity. This provision overturned a Supreme Court ruling that held that it was the complainant's burden to prove that the practice was not related to business necessity.[3]

The Civil Rights Act of 1991 also considered whether provisions of an earlier federal law allowed complainants to sue for damages for racial job discrimination after they were already hired. In a 1989 case, the Supreme Court had interpreted the federal law as applying only to discrimination in hiring and not to discrimination in dismissals, promotions, and other actions taken after an individual was hired.[4] The Civil Rights Act of 1991 rejected this Supreme Court interpretation and applied discrimination protections to actions taken after the point of being hired. This act further enhanced the ability of those who feel they have been discriminated against in employment to seek redress in the courts and to receive compensation when their complaint of discrimination is proved valid.

The Civil Rights Act of 1991 demonstrated several interesting features of the game of politics. First, this act resulted largely from Congress and the president disagreeing with Supreme Court interpretations of earlier civil rights laws. They signaled their disagreement and provided clearer directions to the federal courts with new, stronger statutory language that clarified legislative intent. Second, the prolonged controversy over the passage of this act—in which members of Congress and the president engaged in heated oratory, making charges and calling names—illustrated how politics related to race issues remain divisive in America. George H. Bush's frequent reference to the quota bill, even when language was added to the bill to specifically outlaw quotas, shows the political power of symbolic language related to race and affirmative action.

20-1d The Battle for School Desegregation

The *Brown v. Board of Education of Topeka* case was both a major catalyst to the civil rights movement in general and a call to arms for desegregating public schools across the United States. Writing for the unanimous majority, Chief Justice Earl Warren wrote:

> We conclude that in the field of public education the doctrine of 'separate but equal' has no place. Separate educational facilities are inherently unequal.[5]

When the Court issued instructions in 1955 on the process of desegregating public schools;[6] some criticized these instructions as providing local school systems with too much latitude. This case was followed by many others in the federal courts that resulted in segregated school districts being ordered to desegregate. Implementation of these orders was often slow, however, since many state and local authorities resisted compliance. The most prominent form of defiance was the policy of **massive resistance,** where some southern school districts refused to integrate and went so far as to close down all public schools. Many Southern colleges, too, refused to admit African Americans.

massive resistance *Policies pursued in southern states to avoid compliance immediately after receiving order to desegregate public schools.*

In 1957 rioting broke out in Little Rock, Arkansas, when Governor Orvil Faubus used the Arkansas National Guard to prevent integration in local public schools. Although the federal government was initially wary of entering into this dispute, President Dwight D. Eisenhower, as commander-in-chief of the armed forces, eventually took control of the National Guard and prevented its interference with school integration. Racist tactics and public defiance of constitutional principles provoked the president to show strong federal determination to enforce desegregation.

Throughout late 1950s, local resistance to integration of southern schools was manifest across the South. Within a decade, however, most massive resistance strategies were abandoned as school systems accepted and began to execute plans to desegregate public schools and universities. Once the general principle of integration was accepted, the next question was one of strategy: How were schools to be integrated? This question was relevant not only to southern school districts but also to many in the North, where separate schools for whites and blacks resulted not from laws but from segregating living patterns of urban residents. A voluntary pattern of integration was tried in New Kent County, Virginia, where the school board devised a plan in which every student would be allowed to attend the school of his or her choice. The results were that practically all white students remained in their predominantly white school and most of the African American students stayed in their predominantly black school—so there was practically no integration. The Supreme Court struck down this plan in 1969, holding that the voluntary arrangement did not produce the intended objective of integration.[7]

Given that African Americans and whites in both the North and South lived separately from each other, one predominant strategy to pursue integration was busing. Children in public schools could be integrated—mixed together—by busing students to different parts of town than where they lived. The Supreme Court in 1971 recognized the power of district courts to fashion plans for school desegregation that included busing as well as reassigning teachers and altering school district lines.

Substantial controversy has continually surrounded the practice of busing to achieve integration. Some opposition has come from those who oppose the idea of school integration. But even for many who support the integration objective, long rides for small children on noisy buses has been a difficult and unpleasant price to pay. Given widespread public antipathy to busing as well as divided views within the judicial community, the federal courts have moved back from earlier stances that view widespread mandatory busing as the best and only way to achieve integration. The courts have looked favorably upon other strategies such as magnet schools that offer extra teachers, computers, and better resources as means to attract diverse student bodies and enhance student achievement.[8] Given shifting judicial views and court rulings, many school districts have sought release from mandatory busing activities that were initially mandated as part of judicial orders for desegregation.

Studies show both mixed public views about integration and mixed evidence on the impact of past desegregation policies. The proportion of African-American students who were being educated in schools with predominantly minority students declined from 77 percent in 1968–69 to 63 percent in 1980–81; this figure has risen, however, to 66 percent, showing a trend away from integration.[9] A 1991 survey by the National Opinion Research Corporation showed that more than 90% of white Americans support school integration in general, up from 40% in 1959. At the same time, however, no more than 5% of white parents would voluntarily move their child to a minority school, unless it was a specialized facility with innovative teachers and special resources.[10]

Contemporary issues associated with public school desegregation were evident in Hartford, Connecticut, where the school system in the mid-1990s was 94% African American or Latino, nearly 3 out of 4 students were poor, and the high school dropout rate was more than three times the state average. Recognizing its problems, the state allocated millions of dollars to the school system, which began to spend more money per pupil—nearly $9,000—than almost any other district.[11] The district devised specialized educational programs and magnet schools, but educational achievement has remained very low. A possible quick fix to this situation would have been to bus pupils across school district lines, taking some students to other nearby school districts where white children were predominant. The Connecticut Supreme Court struck down this plan because it was not shown that the state created the segregation that currently exists. Forced busing across school district lines was therefore not required. Hartford, like other many other urban school systems in the North and South, continues to look for means of improving educational achievement and pursuing integration within the context of districts whose residents are largely members of minorities.

By 2000, with some federal court orders to integrate school systems being lifted, some communities began to move away from busing and return to a neighborhood school approach—where many students attend a school close to their home. With this approach, the need for school busing is greatly reduced; busing is used only to transport students to specialty schools that focus on such curriculum areas as the arts or foreign language. Milwaukee's public school system was one of those to embrace neighborhood schools at the start of the 21st century. Under the Milwaukee plan, monies formerly used to bus students will be used to finance bonds that will provide monies to build new schools in dense urban neighborhoods that do not have enough classroom space for the neighborhood's student population.

20-1e Voting Rights Laws

Despite Americans' strong heritage of popular government based on the will of the people, the franchise (the right to vote) has only recently been extended to all adult citizens in the nation. The franchise is central to American democracy because it affects the selection of the presidents, members of Congress, and over eighty thousand elected officials at the state and local level. Because the Constitution contains no specific provisions about voting (the Founders decided to leave this responsibility in the hands of the states), the regulation of voting practices was traditionally viewed as a function of state governments. Early in America's history, voting in many states was restricted to male property owners. By the administration of Populist president Andrew Jackson, however, most states had enacted laws that allowed male citizens to vote.

After Reconstruction, southern states faced the prospect of large numbers of new African-American voters. Fearing the political power of African Americans, several southern states enacted provisions that made it harder for African Americans and other poor individuals to vote in party primaries to select candidates for the general election. Some states only allowed whites to vote in party primaries. Some also used the poll tax, requiring that voters pay a nominal sum to vote, or the *literacy test*, requiring potential voters to demonstrate their ability to read and write, as mechanisms to restrict voting by African Americans and poor whites.

Since the 1940s both judicial decisions and federal laws have eliminated these obstacles to African-American participation in voting. In 1944 the Supreme Court considered the argument of the Democratic Party of Texas that primaries were voluntary associations that had the right to exclude African-American participants. The Court ruled against the Texas political party and held that all-white primaries were unconstitutional.[12]

Federal legislation and a constitutional amendment have extended voting participation rights to African-American Americans. The 24th Amendment, ratified in 1964, struck down the poll tax. On the heels of the civil rights protests, Congress enacted the **Voting Rights Act of 1965.** This legislation, extended and strengthened since 1965, prohibits discrimination in registration and voting and forbids the use of literacy tests. In a move that extends federal government power directly into state affairs, the act allows the federal government to register voters and to oversee voter participation in areas with a record of voting discrimination.

Voting Rights Act of 1965
Law passed by Congress to prohibit discrimination in voting and registration.

20-1f African Americans in Contemporary Politics

With most legal impediments to basic voting rights and other rights of citizenship removed and basic prohibitions against discrimination in place, leaders of African-American and other minority groups have moved away from civil disobedience and adopted more traditional strategies to pursue civil rights in America. In the last two decades, African Americans have made substantial gains in achieving elected office at the state and local levels (see Chapter 18). At the national level, such leaders as Jesse Jackson have worked to keep the spotlight on social injustice and to aggressively register minority group members so that the electoral franchise can be used as a political strategy.

Many contemporary issues being considered by the nation's lawmakers are of importance to African Americans. Welfare and health care reform will hit African Americans harder than others, since this group is disproportionately represented in those receiving welfare assistance. (Chapter 19 surveys the changes taking place in social policy.) Given the strong urban residential patterns of African Americans, urban policies—and changes in them caused by federal spending cutbacks and transformation of entitlement programs into block grants—will be another key area of interest for this group of Americans.

20-2 Other Groups in American Politics

The American melting pot is composed of many groups of people of different races, ethnicities, and countries of origin. In addition to African Americans, other ethnic groups—including Latino Americans, Asian Americans, and Native Americans—have key interests in public policy, and a growing number of political organizations are representing group interests in the political games of American politics. As noted at the start of this chapter, it is important to recognize that each of these groups is diverse and that not all group members share the same political ideology, party affiliation, views about public policy, or strategies for political participation.

20-2a Latino Americans

The term *Latino American* is a label applied to individuals who trace their origins to Spain or to many nations in Central and South America. The U.S. Census Bureau estimated the Latino population to be just less than 40 million, representing 14% of the total U.S. population. This number is expected to increase to 41 million by the year 2010 as Latino Americans become a proportionally larger demographic segment of American society. For the Census Bureau, Latino is an ethnicity category and those classifying themselves as Latino can be either white or African American. Among Latinos, the most frequently claimed countries of origin are Mexico, Puerto Rico, and Cuba, respectively.

Like other immigrant groups coming to the United States, Latinos tend to concentrate in large metropolitan areas. Initially, Los Angeles and New York were popular destinations for Latinos entering the nation. In the past two decades, Miami, Washington, D.C., and San Francisco have also witnessed the growth of large Latino populations. Life in southwestern border states is clearly flavored by residents of Latino background as is evident in cities like San Antonia, Texas; Santa Fe, New Mexico; and Phoenix, Arizona.

Some Latino Americans have lived a more rural existence. Throughout the century, Mexican-American workers have played a key role in agriculture working as field hands and migratory workers, moving from area to area to assist with planting and harvest. The conditions faced by these workers were often harsh, with low wages and poor living quarters. Because of their need to be mobile, the migrant workers seldom had access to public services and their children often received little schooling. In an effort to improve the wages paid to these workers and to enhance their working conditions, Mexican Americans pressed for legislation. Cesar Chavez—a Mexican American whose family lost their family farm and were forced to become migrant workers—led a national movement in the 1960s to create a national farm workers' union. A strike by grape pickers and a nationwide boycott of table grapes in 1966 brought Chavez and his cause to national visibility, bringing attention to this growing population in the U.S. and the poor treatment that many migratory workers received.

Immigration has been an issue of persistent importance to many Latino Americans. The close proximity of Mexico, Cuba, and other Latin American nations to the U.S. border, and the relative prosperity of the American economy, have worked to attract continued immigration into the United States. American immigration laws have allowed many people from these nations to migrate to the U.S., although immigration quotas were not large enough to admit all who wanted to come. For this reason, a substantial proportion of migrants from Mexico and nearby nations have entered the nation illegally, often joining family members who have already settled in the U.S. Despite efforts to tighten the boundary, illegal immigrants continue to enter the United States in substantial numbers.

With the exception of the right to vote, most constitutional rights extend to **aliens** in the United States. However, their residency may be conditioned by government regulations (e.g., visa requirements).[13] Yet despite the general principle that aliens—including those emigrating to the U.S. from Central and South America and from Asian nations—have basic rights and liberties, federal and state laws have discriminated against aliens. Underlying these discriminatory practices has been a sense on the part of some policy makers that aliens should not receive all the benefits that are available to citizens. Through a series of cases making their way to the Supreme Court, aliens have fought discrimination and won legal protections. Court decisions, for example, have struck down state laws that conditioned welfare benefits on citizenship and duration of residency,[14] barred aliens from practicing the law,[15] and prohibited aliens from being employed by state civil servants.[16]

aliens *A legal visitor or resident in a nation of which he or she is not a citizen; a citizen of one nation living in another.*

Greater problems are faced by aliens who have illegally entered the nation. Concern about illegal immigration coupled with worries about government spending—both generally and on social services for illegal aliens—led to a major political backlash in 1994. The backlash was centered in California, the state estimated to have the largest number of illegal aliens. In a measure termed "Save Our State" by its sponsors, a ballot initiative was developed that would render undocumented illegal aliens ineligible for welfare services, public school education, and nonemergency medical care. State offices providing health, welfare, and public education services would be required under the initiative to report suspected illegal aliens. Supporters received a sufficient number of signatures of eligible voters to place the initiative on the state's 1994 election ballot. The measure—known as Proposition 187—received strong public support and was approved by a 3 to 2 ratio.

Republican Governor Pete Wilson, a strong proponent of the initiative, ordered state agencies to develop regulations to enforce the anti-illegal immigrant policy immediately following the election. To date, however, the measure has not yet been enforced. It was challenged in the courts on the grounds that it violated the constitutional rights of aliens. From the start, the constitutionality of Proposition 187 was in doubt, particularly given a Supreme Court decision in 1982 that struck down a Texas law that authorized local public schools to exclude undocumented (i.e., illegal) aliens. The federal courts ultimately struck down most provisions of Proposition 187 as unconstitutional.

Language differences is another issue of concern to some Latino groups. This group of Americans—particularly those who have recently immigrated to the U.S.—often speak little English and have Spanish as their native language. The politics of language has played out in many areas. One is public education. Some advocates for Latino children argued that English language deficiency deprived these children from receiving an adequate education. Congress responded in 1968 by creating the Bilingual Education Act to aid schools in developing educational programs that included instruction in Spanish and English. The program was strengthened in 1974 by requiring school districts that applied for bilingual funds to require native-language instruction. The program has continued since that time although legislation changes in 1984 eased the native-language requirement, allowing districts to use other methods to compensate for English-language deficiency.

The issue of language has for some time touched other undercurrents in American politics. Conservative politicians have felt strongly that English should serve as the nation's fundamental language and that proficiency in the language was a necessary prerequisite for success in American society. Pursuing a common national language was seen as a uniting force in society. It was also seen by conservatives as a means to weaken the unity of minority groups who traditionally ally themselves with liberals and the Democratic Party (see Chapter 8). Through Proposition 227, enacted by voters by a 61%–39% margin in 1998, California replaced bilingual education programs with English-immersion programs. The argument behind this proposition is that students whose first language is not English will do better by becoming proficient in English as quickly as possible—rather than learning through their native language. This policy, which angered many Latino residents in California at the time, has shown some positive gains in academic achievement for California's 1.4 million limited-English immigrant students.

20-2b Asian Americans

Americans who trace their origin to Asian nations and the Pacific Islands comprise just over 4% of the nation's population in 2003. California is the state with the highest number of Asian Americans, followed by New York, Texas, and New Jersey.

One of the first waves of immigration from Asia consisted of Chinese who came to America in the mid-1800s in search of opportunity and advancement. Many took jobs in farming, railroad construction, and mining. The cultural and language differences of the Chinese, and other Asians to follow, led to discrimination and being ostracized. Oftentimes, Asians lived largely among themselves; in large cities, their enclaves became known as *Chinatowns*, places rich with heritage and attractive to outsiders looking for authentic food, culture, and goods. The Chinese were then joined by the Japanese, Koreans, and Filipinos. More recently, arrivals are individuals and families from nations of southeast Asia including Vietnam, Laos, and Thailand—nations connected to the U.S.

through American military action in the Vietnam War. These groups, including Hmong groups from Laos and Cambodia, are settling in cities across the nation and are sometimes sponsored in their relocation by local organizations.

Like other minority groups in American society, Asian Americans have encountered prejudice and discrimination. Perhaps the most striking example was the internment of Japanese Americans during World War II. At the outbreak of war in 1941, soon after much of the nation's naval fleet was destroyed by surprise attack by the Japanese at Pearl Harbor, fears arose about the loyalty of individuals of Japanese background. Based on fear and prejudice, rather than evidence, policy makers feared that Japanese Americans, especially those concentrated on the West Coast, would be sympathetic to the Japanese cause and become likely participants in espionage and sabotage. German Americans and those of Italian descent did not receive similar suspicion despite the fact that Germany and Italy were among the nations at war with the United States.

Responding to the fears and prejudice, President Franklin D. Roosevelt approved Executive Order 9066 in 1942, which set up camps inland and away from the West Coast to which Japanese Americans were forced to relocate. People had to sell their homes and businesses quickly and move to these detention camps, which sometimes were surrounded by barbed wire and armed soldiers. About 110,000 people of Japanese ancestry were interned by this order. The relocation process began with movement to temporary assembly centers, including the Santa Anita racetrack, where internees lived in stables formerly occupied by race horses. Next, they were moved to camps in California, Arizona, Utah, Colorado, and other states. The Supreme Court upheld the internment decree, citing the special conditions of war. The practice, however, has since become an embarrassment. In 1988, in partial compensation for the internment action, Congress awarded $20,000 to each victim in recognition of the economic loss and personal suffering incurred.

Like other minorities, Asian Americans work to achieve equal rights and combat discrimination when it arises. Some Asian Americans face a rather unusual situation, however, one based upon their relative success in assimilating into American society. Many Asian Americans, over a relatively short period of time, have adapted to American life, enhanced their economic and social position, and seen their children make strong achievements in school. These achievements have reached the point, for example, that if only test scores and grades were considered, Asian Americans would receive the greatest number of slots in colleges and universities. At the University of California at Berkeley, for example, Asian Americans already are the largest group on campus. This trend has caused some backlash against Asian Americans. Some whites feel that affirmative action to help strong-performing Asian Americans represents reverse discrimination. Other ethnic and racial minorities have voiced concern about Asian Americans taking the greatest proportion of affirmative action slots. These tensions contribute to overall concerns about affirmative action policies.

20-2c Native Americans

Too often, public views about Native Americans have been shaped by western films that often depict inaccurate and misleading pictures of Indian groups. In recent years, museums and traveling exhibits, television documentaries, books, and other media have been broadening public appreciation of the diversity and richness of the many distinct Indian cultures. Figure 20-1 lists the prominent Native American tribes in America today.

Native American civilizations date back some 30,000 years and were spread over the land area that came to be the United States. Early interactions between settlers from Western Europe and the Indians were sometimes positive—remember the first Thanksgiving where both groups celebrated the first real harvest—and sometimes negative.

The cultures and attitudes of settlers and Native Americans were generally at odds. The culture of most Indian tribes stressed communality—working for and with the group to achieve group objectives. This ethos differed from the individualistic spirit of the European political culture that was transferred to the New World. Native American cultures have typically placed high value in nature—believing that the natural environment is a resource to be appreciated and used wisely to satisfy needs for food, clothing, and shelter.

Figure 20-1
Native American Tribes

The tribal origins of Native Americans are many, as demonstrated in the number of tribes listed in this figure. Each tribe has its own heritage and customs. One measure of the rich heritage and diversity of American Indians is their tribal connections and histories. The data provide a breakdown of Native American tribes living on selected reservations and trust lands with more than 10,000 in population.

Source: U.S. Bureau of the Census, *2000 Census of Population, General Population Characteristics.* (Washington, D.C.: GPO), 2000.

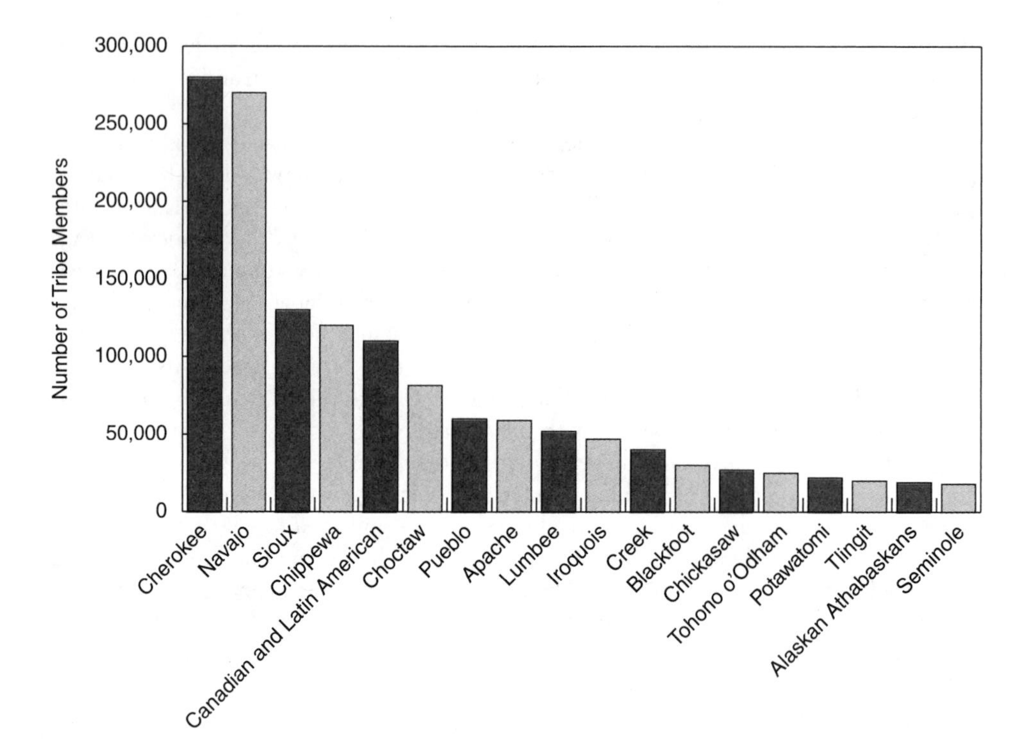

These beliefs ran counter to the settlers' mission to tame the land and aggressively utilize the natural resources without attention to long-term environmental impacts. Many Indian groups were nomadic, moving with the change of seasons and the movement of game and wildlife. Settlers preferred to be more stationary, at least in the short run, cutting down trees and erecting fences to designate parcels of private property. To Indians the land was a common asset for all to enjoy.

These cultural differences were profound and served as the root of persistent conflict. In a pattern known as manifest destiny, waves of settlers pushed forward across the North American continent in search of new lands to settle and farm and new opportunities to earn a living. As they moved, they claimed the land and proceeded to erect settlements. The rights of Native Americans to land were seldom recognized.

The conflicts that arouse often turned bloody—sometimes resulting in substantial loss of life on both sides. They ended with temporary truces and then negotiation of treaties granting Native Americans some plots of land in exchange for much larger tracts being opened for settlement. In the end, Native Americans were pushed into a few reservations—tracts of land ceded by the federal government to tribes.

assimilation *The process by which immigrants adopt the American political culture, the English language, the social customs and move away from their native language, customs, and traditions. The process of becoming "Americanized."*

Government policy pushed for **assimilation,** pressing Native Americans to adopt the predominant culture's values and customs, and downplayed the traditional spirit and richness of the Native American culture. The usual results have been poverty and disillusionment.

Reservation life fostered dependency, replacing ancestral languages with English and eroding traditional religion in favor of Christianity. Officials transferred many children from their parents to boarding schools, operated by the Bureau of Indian Affairs, where they were resocialized as Americans. The U.S. government also gave local control of reservations to the few Native Americans who supported such policies, and officials distributed reservation land—traditionally held collectively—as private property of Indian families.[17]

In the past few decades, a new spirit and vitality has begun to move through Native Americans. Appreciation for the fundamental principles of traditional Native American cultures is growing. Native Americans themselves are revisiting their customs and traditions and finding solidarity. Some enterprising tribes have established gambling casinos on tribal lands—an innovation that has generated substantial new incomes for some Native American tribes and created tensions with state officials. Native Americans have been able to create these gaming facilities in states that otherwise have outlawed casino gambling because tribal land is legally considered tribal property regulated by the federal government—and outside of state government control. Growing social cohesion among Native American tribes and increasing inter-tribal cooperation are translating into greater political power for this group of Americans, who have begun to press government for policies to end discrimination and enhance employment opportunities.

20-2d Gays and Lesbians

Another group of Americans that has become an important political force is gay men and lesbians. Like other minority groups, homosexuals have faced persistent discrimination throughout the nation's history. On the other hand, sexual preference is a factor that manifests itself in feelings and behavior—not necessarily through immediate appearance. For this reason and because of discrimination, many gay men and lesbians have chosen to "live in the closet," sometimes conducting their lives so that friends and colleagues do not know of their sexual preference. Increasingly in the past two decades, they have come out of the closet. Many proudly note their homosexuality and press for political rights and elimination of discrimination.

The non-gay American public continues to come to terms with homosexuality and the political activities and objectives of gay rights activists. The Gallup Poll in 1993 asked a random sample of Americans whether they agreed or disagreed with the statement that homosexuals should remain in the closet and not reveal their sexuality. Fifty-six percent of all of those responding disagreed.[18] Tolerance was greater among women. Sixty-three percent of women as opposed to 48% of men disagreed with the statement that homosexuals should remain in the closet.

Within the past two decades, an increasing number of openly gay legislators have been elected to national, state, and local offices. At the national level, Representatives Barney Frank (D-MA) and Tammy Baldwin (D-WI) for example, have acknowledged their sexual orientation and have become spokespeople on important gay-related political issues. The Gay and Lesbian Victory Fund, a political action committee supporting the election of homosexuals to public office, reported receiving requests for financial assistance from the campaigns of over 130 candidates nationwide in 1994.[19] One prominent illustration of the growing power of homosexuals in America was provided by a march on Washington in April 1993. Hundreds of thousands of people from around the nation gathered to openly proclaimed their homosexuality, listen to entertainment, and voice support for gay rights.

State governments have taken the lead in designing policies dealing with homosexuals. Many states historically sought to criminalize homosexuality by passing laws that prohibit what politicians of the day saw as crimes against nature. Typically, such statutes outlaw homosexual behavior similar to the way they outlaw many types of sexual practices among heterosexual couples. Although most of these laws have seldom been enforced in recent decades, their existence testifies to the historical prejudice against homosexuality. The federal courts have traditionally tended to uphold the right of states to enact laws concerning sexual practices in the name of public health and safety. As recently as 1986, the Supreme Court upheld the right of states to create laws banning homosexuality and refused to grant a right of privacy protection on homosexual behavior.[20]

In recent years, state legislatures and city halls have become active battlegrounds for the rights of homosexuals. As of 2004, 20 states had adopted laws prohibiting employment discrimination based on sexual orientation and 10 states had laws offering state employees domestic partner benefits. Battles over gay rights became an issue in the 2004 presidential campaign after the State of Massachusetts and cities like San Francisco allowed gays to register for marriage or civil union.

Thus far, federal law provides practically no specific protections for gay men and lesbians. The phrases *sexual preference* or *sexual orientation* are not to be found in civil rights laws that prohibit discrimination on the basis of gender, race, ethnicity, color, national origin, or religion. Gay and lesbian political organizations continue to work to have federal laws amended to include homosexual rights. Several current policy issues remain active on the gay and lesbian agenda. Most generally, this group of Americans is pushing for expanded legal protections against discrimination in employment, education, access to medical care, and housing.

In some states, recent political battles have shown a backlash against gay rights. In 1992 residents of Colorado approved a referendum to change the state constitution to bar all measures protecting homosexuals against discrimination. The referendum sought to invalidate ordinances in cities including Denver, Boulder, and Aspen that barred discrimination against gays and lesbians. This move led gay men and lesbians—with support from celebrities like actress Barbra Streisand—to press for a boycott of the state and its ski resorts. Soon after enactment, the law was challenged; the Supreme Court agreed to consider the case. The Supreme Court ultimately struck down this law on the grounds that handicapping a specific group from protections violated the Equal Protection and Due Process rights of the U.S. Constitution (14th Amendment).

The issue of homosexual rights in American society took center stage in 1993 as newly elected President Bill Clinton announced plans to lift the ban on homosexuals in the nation's armed forces (see Time Out 20-1: Gays in the Military: A High-Powered Political Game). The controversy that surrounded this plan, and the vehemence that was expressed by opponents, led Clinton to announce a 6-month delay in lifting the ban. Clinton requested that Secretary of Defense Les Aspin study the issue and devise a plan. At the end of the 6 months, after congressional hearings were held on the issue, the Defense Department announced an alternative to lifting the ban. The *Don't Ask/Don't Tell* policy prohibited the armed services from asking members of the military about their sexual orientation. It also banned service personnel from engaging in homosexual conduct or identifying themselves as homosexual. This policy, played up by the Clinton administration as a compromise, dissatisfied many gay and lesbian rights groups who preferred the original plan to eliminate the ban altogether.

Besides homosexual rights, gay men and lesbians have other policy interests. One set of policy concerns focuses on the AIDS (Acquired Immune Deficiency Syndrome) epidemic. While the AIDS crisis affects all segments of American society, its impact has been felt most strongly among gay men. At first, the federal government was slow to

Time Out 20-1

Gays in the Military: A High-Powered Political Game

Background

As a presidential candidate, Bill Clinton pledged to do away with the government's ban on gays in the military. Soon after taking the oath of office, Clinton proceeded to make good on his pledge. Under the policy in place when Clinton took office, the military could discharge any member found to have engaged in homosexual conduct or to have simply declared his or her sexual orientation. This policy, issued by the Defense Department in 1982, stated that "homosexuality is incompatible with military service. The presence in a military environment of persons who engage in homosexual conduct or who, by their statements, demonstrate a propensity to engage in homosexual conduct, seriously impairs the accomplishment of the military mission."[a] In the decade since the directive was issued, the military had charged about 14,000 personnel on the grounds of homosexuality, with about 1,500 people a year discharged for this reason. When Clinton announced his plan to lift the ban on homosexuals in the military, a major political game unfolded, with many players taking sides in a divided debate about Clinton's proposal.

Questions

1. What do you think the primary arguments were for creating the ban on gays in the military in the first place? What reasons do you think opponents gave for ending the ban?
2. What rules allow action on this issue? What players would you expect to be actively involved in the debate about lifting the ban? Why would they be involved? What stakes did they have in the game? What impact would popular opinion have?

---

a. U.S. Department of Defense, Directive 1332.14, issued January 28, 1992.

respond to the crisis, as medical experts sought to understand the nature of the disease and its transmission. With the seriousness of the epidemic becoming clear, and with major figures like actor Rock Hudson dying from AIDS, Congress took limited action in the mid-1980s by authorizing funding for research on the disease. In 1987 President Ronald Reagan appointed a national commission to study the AIDS crisis and recommend federal government policy responses.

The100th Congress was the first to initiate a federal response to the AIDS crisis. In 1988, as part of the Omnibus Health Bill, Congress appropriated funds for education on the disease, voluntary disease testing and counseling programs, and home- and community-based health care for those suffering from AIDS and those testing positive for the human immunodeficiency virus (HIV). With this legislative measure, governmental response to the crisis moved from research funding to more active strategies. In the same year, the presidential commission on AIDS—headed after initial turmoil by retired admiral James D. Watkins—announced its findings. Chief among the commission's findings was that discrimination against persons who tested positive for HIV, the cause of AIDS, was the single foremost obstacle to fighting the disease. The panel pressured for a strong anti-discrimination policy in response. This proposal was not well received by conservatives, and President Reagan refused to embrace the commission's recommendations. For this reason, the anti-discrimination plan did not enter the policy-making agenda.

In 1990 Congress moved further in fashioning a federal response to the AIDS epidemic by passing the Ryan White Comprehensive AIDS Resources Emergency Act of 1990. The bill was named after a young Indiana boy who was barred from attending his local school after he contracted AIDS from a blood transfusion. The case received national attention and personified the plight of people suffering from the disease. This legislation created a new grant program of emergency relief for areas hardest hit by the epidemic and expanded grant funds for community-based agencies and hospices to provide care to persons with AIDS. It provided still other funds for early intervention services for persons with the disease, persons testing positive for HIV, and those at increased risk of contracting the disease.

Perhaps the primary gay rights issue at the turn of the century concerned same-sex marriage—an issue that strikes deeply into the area of personal values and morals. The issue came to national attention in 1996 as state courts in Hawaii ruled that the state had no compelling interest, under the state's constitution, to prevent same-sex marriages. This ruling raised the fear of many conservatives across the nation that gay couples would travel to Hawaii, become married under Hawaiian law, return to their home community, and expect the marriage to be considered legal (as is the case with marriages of heterosexual couples). Such recognition would mean, among other things, that gay spouses would be eligible for health insurance and other benefits through their partner's private or public sector employment. Several states, in response, worked to ensure that same-sex marriages would not be legally recognized in their state. The U.S. Congress became involved in 1996 and enacted a law that stipulated that no state would be required to recognize a same-sex marriage sanctioned in another state.

Gay rights emerged as a Supreme Court issue in 2003 as the nation's top court was asked to rule on the constitutionality of a Texas state law that made it illegal for persons of the same-sex to engage in sexual relations (*Lawrence v. Texas*). The case dated back to 1996, when police officers entered the home of John Lawrence, in response to a false report of a weapons disturbance, and found Mr. Lawrence having sex with Tyron Garner. The responding officers jailed the two men, charging them with violating the Texas homosexual conduct law that makes it a crime for same-sex couples to engage in sex. The two men challenged the arrest, arguing that the state law under which they were prosecuted violated their constitutional rights to privacy and equal protection under the law (14th Amendment).

In 1986, in *Bowers v. Hardwick*, the Supreme Court held that the Constitution affords no privacy protection to consensual homosexual conduct. In a dramatic decision in 2003 the Supreme Court reversed its early ruling and struck down state laws that make it criminal for individuals of the same gender to engage in sexual relations. This ruling was hailed as a major victory for gay rights activists, who claimed that private sexual behavior was not a matter appropriately regulated by the government (*Lawrence and Garner v. Texas, 02-0102*).

Answers to Time Out 20-1

The political debate over lifting the ban on homosexuals in the military was a flashpoint in the very early days of the Clinton administration. In many ways, lifting the ban would be easy. Clinton could do this through presidential directive. However, intense opposition arose immediately to the proposal to lift the ban, and that opposition was often bipartisan. For example, conservatives from both parties in Congress threatened to write the military's regulation barring homosexuality into law. (Elevating the policy from agency to directive to public law would strengthen it and prevent Clinton from lifting the ban through presidential order). Public reaction was strong as well. Gay rights groups pressed the new president hard to follow through on his campaign pledge, while a national opinion poll said that Americans were largely split on lifting the ban on gays in the military.[a] The military with great unanimity opposed lifting the ban, offering the argument that the presence of homosexuals adversely affects the ability of military services to maintain discipline, trust, order, and morale among its members.

Clinton recognized within days that a major political battle was at hand—one that he had not fully anticipated. He was reluctant to force a showdown on this issue early in his administration, perhaps using up political support that could be used to press forward other policy objectives. In an effort to quell the dispute for the moment, and preempt Congress from taking action, Clinton announced a 6-month delay in lifting the ban and also a moratorium on actions to dismiss homosexuals. During the 6 months, an effort would be made to devise a compromise policy. Defense Secretary Les Aspin—until recently a Representative from Wisconsin—was charged with developing the policy.

Politics continued during the 6-month interim. Congress decided to hold hearings on the issue. Military leaders testified that they believed the introduction of openly homosexual individuals into small units would polarize those units and destroy the bonding that is so important to survival in time of war. Other military officers echoed the general's sentiments, while other military personnel said they did not see homosexuality as a substantial problem in military service. In touching testimony, Marine colonel Frederick C. Peck told the committee that one of his sons was homosexual but that he would oppose permitting him to join the military. He said that his son would be in jeopardy if he enlisted. Groups representing gay rights continued to press their point that gays have served in the military throughout the nation's history without major problems. Even conservative Senator Strom Thurmond of South Carolina, while stating his support for the ban, applauded the gay servicemen and women saying that "The record is replete with instances of dedicated and heroic service by many gays in the ranks of our armed forces."

After protracted debate, a policy compromise was reached—one quite far from the president's initial plan to lift the ban. Under this plan, announced by Clinton in July 1993, the Pentagon would be banned from asking members of the armed services to disclose their sexual orientation. It also banned efforts to catch and identify homosexuals within military units. At the same time, the plan reaffirmed the Pentagon's strict proscription of homosexual behavior and forbid military personnel from even disclosing their sexual orientation to their friends. This plan became known as the *Don't Ask/Don't Tell* policy. Gay rights groups were contemptuous of the plan, while then-Joint Chiefs of Staff Chairman General Colin L. Powell, Jr., called the policy an honorable compromise. Ultimately, Congress enacted legislation that repeated its intent that gays not serve in the military, while basically adopting the compromise plan devised by Aspin and Clinton.

As with most policy games, this was not the last round. Gay and civil rights groups turned to the courts for help in overturning the Don't Ask/Don't Tell Policy. They asked the U.S. District Court for the District of Columbia to block implementation of the policy, arguing that it violated the free speech and association rights of the 14th Amendment. Then, acting in the case of a gay sailor in California, a U.S. District Judge in California ruled against the policy, and this decision was upheld in the Ninth Circuit Court of Appeals. In response to the court's ruling, the Pentagon suspended enforcement of the ban on gays in the military. The policy question remains open as the federal judiciary decides whether a ban on homosexuals in the military violates constitutional rights and liberties. In the meantime, glad the issue was decided for the moment, the Clinton administration moved on to other items on its policy agenda.

---

a. Lydia Saad and Leslie McAneny, "Americans Deeply Split Over Ban on Gays in Military," *Gallup Poll Monthly*, February 1993, 6–11.

20-2e People with Disabilities

People with mental or physical disabilities face many obstacles to enjoying the full benefits of modern society. These individuals often are confronted with public misconceptions and negative stereotypes about their abilities and needs. For people with disabilities, many barriers to participation in mainstream society have resulted from decisions in the public and private sectors.

One major obstacle has been the built environment, that is, the design and construction of public buildings and facilities. The designs of many architects and planners have included features that prevent people with physical disabilities from gaining access. In an effort to remove these tangible obstacles, Congress enacted the Architectural Barriers Act of 1968, requiring that buildings constructed with federal funds be accessible to individuals with disabilities, including persons using wheelchairs.

Section 504, a provision of an act that reauthorized the Rehabilitation Act in 1973, stated that recipients of federal funds may not discriminate on the basis of handicap. This provision has been translated into federal regulations that require employers who receive federal funds (including state and local governments) to provide reasonable accommodations in the workplace to enhance the employment of workers with disabilities. Section 504 also led the Department of Transportation to require local transit authorities to provide persons with disabilities with transportation services comparable to those provided to other transit riders.

Capping a decade of effort, Congress enacted legislation in 1990 that provided even greater protections for persons with disabilities. The Americans with Disabilities Act (ADA) bars discrimination on the basis of disability in public and private employment, public transportation, public accommodations (for example, hotels, retail stores, and restaurants), and telecommunications. By extending protections into the private sector, the act made civil rights for individuals with disabilities comparable to those provided to women and racial minorities. For many people, disability rights laws literally opened their world to opportunities that were unimaginable only a few years before. One writer, describing the effect of the ADA, noted:

> The law's [ADA] mandate requiring universal access to public buildings, transit systems and communications networks has made a once daunting world more navigable. Curb ramps, lift-equipped buses and extrawide restroom stalls for wheelchair users are now as common a feature of the American landscape as are close-captioned TV titles.[21]

Preliminary evidence on implementation of the act demonstrates that some accommodations can be achieved easily and with little expense. Other accommodations, however, do require significant expenditures to achieve compliance with ADA requirements, a situation that has generated some hostility from local and state officials. Their concerns focus on the compliance costs and what they see as a strong yet unfunded federal mandate (see Chapter 3). For their part, private companies have begun the process of implementation. A study of 404 corporate executives by Louis Harris & Associates in 1995 found that 81% had modified their offices since enactment of the ADA. The median cost of making the workplace more accessible was found to be $223 dollars per disabled person, and two-thirds of the businesses said the ADA had not increased lawsuits.[22] The rate of employment of people with disabilities in these companies, however, has remained quite low.

Political issues about disability-focused rights found their way into the federal courts by the late 1990s, nearly a decade after passage of the Americans with Disabilities Act. In separate cases, the Supreme Court issued rulings that tended to limit the types of conditions that were covered by the ADA, thereby reducing the overall scope of protections provided by the ADA. Some critics saw these legal decisions as evidence of a backlash against disability rights mandates.[23] Clearly, questions about the full meaning and application of the ADA will continue for some time.

20-3 Civil Rights and Women

In recent decades, women in the United States have achieved greater equality and have moved into economic, social, and political positions that at one time were almost exclusively the province of men. Their gains have resulted from several factors, including efforts by women's groups to press both the government and society to recognize equal rights for women. One significant achievement was ratification of the 19th Amendment, which granted women the right to vote. The status of women in society was subsequently enhanced with their entry into the workforce, beginning in World War II and continuing in the postwar period. A contemporary picture of public views on the status of women is provided through public opinion poll results in Box 20-3.

20-3a Women Win the Vote

One early issue that rallied the cause of women and stimulated the formation of political groups for women concerned the vote. Women, like other groups in American society, were forced to enter the political game in order to obtain the right to vote. Leaders like Alice Paul, head of the National Women's Party, fought hard and strong to push for women's right to vote. The franchise was extended to women in 1920 after many years of protests by suffragettes, who argued that women were citizens who deserved the right to vote. In response to their protests, the 19th Amendment, adopted in 1920, guarantees women's voting rights.

20-3b Equal Pay for Women in the Workplace

One of the most important political issues affecting women has been the controversy over privacy rights and abortion (as described earlier in Chapter 4). Another leading women's rights issue today concerns the often lower pay that women earn in the workforce as compared with male workers. Recognizing an imbalance in the wages paid to women, Congress enacted, and President John F. Kennedy signed into law, the Equal Pay Act of 1963, which requires employers to pay men and women performing equal work an equivalent salary. This legislation marked the first action by the federal government to safeguard the right of women to hold jobs on the same basis as men.[24]

The Equal Pay Act prohibits employers from discriminating among employees on the basis of gender by paying wages to some employees at a lower rate than those paid to employees of the opposite sex for equal work on the job. Exceptions to this principle may be allowable if wage differentials result from (1) a company's seniority policy, (2) a merit system, (3) a system that measures earnings by quantity or quality or production, or (4) any other factor other than sex.[25] As the result of legislation since 1963, the Equal Pay Act now extends to federal, state, and local government employees.

To charge that a company wage plan is violating the Equal Pay Act, the plaintiff (the person bringing the charges of an unfair pay differential) must make the case that his or her work is substantially equal to that of employees of the opposite sex.[26] If this claim is substantiated, then the burden shifts to the employer, who must demonstrate that the pay differential results from one of the four exceptions listed previously that are permitted under the act.

Despite the Equal Pay Act, wage differentials between men and women continued into the 1990s. Some groups, including many feminist organizations, argue that wage differentials result from segregation practices in the workplace that channel women into lower-paying, lower-responsibility positions. This channeling is seen as reducing the earnings and employment potential of female employees. Other analysts, including some prominent conservatives, hold that wage differentials between men and women result not from discrimination but from other factors unrelated to gender. Reflecting this perspective, the U.S. Commission on Civil Rights concluded in 1985 that male-female wage differences resulted from low job expectations on the part of women, educational choices

Women suffragists picketing in front of the White House, 1917.
Source: Library of Congress, Prints & Photographs Division [LC-USZ62-31799]

leading to jobs that can accommodate childbearing and child-rearing activities, and interruptions in employment due to pregnancy and child-rearing.[27]

The answer to the wage differential issue, according to many advocate groups for women, is a policy of **comparable worth,** the idea that men and women working in jobs of comparable skill, effort, responsibility, and conditions deserve comparable pay. The notion

comparable worth *The view that women should receive equal pay for jobs that are comparable to those held by men, when they have equivalent education and job experience.*

Box 20–3 *Gender Equality in America*

According to a poll conducted by the Gallup Organization in 1993, the challenges of being a woman are increasingly more daunting. Although an increasing number of women are entering the workforce, Americans in 1993 were less likely than in 1975 to say that women have equal job opportunities. The poll also indicates that the public has become more likely to believe that males enjoy a better life in this country than do females. Poll results reflect this story.

1. Do you think society generally favors men and women equally, or does it favor women over men, or men over women?

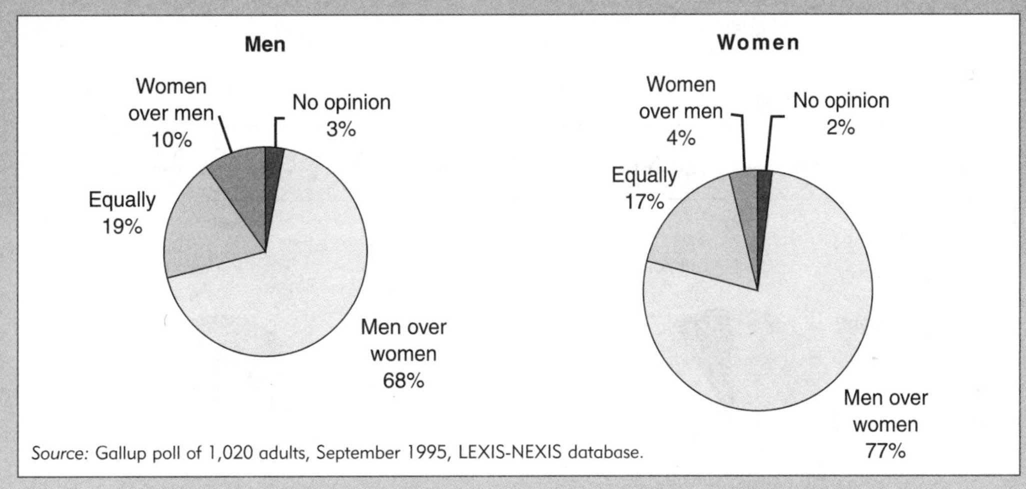

Source: Gallup poll of 1,020 adults, September 1995, LEXIS-NEXIS database.

2. Is it generally better for society if the man is the achiever outside the home, and the woman takes care of the home and family?

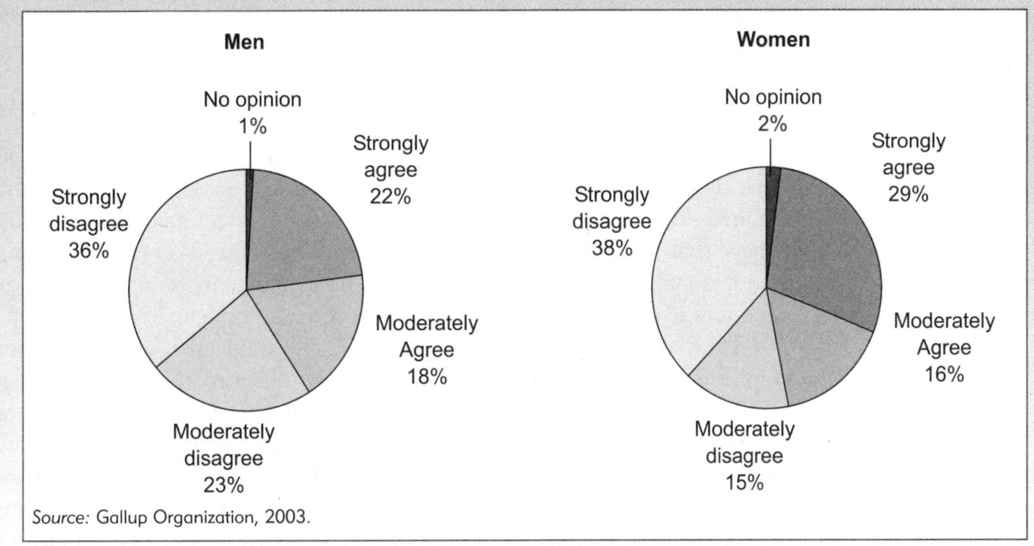

Source: Gallup Organization, 2003.

continued

Box 20-3 Gender Equality in America

—*Continued*

3. Do you think the changes brought about by the women's movement have made men's lives easier or harder than they were 20 years ago?

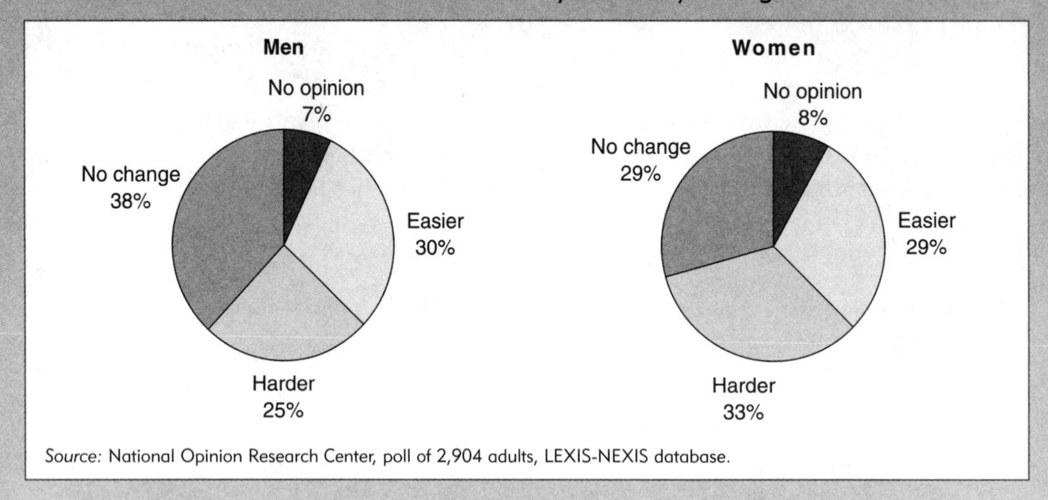

Source: National Opinion Research Center, poll of 2,904 adults, LEXIS-NEXIS database.

4. All things considered, who has a better life in this country—men or women?

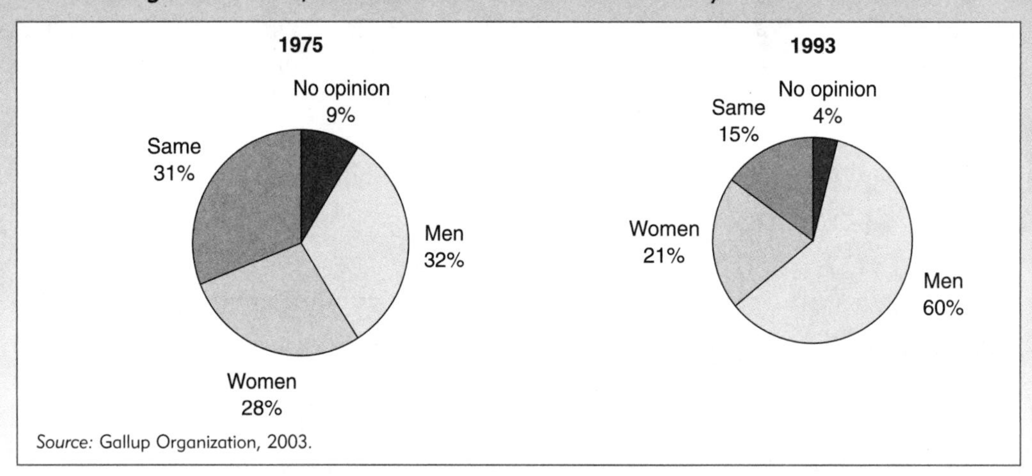

Source: Gallup Organization, 2003.

of comparable worth goes beyond the provisions of the Equal Pay Act by broadening the focus of protections beyond substantially equivalent jobs to jobs in which the levels of required skill, energy, and responsibility are comparable. Opponents of comparable worth believe that this policy is inappropriate because it is based on false assumptions about the causes of male-female wage differentials. These opponents generally prefer to rely on market forces to determine the wage rates of both male and female employees.

Thus far, the federal courts have not upheld comparable worth claims on the basis of constitutional provisions; they have, however, indicated that such claims may be valid, based on various civil rights laws enacted by Congress. Comparable worth remains at the forefront of civil rights issues pursued by groups representing women, who are fighting not only in the courts but in legislative arenas to advance their cause. Whether these legislative proposals will impact the wages of female employees in the workplace remains to be seen.

Besides wages, women have also been concerned about equal opportunity in employment. They believe that their opportunities for employment and advancement should be

Box 20-4 Women Identify Barriers They Face in the Workplace

Every 5 years the Virginia Slims brand of the Philip Morris Company conducts a survey of American women concerning their view of the workforce. The survey conducted in 1995 found that 84% of women interviewed agreed that regardless of changes that may have occurred, women still face more restrictions in life than do men. Seventy-seven percent said that sexual discrimination, while more subtle than in the past, continues to be a serious problem. Over 75% said there was some or a lot of sexual harassment in the workplace.

In this poll, women were asked to give reasons that account for the slow progress of women in the workforce. Their responses offer the following varied explanations:

45%: Women are mostly given lower mid-level jobs, while men hold the real power

44%: Women continue to face the "old boy network" in major corporations

44%: Women are held to higher standards than are men

38%: The doors have not been open long enough for many women to have made it to the top

37%: Women are discriminated against in life, and business is no exception

34%: There are few women in high corporate positions to inspire others

34%: The business world lags behind the rest of society when it comes to equality

25%: Young girls are not encouraged to aspire to careers as managers

---

Source: Roper Starch Worldwide Poll of 3,000 American women conducted in 1995 for the Virginia Slims branch of Philip Morris USA. The poll is described in Judith H. Dobryznski, "Women More Pessimistic About Work," *New York Times*, September 12, 1995, C2.

equivalent to those of men when both have the same level of education and experience. A comprehensive study by the federal Glass Ceiling Commission explored employment patterns of women over several decades. The Commission found that while the female composition of the American workforce has grown in the past three decades, increasing from about 30 to 40%, women continue to face obstacles in obtaining access to top positions in the private sector. This barrier—known as the **glass ceiling**—was demonstrated by the fact that women constitute less than 10% of senior management positions across the nation.[28]

glass ceiling *The concept that invisible forms of discrimination prevent women from rising to top positions in business and government.*

Several reasons for the difficulties of women in the workplace have been voiced by women themselves. A recent national study of women identified specific barriers to their advancement in employment (see Box 20-4: Women Identify Barriers They Face in the Workplace). Also, according to the study, women see that sex discrimination continues in the nation, although it is less obvious than in the past.

20-3c The Equal Rights Amendment

Women's groups spearheaded the **Equal Rights Amendment (ERA)** in the early 1970s in a broad-scale effort to guarantee equal rights to women. This proposed amendment initially was quite popular, passing the House of Representatives and Senate with overwhelming support. President Richard Nixon, a conservative, supported this addition to the Constitution. During the process of state review, however, resistance began to grow. Opposition arose from people with traditional beliefs, who argued that women should be treated differently than men with regard to such issues as the military draft, employment, and the family.[29] Ultimately, only 35 states approved the amendment, three short of the 38 required for ratification.

Equal Rights Amendment (ERA) *Constitutional amendment that was considered but never adopted, in the 1970s. Intended to provide equal rights for women.*

Although the ERA was not ratified, the movement that spawned it stimulated federal laws and court decisions prohibiting many forms of gender discrimination. The Supreme Court has held, for example, that employers may not advertise job listings under the headings "Male Interest" and "Female Interest";[30] nor can firms make promotions based solely on gender. Under similar rulings, states and localities have been prohibited from establishing different ages for majority status (legal status as an adult) for men and women.

20-3d Sexual Harassment

Another prominent issue concerning the civil rights of women concerns sexual harassment—sex-related actions in the workplace that harm or demean employees. Either gender can be sexually harassed, but most complaints about harassment have been made by females about male coworkers or supervisors. National attention to this issue was heightened in 1991 during the confirmation hearings of Judge Clarence Thomas to the Supreme Court when a former employee stated that Thomas had sexually harassed her. The nationally televised hearings of the Senate Judiciary Committee amounted to a forum for examination of sexual harassment in high levels of government. The spirit of questioning by some male members of the committee proved to be insensitive and raised questions in the minds of some about the Senate itself as a male-dominated bastion.

Until the last three decades, sexual harassment was largely an ignored problem in American society. Women often found it difficult to make complaints about harassment because of embarrassment and fear of retaliation. Title VII of the Civil Rights Act of 1964 made it illegal for any employer to discriminate against anyone with respect to compensation, terms, or conditions of employment because of the person's gender. How these provisions related to sexual harassment, however, was not immediately clear.

In 1980, as part of its responsibility to oversee implementation of the federal prohibitions against discrimination on the basis of race and gender, the Equal Employment Opportunity Commission issued guidelines about sexual harassment. These guidelines, linking sexual harassment to the nondiscrimination provisions of the Civil Rights Act of 1964, state that:

> Unwelcome sexual advances, requests for sexual favors, and other verbal or physical conduct of a sexual nature constitute sexual harassment when (1) submission to such conduct is made either explicitly or implicitly a term or condition of an individual's employment, (2) submission to or rejection of such conduct by an individual is used as a basis for employment decisions affecting such an individual, or (3) such conduct has the purpose or effect of unreasonably interfering with an individual's work performance or creating an intimidating, hostile, or offensive working environment.[31]

These guidelines remain the clearest statement of what actions constitute sexual harassment. Such harassment includes not only requests for sexual favors but also statements or actions concerning sex that create a hostile or intimidating work environment.

In the 1986 case of *Meritor Savings Bank v. Vinson*, the Supreme Court ruled that sexual harassment was a form of discrimination based on sex under Title VII of the 1964 Civil Rights Act.[32] This decision extended the protections and remedies provided in the Civil Rights Act to include discrimination resulting from sexual harassment.

In the mid-1990s, national attention was again drawn to the issue of sexual harassment in a highly visible case that, ironically, again played out in the U.S. Senate. This case involved allegations by several women that Senator Robert Packwood of Oregon had engaged in harassing behavior toward several women over a course of many years. Other allegations that the senator used influence to find work for his estranged wife and that he altered personal diaries were used as evidence in the case. All allegations were reviewed by the Senate Ethics Committee composed of three Republicans and three Democrats. The committee's deliberations were slow and spanned several years. Many women's groups were outraged when first the Ethics Committee, and then the Senate, decided not to hold public hearings on the allegations. In the end, however, the Ethics Committee found sufficient compelling evidence that it voted unanimously for the unprecedented action of expelling Packwood from the Senate for sexual and official misconduct. While initially contemptuous of the Ethic Committee's recommendation, Packwood quickly resigned from the Senate to avoid the likelihood of being expelled. This was seen as a victory by many women's groups, who perceived that a visible blow had been struck against sexual harassment in the nation.

20-3e Women's Issues in the New Millennium

Other important issues on America's policy agenda in the 1990s are of key concern to women and the groups that represent them. Included here are the issues of abortion and welfare reforms—prime targets for conservatives.

Chapter 4 chronicled the issue of abortion in American politics and the role of the federal courts in identifying the right to privacy as guaranteeing women the right to have an abortion in certain circumstances. In the landmark *Roe v. Wade* case in 1973, the Supreme Court struck down state laws that prohibited women from receiving abortions. Through subsequent decisions the Court has upheld the right of women to have an abortion but has also allowed states greater capacity to regulate abortion practices. For example, in an important 1990 case, the Court upheld the right of states to require women to wait 24 hours after receiving information on abortion and alternatives before receiving the procedure. The Court also upheld state requirements that teens seeking an abortion receive the consent of a parent or judge.

The issue of abortion remains one of the most volatile in American politics. Despite Supreme Court rulings, the issue of whether abortion should be prohibited is one that deeply divides the nation and touches upon religious beliefs and political ideology. Abortion protests continue across the nation, with a few becoming violent. Religious and conservative groups press forward with their objective to eliminate abortion, while pro-choice groups contend that women have a constitutionally protected right to have an abortion. Undeterred by judicial rulings, abortion foes are supporting candidates who pledge to fight against the practice. Congress is being pressed to enact legislation to commence a process to ratify an amendment to the Constitution that prohibits abortion within the nation. Women's groups across the nation are actively involved in debates and politics concerning abortion policy, and this involvement is likely to continue throughout the decade.

Women are also directly affected by welfare reform initiatives enacted by Congress. Women are, by program design, the primary beneficiaries of key welfare programs like Aid to Families with Dependent Children (AFDC) and the WIC (Women, Infants and Children) program. The elimination of these programs as entitlements, the shift of federal grant dollars to state control through block grants, and overall spending reductions in welfare programs all point to reduced welfare benefits. Other welfare reform initiatives contain stronger requirements that welfare recipients find work or engage in employment training programs in order to receive whatever benefits remain. Despite little attention to the impact of these reforms on women, there is no question that women will feel the greatest consequences of welfare program changes. For this reason, groups representing women have entered the debate to sustain as many welfare-related benefits for women and children as possible and to ensure that new programs include provisions for day care that will enhance the ability of mothers to work or enroll in job training programs.

20-4 Affirmative Action: The Contemporary Battleground over Civil Rights

In the past decade, the greatest hotspot in the political debate and controversy in the area of civil rights focused on *affirmative action* policies. Affirmative action refers to a variety of practices and requirements that together are intended to increase the employment and opportunities of women and people of color. In other words, affirmative action policies require taking race, ethnicity, gender, and disability explicitly into account when decisions are made. For example, affirmative action can require that agencies take additional efforts to inform target groups that have traditionally been underrepresented in the federal work force (racial minorities, Latinos, women, and persons with disabilities) about job openings and to assist persons in these groups with applications. There are three key areas where affirmative action has been applied and where substantial controversy has arisen: employment practices, the award of federal construction and supply contracts, and admission into public colleges and universities (see Box 20-5: A Campus Abandons Affirmative Action).

20-4a The Evolution of Federal Affirmative Action Policy

Affirmative action policies by the federal government date back to the 1960s, a decade when civil rights policies remained persistent on the policy agenda of lawmakers. This was the period of large-scale urban riots, strong political battles for civil rights, and the

Box 20–5 A Campus Abandons Affirmative Action

A well-publicized battle concerning affirmative action took place on one of the nation's leading college campuses, the University of California at Berkeley. In some ways, it was ironic that this campus was a battlefield over this policy, since this campus was one of the early leaders to embrace elements of affirmative action in its admissions process. By 1995 the UC-Berkeley campus had one of the most diverse student bodies of any college or university across the nation: 32% of the student body were whites, 39% were Asian Americans, 14% were Latinos, and 5.5% were African Americans.

In 1995, the university's Board of Regents—the campus' governing body composed of individuals appointed by the governor on staggered terms—considered a plan that would abandon affirmative action and prohibit the use of race and ethnicity as factors in admissions. This plan generated controversy, with many different players entering the political arena to support or oppose the policy. The regents were first urged to revisit affirmative action in admissions by the Republican governor of California and presidential candidate, Pete Wilson, a strong opponent of state affirmative action policies. Abolition of the race-conscious admission policy at UC-Berkeley was advocated by an African-American member of the board of regents and was strongly opposed by the campus' Asian-American chancellor, Chang-Lin Tien. As the date for the regents' decision neared, President Bill Clinton declared support for the general principle of affirmative action and civil rights activist Rev. Jesse Jackson visited the campus to meet with the regents and to press the case for continuing affirmative action in college admissions.

On June 8, 1995, the UC-Berkeley Board of Regents made its decision, and its impact was felt across the colleges and universities of the United States. The governor, exercising his prerogative to serve as chairman of the 26-member board, presided and urged the board to abandon affirmative action. With Jackson and student protesters singing "We Shall Overcome" echoing in the background, the regents moved to another room to continue their debate in a quieter setting. In the end, on a 15–10 vote, the regents decided that the campus would abandon affirmative action hiring practices and race-based admissions. This decision, widely watched across the nation, was seen as potent evidence of shifting public attitudes against the principle of affirmative action as a strategy to compensate for past discrimination.

enactment of important civil rights legislation. In civil rights battles of the period a consistent theme was that employment discrimination severely limited the job opportunities of minorities. For this reason, an early target of affirmative action policies was employment. In 1961, President John F. Kennedy signed an executive order requiring that federal contractors—companies doing business with the federal government through contracts—make special efforts to ensure that workers were hired and treated without regard to race or ethnicity. The intent here was to eliminate discriminatory practices that had hindered the employment of racial and ethnic minorities. In 1965, one year after enactment of the Civil Rights Act of 1964, President Lyndon Johnson signed Executive Order 11246. This measure expanded the mandate initiated by Kennedy by requiring that federal contractors adopt affirmative action plans for all of their operations. Such plans were to include goals and timetables for increased hiring of minorities. (A time line noting trends in the evolution of affirmative action policy is included as Table 20-2.)

Affirmative action was not an agenda item only for Democratic presidents. Republican president Richard M. Nixon, elected to office in 1968, continued the federal government's strategy of designing and strengthening affirmative action policies. In 1969, Nixon and Secretary of Labor George Schultz inaugurated the "Philadelphia Plan," which forced building contractors in Philadelphia to set goals for hiring members of minority groups as a condition for working on federally funded projects. The use of goals and timetables for increasing the employment of women and minorities represented a stronger strategy for pursuing affirmative action.

Still another affirmative action strategy involved provisions for set-asides as part of federal contracts. These set-aside provisions of federal programs stipulate that a certain

Table 20-2 Time Line of the Affirmative Action Policy

The national government's affirmative action policy first grew and expanded, then was challenged in the federal courts, and more recently has been a prominent subject of policy debate among federal lawmakers. The time line demonstrates the widespread players involved in defining affirmative action policy and how policy evolution often moves through multiple political arenas.

Federal affirmative action continues to evolve from its origins in the 1960s. Key events that have influenced the content and direction of affirmative action policy are shown in this time line.

1961: President John F. Kennedy issues Executive Order 10925 urging contractors with the federal government to hire more minority employees. The phrase *affirmative action* is attributed to Hobart Taylor, Jr., an African-American lawyer who was asked by Vice President Lyndon Johnson to aid in drafting the executive order.

1964: President Johnson signs the Civil Rights Act of 1964 barring discrimination in the workplace. Although the act did not establish or explicitly require affirmative action, Title VII of the law did set out principles of nondiscrimination in employment and mechanisms for enforcement.

1965: In the wake of a riot in the Watts district of Los Angeles, California, President Johnson signs Executive Order 11246, which requires contractors to undertake affirmative action to employ racial minorities. The order also transferred responsibility for nondiscrimination in employment from the White House to the Department of Labor.

1969: President Richard Nixon and Secretary of Labor George Schultz inaugurate the "Philadelphia Plan," forcing building contractors in Philadelphia to set goals for hiring members of minority groups as a condition for working on federally funded projects.

1971: In the case *Griggs v. Duke Power Company*, the Supreme Court holds that employers are prohibited from discriminatory practices against minorities and disallows tests and educational requirements for jobs that are not shown to be job-related.

1977: Congress enacts legislation to set aside 10% of public works funds for "minority business enterprises."

1978: In the case *Bakke v. California*, the Supreme Court rules that colleges and universities may consider race as a factor in admissions policies but cannot establish firm quotas for admitting a certain percentage of students from minority groups.

1979: In another case, *United Steelworkers v. Weber*, the Supreme Court upholds the use of voluntary affirmative action plans by private employers.

1980: The action of Congress to create minority set-aside programs for minority businesses is upheld as constitutional by the Supreme Court in *Fullilove v. Klutnick*.

1985: Conservatives in the Reagan administration consider dismantling Executive Order 11246. Public outcry results, and the move to eliminate the order is abandoned.

1989: The Supreme Court strikes down a municipal minority set-aside program in Richmond, Virginia, and holds that an employment practice with discriminatory effects may be justified if it "serves the legitimate goals" of the employer in a substantial way. These rulings by the conservative Rehnquist Court raised questions about this court's views about affirmative action.

1991: Congress enacts and President George H. Bush signs into the law the Civil Rights Act of 1991, which reverses some effects of the Rehnquist court rulings of 1989.

1995: The Regents of the University of California vote to end affirmative action policies on all campuses.

1996: California's Proposition 209 passes by a narrow margin, abolishing all public sector affirmative action programs in the state in employment, education, and contracting.

1996: In *Texas v. Hopwood (58 U.S. 1033)* the U.S. Court of Appeals for the Fifth Circuit rules against the University of Texas, deciding that its law school's policy of considering race in the admissions process was a violation of the equal protection clause.

2003: The U.S. Supreme Court holds that that University of Michigan's use of race among other factors in its law school's admission program is constitutional because the program furthered a compelling interest in obtaining an educational benefit that flows from student body diversity.

Source: Material for was drawn from Nicholas Lemann, "Taking Affirmative Action Apart," *New York Times Magazine* (June 11, 1995), 36–66.

proportion of funds be given to enterprises owned and operated by women or minorities. Set-aside provisions work as a type of quota, targeting federal monies toward companies that are owned predominantly by women or people of color.

A study conducted by the Congressional Reference Service in 1995 documented the level of federal affirmative action policies. This study, requested by then-senator Robert Dole (R-Kan.), chronicled 160 laws, regulations, programs, and executive orders that grant a preference to individuals on the basis of race, sex, national origin, or ethnic background. Included in that report were the following policies:[33]

- The Pentagon had a goal that 5% of all its procurement budget ($112 billion in 1994) be awarded to firms owned by "socially and economically disadvantaged individuals," meaning women and minorities.
- The Environmental Protection Agency required state and local governments that win EPA grants to make positive efforts to use small businesses and minority-owned business sources of supplies and services.
- When awarding grants for teacher training, the Department of Education was required to give special consideration to historically black colleges and universities, and to schools with at least 50% minority enrollment.
- For the Department of State, not less than 10% of money appropriate for diplomatic construction was to be allocated to the extent possible to minority contractors.
- The Surface Transportation and Uniform Relocation Assistance Act of 1987 required that the Department of Transportation provide not less than 10% of appropriated funds to socially and economically disadvantaged individuals.

Each federal agency assigns personnel to oversee implementation of affirmative action policies relevant to that agency. In addition, other federal agencies play a role in policy implementation. The Equal Employment Opportunity Commission (EEOC) is responsible for administering programs to fight discrimination and pursue affirmative action within the agencies of the federal government. The EEOC works with federal agencies as they devise and implement employment practices; it also investigates complaints concerning discrimination in federal agencies.[34] The Office of Federal Contract Compliance Programs (OFCCP) in the Department of Labor oversees nondiscrimination and affirmative action policies of federal contractors.

20-4b Affirmative Action in Subnational Governments and the Private Sector

Affirmative action policies have been pursued in playing fields other than the federal government. Many state and local governments adopted affirmative action policies in an effort to enhance the employment of women, people of color, and people with disabilities. Such policies also moved beyond the realm of employment. For example, colleges and universities across the nation engaged in affirmative action designed to increase the enrollment of targeted groups. Here, affirmative action involved many types of activities, from more aggressive recruitment of minority students to setting enrollment targets that, if met, would mean substantial increases in the number of people of color entering the nation's higher education institutions. A few schools went so far as to establish **quotas** for enrollment—that is, to set aside a percentage of slots for incoming students for one or more minority groups. This strategy, as described in the following section, encountered strong political reaction and was seen by some as *reverse discrimination*—the view that certain policies unfairly disadvantage males and non-minorities.

quota *The practice of setting aside a set number of jobs, training slots, or college admissions openings to a specified target group like women or minorities.*

Some private firms also devised affirmative action policies for their employees. While some of the private sector plans were stimulated by federal requirements placed on federal contractors, many firms not so required also developed plans to enhance the hiring and promotion of women and minorities. In many cases, these plans arose from negotiations between major companies and labor unions representing workers.

20-4c Affirmative Action and Conflicting Policy Values

Contemporary battles over affirmative action result in part from different and oftentimes conflicting views about *equity* (see Chapter 19). Some individuals and groups hold dearly to the notion of *equality of opportunity*, while others advocate that public policies should strive for *equality of outcome*. The equality of opportunity camp, for example, is generally supportive of recruitment efforts to increase applications from women and minority groups. Such action increases the opportunity of these disadvantaged groups to compete for job positions. At the same time, members of this camp chafe at the idea of set-aside programs that automatically channel federal funds toward companies owned by women or minorities. This channeling is seen as increasing the opportunities of some (e.g., disadvantaged groups) while diminishing the opportunities of others (e.g., companies owned by white males).

Advocates of set-aside programs, on the other hand, see them as a primary means of moving American society toward equal outcomes, because the set-asides ensure that firms owned by women and minorities will receive a piece of the federal funding pot. For these Americans, public policies such as affirmative action should have, as their ultimate objective, an equalization of the social, political, and economic status among all groups in society. Underlying the arguments and debates about the future of affirmative action—including those about whether it should continue and what form it should take—is a very real difference in policy values concerning how equity should be achieved in America.

20-4d Affirmative Action and the Courts

As with so many policy controversies, conflicting players turned to the judicial arena to resolve differences among themselves and among unsettled legal questions about affirmative action. The courts' rulings have had a mixed effect on the design and implementation of affirmative action policies.

One key conflict centered on the use of quotas to pursue affirmative action. The Medical School at the University of California at Davis was among the nation's higher education programs that adopted quotas in the 1970s as a means to pursue affirmative action in enrolling people of color. This school had two admissions programs: a regular program and a "specialized" one for disadvantaged minorities (African Americans, Latinos, Asians, and Native Americans). Out of 100 openings for a class entering the medical school, 16 were reserved for special admissions, where a lower set of admissions standards was used. Allan Bakke, a white applicant, was twice denied admission to the medical school, despite the fact that some minority students with lower scores on the medical admissions test and with lower undergraduate grade point averages were admitted through the special program. In Bakke's opinion, and that of others concerned about affirmative action, the admissions quotas worked as a form of reverse discrimination against white applicants.

Bakke's case eventually reached the U.S. Supreme Court, and the nation's highest court ruled in his favor. The Court ruled that the Equal Protection Clause of the 14th Amendment required that "no applicant may be rejected because of his race, in favor of another who is less qualified, as measured by standards applied without regard to race."[35] In other words, it was unconstitutional to use a quota system. The UC-Davis special admissions program, where whites, despite academic achievement, had no possibility of access to the 16 spaces reserved for the program, violated the equal protection rights of Bakke. When the University of California conceded that it could not prove that Bakke would not have been admitted even in the absence of the special admissions program, it was directed to admit Bakke to medical school. Through this ruling, the Supreme Court struck down the use of rigid quotas to pursue affirmative action.

This judicial ruling was not a complete setback for affirmative action policies, however. In its ruling in the Bakke case, the Court held that race is a permissible factor in promoting diverse student bodies, thereby recognizing that race can be explicitly considered in admissions policies so long as a rigid quota system is not used.

In the following year, the Supreme Court considered a case involving an affirmative action plan being used in the private sector. Through a labor agreement, Kaiser Aluminum and the United Steelworkers had agreed upon a plan to increase the number of African Americans in well-paying crafts jobs that required certain skills. It had been the traditional practice in many industries to hire as craft workers only persons with prior craft work experience. African Americans, generally excluded from the craft unions, thus had little opportunity to move into the better-paying craft jobs. To increase the representation of African Americans in craft jobs, Kaiser set aside 50% of craft-training positions for

Box 20–6 Public Views on Affirmative Action

The Gallup Poll Organization conducted a telephone survey of 1,003 randomly selected adults from across the United States in late February 1995 to assess their views on affirmative action.

Respondents were asked the following question, which had two versions: one concerning women and the other being applied to racial minorities.

> *As you know, some affirmative action programs are designed to give preferential treatment to [women/racial minorities] in such areas as getting jobs and promotions, obtaining contracts, and being admitted to schools. Do you generally approve or disapprove of such affirmative action programs?*

Those respondents who said they approved of such programs were asked:

> *Do you approve of affirmative action programs that use quotas—by requiring specific numbers of [women/racial minorities] to be given jobs or admitted to schools—or do you approve of affirmative action programs only if they do not use quotas?*

Respondent answers to these questions paint a contemporary picture of how the American public views affirmative action policies. The public is almost equally split on the issue with regard to women, with 50% approving of affirmative action for women and 45% disapproving. For racial minorities, only 40% favored affirmative action and 56% disapproved. Support among those who approve is much stronger for policies that do *not* use quotas.

Views on Affirmative Action

	For women	For racial minorities
Approve	50%	40%
with quotas	10	13
no quotas	40	27
Disapprove	45	56
No opinion	5	4
Total	100%	100%

Approval and disapproval of affirmative action for women and for racial minorities can be broken down by the sex, race, and party affiliation of respondents, as shown in the following two tables. As the data demonstrate, support for affirmative action policies is greater among women and among non-white respondents and disapproval was greatest among whites and males.

Views on Affirmative Action for Women

	Approve with quotas	Approve with no quotas	Disapprove	No Opinion
Sex				
Men	7%	38%	51%	4%
Women	12	43	40	5
Race				
White	8	38	49	5
Non-White	23	55	16	6
Party				
Republican	9	30	55	6
Independent	5	50	38	7
Democrat	17	40	42	1

Views on Affirmative Action for Racial Minorities

	Approve with quotas	Approve with no quotas	Disapprove	No Opinion
Sex				
Men	11%	26%	61%	2%
Women	14	29	52	5
Race				
White	9	27	61	3
Non-White	33	33	30	4
Party				
Republican	7	26	65	2
Independent	10	25	60	5
Democrat	22	33	42	3

Finally, those questioned in the Gallup Poll were asked: Today do you think affirmative action programs are needed to help [women/racial minorities] overcome discrimination, or are they not needed today? More people thought that affirmative action was not necessary today than thought it was needed to overcome discrimination.

Affirmative Programs Still Needed?

	For women	For racial minorities
Needed	31	41%
Not needed	57	56
No opinion	2	3

You can compare these survey results with your own views about and assessment of affirmative action.

Source: David M. Moore, "Are Americans Today Dubious About Affirmative Action?" *The Gallup Poll Monthly*, March 1995, 36–38.

African-American employees until the percentage of African-American employees equaled the percentage of African Americans in the labor force. A white worker at Kaiser was denied entry into the training program, even though an African-American employee with less seniority was admitted. The employee, Brian Weber, filed a class-action suit claiming that the plan discriminated against whites on the basis of race. The suit claimed that Kaiser's training program plan violated Title VII of the Civil Rights Act, which makes it unlawful to discriminate on the basis of race in hiring and in the selection of apprentices for training programs. The Supreme Court ruled against Weber, holding that Title VII does not prohibit private, voluntary, race-conscious affirmative action programs designed to overcome past discrimination.[36] This judicial decision boosted the legitimacy of affirmative action programs in the private sector.

The federal courts next considered the issue of the constitutionality of set-asides for women and minorities. In 1980 the Supreme Court upheld the constitutionality of set-aside provisions as an acceptable exercise of congressional spending power.[37] The Court took a different position in a case involving a local law in Richmond, Virginia, that required contractors receiving city construction contracts to subcontract at least 30% of funds to minority business enterprises. The Supreme Court ruled that Richmond's set-aside program was unconstitutional.[38] The Court held that the plan was not narrowly tailored to accomplish a specific remedial purpose, such as increasing the representation of African Americans in the crafts trade from which they had been denied entry. The majority opinion also noted that the 14th Amendment authorizes Congress—not cities or states—to act against racial discrimination. Box 20-6: Public Views on Affirmative Action shows the public's reaction to affirmative action in the mid-1990s. Time Out 20-2: Where Do You Stand? asks for your opinion on these issues.

20-4e Battles over Affirmative Action Heighten

Political controversy concerning affirmative action reached new heights with the election of the 104th Congress, when Republicans and conservatives took control of both houses. The 1994 elections shifted the policy agenda toward the right and opened **policy windows** for debate on affirmative action. At the same time, other developments in the states and in the courts suggested that support for affirmative action as a remedy for discrimination was eroding across the nation. Probably the most dramatic political decision about affirmative action in the second half of the 1990s emanated from California. In 1996, California voters approved Proposition 209, placed on the ballot through the initiative process. This proposition, spearheaded by California businessman Ward Connerly and known as the California Civil Rights Initiative, prohibits state and local governments,

policy windows *Advantageous times which response to a policy initiative is likely to be positive and placed upon the decision-making agenda.*

Time Out 20-2

Where Do You Stand?

National surveys assess public opinion on key policy issues both in the abstract and in relation to specific conditions. Responses reflect what people are willing to say publicly at a particular point in time. In order to make responses comparable, respondents are given a limited number of options which admittedly do not reflect all the nuances of an issue area. Although results depend on the nature of the question and what is going on in the world, the relative positions of various demographic groups are relatively consistent. Choose the response to the following question that best reflects your view, and see who among the public tends to agree and disagree with you:

> **Some people think that if a company has a history of discriminating against blacks when making hiring decisions, then they should be required to have an affirmative action program that gives blacks preference in hiring. What do you think? Should companies that have discriminated against blacks be required to have an affirmative action program?**
>
> -YES
>
> -NO

Answers to Time Out 20-2

If you said yes, based on the 2000 National Election Study, you agree with the 52% of respondents who supported affirmative action when a history of discrimination was evident. The type of people most likely to agree with your support of affirmative action in this situation were:

	(percent *supporting* affirmative action when a history of discrimination was evident)
Blacks	82%
Liberals	63%
Democrats	61%
People under 30 years of age	60%
Women	55%
People 30–40 years of age	53%
Independents	52%
National Average	52%

If you said no, based on the National Election Study for the 2000 election, you agree with the 48% of respondents who opposed affirmative action when a history of discrimination was evident . The type of people most likely to agree with your lack of support of affirmative action were:

	(percent *opposing* affirmative action despite a company's past history of discrimination)
Conservatives	64%
Republicans	61%
Whites	54%
Males	52%
People over 50 years of age	52%
Moderates	49%
National Average	48%

public universities and schools, and other public entities in the state from discriminating against or giving preferential treatment to any individual or group in public employment, public education, or public contracting on the basis of race, sex, color, ethnicity, or national origin. The impact of this proposition, which became law when approved by voters, is to eliminate public sector affirmative action policies in the state—including those related to admissions and financial aid in California's universities and colleges.

The impact of this measure spread far beyond California, as this major stroke against affirmative action was considered in other states and localities across the nation. Those against affirmative action saw Proposition 209 as removing preferential treatment (what they saw as *reverse discrimination*) and balancing the playing field. Those who see value in affirmative action as a means to overcome the results of past discrimination, including the American Civil Liberties Union, saw Proposition 209 as a severe threat to the future of affirmative action policy. Proposition 209 was immediately challenged in state and federal courts, delaying its implementation. In 1997, the U.S. Supreme Court failed to take up an appeal of a lower court's decision that upheld the constitutionality of Proposition 209 under the U.S. Constitution, thereby allowing the new policy to become law and be enacted. Other states, including Nevada, have considered similar legislation. The U.S. Congress similarly considered a Proposition 209-like policy, but it did not enact the policy.

Controversy over affirmative action remained strong in the early 21st century. The U.S. Supreme Court reentered the political fray over affirmative action in 2003 when it agreed to hear a case concerning undergraduate and law school admissions at the Ann Arbor campus of the University of Michigan. The dispute here focused on admissions policies that use a point system that allocates points for factors such as SAT scores, athletic skills, or being a child of a University of Michigan graduate. This system also gave 20 points to applicants who are African American, Mexican American, or Native American—a measure to increase diversity in the undergraduate level and law school student bodies. A group of white applicants denied admission to the University of Michigan sued

Box 20-7 An Affirmative Action Fight Goes Online

One prominent attack on affirmative action policy in the mid-1990s was the effort in the State of California to create a ballot initiative that would require the state to abandon all state-sponsored affirmative action programs aimed at minority hiring, education, and government contracting. The ballot initiative is a feature of California politics that allows measures known as initiatives to be placed on state election ballots where citizens can vote the measure up or down. This mechanism is designed to enhance citizen involvement in policy formation. It also allows citizens a route to policy formation that bypasses their elected officials in the state legislature. In order for a proposed initiative to be placed on the ballot, a certain number of registered voters must sign petitions supporting it. In California, nearly 700,000 valid signatures of registered voters are needed for a ballot initiative to qualify.

Strategists working to gain sufficient support to place the anti-affirmative action initiative on the ballot devised a new resource to reach citizens and gain initiative support: going online through the Internet. State election officials said that this was the first time in state history that a referendum campaign was waged electronically through computer email systems.

The strategy works as follows: computer users will be able to access and print out a standardized signature form supporting the ban on state affirmative action policies. These users will then sign the form and send it back to initiative organizers by mail. (Thus far, an electronic reply directly to organizers would not constitute a legal signature.) Strategists found this means of reaching voters as quick and cost-effective as compared with regular mail campaigns and signature drives. As one analyst noted, this electronic strategy to garner public support for a ballot initiative "takes us from an age of carbon paper and show leather into truly high-tech times."

Source: Kevin Johnson, "On-line: Affirmative Action Fight," *USA Today*, July 24, 1995, 6A.

the university on the grounds that the admissions policy violated their rights to equal protection under the law.

The Michigan case caught substantial national attention. President George W. Bush agreed with the students, stating that "racial preferences" should be ruled unconstitutional; he urged universities to adopt "race neutral" admission policies. Many conservative groups joined in the call for ending affirmative action programs that give special treatment of standing to racial groups. A *Los Angeles Times* poll found that many Americans concurred with the president; 55% of poll respondents said that they approved of the president's position, while 27% disapproved.[39] On the other side of the political spectrum, many large corporations, labor leaders, college and university leaders, and the American Bar Association submitted *amicus curiae* briefs supporting Michigan's admission policy and its objective of promoting affirmative action. The Supreme Court ruled on the case in 2003, upholding the University of Michigan law school's use of race in admissions decisions because the policy obtained "an educational benefit that flows from student body diversity," and because the policy was narrowly tailored and flexible, and it provided a "holistic approach" to the admission's review of each applicant (*Gratz v. Bollinger*, 539 *U.S.*). Affirmative action issues are likely to remain an issue of political controversy for some time (see Box 20-7: An Affirmative Action Fight Goes Online).

20-5 Future Civil Rights Policy: Questions about Objectives and Strategies

The start of the new century finds civil rights groups at an interesting juncture—one that is causing some civil rights groups to assess the goals and objectives of future political games. Some groups have made substantial progress toward long-term objectives. African Americans and other racial and ethnic minorities have, over the course of three decades, seen laws and ordinances supporting segregation struck down. In their place, new anti-discrimination laws have been enacted to end discrimination and open up the opportunities of American society to all Americans. This does not mean that discrimination and prejudice have been eliminated. What can be said is that most racial and ethnic groups have won important battles to increase their rights and opportunities.

Many African-American leaders have in recent years been searching for new strategies to rally supporters and achieve further strides in ending the negative impacts of discrimination and prejudice. The National Association for the Advancement of Colored People (NAACP), once a leader in civil rights struggles for African Americans, had by the early 1990s found itself adrift, unclear about future direction and even the support of its dwindling membership. Several factors—including the attack on affirmative action, the Supreme Court's striking down of a Congressional districting plan in Georgia that created a minority dominated district, and budget cuts in social welfare programs—served as catalysts to the NAACP and other organizations representing racial and ethnic minorities.

As part of a strategy of rejuvenation, the NAACP selected a new leader in 1995: Myrlie Evers-Williams, wife of slain civil rights leader Medgar Evers. Upon taking office, she outlined a plan for a new civil rights movement:

> If the civil rights movement is to make its clout felt into the 21st century, it must focus on four moral imperatives—stewardship, inclusiveness, concern for the disadvantaged, and re-dedication to principles of non-violence—as both ethnical and effective tools for the struggle.[40]

According to this plan better use of organizational resources (stewardship), coalition-building and resource pooling to promote fairness, concern about children and disadvantaged people, and a renewed pledge to active, but non-violent, action were the best means to push the civil rights movement forward into the next century.

For other groups who have only recently obtained protection under the law, the next step is to press for aggressive implementation and enforcement. This is the case with the sweeping Americans with Disabilities Act. The large number of public and private organizations affected makes it difficult to monitor compliance, document non-compliance, and evaluate the impact of the act. Organizations representing people with disabilities are devoting energies to monitoring progress in implementation, negotiating with public and private organizations seeking to achieve compliance, and bringing legal action against those seen as failing to live up to the accessibility and fairness mandates of the ADA.

For homosexuals the battle lines are still set around policy formation. Groups representing gay men and lesbians are fighting to convince national policy makers to provide them legal protection under the law. At the state and local levels, homosexuals are making progress in some areas and losing ground in others. In the past few years, lesbians and gay men have fought statewide initiatives to prevent states and localities from including gay rights provisions in laws and ordinances, with some battles won and others lost. The courts are playing an increasingly important role in struggles over the legal rights of homosexuals in American society through their evaluation of policies for gays in the military and for legal protections based upon sexual orientation.

The women's movement is at an interesting junction. Of all groups in American society, women have perhaps made the most progress in achieving goals that started with the right to vote and focus today on equal status in the workplace. This movement lost the major battle over ratification of the Equal Rights Movement but has seen victories in many other areas including increasing representation of women in legislative bodies at the national, state, and local levels. Equal pay, opportunities for promotion, sexual harassment, and abortion remain prime issues for women. Perhaps most important, however, is the broader issue of the roles of women in American life—roles that include family responsibilities as well as economic and political participation. Since the end of World War II, America has struggled with redefinitions of these roles, and the struggle continues even as women assume more visible and important positions in the public and private sectors.

Two issues related to civil rights and the access to opportunities in American life are certain to remain at the center of contemporary political games: affirmative action and immigration policy. At the root of affirmative action is the basic question of how rights and opportunities should be allocated in American society and the extent to which past discrimination requires remedial action today. Americans do not agree on this. Conservatives seek to end affirmative action completely, saying its time has passed. Liberals and moderates have greater toleration for affirmative action but increasingly see it more as a short-term strategy to enhance fairness rather than a permanent feature of American life. These conflicting views have catapulted affirmative action to the lead civil rights question of the day.

Debates about immigration policy, and the rights and opportunities that are available to legal and illegal aliens, point out some of the conflicting views in American society. Despite the country's history as a nation of immigrants, popular opinion in the United States has continually vacillated between the question of whom the government is meant to serve—its people or just its citizens. At times, the government mandate has been broadly inclusive. At other times, it has been read narrowly.[41]

Public opinion polls show that Americans support the rather abstract idea of the United States as a melting pot. At the same time they are concerned about the level of illegal immigration and the demands that both legal and illegal aliens place on public sector budgets, particularly in the areas of education and social services. Some Americans are also threatened by what they see as the growing size and social influence of ethnic and racial minorities in U.S. society. Policy makers at the start of the 21st century find themselves in the middle of this political maelstrom. It remains to be seen how America will respond to the challenges of immigration and social diversity; it is clear that these issues will reverberate through the political system for some time.

Conclusion

A hallmark of American society is its social diversity. From the inception of the nation, American culture has evolved as different groups of immigrants came to the United States, joining the Native Americans who lived here at the start. The waves of immigration came first from western Europe and then shifted to eastern and central Europe. These waves were followed by immigrants from Asia and Latin and Central America.

The melting pot nature of American society can be viewed from different perspectives. On the one hand, Americans are proud of the image of America as the land of opportunity. Here, persons suffering social, political, or religious persecution in other nations could come to stake their claim to a new life. Individual Americans have often been proud of their personal heritage, documented by such things as the proliferation of ethnic festivals across the nation.

The immigration of new ethnic and racial groups has also been associated with social tensions, prejudice, and discrimination. While generally appreciating the melting pot idea, Americans throughout history have often been suspicious of people who are different from themselves—people with different languages, appearances, customs, and food. They have sometimes worried that newer immigrant groups entering the nation will take away jobs and economic opportunities. These fears and concerns have spawned prejudice and discrimination, and some of this discrimination was formalized through federal, state, and local governments and policies.

Women in the United States have experienced discrimination based upon gender. In the early years of the nation, women were seen as having little political or governmental role. Gradually, after protracted struggle, women have been able to gain rights allowing them to substantially enhance their position in American society. Winning the vote, in 1920, was a landmark event for women who have since successfully pressed for political and social reforms to remove social, political, and economic barriers. Contemporary civil rights issues for women include equality in the workplace, fighting sexual harassment and gender discrimination, and legal policies concerning abortion.

The political struggles of women and minorities to achieve equal rights and opportunities have been waged in multiple political arenas. They have included such strategies as political protest, civil disobedience, formation of interest groups, media involvement in demonstrating discrimination, and legislative reforms to prohibit discriminatory practices. The battle is not over for many groups that perceive contemporary barriers to full opportunities for employment, political participation, and social acceptance within the American culture.

Affirmative action has been the most recent battleground for civil rights policies. The sides are strongly divided. Some see affirmative action as a set of policies that have achieved important objectives and that are still necessary to overcome persistent discrimination based on race, ethnicity, gender, and disability status. Others feel affirmative action has gone too far by unfairly giving advantages based upon these social characteristics. These critics see affirmative action as reverse discrimination against white males. Public opinion shows the majority of Americans see problems with at least some attributes of affirmative action policy. Sensing this political opportunity, conservatives at all levels—federal, state, and local—are pushing for constraints on or abolition of affirmative action as the nation moves into the 21st century.

Key Terms

aliens
assimilation
civil disobedience
Civil Rights Act of 1964
comparable worth
Equal Rights Amendment (ERA)
glass ceiling
Jim Crow laws
massive resistance
Plessy v. Ferguson
policy windows
quota
reconstruction
Voting Rights Act of 1965

Practice Quiz

1. Jim Crow laws refer to laws that
 a. first created environmental policy at the national level.
 b. outlawed the secession of southern states.
 c. enforced separate facilities for whites and blacks.
 d. outlawed affirmative action.

2. Rosa Parks gained fame in the civil rights movement by
 a. engaging in civil disobedience.
 b. leading militant clashes with police.
 c. refusing to confirm with laws dictating that she, as an African-American, ride in the back of the bus.
 d. both a and c

3. Massive resistance refers to
 a. secession of the southern states as they left the Union at the start of the Civil War.
 b. civil rights marches in urban areas during the 1960s.
 c. refusal of some public schools in southern states to integrate.
 d. protests against affirmative action programs in federal government employment.

4. In *Plessy v. Ferguson*, the Supreme Court
 a. upheld segregation as constitutional.
 b. struck down segregation as unconstitutional.
 c. affirmed the right of U.S. colleges to use affirmative action.
 d. upheld the right of women to vote.

5. A key provision of the Voting Rights Act of 1965 was
 a. providing women with the right to vote.
 b. outlawing literacy tests as a requirement for voting.
 c. providing African Americans with the right to vote.
 d. both a and c

6. Which is true about the Equal Rights Amendment?
 a. It was enacted as a constitutional amendment in 1982.
 b. It struck down facilities segregated by race and ethnicity.
 c. It protects gays and lesbians in the military.
 d. It failed to receive ratification as a constitutional amendment.

7. The "ADA" refers to a national government law designed to protect which group of citizens?
 a. African Americans
 b. gays and lesbians
 c. people with disabilities
 d. new immigrants to the nation

8. What is true about the right of women to vote in national elections?
 a. The right was conferred by a constitutional amendment.
 b. The suffrage movement advocated strongly in support of the women's right to vote.
 c. The right was included in the 14th Amendment.
 d. both a and b

9. When did citizens ages 18–21 obtain the right to vote?
 a. As part of the Constitution ratified in 1789
 b. In the 1970s through a constitutional amendment
 c. In 1945 following the end of World War II
 d. Immediately following the Civil War

10. The *Bakke v. California* decision by the U.S. Supreme Court
 a. upheld all forms of affirmative action.
 b. struck down all forms of affirmative action.
 c. upheld all race-focused affirmative action.
 d. struck down affirmative action policies based on rigid quotas.

You can find the correct answers to these questions by taking the quiz and then submitting your answers in the Online Edition. The program will automatically score your submission. Where you miss a question, the program will provide the correct answer, a rationale for the answer, and the section number in the chapter where the topic is discussed.

Further Reading

An overview of current race and ethnic relations issues is provided in several books that include: Martin N. Marger, *Race and Ethnic Relations: American and Global Perspectives* (Florence: KY: Wadsworth Publishers, 1999); Robert M. Entman and Andrew Rojecki, *The Black Image in the White Mind: Media and Race in America* (Evanston, IL: University of Chicago Press, 2000); and Scott L. Malcomson, *One Drop of Blood: The American Misadventure of Race* (New York: Farrar, Straus and Giroux, 2000).

An interesting book reference work in the area of civil rights and race relations is presented in Ernest Cashmore and Ellis Cashmore, *Dictionary of Race and Ethnic Relations*, 4th ed. (New York: Routledge, 1997).

The civil rights movement in the United States has been chronicled in many books, including Sanford Wexler, *The Civil Rights Movement: An Eyewitness History* (New York: Facts on File, 1993); Fred Powledge, *Free at Last? The Civil Rights Movement and the People that Made It* (Boston, MA: Little, Brown and Company, 1991); David R. Garrow, *We Shall Overcome: The Civil Rights Movement in the United States in the 1950's and 1960's* (Brooklyn, NY: Carlson Publishers, 1989); Briadys Butler, Marymal Dryden and Melissa Walker, ed. *Women in the Civil Rights Movement: Trailblazers and Torchbearers, 1941-1965* (Brooklyn, NY: Carlson Publishers, 1990; and Angela Shelf Madearis, *Dare to Dream: Coretta Scott King and the Civil Rights Movement* (New York: Lodestar Books, 1994); Adolph L. Reed et al., eds. *Stirrings in the Jug: Black Politics in the Post Segregation Era* (Minneapolis, MN: University of Minnesota Press, 1999).

For biographies of Dr. Martin Luther King, Jr., see Flip Schmulke, *He Had a Dream: Martin Luther King and the Civil Rights Movement* (New York: W.W. Norton, 1995) and John White, *Martin Luther King, Jr., and the Civil Rights Movement in America* (London: British Association for American Studies, 1991).

A book that critically examines the practice of busing to promote racial integration is David J. Armor, *School Desegregation and the Law* (New York: Oxford University Press, 1995).

Among the works on the women's movement, see Cynthia Harrison, *On Account of Sex: The Politics of Women's Issues, 1945–1968* (Berkeley, CA: University of California Press, 1988); Bell Hooks, *Feminism Is for Everybody: Passionate Politics* (Cambridge, MA: South End Press, 2000).

For contrasting views on affirmative action policy, see David K. Shipler, *A Country of Strangers: Blacks and Whites in America* (New York: Vintage Books, 1998) and Abigail Thermstrom and Stephan Thermstrom, *America in Black and White: One Nation, Indivisible* (New York: Simon and Schuster, 1997) (which argues for a color-blind society).

An examination of the politics surrounding the Equal Rights Amendment is presented by Janet K. Boles, *The Politics of the Equal Rights Amendment* (New York: Longman, 1977).

A provocative look at the experiences of ethnic and racial minorities in America is presented in Ronald Takaki's *A Different Mirror: A History of Multicultural America* (Boston, MA: Little, Brown and Company, 1993). Other books dealing with race and ethnicity in America include Ronald Takaki, ed., *From Different Shores: Perspectives in Race and Ethnicity in America* (New York: Oxford University Press, 1987); Lawrence W. Fuchs, *The American Kaleidoscope: Race, Ethnicity, and the Civil Culture*

(Middleton, CT: Wesleyan University Press, 1990); Norman R. Yetman, *Majority and Minority: The Dynamics of Race and Ethnicity in American Life*, 5th ed. (Boston, MA: Allyn and Bacon, 1991).

Among the growing literature on Latino politics are the following: Frank Bonilla, Edwin Melendez, Maria de Los Angeles Torres, and Rebecca Merales, eds., *Borderless Borders: U.S. Latinos, Latin Americans, and the Paradox of Interdependence* (Philadelphia, PA: Temple University Press, 1998); Linda Chavez, *Out of the Barrio: Toward a New Politics of Hispanic Assimilation* (New York: Basic Books, 1991); Rodolpho O. De la Garza, Martha Menchaca, and Louis DeSipio, *Barrio Politics: Latino Politics in the 1990 Elections* (Boulder, CO: Westview Press, 1994); and Carol Hardy-Fanta, *Latina Politics, Latino Politics: Gender, Culture, and Political Participation in Boston* (Philadelphia, PA: Temple University Press, 1993).

A history of Asian Americans is provided in Ronald Takaki, *Strangers from a Different Shore: A History of Asian Americans* (Boston, MA: Little, Brown and Company, 1989). Examination of the internment of Japanese Americans during World War II is presented in Donna K. Nagata, *Legacy of Injustice* (New York: Plenum Press, 1993) and Sandra C. Taylor, *Jewel of the Desert: Japanese American Internment at Topaz* (Berkeley, CA: University of California Press, 1993). For a very readable, poignant study of the internment of Japanese Americans during the Second World War, see Jane Wakatsuki Houston and James Houston, *Farewell to Manzanar: A True Story of Japanese American Experience During and After World War II Internment* (New York: Bantam Starfire, 1983).

The experiences of gays and lesbians in American Society and their connections to politics are presented in several works: Craig A. Rimmerman, *The Politics of Gay Rights* (Chicago: University of Chicago Press, 2000); Brian McNaught, *Gay Issues in the Workplace* (New York: St. Martin's Press, 1993); James D. Woods with Jay H. Lucas, *The Corporate Closet: The Professional Lives of Gay Men in America* (New York: Free Press, 1993); Simon Shepherd and Mick Wallis, *Gay Politics and Culture* (Boston, MA: Unwin Hyman, 1989); Mark Blasius, *Gay and Lesbian Politics: Sexuality and Emergency of a New Ethic* (Philadelphia, PA: Temple University Press, 1994); Shane Phelan, *Getting Specific: Postmodern Lesbian Politics* (Minneapolis, MN: University of Minnesota Press, 1994).

Recent books have explored the AIDs epidemic and the politics surrounding the formulation of public policies to respond to the crisis. These include Randy Shilts, *And the Band Played On: Politics, People and the AIDS Epidemic* (New York: Penguin Books, 1988); Cindy Patton, *Sex and Germs: The Politics of AIDS* (Boston, MA: South End Press, 1995); and Philip M. Kayal, *Bearing Witness: Gay Men's Health Crisis and the Politics of Aids* (Boulder, CO: Westview Press, 1993). An examination of gays and lesbians in the military is presented in Randy Shilts, *Conduct Unbecoming: Lesbians and Gays in the U.S. Military—Vietnam to the Persian Gulf War* (New York: St. Martin's Press, 1993).

Perspectives on the civil rights movement for persons with disabilities are presented in Richard Scotch, *From Goodwill to Civil Rights: Transforming Federal Disability Policy* (Philadelphia, PA: Temple University Press, 1986); Robert Katzmann, *Institutional Disability* (Washington, D.C.: Brookings Institution, 1986); Stephen L. Percy, *Disability, Civil Rights and Public Policy: The Politics of Implementation* (Tuscaloosa, AL: University of Alabama Press, 1989); and *No Pity: People with Disabilities Forging a New Civil Rights Movement* (New York: Times Books, 1993).

Works on Native Americans and civil rights include: Clifford M. Lytle and Deloria Vine, *The Nations Within: The Past and Future of American Indian Sovereignty* (Austin, TX: University of Texas Press, 1999); Deloria Vine, *American Indian Policy in the Twentieth Century* (Norman, OK: University of Oklahoma Press, 1992); and James Olson, Mark Baxter, Darren Pierson, and Jason M. Tetzloff, *Encyclopedia of American Indian Civil Rights* (Westport, CT: Greenwood Publishing Group, 1997).

Endnotes

1. *Plessy v. Ferguson*, 163 U.S. 537 (1896).
2. *Brown v. Board of Education of Topeka*, 347 U.S. 483, 492 (1954).
3. *Wards Cove Packing v. Antonio*, 490 U.S. 642 (1989).
4. *Patterson v. McLean Credit Union*, 491 U.S. 164 (1989).
5. *Brown v. Board of Education of Topeka*, 347 U.S. 483, 492 (1954).
6. *Brown v. Board of Education of Topeka*, 349 U.S. 294 (1955).
7. *Green v. County School Board*, 391 U.S. 430 (1969).
8. Louis Fischer, *Constitutional Rights: Civil Rights and Civil Liberties*, 2nd ed. (New York: McGraw-Hill, 1995), 1010.
9. Susan Phillips, "Racial Tensions in Schools," *CQ Researcher* (January 7, 1994), 6.
10. Cited in Phillips, "Racial Tensions in Schools," 3.
11. Elizabeth Gleick, "Segregation Anxiety: A Court Rules that Hartford's Troubled Schools Cannot Look to the White Suburbs for Salvation," *Time* (April 24, 1995), 63.
12. *Smith v. Allwright*, 321 U.S. 649 (1944).
13. David M. O'Brien, *Constitutional Law and Politics: Volume II: Civil Rights and Civil Liberties* (New York: W.W. Norton, 1991), 1483–84.
14. *Graham v. Richardson*, 403 U.S. 532 (1971).
15. In *re Griffiths*, 413 U.S. 717 (1973).
16. *Sugerman v. Dougall*, 413 U.S. 634 (1973).
17. John J. Macionis, *Society: The Basics*, 2nd ed. (Englewood Cliffs, NJ: Prentice Hall, 1994), 217.
18. "Should Homosexuals Come Out?" *The Gallup Poll Monthly* (April 1993), 34.
19. David W. Dunlap, "The Struggle Over Gay Rights Moves to Statewide Level," *New York Times* (November 6, 1994), A10.
20. *Bowers v. Hardwick*, 478 U.S. 186 (1986).
21. Jill Smolowe, "Noble Aims, Mixed Results," *Time* (July 31, 1995), 54.
22. Cited in Smolowe, "Noble Aims, Mixed Results," 55.
23. See, for example, Stephen L. Percy, "Administrative Remedies and Legal Disputes; Evidence on Key Controversies Underlying Implementation of the Americans with Disabilities Act," *Berkeley Journal of Employment and Labor Law*, Vol. 14, No. 1, 413–436.
24. Cynthia Harrison, *On Account of Sex: The Politics of Women's Issues, 1945–1968* (Berkeley, CA: University of California Press, 1988), 104.
25. The Equal Pay Act, 29 U.S.C. Section 206(d) (1).
26. The Third U.S. Circuit Court of Appeals established the principle that, in cases involving the Equal Pay Act, plaintiffs need show only that their work is "substantially equal" to that of members of the opposite sex and not that it is identical. See *Schultz v. Wheaton Glass*, 421 F.2d 259, 265 (3d Cir. 1970).
27. U.S. Commission on Civil Rights, *Findings and Recommendations* (April 11, 1985).
28. These findings presented in a report by the Glass Ceiling Commission, "Good for Business: Making Full Use of the Nation's Human Capital," released on March 15, 1995. The report is based upon 1990 census data and surveys conducted by the commission.
29. A study of the Equal Rights Amendment is presented in Janet K. Boles, *The Politics of the Equal Rights Amendment* (New York: Longman, 1977).
30. *Pittsburgh Press Co. v. Human Relations Commission*, 413 U.S. 376, 392 (1973).
31. 29 C.F.R. Section 1604.11(a). For more discussion of the issue, see Steward Oneglia and Susan French Cornelius, "Sexual Harassment in the Workplace: The Equal Opportunity Commission's New Guidelines," *Saint Louis Law Journal* 26 (1981).
32. *Meritor Savings Bank v. Vinson*, 477 U.S. 57 (1986).
33. "Compilation and Overview of Federal Laws and Regulations Establishing Affirmative Action Goals or Other Preference Based on Race, Gender or Ethnicity," Report to Senator Robert Dole prepared by the American Law Division, Congressional Research Service, The Library of Congress, February 17, 1995.
34. The activities of the Equal Employment Opportunity Commission in fighting employment discrimination and pursuing affirmative action in federal government employment are presented in the *Annual Report on Employment of Women, Minorities & Individuals with Handicaps in the Federal Government* published by the U.S. Equal Employment Opportunity Commission, Washington, D.C.
35. *Regents of the University of California v. Bakke*, 438 U.S. 265 (1978).
36. *United Steelworkers v. Weber*, 443 U.S. 193 (1979).
37. *Fullilove v. Klutznick*, 448 U.S. 448 (1980).
38. *Richmond v. Croson Co.*, 488 U.S. 469 (1989).
39. Davide Savage, "Bush's Opposition to Racial Preferences Gets Big Support," *Los Angeles Times*, February 16, 2003.
40. Myrlie Evers-Williams, "NAACP's Vision for the Future," *USA Today* (May 25, 1995), 13A.
41. Robert Pear, "Deciding Who Gets What in America," *New York Times* (November 27, 1994), E5.

21

American Politics in an Interdependent World

Key Points

- **The American political system's connection to the governments and societies of other nations.**
- **Linking the American economy to the economies of other nations around the world.**
- **Viewing governance as not only attention to internal affairs but also as a response to the actions and peoples of other nations.**
- **Strategies to promote the nation's economy in the international marketplace, including tariffs, trade agreements, and monetary cooperation.**
- **Foreign policy strategies used to advance and protect American interests abroad.**
- **National defense as a key responsibility of the national government.**
- **Achieving interdependence means that Americans must use economic strategy, foreign policy, diplomacy, and national defense policies to protect the nation's political, social, and economic needs.**

Preview: Foreign Aid IQ

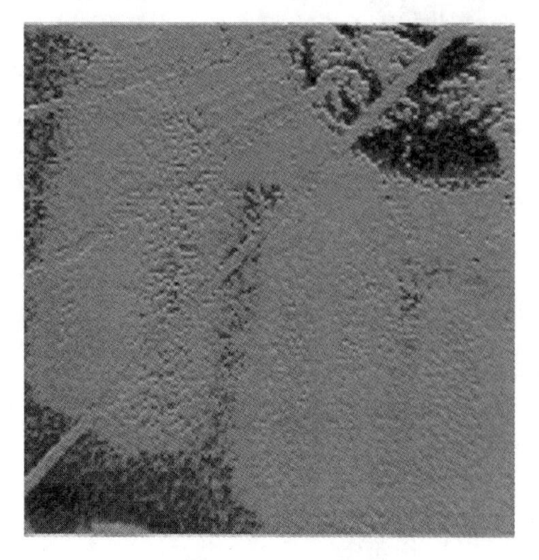

In the last years of the 20th century, public tide turned against American provision of foreign aid to other nations. Americans questioned whether foreign aid was achieving any identifiable objective in the post-cold war area and worried that foreign aid was among the culprits behind ever-growing federal government spending and budget deficits. Public attitudes about foreign aid were documented in a survey conducted by the Program on International Policy Attitudes at the University of Maryland in 1995.

When asked whether the amount the U.S. spends on foreign aid is too much, too little, or about right, three quarters of

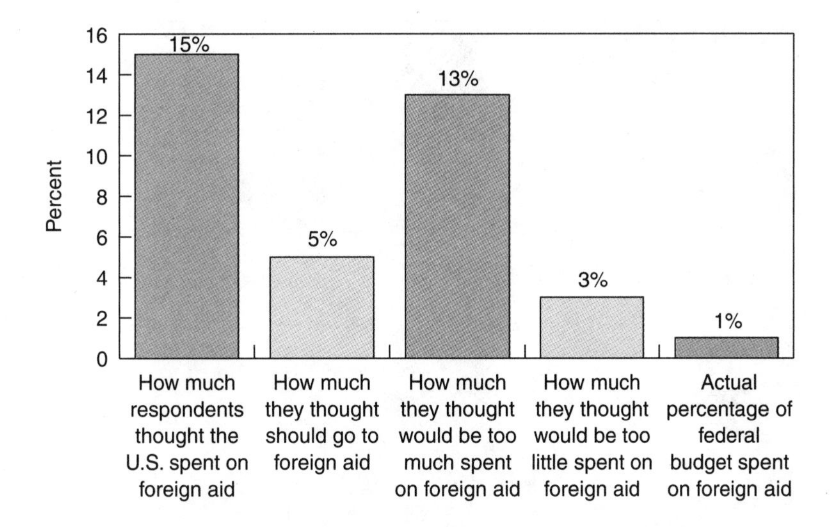

Figure 21-1
Public Opinion about Foreign Aid

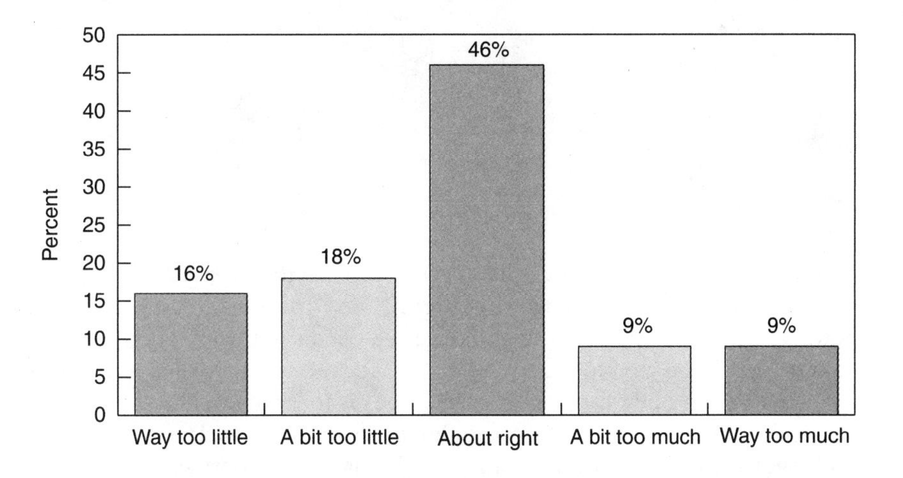

Figure 21-2
Public Opinion about Foreign Aid as Part of the Budget

respondents said it was too much. Sixty-four of these persons said foreign aid should be cut. Americans clearly had an overall negative view of foreign aid. But, was this view based on a clear picture of reality? Perhaps not.

Respondents in the survey were asked to estimate foreign aid expenditures as a percentage of the federal government budget. Their median responses are shown in Figure 21-1.

Americans are generally misinformed about the percentage of federal monies spent on foreign aid. It amounts to only about one percent of the budget. More recent surveys show a similar pattern of misperception. A 2002 Harris poll indicated that the median percentage of foreign aid assumed by the public was 20 percent of the U.S. budget while they would find 8 percent appropriate.

The survey contained a follow-up question aimed at reassessing public views given more accurate information on foreign aid as a portion of the federal budget. Respondents were asked: Imagine that you found out that the U.S. spends 1 percent of the federal budget on foreign aid. Would you feel that this is too much, too little, or about right? Respondents' answers are shown in Figure 21-2.

These results suggest that there may be more public support for foreign aid than originally expected. Given information about the actual portion of the federal budget spent on foreign aid, 34 percent of respondents said this was way too little or a bit too little and 46 percent said it was about the right amount. With accurate information on spending, Americans are less interested in cutting back foreign aid.

Willingness to commit U.S. funds to foreign aid is related to domestic economic conditions and world events. During times of budget deficits, the public thinks about domestic needs first. On the other hand, the American public was quite willing to extend large amounts to help rebuild Iraq after the 2003 war, as it had been about rebuilding other countries after previous wars.

Source: "Foreign Aid: Under Siege in the Budget Wars," *New York Times* (April 30, 1995), E4; and Harris Interactive poll of 3,262 adults, June 2002, LEXIS-NEXIS database.

The Golden Rule (SEP 4/1/61) Printed by permission of the Norman Rockwell Family Agency. Copyright © 1961 the Norman Rockwell Family Entities.
UN/DPI Photo by Norman Rockwell

Earlier in its history, the United States generally tried to remain aloof from the economic and military conflicts that engulfed other nations, particularly those in Europe. Today, however, American politics can no longer be conducted in isolation from the broader political and economic forces in the world. Technological advances in transportation, communications, and weaponry mean that the great oceans no longer protect the United States from the invasion of foreign armies, products, or ideas. The American economy is no longer enclosed within the borders of the nation or continent. Instead it functions within a complex web involving financial interests and investments throughout the world. Even with regard to military power, something Americans have viewed with great pride for the past half-century, the U.S. does not have sufficient resources of its own to police the world and maintain world peace. Like it or not, American politics is *interdependent* on politics and governments of nations throughout the world. In short, **globalism** prevails, and the nations of the world are now unavoidably linked in social, economic, and political ways. Understanding globalism and its implications is key to managing foreign affairs in the contemporary world.

globalism *Recognition that the nations of the world are increasingly interconnected by economic, social, and political forces.*

Traditionally, public policy has been thought of as either domestic, addressing internal problems, or foreign, dealing with relationships with other nations. In today's world, these lines have been blurred. Interdependence means that U.S. domestic affairs—both economic and political—are influenced significantly by the actions taken by the governments and peoples of other nations. At the same time, the peoples and governments of other countries are affected by U.S. economic and political policies.

Interdependence provides both opportunities and threats. On the positive side, close relations with other nations allow the United States to engage in important foreign trade—both to export manufactured goods and to import raw materials required for industrial production. They allow American citizens to travel across the globe to enjoy the wonders of both the ancient and modern worlds. Harmonious relations also enable the United States to share wisdom, culture, entertainment, scientific discoveries, and other achievements with world nations. Strong relationships may also reduce the chance for war or military hostility with other countries.

Interdependence also means relying on the people, institutions, and governments of foreign nations, and such dependence can represent a threat. As Americans have seen in the last quarter century, both their life-style and prosperity depend on the regular production and importation of oil from Middle Eastern nations. When this vital oil connection is severed, for economic or political reasons, the nation is adversely affected.

Similarly, in the 1980s, when the Philippine government announced that it wanted to eliminate U.S. military bases within its borders, the United States was faced with reduced military capability in Southeast Asia. This move was a threat to American military power because it eliminated the place from which the U.S. could deploy military forces in response to threats and problems in Southeast Asia and the Pacific. In response, the U.S. was forced to redeploy its forces to other debarkation points in the region.

Interdependence with foreign nations and governments can, furthermore, have mixed impacts on the United States. American consumers, for example, have long appreciated the high-quality, reasonably priced electronic goods manufactured in Japan, but as consumers have come to favor these foreign products, American corporations and jobs that make electronic goods have declined. Importing these goods has been beneficial to one set of players and harmful to others.

The "peace dividend" is another example of how interdependence can have varied impacts on players and businesses within the nation. The closing of the long-term Cold War with the Soviet Union in about 1990 meant that the U.S. no longer required a huge military capable of responding to Soviet military action anywhere around the globe. For this reason American armed forces, military bases, and armaments were pared back during much of the 1990s. These reductions in American military capacity, termed a "peace dividend" by some analysts, sounded good to policy makers seeking to cut federal spending and curb budget deficits—a boon to American taxpayers. These same cutbacks, however, resulted in base closures and reduced orders for submarines and aircraft—all of which meant civilian layoffs at bases and arms-producing companies. A weakened economy associated with the attacks of September 11, 2001, the war on terrorism, the war with Iraq, and the costs of rebuilding Iraq all combined to erase the peace dividend, with new demands for funds competing with domestic needs.

This chapter explores how interdependence with other nations of the world has had an impact on American politics, American government, and the American way of life. It begins by considering fundamental and enduring objectives of American **foreign policy,** that is, its relations with other nations. The chapter then considers interdependence in three critical policy areas: the world economic game, foreign policy, and national defense. In each policy area, the nature of American interdependence with other nations is explored along with strategies that can and have been used to cope with interdependencies. As will become apparent as we move through this chapter, economic, foreign policy, and defense issues today are often intertwined, raising many challenges for conducting diplomacy with other nations.

> **foreign policy** *The policies of a nation that relate to economic, political, or military relationships with other nations in the world.*

21-1 Managing Interdependence: Goals and Objectives

Managing interdependence requires the execution of political strategies in an international rather than a merely domestic context. A primary difficulty with political strategies in the international environment is that there is no fundamental rulebook, no "international constitution," to govern the behavior of political players or to protect violations of rights. The basic players—individual **nation-states**—must fend for themselves, using whatever resources they have in pursuing relations with other countries. A nation's foreign policy is determined on the basis of the country's particular needs, and its **diplomatic** efforts involve the use of economic, political, and military resources.

> **nation-state** *A legally recognized nation. Refers to the prominent use of nations as the primary building blocks of the world order.*

> **diplomacy** *The foreign relations that independent nations maintain with each other, often through discussions and negotiations, and sometimes through threats.*

21-1a Protection of Sovereignty

The principal goal of the United States and other nations of the world is to maintain **sovereignty**. A nation is generally conceived to be sovereign when other nations of the

> **sovereignty** *The right to exercise governing powers over a specified territory.*

world recognize it as a legitimate state. Once a nation is seen as sovereign, it has the right to govern citizens within its national boundaries.

Achieving sovereignty often requires significant struggle. The American colonists achieved sovereign control only after the Revolutionary War with England. Other nations have similarly achieved independence and sovereign rights through armed conflict against ruling powers. Sometimes, sovereign control is gained through peaceful means, although some form of political protest is usually necessary to convince occupying powers to yield governing control. Great Britain granted independence to India, for example, but only after years of political protest inspired by Mahatma Gandhi and other leaders.

Sometimes, claims about sovereignty are conflicting, and ascertaining which of the claims is most legitimate is difficult. Such was the case in the early 1990s in Yugoslavia, where republics within the nation sought independence. From World War II to 1990, Yugoslavia—composed of multiple republics, including Bosnia, Serbia, Slovenia, and Croatia—was tightly ruled by a central communist government based in Serbia. Following the breakdown of the central government in 1991, the republics of Slovenia and Croatia sought independent status. These republics have ethnic populations and cultures different from those in Serbia. The leaders of these republics claimed that they, not the central authorities, had the legitimate right to exercise sovereign control in their republics.

More recently we have seen the issue of sovereignty arise in post-war Iraq, where the leadership of Saddam Hussein was replaced with that of U.S.-backed Prime Minister Ayad Alawi. This leadership was challenged by religious and ethnic groups who sought to assert leadership over specific regions of Iraq rather than be governed by one central government.

Protecting sovereignty in the modern world cannot be achieved by erecting a wall around the nation and keeping others out. Every nation needs trading partners, and the companies of the world need raw materials for production. In addition, every nation can benefit from the ideas and technological innovations arising in other countries. Protecting sovereignty therefore must include recognition of interdependence and can no longer be achieved as it has been in earlier times in history by the erection of large walls or barriers. Global communications, rapid international transportation, intertwined national economies, and international problems such as environmental pollution all reiterate the interdependencies faced by nations of the world. Protecting national interests today, therefore, requires that nations work together to solve common problems and pursue shared opportunities. This cooperation—illustrated by the North Atlantic Free Trade Agreement described in Chapter 1—requires negotiation and the search for common

The Great Wall of China is an example of efforts to protect sovereignty with physical barriers.
Getty Images/The Image Bank

interest and benefit. In the end, to achieve national objectives a nation may yield a bit of its sovereignty by agreeing to share decisions and actions with other nations—as the U.S. did in agreeing to ease restrictions it had on trade with Mexico and Canada.

21-1b Stability

A second important objective of American foreign policy is stability. Not only do Americans wish to protect sovereignty, but they also wish to live their lives and conduct business without constant threat against their nation or its government. To maintain political stability, the U.S. government works with other nations to prevent terrorism and other hostile actions. The nation's leaders also seek to regularize contacts and discussions with other nations so that mutual interests can be commonly sought and conflicts resolved or minimized.

21-1c Economic Prosperity

Protecting sovereignty and national well-being means more than just protecting one's boundaries from invasion. The United States, like other nations, seeks to protect its economy from disruptions caused by the actions of other countries. The people of a nation can be harmed directly through economic means, even if no military action is involved. If vital resources normally imported into the United States from other nations are cut off, or if the usual markets for produced goods are closed to American exports, then the U.S. economy can suffer severe dislocations. Companies may close, workers may lose their jobs, and the economic vitality of the nation will be harmed. As the economies of world nations have become increasingly intertwined, the efforts of individual nations to manage economic interdependencies and protect their economies have become more complex.

International trade is at the heart of prosperity in an international economy. When nations are free to trade, each may seek the raw materials it needs, and each may sell its produced goods in a competitive international marketplace. When one nation restricts or prohibits trade with other nations, interdependence becomes more a problem than an opportunity. In the last two decades, many analysts and American companies have charged China with unfair trade practices, specifically with creating government regulations that make it difficult for American firms to enter the Chinese marketplace with their goods. These restrictive trade policies have caused political turmoil within the United States and strained diplomatic relations with China.

21-1d Protecting and Fostering Democracy

Deeply embedded within the American political culture is a strong belief in the value of democracy. As shown in this chapter, democracy and liberty are widely held values. So highly esteemed are these values that Americans want democracy not only for themselves, but also for other peoples in the world. At the very least, Americans believe that a people should have the right to choose a nation's form of government. This principle of **self-determination** was included among the **Fourteen Points** articulated by Woodrow Wilson as a blueprint for peace following World War I. Many presidents have restated it since that time.

A traditional U.S. foreign policy has been to encourage the development of democratic political institutions and systems in other nations. The United States has committed **foreign aid,** offered favorable trade agreements, and granted other inducements to stimulate the growth of democracy abroad. Sometimes these economic strategies have been successful, and sometimes they have failed to achieve their objective. In extreme circumstances, the United States has committed military forces toward achievement of this objective.

American efforts to promote democracy conflicted with the actions of the Soviet Union to spread Marxist-Leninist doctrine. Military, economic, and political tensions between the United States and the Soviet Union developed into the **Cold War.** The period from the end of World War II (1945) to 1991 saw the United States and the Soviet Union engaged in nonmilitary confrontations waged through economic, political, and

self-determination *The right of a people of a territory to govern themselves by a government system they freely select for themselves.*

Fourteen Points *Principles for world peace outlined by President Woodrow Wilson at the culmination of World War I; included provision for a League of Nations (the first effort at an international tribunal designed to maintain world peace).*

foreign aid *The provision of currency, grants, or loans from one nation to another, often for the purposes of economic and industrial development; can be given for general purposes or to support particular projects like dams, schools, or hospitals.*

Cold War *The period of conflict between the United States and the Soviet Union from roughly 1945 through 1990. Confrontations were based on economic, political, and diplomatic strategies and not military battles.*

diplomatic means. Indirectly, Cold War rivalries contributed to military conflicts in Korea, Vietnam, and Afghanistan. Since the Soviet Union first liberalized internal politics and broke into separate, independent republics in the early 1990s, relations with the United States have improved, leading to the demise of the Cold War.

Despite its interest in fostering democratic governments around the world, the United States has often developed strong relations with nondemocratic leaders and governments. For example, in the past, the United States maintained solid relations with the Shah of Iran, General Manuel Noriega of Panama, and Ferdinand Marcos of the Philippines—all strong leaders who used military power (and sometimes political terrorism) to maintain their positions. American relations with these regimes were defended on the grounds that these leaders supported vital American interests.

In the Philippines, for example, the United States sought to maintain two major military bases on Philippine territory, thereby establishing an American military presence in Southeast Asia. Because Marcos accepted the American military presence and forces against Marcos opposed the U.S. bases for many years, American leaders felt that supporting the Marcos regime was appropriate. It was only when President Marcos rejected the results of a free and democratic election that the United States withdrew its support from Marcos.

Foreign policy analysts and politicians often debate the basic principles and orientations that should guide the conduct of U.S. foreign policy. One prominent theory of international relations emphasizes the idea of *realism*—a perspective that sees nations as the primary actors in world affairs and international relations focused upon strategies to enhance and maintain national power.

Realism recognizes that power—most nakedly expressed in the threat of war—is the ultimate currency in world affairs; hence the state will by its very nature be fundamentally preoccupied by the question of how power is organized in the international system in terms of its own survival. The concept of national security as the organizing principle of a state's foreign policy is well articulated in realist theory.[1]

From the vantage point of individual nation-states, the principal objective in international affairs is to protect sovereignty, while world order is seen as emerging from the balance of power among nation-states. Pursuit of international relations, according to the realist school, focuses on the development of rational strategies to optimize power positions within the international sphere. During many periods of American history, national leaders seeking to protect U.S. interests and sovereignty have pursued a realist approach to international relations.

Another theoretical view on international relations has been identified by the terms *liberalism* or *idealism*. This perspective—which reached a watermark during Woodrow Wilson's tenure as president and as the world sought to pull itself together after World War I—emphasized the moral importance of fostering democracy around the world. Wilson and other idealists saw democracy as a type of panacea that would enhance the lives of people around the world and the capacity of nations to work together. Wilson articulated this view in his Fourteen Points plan for world peace, including the principle of self-determination.

In some instances the realism and idealism theories can be compatible. This would be the case where fostering democracy in some area abroad could be directly linked to the objective of strengthening America's power position abroad. The U.S. military action in Panama that unseated General Noriega could be seen as consistent with idealism, for it removed a military dictator from power. At the same time it allowed the U.S. to flex its military might and demonstrate its interest in political relations in Central America. At other times, realism and idealism can conflict. For example, many analysts viewed Wilson's plan to promote democracy around the world as utopian dreaming that failed to recognize the ongoing power struggles between nations that would shape future international relations.

In addition to the major schools of realism and idealism, there are still other approaches to the conduct of foreign relations. One such approach emphasizes the promotion of human rights as a fundamental foreign policy objective that the U.S. should aggressively pursue. Of modern presidents, Jimmy Carter was probably the most committed to an idealist foreign policy approach. The Carter administration often held, for example, that American economic and military aid should be used to push other nations to improve their human rights record. More recently, the human rights record of China has been a major concern for the United States. Through both political and economic pressure, the U.S. has pressed China to improve its human rights record.

Still another foreign policy perspective, one growing in importance today, focuses upon economic relations among nations. Given the growing interdependence of national economies on worldwide economic trends and the ending of the Cold War, it is not surprising that contemporary relations among nations focus prominently on economic issues and objectives. For this reason, major foreign policy concerns of the United States focus on the access of American producers to foreign markets, export of American jobs abroad as U.S. companies shift manufacturing facilities to other nations where labor is cheaper, balance of trade, and the value of the U.S. dollar on foreign currency exchanges.

These approaches to foreign policy together indicate the diversity of objectives that the United States can and does pursue when relating to other nations. At different points in history, different approaches have been more dominant. As noted above, economic issues are of prime importance today. During the world wars, on the other hand, protecting national sovereignty was the overriding objective.

21-2 U.S. Players in the Global Game of Interdependence

Managing the interdependence of the American political system with the systems of other nations of the world is accomplished through a large set of players and governing institutions through which economic relations are monitored and negotiated, foreign policy is conducted, and national security is preserved. Players within the U.S. are matched by those of other nations who engage in political and economic games that significantly influence American life. Many of the American players are located in the Executive Branch, although Congress and even the private sector play some role. Current trends toward increased interdependence among nations have led to more interconnections among the American players involved in world economic games, foreign policy, and national defense. More and more, these players must work together to achieve the broad national interests of the United States in the international sphere.

21-2a Executive Branch Players

The Constitution grants the president substantial responsibilities related to foreign policy and national defense. Today, presidents and other officials throughout the federal bureaucracy play key roles in managing global interdependence and protecting America's economic, political, and national defense interests.

Presidential Roles

The U.S. Constitution identifies the president as the pivotal player in the conduct of foreign relations. Section 2 of Article II empowers the president to be the chief diplomat, responsible for negotiating treaties with foreign powers. The president determines when treaties are necessary and initiates the diplomatic meetings for conducting negotiations.

Presidents seldom personally engage in treaty negotiations. Instead, they send representatives to meet with foreign leaders, discuss mutual interests, and negotiate policies acceptable to all parties. These representatives are often officials in the Department of State, although sometimes the president appoints special envoys to engage in specific negotiations. In the case of major treaties, presidents may meet with leaders of other nations in summit conferences to sign treaties that have been largely negotiated prior to the meeting. Such meetings give visibility both to the treaty or international agreement and to the leaders of the nations involved.

Department of State

Officials in the Department of State conduct daily activities associated with directing American foreign policy. The head of this organization—the secretary of state—is recognized as a powerful player within the nation and around the world. The secretary is assisted by a staff of advisers and analysts, some of whom are political appointees. A special type of federal bureaucrat—the **foreign service officer**—handles most of the daily work of American diplomacy. Currently, there are about thirty-seven hundred foreign service officers. These persons, trained as generalists, with skills in foreign relations and diplomacy, are frequently rotated to assignments in different nations, where they staff embassies, facilitate communication between American leaders and those of foreign governments, and monitor and report back to Washington what is happening in other nations.

foreign service officer *An individual who is trained in generalist foreign service skills and enters the civil service in a special classification for public officials engaged in diplomatic service.*

The United States has **embassies** in most nations of the world with whom it has diplomatic relations. Heading each embassy is the **ambassador,** appointed by the president. He or she may be a career foreign service officer or an individual with political connections to the president. Ambassadors are assisted by diplomatic staff, some of whom are specialists in the political workings of the nation in which they are assigned. While nominally responsible to the president as chief executive, ambassadors operate as components of the Department of State.

embassy *The diplomatic offices of one nation located within the boundaries of another nation. Headed by an ambassador and managed by diplomatic staff.*

ambassador *The top official in a U.S. foreign embassy; appointed by the president and confirmed by the Senate.*

Ambassadors represent the fundamental connection between the United States and foreign nations, relaying information back and forth. This role of ambassadors was transformed somewhat during the Persian Gulf War as the Cable News Network (CNN) in some cases replaced diplomatic channels (see Box 21-1: CNN Changes Communication of Diplomatic Information). Staff in American embassies gather information on political and economic developments in their host nations and assist American citizens who are visiting there. There are numerous specialists, especially in the larger embassies, responsible for such things as facilitating business and trade with the U.S.

The National Security Council

The National Security Act of 1947 created a National Security Council (NSC) within the Executive Office of the President. Its purpose is to advise the president about the integration of domestic, foreign, and military policies relating to national security. Because of its location outside of individual cabinet departments, the NSC can provide broad guidance and advice on a full range of national security issues.

national security adviser *Presidential assistant who directs the National Security Council and advises the president on national security issues.*

In several modern administrations, the head of the NSC staff—the **national security adviser**—has become a major player in making and executing foreign policy. Prominent examples include Henry Kissinger, who served under presidents Nixon and Ford, and Zbigniew Brzezinski, appointed by President Jimmy Carter. The power of these individuals arose from their close personal connection to presidents who trusted their wisdom and counsel. On occasion, these advisers went to foreign nations on diplomatic missions defined by the president. It was in this capacity that Henry Kissinger visited the People's Republic of China in 1972 as a prelude to the thaw in relations with the United States.

The position of national security advisor, with its close ties to the president, remains key to American foreign policy in the 21st century. Upon taking office in 2001, President George W. Bush nominated Condoleezza Rice to serve as his national security advisor. She has accompanied President Bush on trips abroad and acts as a key advisor on foreign policy issues. Because of the war in Iraq, much of her attention has focused on America's interests in Iraq and diplomacy among the nations that have supported the United States in this war. When Colin Powell announced his resignation as Secretary of State in November 2004, President Bush announced his intention to nominate her to succeed Powell in the Secretary of State position.

Given their close access to presidents and top foreign policy decision-making, some national security advisers have been seen as rivals to the secretary of state as the principal foreign policy player. This rivalry was clear during the Nixon administration, when Henry Kissinger served as national security adviser and William Rogers as secretary of state. Under presidents Reagan, George H. Bush, and Clinton, the secretary of state regained the primary position, with the National Security Council playing a supporting, rather than a dominating, role in American foreign policy.

Box 21–1 CNN Changes Communication of Diplomatic Information

Nations have typically communicated information to each other through "diplomatic channels," that is, via special telephone and communications lines that allow for the transfer of sensitive information. Diplomatic telephone lines are designed to be "secure," meaning that they cannot be tapped by outside parties. Nations use such channels to dispatch "cables" designed to inform each other about recent developments, the viewpoints of their leaders, and official foreign policy positions.

The Cable News Network (CNN), headquartered in the United States but with offices around the globe, has transformed much of the communications among nations. CNN is unique among television broadcasting networks because of its extensive use of satellites to rapidly relay video transmissions around the world, the number of foreign broadcasters subscribing to CNN's news service (now over 140), and its extensive set of international reporters.

CNN's technological impact was dramatically apparent during the Persian Gulf War. Leaders of nations throughout the world simply watched CNN and learned almost instantly of war developments. These transmissions proceeded much more rapidly than did diplomatic cables. Thus, many leaders learned about the effectiveness of American military action through worldwide television instead of via diplomatic cables.

Perhaps the most striking revelation about the impact of CNN was that it allowed enemy leaders to communicate with each other—and with the American public and decision makers—through public statements broadcast on the CNN network. Nations at war have few direct forms of communication. Instead, they have traditionally relied on indirect communication through third-party nations. CNN changed that practice. During the conflict, both President George H. Bush and President Saddam Hussein of Iraq made public statements intended to send messages to each other.

Worldwide television provides a new form of international communication and may necessitate changes in the way diplomats conduct their business. One American diplomat described the necessary changes as follows:

"Reporting what was going on was once important. Now diplomatic activity has to adapt itself to new situations. You have to do it differently. Now diplomats have to put their emphasis on analyzing, negotiating—and selling your country's policies."

Mobile transmission by CNN during the Persian Gulf War brought almost instantaneous news to the viewing public around the world. Both Bush and Hussein appeared live on CNN during the Persian Gulf War—finding a new way to communicate with world leaders and each other.

The 2003 Iraq war added a new twist. Over seven hundred journalists were imbedded with the coalition troops using videophones and satellite connections to provide front-line coverage in real time. The emergence of a competing Arab-based network (al-Jazeera) allowed the world to see how the war was being covered from another perspective. In addition, Western sources used footage from al-Jazeera, while millions took advantage of their webcasts.

Central Intelligence Agency

The Central Intelligence Agency (CIA), also created in 1947, plays an important yet low-profile role in foreign policy. The CIA gathers political, economic, and military information about other nations, analyzes these data, and disseminates findings to decision makers. Information gathering takes many forms, such as the systematic review of foreign newspapers and journals, scans of military installations through spy satellites, and espionage (actions designed to obtain diplomatic or military secrets through secret means). CIA-provided information allows the president and other foreign policy players to be more effective in conducting diplomatic relations. American leaders can determine, for example, how honest other nations are being about their needs and resources. CIA information may allow American decision makers to better predict the future needs and political moves of other countries.

The CIA engages in **covert action,** activities intended to gather information about the intentions and capabilities of other nations through such actions as infiltration of their political decision-making or military operations.[2] Covert activities may also include direct actions in foreign lands to achieve political or military purposes. During periods of

covert action *Activities intended to gather information about the intentions and capabilities of other nations through infiltration of their political decision making or military operations.*

military conflict, the United States may send trained agents into foreign nations to interrupt the enemy government's operations or military activities. Americans may never learn about these covert activities or may learn about them many years after the fact.

The President as Commander-in-Chief

The president is identified in Article II of the U.S. Constitution as the commander-in-chief of the armed forces. This provision places control of the military in the hands of civilian authority and empowers the president to command military preparedness and action. As described elsewhere in this chapter, this power has clashed with the constitutional power of Congress to declare war.

The Department of Defense

The U.S. military establishment is one of the largest organizations in the world, with personnel assigned to locations around the globe. In 2002, the military was composed of 1.7 million active-duty personnel, over 1.2 million reservists, and thousands of civil employees. Managing and directing this large bureaucracy and its role in the world is a complex task performed by several players clustered within the Department of Defense.

Following World War II, the American military services were unified under one cabinet agency, the Department of Defense (DOD). By law, this department is headed by a civilian secretary of defense, who is second only to the president in directing military affairs. Within the DOD, each military service—the Army, Navy, Air Force, and Marines—has its own department headed by a secretary. Most of the American military command is based at the Pentagon, an enormous five-sided building complex located in Virginia across the Potomac River from Washington, D.C.

Joint Chiefs of Staff *Primary military advisors to the president and secretary of defense. Members represent branches of the military service and are appointed by the president.*

Under the authority of the president, the secretary of defense and the **Joint Chiefs of Staff** direct military command. The joint chiefs are composed of representatives of each military service, who are expected to put aside the narrow goals of their service branch and look out for national defense as a whole. The president appoints each joint chief and selects the chairperson. These officers are key presidential advisors and have responsibility for devising long-range national defense policy. The chiefs have also become vital players in recent military actions where U.S. troops have participated with armed forces of other nations in military operations, many of which have been organized by the United Nations.

Congressional Role in Managing Interdependence

In addition to the Executive Branch, Congress plays a role in foreign policy. One duty of Congress is to ratify treaties negotiated by the president and members of the Executive Branch, with the secretary of State often playing a key role. The president's power to negotiate treaties and otherwise conduct foreign relations is not absolute. Under the Constitution, once the president negotiates treaties, they must be ratified by a two-thirds vote of the Senate. Given the expertise of foreign policy specialists in the executive branch and the president's prominent role as manager of foreign affairs, the Senate often defers to the president and ratifies treaties. Only rarely has the Senate rejected treaties negotiated by the president (see Box 21-2: A Major Presidential Loss in the Treaty-Making Game).

In addition to the Senate's ratification power, Congress also participates in foreign policy through the *power of the purse*, the prerogative to appropriate public funds. Presidents can request that economic or military aid be given to foreign nations as part of American foreign policy initiatives. Only Congress, however, can appropriate foreign aid funds. Oftentimes, Congress awards economic aid on the condition that recipient nations either perform or cease specified activities. For example, Congress has stipulated that certain nations may receive aid only on the condition they improve their human rights record or cooperate in an effort to stop the flow of illegal drugs.

Congress can also use the power of the purse to restrain foreign policy actions that the president and presidential advisers may wish to take. This congressional power was activated in 1982 with the Boland Amendment, which forbade the provision of funds to support the Contra movement in its effort to overthrow the Sandinista government in

Box 21–2 A Major Presidential Loss in the Treaty-Making Game

Woodrow Wilson and the League of Nations

At the end of World War I, Democratic president Woodrow Wilson traveled to Versailles, outside of Paris, France, to participate in negotiating a peace treaty. Wilson advocated the national right of self-determination in a famous speech where he outlined "Fourteen Points"—a blueprint for world peace following the war. Included in the Fourteen Points was a plan to create a League of Nations where all nations could come together to resolve differences and avoid war. The Treaty of Versailles, formally ending World War I and setting the terms of German defeat, was signed in June 1919. This treaty included the call for self-determination and creation of the League of Nations.

Wilson returned to the United States, where he presented the Versailles treaty to the Senate. Since the end of the war, Republicans had taken control of the Senate and a wave of isolationism had swept the nation. Senate Republicans voiced concerns about the treaty, particularly about the proposed League of Nations. A predecessor to the United Nations, the League of Nations was intended to be an international body with a mission to preserve world peace. Republicans argued that the collective security provision of the league charter would serve to (1) draw the United States into future wars among other nations, (2) interfere with the constitutional power of Congress to declare war, and (3) make it difficult for the United States to conduct its own foreign policy.

Upset and angry about the Senate's unwillingness to ratify the treaty without extensive modifications, President Wilson launched a national speaking campaign. He hoped to rouse the public to support the League of Nations and to press the Senate to ratify the Versailles treaty. Exhausted by the campaign, Wilson collapsed, never fully recovering. In the end, the Senate failed to approve American entry into the League of Nations.

Nicaragua. Congress took this action because of a concern about Reagan administration initiatives to support the Contras as a means of removing Daniel Ortega and the Sandinistas from power. The Iran-Contra scandal that emerged during the Reagan administration resulted from violation of the Boland Amendment when Oliver North and others channeled funds from Iranian arms sales to the Contras in Nicaragua.

The views of Congress about foreign policy and diplomacy changed during the mid-1990s as the Republicans took control of Congress. Republican leaders articulated a more limited role in international affairs—a step back from the prominent superpower role the U.S. has exercised since World War II. The elements of the Republican agenda included reducing foreign aid (partially in the name of budgetary savings), U.S. involvement in the United Nations, and American willingness to become militarily involved in regional conflicts.

The War in Iraq led by the United States commencing in 2002 was aimed at removing Iraqi president Saddam Hussein from power. The Bush administration argued that Iraq possessed weapons of "mass destruction"—including nuclear and chemical weapons—that represented threats to U.S. and international security. The administration also linked the terrorist actions of Osama Bin Laden and the al Qaeda terrorist network to Iraq. Based upon these contentions, the U.S. Congress generally supported the war and appropriated funds to support the military action. After the invasion was complete, congressional support waned when no weapons of mass destruction were found, when no link between Iraq and al Qaeda was documented, and when post-war military action claimed substantial resources and many American lives,

Congress and Questions about War Powers

Concerns about war-making powers represent a much longer tension between presidents and Congress. In the U.S. Constitution, the Founders created a dual mechanism for decision making concerning American involvement in wars with other nations. While Article II designates the president as commander-in-chief of the armed forces, Article I grants

Table 21-1 Declared and Undeclared Wars

Popular Name of Military Action	Opponent	Declared or Undeclared
Grenada (1983)	Grenadan government	Undeclared
Gulf War (1991)	Iraq	Undeclared
Iraq War (2003)	Iraqi government	Undeclared
Korean War (1950–53)	North Korea	Undeclared
Mexican War (1848)	Mexico	Declared
Philippine Island Conquest (1899–1901)	Filipinos	Undeclared
Spanish American War (1898)	Spain	Declared
Vietnam War (1964–73)	North Vietnam	Undeclared
War of 1812	Britain	Declared
World War I (1917–18)	Germany	Declared
World War II (1941–45)	Axis Powers	Declared

Congress the power to declare war and to appropriate funds to support the military (see Table 21-1).

As the bar graph in Figure 21-3 indicates, the use of military force without declarations of war has increased in recent years, putting pressure on Congress to find new ways to maintain its role in the separation of power scheme. This two-branch mechanism has often proven difficult in practice. Since World War II, the president has evolved as the dominant player in national defense and world affairs, and on many national defense issues, Congress has deferred to the president. The tricky question has concerned the president's power to commit American forces to military actions abroad.

Given the technological nature of modern warfare, some decisions committing military forces must be made within minutes. Should a missile attack be launched against the United States, the president does not have time to convene Congress and wait for a legislative declaration of war. Not all military action, of course, requires such immediate response. The potential for nuclear attack, however, makes it possible that a "within minutes" response may be required in some circumstances.

In a variety of situations, including military actions in Korea, Vietnam, Lebanon, Grenada, Panama, and the Middle East, American presidents have committed U.S. military forces without Congress declaring war. Presidents have termed these actions as "military" actions" or "engagements" that fall short of war and therefore do not require a declaration of war by Congress. World War II is the last time that Congress formally declared the United States to be at war with other nations.

While recognizing the president's lead in foreign policy matters and the need for prompt reaction to some military threats, Congress is concerned about presidential power to commit military forces without congressional consent. This issue came to a head over the Vietnam War, which was not a formally declared war but a "military action" ordered by American presidents. In the early stages of this conflict, Congress supported the president. Recognizing military hostility against the United States in Vietnam, Congress resolved in 1964, through the Gulf of Tonkin Resolution, to allow the president "to take all necessary measures to repel any armed attack against the forces of the United States and to prevent further aggression."[3] As the Vietnam conflict continued and American casualties mounted, support within Congress for military action in Southeast Asia eroded. Following secret military bombings of Cambodia, Congress repealed the Gulf of Tonkin Resolution, sending a strong signal of displeasure to President Richard Nixon regarding the conduct of the war and continued American military action in Vietnam.

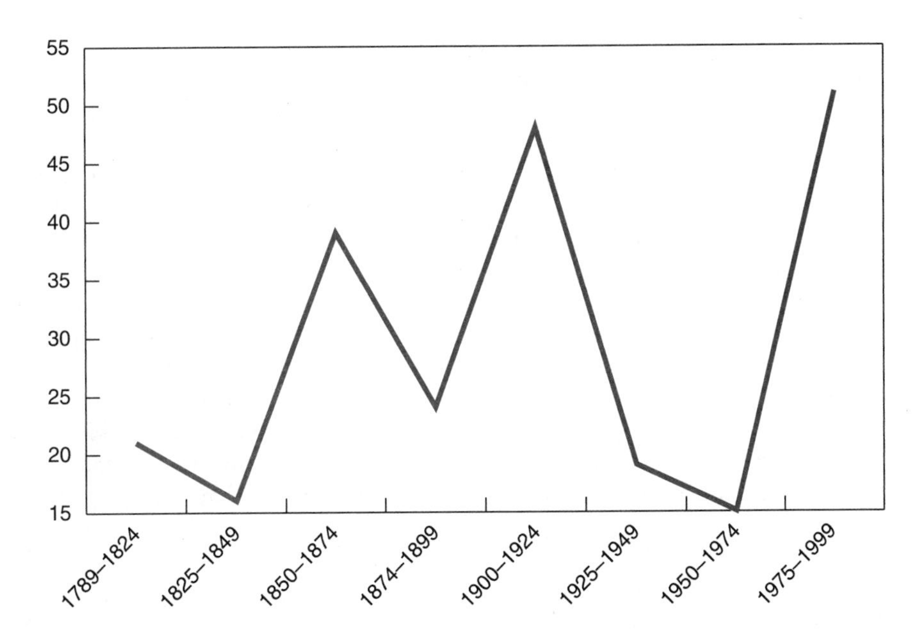

Figure 21-3
Undeclared Wars, 1789–1999

Source: www.fas.org/man/crs_931007.htm (Ellen Collier, CRS Issue Brief, *Instances of Use of United States Forces Abroad, 1798–1993.*)

The War Powers Resolution of 1973 represented an initiative by Congress to restrain presidential power to commit U.S. forces for indefinite periods to military engagements in foreign lands. The intent of the resolution was to craft a balance between the right of Congress to declare war and the president's power as commander-in-chief. The provisions of the War Powers Resolution are relatively straightforward:

1. The president may commit troops to armed combat abroad but must notify Congress of such action within forty-eight hours after such conflict begins, informing legislators, in writing, about the nature of circumstances involved and the scope of military action being taken. If possible, Congress should be notified prior to the commencement of military action.
2. The use of American troops in armed combat must terminate within sixty days of the notice to Congress unless Congress authorizes military involvement for a longer period. This deadline may be postponed for thirty additional days if the president certifies that this time is necessary for a safe evacuation of troops. These deadlines can be enforced by the power of Congress to cut off appropriations to fund military action.
3. Within the sixty- or ninety-day periods defined in the provision 2, Congress may order an immediate withdrawal of U.S. troops by adopting a concurrent resolution, which is not subject to presidential veto.

The War Powers Resolution, despite its intent, has not resolved long-term tensions between presidents and Congress about control of military involvements abroad. President Nixon opposed the resolution, vetoing it because he felt it violated presidential powers as commander-in-chief. Congress overrode the veto. Since that time, the War Powers Resolution has seldom been invoked. Presidents have continued to commit military forces in limited engagements without formal approval by Congress. Often, presidents voluntarily inform Congress about military action but simultaneously argue that the situation is not relevant to war power provisions.

Congress faces both legal and political constraints regarding the exercise of war powers. At a broad level, questions remain about whether the War Powers Resolution interferes with presidential prerogatives as commander-in-chief of the armed forces. More narrowly, a question exists about the constitutionality of the portion of the resolution that allows Congress to order immediate withdrawal of armed forces through concurrent resolution. Some constitutional analysts contend that the concurrent resolution represents a form of legislative veto over executive actions. In a different context, the Supreme Court has ruled the legislative veto as unconstitutional,[4] which thus raises questions about the constitutionality of Congress ordering troop withdrawals during the sixty- to ninety-day period that presidents are allowed to commit military forces abroad.

Even if all constitutional questions about the War Powers Resolution were answered, it still might be difficult for Congress to order troop withdrawal or to cut off funding of military action that is in progress. Such action might appear to undercut presidential authority and could be seen as playing politics with the lives of American military personnel. Congress is unlikely to cut off funds or order withdrawal if such action would endanger military forces.

The War Powers Resolution has been invoked only once, when President Ronald Reagan committed American troops to Lebanon in 1982. Congress became uneasy about this placement of troops, even though the military mission was basically one of maintaining order in the region. Under persistent pressure from Congress, Reagan agreed to a compromise. In September 1983, Congress formally invoked the War Powers Resolution and authorized the continued deployment of U.S. Marines in Lebanon for a period of eighteen months. Before the deadline was reached, Reagan ordered military forces out of Lebanon.

President George H. Bush faced a similar quandary about war powers in 1991 when he contemplated armed action as part of the UN coalition to remove Iraq from Kuwait. For several months prior to military action, Bush maintained that action against Kuwait would not fall under the War Powers Resolution. Many in Congress disagreed and argued that the commitment of military troops in the Middle East was sufficient to trigger war powers requirements.

Prior to the UN deadline of January 15, 1991, for Iraqi withdrawal, George H. Bush asked Congress to pass a resolution supporting the use of American troops to enforce UN Security Council resolution 678. Even though he maintained that the War Powers Resolution had not been triggered, Bush wanted congressional support prior to the commencement of military action. Both houses of Congress supported the resolution, although the margin of passage in the Senate was slim (52 to 47).

21-2b Other Players: The Military-Industrial Complex

Providing national defense for the United States requires more than military personnel and leadership. It also requires resources. Defense spending is a big ticket item for the national government. It necessitates the production of a complex array of sophisticated, high-technology weapons. Large private sector companies that manufacture specialized weapons ordered by the government produce these weapons. The military establishment also relies on a large set of players for information, research, and technology. These players include universities, multinational corporations, research think tanks, and consulting firms.

In a major speech prior to leaving office, President Dwight D. Eisenhower warned the nation about the influence of the "military-industrial complex" on military decisions and foreign policy. By this, he meant to alert policy makers and the public to the influence of defense contractors, researchers, think tanks, and others with a stake in decisions about military policy.[5]

As Figure 21-4 illustrates, federal government spending for defense has been highest during times of major military action (World War II in the early 1940s, the Korean War in the early 1950s, and the Vietnam War in the late 1960s and early 1970s). Spending for human resources grew substantially beginning in the mid-1960s with the launching of social programs as part of the Great Society initiative. As the national debt grew, so did federal spending to pay interest on that debt.

In 2000 defense contractors received over $48 billion in procurement hardware contracts and another $37 billion for research, development, testing, and evaluation of military policy.[6] These contractors have a clear and direct stake in military policy, particularly as it concerns the selection of new weapons systems. For this reason, they use lobbyists and their access to influence the Congressional committees responsible for deciding what military equipment and hardware will be purchased. Contractors seek to

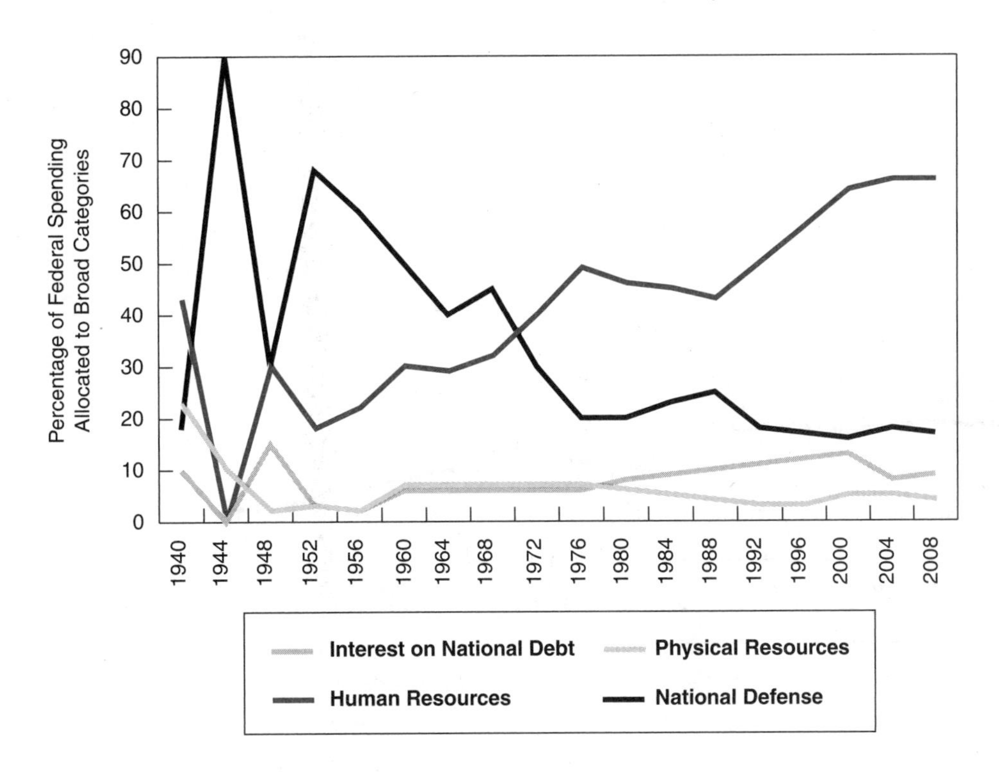

Figure 21-4
Total Federal Government Spending on Defense and Other Purposes, 1940–2008

Sources: Office of the President of the United States, *Budget of the United States Government for Fiscal Year 1996* (Washington, D.C.: U.S. Government Printing Office, 1995), Table 3.1, pp. 36–42) and *Budget of the United States Government for Fiscal Year 2004* (Washington, D.C.: U.S. Government Printing Office, 2003 Table 3.1, pp. 50–51).

participate actively in policy making in order to convince military leaders and members of Congress that their products are essential to the nation's overall arsenal of military power.

Several defense contractors received a strong boost in credibility as a result of the Persian Gulf War in 1991. Prior to the war, contractors were often criticized for cost overruns and production delays for weapons that had not been tested in combat conditions. These criticisms lead to the cancellation of certain weapons systems, including the A-12 fighter and the Bradley Fighting Vehicle. The Persian Gulf War provided the U.S. military with the opportunity to demonstrate the reliability and accuracy of other high-technology weapons, including cruise missiles, cluster bombs, Patriot surface-to-air defense missiles, and the stealth fighter. The weapons generally proved effective, particularly in their ability to strike pinpoint blows on identified military targets.

21-3 Strategies in the World Economic Game

Economic interdependence among the world's nations presents many challenges to the United States. Indeed, economic issues in the global economy have stimulated the formation of many foreign policy initiatives. The challenge for policy makers managing economic relations with other nations is made greater by the many economic exchanges between nations that are made by private companies acting on their own, outside of government. Thus, the government is seeking to manage not only economic relations between governments but also the transactions made by **multinational corporations** that conduct business throughout the world.

multinational corporation *Corporations that conduct business in multiple nations simultaneously.*

The degree of interconnection between national economies can be demonstrated by several measures. One important indicator is international trade. As shown in Figure 21-5, the United States is a major exporting nation, sending $616 billion of goods abroad in 2002.[7] The health of the American economy depends on foreign nations continuing to purchase U.S. goods. Canada and Mexico are the most active trading partners with the United States.

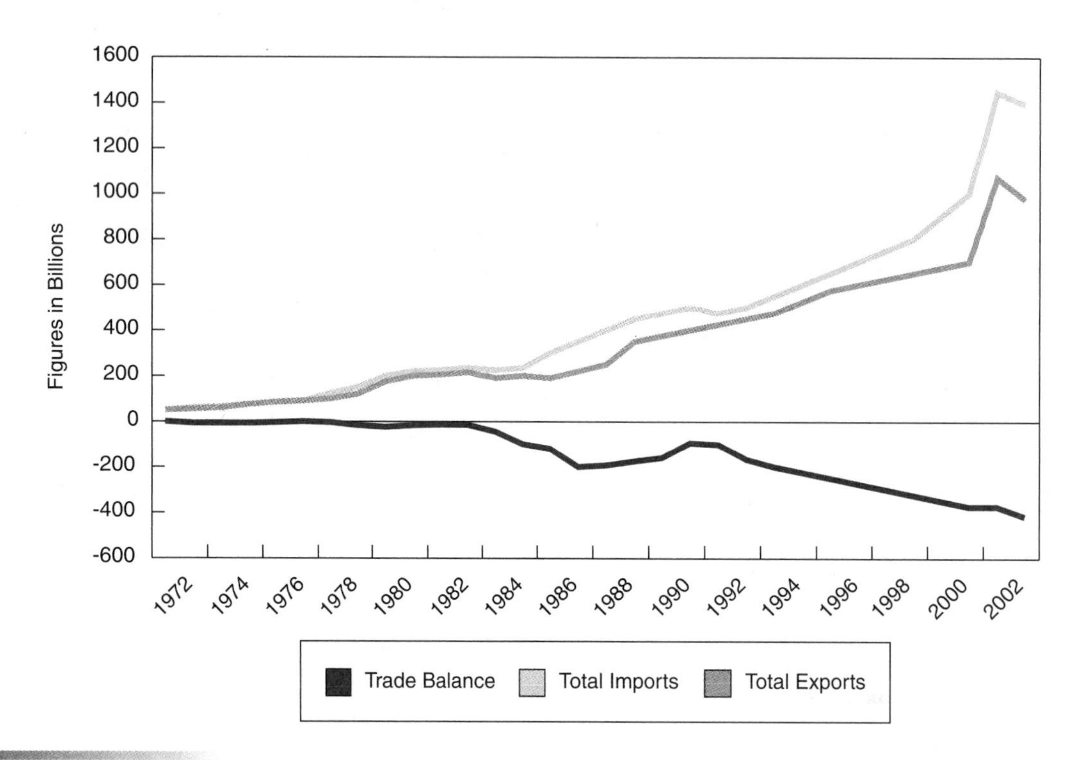

Figure 21-5
United States Exports, Imports, and Trade Balance 1970–2002

Source: U.S. Bureau of the Census, *Statistical Abstract of the United States*. Washington, D.C.: GPO, 2003, Table 1294, p. 813.

trade deficit *The net loss in foreign trade that occurs when the value of goods imported into a nation from abroad exceeds the value of goods exported to other nations.*

America is also an importing nation; it currently imports goods from other nations at a rate of over $1.1 trillion a year.[8] One problem in American foreign trade in the last decade is that imports have consistently exceeded exports, meaning that there is a net loss of capital from the United States. Although an occasional **trade deficit** is seldom a cause for concern, a persistent deficit is indicative of a national economy that is becoming less competitive in the world marketplace. By 2003 the trade deficit exceeded $500 billion.

Another indicator of economic interdependence is the extent of ownership of companies in other nations by citizens of the United States and the ownership of U.S. companies by foreign interests. In 2000, the federal government estimated that almost 6 percent of U.S. businesses had at least one foreign owner (individual, partnership, or government) that owned 10 percent or more of the company.[9]

The idea of the U.S. government engaging in activity to manage economic interdependence may seem to contradict some national values. Within U.S. political culture, a strong element of laissez-faire philosophy remains—that is, a belief that government should avoid interference in the private sector. In the late twentieth and early twenty-first centuries, Americans have come to accept government regulation intended to maintain marketplace competition and protect workers and consumers. Thus there has been some erosion in the earlier hands-off philosophy. Nevertheless, a strong belief remains in the utility of an economy run by private entrepreneurs. As it seeks to manage interdependencies that threaten the vitality of the overall American economy, the government works to avoid excessive intrusion into the affairs of individual corporations. (Chapter 5 examines the economic culture and the importance of private enterprise.)

21-3a Tariffs and Trade Barriers

"Free trade"—the effort to eliminate trade barriers between nations—has been a principle of U.S. policy since the end of World War II. The rationale for this policy is that foreign trade will be most efficient overall if nations of the world refrain from creating government policies that inhibit trade or impose costs. Former president George H. Bush extolled the free trade stance during a visit to Japan in 1992 when he said, "I am strongly convinced that free and open commerce is not a zero-sum game. Free trade on a level playing field creates jobs and lifts standards in both of our countries."[10] Generally, the level of trade between nations and the relative magnitude of exports and imports are determined by economic rather than political forces.

Achieving free trade is difficult, however, because nations often see how restricting trade with other nations can be advantageous to their own economy. Nations may seek to restrict the importation of goods that, because of their cost or quality, threaten domestic producers of the same goods. For example, many Americans, particularly those involved in the auto industry, have pressed Congress and the president to restrict the importation of Japanese automobiles that today represent a substantial market share of cars purchased in the U.S. For their part, Japanese rice producers, subsidized by the Japanese government, have sought to restrict the importation of rice grown in America. In both cases, producers in one nation sought to protect themselves from being financially harmed by the purchase of goods produced abroad.

The most frequent mechanism for restricting trade is the tariff, a duty (tax) placed on merchandise imported from abroad. A tariff works to raise artificially the price of the imported good, making it less price-competitive with its domestically produced counterparts.

Trade restrictions and protective tariffs have frequently been associated with American trade with Japan. From its near destruction as the result of World War II, the Japanese economy has been rebuilt and restructured so as to be the envy of much of the world. As part of this restructuring, Japan focused on sophisticated production technologies and innovative management practices that cumulatively have resulted in substantial improvements in both production efficiency and quality.

Also as part of restructuring, the Japanese government created an intricate system governing the importation of foreign goods, a system that has made it difficult for many American producers to secure a foothold in the Japanese marketplace. In the last three decades, Japanese producers have recognized the potential of American markets. They have systematically increased exports to the United States while maintaining several barriers that prevent American firms from entering Japanese markets.

Nowhere has the impact of Japanese exports and technology been felt more acutely than in automobile production. Throughout the 1970s and 1980s, American automobile manufacturers such as General Motors, Ford, and Chrysler watched a flood of Japanese imports directly compete with American models and experienced a steady erosion in market share (that is, the percentage of all cars purchased in the United States and manufactured by American-owned companies). Feeling the economic pinch, automakers and unions representing autoworkers pressed for protection from Japanese automobile imports.

This pressure for protective tariffs conflicted with the general U.S. preference for free-trade policies. After extensive negotiations, Japanese automobile makers agreed to voluntarily place a trade quota on the number of cars exported to the United States. This agreement limited the supply of imports, thereby raising their price relative to American-made automobiles. Recognizing the political sentiments against foreign-manufactured cars, Japanese companies such as Toyota, Honda, and Nissan have built manufacturing plants inside the United States, employing American workers to produce some models and thus bypassing the quota limitation. Another strategy, threat of tariff imposition, was used successfully by the Clinton administration in 1995 as a strategy to obtain trade concessions during negotiations with Japan about opening up Japanese markets to American-made cars and auto parts (see Time Out 21-1: Using Tariff Threats as a Strategy for Economic Leverage).

The basic problem with the application of protective tariffs is that they invite retaliation. When one nation places a tariff on the second, the latter may respond by imposing its own tariffs, and extensive trade barriers make all types of foreign trade more expensive.

21-3b Trade Agreements

The United States has taken the lead in calling for regular meetings among nations to negotiate policies that reduce trade restrictions. The General Agreement on Tariffs and Trade (GATT) was created at the end of World War II, as the world braced itself for a

Time Out 21-1

Using Tariff Threats as a Strategy for Economic Leverage

America can use a variety of strategies to pursue its economic interests abroad. Several of these strategies have been used during economic relations with Japan—a strong but troublesome trading partner with the U.S.

Background: Repeatedly in the last three decades of the twentieth century, the United States found itself at odds with Japan over trade policy. For Japan, America is a prime market for electronic goods and automobiles. Over time, American industry has lost out to Japanese producers, who often made less expensive goods that U.S. consumers were more than willing to buy. This lead to a persistent trade deficit with Japan where Americans bought far more goods from Japan than Japanese consumers bought from America.

American manufacturers have complained that trade regulations and bureaucratic procedures have often made it difficult for them to find markets in Japan. The imbalance in trade was very apparent in the field of cars, trucks, engines, and auto parts. In 1994, the U.S. imported $40.4 billion worth of these automobile-related goods from Japan while the Japanese bought only $3.1 billion worth of American-made counterparts. Under pressure from automobile and auto parts manufacturers, the Clinton administration felt compelled to respond to the trade deficit in this industry.

Here are some questions to consider from the different perspectives of the U.S. government and the Japanese government:

From the U.S. perspective:

What strategies could the Clinton administration have used to deal with the trade imbalance situation? What are the strengths and weaknesses of each strategy, given the U.S. situation in the case? What single strategy would you have recommended that the Clinton administration use?

From the Japanese perspective:

How does American trade affect your nation? What threat do trade difficulties with Americans pose for the Japanese economy? If the U.S. decided to take strong action to deal with the trade deficit in the auto-related industry, what response should your government make?

new era of peace and international cooperation. The free-trade mission of GATT was designed around a set of important principles:

1. Nondiscrimination—nations should treat all others the same with regard to trade policies,
2. New barriers to imports should be avoided while existing tariffs should be phased out, and
3. Nations should not seek to protect domestic industries through protective tariffs except for short periods during emergency conditions.[11]

Prior to the 1980s six GATT agreements had been reached among world nations, each of which took steps forward in eliminating trade barriers. The most recent round of GATT negotiations began in September of 1986 in Punta del Este, Uruguay; based on the place of its opening, these negotiations that continued through 1994 are known as the "Uruguay round." After several years of protracted meetings and negotiations, an agreement in the Uruguay round was concluded in Geneva, Switzerland, in December 1993. According to this agreement, tariffs were to be cut on about 85 percent of world trade and eliminated on a range of goods, including construction and agricultural equipment, paper, steel, pharmaceuticals, and beer and liquor. For the first time the GATT agreement would include agricultural products, an area sensitive to many nations that subsidize farmers and agricultural interests. The agreement also replaced the previous GATT organization located in Geneva with the World Trade Organization.

The United States in 1993 took another step forward toward free trade through the North American Free Trade Agreement (NAFTA) made with Canada and Mexico. Through this agreement all three nations agreed to a plan that would ultimately eliminate all tariffs on goods produced and sold in North America (see Chapter 1). Some tariffs were eliminated immediately, and others where scheduled for phase out over several years. The agreement also obligated all three partners to work toward common standards to protect food quality and to make efforts to improve the environment.

NAFTA became a controversial issue in American politics, and the political battles surrounding this agreement illustrate conflicting views about international trade agreements. At the urging of the Mexican government, President George H. Bush in 1990 called for the U.S. to sit down with Mexico and Canada to negotiate an agreement to enhance trade and eliminate trade restrictions and tariffs. All three nations agreed to begin negotiations, which began in 1991, and a free trade plan among the North American nations was completed the following year.

The next step was for all three nations to approve the plan. President Bill Clinton supported the agreement and called upon Congress to ratify NAFTA. Strong opposition quickly arose both in the halls of Congress and in states across the nation. One vocal source of opposition came from populist political figures who spoke around the nation about the dangers they claimed the agreement posed to American workers. Ross Perot—the third-party candidate who received 19 percent of the popular vote in the 1992 presidential election— fought long and hard to defeat NAFTA. He went so far as to write and publish an anti-NAFTA book, *Save Your Job, Save Our Country*, which received widespread public attention. The arguments of Perot, Jesse Jackson, and other opponents linked claims about adverse economic impacts of the agreement to themes of nationalism and protecting sovereignty. Business groups gave the agreement mixed reviews. Industries whose leaders saw the agreement as offering new markets for American-made goods supported the plan, while those who feared increased competition voiced concern and opposition. Environmentalists wanted to take the opportunity to press Mexico to be more aggressive in actions to protect the environment and eliminate industrial pollution.

The deep split within the nation about NAFTA was evident as Congress considered legislation in 1993 to implement the NAFTA agreement. Even the leadership in the House of Representatives was divided. Then Speaker Thomas Foley joined President Clinton in supporting NAFTA, while Majority Leader Richard Gephardt and Democratic Whip David E. Bonior worked to defeat the agreement. To overcome opposition and gain enough votes for passage of legislation to support NAFTA, Clinton led the fight for NAFTA. He called together three former presidents—Gerald R. Ford, Jimmy Carter, and George H. Bush—to join him on the stage as he made an emotional appeal for NAFTA support. After intense debates in both houses and after side bargains were made to garner support, Congress approved NAFTA in late 1993, giving way to a new area in free trade among North American nations.

21-3c Monetary Cooperation

Economic interdependence relates not only to trade but also to monetary conditions, currency exchange rates, and the availability of capital for investment. Contemporary communications technology makes it almost as easy to trade on foreign stock markets as on U.S. financial markets. Financial investments now regularly cross national lines, as investors throughout the world seek the most lucrative investments at home and abroad. The stock exchanges throughout the world are now psychologically linked, as the rise or fall of stock prices on one exchange are instantaneously communicated and serve as a signal to investors in other exchanges.

No single nation or international organization controls monetary policies throughout the world. Countries regulate their own domestic monetary and banking systems. In the United States, this function is performed primarily by the Federal Reserve System (see Chapter 22). At the international level, the International Monetary Fund (IMF) serves as a forum for the world's nations to discuss monetary issues and to develop cooperative

Answers to Time Out 21-1

Answers to the questions posed in Time Out 21-1: The Clinton administration began its work with Japan in handling the trade deficit in 1993 through a strategy of negotiation—sitting down at the bargaining table with the intent of convincing Japanese that a trade deficit problem existed and requesting their assistance in changing Japanese policies to reduce and eliminate restrictions that keep out American products. The talks were not fruitful, and, after two years of negotiation, the Clinton administration decided to adopt a second, more potent strategy. President Clinton announced that he would invoke a large tariff on Japanese-built luxury cars imported into the United States within a few weeks if a trade agreement was not reached. This move would greatly increase the price of these cars on American showroom floors. The tariff threat was thus intended to place pressure on the Japanese to make trade concessions to the U.S.

The tariff was a clever one. In actuality, the number of automobiles that would be affected was relatively small, since the tariff was limited to luxury models and not extended to less-expensive and more popular models. In this way, only wealthy Americans interested in luxury cars might be hurt by the tariff. (The incidence would have been much greater had all Japanese cars been included under the tariff.) Also, the tariff hit Japanese automakers in an area of production that provided the largest profit: the luxury market. Perhaps more importantly, the tariff demonstrated the willingness of the United States to flex its economic muscle to achieve the trade concessions it wanted. And, for the Japanese, there was simply no question that exporting goods to America—particularly of automobiles—is critical to the Japanese economy.

After further negotiations and threats on both sides to wage a trade war, negotiations reached a successful conclusion. Japanese negotiators agreed to a plan that would lead to more U.S. auto parts being purchased by Japanese companies and widened access of U.S. automakers to Japan. With news of the agreement, Clinton canceled the planned tariff, just hours before it was to be imposed.

strategies to deal with monetary problems, particularly those related to monetary exchange rates. The IMF emerged from discussions held among forty-four nations in Breton Woods, New Hampshire, in 1944 concerning monetary relations in the postwar period.

The United States also participates in the International Bank for Reconstruction and Development—the World Bank—which provides funds to developing nations to stimulate economic growth and to maintain their economic and political stability. The United States has been a steady contributor to the World Bank, adding funds to the pool of financial resources that can be used for loans to third-world countries. In recent years, the World Bank has focused on the serious economic problems of developing nations and on the frequent occurrence of nations being unable to repay their loans to the World Bank and to other financial institutions.

21-3d The Challenge of Managing Economic Interdependence

Of all forms of interdependence facing the United States, economic interdependence is perhaps the most difficult to manage and control. While America is the top military power at the beginning of the twenty-first century, it is only one of several strong economic powers. On several measures, American economic power appears to be waning. The United States of the 1990s faced regular trade deficits and the resulting outflow of investment capital, a large national budget deficit, an expensive work force when contrasted with other labor markets in the world, and problems with maintaining a competitive edge in several key industries. In the early years of the twenty-first century, economic interdependence remains a major challenge to the United States. While trade deficits continue, a larger emerging problem is the shifting of manufacturing jobs from the U.S. to other nations, particularly China. The lower labor costs in many other nations makes American workers less competitive in the global marketplace. The U.S. remains a leader in newly emerging information technology fields but is losing its place as a major manufacturing nation. This, in turn, impacts domestic politics, as demonstrated in the 2004 presidential campaign by Senator John Kerry, who regularly criticized the Bush administration's record on job loss, including loss of jobs to other countries.

The international marketplace results from decisions made by investors and companies around the globe, who grow increasingly interconnected through modern transportation and communications technology. Investors, most of whom are private rather than public, are motivated not by national interests but by investment returns. While the United States has influence in the GATT talks, World Bank, and International Monetary Fund, these organizations regulate only a few components of the overall economic picture. At best, national governments, including that of the United States, can seek to protect their nations only from specific, harmful, external influences on their economies. Managing economic interdependence remains a substantial challenge to American leaders.

21-4 Strategies for Foreign Policy Games

The United States uses multiple strategies when conducting relations with foreign nations. Often, both the United States and another nation each need something that the other can provide, making reciprocal arrangements an appropriate diplomatic strategy. Such cases represent positive-sum games, where both sides benefit from greater interdependence. For example, western nations all face threats from radical Islamic groups in the Middle East. In response to the September 11, 2001 terrorist attack on the United States, many nations have banded together to directly share intelligence about terrorism with the expectation that collaboration will help all partners to respond more effectively to the threat of terrorism.

When parties engaged in diplomatic relations have unequal interests, mere trading may not be enough to allow them to reach an agreement. In these circumstances, the United States seeks to persuade leaders of other nations to take actions that are advantageous to U.S. interests. The president and the president's representatives may try to persuade foreign leaders to agree to treaties or diplomatic proposals on the basis of merit. This type of appeal may or may not be effective, depending on the interests and perspectives of the other nations involved. Often, additional diplomatic strategies are used to obtain the support of foreign leaders. These may include economic strategies, the supply of arms and military technology, and the intervention of the United Nations. Table 21-2 presents an overview of significant events in American foreign policy.

21-4a Financial and Economic Aid Strategies

The United States can use foreign aid—the grant of money to foreign nations for economic, social, or military purposes— to bring parties to the negotiating table and to leverage support for U.S. policy interests. In 2003 the United States provided $23.6 billion in economic aid and humanitarian assistance, a substantial figure but a very small component of the overall federal budget.[12] Because many nations wish to receive or maintain the flow of economic aid, they have incentive to cooperate with the United States in diplomatic initiatives.

The foreign aid strategy came under some attack in the mid-1990s, as public support ebbed (see the Preview to this chapter) and as conservatives in Congress questioned whether such aid achieved any measurable benefits for the U.S. Foreign aid budgets, like those for many other domestic and foreign policies, came under close scrutiny as Congress sought to reduce federal government spending to reach targets designed to eliminate the budget deficit over a number of years.

Favorable access to the American economy is another powerful bargaining tool in foreign relations. Under the law, the U.S. government has created a system of differential tariffs charged on foreign imports, with the differential depending on the trade status designation given to particular foreign nations. The government can grant **most-favored nation (MFN)** trade status to nations, whereby they pay the lowest tariffs and otherwise have the most advantageous trade position with the United States. By promising to grant or threatening to rescind MFN status, the United States can sometimes gain leverage in negotiations.

most-favored nation (MFN) *International trade policy in which nations agree to give each other the most favorable trade concessions available to foreign countries.*

Table 21-2 Significant Events in American Foreign Policy

1796	In his farewell address as president, George Washington warns the nation to avoid entangling alliances that might threaten the nation's security. Nonalignment and isolationism are dominant U.S. foreign policy positions throughout much of the nineteenth and early twentieth centuries.
1803	Under the lead of President Thomas Jefferson, the United States purchases a vast tract of land—the Louisiana Territory—from France, doubling the size of the nation.
1812–1815	The United States engages in war with Britain (War of 1812) over clashes in the Northwest Territory and naval engagements in which American soldiers are impressed into duty in the British navy.
1823	President James Monroe articulates a foreign policy position, known as the Monroe Doctrine, in which he couples American neutrality in the affairs of European nations with the requirement that European nations cease all efforts to colonize in North and South America.
1800s	Manifest Destiny, the effort of Americans to explore, settle, and develop their nation from coast to coast—captures much of the nation's energy during the nineteenth century. The force of Manifest Destiny led the nation into conflicts and wars with other nations and with native Indians living across the continent.
1846–1848	The United States and Mexico go to war over conflicting claims to Texas and other western territories (Mexican-American War). At the conclusion, Mexico recognizes the American title to Texas and grants the New Mexico and California territories (Mexican Cession) to the United States.
1898	In the Spanish-American War, the victorious United States wins freedom for Cuba and receives Puerto Rico, Guam, and the Philippines as territories.
1899	The United States, emerging as an important world power, announces the Open Door Policy, in which the United States seeks to strengthen its own commercial position in foreign trade with China by limiting the power of other foreign nations.
1917–1919	The United States enters World War I (which had begun in 1914 in Europe) on the side of the Allies (France, Britain, and Russia). American military power tips the scales, resulting in German defeat. In 1918, President Woodrow Wilson announces his Fourteen Points, a statement of the Allied war aims. Included in these points, which were used as a basis for the treaty ending the war, is an appeal for self-determination (whereby nations would determine their own political destiny) and a plan for a League of Nations, where international disputes could be settled in an international forum.
1919–1933	Isolationism runs strong in the United States, which prefers to ignore international disputes and focus attention on domestic issues. In this period, the U.S. Senate, led by Republicans, refuses to ratify the plan for the United States to join the League of Nations.
1933	President Franklin D. Roosevelt strongly endorses the Good Neighbor Policy, which calls for improved relations among countries in North and South America and reduced trade restrictions among these nations.
1941–1945	With the bombing of Pearl Harbor on December 7, 1941, the United States declares war on Germany and Japan (World War II). The nation's productive energy shifts to a war economy, as the U.S. military joins its allies to defeat its enemies. In 1945, the United States drops two atomic bombs on Japan, ending the war and launching the world into the nuclear era.
1945	The United Nations, an international organization dedicated to world peace, is created.
1945–1991	The Cold War is a period of superpower rivalry and competition between the United States and the Soviet Union, the two strongest powers to emerge from World War II. Each nation develops strong nuclear arsenals and perceives the other as a substantial threat to national security.
1947	President Harry S. Truman announces a U.S. commitment, known as the Truman Doctrine, to support free peoples of the world in resisting communist expansionism. This commitment results in a policy of containment, a plan to stop the spread of communism, which already has engulfed Eastern Europe.
1947	Secretary of State General George C. Marshall proposes a plan (known as the Marshall Plan) whereby the nations of Europe come together, develop a long-range plan for postwar recovery and economic development, and request U.S. financial support to finance the redevelopment. The United States ultimately pours billions of dollars into the rebuilding and economic revitalization of Western Europe.
1949	The North Atlantic Treaty Organization (NATO), a defense pact and military alliance between the United States and Western European nations, is created as a means of enforcing the containment doctrine.

Table 21-2 *(continued)*

1950–1953	Under a mandate from the United Nations, the United States and other nations engage in the Korean War in an effort to prevent communist-controlled North Korea from taking military control of South Korea. The Soviet Union provides military and economic support to the North Koreans, while Chinese troops enter the war in support of the South Koreans. The war ends with a truce and a demilitarized zone between the two nations.
1962	In the Cuban Missile Crisis, the United States takes action to stop the Soviet Union from deploying missiles in Cuba. In the superpower confrontation, the United States places a naval blockade around Cuba and prevents Soviet ships from bringing in arms and equipment to complete the missile installations. After several days of high tension, the Soviet Union agrees to remove its missiles from Cuba.
1965-1975	In the Vietnam War, the United States sides with South Vietnam in its war with communist-led North Vietnam. This war pitches American military technology against jungle and guerrilla warfare. The United States withdraws in 1973, hoping that South Vietnam is capable of defending itself. The North Vietnamese succeed in defeating the South and in merging the two Vietnams in 1975.
1972	A brief period of superpower **détente** emerges when the Soviet Union and United States ease Cold War tensions and successfully negotiate an arms control treaty.
1985	Mikhail Gorbachev takes over as the leader of the Soviet Union and boldly moves the country toward *perestroika*, a restructuring of the Soviet economy and foreign policy, and *glasnost*, an opening of discussion and criticism of Soviet governance.
1991	A coup attempt by conservative elements is foiled as the superstructure of the Soviet Union disintegrates. By the end of the year, the Soviet Union is dissolved and is replaced by a loose confederation of former Soviet republics.
1991	The United States, with a coalition of allies, enforces a United Nations resolution that requires Iraqi forces, which had invaded Kuwait in 1990, to return to Iraq. After protracted air attack, allied ground troops achieve success in a few days.
1991–1995	Armed conflict among peoples in regions of the former nation of Yugoslavia attracts United Nations intervention for humanitarian and peacekeeping purposes.
2001	The United States, seeking to increase protection from missile attack (especially from terrorists) proposes creating a new anti-ballistic missile defense system that will violate the 1972 U.S.-Soviet Union arms control treaty.
	Terrorists hijack four U.S. passenger jets and crash them into the twin towers of the World Trade Center in New York City and the Pentagon outside Washington, D.C. The U.S. begins a war on terrorism, invading Afghanistan in an effort to destroy the Al Qaida terror network based there.
2003	U.S. and a coalition of allies invade Iraq, claiming that Saddam Hussein's regime failed to eliminate weapons of mass destruction. Some U.S. allies, including Germany and France, block an effort by the United Nations Security Council to create UN support for the military invasion.

21-4b Arms and Military Power

détente *A period when strained international relations give way to a lessening of military and diplomatic tensions.*

The U.S. government can sometimes influence other nations by permitting them to purchase American-made arms and military technology. The federal government closely scrutinizes these sales, all of which must be approved by the departments of Defense and Commerce. Many nations of the world seek to buy sophisticated U.S.-made weapons. The United States can use its ability to approve or stop arms sales when seeking to convince foreign leaders to accept a foreign policy initiative.

The United States can also finance another country's purchase of weapons and military technology through loans and grants. In 2000, the United States provided $5.2 billion in military aid and loans to foreign nations.[13] The nations receiving the highest amounts of military aid were Israel, Egypt, Jordan and Bosnia Herzegovina.

U.S. military power is another potential resource for diplomatic negotiations. The United States protects other nations, many of which have formal alliances with the

United States. Most of these nations desire to maintain protection under the American "defense umbrella" and, therefore, have incentive to seriously consider American ideas during diplomatic talks. Box 21-3: American Diplomacy in Action describes how the "defense umbrella" was one of the strategies used to create the coalition against Iraq in the 1991 Persian Gulf War.

21-4c The United Nations and International Organization

The United States seeks to achieve its foreign policy goals through its participation in the international organizations, most notably with the United Nations. The United Nations was created in 1945 immediately following World War II and is now composed of over 165 member nations. According to the UN charter, the fundamental objective of the United Nations is to maintain and foster peaceful relations among nations of the world

Box 21-3 American Diplomacy in Action

Creating a Coalition to Force Iraqi Departure from Kuwait

In its efforts to draw a group of nations into a coalition to enforce the 1990 United Nations resolution requiring Iraq to pull out of Kuwait, the United States employed several diplomatic strategies. Creating such an alliance, especially one that included Arab nations that had long been suspicious of American interests in the Middle East, required extensive diplomatic efforts. Among the strategies used were the following:

Persuasion

Appeals to belief in sovereignty: All nations sought for membership in the coalition were participants in the United Nations, which has accepted self-determination as a fundamental right of nations. In seeking support for the coalition, President George H. Bush and his representatives argued that a collective response was necessary to deal with Iraqi aggression that violated the sovereignty of Kuwait.

Rewards and Sanctions

Foreign aid as a diplomatic resource: As an incentive for Egyptian participation in the coalition, the United States agreed to "forgive" loans given to Egypt for the purchase of military weapons. Commitments of future foreign aid may have been made to other coalition participants.

Arms and arms sales: As part of the arrangement with the Saudi Arabian government to allow an American military presence in the Persian Gulf, the United States agreed to sell to Saudi Arabia additional weapons and technology. The United States also provided additional arms to Israel, including Patriot missiles, as an incentive to keep Israel from undertaking military action against Iraq, an action that threatened the stability of the anti-Iraq coalition.

Reminder of the American "defense umbrella": Germany and Japan regularly consume oil from the Middle East, and both have been protected for several decades from communist expansionism by the American military. Neither nation was anxious to become involved in the coalition against Iraq. However, the United States strongly reminded both parties of their long-term protection by the U.S. military and their responsibility to contribute to the world order. In response, both nations pledged billions of dollars to support the military coalition.

Authority

The United Nations and legitimacy: To give legitimacy to the plan to counteract Iraqi occupation of Kuwait, the United States worked actively in the United Nations to ensure that UN resolutions condemned the invasion and allowed the use of force to free Kuwait. By placing the authority of the premier international body—the United Nations—behind the effort to stop Iraq, the United States enhanced the legitimacy of its foreign policy objective.

Personal Leadership

George H. Bush takes charge: From the start, President Bush took an active and personal role in the diplomatic efforts to rally an international response to Iraq's invasion of Kuwait. Bush sent his top representatives to foreign nations to plead his case and spent countless hours on the telephone with foreign leaders. Bush used U.S. resources and personal energy to mold the coalition of partners that opposed Iraq.

in order to "save succeeding generations from the scourge of war," "reaffirm faith in fundamental human rights," and "promote social progress and better standards of life in larger freedom."[14]

The United Nations has two chambers of unequal power and responsibility. The **General Assembly** is composed of one representative from each of the member nations. Each member has one vote. While the General Assembly has no power to compel action by any government, it represents the one international forum where nations stand together as equal players. The influence of this body arises from the weight of its recommendations as an expression of world opinion.

General Assembly *The body in the United Nations where all member nations are represented and have one vote. The chamber has no power to make decisions that compel action by member nations.*

The real power of the United Nations is located, by design, in the **Security Council,** which has the primary responsibility for the maintenance of international peace and security. The Security Council is composed of five permanent members—China, France, Russia, the United Kingdom, and the United States—and ten nonpermanent and rotating members. The Security Council alone has the power to make decisions that all member states are obligated to accept and carry out.

Security Council *The body in the United Nations empowered to make decisions binding upon member nations. Composed of five permanent members—China, France, the Soviet Union, the United Kingdom, and the United States—plus ten nonpermanent and rotating members. Permanent members have veto power.*

One important decision rule operates in the Security Council: All permanent members must agree on policy matters before an action can be approved. This "rule of great power unanimity" gives each permanent player on the Security Council important veto power. Throughout the Cold War period, permanent members used this veto power to stop the United Nations from adopting policy interests favorable to their rivals. All permanent members have used their veto to protect their own interests. Rivalry between the United States and the Soviet Union made it difficult for the United States to use the United Nations to achieve its diplomatic goals; U.S.-backed proposals were often vetoed by the Soviet Union.

During the Cold War (and before what is now termed the "New World Order"), regional crises and conflicts became part of superpower rivalries. Superpowers sometimes used conflicts for their own purposes. The Soviet Union, for example, provided resources to the North Vietnamese during the Cold War in part to check American influence in Southeast Asia. Conversely, the U.S. funneled arms to the Afghans during their war with the Soviet Union in order to embarrass the leading communist power and foster more independence within the Soviet sphere of influence. These rivalries coupled to superpower vetoes in the Security Council blocked the UN from launching initiatives in regional conflicts around the world. With the ebbing of the Cold War and superpower rivalry, new hope arose for the United Nations to serve as an effective mechanism for international security.

During the four decades of the Cold War, the UN's role in maintaining global peace and stability was marginalized by the intense competition that characterized the superpower rivalry. Multilateralism had little place in a world dominated by "zero-sum" realities of the Cold War . . . The end of bipolarism created a power vacuum, and for the fist time since the United Nations was established, nations of the world began to look to the world body and the doctrine of collective security—rather than superpower rivalry—for protection.[15]

Easing of Cold War tensions was expected to create an opportunity to rejuvenate the United Nations as a mechanism for developing strategies for collective security. No longer would Cold War divisions lead one side to veto the actions of the other. However, despite the end of the Cold War, the U.S. has found itself at odds with the United Nations, which has questioned elements of the U.S. invasion of Iraq and the subsequent military action to suppress violence and resistance to America's presence. The Bush administration argued that the United States needs to protect itself in the war on terror, even if it means disagreement with the United Nations.

The United Nations—working in cooperation with several world powers—has increased its **peacekeeping** efforts around the world. Traditionally, peacekeeping was organized with the consent of all parties involved in a conflict and usually employed lightly armed forces whose job it was to monitor an existing peace settlement and help avoid further bloodshed. Another variant of peacekeeping is known as "peace enforcement." Here, the consent of all parties is not required and the focus can be humanitarian assistance, economic and military sanctions, blockade, and even direct military action—

peacekeeping *The practice of using forces from outside nations—often in teams of forces organized through the United Nations—to intervene with the objective of restoring peaceful conditions* all designed to restore the peace.[16] During the 1990s, the United Nations was extensively involved in trouble spots across the globe. In places like Cyprus and the Israeli borders, the UN provided peacekeeping personnel to maintain a peaceful settlement between formerly combative parties. In other conflicts including Bosnia and Kuwait, UN actions involved collective military action to end conflict and aggression.

The capacity of the United Nations to foster collective action to protect security was tested during the 2003 Iraq War. While the UN backed a resolution calling for Iraq to eliminate weapons of mass destruction and to allow the weapon inspectors back into the nation, the organization's Security Council was not able to agree upon the use of military invasion as a means to enforce its prohibition. Ultimately, the United States gathered a set of nations, most notably, the United Kingdom, to join forces to invade Iraq. France, Germany and Russia opposed military action and threatened to veto a Security Council resolution endorsing such action. This rift among the superpowers, many of whom have traditionally been strong U.S. allies, raises questions about the future capacity of the United Nations to reach collective decisions about world security issues.

21-4d The Move Toward Multilateral Foreign Policy

From the U.S. perspective, greater peacekeeping operations by the United Nations would present several advantages. First, such operations ease the military and financial burden to the United States of maintaining security in trouble spots around the world. Perhaps more importantly, peacekeeping organized by an international organization representing all nations of the world represents a **multilateral** or multi-sided approach to world diplomacy and resolving regional security problems. Rather than the U.S. taking **unilateral** action on its own, this new approach envisions the United Nations as an instrument for planning and orchestrating the actions of military forces and peacekeepers. In this way, the U.S. moves away from making unilateral security guarantees to nations throughout the world. Through partnerships, America is seeking to reduce its commitments abroad and to design new shared commitments with other world nations to achieve common objectives of peace and security.

multilateralism *The strategy of pursuing foreign policy objectives through cooperative relationships with other nations, often through international organizations like the United Nations.*

unilateralism *An approach to conducting foreign policy whereby a nation tends to rely upon itself and take action on its own to achieve its objectives. Little cooperation is sought with other nations.*

George H. Bush and the United Nations used multilateral foreign policy as they crafted international solutions to trouble spots in world affairs. Nowhere has this approach been more apparent than in the efforts of several major powers, including the United States, to work together through the United Nations to deal with the widespread war and violence taking place in former republics that once constituted Communist Yugoslavia.

Conflict in Bosnia erupted in 1991 when two of the six republics that had formed communist Yugoslavia—Slovenia and Croatia—declared independence from the federation in 1991 as the communist government lost control. At this time long-standing political rivalries between the republics and ethnic tensions among groups living in the republics served as catalysts to armed conflict. The new Yugoslavian government, under control of the federation's largest ethnic group, the Serbs, allowed Slovenia to leave without much opposition. Croatia, however, was a different case. Ethnic Serbs living in Croatia rejected the idea of secession from the Yugoslav federation, fearing the Croatian nationalists who would control the new independent republic. With the military help of Yugoslav Serbs, the Serbs in Croatia seized control. Armed action in Croatia was halted by virtue of a United Nations-monitoring effort in early 1992, but skirmishes continue. In 1992, hostilities shifted to the Bosnian republic when the population elected a Muslim-dominated government and Serbs within the republic, again with Yugoslav Serb support, sought to take control.

By the mid-1990s, the tragedy of the Balkan conflict among former republics of Yugoslavia was constantly a worldwide news story. Gripping pictures of residents in Sarajevo dodging mortar shells and documented evidence of atrocities shocked and alarmed the world, stimulating humanitarian groups to advocate for international intervention. The United States, during the George H. Bush administration, sought to avoid engagement in what it perceived as a largely "European" question. Ultimately, however, the U.S. joined European nations in a UN-led mission to restore peace. One strategy to restore peace was an arms embargo to nations in the region. This approach did little to end the hostilities, and some analysts claimed this harmed the Bosnians, whose military might was far less than that of the Serbs at the start.

Another multilateral strategy was to force the Serbian forces to withdraw their military forces and weaponry from key trouble spots like the devastated city of Sarajevo. The Serb forces—with continuous backing from Serbian-controlled Yugoslavia—were generally steadfast in refusing to back away. Some progress was made in the fall of 1995 as the United Nations coalition used repeated air strikes on Serbian military strongpoints to convince their leaders to back down. Ultimately, the Serb forces did withdraw under pressure, providing a new opportunity to initiate peace talks where both sides recognized a strong multilateral willingness to use military means to end the conflict. Multilateral efforts to resolve the conflict continue although the deep-seated ethnic tensions in the region made finding a long-term, workable peace strategy very difficult to achieve.

While multilateral approaches to U.S. foreign policy remain active, some challenges to them arose during the 1990s, particularly among conservatives in the Republican-controlled Congress. These politicians distrusted multilateral cooperation, which they saw as leading the U.S. into foreign crises the nation might better avoid. The foreign policy perspectives of conservatives echoed the more isolationist views of the past. Both foreign aid and extensive American military commitments abroad remained unpopular with these conservatives, who preferred that America pay greater attention to domestic problems. This foreign policy perspective represents a major departure for conservatives who, until recently, had been champions of strong diplomatic and military action to curb Soviet power. With the demise of the Cold War adversary, however, conservatives for the first time in a quarter century found themselves defining a new foreign policy perspective. Other foreign policy experts continued to see a need for multilateral approaches in diplomatic and military relations with other nations. For them, partnership and cooperation provide more comprehensive strategies for resolving dispute. (Box 21-4: Competing Views on Multilateralism presents two contrasting views on the value of multilateralism in contemporary American foreign policy.)

21-5 Strategies for National Defense

National defense is a prominent objective of all nations that seek to protect sovereignty and prevent invasion or undue external influence by foreign nations. The national defense of the United States relies in large measure on military power that is exercised through a variety of players and defense strategies. Government players can use different strategies to achieve the objective of national defense. The appropriate strategy at any given point in time depends on the magnitude and nature of external threats and the level of resources (military and otherwise) available to respond to them.

Defense strategies can be arrayed on a continuum that measures the level of American involvement with other nations in achieving its defense objectives. At one end are strategies like isolationism and nonalignment, where the United States has sought to protect itself by staying outside the conflicts of other nations. These strategies, workable at earlier times in American history, are difficult to use today because of the dominant position of the U.S. within the world of nations and the substantial economic, political, and social interdependence that links modern nations. Other defense strategies involve strong relations with other nations who work together to achieve a mutual defense network; these relationships are generally known as military alliances. Still other defense strategies involve the acquisition of a strong military with powerful weapons, extensive personnel, and state-of-the art communications technology. Defense alliances and powerful military forces are strategies used more recently by the United States in its quest to provide national security.

21-5a Nonalignment

One strategy for national defense is **nonalignment.** A nation may seek to remain neutral and avoid taking sides with other nations that have antagonistic relationships. Isolation from the disagreements and battles among other nations reduces threats to national security.

nonalignment *A military strategy whereby a nation avoids alliances with superpowers to avoid becoming entangled in superpower struggles.*

Box 21–4 Competing Views on Multilateralism

The movement of American foreign policy toward multilateral relations with other nations through such organizations as the United Nations has raised questions within the diplomatic community. The two passages below—one supporting American reliance upon multilateral foreign policy strategies and the other warning about such strategies—were prepared by the U.S. Representative to the United Nations and a prominent foreign policy analyst. Together they demonstrate varied perspectives on the utility of multilateral strategies for future American foreign policy.

Should the United States rely more heavily on multilateral institutions like the United Nations in conducting foreign policy?

Yes

Madeleine K. Albright, U.S. representative to the United Nations. From Testimony before the House Foreign Affairs Subcommittee, June 24, 1993.

I see about four categories of states emerging within the United Nations. They include . . . first, a significant number of states that I believe have a stake in the United Nations and the international community as a whole. [Second] are the emerging democracies trying to play a constructive role but struggling with international political and economic turmoil. [Third] are other states and factions that are at war with the international norms and institutions . . . the defiant regimes. [T]he fourth group are the failed societies, the ones where effective government has collapsed or anarchy reigns or the economy is hopeless or humanitarian calamity overwhelms the country . . .

Much of our credibility as a superpower, and we must, in my view, remain one, will depend upon our ability to manage our approach to these four groups. Though sometimes we will act alone, our foreign policy will necessarily point towards multilateral engagement. But unless the United States also exercises leadership within collective bodies like the U.N. there is a risk that multilateralism will not serve our national interests well. In fact, it may undermine our interests.

These two realities, multilateral engagement and U.S. leadership within collective bodies, require an "assertive multilateralism" which would advance U.S. foreign policy goals. Preventive diplomacy, I believe, is the linchpin of assertive multilateralism . . .

It has been my sense that the United States has three options . . . [W]e can be the world's cop, which, frankly, most of the world would like us to be because we're so good at it. But you know...that our people don't want us to do that alone. We could be an ostrich, which a lot of our people would like us to be, because we do have such a very large domestic agenda. But . . . we know from looking at the problems out in the world that that is impossible. So our option here is to be a partner . . .

And I believe that my job at the U.N. . . . is to put an adjective with the partner-"senior," "managing," "leading"—whatever way you want to phrase it. So the "assertive mulitlateralism" comes from having a leadership role within multilateral setting to deal with the problems that we have to deal with . . .

So "assertive multilateralism" is, to me, using the new setting of an international community to bring about agendas that are good, not only for the United States but the entire world . . .

No

Ted Galen Carpenter, Director of Foreign Policy Studies, CATO Institute. From "A Search for Enemies: America's Alliances after the Cold War," 1992, CATO Institute.

The desirability of maintaining a maximum amount of flexibility and decision-making autonomy . . . makes it ill-advised for the United States to support proposals to strengthen the peace-keeping and enforcement powers of the United Nations. An interventionist policy within a global collective security arrangement may be the worst of all possible policy alternatives for the United States. Unilateral interventionism at least leaves the U.S. official the latitude to determine when, where and under what conditions to use the nation's armed forces. Working through the U.N. Security Council to reach such decisions reduces that flexibility and creates another layer of risk. That is certainly true if Washington is serious about collaborating in genuine collective security operations and does not merely seek to use the United Nations as a multilateral façade for U.S. policy objectives . . .

The differing security agendas of the principal international actors create an enormous potential for diplomatic "log rolling" in the Security Council. U.N. partisans invariably argue that there is no danger that the United States will be drawn into peace-keeping or peace-enforcement operations against its will, since all permanent member share veto powers. That is an excessively structuralist interpretation, and it ignores the role of incentives and other aspects of how a political organization such as the United Nations operates in practice.

Theoretically, Washington could, of course, veto any action that might entangle it in an unpalatable collective security venture. But the "go-along-to-get-along" incentives that exist in all legislative bodies will be increasingly present in U.N. deliberations. If the United States wants U.N. support for operations that further U.S. policy objectives, it will find itself under enormous pressure to support operations that other council members deem important—even those ventures are irrelevant to U.S. interests or are potentially dangerous . . .

Maximizing decision-making autonomy must be an important feature of post-Cold War U.S. security strategy . . . Avoiding alliances and other entanglements does not necessarily mean that the United States will automatically refrain from intervening. There may well be instances in which intervention is advisable or even imperative to protect vital security interests. The point is that the United States should always make such fateful decisions for itself; they should not be dictated or influenced by elaborate treaty obligations.

Source: "At issue: Should the United States rely more heavily on multilateral institutions like the United Nations in conducting foreign policy?" *CQ Researcher* (August 20, 1993), 737.

Nonalignment was one of the first strategies of the young United States used for national defense. In a farewell address at the end of his presidency in 1796, George Washington urged the nation to avoid "entangling alliances" with European nations. Washington recognized that nations in Europe—including England, France, and Spain—wished to involve the United States in their ongoing political and military battles. Washington hoped that by staying out of these conflicts the United States could steer clear of foreign wars and concentrate on its own growth and expansion. Throughout much of the nation's history prior to World War I, nonalignment was a common U.S. foreign policy strategy.

A nonalignment strategy works best for a nation not located between other disputing nations and not possessing a vital resource needed by one or more of the disputants. America was able to avoid much of the foreign intrigue in its early years because it was separated from warring nations by large oceans and did not possess any resource of critical need to European nations.

21-5b Staking a Claim

When a nation's vital interests are threatened by other nations, a policy of nonalignment is often insufficient to achieve national defense. A more active posture is needed. One type of active defense policy is to stake a claim to some identified geographic area or policy. The intent of this strategy is to unequivocally signal potential adversaries about the importance of this territory or policy to the nation. Other nations are warned that interference within the identified domain will not be tolerated.

The United States modified its early strategy of nonalignment and staked a claim through the **Monroe Doctrine** articulated in 1823. In this declaration, made in his annual address to Congress, President James Monroe stated that U.S. nonalignment in European affairs would continue only if European nations avoided further involvement in North and South America. Specifically, Monroe announced that the Americas were no longer "subject for further colonization" by nations of Europe. This policy was as much bluster as it was intention, because the United States did not have an extensive military capable of expelling foreign powers from all areas of North and South America.

Monroe Doctrine *Assertion by President James Monroe in 1823 that the Western hemisphere was close to colonization and aggressive actions by European nations. The United States promised not to interfere in the concerns of Europe.*

Another prominent example of claim staking was the **Truman Doctrine** (1947), announced soon after World War II and intended to blunt the expansion of communism and totalitarian rule through Soviet military and political power. Truman stated, "I believe that it must be the policy of the United States to support free peoples who are resisting subjugation by armed minorities or by outside pressures."[17] (Through this doctrine, Truman and subsequent presidents sought to achieve two policy goals: national defense and the protection of democracy throughout the world.)

Truman Doctrine *Policy articulated by President Harry S. Truman in 1947 for giving economic and military and economic aid to nations seeking to resist totalitarian aggression. This doctrine became the centerpiece of containment policy.*

Claim staking works best when the nation making the claim has a strong military force or when the stake itself is of little interest to other nations. The Truman Doctrine, as pursued through a series of alliances, was effective because of the strong military power (including a nuclear arsenal) that backed up the claim that the U.S. intended to check communist expansion. The Monroe Doctrine met with success largely because colonial settlements in the New World were not the top priority of European nations at the time the declaration was issued.

21-5c Economic Strategies

When national interests are threatened, another set of defense strategies center on economic action. One primary strategy in this regard is the economic **embargo,** through which one party seeks to reduce or eliminate all trading activity—that is, imports to and exports from a targeted nation. Sometimes, the embargo focuses on particular items, as reflected in the U.S. Cold War policy that forbade the sale of sophisticated computer technology to the Soviet Union and other communist-bloc nations. This embargo was intended to maintain American superiority in computerized weapons systems by reducing the Soviet Union's access to the requisite technology. Box 21-5: American Use of the Embargo Strategy describes two other situations in which the United States employed an embargo strategy.

embargo *An economic action designed to achieve diplomatic objectives. The reduction or elimination of trade with a nation in order to place economic pressure on that nation.*

A more potent use of the embargo is to undertake actions intended to cut off *all* of a nation's foreign trade. If successful, total trade embargoes can have a devastating impact

Box 21-5 American Use of the Embargo Strategy

Two Case Studies

American leaders have used targeted embargoes as a strategy to achieve U.S. foreign policy. Two case studies of the embargo strategy follow. In one instance, the embargo was effective; in the other, it was not.

Case 1: The Cuban Missile Crisis

In the early 1960s, American intelligence agencies were able to document the construction of missile-launching sites in Cuba. U.S. military planners were very concerned about the close proximity of these bases to the U.S. mainland. After consultation with military and political advisors, President John F. Kennedy decided that the United States could not tolerate the presence of Soviet missile bases in Cuba. After ruling out a military strike to remove the bases, the United States chose to place an embargo on the importation of Soviet missiles and missile-launching equipment into Cuba.

To enforce this embargo, the United States sent warships into the Caribbean Sea with orders to stop and inspect all ships entering Cuban waters. The warships were instructed to turn back any ships containing missiles or related military equipment. On one tense day, a Soviet ship reportedly carrying missiles approached the American warships. Ultimately, the ship changed course and returned to the Soviet Union.

The embargo was effective because it was enforced with what the Soviets saw as a credible military force. Rather than risk an outbreak of military hostilities with the United States, Soviet leaders decided to avert the crisis by not challenging the naval vessels assigned to enforce the embargo.

Case 2: Afghanistan

When the Soviet Union invaded Afghanistan in 1979, President Jimmy Carter sought strategies to demonstrate American dissatisfaction. In 1980, Carter imposed an embargo on the sale of wheat and other grain to the Soviet Union. This move was taken with the recognition that Soviet grain production had recently declined and that the Soviets intended to purchase American grain to make up for the shortfall. Carter expected the embargo to reduce Soviet grain supplies and to put domestic pressures on Soviet leaders.

Most analysts concur that this embargo action was not successful. The Soviets were able to acquire the grain they needed from other nations, who appreciated the opportunity to sell more grain. The embargo also generated negative reactions at home, as both grain-producing farmers and the International Longshoremen's Association protested the embargo's negative domestic impacts.

on the economy of the targeted nation, although the effect is seldom immediate. Total embargoes are sometimes used as a prelude to or substitute for military action. As one example, the United States and other members of the UN coalition imposed a complete embargo on foreign trade with Iraq after Iraq's invasion of Kuwait in 1990. Iraq survived the embargo for several months prior to the outbreak of military hostilities, although it suffered economically and militarily from the action.

The effectiveness of the trade embargo strategy depends on several factors. If the targeted nation has substantial internal resources, then it will take longer for the embargo to have an impact. Effectiveness also depends on the ability of the embargoing nations to completely cut off trade via air, sea, and land routes. Halting all trade is difficult and generally requires the use of military force to prohibit efforts to transport goods in and out of the targeted nation.

21-5d Military Power

A common defense strategy for nations around the world has been to build a military force with which to repel enemy attacks or other threats to national security. This strategy requires the acquisition of weapons and the training of military personnel. New and evolving weapons technology has meant that the relative effectiveness of military weapons changes frequently and that weapons manufactured a few years ago face potential obsolescence. For this reason, the military "buildup" strategy requires continuous upgrading of weapons and ongoing expenditures of national resources to acquire these weapons. It also necessitates the maintenance of a standing military force, whose personnel are recruited through volunteer programs or conscription.

The advent of nuclear weapons during World War II represented a quantum leap in warfare technology. These forces of mass destruction are so potent that they threaten annihilation not only of the targeted enemy but, potentially, of life on the entire planet. For the last three decades of the twentieth century, the United States and the Soviet Union sought to restrain the proliferation of nuclear weapon technology. They were only partially successful in this mission, however, as several other nations in the meantime joined the "nuclear club." The nonproliferation objective was moved forward in 1995 when 170 nations agreed to extend permanently a 1970 treaty intended to limit the spread of nuclear arms.

Despite treaties that have substantially reduced the likelihood of full-scale nuclear war, the nuclear threat remains. As of 2004, the nations with nuclear capability include India, Pakistan, North Korea, and Israel; other nations such as Iran are seen as capable of developing this capacity. The concern here is that regional conflicts—for example, between India and Pakistan—could escalate into nuclear war. Further, there is a growing worry that nuclear weapons may fall into the hands of terrorists who could employ them in international terrorist action. The breakup of the former Soviet Union created challenges in monitoring all nuclear weapons that were installed across the nation. Some of these have disappeared, possibly to a black market in nuclear weapons that could be accessed by terrorist groups. The proliferation of nuclear weapons to a larger number of nations, and the potential for them being acquired by terrorist groups, represent major foreign policy challenges to the United States today.

21-5e Alliances: Expanding the Set of Defense Players

Throughout history, nations have sought to enhance national security through military alliances. Through such alliances, nations form a collective agreement to use military power to aid allied partners who are attacked. Alliances allow nations to employ their forces collectively to respond to external invasion.

The **North Atlantic Treaty Organization** (NATO) is an example of an important military alliance of which the United States is a member. NATO was created in 1949 by the United States and several European nations as a means of countering the military force of the Soviet Union and the spread of communism to nations of Eastern Europe. This enduring alliance combines military units from several nations under a single NATO command (headquartered in Brussels, Belgium) and has effectively protected member nations from military invasion or communist revolution.

North Atlantic Treaty Organization (NATO) *Military alliance between the United States, Canada, and many nations of Western Europe intended to check the spread of communism and the threat of Soviet military power.*

NATO was created as part of a broader strategy known as **containment.**[18] The nations of the free world, particularly the United States and Western European countries, would, through a set of alliances "ring in" communist nations and prevent their expansion. While NATO was the most prominent alliance in this ring, containment also included other alliances, such as the South East Asia Treaty Organization (SEATO).

containment *A foreign policy plan to halt the spread of communism and the influence of the Soviet Union through mutual defense alliances with nations having borders with the Soviet Union and the communist nations of Eastern Europe and Asia.*

With the lessening of Cold War tensions and diminished threat of nuclear attack, the future role of NATO has become unclear. As of 2004, NATO includes 19 nations, several of which were formerly under the control of the Soviet Union (e.g., Hungary, Czech Republic, and Poland). NATO expansion raises questions that remain unanswered, the primary one being *who* is the threat that the expanded military alliance is expected to counter and protect against? Other questions concern the extent of military commitment to be made by NATO to those nations seeking to enter the alliance and the level of military support that the U.S. and Western European nations would provide to them. While there are obvious political advantages to expanded ties between nations of Europe, the future role of NATO—with or without new members—has yet to be determined.

The problem with all military alliances—as anyone who has played a board game such as "Risk" or "Diplomacy" well knows—is that they may quickly disappear when member nations see advantages in leaving them. The Soviet Union learned this lesson the hard way in 1941 when Adolph Hitler ended a two-year nonaggression pact by invading his alliance partner. Having already conquered much of Western Europe, Hitler's war objectives turned to the east and the Soviet Union.

A related national defense strategy is to break up the alliances of other nations, particularly those hostile to your own. Saddam Hussein tried this in 1991 when he sought to break apart the coalition of nations seeking to enforce the UN resolution that Iraq withdraw from Kuwait. Hussein recognized that the coalition contained Arab partners (Egypt, Morocco, Syria, and Saudi Arabia), who traditionally were opposed to the nation of Israel and to American involvement in the Middle East. Hussein reasoned that, if he could bring Israel into the war against Iraq, then the Arab members of the coalition would depart the alliance and side with Iraq. The plan to bring Israel into the war involved the launching of missiles into populated Israeli cities, with the expectation that this would stimulate an Israeli counterattack. This strategy did not work as the Israelis chose, under considerable U.S. pressure, not to take military action. The United States, too, has sought to disrupt alliances including measures taken during World War II to weaken the Axis Alliance between Germany, Italy, and Japan.

21-5f Deterrence

deterrence *A strategy of national defense whereby a strong military force maintained by one nation is expected to convince other nations against the wisdom of engaging in a military attack.*

Other strategies to achieve national defense focus on **deterrence,** convincing potential enemies that attacks will be difficult and costly, thus discouraging them from contemplating military attack. Deterrence only works if it is credible— that is, if potential enemies believe that a nation has adequate military power and the resolve to use it if attacked. Sometimes nations have the military power to stop aggression by another nation but decide, for a variety of reasons, not to intervene. Such was the case with both France and England during the late 1930s. These nations, which initially had far stronger military forces than Germany, did not use their military power to halt German expansion into the Sudatenland, Austria, Czechoslovakia, and Poland. The German leader, Adolph Hitler, was not deterred from taking control of these nations—both by diplomatic and military means—because he believed (correctly, as it turned out) that neither France nor England had the resolve to act militarily against German aggression.

nuclear deterrence *A strategy of national defense whereby a strong arsenal of nuclear weapons is maintained by one nation to convince other nations against the wisdom of engaging in a military attack.*

Since World War II, strategies of deterrence have been closely linked to the technology of warfare. The idea of **nuclear deterrence** emerged as the Soviet Union and the United States developed large nuclear arsenals. The strategy held that neither superpower would attack the other, given the risk that launching a nuclear war would be devastating to both sides.

The strategy of nuclear deterrence shifted over time from an assessment of the damages likely to occur from nuclear attack to whether or not one side could survive a first strike and still be able to retaliate. Mutual deterrence focused on building weapons stockpiles. Each side recognized that, if it launched a surprise attack, its opponent could sustain the blow and remain capable of launching a deadly return salvo of nuclear warheads. In this strategy, eventually known as *mutual assured destruction*, a military stalemate between two superpowers with huge nuclear arsenals was expected to prevent either from striking. The national defense of each side was enhanced. The danger of this system was that the irrational actions of some military commander, mistakes in communication, or some technological flaw might commence military action. Nuclear destruction would be unleashed, without any possibility of turning back.

21-5g Mutual Arms Reduction

Since the 1970s, the superpowers have engaged in a national defense strategy that is, for the most part, unprecedented in human history: seeking peace and stability through limiting and reducing rather than augmenting armament supplies. For multiple reasons this strategy is seen as rational for both sides. Given that both sides have the military capacity to destroy each other several times over, there seems little need to continue further arms buildup. In addition, weapons purchases and the maintenance of large military forces drain money from national budgets that could be used for other purposes.

Superpower discussions concerning military weapons began with treaties negotiated in the 1960s. In 1963 the United States and Soviet Union signed a Limited Test Ban

Treaty in which each pledged to end the testing of nuclear weapons in the atmosphere. Later in the decade, both nations signed a Nonproliferation Treaty, which banned the spread of nuclear weapons to other nations.

Negotiations to limit and reduce the number of nuclear weapons on each side were successfully concluded in the 1970s. In 1972 the United States and Soviet Union participated in strategic arms limitations talks (SALT). In the first SALT treaty, the superpowers agreed to limit the number of fixed launchers for ICBMs (intercontinental ballistic missiles) and the number of SLBM (submarine-launched ballistic missile) launchers. Interestingly, President George W. Bush argued almost thirty years later that the United States should build a missile defense system for national protection—an action that would undoubtedly violate the terms of the 1972 agreement.

In the next round of talks—SALT II—the superpowers expanded limitations on nuclear missile launchers and the number that could contain multiple warheads (these are known as MIRVs, multiple independently targeted reentry vehicles). Limitations on strategic bombers were also included in this agreement. Upon presenting this treaty to the Senate, President Jimmy Carter encountered opposition. The intervening Soviet military operation in Afghanistan angered members of the Senate and renewed worries about Soviet expansionism. Some senators also felt that the United States was giving up more than it was gaining through the arms reduction treaty. The Senate indefinitely postponed ratification of the treaty, although the United States and Soviet Union voluntarily abided by its terms for several years.

During the Reagan and George H. Bush administrations, the United States continued arms reductions talks with the Soviet Union. In 1987 both parties agreed to an intermediate-range nuclear forces (INF) agreement that required both nations to dismantle a specified number of intermediate-range weapons. Both sides also engaged in negotiations aimed at further reducing their stores of long-range nuclear weapons through the strategic arms reductions talks (START).

One problem with agreements to eliminate arms is that it is difficult to determine that the other side has complied. To deal with this issue, both the United States and the Soviet Union agreed to on-site inspections of the other's weapons locations. This arrangement, requiring trust and openness on both sides, was recognized as a substantial step forward in the long-term process of nuclear arms reductions. The problem of verifying the development of nuclear weapons was recently evident in both North Korea and Iraq, where world powers had difficulty ascertaining the progress of these nations in producing their own nuclear capability.

In 1991 the United States and the Soviet Union successfully negotiated a landmark START treaty that, for the first time in the atomic age, reduced the arsenals of long-range nuclear weapons on both sides. The treaty called for both nations to make substantial cuts in ballistic missile warheads and to reduce strategic offensive delivery systems.[19] This treaty was made possible, after 9 years of negotiation, by the lessening of tensions between the Soviet Union and the United States. Table 21-3 presents a historical overview of U.S./Soviet arms control agreements.

Since the breakup of the Soviet Union, the United States and the new nations formed from former Soviet republics—most notably Russia—have continued discussions about further reductions in nuclear arms. Negotiations have become more difficult because several governments now control the nuclear weapons that once were controlled by the central Soviet Union government. These negotiations are important to the United States not only because arms reduction reduces the risk of nuclear war but also because of the U.S. fear that nations such as the Ukraine and Russia might sell nuclear arms to other nations. Such arms sales could increase the number of "nuclear players" and potentially cause greater instability in the international sphere.

21-5h Preemptive Strike

Responding to both fears about terrorist attacks and proliferation of nuclear weapons in developing nations, President George W. Bush identified a new strategy of national defense—one focused on acting before harm is inflicted by others. The terrorist attacks

Table 21-3 U.S./Soviet Arms Control: An Historical Overview

1972	Antiballistic Missile Treaty: Signed in Moscow. Each side was limited to two defensive antiballistic missile (ABM) sites with as many as one hundred antiballistic missile launchers and one hundred interceptor missiles each. Later, this agreement was amended to allow only one ABM site per nation.
1972	Strategic Arms Limitation Treaty: Signed in Vienna. Often referred to as SALT II, the treaty set an initial overall limit of twenty-four hundred intercontinental ballistic missile (ICBM) launchers, submarine missile launchers, heavy bombers, and surface-to-air missiles, with the ceiling to be lowered in later stages. After Soviet troops moved into Afghanistan, this treaty, negotiated by President Jimmy Carter, was withdrawn from the Senate. Even though not ratified, both the United States and the Soviet Union informally agreed to observe the limits set on nuclear weapons. In November 1986, the United States exceeded one category of weapons limitations by deploying an additional B-52 bomber modified to carry cruise missiles. President Ronald Reagan defended the action on the grounds that the Soviet Union had violated terms of the treaty by developing a new missile.
1987	Intermediate-Range Nuclear Forces Treaty: Signed in Washington. This treaty, negotiated over 6 years, provided for the dismantling of all Soviet and American medium- and short-range missiles and established an extensive system of weapons inspection. It was ratified by the Senate in 1988.
1991	Strategic Arms Reductions Treaty: Announced in London. After several years of on-again, off-again negotiations, both sides agreed to unprecedented reductions in their nuclear arsenals. Each nation agreed to cut its nuclear force to six thousand "accountable" warheads seven years after treaty ratification.
1992	Strategic Arms Reductions Treaty Expanded: Announced in Washington. Nuclear arms reductions talks continued after the dissolution of the Soviet Union. Treaty negotiations between President George H. Bush and Russian president Boris Yeltsin resulted in further cuts in nuclear arsenals, including an agreement by both sides to reduce their long-range nuclear arsenals to about one-fourth of their 1990 level by the year 2003. The treaty also bans missiles with multiple warheads.

organized by Al Qaida, which brought hijacked U.S. passenger airliners crashing into the twin World Trade Center towers in New York City and the Pentagon outside of Washington, D.C., created a shock from which the nation is still reeling. While the U.S. had experienced isolated terrorist attacks in the past, never had the American people been subjected to the horror of seeing its own airliners used as weapons to attack populated office towers and the center of America's defense services. With strong organization, but little in the way of weapons, a limited set of terrorists took action that challenged the fundamental safety of Americans, raising questions about whether terrorism would become a common part of American life.

President George W. Bush responded by organizing a coalition of nations to invade Afghanistan, the stronghold of the Al Qaida network and home base for the terror organization's leader, Osama Bin Laden. This military action led to strong damage to the terrorist organization and the creation of a fledgling democracy in Afghanistan.

Next, President George W. Bush turned his attention to Iraq (see Time Out 21-2: What Did You Think About the War in Iraq?). About a dozen years earlier, his father, the first President Bush, organized a military coalition in response to Iraq's invasion and occupation of the sovereign nation of Kuwait. That military action forced the Iraqi military out of Kuwait and weakened the Iraqi military, but Iraq's dictator, Saddam Hussein, remained in power. As part of the peace agreement negotiated at the end of this military conflict, Iraq agreed not to produce or acquire weapons of mass destruction and to allow UN inspectors to work in the nation to ensure that existing weapons of mass destruction were destroyed. However, by the late 1990s, the weapons inspectors had been dismissed from Iraq by Saddam Hussein and U.S. intelligence claimed that Iraq continued to produce destructive weapons that threatened the security of the region, including access to the large supplies of petroleum produced in the Middle East.

preemptive strike The doctrine of engaging in military efforts to protect from external threats prior to any threats being carried out.

In September 2002, President George W. Bush outlined a new plan for national security. A key element of this plan was the **preemptive strike**—the willingness to use force to protect the U.S. and world security by unleashing military action against documented

Time Out 21-2

What Did You Think About the War in Iraq?

Where Do You Stand?

Try to transport yourself back to middle of the 2003 war with Iraq and consider what you thought THEN. Even if you cannot remember exactly, make your best guess, and you can then see who in the population would have agreed with you.

> **Do you support or oppose the United States having gone to war with Iraq in 2003?**
>
> **-SUPPORT**
>
> **-OPPOSE**

security threats *prior* to any action being taken against the U.S. or other nations. The president articulated the preemptive strike doctrine as follows:

> "We must deter and defend against the threat before it is unleashed." This national security plan also called for efforts to aggressively pursue nonproliferation of nuclear weapons, especially seeking to keep these weapons out of the hands of "rogue" states and terrorists.

In 2003, the U.S. exercised a preemptive strike when the U.S. military, joined by forces of several other nations (but opposed by France, Germany, Russia, and other nations) invaded Iraq with the purpose of removing Saddam Hussein from power, destroying weapons of mass destruction, and creating a democratic government in Iraq. Within about three weeks, the coalition forces were able to suppress most military resistance in the nation.

With the defeat of the Iraqi military the U.S. military and coalition partners faced new challenges: restoring Iraq's utilities and infrastructure, eliminating pockets of resistance, maintaining public order, and facilitating the creation of a democratic government in a nation long ruled by dictatorship. In an effort to rebuild the nation, the president asked Congress to provide over $70 billion dollars to help rebuild the parts of Iraq heavily damaged by the war. Just how long the United States will remain in Iraq and how long

AFP/Getty Images

Answer to Time Out 21-2

If you supported the war, you agreed with the majority in April 2003. Based on an April 2–6, 2003, Washington Post-ABC News poll, 77 percent of the respondents supported having gone to war. The type of people most likely to agree with your support of the war were:

	(percent *supporting* having gone to war with Iraq)
Republicans	95%
Liberals	88%
People 45–54 years of age	87%
Men	82%
Whites	81%
Moderates	78%
People 35–44 years of age	77%
NATIONAL AVERAGE	77%

If you opposed the war, you were among the minority in April 2003. Based on an April 2–6, 2003, Washington Post-ABC News poll, 33 percent of the respondents opposed having gone to war. The type of people most likely to agree with your opposition to the war were:

	(percent *opposing* having gone to war with Iraq)*
Liberals	47%
Democrats	45%
People 45–65 years of age	39%
Women	38%
People 18–34 years of age	33%
NATIONAL AVERAGE	33%

*or having no opinion

it will take to create a stable democratic government remain unknown, especially as armed resistance continues from insurgents who are resisting U.S. efforts to create a new democratic regime in Iraq.

21-5i Multiple Needs and Multiple Strategies

At any point in time, the United States has multiple national defense interests and is likely to employ various defense strategies simultaneously. No one strategy can be effective in all types of defense situations. When enmity and imminent hostility characterize relations with other nations, some combination of military power, alliances, and deterrence may be the most effective strategy for national defense. When competing nations recognize common interests and the wisdom of reducing military expenditures, then arms reduction is a useful approach to international relations.

Since the collapse of the Soviet Union and the end of the Cold War, both military and civilian leaders are finding it a challenge to develop an effective policy for future diplomacy and national defense. As one defense analyst has noted,

> Today, instead of a well-defined threat to anchor U.S. foreign policy, pervasive uncertainty faces the world's sole remaining superpower as it attempt to anticipate the future foreign policy environment, establish a new psychological basis for engaging the nation in the world, and develop principles to guide the use of diplomatic, economic, and military tools abroad. For the United States, the post-Cold War is characterized first and foremost by threat uncertainty—the disappearance of a known and familiar adversary. Certainty about the enemy has been supplanted by questions about the identity of future adversaries, their goals and capabilities, and the time frame within which future challengers are likely to arise.[20]

America's national defense already has faced a number of challenges in the post-Cold War era. Within the last two decades, American presidents have identified activities in Iran, Grenada, Panama, Iraq-Kuwait, Haiti, and Bosnia as threats to the United States and other world nations. America has used both its diplomatic power and military might to intervene in these situations. The military intervention has typically been very limited in nature—focusing on well-orchestrated air strikes, for example—as opposed to the major level of military commitment made by the U.S. during World War II and in the Korean and Vietnam wars. The Persian Gulf War is the most recent example of wide-scale U.S. military involvement abroad involving substantial numbers of ground forces.

Policy makers recognize that some future threats will require well-coordinated, limited military strikes aimed at specialized targets. America received a taste of this need when U.S. citizens were taken hostage in Iran in 1979. A military action intended to free the hostages, ordered by President Jimmy Carter, collapsed in process due to technical failures, raising questions about U.S. military capability to make a tactical strike. Recognizing the threats that smaller nations and terrorists can make against American citizens and interests, the American military has sought to enhance its ability to execute swift, targeted, military strikes and to bolster its military capability to intervene in smaller, limited, military actions throughout the world. The U.S. has also in recent years expanded its use of multilateral strategies for national defense, working through alliances or through international organizations like the United Nations to develop cooperative military responses in trouble spots like Bosnia.

The challenge of future defense policy will be to provide broad protection of the United States as well as the capacity to intervene in regionalized, smaller-scale conflicts. Future defense policy must also address future threats. One potential source of threat is nations that possess nuclear weapons and who might use them in a regional conflict. To avoid this problem, the U.S. and other world powers have sought to prevent nuclear proliferation. The best strategy to achieve the nuclear nonproliferation objective focuses on diplomacy and negotiation rather than military might, again underscoring the interdependence between foreign policy and military power in achieving national defense.

Another fundamental defense question is an easy one to ask and a tough one to answer: how large should America's military capacity be? For several decades this question was answered with regard to how strong a military was needed to deter Soviet military action and nuclear attack. With the demise of the Cold War, the question of military size is more problematic. The American defense establishment has faced pressures to shrink as the nation has sought to cash in on the "peace dividend," thereby reducing military expenditures and easing pressures on the deficit. Between 1985 and 1998, for example, spending on military weaponry—including aircraft, ships, and tanks—dropped substantially, and the number of armed services personnel also declined.[21] These cutbacks led some analysts to question the readiness of the military to respond to future national defense needs. The questions have stimulated debates about whether the military has become too small, whether the nation can respond militarily to two or more regional crises, and whether funding for the military should be increased. These questions are likely to continue for some time as America develops a long-term strategy for national defense in the post cold-war period.

Finally, terrorism as a threat to national security will be a fact of life for national defense for some time to come. Rather than fighting the military forces of nations, defense against terrorism requires tracking well-organized units of people who are highly mobile and seldom located within a single nation. Intelligence gathering is key to being prepared to respond to terrorist attacks, as is the capacity to launch preemptive strikes to protect national security.

Conclusion

Contemporary American politics is interdependent with political and economic forces throughout the world. Interdependency requires ongoing efforts to manage relations with other nations. Through foreign policy, the United States seeks to maintain peaceful relations with other nations and to pursue collective strategies to deal with joint problems. In the last half century, the United States has sought to protect itself with a strong military arsenal, a set of economic strategies, and effective military alliances.

The American economy continues to face threats from other nations that seek to manufacture goods of higher quality and lower cost than those produced in the United States. If the United States moves toward greater protectionism, then it abandons its long-term preference for free trade and invites protectionist reaction from other nations. In the last decade, American industry has made great gains in improving its productivity, which helps to prevent further erosion of America's economic position in the world marketplace.

With Cold War tensions diminished, many questions arise about future American defense policy. One primary question concerns how much the United States should reduce its military force in light of the dissolution of the Soviet Union. Should the United States prepare for the possibility that a totalitarian regime will reemerge in the republics of the former Soviet Union? Certainly, U.S. officials intend to be prepared for any threat to American security. However, reducing military spending is appealing in times of persistent budget deficits and substantial domestic problems.

Another important question, one highlighted by the Persian Gulf War, concerns how the United States should prepare itself to respond to regional conflicts where large nuclear arsenals are not effective. Regional conflicts and terrorist incidents require rapid intelligence, quick coordination of efforts with other nations, and speedy deployment of trained personnel and sophisticated technology.

Exploiting a dominant military position to become the superpower may be an inviting role for the United States. Without the effective blocks frequently imposed by the now dissolved Soviet Union and its former allies on American foreign policy initiatives, the United States might begin to see itself as capable of achieving many long-term diplomatic goals. For example, since the Persian Gulf War, the United States has sought to use its enhanced position to push Middle East nations to the conference table, where they can negotiate long-term disputes.

There is, however, a major cost to being the world's superpower. This strategy would require the United States to maintain an extensive military force, and it might lead other nations to expect U.S. military intervention in future international disputes. In addition, many nations might expect the United States to be a regular provider of foreign aid and other economic inducements. Maintaining a strong military and providing economic aid packages are costly endeavors, ones that are difficult for the United States to finance, given a protracted federal budget deficit. American efforts to play a larger role in world affairs will need to be balanced against the nation's economic capability of financing that role.

Effective management of future interdependence, whether political or economic, likely will require greater cooperation among nations of the world. One way to achieve international cooperation is to create some form of "international government." While the current United Nations is a small step in this direction, it is far from a formal governing structure designed to make daily decisions that are binding throughout the world. In a truly international government, individual nations would cede some, maybe all, national sovereignty and agree to be governed by a central international government. Not surprisingly, many nations are reluctant to yield sovereign control.

Harland Cleveland—a former university professor, assistant secretary of state, and U.S. ambassador to NATO—suggests a different approach to increasing international cooperation. He compares the current world situation to the founding of America and sees advantage to developing means whereby nations can retain their sovereignty but also work more effectively to identify common problems and resolve together to solve them through collaborative strategies:

> Our challenge is strikingly similar to the one successfully confronted by Thomas Jefferson, James Madison, Alexander Hamilton, and the other founders of the United States. In America, we not long ago celebrated the 200th anniversary of the Constitution, which was written to govern a large, diverse, developing nation through institutions crafted to ensure that no one would be in general charge.
>
> The real-life management of peace worldwide is likely to mean a Madisonian world of bargains and accommodations among national and functional "factions," a world in which peoples are able to agree on what to do next together without feeling the need (or being forced by global government) to agree on religious creeds or political credos. A practical pluralism, not a unitary universalism, is the likely destiny of the human race.[22]

With the Cold War ended, the potential for greater international cooperation grows. Questions of how the world's nations might play the military and economic games to resolve their interdependent problems will be widely debated and discussed.

Key Terms

ambassador
Cold War
containment
covert action
détente
deterrence
diplomacy
embargo
embassy
foreign aid
foreign policy
foreign service officer
Fourteen Points
General Assembly
globalism
Joint Chiefs of Staff
Monroe Doctrine
most-favored nation (MFN)
multilateralism
multinational corporation
nation-state
national security adviser
nonalignment
North Atlantic Treaty Organization (NATO)
nuclear deterrence
peacekeeping
preemptive strike
Security Council
self-determination
sovereignty
trade deficit
Truman Doctrine
unilateralism

Practice Quiz

1. The "peace dividend" refers to the
  a. formation of NATO following World War II.
  b. cost of operating the United Nations.
  c. reduction in national defense costs resulting from the end of the Cold War.
  d. rebuilding of war-torn Europe following World War II.

2. Sovereignty most generally refers to a nation's ability and authority to
  a. join military alliances like NATO.
  b. regulate environmental conditions.
  c. leave alliances at will.
  d. govern itself free from outside interference.

3. The Cold War was a conflict that involved
   a. conflict between capitalism and communism economic philosophies.
   b. the military power of the U.S. and U.S.S.R.
   c. the threat of strong nuclear response in case of war.
   d. all of the above

4. The primary role of an ambassador is to
   a. represent the U.S. government in relations with the governments of other nations.
   b. levy taxes on multinational corporations.
   c. guide military action against opponents.
   d. decide judicial disputes among nations.

5. Covert action refers to
   a. threats to use nuclear arms.
   b. secret action including espionage.
   c. alliances among nations to create security.
   d. the prevention of the proliferation of nuclear arms.

6. Which agency of the national government has primary responsibility for covert action?
   a. Internal Revenue Service
   b. Department of State
   c. Central Intelligence Agency
   d. Department of Defense

7. The U.S. Congress enacted the War Powers Act in response to which military action?
   a. World War II
   b. Cold War
   c. Korean War
   d. Vietnam War

8. A tariff is
   a. a tax levied on goods imported from abroad.
   b. the legal right of individuals to immigrate.
   c. a tax on foreign nations entering the U.S.
   d. both a and c

9. NAFTA refers to
   a. treaties to reduce nuclear weapon arsenals.
   b. a trade agreement between the U.S., Canada, and Mexico.
   c. NATO's humanitarian efforts and projects.
   d. The United Nations' humanitarian efforts and projects.

10. "Most-favored nation" states relates to
   a. favorite trade states between the U.S. and other nations.
   b. U.S. alliances with NATO.
   c. nations that joined the U.S.-led coalition against Iraq in 2003.
   d. nations with seats in the UN Security Council.

11. Which of the following statements is true of the UN General Assembly?
   a. It has veto power over the Security Council.
   b. It has the power to tax member nations.
   c. It is the body where every member nation is represented.
   d. It is located in Zurich, Switzerland.

12. Which nation does *not* have a permanent seat in the UN Security Council?
   a. France
   b. Canada
   c. United Kingdom
   d. Russia

You can find the correct answers to these questions by taking the quiz and then submitting your answers in the Online Edition. The program will automatically score your submission. Where you miss a question, the program will provide the correct answer, a rationale for the answer, and the section number in the chapter where the topic is discussed.

Further Reading

Globalism—the idea that the nations of the world are growing together into an integrated system—is explored by Thomas L. Friedman in *The Lexus and the Olive Tree: Understanding Globalization* (New York: Anchor Books, 2000) and by Frank Lechner and John Boli (eds.) in *The Globalization Reader* (Malden, MA: Blackwell Publishers, 1999).

Contemporary treatments of American foreign policy are presented by Henry Kissinger in *Does America Need a Foreign Policy?* (Riverside, NJ: Simon & Schuster, 2001) and by Tony Smith in *America's Mission: The United States and the Worldwide Struggle for Democracy in the Twentieth Century* (Princeton, NJ: Princeton University Press, 1994).

Interesting work on evolving U.S. military policy is presented in Thomas M. Barrett, *The Pentagon's New Map: War and Peace in the 21st Century* (New York: Putnam Publishing Group, 2004) and John Lewis Gaddis, *Surprise, Security and the American Experience* (Cambridge, MA: Harvard University Press, 2004).

An intriguing inside perspective on the role of the national security advisor to the president is presented by Zbigniew Brzezinski, who served as national security advisor under President Jimmy Carter, *in Power and Principle: Memoirs of the National Security Advisor, 1977–1981* (New York: Farrar, Straus, Giroux, 1983).

A thorough treatment of containment as a military and political strategy is presented by John Lewis Gaddis in *Strategies of Containment: A Critical Appraisal of American National Security Policy* (New York: Oxford University Press, 1982) and in his article "Containment: Its Past and Future," *International Security* 5 (1981): 73–102.

For perspectives on the challenge of U.S. foreign affairs after the end of the Cold War, see William Blum, *Rogue State: A Guide to the World's Only Superpower* (Common Cause, 2000), Stephen F. Cohen, *Failed Crusade: America and the Tragedy of Post-Communist Russia* (New York: W. W. Norton, 2000), Raymond Tanter, *Rogue Regimes: Terrorism and Proliferation* (New York: Palgrave, 1999), and Ted Galen Carpenter, ed., *NATO's Empty Victory* (Washington, D.C.: CATO Institute, 2000).

For a variety of perspectives on the international political economy—the impact of economic interdependence on political relations—see Robert Gilpin and Jean M. Gilpen, *Global Political Economy: Understanding the International Economic Order* (Princeton, NJ: Princeton University Press, 2001), Benjamin J. Cohen and Charles Lipson (eds.), *Issues and Agents in International Political Economy* (Cambridge, MA: MIT Press, 1999), and Jeffery A. Frieden and David A. Lake, eds., *International Political Economy: Perspectives on Global Power and Wealth*, 2nd ed. (New York: St. Martin's Press, 1991). See also Theodore H. Moran, *American Economic Policy and National Security* (New York: Council on Foreign Relations Press, 1993).

Treatments of recent trade agreements include: Alan M. Rugman, ed., *Foreign Investment and NAFTA* (Columbia, SC: University of South Carolina Press, 1994); Steven Globerman and Michael Wacker, *Assessing NAFTA: A Trinational Analysis* (Vancouver, British Columbia, Canada: Fraser Institute, 1993); and Ralph Nader et al., *The Case Against Free Trade: GATT, NAFTA, and the Globalization of World Power* (San Francisco, CA: Earth Island Press, 1993).

The role of the United Nations in peacekeeping initiatives is explored in William J. Durch, ed., *The Evolution of UN Peacekeeping: Case Studies and Comparative Analysis* (New York: St. Martin's Press, 1993) and Fariborz Mokhtari, ed., *Peacemaking, Peacekeeping and Coalition Warfare* (Washington, D.C.: National Defense University Press, 1994).

A study of the impact of the September 11, 2001 terrorist attack on U.S. foreign policy is presented in Phyllis Bennis, *Before & After: U.S. Foreign Policy and the September 11th Crisis* (Brooklyn, NY: Olive Branch Press, 2003).

A detailed study of the national security assistant and his or her role in American foreign policy is presented by Joseph G. Bock in *The White House Staff and the National Security Assistant: Friendship and Friction at the Water's Edge* (New York: Greenwood Press, 1987).

Students who enjoy international affairs and would like to explore a possible career in this field should consult Maria Pinto Carland et al. (eds), *Careers in International Affairs* (Washington, D.C.: Georgetown University Press, 1997).

A fascinating historical examination of Woodrow Wilson's presidency and his quest to bring the United States into the League of Nations is presented in Gene Smith, *When the Cheering Stopped: The Last Years of Woodrow Wilson* (New York: Morrow, 1964). See also Robert S. McNamara and James G. Blight, *Wilson's Ghost: Reducing the Risk of Conflict, Killing, and Catastrophe in the 21st Century* (Cambridge, MA: Public Affairs, 2001).

A thorough treatment of the Central Intelligence Agency and the U.S. system for gaining foreign intelligence is presented in Scott D. Breckinridge, *The CIA and the U.S. Intelligence System* (Boulder, CO: Westview Press, 1986). See also Robert Baer, *See No Evil: The True Story of A Ground Soldier's War on Terrorism* (New York: Three Rivers Press, 2002).

A remarkable, concise overview of the structure and operations of the United Nations is presented in *Everyone's United Nations* (New York: United Nations, 1972).

The issue of arms control is explored in Kenneth W. Thompson, ed., *Arms Control: Alliances, Arms Sales, and the Future* (Lanham, MD: University Press of America, 1993).

Strategies for enhancing national security in the United States are explored in John J. Weltman et al., eds., *Challenges to American National Security in the 1990s* (New York: Plenum Press, 1991). See also Walter R. Thomas and Howard E. Shuman, eds., *The Constitution and National Security: A Bicentennial View* (Washington, D.C.: National Defense University Press, 1990).

Contemporary debates about the war-making power of modern presidents are examined by Louis Fischer in *Presidential War Power* (Lawrence, KS: University of Kansas Press, 1995).

Endnotes

1. Tony Smith, *America's Mission: The United States and the Worldwide Struggle for Democracy in the Twentieth Century* (Princeton, NJ: Princeton University Press, 1994), 31.
2. John Prados, *President's Secret Wars: CIA and Pentagon Covert Operations Since World War I* (New York: Morrow, 1986); Robert A. Falk, "CIA Covert Action and International Law," Society 12 (March/April 1975): 39–44.
3. *Gulf of Tonkin Resolution*, 78 Stat. 384 (1964).
4. *Immigration and Naturalization Service v. Chadha*, 462 U.S. 919 (1983).
5. Gregg Walker, David A. Bella, and Steven J. Sprecher, *The Military Industrial Complex: Eisenhower's Warning Three Decades Later* (New York: Peter Lang Publishing, 1991).
6. U.S. Census Bureau, *Statistical Abstract of the United States* 194 (Washington, D.C.: U.S. Department of Commerce, 2000), Table 566, 818.
7. U.S. Census Bureau, *Statistical Abstract of the United States 2000* (Washington, D.C.: U.S. Department of Commerce, 2000), Table 1323, 791.
8. U.S. Census Bureau, *Statistical Abstract of the United States 2000* (Washington, D.C.: U.S. Department of Commerce, 2000), Table 1323, 791.
9. U.S. Census Bureau, *Statistical Abstract*, Table 1315, 785.
10. Statement made by President George H. Bush to students in Kyoto, Japan, January 7, 1992.
11. Thomas R. Graham, "Revolution in Trade Politics," *Foreign Affairs* 26 (Fall 1979): 49–63.
12. U.S. Census Bureau, *Statistical Abstract*, Table 1315, 785.
13. U.S. Census Bureau, *Statistical Abstract*, Table 1318, 787.
14. Preamble, Charter of the United Nations, signed by original members in San Francisco in 1945.
15. Nick Birnback, "Beyond Peacekeeping," In John Tessitore and Susan Wollfson, eds., *Issues Before the United Nations, 49th General Assembly, 1994–95* (Lanham, MD: University Press of America, 1994.
16. Nick Birnback, "Beyond Peacekeeping," 4–5.
17. This doctrine was articulated by President Harry S. Truman in 1947 in his address to a joint session of Congress in support of a Greek-Turkey aid bill.
18. The strategy of containment was first articulated by George F. Kennan in an article in *Foreign Affairs* (June 1947). The authorship was originally listed as "X" because Mr. Kennan, a foreign service officer at the time, did not feel it appropriate to directly recommend foreign policy strategy.
19. David F. Hoffman and John E. Yang, "Hallway Huddle Caps Years of Arms Bargaining," *Washington Post National Weekly Edition*, July 22–28, 1991, 14–15.
20. Larry Berman and Emily O. Goldman, "Clinton: Foreign Policy at Midterm," In Colin Campbell and Bert A. Rockman, eds., *The Clinton Presidency: First Appraisals* (Chatham, NJ: Chatham House Publishers, 1996), 293.
21. Eric Schmitt, "Worries about Military Readiness Grow," *New York Times* (April 3, 1995), A9.
22. Harlan Cleveland, "The Management of Peace," The GAO Journal, Winter 1990/91, 4–23.

Epilogue

The Future of American Politics

Key Points

- To reiterate the applicability of the game analogy to American politics and to recognize the continuous nature of the process.
- To develop an understanding of cross-institutional teams necessary for policy making.
- To summarize the commonalities in rules, players, strategies, and patterns of winning and losing across political arenas.
- To assess the impact of social changes, technological innovation, and structural reform on the American political process.

Preview: Who Needs Government Anyway?

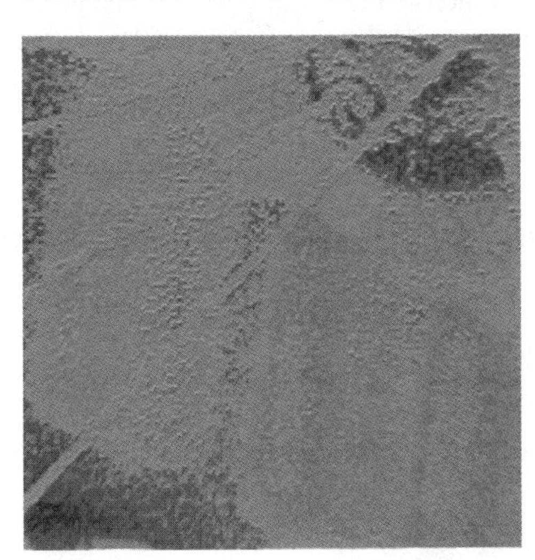

The common Washington dictum that there is "nothing so permanent as a temporary government agency" was taken to heart by Charles H. Duell. Decrying government waste and the need to cut back on unnecessary government activity, Mr. Duell sent a letter of resignation to President William McKinley in 1899 suggesting that his office and department be abolished. Mr. Duell's unselfish willingness to sacrifice his power and position strikes a responsive chord to many people in contemporary America who see growing involvement of government in our lives as both intrusive and an expensive burden. As the old joke goes, "It is a good thing that we don't get all the government we pay for." More creatively, cries for privatization of services and deregulation regularly emerge through the political process. Tax cut promises and attempts to cut back on government expenditures dominate the rhetoric of politicians across the entire political spectrum, so it seems Charles Duell the unselfish bureaucrat should stand out as a fine example to modern advocates of better and more limited government.

In reality, a special place in American history goes to Charles H. Duell for lack of foresight. In 1899 he was Commissioner of Patents, and his reason for suggesting that his agency be closed was his strongly held belief that "everything that can be invented has been invented." The derision of this misguided bureaucrat is compounded when we realize that this statement came prior to the patents for such items as television, airplanes, fax machines, and computers. In fact, almost four million patents have been granted since Charles Duell's foolish comment. Without government monitoring and registering of this creative explosion, both society as a whole and individual inventors would be worse off.

While Duell's desire to get the job done and close the office may initially sound appealing, the flow of inventions is much like the demands for government activity. New needs and opportunities create demands for new policies or the revision of old ones. Just as one invention often contains the seeds of a new one, the passage of one government policy leads to consequences that encourage expansion or require amelioration. Governing is a continuous process, not a discrete task to be completed once and for all. The burning question is not whether we have enough policies, but rather whether we have the right policies. We need the Charles Duells of the world to make us face questions about the necessity of particular government programs, but we owe an equal debt to those nameless government officials who recognized that in this particular case, continued government activity was both necessary and desirable.

"One of the enduring lessons of the Washington power game is that agreement does not equal solution. It is merely a transition point to a new struggle, the winners trying to secure their gains, the losers trying to undo them,"[1] wrote author Hedrick Smith. As former secretary of State and Treasury George Schultz put it, "Nothing ever gets settled in this town. It's not like running a company or even a university. It's a seething debating society in which the debate never stops, in which people never give up, including me, and that's the atmosphere in which you administer."[2]

The American political process is a continuous game, with numerous rounds played in different arenas. Some rounds, like elections and the submission of the president's budget, occur according to a fixed schedule. However, the closeness of the 2000 presidential election and the battle over recounts stretched the normal time schedule for knowing the outcome. Other rounds, such as introducing a bill in Congress or challenging the administration of a policy in the courts, are initiated by the players themselves on no regularized schedule. Players generally stay active from one round to the next because they realize the importance of the stakes. Unlike recreational games, where pride, honor, or relatively small amounts of money are at stake, the political process determines who is able to play the game and who benefits or loses from government actions. Every govern-

Information transmission is the core technology of politics. Changes in communications technology affect the nature of what is transmitted and who can receive it.

ment decision or action results in winners and losers. Players remain active in the games of American politics to increase the likelihood of being winners more often than losers.

Earlier chapters of this text explored the playing fields, rules, players, strategies, and the nature of winners and losers in individual arenas, such as the presidency, the Congress, the courts, and the executive branch. This final chapter adopts a broader perspective, returning to the basic questions identified in Chapter 1:

- How does the nature of the playing field affect how the game is played?
- What are the nature and impact of the rules governing the American political game?
- What are the motivations, resources, skills, and consequences of those who play in the various political games?
- Which strategies are allowable and effective in each political arena?
- What is the pattern of winning and losing in American politics and government?

An exploration of these questions requires investigating broad patterns of political activity that cut across government arenas and profiling the behavior of various players in the governing processes.

E-1 The Playing Field

The American political game is played in a unique context. Our traditions, historical perspectives, and experiences have created a national political culture that defines long-term expectations of the "right" and "wrong" way to do things. Public opinion defines acceptable short-term political goals. To the degree that culture and public opinion are widely shared, they create a set of informal rules by which political players must abide. Each institution of government exists within a unique arena, which operates under both a national culture and a set of local variations. Knowing how to play the game in one arena may not equip an individual with the skills, resources, and perspectives necessary for effective play in another arena. State and local politicians often founder when they attempt to influence national politics. Effective legislators often falter when they attempt to become a driving force in executive branch politics. Since policy making often involves a variety of arenas, effective players attempt to play the key rounds of the game on a field that grants advantages to their particular skills or resources.

Changes in the general playing field can modify the way the political game is played. Changed societal attitudes, evolving social and economic conditions, and emerging technologies all harbor the potential for upsetting established patterns.

E-1a Changed Societal Conditions

America at the dawn of the 21st century differs significantly from the America of the Founders. While conflict has always been part of our society—and even a requirement for true democracy—the level and nature of conflict has changed. In earlier periods, much of the conflict was over the *means* of reaching agreed-upon goals. Today, more of the arguments are over the very *ends* for which government was established.

Waves of immigration and unique life experiences have created a population that shares some basic orientations but view politics and government in dramatically different ways. As the goal of the American "melting pot" gave way to the desire for respect for diversity, the potential for cultural conflict increased. When cohesive groups with their own culture and opinions see society in entirely different ways, political solutions based on compromise and accommodation are much more difficult to reach. Emerging lines of conflict cover a wide variety of policy areas. For some Americans the idea of armed militias in conflict with a government seen as the enemy has become a natural outlook, while others find such anti-government attitudes appalling. After generations of dependence on government, some Americans now couch even the most esoteric demands in the framework of absolute rights, while others eschew such governmental paternalism. For some Americans a primary goal of government is the reduction of violence, while others see violence as a natural method of self-survival. The ability of government to breech such wide gaps of opinion and cultural outlooks while maintaining the basic civil liberties of a democracy will be a significant challenge for future decision makers.

E-1b Technology and the Changing Playing Field

Few technologies are created with the hope of changing the political process, but technologies created for other purposes often upset the traditional way of doing things and reduce the likelihood of "politics as usual" (see Box E-1: Evolving Communications Technology Influences the Play of American Politics).

Communications technologies change the way cultural values and opinions are transmitted. Person-to-person learning in families, schools, and churches now face tremendous competition from radio, television, compact disc players, and the Internet. Mass media technologies have the potential for almost instantly transmitting information to the vast majority of Americans, providing the building blocks for the development of common cultural values and opinions. Millions of Americans had their view of the American justice system permanently transformed by the O.J. Simpson trial and the battle over President Bill Clinton's impeachment.

Dramatic television footage has had a significant impact on Americans' views of war since the mid 1960s. In 2003, during the Iraq War, hundreds of journalists were embedded into military units traveling with them into battle. Miniature cameras, videophones, and satellite dishes allowed them to bring the war into the living rooms of the world with riveting real-time sound and images. The post-war reconstruction efforts and the terrorism that accompanied them were also covered in real time, heightening the drama of the ongoing conflict.

Mass communications technologies provided audiences with a wide range of information, mixing sports, news, and entertainment. While existing and emerging technologies continue to exist, the proliferation of specialized channels of communication through cable television and computer networks challenge the political process. The ability to choose from a wide range of information allows individuals to limit their intake of information to areas of personal interest.

Whereas democratic politics is a socially binding activity based on interaction between individuals with differing outlooks, many of the emerging technologies may lead to social fragmentation. The individuals spending their energies on televised sports and sports oriented computer forums may find little common ground for political activity with individuals using the same technologies to specialize in rock music or public affairs. The ability to talk *with* each other and develop a common culture is threatened by a completely different set of experiences and information causing individuals to talk *past* each other.[3]

Technological advances also affect politics by introducing new issues to the political agenda. Medical advances, such as organ transplants and genetic engineering, force governments to determine who should receive such services and at whose expense. The ability of computers to monitor telephone calls, bank deposits, and other personal transactions raises questions about the individual's right to privacy. The capability of producing nuclear, chemical, and biological weapons requires governments to take moral stands to control the spread and manage the use of such weapons.

New technologies often challenge the applicability and appropriateness of existing political routines. The Founders and early Supreme Court justices did not anticipate that the right to privacy might someday be applied to electronic devices like "caller ID" and issues like abortion. Copyright and intellectual property rights policies were developed with the printing press in mind. The cost and difficulty of stealing another's work made infringements unlikely. Such regulations face new challenges in the day and age of photocopiers, video cameras, tape-recording devices, and computer digitization and dissemination. "Breaking and entering" takes on a new meaning when it no longer involves physical entry and must take into account the impropriety of a hacker breaching the security of a computer system to disrupt business or to steal or corrupt information.

Another perplexity about technology concerns its proliferation. Technology can translate to power. Nuclear weapons technology, for example, gives a few nations a strong world military position. Those nations with the technology seek to prevent its transmission to

Box E–1 *Evolving Communications Technology Influences the Play of American Politics*

Nothing was more constant in the twentieth century than the relentless change in communications technology. One generation relied upon newspapers, the next marveled at radio, and the next watched television programming dominated by only a few networks. The current generation in the twenty-first century watches modern television connected to cable stations with specialized programming on dozens of channels. Communications also have been enhanced by computers that not only process bits of information rapidly but also allow rapid communication of information to locations throughout the world. Richard Armstrong and Richard Davis, analysts of changing communications technology, have identified evolving technologies and applications that will influence the future playing of American politics:

BIDIRECTIONAL CABLE: The proliferation of cable television provides opportunities for viewers to enjoy programming compatible with their interests. One recent cable innovation has been television shopping networks. The next generation of this technology will include a two-way communication system, whereby viewers will be able to send messages to the cable company as well as to receive cable signals. Through such systems, citizens might vote for electoral candidates or express views on policy issues.

BULLETIN BOARD SYSTEMS (BBS): Computer bulletin boards are services whereby messages are recorded and made available to other users. Using a LAN (Local Area Network) or modem connection, users gain access to a bulletin board and can search for relevant information and leave messages for others. Such systems hold the potential for rapid mobilization of new interest groups. Automated LISTSERVE (List serves) technology allows users to sign up for email messages on a desired topic.

BLOGS (abbreviation for "Weblogs"): These personal diaries of the thoughts and opinions of individuals are shared on a continuing basis. The appeal of tapping into the "private" thoughts of a candidate could be an appealing way to stimulate interest in his or her website. During the 2004 presidential campaign the authenticity of documents used by Dan Rather on CBS to question George W. Bush's military record was successfully challenged by blog activists.

CD-ROMs (Compact Disc, Read Only Memory): Like a floppy diskette or tape cassette, the CD-ROM videodisc is a device on which images and data can be stored. Through the use of laser technology, thousands of images can be stored, recreated, and sent to a printer or television screen via a CD-ROM. Mastering of disks was initially very expensive and users had a "read only" capability. The low cost of rewritable CDs now makes them feasible for the consumer market.

COOKIES: Cookies allow site administrators to gather information on users and communicate back to their targeted audience. While increasing the efficiency of getting the right information to the right people, the capability raises serious questions of privacy. Politicians and businesses can now monitor their site traffic and use that information.

CHAT ROOMS: These online discussion areas provide real-time interactive opportunities for individuals with common interests. While politics is one of the least popular chat room subjects, it does offer intensive interaction for some of the most interested potential political activists.

ELECTRONIC MAIL (EMail): Email is a process whereby messages are transmitted between computer users. The day may soon come when mail carriers will be obsolete. Instead, everyone will own a computer and will receive messages, bills—and, unfortunately, even junk mail—via electronic communications. In recent elections, candidates have used email to raise funds, coordinate staff, communicate with the media, and activate supporters.

INFORMATION UTILITIES: Information utilities are large data banks stored on mainframe computers. These utilities are made available, sometimes at a charge, to users who can make a connection via the web. The information in such utilities is frequently updated so that users can have the most current data possible. Database utilities allow political activists to monitor government operations—including such things as regulations published in the *Federal Register*—more effectively. Newspapers allow searching the full text of their stories, and government agencies advertise their services and available data.

These and other technologies—like radio and television in previous generations—are likely to affect our lives and the way political games are played. Increasingly the lines between formats are being erased. Only a few years ago sources were limited to text, video, or audio. Contemporary websites often mix the three formats, increasing the utility of each. Effective political players of the future may well be those who learn to use these new technologies and applications in ways that support their political ambitions.

Source: Data from Richard Armstrong, *The Next Hurrah: The Communications Revolution in American Politics*, pp. 251–283 (New York: Morrow Books, 1988) and from Richard Davis, *The Web of Politics: The Internet's Impact on the American Political System*, New York: Oxford University Press, 1999, passim).

Technological changes in communications have influenced how Americans receive information and entertainment. Newspapers and radio (top right) gave way to television (right), initially with a few networks, and then to cable television with a multiplicity of choices. The shift to the Internet (top left) as a major information source led to even more individualized information gathering.

Top left: Photodisc/Getty Images

Top right: Library of Congress, Prints & Photographs Division [LC-USZ62-109738]

Right: Library of Congress, Prints & Photographs Division, [LC-G613-57609]

others. Thus, the United States has sought to prevent the spread of information about the production of nuclear weapons and the manufacture of sophisticated computers to other nations, particularly those perceived to be adversaries. The predicament is that controlling the spread of information, particularly in a society that values the free expression of ideas, is very difficult.

Despite the clear differences between playing fields in terms of the variable impact of changing social conditions and technologies, the similarities tend to outnumber the variations. While previous chapters emphasized the differences, this chapter will focus on the commonalities. To a large degree all the institutions of government are facing challenges from changing political culture and technologies. Key aspects of the rules, players, strategies, and patterns of winning and losing cross institutional boundaries and present a unified picture of how contemporary American politics works.

E-2 The Rules

The complexity of rules across political arenas makes the knowledge of applicable rules a significant power resource. Politics no longer leaves much room for the untrained amateur. Rather it favors those who have mastered the rules and have sufficient resources to remain active players.

E-2a Nature of the Rules

While establishing the basic divisions of power and some features of the decision-making process, the U.S. Constitution remains a general rulebook. Laws enacted by Congress and informal rules within individual arenas carry almost equal weight in defining the American political game.

Formal Rules, Operating Rules, and Informal Norms

The Constitution stipulates that two representative assemblies—the House of Representatives and the Senate—must pass a piece of legislation before it becomes law. The internal rules of each house influence the behavior of individual players and policy outcomes. Among the relevant rules are those concerning seniority, assignment of committee chair positions, assignment of bills to committees, guidelines for legislative debates, and selection of congressional leadership. Informal norms of behavior, as well as constitutional rules for decision making, influence legislative outcomes.

The pattern is much the same in other government arenas. Formal rules outlined in the Constitution are coupled with operating rules and informal behavior norms, all of which influence decision making in the arena. Judges on the federal bench, for example, rely on constitutional language, legal precedent, and less formal rules about judicial process as they consider questions concerning constitutional meaning and the legality of federal government actions.

Redundant Nature of Decision Making

Rules about government decision making are designed to balance the need for decisive action based on majority rule and the desire to protect minority rights. The process is, by design, redundant. Most decisions require approval by more than one branch of government, and many go through a series of steps within each institution. Multiple opportunities are provided to reconsider past decisions. In Congress, committees reconsider subcommittee decisions, only to have their decisions reconsidered on the floor by the full House or Senate membership. Congressional and presidential decisions are reviewed and refined by bureaucrats, who, in turn, may see their decisions reconsidered by the courts. Conflict, usually followed by compromise, results from a system in which separate institutions share power. Only under rare conditions, when almost universal support is evident, can the rules be modified to allow a quick decision.

The redundant nature of decision making offers several advantages, even though it slows the process. The requirement that policies be approved by multiple parties may enhance error correction. Public policies may fail to include important elements or may contain features that will generate unintended consequences. Redundancy increases the number of times a policy is reviewed, as well as the perspectives from which it is evaluated. In addition, redundancy may enhance accountability by increasing the number and types of players who participate in policy formation, enactment, and implementation.

Incrementalism

To a large degree, the rules governing the conduct of American politics favor the status quo. Small, incremental decisions are more likely than broad, sweeping changes. Many of the rules protect the current power holders, providing some measure of stability but most likely inhibiting creativity and change. Incumbent bureaucrats, protected by the civil service system, may be removed from their positions only for gross violation of official responsibilities. Federal judges are protected by rules that give them life tenure, providing isolation from everyday politics.

E-2b Changing the Rules

The nature and impact of political rules do not remain fixed. Players constantly attempt to change the rules to promote their personal agenda.

Crises, in particular, may generate a reexamination of existing rules and place pressure for rule changes on leaders. For example, after becoming dissatisfied with American military involvement in Southeast Asia, Congress enacted the War Powers Resolution in 1973, with the intent of limiting the president's ability to commit U.S. troops in foreign nations. After the September 11, 2001 terrorist attacks, Congress passed the Patriot Act designed to strengthen FBI access to personal records of potential terrorists. While some saw this as necessary for effective deterrence, others felt it posed a significant threat to personal liberty.

As another example, the rules used by the federal government to distribute information and reports have changed as the result of technological innovations. Traditionally, the federal government distributed all information in written form through the U.S. Government Printing Office (GPO). With the advent of computer technology, the distribution of paper documents has proven to be comparatively inefficient and expensive. The GPO has begun to distribute information and data on computer tapes, diskettes, and CD-ROMs as well as online. The arrival of the Internet has put pressure on government to utilize its capabilities to expand public access to timely information.

Intentional Rule Reform

reform *Planned modifications of a rule or procedure that are designed to achieve specific purposes or outcomes in future political games.*

Planned reform involves an attempt by players to manage change in a way beneficial to their cause. **Reform** alters the playing field, affects the nature of the players, defines accepted strategies, and ultimately determines the winners and losers. For example, since the early 1990s, Congress has debated a substantial revision of campaign finance laws, motivated in part by public concern about the financial contributions legislators were receiving from businesses and interest groups. While limited in the amount of direct campaign contributions they could make, corporations and interest groups had no limits on fees they might pay legislators for speaking engagements. The public quickly recognized speaker fees as an indirect means of funneling financial support to members of Congress. Aware of the growing public dissatisfaction, members of Congress saw it in their own interest to revise campaign finance rules to eliminate fees they could charge for speaking to groups. Other aspects of campaign finance proved more difficult to change as the players recognized the benefits of the existing rules. This debate went on for years. Congress weighed the positive and negative impact of reform against individual members' agendas. No one was completely satisfied with the results, and the players ended up in the courts for another round of resolution.

Rules for Rule Reform

The most fundamental rules, those based in the Constitution, can be reformed in only two ways. Congress can recommend constitutional amendments, which take effect only if approved by three-fourths of the states. Twenty-seven amendments have been enacted in this way. Alternatively, at the behest of two-thirds of the states, Congress can call a constitutional convention that could reevaluate and reform the basic rulebook more comprehensively. These changes are ratified if approved by three-fourths of the states. The constitutional convention route for change has never been taken, and calls for such a convention seldom have been seriously considered.[4] A constitutional convention, where the rule book of American politics could be substantially revised, or even entirely revamped, is perceived as too threatening by most players, who are content with most features of the existing Constitution.

Other rules in the game of American politics are based in public laws, in the operating procedures of political institutions, and in informal political norms. While these rules are more easily changed than are constitutional provisions, they, too, remain relatively stable. The tendency to prefer the status quo to uncertain revised rules works to restrain massive revisions.

Significant rule reforms are usually motivated by widespread concerns about current rules and dissatisfaction with their outcomes. The Constitution was amended early in the twentieth century to allow the direct election of senators and to establish a national income tax. Both amendments followed extensive debate, during which leaders convinced the nation that direct election was a more democratic method of selecting senators and that an income tax was necessary for the federal government to raise sufficient revenues to cover the costs of expanding government programs.

On occasion, Congress has modified its internal operating rules, but again, only upon recognition of serious problems. In 1910, for example, the House of Representatives responded to what was seen as excessive control by the Speaker of the House by adopting new rules that reduced the Speaker's leadership control. During the 1970s, the House of Representatives revised the seniority rule for selecting committee chairs in response to the excessive power wielded by unresponsive committee leaders.

E-2c Strategies for Rule Reform

The need for specific reforms is not always evident, and the likelihood of reform adoption is not a foregone conclusion. Individuals and groups carefully evaluate the implications and impact of proposed reforms for their policy and career preferences. Successful reform requires clever strategies that persuade players their interests will be served by reforms in governing rules.

Reform is most likely to be considered after the influx of a large group of new players with little perceived stake in the traditional ways of doing things. The 1994 election brought to Congress a significant number of new Republican legislators, promoting the Republican Party into majority status. After complaining for years about the inadequacies of how Congress was run, they were primed for passing significant internal reforms. Their efforts included restructuring committees, banning proxy (absentee) voting, and limiting the terms of office of committee chairs. New presidents are more likely to reform White House operations immediately after taking office than after a few years of adapting to a particular set of operating procedures.

The importance of governing rules is verified by the political battles fought over seemingly minor interpretations or revisions of them. Lowering the voting age from 21 years to 18 years (26th Amendment) generated extensive debate as Republican and Democratic party leaders anticipated how expanding the electorate would help or hurt their potential for winning elections. Recent state initiatives to limit the number of terms state legislators may serve have stimulated attempts to apply similar limitations to members of Congress. Since most members of Congress follow strategies designed to maintain their position, such a rule change would dramatically affect congressional players and the way they behave. Control over the rules often determines who can play the game, the strategies they can pursue, and the probable outcomes for future rounds (see Box E-2: A Strategy Primer for Reform).

The American political system has seen relatively few substantial reforms in the rules concerning government decision making. Existing players often seek to protect the status quo due to the fear their political position and power may be weakened as the result of rule changes. Even when most players agree that current rules are improper or insufficient to achieve their purpose, attaining consensus on the nature of rule modifications is difficult at best. The Electoral College is a relevant example. While many players are uncomfortable with this method of presidential selection, its stability and reinforcement of the two-party system have thus far discouraged wholesale Electoral College reform. The uncertain and mixed results of the 2000 presidential election with Al Gore winning the popular vote and George W. Bush winning the Electoral College vote gave the wheel of Electoral College reform another spin. Traditionalists, the representatives of small states (who felt that direct election would encourage candidates to bypass their voters in favor of national media campaigns) combined with those seeing a partisan benefit to the current system to serve as a powerful impediment to change. The clear outcome of the 2004 presidential contest dampened the pressure for change.

Difficulty in modifying rules of the game is evident in campaign finance reform. Most players concur that the current rules allow abuses and potentially unethical practices. Yet, despite agreement on the problem, there is great debate about how to resolve it. None of the players want to adopt new rules that restrain their ability to gather campaign funds or give an edge to political opponents. Democrats, dependent on political action committee

Box E-2 A Strategy Primer for Reform

Reform involves planned change and usually requires one or a combination of common strategies. Whether you desire to modify the election process by promoting public financing for congressional elections, hope to create a new committee structure in your club, or yearn for a different family dinner menu, success is more likely if you pay attention to the following strategies.

The Rhetoric of Reform I: Be Wary of Reformers Bearing Gifts
Successful reformers sell their reform proposals through rhetoric and symbolism. Reforms are linked to widely held values, such as "equality," "fairness," and "efficiency," even though the true motivations might be quite different. Reformers tend to oversell the benefits and downgrade the potential detriments of the desired reform.

The Rhetoric of Reform II: Be Wary of Doomsayers Opposing Reform
The energy with which reformers proclaim the value of reform initiatives is often matched by the diligence with which others oppose reform by proclaiming its doom. Doomsayers often paint a bleak picture of reform consequences in order to stop an effort that will in some way harm their position. For example, opponents of the Equal Rights Amendment exaggerated the impact of this reform, claiming that it would force men and women to use public unisex bathrooms and require sports teams to include female players. One of the most practiced, and often effective, means today to doom a political reform is to claim that it will "raise taxes." With taxpayer revolts common and public willingness to pay new taxes at an all-time low, the cry of "higher taxes" is often enough to sink a ship of proposed reform, even if the cry is untrue.

Timing: Using the Well-Timed Crisis
Effective reformers attempt to portray the status quo not only as undesirable, but also as a crisis that needs immediate and intensive attention. During times of apparent national crisis (for example, war, economic depression, revolution), reform of the rules demonstrates that something is being done. Lacking an obvious crisis, reformers rely on predicting an impending crisis, whose solution lies in adopting the proposed reform.

Targets: You Can Teach a New Dog New Tricks
New members of an institution are more likely to be responsive to reforms than are those players who have become accustomed to the traditional way of doing things. The incumbent players often benefit from existing rules and practices. Incumbents, therefore, may have little incentive to innovate. Reform is most likely when there has been a significant turnover of players, meaning that fewer players have a stake in maintaining the status quo.

Size: Big Enough to Fight for, but Not So Big That You'll Choke on It
Promoting a minor reform with little obvious impact decreases the likelihood that many players will make the effort to promote the change. On the other hand, the unknown consequences of a major reform may also dampen enthusiasm. The most likely reforms are those big enough to fight for, but small enough that most of the consequences are understood and desired by a majority of players.

(PAC) contributions, opposed limiting PACs and large "soft money" contributions to parties, while Republicans, supported by relatively affluent party organizations, sought to maintain their right to use party-generated funds. The 2002 Bipartisan Campaign Reform Act succeeded by focusing on only a few of the concerns (especially the use of "soft money" by political parties). The large amounts of money spent in 2004 by "527" interest groups (named for the section of the law under which they operated) raised significant new questions. New rounds of reform will be needed to address remaining concerns and take up the negative unintended consequences of the last round of reform.

E-3 The Players

Participants in the American political game are not a random sample of the American population. Differing motivations and skills combine with informal traditions and formal rules to distinguish between spectators and players.

E-3a A General Profile

Participants in most political arenas tend to be drawn from the better educated, informed, and economically advantaged segments of the American population. Joining the political game requires such resources as time, information, education, leadership skills, and often money; these resources are more likely possessed by society's "haves" than by its "have-nots."

Despite these limitations, the American political game is relatively **inclusive,** providing opportunities for new individuals, groups, and organizations seeking to reach their goals through politics—especially if they represent or can influence a substantial block of voters and/or contributors. In recent years, groups as divergent as blacks, women, Hispanics, gays, antiabortion activists, and advocates for the homeless have become significant players in American politics, seeking to influence government policies on such issues as civil rights, AIDS research, sexual harassment, and housing.

inclusive games *Games that welcome or allow the entry of new players.*

Reduced participation rates for some political activities, such as voting, worry observers who fear the implications of citizen noninvolvement. Technologies such as television and the Internet hinder the traditional role of political parties by allowing candidates to bypass party organizations and appeal directly to the voters. As discussed earlier, the growth of specialized media and targeted communications makes it more likely that individuals will be better informed, but about fewer issues. This leads to fragmentation of the political system, as voters lose sight of broad issues and focus on narrow interests. The increased capacity of the news media to instantly inform and entertain the public is balanced against the potential danger of citizens turning politics into a detached spectator sport. If the media make it easier and more entertaining to watch the game than to participate in it, the essential element of democracy—active citizen involvement in governance—is endangered.

E-3b Games for Selecting Players

Within the American political system, an assortment of distinctive games is used to select government players. The selection games, each governed by a set of operational rules, vary according to the nature of player position and the role players are expected to perform.

The Chief Executive Election Game

Chief executives, such as presidents, governors, and mayors, gain office in America through the "chief executive election game." Nominees must present themselves to the electorate in regularly scheduled contests. Turnover among these executives is increased through rules limiting the number of terms an individual can serve in office (for example, presidents are limited to two terms, and some governors may serve only one or two consecutive terms in office). Chief executives are expected to be more than neutral administrators; citizens rely on them to exercise political leadership and to recommend policy proposals relating to current problems or crises.

The Representative Election Game

The "representative election game" is used to select members of Congress, as well as state legislators and city council members. According to this game, residents of a geographic territory are entitled to periodically elect legislators to "re-present" their viewpoints. This form of player selection allows individual voters to convey their interests and preferences to an elected legislator, who is then motivated to look out for his or her constituents' interests in the policy-making process. Accountability, the linchpin of democracy, is sought through frequent elections, whereby representatives ask their constituents for permission to remain in office and challengers seek the opportunity to replace incumbents.

The Nomination Appointment Game

The "nomination appointment game" is used to select political executives. The right of appointment allows presidents, governors, and mayors to create a team of advisors and subordinates committed to their leadership and policies. Most presidential appointees must be confirmed by the Senate, which allows the national legislature to review the qualifications and policy preferences of nominees. Although the Senate usually confirms presidential nominations, the process requires the president to anticipate senatorial objections. The nomination appointment game also allows presidents to remove political executives with whom they are dissatisfied.

A similar but distinct game is used to select judges for the federal bench. As with top administrators, the president nominates and the Senate confirms. However, presidents are not allowed to remove judges from the bench. Judges serve in office as long as they wish, under the condition that they commit no gross violation of official duties and responsibilities. Should such violations occur, judges can be removed through the formal process of impeachment and conviction. The rules of the judicial selection game were purposely designed to isolate federal judges from daily political struggles so they could provide objectivity and fairness in judicial decisions. At state and local levels, judges may be either appointed or popularly elected.

The Merit Appointment Game

Another game is used to select bureaucratic players in government agencies. In response to abuses that arose through patronage and machine politics, the process for selecting government employees became a "merit appointment game," in which skill and competence are the guiding principles for selection, retention, and advancement. Competitive examinations and evaluation, rather than political loyalty, determine the players. Neutral competence is expected to increase the efficiency of government operations and the fairness of government job and resource allocations.

E-3c Emergence of Cross-Institutional Teams

Descriptions in previous chapters of individual political arenas may have left the false impression that each arena has a fixed boundary and that players are active in only one arena. In reality, the checks and balances design of American government, enforced by the separation of powers and federalism, requires players in each institutional arena to work with those in other arenas. Some players—notably, interest groups—seek to play in multiple arenas because they have stakes in policy decisions made in those arenas. For example, dairy farmers have a stake in policy decisions made by Congress (when enacting legislation to provide price supports for milk), the Department of Agriculture (when implementing price support policies), and perhaps even the courts (should the constitutionality of price support policies be questioned).

Political Party Teams

Political parties have traditionally provided a basis for cooperation across arena boundaries by players who share outlooks and ideologies. Presidents, as well as governors and mayors, use partisanship to build coalitions with legislators in the process of debating and enacting public policy. Chief executives also use partisanship for selecting loyal political executives and for increasing the likelihood that appointed judges will support proposed policies. The decline of parties as a force in elections and the movement away from partisan appointments toward more personal-based appointments have, however, reduced party power to reinforce policy coordination.

Partisan teams play important roles in legislative politics. The organization of congressional leadership is based, in large measure, on partisan strength in each house. During policy debates, individual representatives often coalesce around a party position to collectively achieve a legislative victory. A primary objective of congressional party leaders is to make partisan teams work effectively by convincing individual party members to support the party position. After years of decline, the 1980s and 1990s revealed a new emphasis on partisan distinctiveness. Divided government control of Congress and the presidency which has dominated the post-war period combined with increased party distinctiveness to make it more difficult to create the necessary bi-partisan coalitions for enacting policy. George W. Bush emerged from the 2000, 2002, and 2004 elections with small Republican majorities in both chambers, but there was no guarantee he could regularly dominate the policy process. Lack of Republican cohesion led to a campaign finance law he did not prefer and limited his tax cut goals.

Issue Networks

In addition to partisanship, other types of cross-institutional teams have developed on the basis of common policy interests. In many policy realms, administrative officials, legislators, interest groups, and other players are linked together in an issue network. Interest groups push for specific policies and attempt to influence congressional subcommittee members who draft public laws and bureaucrats who will administer them. Subcommittee members need information from the bureaucrats and campaign support from interest groups. Bureaucrats depend on congressional subcommittees for their direction and funding and on interest groups for support. The same groups of players face each other year after year, often without significant oversight by the media, the public, or other government players. The dominance of issue networks in particular policy areas may lead to cozy "**closed games,**" with a small set of players linked by their mutual interests making most policy decisions.[5]

closed games *Games that attempt to exclude new players.*

When the interests of many citizens and organizations are affected by public policies, deliberations about policy formation and execution tend to be more open. In this context, issue networks can be observed in action. These networks include not only representatives of subcommittees, bureaus, and regulated interest groups, but also broader groups whose members are affected by the policy debate. Recent policy debates on civil rights and military policies have brought diverse players into political games. Relatively new to policy debates are public interest lobbies that seek to represent broader public concerns rather than the narrow interests of specialized groups.

E-4 The Strategies

Public policies are the stakes in the American political game. Without significant stakes, few players would take interest or expend time and energy in political pursuits. Various levels and stages in the policy game involve different players and utilize a wide set of strategies. A number of successful strategies distinguish the winners and losers in the policy game.

The appropriateness of strategies for playing political games varies by political arena. What works in Congress, city councils, or the White House may be either ineffective or illegal in the courts or the bureaucracy. Some common strategies, however, cross institutional boundaries.

E-4a Building Coalitions among Players

Proponents and opponents of particular policies seek to build broad-based coalitions to facilitate, revise, or kill the policy option in question. The multiple stages in the policy process mean that attaining a policy goal requires success at each step, while opponents have many opportunities to stop a policy proposal. Coalition building relies on strategies that vary depending on whether the goal involves passing or defeating a policy.

Divide and Conquer

Opponents try to "divide and conquer" the opposition, while proponents must keep the coalition together through persuasion, leadership, and bargaining. The more specific a policy proposal is, the easier it is for opponents to drive a wedge between supporters with differing specific goals.

coalition of mixed expectations *A group of political players agreeing to a particular policy initiative but having varying reasons for giving support and different expectations about policy outcomes.*

Coalesce and Compromise

Proponents attempt to weave a broad **coalition of mixed expectations**, keeping the goals vague and recognizing that members can agree on a final outcome without agreeing on specific details.

compromise *The mutual accommodation among players with competing interests that allows a decision to be made.*

Since American politics is based on separate arenas that share power, **compromise** is a key strategy. Each team of players pushes for its position but generally recognizes that nothing will be accomplished without some accommodation to the opposition. Straying from an absolute goal is justified with statements such as "Half a loaf is better than nothing at all," "If you can't lick them, join them,"[6] or, as former president Gerald Ford put it, "Compromise is the oil that makes governments go."[7]

Beckon and Bargain

Existing players are often happy to play a closed game among themselves. By excluding other players, they may be able to design policies more favorable to themselves and acquire more of the benefits distributed through public policies. In a democracy, however, the potential for bringing new players into the game invites coalition strategies to increase the player base. Coalition players change the nature of the game by bringing in new participants, rather than by changing the views of existing ones. New coalition members may have to be promised policy benefits to stimulate their participation.

New technology has expanded the ways in which potential coalition members can be informed. Television allows coalition managers to bypass many of the traditional players to appeal directly to the voters. Computer networks have been used to both inform and activate like-minded individuals. Political strategists work on the assumption that the inclusiveness of the American political system will welcome almost any cause that can stimulate a proponent and find a constituency among the public (see Box E-3: The Origins of Policies).

Box E-3 The Origins of Policies

Think about the key problems you see facing American society either on the local or national level. Consider which of these problems is amenable to solution by changes in public policy. Government is limited to solving problems that can be rectified by distributing some benefit, redistributing some resources, or regulating certain behaviors. Within each category of solution there are finite limits as to how far the government can go.

Once you have identified some problems in American society, list a specific piece of public policy you would like to see the government take action on immediately. Indicate the types of people who would likely support your policy and those who would oppose its passage.

In a democracy, everyone has the right to identify problems and propose solutions. *Every* piece of public policy initially began with someone going through an exercise like this one, and you have as much right as anyone else to make demands on government. Your success will depend on a number of factors. Your willingness to actively play the political game will to a large degree determine whether your ideas will be heard. Your skill at presenting your solutions in a way that will draw the support of others will determine whether a supporting coalition will develop. The nature and strengths of opposing players will determine whether your proposals have a chance of passage.

The history of important public policies in America is often marked by one individual who made the effort to identify a problem, frame a solution, and act on it. Thousands of individuals have saved millions of lives by identifying street corners in need of stop signs. Women were allowed to enter the U.S. military academies because one woman wrote a letter complaining that she was denied equal treatment by being excluded. The pensions of American workers are protected by the federal government because one individual complained that workers in his company were being let go just before retirement and losing benefits. Civil rights in America will forever be changed because one woman refused to go to the back of a bus. Pressure for gun control was stimulated by one individual who lost his son to gun violence and began writing the families of other gun victims to create an interest group. The examples of significant action by ordinary individuals would fill many volumes.[a]

The action one needs to take might be as simple as writing a letter to a public official or speaking up in a public meeting. Winning the game is not easy, but by not playing one cedes victory to others from the outset. Perhaps it is time for you to suit up and join the game.

---

a. For examples of individual citizens who made a difference in affecting national public policy, see Stephen Frantzich, *Citizen Democracy: Political Activists in a Cynical Age* (Lanham, MD: Rowman and Littlefield Publishers, 2005).

Former President Bill Clinton presents James Brady with a replica of the plaque that will be hung permanently in the James S. Brady Press Briefing Room.
Clinton Presidential Library

E-4b Shifting Coalitions

Coalitions in American politics are seldom stable. Although Republicans are most likely to support fellow Republicans, and Democrats to support fellow Democrats, the margin of victory often depends on defectors from the opposing partisan or ideological team. A coalition formed over one policy issue or in one election may look very different than a coalition formed in another election or policy battle. The adage that "politics makes strange bedfellows" discourages politicians from writing off potential supporters. Since politics is a continuous game, coalition builders recognize that making long-term enemies makes little sense. Today's opponent may be tomorrow's ally.

Shifting coalitions affected gun control legislation during the 1990s. Conservatives generally, and former president Ronald Reagan specifically, had long opposed gun control legislation. In 1991, however, Reagan had a change of heart. Congress was considering the "Brady Bill," sponsored by a group led by James Brady, Reagan's first press secretary, who was badly wounded during an assassination attempt on Reagan. After an appeal from Brady and supporters, Reagan changed his stance and supported legislation that would require a waiting period before a handgun could be purchased. Sensing a change in the players after the 1994 election, the National Rifle Association used aggressive rhetoric to condemn federal agents enforcing gun control laws as part of its strategy to rescind recent gun control legislation. The rhetoric offended high profile supporters such as former president George Bush, who canceled his membership and weakened support for the NRA. The 1995 bombing of the federal building in Oklahoma City by a member of a gun supporting citizen militia, although clearly condemned by the NRA, dampened public ardor for making guns more available. The rash of school shootings in places such as Littleton, Colorado's Columbine High School increased pressure to make guns less available, while re-energizing the NRA in its fight to protect the right to bear arms.

E-5 Determining the Winners and Losers

In the long run, players, rules, and strategies mean little in isolation. The true importance of a political system lies in understanding the nature of the public policies it produces and delivers to its citizens. Several factors determine whose policy preferences prevail and whose desires are fulfilled by the American political game.

E-5a You Can't Win If You Don't Play

> The only thing necessary for the triumph of evil is for good men to do nothing. (Attributed to British parliamentarian Edmund Burke)

> The penalty good men pay for indifference to public affairs is to be ruled by evil men. (Attributed to Plato)

Groups and individuals who take an active role in the American political process tend to achieve their policy objectives more often than do groups or individuals lacking the knowledge, motivation, resources, or skills to participate. Since political participation is dominated by individuals from higher socioeconomic levels, the political system responds to their wishes and needs more effectively than to the needs of individuals with less income and education.

E-5b You Can't Know the Players without a Program

In 1822, James Madison wrote:

> A popular Government without popular information . . . is but a Prologue to a Farce or a Tragedy. . . . Knowledge will forever govern ignorance: And people who mean to be their own Governors, must arm themselves with the power which knowledge gives.[8]

Winning in politics involves applying the right power resource at the appropriate time. If players do not know when, where, and by whom a decision is to be made, their potential for having a significant impact decreases. An organized group of citizens has little likelihood for success unless its views are communicated before key decisions are made. A president lacking information on the motivations of a member of Congress, the goals of a foreign leader, or the perspectives of an executive branch appointee will be less likely to succeed than will a president with relevant intelligence on other key players. Those individuals and groups who effectively monitor the political process and anticipate upcoming decisions gain their objective more often than those who react after the fact.

While information has always been a significant political power resource, the proliferation of government functions and the new technologies for monitoring official actions grant those players capable of harnessing technology to monitor the process a significant advantage.

E-5c Quitters Never Win and Winners Never Quit

> The opera ain't over till the fat lady sings. (Dan Cook, sportscaster[9])

As a continuous game in which the players have almost unlimited ability to review and revise past decisions, American politics rewards groups and individuals who persist in the process round after round. Groups and individuals seldom win unless they remain on the field until the game is over. In politics, it is rare for an issue to be settled once and for all. Players expecting immediate satisfaction and quick policy victories will almost certainly experience frustration. The ultimate winners in the policy process recognize that victory requires constant vigilance. Winners must protect their gains, while losers in an initial round look for ways to redeem their cause and win future rounds.

E-5d Everybody Loves a Winner

Author Hedrick Smith wrote:

> Politics is like football: The team with forward motion gets the breaks and gains the extra yardage; the team on its heels loses and becomes dispirited.[10]

Winners develop a reputation for winning that encourages them to try again, while losers often get discouraged and lose faith in their potential to win.[11] Many incumbent officeholders win their next election by looking so invulnerable that only weak candidates challenge them. After winning a number of key victories in Congress or the courts, presidents find members of Congress and justices less willing to challenge them. On the other hand, a string of losses may encourage other players to "kick the victim while he or she is down."

The "winner syndrome" was evident in early 1991, as Democrats began to consider challenging George H. Bush in the 1992 presidential election (they anticipated the incumbent president would run for reelection). Usually in the year preceding a presidential election year, challengers begin to announce their intention to run and commence plans to compete in their party's primaries. This pattern was slow to emerge in 1991, in large measure because Bush was perceived as a "winner" as a result of the Persian Gulf War. Bush's popularity at the polls reached an all-time high following this military action, primarily because the United States was able to achieve most of its objectives in a dramatic way without substantial loss of American lives. Potential challengers were wary of taking on a popular, incumbent president. They worried that challenging the "winner" would likely make them the loser. One challenger who entered the race—Governor Bill Clinton of Arkansas—had little to lose politically and sensed that Bush was politically vulnerable in the upcoming election. His instincts were correct, particularly as a weakened national economy ultimately contributed to difficult races for most incumbents in 1992.

The reluctance of Democratic challengers diminished late in 1991, as economic and social issues replaced foreign affairs as dominant policy concerns of Americans. By the fall of 1991, it was apparent that the economic recession plaguing the nation was not abating and that the Bush administration was unable to provide a popular policy agenda to deal with economic and social problems. By late 1991, not only had several Democrats announced plans to challenge Bush, but also some Republicans. But Bill Clinton had a head start, and challengers could not catch up to his nomination bandwagon.

The pattern reversed as the 1996 election approached. Bill Clinton was seen as vulnerable, and a bumper crop of Republicans entered the fray. Even within his own party, leaders like Jesse Jackson toyed with running. With Bill Clinton having to leave office after the 2000 election, an open seat presidency drew significant challenges among both major political parties. Vice president Al Gore had to fend off former senator Bill Bradley, while Texas governor George W. Bush had to defeat Senator John McCain, before they could face each other in the most expensive presidential campaign in history. Whenever a politician, political party, or political cause seems to be on the ropes, or is forced to leave the ring, opportunistic players generally emerge.

After the 2003 Iraq War, George W. Bush emerged as a winner with validation of his military strategy and high public opinion ratings. He attempted to learn from his father and quickly turned to domestic issues to secure an advantage in the 2004 race. The Democrats also seemed to have learned a lesson. Rather than standing back assuming Bush was invincible, a large group of contenders emerged. Most ignored the war issue during the primaries and sought to turn public attention back to domestic and economic issues. The eventual Democratic nominee, John Kerry, turned the attention back to foreign policy by emphasizing his war record, a strategy many felt backfired.

E-5e Some Abiding Game Plans

Amidst changing players, arenas, and rules, certain game plans have an abiding place in the American political system. These include capitalism, respect for private property, promotion of equality, and emphasis on fair play.

Capitalism and the Respect for Property

Underlying much of the American political game is a deep respect for capitalism and the ownership of property. The American Revolution was fought and the U.S. Constitution written with the protection of property as a basic goal. The shift in the former Soviet Union and Eastern European countries toward more capitalist systems bolsters the belief that the opportunity to acquire property serves as a key motivator of individuals.

American public policy reflects capitalist orientations. Tax laws favor individuals and businesses who use their past economic successes to bolster the economy. The tax cut discussion during the 2000 presidential campaign was instructive. While the candidates differed on who would receive their tax cut, both reflected the view that citizens have the rights to the economic fruits of their labor except when government can make a good case that some of it is needed for collective public benefits. The burden of proof is on the government. Recent moves toward privatizing government functions reveal a distrust of government and a laudatory image of the private sector, which can achieve more with fewer resources. During the 2004 campaign, President George W. Bush took a strong stand in favor of allowing workers to invest some of their Social Security contributions in the private sector, a major potential change in the more than 60 year old program.

Equality: An Elusive Goal

Alongside capitalism's acceptance of inequality, based on differences in motivation and skills, lies an American commitment to equality. Largely rejecting the goal of equality of condition in which winners would look very much like losers, Americans emphasize equality of opportunity, in which everyone is given an equal chance to play and win political games. In the American ethos, everyone should be given an even opportunity, from which he or she is responsible for crafting success or failure. The battle over affirmative action hinges on a disagreement about *when* equality of opportunity should begin.

Fair Play

Americans expect fair play in their lives, and in politics. They will rally around an electoral underdog for no other reason than they feel it is unfair for one candidate to be too dominating. Americans also respond negatively to reports that a candidate or public official has played a political game unfairly. The Watergate scandal, for example, hurt President Richard Nixon, in large measure because Americans felt that breaking into an opponent's headquarters to learn his game plans was not fair. Moves to investigate former president Ronald Reagan's 1980 presidential campaign for allegedly attempting to delay the return of American hostages in Iran until after the election fall into the same category. The investigation into Bill Clinton's investments into the Whitewater land deal revolved around a perception that he was treated more favorably because of his political position, thus seemingly being unfair to others.

Political strategists must be wary not to offend popular notions of fair play. In electoral campaigns, strategists have an incentive to exaggerate the positive qualities of their candidate and the flaws of his or her opponents. If the exaggeration goes too far, however, citizen sensibilities about fair play may be upset, resulting in a negative backlash. During the battles of the recount after the 2000 election, both candidates framed their position in terms of fairness to the public and the nation. Realization of confusing ballots, significant voter errors, and wide disparity by election officials in invalidating ballots led to loud outcries of unfairness resulting in new legislation and administrative procedures. Even the most partisan activist can accept losing if the game is not seen as rigged.

E-5f Changing the Underlying Dimensions of the Game

In response to major or emerging problems, changing social or economic perspectives, or technological changes, the dimensions of political games can change.

Reestablishing Game Boundaries

During much of the twentieth century, the American political game has shifted from the states and localities to Washington, D.C., while such themes as "energy independence" have lured many Americans into the feeling that the United States as a nation could go it alone. Both of these developments are being challenged in the twenty-first century.

The national government has proven either incapable of or financially unable to provide the goods and services demanded by the public. Technology-generated problems, such as pollution, energy dependence, and nuclear waste, fail to honor traditional geographic boundaries. Other problems, such as drug abuse, crime, and disease have defied nationally defined solutions. New pressure is being placed on state and local governments to pick up the slack and forge new policy alliances between themselves and the national government.

On the international front, America finds itself enmeshed in an increasingly interdependent world. The markets for American products and U.S. sources of raw materials cover the globe. Multinational corporations dominate world commerce, with only limited concern for purely American interests. Much of American productivity is based on foreign investment. Modern communications and transportation make problems in far corners of the world drop on America's doorstep. When Iraq invaded Kuwait, America became involved to protect world access to oil, to contain a power-hungry despot, and to reinforce acceptable standards for relations among nations. The days in which it was possible to clearly distinguish domestic and international games are gone. Globalization is a fact of life, with the U.S. thrust into a leadership position because of its human, material, and technological resources.

Redefining the Nature of Winning and Losing

From the 1950s to the 1970s, unprecedented economic growth and American optimism about the ability of government to solve social problems undergirded a dramatic expansion of government activity, especially at the national level. Politics was often a positive-sum game in which the growth of each year's budget and the addition of each new program meant that most players gained at least some of their objectives. The federal government became a referee among competing interests, assuring that no one interest won too much, but that everyone won at least something.[12]

The exploding costs of government programs and a growing recognition of the limits of government intervention have more recently led to a different set of games. Attempts to manage the budget deficit by making expenditures more closely match tax revenues require some combination of tax increase and expenditure cuts. In many arenas, politics has become a negative-sum game in which all players lose to some degree. At best under such conditions, politics is a zero-sum game, in which the gains of one set of players are made up through the budgetary losses of others. As players begin to see politics as more of a zero-sum game, many of the motivations for bargaining and compromise evaporate. Conflict increases as proponents of different government programs begin seeing every other program as a possible competitor. For example, when the Soviet Union began to collapse as a viable threat to American national defense, proponents of domestic programs touted the "peace dividend" and began planning to cut into the defense piece of the overall budget "pie." In the domestic realm, entire programs such as the Corporation for Public Broadcasting and the National Endowment for the Arts were targeted for significant cuts in order to maintain funding for other programs.

The politics of surpluses that began in the late 1990s changed the environment again to a positive-sum game, with all parties fighting for either tax cuts or capturing the surplus to support expanded programs in their area of interest. The Republicans and President George W. Bush won an early victory in 2001 for cutting taxes and returning much of the surplus to the taxpayers. The Democrats held out for a smaller tax cut and bolstering social service and education programs. In a classic positive-sum game statement, President Bush argued that his program would do both by "return[ing] money to the taxpayers and provid[ing] reasonable spending increases."[13]

The return of deficits after the economic dislocation of the September 11th terrorist attacks and the extensive expenditures on the Iraq War and reconstruction shifted the definition of winning once again. Holding on to funding for one's preferred government programs returned as a sign of victory, while expansion in funding seemed like an elusive dream. Playing good defense became much more important than a creative offense for the foreseeable future. Politically, the negative-sum game era was back, with all the conflict that implies. Politicians faced a public that had been willing to accept an understandable economic downturn and a large commitment of resources to increase homeland security, but were now ready to get back to normal.

From an observer's perspective, such changes in winning or losing the game make watching more interesting. From the perspective of the players, the changes present challenges that determine how long and in what role they will perform on the playing field. For individuals subject to American government decisions, the consequences are even more important. Whether one is a participating citizen, political constituent, government client, or invisible victim, winning and losing have direct consequences, affecting gaining or losing jobs, welfare checks, opportunities for education, cultural programs, protection from criminals, highway maintenance, and taxes. It is these goods, services, costs, and protections for which government was formed and that politics is all about.

E-6 The Game Goes On

As author Hedrick Smith noted:

> It's a new ball game, with new sets of rules, new ways of getting power leverage, new types of players, new game plans, and new tactics that affect winning and losing.[14]

While the American political game retains many of its abiding characteristics, changes in the playing field affect the potential players, encourage reform of the rules, determine the effectiveness of various strategies, and influence who wins the game. Although the causes of change are numerous, new technologies represent an enduring influence on American politics. The contours of contemporary American politics are hard to imagine without television, computer-generated mail, public opinion polling, and an efficient national transportation system. Anticipating what the next wave of technological changes will bring is more difficult. On the immediate horizon for political applications are the Internet, 500 channel cable TV systems, cellular telephones, and high-definition television. The players who can effectively harness that next wave of technology for political purposes will benefit the candidates they support and the causes they pursue.

Players in the American political system can be expected to continue their ongoing struggle to influence policy making in order to increase the flow of benefits in their direction and to deflect costs and government regulation. American politics is a game, but sometimes this recognition is disturbing to citizens. Government decisions are not reached through an objective process in which officials examine all possible courses of action and select what is best for the nation as a whole. Instead, government policies result from continuous political games that match self-interested (and sometimes altruistic), but often unequal, teams of players. Public policies emerge as some players win rounds of the policy game. These policies will likely change in future rounds as other players join the game, or existing players utilize new resources to challenge the winners of the last round. While the future of the American political system cannot be precisely predicted, one firm and fast prediction is possible: The game will go on!

Key Terms

closed games
coalition of mixed expectations
compromise
inclusive games
reform

Practice Quiz

1. Which is *not* an example of incremental decision making?
  a. The invasion of Afghanistan to find and destroy terrorists responsible for the September 11, 2001 attack
  b. Approving budgets after review of changes from a previous year's budget
  c. Semi-annual review and minor clarification of administrative rules
  d. All of the above

2. Merit appointment is designed as a strategy for which group of officials?
  a. Appointed cabinet secretaries
  b. Bureaucrats selected via civil service
  c. Senators and representatives
  d. Federal judges

3. Which is an example of checks and balances?
- a. Nomination of federal judges by the chief executive
- b. Veto power of the chief executive
- c. Ability of Congress to override chief executive vetoes
- d. All of the above

4. Which of the following is not a long-term "game plan" of American politics?
- a. Capitalism
- b. Respect for private property
- c. Belief in fair play and opportunities
- d. Massive resistance

5. Efforts to "privatize" governmental services are often pursued in the belief that privatized services will
- a. merge public and religious institutions.
- b. cost less to deliver.
- c. utilize civil service systems.
- d. end discrimination.

6. Federalism as a governing system is based upon
- a. universal franchise.
- b. equal protection.
- c. sharing of governing powers among layers of government.
- d. progressive taxation.

7. Which player is not usually a part of "issue networks"?
- a. Legislators on subcommittees
- b. Administrative officials in agencies
- c. Federal judges
- d. Interest groups

You can find the correct answers to these questions by taking the quiz and then submitting your answers in the Online Edition. The program will automatically score your submission. Where you miss a question, the program will provide the correct answer, a rationale for the answer, and the section number in the chapter where the topic is discussed.

Further Reading

The bicentennial of the U.S. Constitution led to a number of writings about the future of the American system. *Reforming American Government: The Bicentennial Papers of the Committee on the Constitutional System* (Boulder, CO: Westview Press, 1985), edited by Donald Robinson, brought together a series of academics and practitioners to analyze the state of American government after two hundred years and to propose some changes.

The New American Political System (Washington, D.C.: American Enterprise Institute, 1990), edited by Anthony King, includes a set of essays about contemporary changes in key political institutions. William Hudson's *American Democracy in Peril* (Chatham, NJ: Chatham House, 1998) outlines the key challenges facing America during the upcoming decades. Robert Putnam's *Bowling Alone* (New York: Simon and Schuster, 2000) takes on the issue of citizen participation with extensive empirical data, while Joseph Nye et al. analyze cynicism in *Why People Don't Trust Government* (Cambridge, MA: Harvard University Press, 1997). Robert Putnam and Lewis Feldstein provide examples of individuals and groups overcoming cynicism in Better Together (New York: Simon and Schuster, 2003).

Richard Davis' *The Web of Politics: The Internet's Impact on the American Political System* (New York: Oxford University Press, 1999) and Robert J. Klotz's *The Politics of Internet Communication* (Lanham, MD: Rowman and Littlefield Publishers, 2004) outline contemporary research on the use and impact of new technology on the political process. In *The Electronic Commonwealth: The Impact of New Technologies on Democratic Politics* (New York: Basic Books, 1988), Jeffrey Abramson, Christopher Arterton, and Gary R. Orren discuss the link between technology and democracy. Futurists Alvin and Heidi Toffler outline their view of the changing dynamics of American politics and society in *Creating a New Civilization: The Politics of the Third Wave* (Atlanta, GA: Turner Publishing, Inc., 1995). Stephen Frantzich's *Cyberage Politics 101: Mobility, Technology and Democracy* (New York: Peter Lang , 2002) explores the impact of the Internet in dampening political involvement.

Endnotes

1. Hedrick Smith, *The Power Game* (New York: Random House, 1988), 545.
2. Quoted in Smith, *The Power Game*, 566.
3. Stephen Frantzich, *Cyberage Politics 101: Mobility, Technology and Democracy* (New York: Peter Lang , 2002), 57–59, 89–90.
4. In 1967, thirty-three states petitioned Congress to call a constitutional convention. This number was one short of the required two-thirds of the states.
5. Dorothy B. James, *The Contemporary Presidency*, 2nd ed. (Indianapolis, IN: Bobbs-Merrill, 1974); Roger H. Davidson, "Breaking Up Those 'Cozy Triangles': An Impossible Dream?" in *Legislative Reform and Public Policy*, ed. Susan Welch and John G. Peters (New York: Praeger, 1977), 30–53.
6. Attributed to Senator James E. Watson by Suzy Platt, *Respectfully Quoted* (Washington, D.C.: Library of Congress, 1989), 53. This book of the quotes most often requested by members of Congress has two pages of quotes dealing with compromise.
7. U.S. Congress, House Committee on the Judiciary, Nomination of Gerald Ford to Be Vice President of the United States, 93rd Congress, first session (1973).
8. James Madison, letter to W. T. Barry, August 4, 1822. Quoted in Platt, *Respectfully Quoted*, 186.
9. Platt, *Respectfully Quoted*, 341.
10. Smith, *The Power Game*, 520.
11. The idea of reputation as a basis of presidential power was first discussed by Richard Neustadt, *Presidential Power* (New York: Wiley, 1960).
12. For a more complete discussion of this view, see Theodore J. Lowi, *The End of Liberalism* (New York: Norton, 1979).
13. Quoted in Karen Masterson, "House approves GOP budget; tight Senate vote approaches," *Houston Chronicle*, May 10, 2001, p. A8.
14. Smith, *The Power Game*, xv.

Appendix A
The Declaration of Independence[1]

In Congress,[2] July 4, 1776[3]

The Unanimous[4] Declaration of the Thirteen United States of America[5]

When in the Course of human events, it becomes necessary for one people to dissolve the political bands which have connected them with another,[6] and to assume among the Powers of the earth, the separate and equal station to which the Laws of Nature and of Nature's God entitle them, a decent respect for the opinions of mankind requires that they should declare the causes which impel them to the separation.

We hold these truths to be self-evident,[7] that all men are created equal, that they are endowed by their Creator with certain unalienable Rights,[8] that among these are Life, Liberty and the pursuit of Happiness.[9] That to secure these rights, Governments are instituted among Men, deriving their just powers from the consent of the governed. That whenever any Form of Government becomes destructive of these ends, it is the Right of the People to alter or to abolish it, and to institute new Government, laying its foundation on such principles and organizing its powers in such form, as to them shall seem most likely to effect their Safety and Happiness.[10]

Prudence, indeed, will dictate that Governments long established should not be changed for light and transient causes; and accordingly all experience hath shown, that mankind are more disposed to suffer, while evils are sufferable, than to right themselves by abolishing the forms to which they are accustomed. But when a long train of abuses and usurpations, pursuing invariably the same Object evinces a design to reduce them under absolute Despotism, it is their right, it is their duty, to throw off such Government, and to provide new Guards for their future security.

—Such has been the patient sufferance of these Colonies;[11] and such is now the necessity which constrains them to alter their former Systems of Government. The history of the present King[12] of Great Britain is a history of repeated injuries and usurpations,[13] all having in direct object the establishment of an absolute Tyranny over these States. To prove this, let Facts be submitted to a candid world.[14]

He has refused his Assent to Laws, the most wholesome and necessary for the public good.

He has forbidden his Governors to pass Laws of Immediate and pressing importance, unless suspended in their operation till his Assent should be obtained; and when so suspended, he has utterly neglected to attend to them.

He has refused to pass other Laws for the accommodation of large districts of people, unless those people would relinquish the right of Representation in the Legislature, a right inestimable to them and formidable to tyrants only.

He has called together legislative bodies at places unusual, uncomfortable, and distant from the depository of their Public Records, for the sole purpose of fatiguing them into compliance with his measures.

He has dissolved Representative Houses repeatedly, for opposing with manly firmness his invasions of the rights of the people.

He has refused for a long time, after such dissolutions, to cause others to be elected; whereby the Legislative Powers, incapable of Annihilation, have returned to the People at large for their exercise; the State remaining in the meantime exposed to all the dangers of invasion from without, and convulsions within.

He has endeavored to prevent the population of these States; for that purpose obstructing the Laws for Naturalization of Foreigners; refusing to pass others to encourage their migration hither, and raising the conditions of new Appropriations of Lands.

He has obstructed the Administration of Justice, by refusing his Assent to Laws for establishing Judiciary Powers.

He has made Judges dependent on his Will alone, for the tenure of their offices, and the amount and payment of their salaries.

He has erected a multitude of New Offices, and sent hither swarms of Officers to harass our People, and eat out their substance.

He has kept among us, in times of peace, Standing Armies without the Consent of our legislature.

He has affected to render the Military independent of and superior to the Civil Power.

He has combined with others to subject us to a jurisdiction foreign to our constitution, and unacknowledged by our laws; giving his Assent to their acts of pretended Legislation;

For quartering large bodies of armed troops among us;

For protecting them, by a mock Trial, from Punishment for any Murders which they should commit on the Inhabitants of these States;

For cutting off our Trade with all parts of the world;

For imposing taxes on us without our Consent;

For depriving us in many cases, of the benefits of Trial by Jury;

For transporting us beyond Seas to be tried for pretended offenses;

For abolishing the free System of English Laws in a neighboring Province, establishing therein an Arbitrary government, and enlarging its Boundaries so as to render it at once an example and fit instrument for introducing the same absolute rule into these Colonies;

For taking away our Charters, abolishing our most valuable Laws, and altering fundamentally the Forms of our Government;

For suspending our own Legislature, and declaring themselves invested with Power to legislate for us in all cases whatsoever.

Annotated by Howard Ernst (Associate Professor of Political Science at the United States Naval Academy and Senior Scholar at the University of Virginia Center for Politics). Ernst is a co-editor of *Dangerous Democracy? The Battle Over Ballot Initiatives in America* (2001) and author of *Chesapeake Bay Blues: Science, Politics, and the Struggle to Save the Bay* (2003).

He has abdicated Government here, by declaring us out of his Protection and waging War against us.

He has plundered our seas, ravaged our Coasts, burnt our towns, and destroyed the lives of our people.

He is at this time transporting large armies of foreign mercenaries to compleat the works of death, desolution and tyranny, already begun with circumstances of Cruelty & perfidy scarcely paralleled in the most barbarous ages, and totally unworthy the Head of a civilized nation.

He has constrained our fellow Citizens taken Captive on the high Seas to bear Arms against their Country, to become the executioners of their friends and Brethren, or to fall themselves by their Hands.

He has excited domestic insurrections amongst us, and has endeavored to bring on the inhabitants of our frontiers, the merciless Indian Savages, whose known rule of war-fare, is an undistinguished destruction of all ages, sexes and conditions.[15]

In every stage of these Oppressions We have Petitioned for Redress in the most humble terms: Our repeated Petitions have been answered only by repeated injury. A Prince, whose character is thus marked by every act which may define a Tyrant, is unfit to be the ruler of a free People.

Nor have We been wanting in attention to our British brethren. We have warned them from time to time of attempts by their legislature to extend an unwarrantable jurisdiction over us. We have reminded them of the circumstances of our emigration and settlement here. We have appealed to their native justice and magnanimity, and we have conjured them by the ties of our common kindred to disavow these usurpations, which would inevitably interrupt our connections and correspondence. They too have been deaf to the voice of justice and of consanguinity. We must, therefore, acquiesce in the necessity, which denounces our Separation, and hold them, as we hold the rest of mankind, Enemies in War, in Peace Friends.

We,[16] therefore, the Representatives of the United States of America, in General Congress, Assembled, appealing to the Supreme Judge of the world[17] for the rectitude of our intentions, do, in the Name and by Authority of the good People of these Colonies, solemnly publish and declare, That these United Colonies are, and of Right ought to be Free and Independent States; that they are Absolved from all Allegiance to the British Crown, and that all political connection between them and the State of Great Britain, is and ought to be totally dissolved; and that as Free and Independent States, they have full Power to levy War, conclude Peace, contract Alliances, establish Commerce, and to do all other Acts and Things which Independent States may of right do. And for the support of this Declaration, with a firm reliance on the Protection of Divine Providence, we mutually pledge to each other our lives, our Fortunes and our sacred Honor.[18]

Annotations

1. The Declaration of Independence is comprised of four distinct sections. (1) The first paragraph of the Declaration functions as the document's "preamble"—its introductory section that states the reasons the document was written. (2) The second and third paragraphs of the Declaration assert the political philosophy on which the document is based. (3) The bulk of the Declaration, from paragraph four through the second to last paragraph, consists of a long list of grievances the colonists suffered at the hands of King George III. (4) The final paragraph is the document's legal declaration—the section where independence is formally declared.
2. During the summer of 1776, delegates from the Continental Congress met at Pennsylvania's State House in Philadelphia. The modest building, commonly referred to as Independence Hall, served as the birthplace of the nation.
3. According to Jefferson's notes, the high temperature for the day was 76 degrees, the low was 68 degrees, and the prevailing wind was from the southeast. It was part of Jefferson's daily ritual to record weather observations, and July 4, 1776 was to be no exception.
4. Thomas Jefferson is often credited as being the author of the Declaration of Independence. While he is the document's primary author, and he penned the first draft of the Declaration, Jefferson was but one member of a five-person committee that was responsible for creating the Declaration. Other members of the committee included John Adams, Benjamin Franklin, Robert R. Livingston, and Robert Sherman. Jefferson, who was only thirty-three years of age when he drafted the Declaration, never claimed to be the primary source of the revolutionary ideas found in the Declaration. In fact, Jefferson was initially so displeased with the version of the Declaration that emerged from the committee that he frequently sent copies of his original draft, along with the committee's final draft, to his close friends so that they would not confuse his work with that of the committee. Later in life, Jefferson more fully appreciated the significance of the document and his role in its creation, and requested that "Author of the Declaration of Independence" be the first accomplishment inscribed on his tombstone.
5. This represents the first usage of the phrase "United States of America" in a formal document.
6. A contentious point among historians who study this period concerns the point in time when the "American identity" was born (i.e., the point when the colonists became a distinct people, separate from their British identity). In fact, the colonists themselves where not of like mind concerning this issue, with some clinging to their British identity even as the Revolution unfolded around them. While the Declaration, with its bold claims of independence, severed political ties with Britain, it would take some time for the former colonists to sever their psychological ties to the motherland.
7. In Jefferson's original draft, he referred to these truths as "sacred and undeniable."
8. This is one of the most important phrases in the Declaration. It establishes that people have basic rights that cannot legitimately be denied by government. The founding concept of unalienable rights, or natural rights, has evolved into the contemporary concept of "human rights," rights that all people are entitled to regardless of their particular form of government or their status in society.
9. Ironically this passage is one of the most famous and least original phrases in the Declaration of Independence. Well before Jefferson penned the phrase, John Locke wrote in his Second Treatise on Government (1690) of the pursuit of "life, liberty and property." And George Mason, when drafting the Virginia Declaration of Rights, also published before the Declaration of Independence (June of 1776) and read by Thomas Jefferson, states a nearly identical phrase:

    > That all men are by nature equally free and independent and have certain inherent rights, of which, when they enter into a state of society, they cannot, by any compact, deprive or divest their posterity; namely, the enjoyment of life and liberty, the means of acquiring and possessing property, and pursuing and obtaining happiness and safety.

    When the New England Federalist, Timothy Pickering, questioned the originality of Jefferson's contribution to the Declaration, Jefferson insisted that he referred to no books or pamphlets when drafting the document, but he never denied being influenced by earlier works.

10. In this timeless passage, the Declaration affirms the principle of "popular sovereignty" for the new country and marks a turning point in world history. Since 1776, these words have served as inspiration for oppressed people around the globe. Part of the universal power of the passage is that it declares its truths to be "self evident" and that they apply to "all" people.
11. In this section, Jefferson downplayed the numerous acts of rebellion and defiance that had fueled the flames of independence throughout the mid-1700s. Some of the most significant early acts of defiance included: the formation of the Stamp Act Congress in New York (1765), the creation of the Boston Boycott Agreement (1768), the formation of the Sons of Liberty (a rebellious group of anti-British dissenters led by Samuel Adams), the burning of the British customs vessel "Gaspee" (1772), the Boston Tea Party (1773), the meeting of the First Continental Congress (1774), the publication of Jefferson's paper "A Summary View of the Rights of British America" (1774), Patrick Henry's famous speech demanding "liberty or death" (1775), firing on British troops at Lexington and Concord (1775), the meeting of the Second Continental Congress (1775), and the publication of Common Sense by Thomas Paine (1776).
12. Note that the Declaration is intended for the King, not the British Parliament. The colonists had long held that they were subjects of the King, not the Parliament in which they had no formal representation. Though not mentioned by name, the "King" referred to in this section was George III, who ascended to the throne in 1760. King George's heavy-handed treatment of the colonies was a primary factor that drove the colonists down the path of independence. The erratic behavior and often-irrational decisions of George III have led several scholars to question his sanity during the critical years from 1760–1776.
13. When reading this section, it is important to keep in mind the political context of the time. Following the French and Indian War (1756–1763), a war in which Britain and its North American colonies defeated France and its Indian allies, relations between Britain and the colonies had steadily deteriorated. Some of the key actions taken by Britain that contributed to increased tensions with the colonies included: the Sugar Act (1764), the Stamp Act (1765), the Tea Act (1773), the Boston Massacre (1770), the Intolerable Acts (1774), the firing of shots at Lexington and Concord (1775), and the rejection of the Olive Branch Petition (1775).
14. This section of the Declaration, which lists specific grievances against Britain and is perhaps the least important from a historical perspective, closely resembles the preamble of a proposed constitution that Jefferson drafted in June of 1776.
15. In Jefferson's original draft, this section was followed by a lengthy paragraph that accused the king of suppressing legislative attempts by the colonies to end the slave trade, which Jefferson referred to as "a war against human nature itself, violating its most sacred rights of life & liberty." Opposition from delegates from both the south and the north forced Jefferson's paragraph to be deleted from the final draft.
16. On July 4, 1776 only two people signed the Declaration of Independence, John Hancock, who served as the President of the Congress, and Charles Thomson, who was the Secretary of the Congress and signed only as a witness to the authenticity of Hancock's signature. The original Declaration of Independence, signed by Hancock and Thomson on July 4, 1776, was lost after being sent to the printer and has not since been located. It was not until August 2, 1776 that the engrossed, or parchment, Declaration was signed by most of the delegates. It is also worth noting that several of the delegates who signed on August 2, 1776 were not present at the earlier vote in July and, likewise, some of the delegates who voted in favor of independence were not available to sign the document in August. The Declaration of Independence that is carefully stored and exhibited in Exhibition Hall at the National Archives Building in Washington, D.C. is the parchment copy signed on August 2, 1776.
17. Interestingly, the Declaration makes two references to the divine. In the second paragraph of the Declaration the "Creator" is mentioned as the source of unalienable rights, and in this section the Declaration appeals to the "Supreme Judge of the world." These references distinguish the Declaration from the Constitution and many of the nation's other founding documents, which are devoid of references to the divine.
18. Two of the most interesting stories concerning the signing of the Declaration relate to John Hancock and Benjamin Franklin. Legend has it that Hancock was adamant that the signers be unanimous in their support. Responding to Hancock's plea, Franklin is reported to have said, "Yes, we must indeed all hang together, or most assuredly we shall hang separately." It is also alleged that Hancock signed his name large enough for King George III to be able to read it without having to wear glasses. Hancock's flamboyant signature has made his name synonymous with the act of signing documents.

Appendix B
The Articles of Confederation[1]

March 1781[2]

To all to whom these presents shall come, we the undersigned delegates of the states affixed to our names, send greeting:

Whereas the delegates of the United States of America in Congress[3] assembled,[4] did, on the fifteenth day of November in the year of our Lord seventeen seventy-seven, and in the second year of the Independence of America, agree to Certain Articles of Confederation and perpetual union between the states of New Hampshire, Massachusetts Bay, Rhode Island and Providence Plantations, Connecticut, New York, New Jersey, Pennsylvania, Delaware, Maryland, Virginia, North Carolina, South Carolina and Georgia in the words following, viz:

The Articles of Confederation and Perpetual Union Between the States of New Hampshire, Massachusetts Bay, Rhode Island and Providence Plantations, Connecticut, New York, New Jersey, Pennsylvania, Delaware, Maryland, Virginia, North Carolina, South Carolina and Georgia.[5]

ARTICLE I. The style of this Confederacy shall be "The United States of America."[6]

ARTICLE II. Each state retains its sovereignty,[7] freedom and independence, and every power, jurisdiction and right which is not by this Confederation expressly delegated to the United States in Congress assembled.

ARTICLE III. The said states hereby severally enter into a firm league of friendship with each other for their common defence, the security of their liberties, and their mutual and general welfare, binding themselves to assist each other against all force offered to, or attacks made upon them, or any of them, on account of religion, sovereignty, trade, or any other pretence whatever.

ARTICLE IV. The better to secure and perpetuate mutual friendship and intercourse among the people of the different States in this Union, the free inhabitants of each of these states, paupers, vagabonds and fugitives from justice excepted, shall be entitled to all privileges and immunities of free citizens in the several states; and the people of each state shall have free ingress and regress to and from any other state, and shall enjoy therein all the privileges of trade and commerce, subject to the same duties, impositions and restrictions as the inhabitants thereof respectively; provided, that such restrictions shall not extend so far as to prevent the removal of property imported into any state, to any other state of which the owner is an inhabitant; provided also, that no imposition, duties or restriction shall be laid by any state on the property of the United States, or either of them.

If any person guilty of or charged with treason, felony, or other high misdemeanor in any state, shall flee from justice, and be found in any of the United States, he shall upon demand of the governor or executive power of the state from which he fled, be delivered up and removed to the state having jurisdiction of his offense.

Full faith and credit shall be given in each of these states to the records, acts and judicial proceedings of the courts and magistrates of every other state.

ARTICLE V.[8] For the more convenient management of the general interests of the United States, delegates shall be annually appointed[9] in such manner as the legislature of each state shall direct, to meet in Congress on the first Monday in November, in every year, with a power, reserved to each state, to recall its delegates, or any of them, at any time within the year, and to send others in their stead, for the remainder of the year.

No state shall be represented in Congress by less than two, nor by more than seven members; and no person shall be capable of being a delegate for more than three years in any term of six years;[10] nor shall any person, being a delegate, be capable of holding any office under the United States, for which he, or another for his benefit receives any salary, fees or emolument of any kind.[11]

Each state shall maintain its own delegates in a meeting of the states,[12] and while they act as members of the committee of the states.

In determining questions in the United States, in Congress assembled, each state shall have one vote.[13]

Freedom of speech and debate in Congress shall not be impeached or questioned in any court, or place out of Congress, and the members of Congress shall be protected in their persons from arrests and imprisonments, during the time of their going to and from, and attendance on Congress, except for treason, felony, or breach of the peace.

ARTICLE VI.[14] No state without the consent of the United States in Congress assembled, shall send any embassy to, or receive any embassy from, or enter into any conference, agreement, alliance or treaty with any king, prince or state; nor shall any person holding any office of profit or trust under the United States, or any of them, accept of any, present, emolument, office or title of any kind whatever from any king, prince or foreign state; nor shall the United States in Congress assembled, or any of them, grant any title of nobility.

No two or more states shall enter into any treaty, confederation or alliance whatever between them, without the consent of the United States in Congress assembled, specifying accurately the purposes for which the same is to be entered into, and how long it shall continue.

No state shall lay any impost or duties, which may interfere with any stipulations in treaties, entered into by the United States in Congress assembled, with any king, prince or state, in pursuance

---

Annotated by Howard Ernst (Associate Professor of Political Science at the United States Naval Academy and Senior Scholar at the University of Virginia Center for Politics). Ernst is a co-editor of *Dangerous Democracy? The Battle Over Ballot Initiatives in America* (2001) and author of *Chesapeake Bay Blues: Science, Politics, and the Struggle to Save the Bay* (2003).

of any treaties already proposed by Congress to the courts of France and Spain.

No vessels of war shall be kept up in time of peace by any state, except such number only as shall be deemed necessary by the United States in Congress assembled, for the defence of such state, or its trade; nor shall any body of forces be kept up by any state, in time of peace except such number only, as in the judgment of the United States, Congress assembled, shall be deemed requisite to garrison the forts necessary for the defence of such state; but every state shall always keep up a well regulated and disciplined militia, sufficiently armed and accoutered, and shall provide and constantly have ready for use, in public stores, a due number of field pieces and tents, and a proper quantity of arms, ammunition and camp equipage.

No state shall engage in any war without the consent of the United States in Congress assembled, unless such state be actually invaded by enemies, or shall have received certain advice of a resolution being formed by some nation of Indians to invade such state, and the danger is so imminent as not to admit of a delay, till the United States in Congress assembled can be consulted: nor shall any state grant commissions to any ships or vessels of war, nor letters of marque or reprisal, except it be after a declaration of war by the United States in Congress assembled, and then only against the kingdom or state and the subjects thereof, against which war has been so declared, and under such regulations as shall be established by the United States in Congress assembled, unless such state be infested by pirates, in which case vessels of war be fitted out for that occasion, and kept so long as the danger shall continue, or until the United States in Congress assembled shall determine otherwise.

ARTICLE VII. When land forces are raised by any state for the common defence, all officers of or under the rank of colonel, shall be appointed by the Legislature of each state respectively by whom such forces shall be raised, or in such manner as such state shall direct, all vacancies shall be filled up by the state which first made the appointment.

ARTICLE VIII.[15] All charges of war, and all other expenses that shall be incurred for the common defence or general welfare, and allowed by the United States in Congress assembled, shall be defrayed out of a common treasury, which shall be supplied by the several states, in proportion to the value of all land within each state, granted to or surveyed for any person, as such land and the buildings and improvements thereon shall be estimated according to such mode as the United States in Congress assembled, shall from time to time direct and appoint.

The taxes for paying that proportion shall be laid and levied by the authority and direction of the legislatures of the several states within the time agreed upon by the United States in Congress assembled.

ARTICLE IX.[16] The United States in Congress assembled, shall have the sole and exclusive right and power of determining on peace and war except in the cases mentioned in the sixth article; of sending and receiving ambassadors; entering into treaties and alliances; provided that no treaty of commerce shall be made whereby the legislative power of the respective states shall be restrained from imposing such imposts and duties on foreigners, as their own people are subjected to, or from prohibiting the exportation or importation of any species of goods or commodities whatsoever; of establishing rules for deciding in all cases, what captures on land or water shall be legal, and in what manner prizes taken by land or naval forces in the service of the United States shall be divided or appropriated; of granting letters of marque and reprisal in times of peace; appointing courts for the trial of piracies and felonies committed on the high seas and establishing courts for receiving and determining finally appeals in all cases of captures, provided that no member of Congress shall be appointed a judge of any of said courts.

The United States in Congress assembled[17] shall also be the last resort on appeal in all disputes and differences now subsisting or that hereafter may arise between two or more states concerning boundary, jurisdiction or any other cause whatever; which authority shall always be exercised in the manner following. Whenever the legislative or executive authority or lawful agent of any state in controversy with another shall present a petition to Congress, stating the matter in question and praying for a hearing, notice thereof shall be given by order of Congress to the legislative or executive authority of the other state in controversy, and a day assigned for the appearance of the parties by their lawful agents, who shall then be directed to appoint by joint consent commissioners or judges to constitute a court for hearing and determining the matter in question: but if they can not agree, Congress shall name three persons out of each of the United States, and from the list of such persons each party shall alternately strike out one, the petitioners beginning, until the number shall be reduced to thirteen; and from that number not less than seven, nor more than nine names, as Congress shall direct, shall in the presence of Congress be drawn out by lot, and the persons whose names shall be so drawn or any five of them, shall be commissioners or judges, to hear and finally determine the controversy, so always as a major part of the judges who shall hear the cause shall agree in the determination: and if either party shall neglect to attend at the day appointed, without showing reasons, which Congress judge sufficient, or being present shall refuse to strike, the Congress shall proceed to nominate three persons out of each state, and the Secretary of Congress shall strike in behalf of such party absent or refusing; and the judgment and sentence of the court to be appointed, in the manner before prescribed, shall be final and conclusive; and if any of the parties shall refuse to submit to the authority of such court, or to appear or defend their claim or cause, the court shall, nevertheless proceed to pronounce sentence, or judgment, which shall in like manner be final and decisive, the judgment or sentence and other proceeds being in either case transmitted to Congress, and lodged among the acts of Congress for the security of the parties concerned: provided that every commissioner, before he sits in judgment, shall take an oath to be administered by one of the judges of the supreme or superior court of the state where the cause shall be tried, "well and truly to hear and determine the matter in question, according to the best of his judgment without favor, affection, or hope of reward": provided also that no state shall be deprived of territory for the benefit of the United States.

All controversies concerning the private right of soil claimed under different grants of two or more states, whose jurisdiction as they may respect such lands, and the states which passed such grants are adjusted, the said grants or either of them being at the same time claimed to have originated antecedent to such settlement of jurisdiction, shall on the petition of either party to the Congress of the United States, be finally determined as near as may be in the same manner as is before prescribed for deciding disputes respecting territorial jurisdiction between the different states.

The United States in Congress assembled shall also have the sole and exclusive right and power of regulating the alloy and value of coin struck by their own authority, or by that of respective state fixing the standard of weights and measures throughout the United States regulating the trade, and managing all affairs with the Indians, not members of any of the states, provided that the legislative right of state within its own limits be not infringed or violated; establishing and regulating post offices from one state to another, throughout all the United States, and exacting such postage on the papers passing through the same as may be requisite to defray the expenses of the said office; appointing all officers of the land forces, in the service of the United States, excepting regimental officers; appointing all the officers of the naval forces, and commissioning all officers whatever in the service of the United States; making rules for the government and regulation of said land and naval forces, and directing their operations.

The United States in Congress assembled shall have authority to appoint a committee, to sit in the recess of Congress, to be denominated "a Committee of the States," and to consist of one delegate from each state; and to appoint such other committees and civil officers as may be necessary for managing the general affairs of the United States under their direction; to appoint one of their number to preside, provided that no person be allowed to serve in the office of president more than one year in any term of three years; to ascertain the necessary sums of money to be raised for the service of the United States, and to appropriate and apply the same for defraying the public expenses; to borrow money, or emit bills on the credit of the United States, transmitting every half year to the respective states an account of the sums of money so borrowed or emitted; to build and equip a navy; to agree upon the number of land forces, and to make requisitions from each state for its quota, in proportion to the number of white inhabitants in such state; which requisition shall be binding, and therepon the legislature of each state shall appoint the regimental officers, raise the men and clothe, arm and equip them in a soldierlike manner, at the expense of the United States; and the officers and men so clothed, armed and equipped shall march to the place appointed, and within the time agreed on by the United States in Congress assembled: but if the United States in Congress assembled shall, on consideration of circumstances judge proper that any state should not raise men, or should raise a smaller number than its quota, and that any other state should raise a greater number of men than the quota thereof, such extra number shall be raised, officered, clothed, armed and equipped in the same manner as the quota of such state, unless the legislature of such state shall judge that such extra number can not be safely spared out of the same, in which case they shall raise, officer, clothe, arm and equip as many of such extra number as they judge can be safely spared. And the officers and men so clothed, armed and equipped, shall march to the place appointed, and within the time agreed on by the United States in Congress assembled.

The United States in Congress assembled[18] shall never engage in war, nor grant letters of marque and reprisal in time of peace, nor enter into any treaties or alliances, nor coin money, nor regulate the value thereof, nor ascertain the sums and expenses necessary for the defense and welfare of the United States, or any of them, nor emit bills, nor borrow money on the credit of the United States, nor appropriate money, nor agree upon the number of vessels of war, to be built or purchased, or the number of land or sea forces to be raised, nor appoint a commander-in-chief of the army or navy, unless nine states assent to the same: nor shall a question on any other point, except for adjourning from day to day be determined, unless by the votes of a majority of the United States in Congress assembled.

The Congress of the United States shall have power to adjourn to any time within the year, and to any place within the United States, so that no period of adjournment be for a longer duration than the space of six months; and shall publish the journal of their proceedings monthly, except such parts thereof relating to treaties, alliances or military operations, as in their judgment require secrecy; and the yeas and nays of the delegates of each state on any question shall be entered on the journal, when it is desired by any delegate; and the delegates of a state, or any of them, at his or their request, shall be furnished with transcript of the said journal, except such parts as are above excepted to lay before the legislatures of the several states.

ARTICLE X. The Committee of the States, or any nine of them shall be authorized to execute, in the recess of Congress, such of the powers of Congress as the United States in Congress assembled, by the consent of nine states, shall from time to time think expedient to vest them with; provided that no power be delegated to the said committee for the exercise of which, by the Articles of Confederation, the voice of nine states in the Congress of the United States assembled is requisite.

ARTICLE XI.[19] Canada acceding to this Confederation, and joining in the measures of the United States, shall be admitted into, and entitled to all the advantages of this Union: but no other colony shall be admitted into the same, unless such admission be agreed to by nine states.

ARTICLE XII. All bills of credit emitted, moneys borrowed and debts contracted by, or under the authority of Congress, before the assembling of the United States, in pursuance of the present Confederation, shall be deemed and considered as a charge against the United States, for payment and satisfaction whereof the said United States and the public faith are hereby solemnly pledged.

ARTICLE XIII. Every state shall abide by the determinations of the United States in Congress assembled, on all questions which by this Confederation are submitted to them. And the Articles of this Confederation shall be inviolably observed by every state, and the Union shall be perpetual; nor shall any alteration at any time hereafter be made in any of them, unless such alteration be agreed to in a Congress of the United States, and be afterwards confirmed by the legislatures of every state.[20]

AND WHEREAS it hath pleased the Great Governor of the world to incline the hearts of the legislatures we respectively represent in Congress, to approve of, and to authorize us to ratify the said Articles of Confederation and perpetual Union. Know ye that we the undersigned delegates, by virtue of the power and authority to us given for that purpose, do by these presents, in the name and in behalf of our respective constituents, fully and entirely ratify and confirm each and every of the said Articles of Confederation and perpetual Union, and all and singular the matters and things therein contained: and we do further solemnly plight and engage the faith of our respective constituents, that they shall abide by the determinations of the United States Congress assembled, on all questions, which by the said Confederation are submitted to them. And that the articles thereof shall be inviolably observed by the states we respectively represent, and that the Union shall be perpetual.

IN WITNESS WHEREOF we have hereunto set our hands in Congress. Done at Philadelphia in the State of Pennsylvania the ninth day of July in the year of our Lord one thousand seven hundred and seventy-eight, and in the third year of the independence of America.

On the part & behalf of the State of New Hampshire:

JOSIAH BARTLETT

JOHN WENTWORTH JUNR. August 8th 1778

On the part and behalf of The State of Massachusetts Bay JOHN HANCOCK SAMUEL ADAMS ELBRIDGE GERRY FRANCIS DANA JAMES LOVELL SAMUEL HOLTEN

On the part and behalf of the State of Rhode Island and Providence Plantations WILLIAM ELLERY HENRY MARCHANT JOHN COLLINS

On the part and behalf of the State of Connecticut ROGER SHERMAN SAMUEL HUNTINGTON OLIVER WOLCOTT TITUS HOSMER ANDREW ADAMS

On the Part and Behalf of the State of New York JAMES DUANE FRANCIS LEWIS WM DUER GOUV MORRIS

On the Part and in Behalf of the State of New Jersey November 26, 1778 JNO WITHERSPOON NATHANIEL SCUDDER

On the part and behalf of the State of Pennsylvania ROBT MORRIS DANIEL ROBERDEAU JOHN BAYARD SMITH WILLIAM CLINGAN JOSEPH REED 22nd July 1778

On the part & behalf of the State of Delaware THO McKEAN February 12, 1779 JOHN DICKINSON May 5th 1779 NICHOLAS VAN DYKE

On the part and behalf of the State of Maryland JOHN HANSON March 1 1781 DANIEL CARROLL do

On the Part and Behalf of the State of Virginia RICHARD HENRY LEE JOHN BANISTER THOMAS ADAMS JNo HARVIE FRANCIS LIGHTFOOT LEE

On the part and Behalf of the State of No Carolina JOHN PENN July 21st 1778 CORNs HARNETT JNo WILLIAMS

On the part & behalf of the State of South Carolina HENRY LAURENS WILLIAM HENRY DRAYTON JNo MATHEWS RICHD HUTSON THOs HEYWARD Junr

On the part & behalf of the State of Georgia JNo WALTON 24th July 1778 EDWD TELFAIR EDWD LANGWORTHY

Annotations

1. While the Declaration of Independence was being debated in Philadelphia in the summer of 1776, plans for a post-independence government were already underway. On June 7, 1776, a committee of the Continental Congress, led by John Dickinson of Pennsylvania, was formed to draft the nation's first governing document. By the winter of 1777, Congress had approved a greatly revised version of Dickinson's original plan. It would take another four years for the Articles of Confederation to be ratified by the final state (Maryland) and for the document to become the law of the land on March 1, 1781.
2. The biggest sticking point in the debate over ratification, a point that stalled ratification for several years and had little to do with constitutional governance, was the parochial concern over who would control western lands. Several states wanted western lands to be controlled by the federal government, while the seven states that had claims to western territories demanded that the states control western expansion. Since ratification required unanimous approval by the states and neither side was initially willing to relinquish their position, this single issue stalled the ratification process and, more importantly, threatened the success of the nascent republic. Eventually, the states without land claims won the debate, as each state relinquished its land claims, opening the door for ratification of the Articles of Confederation.
3. Though lacking the written authority of a constitution, the Continental Congress functioned as the de facto national government from September 5, 1774, when the First Continental Congress met, to March 1, 1781, when the Articles of Confederation were ratified. This remarkable legislative body was able to successfully declare independence from Britain, raise an army, repel one of the most powerful naval forces in history, negotiate with foreign nations, and lay the foundations for economic growth.
4. Note the peculiar phrase "delegates of the United States of America in Congress assembled." This telling passage suggests the extent to which the states desired to retain their sovereignty under the Articles of Confederation. The "delegates" were acting on behalf of the sovereign "states," and did not claim to take their authority directly from the American people. Moreover, the term "United States of America in Congress assembled" gives primacy to the states and presents Congress, the sole branch of the federal government, as a transient body that assembles from time to time. Compare this opening line to that of the Constitution, which states "We the People of the United States, in Order to form a more perfect Union...do ordain and establish this Constitution for the United States of America."
5. While the states had achieved several successes under the Articles of Confederation (e.g., defeated the British, negotiated the Treaty of Paris, and protected individual liberties), rule under the Articles of Confederation was rife with problems by the late 1780s. Since action under the articles required approval from nine of the thirteen states and amending the articles required approval by all thirteen states, governmental action and reform was exceedingly difficult to achieve. Moreover, Congress did not have the power to collect taxes from individuals or to regulate interstate commerce, further limiting its ability to act. Under the Articles of Confederation, British troops remained on western lands; Spanish troops threatened the Mississippi; states began to print their own currency and failed to contribute their share to the national treasury. Moreover, the Federalist advocates of a stronger constitution pointed to Shays's Rebellion, a 1786 Massachusetts rebellion led by Daniel Shays that aimed to forcibly halt foreclosures on farms by closing the state court, as an example of the growing economic turmoil and military weakness that plagued the nation.
6. Still a relatively novel term in the late 1770's, the phrase "United States of America" was made popular just a few years earlier by the Declaration of Independence.
7. Article Two of the Articles of Confederation explicitly states a general principle that runs throughout the document. It explains that each state "retains its sovereignty." This aspect of the Articles of

Confederation has led scholars to compare the Articles to a treaty among nations, in which each nation, or in this case each state, agrees to certain terms of the treaty but does not relinquish its sovereign authority. Compare this article to the Constitution's weaker statement of states' rights—the 10th Amendment—, which states "The powers not delegated to the United States by the Constitution, nor prohibited by it to the States, are reserved to the States respectively, or to the people."

8. The Articles of Confederation established a "unicameral" legislature (i.e., a legislative body that is not divided into distinct branches). In contrast, the Constitution created a bicameral legislature (i.e., a legislative body divided into two distinct branches—the House and Senate).
9. There are two important points to note here. First, under the Articles, representatives to Congress served one-year terms. In contrast, under the U.S. Constitution, members of the House serve two-year terms and members of the Senate serve six-year terms. Second, the word "appointed" is used instead of elected or another more democratic term. The Articles of Confederation left it entirely up to the state legislatures to appoint representatives to Congress. This arrangement reaffirmed the fact that the states retained their sovereignty, and that without direct state support Congress could not even select members.
10. Unlike the Constitution, The Articles of Confederation provided for a form of "term limits," with no person permitted to serve more than three out of every six years.
11. The Articles of Confederation also differed from the Constitution in that it did not articulate a specific scheme for congressional representation. The Constitution specified that each state would be allowed two senators and that representation in the House would be based on each state's population. In contrast, the Articles of Confederation only established general parameters for representation (at least two members from each state and no more than seven from a particular state) and left it up to the state legislatures to appoint members of Congress. Since the Articles of Confederation gave each state equal representation in Congress (i.e., one voter per state), the size of each state's congressional delegation was less important than it became under the Constitution.
12. To guard against power flowing to the federal government, the Articles of Confederation called on the states, not the federal government, to provide for congressional pay.
13. Since each state retained its sovereignty under the Articles of Confederation, it made sense that each state would be given equal representation. This arrangement is comparable to international agreements in which each country is allocated a single vote, regardless of each nation's relative economic status or population.
14. Article VI enumerates several prohibitions placed on the states by the Articles of Confederation. Some of the barred activities included: establishing foreign embassies, entering in foreign treaties, accepting foreign titles, entering into inter-state treaties, possessing vessels of war during peacetime, and engaging in offensive military campaigns.
15. Though each state was politically equal under the Articles of Confederation, they were not equally responsible for contributing to the national defense. Wealthier states, which had more disposable resources and more to lose from a foreign invasion, were expected to pay a larger share for the national defense than less affluent states.
16. This paragraph outlines several specific legislative powers under the Articles of Confederation (including the power to make war, receive ambassadors, and enter into foreign treaties). Lacking an executive branch, Congress was solely responsible for providing for the nation's defense and for promoting international agreements.
17. Not only did Congress possess powers commonly thought of as executive powers, Congress also possessed important judicial powers under the Articles of Confederation. Namely, Congress had the sole authority to resolve interstate disputes; a power that would rest with the Supreme Court after the Constitution was adopted.
18. It is interesting to note that the Articles of Confederation did not strictly adhere to the concept of majority rule. For many of the most controversial and arguably most important functions of government, the Articles of Confederation required a super majority (i.e., support from nine out of the thirteen states). This conservative feature of the Articles assured that important decisions could not be made without widespread support within Congress.
19. In this Article, Canada was offered an open invitation to join the Confederation. Not even a vote from Congress would have been required for Canada to become part of the United States.
20. Though the Articles of Confederation clearly state that the union shall be "perpetual" and that amending the agreement would require confirmation from each state, America's founding fathers disregarded this aspect of the Articles when they framed and ratified the Constitution.

Appendix C

The Constitution of the United States of America[1]

Ratified June 21, 1788[2]

We the People[3] of the United States,[4] in Order to form a more perfect Union,[5] establish Justice, insure domestic Tranquility, provide for the common defence, promote the general Welfare, and secure the Blessings of Liberty to ourselves and our Posterity,[6] do ordain and establish this Constitution[7] for the United States of America.[8]

Article. I.[9]

Section. 1.

All legislative Powers herein granted shall be vested in a Congress of the United States, which shall consist of a Senate and House of Representatives.[10]

Section. 2.

Clause 1: The House of Representatives shall be composed of Members chosen every second Year by the People of the several States, and the Electors in each State shall have the Qualifications requisite for Electors of the most numerous Branch of the State Legislature.

Clause 2: No Person shall be a Representative who shall not have attained to the Age of twenty five Years, and been seven Years a Citizen of the United States, and who shall not, when elected, be an Inhabitant of that State in which he shall be chosen.

Clause 3: Representatives and direct Taxes shall be apportioned among the several States which may be included within this Union, according to their respective Numbers, which shall be determined by adding to the whole Number of free Persons, including those bound to Service for a Term of Years, and excluding Indians not taxed, three fifths of all other Persons. The actual Enumeration shall be made within three Years after the first Meeting of the Congress of the United States, and within every subsequent Term of ten Years, in such Manner as they shall by Law direct. The Number of Representatives shall not exceed one for every thirty Thousand, but each State shall have at Least one Representative; and until such enumeration shall be made, the State of New Hampshire shall be entitled to chuse three, Massachusetts eight, Rhode-Island and Providence Plantations one, Connecticut five, New-York six, New Jersey four, Pennsylvania eight, Delaware one, Maryland six, Virginia ten, North Carolina five, South Carolina five, and Georgia three.

Clause 4: When vacancies happen in the Representation from any State, the Executive Authority thereof shall issue Writs of Election to fill such Vacancies.

Clause 5: The House of Representatives shall chuse their Speaker and other Officers; and shall have the sole Power of Impeachment.

Section. 3.

Clause 1: The Senate of the United States shall be composed of two Senators from each State, chosen by the Legislature thereof, for six Years; and each Senator shall have one Vote.

Clause 2: Immediately after they shall be assembled in Consequence of the first Election, they shall be divided as equally as may be into three Classes. The Seats of the Senators of the first Class shall be vacated at the Expiration of the second Year, of the second Class at the Expiration of the fourth Year, and of the third Class at the Expiration of the sixth Year, so that one third may be chosen every second Year; and if Vacancies happen by Resignation, or otherwise, during the Recess of the Legislature of any State, the Executive thereof may make temporary Appointments until the next Meeting of the Legislature, which shall then fill such Vacancies.

Clause 3: No Person shall be a Senator who shall not have attained to the Age of thirty Years, and been nine Years a Citizen of the United States, and who shall not, when elected, be an Inhabitant of that State for which he shall be chosen.

Clause 4: The Vice President of the United States shall be President of the Senate, but shall have no Vote, unless they be equally divided.

Clause 5: The Senate shall chuse their other Officers, and also a President pro tempore, in the Absence of the Vice President, or when he shall exercise the Office of President of the United States.

Clause 6: The Senate shall have the sole Power to try all Impeachments. When sitting for that Purpose, they shall be on Oath or Affirmation. When the President of the United States is tried, the Chief Justice shall preside: And no Person shall be convicted without the Concurrence of two thirds of the Members present.

Clause 7: Judgment in Cases of Impeachment shall not extend further than to removal from Office, and disqualification to hold and enjoy any Office of honor, Trust or Profit under the United States: but the Party convicted shall nevertheless be liable and subject to Indictment, Trial, Judgment and Punishment, according to Law.

Section. 4.

Clause 1: The Times, Places and Manner of holding Elections for Senators and Representatives, shall be prescribed in each State by the Legislature thereof; but the Congress may at any time by Law make or alter such Regulations, except as to the Places of chusing Senators.

Clause 2: The Congress shall assemble at least once in every Year, and such Meeting shall be on the first Monday in December, unless they shall by Law appoint a different Day.

Section. 5.

Clause 1: Each House shall be the Judge of the Elections, Returns and Qualifications of its own Members, and a Majority of each shall constitute a Quorum to do Business; but a smaller Number may adjourn from day to day, and may be authorized to compel the Attendance of absent Members, in such Manner, and under such Penalties as each House may provide.

Annotated by Howard Ernst (Associate Professor of Political Science at the United States Naval Academy and Senior Scholar at the University of Virginia Center for Politics). Ernst is a co-editor of *Dangerous Democracy? The Battle Over Ballot Initiatives in America* (2001) and author of *Chesapeake Bay Blues: Science, Politics, and the Struggle to Save the Bay* (2003).

Clause 2: Each House may determine the Rules of its Proceedings, punish its Members for disorderly Behaviour, and, with the Concurrence of two thirds, expel a Member.

Clause 3: Each House shall keep a Journal of its Proceedings, and from time to time publish the same, excepting such Parts as may in their Judgment require Secrecy; and the Yeas and Nays of the Members of either House on any question shall, at the Desire of one fifth of those Present, be entered on the Journal.

Clause 4: Neither House, during the Session of Congress, shall, without the Consent of the other, adjourn for more than three days, nor to any other Place than that in which the two Houses shall be sitting.

Section. 6.

Clause 1: The Senators and Representatives shall receive a Compensation for their Services, to be ascertained by Law, and paid out of the Treasury of the United States. They shall in all Cases, except Treason, Felony and Breach of the Peace, be privileged from Arrest during their Attendance at the Session of their respective Houses, and in going to and returning from the same; and for any Speech or Debate in either House, they shall not be questioned in any other Place.

Clause 2: No Senator or Representative shall, during the Time for which he was elected, be appointed to any civil Office under the Authority of the United States, which shall have been created, or the Emoluments whereof shall have been encreased during such time; and no Person holding any Office under the United States, shall be a Member of either House during his Continuance in Office.

Section. 7.

Clause 1: All Bills for raising Revenue shall originate in the House of Representatives; but the Senate may propose or concur with Amendments as on other Bills.

Clause 2: Every Bill which shall have passed the House of Representatives and the Senate, shall, before it become a Law, be presented to the President of the United States; If he approve he shall sign it, but if not he shall return it, with his Objections to that House in which it shall have originated, who shall enter the Objections at large on their Journal, and proceed to reconsider it. If after such Reconsideration two thirds of that House shall agree to pass the Bill, it shall be sent, together with the Objections, to the other House, by which it shall likewise be reconsidered, and if approved by two thirds of that House, it shall become a Law. But in all such Cases the Votes of both Houses shall be determined by yeas and Nays, and the Names of the Persons voting for and against the Bill shall be entered on the Journal of each House respectively. If any Bill shall not be returned by the President within ten Days (Sundays excepted) after it shall have been presented to him, the Same shall be a Law, in like Manner as if he had signed it, unless the Congress by their Adjournment prevent its Return, in which Case it shall not be a Law.

Clause 3: Every Order, Resolution, or Vote to which the Concurrence of the Senate and House of Representatives may be necessary (except on a question of Adjournment) shall be presented to the President of the United States; and before the Same shall take Effect, shall be approved by him, or being disapproved by him, shall be repassed by two thirds of the Senate and House of Representatives, according to the Rules and Limitations prescribed in the Case of a Bill.

Section. 8.

Clause 1: The Congress shall have Power To lay and collect Taxes, Duties, Imposts and Excises, to pay the Debts and provide for the common Defence and general Welfare of the United States; but all Duties, Imposts and Excises shall be uniform throughout the United States;

Clause 2: To borrow Money on the credit of the United States;

Clause 3: To regulate Commerce with foreign Nations, and among the several States, and with the Indian Tribes;

Clause 4: To establish an uniform Rule of Naturalization, and uniform Laws on the subject of Bankruptcies throughout the United States;

Clause 5: To coin Money, regulate the Value thereof, and of foreign Coin, and fix the Standard of Weights and Measures;

Clause 6: To provide for the Punishment of counterfeiting the Securities and current Coin of the United States;

Clause 7: To establish Post Offices and post Roads;

Clause 8: To promote the Progress of Science and useful Arts, by securing for limited Times to Authors and Inventors the exclusive Right to their respective Writings and Discoveries;

Clause 9: To constitute Tribunals inferior to the supreme Court;

Clause 10: To define and punish Piracies and Felonies committed on the high Seas, and Offences against the Law of Nations;

Clause 11: To declare War, grant Letters of Marque and Reprisal, and make Rules concerning Captures on Land and Water;

Clause 12: To raise and support Armies, but no Appropriation of Money to that Use shall be for a longer Term than two Years;

Clause 13: To provide and maintain a Navy;

Clause 14: To make Rules for the Government and Regulation of the land and naval Forces;

Clause 15: To provide for calling forth the Militia to execute the Laws of the Union, suppress Insurrections and repel Invasions;

Clause 16: To provide for organizing, arming, and disciplining, the Militia, and for governing such Part of them as may be employed in the Service of the United States, reserving to the States respectively, the Appointment of the Officers, and the Authority of training the Militia according to the discipline prescribed by Congress;

Clause 17: To exercise exclusive Legislation in all Cases whatsoever, over such District (not exceeding ten Miles square) as may, by Cession of particular States, and the Acceptance of Congress, become the Seat of the Government of the United States, and to exercise like Authority over all Places purchased by the Consent of the Legislature of the State in which the Same shall be, for the Erection of Forts, Magazines, Arsenals, dock-Yards, and other needful Buildings;—And

Clause 18: To make all Laws which shall be necessary and proper for carrying into Execution the foregoing Powers, and all other Powers vested by this Constitution in the Government of the United States, or in any Department or Officer thereof.

Section. 9.

Clause 1: The Migration or Importation of such Persons as any of the States now existing shall think proper to admit, shall not be prohibited by the Congress prior to the Year one thousand eight hundred and eight, but a Tax or duty may be imposed on such Importation, not exceeding ten dollars for each Person.

Clause 2: The Privilege of the Writ of Habeas Corpus shall not be suspended, unless when in Cases of Rebellion or Invasion the public Safety may require it.

Clause 3: No Bill of Attainder or ex post facto Law shall be passed.

Clause 4: No Capitation, or other direct, Tax shall be laid, unless in Proportion to the Census or Enumeration herein before directed to be taken.

Clause 5: No Tax or Duty shall be laid on Articles exported from any State.

Clause 6: No Preference shall be given by any Regulation of Commerce or Revenue to the Ports of one State over those of another: nor shall Vessels bound to, or from, one State, be obliged to enter, clear, or pay Duties in another.

Clause 7: No Money shall be drawn from the Treasury, but in Consequence of Appropriations made by Law; and a regular Statement and Account of the Receipts and Expenditures of all public Money shall be published from time to time.

Clause 8: No Title of Nobility shall be granted by the United States: And no Person holding any Office of Profit or Trust under them, shall, without the Consent of the Congress, accept of any present, Emolument, Office, or Title, of any kind whatever, from any King, Prince, or foreign State.

Section. 10.

Clause 1: No State shall enter into any Treaty, Alliance, or Confederation; grant Letters of Marque and Reprisal; coin Money; emit Bills of Credit; make any Thing but gold and silver Coin a Tender in Payment of Debts; pass any Bill of Attainder, ex post facto Law, or Law impairing the Obligation of Contracts, or grant any Title of Nobility.

Clause 2: No State shall, without the Consent of the Congress, lay any Imposts or Duties on Imports or Exports, except what may be absolutely necessary for executing it's inspection Laws: and the net Produce of all Duties and Imposts, laid by any State on Imports or Exports, shall be for the Use of the Treasury of the United States; and all such Laws shall be subject to the Revision and Controul of the Congress.

Clause 3: No State shall, without the Consent of Congress, lay any Duty of Tonnage, keep Troops, or Ships of War in time of Peace, enter into any Agreement or Compact with another State, or with a foreign Power, or engage in War, unless actually invaded, or in such imminent Danger as will not admit of delay.

Article. II.[11]

Section. 1.

Clause 1: The executive Power shall be vested in a President[12] of the United States of America. He shall hold his Office during the Term of four Years, and, together with the Vice President, chosen for the same Term, be elected, as follows

Clause 2: Each State shall appoint, in such Manner as the Legislature thereof may direct, a Number of Electors, equal to the whole Number of Senators and Representatives to which the State may be entitled in the Congress: but no Senator or Representative, or Person holding an Office of Trust or Profit under the United States, shall be appointed an Elector.

Clause 3: The Electors shall meet in their respective States, and vote by Ballot for two Persons, of whom one at least shall not be an Inhabitant of the same State with themselves. And they shall make a List of all the Persons voted for, and of the Number of Votes for each; which List they shall sign and certify, and transmit sealed to the Seat of the Government of the United States, directed to the President of the Senate. The President of the Senate shall, in the Presence of the Senate and House of Representatives, open all the Certificates, and the Votes shall then be counted. The Person having the greatest Number of Votes shall be the President, if such Number be a Majority of the whole Number of Electors appointed; and if there be more than one who have such Majority, and have an equal Number of Votes, then the House of Representatives shall immediately chuse by Ballot one of them for President; and if no Person have a Majority, then from the five highest on the List the said House shall in like Manner chuse the President. But in chusing the President, the Votes shall be taken by States, the Representation from each State having one Vote; A quorum for this Purpose shall consist of a Member or Members from two thirds of the States, and a Majority of all the States shall be necessary to a Choice. In every Case, after the Choice of the President, the Person having the greatest Number of Votes of the Electors shall be the Vice President. But if there should remain two or more who have equal Votes, the Senate shall chuse from them by Ballot the Vice President.

Clause 4: The Congress may determine the Time of chusing the Electors, and the Day on which they shall give their Votes; which Day shall be the same throughout the United States.

Clause 5: No Person except a natural born Citizen, or a Citizen of the United States, at the time of the Adoption of this Constitution, shall be eligible to the Office of President; neither shall any Person be eligible to that Office who shall not have attained to the Age of thirty five Years, and been fourteen Years a Resident within the United States.

Clause 6: In Case of the Removal of the President from Office, or of his Death, Resignation, or Inability to discharge the Powers and Duties of the said Office (See Note 9), the Same shall devolve on the Vice President, and the Congress may by Law provide for the Case of Removal, Death, Resignation or Inability, both of the President and Vice President, declaring what Officer shall then act as President, and such Officer shall act accordingly, until the Disability be removed, or a President shall be elected.

Clause 7: The President shall, at stated Times, receive for his Services, a Compensation, which shall neither be encreased nor diminished during the Period for which he shall have been elected, and he shall not receive within that Period any other Emolument from the United States, or any of them.

Clause 8: Before he enter on the Execution of his Office, he shall take the following Oath or Affirmation:—"I do solemnly swear (or affirm) that I will faithfully execute the Office of President of the United States, and will to the best of my Ability, preserve, protect and defend the Constitution of the United States."

Section. 2.

Clause 1: The President shall be Commander in Chief of the Army and Navy of the United States, and of the Militia of the several States, when called into the actual Service of the United States; he may require the Opinion, in writing, of the principal Officer in each of the executive Departments, upon any Subject relating to the Duties of their respective Offices, and he shall have Power to grant Reprieves and Pardons for Offences against the United States, except in Cases of Impeachment.

Clause 2: He shall have Power, by and with the Advice and Consent of the Senate, to make Treaties, provided two thirds of the Senators present concur; and he shall nominate, and by and with the Advice and Consent of the Senate, shall appoint Ambassadors, other public Ministers and Consuls, Judges of the supreme Court, and all other Officers of the United States, whose Appointments are not herein otherwise provided for, and which shall be established by Law: but the Congress may by Law vest the Appointment of such inferior Officers, as they think proper, in the President alone, in the Courts of Law, or in the Heads of Departments.

Clause 3: The President shall have Power to fill up all Vacancies that may happen during the Recess of the Senate, by granting Commissions which shall expire at the End of their next Session.

Section. 3.

He shall from time to time give to the Congress Information of the State of the Union, and recommend to their Consideration such Measures as he shall judge necessary and expedient; he may, on extraordinary Occasions, convene both Houses, or either of them, and in Case of Disagreement between them, with Respect to the Time of Adjournment, he may adjourn them to such Time as he shall think proper; he shall receive Ambassadors and other public Ministers; he shall take Care that the Laws be faithfully executed, and shall Commission all the Officers of the United States.

Section. 4.

The President, Vice President and all civil Officers of the United States, shall be removed from Office on Impeachment for, and Conviction of, Treason, Bribery, or other high Crimes and Misdemeanors.

Article. III.[13]

Section. 1.

The judicial Power of the United States, shall be vested in one supreme Court, and in such inferior Courts as the Congress may from time to time ordain and establish. The Judges, both of the supreme and inferior Courts, shall hold their Offices during good Behaviour, and shall, at stated Times, receive for their Services, a Compensation, which shall not be diminished during their Continuance in Office.

Section. 2.

Clause 1: The judicial Power shall extend to all Cases, in Law and Equity, arising under this Constitution, the Laws of the United States, and Treaties made, or which shall be made, under their Authority;—to all Cases affecting Ambassadors, other public Ministers and Consuls;—to all Cases of admiralty and maritime Jurisdiction;—to Controversies to which the United States shall be a Party;—to Controversies between two or more States;—between a State and Citizens of another State;—between Citizens of different States,—between Citizens of the same State claiming Lands under Grants of different States, and between a State, or the Citizens thereof, and foreign States, Citizens or Subjects.

Clause 2: In all Cases affecting Ambassadors, other public Ministers and Consuls, and those in which a State shall be Party, the supreme Court shall have original Jurisdiction. In all the other Cases before mentioned, the supreme Court shall have appellate Jurisdiction, both as to Law and Fact, with such Exceptions, and under such Regulations as the Congress shall make.

Clause 3: The Trial of all Crimes, except in Cases of Impeachment, shall be by Jury; and such Trial shall be held in the State where the said Crimes shall have been committed; but when not committed within any State, the Trial shall be at such Place or Places as the Congress may by Law have directed.

Section. 3.

Clause 1: Treason against the United States, shall consist only in levying War against them, or in adhering to their Enemies, giving them Aid and Comfort. No Person shall be convicted of Treason unless on the Testimony of two Witnesses to the same overt Act, or on Confession in open Court.

Clause 2: The Congress shall have Power to declare the Punishment of Treason, but no Attainder of Treason shall work Corruption of Blood, or Forfeiture except during the Life of the Person attainted.

Article. IV[14]

Section. 1.

Full Faith and Credit shall be given in each State to the public Acts, Records, and judicial Proceedings of every other State. And the Congress may by general Laws prescribe the Manner in which such Acts, Records and Proceedings shall be proved, and the Effect thereof.

Section. 2.

Clause 1: The Citizens of each State shall be entitled to all Privileges and Immunities of Citizens in the several States.

Clause 2: A Person charged in any State with Treason, Felony, or other Crime, who shall flee from Justice, and be found in another State, shall on Demand of the executive Authority of the State from which he fled, be delivered up, to be removed to the State having Jurisdiction of the Crime.

Clause 3: No Person held to Service or Labour in one State, under the Laws thereof, escaping into another, shall, in Consequence of any Law or Regulation therein, be discharged from such Service or Labour, but shall be delivered up on Claim of the Party to whom such Service or Labour may be due.

Section. 3.

Clause 1: New States may be admitted by the Congress into this Union; but no new State shall be formed or erected within the Jurisdiction of any other State; nor any State be formed by the Junction of two or more States, or Parts of States, without the Consent of the Legislatures of the States concerned as well as of the Congress.

Clause 2: The Congress shall have Power to dispose of and make all needful Rules and Regulations respecting the Territory or other Property belonging to the United States; and nothing in this Constitution shall be so construed as to Prejudice any Claims of the United States, or of any particular State.

Section. 4.

The United States shall guarantee to every State in this Union a Republican Form of Government, and shall protect each of them against Invasion; and on Application of the Legislature, or of the Executive (when the Legislature cannot be convened) against domestic Violence.

Article. V.[15]

The Congress, whenever two thirds of both Houses shall deem it necessary, shall propose Amendments to this Constitution, or, on the Application of the Legislatures of two thirds of the several States, shall call a Convention for proposing Amendments, which, in either Case, shall be valid to all Intents and Purposes, as Part of this Constitution, when ratified by the Legislatures of three fourths of the several States, or by Conventions in three fourths thereof, as the one or the other Mode of Ratification may be proposed by the Congress; Provided that no Amendment which may be made prior to the Year One thousand eight hundred and eight shall in any Manner affect the first and fourth Clauses in the Ninth Section of the first Article; and that no State, without its Consent, shall be deprived of its equal Suffrage in the Senate.

Article. VI.[16]

Clause 1: All Debts contracted and Engagements entered into, before the Adoption of this Constitution, shall be as valid against the United States under this Constitution, as under the Confederation.

Clause 2: This Constitution, and the Laws of the United States which shall be made in Pursuance thereof; and all Treaties made, or which shall be made, under the Authority of the United States, shall be the supreme Law of the Land; and the Judges in every State shall be bound thereby, any Thing in the Constitution or Laws of any State to the Contrary notwithstanding.

Clause 3: The Senators and Representatives before mentioned, and the Members of the several State Legislatures, and all executive and judicial Officers, both of the United States and of the several States, shall be bound by Oath or Affirmation, to support this Constitution; but no religious Test shall ever be required as a Qualification to any Office or public Trust under the United States.

Article. VII.[17]

The Ratification of the Conventions of nine States, shall be sufficient for the Establishment of this Constitution between the States so ratifying the Same.

done in Convention by the Unanimous Consent of the States[18] present the Seventeenth Day of September in the Year of our Lord one thousand seven hundred and Eighty seven and of the Independence of the United States of America the Twelfth In witness whereof We[19] have hereunto subscribed our Names,[20]

GO WASHINGTON—Presidt. and deputy from Virginia

[Signed also by the deputies of twelve States.]

Annotations

1. Ratification of the U.S. Constitution in 1788 marked the successful completion of a long and arduous struggle for a functional, independent, national government for the thirteen former British colonies. One of the first steps along the path to national governance was formation of the Stamp Act Congress in 1765. At this meeting, representatives from nine of the thirteen colonies met to draft a document listing the many rights that the King had violated. Momentum for independence grew with the formation of the First Continental Congress in 1774, which represented the second organized meeting of delegates from the colonies—only Georgia chose to not send delegates. The Second Continental Congress convened in 1775 and authorized the formation of an army led by George Washington. Following the Declaration of Independence in 1776 and in the midst of the Revolutionary War, the Articles of Confederation were written in 1776 and ratified in 1781, creating the nation's first formal attempt at a permanent governmental structure. The articles served as little more than a loose alliance among the sovereign states—a league of friendship. Frustrated that the Articles of Confederation had failed to provide the economic and security structures believed necessary for the nation to prosper, a congressional committee, in 1785, recommended altering the articles. In 1786, representatives from five states (Delaware, New York, New Jersey, Pennsylvania, and Virginia) met in Annapolis, Maryland to discuss ways to improve the articles. On February 21, 1787, Congress gave its approval to hold a convention for the purpose of revising the articles. In May of 1787, the Constitutional Convention was convened in Philadelphia and met for four months before producing the nearly 5,000-word document that would become the U.S. Constitution.
2. The Constitution was adopted by delegates at the Constitutional Convention on September 17, 1787 and sent to the various states for ratification. The states ratified the Constitution in the following order: Delaware (December 7, 1787); Pennsylvania (December 12, 1787); New Jersey (December 18, 1787); Georgia (January 2, 1788); Connecticut (January 9, 1788); Massachusetts (February 6, 1788); Maryland (April 28, 1788); South Carolina (May 23, 1788); and New Hampshire (June 21, 1788). The Constitution took effect after ratification by the ninth state, New Hampshire. Following ratification, the Constitution was adopted by Virginia on June 25, 1788; New York on July 26, 1788; North Carolina on November 21, 1789; Rhode Island on May 29, 1790; and Vermont on January 10, 1791.
3. Spelling and punctuation have been retained from the engrossed copy of the Constitution housed in the National Archives.
4. Congress did not authorize delegates at the Philadelphia Convention to draft an entirely new constitution. Congress explicitly stated that delegates should meet "for the sole and expressed purpose of revising the Articles of Confederation and reporting to Congress and the several legislatures such alterations and provisions therein as shall, when agreed to in Congress and confirmed by the states, render the federal constitution adequate to the exigencies of Government & the preservation of the Union." Not only did the delegates overreach the authority granted to them by Congress when they created an entirely new constitution, they also ignored the instruction to submit their proposal to the state legislatures through Congress. Instead, the delegates chose to submit the Constitution to special ratification conventions within each state. Moreover, they called for the Constitution to go into effect after being approved by only three-fourths of the states (i.e., nine), rejecting the requirement of unanimity specified by the Articles of Confederation. The questionable authority of the delegates and the rejection of accepted procedures, has led many scholars to describe the process by which the Constitution was framed and adopted as the nation's second revolution.
5. While the states had achieved several successes under the Articles of Confederation (e.g., defeated the British, negotiated the Treaty of Paris, and protected individual liberties), rule under the Articles of Confederation was rife with problems by the late 1780s. Since action under the articles required approval from nine of the thirteen states and amending the articles required approval by all thirteen states, governmental action and reform was exceedingly difficult to achieve. Moreover, Congress did not have the power to collect taxes from individuals or to regulate interstate commerce, further limiting its ability to act. Under the Articles of Confederation, British troops remained on western lands; Spanish troops threatened the Mississippi; states began to print their own currency and failed to contribute their share to the national treasury. Moreover, the Federalist advocates of a stronger constitution pointed to Shays's Rebellion, a 1786 Massachusetts rebellion led by Daniel Shays that aimed to forcibly halt foreclosures on farms by closing the state court, as an example of the growing economic turmoil and military weakness that plagued the nation.
6. The Constitution was as much a rejection of the weaker national arrangement in place under the Articles of Confederation as it was an experiment in mostly untested governmental principles. In this section of the Constitution, the new government's primary objectives, objectives that were not being adequately fulfilled under the articles, are explicitly mentioned.
7. The Constitution is divided into seven articles. The first three articles establish the institutional structure of the new government (Article I establishes Congress, Article II establishes Presidency, and Article III establishes the Court System). Article IV covers state relations; Article V addresses constitutional change; Article VI defines national authority; and Article VII describes the ratification process for the Constitution.

8. When reading the Constitution, try to identify examples of the nation's founding principles—i.e., federalism (i.e., a division of power between the states and the federal government in which both levels of government retain a degree of independence), separation of powers (the idea that independent governmental institutions with overlapping powers will help to guard against tyranny), representative democracy (the principle that representatives of the people, not the people themselves, should carry out the daily functions of government), rule of law (the idea that the U.S. is a nation governed by laws and that no person or group of people is above the law), and popular sovereignty (the idea that government derives its ultimate authority directly from the governed and that citizens have an active role to play in guarding against tyranny).
9. Article I of the Constitution describes the powers and structure of Congress. It is no coincidence that this is the first, longest, and most detailed article in the Constitution. The framers believed that the lawmaking branch of government would naturally have the most power and therefore spent a great detail of time debating and outlining the powers of the legislative branch.
10. A legislative body with two distinct branches is known as a bicameral legislature.
11. Article II, the executive article, outlines the powers of the president. Creating the executive branch was a particularly difficult task for the framers of the Constitution. On the one hand, the delegates at the Philadelphia Convention did not desire to establish a monarch for the new world, having recently rebelled against the King of England. On the other hand, the framers desired for the new government to possess an independent executive branch that would provide the government with energy and leadership, something that was missing from the Articles of Confederation. What they created was something uniquely American—a chief executive that was neither monarch nor prime minister, that was linked to the legislature but not controlled by it, that represented the entire nation but was not an instrument of public opinion.
12. The New Jersey Plan, a plan proposed at the Constitutional Convention by a group of delegates from small states, called for a multi-person executive. The framers eventually rejected the idea for a multi-person executive, hoping that a single executive would help provide the office energy and direction. See Federalist 70 for Alexander Hamilton's eloquent defense of a strong, unified executive office.
13. Article III outlines the federal court system. It is by far the shortest of the Constitution's three institutional articles, containing only 389 words. In comparison, Article I, the legislative article, contains 2,372 words, and Article II, the executive article, contains 1,050 words. It is also far more vague than the other institutional articles and received comparatively little discussion and debate at the Constitutional Convention. In fact, the article relied on Congress at an unspecified future date to create inferior federal courts. Alexander Hamilton in Federalist Paper 78 explained the general sentiment of many of the framers when he wrote that the judiciary, lacking the power of the "sword" and the power of the "purse," was to be the "least dangerous" and the least powerful branch of federal government. For the most part, the court did play a relatively minor role in national politics until 1803 when the fourth Chief Justice of the Supreme Court, John Marshall, made his famous ruling in *Marbury v. Madison* in which the court boldly declared a legislative act void and affirmed the court's right to judicial review.
14. Article IV discusses state relations and provides insights into the form of federalism that the framers intended to create. Political scientists commonly discuss three general types of federal/state power sharing arrangements. In a unitary system, such as the British system, state and local governments derive their power from the federal government and operate at the will of the central government. In a confederated system, as was the case under the Articles of Confederation, the states are the highest level of government and actions of the federal government must be enacted through the sovereign states. In the system the framers created, a federal system, power is shared between the national government and the state governments, with both levels of government deriving their power directly from the people. American federalism was one of the most novel aspects of the Constitution and has been adopted by several other nations (e.g., India, Mexico, and Switzerland).
15. Article V discusses the amendment process. The Constitution stipulates two ways to propose constitutional amendments. Amendments can be proposed by a vote of two-thirds of the states or by a two-thirds vote in Congress. To date, no amendment has been successfully proposed by the states. The Constitution also allows for two ways to ratify amendments. Ratification can be accomplished by gaining approval of three-fourths of the state legislatures or by the approval of special conventions in three-fourths of the states. Only one amendment, the 21st Amendment (repealing prohibition), was ratified by special convention in the states. Twenty-six of the twenty-seven amendments to the U.S. Constitution were proposed by Congress and ratified by the state legislatures.
16. Article VI contains three distinct clauses. Clause one is of little relevance today and simply guaranteed that any debts owed under the Articles of Confederation would be assumed under the Constitution. The second clause has had far more lasting importance. It explicitly states that the Constitution, federal laws, and national treaties shall be the supreme law of the land. Moreover, the Supremacy Clause binds state judges to the Constitution and federal laws, providing the federal government with a level of authority unprecedented under the Articles of Confederation. The last clause requires an oath of affirmation to the Constitution from key state and federal officers. It also protects federal officers against religious requirements, providing a protection against religious establishment even before ratification of the 1st Amendment to the Constitution.
17. What might appear to some as merely a procedural article with little lasting importance, Article VII of the Constitution is particularly important. This article, more than any other section of the Constitution, reveals the framers as revolutionaries. In this section, they reject their instructions from Congress, reject the accepted procedures of the Articles of Confederation, and call on conventions in each state to ratify the Constitution. They appeal to the states and directly to the citizens of the states to legitimize the new government.
18. By today's standards, the fifty-five delegates who attended the Philadelphia Convention were a fairly homogeneous group. Most of the delegates came to the convention with a common intellectual background, many having read the classic works of Locke, Montesquieu, Rousseau, Aristotle, Plato and others. They also shared common experiences (twenty-one served in the American Revolution, thirty-nine had been members of the Continental Congress, and seven had been governors). The delegates were relatively young—six under the age of thirty. James Madison, who played a prominent role at the convention, was only thirty-six years old. The delegates were all white, all male, all of European lineage, and all relatively affluent.
19. Not all of the delegates chosen to attend the convention played active roles. In fact, nineteen of the delegates selected for the convention failed to attend or left the convention before it adjourned. More than a dozen of the delegates in attendance played relatively minor roles. Of the active delegates, a few of the most energetic attendees included James Madison, Edmund Randolph, James Wilson, and Benjamin Franklin. James Madison, who is often considered the father of the U.S. Constitution, was particularly active at the convention. He sat at the front of the hall, took detailed notes on the proceedings, and, along with his fellow Virginians, helped to draft the Virginia Plan, which greatly influenced the Constitution.
20. Several of the nation's revolutionary heroes were not present at the Constitutional Convention. Patrick Henry refused to attend. Thomas Jefferson, Thomas Paine, and John Adams were abroad. John Hancock and Samuel Adams were not selected by their states as delegates. And the state of Rhode Island chose not to send any delegates to the Philadelphia Convention.

Appendix D
Federalist No. 10[1]

November 22, 1787[2]

James Madison[3]

To the People of the State of New York:[4]

AMONG the numerous advantages promised by a well constructed Union, none deserves to be more accurately developed than its tendency to break and control the violence of faction. The friend of popular governments never finds himself so much alarmed for their character and fate, as when he contemplates their propensity to this dangerous vice. He will not fail, therefore, to set a due value on any plan which, without violating the principles to which he is attached, provides a proper cure for it. The instability, injustice, and confusion introduced into the public councils, have, in truth, been the mortal diseases under which popular governments have everywhere perished;[5] as they continue to be the favorite and fruitful topics from which the adversaries to liberty derive their most specious declamations. The valuable improvements made by the American constitutions on the popular models, both ancient and modern, cannot certainly be too much admired; but it would be an unwarrantable partiality, to contend that they have as effectually obviated the danger on this side, as was wished and expected. Complaints are everywhere heard from our most considerate and virtuous citizens, equally the friends of public and private faith, and of public and personal liberty, that our governments are too unstable, that the public good is disregarded in the conflicts of rival parties, and that measures are too often decided, not according to the rules of justice and the rights of the minor party, but by the superior force of an interested and overbearing majority. However anxiously we may wish that these complaints had no foundation, the evidence, of known facts will not permit us to deny that they are in some degree true. It will be found, indeed, on a candid review of our situation, that some of the distresses under which we labor have been erroneously charged on the operation of our governments; but it will be found, at the same time, that other causes will not alone account for many of our heaviest misfortunes; and, particularly, for that prevailing and increasing distrust of public engagements, and alarm for private rights, which are echoed from one end of the continent to the other. These must be chiefly, if not wholly, effects of the unsteadiness and injustice with which a factious spirit has tainted our public administrations.

By a faction, I understand a number of citizens, whether amounting to a majority or a minority of the whole, who are united and actuated by some common impulse of passion, or of interest, adverse to the rights of other citizens, or to the permanent and aggregate interests of the community.[6]

There are two methods of curing the mischief of faction: the one, by removing its causes; the other, by controlling its effects.

There are again two methods of removing the causes of faction:[7] the one, by destroying the liberty which is essential to its existence; the other, by giving to every citizen the same opinions, the same passions, and the same interests.[8]

It could never be more truly said than of the first remedy, that it was worse than the disease. Liberty is to faction what air is to fire, an aliment without which it instantly expires.[9] But it could not be less folly to abolish liberty, which is essential to political life, because it nourishes faction, than it would be to wish the annihilation of air, which is essential to animal life, because it imparts to fire its destructive agency.

The second expedient is as impracticable as the first would be unwise. As long as the reason of man continues fallible, and he is at liberty to exercise it, different opinions will be formed. As long as the connection subsists between his reason and his self-love, his opinions and his passions will have a reciprocal influence on each other; and the former will be objects to which the latter will attach themselves.[10] The diversity in the faculties of men, from which the rights of property originate, is not less an insuperable obstacle to a uniformity of interests. The protection of these faculties is the first object of government. From the protection of different and unequal faculties of acquiring property, the possession of different degrees and kinds of property immediately results; and from the influence of these on the sentiments and views of the respective proprietors, ensues a division of the society into different interests and parties.

The latent causes of faction are thus sown in the nature of man; and we see them everywhere brought into different degrees of activity, according to the different circumstances of civil society. A zeal for different opinions concerning religion, concerning government, and many other points, as well of speculation as of practice; an attachment to different leaders ambitiously contending for pre-eminence and power; or to persons of other descriptions whose fortunes have been interesting to the human passions, have, in turn, divided mankind into parties, inflamed them with mutual animosity, and rendered them much more disposed to vex and oppress each other than to co-operate for their common good. So strong is this propensity of mankind to fall into mutual animosities, that where no substantial occasion presents itself, the most frivolous and fanciful distinctions have been sufficient to kindle their unfriendly passions and excite their most violent conflicts.[11] But the most common and durable source of factions has been the various and unequal distribution of property. Those who hold and those who are without property have ever formed distinct interests in society. Those who are creditors, and those who are debtors, fall under a like discrimination. A landed interest, a manufacturing interest, a mercantile interest, a moneyed interest, with many lesser interests, grow up of necessity in civilized nations, and divide

---

Annotated by Howard Ernst (Associate Professor of Political Science at the United States Naval Academy and Senior Scholar at the University of Virginia Center for Politics). Ernst is a co-editor of *Dangerous Democracy? The Battle Over Ballot Initiatives in America* (2001) and author of *Chesapeake Bay Blues: Science, Politics, and the Struggle to Save the Bay* (2003).

them into different classes, actuated by different sentiments and views. The regulation of these various and interfering interests forms the principal task of modern legislation, and involves the spirit of party and faction in the necessary and ordinary operations of the government.[12]

No man is allowed to be a judge in his own cause, because his interest would certainly bias his judgment, and, not improbably, corrupt his integrity. With equal, nay with greater reason, a body of men are unfit to be both judges and parties at the same time; yet what are many of the most important acts of legislation, but so many judicial determinations, not indeed concerning the rights of single persons, but concerning the rights of large bodies of citizens? And what are the different classes of legislators but advocates and parties to the causes which they determine? Is a law proposed concerning private debts? It is a question to which the creditors are parties on one side and the debtors on the other. Justice ought to hold the balance between them. Yet the parties are, and must be, themselves the judges; and the most numerous party, or, in other words, the most powerful faction must be expected to prevail. Shall domestic manufactures be encouraged, and in what degree, by restrictions on foreign manufactures? Are questions which would be differently decided by the landed and the manufacturing classes, and probably by neither with a sole regard to justice and the public good? The apportionment of taxes on the various descriptions of property is an act which seems to require the most exact impartiality; yet there is, perhaps, no legislative act in which greater opportunity and temptation are given to a predominant party to trample on the rules of justice. Every shilling with which they overburden the inferior number, is a shilling saved to their own pockets.

It is in vain to say that enlightened statesmen will be able to adjust these clashing interests, and render them all subservient to the public good.[13] Enlightened statesmen will not always be at the helm. Nor, in many cases, can such an adjustment be made at all without taking into view indirect and remote considerations, which will rarely prevail over the immediate interest which one party may find in disregarding the rights of another or the good of the whole.

The inference to which we are brought is, that the CAUSES of faction cannot be removed, and that relief is only to be sought in the means of controlling its EFFECTS.[14]

If a faction consists of less than a majority, relief is supplied by the republican principle, which enables the majority to defeat its sinister views by regular vote.[15] It may clog the administration, it may convulse the society; but it will be unable to execute and mask its violence under the forms of the Constitution. When a majority is included in a faction, the form of popular government, on the other hand, enables it to sacrifice to its ruling passion or interest both the public good and the rights of other citizens.[16] To secure the public good and private rights against the danger of such a faction, and at the same time to preserve the spirit and the form of popular government, is then the great object to which our inquiries are directed. Let me add that it is the great desideratum by which this form of government can be rescued from the opprobrium under which it has so long labored, and be recommended to the esteem and adoption of mankind.[17]

By what means is this object attainable? Evidently by one of two only. Either the existence of the same passion or interest in a majority at the same time must be prevented, or the majority, having such coexistent passion or interest, must be rendered, by their number and local situation, unable to concert and carry into effect schemes of oppression. If the impulse and the opportunity be suffered to coincide, we well know that neither moral nor religious motives can be relied on as an adequate control. They are not found to be such on the injustice and violence of individuals, and lose their efficacy in proportion to the number combined together, that is, in proportion as their efficacy becomes needful.[18]

From this view of the subject it may be concluded that a pure democracy, by which I mean a society consisting of a small number of citizens, who assemble and administer the government in person, can admit of no cure for the mischiefs of faction. A common passion or interest will, in almost every case, be felt by a majority of the whole; a communication and concert result from the form of government itself; and there is nothing to check the inducements to sacrifice the weaker party or an obnoxious individual. Hence it is that such democracies have ever been spectacles of turbulence and contention; have ever been found incompatible with personal security or the rights of property; and have in general been as short in their lives as they have been violent in their deaths.[19] Theoretic politicians, who have patronized this species of government, have erroneously supposed that by reducing mankind to a perfect equality in their political rights, they would, at the same time, be perfectly equalized and assimilated in their possessions, their opinions, and their passions.

A republic, by which I mean a government in which the scheme of representation takes place, opens a different prospect, and promises the cure for which we are seeking. Let us examine the points in which it varies from pure democracy, and we shall comprehend both the nature of the cure and the efficacy which it must derive from the Union.

The two great points of difference between a democracy and a republic are: first, the delegation of the government, in the latter, to a small number of citizens elected by the rest; secondly, the greater number of citizens, and greater sphere of country, over which the latter may be extended.

The effect of the first difference is, on the one hand, to refine and enlarge the public views, by passing them through the medium of a chosen body of citizens, whose wisdom may best discern the true interest of their country, and whose patriotism and love of justice will be least likely to sacrifice it to temporary or partial considerations. Under such a regulation, it may well happen that the public voice, pronounced by the representatives of the people, will be more consonant to the public good than if pronounced by the people themselves, convened for the purpose. On the other hand, the effect may be inverted. Men of factious tempers, of local prejudices, or of sinister designs, may, by intrigue, by corruption, or by other means, first obtain the suffrages, and then betray the interests, of the people. The question resulting is, whether small or extensive republics are more favorable to the election of proper guardians of the public weal; and it is clearly decided in favor of the latter by two obvious considerations:

In the first place, it is to be remarked that, however small the republic may be, the representatives must be raised to a certain number, in order to guard against the cabals of a few; and that, however large it may be, they must be limited to a certain number, in order to guard against the confusion of a multitude. Hence, the number of representatives in the two cases not being in proportion to that of the two constituents, and being proportionally greater in the small republic, it follows that, if the proportion of fit characters be not less in the large than in the small republic, the former will present a greater option, and consequently a greater probability of a fit choice.

In the next place, as each representative will be chosen by a greater number of citizens in the large than in the small republic, it will be more difficult for unworthy candidates to practice with success the vicious arts by which elections are too often carried; and the suffrages of the people being more free, will be more likely to centre in men who possess the most attractive merit and the most diffusive and established characters.

It must be confessed that in this, as in most other cases, there is a mean, on both sides of which inconveniences will be found to lie. By enlarging too much the number of electors, you render the representatives too little acquainted with all their local circumstances and lesser interests; as by reducing it too much, you render him unduly attached to these, and too little fit to comprehend and pursue great and national objects. The federal Constitution forms a happy combination in this respect; the great and aggregate interests being referred to the national, the local and particular to the State legislatures.

The other point of difference is, the greater number of citizens and extent of territory which may be brought within the compass of republican than of democratic government; and it is this circumstance principally which renders factious combinations less to be dreaded in the former than in the latter. The smaller the society, the fewer probably will be the distinct parties and interests composing it; the fewer the distinct parties and interests, the more frequently will a majority be found of the same party; and the smaller the number of individuals composing a majority, and the smaller the compass within which they are placed, the more easily will they concert and execute their plans of oppression. Extend the sphere, and you take in a greater variety of parties and interests; you make it less probable that a majority of the whole will have a common motive to invade the rights of other citizens; or if such a common motive exists, it will be more difficult for all who feel it to discover their own strength, and to act in unison with each other. Besides other impediments, it may be remarked that, where there is a consciousness of unjust or dishonorable purposes, communication is always checked by distrust in proportion to the number whose concurrence is necessary.

Hence, it clearly appears, that the same advantage which a republic has over a democracy, in controlling the effects of faction, is enjoyed by a large over a small republic,—is enjoyed by the Union over the States composing it. Does the advantage consist in the substitution of representatives whose enlightened views and virtuous sentiments render them superior to local prejudices and schemes of injustice? It will not be denied that the representation of the Union will be most likely to possess these requisite endowments. Does it consist in the greater security afforded by a greater variety of parties, against the event of any one party being able to outnumber and oppress the rest? In an equal degree does the increased variety of parties comprised within the Union, increase this security? Does it, in fine, consist in the greater obstacles opposed to the concert and accomplishment of the secret wishes of an unjust and interested majority? Here, again, the extent of the Union gives it the most palpable advantage.

The influence of factious leaders may kindle a flame within their particular States, but will be unable to spread a general conflagration through the other States. A religious sect may degenerate into a political faction in a part of the Confederacy; but the variety of sects dispersed over the entire face of it must secure the national councils against any danger from that source. A rage for paper money, for an abolition of debts, for an equal division of property, or for any other improper or wicked project, will be less apt to pervade the whole body of the Union than a particular member of it; in the same proportion as such a malady is more likely to taint a particular county or district, than an entire State.

In the extent and proper structure of the Union, therefore, we behold a republican remedy for the diseases most incident to republican government. And according to the degree of pleasure and pride we feel in being republicans, ought to be our zeal in cherishing the spirit and supporting the character of Federalists.

PUBLIUS.[20]

Annotations

1. *The Federalist Papers*, comprised of 85 essays written by Alexander Hamilton, James Madison, and John Jay, were written in support of ratification of the U.S. Constitution. Though originally conceived as federalist propaganda to help persuade the state of New York to ratify the Constitution, or perhaps more accurately as a defense against the anti-federalist propaganda circulating throughout New York, the essays have come to be considered the nation's most thoughtful and thorough defense of its Constitution. To this day, the *Federalist Papers* are widely considered the single best guide to the thoughts and desires of the nation's founders.
2. *Federalist 10* was first published in the *New York Daily Advertiser* on November 22, 1787. It was reprinted the following day in the *New York Independent Journal*.
3. The tenth of the 85 *Federalist Papers*, *Federalist 10* was the first of the essays authored by James Madison. Madison went on to write 29 *Federalist Papers* (from November 1787 through February 1788) before returning to Virginia on March 4, 1788 to campaign for the Constitution in his home state. Though the idea of producing the *Federalist Papers* was hatched by Hamilton, and Hamilton wrote a larger number of the essays than Madison (51 to 29), the quality of Madison's writing and clarity of his arguments (*Federalist 10*, *45*, and *51* in particular) have helped to make Madison's essays the most famous of the *Federalist Papers*. John Jay, who was struck by severe rheumatism during the winter of 1787, completed only five of the essays. William Duer, who offered to help with the project, had his essays rejected by Madison.
4. At the time the Constitution was being debated, Congress met in New York, making it the nation's capital and a key state in the ratification process. The state of New York was slow to support the Constitution, ratifying only after a successful ratification vote in Virginia and after the state had been promised a bill of rights. New York became the eleventh state to ratify the Constitution on July 26, 1788.
5. Early in the essay, Madison aims to establish the importance of his central concern—the threat of factions to popular governance. Madison believed that the future of the young nation depended on implementing mechanisms to guard against the mischief of factions.
6. This is an interesting and expansive definition of faction. Notice that Madison does not limit his definition to groups that represent what we now commonly consider "special interests." Political parties, interest groups, labor unions, corporations, and just about all groups organized for collective action satisfy Madison's broad definition of faction.
7. Here Madison discusses two ways to "remove the causes" of faction. Later he will argue that neither of the two methods of removing factions is acceptable and that the nation's best hope resides in seeking

protections from the mischief of factions, something that he believed the new Constitution accomplished.

8. One cure for the problem of factions considered by Madison was to destroy the liberty upon which factions flourish, a cure Madison argued was worse than the problem. Another cure discussed by Madison was giving people the same opinions, passions, and interests; a cure Madison viewed as impossible since he believed human reason was flawed and inextricably linked to self-interest.
9. Quotes like these have earned Madison a reputation as one of the nation's great rhetoricians.
10. Note the assumptions about human nature and human reason that are built into this passage. Madison argues that reason is flawed in that it is distorted by self-interest. Here he challenges one of the central assumptions of democracy—i.e., the notion that a well-informed public will reach a consensus regarding the common interests of a nation.
11. In this passage Madison provides further insights into his rather chilling view of human nature. His belief that "frivolous and fanciful distinctions" are sufficient to incite the "most violent conflicts" is similar to the philosophy described by Thomas Hobbes in his classic work *The Leviathan*. In contrast, other prominent thinkers of the time, like Thomas Jefferson, argued that people are driven by an inborn moral sense and that the general public is more likely to quietly suffer injustices than they are to rise up in violence.
12. The economic determinism discussed in this section (i.e., the idea that unequal division of property is a primary factor leading to competing interests in society) is remarkably similar to the economic determinism championed by Karl Marx roughly a century later. A fundamental difference between the two thinkers is the manner in which they chose to address the problem of factions. Marx called on government to secure a more equitable distribution of property, thereby eliminating the primary cause of factions and social inequality. Madison, on the other hand, did not aim to upset social order and argued instead for the protection of private property, calling on government to regulate the various interests that are produced by competing economic interests.
13. Here Madison disagrees with the assertion that enlightened statesmen can be relied on to overcome the spirit of faction and pursue the public good. Hence, Madison concludes that there are no easy "cures" for the problem of factions.
14. Applying a disease metaphor to help explain this passage is particularly useful. Madison suggests that since the disease of faction, a disease that has proven fatal to democracies across the globe, cannot be cured, steps must be taken to treat the symptoms. He views the Constitution that emerged from Philadelphia in 1787 as a particularly useful therapy for the symptoms of faction.
15. The "republican principle" that Madison refers to in this passage is perhaps best understood today as a "democratic principle" (i.e., the notion that decisions should be made through a majority vote, thereby reducing the threat of minority factions). It is also important to keep in mind that the term "republican," used throughout Madison's essays, does not refer to the Republican Party, which of course did not exist at the time Madison was writing.
16. Here Madison states a chief concern regarding the risk of factions. Madison's greatest fear was not that a minority faction would form and somehow seize control of government. His most pressing concern was that a majority faction would form around an issue that was adverse to the public good or to private rights.
17. The word desideratum is a noun that means "something that is needed." The word opprobrium is a noun that refers to "the disgrace caused by shameful conduct."
18. In the following section, Madison explains how the Constitutional arrangement that he promoted would provide protections against the effects of factions. Essentially, he argues that since the impulse to form factions cannot be overcome, the best approach is to reduce the opportunity for a dominant faction to form by expanding the size of the nation and the number of citizens who participate in elections. He suggests that the size of the new nation and the number of people represented in government would make it difficult for factions to form in general and extremely difficult for majority factions to form in particular. It is interesting to consider if the impediments to the formation of factions that Madison considered in 1787 remain relevant in the modern context.
19. Often considered the "Father of the U.S. Constitution" and a strong advocate for popular sovereignty, Madison was not a champion of direct democracy. Though Madison believed that government derived its rightful authority from the consent of the governed, he also remained fearful of the unchecked passions of the populace. He desired a system that was legitimized through popular sovereignty and that "refined and enlarged" public views. He believed that the Constitution would elevate public views and promote the public good in a number of ways: A) Wise, impartial, justice loving representatives of the people would serve as better arbiters of the public good than the citizens themselves. B) A government comprised of the proper number of representatives would promote meaningful deliberation. C) The selection process for representatives would help to promote the selection of only the most worthy representatives. D) The size of the territory would make it difficult for factions to form. E) In later *Federalist Papers* (*Federalist 51* in particular), Madison also discusses the advantages derived from the Constitution's separation of powers.
20. To preserve the anonymity of the authors and to promote the appearance of unity, each of the Federalist Papers was written under the pseudonym Publius. Publius Valerius Publicola was a Roman noble credited with helping to found and defend the ancient republic. Interestingly, Madison and Hamilton had rather distinct political philosophies and neither wholeheartedly endorsed the Constitution that emerged from Philadelphia. What united them was their common belief that rule under the Constitution, even with its imperfections, would be far superior to continuing under the Articles of Confederation.

Appendix E
Federalist[1] No. 51[2]

February 8, 1788

James Madison[3]

To the People of the State of New York:[4]

To WHAT expedient, then, shall we finally resort, for maintaining in practice the necessary partition of power among the several departments, as laid down in the Constitution?[5] The only answer that can be given is, that as all these exterior provisions are found to be inadequate,[6] the defect must be supplied, by so contriving the interior structure of the government as that its several constituent parts may, by their mutual relations, be the means of keeping each other in their proper places. Without presuming to undertake a full development of this important idea, I will hazard a few general observations, which may perhaps place it in a clearer light, and enable us to form a more correct judgment of the principles and structure of the government planned by the convention.

In order to lay a due foundation for that separate and distinct exercise of the different powers of government, which to a certain extent is admitted on all hands to be essential to the preservation of liberty, it is evident that each department should have a will of its own; and consequently should be so constituted that the members of each should have as little agency as possible in the appointment of the members of the others.[7] Were this principle rigorously adhered to, it would require that all the appointments for the supreme executive, legislative, and judiciary magistracies should be drawn from the same fountain of authority, the people, through channels having no communication whatever with one another. Perhaps such a plan of constructing the several departments would be less difficult in practice than it may in contemplation appear. Some difficulties, however, and some additional expense would attend the execution of it. Some deviations, therefore, from the principle must be admitted. In the constitution of the judiciary department in particular, it might be inexpedient to insist rigorously on the principle: first, because peculiar qualifications being essential in the members, the primary consideration ought to be to select that mode of choice which best secures these qualifications; secondly, because the permanent tenure by which the appointments are held in that department, must soon destroy all sense of dependence on the authority conferring them.

It is equally evident, that the members of each department should be as little dependent as possible on those of the others, for the emoluments annexed to their offices. Were the executive magistrate, or the judges, not independent of the legislature in this particular, their independence in every other would be merely nominal.

But the great security against a gradual concentration of the several powers in the same department, consists in giving to those who administer each department the necessary constitutional means and personal motives to resist encroachments of the others.[8] The provision for defense must in this, as in all other cases, be made commensurate to the danger of attack. Ambition must be made to counteract ambition.[9] The interest of the man must be connected with the constitutional rights of the place. It may be a reflection on human nature, that such devices should be necessary to control the abuses of government. But what is government itself, but the greatest of all reflections on human nature? If men were angels, no government would be necessary. If angels were to govern men, neither external nor internal controls on government would be necessary.[10] In framing a government which is to be administered by men over men, the great difficulty lies in this: you must first enable the government to control the governed; and in the next place oblige it to control itself. A dependence on the people is, no doubt, the primary control on the government; but experience has taught mankind the necessity of auxiliary precautions.[11]

This policy of supplying, by opposite and rival interests, the defect of better motives, might be traced through the whole system of human affairs, private as well as public. We see it particularly displayed in all the subordinate distributions of power, where the constant aim is to divide and arrange the several offices in such a manner as that each may be a check on the other that the private interest of every individual may be a sentinel over the public rights. These inventions of prudence cannot be less requisite in the distribution of the supreme powers of the State.[12]

But it is not possible to give to each department an equal power of self-defense. In republican government, the legislative authority necessarily predominates.[13] The remedy for this inconveniency is to divide the legislature into different branches; and to render them, by different modes of election and different principles of action, as little connected with each other as the nature of their common functions and their common dependence on the society will admit. It may even be necessary to guard against dangerous encroachments by still further precautions. As the weight of the legislative authority requires that it should be thus divided, the weakness of the executive may require, on the other hand, that it should be fortified. An absolute negative[14] on the legislature appears, at first view, to be the natural defense with which the executive magistrate should be armed. But perhaps it would be neither altogether safe nor alone sufficient. On ordinary occasions it might not be exerted with the requisite firmness, and on extraordinary occasions it might be perfidiously abused. May not this defect of an absolute negative be supplied by some qualified connection between this weaker department and the weaker branch of the stronger department, by which the latter may be led to support the constitutional rights of the former, without being too much detached from the rights of its own department?

If the principles on which these observations are founded be just, as I persuade myself they are, and they be applied as a criterion

---

Annotated by Howard Ernst (Associate Professor of Political Science at the United States Naval Academy and Senior Scholar at the University of Virginia Center for Politics). Ernst is a co-editor of *Dangerous Democracy? The Battle Over Ballot Initiatives in America* (2001) and author of *Chesapeake Bay Blues: Science, Politics, and the Struggle to Save the Bay* (2003).

to the several State constitutions, and to the federal Constitution it will be found that if the latter does not perfectly correspond with them, the former are infinitely less able to bear such a test.

There are, moreover, two considerations particularly applicable to the federal system of America, which place that system in a very interesting point of view.[15]

First. In a single republic, all the power surrendered by the people is submitted to the administration of a single government; and the usurpations are guarded against by a division of the government into distinct and separate departments. In the compound republic of America,[16] the power surrendered by the people is first divided between two distinct governments, and then the portion allotted to each subdivided among distinct and separate departments. Hence a double security arises to the rights of the people. The different governments will control each other, at the same time that each will be controlled by itself.

Second. It is of great importance in a republic not only to guard the society against the oppression of its rulers, but to guard one part of the society against the injustice of the other part. Different interests necessarily exist in different classes of citizens. If a majority be united by a common interest, the rights of the minority will be insecure. There are but two methods of providing against this evil:[17] the one by creating a will in the community independent of the majority that is, of the society itself; the other, by comprehending in the society so many separate descriptions of citizens as will render an unjust combination of a majority of the whole very improbable, if not impracticable. The first method prevails in all governments possessing an hereditary or self-appointed authority. This, at best, is but a precarious security; because a power independent of the society may as well espouse the unjust views of the major, as the rightful interests of the minor party, and may possibly be turned against both parties. The second method will be exemplified in the federal republic of the United States. Whilst all authority in it will be derived from and dependent on the society, the society itself will be broken into so many parts, interests, and classes of citizens, that the rights of individuals, or of the minority, will be in little danger from interested combinations of the majority.[18] In a free government the security for civil rights must be the same as that for religious rights. It consists in the one case in the multiplicity of interests, and in the other in the multiplicity of sects. The degree of security in both cases will depend on the number of interests and sects; and this may be presumed to depend on the extent of country and number of people comprehended under the same government. This view of the subject must particularly recommend a proper federal system to all the sincere and considerate friends of republican government, since it shows that in exact proportion as the territory of the Union may be formed into more circumscribed Confederacies, or States oppressive combinations of a majority will be facilitated: the best security, under the republican forms, for the rights of every class of citizens, will be diminished: and consequently the stability and independence of some member of the government, the only other security, must be proportionately increased. Justice is the end of government. It is the end of civil society.[19] It ever has been and ever will be pursued until it be obtained, or until liberty be lost in the pursuit. In a society under the forms of which the stronger faction can readily unite and oppress the weaker, anarchy may as truly be said to reign as in a state of nature, where the weaker individual is not secured against the violence of the stronger; and as, in the latter state, even the stronger individuals are prompted, by the uncertainty of their condition, to submit to a government which may protect the weak as well as themselves; so, in the former state, will the more powerful factions or parties be gradually induced, by a like motive, to wish for a government which will protect all parties, the weaker as well as the more powerful. It can be little doubted that if the State of Rhode Island was separated from the Confederacy and left to itself, the insecurity of rights under the popular form of government within such narrow limits would be displayed by such reiterated oppressions of factious majorities that some power altogether independent of the people would soon be called for by the voice of the very factions whose misrule had proved the necessity of it. In the extended republic of the United States,[20] and among the great variety of interests, parties, and sects which it embraces, a coalition of a majority of the whole society could seldom take place on any other principles than those of justice and the general good; whilst there being thus less danger to a minor from the will of a major party, there must be less pretext, also, to provide for the security of the former, by introducing into the government a will not dependent on the latter, or, in other words, a will independent of the society itself. It is no less certain than it is important, notwithstanding the contrary opinions which have been entertained, that the larger the society, provided it lie within a practical sphere, the more duly capable it will be of self-government. And happily for the REPUBLICAN CAUSE, the practicable sphere may be carried to a very great extent, by a judicious modification and mixture of the FEDERAL PRINCIPLE.

PUBLIUS.[21]

Annotations

1. Considered by many scholars as the single best guide to the thoughts and desires of the nation's founders, the *Federalist Papers* are comprised of eighty-five essays written by Alexander Hamilton, James Madison, and John Jay. The essays were written as a defense of the proposed Constitution from anti-federalist attacks. The essays have come to be considered the nation's most thoughtful and thorough explanation of its constitutional arrangement.
2. In this essay, Madison continues a line of argument he began in earlier *Federalist Papers*, explaining the Constitution's structural improvements over the Articles of Confederation. Chief among these design improvements is the Constitution's creation of separate governmental institutions with overlapping powers. In *Federalist 47*, Madison explained that "The accumulation of all powers legislative, executive, and judiciary in the same hands, whether of one, a few or many, and whether hereditary, self appointed, or elective, may justly be pronounced the very definition of tyranny." By dividing governmental authority into distinct branches and giving each branch the authority to check the power of the others, Madison hoped the Constitution would provide safeguards against tyranny, safeguards missing from the Articles of Confederation.
3. Between November 1787 and February 1788, Madison wrote 29 of the 85 *Federalist Papers*. Though Hamilton wrote far more of the essays, 51 to Madison's 29, the clarity and power of Madison's prose has secured his reputation as the federalist bard of the U.S. Constitution. Of the seven most commonly cited *Federalist Papers* (i.e., Nos. 10, 37, 39, 47, 51, 70 and 78), Madison authored five (Nos. 10, 37, 39, 47, and 51) and Hamilton authored two (Nos. 70 and 78).
4. At the time the Constitution was being debated, Congress met in New York, making it the nation's capital and a key state in the ratification process. The state of New York was slow to support the Constitution,

ratifying only after a successful ratification vote in Virginia and after the state had been promised a bill of rights. New York became the eleventh state to ratify the Constitution on July 26, 1788.

5. In this section, Madison introduces the main topic of *Federalist 51*, the constitutional protections that guard against tyranny.
6. By "exterior provisions," Madison means the checks that are placed on popular government through elections and other forms of public control.
7. The idea of "checks and balances" did not originate with James Madison or the U.S. Constitution. In *Federalist 47*, Madison credits the great French political philosopher Montesquieu (1689–1755) as the oracle to be cited when discussing separation of powers. Moreover, the concept was familiar to the framers of the U.S. Constitution since it had been practiced in the British governmental structure of the time and in the state constitutions.
8. Madison did not trust that dividing government into independent departments would adequately provide the necessary protections from tyranny. He believed that separate institutions with overlapping powers served as the best internal check. It was in the overlap of authority that each branch of government would be empowered to check the authority of other branches. In such an arrangement, no branch of government could adequately function without some degree of cooperation from the others. For example, legislation passed by Congress could be vetoed by the President; legislation vetoed by the President could be overridden by Congress; treaties negotiated by the President could only be ratified by Congress; enforcement of judicial decisions could only be accomplished through executive action; military conflicts directed by the President could only be declared wars and funded through action by Congress; federal court justices could only be nominated by the President and confirmed by Congress; and so on. This web of interdependence was to serve as the primary internal check against tyranny.
9. Here Madison explicitly states his general strategy for guarding against tyranny—pit the ambition of one would-be-tyrant against the ambition of other power seekers. Ambition, the very trait that causes people to engage in the endless pursuit of power and which threatens the liberty of all people, would be harnessed to protect civil society.
10. This is one of Madison's most famous passages. It reveals far more than his skill as a writer; it provides insights into his view of human nature. The Hobbesian view of human nature and the system of checks and balances that logically flows from this perspective lies at the heart of Madison's political philosophy. It was also this view of human nature that lies at the heart of the anti-federalist opposition to the Constitution. Samuel Bryan, Melancton Smith, Patrick Henry, and other prominent anti-federalists argued that a responsive government held accountable by a virtuous citizenry through frequent elections and clear lines of accountability was far superior to a complex system of checks and balances. They argued that numerous internal divisions within government and overlapping governmental powers would likely reduce the public's ability to control government and, consequently, weaken the best guard against tyranny—a vigilant, well informed public. For a more recent critique of Madison's view, see Richard Matthews' influential work, *If All Men Were Angels: James Madison & the Heartless Empire of Reason* (1995). Building on the work of the anti-federalists, Matthews argues that founding a political system based on such a pessimistic view of human nature promotes a level of political conflict and distrust that might have otherwise been avoided.
11. Madison did not believe that separation of powers was the first or most important check against tyranny. Similar to the anti-federalists, Madison believed that a dependence on the people was the primary check against tyranny. But unlike the anti-federalists, Madison had little confidence that elections and popular oversight would be sufficient to guard against the ambitions of tyrants. Consequently, he argued that auxiliary checks, such as separation of powers, were necessary precautions.
12. In *Federalist 10*, Madison applied the same logic to curing the "mischief of factions." Instead of arguing against factions, or denying the qualities of human nature that assure factions would form, Madison welcomed the formation of such groups. He believed that the formation of many competing groups would serve as the best protection from the formation of one dominant group.
13. The idea of "checks and balances" does not assume that each branch of government is equal in power. Madison believed that the legislative branch, the law-giving branch, would be the most powerful. Because of its innate power, special attention was given to provide internal checks on the legislative branch. Dividing the legislature into two houses and providing the executive with veto power provided auxiliary checks on this most powerful branch of government.
14. By "absolute negative," Madison was referring to an absolute veto (i.e., a presidential veto that could not be overridden by the legislature). Though the executive was not given such authority, its powers were concentrated in the hands of a single person, the president. Concentrating power in the executive, just like dividing it in the legislative department, was part of the larger strategy to ensure that no one branch of government would become dominant.
15. In the section that follows, Madison outlines several checks and balances provided in the proposed constitutional arrangement. Chief among these checks are the division of power between the federal government and the state governments, the creation of many competing societal factions, the division of the federal government into three distinct branches, and the division of the legislative branch into two separate houses.
16. Here Madison is referring to the nation's "federal system" or "American federalism" (a political system in which power is shared between the national government and the state governments, with both levels of government maintaining a degree of independence and deriving their power directly from the people).
17. As was the case in *Federalist 10*, Madison reveals his distaste for classic democracy or majority rule. He argued that majority rule threatens the rights of minor groups and therefore is an "evil" to be guarded against. It is important not to confuse Madison's concern for minority rights with the modern notion of minority advocacy (i.e., the concern for the rights of underprivileged groups in society). As the anti-federalists were quick to point out, Madison was raised on a four thousand acre tidewater plantation and was part of Virginia's slaveholding elite. His concern for minority rights was most likely tied to his desire to secure the property rights of the few against the mass ambitions of the majority.
18. In this section, Madison rejects the creation of a ruling class (i.e., a hereditary or self-appointed authority) for the protection of minority interests in society. Instead, Madison argues that a division of authority within government and a division of factions external to government would provide the surest security against a majority faction. For more on Madison's beliefs regarding factions, see *Federalist 10*.
19. Here Madison states that the "end," or primary objective, of civil society and civil society's offspring—government—is justice. For Madison, a properly functioning government serves as an objective umpire between competing interests. Justice, according to Madison, naturally occurs when government functions as a judicious broker between competing interests. Hence, Madison argued, the secret to achieving a just society was to structure government in such a way that no special weight was given to any one faction, even a majority faction.
20. Here Madison restates his argument from *Federalist 10*, claiming that enlarging the sphere of the national government would provide valuable protections from the formation of a dominant faction.
21. To preserve the anonymity of the authors and to promote the appearance of unity, each of the Federalist Papers was written under the pseudonym Publius. Publius Valerius Publicola was a Roman noble credited with founding and defending the ancient republic.

Glossary

A

abolition The complete removal of the practice of slavery.

access The ability to get the attention of policy makers to present one's position.

accountability The process by which voters are given the opportunity to judge the actions of government officials and affect the officials' power and career.

ad hoc committee A body such as an investigating committee formed to serve a specific purpose only.

adjudication A quasi-judicial process used to make rules that have a major impact on a limited number of parties.

administrative rules The guidelines and procedures (also known as administrative regulations) designed by agencies of the executive branch to implement public laws; agencies rely upon the statutes enacted by Congress when designing administrative rules.

adversarial reporting An approach to covering news stories in which the reporter refuses to accept the position expressed by the participants and, instead, aggressively delves into the situation, with little regard for embarrassing the subjects.

advice and consent The constitutional right of the Senate to approve major presidential appointments, such as cabinet members, ambassadors, and Supreme Court nominees.

affirmative action Policies designed to enhance the employment of women and minorities and to undo past discriminatory practices.

agenda A set of problems a decision maker either chooses or is forced to take action on.

Aid to Families with Dependent Children (AFDC) A federal program that provides income support payments to poor families with children.

alien A legal visitor or resident in a nation of which he or she is not a citizen; a citizen of one nation living in another.

ambassador The top official in a U.S. foreign embassy; appointed by the president and confirmed by the Senate.

***amicus curiae* brief** "Friend of the court" brief in which an outside party presents arguments on one side or another of a case being considered by the court.

Anti-Federalists Historically, individuals who opposed all or portions of the proposed Constitution and encroachment on local power.

antitrust policies Federal government policies that seek to sustain competition in the economy by breaking up or regulating monopolistic industries.

appellate jurisdiction The power to consider court cases that are being appealed from lower courts.

appropriations The monies approved by Congress from the public treasury for funding federal agencies and operating federal programs.

arena Location where the game is played. Often tied directly to political institutions, such as the presidency or Congress, where players make policy.

Articles of Confederation Legal basis for the first plan of government for the United States (1776; replaced by the Constitution upon its ratification in 1788).

assimilation The process by which immigrants adopt the American political culture, the English language, the social customs and move away from their native language, customs, and traditions. The process of becoming "Americanized."

at-large elections Elections in which candidates run for office on a citywide basis rather than from wards or electoral districts within cities.

attitudes Long-term and deeply held perspectives about what is important and how society works. See also *opinions* and *values*.

authoritarian system System of government whereby power is concentrated in a leader or an elite without accountability.

authority Power that some players have over others as the result of their rank or position.

autocratic Rule by one having complete and unlimited power.

B

Baker v. Carr A 1962 Supreme Court case affirming the Court's jurisdiction over redistricting and affirming the lack of one-man, one-vote as a violation of the equal protection clause of the 14th Amendment.

balance of trade The sum total of imports and exports, with special concern for the degree to which a country spends more on importing goods and services than it earns from other nations.

balanced budget A state of national income and expenses in which government receipts equal or exceed outlays.

balancing the ticket Increasing the political appeal of a party's candidates by including candidates popular with different geographical, ethnic, social, and/or ideological groups.

bandwagon effect Encouraging socially motivated voting by implying that everyone else is jumping on the bandwagon and that the voter should not be left behind.

bicameral legislature A legislature with two chambers.

bill of attainder Legislative act that declares an individual guilty of a crime without a trial and punishes the person.

Bill of Rights The first ten amendments to the Constitution that spell out many civil rights and liberties of citizens.

bipartisan Support for a course of action not split exclusively along party lines.

blanket primary Nomination elections in some states that allow voters to shift among parties for different offices. See also *open* and *closed primary*.

bloc voting Highly unified voting by elected officials from one political party.

block grants Federal grants to state or local governments for a broad program area.

bought coalition A group of individuals agreeing to support a position only after a change in the substance of the legislation or in exchange for some other benefit.

boycott Political action of not purchasing the goods of a nation, group, or individual, to protest its policies; the use of economic pressure to exert political influence.

bribery The direct exchange of items of value for a public official's vote or support.

broad constructionist view A judicial philosophy that holds that constitutional interpretation should be based not only upon constitutional language and an appreciation for the intent of the Founders in designing its provisions, but also upon evolutionary ideas about civil rights and social justice.

brokerage politics Form of politics whereby elected officials obtain support by providing tangible benefits to constituents, who return the favor by providing votes for elected officials.

Brown v. Board of Education of Topeka Landmark Supreme Court case that ruled that segregated public schools were unconstitutional under the equal protection clause of the Constitution.

bundling A campaign fund-raising technique in which a group identifies worthy recipients and serves as a collection point for contributions and hands over a "bundle" of checks.

bureau Generic term used to describe organization units within agencies; may also carry such names as Office, Administration, or Division.

bureaucratic A method of organization marked by formal rules, hierarchical structure, and delegation of authority.

C

cabinet A body of advisers to the president who are appointed by the president.

cabinet secretaries Presidential appointees chosen to administer the major departments of government, who together report to and advise the chief executive.

candidate-centered campaign Campaigns dominated by the personal organization of the candidate, in which voters judge candidates more on their personal characteristics than on their party.

canon An accepted rule, standard, or criterion.

capital The private accumulation of goods used in the production of derivative goods.

capitalism An economic system based on the widespread private ownership of the means of production and trade, combined with an unrestricted marketplace for goods and services.

carpetbagging A derisive term used to describe opportunist politicians moving into a new electoral district and running for office.

casework The individualized services done by elected and appointed officials to help solve the problems of constituents.

categoric group Individuals with common characteristics, but who see no way those characteristics are related to some interest that might be pursued in the political realm. See also *potential group* and *interest group*.

caucus A meeting of party activists to select nominees, choose leaders, determine party policy, or plan strategy.

Charles Montesquieu (1689–1755) French philosopher and jurist who proposed that governments be created with a formal separation of executive, legislative, and judicial powers.

checks and balances Assignment of government powers so that the powers of one branch of government may be used to limit the powers of another branch.

chief diplomat The president's role as manager of U.S. relations with other countries.

chief executive The president's role as the administrator of the federal government.

chief legislator The extra constitutional role of the president in defining problems worthy of legislative action and suggesting the preferred legislative solution.

chief of staff The top presidential aide, charged with controlling access to the president and managing the White House staff.

chief of state The role of the president as the symbolic leader of the country, representing the United States at official events and embodying national goals and aspirations.

city manager A professionally trained executive hired by a municipality to oversee the daily administration of local government.

civic duty The sense of obligation to participate in the political process.

civil case A dispute between private parties, not involving a governmental body.

civil disobedience The political protest strategy of purposefully disregarding laws and failing to comply with them in order to show opposition to them. Usually involves peaceful protest.

civil liberties Fundamental freedoms provided to American citizens in the Constitution and the Bill of Rights. Includes freedoms of speech, the press, religion, and assembly.

Civil Rights Act of 1964 Important legislation that prohibits discrimination in public accommodations and employment on the basis of race, national origin, religion or sex.

civil servants Public-sector employees selected for their jobs through a civil service system, usually involving a process of competitive examination or competitive evaluation of applications.

civil service A system for selecting government employees on the basis of merit rather than political connection or patronage.

class action suit The joint action of similarly affected individuals in taking a case to court even though the individual impact of the situation may be minimal.

clients Individuals taken care of by government but not expected to participate in the political process.

closed games Games that attempt to exclude new players.

closed primary Nomination elections involving only affiliates of the party. See also *blanket* and *open primary*.

closed shop Requirements that all employees of a company are union members in good standing.

cloture Cutting off debate during a filibuster by acquiring a three-fifths vote of those present and voting (used in the Senate only).

coalition A temporary group of often diverse members who agree to support a particular policy position.

coalition of mixed expectations A group of political players agreeing to a particular policy initiative but having varying reasons for giving support and different expectations about policy outcomes.

coattail effect The ability of candidates on the top of the party ticket to affect races at lower levels, either by changing the composition of the electorate or by directly encouraging voters.

Cold War The period of conflict between the United States and the Soviet Union from roughly 1945 through 1990. Confrontations were based on economic, political, and diplomatic strategies and not military battles.

collective bargaining The process by which workers in plants or industries come together, usually through labor unions, to negotiate pay, benefits, and working conditions.

collective benefits Those goods, services, and rewards that cannot be limited to members of a particular group. See also **selective benefits.**

Commander-in-Chief The president's role as manager of the U.S. armed services.

commerce clause Provision in the U.S. Constitution that empowers the national government to regulate interstate commerce.

common law A cumulative body of law that evolved in England over several centuries and that is based primarily on judicial decisions and precedent rather than laws written by legislative bodies.

communism A political and economic ideology based on the elimination of private property, with goods owned in common and distributed on the basis of need.

compact theory Theory of federalism that sees the national government and the U.S. Constitution as legally based on the consent of sovereign state governments.

comparable worth The view that women should receive equal pay for jobs that are comparable to those held by men, when they have equivalent education and job experience.

compartmentalizing Isolating attitudes, opinions, and/or behavior into categories (compartments) without recognizing the connection between them.

competitive bidding Process whereby local governments award contracts. Bidders are required to submit closed bids prior to a specified date, at which time the bids are opened and the contract is generally awarded to the lowest bidder thought to be capable of fulfilling contract requirements.

competitive evaluation The civil service system practice of measuring the competence of job applicants through a process in which applications and resumes are competitively rated by a review team to identify the most qualified applicants; most common in midlevel managerial job positions.

competitive examination The civil service system practice of measuring the competence of job applicants through a standardized test designed to assess information and talents relevant to job performance; most common in lower-level and specialized job functions.

competitive federalism Period of federal relationships, roughly 1980 to the present, characterized by cutbacks in federal aid, re-sorting of program responsibilities, and the increased use of regulatory mandates.

complete citizens Individuals who fully relate to the political process in a deep and continuing manner; they are more than simply legal residents of a political unit.

compromise The mutual accommodation among players with competing interests that allows a decision to be made.

Compromise of 1850 Compromise reached by Congress, admitting California as a free state and including a strict policy regarding the return of runaway slaves.

concurring opinion Opinion by one or more justices who agree with the majority decision in a case but disagree with the legal reasoning of the majority.

confederation A plan by which a league of sovereign states delegates limited powers to a central government.

conference committee A joint House and Senate committee established to reconcile differences between two different versions of the same legislation.

conservatives Supporters of a political ideology that distrusts human nature, who envision a limited role for government, require significant justification for change, emphasize order over freedom, and assume a natural hierarchy in society.

constituents Persons who elect a person to office or to whom an appointed official is accountable.

containment A foreign policy plan to halt the spread of communism and the influence of the Soviet Union through mutual defense alliances with nations having borders with the Soviet Union and the communist nations of Eastern Europe and Asia.

continuous games Games with no clear ending point and with many rounds. See also *discrete games*.

contract theory Theory of federalism that sees the national government and Constitution as legally based on the consent of the people.

cooperative federalism In response to the Depression and World War II, the national, state, and local levels of government exercised more direct cooperation.

cooptation Development of close ties between an agency and the organizations and companies it is intended to regulate; may interfere with enforcement of the agency's regulatory responsibilities.

coproduction Residents taking on activities often performed only by government, if at all, to enhance the level and quality of community services.

cost-of-living adjustment (COLAs) Automatic adjustments made to social programs that annually increase benefits according to the Consumer Price Index in order to compensate for inflation.

council-manager plan A plan of local government whereby the city council is responsible for major policy decisions, and daily administration is managed by a professionally trained executive hired by the council.

county Unit of local government originally designed as an administrative subunit of state government; provides state-designated and other local services.

covert action Activities intended to gather information about the intentions and capabilities of other nations through infiltration of their political decision making or military operations.

creative federalism Period when national, state, and local governments cooperatively initiated bold and creative social programs.

cross-pressures Conflicting attitudes that make it difficult to form an opinion or to take satisfying and consistent action on them.

cultural diversity The coexistence of a variety of cultures that are accepted as worthy and legitimate.

culture Those aspects of a society's history, artistic accomplishment, and attitudes toward the world deemed worthy of transmission from one generation to the next.

cyberdemocracy Political strategies using new computer-based technological tools, such as e-mail and the Internet.

cyberspace The area of communication created by new computer-based technologies.

D

dealignment A decline in political party loyalty and a rise in voting independence.

deficit The shortfall between government expenditures and income.

delegate A style of representation in which the person represents the views of others, no matter what he or she might prefer. See also *trustee*.

delegation doctrine Process whereby Congress enacts laws that give general policy directions and instruction, leaving specific policy execution to designated federal agencies.

demand-side economic policy Policies benefiting the demand segments of the economy (workers, consumers, and so on) to stimulate economic growth starting at the bottom and working its way up.

dependent voters Voters using a relatively fixed set of criteria, such as party identification or ethnic background, to differentiate candidates. See also *responsive voters*.

deregulation An initiative to lessen or remove the impact of regulatory mandates placed on the private sector and on state and local governments.

détente A period when strained international relations give way to a lessening of military and diplomatic tensions.

deterrence A strategy of national defense whereby a strong military force maintained by one nation is expected to convince other nations against the wisdom of engaging in a military attack.

deviating election An election in which the candidate of the minority party wins by gaining enough votes from voters identifying with the majority party.

devolution The transference of authority and control by a national government to local governments (including states).

Dillon's rule Legal interpretation that state governments have full powers over city governments.

diplomacy The foreign relations that independent nations maintain with each other, often through discussions and negotiations, and sometimes through threats.

disclosure laws Legislation requiring groups or individuals to publicly report various aspects of their behavior, with the expectation that the fear of public embarrassment will stop illegal or undesirable actions.

discrete games Games that have a clear ending point; games with either one or a limited number of rounds.

discretion The legal ability of federal officials to employ experience and personal judgment in executing public policies. Restrained and limited by statutes and administrative rules.

dissenting opinion Opinion by one or more justices who voted with the minority (against the majority) on a given case.

distribution The way public preferences are arrayed across the various alternatives.

distributive policy Public policies that distribute goods and services widely among the population with no significant bias toward particular groups.

divided government When one co-equal branch of government is controlled by one party and the other branch or branches are controlled by the opposing party. Usually relates to the partisan split between the president and Congress.

dual federalism Each level of government operated more or less separately from the other.

due process Legal proceedings conducted in a proper manner, ensuring protection of individual rights.

E

economic culture Widely shared fundamental beliefs, attitudes, and perspectives about how the economy should work.

economies of scale The ability to reduce the per unit cost of a produced item by expanding the size of the production process and thus reducing administrative overhead, equipment, and other fixed costs.

effectiveness An evaluative criterion that compares the goals of public policies with the impacts that result from the implementation of those policies.

efficacy The feeling that involvement in politics makes sense and is an efficient use of one's time.

efficiency An evaluative criterion that compares the costs of public policies with the benefits that result from the implementation of those policies.

Electoral College The collective name for individuals chosen by majority vote in each state to cast that state's ballots for president.

electors The individuals chosen to serve in the electoral college and to cast votes electing a president.

elitism Theory of political power in which key political decisions are made by a small number of skilled, committed persons.

Emancipation Proclamation Formal declaration by President Abraham Lincoln in 1863, freeing all slaves in the Confederate States; continuing rebellion prevented implementation.

embargo An economic action designed to achieve diplomatic objectives. The reduction or elimination of trade with a nation in order to place economic pressure on that nation.

embassy The diplomatic offices of one nation located within the boundaries of another nation. Headed by an ambassador and managed by diplomatic staff.

emulation The patterning of one's attitudes, outlooks, and behavior after parents, friends, or other respected individuals.

enfranchisement Having the legal right to vote.

entitlement programs Programs in which persons automatically qualify to enroll in the program and receive benefits if they satisfy eligibility requirements.

environmental impact statement Reports that federal agencies must prepare for any project expected to have some impact on the environment. These reports, required by the National Environmental Policy Act, describe how projects will affect the environment.

equal protection clause The provision of the 14th Amendment that forbids states from abridging the constitutional rights of citizens and requires equal enforcement of the law for all citizens.

Equal Rights Amendment (ERA) Constitutional amendment that was considered but never adopted, in the 1970s. Intended to provide equal rights for women.

equal time rule Legislation enforced by the Federal Communications Commission that requires radio and television stations offering or selling time to one candidate or party to offer equal time at equal rates to all other candidates or parties in a particular race.

equality of opportunity The guarantee that all participants in the political process begin with an equal chance to win. See also *equality of outcome*.

equality of outcome (or condition) The result of a political (or economic) game in which all players end up the same. See also *equality of opportunity*.

equity An evaluation criterion that considers the extent to which the impacts of public policy are equally distributed.

establishment clause Provision of the 1st Amendment that holds that "Congress shall make no law respecting an establishment of religion."

ethnocentrism The emphasis on and unthinking support for the values and institutions of one's own society to the exclusion of the contributions of other societies.

evaluative criteria Standards used to measure and assess the impacts that result from public policy implementation.

ex post facto law Law that makes some action taken in the past illegal and punishable at the time the law is enacted.

exclusionary rule Constitutional ruling, premised on the 4th Amendment, that evidence obtained through an illegal search or seizure may not be used in a criminal trial.

Executive Office of the President (EOP) Set of agencies and advisers created to provide advice and assistance to the office of the president as the president directs and manages the executive branch.

executive order A rule or regulation issued by the president without the formal approval of Congress but having the force of law.

executive privilege A president's right to withhold information from the other branches of government in order to guarantee receiving candid advice from presidential advisers or to protect national security.

exit poll Informal survey of voting patterns based on interviews of those who are exiting election sites.

externalities Consequences of political strategies and games that affect other players not directly involved in the game.

F

faction A subgroup within a larger organization or society.

fairness doctrine Enforced by the Federal Communications Commission until 1987, this rule required radio and television stations to be fair to all sides of political issues by fairly presenting opposing views.

faithless elector A member of the electoral college who is selected as a supporter of one candidate but who votes for another.

"family values" A set of moral principles that could include, but is not limited to, opposition to abortion, birth control, and premarital sex, and support for prayer in public schools, introduced as a political slogan by Dan Quayle.

Federal Election Campaign Act (FECA) Law passed in 1972 and amended in 1974, 1976, and 1979 establishing the rules for campaign financing of federal elections. The act establishes reporting requirements for the Federal Elections Commission for all federal races and provides for public financing of presidential races.

federalism Pattern of government in which a national, overarching government shares power with subnational or state governments.

Federalists Individuals who supported the ratification of the Constitution as drafted in Philadelphia in 1787.

fiscal federalism Financial arrangements and transfers among governments at different levels in the federal system.

filibuster A delaying tactic used by a legislative minority to control floor proceedings until a compromise is reached. Allowed in the U.S. Senate only.

First Continental Congress The 1774 meeting of delegates from the colonies to discuss what were seen as negative actions by Parliament.

fiscal policy Policy designed to maintain economic growth and stability through government finance policies related to taxing and spending.

flat tax A taxation method in which everyone who earns enough to be taxed pays the same percentage of their income in tax.

floor Referring to the main level of a legislative chamber, the arena for voting and other formal business.

foreign aid The provision of currency, grants, or loans from one nation to another, often for the purposes of economic and industrial development; can be given for general purposes or to support particular projects like dams, schools, or hospitals.

foreign policy The policies of a nation that relate to economic, political, or military relationships with other nations in the world.

foreign service officer An individual who is trained in generalist foreign service skills and enters the civil service in a special classification for public officials engaged in diplomatic service.

format The manner of presentation distinctive for each medium, which affects its use and impact.

formula grant Federal grant to states or localities that is distributed on the basis of a prespecified formula.

Fourteen Points Principles for world peace outlined by President Woodrow Wilson at the culmination of World War I; included provision for a League of Nations (the first effort at an international tribunal designed to maintain world peace).

fragmentation The breaking of a society (or audience) into groups of individuals with narrow and competing interests.

franchise The right to vote.

franking privilege The right of legislators to send out official mail at no cost.

free exercise clause Provision of the 1st Amendment that prevents Congress from prohibiting the free exercise of religious practice.

Freedom of Information Act Legislation requiring agencies to publish a classification scheme for their documents and to establish a procedure for requesting documents that does not compromise national security, trade secrets, or personal privacy.

G

Gallup Poll A widely recognized national opinion polling company that asks standard questions on a regular basis.

gatekeeper An individual or organization controlling access to a desired resource such as publicity or a nomination for public office.

general assembly The body in the United Nations where all member nations are represented and have one vote. The chamber has no power to make decisions that compel action by member nations.

general revenue sharing Federal grant with few strings attached; this type of grant was common from 1972 to 1986.

gerrymandering The process of designing political districts for partisan or group advantage. The term derives from an elongated set of districts created by Governor Elbridge Gerry of Massachusetts, which eighteenth-century political cartoonist Elkanah Tinsdale drew as a salamander and dubbed a "Gerrymander."

glass ceiling The concept that invisible forms of discrimination prevent women from rising to top positions in business and government.

globalism Recognition that the nations of the world are increasingly interconnected by economic, social. and political forces.

government The formal set of institutions having the legitimate right to make collective decisions on the part of an organized society.

government-in-sunshine laws Laws that require government agencies to conduct their meetings open to the public, except in specified situations such as discussions that might violate national security interests or the privacy of individuals.

grassroots lobbying Calling on group membership to take concrete actions, such as writing or calling decision makers, in support of an interest group policy.

Great Compromise Agreement at the Constitutional Convention concerning representation of the states; creation of a two-house legislature, the Senate with equal representation and the House of Representatives with representation based on population.

Great Society The label for the social policies promoted by President Lyndon Johnson and enacted by Congress in the 1960s as part of the War on Poverty. These policies were premised on the belief that social and economic problems can be solved through programs orchestrated by the federal government.

gross domestic product (GDP) The monetary value of all goods and services produced in a nation in a given year. Important indicator of economic performance.

group entrepreneur An individual who sensitizes potential group members to their interests and attempts to organize them. See also *potential group* and *interest group*.

H

Hatch Act A law designed to limit the partisan political activities of government employees.

hate speech Words related to race, religion, or creed intended to incite anger or violence.

hearing A committee meeting in which experts are brought in to testify about proposed legislative action.

home rule Powers of self-government granted to municipalities; the extent of the powers is often determined by the size and classification of the city.

I

ideology A comprehensive set of beliefs about the proper nature of people and society.

immunity Doctrine that public officials cannot be held personally accountable or sued for official actions and decisions; recent court decisions allow limited immunity.

impeach To indict a government official for improper acts and in the process to verify that enough evidence exists to go forward with a proceeding that could lead to removal from office. In the case of federal government officials such as the president and judges, the House of Representatives impeaches and the Senate tries the case.

impeachment The formal bringing of charges against a government official that could lead to that official's removal from office.

implied power The authority that, though not explicitly granted by the U.S. Constitution, is inferred based on a broad interpretation of the necessary and proper clause.

impoundment A president's refusal to spend money appropriated by Congress.

inclusive games Games that welcome or allow the entry of new players.

inclusiveness An organization's strategy of including, rather than excluding, potential supporters by making organization positions more appealing to them.

income tax A tax levied on the incomes of individuals, families, and corporations. Usually, a progressive tax; that is, tax rates increase with income.

incorporate To obtain the legal corporate status of municipality through procedures specified in state laws and constitutions.

incrementalism Breaking large problems into small segments and taking limited actions designed to correct the most troublesome aspects.

independent expenditures The purchase of goods or services in support of a candidate without any consultation or coordination with the candidate or the campaign staff.

independent regulatory commissions Federal agencies charged with regulation for private-sector activities that directly affect the public; designed to be partially insulated from political forces.

inflation The rate at which the costs of goods and services increase or an economic period where prices are rising relatively, rapidly eroding purchasing power.

infomercial An advertisement designed to look like an information program.

informal rulemaking A process to devise administrative rules with broad application; proposed rules must be published in the *Federal Register* and public comments solicited before issuing rules in final form.

infrastructure The buildings, utilities, power and water lines, and other constructed features of urban areas.

initiative A procedure allowing voters to propose and vote directly on legislation.

in-kind contributions The direct provision of goods and services, such as computer time, office supplies, and transportation, to a preferred candidate.

insider trading The illegal use of inside information by corporate officials to plan effective investment strategies.

instrumental voting A voting choice motivated by the match between the voter's policy goals and the candidate's promises. See also *social needs* and *psychological needs voting*.

intensity The depth to which opinions are held and the emotional tie that individuals have to those opinions.

interest group Individuals who are aware of the interests they share with others and who have expended the resources necessary to create an organization that attempts to influence government policy. See also *categoric group* and *potential group*.

iron triangles Enduring relationships among members of federal agency bureaus, congressional committees, and interest groups who share an interest in a specific area of public policy. Participants generally discourage outsiders from joining their closed game.

issue networks The natural and continuous interaction of government and private players with an interest in a specific policy area. These relationships involve members of federal agency bureaus, congressional committees, and interest groups who share an interest in a specific area of public policy. They are sometimes also called "iron triangles."

issue publics That portion of the population that has given serious consideration to an issue or a candidate and has a well-thought-out preference.

J

Jim Crow laws State and local laws that established segregation in public facilities and public schools. Initially upheld under "separate but equal" doctrine.

Joint Chiefs of Staff Primary military advisors to the president and secretary of defense. Members represent branches of the military service and are appointed by the president.

joint committees Permanent committees made up of both House and Senate members.

judicial activism Using powers of judicial review and statutory interpretation to expand the role of the judiciary in defining public policy.

judicial conference Closed meeting in which members of the Supreme Court discuss cases and make decisions about them.

judicial restraint Belief in a limited role for the federal courts in defining public policy.

judicial review The authority of the federal courts to consider the constitutionality of laws enacted by Congress and the actions taken by officials in the executive branch.

jurisdiction The types of matters that a given court is empowered to consider.

jury profiling An attempt to research the type of juror who would be most favorable to one's cause. Based on the right of lawyers to challenge the right of a certain number of potential jury members to sit on the jury.

K

Kentucky Resolution Law Passed by the Kentucky State Legislature in 1798 that held that the Alien and Sedition Acts were void and of no force; an early expression of the states' rights philosophy.

kickback Payoff made to a public official from a company or individual who received favorable treatment as the result of intervention by the official.

L

laissez-faire The economic doctrine, often associated with economist Adam Smith, that holds that individuals and companies should be free to make decisions about investment, production, and distribution without government interference.

latent interests Common outlooks and policy goals that could be activated and stimulate political involvement.

layer-cake federalism Period of dual federalism when the national and state governments operated separately from each other with little mixing of governing responsibilities.

leader of the free world The president's position as spokesperson and coordinator of joint efforts by the noncommunist nations.

leadership The ability to influence others as a result of demeanor, trust, or personal charisma.

leak (news) A government official's deliberate disclosure of secret information to embarrass others or to promote a particular policy.

legislative caucus The meeting of party members in a legislature to choose leadership and set policy direction.

legislative veto Federal law that requires congressional approval of actions before the actions can be taken by federal agencies; ruled unconstitutional by the Supreme Court in 1983.

legitimacy Public perception that an individual is the rightful occupant of a position of power and/or the feeling that the political process deserves public respect.

libel Malicious and intentional use of untrue written statements that damage an individual's reputation. See also *slander*.

liberals Supporters of a political ideology that trusts human nature, who see an active role for government, welcome change, emphasize freedom over order, and strive for complete equality in society.

libertarians Advocates of a political philosophy marked by a distrust of all government and a desire for maximum individual freedom and approval of those government actions that protect one individual or country from another.

line-item veto The power given a governor or president to disapprove specific sections of legislation otherwise approved.

literacy test Examinations of a potential voter's ability to read and write; was often used to deny the rights of members of minorities to vote.

litmus test Borrowed from a test in chemistry, a stand on a specific political issue that defines a person or group.

lobbyists Individuals, often paid by an interest group, who communicate group interests to government officials. The term originates from the practice of waiting in the "lobby" of legislative chambers to attempt to persuade legislators before a vote.

local color Aspects of a story that have special meaning for a local rather than a national audience.

Locke, John (1632–1704) English writer and philosopher who espoused the belief that men are born with inalienable rights—including rights to life, liberty and property—that the government should not have the power to restrict. Locke's work heavily influenced Thomas Jefferson as he crafted the American Declaration of Independence.

logrolling The cooperation among politicians as they attempt to build a coalition by trading favors. The term is derived from the necessary cooperation among lumberjacks when they attempt to move logs on the water.

M

maintaining election An election in which the candidate of the majority party in the electorate wins.

majority leader The head of the majority party in each house of Congress.

majority opinion The written rationale explaining the views of the justices who were in the majority when voting on an individual case.

majority-minority district An electoral district designed so that an ethnic minority has a numerical majority.

mandate The message implied in an election result endorsing a particular set of public policy choices.

marble-cake federalism Pattern of relationships among the national, state, and local governments that features extensive sharing and intermingling of governing responsibilities.

Marbury v. Madison Supreme Court decision in 1803 that established the Supreme Court's prerogative to perform judicial review of laws enacted by Congress and of actions taken by federal officials.

massive resistance Policies pursued in southern states to avoid compliance immediately after receiving order to desegregate public schools.

matching funds Monies that state and local governments are required to contribute to participate in federal grant programs; intended to increase state and local stake in federal programs.

Mayflower Compact Agreement signed by the Pilgrims on the *Mayflower* in 1620 concerning the governance by majority rule of the Plymouth Plantation.

media The generalized term for all commercial communications that attempt to reach a mass audience with newsworthy information or entertainment.

Medicaid Created in 1965, this program provides funds to subsidize the medical and hospital care of poor persons served though state health programs.

Medicare A federal program created in 1965 that subsidizes the health care costs of senior citizens; consists of separate parts covering (a) some of the cost of hospital care for retired and disabled people covered by social security and (b) the costs of physicians' fees for persons 65 or over and disabled social security beneficiaries (who pay the premiums).

melting pot A description of the American experience of welcoming successive waves of immigrants and integrating them into the dominant culture.

mercantilism Philosophy that colonies perform a subservient role to the economy of the mother country by providing raw materials and by serving as a base for the purchase of manufactured goods.

merit principle Belief that jobs should be awarded on the basis of education and job skill (merit) as opposed to political connection or favoritism.

Metropolitan Statistical Area (MSA) The U.S. Census Bureau designation of a central city with a population of 50,000 or more and its surrounding county, plus other counties economically tied to the core county.

minimum winning coalition The minimum number of coalition members required to achieve a particular policy goal. The number involved, usually a simple majority, varies from case to case but as a general rule represents the maximum size of managed or bought coalitions.

minority leader The head of the minority party in each house of Congress.

Miranda rule Due process requirement that suspects be informed of their rights.

Missouri Compromise of 1820 Agreement reached in Congress allowing the admission of Missouri as a slave state and Maine as a free state and prohibiting slavery north of the 36°30' parallel line.

moderates Individuals whose views fall between those of liberals and conservatives. Moderates often hold their views less fervently than individuals with more extreme opinions.

monetary policies Federal government policies designed to maintain economic growth and stability through control of the money supply, interest rates, and credit.

Monroe Doctrine Assertion by President James Monroe in 1823 that the Western hemisphere was close to colonization and aggressive actions by European nations. The United States promised not to interfere in the concerns of Europe.

most-favored nation (MFN) International trade policy in which nations agree to give each other the most favorable trade concessions available to foreign countries.

multilateralism The strategy of pursuing foreign policy objectives through cooperative relationships with other nations, often through international organizations like the United Nations.

multinational corporation Corporations that conduct business in multiple nations simultaneously.

municipality General-purpose local government that provides an array of public services to residents of the jurisdiction; requires population concentration and incorporation under state laws and constitutions.

N

national party convention The quadrennial (every fourth year) meeting of party members to choose the party's presidential nominee, establish policy goals, and decide on party rules.

national security adviser Presidential assistant who directs the National Security Council and advises the president on national security issues.

nation-state A legally recognized nation. Refers to the prominent use of nations as the primary building blocks of the world order.

natural coalition A group of individuals agreeing to support a particular position without any additional inducement.

natural dualism The view that all major issues divide into two alternatives (liberal/conservative, "ins/outs," pro/con, and so on.).

natural rights Rights to life, liberty, property, and pursuit of happiness; based on the philosophical position that every individual is entitled to them.

natural-born citizens Individuals born in the United States or children born abroad of U.S. citizens. The presidency is the only elective office that specifies that candidates be natural-born citizens.

necessary and proper clause Provision of the Constitution empowering the national government to enact laws required to enforce the powers granted to it in Article I, Section 8; known also as the elastic clause.

needs test The examination of the financial, medical, or social situation of individuals and families seeking to receive benefits through social welfare programs compared with governmental standards that define eligibility for assistance.

negative advertising Campaign ads that directly question the behavior and/or consistency of one's opponent as opposed to touting one's own virtues.

negative-sum games Games in which most, if not all, the players lose something as a result of playing the game. See also *positive* and *zero-sum games*.

New Deal Series of policy initiatives proposed by President Franklin D. Roosevelt to lead the nation out of the Great Depression. Included policies to regulate the economy and to stimulate economic growth.

New Jersey Plan Submitted by William Patterson of New Jersey on behalf of smaller states at the Constitutional Convention. It called for equal representation of states in a one-house legislature.

new politics A set of political strategies relying on new communications technologies and the personal appeal of candidates.

news hole The amount of room in a publication or in a broadcast given over to covering the news.

news hook The characteristic of a news event on which one hangs the story. This is often an individual whom the media feel is newsworthy.

news leaks A government official's deliberate disclosure of secret information to embarrass others or to promote a particular policy.

NIMBY The acronym for "not in my backyard," referring to the hesitancy of residents to accept relatively undesirable government facilities in their area.

nomination The stage in the election process during which the official competing candidates are chosen.

nonalignment A military strategy whereby a nation avoids alliances with superpowers to avoid becoming entangled in superpower struggles.

nonpartisan elections Electoral contests in which candidates do not campaign as party representatives; no party affiliations are listed on ballots.

norms The informal social rules that guide the behavior of an institution and its members.

North Atlantic Treaty Organization (NATO) Military alliance between the United States, Canada, and many nations of Western Europe intended to check the spread of communism and the threat of Soviet military power.

nuclear deterrence A strategy of national defense whereby a strong arsenal of nuclear weapons is maintained by one nation to convince other nations against the wisdom of engaging in a military attack.

nullification doctrine Claim of some states that they had the right to review laws passed by Congress and to nullify those they felt were inappropriate.

O

Office of Management and Budget (OMB) The agency of the Executive Office of the President supporting the development of the president's budget.

office-bloc ballot Arranging names on the ballot by office to encourage voting on the basis of the characteristics of specific candidates. See also *party-column ballot*.

omnibus legislation A wide variety of often unrelated legislation included within a single and very complex bill.

one-person, one-vote The attempt to make all citizens' votes count the same by creating districts of roughly equal population size.

open games Games that allow most interested individuals the ability to participate.

open primary Nomination elections allowing voters to choose on Election Day in which party's nomination process they wish to participate. See also *blanket* and *closed primary*.

opinion leaders Individuals who command enough respect and/or knowledge that others use their opinions as models to follow.

opinions Short-term expressed preferences between alternative courses of action. See also *attitudes* and *values*.

original jurisdiction The power of a court to be the first judicial tribunal in which a case is considered.

oversight Congress's formal review of the expenditures and performance of the executive branch.

P

pack journalism A defensive strategy used by journalists comparing their coverage with that of competing media, which results in uniformity of coverage.

parliamentary system A government system in which voters select the legislature (parliament), which in turn elects the chief executive (prime minister) from its ranks. Most democratic systems in the world use a parliamentary system rather than its chief alternative, the presidential system.

parochialism The tendency to look out for the narrow interests of one political group or geographic area.

participatory (direct) democracy Democratic political game in which all or most players participate directly in all political decisions.

partisan Favoring the interests of one party over another.

party-column ballot Arranging the names on the ballot by party to encourage party-line voting.

party discipline The willingness of members of a legislative party to follow the wishes of the majority of their party when voting.

party identification The sense of affinity or feeling of belonging to one of the political parties.

party-in-the-electorate Those voters who psychologically identify with one of the parties and tend to vote for its nominees.

party leader The president's informal status as the spokesperson and agenda setter for his or her political party.

party machine Sophisticated and carefully crafted organizations that controlled city politics by awarding favors (that is, patronage jobs or city licenses) in return for electoral support.

party platform The official statement of party policy goals and the means for reaching those goals.

patronage The practice of bestowing public-sector jobs as a reward for political support or personal loyalty.

peacekeeping The practice of using forces from outside nations—often in teams of forces organized through the United Nations—to intervene with the objective of restoring peaceful conditions.

persuasion The ability to convince others to follow a desired course of action.

players Persons who actively participate in political games.

playing field Context in which political games are played, including political culture and public opinion.

Plessy v. Ferguson Supreme Court case in 1898 that upheld segregated facilities if facilities were "equal." Legitimized "separate but equal doctrine." Overturned in *Brown v. School Board of Topeka* in 1954.

pluralism Political game with multiple opportunities for participation.

plurality The category (or set of categories) having the greatest number of responses—not necessarily more than one-half (a majority).

policy entrepreneur Individual or group among decision makers who devotes time and energy to promoting a policy or set of policies.

policy windows Advantageous times which response to a policy initiative is likely to be positive and placed upon the decision-making agenda.

Political Action Committee (PAC) A group of citizens who voluntarily combine their individual campaign contributions and support favored candidates, often with the encouragement of organized interest groups or corporations.

political boss An individual, who might or might not be an elected official, who headed a political machine and wielded strong influence in local government politics.

political culture Widely shared fundamental beliefs, attitudes, and perspectives concerning how political games should be played.

political executives Officials appointed by the president to manage federal government agencies; they include cabinet secretaries and about 600 officials who hold top positions in federal agencies.

political party An organized group of individuals with similar ideologies, joined together to control the personnel and policies of government through elections.

political socialization The process by which political attitudes and outlooks of society are transmitted from one generation to the next through teaching or emulation.

politics Efforts of individuals and groups to secure the benefits, services, and protections provided by governments.

polity An organization with an agreed-upon form of government.

poll tax A special tax required before a person could vote; was often used to discourage low-income individuals, and particularly members of minorities, from voting.

popular vote The actual number of votes cast for a candidate.

population density The number of people per square mile of a geographic territory (for example, city, county, or state).

population The individuals (or entities) about which one wishes to make generalizations in a public opinion poll.

populist Member of a party claiming to represent the rights of the common people; formed in 1891 to further agrarian interests. Currently used for politicians emphasizing the interests of the common person.

pork barrel Legislation favoring the districts of particular members of Congress by guaranteeing them public works projects, defense contracts, and other government programs.

positive-sum games Games in which most, if not all, of the players gain as a result of playing the game.

postindustrial society Economy based on the production of services rather than goods, where the professional and technical classes dominate and where new technologies change the nature of social interaction.

potential group Individuals who recognize a common interest and have some awareness of who they share the interest with. See also *categoric group* and *interest group*.

power of the purse The prerogative of Congress to appropriate public funds.

power The ability to get others to follow your wishes by employing resources such as threats, promises, personal charisma, or information.

pragmatism A practical approach to politics in which slavish commitment to ideology or past loyalties is replaced with a more realistic acceptance of flexibility.

precedent The decision or guideline established in a case that will be used by the courts in determining future decisions.

preemptive strike The doctrine of engaging in military efforts to protect from external threats prior to any threats being carried out.

President Pro Tempore The presiding officer in the Senate when the vice president is not in attendance.

presidential program The package of policy initiatives proposed by a president for legislative or administrative action.

price fixing A conspiracy among companies to subvert the free market and agree on a price for a product or service.

primary election A preelection selection process to determine the official nominees of a party when more than one candidate has filed.

prior restraint Forbidding the publication or broadcast of material before it is written or aired.

prioritizing Choosing among competing attitudes to establish an opinion with the potential for action.

private interest group A group looking out for the interests of one segment of society.

privatization Shifting the management of government programs to private-sector firms and nonprofit organizations.

probable cause Reasonable grounds that a criminal act has been committed.

progressive tax rates Tax rates requiring wealthier individuals and corporations to pay a higher percentage of their income than that paid by poorer individuals and corporations.

Progressives A political movement flourishing in America between 1890 and 1920 that promoted progress in government.

project grants Federal grant programs that require states and localities to submit a project proposal for review by the federal agency overseeing the grant program.

property tax A tax levied by a local government on the owners of private property in the jurisdiction according to the value of the property.

proportional representation A system of electing representatives from lists nominated by the political parties in which more than one representative is selected from each district.

Protestant ethic The theologically supported precepts of individualism, hard work, frugality, and respect for material success as a sign of God's favor.

proxy voting Allowing one individual to cast the vote of another.

psychological needs voting A voting choice based on the attempt to use one's vote as a verification of one's self-image. See also *instrumental* and *social needs voting*.

public funding Government provision of funds for the running of a political campaign.

public interest group A group advocating the broader interests of society as opposed to the narrower economic interests promoted by most business and professional interest groups.

public opinion Short-term attitudes about political players or particular public policies that are important enough to generate widespread interest.

public policy Outcomes of political games that distribute benefits or sanctions to players and others. Generally characterized as regulatory, distributive, or redistributive.

public-private partnerships Partnerships of governments and businesses to design and operate programs with broad benefits.

Q

quorum The necessary number of individuals to legally carry out business in a legislature or other meeting.

quota The practice of setting aside a set number of jobs, training slots, or college admissions openings to a specified target group like women or minorities.

R

Rainbow Coalition An organization that attempts to weave together peoples of all races and genders into a viable political force for progressive policies.

randomness A process for selecting a sample from a population in which every individual (or entity) has an equal chance of being selected.

ratification Formal approval of a legal document, for example, the Constitution.

ratings The measurement of the relative size and composition of the audience watching or listening to a particular network or station.

rationalizing Explaining away inconsistencies between attitudes, opinions, and/or behavior in an attempt to erase the apparent conflict.

realigning election Election in which individual party identification shifts toward one party.

realignment A dramatic change in the balance between the political parties involving a shift in the way major social groups vote.

real-time politics Monitoring political events as they happen without delay or mediation.

reapportionment The allocation of legislative seats to each state after a census.

recall The procedure by which voters may submit a petition and vote as to whether an elected official should be removed from office.

recession An economic period characterized by negative economic growth and unemployment.

reconstruction The period immediately following the Civil War when the politics of Southern States were dominated by politicians from the North.

redistributive policies Public policies that transfer wealth, rights, duties, responsibilities, or other values from one group to another. See also *distributive policies* and *regulatory policies*.

redistricting The process of redrawing constituency boundaries for electoral districts.

referendum An election in which state or local officials submit a proposed legislative or constitutional change to the public for a vote.

reform Planned modifications of a rule or procedure that are designed to achieve specific purposes or outcomes in future political games.

regulatory federalism Pattern of regulatory requirements imposed by a government at a higher level in the federal system upon lower-level governments.

regulatory mandates Actions either required of or prohibited to state and local governments if they are to receive federal funds or avoid legal penalties.

regulatory policies Public policies that place government limits on or establish guidelines for the behavior of individuals, groups, and organizations within the political system.

representation The process of taking into account the interests of others (often constituents) and of fighting for those interests.

representative government Theory of political power in which citizens or constituents choose others to represent their interests in government decision making.

representativeness The degree to which the personal characteristics of the members of an institution match the characteristics of the general population that the institution represents.

republicanism Democratic political game in which groups of citizens are constituents who choose others (elected representatives) to look after their interests in government decision making.

reserve powers Powers not granted to the national government in the Constitution and retained by the states and the people.

responsible party model An idealized party system marked by clearly differentiated parties, party-oriented voters, candidates committed to party goals, and cohesive support for the party by elected and appointed officials.

responsive voters Voters amenable to having their voting decision affected by campaign communications. See also *dependent voters*.

responsiveness An evaluative criterion that compares the policy preferences of citizens with the nature and impact of public policies implemented by governments.

reverse discrimination Hurting one group in society in the process of attempting to help another group by giving them a special preference.

rewards Positive payoffs received for successfully playing political games.

right-to-work laws State laws that prohibit unions from including provisions for compulsory union membership in collective bargaining agreements.

Roe v. Wade Major Supreme Court decision in 1973 that upheld the right of women to have abortions.

roll call vote A legislative vote in which the position of each member of Congress is recorded.

Rousseau, Jean-Jacques (1712–1778) European philosopher who articulated the concept of a "social contract," that is, an agreement among people that sets the conditions and expectations for being a member of a society.

rule of four Rule used by the Supreme Court stipulating that a minimum of four judges must vote to consider an appeals case before it can be selected for consideration and placed on the Court's schedule.

rule of unanimity All eligible voters or voting units must vote in favor of a proposed measure before it is formally approved.

rules Guidelines that determine how political games will be conducted, who gets to play, and the information the players will receive during the game.

S

sales tax A tax using one rate and applied to the sale of most consumer goods; housing and food are often exempt.

sample A subset of individuals (or entities) that serves as the basis for making generalizations about a population.

sanctions Negative payoffs received for playing political games.

secession Move of states to formally and legally become separate from the Union.

Second Continental Congress Second meeting of colonial delegates; 1775, voted to send the "Olive Branch Petition" to the king; 1776, approved the Declaration of Independence; 1777, approved the Articles of Confederation.

secularization Emphasizing worldly concerns as opposed to religious or moral ones.

Security Council The body in the United Nations empowered to make decisions binding upon member nations. Composed of five permanent members—China, France, the Soviet Union, the United Kingdom, and the United States—plus ten nonpermanent and rotating members. Permanent members have veto power.

sedition Incitement of rebellion against governmental authority.

segregation The enforced separation of a group (such as a racial one) from the rest of society.

select committee A congressional committee established to deal with a temporary task or emerging problem. Sometimes called a special committee.

selective attention The process of picking and choosing among sources and messages in a consistently biased manner.

selective benefits Those goods, services, and rewards that can be limited to members of a particular group. See also *collective benefits*.

selective exposure The decision to use a particular mass communications media.

selective incorporation The process through which freedoms and protections of the Bill of Rights have been extended to state and local levels.

selective perception The way in which an individual interprets and categorizes the content of new information.

self-determination The right of a people of a territory to govern themselves by a government system they freely select for themselves.

senatorial courtesy A practice whereby presidents consult with senators from a state when considering the nomination of federal judges to positions in that state. Also, members of the Senate tend to defer to their colleagues from the state in which the appointment is being made.

Senior Executive Service (SES) Program created in the late 1970s to develop top-quality managers within the executive branch and to discourage them from leaving the public sector for better-paying jobs in the private sector.

seniority The process of choosing congressional committee chairs on the basis of their length of service on the committee.

separation of powers The allocation of governmental powers among the three branches of government so that they are a check on one another.

side payments Benefits having nothing to do with the issue at hand but that are given to an individual joining a coalition.

silent majority A term used by politicians that refers to views held by a large number of individuals who fail to make their preference known through dramatic political action.

single-member district A process of distributing seats so that each geographic district has one, and only one, elected official representing it.

slack resources Political resources, such as time and money, that are left over after the basic necessities of life are taken care of.

slander Malicious and intentional use of untrue verbal statements that damage an individual's reputation. See also *libel*.

slate The group of candidates nominated by a party running as a team.

social contract Agreement among individuals to form a polity.

social needs voting A voting choice based on the influence of friends or relatives.

Social Security A federal program that provides retirement benefits to senior citizens. Workers and employers pay payroll taxes to support the program.

socialization The process by which political attitudes and outlooks of society are transmitted from one generation to the next through teaching or emulation.

socioeconomic status (SES) A composite measure of one's level of education, income, and occupational status. These three variables are highly, but not perfectly, correlated.

soft money Contributions and expenditures given by national parties to state parties to encourage voter participation through registration, party building, and get-out-the-vote drives.

Solicitor General The chief attorney representing the United States in cases before the Supreme Court in which the national government is a party.

Sons of Liberty Groups of colonists who protested coercive acts of Parliament in the period prior to the American Revolution.

sound bite A short segment of a speech or an interview used in a radio or television news story—usually with strong symbolism and/or wording.

sovereign Undisputed, supreme power as a political unit.

sovereignty The right to exercise governing powers over a specified territory.

Speaker The presiding officer in the House of Representatives.

special district Single-purpose unit of local government that provides one basic service or function.

spending power The ability of the federal government to influence the actions and programs of state and local governments because of the provision of federal funds to support such programs.

spin The attempt to portray potentially negative events in the most positive light so that they will not "spin out of control."

spoils system A comprehensive method of distributing jobs and government benefits to supporters of a particular party or candidate while discriminating against individuals who either remain neutral or support the opposition.

spot advertising A short—usually 30- or 60-second—promotion for candidates or causes on radio or television.

stability (of public opinion) The degree to which the distribution of public opinions remains consistent over time.

standing committee A permanent committee of one house of Congress assigned the responsibility of dealing with bills in a particular policy area.

standing The right to initiate legal action based on direct involvement in controversy and injury sustained from the controversy.

state delegation The members of Congress from a particular state. Some delegations meet on a bipartisan basis, while members from other states meet separately as Republicans or Democrats.

State of the Union Message The annual message to Congress in which the president lays out the presidential legislative agenda. Nineteenth-century presidents sent a written message, while modern presidents personally promote their policy goals.

states' rights The position that states have clear rights and privileges under the Constitution, onto which actions of the federal government may not infringe.

statutory intent The goals and objectives of Congress outlined in public laws, which are intended as instructions to the federal agencies that engage in policy implementation.

statutory law Written laws enacted by legislative bodies such as Congress, state legislatures, and city councils.

strategy Preconceived plan of action intended to achieve victory in political games; action taken to enhance the probability of winning. Also called game plans, tactics, procedures.

strict constructionist view A judicial philosophy that holds that constitutional interpretation should be limited to the language of the Constitution and to the interpretation of the Founders' intentions.

strong mayor A plan of local government in which the city council operates as the local legislature and the elected mayor serves as the local chief executive to residents.

structural bias Potential distortion that is built into the news gathering and reporting process but that is not intended by the journalists or editors.

stumping Campaigning for a candidate. The term comes from the practice in old-time campaigns of standing on a stump to give a speech in order to be seen and heard.

subcommittee A specialized unit of a full congressional committee that deals with the details of legislation before passing it on to the full committee for its approval.

subculture A divergent set of social outlooks held by an identifiable minority group within a society.

suffrage The legal right to vote.

suffragettes Women advocating and demonstrating for extension of enfranchisement to women.

supply-side economic policy Policies benefiting the supply segments of the economy (investors, corporations) to stimulate economic growth by having the results "trickle down."

supremacy clause Constitutional provision declaring that, should the Constitution, treaties, or laws of the national government clash with those of state governments, the national ones shall be supreme.

symbiotic A relationship between two entities in which each needs the other for some purpose.

symbolic speech Expression of ideas and beliefs through symbols or symbolic actions.

T

tariff A tax levied on products being imported into the country.

tax expenditures Tax breaks given to individuals, families and corporations that represent forgone tax revenues that would be otherwise collected. Tax breaks are given to achieve social and economic objectives.

technology Specialized knowledge and tools, often scientific in nature, facilitating the conduct of everyday life and activities, including politics.

teleconferencing An interactive technology using computer-based digitized video to allow a two-way conversation between individuals or groups.

teledemocracy The harnessing of techniques, such as televised town meetings with the capability of two-way communication and remote voting, to increase citizen participation.

ticket splitting The abandonment of a straight party-line vote in favor of picking and choosing among the candidates of different parties.

township Unit of local government found in some states and based on geographic territory rather than population concentration.

tracking polls A series of polls taken at short intervals that attempt to measure changes in opinion.

trade deficit The net loss in foreign trade that occurs when the value of goods imported into a nation from abroad exceeds the value of goods exported to other nations.

Truman Doctrine Policy articulated by President Harry S. Truman in 1947 for giving economic and military aid to nations seeking to resist totalitarian aggression. This doctrine became the centerpiece of containment policy.

trustee A style of representation in which the person uses his or her individual judgment in looking out for the interests of others. See also *delegate*.

U

unanticipated consequences The unplanned results of government policies. These consequences may stimulate policy changes.

uncoordinated expenditures Campaign advertising done without the knowledge and/or cooperation of the candidate. Such expenditures do not fall under the normal campaign contribution limitations.

unicameral legislature Legislature that has one house.

unilateralism An approach to conducting foreign policy whereby a nation tends to rely upon itself and take action on its own to achieve its objectives. Little cooperation is sought with other nations.

union shop Requirement that all employees that join a company be required to join a union within a specified time period.

unitary political system Governing system in which a national government governs with little or no use of regional or state governments.

urban reform movement A reform initiative, dating from the late 1800s, in which reformers sought to change, modernize, and professionalize local government and to reduce corruption and the power of political machines.

user fees Charges made by local government on individuals or businesses that consume specific city services, including fees to use recreational and other city-provided services.

V

values Attitudes referring to the desired goals for individual or societal accomplishment. Our visions of the good life and the perfect society. See also *attitudes* and *opinions*.

veteran's preference Practice within the civil service system that adds points to competitive examinations and evaluations for all applicants who are military veterans.

veto The president's (or governor's) formal refusal to approve a piece of legislation, requiring it to go back to Congress (or the state legislature) for reconsideration.

victims Individuals affected by government policies whose interests are not taken into account in the policy process.

Virginia Plan Proposal drafted by James Madison and presented at the Constitutional Convention that reflected the interests of larger states.

virtual representation The view that a government official can look out for the interests of a specified group of individuals even though the individuals have no control over the official's actions.

voice vote A method of voting in Congress in which members orally answer yes or no to a proposal.

Voting Rights Act of 1965 Law passed by Congress to prohibit discrimination in voting and registration.

vouchers Certificates provided by the government that allow recipients to purchase specific items. Food stamps are an example.

W

War on Poverty Set of programs including food stamps and urban redevelopment designed by the administration of President Lyndon Johnson and enacted by Congress in the mid-1960s.

War Powers Resolution The 1973 act of Congress designed to limit presidentially initiated military actions by requiring consultation with Congress and congressional approval.

ward Electoral unit within city boundaries where residents are entitled to elect representatives to the city council.

welfare state A political system in which it is public policy that government strives to provide a broad set of health and social programs to all citizens—generally in exchange for high public sector taxes.

whip A party official with the responsibilities of assessing member preferences, presenting the party position, and getting supporters of the party position to the floor for voting.

wire services Commercial reporting services, such as the Associated Press (AP) and United Press International (UPI), that provide objective stories focusing on national and international events. Local editors choose which stories to include, edit their length, and introduce them with headlines.

writ of certiorari An order from a higher court demanding that a lower court send up the record of a specified case for review. This signals that the Supreme Court will hear a case appealed from lower federal courts.

writ of habeas corpus Legal order directing a person or authority holding someone as prisoner to bring that person before judicial authority to determine the lawfulness of imprisonment.

Z

zero-sum games Games with a finite payoff in which a player's winnings are gained at the expense of the other player or players. See also *negative* and *positive-sum games*.

Index

Page numbers in italics identify illustrations. An italic *t* next to a page number (e.g., 241*t*) indicates information that appears in a table. An italic *n* and number following a page number (e.g., 241*n*13) indicate information that appears in an end-of chapter note and the number of the note where the material can be found. A page number followed by an italic *n* with no note number (e.g., 241*n*) indicates an on-page note reference.